A BIBLIOGRAPHY OF
PRINTED WORKS RELATING TO
THE UNIVERSITY
OF OXFORD

A BIBLIOGRAPHY OF PRINTED WORKS RELATING TO THE UNIVERSITY OF OXFORD

By

E. H. CORDEAUX, M.A.

SUPERINTENDENT, BODLEIAN LAW LIBRARY

and

D. H. MERRY, M.A.

OXFORD

AT THE CLARENDON PRESS

1968

Oxford University Press, Ely House, London W. 1

GLASGOW NEW YORK TORONTO MELBOURNE WELLINGTON
CAPE TOWN SALISBURY IBADAN NAIROBI LUSAKA ADDIS ABABA
BOMBAY CALCUTTA MADRAS KARACHI LAHORE DACCA
KUALA LUMPUR HONG KONG TOKYO

PRINTED IN GREAT BRITAIN

FOREWORD

MR. CORDEAUX and MR. MERRY are already well known as the compilers of *A Bibliography of Printed Works relating to Oxfordshire*, which was published by the Oxford Historical Society in 1955. This excellent work was very well received and has proved an admirable working tool for scholars, whether professional or amateur, working on the history of the County of Oxford. The appeal of the present publication is likely to be even more extensive. Much work has in recent years been done on the history of the University, and more is in progress or envisaged and will be greatly facilitated by the availability of this bibliography.

The authors are both senior members of the staff of the Bodleian Library, but this publication is their own and does not appear with the *imprimatur* of the Library. It is nevertheless a work of which the Library is proud and for which its readers will be grateful. A glance at the pages shows that a large number of the items listed are official or semi-official documents, with no named author and no particularly revealing title: publications, in fact, which task to the limit the patience of the users of catalogues and the potentialities of the catalogues themselves. Here they are shown with their Bodleian shelfmarks and classified with precision. As a result, a great area of the resources of the Bodleian and an area in which, in the nature of things, the Bodleian is exceedingly rich, is made far more accessible than it was before. Since the bibliography is published, moreover, instead of existing only in a unique copy on the Library's premises, scholars outside Oxford can prepare fully in advance for a visit to the Bodleian, or can order photographic reproductions without the need to come here at all. A published, specialized bibliography, listing articles in periodicals as well as books, is more attuned to the needs of modern scholarship than the old-fashioned general subject catalogue.

The best thanks of the Library and of the University and of all who are interested in the history of the University are due to Mr. Cordeaux and Mr. Merry.

ROBERT SHACKLETON
Bodley's Librarian

1 January 1967

PREFACE

THE bibliography has a limiting date of 1965/6. It honours the pledge we made in the preface to our *Bibliography of Oxfordshire* published in 1955, and is governed by the general principles followed in that work. We do not claim that it is comprehensive. Indeed we have deliberately excluded some items, and some types of material; sheer bulk has made this necessary. We have tried, however, to record any item of intrinsic interest notwithstanding its size or provenance. For example, although we have excluded some 'potted' histories and the like, we have included a large amount of ephemeral literature which reflects University policy and politics. Much of this literature is probably unknown and unavailable outside the Bodleian, but any research into University history, particularly in the eighteenth and nineteenth centuries, would need to take account of it. We have also included formal entries for Bodleian 'scrap-book' collections, if these seemed to have a value. This applies particularly to material relating to university societies. We have sometimes recorded a trivial item in order to establish the existence and date of a society.

Religion provides another example of selection. Works about the nineteenth-century Oxford Movement which describe its impact on the nation as a whole have not been included. Those which affect Oxford, and particularly those recording the beginnings of the Movement, have been noted. No items concerned with theological doctrine or controversy have been accepted unless they have specifically involved the University.

Maps, prints, and plans, when not in book form have generally been excluded, but Bodleian guardbooks of views have been listed, because as collections they seemed to us to have a definite value. A card index to individual views and plans is available in the Bodleian.

Newspapers have not been analysed, but a large number of periodicals have been examined and significant articles have been given entries. Many isolated articles from periodicals not otherwise examined have also been included.

Acts of Parliament on specific aspects of, or subjects affecting, the University and colleges have been included, but general acts which have a 'saving clause' for University privilege have been excluded: these can be found in Shadwell's Enactments (no. 956).

Parliamentary accounts and papers and the Reports of Commissioners have also been examined and, where it seemed profitable, recorded.

Prize essays, prize poems, and University sermons have not been listed unless their subject-matter relates to the University. Lists of prize winners are included in the Historical Register (no. 1579).

The section 'Biography' caused some difficulty. It is obviously impossible, even if desirable, to include the biographies of all Oxford men. It seemed therefore reasonable to list the biographies of Oxford worthies rather than of worthies who happened to be Oxford men. To this end we have tried to find biographies of all those listed in the Historical Register as having held a University appointment, in addition to those whom, in the course of compiling the bibliography, we came to recognize as worthies. In the field of autobiography and reminiscence we accepted all the items we found: these we regard as an important source for the social history of the University and they are listed under the heading Life and Manners. Because it was not found practicable to list them in a strict chronological sequence of the period covered, they are divided by century, and within the century arranged by the date of publication.

It should be noted that the Faculty headings include any item concerned with the subjects currently supervised by a Faculty, even though the date of an item may precede the foundation of the Faculty.

The sections Government and Reform to a certain extent overlap, and some items receive a full entry under both headings. Reform covers general ground; when a particular subject, faculty, or department is the object of reform, the entries are to be found under the relevant heading.

Bibliographical details have been kept to the minimum consistent with accurate identification, and in the case of the fifteenth to seventeenth centuries reference is made to Falconer Madan's *Oxford Books*. Bodleian shelfmarks have been added throughout, and where the Bodleian is without a copy we have tried to indicate where a copy may be found. In some cases it has not been possible to compile a complete entry. Information enabling more complete entries to be made would be welcomed. No attempt has been made to standardize authors' names in the entries. They normally appear in the form given on the item described.

Many items listed are concerned with more than one aspect of the University. Normally we have included a full entry under the main subject of the study and by a series of cross-references ensured that any other aspect involved is adequately identified.

In addition to the index of personal names and index of subjects, we have also compiled a 'title or first-line' index of anonymous works which do not clearly indicate their subject-matter in the title.

In acknowledging the help we have received from many people, we again pay tribute to the late Strickland Gibson. We should like to thank the many members of the Bodleian staff who, from time to time during the last ten years, have drawn our attention to Oxford references. In particular we are grateful to Miss Pamela Boult for clerical assistance, to Mrs. Hilary Cornwell and Mrs. Jane Venis for their help with the recording of Oxford fiction, and to the staff of the Clarendon Press for patient skill devoted to a tedious undertaking.

E. H. C.

D. H. M.

KEY TO LIBRARIES

WHEN a work is not in the Bodleian, the Library known to possess a copy
is indicated in the space where the Bodleian shelfmark would otherwise
appear by the use of the following initials and abbreviations.

All Souls coll.	All Souls College, Oxford
B.M.	British Museum
B.N.	Bibliothèque Nationale
B.N.C.	Brasenose College, Oxford
C.C.C.	Corpus Christi College, Oxford
Ch. Ch.	Christ Church, Oxford
Ex. coll.	Exeter College, Oxford
Harvard	Harvard University Library
Honnold	Honnold Library, Claremont, Cal.
Ind. Inst.	Indian Institute, Oxford
L. of C.	Library of Congress
L.L.	Bodleian Law Library, Oxford
Lambeth	Lambeth Palace Library
Mag. coll.	Magdalen College, Oxford
Manch. coll.	Manchester College, Oxford
O.C.L.	Oxfordshire County Library
O.P.L.	Oxford City Public Library
O.U.A.	Oxford University Archives
O.U.P.	Clarendon Press, Oxford
P.C.O.	Privy Council Office
P.R.O.	Public Records Office
Queen's coll.	Queen's College, Oxford
Radcl.	Radcliffe Science Library, Oxford
R.H.	Rhodes House Library, Oxford
S. of A.	Society of Antiquaries, London
St. B.T.L.	St. Bride Typographical Library, London
St. John's	St. John's College, Oxford
Taylor	Taylor Institution, Oxford
Worc. coll.	Worcester College, Oxford

CLASSIFICATION SCHEME

HISTORY

GENERAL SOURCES
(INCLUDING DOCUMENTS AND RECORDS)

See 1106 [Oxford University gazette. 1870–].

1. Statutes of the colleges . . . and Catalogues of documents relating to the University preserved in the Public Record Office. Vol. 3. Oxf. &c., 1853, 8°. 111 pp.   G.A. Oxon 8° 26=R.

2. PULLING, A., The law reports. Index to Orders in Council, proclamations, Royal commissions of inquiry [&c.] publ. in the London gazette, 1830–1883. Lond., 1885, 4°.   22858 d. 63

3. MADAN, F., An outline of a Bibliotheca Oxoniensis [signed Locrinides]. (Oxf. mag., 1885, vol. 3, p. 62, 63.)   Per. G.A. Oxon 4° 141

4. MADAN, F., Rough list of manuscript materials relating to the history of Oxford, contained in the printed catalogues of the Bodleian and college libraries. Oxf., 1887, 8°. 170 pp.   G.A. Oxon 8° 428

5. MADAN, F., Oxford, a subject- and alphabetical index. Oxf., 1887, 8°. 53 pp.   G.A. Oxon 8° 449

6. MADAN, F., Oxford books, a bibliography of printed works relating to the University and City of Oxford, or printed or published there.
— Vol. 1. The early Oxford press, 1468–1640. [See note in no. 6379.] Oxf., 1895, 8°. 365 pp.   25823 d. 192 (1) = R.
— Vol. 2. Oxford literature, 1450–1640 and 1641–1650. Oxf., 1912, 8°. 712 pp.   25823 d. 192 (2) = R.
— Vol. 3. Oxford literature, 1651–1680. Oxf., 1931, 8°. 621 pp.
                         25823 d. 192 (3) = R.

General

7. HARRISON, W., An historicall description of the Islande of Britayne. (Book 2, ch. 6, Of universities, f. 78ᵛ–80ᵛ.) (Holinshed's Chronicles, vol. 1, 1577.)   Douce H 240
— [Another ed.] (Book 2, ch. 3, p. 148–53.) (Holinshed's Chronicles, vol. 1, 1586.)   Σ III 44
— [Another ed., *entitled*] Harrison's Description of England in Shakspere's youth. (New Shakspere soc., 1876, ser. 6, p. 70–89.)
                     Soc. M. adds. 58 d. 3 = A.

8. WINDSOR, M., Academiarum totius Europæ catalogus. Lond., 1586. 2 sheets.   C.C.C.
— [Another ed. Signed M.W. Pp. 28–48 contain an account of Oxford.] [Madan 111.] Lond., 1590, 4°.   A 17. 8 Linc.

— [Another issue.]   B.M.
— [Another ed., *entitled*] Europæi academiæ celebriores . . . [Imperf.
proof sheets only.] [Oxf., 1592.] 2 sheets.   C.C.C.

9. FITZHERBERT, N., Nicolai Fierberti Oxoniensis . . . Academiæ
   descriptio. [Madan 211.] Romæ, 1602, 8°. 55 pp.   Gough Oxf. 9 (2)
   — Repr. (Elizabethan Oxford. Oxf. hist. soc., vol. 8.) 1887.
                                                      G.A. Oxon 8° 360 = R.

10. TWYNE, B., Antiquitatis Academiæ Oxoniensis apologia. [Madan 302.]
    Oxon., 1608, 4°. 384+[72] pp.   4° T 22 Art. Seld.
    — Vltima ed. [Madan 484.] 1620.   G.A. Oxon 8° 271

11. STOW, J., The annales, or Generall chronicle of England . . . augmented
    by E. Howes. (An appendix . . . of the . . . universities, p. 956, 57.)
    [Madan 424.] Lond., 1615, fol.   K 5. 14 Art.
    — [Another ed.] 1631. (p. 1061, 62.)   D 1. 5 Art.

12. FULMAN, W., Academiæ Oxoniensis notitia [by W. Fulman]. [Madan
    2689.] Oxon., 1665, 4°. 56 pp.   4° T 98 (1) Th.
    — [Another issue.] [Madan 2690.]   Wood 513 (3)
    — [Another ed., *entitled*] Notitia Oxoniensis academiæ. [Madan 3036.]
    Lond., 1675, 4°. 112 pp.   Gough Oxf. 75

13. WOOD, A., Historia et antiquitates Universitatis Oxoniensis duobus
    voluminibus comprehensæ. [Tr. by R. Peers and R. Reeves.] [Madan
    2996.] Oxon., 1674, fol. 414 pp.   Wood 430
    — [Another, University presentation copy, with Loggan's Oxonia
    illustrata (no. 284) interleaved.]   Vet. A 3 b. 21, 22

14. WOOD, A., The history and antiquities of the University of Oxford,
    now first publ. in English by J. Gutch. 2 vols. [in 3]. Oxf., 1792–96, 4°.
                                                       Vet. A 5 d. 771 = R.
    [See also no. 6403.]

15 WOOD, T., A vindication of the historiographer of the University of
    Oxford [A. à Wood], and his works, from the reproaches of the lord
    bishop of Salisbury [G. Burnet] in his letter . . . concerning . . . A
    specimen of some errors and defects in the history of the Reformation
    of the Church of England, by Anthony Hurmer [i.e. H. Wharton].
    Written by E.D. Lond., 1693, 4°. 30 pp.   Gough Oxf. 142 (2)

    See 1606 [Wood, A., Fasti or Annals. 1691 &c.].

16. BENTHEM, H. L., Engeländischer Kirch- und Schulen-Staat. [Oxford
    univ., p. 294–351.] Lüneburg, 1694, 8°.   8° N 53 Art.

17. HEARNE, T., An account of several antiquities in and about the Uni-
    versity of Oxford. (The Itinerary of John Leland, 1711, vol. 2, p. 64–
    94.)   Mus. Bibl. II 25
    — (The Itinerary, 1744, 2nd ed., vol. 2, p. 86–121.)   Mus. Bibl. II 33

    See 163–66 [J. Ayliffe's The antient and present state of the University, 1714
    &c., and comment thereon].

18. HUTTEN, L., Antiquities of Oxford (p. 273–410 of Textus Roffensis, ed. T. Hearnius). Oxon., 1720, 8°.   Mus. Bibl. II 66
— Repr. (Elizabethan Oxford. Oxf. hist. soc., 8.) 1887.
        G.A. Oxon 8° 360 = R.

19. WOOD, A., Some notes relating to the history of Oxford, and the places thereabouts. (Libri nigri Scaccarii volumen secundum, ed. T. Hearnius, 1728, p. 571–94.)   Mus. Bibl. II 88
— (Liber niger Scaccarii, ed. altera, 1771, vol. 2, p. 571–94.)
        Mus. Bibl. II 88**

20. SALMON, T., The present state of the universities . . . (Oxf. univ., p. 25–460.) Lond., 1744, 8°.   G.A. Oxon 8° 65

[See no. 295 for an extract of this work.]

21. POINTER, J., Oxoniensis Academia: or, The antiquities and curiosities of the University of Oxford. Lond., 1749, 12°. 254 pp.
        Gough Oxf. 15, 16

22. PESHALL, SIR J., The history of the University of Oxford, from the death of William the conqueror to the demise of queen Elizabeth [by sir J. Peshall, bart.]. Oxf., 1773, 4°. 264 pp.   Gough Oxf. 139

23. WALKER, J., Oxoniana [by J. Walker]. 4 vols. Lond., [1809], 8°.
        G.A. Oxon 8° 35–38

24. CHALMERS, A., A history of the colleges, halls and public buildings attached to the University of Oxford. Illustr. by a series of engravings. 2 vols. Oxf., 1810, 4°.   G.A. Oxon 4° 26, 27

25. ACKERMANN, R., A history of the University of Oxford, its colleges, halls and public buildings [by W. Combe, and publ. by R. Ackermann]. 2 vols. Lond., 1814, fol.   G.A. Oxon b. 109

[See also no. 450 Ackermann's Oxford, with notes by H. M. Colvin. A selection of plates . . . 1954.]

26. INGRAM, J., Memorials of Oxford. 3 vols. Oxf., 1837, 8°.
        G.A. Oxon 8° 18–20

[See also no. 450. Ackermann's Oxford, with notes by H. M. Colvin. A selection of plates from . . . James Ingram's Memorials. 1954.]

27. INGRAM, J., General history of the University and City. (Memorials of Oxford, 1837, vol. 3. 32 pp.)   G.A. Oxon 8° 20
— [Reissued.] (Memorials of the public buildings of Oxford. 1848.)
        G.A. Oxon 8° 17

28. HUBER, V. A., The English universities, from the Germ. of V. A. Huber, an abridged tr., ed. by F. W. Newman. 2 vols. [in 3]. Lond., 1843, 8°.   43. 1404–06
[The Germ. ed. was publ. at Cassel in 1839, 40: Mason R. 135, 136.]

29. INGRAM, J., Memorials of the public buildings of Oxford. New ed. [10 pt., of which one is publ. for the first time. The remainder appeared in vol. 2, 3 of the Memorials of Oxford, 1837 (no. 26).] Oxf. &c., 1848, 8°.   G.A. Oxon 8° 17

30. History, gazetteer and directory of the county of Oxford. (R. Gardner.) (Univ. and city, pp. 1–392.) Peterborough, 1852, 8°. G.A. Oxon 8° 64

31. KIRKPATRICK, E., The historically received conception of the university considered with especial reference to Oxford. Lond. &c., 1857, 8°. 309 pp. G.A. Oxon 8° 99

32. SMITH, G., Subjects for inquiry connected with the history of the University and its colleges. (Proc., Oxf. architect. and hist. soc., 1861, N.S., vol. 1, p. 16–21.) Per. G.A. Oxon 8° 498 = R.

33. GRANT, SIR A., Oxford, a lecture. Bombay, 1864, 8°. 40 pp. G.A. Oxon 8° 611 (25)

34. Oxford and its colleges. (Leisure hour, 1866, vol. 15, p. 279 &c.) Per. 2705 d. 33

35. BURROWS, M., The national character of the old English universities. (Blackwood's Edinb. mag., 1868, vol. 103, p. 326–48.) Per. 2705 e. 486

36. JEAFFRESON, J. C., Annals of Oxford. 2 vols. Lond., 1871, 8°. G.A. Oxon 8° 166, 167

37. Old and new annalists of Oxford. [Comparisons between Wood and others, and J. C. Jeaffreson's Annals.] (Blackwood's Edinb. mag., 1871, vol. 109, p. 718–39.) Per. 2705 e. 486

38. LANG, A., Oxford. (Portfolio, 1879, p. 4–9, 26–32, 42–48, 62–67, 77–82, 94–99, 115–19, 131–35, 146–50, 162–66.) Per. 170 c. 2
— 2nd ed. [Publ. in book form, *entitled*] Oxford, brief historical and descriptive notes. Lond., 1882, fol. 56 pp. G.A. fol. A 327
— [Another ed.] Lond., 1890, 8°. 282 pp. G.A. Oxon 8° 462
— [Another ed.] Lond., 1916, 4°. 223 pp. G.A. Oxon 4° 332

39. GOLDIE, F., A bygone Oxford. (Month, 1880, vol. 40, p. 27–59.) Per. 11132 d. 17

40. LYTE, H. C. MAXWELL, A history of the University of Oxford, to the year 1530. Lond. &c., 1886, 8°. 504 pp. G.A. Oxon 4° 760 = R.

41. BRODRICK, G. C., A history of the University of Oxford. (Epochs of Church hist.) Lond., 1886, 8°. 235 pp. G.A. Oxon 8° 1201

42. BOASE, C. W., Oxford. (Historic towns.) Lond., 1887, 8°. 230 pp. G.A. Oxon 8° 914

43. A chat about Oxford. (All the year round, 1888, new ser., vol. 43, p. 326–32.) G.A. Oxon 4° 586 (37)

44. HULTON, S. F., Rixae Oxonienses. Oxf. &c., 1892, 8°. 170 pp. G.A. Oxon 8° 479

45. CLARKE, A. M., Oxford university. (Cath. world, 1895, vol. 61, p. 491–511.) Per. 2714 d. 1

46. GLADSTONE, W. E., An academic sketch [of the history of the University]. (Romanes lect., 1892.) Oxf., 1892, 8°. 47 pp.
G.A. Oxon 8° 535

46.5. MILBURN, J. B., The Church and the universities: Oxford. (Dublin review, 1899, N.S., vol. 124, p. 314–41.) Per. 3977 e. 199

47. FREMANTLE, A. E. S., Oxford, a retrospect from South Africa. Lond. &c., 1900, 8°. 43 pp. G.A. Oxon 8° 659 (19)

48. GREEN, J. R., Oxford studies, ed. by mrs. J. R. Green and K. Norgate. Lond. &c., 1901, 8°. 302 pp. G.A. Oxon 8° 686

49. HEADLAM, C., Oxford and its story. Lond., 1904, 4°. 366 pp.
G.A. Oxon 4° 229
— [Another ed., *entitled*] The story of Oxford. (Mediæval town ser.) Lond., 1907, 16°. 436 pp. G.A. Oxon 16° 97
— [Another ed., *entitled*] Oxford and its story. Lond. &c., 1912, 4°. 366 pp. G.A. Oxon 4° 317

50. GEM, S. H., The early days of the University of Oxford. Oxf. &c., 1905, 16°. 36 pp. G.A. Oxon 16° 33 (22)

51. Chronological tables. A. Of existing foundations, &c. in Oxford, with some few notes of early historical events. B. Of existing buildings in Oxford. (Meeting of Assoc. booksellers at Oxf., 1906.) [Oxf.], 1906, 8°. 12 pp. G.A. Oxon 4° 247

52. MARRIOTT, J. A. R., Oxford & its place in national history, lecture. Oxf. &c., 1907, 8°. 35 pp. G.A. Oxon 8° 744 (13)
[See also no. 66.]

See 390 [Durand, R., Oxford, its buildings and gardens. 1909].

53. AYNARD, J., Oxford & Cambridge. (Villes d'art célèbres.) Par., 1909, 4°. 131 pp. G.A. Oxon 4° 263

54. HENDERSON, P. A. WRIGHT-, Oxford past and present, by the warden of Wadham college. (Blackwood's mag., 1909, vol. 185, p. 181–91.)
Per. 2705 d. 386
— [Repr.] (Glasgow & Balliol and other essays, p. 82–104.) Oxf. &c., 1926, 8°. G.A. Oxon 8° 1050

55. DAWSON, C. B., The mirror of Oxford. Lond. &c., 1912, 8°. 265 pp.
G.A. Oxon 8° 846

56. Oxford in war-time, 1642–1914. (Oxf. mag., 1914, vol. 33, p. 54, 55.)
Per. G.A. Oxon 4° 141

57. MANSBRIDGE, A., The older universities of England, Oxford & Cambridge. Lond. &c., 1923, 8°. xxiv+296 pp. 2625 d. 65

58. SPIERS, R. A. H., Round about 'The Mitre' at Oxford, episodes of the University, city and hotel [by R. A. H. Spiers]. Oxf., [1923], 4°. 150 pp. G.A. Oxon 4° 451
— 2nd ed. 1929. 157 pp. G.A. Oxon 4° 497

59. BUCHAN, J., Thoughts on a distant prospect of Oxford [historical survey]. (Blackwood's mag., 1923, vol. 214, p. 548–60.)
Per. 2705 d. 386
[Also publ. in Buchan's Homilies and recreations. 1926.]

60. MALLET, C. E., A history of the University of Oxford. 3 vols. Lond., 1924–27, 8°. G.A. Oxon 4° 758 = R.

61. HENDERSON, P. A. WRIGHT-, Glasgow & Balliol, and other essays [An old Oxford common room; Oxford past and present; the Oxford undergraduate past and present]. Lond. &c., 1926, 8°. 145 pp.
G.A. Oxon 8° 1050
[The second item was publ. in 1909: cf. no. 54.]

62. MYRES, SIR J. L., Oxford in the making. (Univ. of California chronicle, July 1927, p. 283–305.)
— [Repr.] G.A. Oxon 4° 667
— [Another ed.] (Amer. Oxon., 1928, vol. 15, p. 140–60.)
Per. G.A. Oxon 8° 889

63. DE BRISAY, A. C. DELACOUR, L'Université d'Oxford et la vie universitaire en Angleterre. Par., 1928, 8°. vi+167 pp. G.A. Oxon 8° 1063

64. MAYCOCK, A. L., An Oxford note-book. Edinb. &c., 1931, 8°. 304 pp.
G.A. Oxon 8° 1088

65. Oxford university in the centenaries of 1932. (Oxf. mag., 1932, vol. 50, p. 552–54.) Per. G.A. Oxon 4° 141

66. MARRIOTT, SIR J. A. R., Oxford, its place in national history. Oxf., 1933, 8°. 206 pp. G.A. Oxon 8° 1100
[An expansion of his earlier work, no. 52.]

67. Oxford, 1935: a souvenir of the World educational conferences. Oxf., 1935, 8°. 316 pp. G.A. Oxon 8° 1150

68. The book of Oxford. (British med. assoc.) Oxf., 1936, 8°. 243 pp.
G.A. Oxon 8° 1163

69. BUTCHER, H. T., Oxford in the '37s. (Oxf. mag., 1937, vol. 55, p. 598, 99.) Per. G.A. Oxon 4° 141

70. HOBHOUSE, C., Oxford, as it was, and as it is to-day. Lond., 1939, 8°. 120 pp. G.A. Oxon 8° 1176
— 2nd ed. 1941. B.M.
— 3rd ed. 1944. B.M.
— 4th ed. 1948.
— 5th ed. 1952. G.A. Oxon 8° 1256

71. PLOWMAN, H., Some historical observations on town and gown. (Oxford, 1949, special no., p. 55–67.) Per. G.A. Oxon 8° 1141

72. The history of the University of Oxford, guide to an exhibition held in 1953 [in the Bodleian]. Oxf., 1953, 8°. 36 pp.+4 pl.
2590 e. Oxf. 1. 37 = R.

73. The University of Oxford. (Victoria history of the county of Oxford, vol. 3.) Lond., 1954, fol. 382 pp. G.A. Oxon c. 331 (3) = R.

74. MARTIN, A. F., and STEEL, R. W., ed., The Oxford region, a scientific and historical survey. Oxf., 1954, 4°. 202 pp. G.A. Oxon 4° 722

75. SPARROW, J., Oxford in politics [in history. An article and a review of no. 160]. (Listener, 1958, vol. 59, p. 1049–51.) Per. 2705 c. 60

76. CURTIS, M. H., Oxford and Cambridge in transition, 1558–1642, an essay on changing relations between the English universities and English society. Oxf., 1959, 8°. 314 pp. 26011 e. 344

Foundation to end of Twelfth century

77. CAIUS, J., De antiquitate Cantabrigiensis academiæ libri duo, in quorum secundo de Oxoniensis quoq; gymnasij antiquitate disseritur & Cantabrigiense longe eo antiquius esse definitur. Londinensi [i.e. J. Caius] authore. Adiunximus assertionem antiquitatis Oxoniensis academiæ, ab Oxoniensi quodam [i.e. T. Caius] conscriptam. [Madan 47.] Lond., 1568, 8°. 364 pp. 8° A 50 Art. Seld.
— [Another ed.] [Madan 51.] 1574, 4°. 268 pp. Wood 480
— [Another ed., entitled] Thomæ Caii . . . Vindiciæ antiquitatis academiæ Oxoniensis contra Joannem Caium. In lucem emisit T. Hearnius. 2 voll. [The work of J. Caius is included.] Oxonii, 1730, 8°.
Douce H H 174, 175

78. SCOT, J., The foundation of the Vniversitie of Oxford. [Madan 501.] [Cambr.], 1622, fol. 2 sheets. S. of A.
— [Another ed.] [Madan 771.] 1634. Gough Maps 43 (f. 139, 140)
— [A transl., entitled] Fundatio academiae Oxoniensis. [Cambr.], 1622, s. sh. S. of A.

79. D'EWES, SIR S., Two speeches spoken by sir Simonds D'Ewes, the first touching the antiquity of Cambridge . . . [supporting its historical precedence over Oxford. Another report of this speech is to be found in The severall votes and resolutions . . . by Parliament die Martij 15. 1642. Cf. Madan 967.] Lond., 1642, 4°. Wood 514 (8)

80. LANGBAINE, G., The foundation of the Universitie of Oxford . . . [by G. Langbaine]. [Madan 2150.] Lond., 1651, 4°. 17 pp. Gough Oxf. 109

81. PESHALL, SIR J., The history of the University of Oxford to the death of William the conqueror [by sir J. Peshall, bart.]. Oxf., 1772, 8°. [36 pp.] Gough Oxf. 72 (3)
— [Another issue.] [37 pp.] Gough Oxf. 109 (5)
— [Another issue.] [37 pp.] Bliss B 182

82. KILNER, J., Of the two universities before and after their incorporation: with something more of the very first . . . of those particular bodies of scholars now incorporated [Merton]. (The account of Pythagoras's school in Cambridge [by J. Kilner] suppl. p. 123–31.) n. pl., [1790?], fol. Gough Cambr. 97

83. Pre-historic Oxford. (Dublin univ. mag., 1867, vol. 70, p. 603–19.)
G.A. Oxon 4° 580 (3)

84. GREEN, J. R., The early history of Oxford. i. The Town. ii. Town and
Gown. (Macmillan's mag., 1871, vol. 24, p. 443–51; vol. 25, p. 32–
40.)   Per. 2705 d. 254

85. PARKER, J., The early history of Oxford, 727–1100. (Oxf. hist. soc., 3.)
Oxf., 1885, 8°. 420 pp.   G.A. Oxon 8° 360 = R.

86. RASHDALL, H., and HOLLAND, T. E., The origin of the University of
Oxford. [Letters exchanged.] (Academy, 1888, vol. 33, p. 378, 79;
vol. 34, p. 40, 41, 104.)   N. 2696 d. 4

87. RASHDALL, H., The first Oxford school. (Academy, 1889, vol. 35,
p. 360, 61.)   N. 2696 d. 4

88. HOLLAND, T. E., The University of Oxford in the twelfth century.
(Oxf. hist. soc., 1890, vol. 16, p. 137–92.)   G.A. Oxon 8° 360 = R.

89. HOLLAND, T. E., The origin of the University of Oxford. (Eng. hist.
rev., 1891, vol. 6, p. 238–49.)   Per. 2231 d. 342 = K.

90. LEACH, A. F., Origin of Oxford. (Nat. rev., 1896, vol. 28, p. 93–102.)
Per. 22775 d. 14

Medieval (1200–1499)

91. Rotuli Parliamentorum ut et petitiones et placita in Parliamento tempore Edwardi r. i. (–Henry vii). [Ed. by J. Strachey.] 6 vols. [Lond.,
1767–77], fol.   Vet. A 5 b. 46 = R.
— Index [ed. in part by J. Strachey and J. Pridden, and completed by
E. Upham]. Lond., 1832, fol.   Vet. A 5 b. 46 = R.

92. PAULI, R., Bischof Grosseteste und Adam von Marsh, ein Beitrag zur
älteren Geschichte der Universität Oxford. (Verzeichniss d. Doctoren
. . . in Tübingen, 1863–64.) Tübingen, 1864, 4°. 44 pp.
Diss. Y 1 (27)

93. ANSTEY, H., ed., Munimenta academica, or Documents illustrative of
academical life and studies at Oxford. Pt. 1. Libri cancellarii et procuratorum. Pt. 2. Libri cancellarii et procuratorum, accedunt Acta
Curiæ cancellarii et memoranda ex registris nonnulla. (Rerum Britanni-
carum medii ævi scriptores, vol. 50.) 2 vols. Lond., 1868, 8°.
Rolls ser. 50

94. GASCOIGNE, T., Loci e libro veritatum: passages selected from Gascoigne's Theological dictionary illustrating the condition of Church
and State, 1403–58, ed. J. E. Thorold Rogers. (Oxford univ. *passim*.)
Oxf., 1881, 8°. xiv+254 pp.   Clar. Press 31 a. 144

95. HENSON, H. H., ed., Letters relating to Oxford in the 14th century,
from originals in the Public Record Office and British Museum. (Oxf.
hist. soc., 1885, vol. 5, p. 1–56.)   G.A. Oxon 8° 360 = R.

96. BRODRICK, G. C., Oxford in the Middle Ages. (Macmillan's mag., 1887, vol. 56, p. 150–60.) Per. 2705 d. 254

97. BREWER, H. W., Mediæval Oxford. Lond., 1891, obl. 8°. 16 pp.
G.A. Oxon 8° 987

98. PROTHERO, R. E., 1st baron Ernle, Oxford before the Reformation [by R. E. Prothero]. (Quarterly review, 1892, vol. 174, p. 1–32.)
Per. 3977 e. 191

99. RASHDALL, H., The universities of Europe in the Middle ages. (Oxford, vol. 2, pt. 2.) Oxf., 1895, 8°. 260 d. 22
— New ed., ed. by F. M. Powicke and A. B. Emden. (Oxford, vol. 3.) Oxf., 1936, 8°. 2625 d. 159 = R.

100. Oxford in the 13th century. (Macmillan's mag., 1895/96, vol. 73, p. 99–105.) Per. 2705 d. 254

101. Parliamentary petitions relating to Oxford, ed. by L. Toulmin Smith. (Oxf. hist. soc., 1896, vol. 32, p. 77–161.) G.A. Oxon 8° 360 = R.

102. ANSTEY, H., ed., Epistolae Academicae Oxon. (Registrum F.) A collection of letters and other documents illustrative of the academical life and studies at Oxford in the 15th century (1421–1509). 2 pt. (Oxf. hist. soc., vol. 35, 36.) Oxf., 1898, 8°. G.A. Oxon 8° 360 = R.

103. MILBURN, J. B., University life in mediæval Oxford. (Dublin review, 1901, N.S., vol. 129, p. 72–97.) Per. 3977 e. 199

104. SALTER, H. E., The Stamford schism. (Eng. hist. review, 1922, vol. 37, p. 249–53.) Per. 2231 d. 342 = K.

105. SALTER, H. E., ed., Snappe's Formulary, and other records. (Oxf. hist. soc., vol. 80.) Oxf., 1924, 8°. 404 pp. G.A. Oxon 8° 360 = R.

106. SALTER, H. E., History revision. The medieval university of Oxford. (History, 1929, vol. 14, p. 57–61.) Per. 26333 d. 106 = S.

107. SALTER, H. E., ed., Registrum cancellarii Oxoniensis, 1434–1469. 2 vols. (Oxf. hist. soc., vol. 93, 94.) Oxf., 1932, 8°.
G.A. Oxon 8° 360 = R.

108. SCHACHNER, N., The mediaeval universities. (Oxford passim.) Lond., 1938, 8°. 388 pp. 260 e. 126

109. Formularies which bear on the history of Oxford, c. 1204–1420, ed. by H. E. Salter, W. A. Pantin, H. G. Richardson. 2 vols. (Oxf. hist. soc., N.S., vol. 4, 5.) Oxf., 1942, 8°. G.A. Oxon 8° 360 = R.

110. POWICKE, F. M., The alleged migration of the University of Oxford to Northampton in 1264. (Oxoniensia, 1943/44, vol. 8/9, p. 107–11.)
Per. G.A. Oxon 4° 658 = R.

111. HILL, R. M. T., Oliver Sutton, bishop of Lincoln, and the University of Oxford. (Trans., Roy. hist. soc., 1949, ser. 4, vol. 31, p. 1–16.)
Per. 2262 e. 99 = K.

112. POWICKE, F. M., Ways of medieval life and thought. (Oxford *passim*.) Lond., [1950], 8°. 255 pp.   22215 e. 14

113. EDWARDS, K., The activities of some fellows of De Vaux college, Salisbury, at Oxford and elsewhere. (Oxoniensia, 1955, vol. 19, p. 61–91.)   Per. G.A. Oxon 4° 658 = R.

114. MITCHELL, R. J., John Free, from Bristol to Rome in the 15th century. (Chapter 2, Oxford: 1445–1456.) Lond. &c., 1955, 8°.
                                                              2998 e. 90

115. KIBRE, P., Scholarly privileges in the Middle ages: the rights, privileges and immunities of scholars and universities at Bologna, Padua, Paris, and Oxford. (Medieval acad. of America, 72.) Lond., 1961, 4°. 446 pp.   Soc. 3974 d. 332 (72)

Sixteenth century

116. PLUMMER, C., *ed.*, Elizabethan Oxford, reprints of rare tracts [i. N. Fierberti Oxoniensis academiæ descriptio, 1602. ii. L. Hutten on The antiquities of Oxford. iii. Queen Elizabeth at Oxford, 1566. A. Johannis Berebloci Commentarii. B. Academiæ Oxoniensis topographica delineatio per T. Nelum. C. Of the Actes done at Oxford by N. Robinson. D. A brief rehearsal, by R. Stephens. iv. Queen Elizabeth at Oxford, 1592. v. Apollinis et musarum eidyllia per J. Sanfordum, 1592]. (Oxf. hist. soc., vol. 8.) Oxf., 1887, 8°. 316 pp.
                                              G.A. Oxon 8° 360 = R.

117. A University entertainment in 1583. [Transcript of a bill of accounts incurred by the University in entertaining Albert Laski, prince of Sieradz.] (Oxf. mag., 1911, vol. 30, p. 85, 86.)   Per. G.A. Oxon 4° 141

117.5. ROTH, C., Oxford starrs. (Oxoniensia, 1957, vol. 22, p. 63–77.)
                                              Per. G.A. Oxon 4° 658 = R.

See 76 [Curtis, M. H., Oxford and Cambridge in transition, 1558–1642. 1959]. See also 282, 291, 546–49.

Seventeenth century
General

118. PATTISON, M., A chapter of university history [in the 17th century]. (Macmillan's mag., 1875, vol. 32, p. 237–46; 308–13.)
                                                        Per. 2705 d. 254

119. Thomas Baskerville's Account of Oxford, written in 1683–6, ed. by H. Baskerville. (Oxf. hist. soc., 1905, vol. 47, p. 175–226.)
                                              G.A. Oxon 8° 360 = R.

120. A seventeenth century visitor to Oxford [Joachim Moors or Morsius]. (Oxf. mag., 1932, vol. 50, p. 388, 89.)   Per. G.A. Oxon 4° 141

121. PECOVER, R. A., Haydn's visit to Oxford. (Oxf. mag., 1932, vol. 50, p. 586, 87.)   Per. G.A. Oxon 4° 141

122. WOOD, A. à, The life and times of Anthony Wood, antiquary of Oxford, 1632–1695, described by himself, collected from his diaries and other papers by A. Clark. 5 vols. (Oxf. hist. soc., 19, 21, 26, 30, 40.) Oxf., 1891–1900, 8°.   G.A. Oxon 8° 360 = R.

123. WOOD, A. à, The life and times of Anthony à Wood, abridged from A. Clark's edition, and with an intr. by L. Powys. Lond., 1932, 4°. 319 pp.   G.A. Oxon 4° 515

124. The life and times of Anthony à Wood, abridged from Andrew Clark's edition, with an intr. by L. Powys. (World's classics.) Lond. &c., 1961, 16°. 372 pp.   G.A. Oxon 16° 234

See 76 [Curtis, M. H., Oxford and Cambridge in transition, 1558–1642. 1959].

Civil War and Commonwealth

125. His majesties two letters, one to the . . . Vniversity of Oxford: the other to the high sheriff of the county and to the major of the city of Oxford. [Thanks for a loan of money; promises of protection. The second letter commends the protection of the University to the sheriff and mayor.] [Madan 1016.] Lond., 1642, 4°. 8 pp.
Antiq. e. E. 1642. 16

126. True news from Oxford, a relation of the magnificent valour of the scholars . . . [Madan 1029.] Lond., 1642, 4°. 8 pp.
Antiq. e. E. 1642. 18

127. Exceeding true newes from Boston, Sherbourne castle, Oxford . . . [Madan 1035.] Lond., 1642, 4°. 8 pp.   B.M.

128. Vniversity newes, or, The vnfortunate proceedings of the cavaliers in Oxford, wherein is declared the severall misdemeanors and uncivill behaviour of the . . . troopers which came . . . to assist the schollers against the Parliament . . . [Madan 1037.] Lond., 1642, 4°. 8 pp.
Antiq. e. E. 1642. 119 (2)

129. PINKE, R., A letter sent from the provost vice-chancellour of Oxford to the . . . earle of Pembrooke, lord chancellour of Oxford. Together with his lordships answer. [Madan 1038.] Lond., 1642, 4°. 5 pp.
Gough Oxf. 8 (10)

130. [Relation of the capture of Oxford scholars by London troopers. Also an account of the entry into the city and the damage done by the troopers.] (The Cavalliers advice to his maiesty, p. 3–6.) [Madan 1039.] Lond., 1642, 4°.   B.M.

131. A perfect diurnall of the passages of the souldiers that are under the command of the lord Say in Oxford. From the 9th of Septemb. to the 6th of Octob. [Madan 1042.] Lond., 1642, 4°. 8 pp.   B.M.

132. TOLSON, J., Mr. Vice-chancellors speech to his majestie at Christ Church . . . on new yeares day: when, in the name of the whole

Vniversitie, he presented . . . a faire guilt cup and two hundred pounds
of gold in it. [Madan 1159.] Oxf. [really Lond.], 1643, 4°. 8 pp.
                                                    Antiq. e. E. 1643. 114
— [Repr.] (Somer's tracts, 1750, vol. 2, p. 126.)   GG 137 Art.
— [Repr.] (Somer's tracts, 2nd ed., 1810, vol. 4, p. 484.)   Σ III 14

133. A speech delivered by the kings . . . majestie, in the Convocation
     house . . . expressing his intentions of abiding there . . . [Madan 1170.]
     Oxf. [really Lond.], 1643, 4°. 8 pp.   Antiq. e. E. 1643. 3

134. [Begin.] Charles R. His majesty taking into his princely consideration
     . . . [An official order for collections to be made in college chapels and
     city churches, for the relief of wounded soldiers.] [Madan 1345.] Oxf.,
     1643, s. sh.   Wood 276 a (126)

135. [Begin.] His majesty pittying . . . [Notice by the king ordering a
     general collection on Sunday Oct. 1, 1643, in all churches and chapels
     in Oxford at morning prayer, for sick and maimed soldiers.] [Madan
     1457.] Oxf., (1643), s. sh.   MS. Rawl. D 399 (f. 207)

136. By the king. A proclamation touching the lodgers in the Vniversity
     and City of Oxford. [Madan 1461.] Oxf., (1643), s. sh.   P.C.O.

137. By the king. A proclamation for the speedy clearing of lodgings
     for accommodation of the members of both Houses, summoned to
     assemble in Oxford, the two and twentieth day of . . . Ianuary.
     [Madan 1514.] Oxf., 1643, s. sh.   Don. b. 4 (29)

138. By the king. A proclamation for the better defence of the kings royall
     person, and of the Vniversity and City of Oxford. [Madan 1617.] Oxf.,
     1644, s. sh.   Sutherland 80 (366)

139. By the king. A proclamation for the better defence of the kings royall
     person, and of this Vniversitie and City. [Madan 1646.] Oxf., 1644,
     s. sh.   P.C.O.

140. DUPPA, B., Two prayers; one for the safety of his majesties person;
     the other for the preservation of this University and City of Oxford.
     [Madan 1648.] Oxf., 1644, 4°. 8 pp.   Wood 514 (14)

141. [Begin.] Having taken speciall notice . . . [An order that all suitable
     persons at Oxford shall enlist forthwith in the Lord keeper's or the earl
     of Dover's regiment during the king's short absence.] [Madan 1689.]
     Oxf., (1644), s. sh.   MS. Tanner 61 (f. 165)

142. An humble petition of the Vniversity and City of Oxford; lately
     presented to his majestie for a speedy accommodation of peace,
     between himselfe and his high court of Parliament. Together with
     his majesties gracious answer. [Madan 1754.] Lond., [1644], 4°.
     8 pp.   G. Pamph. 2288 (8)

143. An account of the musterings of the University of Oxford, with other
     things that happened there, from Aug. 9. 1642 to July 15th, 1643 in-
     clusively. From an original MS. . . . written as it seems by mr. Brian

Twyne. (Chronicon sive annales prioratus Dunstaple, T. Hearnius descripsit, 1733, tom. 2, p. 737–87.)   Mus. Bibl. II 98

144. RIGAUD, G., The lines formed round Oxford, with notices of the part taken by the University in behalf of the royalist cause, between 1642 and 1646. (Archaeol. journ., 1851, vol. 8, p. 366–82.)
G.A. Gen. top. 8° 529 = R.
See also Visitations, 1526–63.

145. Sundry things from severall hands concerning the University of Oxford: viz. i. A petition from some well-affected therein. ii. A modell for a colledge reformation [Christ Church is selected as a specimen]. iii. Queries concerning the said University and several persons therein. [Madan 2430.] Lond., 1659, 4°. 12 pp.   Wood 515 (22)
— [Another ed.] (Harl. misc., vol. 6, p. 79.) 1745.   GG 129 Art.
— [Another ed.] (Harl. misc., vol. 6, p. 86.) 1810.   Σ III 6

See 1562 [Burrows, M., Some account of the state of the University during the Commonwealth, 1881].

146. Oxford under the Puritans. (Quarterly review, 1882, vol. 154, p. 469–94.)   Per. 3977 e. 191

Restoration and James II

147. CHAMBERLAYNE, E., The second part of The present state of England. 2nd ed. [First publ. with the 5th ed. of part 1.] (Oxf. univ., p. 283–95.) Lond., 1671, 12°.   Hope adds. 174
[Other eds. publ. up to the 38th ed. in 1755: Hope adds. 175–205. The 21st ed. onwards continued by J. Chamberlayne.]

148. Correspondence of Henry, earl of Clarendon and James, earl of Abingdon, chiefly relating to the Monmouth insurrection, 1683–1685. (Oxf. hist. soc., 1896, vol. 32, p. 245–78.)   G.A. Oxon 8° 360 = R.

149. NEALE, C. M., Oxford annals, 1st draft of a specimen year (1687). Oxf., 1914, 8°. 9 pp.   G.A. Oxon 8° 892

William III and Anne

150. HARTSHORNE, A., Oxford in the time of William III and Anne, 1691–1712. Some notes on a collection of letters. [Pt.] 1–3. (Oxf. mag., 1910, vol. 29, p. 27, 28; 41–44; 59–62.)   Per. G.A. Oxon 4° 141

Eighteenth century

General

151. WENDEBORN, G. F. A., Beyträge zur Kenntnis Grosbritanniens vom Jahr 1779 [by G. F. A. Wendeborn] herausg. von G. Forster. (Oxford *passim*.) Lemgo, 1780, 8°.   B.M.
— [Another ed., *entitled*] Der Zustand des Staats, der Religion . . . gegen das Ende des 18. Jahrhunderts. 4 Th. Berl., 1785–88, 8°.   B.M.

— Tr. by the author. [*Entitled*] A view of England . . . (Universities,
vol. 2, p. 139–71.) Lond., 1791, 8°.   Douce W 186
— 2nd ed. Dubl., 1791.

152. Reliquiae Hearnianae: The remains of Thomas Hearne, extr. from
his MS. diaries by P. Bliss. 2 vols. Oxf., 1857, 8°.
                                         Mus. Bibl. II 112, 113
— 2nd ed., enlarged. 3 vols. Lond., 1869, 8°.   Mus. Bibl. II 114–16

153. Remarks and collections of Thomas Hearne [1705–35], ed. by C. E.
Doble (D. W. Rannie, H. E. Salter). 11 vols. (Oxf. hist. soc., vol. 2, 7,
13, 34, 42, 43, 48, 50, 65, 67, 72.) Oxf., 1885–1921, 8°.
                                         G.A. Oxon 8° 360 = R.

154. ROBERTSON, G., and GREEN, J. R., Oxford during the last century,
being two series of papers published in the Oxford Chronicle & Berks
& Bucks gazette during the year 1859. [By G. Robertson and J. R.
Green.] Oxf., 1859 [and 1860], 4°. 131 pp.   G.A. Oxon 4° 18

155. GREEN, J. R., and ROBERTSON, G., Studies in Oxford history, chiefly
in the 18th century, ed. by C. L. Stainer. [Papers additional to the
publication in 1859 are included.] (Oxf. hist. soc., vol. 41.) Oxf., 1901,
8°. 361 pp.   G.A. Oxon 8° 360 = R.

156. HAVERFIELD, F. J., Extracts from the 'Gentleman's magazine' relating to Oxford, 1731–1800. (Oxf. hist. soc., 1890, vol. 16, p. 417–48.)
                                         G.A. Oxon 8° 360 = R.

157. GODLEY, A. D., Oxford in the eighteenth century. Lond., 1908, 8°.
291 pp.   G.A. Oxon 8° 760

158. WOODFORDE, J., The diary of a country parson, 1758 (–1802) ed. by
J. Beresford. 5 vols. Lond., 1924–31, 8°.   211 d. 183

159. WOODFORDE, J., Woodforde. Passages from the five volumes of the
Diary of a country parson, 1758–1802, selected and ed. by J. Beresford.
Lond., 1935, 8°. 534 pp.   211 d. 371

160. WARD, W. R., Georgian Oxford: University politics in the eighteenth
century. Oxf., 1958, 8°. 296 pp.   G.A. Oxon 8° 1360 = R.

1714–1717 Jacobite disturbance

161. [*Begin.*] At a general meeting of the vice-chancellor, heads of houses
. . . Aug. 4. 1714. [Offering a reward for the discovery of the author of
a treasonable letter directed to the mayor of the City.] [Oxf.], (1714),
s. sh.   MS. Hearne's Diaries 51 (45e)

162. The Jacobite memorial: a true copy of the letter sent to mr. Broad-
water, mayor of Oxford, with the proceedings of that loyal University
and City relating thereunto. Lond., 1714, 8°. 8+31 pp.
                                         G.A. Oxon 8° 68 (1)

163. AYLIFFE, J., The antient and present state of the University of
Oxford. 2 vols. Lond., 1714, 8°.   Gough Oxf. 1, 2
—[Another ed.] 1723.   G.A. Oxon 8° 1096, 1097

164. The case of dr. Ayliffe at Oxford, giving First, An account of the . . .
prosecution of him . . . for . . . a book entituled The ancient and present
state of the University of Oxford: and, Secondly, An account of the
proceedings had against him in his own college. Lond., 1716, 8°.
xxvi+98+xiv pp.   G.A. Oxon 8° 59 (5)

165. An answer to some passages in The case of dr. Ayliffe at Oxford.
n. pl., [c. 1716], 4°.   Gough Oxf. 136 (10)

166. A brief state of dr. Ayliffe's case at Oxford. n. pl., [1716], s. sh.
                                             MS. Rawl. J fol. 2 (f. 112)

167. RAWLINSON, R., A full and impartial account of the Oxford-riots. In
a letter from a member of the University [R. Rawlinson]. Lond., 1715,
8°. 24 pp.   G.A. Oxon 8° 59 (7)

168. The speech of a member of the Constitution-club at Oxford, Feb. 9.
1715–16, being his defence against certain articles exhibited against
him and several other gentlemen in the Chancellor's court there.
Lond., 1716, 8°. 35 pp.   Gough Oxf. 113 (6)

169. GINGLE, J., The severall depositions concerning the late riot in Oxford. [By J. Gingle.] Lond., 1716, 8°. 38 pp.   G.A. Oxon 8° 59 (8)

170. GARDINER, B., A plain relation of some late passages at Oxford. Part
the first. [With] Appendix. [By B. Gardiner.] Oxf., 1717, 4°. 14+16 pp.
                                                 Gough Oxf. 105 (12)

171. The severall papers which were laid before . . . the Lords . . . in
Parliament . . . relating to the riots at Oxford . . . with the resolutions
of the House thereupon. Lond., 1717, fol. 36 pp.
                                                 Gough Oxf. 103 (24)

172. Reasons for a royal visitation; occasion'd by the present great defec-
tion of the clergy from the government shewing the absolute necessity
of purging the universities and restoring discipline to the Church.
Lond., 1717, 8°. 64 pp.   Gough Oxf. 113 (7)

1745–1755 Jacobite disturbance

173. Epistola objurgatoria ad Guilielmum King. [*Followed by*] Epistola
canonici reverendi admodum ad archidiaconum reverendum admodum. [Really by W. King]. Lond., 1744, 4°. 30 pp.
                                                 Gough Oxf. 144 (2)
— [Another ed. No 'Eratum' on p. 30].   Gough Oxf. 81 (3)

174. A letter to a friend occasioned by Epistola objurgatoria, &c. By
S.P.Y.B. [i.e. S. Parker, Yeoman Bedel, but probably by W. King].
Lond., 1744, 4°. 15 pp.   Gough Oxf. 144 (3)

175. A chiding letter to S.P.Y.B. [Samuel Parker, Yeoman Bedel] in defence of Epistola objurgatoria [by W. King]. Lond., 1744 [45], 8°. 19 pp.   G.A. Oxon 8° 219 (2)

176. BENTHAM, E., A letter to a young gentleman of Oxford. [An anti-Jacobite pamphlet.] Oxf., 1748, 8°. 30 pp.   G.A. Oxon 8° 232 (1)
— 2nd ed. 1749. 32 pp.   G. Pamph. 204
— 3rd ed. 1749. [The Bodleian copy is imperf.]   G.A. Oxon 8° 61

177. KING, W., A proposal for publishing a poetical translation both in Latin and English of . . . tutor Bentham's Letter to a young gentleman of Oxford. By a master of arts. [W. King.] Lond., 1748, 8°. 32 pp.
                                                            G. Pamph. 88 (3)
— 2nd ed. 1749. 40 pp.   G.A. Oxon 8° 61 (6)

178. KING, W., A poetical abridgement both in Latin and English, of . . . mr. tutor Bentham's Letter to a young gentleman of Oxford. To which are added Some remarks on the letter to a fellow of a college. By the author of the Proposal, &c. [W. King.] Lond. 1749, 8°. 61 pp.
                                                            G.A. Oxon 8° 6 (6)

179. BENTHAM, E., A letter to a fellow of a college, being the sequel of a Letter to a young gentleman of Oxford. Lond. &c., 1749, 8°. 72 pp.
                                                            G. Pamph. 88 (4)

180. A certain proposal of a certain little tutor [E. Bentham] for making certain reformations in a certain method of education most certainly practis'd in a certain university. [In verse.] Lond., [c. 1749], 8°. 7 pp.
                                                            G.A. Oxon 8° 165 (10)

181. A case of conscience, humbly put to the . . . University of Oxford. Whether one may take the oaths to king George: and yet, consistently with honour . . . do all one can in favour of the Pretender? Lond., [1749], 8°. 28 pp.   Vet. A 4 e. 422 (4)
— 2nd ed., with additions [*entitled*] Oxford honesty: or, A case of conscience . . . Lond., [1749], 8°. 39 pp.   G.A. Oxon 8° 62 (2)
— 3rd ed. [1749].   G.A. Oxon 8° 1000 (9)

182. COADE, G., A blow at the root: or, An attempt to prove that no time ever was . . . so proper and convenient as the present, for introducing a further reformation into our national church, universities and schools, by an impartial hand. [By G. Coade. Oxf. univ. *passim*.] Lond., 1749, 4°. 87 pp.   Gough Oxf. 68 (15)

183. KING, W., Oratio in Theatro Sheldoniano habita idibus Aprilibus, MDCCXLIX, die dedicationis Bibliothecæ Radclivianæ. Lond. &c., (1749), 4°. 34 pp.   Gough Oxf. 81 (5)
— [Another ed.] (Opera G. King, vol. 1.) [1754].   GG 43 Art.

184. Carmen rhythmicum, monachicum, Momo dicatum, a rusticante Oxoniensi in honorem literatissimi ******** conscriptum. Lond., 1749, 8°. 24 pp.   Gough Oxf. 81 (6)

185. SQUIRE, S., Remarks on dr. K---- 's speech . . . at the dedication of
dr. R-----'s library, xiiith of April, MDCCXLIX. By Phileleutherus
Londinensis [S. Squire. Sometimes ascr. to J. Burton]. Lond., 1750,
8°. 45 pp.   Gough Oxf. 81 (7)

186. KING, W., A translation of a late celebrated oration [no. 183] occasioned by a lible, entitled Remarks on doctor K—g's speech. Lond.,
1750, 8°. 54 pp.   G.A. Oxon 8° 62 (3)

187. BURTON, J., An answer to dr. King's speech. Oxf., [c. 1750], s. sh.
                                                    Gough Oxf. 81 (8)
— 3rd ed., enlarged. s. sh.   Gough Oxf. 81 (9)

188. The old lady in her tantarums; or, Mother Oxford ranting at her
eldest son K--ng, being a translation of part of an epistle lately published by J. B[urton]. By a school-boy at Eton [W. King?]. Eton, 1750,
8°. 28 pp.   Gough Oxf. 81 (16)

189. KING, W., Elogium famæ inserviens Jacci Etonensis, sive Gigantis;
or, The praises of Jack of Eton, commonly called Jack the Giant [i.e.
J. Burton]. By a master of arts [W. King]. Oxf., 1750, 8°. 96 pp.
                                                    G.A. Oxon 8° 6 (9)

190. KING, W., The wonder of wonders, or, Fresh intelligence from Eton,
a character of . . . John Burton [by W. King]. [Oxf., 1750], s. sh.
                                                    G. Pamph. 1675 (31)

191. WALPOLE, H., Delenda est Oxonia [ed. by P. Toynbee. A pamphlet
written in 1749 aimed at asserting the liberties of the University by
suggesting a parallel between the actions of James II and the resolution
of the Ministry to vest the nomination of the Chancellorship of the
University in the king]. (Engl. hist. review, 1927, vol. 42, p. 95–108.)
                                                    Per. 2231 d. 342 = K.

192. HENLEY, J., Law and arguments in vindication of the University of
Oxford: in two seasonable discourses. i. On the question whether the
law of England countenances the interposition of extrinsecal authority,
in . . . universities and colleges . . . ii. A detection of the main primary
author [N. Amhurst] of the imputation of Jacobitism in the University
of Oxford. [By J. Henley.] Lond., [1749], 8°. 29 pp.
                                                    Gough Oxf. 44 (4)

193. BROOKE, H., A letter to the Oxford Tories, by an Englishman [H.
Brooke]. Lond., 1750, 8°. 26 pp.   G. Pamph. 204 (4)

194. BLACOW, R., A letter to William King . . . containing a particular
account of the treasonable riot at Oxford, in Feb. 1747. Lond., 1755,
8°. 48 pp.   Gough Oxf. 131 (10)
—2nd ed. 1755.   G.A. Oxon 8° 60 (2)

195. A letter [signed A.M.] from a member of the University of Oxford to
a gentleman in the country; containing a particular of a watch-plot
lately discovered there . . . Lond., 1755, 8°. 16 pp.
                                                    Gough Oxf. 131 (9)

196. Informations and other papers relating to the treasonable verses
found at Oxford, July 17. 1754. Oxf., 1755, 8°. 45 pp.
G.A. Oxon 8° 60 (1)

197. A satire upon physicians, or, An English paraphrase, with notes and
references, of dr. King's . . . oration delivered at the dedication of the
Radclivian library in Oxford. To which is added, A curious petition to
an hon. house, in favour of dr. King. Lond., 1755, 8°. 63 pp.
Gough Oxf. 81 (14)

198. Doctor King's apology: or, Vindication of himself from the several
matters charged on him by the Society of informers. Oxf., 1755, 4°.
46 pp.   Gough Oxf. 81 (10)
— 2nd ed. 1755. 47 pp.   Gough Oxf. 81 (11)

199. NEWTON, R., The principles of the University of Oxford as far as relates to affection to the government stated [by R. Newton, who states
that this is a chapter of a larger work, and defends himself against a
'Mr. D.']. Lond., 1755, 8°. 23 pp.   G.A. Oxon 8° 165 (8)

200. A letter to doctor King, occasion'd by his late Apology, and, in particular, by such parts of it as are meant to defame mr. Kennicott,
fellow of Exeter college. By a friend to mr. Kennicott. Lond., 1755,
8°. 148 pp.   Gough Oxf. 81 (12)

201. An answer to mr. B —— w's [Blacow's] apology as it respects his
king, his country, his conscience, and his god, by a student of Oxford.
Lond., 1755, 8°. 30 pp.   G.A. Oxon 8° 60 (3)

See also 7260–65 [Various polemics about the conduct of Exeter college during
the 1754 election].

202. A new speech from the old trumpeter of liberty hall [W. King]; in
English: with a few gentle animadversions. [Signed Oxoniensis, R.
Jenner.] Lond., [1756], 8°. 28 pp.   G.A. Oxon 8° 60 (10)

203. KING, W., Oratiuncula habita in domo Convocationis, Oxon. die
Oct. 27. 1756 [by W. King]. Publ. et illustr. notis criticis, politicis, et
satiricis j. c. prof. reg. [R. Jenner. A mock criticism by W. King of his
own speech [no. 202] parodying Jenner's Latin style.] Oxon. &c.,
1757, 4°. xvi+24 pp.   Gough Oxf. 81 (17)

204. VARLEY, F. J., The treasonable riot outside Oriel college [23rd Feb.,
1747]. (Oriel record, 1929, vol. 5, p. 65–69.)   Per. G.A. Oxon 4° 485

Nineteenth century

205. State of the universities. (Quarterly review, 1827, vol. 36. Oxf.
passim in p. 216–68.)   Per. 3977 e. 191

206. Oxford as it is, a letter to a noble lord, by a foreigner of rank [signed
L. de G. . .]. Lond., 1834, 8°. 40 pp.   G.A. Oxon 8° 1001 (16)

207. State of Oxford university. (Eclectic review, 1837, N.S., vol. 2, p. 1–
27, 121–37.)   Per. 3977 e. 76

208. PERRY, W. C., German views of Oxford and Cambridge. [Remarks on a lecture by prof. Helmholtz on academical freedom in German universities.] (Macmillan's mag., 1878, vol. 37, p. 406–10.)
G.A. Oxon 4° 581 (19)

209. PRAT, F., Oxford — une journée d'étudiant. (Études relig., phil., hist. et litt., publ. par des pères de la Compagnie de Jésus, 1892, tom. 56, p. 82–104.)   G.A. Oxon 4° 419

210. Oxford as seen by a Frenchman. [An account of F. Prat's Oxford, with translated quotations.] (Month, 1892, vol. 75, p. 161–71.)
Per. 11132 d. 17

211. SMITH, GOLDWIN, Oxford revisited. (Fortnightly rev., 1894, vol. 61, p. 149–58.)   Per. 3977 d. 59

212. BIGGE, L. A. SELBY-, Practical Oxford: a reply to professor Goldwin-Smith. (Contemp. rev., 1894, vol. 65, p. 722–34.)   Per. 3977 d. 58

213. BRODRICK, G. C., The University of Oxford in 1898. (Nineteenth cent., 1898, vol. 44, p. 208–23.)   Per. 3977 d. 66

214. KNICKERBOCKER, W. S., Creative Oxford, its influence in Victorian literature. New York, 1925, 8°. ix+224 pp.   G.A. Oxon 8° 1089

215. MACAN, R. W., Oxford in the 'seventies. [Historical retrospect.] (Roy. soc. of lit. of the U.K., The Eighteen-seventies, ed. by H. Granville-Barker, 1929, p. 210–48.)   Soc. 3962 e. 161 = S.

216. VOLLRATH, W., Verschwiegenes Oxford; Matthew Arnold, Goethe und Walter Pater. Heidelberg, [1951], 4°. 52 pp.   G.A. Oxon 4° 675

216.5. WARD, W. R., Victorian Oxford. Lond., 1965, 8°. 431 pp.
G.A. Oxon 8° 1512 = R.

Twentieth century
General

217. WARREN, SIR T. H., Oxford in 1903 [by sir T. H. Warren]. (Edinb. review, 1903, vol. 198, p. 513–33.)   Per. 3977 e. 190

218. MAUDE, H. C., Oxford since 1880: gains and losses. 1, 2. (Oxf. mag., 1931, vol. 50, p. 235–38; 274–76.)   Per. G.A. Oxon 4° 141

219. PHELPS, L. R., Oxford since 1910. (Oxf. mag., 1935, vol. 53, p. 566–68.)   Per. G.A. Oxon 4° 141

220. BARKER, E., Changing Oxford. (Fortnightly review, 1937, vol. 147, p. 175–83.)   Per. 3977 d. 59

221. PROUDFOOT, M., The role of Oxford in the post-war world. (Nineteenth century, 1947, vol. 141, p. 168–73.)   Per. 3977 d. 66

222. Oxford—a future for our university, a statement for discussion prepared by the University branch of the Communist party. Oxf., [1951], 8°. 35 pp.   G.A. Oxon 8° 1230 (1)

223. LENNARD, R., Oxford through half a century. (Quart. review, 1954, vol. 292, p. 72–84.) Per. 3977 e. 191

224. OAKES, G. W., Oxford today. (Amer. Oxonian, 1958, vol. 45, p. 59–62.) Per. G.A. Oxon 8° 889

224.1. GILBERT, E. W., The university town in England and West Germany: Marburg, Göttingen, Heidelberg and Tübingen viewed comparatively with Oxford and Cambridge. (Univ. of Chicago, dept. of geogr., research paper 71.) Chicago, 1961, 8°. 74 pp. 2625 d. 199 = G.

1914–1918 War

225. POOLE, R., Oxford in war time [1914–18]. [Typewritten.] [Oxf., 1918], 4°. 12 pp. G.A. Oxon 4° 556

226. STALLYBRASS, W. T. S., Oxford in 1914–1918. (Oxford, 1939, vol. 6, no. 2, p. 31–45.) Per. G.A. Oxon 8° 1141

227. JOSEPH, H. W. B., Oxford in the last war [signed H.W.B.J.]. I, II. (Oxf. mag., 1941, vol. 59, p. 308–10; 326, 27.) Per. G.A. Oxon 4° 141

1939–1945 War

228. B., D.W., The University and conscription. (Oxf. mag., 1939, vol. 57, p. 561–64.) Per. G.A. Oxon 4° 141

229. NORWOOD, SIR C., Oxford to-day. (Oxford, 1939, vol. 6, no. 2, p. 18–30.) Per. G.A. Oxon 8° 1141

230. BOWRA, SIR C. M., Conditions at Oxford in war-time. (Oxford, 1940, vol. 6, no. 3, p. 36–42.) Per. G.A. Oxon 8° 1141

231. STALLYBRASS, W. T., Oxford in war-time. (Amer. Oxon., 1941, vol. 28, p. 97–101.) Per. G.A. Oxon 8° 889

232. MAIS, S. P. B., Oxford in war-time. (Country Life, 1941, vol. 90, p. 280–82.) Per. 384 b. 6

233. S., R.H., Civil defence in the University and colleges. (Oxf. mag., 1942, vol. 61, p. 6, 7.) Per. G.A. Oxon 4° 141

234. ROWSE, A. L., Oxford in war-time. (Engl. spirit, 1944, p. 260–65.) 27001 e. 1582

Racial and regional groups within the University

235. [Expulsion of the Irish from Oxford.] (1 Hen. V, c. 8, Pub.) (In this volume are contained the statutes made . . . from . . . Henry the thirde vnto the fyrste yere of . . . Henry the viii.) Lond., 1543, fol. L.L.
— 1 Hen. VI, c. 3, Pub.
— 2 Hen. VI, c. 8, Pub.
— 17 Edw. IV. (Rotuli Parl., 1777, vol. 6, p. 192.)

236. LINDSAY, T. M., Scotch students at Oxford 500 years ago. (Macmillan's mag., 1870, vol. 22, p. 230–35.) Per. 2705 d. 254.

237. YOUNG, R. F., Bohemian scholars and students at the English universities from 1347 to 1750. (Engl. hist. review, 1923, vol. 38, p. 72–84.)
Per. 2231 d. 342 = K.
— Repr.   2625 d. 53 (12)

238. JACOBOWSKY, C. V., Svenska studenter i Oxford, *ca.* 1620–1740. (Personhistorisk tidskrift, 1927, p. 105–93.)
— [Repr.] 1928.   G.A. Oxon 8° 1055 (5)

239. YOUNG, R. F., A Bohemian philosopher at Oxford in the 17th century, George Ritschel. Lond., (1924), 8°. 24 pp.   2656 d. 29 (1)

240. YOUNG, R. F., A Bohemian scholar at Heidelberg and Oxford in the 16th century: Jan Bernart of Přerov, 1553–1600. (School of Slavonic studies, Univ. of London.) Lond., 1928, 8°. 20 pp.
G.A. Oxon 8° 1056 (4)

241. BOWEN, I., Cambrians in Oxford history. (Welsh outlook, 1929, vol. 16, p. 358–62.)   Per. 2292 d. 9

242. KIBRE, P., The nations in the mediaeval universities. (Oxford, p. 160–66.) (Medieval acad. of Amer., publ. 49.) Cambr., Mass., 1948, 8°.   Soc. 3974 d. 332 (49)

242.5. USHER, G., Welsh students at Oxford in the Middle Ages. (Univ. of Wales. Bull., Board of Celtic studies, 1956, vol. 16, p. 193–98.)
Soc. 397 d. 55

242.69. ROTH, C., The vicissitudes of the first Oxford Jewish graduate [Sacville Davis, 1862]. (Oxf. mag., 1963, N.S., vol. 3, p. 230–32.)
Per. G.A. Oxon 4° 141

242.7. HINNEBUSCH, W. A., Foreign Dominican students and professors at the Oxford Blackfriars. (Oxf. studies presented to D. Callus; Oxf. hist. soc., 1964, N.S., vol. 16, p. 101–34.)   G.A. Oxon 8° 360 = R.

242.71. EMDEN, A. B., Northerners and Southerners in the organization of the University to 1509. (Oxf. studies presented to D. Callus; Oxf. hist. soc., 1964, N.S., vol. 16, p. 1–30.)   G.A. Oxon 8° 360 = R.

ACCOUNTS BY VISITING TRAVELLERS

243. MALER, J. [An account of his visit to Oxford in 1551 is included in his autobiography in Band 6 of Bekenntnisse merkwürdiger Männer von sich selbst, herausg. von J. G. Müller.] Winterthur, 1810.
— 2e. Aufl. 1822.   B.M.

244. CHYTRAEUS, N., Hodoeporicon. Poematum Nathanis Chytraei praeter sacra omnium libri septendecim. [His visit to Oxford in 1566 is described.] Rostochii, 1579, 8°. 362 pp.   B.M.

245. RATHGEB, J., Kurtze und warhaffte Beschreibung der Badenfahrt. [Account of the visit to England in 1592 of Frederick I, duke of Württemberg.] Tübingen, 1602, 4°.   B.M.

— [Another ed., *entitled*] Warhaffte Beschreibung zweyer Raisen, welcher erste die Badenfahrt genannt . . . (Oxford, fol. 20ʳ–25ᵛ). Tübingen, 1603, 4°. 55 d. 82
— [Another ed.] 1604.
[Engl. transl. in no. 246.]

246. RYE, W. B., *ed.*, England as seen by foreigners in the days of Elizabeth and James i., comprising translations of the journals of the two dukes of Wirtemberg [Frederick and Louis Frederick] in 1592 [the account written by J. Rathgeb] and 1610, with extracts from the travels of foreign princes and others, notes by W. B. Rye. [Oxford univ., p. 20–30, &c.] Lond., 1865, 4°. 226 i. 42

247. LUDWIG, *Prinz von Anhalt-Köthen*, Reisebeschreibung. [A poem describing his visit to England in 1596. The poem is included in Accessiones historiae Anhaltinae, by J. C. Becmann. Zerbst, 1716, fol.] B.M.

247.1. BACHRACH, A. G. H., Sir Constantine Huygens and Britain: 1596–1687. (Oxford *passim*.) (Publ., Sir Thomas Browne inst., Leiden, Gen. ser., 1.) Leiden &c., 1962, 8°. 396 e. 195

248. HENTZNER, P., Itinerarium Germaniæ, Galliæ, Angliæ, Italiæ . . . (Oxford visited in 1598, p. 141–44.) Norinbergæ, 1612, 4°.
Douce HH 282
[Other Latin eds. publ. in 1617, 1629, and 1661.]
— A journey into England [with an Engl. tr. by R. Bentley, ed. by H. Walpole. Oxford, p. 59–65]. Printed at Strawberry-Hill, 1757, 8°.
G.A. Gen. top. 348
[Other eds. in 1761, 62, 65, 71, 97, 1807, 81, 1940.]

249. PLATTER, T., Englandfahrt im Jahre 1599, herausg. von H. Hecht. (Oxford, p. 115–20.) Halle/Saale, 1929, 8°. G.A. Gen. top. 8° 1046
— Thomas Platter's Travels, rendered into English by C. Williams. (Oxford, p. 216–20.) Lond., 1937, 8°. 247123 d. 48

250. GERSCHOW, F., Diary of the journey of . . . Philip Julius, duke of Stettin-Pomerania . . . 1602. [In German and English. Oxford, p. 41–49.] (Trans., Roy. hist. soc., 1892, N.S., vol. 6.) Soc. 2262 e. 45 = K.

251. The travels of Peter Mundy [Oxford, 1639]. (Hakluyt soc., N.S., vol. 55, p. 25–28.) Lond., 1925, 8°. Soc. 2031 d. 4 = G.

252. Landshöfdingen friherre Gabriel Kurcks lefnadsminnen uppteck-nade af honom själf, i tryck utg. af Finlands Statsarkiv genom R. Hausen. [A visit to Oxford in 1654, p. 52–57.] Helsingfors, 1906, 8°.
23994 e. 57

253. MONCONYS, B. DE, Iournal des voyages de monsieur de Monconys. [Oxf. visited in June 1663, pt. 2, p. 48–54.] à Lyon, 1666, 4°.
4° W 16 Art. BS.
— [Another ed.], p. 94–106. Par., 1695, 8°. 8° F 186 Linc.

254. SORBIÈRE, S., Relation d'un voyage en Angleterre [by S. Sorbière].
(Oxf. p. 94–107). Par., 1664, 16°. Wood 166
— [Another ed.] p. 77–88. Cologne, 1666, 12°. Mason FF 15
— [Another ed.] Done into English [*entitled*] A voyage to England.
Lond., 1709, 8°. Gough Gen. top. 326

255. A Frenchman at Oxford in 1665 [*sic*] [extr. from 'A voyage to England'
by Sorbière]. (Oxf. mag., 1889, vol. 7, p. 240, 41.)
Per. G.A. Oxon 4° 141

256. Travels of Cosmo the third, grand duke of Tuscany, through England
. . . 1669, tr. from the Ital. MS. at Florence. (Oxf. univ., p. 251–76.)
Lond., 1821, 4°. 4° BS. 796

257. HERDEGEN, J., Historische Nachricht von dess löblichen Hirten-
und Blumen-Ordens an der Pegnitz Anfang und Fortgang, verfasset
von dem Mitglied dieser Gesellschafft Amarantes [i.e. J. Herdegen.
The account by M. Kempe of his visit to England in 1670/71 is at
p. 293–318]. Nürnberg, 1744, 8°. B.M.

258. EBERT, A., Auli Apronii vermehrte Reise-Beschreibung von Franco
Porto . . . durch Teutschland . . . England . . . [in 1678]. Franco Porto,
1724, 8°. B.M.

259. Sir T. Molyneux. (Gallery of illustr. Irishmen, 13.) [Containing a
letter describing his visit to Oxf. in 1683.] (Dublin univ. mag., 1841,
vol. 18, p. 323–26.) Per. 3977 e. 74

See 16 [Benthem, H. L., Engeländischer Kirch- und Schulen-Staat, 1694. An
account based on his visit to England in 1686/87].

260. ERNDTEL, C. H., C.H.E.D. de itinere suo Anglicano et Batavo annis
1706 et 1707 facto, relatio. (Oxford, p. 68–73.) Amst., 1711, 8°.
Gough Gen. top. 84
— Transl. from the Latin. (Oxford, p. 47–53.) Lond., 1711, 8°.
G. Pamph. 2052 (2)

261. HOLBERG, L. VON, *Baron*, Opuscula quaedam Latina. (Oxf. univ.,
p. 26–35. 1706.) Lips., 1737, 8°. 8° E 189 Art.
— Transl. (p. 19–25.) (Autobiography, vol. 12.) Lond., 1829, 12°.
2106 f. 33

262. UFFENBACH, Z. C. VON, *Baron*. Merkwürdige Reisen durch Nieder-
sachsen, Holland und Engelland. 3 Th. (Oxf. Th. 3, p. 86–184). Ulm,
1753, 54, 4°. 203 a. 280–82
— [Transl. *entitled*] Oxford in 1710, ed. [and tr.] by W. H. and W. J. C.
Quarrell. Oxf., 1928, 8°. 70 pp. G.A. Oxon 8° 1062

263. LE SAGE, G. L., Remarques sur l'Angleterre faites par un voyageur
[G. L. Le Sage] dans les armées [*sic*] 1710 & 1711. [Oxford, p. 42–53.]
Amst., 1715, 12°. Douce A 46

264. The voyage of don Manoel Gonzales . . . to Great Britain [in 1730]. (A general collection of . . . voyages and travels, by John Pinkerton. vol. 2.) [Oxford univ., p. 102–23.] Lond., 1808, 4°.   4° BS. 897

265. KIELMANSEGGE, F. VON, count, Diary of a journey to England, 1761–1762, tr. by countess Kielmansegg. (Oxford, p. 96–114.) New York &c., 1902, 8°.   247125 e. 11

266. Oxford in 1778. [An account of a visit by two 'Scotch gentlemen', ed. by D. G. Ritchie.] (Oxf. mag., 1892, vol. 11, p. 105, 06.)
Per. G.A. Oxon 4° 141

See 151 [Wendeborn, G. F. A., Beyträge zur Kenntnis Grosbritanniens vom Jahr 1779. 1780 &c.].

267. MORITZ, K. P., Reisen eines Deutschen in England im Jahr 1782. (Oxford, p. 155–70.) 2e. Berl., Aufl. 1785, 8°.   G.A. Gen. top. 16° 27 [Other eds. in 1798, 1808, 1886.]
— Tr. by a lady. [Entitled] Travels chiefly on foot, through several parts of England. (Oxford, p. 165–80.) Lond., 1795, 8°.
Gough Gen. top. 293

268. Passages from the English note-books of Nathaniel Hawthorne. Vol. 2 [p. 144–65 concern a visit to Oxford in 1856]. Lond., 1870, 8°.
G.A. Gen. top. 8° 214

269. TAINE, H. A., Notes sur l'Angleterre. Par., 1872, 16°. 395 pp.
Bibl. Nat.
— 2e éd. (Oxf. univ., p. 153–69.) Par., 1872, 16°.   247126 e. 253 [Other eds. in 1872, 74, 80, 83, 85, 90, 95, 99, 1903, 07, 10, 23.]

270. TAINE, H. A., Notes on England, tr. by W. F. Rae. (Oxf. univ., p. 137–52.) Lond., 1872, 8°.   226 j. 172
— Taine's Notes on England, tr. by E. Hyams. (Oxf. univ., p. 114–26.) Lond., 1957, 8°.   247126 e. 262

271. NADAL, E. S., Two visits to Oxford. (Scribner's monthly, 1874, vol. 8, p. 728, &c.)   B.M.

272. A visit to Oxford in 1880 by an American girl. Extracts from the diary of Emily M. Eliot. (Bodl. libr. record, 1960, vol. 4, p. 551–58.)
Per. 2590 d. Oxf. 1.41 = R.

273. BOURGET, P. C. J., Sensations d'Oxford. (La Nouvelle revue, 1883, tom. 24, p. 557–98.)   G.A. Oxon 4° 582 (10)

274. CORBIN, J., Bourget's Impressions of Oxford. (Lamp, 1903, vol. 26, p. 123 etc.)   B.M.

275. WOODS, M. L., French [19th century travellers'] views of an English university. (Nineteenth cent., 1898, vol. 44, p. 991–1003.)
Per. 3977 d. 66

276. PASQUIER, H., Impressions de voyages et de lectures. (Pp. 1–48. Au pays des Plantagenets. Une visite à Oxford.) Angers, 1898, 8°.
27525 e. 1635

277. LULEY, G., Ein Ferienaufenthalt in Oxford. (Jahresb. der Gross-
herzoglichen Realschule zu Wimpfen a. Neckar, 1905/06, p. 17–22.)
G.A. Oxon 4° 186 (29)

278. BORGESE, G. A., Escursione in terre nuove, visioni e notizie. Milano,
1931, 8°. 91 pp. G.A. Oxon 8° 1082

278.3. MAUROIS, A., Trois écrivains français à Oxford. (Oxford, 1935, vol.
I, no. 3, p. 28–33.) Per. G.A. Oxon 8° 1141

279. BADOLATO, F., Oxford: Summer 1960. [Typewritten.] n. pl., (1960),
4°. 6 sh. G.A. Oxon 4° 774

VIEWS, DESCRIPTIONS, AND GUIDES

See also among 6402 etc. [Views etc. of Colleges only].

280. [5 volumes of Photographs by Taunt.] G.A. Oxon a. 102–06

281. JOBST, W., Omnium academiarum et . . . scholarum totius Europæ,
erectiones, fundationes & confirmationes, authore Guolphgango Iusto.
[Account of Oxf. univ., sig. c 4ᵛ–6ᵛ.] Frankophurti a. V., 1554, 12°.
B.M.

282. NEALE, T., Chronographia sive origo collegiorum Oxoniensis academiæ, una cum descriptione eorundem ad . . . Elizabetham . . .
conscripta 1566 [by T. Neale]. (Academiarum quæ aliquando fuere et
hodie sunt in Europa catalogus [by M. Windsore], 1590, sig. F1ᵛ–H3ᵛ.)
Wood 498 (1)
[Subsequently publ. with Bereblock's views, no. 291.]

283. BIBYE, S., Oxoniensis academiæ et collegiorum quæ in eadem nunc
sunt . . . descriptio. [Madan 210.] [A folded broadside illustr. used in
no. 245.] Tubingæ, 1602, s. sh. 55 d. 82

284. LOGGAN, D., Oxonia illustrata, sive Omnium celeberrimæ istius
universitatis collegiorum, aularum, bibliothecæ Bodleianæ, scholarum
publicarum, theatri Sheldoniani; nec non urbis totius scenographia.
[Madan 3035.] Oxon., 1675, fol. 40 plates. Arch. Antiq. A II 13

285. NEW, E. H., The new Loggan prints. Of the Loggan prints. (The Miscellany, 1915, vol. 2, p. 57–66.) G.A. Oxon 4° 498

286. The new Loggan guide to Oxford colleges, illustrations by E. H. New,
letterpress by E. G. Withycombe. Oxf., 1932, 4°. 56 pp.
G.A. Oxon 4° 509

287. CORONELLI, M. V., Oxoniæ atque Cantabrigiæ universitates celeberrimæ a . . . Coronelli . . . imaginibus illustratæ dum Angliæ regnum
peragrauit, ac in tomos xxxxv Universalis suæ bibliothecæ descriptæ.
[Some 48 drawings are of Oxford buildings &c.] [Ven.? 17—], 4°.
G.A. Oxon 4° 10

288. A step to Oxford, in which is comprehended an impartial account of
the University. Lond., 1704, fol. 10 pp. 13Θ39

289. BEEVERELL, J., Les délices de la Grande Bretagne & de l'Irlande. (Oxford, tom. 3, p. 521–88.) à Leide, 1707, 8°.   Douce B 615
— [39 engravings on 11 folio sheets from the plates of the above.]
G.A. Oxon a. 82

290. Iter Oxoniense, 1710. [A diary of a party of Lincolnshire gentlemen. Mainly concerning their journey to and from Oxford.] Communicated by J. Simpson. (Reliquary, 1883/4, vol. 24, p. 168–74.)
Per. 17572 e. 13

291. NEALE, T., Collegiorum scholarumque publicarum Academiæ Oxoniensis topographica delineatio [in Latin verse, with 17 views from drawings by J. Bereblock]. (Henrici Dodwelli de Parma equestri Woodwardiana dissertatio, ed. T. Hearne, 1713, p. 115–50.)
Mus. Bibl. II 43
— [Another ed.] (Nichols's Progresses of q. Eliz., 1788, Text, vol. 1, p. 60–73 of The queen at Oxford, 1566; Plates in vol. 3.)
DD 74, 76 Jur.
— [Another ed., without plates.] (Nichols's Progresses of q. Eliz., 1823, new ed., vol. 1, p. 217–29.)   4° BS. 381 = A.
— [Another ed.] e cod. MS. Bibl. Bodl. arte photozinc. expressa. Oxon., 1882, 4°.   G.A. Oxon 4° 81
— [Another ed., without plates.] (Oxf. hist. soc., vol. 8, p. 151–68.) Oxf., 1887, 8°.   G.A. Oxon 8° 360 = R.
[The description without the views appeared first in 1590. See no. 282.]

292. Oxonia illustrata, of het verheerlykt Oxford vervattende de gezichten der zelve stad, met haare gebouwen lust-huizen, en andere omleggende plaatzen, in 48. prenten afgebeeld. [The plates all come from J. Beeverell's Les délices de la Grande Bretagne, 1707 &c. which in turn are reproductions of Loggan's views.] Amst., [c. 1730], 4°.
G.A. Oxon 4° 494

293. WILLIAMS, W., Oxonia depicta, sive, Collegiorum et aularum in inclyta Academica Oxoniensi ichnographica, orthographica et sceno-graphica . . . delineatio LXV tabulis æneis expressa; cui accedit notitia. n. pl., [1732, 33], fol.   G.A. fol. B 33*

294. A description of the City of Oxford [and colleges]. (London mag., or Gentleman's monthly intelligencer, 1747, p. 418–20, 441–43, 565–67.)
Hope adds. 402

295. The gentleman and lady's pocket companion for Oxford. [Extracted from the work of T. Salmon: see no. 20.] Lond., 1747, 12°. 71 pp.
G.A. Oxon 16° 136 (15)

296. A pocket companion [afterw.] A new pocket companion for Oxford, with an historical account of . . . the colleges . . . Oxf. &c., [1753], 12°.
Gough Oxf. 23
— [Another issue.]   G.A. Oxon 16° 5
[Other eds. in 1756, 1759, 1762, 1763, 1764, 1765, 1766, 1768, 1769, 1772, 1776, 1782, 1783, 1785, 1787, 1788, 1789, 1790, 1793, 1794,

1795, 1796, 1797, 1799, 1800, 1801, 1802, 1803, 1804, 1805, 1806, 1807, 1808, 1809, 1810, 1812, 1814, 1816.]

See 296 [A pocket companion for Oxford. New ed. 1756. G. A. Oxon 8° 290].

297. The new Oxford guide: or, Companion through the University. By a gentleman of Oxford. Oxf. &c., 1759, 8°. G.A. Oxon 16° 27
— 2nd ed. (1759). Gough Oxf. 17 (1)
[Other eds. in 1763, 1764, 1765, 1768, c. 1771/72, 1776, 1777, 1781, 1785, 1786, 1787, 1788, 1792, 1794, 1797, 1803, 1813.]

See 296 [A pocket companion for Oxford. New ed. 1759. G. A. Oxon 8° 176(1)]

298. WARTON, T., A companion to the guide, and a guide to the companion [by T. Warton. A humorous production ridiculing the Oxford Guide]. Lond. &c., [c. 1760], 8°. Douce O 56 (2)
[The 2nd, 3rd, and 4th eds. were publ. without date; a New ed. appeared in 1806.]

See 296 [A pocket companion for Oxford. New ed. 1762. G. A. Oxon 8° 344 (1)].
See 296 [A pocket companion for Oxford. New ed. 1763. G. A. Oxon 8° 345 (4)].

299. MALCHAIR, J. B., XII views consisting chiefly of the environs of Oxford. n. pl., 1763 [–c. 1780], obl. 4°. Vet. A 5 c. 62

300. WELLESLEY, H. [Remarks on the drawings by J. Malchair, illustrative of the topography of Oxford.] (Proc., Oxf. architect. and hist. soc., 1862, N.S., vol. I, p. 148–51.) Per. G.A. Oxon 4° 498 = R.

301. OPPÉ, P., John Baptist Malchair of Oxford. (Burlington mag., 1943, vol. 83, p. 191–97.) Per. 170 c. 25

302. MINN, H., Drawings by J. B. Malchair in Corpus Christi college. (Oxoniensia, 1943/44, vol. 8/9, p. 159–68.) Per. G.A. Oxon 4° 658 = R.

See 297 [The new Oxford guide. 3rd ed. (1763). Douce O 63].
See 296 [A pocket companion for Oxford. New ed. 1764. G.A. Oxon 16° 43].
See 297 [The new Oxford guide. 3rd ed. (1764). G.A. Oxon 16° 38].
See 296 [A pocket companion for Oxford. New ed. 1765. G.A. Oxon 16° 190].
See 297 [The new Oxford guide. 4th ed. (1765).G.A. Oxon 8° 349].
See 296 [A pocket companion for Oxford. New ed. 1766. G.A. Oxon 16° 131].
See 296 [A pocket companion for Oxford. New ed. 1768. G.A. Oxon 16° 2].
See 297 [The new Oxford guide. 5th ed. (1768). G.A. Oxon 8° 175 (1); another 5th ed. G.A. Gen. top. 16° 300].
See 296 [A pocket companion for Oxford. New ed. 1769. G.A. Oxon 16° 7].
See 297 [The new Oxford guide. 6th ed. [c. 1771/72]. G.A. Oxon 8° 175 (2)].
See 296 [A new pocket companion for Oxford. New ed. (1772). G.A. Oxon 8° 213].
See 297 [The new Oxford guide. 6th ed. (1776). G.A. Oxon 8° 347].
See 296 [A new pocket companion for Oxford. New ed. (1776). G.A. Oxon 16° 26].
See 297 [The new Oxford guide. 6th ed. (1777). Douce O 90; another 6th ed. G.A. Oxon 16° 14].
See 297 [The new Oxford guide. 6th ed. [1781]. Vet. A 5 f. 617 (1)].
See 296 [A new pocket companion for Oxford. New ed. 1782. G.A. Oxon 8° 237].

See 296 [A new pocket companion for Oxford. New ed. 1783. G.A. Oxon 8°
929].
See 297 [The new Oxford guide. 7th ed. 1785. G.A. Oxon 8° 175 (3)].
See 296 [A new pocket companion for Oxford. New ed. 1785. G.A. Oxon 8°
291].
See 297 [The new Oxford guide. 7th ed. 1786. G.A. Gen. top. 8° 307 (2)].
See 296 [A new pocket companion for Oxford. New ed. 1787. G.A. Oxon 8°
344 (2)].
See 297 [The new Oxford guide. 7th ed. 1787. G.A. Oxon 8° 225 (1)].
See 296 [A new pocket companion for Oxford. New ed. 1788. G.A. Oxon 8°
176 (2)].
See 297 [The new Oxford guide. 7th ed. (1788). G.A. Oxon 8° 347*].

303. JUNG, P., Guide d'Oxford. Oxf., 1789, 12°. 109 pp.
                                                Gough Oxf. 17 (5)
— 2e éd. 1805. 124 pp.   G.A. Oxon 8° 168

See 296 [A new pocket companion for Oxford. New ed. 1789. G.A. Oxon 8° 94].
See 296 [A new pocket companion for Oxford. New ed. 1790. G.A. Oxon 8°
176 (4)].
See 297 [The new Oxford guide. 8th ed. (1792). G.A. Oxon 8° 175 (4)].
See 296 [A new pocket companion for Oxford. New ed. 1793. Gough Oxf. 17
(4)].
See 297 [The new Oxford guide. New ed. 1794. G.A. Oxon 16° 176].
See 296 [A new pocket companion for Oxford. New ed. 1794. G.A. Oxon 16°
176 (1)].
See 296 [A new pocket companion for Oxford. New ed. 1795. G.A. Oxon 16°
60].
See 296 [A new pocket companion for Oxford. New ed. 1796. G.A. Oxon 8°
295].
See 296 [A new pocket companion for Oxford. New ed. 1797. G.A. Oxon 8°
301].
See 297 [The new Oxford guide. 9th ed. (1797). G.A. Oxon 8° 309].
See 296 [A new pocket companion for Oxford. New ed. 1799. G.A. Oxon 16°
45].
See 296 [A new pocket companion for Oxford. New ed. 1800. G.A. Oxon 8°
345 (1)].
See 296 [A new pocket companion for Oxford. New ed. 1801. G.A. Oxon 16°
123 (2)].
See 296 [A new pocket companion for Oxford. New ed. 1802. G.A. Oxon 16°
205].

304. MALTON, T., Oxford [views]. No. 1–[4]. [24 plates and 6 prints in
outline.] Lond., 1802–10, fol.   G.A. fol. B 38

See 296 [A new pocket companion for Oxford. New ed. 1803. G.A. Oxon 8°
176 (5)].
See 297 [The new Oxford guide. 12th ed. (1803). G.A. Oxon 16° 141].
See 296 [A new pocket companion for Oxford. New ed. 1804. G.A. Oxon 16°
45*].

305. Oxford delineated. No. 1 (2) of A graphic and descriptive tour of the
University of Oxford . . . Views (by C. A. Pugin and J. C. Nattes) with
their history. (Lond.), 1805, fol.
[Bodley has two imperfect copies: G.A. fol. B 81 contains p. 1–16 of
the letterpress; G.A. Oxon a. 98 contains 14 views.]

See 303 [Jung, P., Guide d'Oxford. 2e éd. 1805. G.A. Oxon 8° 168].
See 296 [A new pocket companion for Oxford. New ed. 1805. G.A. Oxon 8°
225 (2)].
See 296 [A new pocket companion for Oxford. New ed. 1806. G.A. Oxon 16°
29].

306. BARKER, H. A., A view of the University and City of Oxford taken
from the Radcliffe Library. Lond., [1807], s. sh. G.A. Oxon 8° 184 (5)

See 296 [A new pocket companion for Oxford. New ed. 1807. G.A. Oxon 16°
16].
See 296 [A new pocket companion for Oxford. New ed. 1808. G.A. Oxon 16°
8].
See 296 [A new pocket companion for Oxford. New ed. 1809. G.A. Oxon 16°
8*].
See 24 [Chalmers, A., A history of the . . . University of Oxford, illustrated.
1810. G.A. Oxon 4° 26, 27].
See 296 [A new pocket companion for Oxford. New ed. 1810. G.A. Oxon 8°
344 (3)].
See 296 [A new pocket companion for Oxford. New ed. 1812. G.A. Oxon 16°
136 (19)].
See 297 [The new Oxford guide. 19th ed. 1813. G.A. Oxon 8° 1179 (2)].
See 25 [Ackermann, R., A history of the University of Oxford. 1814. G.A.
Oxon b. 109].
See 296 [A new pocket companion for Oxford. New ed. 1814. G.A. Oxon 8°
345 (2)].
See 296 [A new pocket companion for Oxford. New ed. 1816. G.A. Oxon 16°
75 (3)].

307. WADE, W. M., Walks in Oxford. 2 vols. Oxf., 1817, 8°.
G.A. Oxon 8° 376, 377
[2 other issues and another ed. also publ. in 1817; 2nd ed., 1818;
another ed. 1824. 2 issues.]

308. The Oxford portfolio. [Views] no. 1–13. Drawn, etched (and published) by G. Cooper. n. pl., 1817, fol. 13 sheets.   G.A. Oxon b. 82

309. The young travellers; or, A visit to Oxford, by a lady. Lond., 1818,
8°. 151 pp.   G.A. Oxon 8° 520
— [Another ed.] 1820.   G.A. Oxon 8° 936

See 307 [Wade, W. M., Walks in Oxford. 2nd ed. 1818. G.A. Oxon 8° 294].

310. The Oxford university and city guide. Oxf., 1818, 12°.
G.A. Oxon 16° 137
— 3rd ed. (1818).   G.A. Oxon 16° 11
[Other eds. in 1819, 1820, 1821, 1822, 1823, 1824, 1825, 1826, 1827,
1828, 1829, 1830, 1834, 1837, 1839, 1849, 1852, 1859, c. 1860.]

See 310 [The Oxford university and city guide. 4th ed. (1819). G.A. Oxon 8°
226].
See 310 [The Oxford university and city guide. New ed. 1820. G.A. Oxon 8°
362].

311. LAMB, C., Oxford in the vacation [signed Elia]. (Lond. mag., 1820,
vol. 2, p. 365–69.)   G.A. Oxon 4° 578 (1)

See 309 [The young travellers; or, A visit to Oxford. 1820. G.A. Oxon 8° 936].

312. The University and City of Oxford; displayed in . . . 72 views drawn
and engraved by J. and H. S. Storer, accompanied with a dialogue . . .
by R. Lascelles. Lond., 1821, 8°. 296 pp.   G.A. Oxon 4° 85

See 310 [The Oxford university and city guide. New ed. 1821. G.A. Oxon 8°
460].

313. The Oxford visitor: or, Picturesque views of all the colleges and halls of the University: public buildings of the City. With historical descriptions. The subjects are drawn and engraved by J. & H. S. Storer. Lond., 1822, 12°. 114 pp.   G.A. Oxon 8° 378

> See 310 [The Oxford university and city guide. New ed. 1822. G.A. Oxon 8° 68 (5)].

314. Views of all the colleges, halls and public buildings in the University and City of Oxford. Oxf., [1823], 16°. 42 plates.   G.A. Oxon 8° 41 [Other eds. publ. in 1824, c. 1830, c. 1834.]

> See 310 [The Oxford university and city guide. New ed. 1823. G.A. Gen. top. 8° 13].

315. SKELTON, J., Oxonia antiqua restaurata . . . 170 engravings. 2 vols. Oxf., 1823, fol.   G.A. fol. A 111, 112
— 2nd ed., with additions. Lond., 1843, fol. 110 pp.+150 pl.
                                                           G.A. fol. A 113 = R.

> See 310 [The Oxford university and city guide. New ed. 1824. G.A. Oxon 8° 229].
> See 307 [Wade, W. M., Walks in Oxford. 1824. G.A. Oxon 8° 302; Manning 8° 119].
> See 314 [Views of all the colleges . . . 1824. G.A. Oxon 16° 206].

316. Mathews's views of colleges in Oxford. n. pl., 1825, 16°. 20 views.
                                                           G.A. Oxon 16° 144

> See 310 [The Oxford university and city guide. New ed. 1825. G.A. Oxon 8° 292].

317. The perambulation of Oxford . . . to which is added an appendix, containing a description of the models in the Picture gallery. New ed. Oxf., 1825, 21, 8°.   G.A. Oxon 8° 599
— [Another ed.] 1826, 21.   G.A. Oxon 8° 599*

> See 310 [The Oxford university and city guide. New ed. 1826. G.A. Oxon 16° 9].
> See 310 [The Oxford university and city guide. New ed. 1827. G.A. Oxon 16° 181].

318. FISHER, J., Scraps of Oxford and its environs; engraved views. No. 1. Oxf., 1827, 4°. 5 views.   G.A. Oxon 4° 358

319. WHITTOCK, N., A topographical and historical description of the University and City of Oxford, with views . . . To which is added, Correct delineations of the costume of the members of the University. [An additional title-leaf reads] The microcosm of Oxford. Lond., 1828, 4°. 102 pp.+42 plates.   G.A. Oxon 4° 92
— [Another ed.] 1829.   G.A. Oxon 4° 101
[The 'Topographical description' and the 'Microcosm' (no. 320) contain almost the same plates, but the former has 102 pp. of text to the latter's 40 pp.]

320. WHITTOCK, N., The microcosm of Oxford, a series of views of the . . . University and City of Oxford. Accompanied with brief notices. Oxf. &c., [c. 1828], 4°. 40 pp.+40 plates.   G.A. Oxon 4° 102

See 310 [The Oxford university and city guide. New ed. 1828. G.A. Oxon 8°
238].
See 310 [The Oxford university and city guide. New ed. 1829. G.A. Oxon 8°
362*].
See 314 [Views of all the colleges . . . c. 1830. G.A. Oxon 16° 228].
See 310 [The Oxford university and city guide. New ed. 1830. G.A. Oxon 8°
293].

321. Oxford delineated; or, A sketch of the history and antiquities, and a
general topographical description of that celebrated University and
City [by T. Joy] illustr. by a series of views [by J. Whessell]. Oxf., 1831
[–33], 4°. 88 pp.+32 plates.   G.A. Oxon 4° 65

See 314 [Views of all the colleges . . . c. 1834. G.A. Oxon 16° 146].
See 310 [The Oxford university and city guide. New ed. 1834. G.A. Oxon 16°
13].

322. DELAMOTTE, W. A., Remains of ancient splendour in Oxford and its
vicinity [6 drawings]. Oxf., 1837, 4°.   G.A. Oxon 4° 50

See 26 [Ingram, J., Memorials of Oxford. 1837. G.A. Oxon 8° 18–20].
See 310 [The Oxford university and city guide. New ed. 1837. G.A. Oxon 8°
386].

323. The stranger's guide through the University and City of Oxford.
Oxf., 1838, 8°.   G.A. Oxon 8° 68 (6)
[Other eds. publ. in 1839, 1847, c. 1849, 1853.]

324. Illustrations of Oxford, select views [by various hands] . . . with
historical and descriptive letter press. Vol. 1. [Publ. by J. Ryman.]
Oxf., 1839, fol.   G.A. Oxon a. 95

See 310 [The Oxford university and city guide. New ed. 1839. G.A. Oxon 8°
940 (1)].
See 323 [The stranger's guide. 2nd ed. 1839. G.A. Oxon 8° 1222].

325. [A folded sheet of Oxford views, c. 1840.]   G.A. Oxon 16° 145

326. A hand-book for Oxford; or An historical and topographical guide to
the University, city and environs, by a graduate. Oxf. &c., 1841, 16°.
179 pp.   G.A. Oxon 16° 103

327. Original views of Oxford, its colleges, chapels and gardens, from
drawings made by W. A. Delamotte, executed in lithography by W.
Gauci: with notices by C. Ollier. Lond., 1843, fol. 26 pp.+26 plates.
G.A. Oxon a. 30

See 315 [Skelton, J., Oxonia antiqua restaurata . . . engravings. 2nd ed. with
additions. 1843. G.A. fol. A 113=R.].

328. G., MISS C., Panorama of Oxford from the roof of the Bodleian
Library. Lond., 1845, s. sh.   G.A. fol. A 128

329. PARKER, J. H., A handbook for visitors to Oxford. [By J. H. Parker.]
Oxf., 1847, 16°. 223 pp.   G.A. Oxon 16° 150
[Other eds. in 1858, 75.]

See 323 [The stranger's guide. 5th ed. 1847. G.A. Oxon 8° 227].

330. The railway traveller's walk through Oxford [by J. H. Parker]. Oxf.,
1848, 16°. 115 pp.   G.A. Oxon 8° 68 (8)
[Other eds. publ. *c.* 1850, *c.* 1858, 1874.]

331. Oxford. (The land we live in, 1848, pt. 8, p. 33–72.)
G.A. Oxon 4° 367

See 310 [The Oxford university and city guide. New ed. 1849. G.A. Oxon 8°
1221].
See 323 [The stranger's guide. 6th ed. *c.* 1849. G.A. Oxon 8° 541].

332. Microcosm of Oxford [views] drawn, engraved and published by N.
Whittock. Lond., [*c.* 1850], s. sh. [folded].   G.A. Oxon 16° 104

See 330 [The railway traveller's walk through Oxford. *c.* 1850. G.A. Oxon 16°
172].

333. An easy guide and directory to the sights of the University and City of
Oxford. Publ. by John Dewe. Oxf., [*c.* 1850], 16°. 18 pp.
G.A. Oxon 8° 147 (13)

334. LORAIN, P., Mémoire sur l'Université d'Oxford. [An extract from
Moniteur universel.] Par., 1850, 8°. 43 pp.   B.N.

335. Views of Oxford [publ. by Rock and co.]. Lond., [1850, 51], 8°.
15 leaves.   G.A. Oxon 8° 920

336. RUNDT, C., A walk round Oxford. [Text in Engl. and Germ.] Berl.,
[1851?], obl. 4°. 8 pp.+16 plates.   G.A. fol. B 88

337. NEATE, C., Introduction au Manuel descriptif de l'Université
d'Oxford, à l'usage des étrangers [by C. Neate]. Oxf. &c., 1851, 16°.
24 pp.   G.A. Oxon 16° 23

See 310 [The Oxford university and city guide. New ed. 1852. G.A. Oxon 8°
1514].

338. RUNDT, C., Views of the most picturesque colleges. Pt. 1, 2. (Berl.),
[1852?], fol.   G.A. Oxon a. 37

339. Knight's excursion companion. No. 8. Oxford. n. pl., [1853], 8°.
24 pp.   G.A. Oxon 4° 578 (6)

See 323 [The stranger's guide. 1853. 2 issues, the 2nd undated. G.A. Oxon 8°
940 (2, 3)].

340. DELAMOTTE, P. H., Views in Oxford, photographed by P. H. Delamotte. Lond. &c., 1857, fol. 41 plates.   G.A. Oxon b. 18

See 329 [A handbook for visitors to Oxford. New ed. 1858. G.A. Oxon 8° 56].
See 330 [The railway traveller's walk through Oxford. New ed. *c.* 1858. G.A.
Oxon 16° 3].
See 310 [The Oxford university and city guide. New ed. 1859. G.A. Oxon 8°
1190].

341. The Oxford guide, a description . . . New ed. Oxf., [*c.* 1860], 8°. 84 pp.
G.A. Oxon 8° 1012 (1)

342. An easy guide to Oxford arranged as a walk. [Publ. and perhaps
written by J. Dewe.] Oxf., [*c.* 1860], 16°. 19 pp.   G.A. Oxon 16° 166

— [Another ed.] Dewe's Easy guide . . . [*c.* 1865].
G.A. Oxon 8° 147 (4)
— [Another ed., *entitled*] Shrimptons' easy guide . . . Revised. Oxf., 1871, 16°. 64 pp. G.A. Oxon 16° 182

343. Dewe's pictorial plan and walk through Oxford. Oxf., [*c.* 1860], 16°. 11 pp. G.A. Oxon 16° 186
[A different itinerary from 342.]

344. Views of Oxford [publ. by Kershaw & son]. Lond., [*c.* 1860], 8°. 12 leaves. G.A. Oxon 8° 921

345. [A collection of Oxford views, *c.* 1860.] G.A. Oxon 4° 38

See 310 [The Oxford university and city guide. New ed. *c.* 1860. G.A. Oxon 8° 280].

346. City of Oxford. [A brief guide with 12 plates.] Lond. &c., [*c.* 1860], 16°. G.A. Oxon 16° 214

347. WALCOTT, M. E. C., Oxford. (Cathedral cities of Engl. and Wales.) Oxf., [1865], 8°. 51 pp. G.A. Oxon 8° 1130* (16)

See 342 [Dewe's Easy guide to Oxford: arranged as a walk. *c.* 1865. G.A. Oxon 8° 147 (4)].
See 342 [Shrimptons' easy guide to Oxford: arranged as a walk. Revised. 1871. G.A. Oxon 16° 182].

348. Without a guide [signed E.P.]. (Fraser's mag., 1872, N.S., vol. 6, p. 686–96.) G.A. Oxon 4° 581 (4)

349. ARNOLD, F., Oxford and Cambridge: their colleges, memories and associations. Lond., [1873], 4°. 400 pp. G.A. Oxon 4° 55

350. Alden's Oxford guide. [1st– ed.] Oxf., 1874– , 16°.
G.A. Oxon 16° 107
[Publ. for the most part annually.]

See 330 [The railway traveller's walk through Oxford. New ed. 1874. G.A. Oxon 16° 3].

351. MOORE, J. J., The pictorial and historical guide to Oxford, by the ed. of the Historical handbook to Oxford [J. J. Moore]. Oxf., 1875, 8°. 84 pp. G.A. Oxon 8° 161 (17)
— 2nd ed. 1875. G.A. Oxon 8° 333
— 5th ed. (Shrimptons' Pictorial guide.) [1889]. G.A. Oxon 8° 453
— 6th ed. [*entitled*] The pictorial and historical gossiping guide, revised by H. Hurst. [1897]. G.A. Oxon 8° 681

See 329 [A handbook for visitors to Oxford. New ed. 1875. G.A. Oxon 8° 203].

352. Oliver's guide to Oxford for use of visitors to the Agricultural show, June 1878. [Oxf.], 1878, 8°. 16 pp. G.A. Oxon 8° 962

353. MOORE, J. J., The historical handbook and guide to Oxford. 2nd ed. Oxf., 1878, 8°. 296 pp. G.A. Oxon 8° 284

See 272 [A visit to Oxford in 1880 by an American girl, E. M. Eliot. 1960].

354. Old Oxford: an appendix to Alden's Sixpenny guide to Oxford.
[Signed G.R.] Oxf., [1880?], 12°. pp. 97–110. G.A. Oxon 16° 136 (18)

355. The Leporello album of Oxford views. n. pl., [1880], 12 views each
7 × 11 cm.   G.A. Oxon 8° 267

356. The visitor's guide to Oxford. New ed. Oxf., (1881), 8°. 136 pp.
                                                    G.A. Oxon 8° 263
[Other eds. publ. in 1883, 88.]

See 290 [Iter Oxoniense, 1710. 1883/84. Per. 17572 e. 13, vol. 24].
See 356 [The visitor's guide. 1883. G.A. Oxon 8° 866].

357. DICKENS, C., *ed.*, A dictionary of the University of Oxford. Lond.,
1884, 16°. 134 pp.   G.A. Oxon 16° 1

358. Photographic view album of Oxford. n. pl., [*c.* 1885], obl. 4°. 16 plates.
                                                    G.A. Oxon 4° 334

See 356 [The visitor's guide. 1888. G.A. Oxon 8° 866*].

359. Catalogue of a collection of drawings of Oxford by J. Fulleylove, now
exhibiting at the Fine art society's, with a note by T. H. Ward. (Lond.),
1888, 8°. 12 pp.   G.A. Oxon 8° 436

See 351 [The pictorial and historical guide. 5th ed. 1889. G.A. Oxon 8° 453].

360. FULLEYLOVE, J., Oxford, with notes by T. H. Ward. Lond., 1889,
fol. xvi+30 pp.+30 plates.   G.A. Oxon b. 3

See 7150 [Handbook to Oxford cathedral, also an account of the colleges &c.
1889. G.A. Eccl. top. 4° 14 (4)].

361. HINKSON, K. T., University of Oxford. (Cath. world, 1890, vol. 50,
p. 607–17.)   Per. 2714 d. 1

362. KING, J. W., Six original lithographs of Oxford. Oxf., [*c.* 1890], fol.
6 plates.   G.A. Oxon b. 39

363. ALDEN, E. C., A day in Oxford, a lecture [by E. C. Alden] to illustrate
a series of slides. (Oxf.), [1891], 8°. 28 pp.   G.A. Oxon 8° 524 (1)

364. Pictorial and descriptive guide to Oxford. (Ward & Lock's guide
books.) Lond. &c., [1893], 8°. 160 pp.   G.A. Oxon 16° 40
— A new . . . guide to Oxford and district. [1st]–4th ed. Lond. &c.,
[1923–49], 8°.   G.A. Oxon 16° 165

365. John Heywood's illustrated guide to Oxford. 1894–[1929]. Lond. &c.,
1894–[1929], 8°.   G.A. Oxon 8° 601

366. Oxford and its University, an illustrated handbook for the use of . . .
the British pharmaceutical conference. [Lond.], 1894, 8°. 48 pp.
                                                    G.A. Oxon 8° 602

367. SMITH, G., Oxford and her colleges. Lond. &c., 1894, 16°. 99 pp.
                                                    G.A. Oxon 16° 44
— [Another ed.] New York &c., 1895. 170 pp.   G.A. Oxon 16° 48

368. Round about 'The Mitre'. 6th ed. Oxf., 1895, 8°. 16 pp.
                                                G.A. Oxon 8° 969 (1)
— 7th ed. 1900.   G.A. Oxon 8° 969 (2)

369. Oxford and her colleges [photographs]. (The Album, suppl. June 24, 1895.) n. pl., 1895, fol. 16 pp.   G.A. Oxon c. 205

370. WHITTAKER, T., Sights and scenes in Oxford city and university, 101 plates. Lond. &c., [1896], 4°. 215 pp.   G.A. Oxon c. 36

371. WELLS, J., Oxford and its colleges. Lond., 1897, 16°. 330 pp.
                                                G.A. Oxon 16° 51
— [Other eds. in 1898, 99, 1901, 02, 04, 06, 08, 11, 14, 19, 23.]
— 13th ed. (Little guides.) Lond., 1926, 16°. 354 pp.
                                            G.A. Oxon 16° 177

See 351 [The pictorial and historical gossiping guide. 6th ed. 1897. G.A. Oxon 8° 681].

372. Handbook to Oxford. (Oxf. tourist comm.) (Lond.), [1898], 8°. 28 pp.
                                            G.A. Oxon 8° 620 (23)

373. DODGSON, C. L., Isa's visit to Oxford, 1888. (Lewis Carroll picture book, 1899, p. 321–31.)   270 e. 1155

374. Album of views of Oxford university. Lond. &c., [c. 1900], obl. 4°. 26 pp.   G.A. Oxon c. 144

See 368 [Round about 'The Mitre'. 7th ed. 1900. G.A. Oxon 8° 969 (2)].

375. Photographs of Oxford. [Oxf., c. 1900], 8°.   G.A. Oxon 8° 691

376. ENGLISH, E., Oxford illustrated. (Mate's illustr. guides.) Oxf. &c., 1901, obl. 8°.   G.A. Oxon 8° 906
— 4th ed. [1904].   G.A. Oxon 8° 757

377. TAUNT, H. W., Pocket guide to Oxford and neighbourhood. Oxf., [1901], 16°. 4 pp.   G.A. Oxon 16° 33 (14)
— [Another issue *entitled*] Oxford and round it. Oxf., [1903], 16°. 4 pp.
                                            G.A. Oxon 16° 33 (15)

378. THOMAS, E., and FULLEYLOVE, J., Oxford, painted by J. Fulleylove, described by E. Thomas. Lond., 1903, 8°. 265 pp. G.A. Oxon 8° 699
— [Another ed.] (Black's popular ser. of colour books.) Lond., 1922, 8°. 268 pp.   G.A. Oxon 8° 1006

See 377 [Taunt, H. W., Oxford and round it. 1903. G.A. Oxon 16° 33 (15)].

379. TAUNT, H. W., Oxford (and its historical associations). (Oxf.), [1905?], 8°. 32 pp.   G.A. Oxon 8° 715 (10)
— [Another issue.] Printed privately for 'Frank Cooper'.
                                            G.A. Oxon 8° 715 (11)

380. PEEL, R., and MINCHIN, H. C., Oxford. Lond., 1905, 8°. 144 pp.
                                            G.A. Oxon 8° 719

381. VAN RUITH, H., Sketches in Oxford. (Artist ser.) n. pl., [c. 1905], 6 plates.   G.A. Oxon 8° 975

382. One hundred and one views. Oxford. Lond., [1906], 4°.
G.A. Oxon 4° 236

383. GRAPPE, G., Les pierres d'Oxford. (Petite collection 'Scripta brevia'.)
Par., 1906, 16°. 56 pp.   G.A. Oxon 16° 84

384. Davis's short guide to Oxford. Oxf., 1906, 16°. 70 pp.
G.A. Oxon 16° 88

385. MASSÉ, H. J. L. J., Oxford. (Langham ser. of art monogr.) Lond.,
1906, 16°. 112 pp.   G.A. Oxon 16° 92

386. Picturesque Oxford, 60 photographs. Oxf. &c., 1907, 16°. 64 pp.
G.A. Oxon 16° 99
— 4th impr. 1915.   G.A. Oxon 16° 99*
— New ed. 1948.   G.A. Oxon 8° 1184 (10)

387. ALDEN, E. C., Oxford: historical, descriptive, pictorial, with notes on
Oxford architecture. Oxf. &c., (1909), obl. 8°. 84 pp.
G.A. Oxon 8° 770
— [Reissued.] (Oxf. chamber of trade. Visit of a delegation of Amer.
and Canad. merchants, May 2nd, 1921.) Oxf., (1921), obl. 8°. 81 pp.
G.A. Oxon 8° 997

388. BELLINGHAM, I., Notes on Oxford, by mother Mary Emmanuel.
Dundalk, 1909, 8°. 34 pp.   G.A. Oxon 8° 761 (19)

389. FLETCHER, H., Oxford and Cambridge, delineated by H. Fletcher,
with . . . notes by various writers. Lond., 1909, 4°. 288 pp.
G.A. Oxon 4° 283

390. DURAND, R., Oxford, its buildings and gardens, with 32 drawings in
colour by W. A. Wildman. Lond., 1909, 4°. 238 pp.
G.A. Oxon 4° 286

391. Mowbrays' guide to Oxford. Lond. &c., 1909, 16°. 64 pp.
G.A. Oxon 16° 33 (28)
— [Another ed.] 1916. 50 pp.   G.A. Oxon 16° 136 (13)

392. Royal archaeological institute. The summer meeting at Oxford, 19th
to 28th July, 1910. [Historical guide, maps, plans &c.] (Archaeol.
journ., 1910, vol. 67, p. 319–66.)   G.A. Oxon 4° 388

393. LANG, E. M., The Oxford colleges. Lond., [1910], 16°. 258 pp.
G.A. Oxon 16° 111

394. Souvenir für den Besuch der Repräsentanten des Deutschen Christ-
lichen Vereins junger Männer. Oxf., 1910, 8°. 24 pp.
G.A. Oxon 8° 900 (5)

395. Oxford, described by F. D. How, pictured by E. W. Haslehurst.
(Beautiful England.) Lond. &c., [1910], 4°. 56 pp. G.A. Oxon 4° 298

396. NORRIS, E., Oxford [by mr. and mrs. E. Norris]. n. pl., [1911], 4°.
6 pp.   G.A. Oxon 4° 504 (5)

397. TAUNT, H. W., Oxford illustrated by camera and pen. Oxf., [1911], 8°.
244 pp.   G.A. Oxon 8° 832

398. MORRIS, J. E., Oxford. (Beautiful Britain.) Lond., 1911, 8°. 63 pp.
                    G.A. Oxon 8° 830

398.1. Fifty water-colour drawings of Oxford [in the late 19th century,
chiefly by W. Matthison], reprod. in colour, with brief descriptive
notes by E. C. Alden. Oxf. &c., [1912], 4°.   G.A. Oxon 4° 788
— [Another ed. 1921.]   G.A. Oxon 4° 441

399. MORE, P. E., The paradox of Oxford. Repr. from the School review,
June 1913. (Michigan univ., University bulletin, N.S., vol. 15, no. 5.
19 pp.)   G.A. Oxon 4° 276 (25)

400. RICHARDS, F., Oxford, a sketch-book. Lond., 1913, 8°. [24 leaves.]
                    G.A. Oxon 8° 880
— [Repr. for the 6th time] with descriptive notes. 1935 [16 leaves].
                    G.A. Oxon 8° 1151

401. Surveyors' institution. Visit . . . to Oxford, 23, 24 May, 1913. Oxf.,
(1913), 8°. 40 pp.   G.A. Oxon 8° 874 (12)

402. Oxford city and county bowling assoc. Visit of the Canadian bowlers,
June 28, 1913. (Souvenir.) [Photographs.] (Oxf.), 1913, 8°. 23 pp.
                    G.A. Oxon 4° 399 (1)

403. The Johnson society. Visit to Oxford. Repr. from Staffordshire advertiser, May 31, 1913. n. pl., (1913), 8°. 12 pp. G.A. Oxon 8° 850 (29)

404. DAVIDSON, N. J., Things seen in Oxford. Lond., 1914, 16°. 258 pp.
                    G.A. Oxon 16° 128
— New & revised ed. Lond., 1927, 16°. 164 pp.   G.A. Oxon 16° 204

   See 386 [Picturesque Oxford. 4th impr. 1915. G.A. Oxon 16° 99*].

405. FLETCHER, C. R. L., A handy guide to Oxford specially written for the
wounded. Oxf., 1915, 8°. 136 pp.   G.A. Oxon 16° 133
— Revised ed. Lond. &c., 1926, 8°. 136 pp.   G.A. Oxon 16° 171

406. Oxford visitors and entertainments committee. Oxford. (Oxf.), 1915,
8°. 14 pp.   G.A. Oxon 8° 611 (8)

407. WILSON, T., Oxford: an appreciation by a working man [signed T.W.
Repr. from 'The Rugby Advertiser' where half the article was de-
leted]. n. pl., [1916], 2 sh.   G.A. Gen. top. 8° 871 (1)

408. Oxford as a place of residence. (The Residential Centres Bureau ser.
of handbooks.) Oxf., [1916?], 16°. 30 pp.   G.A. Oxon 16° 138 (2)

409. Catholic social guild. C.S.G. conference, Oxford, 1916. [Programme
and historical handbook to Oxford.] (Oxf.), 1916, 8°. 39 pp+9 plates.
                    G.A. Oxon 8° 884 (2)

410. FULLEYLOVE, J., Oxford water-colours. Lond., 1916, 8°. [18 plates].
                    G.A. Oxon 8° 910

411. FYFE, D. H., Oxford. (Treasure-house ser.) Lond., 1916, 8°. 287 pp.
                                        G.A. Oxon 8° 911
 — [Another ed.] New York, [1917?].

412. [Collection of postcards, pre 1918.] 2 vols.   G.A. Oxon 4° 548, 549

413. Oxford from the air [5 photographs]. Oxf., [1919?], 4°.
                                        G.A. Oxon c. 255

414. CONWAY, L. R., Oxford, pictures. Lond., [1920], fol. 12 plates.
                                        G.A. Oxon c. 217

415. WELLS, J., The charm of Oxford, illustr. by W. G. Blackall. Lond.,
     1920, 4°. 154 pp.+27 pl.   G.A. Oxon 4° 409
 — New ed. 1934.   G.A. Oxon 4° 546

416. PAINTIN, H., A day in Oxford. Oxf., [1920], 16°. 35 pp.
                                        G.A. Oxon 16° 161
 — [Another ed. 1924.] 23 pp.   G.A. Oxon 8° 1028

    See 387 [Alden, E. C., Oxford . . . with notes on Oxford architecture. 1921.
       G.A. Oxon 8° 997].
    See 398.1 [Fifty water-colour drawings of Oxford [in the late 19th century,
       chiefly by W. Matthison] with brief notes by E. C. Alden. 1921. G.A. Oxon
       4° 441].
    See 378 [Oxford, painted by J. Fulleylove, described by E. Thomas. 1922.
       G.A. Oxon 8° 1006].

417.

418. MADAN, F., Oxford outside the guide books. Oxf., 1923, 8°. 271 pp.
                                        G.A. Oxon 8° 1014

419. TAYLOR, G. R. S., Oxford, a guide to its history and buildings. Lond.
     &c., 1923, 8°. 125 pp.   G.A. Oxon 8° 1020

420. The Associated booksellers of Great Britain and Ireland. Con-
     ference at Oxford, handbook and souvenir. Oxf., 1924, obl. 8°. 81 pp.
                                        G.A. Oxon 8° 1029

    See 416 [Paintin, H., A day in Oxford. 1924. G.A. Oxon 8° 1028].

421. Oxford, the city of spires. [Bell's Guide book. 15 issues.] Oxf., [1922–
     37], 8°.   G.A. Oxon 8° 1003
 — [1938].   G.A. Oxon 8° 1148 (12)

422. STEVENS, H. B., About and around Oxford. ('Borough' guides.)
     Chelt. &c., [1923], 8°. 48 pp.   G.A. Oxon 8° 1021
 — 4th–9th eds. [Publ. anonymously.] 1929–38.   G.A. Oxon 8° 1021

423. Oxford. (N.U.T. conference souvenir.) Lond. &c., [1925], 16°. 148 pp.
                                        G.A. Oxon 16° 168

424. OXLEY, L. RICE-, Oxford renowned. Lond., 1925, 8°. 291 pp.
                                        G.A. Oxon 8° 1042
 — 2nd ed. 1934. 263 pp.   G.A. Oxon 8° 1143
 — 3rd ed. 1947. 263 pp.   G.A. Oxon 8° 1209

425. Oxford: official handbook. Oxf., [1926], 8°. 46 pp.
G.A. Oxon 8° 1002 (13)

See 371 [Wells, J., Oxford and its colleges. 13th ed. 1926. G.A. Oxon 16° 177].
See 405 [Fletcher, C. R. L., A handy guide to Oxford. Revised ed. 1926. G.A. Oxon 16° 171].
See 404 [Davidson, N. J., Things seen in Oxford. New & revised ed. 1927. G.A. Oxon 16° 204].

426. TAYLOR, W. F., Just Oxford, camera pictures selected by W. G. Morris. (Homeland illustr., no. 6.) Lond. &c., 1928, 4°. 32 pp.
G.A. Gen. top. 4° 322 (6)

427. LAMBORN, E. A. GREENING, Oxford, a short . . . guide (written for the Seventeenth International Congress of Orientalists). Oxf., 1928, 8°. 23 pp.   G.A. Oxon 8° 1056 (3)
— [Another ed.] To which is added A brief chronology of the University press. Oxf., 1930, 8°. 24+8 pp.   G.A. Oxon 8° 1056 (17)

428. Oxford arts club. Drawings of Oxford, 1810–1830, by J. C. Buckler, lent by the Friends of the Bodleian. March 2–April 6, 1929. [Catalogue and photographic reproductions of those of Buckler's drawings which were on exhibition.] Oxf., 1929, 4°. 11 pp.+photographs.
G.A. Oxon 4° 625

429. LONG, E. J., Oxford, mother of Anglo-Saxon learning. (Nat. geogr. mag., 1929, vol. 56, p. 563–96.)   Per. 2017 d. 159

See 427 [Lamborn, E. A. G., Oxford, a short guide. 1930. G.A. Oxon 8° 1056 (17)].

430. How to see Oxford. (Pilot guide book.) (Lond.), [1930], 8°. 75 pp.
G.A. Oxon 8° 1075

431. GRAHAME, K., Oxford through a boy's eyes [in the 1860's]. (Country Life, 1932, vol. 72, p. 633–35.)   Per. 384 b. 6

432. Oxford, the colleges and university buildings, with an introduction by C. Hussey. Lond., 1932, 4°. 48 pp.   G.A. Oxon 4° 505 (3)

See 424 [Rice-Oxley, L., Oxford renowned. 2nd ed. 1934. G.A. Oxon 8° 1143].
See 415 [Wells, J., The charm of Oxford. New ed. 1934. G.A. Oxon 4° 546].
See 400 [Richards, F., Oxford. 1935. G.A. Oxon 8° 1151].

433. BETJEMAN, J., An Oxford university chest. Lond., 1938, 4°. 191 pp.
G.A. Oxon 4° 589

434. COLYER, S. W., The spell of Oxford, a book of photographs. Lond. &c., 1940, 4°. 33 plates.   G.A. Oxon 4° 615

435. LEE, R. W., Oxford, what to see and how to see it. (Engl.-speaking union.) n. pl., [1943], 8°. 4 pp.   G.A. Oxon 8° 1175 (15)
— [Another ed.] [1943].   G.A. Oxon 8° 1175 (16)

436. FITZ RANDOLPH, H., Origins of Oxford. Oxf., [1944], 8°. 16 pp.
G.A. Oxon 8° 1325 (1)
— Revised and enlarged ed. [entitled] Oxford university today, with historical notes. Oxf., 1955, 8°. 41 pp.   G.A. Oxon 8° 1255 (17)

437. CHIANG YEE, The silent traveller in Oxford. Lond., 1944, 8°. 183 pp.
G.A. Oxon 8° 1192

438. HARRIS, G. M., Changing Oxford. (Geogr. mag., 1944/45, vol. 17,
p. 70–83.)   Per. 2017 d. 229 = G.

See 424 [Rice-Oxley, L., Oxford renowned. 3rd ed. 1947. G.A. Oxon 8° 1209].
See 386 [Picturesque Oxford. New ed. 1948. G.A. Oxon 8° 1184 (10)].

439. A day in Oxford, what to see and how to see it. Oxf., [1947], 8°. 31 pp.
G.A. Oxon 8° 1184 (4)
— 4th impr. 1949.   G.A. Oxon 8° 1184 (11)

440. CANZIANI, E., Oxford in brush and pen. Lond., 1949, 8°. 203 pp.
G.A. Oxon 8° 1223

441. BURNETT, R. G., and TATTERSALL, E. W., Oxford and Cambridge in
pictures. Lond., 1950, 4°. 181 pp.   G.A. Gen. top. 4° 449

442. GARDINER, G., Oxford, a book of drawings, intr. and described by
L. Fox. Bristol, 1951, 4°. 39 pp.   G.A. Oxon 4° 676

443. WOOLLEY, A. R., Oxford university and city. Lond., 1951, 4°. 208 pp.
G.A. Oxon 4° 659

444. MUIR, D. E., Oxford. (Our beautiful homeland.) Lond. &c., [1951],
4°. 64 pp.   G.A. Oxon 4° 666

445. MAIS, S. P. B., The story of Oxford. Lond. &c., 1951, 8°. 87 pp.
G.A. Oxon 8° 1231

446. BONE, G., Came to Oxford, illustr. by M. Bone. Oxf., 1952, 4°. 133 pp.
G.A. Oxon 4° 696

447. SHARP, T., Oxford observed. Lond., 1952, 4°. 56 pp.
G.A. Oxon 4° 695

448. Pictorial guide to Oxford city and university, ed. by W. A. Stoker,
descriptive writing by L. B. Frewer. Lond., [1952], 8°. 72 pp.
G.A. Oxon 8° 1257

449. MASTERMAN, J. C., To teach the senators wisdom, or, An Oxford
guide-book. Lond., 1952, 8°. 283 pp.   G.A. Oxon 8° 1253

450. Ackermann's Oxford, with notes by H. M. Colvin. A selection of
plates from Rudolph Ackermann's History . . . 1814, and James Ingram's Memorials . . . 1837. (King Penguin books, 69.) Lond., 1954,
8°. 36 pp.+24 plates.   1707 e. 26 (69)

[See also no. 25, 26 for Ackermann and Ingram's original publications.]
See 436 [Fitz Randolph, H., Oxford university today. 1955. G.A. Oxon 8° 1255
(17)].

451. LITTLE, J. P. BROOKE, The University city of Oxford. (Pitkins Pride
of Britain pictorial books.) Lond., [1955], 4°. 24 pp.
G.A. Gen. top. 4° 516 (17)

452. MUIRHEAD, L. RUSSELL, *ed*., Oxford and Cambridge. (Blue guides.) Lond., 1958, 16°. 64 pp.   G.A. Gen. top. 16° 388

453. Look at Oxford, described by A. Rutherford, photographed by R. H. Tilbrook. Norwich, [1959], 4°. 32 pp.   G.A. Oxon 4° 748

453.1. MAGOWAN, R. S., Oxford & Cambridge, a book of photographs [Oxf., p. 1–88]. Lond., 1961, fol.   G.A. Gen. top. 4° 620

453.15. OORTHUYS, C., This is Oxford and Cambridge, 86 photographs by Cas Oorthuys, text by R. Penrose. (Photo books of the world.) Oxf. &c., [1962], 8°.   G.A. Gen. top. 8° 1721

453.2. WOOLLEY, A. R., The Clarendon guide to Oxford. Oxf., 1963, 8°. viii+147 pp.   G.A. Oxon 8° 1468

453.3. OORTHUYS, C., Term in Oxford. [Photographs.] Oxford, 1963, 4°. 144 pp.   G.A. Oxon 4° 794

453.31. Historic buildings of Oxford. [Photographs, seemingly of the 1945–50 era, with alternate pages of text.] Produced as a student exercise at the College of Technology, Oxford. [Oxf., 1963?], 4°.
      G.A. Oxon 4° 799

453.4. MORRIS, J., Oxford. Lond., 1965, 8°. 296 pp.   G.A. Oxon 8° 1505

POETICAL DESCRIPTIONS

454. VAUX, F., Detur pulchriori: or, a poem in the praise of the Vniversity of Oxford [signed F.V.]. [Madan 2372.] [Oxf.], 1658, 4°. 8 pp.
      Wood 515 (18)

455. VERNON, F., Oxonium, poema, authore F.V. [Description of Oxford and neighbourhood in Latin verse.] [Madan 2760.] Oxon., 1667, 4°. 28 pp.
— [Another issue.] [Madan 2761.]   Bliss B 72 (3)

456. SZILÁGYI, G., Acrostichon hoc laudi & honori Universitatis Oxoniensis . . . sincero canebam animo Georgius Szilágyi Ungarus anno 1671. [Madan 2876.] [Lond.?], (1671), s. sh.   Wood 276a (521)

457. BENLOWES, E., Oxonii encomium [4 poems by E. Benlowes]. [Madan 2915.] Oxon., 1672, fol. 20 pp.   Gough Oxf. 90 (14)

458. BENLOWES, E., Oxonii elogia, academicis præcellentioribus [by E. Benlowes]. [Madan 2968.] [Oxf., 1673], s. sh.   Wood 423 (45)

459. TICKELL, T., Oxford, a poem [by T. Tickell]. Lond., 1707, fol. 10 pp.
      G.A. fol. A 240 (1)

460. AMHURST, N., Oculus Britanniæ: an heroi-panegyrical poem on the University of Oxford [signed Philo-musus]. Lond., 1724, 8°. [vi]+64.pp.
      Gough Oxf. 50 (1)

461. HEANY, J., Oxford, the seat of the muses, a poem. Oxf., 1738, 4°.
14 pp.　　　　　　　　　　　　　　　　　Gough Oxf. 90 (12)
— 2nd ed. Lond., 1738.　　　　　　　　　　G. Pamph. 2288 (18)

462. MASON, W., Isis, an elegy. Lond., 1749, 4°. 16 pp.　　　2804 d. 7 (6)

463. WARTON, T., The triumph of Isis, a poem [by T. Warton] occasioned by Isis, an elegy [by W. Mason]. Lond., [1749], 4°. 16 pp.
　　　　　　　　　　　　　　　　　　　　Vet. A 4 d. 74 (2)
— 2nd ed., corrected. Lond., 1750, 4°. 16 pp.　Gough Oxf. 90 (18)
— 3rd ed. 1750.　　　　　　　　　　　　　　G. Pamph. 96 (6)
— [Another ed.] n. pl., 1750, 8°. 16 pp.　　　Vet. A 4 d. 74 (1)
— [Another ed.] (Coll. of poems by several hands, vol. 1.) Lond., 1768,
8°.　　　　　　　　　　　　　　　　　　　Godw. subt. 259

464. GREEN, G. S., The images of the ancients, particularly those in the
University of Oxford . . . a poem. By a tradesman of Oxford [G. S.
Green]. Lond., 1758, 8°. 24 pp.　　　　　　G.A. Oxon 8° 62 (7)

465. AUBRY, M., Oxonii dux poeticus, sive Latinis versibus . . . descriptio,
qua fere publica quæque Oxonii monumenta adumbrantur. Oxonii,
1795, 8°. 64 pp.　　　　　　　　　　　　　Gough Oxf. 17 (6)

466. AUBRY, M., The beauties of Oxford, a tr. of a Latin poem written in
1795 by W. Willes. Louth, 1811, 8°. 70 pp.　　G.A. Oxon 8° 430

467. MONTGOMERY, R., Oxford, a poem. [Engraved title-leaf: Montgomery's Oxford.] Oxf., 1831, 8°. 258 pp.　　G.A. Oxon 8° 113
— 2nd ed. 1831.　　　　　　　　　　　　　　　　280 e. 3956
— 3rd ed. 1831.　　　　　　　　　　　　　　　　280 e. 3957
— 4th ed. 1835.　　　　　　　　　　　　　　　　280 e. 2452

468. PHILO-PURITAN pseud., Three days at Oxford in 1846, in three
fyttes. Lond., 1855, 8°. 71 pp.　　　　　　　　280 r. 524

469. MORRAH, H. A., In college groves, and other Oxford verses, chiefly
repr. from the Oxford magazine. Oxf. &c., 1894, 8°. 101 pp.　280 d. 134

470. Oxford verses, ed. by Rosslyn Bruce. Oxf. &c., 1894, 8°. 80 pp.
　　　　　　　　　　　　　　　　　　　　　2805 e. 154

471. Sphinx pseud. Oxford, a tribute. Oxf. &c., 1913, 8°. 12 pp.
　　　　　　　　　　　　　　　　　　　　28001 e. 1314 (17)

472. RIDLEY, M. R., Oxford, Newdigate prize poem. Oxf. &c., 1913, 8°.
10 pp.　　　　　　　　　　　　　　　　　28041 e. 11 (11)

473. STANIER, M., Culex's guide to Oxford. [Poems.] Abingdon-on-
Thames, 1955, 8°. 51 pp.　　　　　　　　　28001 e. 7885

ANTHOLOGIES

474. Echoes from the Oxford magazine, reprints of seven years. Oxf. &c.,
1890, 8°. 180 pp.　　　　　　　　　　　　　2808 e. 7
— 2nd ed.　　　　　　　　　　　　　　　　　2808 e. 53
— [Another ed.] Lond., 1908, 12°. 159 pp.　　2808 f. 19

475. More echoes from the Oxford magazine, a second series of reprints of seven years. Oxf. &c., 1896, 8°. 158 pp.   2805 e. 169

476. In praise of Oxford. Oxf. &c., [1908], 16°. 20 pp.+6 plates.
                                        G.A. Oxon 16° 33 (29)

477. FIRTH, J. B., ed., The minstrelsy of Isis, an anthology of poems relating to Oxford and all phases of Oxford life. Lond., 1908, 8°. 397 pp.
                                        2805 e. 355

478. BALL, O. H., ed., The Oxford garland, prose & verse in praise of Oxford. Lond., 1909, 8°. 96 pp.   G.A. Oxon 8° 775

479. SECCOMBE, T., and SCOTT, H. S., eds., In praise of Oxford, an anthology in prose and verse. History and topography (Life and manners). 2 vols. Lond., 1910, 12, 8°.   G.A. Oxon 4° 737

480. KNIGHT, W., ed., The glamour of Oxford, verse and prose. Oxf. &c., 1911, 8°. 263 pp.   G.A. Oxon 8° 820

481. LEWIS, C. DAY, and FENBY, C., eds., Anatomy of Oxford, an anthology. Lond., 1938, 8°. 318 pp.   G.A. Oxon 8° 1171

482. HORDER, T. J., 1st baron, ed., In praise of Oxford, an anthology. Lond., 1955, 16°. 56 pp.   2705 f. 403 (41)

ARCHITECTURE AND ALLIED ARTS
General

See 569 [A speech which incidentally describes recent architectural and public works at Oxford. 1624?].

483. TATHAM, E., Oxonia explicata & ornata. Proposals for disengaging and beautifying the University and City of Oxford [by E. Tatham]. Lond., 1773, 4°. 25 pp.   G.A. Oxon 4° 46
— 2nd ed., enlarged. Lond., 1777, 8°. 43 pp. G.A. Oxon 8° 1033 (11)
— New ed., by E. Tatham. Oxf., 1820, 4°. 24 pp. G.A. Oxon 4° 47

484. DALLAWAY, J., Anecdotes of the arts in England; or Comparative remarks on architecture, sculpture, and painting, chiefly illustrated by specimens at Oxford. Lond., 1800, 8°. 526 pp.   Douce D 175

484.1. DALLAWAY, J., Observations on English architecture . . . including a critical itinerary of Oxford and Cambridge. [Oxford univ., p. 110–67.] Lond., 1806, 8°.   Douce D subt. 1

485. Specimens of Gothic architecture . . . selected from ancient buildings at Oxford, &c. Drawn and etched by F. Mackenzie and A. Pugin. Lond., [1816], 4°. 61 plates.   G.A. Oxon 4° 30

See 6576 [New method of refacing buildings. 1829].

486. JEWITT, O., On the late, or debased, Gothic buildings of Oxford from the reign of Elizabeth to the end of the 17th century. (Archaeol. journ., 1851, vol. 8, p. 382–96.)   Per. G.A. Gen. top. 8° 529 = R.
— [Repr.] 16 pp.   G.A. Oxon 8° 72 (9)

487. BRUTON, E. G., Private halls and collegiate additions; their architecture and ecclesiology. With plans. Oxf. &c., 1854, 8°. 16 pp.+3 plans.
G.A. Oxon 8° 71 (5)

488. College and City improvements. (Builder, 1856, vol. 14, p. 586, 87.)
N. 1863 c. 1
[Similarly published in the Builder in the following years: 1867, 1868, 1869, 1870, 1872, 1873, 1874, 1875, 1876, 1878, 1882, 1883.]

489. FREEMAN, E. A., The new buildings in Oxford. (Proc., Oxf. architect. and hist. soc., 1862, N.S., vol. 1, p. 167–72.)
Per. G.A. Oxon 8° 498 = R.

490. PARKER, J., Chronological table of buildings in Oxford [by J. Parker]. (Visit of the Architect soc. of the archdeaconries of Northampton and Oakham, July 17, 1877.) [Oxf.], (1877), 16°. 8 pp.
G.A. Oxon 16° 136 (11)

491. BRUTON, E. G., On post-Reformation architecture in Oxford. (Proc., Oxf. architect. and hist. soc., 1881, N.S., vol. 4, p. 21–27.)
Per. G.A. Oxon 8° 498 = R.

492. WOODS, F. H., Recent buildings in Oxford. (Proc., Oxf. architect. and hist. soc., 1882, N.S., vol. 4, p. 51–58.)   Per. G.A. Oxon 8° 498 = R.

493. Oxford. (Builder, 1890, vol. 59, p. 99–103.)   G.A. Oxon 4° 577 (45)

494. SAINTENOY, P., Notes de voyage. Architecture et archéologie. Kent, Oxfordshire. [Oxford University p. 59–126.] Bruxelles, 1894, 4°.
17356 d. 72

495. HURST, H., Remains of external pargetting in Oxford. (Proc., Oxf. architect. and hist. soc., 1897, N.S., vol. 6, p. 135–40.)
Per. G.A. Oxon 8° 498 = R.
— [Another issue.] (Berks, Bucks & Oxon archaeol. journ., 1898, vol. 4, p. 105–11.)   Per. G.A. Berks 4° 270 = R.

496. PARRY, J. W., The buildings of Oxford, from an engineer's point of view. (Engineering mag., 1898, vol. 16, p. 397–416; 1899, vol. 16, p. 567–86.)   G.A. Oxon 4° 399b (8)

497. GUINEY, L. I., The Gothic afterglow in Oxford. (Mag. of Christian art, 1907, p. 45–53.)   G.A. Oxon c. 317 (23*)
See 387 [Alden, E. C., Oxford . . . with notes on Oxford architecture. 1909].

498. NICHOLSON, E. W. B., Can we not save architecture in Oxford? Oxf. &c., 1910, 4°. 12 pp.   G.A. Oxon 4° 262 (5)

499. LAMBORN, E. A. GREENING, The story of architecture in Oxford stone [the evolution of architecture as illustrated by Oxford]. Oxf., 1912, 8°. 288 pp.   G.A. Oxon 16° 216

500. VALLANCE, A., The old colleges of Oxford, their architectural history illustrated and described. Lond., (1912), fol. xxxiv+133 pp.+ 50 plates.   G.A. Oxon b. 79

501. CORLETTE, H. C., Oxford: a school of architecture. (Journ., Roy. inst. of Brit. architects, 1922/23, 3rd ser., vol. 30, p. 74–86.)
Soc. 17356 d. 27
— Repr. 1923. 13 pp. G.A. Oxon 4° 439
— [Repr. without illustr.] (Oxf. mag., 1923, vol. 41, p. 158–61; 177, 78.) Per. G.A. Oxon 4° 141

502. In Oxford and Cambridge: preliminary glimpses of university additions, by 'mr. Smith'. (Architect's journ., 1929, vol. 69, p. 94–100.)
N. 1863 c. 12

503. PURCHON, W. S., Oxford *versus* Cambridge: an architectural match. (Architect's journ., 1929, vol. 70, p. 90–92.) N. 1863 c. 12

504. BYRON, R., Oxford revisited. (Architectural review, 1929, vol. 65, p. 111–17.) Per. 17356 c. 8

504.5. SMITH, A. H., New buildings in Oxford. (Oxford, 1934, vol. 1, no. 2, p. 33–43.) Per. G.A. Oxon 8° 1141

505. HOLROYD, M., New light [i.e. floodlight] on Oxford architecture [signed M. H.]. (Oxf. mag., 1935, vol. 53, p. 597, 98.)
Per. G.A. Oxon 4° 141

506. HOLROYD, M., Oxford architecture [signed M.H.]. (Oxf. mag., 1936, vol. 55, p. 51, 52.) Per. G.A. Oxon 4° 141

507. An inventory of the historical monuments in the City [and University] of Oxford. (Royal comm. on hist. monuments.) Lond., 1939, 4°. 244 pp. + 216 plates. G.A. Oxon 4° 633 = R.

508. HOLROYD, M., More new buildings in Oxford. (Oxford, 1940, vol. 7, no. 1, p. 41–49.) Per. G.A. Oxon 8° 1141

509. BETJEMAN, J., Gothic revival in Oxford in the nineteenth century. (Oxford, 1940, vol. 6, no. 3, p. 42–57.) Per. G.A. Oxon 8° 1141

510. HARVEY, J. H., The building works and architects of cardinal Wolsey, an essay, based largely on original documents, on the Gothic design of the early 16th century [concerns Balliol, Christ Church, Corpus Christi, & Magdalen colleges; also St. Frideswide's monastery]. (Journ., Brit. archaeol. assoc., 1943, 3rd ser. vol. 8, p. 50–59.)
Per. G.A. Gen. top. 8°. 526 = R.

511. ARKELL, W. J., Oxford stone. Lond., 1947, 8°. 185 pp.
G.A. Oxon 8° 1210

512. DAVIS, R. H. C., The chronology of perpendicular architecture in Oxford. (Oxoniensia, 1946/7, vol. 11/12, p. 75–89.)
Per. G.A. Oxon 4° 658 = R.

513. PANTIN, W. A., The development of domestic architecture in Oxford. (Antiq. journ., 1947, vol. 27, p. 120–50.) Per. 17572 d. 73 = R.

514. Ministry of local government and planning. Provisional list of buildings of architectural or historic interest for consideration in connection
with the provisions of sect. 30 of the Town and country planning act,
1947. City of Oxford [incl. University]. [Reprod. from typewriting.]
n. pl., 1950, fol. 174 pp.   G.A. Oxon c. 322 = R.

515. RICHARDS, J. M., Recent building in Oxford and Cambridge. (Architectural review, 1952, vol. 112, p. 73–79, 413, 14.)   Per. 17356 c. 8

516. RENDEL, H. S. GOODHART-, Oxford buildings criticized. (Oxoniensia,
1952/53, vol. 17/18, p. 200–15.)   Per. G.A. Oxon 4° 658 = R.

517. Stone restoration in Oxford. (Monumental journ., 1956, vol. 23,
p. 503–06.)

518. SHOCK, M., The new face of Oxford. [University building projects.]
(Amer. Oxonian, 1961, vol. 48, p. 105–11.)   Per. G.A. Oxon 8° 889

519. Oxford university design society. New Oxford, a guide to the modern
city. [Descriptions and comments on new buildings.] (Oxf.), [1961], 4°.
58 pp.   G.A. Oxon 4° 477

519.1. ALEXANDER, J. H., A home for dinosaurs. [On Oxford architecture.]
(Essay soc. of St. Edm. Hall, Five essays, 1964, p. 29–50.) 27041 e. 11

519.2. PANTIN, W., The halls and schools of medieval Oxford: an
attempt at reconstruction. (Oxf. studies presented to D. Callus; Oxf.
hist. soc., 1964, N.S., vol. 16, p. 31–100.)   G.A. Oxon 8° 360 = R.

Bells

520. B., W. C., A note on the chimes of Oxford. (Oxf. mag., 1933, vol. 51,
p. 732.)   Per. G.A. Oxon 4° 141

Glass

521. GRINLING, C. H., Ancient stained glass in Oxford. (Proc., Oxf.
architect. and hist. soc., 1883, N.S., vol. 4, p. 111–84.)
                                          Per. G.A. Oxon 8° 495 = R.

522. POOLE, MRS R. L., Early 17th century portraits in stained glass at
Oxford. (Journ., Brit. soc. of master glass-painters, 1929, vol. 3,
p. 13–20.)   Soc. 17031 d. 6

523. LAMBORN, E. A. GREENING, Painted glass in Oxford. (Oxford, 1939,
vol. 5, no. 3, p. 25–36.)   Per. G.A. Oxon 8° 1141

HERALDRY

See also 6492–6500. Colleges: heraldry.

524. [Prints &c. of University arms.]   G.A. Oxon a. 72

See 560 [Sansbury, J., Ilium in Italium. 1608].

525. JACKSON, W., The muses banner, or, a compleat ensign of the arms of the University of Oxford and all the colleges therein. n. pl., [c. 1710], s. sh.   Rawl. prints a. 5 (f. 88)

526. D., J. M., Description of the Oxford University arms. [Oxf.], 1871, s. sh.   G.A. Oxon c. 250 (vii)

527. LANDON, P., Arms of Oxford university. (Antiquary, 1901, N.S., vol. 37, p. 208–12, 230–33.)   Per. 17572 d. 32

528. LAMBORN, E. A. GREENING, The arms of Oxford. (Oxford, 1938, vol. 5, no. 1, p. 31–49.)   Per. G.A. Oxon 8° 1141

529. LITTLE, J. P. BROOKE-, The arms of Oxford University & colleges. (Coat of Arms, 1951, vol. 1, p. 157–61, 198–200, 235–38.)
                                                      Per. 21932 e. 42

530. Representations of the arms of the University of Oxford in use at the University Press and elsewhere. Oxf., 1956, fol. 24 pp.+[4 pp. of Binder's brasses].   21943 c. 6

531. HASSALL, W. O., The Three Kings and the University arms. (Oxoniensia, 1958, vol. 23, p. 143, 44.)   Per. G.A. Oxon 4° 658 = R.

PICTURES, PLATE, AND HISTORIC TREASURES

532. CUST, L., Portraits at the universities. (Fasciculus Ioanni Willis Clark dicatus, Cantab., 1909, p. 423–37.)   3974 d. 121

533. POOLE, MRS R. L., Catalogue of portraits in the possession of the University, colleges, City and County of Oxford. 3 vols. Oxf., 1912, 25, 8°.   17061 d. 44 = S.
— [Another ed.] (Oxf. hist. soc., vol. 57, 81, 82.) Oxf., 1912, 26, 8°.
                                                      G.A. Oxon 8° 360 = R.

534. BELL, C. F., English seventeenth-century portrait drawing in Oxford collections, by C. F. Bell (and R. Poole). 2 pt. (Walpole soc., vol. 5, 14.) Oxf., 1917, 26, 4°.   Soc. 17006 c. 82 (5, 14)

See also 4688–4700. Portraits and Caricatures [of Oxford alumni exclusively].

535. MOFFATT, H. C., Old Oxford plate. Lond., 1906, 4°. 209 pp.+96 pl.
                                                      17551 d. 29

536. HILL, R. H., The University plate in the sixteenth century. (Bodleian quarterly record, 1924, vol. 4, p. 141–44.) Per. 2590 d. Oxf. 1. 41 = R.

537. Treasures of Oxford. Catalogue of the exhibits. (Goldsmiths' hall, London.) [With] Illustrations. Lond., 1953, 8°. 90 pp.+46 plates.
                                                      17581 e. 77

538. HUGHES, G. B., Treasures of Oxford. (Country Life, 1953, vol. 113, p. 1610–12.)   Per. 384 b. 6

EXTERNAL RELATIONS
General

539. BENTHAM, E., The honor of the University of Oxford defended, against the illiberal aspersions of E—d B—e [E. Burke, concerning Convocation's address of 26 Oct., 1775 on the American rebellion]. Tr. from the orig. Lat. of E. B— D.D. Lond., [1781?], 8°. 36 pp.
Gough Oxf. 49 (2)

540. To . . . David Lloyd George, and the other representatives of the British Empire at the peace conference. [Memorial of resident members of the University about the lenient treatment they believe to be intended towards the Turkish Empire.] n. pl., [1919], fol. 5 pp.
G.A. Oxon b. 141 (129)

541. KONOVALOV, S., Oxford and Russia, an inaugural lecture. Oxf., 1947, 8°. 24 pp.
325 d. 9

With the country at large

542. London, Anno Dom. 1647. A brief declaration of those that have accepted the trust of receiving and distributing such sums of money as wel-affected persons shall subscribe towards the maintenance of hopeful students at both the universities for the . . . supply of the Church . . . with . . . ministers . . . [Madan 1919.] (Lond., 1647), s. sh.
Wood 276a (305)

543. To the members of the Convocation of the University of Oxford . . . [Arguments against the manner in which members are asked to contribute to the 'exigencies of the state'.] [Oxf.], (1779), s. sh.
G.A. Oxon b. 111 (62)

544. [Begin.] It having been understood . . . [Announcement of a committee to collect articles of clothing &c. throughout the University for transmission to the Crimea.] [Oxf.], (1854), s. sh.
G.A. Oxon c. 70 (291)

545. University patriotic fund. [Announcement and list of subscribers.] [Oxf.], 1854, s. sh.   G.A. Oxon c. 70 (290)
— Amount of contributions received to . . . Feb. 3, 1855. [Oxf.], 1855, s. sh.   G.A. Oxon c. 71 (348)

545.5. GRIFFIN, J., A neglected moral function of the University [the nation's moral scapegoat.] (Oxf. mag., 1966, p. 220, 21.)
Per. G.A. Oxon 4° 141

With the Crown and Royal family

See also 1367–74. Oaths.

546. BEREBLOCK, J., Commentarii sive ephemeræ actiones rerum illustrium Oxonii gestarum in adventu . . . Elizabethæ (A.D. MDLXVI).

Per J. B. (Historia vitæ et regni Ricardi II, ed. T. Hearnius, 1729, p. 251–96.) Mus. Bibl. II 89
— [Another ed.] (Nichols's Progresses of q. Eliz., 1788, vol. 1, p. 35–59 of The queen at Oxford, 1566.) DD 74 Jur.
— [Another ed.] (Oxf. hist. soc., 8, p. 111–50.) Oxf., 1887, 8°.
G.A. Oxon 8° 360 = R.

See 282 [Neale, T., Chronographia, una cum descriptione, ad Elizabetham conscripta, 1566. 1590; subsequently reissued with Bereblock's views in 1713, no. 291].

547. The queen's progress, 1566 [running title]. The queen at Oxford, 1566. (Nichols's Progresses of q. Eliz., 1788, vol. 1, 110 pp.; vol. 3, p. 107–13, with a reprod. of the Agas map and 17 views by Bereblock.)
DD 74, 76 Jur.
— [Another ed.] (Nichols's Progresses of q. Eliz., 1823, new ed., vol. 1, p. 206–50.) 4° BS. 381 = A.

548. A brief rehearsall of all such things as were done in the University of Oxford during the queen's majesty's abode there [1566]. This exhibited by Richard Stephens, as an extract drawn out of a longer treatise made by mr. Neale. From Harl. MS. 7033, f. 139. (Nichols's Progresses of q. Eliz., 1788, vol. 1, p. 95–100 of The queen at Oxford, 1566.) DD 74 Jur.
— [Another ed.] (Oxf. hist. soc., 8, p. 195–205.) Oxf., 1887, 8°.
G.A. Oxon 8° 360 = R.

549. The queen's journey to Oxford, 1566. Communicated by mr. Gutch from Wood's MSS. (Nichols's Progresses of q. Eliz., 1788, vol. 3, p. 107–14.) DD 76 Jur.
— [Another ed., *entitled*] The queen's entertainment at Oxford. From Wood's MS. corrected by mr. Gough. (Nichols's Progresses, 1823, new ed., vol. 1, p. 206–17.) 4° BS. 381 = A.

550. Ad illustrissimam r. Elizabetham, L. H. [L. Humphrey] vice-can. Oxon. oratio Woodstochiæ habita an. 1572, August 31. [Madan 48.] Lond., 1572, 4°. 24 pp. 8° R 20 (1) Art. BS
— [Another ed.] 1572. Wood 512 (?)

551. Oratio ad sereniss. Angliæ . . . reginam Elisabetham, in aula Woodstochiensi habita a Laurentio Humfredo, Academiæ Oxoniensis procancellario anno 1575. Septemb. 11. [Madan 52.] Lond., 1575, 4°. 52 pp. Gough Oxf. 116 (5)
— [Another ed.] (Nichols's Progresses of q. Elizabeth, 1823, new ed., vol. 1, p. 583, &c.) 4° BS. 381 = A.

552. SANFORD, J., Apollinis et musarum εὐκτικὰ εἰδύλλια in . . . Elizabethæ . . . Oxoniam aduentum . . . MDLXXXXII. [Madan 126.] Oxon., (1592), 4°. 24 pp. B.M.
— [Repr.] (Oxf. hist. soc., vol. 8. Elizabethan Oxford, p. 277–99.) Oxf., 1887, 4°. G.A. Oxon. 8° 360=R.

553. The grand reception and entertainment of queen Elizabeth at Oxford in 1592. From a ms. account originally written by mr. Philip Stringer.

(Nichols's Progresses of q. Eliz., 1788, vol. 2, p. 19–30 of The queen at
Oxford, 1592.)   DD 75 Jur.
— [Another ed.] (Nichols's Progresses &c., 1823, new ed., vol. 3,
p. 149–60.)   4° BS. 383 = A.

554. WOOD, A., [Description of the queen's second visit to Oxford in 1592,
extr. from the Annals.] (Nichols's Progresses of q. Eliz., new ed., 1823,
vol. 3, p. 144–48.)   4° BS. 383 = A.

555. Oxoniensis academiæ funebre officium in memoriam . . . Elisabethæ,
nuper Angliæ, Franciæ, & Hiberniæ reginæ. [Madan 228.] Oxon., 1603,
4°. 188 pp.   4° O 14 Art.
— [Another ed.] (Nichols's Progresses of q. Eliz., 1788, vol. 3, 172 pp.)
                                                                 DD 76 Jur.

556. Academiæ Oxoniensis pietas erga serenissimum . . . Iacobum . . .
regem . . . [Madan 229.] Oxon., 1603, 4°. 212 pp.   4° O 13 (1) Art.
— [Another issue.] [Madan 230.]   Gough Oxf. 54

557. NIXON, A., Oxfords triumph: in the royall entertainement of his . . .
maiestie, the queene and the prince: the 27 of August last, 1605. With
the kinges oration . . . [Madan 261.] Lond., 1605, 4°. 48 pp.   B.M.

558. The preparation at Oxford in August 1605 against the coming thither
of king James, with the queen and the young prince; together with the
things then . . . done . . . (The progresses . . . of king James I, by J.
Nichols, vol. 1, p. 530–59.) Lond., 1828, 4°.   4° BS. 377 = A.

559. WAKE, I., Rex platonicus: sive, De . . . Iacobi . . . regis ad . . . Aca-
demiam Oxoniensem adventu, Aug. 27. anno 1605 narratio. [Madan
288.] Oxon., 1607, 4°. 152 pp.   Gough Oxf. 10
— Ed. 2a. [Madan 291.] 1607. 16°. 250 pp.   Antiq. f. E. 1607.1
— Ed. 3a. [Madan 425.] 1615.   Tanner 367
— Ed. 4a. [Madan 591.] 1627.   Douce W 8
— Ed. 5a [Madan 800.] 1635.   Gough Oxf. 32
— Ed. 6a. [Madan 2628.] 1663.   8° W 7 Art. BS.

560. SANSBURY, J., ed., Ilium in Italium. Oxonia ad protectionem regis
sui omnium optimi filia, pedisequa. [Signed I. S.] [Madan 301.]
Oxon., 1608, 16°. 48 pp.   Gough Oxf. 30

561. Eidyllia [by members of Broadgates hall] in obitum fulgentissimi
Henrici Walliæ principis duodecimi, Romæq; ruentis terroris maximi,
quo nihil maius . . . [Madan 342.] Oxon., 1612, 4°. 36 pp.   Wood 484 (2)

562. Iusta Oxoniensium [poems by members of the University on the
death of Henry, prince of Wales.] [Madan 344.] Lond., 1612, 4°.
124 pp.   Pamph. C 10 (3)
— [Another issue.] [Madan 345.]   4° O 12 Art.

563. Epithalamia, sive Lusus Palatini in nuptias . . . Friderici comitis
Palatini . . . et . . . Elisabethæ Iacobi . . . Britanniæ regis filiæ primo-
genitæ. [Madan 375.] Oxon., 1613, 4°. 128 pp.   4° O 14 (2) Art.
— [Another issue.] [Madan 376.]

564. FENNOR, W., The deciding of the difference betwixt the two universities . . . about the kings entertainement, spoke . . . the xiij. of Iuly, 1615.
By W. F. [Sig. E1—3 of Fennors Descriptions.] [In verse.] [Madan
440.] Lond., 1616, 4°.   4° F 12 (2) Art.

565. Iacobi ara ceu, in Iacobi . . . regis . . . auspicatissimum reditum e
Scotia in Angliam, Academiæ Oxoniensis gratulatoria. [Madan 450.]
Oxon., 1617, 4°. 80 pp.   Mar. 528

566. Academiæ Oxoniensis funebria sacra. Æternæ memoriæ . . . Annæ . . .
Iacobi Magnæ Britanniæ . . . regis . . . sponsæ, dicata. [Madan 470.]
Oxon., 1619, 4°. 144 pp.   4° I 21 Art.

See 5713 [Lyell, J. P. R., King James I and the Bodleian Library catalogue of
1620. 1933].
See 1125 [Oath not to teach, etc., that it is lawful to take up arms against a
Sovereign. 1622].

567. Votiva, sive ad . . . Iacobum Magnæ Britanniæ . . . regem, de auspi-
cato . . . Caroli Walliæ principis in regiam Hispanicam aduentu, pia . . .
Oxoniensium gratulatio. [Madan 509.] Lond., 1623, 4°. 42 pp.
                       4° S 4 (4) Art. BS.

568. Carolus redux [poems to congratulate prince Charles on his safe return from Spain]. [Madan 510.] Oxon., 1623, 4°. 92 pp.
                       4° H 17 (3) Art.

569. PRIDEAUX, J., Alloquium serenissimo regi Iacobo Woodstochiæ
habitum 24. Augusti anno 1624. [A speech, signed I. P., which incidentally describes recent architectural and public works at Oxford.]
[Madan 519.] [Oxf., 1624?], 4°. 8 pp.   Wood 512 (9)
— [Repr. in Prideaux's Perez-Vzzah in 1625, Bliss B29 (2); and in
1637.]

570. Oxoniensis Academiæ parentalia . . . memoriæ . . . Iacobi Magnæ
Britanniæ . . . regis . . . dicata. [Madan 530.] Oxon., 1625, 4°. 96 pp.
                       4° I 21 (9) Art.
— [Another issue.] 104 pp. [Madan 531.]

571. Epithalamia Oxoniensia in auspicatissimum . . . Caroli Magnæ
Britanniæ . . . regis, cum Henretta Maria . . . Henrici . . . Gallorum
regis filia, connubium. [Madan 528.] Oxon., 1625, 4°. 100 pp.
                   Antiq. e. E. 1625. 4
— [Another issue.] [Madan 529.]   4° M 37 (3) Art.

572. Britanniæ natalis [poems on the birth of Charles ii]. [Madan 651.]
Oxon., 1630, 4°. 82 pp.   Wood 484 (3)
— [Another issue.] [Madan 650.]

573. Musarum Oxoniensium pro rege suo soteria. [Madan 725.] Oxon.,
1633, 4°. 72 pp.   Antiq. e. E. 1633. 8
— [Another issue.] [Madan 726.]   Bliss B 38
— [Another issue on large paper.] [Madan 727.]   B.M.

574. Solis Britannici perigæum sive Itinerantis Caroli auspicatissima
periodus. [Madan 728.] Oxon., 1633, 4°. 100 pp.
— [Another issue.] [Madan 729.]
— [Another issue.] [Madan 729*.]   4° I 21 (8) Art.

575. Vitis Carolinæ gemma altera sive auspicatissima ducis Eboracensis
genethliaca decantata ad Vada Isidis. [Madan 730.] Oxon., 1633, 4°.
90 pp.   BB 16 (3) Art. Seld.
— [Another ed.] [Madan 731.] 104 pp.   B 13. 4 (2) Linc.

576. Coronæ Carolinæ quadratura, sive, Perpetuandi imperii Carolini ex
quarto pignore feliciter suscepto captatum augurium [poems on the
birth of princess Elizabeth]. [Madan 815.] Oxon., 1636, 4°. 92 pp.
                                                             Mal. 910
— [Madan 816.]   Ashm. 1032 (6)

577. TAYLOR, A. J., The royal visit to Oxford in 1636. (Oxoniensia, 1936,
vol. i, p. 151–58.)   Per. G.A. Oxon 4° 658 = R.

578. Flos Britannicus veris novissimi filiola Carolo & Mariæ nata xvii
Martii anno M.DC.XXXVI [poems on the birth of princess Anne].
[Madan 840.] Oxon., [1637], 4°. 100 pp.   Antiq. e. E. 1636. 5
— [Another issue.] [Madan 840*.]   Antiq. e. E. 1636. 6
— [Another issue.] [Madan 840**.]   Antiq. e. E. 1636. 7
— [Another issue.] [Madan 840***.]   4° H 17 (5) Art.
— [Another issue.] [Madan 840****.]   Antiq. e. E. 1636. 8
— [Another issue.] [Madan 841.]

579. Musarum Oxoniensium charisteria pro serenissima regina Maria
recens e nixus laboriosi discrimine recepta. [On the birth of princess
Catherine.] [Madan 871] Oxon., 1638, 4°. 88 pp.   Gough Oxf. 54

580. Horti Carolini rosa altera [poems on the birth of prince Henry].
[Madan 931.] Oxon., 1640, 4°. 108 pp.   4° I 21 (4) Art.

581. Προτέλεια Anglo-Batava, plusquam virgineo, Guilielmo Arausi &
Mariæ Britanniarum Academia Oxoniensi procurante. [Madan 964.]
Oxon., 1641, 4°. 68 pp.   Wood 320 (9)
— [Another issue.] [Madan 964*.] 66 pp.   B 13. 4 (8) Linc.

582. Eucharistica Oxoniensia, in . . . Caroli . . . regis . . . e Scotia reditum.
[Madan 965.] Oxon., 1641, 4°. 88 pp.   4° I 12 (6) Art.

583. Musarum Oxoniensium ἐπιβατήρια serenissimæ reginarum [Henri-
ettæ] Mariæ ex Batavia feliciter reduci publico voto d.d.d. [Madan
1418.] Oxon., 1643, 4°. 64 pp.   4° I 21 Art.

584. Musarum Oxoniensium ἐλαιοφόρια, sive ob fædera, auspiciis . . .
Oliveri . . . protectoris, inter rempub. Britannicam & ordines fæderatos
Belgii fæliciter stabilita, gentis togatæ ad vada Isidis celeusma metri-
cum. [Madan 2243.] Oxon., 1654, 4°. 104 [really 84] pp.
                                                         B 13. 4 Linc.

585. IRELAND, T., Momus elencticus or a light come-off upon that serious
piece of drollerie presented by the vice-chancellor of Oxon . .   at

Whitehall, to expell the melancholy of the court [by T. Ireland].
[Madan 2246.] [Lond., 1654], 8°. 8 pp. Wood 515 (13)
[A skit on no. 584.]

586. Britannia rediviva. [Verses on the restoration of Charles II.] [Madan
2466.] Oxon., 1660, 4°. 156 pp. 4° M 16 (1) Art. BS.

587. Epicedia Academiæ Oxoniensis, in obitum . . . Henrici ducis Gloces-
trensis. [Madan 2467.] Oxon., 1660, 4°. 72 pp. Gough Oxf. 54

588. Epicedia Academiæ Oxoniensis, in obitum . . . Mariæ principis
Arausionensis. Oxon., 1660, 4°. 80 pp. Vet. A 3 e. 96
— [Another issue.] [Madan 2543.] Oxon., 1661, 4°. 84 pp.
4° I 21 (1) Art.

589. Domiduca Oxoniensis: sive Musæ Academicæ gratulatio ob auspicatissimum serenissimæ; principis Catherinæ Lusitanæ, regi suo de-
sponsatæ in Angliam appulsum. [Madan 2578.] Oxon., 1662, 4°. 144 pp.
4° M 16 Art. BS.

590. Advertisements from the delegates of Convocation for his majesties
reception, for the heads of houses to deliver with great charge unto
their companies. [Madan 2644.] [Oxf., 1663], s. sh. Don. b. 12 (5)
— [Another issue.] Don. b. 12 (5a)

591. Epicedia Universitatis Oxoniensis in obitum . . . principis Henriettæ
Mariæ reginæ matris. [Madan 2814.] Oxon., 1669, fol. 56 pp.
A 3. 12 Art.

592. Epicedia Universitatis Oxoniensis in obitum . . . principis Henriettæ
Mariæ [really Henrietta Anne] ducissæ Aurelianensis. [Madan 2845.]
Oxon., 1670, fol. 60 pp. AA 52 Art.

593. Orders for the reception of . . . the prince of Orange agreed upon by
the vice-chancellor & delegats . . . [Madan 2858.] [Oxf., 1670], s. sh.
Wood 276a (329)

594. Quæstiones discutiendæ in comitiis Oxonii habitis in honorem . . .
Gulielmi Henrici principis Arausionensis . . . Decemb. 20. An. 1670.
Oxon., 1670, s. sh. Don. b. 12 (14)

595. Epicedia Universitatis Oxoniensis in obitum . . . principis Annæ
ducissæ Eboracensis. [Madan 2869.] Oxon., 1671, fol. 52 pp.
AA 52 Art.

596. Comitia habita . . . Ap. 23. An. 1685. die inaugurationis . . . Jacobi II.
et . . . Mariæ . . . (Oxf.), 1685, s. sh. Wood 276a (408)

597. Pietas Universitatis Oxoniensis in obitum . . . regis Caroli secundi.
[*With*] Supplex recognitio et gratulatio solennis . . . Jacobo secundo . . .
regi . . . Oxon., 1685, fol. 86 pp. H 9. 15 (1) Art.
— [Another issue]. Magd. coll.
[Bodley has an imperf. copy. Pamph. A 170 (16)].

598.

599. The humble address and recognition of the University of Oxford, presented to . . . James II. Oxf., 1685, fol. 4 pp.　　Wood 423 (60)

600. [*Begin.*] To the right worshipfull the heads of the respective colleges . . . [Notice of a convocation in honour of the king's inauguration]. [Oxf.?], MCDLXXXV [really 1685], s. sh.　　Don. b. 12 (34)

601. Advertisements from the Delegates of Convocation for his majesties reception for the heads of Houses to deliver with great charge unto their companies. [Oxf., 1687], s. sh.　　B.M.

602. [*Begin.*] Doctors in all faculty's . . . [List of doctors and masters appointed to meet the king, with regulations respecting the procession.] Aug. 26. [Oxf.?], 1687, s. sh.　　Wood 276a (379)

603. Strenæ natalitiæ Academiæ Oxoniensis in celsissimum principem. [On the birth of James, son of James II.] Oxon., 1688, fol. 88 pp.
G 1. 15 (2) Art.

604. Some select and amusing verses, taken out of the two famous volumes intitul'd, Strenæ natalitiæ Academiæ Oxoniensis in celsissimum principem, &c. (State-amusements . . . exemplified in the abdication of king James the second, p. 35–70.) Lond., 1711, 8°.　　Douce I 216

See 3720 [Hemphill, B., Oxford and James II. The installation of Catholics in Oxford. 1948].

605. Vota Oxoniensia pro serenissimis Guilhelmo rege et Maria regina M. Britanniæ &c. nuncupata . . . Oxon., 1689, fol. 132 pp.
G 1. 15 (1) Art.

606. Comitia habita . . . Apr. 11. An. 1689. die inaugurationis . . . Wilhelmi et . . . Mariæ. (Oxf.) 1689, s. sh.　　Wood 276a (409)

607. Academiæ Oxoniensis gratulatio pro exoptato . . . regis Guilielmi ex Hibernia reditu. Oxoniæ, 1690, fol.　　Pamph. 201 (1)

608. Advertisements from the Delegates of Convocation for his majesties reception . . . [Orders governing the behaviour of members.] Oxf., 1695, s. sh.　　Wood 276a (330)

609. Pietas Universitatis Oxoniensis in obitum . . . reginæ Mariæ. Oxon., 1695, fol. 132 pp.　　Vet. A 3 c. 107

610. Comitia habita . . . Apr. 16. An. Dom. 1696 in die gratulationis publicæ pro salute regis Gulielmi. (Oxf.) ,1696, s. sh.
Wood 276a (404b)

611. Comitia habita . . . Decemb. 2. An. Dom. 1697 in die gratulationis publicæ pro pace Gulielmi regis auspiciis Europæ reddita. (Oxf.), 1697, s. sh.　　Wood 276a (404c)

612. Exequiæ . . . principi Gulielmo Glocestriæ duci ab Oxoniensi academia solutæ. Oxon., 1700, fol. 144 pp.　　AA 64 (1) Art.

613. Pietas Universitatis Oxoniensis in obitum . . . Gulielmi III. et gratulatio in . . . Annæ reginæ inaugurationem. Oxon., 1702, fol. 128 pp.　　AA 64 (2) Art.

614. The royal progress: or The universal joy of her majesty's subjects at Oxford and other places, in her passage . . . to . . . Bath. [In verse.] Lond., [17—], s. sh. Antiq. c. E. 9 (91)

615. Advertisements from the Delegates of Convocation for her majesties reception . . . [Orders governing the behaviour of members.] [Oxf.], 1702, s. sh. Don. b. 12 (42)

616. Comitia philologica in honorem. . . Annæ . . . reginæ habita . . . Julii 16. A.D. 1702. (Oxf.), 1702, s. sh. Don. b. 12 (41)

617. Comitia philologica in honorem . . . Annæ . . . reginæ, habita in Universitate Oxoniensi, Julii 16. A.D. 1702. Oxonii, 1702, fol. 52 pp. AA 64 (4) Art.

618. Comitia philologica in Theatro Sheldoniano 3 Decemb. Anno Dom. 1702 die gratulationis publicæ ob res sub auspiciis . . . Annæ fæliciter terra marique gestas. (Oxf.), 1702, s. sh. G.A. Oxon b. 19

619. Epinicion Oxoniense, sive solennis gratulatio ob res feliciter terra marique gestas a copiis. . . . Annæ contra Gallos pariter ac Hispanos A.D. 1702. Oxon., 1702, fol. 33 pp. AA 64 (5) Art.
— [Another issue.] S 6. 15 (31) Jur.

620. Plausus musarum Oxoniensium; sive Gratulatio Academiæ ob res prospere terra marique gestas in comitiis philologicis habitis in Theatro Sheldoniano calendis Januarii 1704. Oxon., 1704, fol. 52 pp. L 3. 3 (4) Th.

621. Exequiæ . . . Georgio principi Daniæ ab Oxoniensi academia solutæ. Oxon., 1708, fol. 127 pp. S 11. 16 (8) Th.

622. London, April the 28th, 1710. The following address . . . was . . . presented to her majesty . . . The humble address of the University of Oxford [expressing loyalty to the crown, to the succession of the house of Hanover, and to the Protestant religon]. Lond., 1710, s. sh. B 3. 15 Art.

623 An answer to the address of the Oxford University, . . . intituled, The humble address of the University of Oxford, &c. Lond., 1710, 8°. 28 pp. Pamph. 291 (32)

See 1249 [Comitia philologica, 1713; in honorem reginæ Annae.]
See also 161–72 [Jacobite disturbance of 1714 &c.].

624. Pietas Universitatis Oxoniensis in obitum . . . Annæ et gratulatio in . . . Georgii inaugurationem. Oxon., 1714, fol. 168 pp. M 6. 6 (2) Art.

625. [Begin.] At a general meeting of the Vice-chancellor, heads of houses . . . July 26. 1715. [Regulations for preserving good behaviour during the celebrations on the accession of George I.] [Oxf.], (1715), s. sh. 4 Δ 260 (9)

626. The muses fountain clear: or, The dutiful Oxonian's defence of his mother's loyalty to . . . king George. Wherein is fully demonstrated

that the University of Oxford . . . constantly promoted and maintain'd the revolution and Protestant succession. Lond., 1717, 8°. 36 pp.

Gough Oxf. 53 (2)

627. Pietas Universitatis Oxoniensis in obitum . . . Georgii I et gratulatio in . . . Georgii II inaugurationem. Oxon., 1727, fol.   H 9. 19 Art.

628. Epithalamia Oxoniensia (. . . in . . . principum Gulielmi Caroli Henrici Arausionensis, Annæque Britannicæ nuptias . . .). Oxon., 1734, fol.   H 1. 19 (1) Art.

629. Persons appointed to attend at the Theatre during the stay of . . . the prince of Orange . . . [Oxf., 1734], s. sh.   Don. b. 12 (52b)

630. Gratulatio Academiæ Oxoniensis in nuptias . . . Frederici principis Walliæ et Augustæ principissæ de Saxo-Gotha. Oxon., 1736, fol.

Pamph. 406 (5)

631. Pietas Academiæ Oxoniensis in obitum . . . reginæ Carolinæ. Oxon., 1738, fol.   Pamph. 408 (12)

See also 173–204 [Jacobite disturbance of 1745, &c.].

632. The English poems, collected from the Oxford and Cambridge verses on the death of . . . Frederick, prince of Wales. Edinb., 1751, 12°. 183 pp.   2805 f. 526

633. Epicedia Oxoniensia in obitum . . . Frederici principis Walliæ. Oxon., 1751, fol. 192 pp.   H 4. 1 (1) Art.

634. Pietas Universitatis Oxoniensis in obitum . . . Georgii II. et gratulatio in . . . Georgii III. inaugurationem. Oxon., 1761, fol. 250 pp.

H 4. 1 (2) Art.

635. Epithalamia Oxoniensia, sive Gratulationes in . . . Georgii III. et . . . Sophiæ Charlottæ nuptias auspicatissimas. Oxon., 1761, fol. 188 pp.

H 4. 1 (3) Art.

636. Gratulatio solennis Universitatis Oxoniensis ob celsissimum Georgium Fred. Aug. Walliæ principem Georgio III. et Charlottæ reginæ auspicatissime natum. Oxon., 1762, fol. 192 pp.

H 4. 1 (4) Art.

637. [Begin.] At a meeting of the Vice-chancellor, heads of houses and proctors . . . [Notice that some method other than an 'Illumination' be adopted to celebrate the anniversary of the king's accession to the throne.] Oct. 11. [Oxf.], 1809, s. sh.   Don. b. 12 (139)

638. University and City of Oxford. [Notice of the Vice-chancellor and Mayor dissuading people from illuminating their buildings to commemorate the king's accession to the throne; and announcing the enforcement of statutes against the throwing of fire-works, making bonfires etc. in the streets. Oct. 20, 1809.] [Oxf.], 1809, s. sh.

Don. b 12 (140)

639. A correct account of the visit of . . . the prince regent and his illustrious guests, to the City and University of Oxford in June, 1814. Oxf., 1814, 8°. 53 pp.   G.A. Oxon 8° 934 (1)

640. Authentic account of the visit of . . . the prince regent to the University of Oxford, June 14. MDCCCXIV. Oxf., 1814, 8°. 40 pp.
                                          G.A. Oxon 8° 934 (2)

641. An account of the visit of . . . the prince regent and . . . the emperor of Russia and the king of Prussia to the University of Oxford in June 1814. Oxf., 1815, 4°, 78 pp.   Clar. Press 31 b. 93
— [Another ed.] Oxf., 1815, fol. 98 pp.   G.A. Oxon b. 7

642. Europæ pacatores Oxonium invisentes. [In verse. The visit of the prince regent & foreign potentates at the end of the Napoleonic wars.] (Manch.), [1814?], 4°. 8 pp.   G. Pamph. 1735 (13)

643. HUGHES, J., Ode recited amongst others, in the Theatre, Oxford, on the visit of the prince regent and foreign potentates . . . June 15. MDCCCXIV. [Signed J. Hughes.] (Oxf., 1814), 4°. 7 pp.
                                           G.A. Oxon 4° 13 (16)

See 5919 [Plan of Radcliffe Camera with arrangements for banquet. 1814].
See 5920 [Hakewill, An architect and a royal visit to Oxford in 1814. 1880].
See 1379–84 [Proposed indulgence of one term as a compliment to the king. 1820].

644. Lines on the approaching festival; suggested more particularly by the expectation of the presence of . . . the duke of Wellington. [The festival was probably the Oxford celebration of the coronation of George IV.] Oxf., 1820, 4°. 8 pp.   G.A. Oxon 4° 319 (1)

645. LOWE, R., 1st visct. Sherbrooke, Poema canino-anglico-Latinum super adventu recenti serenissimarum principum [the duchess of Kent and her daughter Victoria] non cancellarii præmio donatum aut donandum nec in Theatro Sheldoniano recitatum aut recitandum. [By R. Lowe.] (Oxf.), [1832], 8°. 8 pp.   28041 e. 9 (2)
— Ed. 4a. 1832.   G.A. Oxon 8° 255
— Ed. 5a. 1843 [1833?].   28041 e. 9 (1)
— Ed. 6a. 1835.   G.A. Oxon b. 113 (47)

646. The princess of Wales at Oxford. (Leisure hour, 1863, p. 479).
                                           G.A. Oxon 4° 578 (13)

See 2333 [Speech of the earl of Derby when the degree of D.C.L. was conferred upon the prince of Wales. 1863].

647. A royal year [1859/60, the year of residence of the prince of Wales] at Oxford. by an M.A. of Christ Church, Oxon. (St. James's mag., 1865, vol. 13, p. 493–502.)   Per. 2705 d. 268

648. WILLARD, J. F., The royal authority and the early English universities. Thesis, Pennsylvania. Phila., 1902, 8°. 89 pp.   2625 d. 10 (5)

649. King Edward VIII at Oxford, 1912–1914. (Oxf. mag., 1936, vol. 54, p. 309, 10.)   Per. G.A. Oxon 4° 141

See 5441 [Gibson, S., Royal visits to the Bodleian library. 1946].

650. FREEBORN, M. E., Kings and queens at Oxford. Oxf., 1953, 8°. 137 pp.
G.A. Oxon 8° 1277

With Parliament

University representation, General

651. An act to limit the time for proceeding to election in counties . . . and for polling at elections for the universities of Oxford and Cambridge, and for other purposes. (16 & 17 V., c. 68, Pub.) Lond., 1853, fol. 4 pp.
L.L.

652. University elections. A bill to provide that votes at elections for the Universities may be recorded by means of voting papers. 12 February 1861. [Lond.], 1861, fol. 3 pp.   Pp. Eng. 1861 vol. 4
— As amended by the select committee. 27 May 1861. [Lond.], 1861, fol. 4 pp.   Pp. Eng. 1861 vol. 4
— As amended by the select committee and in committee. 3 July 1861. [Lond.], 1861, fol. 5 pp.   Pp. Eng. 1861 vol. 4

653. Report from the select committee on the University elections bill; together with the proceedings of the committee and minutes of evidence. [Lond.], 1861, fol. viii+22 pp.   Pp. Eng. 1861 vol. 14

654. An act to provide that votes at elections for the Universities may be recorded by means of voting papers. (24 & 25 V., c. 53, Pub.) Lond., 1861, fol. 4 pp.   L.L.
— 31 & 32 V., c. 65, Pub.

655. University elections. Voting papers. A bill to amend the law relating to the use of voting papers in elections for the universities. [Lond.], 1868, s. sh.   Pp. Eng. 1867/68 vol. 5

656. WILLIAMS, W. R., Members for Oxford university. (The parliamentary history of the County of Oxford, 1213–1899, pp. 142–73.) Brecknock, 1899, 8°.   G.A. Oxon 8° 662

657. Franchise and removal of women's disabilities. A bill to establish a single franchise at all elections and thereby to abolish university representation, and to remove the disabilities of women. [Lond.], 1902, s. sh.   Pp. Eng. 1902 vol. 1

658. Franchise and removal of women's disabilities. A bill to establish a single franchise at all elections and thereby to abolish university representation, and to remove the disabilities of women. 3 Feb. 1908. [Lond.], 1908, s. sh.   Pp. Eng. 1908 vol. 2

659. Franchise and removal of women's disabilities. A bill to establish a single franchise at all elections and thereby to abolish university representation, and to remove the disabilities of women. 19 February 1909. [Lond.], 1909, s. sh.   Pp. Eng. 1909 vol. 2

660. Representation of the People act, 1918. Register of Parliamentary electors for the University of Oxford. Sept. 1, 1918–Feb. 1946. Oxf., 1918–46, 8°.
[The Bodleian set wants the Registers for 1942 and 1945: Per. G.A. Oxon 8° 984.]

661. University representation. [Urging the retention of the University franchise.] n. pl., [1930?], 4°. 3 pp.   G.A. Oxon b. 139 (34)

662. SAMUEL, SIR H., University representation. (Oxf. mag., 1931, vol. 49, p. 543–46.)   Per. G.A. Oxon 4° 141

663. A memorandum upon the representation of the universities . . . submitted to the electors of the universities of Oxford and Cambridge, January 1931. (Lond., 1931), 4°. 5 pp.   G.A. Oxon b. 139 (35)

664. MCCALLUM, R. B., University representation [signed] R. B. McC. (Oxf. mag., 1948, vol. 66, p. 311–14.)   Per. G.A. Oxon 4° 141

665. MACLAGAN, M., The University franchise (with a complete list of Oxford burgesses since 1603). (Oxford, 1949, special no. p. 13–36.)
     Per. G.A. Oxon 8° 1141

666. HUMBERSTONE, T. L., University representation [including] Complete biographical index of University members, by I. Grimble. Lond., &c., 1951, 8°. 128 pp.   22772 e. 96

667. JONES, C., The university vote (written in collaboration with P. Jenkin, J. Lemkin, R. Lewis and W. Bankes). (Bow group pamph.) Lond., 1953, 8°. 32 pp.   22772 e. 66 (16)

668. REX, M. B., University representation in England, 1604–1690. [Oxford univ. *passim*.] (Études présentées à la Commission internat. pour l'hist. des Assemblées d'états, vol. 15.) Lond., 1954, 8°. 408 pp.
     24854 d. 15 (15)

University representation, Particular elections

669. MONCK, G., To the . . . vice-chancelour and the . . . convocation in . . . Oxford [soliciting the votes of Convocation for William Lenthall in the election of burgesses]. [Madan 2509.] [Oxf.? 1660], s. sh.
     Wood 423 (33)

670. A true copy of the poll for members of parliament for the University of Oxford, taken March the 21st, 1721. Oxf., 1722, 4°. 14 pp.
     G.A. Oxon 4° 6 (7)

671. HARRISON, S., An account of the late election for the University of Oxford. Together with . . . remarks on the printed poll. By a Master of arts [S. Harrison]. Lond., 1722, 8°. 53 pp.   Gough Oxf. 120 (4)

672. An exact account of the poll, as it stood between . . . mr. Trevor and Wm. Bromley, esq., candidates at the late election of a member for the City and University of Oxford. Lond., [1737], 16°. 40 pp.
     Gough Oxf. 101 (10)

673. A true copy of the poll taken at Oxford, January 31, 1750. With several papers sent to the common rooms of the respective colleges relating to the election of a member of Parliament for the University. Lond., (1750), 4°. 15 pp.   G.A. Oxon 4° 21
— [Another issue.]   G.A. Oxon 4° 97 (2)

674. Copy of a letter sent to a certain b[ishop: T. Sherlock, bp. of London] (on account of a pragmatical interposition in a late election for the U—— of O——). [Lond.?, 1750?], 4°. 8 pp.   Vet. A. 5. d. 256 (7)

675. A letter [from Henry, viscount Cornbury] to the rev. the vice-chancellor of Oxford to be read in Convocation. n. pl., [1750], s. sh.
                                                        G.A. Oxon b. 19

676. A letter to . . . Henry viscount Cornbury, occasioned by a letter from his lordship to the vice-chancellor of Oxford in Convocation. To which is prefix'd his lordship's letter. [Terminating his lordship's representation of the university in parliament.] Lond., 1751, 8°. 23 pp.
                                                        G.A. Oxon 8° 61 (9)

677. BAGOT, WILLIAM, baron, Memorials of the Bagot family [by William, baron Bagot. pp. 86–88 concern the election of sir W. W. Bagot as University burgess in 1762]. Blithfield, 1824, 4°. 2182 B. d. 13

678. An authentic copy of the poll for members to serve in the ensuing Parliament for the University of Oxford, taken March xxiii. MDCC-LXVIII. Oxf., 1768, 4°. 14 pp.   G.A. Oxon 4° 6 (5)

679. To the University of Oxford [paper supporting the candidature of W. Jones for University burgess: with extracts from his works]. 5 May 1780. n. pl., (1780), fol. 4 pp.   Gough Oxf. 96 (66)

680. SHORE, J., 1st baron Teignmouth, Memoirs of the life, writings and correspondence of sir William Jones [pp. 174–85 concern sir W. Jones' candidature for University burgess in 1780]. Lond., 1801, 4°.
                                                        4° BS. 226
— [2nd ed., 1806, other eds. in 1807, 1835.]

681. An authentic copy of the poll for members to serve in the ensuing Parliament for the University of Oxford, taken on the 5th and 6th of November, 1806. Oxf., 1806, 4°. 22 pp.   G.A. Oxon 4° 22 (1)

682. An authentic copy of the poll for a member to serve in the present Parliament for the University of Oxford, taken on the 22d, 23d and 24th of August, 1821. Oxf., 1821, 4°. 31 pp.   G.A. Oxon 4° 22 (2)

683. THOMAS, V., A letter addressed to . . . dr. Tournay, warden of Wadham college [on the latter's support for R. Heber rather than sir J. Nicholl, to represent the University in Parliament]. Oxf., 1821, 8°. 15 pp.   G.A. Oxon 8° 58 (3)

684. [Begin.] Can the members of the University wish to see . . . [A paper, dated July 14, complaining about the way in which the principal of Brasenose college, F. Hodson, has been canvassing for mr. Heber.] Oxf., (1821), s. sh.   G.A. Oxon b. 19

685. An extract from the Oxford Herald of August 18th. Oxford university election. [A paper, signed by J. Wintle, chairman, reiterating the charge of premature canvassing which mr. Heber's committee had denied.] Oxf., (1821), s. sh. G.A. Oxon b. 19

686. An extract from the Oxford Herald of August 18th. Oxford university election. [Another paper, signed Verax, reiterating the charge of premature canvass against mr. Heber.] Oxf., (1821), s. sh.
G.A. Oxon b. 19

687. Occurrences in Convocation. [A paper which recounts mr. Heber's admittance of premature canvass in one instance.] Oxf., (1821), s. sh.
G.A. Oxon b. 19

688. Oxford university election. [A paper, signed A. B., printing a letter which purports to prove premature canvass by mr. Heber.] [Oxf., 1821], s. sh. G.A. Oxon b. 19

689. Oxford election pamphlets. [A list of the octavo pamphlets printed in the 1829 contest.] (The Crypt, 1829, N.S., vol. I, p. 221.) Hope 8° 285

690. An authentic copy of the poll for a member to serve in the present Parliament for the University of Oxford . . . taken on the 26th, 27th and 28th of February, MDCCCXXIX. Oxf., 1829, 8°. 41 pp.
G.A. Oxon 8° 69 (1)

691. An expostulatory letter, addressed to the members of the University of Oxford who voted for the anti-Catholic petition, by Pertinax Peerwell. Lond., 1829, 8°. 22 pp. G.A. Oxon 8° 145 (7)

692. [Begin.] In consequence of a strong feeling . . . for the re-election of mr. Peel, the following members . . . resolved that a committee should be formed for . . . that object. Feb. 12. (Oxf., 1829), s. sh.
G.A. Oxon b. 21

693. GILES, J. A., A reply to 'An expostulatory letter . . . by Pertinax Peerwell', by a Protestant member of the University of Oxford [J. A. Giles]. Feb. 13. Oxf., (1829), 8° 11 pp.
G.A. Oxon 8° 145(8)

694. [Begin.] Mr. Peel having resigned his seat . . . and being deemed by us unfit to be re-elected . . . [Announcement of opposition to Peel, signed by numerous members of the University.] Feb. 13. (Oxf., 1829), s. sh.
G.A. Oxon b. 21

695. [Begin.] Mr. Peel's honourable feeling . . . [A paper, signed by R. Marsham, chairman, announcing the formation of a committee in support of sir R. Peel. Feb. 13.] (Oxf., 1829), s. sh.
G.A. Oxon c. 107 (37)
— [Another ed.] G.A. Oxon b. 21

696. [Begin.] Mr. Peel's honourable abandonment . . . [A paper satirizing no. 695 which it imitates in appearance.] Feb. 13. (Oxf., 1829), s. sh.
G.A. Oxon c. 107 (37)

697. KEBLE, J., [*Begin.*] The undersigned respectfully solicits . . . [6 queries about Peel's opinions concerning the Roman Catholics &c.] Feb. 16. Oxf., 1829, s. sh.   Bliss B 421 (41)
— [Another ed. On the reverse are printed the names of sir R. H. Inglis's committee.] (Lond.), 1829, s. sh.   Bliss B 421 (46)

698. 'Members of Convocation!' Question. 'Is, or is not, sir Robert Inglis . . .?' [Seeking to prove his devotion to the Church of England.] Feb. 18. (Oxf., 1829), s. sh.   G.A. Oxon b. 21

699. 'Nolumus leges Angliæ mutari.' [An electoral squib.] Feb. 19. (Oxf., 1829), s. sh.   G.A. Oxon 8° 145 (12)

700. CAMERON, C. R., A letter in reply to the letters of . . . J. Blanco White and mr. Peel's committee. Feb. 20. n. pl., [1829], 4°. 3 pp.
                                                    Bliss B 421 (40)

701. PHILLPOTTS, H., Copy of a letter from the dean of Chester to . . . dr. Ellerton. Feb. 20. (Oxf., 1829), s. sh.   G.A. Oxon b. 21

702. To the members of the University of Oxford who are opposed to the admission of Roman Catholics into . . . Parliament . . . [signed, A Churchman]. Feb. 23. (Holborn, 1829), s. sh.   G.A. Oxon b. 21

703. Address to the right honourable candidate from mr. Peel's committee in Oxford. [An anti-Peel electoral paper.] Feb. 23. (Oxf., 1829), s. sh.
                                                    G.A. Oxon b. 21

704. To a friend in London. [A paper, signed A friend to emancipation, in support of sir R. H. Inglis.] Feb. 23. Oxf., (1829), 4°. 3 pp.
                                                    Bliss B 421 (62)

705. Advertisement. Signor Capellani, professor of rat-catching . . . [Electoral squib.] Feb. 23. Oxf., [1829], s. sh.   Bliss B 421 (71)

706. DAVISON, J., The following [38] considerations are . . . submitted to the members of Convocation . . . Feb. 23. Oxf., [1829], fol. 4 pp.
                                                    Bliss B 421 (64)
— [Another ed., having 40 considerations, *entitled*] Considerations on the justice and wisdom of conciliatory measures towards Ireland. Oxf., 1829, 8°. 15 pp.   Bliss B 421 (140)

707. HULL, W. W., To Mr. Davison . . . [Answers, signed A lay member of Convocation, to his 40 considerations. By W. W. Hull.] Feb. 26. Oxf., (1829), fol. 3 pp.   Bliss B 421 (65)

708. Grand concert under the patronage of the rev. Thomas Growler for the benefit of mr. Peeligrini . . . February 25, 1829. [Electoral squib.] (Oxf., 1829), s. sh.   G.A. Oxon 8° 145 (17)

709. Arrival of the Plenipot Rat [Henry Phillpotts] . . . [Electoral squib.] Feb. 25. Oxf., 1829, s. sh.   Bliss B 421 (70)

710. The substance of two speeches delivered in Convocation on Feb. 26, 1829 [concerning the election of an M.P. for the University. By Edward Burton]. Oxf., 1829, 8°. 23 pp.   G.A. Oxon 8° 145 (5)

711. GIRDLESTONE, C., Substance of a speech for the Convocation house, Oxford, February 26, 1829. Oxf., 1829, 8°. 8 pp.　　Bliss B 421 (113)

712. Address to the members of Convocation [against the re-election of mr. Peel as the M.P. for the University. Anti-Catholic]. By a member of Convocation. Newport, Mon., 1829, 8°. 14 pp.

G.A. Oxon 8° 145 (1)

713. An old song adapted to new times . . . called the Pope and the devil . . . [Electoral squib.] (Oxf.), [1829], s. sh.　　　　　　G.A. Oxon b. 21

714. Argumentum ad crumenam poetice redditum. To all resident members of Convocation, greeting. [Electoral squib.] (Oxf.), [1829], s. sh.

G.A. Oxon b. 112 (96)

715. A circular letter . . . by the committee for ensuring the reelection of mr. Peel [as M.P. for the University.] Oxf., 1829, 8°. 20 pp.

G.A. Oxon 8° 145 (3)

716. [Begin.] The common room of Ch. Ch. having read . . . of signor Capellani's cats . . . [An electoral squib.] (Oxf.), [1829], s. sh.

G.A. Oxon 8° 145 (14)

717. The following considerations [by J. Davison] or rather questions having been . . . submitted . . . , answers are here . . . submitted . . . [The first 5 considerations only are answered. The piece is inscribed at the foot 'To be continued'.] (Oxf.), [1829], s. sh.　　Bliss B 421 (66)

718. Καλοῖς κἀγαθοῖς. [An electoral squib, signed Εὐήθης.] Oxf., [1829], 4°. 3 pp.　　　　　　　　　　　　　　　　　　Bliss B 421 (60)

719. Letter from . . . J. Blanco White . . . to a friend in Oxford [supporting Peel]. Oxf., [1829], 4°. 3 pp.　　　　　　　　Bliss B 421 (39)

720. Grand menagerie. Mr. Wombwell begs leave . . . [An electoral squib.] (Oxf.), [1829], s. sh.　　　　　　　　G.A. Oxon c. 107 (35)

721. More theatricals. By permission . . . [An electoral squib.] (Oxf.), [1829], s. sh.　　　　　　　　　　　　G.A. Oxon c. 107 (36)

722. MACKLIN, CHARLES, pseud., Plain and cursory thoughts on Catholic Irish emancipation and on the propriety of re-electing mr. Peel a representative of this University. Oxf., 1829, 8°. 16 pp.

G.A. Oxon 8° 145 (4)

723. Reasons from all sides why sir Robert H. Inglis, bart. should not be the representative of the University of Oxford. Lond., 1829, 8°. 32 pp.

Bliss B 421 (51)

724. SEWELL, W., A circular letter of advice and justification from the committee for ensuring the election of sir Robert Inglis [as M.P. for the University. By W. Sewell]. Oxf., 1829, 8°. 44 pp.

G.A. Oxon 8° 145 (2)

725. Theatre royal. Convocation house. The celebrated amateur, mr. Burgess P——l . . . [An electoral squib.] (Oxf.), [1829], s. sh.

G.A. Oxon 8° 145 (16)

726. CRAMER, J. A., A letter to sir Robert Harry Inglis . . . one of the
representatives of the University of Oxford in Parliament, from one of
his constituents [J. A. Cramer]. [Signed A Ch. Ch. Master of arts.]
Oxf., 1829, 8°. 15 pp.   G. Pamph. 2193 (1)
— [Another ed.]   Bliss B 421 (138)

727. A letter to sir R. H. Inglis . . . occasioned by one lately addressed to
him from a Christ Church M.A. [signed Vindex]. (Oxf., 1829), 8°.
14 pp.   Bliss B 421 (139)

727.1. A letter of congratulation and advice to sir R. H. Inglis, by a member of the University of Oxford. Lond., 1829, 8°. 10 pp.   29. 927

728. GASH, N., Peel and the Oxford university election of 1829. (Oxoniensia, 1939, vol. 4, p. 162–73.)   Per. G.A. Oxon 4° 658 = R.

729. TRISTRAM, H., Catholic emancipation: Mr. Peel, and the University
of Oxford. (Cornhill mag., 1929, N.S., vol. 66, p. 406–18.)
                                               Per. 2705 d. 213

730. An authentic copy of the poll for two burgesses to serve in Parliament
for the University of Oxford, taken on the 29th, 30th, 31st July and the
2nd and 3rd of August, MDCCCXLVII. [With] Pairs. Oxf., 1847, 8°.
55 pp.+8 pp.   G.A. Oxon 4° 56

731. At a meeting . . . at the house of the master of Balliol [R. Jenkyns]
. . . May 10, 1847. [Proposals to promote the election of E. Cardwell.]
[Oxf., 1847], s. sh.   G.A. Oxon c. 63 (76b)
— [Another ed., dated May 12, with additional sheet of information
from the committee.]   G.A. Oxon c. 63 (79c)

732. Oxford, May 12. [Resolution to support W. E. Gladstone.] [Oxf.,
1847], s. sh.   G.A. Oxon 4° 56

732.1. Representation of the University [suggesting R. Bullock-Marsham
as a candidate]. [Oxf., 1847], s. sh.   G.A. Oxon c. 63 (81b)

733. The representation of the University of Oxford. Oxford, May 17,
1847. [Resolutions of a meeting to promote the election of C. G.
Round.] [Oxf., 1847], 4°. 3 pp.   G.A. Oxon c. 63 (81c)

734. CHRETIEN, C. P., May 19, 1847. [Begin.] The attention of members of
Convocation . . . [A paper by C. P. Chretien, urging support of
Gladstone.] (Oxf., 1847), 4°. 3 pp.   G.A. Oxon 4° 56

735. Oxford university election. It is attempted . . . [Assertions that C. G
Round was Peel's supporter when advocating Roman Catholic claims
in 1829.] May 22. [Oxf.], 1847, s. sh.   G.A. Oxon c. 63 (82b)

736. Oxford university election. (Private.) A report injurious . . . [Defend-
ing C. G. Round against stories that he is a dissenter.] May 22. [Oxf.],
1847, s. sh.   G.A. Oxon c. 63 (82c)

737. To members of Convocation. The attention of mr. Round's Oxford committee . . . [defending his attachment to the Established church. Signed by C. A. Ogilvie, chairman.] May 24. [Oxf.], (1847), s. sh.
G.A. Oxon 4° 56

738. The following statement of facts with reference to the 'Dissenters' chapels' bill' is respectfully submitted . . . [against Gladstone and in favour of Inglis and Round]. [Oxf.], (1847), s. sh.
G.A. Oxon c. 63 (158)

739. The following (second) statement of facts, with reference to the Dissenters' chapels' bill is respectfully submitted . . . [in favour of Gladstone]. May 27. [Oxf.], (1847), s. sh.   G.A. Oxon c. 63 (159)

740. Extract from the 'Times' June 23, 1847. [Paper answering affirmatively a letter questioning whether C. G. Round voted against Inglis in 1829.] June 24. [Oxf.], (1847), s. sh.   G.A. Oxon c. 63 (160)

741. Oxford university election. [A letter, signed by W. Harrison, C. Sumner, and E. P. Hathaway, comparing the voting record of Gladstone and Round.] July 19. [Oxf.], (1847), s. sh.
G.A. Oxon 4° 56

742. Mr. W. E. Gladstone's committee . . . make the following statement with respect to the course pursued . . . with regard to the censure upon mr. Ward's book 'The ideal of a Christian Church' . . . [Oxf., 1847], s. sh.   G.A. Oxon 4° 56

743. MAURICE, F. D., Thoughts on the duty of a Protestant in the present Oxford election, a letter. July 24. Lond., 1847, 8°. 25 pp.
G.A. Oxon 4° 56

744. GLADSTONE, W. E., [Begin.] In consequence of the occurrence . . . of an attack upon mr. W. E. Gladstone . . . [A reply by Gladstone to no. 741.] July 26. n. pl., (1847), 4°. 3 pp.   G.A. Oxon 4° 56

745. Oxford university election. A letter was addressed a few days since . . . [Comments on Gladstone's reply, no. 744.] [Oxf., 1847], s. sh.
G.A. Oxon 4° 56

746. Et facta, et verba. To members of Convocation. A few facts concerning mr. W. E. Gladstone. [Oxf., 1847], s. sh.   G.A. Oxon c. 63 (156)

747. MACKARNESS, J. F., A few words to the country parsons touching the election for the University of Oxford, by one of themselves [J. F. Mackarness]. Lond., 1847, 8°. 15 pp.   G.A. Oxon 4° 56

748. MICHELL, R., The bishop of Bath and Wells' letter. [Michell's comments on Gladstone's attitude to the Roman Catholics, mentioning in passing R. Bagot's testimony as to Gladstone's 'soundness'.] [Oxf., 1847], s. sh.   MS. Top. Oxon c. 72 (54)

749. Oxford university election: principles involved. (Oxf. Protestant mag., 1847, vol. I, p. 311–14.)   Per. G.A. Oxon 8° 119

750. Representation of Oxford university. (Oxf. Protestant mag., 1847, vol. 1, p. 187–90.)   Per. G.A. Oxon 8° 119

751. The Tractarian triumph [election of W. E. Gladstone]. (Oxf. Protestant mag., 1847, vol. 1, p. 361–69.)   Per. G.A. Oxon 8° 119

752. Tractarian estimate of the University elections. (Oxf. Protestant mag., 1847, vol. 1, p. 407–10.)   Per. G.A. Oxon 8° 119

753. Votes of the three candidates on recent questions bearing on the Church and religion. From the Morning Herald. [Oxf., 1847], 4°. 3 pp.
G.A. Oxon c. 63 (80e)

754. An authentic copy of the poll for two burgesses to serve in Parliament for the University of Oxford, taken on the 10th, 12th, 13th and 14th of July, M.DCCC.LII [*With*] Pairs. Oxf., 1852, 8°. 58+8 pp.
G.A. fol. A 129

755. Extract from the Morning Herald, May 27, 1852 [about the impending election. *Begin.* The time is fast approaching . . .]. n. pl., (1852), 4°. 3 pp.   G.A. fol. A 129

756. Oxford, May 21, 1852. Sir, Allow me to place before you the accompanying declaration signed by an immense majority of the resident body of the University [against a third candidate for representation in Parliament]. [Oxf.], (1852), 4°. 4 pp.   G.A. fol. A 129
— May 25. [An enlarged list of signatures.] [Oxf.], (1852), fol. 3 pp.
G.A. fol. A 129
— May 28. 4 pp.   G.A. fol. A 129
— May 28. 6 pp.   G.A. fol. A 129
— [*Begin.*] We the undersigned resident members . . . [An enlarged list.] [Oxf.], (1852), fol. 6 pp.   G.A. fol. A 129

757. Oxford university election. The committee appointed by a large number of non-resident members . . . for the purpose of resisting the re-election of mr. Gladstone . . . [signed Brook W. Bridges, chairman]. 3 June. n. pl., (1852), 8°. 3 pp.   G.A. Oxon 8° 208

758. Oxford university election. Extract from the Morning Herald of June 4, 1852. n. pl., (1852), 8°. 4 pp.   G.A. Oxon 8° 208

759. [*Begin.*] The undersigned members of Convocation . . . while they deem the practice . . . [justifying the opposition to Gladstone of another candidate, on the grounds of Gladstone's alleged change of opinions]. [Oxf., 1852], s. sh.   G.A. fol. A 129

760. GLADSTONE, W. E., The following letter has been published this morning . . . June 11, 1852 . . . [defending himself against the attacks of no. 759]. n. pl., (1852) s. sh.   G.A. fol. A 129
— [Another ed.]   G.A. fol. A 129

761. KEBLE, J., Letter to sir Brook W. Bridges, bart. June 16. Lond., 1852, 8°. 16 pp.   G.A. fol. A 129

762. [*Begin.*] Tank house, Zoological gardens, June 19, 1852. Dear
Gresswell . . . [An electoral squib, signed The Hippopotamus.]
[Oxf.], (1852), s. sh.   G.A. fol. A 129

763. WOODGATE, H. A., Is mr. Gladstone inconsistent with his former
profession? A question . . . to the members of Convocation. July 1.
Oxf. &c., 1852, 8°. 15 pp.   G.A. fol. A 129
— 2nd ed. 1852.   G. Pamph. 2399 (16)

764. WILSON, B., Twenty-one reasons for the re-election of mr. Gladstone.
July 8. Oxf. &c., 1852, 8°. 16 pp.   G.A. fol. A 129

765. MACKENZIE, H., Is there not a cause? [An electoral paper, signed
One concerned for the honour of the University, i.e. H. Mackenzie.
Anti-Gladstone.] July 12. [Oxf.], (1852), s. sh.   G.A. fol. A 129

766. An authentic copy of the poll for a burgess to serve in Parliament for
the University of Oxford, taken on the 4th [to] 20th of January,
M.DCCC.LIII. [*With*] Pairs. Oxf., 1853, 8°. 55+8 pp.
                                                  G.A. Oxon 4° 57 (43)

767. A copy of the poll for the election of a member to represent the University of Oxford in Parliament taken . . . on the 4th [to] the 20th
days of Jan., 1853. (Lond., 1853), 16°. 36 pp. G.A. Oxon 16° 161 (18)

768. Oriel, Jan. 3, 1853. [A letter, signed C. M., in support of Gladstone.]
[Oxf.], (1853), s. sh.   G.A. Oxon 4° 57 (28)

769. [*Begin.*] It is announced in the Times of this morning . . . January 4
. . . Oxford university election. [Recording that there will be opposition
to Gladstone; printing the text of a letter from the latter; and appealing
for support for him.] [Oxf., 1853], 4°. 3 pp.   G.A. Oxon 4° 57 (4)

770. Oxford university election. Jan. 4, 1853. [*Begin.*] The attention of
Members . . . is earnestly requested to . . . facts extracted from the
Morning Chronicle . . . [Complaints, by Gladstone's committee, of the
manner of introducing an opponent in the election.] [Oxf.], (1853), 4°.
4 pp.   G.A. Oxon 4° 57 (5)

771. Oxford university election. Dr. Lempriere's letter. [Correspondence
about the announcement of lord Chandos as an opponent to Gladstone,
when the former had already declined candidature.] [Oxf.], (1853), 4°.
3 pp.   G.A. Oxon 4° 57 (23)
— [Another ed.] 8°. 4 pp.   G.A. Oxon 4° 57 (24)

772. TUPPER, M. F., Is it right to vote for mr. Gladstone? Jan. 7. [Oxf.],
(1853), 8°. 4 pp.   G.A. Oxon 4° 57 (27)

773. Oxford, January 7, 1853. Mr. Perceval, having been in 1825 . . .
[Brief biogr. details.] [Oxf.], (1853), s. sh.   G.A. Oxon 4° 57 (21)

774. Oxford university election. Mr. Gladstone's committee room . . . Jan.
7, 1853. [An open letter from R. Greswell, and one from Gladstone to
sir W. Heathcote; followed by State of the poll, Friday half-past 2.]
[Oxf.], (1853), 8°. 4 pp.   G.A. Oxon 4° 57 (13)

— [Another ed. State of the poll, Friday, 5 o'clock.]

G.A. Oxon 4° 57 (14)

— [Another ed. State of the poll, Saturday, 5 o'clock.]

G.A. Oxon 4° 57 (15)

775. Oxford, Tuesday morning, Jan. 11, 1853. [Introductory letter from G. A. Denison preceding] Explanation of the Chandos mystery. [Oxf.], (1853), s. sh.   G.A. Oxon 4° 57 (30)

776. Oxford university election. The attention of members of Convocation is . . . called to the following letter [from R. Greswell] with the circulars appended [from C. Lempriere and T. Short, E. W. Rowden] . . . which has been sent for publication . . . tomorrow, January 12. [Oxf.], (1853), s. sh.   G.A. Oxon 4° 57 (31)

777. Oxford university election. Mr. Gladstone's committee room . . . Jan. 11, 1853. [Announcement that polling will continue; State of the poll, Jan. 11, 5 o'clock; and a list of committee members.] [Oxf.], (1853), 4°. 3 pp.   G.A. Oxon 4° 57 (16)

778. Oxford university election. Mr. Gladstone's committee room . . . Jan. 12, 1853. [Announcement that polling will continue; State of the poll, Jan. 12, 5 o'clock; R. Greswell's covering letter complaining of the manner of introducing an opponent to Gladstone, etc.] [Oxf.], (1853), 4°. 4 pp.   G.A. Oxon 4° 57 (17)

779. A few reasons offered by a member of Convocation against the continuance of the present contest . . . [Signed One who is not a member of either committee.] Jan. 13. [Oxf.], 1853, s. sh. G.A. Oxon 4° 57 (36)

780. Mr. Gladstone's committee room . . . Jan. 14, 1853. [Announcement that polling will continue for the full 15 days allowed; and State of the poll, Jan. 14, 5 p.m.] [Oxf.], (1853), s. sh.   G.A. Oxon 4° 57 (18)
— [Another ed. State of the poll, Jan. 15, 4 p.m.] G.A. Oxon 4° 57 (19)
— [Another ed. With a statement from Perceval's committee appended.] [Oxf.], (1853), 8°. 3 pp.   G.A. Oxon 4° 57 (20)

781. Elections for the universities [signed One who has been a 'Writer of the poll']. Jan. 21. [Oxf.], 1853, s. sh.   G.A. Oxon 4° 57 (37)

782. DENISON, G. A., The coalition of 1852, a letter to the electors of the University of Oxford. Lond., 1853, 8°. 8 pp.   G. Pamph. 2404 (6)

783. DENISON, G. A., Oxford university election. The coalition of December, 1852, and the contest of January, 1853, a letter. Lond., 1853, 8°. 14 pp.   G. Pamph. 2404 (5)

784. A few words on the representation of the University of Oxford, addressed to the country clergy, by one of themselves. Oxf., [1853], 8°. 15 pp.   G.A. Oxon 4° 57 (34)

785. HOOK, W. F., The coalition, a letter to a member of Convocation [supporting W. E. Gladstone]. Oxf., 1853, 12°. 7 pp.

G.A. Oxon 4° 57 (35)

786. HAWKINS, E., A letter . . . upon the future representation of the
University of Oxford, by the provost of Oriel. Oxf. &c., 1853, 8°.
16 pp.   G.A. Oxon 4° 57 (41)

787. MACBRIDE, J. D., A reply to the provost of Oriel's letter on the
future representation of the University of Oxford, by the principal of
Magdalene Hall. Oxf. &c., 1853, 8°. 25 pp.   G.A. Oxon 8° 146 (15)

788. NORTHCOTE, SIR S. H., A statement of facts connected with the
election of . . . W. E. Gladstone as member for the University of
Oxford in 1847, and with his re-elections in 1852 and 1853. Oxf. &c.,
1853, 4°. 32 pp.   G.A. Oxon 4° 57 (40)
— [Proof copy.] 8°. 32 pp.   G.A. Oxon 4° 57 (39)

789. An authentic copy of the poll for a burgess to serve in Parliament for
the University of Oxford, taken on the 27th–30th of June, and on the
1st of July, MDCCCLIX. Oxf., 1859, 8°. 55 pp. G.A. Oxon 8° 69 (5)
— [Another issue.]   G.A. Oxon 8° 469 (16)

790. GLADSTONE, W. E., [A letter dated June 17, to the Provost of Oriel
respecting his intended assumption of office as chancellor of the Exchequer.] n. pl., (1859), 4°. 3 pp.   G.A. Oxon 4° 58 (1)

791. KEBLE, J., Letter from . . . John Keble [to dr. Phillimore]. June 22,
1859. n. pl., (1859), s. sh.   G.A. Oxon 4° 58 (5)

792. GRESWELL, R., [A letter dated June 22, to H. L. Mansel, bringing
to his notice errors of fact in indictments against Gladstone.] [Oxf.],
(1859), s. sh.   G.A. Oxon 4° 58 (4)

793. MANSEL, H. L., [A letter dated June 23, to R. Greswell in reply to no.
792.] [Oxf.], (1859), s. sh.   G.A. Oxon c. 75 (242)

794. GLADSTONE, W. E., [A letter, dated June 23, to the Junior proctor
of Christ Church respecting the views of the government on defence.]
n. pl., (1859), s. sh.   G.A. Oxon 4° 58 (6)

795. Shall we reject mr. Gladstone? A letter to the electors of the University of Oxford, by a non-resident member of Convocation. Oxf. &c.,
1859, 4°. 12 pp.   G.A. Oxon 4° 58 (15)

796. Shall we elect mr. Gladstone? A letter to the author of A letter to the
electors of the University of Oxford. By a resident member of Convocation. Oxf., 1859, 8°. 12 pp.   G.A. Oxon 8° 179 (16)

797. Oxford university election. Mr. Gladstone's committee room . . .
June 25, 1859. [Announcement of polling arrangements; and Oxford
committee.] [Oxf.], (1859), 4°. 3 pp.   G.A. Oxon 4° 58 (10)

798. A few words to the country clergy on the Oxford university election,
by a country clergyman. n. pl., [1859], 8°. 8 pp. G.A. Oxon 4° 58 (16)

799. Latest intelligence. Great battle! Victory of the allied armies . . . [An
electoral squib.] [Oxf., 1859], s. sh.   G.A. Oxon c. 75 (244)

800. Misstatements respecting mr. Gladstone. [Oxf., 1859], s. sh.
G.A. Oxon 4° 58 (12)

801. GLADSTONE, T., To the Vice-chancellor of the University of Oxford. [A letter criticizing the method by which the University selects its representative in Parliament.] Jan. 24, 1860. n. pl., (1860), s. sh.
G.A. Oxon c. 76 (23)

802. An authentic copy of the poll for two burgesses to serve in Parliament for the University of Oxford, taken on the 13th, 14th, 15th, 17th and 18th of July 1865. Oxf., 1865, 8°. 99 pp.   G.A. Oxon 4° 430 (3)
— [Revised ed.] 1865.   G.A. Oxon 4° 430 (4)

803. [*Begin.*] Sir, In consequence of the very general dissatisfaction felt at mr. Gladstone's conduct . . . [Announcement of opposition by Gathorne Hardy.] [Oxf.], (1865), 4°. 4 pp.   G.A. Oxon c. 81 (358)
— [Another ed., with additional signatures.]   G.A. Oxon c. 81 (378)

804. Is mr. Gladstone the right man for Oxford university? The question answered in the negative by himself. n. pl., [1865], 8°. 16 pp.
G.A. Oxon 8° 179 (24)

805. CARDWELL, E., To the electors of Oxford. [Electoral address.] (Oxf., 1865), s. sh.   G.A. Oxon c. 81 (362)

806. GLADSTONE, W. E., To the members of Convocation in the University of Oxford. [Letter of farewell to his constituency.] n. pl., (1865), s. sh.
G.A. Oxon c. 81 (354)

807. DODGSON, C. L., The dynamics of a parti-cle, with an excursus on The new method of evaluation as applied to π. [By C. L. Dodgson.] Oxf., 1865, 8°. 28 pp.   Arch. AA e. 33
— 2nd ed. 1865.   250 i. 3 (8)
— 3rd ed. [On wrapper.] Hardy v. Gladstone. In re Jowett. The dynamics of a parti-cle. 1865.   G.A. Oxon c. 82 (391)
— [Another ed.] First pr. in 1865. (Notes by an Oxf. chiel.) Oxf., 1874, 12°.   G.A. Oxon 8° 161 (22)
— [Another ed.] (The Lewis Carroll picture book, ed. by S. D. Collingwood, 1899, p. 59–75.)   270 e. 1155

808. Hendecasyllabics. After Tennyson. [Electoral squib on Gathorne Hardy.] n. pl., [1865], s. sh.   G.A. Oxon c. 81 (355)

809. URQUHART, E. W., The late Oxford university election. Lond. &c., 1865, 8°. 51 pp.   G.A. Oxon 8° 146 (9)

810. CALDICOTT, J. W., Analysis of the poll-book in the recent election of two burgesses to serve in Parliament for the University of Oxford. Lond. &c., 1866, 8°. 16 pp.   G.A. Oxon 8° 92 (7)

See 8677.4 [Campbell, J., Worcester College and the University election of 1865. 1961].

811. Voters (Oxford, &c. universities) . . . Return of the number of voters on the electoral roll . . . on the 1st day of January 1868. [Lond.], 1867, s. sh.   Pp. Eng. 1867/68 vol. 56

812. Sir Roundell Palmer for Oxford. From the 'Guardian' of October 14. n. pl., [1868], 8°. 4 pp.   G.A. Oxon c. 221

813. Oxford university election. Sir Roundell Palmer's committee room . . . Oct. 16, 1868. [Notification of Palmer's willingness to be nominated.] [Oxf.], (1868), s. sh.   G.A. Oxon c. 221

814. Oxford, Nov. 12, 1868. Dear Sir, It has been decided that . . . [Notification that the promises on behalf of Palmer do not warrant his proceeding to a poll.] [Oxf.], (1868), s. sh.   G.A. Oxon c. 221

815. 'Gorilla-Ben-Snip.' [An electoral squib.] [Oxf., 1868], s. sh.
                         G.A. Oxon c. 84 (505)

816. A long time after the destruction of Sennacherib. [Electoral squib.] [Oxf., 1868], s. sh.   G.A. Oxon c. 84 (503)

817. Mr. Hardy's and mr. Mowbray's committee-room . . . Sir, In soliciting your vote . . . [Election manifesto.] [Oxf., 1868], s. sh.
                         G.A. Oxon c. 84 (509)

818. Shoemaker shut the door, a semi-humorous ditty. [Electoral squib.] [Oxf., 1868], s. sh.   G.A. Oxon c. 84 (506)

819. An authentic copy of the poll for a burgess to serve in Parliament for the University of Oxford taken 13th–17th May, 1878. Oxf., 1878, 8°. 99 pp.   G.A. Oxon 4° 430 (5)
— [Revised ed.] 1878.   G.A. Oxon 4° 430 (6)

820. University voters. Returns of the total number of doctors and actual masters of arts in the University of Oxford who have the right of voting at the election of members to serve in Parliament for such university: of the number of electors in Holy orders. [Lond.], 1879, s. sh.
                         Pp. Eng. 1879 vol. 58

821. Report of speech made by earl Percy at the meeting of non-resident graduates . . . 18th June 1909 [proposing a resolution in favour of lord Hugh Cecil's candidature]. n. pl., (1909), 4°. 3 pp.
                         G.A. Oxon b. 139 (5)

822. Executive committee for the promotion of . . . lord Hugh Cecil . . . [Letter and list of signatures.] [Lond.], (1909), 4°. 8 pp.
                         G.A. Oxon 4° 276 (9b)

823. Requisition addressed to mr. Arthur J. Evans [and] Mr. Evans's reply. (Lond.), [1909], 4°. 4 pp.   G.A. Oxon b. 139 (8)

824. Representation of Oxford university. [Exchange of letters between the marquis of Lansdowne and A. J. Evans, in which the latter announces the withdrawal of his candidature.] n. pl., (1909), 8°. 4 pp.
                         G.A. Oxon b. 139 (11)

825. Proposed Labour candidature for Oxford university. [A letter, signed
J. M. MacTavish, in support of H. S. Furniss.] n. pl., (1918), 4°. 4 pp.
G.A. Oxon b. 139 (14)

826. FURNISS, H. S., Oxford university and the Labour party. (Lond.),
[1918], 8°. 8 pp.   G.A. Oxon b. 139 (15a)

827. FURNISS, H. S., Oxford university Parliamentary election. (Lond.,
1918), 8°. 4 pp.   G.A. Oxon b. 139 (15b)

828. [Begin.] The reasons for prolonging the duration of Parliament . . .
[signed by E. Armstrong and 10 others, urging support for lord Hugh
Cecil and Rowland Prothero]. Oxf., (1918), s. sh.
G.A. Oxon b. 139 (13)

829. Oxford university election, 1919. [Announcement of C. W. C.
Oman's candidature.] Oxf., (1919), 4°. 4 pp.   G.A. Oxon b. 139 (19)

830. RILEY, A., To the electors of the University of Oxford. [Electoral
manifesto.] (Lond., 1919), 4°. 4 pp.   G.A. Oxon b. 139 (20)

831. To the electors of the University of Oxford. [Election manifesto in
support of Gilbert Murray.] Oxf., [1919], 4°. 3 pp.
G.A. Oxon b. 139 (21)

832. Oxford university Parliamentary election, 1922. Address to the
electors on behalf of . . . lord Hugh Cecil . . . and sir Charles Oman . . .
Oxf., (1922), 4°. 3 pp.   G.A. Oxon b. 139 (23a)

833. To the electors of the University of Oxford. [Support for Gilbert
Murray.] Oxf., 1922, 4°. 3 pp.   G.A. Oxon b. 139 (23b)

834. Oxford university Parliamentary election, 1923. Address . . . on
behalf of . . . lord Hugh Cecil . . . and sir Charles Oman . . . Oxf., (1923),
4°. 3 pp.   G.A. Oxon b. 139 (29a)

835. To the electors of the University of Oxford. December 1923.
[Support for Gilbert Murray.] Oxf., 1923, 4°. 4 pp.
G.A. Oxon b. 139 (29b)

836. Oxford university Parliamentary election, 1924. Address . . . on
behalf of . . . lord Hugh Cecil . . . and sir Charles Oman . . . Oxf., (1924),
2 leaves.   G.A. Oxon b. 139 (31a)

837. To the electors of the University of Oxford. October 1924. [Support
for Gilbert Murray.] Oxf., (1924), 4°. 3 pp. G.A. Oxon b. 139 (31b)

838. Oxford university Parliamentary election, 1929. Address . . . on
behalf of . . . lord Hugh Cecil . . . and sir Charles Oman . . . Oxf., (1929),
4°. 3 pp.   G.A. Oxon b. 139 (34)

839. Oxford and the National government. [Letters exchanged between
H. A. L. Fisher, chairman of the Liberal committee, and lord Hugh
Cecil and sir Charles Oman, university burgesses; with a statement
from Gilbert Murray that he will not contest the seat at present.] (Oxf.
mag., 1931, vol. 50, p. 51–53.)   Per. G.A. Oxon 4° 141

840. Oxford university Parliamentary election. Professor Stocks' election address [*with*] Letter from professor Gilbert Murray. Oxf., [1935], 4°. 4+2 pp. G.A. Oxon b. 139 (36*a*, *c*)

841. Oxford university Parliamentary election, 1935. Address . . . on behalf of . . . lord Hugh Cecil . . . and C. R. M. F. Cruttwell . . . Oxf., (1935), 4°. 3 pp. G.A. Oxon b. 139 (36*b*)

842. HERBERT, A. P., Letter to the electors of Oxford university. (Lond.), 1935, 8°. 14 pp. G.A. Oxon b. 139 (36*d*)

843. LINDEMANN, F. A., Oxford university Parliamentary representation. [Electoral address.] Oxf., (1936), s. sh. G.A. Oxon b. 139 (161)

844. BUZZARD, SIR E. FARQUHAR, Oxford university Parliamentary election, 1937. To the electors . . . Oxf., (1937), 4°. 3 pp. G.A. Oxon b. 139 (163*a*)

845. Oxford university Parliamentary election, 1937. To the electors . . . [An address in support of sir Farquhar Buzzard.] Oxf., (1937), 4°. 4 pp. G.A. Oxon b. 139 (163*b*)

846. Oxford university representation. Sir Arthur Salter. [An 'all-party' letter of support.] Oxf., [1937], s. sh. G.A. Oxon b. 139 (164*a*)

847. LINDEMANN, F. A., To the electors of Oxford university. Oxf., (1937), 4°. 4 pp. G.A. Oxon b. 139 (166*a*)

848. SALTER, SIR A., Oxford university by-election 1937. Letter to the electors of Oxford university. Oxf., (1937), 4°. 16 pp. 22774 e. 50

849. HERBERT, SIR A. P., Letter to the electors of Oxford university, General election, July, 1945. Lond., 1945, 8°. 8 pp.
22774 e. 37 (10)

With other universities

850. Academiæ Francofurtanæ ad Viadrum encænia secularia Oxonii . . . Apr. 26. anno fundat. 201. annoque Dom. 1706. celebrata. Oxon., 1706, fol. 43 pp. Bliss B 412 (1)

851. English and Scottish degrees. (Scottish mag., 1848, vol. 1, p. 449–55.)
Per. 1132 e. 25
— Repr. [*entitled*] Oxford and the Scottish universities. 1848. 8 pp.
3974 e. 197 (11)

852. BENSON, C. E., Oxford–Cambridge; Cambridge–Oxford. (Quarterly review, 1931, vol. 256, p. 40–50.) Per. 3977 e. 191

853. CASARTELLI, L. C., Oxford and Louvain. (Dublin review, 1903, vol. 132, p. 285–308.) Per. 3977 e. 199

854. To the professors of the arts and sciences and to members of the universities and learned societies in Germany and Austria. [Declaration by many senior members of the University stating their desire for the resumption of normal relations as soon as possible.] [Oxf., 1920], 4°. 3 pp.
G.A. Oxon b. 141 (191*a*)

With Oxford City
General

See also 4560–81 for works on relations between tradesmen and undergraduates.
See 865, 882. St. Scholastica's day, 1354.

855. The humble petition of the major, aldermen, bayliffs and commonalty of the City of Oxon . . . with their grievances annexed, and parliaments answer thereunto. [Madan 2011.] Lond., 1649, 4°. 8 pp.
Gough Oxf. 138 (4)

856. The answer of . . . the Vniversity of Oxford, to the petition, articles of grievance, and reasons of the Citie of Oxon. presented to the honorable committee for regulating the Vniversity of Oxford, the 24. of June, 1649. [Chiefly by G. Langbaine.] [Madan 2019.] Oxf., 1649, 4°. 46 pp.
Wood 614 (6)
— 2nd ed. [Madan 3184.] Oxf., 1678, 4°. 46 pp.   G. Pamph. 56

857. [*Begin.*] This indenture made . . . [A form of indenture binding an apprentice to a member of the University.] [Madan 2518.] [Oxf., 1660?], s. sh.   G.A. Oxon b. 111 (13)

858. [*Begin.*] Whereas Tuesday next . . . [Notice by the vice-chancellor that Jan. 30, 1671/2 is to be observed as a day of fasting, for the martyrdom of Charles i.] [Madan 2932.] [Oxf.], 1672, s. sh.   Wood 276a (360)
— [Another issue.] [Madan 2933.]

859. [*Begin.*] Whereas complaint hath . . . [Proclamation by the vice-chancellor that no boatmen or fishermen are to hire out their boats on Sundays, except in certain circumstances.] July 7. [Madan 2983.] [Bodleian copy mutilated.] [Oxf.], (1673), s. sh. G.A. Oxon b. 111 (22)

860. A defence of the rights and priviledges of the University of Oxford: containing 1. An answer to the petition of the City of Oxford, 1649 [by G. Langbaine]. 2. The case of the University of Oxford, presented to the . . . Commons, Jan. 24. 1689/90 [by J. Harrington]. Oxf., 1690, 4°. 54 pp.   G.A. Oxon 4° 6 (28)

861. WRIGHT, W., The case of the City of Oxford [by W. Wright] shewing how far they are concerned to oppose the confirmation of the charters and pretended priviledges of the University, with an answer to . . . A defence of the rights and priviledges of the University of Oxford. n. pl., [1690], 4°. 11 pp.   Gough Oxf. 138 (6)

862. The case of the University of Oxford . . . [A petition, drawn up by J. Harrington, to the Lords asking that the bill confirming the privileges of the University be committed.] n. pl., [1690], s. sh. Wood 276a (304)

863. HARRINGTON, J., The case of the University of Oxford; shewing that the City is not concern'd to oppose the confirmation of their charters by parliament. [By J. Harrington.] Oxf., 1690, 4°. [p. 37–54 of A defence of the . . . University of Oxford.]   Gough Oxf. 105 (2)

864. WOOD, T., A vindication of the proceedings of the University of Oxford against the allegations of an act of the Council of the City of Oxford, dated Sept. 6. 1703. By a private hand [T. Wood.] n. pl., (1703), 4°. 7 pp. Gough Oxf. 105 (1)

See also 161–72 [Jacobite disturbance of 1714].

865. A relation of the conflict betwixt the scholars and townsmen of Oxford upon the 10th of February, A.D. 1354, made by maister John de Staunton, Feb. 18. 1354, extracted out of the registry of John Synewall, bishop of Lincoln. (Bibl. lit., 1724, no. 9, p. 1–8.) Per. 3974 d. 291 (9)

See 1048 [Controversy in connexion with the amendment of Stat. Tit. II. 9: the simultaneous enjoyment of university and civic privileges. 1759].
See 982, 983 [Proposed amendment of the statute relating to the simultaneous enjoyment of university and civic privileges. 1759].

866. The case of a gentleman [F. Bassett of Queen's college, a freeman of the City] unjustly deprived of his vote at the election of a chancellor of the University [because he had accepted civic honours]. Lond., 1759, 8°. 31 pp. G.A. Oxon 8° 59 (14)

867. Explicatio statuti de privilegiis Universitatis et Civitatis simul non fruendis, Tit. II. sect. 9. n. pl., [1760], s. sh. Caps. 10. 9 (4)

868. A candid remonstrance to the vice-chancellor and members of the University occasioned by a late address to the freemen and other inhabitants of the City of Oxford. By a citizen. Lond., 1764, 8°. 19 pp.
G.A. Oxon 8° 219 (4)

869. [Prospectus of a work to be published June 1, 1779, *entitled*] The cruelty, injustice, and impolicy of the present mode of information and punishment relative to prostitution established in the University. Oxf., 1779, 8°. 10 pp. Gough Oxf. 90 (24)

870. [*Begin.*] In a Convocation to be holden on Tuesday, February 1st. [Jan. 24, 1825. Proposal to affix University seal to an instrument releasing the Mayor and citizens of Oxford from the performance of the acts now required of them on Dies scholastica. With a brief account of the said obligation, &c.] [Oxf.], 1825, fol. 3 pp. G.A. Oxon c. 41 (6)

871. [*Begin.*] An act . . . . [Notice of a Convocation to be held on 13th Feb., 1827, to consider a proposal to indemnify the City for the additional expense incurred by imprisoning prostitutes, under the Act for the better preservation of the peace and good order in the Universities. 6 Geo. IV. c. 97.] Feb. 5, 1827. [Oxf.], 1827, s. sh. G.A. Oxon c. 43 (14)

872. A letter to the rev. the vice chancellor . . . containing a few remarks on certain proctorial power [to commit to safe custody any known prostitute met with on the streets after dark] with reference to a late event at Cambridge. By a non-resident master of arts. Oxf. &c., 1847, 8°. 16 pp.
G. Pamph. 2904 (11)

873. Gown and town in 1848. (Oxf. Protestant mag., 1848, vol. 2, p. 44–48.) Per. G.A. Oxon 8° 119

874. The vote of Wednesday next. The mayor's oath [to observe the privileges of the University. The vice-chancellor will seek from Convocation authority to enforce this by taking legal measures. Signed Clericus]. n. pl., 1858, s. sh.   G.A. Oxon c. 74 (54)

875. [*Begin.*] Whereas the authorities . . . [June 20, 1859. To be proposed in Convocation of June 24, a decree authorizing the vice-chancellor to refrain from opposing a bill introduced into Parliament by the authorities of the City of Oxford, which would relieve the mayor and others from taking the oath to observe the privileges of the University.] n. pl., (1859), s. sh.   G.A. Oxon c. 75 (228)

876. An act to repeal part of an act passed in the thirteenth year of Elizabeth, chapter twenty-nine, concerning the several incorporations of the Universities of Oxford and Cambridge . . . [repealing so much of the act as imposes upon the mayor &c. of Oxford the obligation of taking an oath for the conservation of the privileges of the University of Oxford]. (22 & 23 V., c. 19, Pub.) Lond., 1859, fol. 4 pp.   L.L.

877. Gown and town rows at Oxford and their historical significance. (Dubl. univ. mag., 1868, vol. 71, p. 363–81.)   Per. 3977 e. 74

878. An act to amend the law relating to prisons in England (40 & 41 V., c. 21, Pub.). [Sect. 54 relieves the University of its obligation to contribute towards gaol expenses by virtue of a single payment to the City of £400.] Lond., 1877, 4°.   L.L.

879. WILSON, J. C., [*Begin.*] The unobtrusive decree . . . [Protest against the decree for the appointment of a delegacy 'for the purpose of acting in the long vacation on behalf of the University, in the matter of the bill now before Parliament affecting the local government of the City of Oxford'.] [Oxf.], (1888), s. sh.   G.A. Oxon b. 140 (82*e*)

880. WILSON, J. C., The proposed agreement between the University and the City respecting the local government of Oxford. [Oxf.], (1888), s. sh.   G.A. Oxon b. 140 (82*f*)

881. The sin of our cities. Oxford, by a member of the University. [Observations in favour of restricting the power of the University police and court over Oxford citizens.] (Modern review, 1893, vol. 1, p. 329–39.)   G.A. Oxon 4° 575 (21)

882. Poems relating to the riot between town and gown on St. Scholastica's day, Feb. 10, 1354/5 and two following days. Tryvytlam de laude Universitatis Oxoniæ. Ed. by H. Furneaux. (Oxf. hist. soc., 1896, vol. 32, p. 163–209.)   G.A. Oxon 8° 360 = R.

883. PAINTIN, H., Isaac Grubb and the oath, an episode of Nov. 9th, 1857. [An account of Grubb's refusal to take the oath to the University on his election as Mayor.] Repr. from the Oxf. Chronicle, Nov. 15th, 1907. [Oxf.], (1907), 4°. 3 pp.   G.A. Oxon 4° 186 (26)

884. PLOWMAN, T. F., Gown and Town. (Chambers's journ., 1916, 7th ser., vol. 6, p. 289–92.)   G.A. Oxon 4° 276 (30)

884.2. FOWLER, G. T., University members of the City council. (Oxf. mag., 1961, N.S., vol. 1, p. 371, 72.) Per. G.A. Oxon 4° 141

884.5. BOLTON, J. L., The Barbers' Company, a university gild. (Oxoniensia, 1963, vol. 28, p. 84–86.) Per. G.A. Oxon 4° 658 = R. Top.

Sale of food and drink

885. An acte that purueyors shal not take victuels within fyue miles of Cambridge and Oxforde. (2 & 3 Phil. & Mary, c. 15, Pub.) Lond., 1555, fol. L.L.
— [Another ed.] [Lond., 1555?], fol. 2 leaves. [The Bodleian copy lacks the 2nd leaf: Vet. A 1 b. 4 (225)].

886. [Begin.] Robert, earle of Leicester . . . [43 orders by the chancellor of the University for the Oxford market]. [Madan 53.] [Lond., 1575?], 2 sheets. O.U.A.

887. An acte that purueiours may take grayne, corne or victtuals within five myles of Cambridge and Oxforde in certayne cases. (1571. 13 Eliz., c. 21, Pub.) Lond., 1578, fol. L.L.

888. [Begin.] Thomas baron of Buckurst . . . [Orders for the market of the City of Oxford, issued by the chancellor of the University.] [Madan 197.] [Oxf., 1600?], 2 sheets. B.N.C.

889. [Begin.] Thomas earle of Dorset . . . [Orders for the market of the City of Oxford, by the chancellor of the University.] [Madan 279.] [Oxf., 1606], s. sh. O.U.A.

890. A proclamation [by abp. Laud as chancellor] for the well ordering of the market in the Cittie of Oxford and for the redresse of abuses in weights and measures within the precincts of the Vniversity of Oxford. [Madan 769.] Oxf., 1634, 4°. 6 pp. Wood 276a (310)

891. [Begin.] To all Christian people . . . [Form of licence to ale-house keepers.] [Madan 947.] [Oxf., 1640?], s. sh. Wood 276a (343)

892. [Begin.] To all Christian people . . . [Form of notification by the vice-chancellor, that he has duly licensed a person to keep an ale-house.] [Madan 949.] [Oxf., 1640], s. sh.

893. By the king. A proclamation for the better meanes of making provision for the kings army [allowing butchers to kill and furnish flesh to the markets at Oxford during the Lent then approaching]. [Madan 1236.] [Oxf., 1642/3], s. sh. Arch. G. b. 1 (30)

894. Octob: 21, 1667. Prizes of wines set and appointed by the vice-chancellor. [Madan 2776.] [Oxf., 1667], s. sh. Wood 276a (354)

895. [Begin.] Prizes of wines set and appointed . . . [A programma altering the prices of wine.] [Madan 3017.] [Oxf.], 1674, s. sh. Wood 276a (372)

896. [Begin.] Univers. Oxon. [Notice by the vice-chancellor regulating the prices of provisions in the market.] [Oxf.? 1681], s. sh.
Wood 276a (377)

897. [*Begin.*] Whereas by several letters patents . . . [Vice-chancellor's proclamation listing maximum prices of wine, beer and ale.] July 7th. [Oxf.], 1701, s. sh.   G.A. Oxon b. 19

898. [*Begin.*] We [   ] majesty's justices of the peace . . . [Licence to keep a common ale-house. This form was completed for someone whose name is obliterated, in the parish of St. Mary the Virgin. The J.P.'s who signed were R. Shippen, vice-chancellor, and A. Charlett.] 17[20].   Ashm. 1819 (29)

899. [*Begin.*] At a meeting of the vice-chancellor, heads of houses and proctors . . . 20th of May . . . 1728. Whereas the great number of publick houses . . . [Order for the better regulation thereof.] [Oxf.] 1728, s. sh.   Don. b. 12 (47*a*)

900. [*Begin.*] April 22, 1734. There is now drawn up, in order to be proposed in Convocation, an inhibition to the wine-cellars lately opened in this town. [A memorandum against the proposed inhibition.] n. pl., (1734), fol. 3 pp.   G.A. Oxon 4° 6 (11)
— [Recirculated. July 13, 1741.]   G.A. Oxon b. 19

See 4043 [An act for the more effectual preventing the unlawful playing of interludes within the precincts of the two universities . . . and for explaining . . . An act for laying a duty upon the retailers of spiritous liquors as may affect the privilege of the said universities. 1737].

901. By the vice-chancellor. A programma [enforcing the prescribed number of vintners (3) in the University]. [Oxf.], 1740, s. sh.
                                                    Don. b 12 (55)

902. An act to continue the several laws therein mentioned for preventing theft and rapine on the northern borders of England [&c.] . . . and to prevent the retailing of wine within either of the universities . . . without licence. (17 G. II, c. 40, Pub.) Lond., 1744, fol. 14 pp.   L.L.

903. At a meeting of the heads of houses . . . on the fifth of . . . June 1766, it was ordered [that cooks, coffee-house and inn keepers be enjoined not to send dinners into colleges; that no coffee-house keepers shall receive scholars to dine, sup, or drink wine; etc.]. [Oxf.], (1766), s. sh.
                                                    G.A. Oxon b. 19

904. An alphabetical list of such persons within the University of Oxford . . . as are licensed to vend wine by retail . . . 1828/29–68/69. [Oxf., 1828–68], s. sh.
[The Bodleian set is imperfect: issues for the years 1828/29, 50/51, 53/54, 54/55, 62/63–68/69 are to be found in G.A. Oxon c. 44–85.]

905. An act to amend the laws for the importation of corn. [Inspectors of corn to be appointed for the City by the Chancellor of the University.] (9 G. IV, c. 60, Pub.) Lond., 1828, fol. 22 pp.   L.L.
— 5 & 6 V., c. 14, Pub.
— 45 & 46 V., c. 37, Pub.

906. University and City of Oxford. [Assize of bread. Forms, signed by the clerks of the Market, completed in MS. for the period Oct. 5, 1821–Apr. 2, 1870.]   MS. Top. Oxon d. 68–70

907. [*Begin.*] The Committee . . . [Report of the Committee appointed at the ruri-decanal chapter held on 31 July 1868 'to consider how far a better system of licensing and regulating public-houses and beershops can be devised'.] [Oxf., 1868], fol. 3 pp.   G.A. Oxon b. 32

908. An act to abolish certain rights and privileges of the City of Oxford . . . in connection with the sale of wine and the granting of licences therefor and for other purposes. (12 & 13 G. V, c. 36. L. & P.) (Lond.), 1922, 8°. 5 pp.   L.L.

Carriers and coaches

909. Orders [by the vice-chancellor] concerning the rates and demands of carriers, and their porters, for goods brought, and conveyed betwixt the University of Oxford and City of London. [Madan 2751.] [Oxf., 1666], s. sh.   Wood 276a (352)

910. [*Begin.*] Whereas the appointment . . . [Vice-chancellor's orders regulating the University carriers, T. Moore and R. Stonehill between Oxford and London.] Ap: 5. [Madan 2835.] [Oxf.?], 1669, s. sh.
                                                          Wood 276a (355)

911. [*Begin.*] Whereas Edward Bartlet . . . [Programma issued by the vice-chancellor forbidding all members of the University to make use of Edward Bartlet's flying coach to London, it being unlicenced.] July 20. [Madan 2857.] [Oxf.], 1670, s. sh.   Wood 276a (358)

912. [*Begin.*] Whereas the appointment . . . [Notice by the vice-chancellor that Thomas Moore intends a one-day coach to London, and detailing regulations to be observed.] Apr. 1. [Madan 2894.] [Oxf., 1671], s. sh.
                                                          Wood 276a (359)

913. [Vice-chancellor's notice, quashing the project of an unlicensed coach between London and Oxford.] [Madan 2895.]

914. [*Begin.*] By order from . . . [Notice by the vice-chancellor forbidding members of the University to make use of the flying coach operated by the unlicensed carriers Thomas Dye and John Fosset. Apr. 27, 1671.] [Madan 2897.] [Oxf.], 1671, s. sh.   Wood 276a (365)

915. To London every day [notice that there will be a one-day coach from T. Moore's house to London, every week-day, and one back. May]. [Madan 2898.] [Oxf., 1671], s. sh.   Wood 276a (355*)

916. Oxford one day stage-coach [notice by widow Stonehill and John Fosset to Londoners travelling to Oxford]. [Madan 2910.] [Oxf.? 1671], s. sh.   Wood 276a (363)

917. [*Begin.*] By order from mr. Vice-Chancellor [notice discommoning T. Dye and J. Fosset, who set up a London coach without his licence]. Feb. 22, 1671. [Madan 2934.] [Oxf.], 1672, s. sh.   Wood 276a (362)

— [Another ed.] Feb. 23, 1671.   Don. b. 12 (15)
— [Another ed.] Apr. 22, 1672. [Madan 2936.]   Wood 276a (370)

918. [*Begin.*] Whereas the appointment . . . [Order of the vice-chancellor about T. Moore and E. Bartlet jnr.'s one-day coach to and from London.] Apr. 19. [Madan 2935.] [Oxf.], 1672, s. sh. Wood 276a (369)

919. [*Begin.*] Whereas the carriers . . . [Notice of the vice-chancellor concerning carriers, fares, &c. Dec. 4, 1674.] [Madan 3019.] [Oxf.], 1674, s. sh.   Wood 276a (318)

Discommoning

See also 909–19. Carriers and coaches.

920. [Notices discommoning tradesmen and others.]

17 Dec. 1768. M. Woolfe, a Jew.	G.A. Oxon b. 19
29 June 1804. W. Wise, bookseller.	Don. b. 12 (103)
10 June 1809. T. G. Bennet, barber.	G.A. Oxon b. 19
4 July 1817. T. Austin, stable-keeper.	G.A. Oxon b. 19
21 Nov. 1817. J. Dickeson, coffeehouse keeper.	G.A. Oxon b. 19
21 June 1819. T. Austin, stable keeper.	G.A. Oxon b. 19
10 Oct. 1820. R. Speakman, tailor.	G.A. Oxon b. 19
11 June 1821. W. Shayler, stable keeper.	G.A. Oxon b. 19
16 June 1821. J. Moore, stable keeper.	G.A. Oxon b. 19
21 March 1823. T. Morris, confectioner.	G.A. Oxon b. 19
4 June 1824. W. Shayler, stable keeper.	G.A. Oxon c. 40 (41)
27 May 1825. W. Shayler, stable keeper.	G.A. Oxon c. 41 (63)
28 May 1828. T. Austin, stable keeper.	G.A. Oxon c. 44 (59)
30 April 1830. J. Giles, coffeehouse keeper.	G.A. Oxon c. 46 (38)
15 May 1830. T. Perrin, stable keeper.	G.A. Oxon b. 21
15 May 1830. J. C. Jones, stable keeper.	G.A. Oxon c. 46 (49)
19 May 1836. S. Wild, veterinary surgeon.	G.A. Oxon b. 23
5 April 1837. J. Moore, stable keeper.	G.A. Oxon c. 53 (40)
12 May 1837. J. Sheard, stable keeper.	G.A. Oxon c. 53 (73)
1 March 1839. T. Perrin, livery-stable keeper.	G.A. Oxon c. 55 (39)
10 Feb. 1841. R. Wilkins, butcher.	G.A. Oxon c. 57 (20)
3 June 1843. S. Beesley, stable keeper.	G.A. Oxon c. 59 (73)
29 March 1844. S. Beesley [sentence withdrawn].	G.A. Oxon c. 60 (44)
29 March 1844. C. Tedder & A. Allsop, stable keepers.	G.A. Oxon c. 60 (43)
13 May 1844. I. Batten, stable keeper.	G.A. Oxon c. 60 (74)
22 May 1846. W. Leech, tailor.	G.A. Oxon c. 62 (49)
5 June 1846. W. Leech [sentence withdrawn].	G.A. Oxon c. 62 (56)
25 March 1859. W. Holland, hotel keeper.	G.A. Oxon c. 75 (109)
19 June 1862. J. Reeves, Isis tavern, Wootton.	G.A. Oxon c. 78 (207)

921. WISE, W., An appeal from custom to conscience [in connexion with his discommoning as a stationer because of his activities as a bookseller]. Oxf., [1804], 16°. 15 pp.   2581 f. 31

922. WISE, W., A bone for the booksellers. Oxf., [1804].

GOVERNMENT

GENERAL

See also 1638–1825. Reform.

923. An acte for thincorporation of bothe thunyversities. (13 Eliz., c. 29, Pub.) 1571.
— 22 & 23 V., c. 19, Pub.
[Text in Shadwell's Enactments &c. See no. 956.]
See 191 [Walpole, H., Delenda est Oxonia. 1749].
See 192 [Henley, J., On the question whether the law of England countenances the interposition of extrinsecal authority &c. 1749].

924. WALLIS, J., An abstract of divers privileges and rights of the University of Oxford. (Collectanea curiosa, by J. Gutch, vol. 2, p. 35–48.) Oxf., 1781, 8°.   Gough Oxf. 66

See 1846–49 [Alleged illegality of the present academical system. 1831].

925. Oxford and its governors. (Christ. rememb., 1844, N.S., vol. 7, p. 690–709.)   Per. 971 e. 44

926. [*Begin.*] It is believed that . . . [A scheme for the reform of the constitution of the University, signed by H. Wall and 40 others.] Feb. 15. [Oxf.], (1854), s. sh.   G.A. Oxon c. 70 (53)

927. [*Begin.*] In a Convocation to be holden . . . 24th [Feb.] . . . it will be proposed to affix the University seal to the following . . . petition to the queen's . . . majesty. Feb. 17. [The petition seeks a royal licence to repeal the statute relating to Collectors in Lent, to amend the statute regulating the election of proctors, and to supplement the statute concerned with the constitution and duties of the Hebdomadal board: the details of the proposed new constitution are included.] [Oxf.], (1854), 4°. 4 pp.   G.A. Oxon c. 70 (58)

928. Reasons for voting for the proposed petition [no. 927] on Friday, February 24th. Oxf., [1854], s. sh.   G.A. Oxon c. 71 (311)

929. 'The new constitution.' [Observations, signed A resident, opposing the proposed petition, i.e. no. 927.] [Oxf., 1854], 4°. 3 pp.
            G.A. Oxon b. 27

930. Hints on the Hebdomadal reform bill [signed Non-resident]. Feb. 20 Lond., 1854, 8°. 8 pp.   G.A. Oxon 8° 63 (12)

931. MARRIOTT, C., How are we to vote on the proposed constitution for the universities? [signed C.M.]. Feb. 20. [Oxf.], (1854), 8°. 4 pp.
            G.A. Oxon b. 27

932. [*Begin.*] The attention of members of Convocation is called to the following extract from . . . the Morning Chronicle, Feb. 22, 1854. [A

criticism of the Hebdomadal Board for asking Convocation to support the proposed petition, i.e. no. 927, after it has been privately submitted to and rejected by ministers of the crown.] Feb. 22. n. pl., (1854), s. sh.
G.A. Oxon c. 70 (269)

933. Answer to the statement from the Morning Chronicle, on the intention of Her majesty's ministers [with regard to the proposed petition, i.e. no. 927. Signed One cognizant of facts. Feb. 23]. Oxf., [1854], s. sh.
G.A. Oxon b. 27

934. 'Our liberty is at stake.' [A paper dated Feb. 23, opposing the proposed petition to her majesty, i.e. no. 927.] [Oxf., 1854], s. sh.
G.A. Oxon c. 70 (270)

935. NEATE, C., Reasons for voting against the petition [no. 927] to be submitted to Convocation on the 24th instant [signed C.N.]. Feb. 23. [Oxf.], (1854), s. sh.   G.A. Oxon c. 70 (271)

936. [*Begin.*] The attention of members of Convocation is called to . . . lord Derby's speech in the House of Lords last night [a refutation of no. 933]. Feb. 24. [Oxf.], (1854), s. sh.   G.A. Oxon b. 27

937. BUTLER, G., Concio in Sheldoniano theatro habita Febr. xxiv. [A speech on the proposed petition to her majesty.] n. pl., [1854], 8°. 6 pp.
G.A. Oxon 8° 705 (9)

938. BARRY, H. B., A few words on the constitution to be submitted to the Convocation of the University of Oxford by the Hebdomadal board. Oxf., 1854, 8°. 16 pp.   G.A. Oxon 8° 429

See 1731 [Barry, H. B., Remarks on the three proposals for reforming the constitution of the University. 1854].

939. A bill to make further provision for the good government and extension of the University of Oxford and of the colleges therein. 17 Mar. 1854. [Lond.], 1854, fol. 18 pp.   Pp. Eng. 1854 vol. 5
— As amended in committee. 11 Apr. 1854. 20 pp.
Pp. Eng. 1854 vol. 5
— As amended in committee and on re-commitment. 1 June, 1854. 12 pp.   Pp. Eng. 1854 vol. 5
— As amended in committee on first and second re-commitment, and on consideration of bill as amended. 23 June, 1854. 14 pp.
Pp. Eng. 1854, vol. 5
— As amended by the Lords. 12 pp.   Pp. Eng. 1854, vol. 5

940. An act to make further provision for the good government and extension of the University of Oxford, of the colleges therein . . . (17 & 18 V., c. 81, Pub.) Lond., 1854, fol. 17 pp.   L.L.
— 19 & 20 V., c. 31, Pub.
— 20 & 21 V., c. 25, Pub.
— 32 & 33 V., c. 20, Pub.
— 40 & 41 V., c. 48, Pub.

941. A bill intituled An act to amend the act of the seventeenth and eighteenth years of her majesty, concerning the University of Oxford and

the college of Saint Mary Winchester. 5 June 1856. [Lond.], 1856, fol.
3 pp.   Pp. Eng. 1856 vol. 5
— [Act.] (19 & 20 V., c. 31, Pub.) Lond., 1856, fol.   L.L.

942. A bill intituled An act to continue the powers of the Commissioners
under an act of the 17th and 18th years of her majesty concerning the
University of Oxford . . . and further to amend the said act. [Lond.],
1857, fol. 3 pp.   Pp. Eng. 1857 sess. 2, vol. 3
— [Act.]. (20 & 21 V., c. 25, Pub.) Lond., 1857, fol.   L.L.

943. Universities incorporation act amendment. A bill to repeal part of an
act . . . 13 Eliz. c. 29, concerning the several incorporations of the universities of Oxford and Cambridge, and the confirmation of the charters, liberties, and privileges granted to either of them. 18 July 1859.
[Lond.], 1859, fol. 4 pp.   Pp. Eng. 1859 sess. 2, vol. 2
— [Act.] (22 & 23 V., c. 19, Pub.) Lond., 1859, fol.   L.L.

See 93 [Munimenta academica. 1868].

944. GEORGE, H. B., University legislation. Suggestions for an improved
method of procedure. 19 Apr. [Oxf.], 1869, 4°. 3 pp.
                                        G.A. Oxon c. 85 (409)

945. GRIFFITHS, J., ed., Enactments in Parliament specially concerning
the universities of Oxford and Cambridge. Oxf., 1869, 8°. 369 pp.
                                        Clar. Press 31 a. 64

946. University of Oxford. A bill intituled An act for making further provision respecting the University of Oxford and the colleges therein.
8 May 1876. [Lond.], 1876, fol. 12 pp.   Pp. Eng. 1876 vol. 7

947. A bill to make further provision respecting the Universities of Oxford
and Cambridge. 9 Feb. 1877. [Lond.], 1877, fol. 14 pp.
                                        Pp. Eng. 1877 vol. 6
— As amended in committee. 12 Mar. 1877. 16 pp.
                                        Pp. Eng. 1877 vol. 6
— As amended in committee on re-commitment. 4 June 1877. 19 pp.
                                        Pp. Eng. 1877 vol. 6
— Lords' amendments. 30 July 1877. 9 pp.   Pp. Eng. 1877 vol. 6
— Memorandum respecting Lords' amendments. 21 July 1877. 6 pp.
                                        Pp. Eng. 1877 vol. 6

948. An act to make further provision respecting the Universities of Oxford
and Cambridge, and the colleges therein. (40 & 41 V., c. 48, Pub.)
Lond., 1877, 4°. 21 pp.   L.L.
— 43 & 44 V., c. 11, Pub.

949. Universities of Oxford and Cambridge (Limited tenures). A bill intituled An act to authorize the extension and further limitation of the
tenures of certain university and college emoluments limited or to be
limited by orders of the Oxford and Cambridge commissioners. 7 July
1880. [Lond.], 1880, fol. 3 pp.   Pp. Eng. 1880 vol. 7
— Act. (43 & 44 V., c. 11, Pub.).   L.L.

950. Universities of Oxford and Cambridge (Statutes). A bill intituled An act to make provision respecting certain statutes made by the Commissioners under the Universities of Oxford and Cambridge act, 1877. [Concerns those statutes which may not have been approved by Her majesty in Council before the expiration on 31st Dec., 1881 of the Commissioners' powers.] [Lond.], 1881, fol. 4 pp. Pp. Eng. 1881 vol. 6

951. Universities committee of the Privy council. A bill to amend the constitution of the Universities committee of the Privy council, and for purposes relating thereto. [Lond.], 1882, fol. 4 pp. Pp. Eng. 1882 vol. 6

952. Universities committee of Privy Council. A bill to enlarge the powers and amend the procedure of the Universities committee of the Privy Council. 16 Feb. 1883. [Lond.], 1883, fol. 3 pp.
Pp. Eng. 1883 vol. 10

953. The following memorial was laid before Council on Feb. 9, 1885 [concerning the reform of the legislative constitution and procedure of the University]. [Oxf.], (1885), s. sh.   G.A. Oxon c. 153

954. The following letter [to T. H. Grose] has been received in reply to the Memorial laid before Council on Feb. 9 [signed E. T. Turner]. May 26. [Oxf.], (1885), s. sh.   G.A. Oxon c. 153

955. WILLIAMS, J., The law of the universities. Lond., 1910, 8°. 151 pp.
L.L.

956. SHADWELL, C. L., ed., Enactments in Parliament specially concerning the Universities of Oxford and Cambridge. 4 vols. Oxf., 1912, 8°.
L.L.
— [Another issue.] (Oxf. hist. soc., vol. 58–61.)
G.A. Oxon 8° 360=R.

957. A bill to make further provision with regard to the universities of Oxford and Cambridge and the colleges thereof. 9 March 1914. Lond., 1914, fol. 18 pp.   Pp. Eng. 1914 vol. 6
See 1488 [Act to extend powers. 1915].

958. University of Oxford. Report for the year 1914/15– . Oxf., 1915– , 8°.   G.A. Oxon 8° 1032

959. MONTMORENCY, J. E. G. DE, The future of Oxford and Cambridge. (Edinb. review, 1919, vol. 230, p. 178–89.)   Per. 3977 e. 190

960. A bill to make further provision with respect to the universities of Oxford and Cambridge and the colleges therein. Lond., 1922, 4°. 12 pp.   Pp. Eng. 1923 vol. 3
— Brought from the Lords, 9 May 1923. Lond., 1923, 4°. 13 pp.
Pp. Eng. 1923 vol. 3
— As amended by Standing committee B. Lond., 1923, 4°. 13 pp.
Pp. Eng. 1923 vol. 3

961. An act to make further provision with respect to the Universities of Oxford and Cambridge and the colleges therein. (13 & 14 G. V, c. 33. Pub.) (Lond.), 1923, 8°. 14 pp.   L.L.

— [Evidence (in typewriting) given before the Royal Commission on Oxford and Cambridge, 1922, was presented to Bodley by the secretary to the Commission: MS. Top. Oxon b. 104–09; c. 267.]

962. CASE, T., Letters to 'The Times', 1884–1922, ed. by R. B. Mowat. Oxf., 1927, 8°. 284 pp.   3977 d. 220

963. The government of Oxford. Lond., 1931, 8°. 82 pp.
G. A. Oxon 8° 1087

964. MCCALLUM, R. B., An undergraduate council. (Oxf. mag., 1934, vol. 52, p. 565, 66.)   Per. G.A. Oxon 4° 141

965. A., P. E., 'The mills . . . grind?'—Longfellow. [An article suggesting reforms to strengthen the administrative staff of the University.] (Oxf. mag., 1938, vol. 56, p. 319, 20.)   Per. G.A. Oxon 4° 141

966. LAST, H., University procedure. [A letter occasioned by some points in the speech of the senior proctor, A. Ewart.] (Oxf. mag., 1944, vol. 62, p. 213, 14.)   Per G.A. Oxon 4° 141

967. EWART, A., University procedure. [A letter, answering H. Last.] (Oxf. mag., 1944, vol. 62, p. 226–28.)   Per. G.A. Oxon 4° 141

968. LAST, H., University procedure. [A letter occasioned by the letter of A. Ewart.] (Oxf. mag., 1944, vol. 62, p. 250, 51.) Per. G.A. Oxon 4° 141

969. The [University and employees'] joint committee. (Oxf. mag., 1947, vol. 66, p. 85.)   Per. G.A. Oxon 4° 141

970. CARTLAND, J. B., Should we limit our numbers? [I], II. (Oxf. mag., 1948, vol. 66, p. 276; 314–16.)   Per. G.A. Oxon 4° 141

971. VEALE, SIR D., The administration of the University, an address. (Oxf. mag., 1950, vol. 69, p. 8–10.)   Per. G.A. Oxon 4° 141

972. VEALE, SIR D., University administration. (Fortnightly, 1951, vol. 176, p. 741–46.)   Per. 3977 d. 59
— [Another ed.] (Amer. Oxonian, 1957, vol. 44, p. 5–9.)
Per. G.A. Oxon 8° 889

973. MCCALLUM. R. B., The government of the University. (Oxford, 1954, vol. 13, no. 1, p. 75–79.)   Per. G.A. Oxon 8° 1141

See 115 [Kibre, P., Scholarly privileges in the Middle ages. 1961].

973.3. BARNES, L., Authority in Oxford. (Oxf. mag., 1962, N.S., vol. 3, p. 20, 21.)   Per. G.A. Oxon 4° 141

973.4. VAIZEY, J., Robbins and Oxford. (Oxf. mag., 1963, N.S., vol. 4, p. 62–64.)   Per. G.A. Oxon 4° 141

973.5. HAWKE, D. M., Self-government at Oxford. (Oxf. mag., 1963, N.S., vol. 4, p. 77, 78.)   Per. G.A. Oxon 4° 141

See 6433.51 [Pantin, W., History of the relations between colleges and university in the government of the university. 1964].

973.6. Report of a committee appointed by the Hebdomadal Council to consider points arising out of the Robbins report. Suppl. no. 7 (March 1964), Univ. Gazette, 3191. Oxf., 1964, 8° 11 pp.
Per G.A. Oxon c. 86

973.61. BLAKE, R., The effect of Robbins on Oxford. (Oxford, 1964, vol. 19, p. 60–68.)   Per. G.A. Oxon 8° 1141

CHARTERS

974. Registrum privilegiorum almæ Universitatis Oxoniensis. [Contains the Charters of 1 Ed. IV and 14 Hen. VIII and the Act 13 Eliz. c. 29, Pub.] Oxon., 1770, 4°.   G.A. Oxon 4° 260

975. GIBSON, S., ed., The great charter of Charles i, 3 March 1636. (Bodleian quarterly record, 1932, vol. 8, p. 73–94, 121–32.)
Per. 2590 d. Oxf. 1. 40=R.
— Repr. 40 pp.   G.A. Oxon 4° 505 (5)

CONVOCATION

See 1043, &c. [Power of making statutes vested in Convocation and not in Congregation. 1758].

976. [*Begin.*] The members of Convocation are desired seriously to consider the following most decent, liberal, academical and gentlemanlike performance. [A copy of a protest, signed by P. Pead and 15 other members of Congregation and dated 30 Jun., against the right of the vice-chancellor and proctors to vote in the body of Convocation.] [Oxf., 1758], s. sh.   Gough Oxf. 96 (52)

977. [*Begin.*] A doubt has arisen concerning the legality of the V. Cr's. and Proctors' voting in Convocation . . . [A defence of the protest, no. 976.] [Oxf., 1758], s. sh.   Gough Oxf. 96 (54)

978. [*Begin.*] A protest being a matter of common form . . . [A criticism of no. 976, but in favour of the protest.] [Oxf., 1758], s. sh.
Gough Oxf. 96 (57)

979. [*Begin.*] The house of Congregation consists of three estates . . . [A paper on the voting rights of the vice-chancellor, proctors, and regent and non-regent masters.] [Oxf., 1758], 8°. 4 pp.
G.A. Oxon b. 19

980. [*Begin.*] The gentlemen who have involved themselves . . . [A paper against the protest and an answer to no. 978.] [Oxf., 1758], s. sh.
Gough Oxf. 96 (58)

981. [*Begin.*] The publishing of the late intended protest . . . [A defence of the protest and an answer to no. 980.] [Oxf., 1758], s. sh.
Gough Oxf. 96 (53)

982. De personis, ex quibus constat magna Congregatio sive Convocatio magistrorum regentium & non regentium. [*Followed by*] Explicatio

statuti de privilegiis universitatis & civitatis simul non fruendis.
Present draught. Proposed amendments. n. pl., [1759], s. sh.

Gough Oxf. 96 (47b)

983. De personis, ex quibus constat magna Congregatio sive Convocatio
magistrorum regentium et non regentium. [Followed by] Explicatio
statuti de privilegiis universitatis et civitatis simul non fruendis, tit ii.
sect. 9. [Copy of statute to be promulgated in Congregation, July 7,
1759.] n. pl., [1759], s. sh. Gough Oxf. 96 (47a)

See 1048 [Controversy in connexion with the amendment of Stat. Tit. X. sect.
2. 1759].

984. De personis, ex quibus constat magna Congregatio, sive Convocatio
magistrorum regentium et non regentium. n. pl., [1760]. s. sh.

Caps. 10. 9 (3)

985. The state of the question respecting the votes of the vice-chancellor.
1770.

986. [Begin.] Distinct estates of government . . . [A criticism of no. 985.]
7 June 1770. [Oxf.], (1770), 8°. 12 pp. G.A. Oxon b. 19

987. [Begin.] It has been questioned . . . [A criticism of no. 985.] [Oxf.,
1770], 8°. 4 pp. G.A. Oxon b. 19

988. Reasons for supposing that the vice-chancellor and proctors have
affirmative as well as negative votes in the house of Convocation.
n. pl., [1770], s. sh. Gough Oxf. 96 (46)

989. L., Question of an adjourned Convocation [signed L., i.e. R. Laurence? The question arose during the election for the chancellorship].
Oxf., [1809], s. sh. G.A. Oxon b. 19

990. LAURENCE, R., The question, whether a scrutiny in Convocation
can be adjourned to a second day? considered [signed A member of
Convocation. The question arose during the election for the chan-
cellorship]. Oxf., [1809], fol. 3 pp. G.A. Oxon b. 19

See 1201 [Remarks on the power of the proctors in Convocation, occasioned by
certain passages in the late publications of Mr. Coker and Mr. Copleston.
1810].

991. SEWELL, W., The legislation of the University of Oxford, and the
Hebdomadal board, a speech prepared for the Convocation, April 23,
1850 [asserting that the government of the University is vested in
Convocation]. Oxf. &c., 1850, 8°. 45 pp. Bliss B 218 (3)

992. X.Y.Z. pseud., To members of Convocation. [A paper opposing a
decree which proposes to grant £300 per annum for 3 years for
lectures in English law, and an unspecified salary for lectures on
the Hindustani language, the lecturers to be appointed by the Hebdomadal council. The point of the objection is the manner in which
it is proposed to abrogate the rights of Convocation.] 21 Nov. [Oxf.],
(1855), s. sh. G.A. Oxon b. 28
— To members of Convocation. [Another paper reiterating the previous objections.] Oxf., (1855), s. sh. G.A. Oxon b. 28

993. Register of Convocation. 1860–1936. Oxf., 1860–1936, 8°.
G.A. Oxon 8° 509

See 2601 [A paper by C. L. Shadwell calling attention to Convocation's rights as affected by the resolution on the medical statutes. 1872].
See 1009 [Goodrick, A. T. S., Anecdotes of debates. 1904].

994. FAIRBAIRN, A. M., Oxford and its Convocation [a letter on aspects of its reform, repr. from The Times of Mar. 16]. [Oxf., 1905], 8°. 7 pp.   G.A. Oxon 8° 715 (25)

995. Acts of Convocation. 1907–1926. [Oxf.], 1907–26, fol. 857 pp.
G.A. Oxon c. 243

996. CASE, T., Voting of Convocation, either in person or by voting papers. [Observations on an amendment to the Statutes respecting a poll of Convocation, to be proposed in Congregation on Jan. 28.] [Oxf.], (1913), 8°. 4 pp.   G.A. Oxon c. 310 (119)

See also 5852, &c. Convocation house.

CONGREGATION

See 1043, &c. [Power of making statutes vested in Convocation and not in Congregation. 1758].

997. A register of members of Congregation . . . for the year ending on the 24th day of September, 1855 (–69). [Thereafter publ. in the Oxford university gazette.] [Oxf.], 1854–68, s. sh.   G.A. Oxon c. 70–86

998. Report of the committee of Congregation on its regulations. [Feb.] [Oxf., 1855], s. sh.   G.A. Oxon 4° 255

999. [Begin.] The committee to propose . . . [Regulations, formulated by a committee, for the conducting of the business of Congregation, to be submitted for the approbation of Congregation on 16th Feb., 1855.] Feb. 5, 1855. [Oxf.], 1855, s. sh.   G.A. Oxon c. 80 (91)

See 1032 [Marsham, R. B., Letter, denying the right of the Hebdomadal council to impose regulations on Congregation. 1855].

1000. The following case has been submitted to the attorney general, and is printed with his opinion . . . [to attempt to define 'all residents', who comprise Congregation]. n. pl., [1864], 8°. 3 pp.
G.A. Oxon c. 80 (376)

1001. BERNARD, M., [Begin.] I wish to say a few words . . . [Letter signed M. Bernard, concerning the conduct of business in Congregation.] n. pl., (1868), 4°. 4 pp.   G.A. Oxon c. 84 (48)

1002. Report presented to the Hebdomadal council by the joint committee of Council and Congregation [appointed 'to consider and report on the present provisions with respect to the mode of submitting statutes to Congregation' &c. With other recommendations concerning the meetings and procedure of Congregation]. [Oxf.], (1869), 4°. 7 pp.
G.A. Oxon b. 32

1003. Procedure of Congregation. [Reprint of the statutes passed 4 March 1870.] [Oxf., 1870], 8°. 4 pp.   G.A. Oxon b. 137 (28)

  See 2601 [A paper by C. L. Shadwell calling attention to a precedent which may be established if Congregation and not Convocation is allowed to accept a resolution on the medical statutes. 1872].

1004. Case for opinion on voting in Congregation for members of Council. [Oxf., 1875], s. sh.   G.A. Oxon c. 33 (144)

1005. The proposed rehabilitation of oligarchy and absenteeism. [Letters on the character of the House of Congregation, by E. Cannan, D. B. Monro, C. Oman, R. Marett.] (Oxf. mag., 1893, vol. 11, p. 168, 69, 184, 85, 209.)   Per. G.A. Oxon 4° 141

1006. Reform of Congregation [signed by D. B. Monro and 5 others. With a questionnaire.]. Feb. 8. [Oxf.], (1893), 2 sh.
                                                    G.A. Oxon c. 153

1007. Reform of Congregation [signed by D. B. Monro and 5 others, reporting on the questionnaire sent on Feb. 8]. Apr. 20. [Oxf.], (1893), 2 sh.   G.A. Oxon c. 153

1008. JACKSON, W. W., The reform of Congregation [signed W. W. Jackson]. 21 Apr. [Oxf.], (1893), fol. 4 pp.   G.A. Oxon c. 153

1009. GOODRICK, A. T. S., Congregation and Convocation. [Anecdotes of debates.] (Macmillan's mag., 1904, vol. 90, p. 223–32.)
                                                    Per. 2705 d. 254

1010. Reform of Congregation [by making mere residence in Oxford insufficient qualification for membership]. [Oxf., 1909], s. sh.
                                                    G.A. Oxon c. 153

1011. The proposal to limit Congregation. [A paper against the proposal.] [Oxf., 1909], s. sh.   G.A. Oxon c. 153

1012. The proposed reform of Congregation. [A paper against the proposal.] [Oxf., 1909], s. sh.   G.A. Oxon c. 153

1013. The statute on the constitution of Congregation [arguments against the statute to be presented to the House on Nov. 26, signed by P. S. Allen and 11 others.] Nov. 20. [Oxf.], (1912), s. sh.
                                                    G.A. Oxon c. 310 (113)

1014. Convocation, March 4. The disenfranchising statute, last reading. [Oxf., 1913], s. sh.   G.A. Oxon c. 153

1015. Acts of Congregation. Dec. 2, 1919–1926. [Oxf.], 1919–26, fol. pp. 197–277.   G.A. Oxon c. 245

1016. GIBSON, S., The congregations of the University of Oxford. (Bodleian quarterly record, 1925, vol. 4, p. 296–314.)
                                              Per. 2590 d. Oxf. 1. 40=R.
— Repr. 1926. 19 pp.   G.A. Oxon 4° 403* (12)

1017. SALTER, H., The congregation of artists. (Bodleian quarterly record, 1926, vol. 5, p. 19–22.)   Per. 2590 d. Oxf. 1. 40=R.

1018. Elections in Congregation. [A proposal to amend the rule with regard to voting.] (Oxf. mag., 1932, vol. 50, p. 423, 24.)
Per. G.A. Oxon 4° 141

1018.5. Report of a Committee on business for Congregation. Suppl. no. 3 to the Univ. Gazette (3186, February 1964). Oxf., 1964, 8°. 16 pp.
Per. G.A. Oxon c. 86
See also 6035, &c. Congregation house.

CONGREGATION, ANCIENT HOUSE OF

1019. Acts of the Ancient House of Congregation. [Oxf.], 1916–26, fol. 157 pp.   G.A. Oxon c. 244
[Also to be found both previously and subsequently in the Oxford university gazette.]

HEBDOMADAL COUNCIL

1020. TATHAM, E., A new address to the free and independent members of Convocation [concerning the holding of Hebdomadal meetings and the new examination statute]. By the rector of Lincoln. (June 22nd.) Oxf., 1810, 4°. 26 pp.   G.A. Oxon 4° 13 (17)

1021. TATHAM, E., An address to the members of the Hebdomadal meeting [concerning the time and place of statutable meetings]. (July 5th.) [Oxf.], (1810), 4°. 6 pp.   G.A. Oxon 4° 48

1022. [Begin.] At a meeting of the vice-chancellor, heads of houses and proctors . . . [Statement denying charges made by E. Tatham, that the Hebdomadal board met 'in an artful, collusive or smuggling manner'.] July 9. [Oxf.], (1810), fol. 3 pp.   G.A. Oxon b. 19

1023. TATHAM, E., A particular address to the members of Convocation [championing the statutable Hebdomadal meeting]. (July 10th.) [Oxf.], (1810), s. sh.   G.A. Oxon 4° 48

1024. TATHAM, E., An address to the . . . lord Grenville, chancellor of the University of Oxford, upon great and fundamental abuses [the disregard of statutable meetings of the Hebdomadal board]. By the rector of Lincoln. (June 7.) Oxf., 1811, 4°. 42 pp.
G.A. Oxon 4° 82

See 991 [Sewell, W., The legislation of the University of Oxford, and the Hebdomadal board. 1850].
See 926, &c. [Proposed reform of the Hebdomadal board. 1854].

1025. The coming election of the Hebdomadal council. [Suggestions, signed A member of Congregation, as to the people who should be elected.] [Oxf., 1854], s. sh.   G.A. Oxon b. 28

1026. To members of Congregation. [Arguments signed A real well-wisher to the University, in favour of the election of certain people to serve on the Hebdomadal council.] [Oxf., 1854], s. sh.

G.A. Oxon b. 28

1027. To members of Congregation. [An answer, signed Another well-wisher and a member of Congregation, to no. 1025 and 1026.] [Oxf., 1854], s. sh.   G.A. Oxon b. 28

1028. Oxford, October 24, 1854. [*Begin.*] The vacancy in the Hebdomadal council, caused by the bracketing of mr. Marriott and mr. Pattison . . . [signed 'A lover of fair play' urging that the contest be restricted to these two]. [Oxf.], (1854), s. sh.   G.A. Oxon b. 28

1029. [*Begin.*] There is little doubt . . . Oxford, October 26, 1854. [In favour of mr. Pattison for the seat on the Hebdomadal council.] [Oxf.], (1854), s. sh.   G.A. Oxon b. 28

1030. [*Begin.*] An invidious comparison . . . [In favour of mr. Marriott for the seat on the Hebdomadal council. 27 October 1854.] [Oxf.], (1854), s. sh.   G.A. Oxon b. 28

1031. Regulations to be observed at elections of members of the Hebdomadal council. Jan. 23. [Oxf.], 1855, s. sh.   G.A. Oxon 4° 255

1032. MARSHAM, R. B., [Letter to the vice-chancellor, denying the right of the Hebdomadal council to impose regulations on the House of Congregation. Mar. 13]. [Oxf.], (1855), 8°. 4 pp.

G.A. Oxon 8° 146 (20)

1033. The election of a member of the Council. [The reasons for favouring the nomination of F. C. Plumptre.] Oxf., 1856, s. sh.

G.A. Oxon c. 72 (36)

1034. Rules adopted by the Hebdomadal council for the regulation of its proceedings. [Oxf., 1860], s. sh.   G.A. Oxon c. 76 (333)

1035. SMITH, G., The elections to the Hebdomadal council, a letter to the rev. C. W. Sandford. Oxf. &c., 1866, 8°. 20 pp.

G.A. Oxon 8° 93 (6)

1036. DODGSON, C. L., The elections to the Hebdomadal council; a letter to the rev. C. W. Sandford has been addressed (on this subject) by Goldwin Smith and may possibly reach a second edition. [A satire, in verse by C. L. Dodgson on G. Smith's letter.] Oxf., 1866, 8°. 11 pp.   G.A. Oxon 8° 93 (5)
— [Repr.] (Phantasmagoria and other poems, by Lewis Carroll, p. 129–42.) Lond., 1869, 12°.   280 m. 281
— [Repr. also in no. 1037 in 1874.]

1037. DODGSON, C. L., Facts, figures and fancies relating to the elections to the Hebdomadal council [repr. from Phantasmagoria, and other poems], the offer of the Clarendon trustees [to provide funds for increasing the accommodation for the study of physics] and the proposal

to convert the parks into cricket-grounds. First pr. in 1866–1868. (Notes by an Oxford chiel.) [In verse. By C. L. Dodgson.] Oxf., 1874, 8°. 29 pp.   G.A. Oxon 8°. 161 (23)
— [Another ed.] (The Lewis Carroll picture book, ed. by S. D. Collingwood, 1899, p. 77–95.)   270 e. 1155

1038. Case for opinion on voting in Congregation for members of Council. [Oxf., 1875], s. sh.   G.A. Oxon c. 33 (144)

1039. Rules adopted by the Hebdomadal council for the regulation of its proceedings. [Oxf., c. 1875], s. sh.   G.A. Oxon c. 33 (160)

See 1811 [The constitution of Council. 1909].

1040. The position of professors and readers upon the Hebdomadal council. [Arguments against the statute to be promulgated on Nov. 26, signed by G. C. Bourne and 30 others.] [Oxf., 1912], s. sh.   G.A. Oxon c. 310 (112)

1041. [*Begin.*] The statute that will . . . [Arguments upholding the principle of professorial privilege in respect of membership of the Hebdomadal council, in opposition to the proposed new statute on the constitution of the Council. Signed L. R. Farnell, S. Ball, A. D. Lindsay.] 30 Jan. 1914. [Oxf.], 1914, 4°. 4 pp.   G.A. Oxon c. 309 (10)

1042. The constitution of the Hebdomadal council. [Oxf., 1914], 8°. 4 pp.   G.A. Oxon c. 153
— [Another issue signed by P. E. H. Adams and 40 other professors and readers.]   G.A. Oxon b. 141 (91*b*)

1042.1. The constitution of the Hebdomadal council [signed by W. R. Anson and 6 others]. [Oxf., 1914], s. sh.   G.A. Oxon b. 141 (91*c*)

STATUTES AND DECREES

General

For works on particular statutes, see under the separate subjects.

1043. [*Begin.*] A question having been started . . . [Observations supporting the contention that the power of making statutes is vested in Convocation and not in Congregation.] n. pl. [1758], fol. 4 pp.   Gough Oxf. 96 (51)

1044. WRIGHT, W., and AUSTEN, G., A representation of the conduct of the proctors [W. Wright and G. Austen] with respect to two explanatory statutes proposed by the vice-chancellor to them and to the heads of Houses. [The proctors opposed the view that the University had power to alter or explain royal statutes.] n. pl., [1759], fol. 4 pp.   Gough Oxf. 96 (43)

1045. WRIGHT, W., and AUSTEN, G., An answer [by W. Wright and G. Austen] to the objections made in Convocation to the Representation of the conduct of the proctors. n. pl., [1759], s. sh. Gough Oxf. 96 (45)

1046. [*Begin.*] The two explanatory statutes . . . [Evidence, consisting of a letter to abp. Laud from Convocation, a letter to Convocation from Lord Clarendon, dated 29 Mar., 1662, and a petition by the University to Charles ii, shewing that the prevailing opinion has always been against the University having power to alter or explain royal statutes.] n. pl., [1759], s. sh.   Gough Oxf. 96 (44)

1047. Case [by sir W. Blackstone? of the University with regard to its powers in making, altering or repealing statutes, submitted for the opinion of counsel. *Followed by*] Answer [signed J. Morton, R. Wilbraham. Ju. 2, 1759. Page 1, col. 2 *begin* 'lareque']. n. pl., (1759), fol. 4 pp.   Gough Oxf. 96 (55)
— [Another ed., reissued on Mar. 9, 1773. Page 1, col. 2 *begin* 'reformandis'.] n. pl., [1773], fol. 4 pp.   G.A. Oxon b. 19
— [Another issue of the preceding, with additional paragraph *begin*. It appears by this case as also . . .]   G.A. Oxon b. 17 (20)
— [Amending paragraph, *begin*.] The paragraph subjoined to the case. Mar. 11, 1773. n. pl., (1773), s. sh.   G.A. Oxon b. 17 (21)

1048. A letter to a late member of the U—y of O—d, with respect to the two explanatory statutes proposed to the C————n. [An account of the controversy in connexion with the proctors' opposition to the view that the University has power to alter or explain royal statutes.] n. pl., (1759), 8°. 47 pp.   G.A. Oxon 8° 59 (15)

1049. [*Begin.*] The Convocation will shortly be moved . . . [An argument in favour of the contention that Convocation has the power to amend and explain royal statutes at present in force. June, 1760.] n. pl., [1760], 4°. 4 pp.   Gough Oxf. 96 (50)

1050. [*Begin.*] To obviate the mistakes of an explanatory paper . . . [An answer to no. 1049 disputing the right of Convocation to amend and explain royal statutes at present in force.] July 2d 1760. n. pl., (1760), s. sh.   Gough Oxf. 96 (49)

1051. [*Begin.*] Qu. 1. Has the University . . . [Three questions submitted to counsel with regard to the power of the University to make, alter, or explain statutes. With the answers, signed J. Morton, R. Wilbraham. Ju. 2, 1759. This was repr. from no. 1047 in connexion with the proposed alteration of Stat. Tit. XIV. § 3 in 1770.] n. pl., [1770], s. sh.   Gough Oxf. 73 (2)

    See 1312 [The statute Tit. X. sect. 2. § 2. 1770].

1052. [*Begin.*] It appears by the inspeximus . . . [A paper, dated June 25, 1770 and signed A non-regent, on the obligation of obtaining the royal assent to statutes.] [Oxf.], 1770, s. sh.   Don. b. 12 (84)

1053. [*Begin.*] By the statute Tit. X. 2. 2 . . . [A paper, dated 25 June 1770, on the power of the University to make statutes without royal licence.] [Oxf.], (1770), 4°. 3 pp.   G.A. Oxon b. 19

1054. [*Begin.*] The statute Tit. X. 2. 1 . . . [A paper, dated June 25, 1770, on the power of the University to make statutes without royal licence.] [Oxf.], (1770), s. sh. G.A. Oxon b. 19

1055. An attempt to ascertain the true meaning of the first part of the statute De statutis & decretis in domo Convocationis condendis & interpretandis; wherein the obligation of the restrictive clause relating to the specialis regis ipsius licentia, is considered. n. pl., [1773], s. sh. Gough Oxf. 96 (48)

1056. [*Begin.*] The question whether . . . [the statute De tempore et conditionibus matriculationis is or is not a 'Royal statute']. n. pl., 1773, fol. 4 pp. G.A. Oxon b. 17 (22)

1057. [*Begin.*] The University of Oxford is bringing an accusation . . . [Paper giving the text of four questions on the power of the University to make statutes which would change the Laudian code. With the answers of J. Campbell, the attorney-general, and S. Lushington. These questions arise from the proposed decree against Hampden.] [Oxf., 1836], s. sh. Bliss B 213 (32)

See 3497 [Thomas, V., Oratiuncula . . . Cui subjiciuntur Morton et Wilbraham . . . sententiæ. 1836].

1058. SEWELL, W., [*Begin.*] The statutes of the University contain the following provision. Tit. X. Sect. 2 . . . [A protest against the manner in which the revision of the statutes had been initiated. By W. Sewell?] (Oxf.), [1837], 4°. 4 pp. G.A. Oxon c. 53 (119)

1059. GRESWELL, E., An address to the members of Convocation [objecting to the manner in which the revision of the Statutes had been initiated] by a member of Convocation [E. Greswell]. Oxf., [1837], 8°. 15 pp. G.A. Oxon c. 53 (121)

1060. SEWELL, W., Some reasons by a member of Convocation for objecting to the proposed revision of the University statutes, and to the revised portion of them which has just been published [by W. Sewell]. Oxf., [1837], fol. 4 pp. G.A. Oxon c. 53 (120)

1061. THOMAS, V., Oxford, Nov. 18, 1837. [Protest against the manner in which the revision of the statutes had been initiated. Signed 'Another member of Convocation', i.e. V. Thomas?] (Oxf., 1837), fol. 4 pp. G.A. Oxon c. 53 (118)
— [Another issue.] G.A. Oxon b. 23

1062. COXE, H. O., Oxford, Nov. 21, 1837. [Additions, by H. O. Coxe, to no. 1061. Dated Nov. 18, 1837.] (Oxf., 1837), s. sh. G.A. Oxon c. 53 (122)

1063. SYMONS, B. P., An examination of 'Some reasons by a member of Convocation [W. Sewell] for objecting, &c.' [Signed An experienced member of Convocation, i.e. B. P. Symons.] Nov. 21. (Oxf., 1837), fol. 4 pp. G.A. Oxon c. 53 (126)

1064. JENKYNS, R., [*Begin.*] It is a matter of notoriety . . . [A paper defending the power of the Hebdomadal board to initiate the revision of the statutes without reference to Convocation, signed 'A senior member of Convocation', i.e. R. Jenkyns?] Nov. 21. n. pl., (1837), s. sh. G.A. Oxon c. 53 (123)

1065. GRESWELL, E., Notorious truths, or facts, which may be asserted without much fear of contradiction [concerning the validity of the present general revision of the statutes. By E. Greswell]. Nov. 22. [Oxf., 1837], s. sh. G.A. Oxon b. 23

1066. RIGAUD, S., Considerations submitted to those who are inclined to oppose the measures which will be proposed to Convocation on the 23rd inst. [By S. Rigaud.] Nov. 22. Corrected. n. pl., (1837), s. sh. G.A. Oxon c. 53 (125)

1067. JOHNSON, G. H. S., Remarks [signed A member of Convocation, i.e. G. H. S. Johnson?] on 'An address to the members of Convocation' [by E. Greswell]. Nov. 22. Oxf., 1837, 8°. 13 pp. G.A. Oxon c. 53 (127)

1068. HARRISON, B., A paper has been circulated, with the signature of 'A senior member of Convocation' [R. Jenkyns?] containing some statements on which the following brief remarks are respectfully offered [signed A member of Convocation, 'sequioris ævi', i.e. B. Harrison]. Nov. 22. (Oxf., 1837), fol. 4 pp. G.A. Oxon c. 53 (124)

1069. HARRISON, B., The 'Considerations, &c.' and 'Remarks, &c.' which have just appeared call for a few words on a matter of historical fact. [A paper about the Laudian revision of the statutes, signed Indigator veri, i.e. B. Harrison.] Nov. 23. (Oxf., 1837), fol. 3 pp. G.A. Oxon b. 23

1070. THOMAS, V., Questions [signed 'The other member of Convocation', i.e. V. Thomas, about the validity of the present general revision of the statutes]. Nov. 23. (Oxf., 1837), s. sh. G.A. Oxon b. 23

1071. GRESWELL, E., A letter [signed E. Greswell] to . . . the duke of Wellington . . . on the proceedings in the House of Convocation on Thursday the 23rd inst. [Nov., concerning the general revision of the Statutes.] Oxf., 1837, 8°. 37 pp. 37. 723

1072. THOMAS, V., Reasons for protesting against the principle upon which a general revision of the Statutes of the University has been undertaken, and against the manner in which a portion of the Statutes so revised was submitted to Convocation, November 23, 1837. Oxf., 1838, 4°. 61 pp. G.A. Oxon 4° 90

See 991 [Sewell, W., The legislation of the University of Oxford and the Hebdomadal board. 1850].

1073. A bill to extend the power of making statutes possessed by the

University of Oxford, and to make further provision for the administration of justice in the Court of the Chancellor of the said University. 2 May 1862. [Lond.], 1862, fol. 5 pp.   Pp. Eng. 1862 vol. 3
— [Act.] (25 & 26 V., c. 26, Pub.) Lond., 1862, fol. 4 pp.   L.L.
— 28 & 29 V., c. 55, Pub.

1074. CONINGTON, J., [Begin.] Last week I addressed the following
letter to the vice-chancellor [complaining of laxity on the part of
Council members in explaining terms of statutes, and urging that
statutes promulgated should have attached to them the names of their
proposers etc.]. [Oxf.], (1867), s. sh.   G.A. Oxon b. 32 (17)

See 1002 [Report on the mode of submitting statutes to Congregation. 1869].

1075. The following case as to the validity of the present mode of enacting
University statutes, submitted to sir R. Palmer and mr. Wickens, and
the following opinion thereon received from them are printed for the
information of members of Convocation. Mar. 15. [Oxf.], 1869, 4°.
8 pp.   G.A. Oxon c. 85 (110)

1076. A bill to remove doubts as to the validity of certain statutes [those
submitted for approval in separate portions] made by the Convocation
of the University of Oxford. 28 May, 1869. [Lond.], 1869, fol. 3 pp.
                                                 Pp. Eng. 1868/9 vol. 4
— [Act.] (32 & 33 V., c. 30, Pub.) Lond., 1869, s. sh.   L.L.

1077. Remarks and suggestions in connection with the new statutes made
for the University and colleges by the University of Oxford commissioners, and now lying on the table of the two Houses of parliament. [March 1882.] (Oxf.), [1882], 4°. 16 pp.   G.A. Oxon 4° 72

1078. BERNARD, M., A letter . . . on the statutes of the University of
Oxford commission. Lond., 1882, 8°. 45 pp.   G.A. Oxon 8° 296 (6)

See 1930 [Return of University statutes made since 1877. 1886].
See 3189 [Case, T., A financial danger . . . and the omission of a statute from
   the Statuta Universitatis . . . 1913].
See 1488 [Act extending powers to make statutes. 1915].

1079. GIBSON, S., The earliest statutes of the University of Oxford.
(Bodleian quarterly record, 1921, vol. 3, p. 116–18.)
                                           Per. 2590 d. Oxf. 1. 40=R.

1080. GIBSON, S., A collation of the Corpus statutorum univ. Oxon.
(Bodleian quarterly record, 1925, vol. 4, p. 271–74.)
                                           Per. 2590 d. Oxf. 1. 40=R.

See 1491 [Act extending powers to make statutes. 1939].

Corpus statutorum and collections

See 1093 [G. Darell's codification of early 17th cent. c. 1852].

1081. Corpus statutorum Vniversitatis Oxon. sive Pandectes constitutionum academicarum, e libris publicis et regestis Vniversitatis consarcinatus. [Madan 768.] Oxon., 1634, fol. 264 pp.   Caps. 10. 9 (1)

[These statutes were in force for one year, and necessary alterations were approved by abp. Laud in June 1636. Blank spaces were provided for alterations in MS.; the book itself was not reprinted in 1636.]

1082. The keepers of the Archives, [announcement of] a lecture to be delivered 7 March 1928 by S. Gibson. [The publication consists of Brian Twyne's version of the preface to the 1634 statutes, entitled 'Historia de statutis Vniversitatis recolendis' and 'Præfatio ad lectorem, auctore Petro Turner', the version printed in no. 1081.] Oxf., 1928, 8°. 23 pp.   G.A. Oxon 4° 339a (18)

1083. Statutes of the University of Oxford, codified in the year 1636 under the authority of archbishop Laud, ed. by J. Griffiths, with an intr. on the history of the Laudian code by C. L. Shadwell. Oxf., 1888, 4°. xxxii+339 pp.   G.A. Oxon 4° 753=R. Top.

1084. [Begin.] Nos collegiorum et aularum . . . præfecti . . . [A facs. sheet of signatures to the Laudian statutes of 1636.] [Oxf., 18—], s. sh.
G.A. Oxon b. 147

1085. Synopsis seu Epitome statutorum, eorum præsertim quæ iuventuti Academ. Oxon: maxime expedit pro doctrina & moribus habere cognita. [Madan 797.] Oxon., 1635, s. sh.   Wood 423 (15)

1086. Statuta selecta e corpore statutorum . . . [Madan 873.] [Oxf.], 1638, 16°. 228 pp.   8° O 19 Jur.

1087. Ordinationes collegii Orielensis in quibus et statuta Universitatis Oxonicnsis ab Eduardo VI. lata ac sancita. (Johannis de Trokelowe Annales Eduardi II, divulgit T. Hearnius, 1729, p. 295–372.)
Mus. Bibl. II 90

1088. Statuta selecta e corpore statutorum Universitatis Oxon . . . [Madan 2568.] Oxon., 1661, 12°. 200 pp.   G.A. Oxon 16° 122
— [Another and earlier issue.] [Madan 2569.]   Vet. A 3 f. 969

1089. Parecbolae, sive Excerpta e corpore statutorum . . . Oxon., 1671, 8°.
Gough Oxf. 117
[Other eds. in 1674, 1682, 1691, 1693, 1700, 1705, 1710, 1721, 1729, 1740, 1756, 1771, 1784, 1794, 1808, 1815, 1820, 1828, 1830, 1832, 1835, 1838, 1840–43, 1845, 1846, 1848–51, 1854. All but the following are in Bodley: 1838, 1843, 1846, 1848, 1850, 1851, 1854.]
[For details of shelfmarks, &c., see the Bodleian catalogue.]

1090. [Begin.] Carolus Dei gratia . . . [The Letters patent of Charles I confirming the Laudian code. Followed by] Statuta aularia [etc. A supplement to the Parecbolae, consisting of sig. Gg–Tt, which was printed by dr. Charlett]. [Oxf., c. 1700], 8°. 8+102 pp.
Gough Oxf. 20

1091. Corpus statutorum Universitatis Oxoniensis: sive Pandectes constitutionum academicarum, e libris publicis et regestis Universitatis consarcinatus. [With Addenda.] Oxon., 1768– , 4°.
[For bibliographical details see no. 1080.]   G.A. Oxon c. 17–19

1092. Oxford university statutes, tr. by G. R. M. Ward (and completed under the superintendence of J. Heywood). 2 vols. Lond., 1845, 51, 8°.
G.A. Oxon 8° 27=R.

1093. Transcriptum Statutorum Universitatis Oxon. ex libris. [Perhaps the only surviving copy in a printed form of proof sheets of George Darell's codification (early in the 17th century) of the old statutes of the University. It was put into print for the University Commissioners of 1852–54, but not issued by them.] [Oxf., c. 1852], 8°. 333 [really 363] pp.
Arch. AA d. 17

1094. Statuta Universitatis Oxoniensis. 1857– . Oxon., 1857– , 8°.
Per. G.A. Oxon 8° 645

1095. Ordinances and statutes framed or approved by the Oxford university commissioners, in pursuance of the act, 17 and 18 Vict. c. 81. Oxf., 1878, 8°. 533 pp.
G.A. Oxon 8° 774

1096. Statutes made for the University of Oxford and for the colleges and halls therein, by the University of Oxford commissioners. Oxf., 1882, 8°. viii+793 pp.
S. Ed. 35

1097. New statutes made for the University by the University of Oxford commissioners. Oxf., 1882, 8°. 91 pp.   G.A. Oxon 8° 425=R. Top.

1098. Supplementary statutes made . . . in pursuance of the Universities of Oxford and Cambridge act, 1877. Oxf., 1888, 8°. 36 pp.
G.A. Oxon 8° 645*

1099. Decrees approved by Convocation since Jan. 1, 1870 (Jan. 1, 1865) and in operation on June 30, 1891 (Oct. 10, 1905). [Afterwards publ. as part of the annual volume of Statutes.] Oxf., (1891–1905), 8°.
G.A. Oxon 8° 628

1100. [Orders in Council approving Oxford university statutes. 1906–].
G.A. Oxon c. 200

1101. Statuta antiqua Vniversitatis Oxoniensis, ed. with an intr. by S. Gibson. Oxf., 1931, 8°. 668 pp.   G.A. Oxon 4° 757=R.

1102. University of Oxford. Emergency provisions. 1939, 1940. Oxf., 1939, 40, 8°.
G.A. Oxon 8° 1178

OFFICIAL STATEMENTS, ADDRESSES, ETC.

General

1103. [Miscellaneous collections in the Bodleian of university papers, notices &c.]

1662–	G.A. Oxon b. 19–36, 137–48
1772–1871	G.A. Oxon a. 14–19
1824–69	G.A. Oxon c. 40–85
1831–36	G.A. Oxon 4° 255

1104. [Letter dated Nov. 18 from the vice-chancellor, F. K. Leighton, recounting that 16 professors had attended the meeting which agreed that an official Oxford university gazette be founded; and asking for the views of those professors not present at the meeting.] [Oxf.], (1869), s. sh. G.A. Oxon a. 18

1105. HATCH, E., [Begin.] For the Hebdomadal council only . . . [Copy of a letter addressed to the Delegates of the University press, suggesting the inauguration of the university gazette. Dec. 3?] [Oxf., 1869], 4°. 3 pp. G.A. Oxon c. 85 (485)

1106. Oxford university gazette. Vol. 1– . Oxf., 1870– , fol.
G.A. Oxon c. 86

Complimentary addresses, &c.

See also 546–650, 850–54.

1106.5. Ornatissimis viris, Georgio Beaumont . . . Gulielmo Bromley, Thomæ Sclater . . . & Antonio Keck . . . supremi testamenti Johannis Radcliffe M.D. curatoribus integerrimis. [At end.] Ita precatur devinctissima favoris vestri cultrix, Academia Oxoniensis. n. pl., [1715], s. sh. MS. Ballard 48 (f. 125)

1107. BOONE, J. S., The welcome of Isis, a poem occasioned by the Duke of Wellington's visit to the University. By the author of 'The Oxford spy'. Oxf., 1820, 8°. 31 pp. G.A. Oxon 8° 1345 (7)
— [Another ed.] 1834. G.A. Oxon 8ᵛ 124 (10)

1108. [Begin.] On Saturday, November 10 . . . it will be proposed to Convocation to affix the University seal to an address . . . to the Emperor of Germany on occasion of the four hundredth anniversary of Luther's birth. This proposition will be opposed on the following grounds . . . [Oxf., 1883], s. sh. G.A. Oxon b. 140 (f. 47)

1109. HEURTLEY, C. A., The proposed address . . . on the 400th anniversary of the birth of Luther. Nov. 9. [Oxf.], (1883), s. sh.
G.A. Oxon b. 140 (f. 47)

1110. [A collection in the Bodleian of congratulatory lettters from the University of Oxford. 1887– .] G.A. Oxon a. 32, 32*, 32**

Funeral addresses, &c.

See also 546–650.

1111. WILSON, T., Vita et obitus duorum fratrum Suffolcensium . . . [Contributions by Oxford writers occur on sig. D2–K1.] [Madan 41.] Lond., [1551], 4°. 4° S 23 (1) Art.

1112. Exequiæ illustrissimi equitis d. Philippi Sidnæi, gratissimæ memoriæ ac nomini impensæ. [Madan 87.] Oxon., 1587, 4°. 96 pp.
4° H 17 Art.

1113. Oxoniensium στεναγμός siué, carmina ab Oxoniensibus conscripta, in obitum . . . Christophori Hattoni . . . Academiæ Oxoniensis cancellarii. [Madan 125.] Oxon., 1592, 4°. 24 pp.   Lambeth

1114. Funebria . . . equitis d. Henrici Vntoni, ad Gallos bis legati regij, ibiḱ; nuper fato functi, charissimæ memoriæ, ac desiderio a musis Oxoniensibus apparata [ed. by R. Wright]. [Madan 159.] Oxon., 1596, 4°. 68 pp.   4° H 17 Art.

1115. Iusta funebria Ptolemæi Oxoniensis Thomæ Bodleii . . . celebrata in Academia Oxoniensi mensis Martij 29. 1613. [*Followed by*] Oratio funebris . . . ab oratore publico. [Madan 377.] Oxon., 1613, 4°. 134 [+12] pp.   Gough Oxf. 125 (2)
[The second piece is repr. in no. 5421, Trecentale Bodleianum, 1913, p. 87–103.]

1116. Carmina funebria in obitum . . . Georgii de Sancto Paulo equitis aurati C.C.C. Oxon. olim convictoris & eiusdem benefactoris mundi. [Madan 405.] Oxon., 1614, 4°. 16 pp.   C.C.C.

1117. Vltima linea Savilii sive in obitum . . . Henrici Savilii . . . iusta academica. [Madan 498.] Oxon., 1622, 4°. 58 pp.   Mar. 524

1118. Camdeni insignia. [Verses, &c., in memory of W. Camden.] [Madan 517.] Oxon., 1624, 4°. 76 pp.   4° H 17 (7) Art.

1119. Schola moralis philosophiæ Oxon. in funere Whiti [dr. Thomas White] pullata. [Madan 518.] Oxon., 1624, 4°. 14 pp.   Wood 484 (6)

1120. Epicedia Universitatis Oxoniensis in obitum invictissimi herois Georgii ducis Albemarliæ. Oxon., 1670, fol. 80 pp.   Firth c. 2 (2)
— [Another issue.] [Madan 2844.]   AA 52 (2) Art.

1121. At a general meeting of the Vice-chancellor, heads of houses, and proctors . . . Nov. 27. 1714 . . . [Regulations for the more solemn performance of the funeral rites of dr. John Radcliffe.] [Oxf., 1714], s. sh.
     Wood 276a (577)

1122.

1123. Exequiæ . . . Johanni Radcliffe . . . ab Oxoniensi Academia solutæ. Oxon., 1715, fol. 120 pp.   M 6. 6 (1) Art.

1124. Dr. Radcliffe's obsequies at Oxford, from an original document. (The Crypt, 1828, vol. 3, p. 265, 66.)   Hope 8° 281

Proscriptions

See also 3475–3593.

1125. Decretum Vniversitatis Oxoniensis damnans propositiones [from D. Pareus] neotericorum infra-scriptas [namely that it is lawful to take up arms against a Sovereign] sive Iesuitarum, sive Puritanorum sive aliorum . . . [An oath, to be taken by all graduates, not to teach, defend or hold such principles, is added; together with an order for the public burning of 'Pareus in ep. S. Pauli ad Romanos'.] [Madan 499.] Oxon., 1622, 4°. 12 pp.   4° D 6 Jur.

— [A Dutch transl.] Decreet of besluyt van de Universiteyt van Oxfort
. . . [Followed by a repr. of the Latin version.] [Madan 500.] [Amst.?
1622?], 4°. 16 pp.   Antiq. e. N. 1622. 2

1126. Judicium & decretum Universitatis Oxoniensis latum in Convocatione habita Jul. 21. an. 1683, contra quosdam perniciosos libros
& propositiones impias, quæ capitibus sacratissimorum principum,
eorum statui & regimini, & omni humanæ societati exitium intentant.
(Oxf.), 1683, fol. 9 pp.   H 9.15 (2) Art.

1127. The judgement and decree of the University of Oxford past in their
Convocation, July 21. 1683, against certain pernicious books and
damnable doctrines destructive to the sacred persons of princes, their
state and government, and of all humane society. Rendred into English.
(Oxf.), 1683, fol. 9 pp.   Wood 423 (58)
— [Repr.] (Somers' tracts, 1748, vol. 3, p. 223–27.)   GG 134 Art.
— [Repr.] (Somers' tracts, 2nd ed. 1812, vol. 8, p. 420–24.) Σ III. 18

1128. University loyalty: or, The genuine explanation of the principles
of the English clergy, as established and directed by the decree of the
University of Oxford past in their Convocation 21 July 1683, and
republish'd at the trying of dr. H. Sacheverell for high crimes and mis-
demeanours. Lond., 1710, 8°. 60 pp.   8° L 1 (3) Linc.

1129. The Oxford decree [of 21 July, 1683]: being an entire confutation
of mr. Hoadley's book, of the original of government [Some considerations offered to the bishop of Exeter. 1709]; taken from the London
Gazette. Lond., repr. in 1710, 8°. 8 pp.   8° I 237 (14) BS.

1130. [*Begin.*] Whereas at the Assizes held at Oxford the 13th day of July
1711 . . . [Vice-chancellor's proclamation proscribing The Medley,
no. 41, and The Laity's remonstrance to the late representation of the
Lower H. of C—n.] 27 July. [Oxf.], (1711), s. sh. G.A. Oxon b. 19

OFFICERS AND OFFICES

Chancellor

1131. GIBSON, S., ed., Confirmations of Oxford chancellors in the Lincoln
episcopal registers. (Engl. hist. review, 1911, vol. 26, p. 501–12.)
                                                      Per. 2231 d. 342=K.
— Repr.   G.A. Oxon 4° 299

1132. Confirmations by the bishops of Lincoln of elections made to the
office of chancellor (1290–1369). (Oxf. hist. soc., 1924, vol. 80,
p. 40–89.)   G.A. Oxon 8° 360=R.

1133. A list of the early chancellors and proctors of the University. (Oxf.
hist. soc., 1924, vol. 80, p. 318–36.)   G.A. Oxon 8° 360=R.

1134. MCNULTY, J., William of Rymyngton, prior of Salley abbey,
chancellor of Oxford, 1372–3. (Journ., Yorks. archaeol. soc., 1931,
vol. 30, p. 231–47.)   Per G.A. Yorks 8° 402=R. Top.

1135. The charges of my lord of Leiyster [chancellor of the University of Oxford] his dinner the vth day of September, 1570 [at Oxford]. (Collectanea curiosa, by J. Gutch, vol. 2, p. 4–11.) Oxf., 1781, 8°.
Gough Oxf. 66

1136. Election of a chancellor in 1610. The manner of the Oxford men signifying to my lord chancellor [lord Ellesmere] that they had chosen him their chancellor of Oxford. (Oxf. Protestant mag., 1847, vol. 1, p. 84–87.)
Per. G.A. Oxon 8° 119

1137. LAUD, W., abp. of Canterbury, The true copie of a letter sent from . . . William . . . arch-bishop of Canterbury . . . when he resign'd his office of chancellour. Published by occasion of a . . . forgery that runs under this title. And also the answer of the Vniversity. [Madan 970.] Oxf., 1641, 4°. 12 pp.
Wood 616 (20)
— [Another ed.] (Harl. misc., 1745, vol. 5, p. 535, 36.) GG 128 Art.
— [Another ed.] (Harl. misc., 2nd ed., 1810, vol. 5, p. 570.)
Σ III. 5
— [Another ed.] (Somers' tracts, 2nd ed., 1810, vol. 4, p. 436.)
Σ III. 14

1138. LAUD, W., abp. of Canterbury, The copie of a letter sent from William Laud . . . specifying his willingnesse to resigne his chancellor-ship . . . [A forgery.] [Madan 971.] [Lond.], 1641, 4°. 4 pp. 4° P 82 (16) Th.
— [Another issue.] [Madan 972.]
— [Another issue.] [Madan 973.]
Antiq. e. E. 1641. 9

1139. CARTWRIGHT, W., To . . . Philip earle of Pembroke and Montgomery . . . chancellour of the Vniversity . . . vpon his lordship's election of [i.e. as] chancellor . . . [A poem, signed W. Cartwright.] [Madan 966.] [Lond.], 1641, s. sh.
MS. Tanner 306 (291)

1140. WHITEHALL, R., Illustrissimo domino dno Richardo Cromwel, in honoratissimum cancellarii Oxoniensis officium & dignitatem fœliciter electo anno MDCLVII carmen onomasticon gratularium. [Madan 2326.] [Lond.], (1657), s. sh.
Wood 423 (32)

1140.1. WHITEHALL, R., Viro, favore regio, et meritis suis . . . Eduardo Hide . . . Oxoniæ cancellario . . . carmen gratulatorium [in Lat. and Engl., the former being an acrostic]. [Lond., 1660], s. sh. A 3. 18 Art.

See 191 [Walpole, H., Delenda est Oxonia. 1749].

1141. [Begin.] Tit. II. De matricula universitatis . . . [Opinions of C. Pratt, R. Wilbraham, and of J. Morton, concerning the qualifications of an unspecified candidate [lord Lichfield] for the office of chancellor. Dec. 22, 26.] n. pl., (1758), fol. 4 pp.   Gough Oxf. 96 (61b)

1142. [Begin.] Copies of the opinions of three very eminent and learned gentlemen . . . [Observations, by sir W. Blackstone?, on no. 1141. Dec. 30.] (Oxf., 1758), fol. 4 pp.   Gough Oxf. 96 (61a)

1143. Some considerations submitted to the members of Convocation [about the qualifications of a person proposed as chancellor, who had been a freeman of the City]. [Oxf., 1758], fol. 3 pp.

G.A. Oxon b. 19

See 866 [The case of a gentleman unjustly deprived of his vote at the election of a chancellor. 1759].

1144. Orders for the reception of . . . John, earl of Westmorland &c., and chancellor of the University of Oxford . . . [Oxf.], 1759, s. sh.

G.A. Oxon b. 19

1145. WILKES, J., The North Briton. No. 29, Dec. 18, 1762 [by J. Wilkes. An allegory on the election of lord Lichfield as chancellor of the University]. (Lond.), 1762, fol. Hope fol. 56

1146. Duæ oratiunculæ habitæ in Encæniis celebratis, A.D. 1773, Oxonii in honorem . . . domini North, cancellarii. n. pl., (1773), 8°. 8 pp.

G.A. Oxon 4° 351

See 6403 [Wood, A., A commentary on the supreme magistrates. 1790].

1147. CLARKE, G. S., Verses on the installation of . . . the duke of Portland, chancellor of the University. Oxf., 1793, 4°. 7 pp.

Gough Oxf. 90 (38)

See 989, 990 [Procedure in Convocation relating to the election of a chancellor. 1809].

1148. University of Oxford. A letter from a master of arts of the University of Oxford. (Nov. 29.) [Followed by] A second letter to the members of Convocation from an independent Master of arts. (Dec. 5.) Oxf., (1809), fol. 4 pp. G.A. Oxon b. 19

1149. Oxford chancellorship. [Letters by Oxoniensis supporting Lord Grenville's candidature, repr. from the Bath Chronicle and Bath Herald.] (Bath, 1809), s. sh. G.A. Oxon b. 111 (125)

1150. HODSON, F., [Begin.] A letter having appeared . . . signed Oxoniensis . . . [A denial of that portion of no. 1149 which purported to quote a letter from lord Grenville to F. Hodson.] Dec. 6. (Oxf., 1809), s. sh. G.A. Oxon b. 19

1151. [Begin.] The principal of Brasenose college . . . [A letter, signed A member of Convocation, challenging no. 1150.] Dec. 6. Oxf., 1809, s. sh. G.A. Oxon b. 19

1152. University of Oxford. The third and last letter to the members of Convocation, from an independent master of arts. (Dec. 9.) Oxf., [1809], s. sh. G.A. Oxon b. 19

1153. A case of singular distress. [Skit on no. 1152.] Oxf., [1809], s. sh. G.A. Oxon b. 19

1154. [Begin.] A poor gentleman . . . [Answer to no. 1152. Signed The poor gentleman.] Dec. 13. Oxf., 1809, s. sh. G.A. Oxon b. 19

1155. To the members of Convocation. [A paper, *begin.*] A letter inserted in the Courier [and signed A friend to toleration, dated Dec. 11]. Oxf. (1809), s. sh.   G.A. Oxon b. 19

1156. The judgment of Apollo, a fragment [in verse, on the election]. Oxf., [1809], 4°. 3 pp.   G.A. Oxon b. 19

1157. To the members of Convocation. [*Begin.*] Conceiving as I do . . . [Observations on the expediency of reserving votes in the present contest, signed A country clergyman.] Dec. 12. Oxf., 1809, s. sh.   G.A. Oxon b. 19

1158. To the members of Convocation. [*Begin.*] A proposal having been made . . . [A protest against no. 1157. Signed Another country clergyman.] Dec. 12. Oxf., 1809, s. sh.   G.A. Oxon b. 19

1159. To the members of Convocation. [*Begin.*] During the whole of the present contest . . . [A paper from lord Grenville's friends.] Dec. 12. Oxf., 1809, fol. 3 pp.   G.A. Oxon b. 19

1160. [*Begin.*] As some of the members of Convocation . . . [A reminder of the oath taken by voters, signed A member of Convocation.] Oxf., [1809], s. sh.   G.A. Oxon b. 19

1161. Memento. [Extracts from the various proceedings in Parliament, &c. shewing the part played by lord Grenville in the fight for Catholic emancipation, and the opposition thereto of the University of Oxford.] Lond., [1809], 8°. 23 pp.   G.A. Oxon b. 19
— [Another issue.] 24 pp.   G.A. Oxon b. 19

1162. [*Begin.*] At a meeting of independent members . . . [A satire on no. 1161. Signed Memento, chairman. *c.* Dec. 13.] Oxf., [1809], s. sh.   G.A. Oxon b. 19

1163. COKER, J., A letter to the electors of the University of Oxford upon the present contest for the chancellorship. By a member of Convocation [J. Coker]. Oxf., (1809), 8°. 9 pp.   G.A. Oxon 8° 58 (7)
— [Another ed.] (1809), 12°. 9 pp.   3974 e. 100 (13)

1164. List of the members of the University [no. 1573]. [Interleaved for use of canvassers in the election for chancellor in December 1809. This copy has been completed in MS., apparently by Lord Grenville's committee.]   MS. Top. Oxon b. 252

1165. TWISS, H., The public and private life of lord chancellor Eldon. 3 vols. [Chapter 29 of vol. 2, p. 107–15, deals with Eldon's candidature for chancellor of the University in 1809.] Lond., 1844, 8°.   44. 1595

1166. COKER, J., Some reflections on the late election of a chancellor of the University of Oxford. Maidstone, [1810], 8°. 28 pp.   G.A. Oxon 8° 9
— 2nd ed. 1810. 24 pp.   G. Pamph. 1098 (4)

1167. COPLESTON, E., A letter to John Coker . . . on his second edition of Reflections on the late election of a chancellor of the University of Oxford. [Signed E. Copleston.] Oxf., 1810, 8°. 20 pp.

G.A. Oxon 8° 58 (8)

1168. COKER, J., An answer to a letter addressed by . . . Edward Copleston to John Coker upon the subject of his Reflections on the late election of a chancellor [signed J. Coker]. Maidstone &c., (1810), 8°. 28 pp.

G.A. Oxon 8° 58 (9)

1169. COPLESTON, E., A second letter to John Coker . . . upon the subject of his Reflections on the late election of a chancellor [signed E. Copleston]. Oxf., 1810, 8°. 22 pp.   G.A. Oxon 8° 58 (10)

1170. COKER, J., An answer to a Second letter from . . . Edward Copleston [signed J. Coker]. Oxf., 1810, 8°. 16 pp.   G.A. Oxon 8° 58 (11)

See 1201 [Remarks on the power of the proctors in Convocation, occasioned by certain passages in the late publications of mr. Coker and mr. Copleston. 1810].

1171. [Notice of a proposed aerial voyage of an aerostatic machine and car which mr. Sadler proposes to make at Oxford to commemorate the installation of lord Grenville as chancellor.] (Oxf.), [1810], s. sh.

G.A. Oxon b. 111 (126)

1172. [Jan. 14, 1834. List of supporters of the duke of Wellington as chancellor.] (Oxf.), 1834, s. sh.   G.A. Oxon c. 50 (112)

1173. Chancellorship of the University of Oxford . . . [A list of Wellington's supporters.] [Oxf., 1834], s. sh.   G.A. Oxon c. 50 (113)

1174. CRAMER, J. A., Oratio habita coram . . .. Arturo duce de Wellington cancellario . . . Londini die Februarii VII°. (in theatro Sheldoniano die Junii decimo) MDCCCXXXIV. a publico oratore [J. A. Cramer]. (Oxon., 1834), 4°. 13 pp.   2 Δ 189

1175. Installation of the chancellor. Oxford, Feb. 15, 1834. [An account of the duke of Wellington's installation at Apsley house, London on Feb. 7.] n. pl., (1834), s. sh.   G.A. Oxon b. 111 (263)

1176. Congratulatory addresses . . . at the installation of . . . the duke of Wellington, chancellor of the university. Oxf., 1834, 8°. 69 pp.

3967 f. 23

— 2nd ed. 1834. 69 pp.   G.A. Oxon 8° 147 (2)

1177. KEBLE, J., Ode for the Encænia at Oxford, June 11, 1834 in honour of . . . Arthur, duke of Wellington, chancellor of the University. [By J. Keble.] Oxf., 1834, 8°. 8 pp.   G.A. Oxon b. 113 (45)

1178. BARMBY, J., The duke of Wellington's encaenia, 1834. [Excerpts from diary of rev. James Barmby.] (Oxf. mag., 1934, vol. 52, p. 823, 24.)   Per. G.A. Oxon 4° 141

1179. GASH, N., Oxford politics in the chancellor's election of 1834. (Oxf. mag., 1938, vol. 56, p. 543, 44; 574, 75.)   Per. G.A. Oxon 4° 141

1180. SEWELL, W., Misgivings on the requisition to lord Derby, by a conservative member of Convocation [signed W.S.]. n. pl., [1852], 8°. 8 pp.   G.A. Oxon 8° 106

1181. MICHELL, R., Oratio habita coram . . . Eduardo comite de Derby cancellario . . . Londini die Octobris XXImo. MDCCCLII a publico oratore [R. Michell]. (Oxon., 1852), 4°. 6 pp.   G.A. Oxon 4° 94

1182. Congratulatory addresses recited in the Theatre . . . at the installation of the . . . earl of Derby, chancellor . . . MDCCCLIII. Oxf., 1853, 8°. 40 pp.   G.A. Oxon 8° 232 (5)

1183. CLAUGHTON, T. L., bp. of St. Albans, Installation ode [on the earl of Derby as chancellor. By T. L. Claughton]. [Oxf.], 1853, 4°. 7 pp.
                                                       G.A. Oxon 4° 319 (2)

1184. The proceedings at the installation of . . . the earl of Derby, chancellor of the University of Oxford, with congratulatory odes. Oxf., 1853, 8°. 93 pp.   G.A. Oxon 8° 44

1185. Proceedings in Convocation in 1869 at the election of a chancellor [the marq. of Salisbury. In Lat.]. [Oxf.], 1903, 8°. 5 pp.
                                                       G.A. Oxon 8° 683 (27)

1186. Congratulatory addresses, recited in the Theatre, at the installation of the . . . marquis of Salisbury, chancellor of the University, June 21, 1870. Oxf., 1870, 4°. 15 pp.   G.A. Oxon 4° 13 (1)

1187. Proceedings at the installation of the chancellor [visct. Goschen]. [Oxf.], (1903), s. sh.   G.A. Oxon 8° 623 (28)

1188. The chancellorship of the University of Oxford. The undermentioned undertake to give lord Rosebery their support. [Oxf., 1907], 4°. 4 pp.   G.A. Oxon 4° 254

1189. CURZON, G. N., 1st marq. Curzon of Kedleston, Oratio cancellarii [lord Curzon] ad admissionem A. D. V. Id. Mai A.S. MCMVII. [In Lat. and Eng.] [Oxf.], 1907, 4°. 6 pp.   G.A. Oxon 4° 250

1190. Admission and installation of the chancellor [visct. Halifax] 7 Dec. 1933. [Oxf.], (1993), 4°. 3 pp.   G.A. Oxon b. 138 (f. 32)

1191. BROCK, M. G., The University chancellorship. (Amer. Oxonian, 1960, vol. 47, p. 105–09.)   Per. G.A. Oxon 8° 889

High Steward

1192. Historical notes on the office of high steward of the University. (Oxford, 1954, vol. 13, no. 2, p. 11–15.)   Per. G.A. Oxon 8° 1141

Vice-Chancellor

1193. A pandarique ode on the vice-chancelor's [J. Lloyd] return to Oxon: (Lond.), 1683, s. sh.   Wood 423 (57)

1194. A hymn to St. Tack, sung at the election of the new vice-chancellour [W. Lancaster] of Oxford. [Lond.], 1706, s. sh.   Antiq. c. E. 9 (23)

See 976, &c. [Right to vote in body of Convocation. 1758, &c.].
See 6403 [Wood, A., A commentary on the supreme magistrates. 1790].

1195. SIMMONS, J. S. G., The duke of Wellington and the vice-chancellorship in 1844. (Bodleian library record, 1954, vol. 5, p. 37–52.)
Per. 2590 d. Oxf. 1. 41=R.

1196. LIVINGSTONE, R. W., Should Oxford have a permanent vice-chancellor? (Oxford mag., 1934, vol. 53, p. 149–51.)
Per. G.A. Oxon 4° 141

1197. YANG HUEI-LI, On permanent vice-chancellors. (Oxf. mag., 1934, vol. 53, p. 246, 47.)   Per. G.A. Oxon 4° 141

1198. A., P. E., What now? [Discussion on the appointment by election or selection of a vice-chancellor.] (Oxf. mag., 1938, vol. 57, p. 174–77.)
Per. G.A. Oxon 4° 141

Oration

See 8509 [Bathurst, R., Vice chancellor's oration, 1673–76. 1761].

1199. HODGES, W., Oratio habita in venerabili Domo Convocationis Octob. 5to, 1744, cum vice-cancellarii officium tertia & postrema vice deposuerit. [Oxf.], (1744), 8°. 22 pp.   G.A. Oxon 8° 233 (3)

[The text of the vice-chancellor's annual oration from 1870 is to be found in the University gazette. These have occasionally been reprinted: the Bodleian has reprints of speeches for 1908, 18, 21–23.]

Proctors

See also Police, 1349–66.

1200. Ordo sive series electionis Procvratorum in singulis coll: Academiæ Oxoniensis. [Madan 628.] [Oxf., 1629], s. sh.   Wood 423 (14)
— Statuta. [Madan 629.] Oxon., 1629, s. sh.   Wood 276a (410)

See 976, &c. [Right to vote in body of Convocation. 1758, &c.].
See 6403 [Wood, A., A commentary on the supreme magistrates. 1790].

1201. Remarks on the power of the proctors in Convocation, occasioned by certain passages in the late publications of mr. Coker and mr. Copleston. By a member of Convocation. Oxf., 1810, 8°. 16 pp.
G.A. Oxon 8° 1130 (1)

See 1328 [Walker, J., Observations on the procuratorial office. 1822].
See 927, &c. [Proposed amendment of the statute regulating the cycle for the election of proctors. 1854].

1202. Concio procuratoria (Oratio procuratoria). 1854. Oxon., 1854, 8°. 16 pp.   Bliss B 220 (1)
— 1863.   G.A. Oxon c. 79 (432)
[From 1870 onwards the proctor's speech is printed in the University gazette. Some speeches were printed separately: the Bodleian has those of 1874, 86, 91, 94, 97, 1903, 06–08, 26, 32.]

1203. Nov. 25, 1856. [*Begin.*] The attention of members of Convocation
. . . [Observations on the proposed statute De procuratorum elec-
toribus, concerning the basis of the new college cycle for election
of the proctors.] Oxf., 1856, s. sh.   G.A. Oxon. c. 72 (345)

1204. DODGSON, C. L., The proposed procuratorial cycle to be submitted
to Congregation, on Oct. 27, 1885 [*and*] Postscript. Oct. 24. Oxf.,
(1885), 4°. 4 pp.   G.A. Oxon b. 140 (61*b*)

1205. DODGSON, C. L., The proctorial cycle to be voted on in Congregation on Tuesday, Nov. 10, 1885. Nov. 6. [Oxf.], (1885), 4°. 3 pp.
                                                    G.A. Oxon b. 140 (62*a*)

1206. DODGSON, C. L., Suggestions as to the elections of proctors. Oxf.,
1886, 4°. 10 pp.   G.A. Oxon 4° 106

1207. LIVINGSTONE, R. G., Statute on the proctorial cycle, in Convocation Tuesday, Feb. 8, at 2 p.m. [By R. G. Livingstone?] [Oxf., 1887],
s. sh.   G.A. Oxon b. 140 (68*c*)

1208. The new Proctorial statute [letter against, signed 'Conservative'].
(Oxf. mag., 1893, vol. 11, p. 281, 82.)   Per. G.A. Oxon 4° 141

See 3797 [Proctorial reminiscences].

1209. A list of the early chancellors and proctors of the University. (Oxf.
hist. soc., 1924, vol. 80, p. 318–36.)   G.A. Oxon 8° 360=R.

See 242.71 [Emden, A. B., Northerners and Southerners . . . *Appendix I*
entitled A list of Northern and Southern proctors to 1509. 1964].
See 1335.6 [Pantin, W., The jurisdiction and discipline of the University.
1966].

1209.4. BUXTON, R., The proctors. (Oxf. mag., 1965, N.S., vol. 5,
p. 188–90.)   Per. G.A. Oxon 4° 141

Public Orator

1210. MICHELL, R., The office of Public orator. (Orationes Crewianæ,
1878, p. 166–75.)   G.A. Oxon 4° 62

1211. [The text of some speeches by Public orators from 1870 onwards
may be found in the University gazette. Some have been reprinted:
a made-up volume in the Bodleian covers the period 1925–51; G.A.
Oxon b. 117].

See 2339 [Brioche, G. E., Une antique institution d'Oxford [Public orator].
1927].
See also 1110 [Congratulatory letters].
See also 1262 [Crewe benefaction].
See also 2329, &c. [Honorary degrees].

Registrar

1212. CHASE, D. P., The registrarship of the University; suggestions
addressed to members of Congregation. Oxf., (1870), 8°. 7 pp.
                                                    G.A. Oxon 8° 250 (12)

1213. Some reasons for rejecting the preamble of the Statute to be submitted to Congregation . . . March 9th, for taking the appointment of the Registrar out of the hands of Convocation [signed by J. Bellamy and 5 others]. [Oxf., 1897], s. sh.   G.A. Oxon c. 153

See also 6401, University registry.

Bedels

1214. LICHFIELD, L., [Supplication for votes for the place of 'Yeoman beadle'. Lichfield writes that his ancestors lost £1094 by printing proclamations etc. for Charles i, and that he suffers from 'the great inclination of authors . . . to have their books printed at the famous Clarendon printing office . . .'.] [Oxf., c. 1730], s. sh.
MS. Eng. lett. d. 77 (f. 169)

1215. [Begin.] The statute De bedellis . . . [Observations against the proposed reduction in the establishment of Esquire bedels.] Feb. 9. (Oxf., 1856), 4°. 3 pp.   G.A. Oxon c. 72 (49)

1216. Bedels' statute. [Begin.] Members of Congregation will do well to consider before they determine to vote against the Bedels' statute . . . [Feb. 23.] [Oxf., 1856], s. sh.   G.A. Oxon c. 72 (79)

1217. Is it expedient to reduce the stipends of the Superior bedels? [Observations, signed A member of Congregation, on no. 1216.] Feb. 25. [Oxf.], (1856), s. sh.   G.A. Oxon c. 72 (82)

1218. The proposed statute 'De bedellis, &c.' [An answer to no. 1216.] Feb. 27. (Oxf., 1856), 4°. 4 pp.   G.A. Oxon c. 72 (85)

1219. Bedells' statute. [Begin.] The real question of principle . . . [Observations by E. P. Pusey. Feb. 27.] Oxf., [1856], 4°. 3 pp.
G.A. Oxon c. 72 (50)

1220. Oxford, February 27, 1856. [Begin.] Mr. G. V. Cox having received . . . [Extracts &c. from a letter by a Cambridge university bedell, supporting mr. Cox in his efforts to oppose the new Bedels' statute.] Oxf., (1856), s. sh.   G.A. Oxon c. 72 (84)

1221. Bedells' statute. [Begin.] The votes on the Statute De bedellis in the last term . . . [Statement, signed A member of Congregation, in favour of re-introducing the amendment to the statute. May.] Oxf., [1856], s. sh.   G.A. Oxon c. 72 (210)

1222. [Begin.] Wednesday, May 14, 1856. Amidst the many notices . . . [A paper, signed A member of Congregation, urging the rejection of the proposed Bedels' statute.] [Oxf.], (1856), s. sh.
G.A. Oxon c. 72 (209)

1223. Statute 'De bedellis'. [A paper, dated 19 May 1856 and signed A member of Convocation, urging the rejection of the proposed economies in the bedels.] [Oxf.], (1856), s. sh.   G.A. Oxon b. 28

Clerks of the Market

See 855, &c.

Coroner

1224. In the Queen's bench. In the matter of the election of a coroner for the University of Oxford. Motion to the court [on behalf of J. M. Davenport for a 'mandamus' to admit him to the office in place of the elected candidate, C. M. Owen]. 9th Nov. n. pl., (1866), fol. 4 pp.
G.A. Oxon c. 82 (390)

1225. DAVENPORT, J. M., To the members of Convocation . . . [A letter explaining his recent proceedings with regard to the office of University coroner.] n. pl., (1866), s. sh.   G.A. Oxon c. 82 (395)

Delegates of Privileges

1226. GIBSON, S., The Delegates of privileges. (Oxford, 1943, vol. 8, no. 2, p. 30–35.)   Per. G.A. Oxon 8° 1141

Preachers

See 3768–95 Religion.

CEREMONIES

General

1227. BUXTON, L. H. D., and GIBSON, S., Oxford university ceremonies. Oxf., 1935, 8°. 168 pp.   G.A. Oxon 8° 1392=R.

Degree ceremonies

See 2318 [Holland, T., Oratio Sarisburiae [&c.] 1599. Account of degree ceremony for D.D.].

1228. Formulæ of conferring degrees. [Oxf., 1864], s. sh.
G.A. Oxon c. 80 (114)

1229. Candidates for degrees are requested . . . [Regulations.] [Oxf., 1864], s. sh.   G.A. Oxon c. 80 (113)

1230. Degree statute, Tit. VI. (IX). iii–vii. [*Begin.*] The changes proposed . . . are meant solely to shorten and simplify the ceremony of granting degrees . . . n. pl., [1864], s. sh.   G.A. Oxon c. 80 (84)

1231. WELLS, J., The Oxford degree ceremony. Oxf., 1906, 8°. 98 pp.
G.A. Oxon 16° 231=R.

1232. WIBLIN, J. G., The degree ceremony [by J. G. Wiblin]. Oxf., 1930, 8°. 4 pp.   G.A. Oxon 8° 1056 (9)

1233. GIBSON, S., Innovations in the degree ceremony. (Oxford, 1938, vol. 4, no. 3, p. 31–35.)   Per. G.A. Oxon 8° 1141

1234. Guide to the Oxford degree ceremony. Oxf., 1949, 8°. 11 pp.
G.A. Oxon 8° 1184 (12)

1235. MAWDSLEY, W. N. HARGREAVES-, Grand compounders. (Oxoniensia, 1957, vol. 22, p. 110, 11.)   Per. G.A. Oxon 4° 658=R.

1235.4. PANTIN, W. A., Latin [in degree ceremonies]. (Oxf. mag., 1965, N.S., vol. 5, p. 225.)   Per. G.A. Oxon 4° 141

Act or Encaenia

See also 5010, &c. Terrae filius.

1236. Of the Actes done at Oxford, when the queen's majesty was there; so collected and noted by Nicholas Robinson. From Harl. MS. 7033, f. 131. (Nichols's Progresses of q. Eliz., 1788, vol. 1, p. 81–94 of The queen at Oxford, 1566.)   DD 74 Jur.
— [Another ed.] (The Progresses, &c., 1823, new ed., vol. 1, p. 229–47.)   4° BS. 381=A.
— [Another ed.] (Oxf. hist. soc., 8, p. 169–91.) Oxf., 1887, 8°.
G.A. Oxon 8° 360=R.

1237. WHITEHALL, R., Τεχνηπολιμογαμία: or, The marriage of armes and arts, July 12. 1651, an accompt of the Act at Oxon. By R. W. [Madan 2163.] Lond., 1651, 8 pp.   Bliss B 66

1238. [*Begin.*] Oxon. Iuly 5th. 1652. [Notice by the vice-chancellor and heads of houses against disturbance of the Act by 'humming' and other noises.] [Madan 2187.] Oxf., 1652, s. sh.   Wood 276a (345)

1239. [*Begin.*] To the . . . heads of the respective colleges . . . [Orders and regulations for the Encaenia and Act.] [Madan 3292.] [Oxf.], 1669, s. sh.   Wood 276a (384)
[Issues for 1671-75, 83; c. 1690, 93, 1702, 03, 33, 50, 51, 54–56, 63, 88, 93, &c. are to be found in the following shelfmarks: Wood 276a; Don. b. 12; G.A. Oxon a. 14–19; G.A. Oxon b. 19–36; G.A. Oxon b. 111; G.A. Oxon c. 40–85.]

1240. OWEN, C., Carmen Pindaricum in Theatrum Sheldonianum in solennibus magnifici operis Encænis recitatum Julii die 9° anno 1669. [Madan 2816.] Oxon., 1669, 4°. 32 pp.   Gough Oxf. 109

1241. [*Begin.*] Whereas formerly . . . [Vice-chancellor's notice that the disturbance caused by persons pressing in within the rail at the performance of practical music on Act Saturday, is forbidden in the future.] July 6. [Madan 2900.] [Oxf., 1671], s. sh.   Wood 276a (367)

See 1260 [Order of proceedings. 1674-].

1242. Theatri Oxoniensis encænia, sive Comitia philologica. Julii 6. Anno 1677. celebrata. [Madan 3148.] Oxon., 1677, fol. 60 pp.
G 1. 10 Jur.

1243. Orders for the reception of . . . James, duke of Ormond . . . agreed
upon by the vice-chancellor and delegates . . . [Madan 3150.] [Oxf.,
1677], s. sh.   Don. b. 12 (27)
— [Proof.]   Wood 276a (324)

1244. Comitia philologica in gratulatione . . . Academiæ Oxon: ob . . .
cancellarii adventum expectatissimum. Aug. 6, Aº. 1677 celebrata.
[Madan 3151.] Oxon., 1677, s. sh.   Wood 276a (406a)

1245. Comitia philologica, habita Aug. 6. anno 1677. In gratulatione
solenni ob adventum expectatissimum illustrissimi principis Jacobi
Ormondiæ ducis Hibenia [sic] . . . cancellarii . . . [Madan 3152.]
[Oxf., 1677], fol. 18 pp.   Wood 423 (53)
— [Another issue.] 20 pp. [Madan 3153.]

1246. Theatri Oxoniensis encænia, sive Comitia philologica Julii 7, anno
1693. celebrata. Oxon., 1693, fol.   Pamph. 213 (1)

1247. The Oxford-act: a poem. Lond., 1693, 4º. 22 pp.
                                                         Gough Oxf. 59 (5)
[Some copies have the misprint 1613: C 6. 14 Linc.]

1248. The Oxford treatment of their Cambridge friends at the Act, in a
dialogue between Eugenius and Crites. Lond., 1705, fol. 10 pp.
                                                         Firth c. 9 (2)

1249. Academiæ Oxoniensis comitia philologica in Theatro Sheldoniano
decimo die Julii, 1713 celebrata: in honorem . . . reginæ Annæ pacificæ.
Oxon., 1713, fol.   Pamph. 311 (47)

1250. Oxford act: an epistle to a noble lord [in verse]. Lond., 1714, 8º.
vii+7 pp.   G.A. Oxon 8º 926 (4)

1251. Ordo comitiorum philologicorum. [Oxf.], 1733, s. sh.
                                                         G.A. Oxon b. 111 (40)

1252.

1253. The Oxford act, a new ballad opera, as it was perform'd by a
company of students at Oxford. Lond., 1733, 8º. 44 pp.
                                                         Gough Oxf. 59 (6)

1254. COURAYER, P. F., An oration spoken in the Theatre . . . at the
publick act, 1733, tr. by a gentleman of the University of Oxford.
Lond., 1734, 8º. 23 pp.   Gough Oxf. 113 (2)

1255. The Oxford act, A.D. 1733, a particular and exact account of that
solemnity: wherein is inserted an imitation of Bellus homo & academicus. A letter. Lond., 1734, 8º. 75 pp.   G.A. Oxon 8º 61 (2)

1256. Part of a letter from a gentleman on a journey, giving an account of
the Encænia at Oxford. (Gents. mag., 1763, vol. 33, p. 348, 49.)
                                                         Per. 22863 e. 193=A.

1257. COPLESTON, E., bp. of Llandaff. Ode for the Encænia at Oxford,
July 3, 1810 [by E. Copleston]. Oxf., (1810), 4º. 4 pp. 4º BS. 175 (4)

1258. A song of the Encænia. Oxf., 1853, 8°. 12 pp. G.A. Oxon 8° 286 (9)

1259. To the undergraduate members of the University. [An appeal, signed A tutor, for better behaviour in the Theatre on the Day of Commemoration.] [Oxf., 1852], s. sh. G.A. Oxon c. 68 (114)

1260. Theatri Oxoniensis encænia Jul. 10 [&c.] An. 1674 (76, 77, 79–84, 93, 1703) celebrata. [Order of proceedings.] [Madan 3293.] Oxf., 1674–1703, s. shs. Wood 276a (394–404a); Don. b. 12 (45)

1261. Encaenia [order of proceedings]. 1879– . (Oxf., 1879–), 4°. [The following are in Bodley: 1879, 81, 83, 85, 87–90, 94–97, 99, 1902–08, 11–16, 19–23, 25–29, 31–34, 36–39, 46, 48, 50, 52– .
G.A. Oxon b. 138 (19–34); c. 316].

Creweian oration

1262. Oratio Creweiana.
1751. Lowth, R., Oratio anniversaria . . . ex instituto Nathanielis domini Crewe . . . (De sacra poesi Hebræorum, 1753, p. 353–67.)
CC 55 Th.
1788. Crowe, W., Oratio ex instituto . . . Nathanielis dom. Crew . . . Oxon., (1788), 4°. 11 pp. Gough Oxf. 90 (28)
1800. Crowe, W., Oratio Creweiana. Oxon., 1800, 4°. 19 pp.
Gough Oxf. 89 (4)
1849–75 [alternate years]. Michell, R., Orationes Creweianæ. Lond. &c., 1878, 4°. 187 pp. G.A. Oxon 4° 62
1862. Arnold, M., Oratio anniversaria . . . [Oxf.], (1862), 8°. 8 pp.
G.A. Oxon 8° 124 (18)
1881–89 [alternate years], 1890–1904 [alternate years], and 1908. Merry, W. W., Orationes tum Creweianae tum gratulatoriae . . . Oxon., 1909, 4°. 102 pp. G.A. Oxon 4° 261
In 1904, 07 and 1911 the oration was included in the Encaenia programme: G.A. Oxon c. 218; G.A. Oxon 4° 252; G.A. Oxon b. 32/1911.
1913 [Bodley has a summary of the speech: G.A. Oxon b. 138 (26)].
1915, 17 [Text: G.A. Oxon c. 309 (49, 60)].
1919 [Bodley has a summary: G.A. Oxon b. 138 (34)].
1925, 27 [Text: G.A. Oxon b. 138 (34, 30)].
1929 [Text: G.A. Oxon c. 316].
1934, 36 [Text: G.A. Oxon b. 138 (33, 34)].
1948, 54 [Text: G.A. Oxon c. 316].
[From 1924 the Oration is printed in the Oxford University gazette.]

1263. Memoirs of Nathaniel, lord Crewe, ed. by A. Clark. (Camden misc., 1893, new ser., vol. 9, no. 6). [Lond.], 1893, 8°. 48 pp.
2233 e. 54=K.

1264. MUNRO, M. C. N., Nathaniel lord Crewe, 'time-serving favourite of James II'. (Oxf. mag., 1937, vol. 55, p. 727–29.)
Per. G.A. Oxon 4° 141

DISCIPLINE
General

1265. [Certain scholars of Oxford to be banished the University.] (9 Hen.
V, c. 8, Pub.) (In this volume are conteined the statutes made . . .
from . . . Henry the thirde vnto the fyrste yere of . . . Henry the viii.)
Lond., 1543, fol.   L.L.

1266. [*Begin.*] Jan. 9. 1651. By the Vicechancellour . . . [Notice seeking
to prevent members from riotous attacks on persons 'of godly conversation'.] [Madan 2155.] Oxf., 1651[2], s. sh.   Wood 276a (319)

1267. [*Begin.*] March 22. 1651. By the Vice-Chancellour . . . [Order
prohibiting coursing in the public schools and disorders in the streets.]
[Madan 2156.] Oxf., 1651/2, s. sh.   Wood 276a (344)
— [Another ed.] 1653[4].]Madan 2220.]   O.U.A.

1268. [*Begin.*] Quandoquidem compertum est . . . [Notice by the vice-
chancellor against turbulent conduct of members in public.] Jan. 29.
[Madan 2268*.] Oxf., 1655, s. sh.   O.U.A.

1269. [*Begin.*] Quandoquidem compertum est . . . [Notice by the vice-
chancellor to members to abstain from unseemly tumult and noise.]
Feb. 22. [Madan 2366.] Oxon., (1658), s. sh.

1270. [*Begin.*] Quandoquidem compertum est . . . [Notice by the vice-
chancellor against turbulent conduct of members in public.] Mar. 20.
[Madan 2426.] Oxon., 1660[1], s. sh.   G.A. Oxon b. 111 (1)
— [Repr.] Feb. 18. [Madan 2604.] [Oxf.], (1662), s. sh.

1271. [1671. Notice issued Jan. 27, by the vice-chancellor for the proper
observance of the anniversary of the day of execution of Charles i,
January 30.] [Madan 2892.]
— [Another issue.] [Madan 2893.]

1272. [*Begin.*] By order from mr. Vice-Chancellor. Whereas complaint . . .
[Notice against disorders committed 'in and about the new tennis-
court where . . . the duke of York's servants now act'. July 10, 1671.]
[Oxf.], 1671, s. sh.   Don. b. 12 (18)

1273. December 3. 1678. [Vice-chancellor's notice that no member be
uncivil to the soldiers if taken or apprehended by them.] [Madan
3191.] [Oxf.], 1678, s. sh.   Don. b. 12 (31)

1274. Orders to be observed while his majestie or . . . Parliament continue
in Oxford . . . [Oxf.? 1681], s. sh.   Wood 276a (328)

1275. The experiences of mr. pro-proctor Charlett, 1683. (Oxf. mag.,
1892, vol. 10, p. 444, 45.)   Per. G.A. Oxon 4° 141

1276. At a general meeting of the vice-chancellor, heads of houses, and
proctors . . . [Proclamation, dated 7 Nov. 1704, enforcing more rigid
discipline.] [Oxf.], (1704), s. sh.   G.A. Oxon b. 19

— Jan. 14, 1733/4.   G.A. Oxon b. 19
— Dec. 11, 1738.   G.A. Oxon b. 19
— Feb. 23, 1746/7.   G.A. Oxon b. 19
— Apr. 11, 1748.   G.A. Oxon b. 19

1277. [*Begin.*] All persons are . . . [Vice-chancellor's order forbidding any member to partake in cock-fighting. Apr. 16, 1739.] [Oxf.], 1739, s. sh.   Don. b. 12 (54)

1278. [*Begin.*] July 28th. 1747. Whereas complaint . . . [Vice-chancellor's notice about unruly behaviour at the time of the Assizes.] [Oxf.], 1747, s. sh.   Don. b. 12 (57)

1279. [*Begin.*] Whereas certain undergraduate scholars . . . [Vice-chancellor's and proctors' notice that no leniency will be granted to persons insulting the procuratorial office. May 5, 1750.] [Oxf.], 1750, s. sh.   Don. b. 12 (59a)

1280. At a meeting of the Heads of Houses . . . on the fifth day of . . . June, 1766, it was agreed [that undergraduates, civilian or bachelor of arts must attend meals in the common refectory; that cooks of colleges &c. be charged to send no dinners into the private chambers of any under M.A. or B.L.]. [Oxf.], (1766), s. sh.   G.A. Oxon b. 19

1281. To the Vice-chancellor of the University . . . [A letter, signed A member of Convocation, asking the vice-chancellor to exercise his veto on a paragraph in the 16th section of the amended statute De moribus conformandis, when it is proposed in Convocation on Mar. 28.] Mar. 19. (Oxf., 1838), s. sh.   G.A. Oxon c. 54 (38)

1282. [*Begin.*] 'A member of Convocation' having requested the vice-chancellor to . . . veto . . . [A reply, signed Another member of Convocation, to 1281.] Mar. 21. Oxf., 1838, s. sh.   G.A. Oxon c. 54 (49)

1283. [*Begin.*] At a numerous meeting . . . [Memorial, signed by W. H. Butler and 4 others representing the Oxford tradesmen, recording some objections to the amended statute De moribus conformandis, about to be proposed in Convocation.] Mar. 21. [Oxf.], (1838), s. sh.   G.A. Oxon c. 54 (50)

1284. JONES, O. S., Discipline at Oxford university. (Idler, 1896, vol. 10, p. 464–67.)   Per. 2705 d. 238

1285. Memorandum to undergraduates on matriculation. n. pl., [1904?], s. sh.   G.A. Oxon c. 107 (3)

See 3351 [Rules of discipline in force for the women students. 1909].

1286. Memorandum [*afterw.*] Proctors' memorandum on the conduct & discipline of junior members of the University. Mich. term, 1926– . Oxf., 1926– , 4°.   G.A. Oxon 4° 632

1287. K., K.M., Proctorial regulations. (Oxf. mag., 1946, vol. 64, p. 193, 94.)   Per. G.A. Oxon 4° 141

1287.1. Report of the Committee on the disciplinary powers of the vice-chancellor and proctors. (Suppl. no. 2, Univ. gazette, 1965, vol. 96.) [Oxf.], 1965, 8°. 9 pp.   Per. G.A. Oxon c. 80

Specific incidents and misdemeanours

1288. [Begin.] Whereas on Friday last . . . [Notice by the vice-chancellor in consequence of the breaking of windows of colleges and private houses on April 14, 1676, offering a reward for information leading to the discovering of the culprits.] [Madan 3115, 3116.] [Oxf., 1676], s. sh.   Wood 276a (374)

1289. An account of mr. [James] Parkinson's expulsion [for anti-royalist sentiments] from the University of Oxford in the late times, in vindication of him from the false aspersions cast on him in a late pamphlet, entituled The history of passive obedience. Lond., 1689, 4°. 20 pp.
                                                              Gough Oxf. 69

See 8642 [A faithful narrative of the proceedings . . . wherein the reasons that induced mr. Baker to accuse mr. Swinton of sodomitical practices are set down . . . 1739].

1290. A letter [signed Terrafilius] to the heads of the University of Oxford on a late very remarkable affair [the alleged murder, in a flight of revelry, of a college servant by a group of wealthy idlers: and a plea for stricter discipline]. Lond., 1747, 8°. 32 pp. G.A. Oxon 8° 59 (18)

1291. [Begin.] March 20. 1749–50. Whereas on Friday evening . . . [Vice-chancellor's and proctors' notice offering a reward of ten guineas for information leading to the arrest of a person who threw a large stone at the senior proctor, hitting him on the head.] [Oxf.], 1750, s. sh.
                                                              Don. b. 12 (59b)

1292. WILMOT, G., A serious inquiry into some late proceedings in vindication of the honour, credit and reputation of the University of Ox---d relative to an offence of a certain member of the same [W. Lewis. By G. Wilmot]. Lond., 1751, 8°. 55 pp. G.A. Oxon 8° 60 (4)

1293. LEWIS, W., An answer [by W. Lewis] to the Serious inquiry [by G. Wilmot] into some proceedings relating to the University of Ox---d. Lond., [1751], 8°. 47 pp.   G.A. Oxon 8° 60 (5)

1294. WILMOT, G., A letter to ******* **** M.D. heretofore of ****** ****** college . . . [Signed Olim Oxoniensis. An answer to no. 1293.] Lond., 1752, 4°. 16 pp.   Gough Oxf. 110 (5)

1295. SCROPE, R., A letter to — —, esq., occasioned by a late misrepresentation of the circumstances of a prosecution commenced A.D. 1763 by the proctors of the University . . . against W. C— [Craven] . . . with brief reflections upon academical discipline. Salisbury, &c., 1773, 4°. 30 pp.   Gough Oxf. 60 (8)

1296. [Begin.] Whereas yesterday evening . . . [Notice, signed Michael Marlow, vice-chancellor, offering reward for evidence to convict the offender who attacked dr. Cooke, president of C.C. college; and any other person who committed acts of violence during the rioting on the evening of Oct. 8.] Oct. 9. [Oxf.], (1800), s. sh. G.A. Oxon b. 111 (90)

Costume

1297. [A made-up volume in the Bodleian of Prints, &c. of University costume.] G.A. Oxon a. 72

1298. [*Begin.*] Paul Hood . . . [Peremptory order by the vice-chancellor that academical costume be worn in public by all members, especially at sermons and other scholastic exercises.] Oct. 8. [Madan 2516.] [Oxf., 1660], s. sh. Wood 276a (347)

1299. [*Begin.*] May the 31. 1661. Paul Hood . . . [Vice-chancellor's order that academical costume be worn in public.] [Oxf.], 1661, s. sh.
Don. b. 12 (6b)

1300. [*Begin.*] Robert Say . . . [Notice by the vice-chancellor calling on every graduate to 'appear in his formalities at sermons and elsewhere' and undergraduates in their proper academical costumes.] 13 Feb. [Madan 2749.] [Oxf.], (1666), s. sh. Wood 276a (350)

1301. [*Begin.*] Cum de vestitu & habitu scholastico . . . [Orders by the vice-chancellor concerning academic dress. 27 Aug.] [Madan 2750.] Oxon., (1666), s. sh. Wood 276a (320)

1302. EDWARDS, G., Reverendis et eruditis viris in theologia, medicina, et jure civili doctoribus Academiæ Oxoniensis, hæc, omnium ordinium [*sic*] habituumqȝ, academicorum exemplaria . . . [Madan 2997.] [Oxf.? 1674], fol. 12 plates. Wood 276b (19)
— [Another ed., *entitled*] Habitus academicorum Oxoniensium a doctore ad servientem. [1679/80?] [Madan 2997*.] G.A. Oxon 4° 483

1303. [*Begin.*] Cum statutum Universitatis . . . [Vice-chancellor's notice about dress, long hair, and preaching from memory.] Nov. 24. [Madan 3018.] [Oxf.], (1674), s. sh. Wood 276a (322)

1304. [*Begin.*] 'Sir, I do most earnestly desire you . . . [Notice signed Joh. Nicholas Vice-can. asking heads of houses to co-operate with him 'in removing the neglect of wearing University habits' at statutable times.] [Madan 3189.] [Oxf., 1678], s. sh. G.A. Oxon b. 111 (23)

1305. [*Begin.*] At a meeting of the heads of houses. Mar. 22. 1688. Whereas the gowns . . . [Order requiring a stricter observance of the forms of academic dress.] [Oxf.? 1689], s. sh. Wood 276a (380)

1306. At a meeting of the heads of houses, April 28. 1690 . . . Models and patterns of scholastical habit. [Oxf.], (1690), s. sh.
G.A. Oxon b. 19

1307. To the . . . Vice-chancellor and the heads of houses. [A letter on innovation in academical habits. Signed Members of Convocation, March 13, 1770.] [Oxf.], 1770, s. sh. Don. b. 12 (70)

1308. [*Begin.*] 1. Clerks servientes, servitors . . . [A paper of March 29, 1770, quoting statutes relating to academic costume, and appending 6 observations thereon.] [Oxf.], 1770, s. sh.   Don. b. 12 (71*a*)

1309. Observations upon the statute Tit. xiv. De vestitu & habitu scholastico . . . [Oxf., 1770], fol. 4 pp.   Don. b. 12 (71*b*)

1310. Remarks on some strictures lately published, entitled Observations upon the statute Tit. xiv. De vestitu et habitu scholastico: with a brief state of the controversy which gave occasion to them. Oxf., 1770, 4°. 26 pp.   Gough Oxf. 80 (23)

1311. HALLIFAX, B., Remarks on Observations upon the statute De vestitu et habitu scholastico [signed A regent, i.e. B. Hallifax]. Apr. 17. (Oxf., 1770), 4°. 12 pp.   Gough Oxf. 80 (24)

1312. [*Begin.*] The statute Tit. x. Sect. 2. §. 2. [Observations against the proposed amendment of statute Tit. xiv. De vestitu et habitu scholastico.] June 21. n. pl., (1770), 8°. 4 pp.   Gough Oxf. 73 (1)

1313. The following amendments of the form of a new statute De habitu academico will be . . . offered in Convocation by a member of the house . . . 4 July 1770. [Oxf.], 1770, s. sh.   Don. b. 12 (73*b*)

1314. [Academical dress according to the changes agreed upon in Convocation 13 July 1770. 25 plates.]   MS. Top. Oxon c. 16 (f. 20–45)

1315. The academic costume of the University of Oxford, engraved and published by Taylor. Oxf., [1807], 16°. 25 pl.   G.A. Oxon 16° 21

1316. The costume of the University of Oxford, illustr. by a series of engravings from original drawings by T. Uwins: to which is prefixed a brief account of the members and officers of that University [by W. Combe]. Lond., 1815, fol. 18 pp.+17 plates   G.A. Oxon c. 267

1317. Reasons for the non placet given in the House of Convocation, Tuesday, November 26, 1816 [on the proposed amendment of the statute De habitu &c.]. Oxf., 1816, 8°. 15 pp.   G.A. Oxon 8° 1382

1318. The costumes of the members of the University of Oxford, drawn, engraved & publ. by N. Whittock. Lond., [*c.* 1840], s. sh. folded. 17 plates.   G.A. Oxon 16° 4
— [Another ed. 18– .]   G.A. Oxon 16° 4*

1319. December 9, 1857. [*Begin.*] The question has been raised . . . [A paper, signed Suasor legis, on the proposed change in the academical costume of the undergraduate.] Oxf., (1857), s. sh.
G.A. Oxon c. 73 (332)

1320. The demi-semi-pro-proctors. [A paper attacking certain alterations in the commoner's gown brought in by the new statute De habitu academico.] Oxf., 1857, s. sh.   G.A. Oxon c. 73 (318)

1321. Shrimpton's Series of the costumes of the members of the University of Oxford. [Coloured plates.] Oxf., 1885, fol.   B.M.

1322. FRANKLIN, C. A. H., Academic costume. (Oxf. mag., 1930, vol. 48, p. 423–28; 464–67.)   Per. G.A. Oxon 4° 141

1323. FLEMING, U., The Oxford gown [history of]. (Britain to-day, 1948, no. 151, p. 35–37).   Per. 22893 d. 24

1324. MAWDSLEY, W. N. HARGREAVES-, The commoner's gown. (Oxoniensia, 1957, vol. 22, p. 111.)   Per. G.A. Oxon 4° 658=R.

1325. MAWDSLEY, W. N. HARGREAVES-, Academical dress. (Oxf. mag., 1957, vol. 76, p. 132–34, 148.)   Per. G.A. Oxon 4° 141

1326. VENABLES, D. R., and CLIFFORD, R. E., Academic dress of the University of Oxford. Oxf., 1957, 8°. 32 pp.   21994 e. 55

1326.3. MAWDSLEY, W. N. HARGREAVES-, A history of academical dress in Europe until the end of the eighteenth century. [Oxf., p. 60–106.] Oxf., 1963, 8°.   21994 e. 60

Courts

General

1327. [Blank form of summons used by the vice-chancellor as magistrate. 179—.]   G.A. Oxon c. 250 (vii. 126)

1328. WALKER, J., Curia Oxoniensis: or, Observations on the statutes which relate to the University court; on the illegality of searching houses; on the procuratorial office; and on the University police act [by J. Walker]. 2nd ed. Oxf., 1822, 8°. iv+74 pp.
     G.A. Oxon 8° 219 (14)
— 3rd ed. 1825. 80 pp.   G.A. Oxon 8° 1046 (14)
— [Another issue.] 3rd ed. 1826.   G. Pamph. 203

1329. SEWELL, R. C., An inquiry into the constitution and practice of the Chancellor's court. Oxf. &c., 1839, 8°. 55 pp.   Bliss B 215 (1)

1330. LATIMER, D., The Chancellor's court . . . and the position of persons prosecuted for libel therein. (Oxf.), 1860, 8°. 11 pp.
     G.A. Oxon 8° 124 (20)

See 1922 [Bill enabling the University to retain the custody of certain testamentary documents. 1860].
See 1073 [Act making further provision for the administration of justice in the Court of the chancellor. 1862].

1331. GRIFFITHS, J., An index of wills proved in the Court of the chancellor of the University of Oxford, and to such of the records and other instruments and papers of that court as relate to matters or causes testamentary. Oxf., 1862, 8°. 88 pp.   G.A. Oxon 8° 331=R.

1332. In the Chancellor's court of the University of Oxford. Scale of fees. n. pl., [1865], s. sh.   G.A. Oxon c. 81 (159)

See 93 [Acta Curiae cancellarii. 1868].
See 881 [The sin of our cities. Oxford. Observations favouring restricting the power of University police and court over citizens. 1893].

1333. University jurisdiction. (Oxf. mag., 1893, vol. 11, p. 413, 14.)
Per. G.A. Oxon 4° 141

1334. An act to consolidate certain enactments relating to county courts.
(24 & 25 G. V, c. 53, Pub.) [Sect. 192 (8) preserves University privileges and jurisdiction.] (Lond.), 1934, 8°. 115 pp.   L.L.

1335. PHILIP, I. G., The Court Leet of the University of Oxford. (Oxoniensia, 1950, p. 81–91.)   Per. G.A. Oxon 4° 658=R.

1335.6. PANTIN, W., [The jurisdiction and discipline of the University.]
(Delegates of privileges, Annual rept., 1964/65. Oxf. Univ. Gazette,
1966, vol. 96, suppl. no. 4, p. 1–14.)   Per. G.A. Oxon c. 80

Rules

1336. Chancellor's court of the University of Oxford . . . [Rules for the
better regulation of the court, laid down by the Vice-chancellor and
the Assessor. 6 January 1755.] [Oxf.], 1755, s. sh.   Don. b. 12 (64)

1337. Rules of the Chancellor's court of the University of Oxford to come
into operation 1st March, 1865. n. pl., (1864), 8°. 26 pp.
G.A. Oxon 8° 92 (4)

1338. Rules of the Chancellor's court. Oxf., 1891, 4°. 27 pp.
G.A. Oxon 4° 504 (8)

1339. [Order in Council 1894 no. 212, applying the enactments and rules
of the Supreme court relating to appeals from county courts, to the
Vice-chancellor's court.] [Lond.], 1894, s. sh.   G.A. Oxon c. 25 (11)

1340. Rules of the Chancellor's court, 1908. Oxf., (1908), 8°. 30 pp. L.L.

1341. Rules of the Chancellor's court. Oxf., 1933, 8°. 29 pp.   L.L.

Cases

See 6621 [William Powell plantiffe; the warden and fellows of All-soules
colledge, defendants. In the Chancellors court. 1656].

1341.5. Peter de Walpergen against the executors of John Fell, 1687–88.
(Double Crown club anecdote, 1.) Oxf., (printed in types bequeathed
by Fell, and given to the Double Crown club at Corpus Christi
college, by Harry Carter), 1964, 8°. 20 pp.   25823 e. 139

1342. The libel [against Edward Hyde] issu'd out of the Chancellor's
court of the University of Oxford against mr. Anthony à Wood [in
his Athenae Oxonienses, vol. 2] . . . by . . . Henry Hyde, late earl of
Clarendon, with mr. Wood's answer, and the sentence given after the
tryal begun March 3. 1692/3, finished July 29. 1693. n. pl., [c. 1695],
fol. 4 pp.   G 2. 1 Jur.
— [Another copy on vellum.]   M 4. 16 Jur.
— [Another ed.] (Miscellanies on several curious subjects, 1714, p. iii–
xxviii.)   8° F 73 Jur.

1343. EDWARDS, J., The substance of two actions and proceedings therein
[R. Hopkins v. J. Edwards] in the University court of Oxford. [By
J. Edwards?] Lond., [1749], 8°. 46 pp.   G.A. Oxon 8° 62 (5)
— [Another issue.] 1749.   G.A. Oxon 8° 62 (6)

1344. KYNASTON, J., A collection of papers relative to the prosecution
now carrying on in the Chancellor's court in Oxford . . . against mr.
Kynaston by Matthew Maddock . . . for the charge of adultery alledged
against the said Matthew Maddock. [With] Appendix. Lond., 1764,
8°. 29+7 pp.   Gough Oxf. 113 (12)

1345. KYNASTON, J., Copy of a letter [to] Robert Jenner late of Brazen
Nose college, Oxford. [Followed by] Copy of a letter to mr. Samuel
Malbon . . . [and] To the gentlemen of the University [relative to the
prosecution in the Chancellor's court of J. Kynaston by M. Maddock].
n. pl., [1765], fol. 4 pp.   G.A. Oxon 4° 6 (22)

1346. Proceedings in the Vice-chancellor's court . . . in the case of
Williams versus Brickenden for false imprisonment. To which is prefixed, The case of mr. Williams as submitted to mr. serjeant Williams
and mr. Holroyd, with their respective opinions. Oxf., 1811, 8°. 85 pp.
                                                 G.A. Oxon 8° 219 (9)

1347. John Parkinson, M.A., versus The Proctors. Judgement [concern-
ing an appeal against a conviction for taking part in a horse-race on
Port Meadow]. 5 Dec., 1859. n. pl., (1859), 8°. 12 pp.
                                                 G.A. Oxon 8° 146 (18)

1348. Pusey and others v. Jowett. The argument and decision as to the
jurisdiction of the Chancellor's court at Oxford. Oxf. &c., [1863],
8°, 41 pp.   G.A. Oxon 8° 70 (40)

Police

See also 1200–09, Proctors.

1349. [Begin.] Civitas ⎱ Ad general. quart. session.
              Oxon ⎰
[Notice commanding all constables 'to make diligent search for all
vagrants and sturdy beggars who shall lurke within the said city,
and to apprehend, punish and convey them according to the direction
of the . . . acts'.] Jan. 22. 1707/8. [Oxf.], 1708, s. sh.   G.A. Oxon b. 19

1350. At a meeting of the Vice-chancellor, Heads of Houses . . . Jan.
28. 1799. [Rules of an Association for the protection of persons and
property.] [Oxf.], (1808), s. sh.   G.A. Oxon b. 13

1351. A bill for the better preservation of the peace and good order in the
universities of England. 3 June. [Lond.], 1825, s. sh.
                                                 Pp. Eng. 1825 vol. 3
— [Act]. (6 G. IV, c. 97, Pub.) Lond., 1825, s. sh.   L.L.

1352. [*Begin.*] The following plan . . . will be submitted to [Convocation] . . . Plea for the establishment of a police within the precincts of the University and City of Oxford. June 1, 1829. [Oxf.], 1829, 4°. 4 pp.

G.A. Oxon c. 45 (54)

1353. The following account of monies received and paid on account of nightly police . . . June 5, 1829–Oct. 1, 1830 (–54/55) has been approved. [Oxf.], (1830–56), s. sh.   G.A. Oxon c. 46–72

1354. University police. General instructions. [Oxf., 1829], 12°. 3 pp.

G.A. Oxon c. 45 (74)

1355. University police. Inspectors' instructions. [Oxf., 1829], 12°. 4 pp.

G.A. Oxon c. 45 (75)

1356. University police. Constables' instructions [Oxf., 1829], 12°. 4 pp.

G.A. Oxon c. 45 (76)

1357. University police. General instructions. (Inspectors' instructions. Constables' instructions.) [Oxf., *c.* 1840], 8°. 12 pp.

G.A. Oxon 8° 828 (7)

1358. [Form of appointment to the office of constable by the vice-chancellor.] [Oxf., 1830], s. sh.   G.A. Oxon b. 111 (242)

1359. A letter . . . containing a few remarks on certain proctorial power [to commit to safe custody any known prostitute met with on the streets after dark] with reference to a late event at Cambridge. By a non-resident master of arts. Oxf. &c., 1847, 8°. 16 pp.

G. Pamph. 2904 (11)

1360. Report of the committee of [the Hebdomadal] Council appointed to inquire into the state of the police, 30th June 1862. n. pl., 1862, 8°. 4 pp.   G.A. Oxon c. 78 (219)

1361. Police of Oxford. [Statement by the Hebdomadal Council on the proposed consolidation of the University and City police forces.] [Oxf.], (1867), 8°. 7 pp.   G.A. Oxon 8° 105 (13)

1362. Report from the Committee appointed by the Council of the City of Oxford for conferring with the authorities of the University on the amalgamation of the police, to the Watch and ward committee. [Oxf.], 1867, fol. 3 pp.   G.A. Oxon c. 229 (5)

1363. For use of the Police committee [of the City of Oxford] only. Draft copy of Bill to establish a united constabulary force in Oxford and for other purposes. n. pl., [1867], 4°. 4 pp.   G.A. Oxon c. 229 (4)

1364. A bill for the establishment of a united constabulatory force in and for the University and City of Oxford. (Lond., 1868), fol. 11 pp.

G.A. Oxon c. 84 (552)

— Act. (31 & 32 V., c. 59, L. & P.) London., 1868, fol. 10 pp.   L.L.

— 44 & 45 V., c. 39, L. & P.

See 5849 [Transfer to General fund of the Police pension fund. 1869].

1365. Regulations for the proctors' servants. [Oxf.], 1875, s. sh.

G.A. Oxon c. 33 (170)

1366. For the Hebdomadal council only. Recommendations of the Vice-chancellor, pro-vice-chancellor and proctors [concerning the organiza-tion &c. of the proctors' police force]. [Feb. 23.] [Oxf., 1869], s. sh.

G.A. Oxon a. 18

— Committee on report of septem viri [March 4]. [Oxf.], (1869), s. sh.

G.A. Oxon a. 18

See 881 [The sin of our cities. Oxford. [Observations favouring restricting the power of University police and court over citizens.] 1893].

Oaths

See also 3594, &c. Religious Tests.
See 1125 [Oath to be taken by all graduates not to teach, &c. that it is lawful to take up arms against a Sovereign. 1622].

1367. 5. Elizabeth. The oath of supremacy to be taken by every one that is matriculated being sixteen years of age or more . . . [Madan 565.] [Oxf., c. 1625], s. sh.   Wood 515 (1)
— [Repr. c. 1640.] [Madan 948.]

1368. [A form certifying that the oaths appointed instead of the oath of allegiance and supremacy, have been taken and subscribed.] [Oxf., 17—], s. sh.   MS. Eng. lett. d. 77 (f. 100)
[The form referred to has been completed in the name of Rev. John Pointer, chaplain of Merton, in 1723/4.]

See 181 [A case of conscience, whether one may take oaths to King George, and yet favour the Pretender. 1749].

1369. Report of the committee appointed Nov. 16, 1835, 'to report to the Hebdomadal board whether any or what oaths in the Corpus statu-torum might with advantage be either altered or abrogated'. Dec. 12. [Oxf.], (1835), 4°. 3 pp.   G.A. Oxon 4° 188

1370. [Preliminary draft of copies of all oaths and forms of applications for graces &c., prepared in response to a House of Lords' order, and circulated to Heads of Houses before submission.] [Oxf., 1835], 4°. 7 pp.   G.A. Oxon b. 111 (280)

1371. [Order of the House of Lords, 6 Mar., 1835 requesting copies of all oaths and forms of application for graces. With the Report of the University.] [Oxf., 1835], fol. 7 pp.   G.A. Oxon c. 51 (119)
— [Another ed. With translations. Entitled] Report from the Univer-sity to an order of the House of Lords [&c.] 19 Mar., 1835. 10 pp.

G.A. Oxon c. 25 (9)

— [Another ed.] 31 Mar., 1835. 8 pp.   G.A. Oxon b. 22

1372. The following hints upon the alterations proposed in the statutes relating to oaths are respectfully submitted to members of Convoca-tion, by one of their body. Oxf., [1836], 4°. 3 pp.

G.A. Oxon c. 52 (29)

1373. SEWELL, W., Oaths to obey statutes, a sermon. Oxf. &c., 1852,
    8°. 34 pp.   100 i. 87 (14)

1374. For the Hebdomadal council only. Oaths and declarations committee
    . . . The committee recommend the following alterations in the statutes
    . . . [Oxf., 1868], fol. 6 pp.   G.A. Oxon a. 18

RESIDENCE

General

See also Degrees, 2274, &c. Handbooks, 1566 &c.

1375. [*Begin.*] William Shipley, B.A., of Christ-church . . . [Queries
    about residence, discipline, &c. arising from the application of William
    Shipley, B.A., for a dispensation for the absence of three terms in
    order to proceed to M.A.]. June 14, 1700 [really 1770]. [Oxf., 1770],
    s. sh.   Don. b. 12 (78)

1376. NAPLETON, J., Considerations on the residence usually required for
    degrees in the University of Oxford [by J. Napleton]. Oxf., 1772, 8°.
    24 pp.   G.A. Oxon 8° 61 (14)

1377. [A collection in the Bodleian of printed forms for use in applications
    for dispensations of residence etc. for degrees; in use during the 19th
    century.   G.A. Oxon 4° 220; G.A. Oxon b. 111 (237, 8).]

1378. Queries submitted to the members of Convocation. [9 queries
    about terms which should be kept by a B.A. wishing to become M.A.]
    Oxf., [c. 1800], s. sh.   G.A. Oxon b. 19

1379. COPLESTON, E., [*Begin.*] A member of Convocation, who . . .
    [A paper by E. Copleston against the decree to be proposed in
    Convocation on 20 Mar. for an indulgence of one term as a compliment
    to the king.] 21 Mar. Oxf., [1820], 4°. 3 pp.   G.A. Oxon b. 19

1380. TATHAM, E., [*Begin.*] The rector of Lincoln presents . . . [A paper
    opposing the proposed indulgence.] 21 Mar. Oxf., 1820, s. sh.
                                                            G.A. Oxon b. 19

1381. [*Begin.*] A member of Convocation having printed . . . [An answer
    to no. 1379.] 22 Mar. Oxf., 1820, 4°. 4 pp.   G.A. Oxon b. 19

1382. To the member of Convocation. [*Begin.*] In reply to certain ques-
    tions . . . [Another answer to no. 1379.] 22 Mar. Oxf., 1820, s. sh.
                                                            G.A. Oxon b. 19

1383. Members of Convocation cross-examined. [A paper signed 'q.' in
    favour of the proposed indulgence.] 22 Mar. Oxf., 1820, s. sh.
                                                            G.A. Oxon b. 19

1384. [*Begin.*] Most heartily concurring . . . [A paper against the proposed
    decree.] 23 Mar. Oxf., 1820, s. sh.   G.A. Oxon b. 19

1385. HEURTLEY, C. A., The proposed abrogation of the statute which required three weeks' residence for the degree of M.A. Oxf., (1859) 8°. 3 pp.   G.A. Oxon c. 75 (326)

1386. Memorandum on the boundaries of the University of Oxford, for the use of the Delegacy of unattached students [signed J. E. Thorold Rogers, G. S. Ward]. Nov. 6. [Oxf.], (1875), s. sh.
G.A. Oxon c. 33 (124)

1387. KITCHIN, G. W., Case for the decision of the question. What are the limits [i.e. boundaries] of residence, with a view to the keeping of Terms within the University? [signed G. W. K.]. [Oxf., 1875], 8°. 7 pp.
G.A. Oxon c. 33 (126)

1388. DYER, L., Oxford as it is, a guide to rules of collegiate residence and University requirements for degrees. Lond. &c., 1902, 8°. 42 pp.
G.A. Oxon 8° 683 (20)

1389. Absence of members of the University on military service or for reasons arising out of the war. Decrees and regulations. August 1915. [Oxf.], 1915, 8°. 11 pp.   G.A. Oxon 8° 1130* (1)
— May 1916.   G.A. Oxon 8° 1130* (2)

1390. General information concerning admission, residence [&c.]. Oxf., 1918– , 8°.   Per. 2626 e. 392

1391. Privileges granted on account of war service. [Regulations concerning residence and examinations.] [Oxf., 1919], 8°. 4 pp.
G.A. Oxon 8° 884 (9)

1392. University of Oxford. Absence due to the war; decrees and regulations in operation, Feb. 11, 1919. Oxf., 1919, 8. 20 pp.
G.A. Oxon 8° 884 (20)

1393. LEVENS, R. G. C., Residence for war degrees. (Oxf. mag., 1940, vol. 58, p. 335, 36.)   Per. G.A. Oxon 4° 141

See 6433.51 [Pantin, W., History of the relations of colleges with university in the matter of accommodation. 1964].

Matriculation

See also 3594, &c. Religious tests.
See 1367 [5. Elizabeth. The oath of supremacy to be taken by every one that is matriculated . . . c. 1625, &c.].
See 1056 [Observations on whether the statute De tempore et conditionibus matriculationis is or is not a 'Royal statute'. 1773].

1394. Congregation, Tuesday, May 22nd. [Statement on behalf of the Department for the training of teachers, urging the rejection of a proposed statute compelling all students, except members of Ruskin college, reading for a Diploma, to matriculate.] [Oxf., 1923], 4°. 2 pp.
G.A. Oxon b. 141 (143a)

See also 6433.38, &c.

1395.

Migration

1396. NEWTON, R., University education: or, An explication and amendment of the statute which . . . prohibits the admission of scholars going from one society to another, without the leave of their respective governors, or of their chancellor. Lond., 1726, 8°. 207 pp.
G. Pamph. 206 (1)
— 2nd. ed. Lond., 1733, 8°. 272 pp.   G.A. Oxon 8° 196

1397. AMHURST, N., A letter to . . . dr. Newton . . . occasion'd by his book entitled, University education, &c. (Appendix, Terrae-filius, 1726, vol. 2, p. 289–337)   Hope adds. 324
— (Appendix, Terrae-filius, 1726, vol. 2, 2nd ed., p. 129–181.)
Hope 8° 986
— (Appendix, Terrae-filius, 1754, 3rd ed., p. 277–324.)
G.A. Oxon 8° 307

1398. VARLEY, F. J., The case of William Seaman [who migrated from Hart Hall to Oriel college. Signed F. J. V.]. (Oriel record, 1928, vol. 5, p. 32–34.)   Per G.A. Oxon 4° 484

Incorporation

1399. GRIFFITHS, J., [Begin.] An official notice . . . [Comments on certain amendments proposed to be made to Tit. VI (IX), Sect. VII, De incorporatione et admissione exterorum.] Apr. 26. n. pl., (1861), s. sh.   G.A. Oxon c. 77 (143)

1400. Incorporation. [Regulations and fees.] [Oxf., 1864], s. sh.
G.A. Oxon c. 80 (410)

Terms and Vacations

1401. HARMAR, J., Vindiciæ Academiæ Oxoniensis, sive, Oratio apologetica, qua exercitiorum academicorum in trimestre vacatio a crimine vindicatur . . . [Madan 2581.] Oxon., 1662, 12°. 58 pp.   8° C 509 Linc.

1402. Alteration of Easter and Trinity terms [under the proposed statute. With table of dates, 1860–87]. [Oxf., 1860], s. sh.
G.A. Oxon c. 76 (79)

1403. The summer terms. The vote of Friday next [13th June, signed A college tutor]. [Oxf.], (1862), fol. 2 leaves.   G.A. Oxon b. 30

1404. Some objections to the 'proposed revolution' in connection with the summer term. [Oxf., 1862?], s. sh.   G.A. Oxon a. 29

1405. KITCHIN, G. W., A letter . . . on the summer term and commemoration week [and proposals to avoid the time wasted in revelry by readjusting the terms and examinations]. Oxf., (1869), 8°. 8 pp.
G.A. Oxon 8° 250 (13)

See 1888–91 [Discussion about re-arrangement of examinations in the summer term].

Lodging Houses, &c.

1406. Regulations of lodging houses for junior members of the University. n. pl., [1852], s. sh.   G.A. Oxon c. 68 (151)
— [c. 1855]   G.A. Oxon b. 21

1407. The Hebdomadal council and the Lodging statute. [Oxf.], (1867), 4°. 4 pp.   G.A. Oxon c. 83 (428)

1408. Lodging-house regulations [and] Application for lodging-house licence. [Provisionally adopted, 24 July 1868.] [Oxf.], (1868), 3 sh.
                                                    G.A. Oxon c. 84 (496)
— [Final form of regulations and licence.]   G.A. Oxon c. 84 (500)

1409. Lodger regulations. [A parody of the regulations issued by the Delegacy of lodging houses.] n. pl., [1868], fol. 2 sh.
                                                    G.A. Oxon c. 84 (490)

1410. [Begin.] This paper is issued by the Delegates for licensing lodging-houses, to supply information respecting the admission of unattached students, and the residence of students in lodgings. Aug. 5, 1868. (Oxf., 1868), 8°. 4 pp.   G.A. Oxon c. 84 (268)

1411. Lodging-houses licensed. Mich. term, 1868–Mich. term, 1916. [Oxf.], 1868–1916, fol. & 4°.   G.A. Oxon 4° 245

1412. For the use of the Hebdomadal council. Committee on the delegacy of lodging houses. [Recommended alterations to the statutes.] [Oxf., 1869], 4°. 4 pp.   G.A. Oxon a. 18

1413. For the use of the Hebdomadal council. Committee on the delegacy for licensing lodgings. [Another form of no. 1412.] [Oxf., 1869], 4°. 3 pp.   G.A. Oxon a. 18

1414. Report of the Delegati ad aedes licentiandas. Oxf., 1869, 8°. 16 pp.
                                                    G.A. Oxon 8° 250 (9)

1415. BURGON, J. W., Strictly private . . . Our present lodging-house system, immoral: and requiring reform. n. pl., (1876), 8° 7 pp.
                                                    G.A. Oxon b. 140 (34e)

1416. BURGON, J. W., The late vicar of S. Mary's in explanation; a few words on the lodging-house question, a letter. Oxf., 1876, 8°. 8 pp.
                                                    G.A. Oxon 8° 164 (11)

1417. Saint and soubrette, or 'Chops and tomato sauce!' A brief reply to Mr. Burgon's attack on the Oxford lodging-houses. Oxf., 1876, 8°. 8 pp.   G.A. Oxon 8° 286 (4)

1418. GRIFFITH, E. F. G. University of Oxford. Lodging-house delegacy. Report on the sanitary condition of the lodging-houses. Oxf., 1881, 8°. 36 pp.   G.A. Oxon 8° 296 (4)

1419. Report of the Delegacy for licensing lodging-houses on the sanitary inspection of lodging-houses, 1881–82. Oxford, (1882), 8°. 44 pp.
                                                    G.A. Oxon 4° 399a (8)

1420. SHADWELL, C. L., Residence in lodgings. [Historical account by
C. L. Shadwell.] [Oxf., 1900], fol. 2 leaves.   G.A. Oxon b. 14

1421. [Form of] Memorandum of agreement . . . between . . . [the]
holder of a licence issued by the Delegates of lodging houses . . . and
. . . [the] undergraduate student . . . [Oxf., 1915], s. sh.
G.A. Oxon c. 249 (1)

1422. CHILD, G. W., The proposed statute on lodging houses. [A letter
signed G. W. Child.] [Oxf., 1881], 8°. 8 pp.   G.A. Oxon 8° 1055 (12)

1423. Accommodation in Oxford after the war. (Oxf. mag., 1945, vol. 63,
p. 160–62.)   Per G.A. Oxon 4° 141

1423.5. WENDEN, D. J., The new graduate flats. (Oxf. mag., 1966,
p. 361–63).   Per G.A. Oxon 4° 141

ECCLESIASTICAL PREFERMENT AND PATRONAGE

1424. An act to vest in the two universities the presentations of benefices
belonging to papists. (1 W. & M., sess. 1, c. 26, Pub.) Lond., 1689,
fol. 8 pp.   L.L.
— 12 Anne, sess. 2, c. 14, Pub.
— 1 & 2 V., c. 106, Pub.
— 32 & 33 V., c. 109, Pub.

See 7047, 7048 [Presentation to livings. 1889].

1424.5. PHILIP, I. G., Queen Mary Tudor's benefaction [of three impropriate rectories] to the University. (Bodleian library record, 1954,
vol. 5, p. 27–37.)   Per 2590 d. Oxf. 1. 41=R.

See also 6468–70.

FINANCE AND PROPERTY

General

See also 6134, &c. University chest.

1425. An act for enabling the two universities [&c.] to hold in perpetuity
their copy right in books given or bequeathed to the said universities.
(15 G. III, c. 53, Pub.) Lond., 1775, fol. 10 pp.   L.L.

1426. An act for granting to his majesty an additional duty upon almanacks . . . and for allowing a certain annual sum . . . to each of the
universities of Oxford and Cambridge in lieu of the money heretofore
paid . . . by the Company of stationers . . . for the privilege of printing
almanacks. (21 G. III, c. 56, Pub.) Lond., 1780, fol. 8 pp.   L.L.

1427. [Convocation notice of 22 March 1841 proposing to discharge the
estate of Langdon Hills from the obligation of £1,846. 5s. 4d. advanced
as a loan, and to pay the several readers in moral philosophy their full
annuity of £100 for the last 8 years, which the estate is intended to
provide.] [Oxf.], 1841, s. sh.   G.A. Oxon 4° 255

1428. PUSEY, E. B., On the proposed vote of £53,100 [signed A doctor of divinity, i.e. E. B. Pusey]. [Oxf.], (1851), 4°. 4 pp. G.A. Oxon b. 27

1429. [*Begin.*] On Thursday, Oct. 25th . . . [Circular protesting against a proposed statute sanctioning the investment of University funds in securities other than Consols and Exchequer bills.] [Oxf., 1860], s. sh.
G.A. Oxon c. 76 (298)

See 1764 [Report of commissioners appointed to inquire into the property and income of the Universities of Oxford and Cambridge. 1874].
See 1926 [Statistics relating to the Press fund. 1876].

1430. An account [*afterw.*] Register of the estates and other properties of the University of Oxford administered by the curators of the University chest. Oxf., 1879– , 4°.
[The Bodleian set is imperfect: G.A. Oxon c. 32.]

See 1930 [Common university fund. 1886].

1431. Contemporary statistics. [A defence of University expenditure from an attack by Joseph King in The Contemporary Review, no. 1794.] (Oxf. mag., 1892, vol. 11, p. 65, 66.) Per. G.A. Oxon 4° 141

See 1811 [Finance. 1909].

1432. Licence in mortmain to the Chancellor, masters and scholars of the University of Oxford [to hold lands &c. to the value of £10,000 a year beyond those already possessed. 20 Apr., 1860]. [Oxf., 1909], fol. 4 pp.
G.A. Oxon c. 107 (6)

See 2454 [Stewart, J. A., Notes on Amendments from the point of view of a delegate of the Common university fund. 1910].

1433. The War budget and the University. (Oxf. mag., 1914, vol. 33, p. 40, 41.) Per. G.A. Oxon 4° 141

1434. MCCALLUM, R. B., Oxford and the financial crisis. (Oxf. mag., 1931, vol. 50, p. 13, 14.) Per. G.A. Oxon 4° 141

1435. W3 *pseud.*, Accounts. [A humourous article.] (Oxf. mag., 1938, vol. 56, p. 639, 40.) Per. G.A. Oxon 4° 141

1436. THOMPSON, J. H. C., University finance. [An account of its administration.] (Oxford, 1954, vol. 13, no. 2, p. 54–62.)
Per. G.A. Oxon 8° 1141

1436.3. BLEANEY, B., University finance. (Oxf. mag., 1965, N.S., vol. 5, p. 408, 09.) Per. G.A. Oxon 4° 141

1436.31. KEEN, H. H., University finance. (Oxf. mag., 1965, vol. 6, p. 8, 9.) Per. G.A. Oxon 4° 141

Accounts

1437. Computus [&c. University revenue and expenditure 'memorandum' book. *c.* 1700]. Bliss B 411

1438. The general account of the University from Nov. 6, 1855 to Nov. 6, 1856. [Oxf.], 1856, fol. 4 pp.   G.A. Oxon c. 72 (380)

See 1929 [Statute concerning the form, audit, and publication of the accounts of the University. 1882].

1439. Abstracts of the accounts of the curators of the University chest and of University institutions, together with the accounts of the colleges for the year ending Dec. 31, 1883– . Oxf., 1884– , fol.
G.A. Oxon c. 86, 87

1440. GIBSON, S., ed., The oldest account book of the University of Oxford [1357, 1358]. (Engl. hist. review, 1909, vol. 24, p. 735–43.)
Per 2231 d. 342=K.
— Repr.   G.A. Oxon 4° 281

1441. PHILIP, I. G., Early accounts of the University of Oxford. (Accountant, 1953, p. 131–35.)   Per 1808 d. 24

1442. PHILIP, I. G., [Notes on some financial documents of the University, 15th–18th century]. (Annual report, Delegates of Privileges, 1965/66. 7 pp. Suppl. 3 to the Univ. Gazette, vol. 97, Dec. 1966.)
Per. G.A. Oxon c. 86

Appeals

1443. Statements of the needs of the University, being replies to a circular letter addressed by the vice chancellor on Feb. 20, 1902, to heads of institutions and departments, to boards of faculties and to professors and readers. Oxf., 1902, 8°. 168 pp.   G.A. Oxon 8° 692

1444. [Begin.] The following statement . . . [by various professors and heads of departments of the cost at which, in their opinion, the most conspicuous existing deficiencies may be met]. [Oxf., 1902], 8°. 14 pp.
G.A. Oxon b. 141 (23c)

1445. The needs of our oldest university. (Nature, 1905, vol. 72, p. 231, 32.)   Radcl.

1446. Strictly confidential. The needs of Oxford. [Outline of scheme to assist the University to raise £250,000 over the next few years.] [Oxf., 1907], fol. 4 pp.   MS. Top. Oxon c. 236 (f. 74, 75)
— [Proof sheets. Nov. 1906.]   MS. Top. Oxon c. 236 (f. 73)

1447. Oxford university appeal fund. Report of London meeting, May 16, 1907. Lond., 1907, 8°. 36 pp.   G.A. Oxon c. 116

1448. Oxford university appeal fund. [Miscellaneous papers, 1907–1909.]
G.A. Oxon c. 116

1449. The Oxford University endowment fund. [Report, and articles thereon, after the first quinquennium.] (Oxf. mag., 1913, vol. 32, p. 10, 11; 41, 42; 104, 105; 125.)   Per G.A. Oxon 4° 141

1450. Financial needs of the University. [Review by the Hebdomadal council setting out statements made by the Boards of Faculties.] [Oxf., 1932], 8°. 20 pp.   G.A. Oxon b. 141 (181*a*)

1451. Oxford university appeal. Needs of the University [and] Statement from the American appeal committee. (Amer. Oxon., 1937, vol. 24, p. 1–15.)   Per G.A. Oxon 8° 889

1452. Oxford university, a programme of development. A short account of what has so far been achieved and what the University still hopes to do. [Appeal for money.] Oxf., 1938, 8°. 20 pp.   G.A. Oxon 8° 1132 (21)

1453. The Oxford historic buildings appeal. [June.] (Oxf., 1957), 4°. 4 pp.   G.A. Oxon 4° 744
— [Another appeal, with same title.] 1 November. (Oxf., 1957), s. sh.
                                               G.A. Oxon 4° 744

1454. DICK, M. W., Oxford historic buildings appeal. [Historical account to accompany the appeal. Signed M. W. D.] (Oxf.), [1957], 4°. 8 pp.
                                               G.A. Oxon 4° 744

1455. Oxford historic buildings fund. First (–   ) Report of the Trustees. [Oxf., 1959–], 4°.   Per G.A. Oxon 4° 782

1455.3. The work of the Oxford historic buildings appeal. (Oxford, 1963, vol. 18, p. 70–80.)   Per G.A. Oxon 8° 1141

Board of finance

1456. The proposed Board of finance. [Arguments against the proposed statute signed by A. J. Butler and 4 others, representing a committee of college bursars. May 10.] [Oxf.], (1911), s. sh.
                                               G.A. Oxon c. 310 (63)

1457. CASE, T., The relation of the proposed statute on finance to the Commissioners' statutes for the University and colleges under the Universities . . . act, 1877. [Oxf., 1911], 8°. 11 pp.
                                               G.A. Oxon b. 140 (181*b*)

1458. CASE, T., The proposed statute concerning a Board of finance [signed T. Case]. Feb. 10, 1912. [Oxf.], (1912), 8°. 45 pp.
                                               G.A. Oxon c. 310 (82)

1459. CASE, T., The proposed statute concerning a Board of finance and the opinion of the standing counsel of the University [signed T. Case]. Feb. 24, 1912. [Oxf.], (1912), 8°. 18 pp.   G.A. Oxon c. 310 (84)

1460. ANSON, SIR W. R., and GELDART, W. M., The proposed Board of finance. [An answer to T. Case, signed W. R. A. and W. M. G.] Mar. 1 [Oxf.], (1912), 8°. 7 pp.   G.A. Oxon c. 310 (90)

1461. CASE, T., A conspectus of the legal powers of the University in matters of finance and the proposed statute concerning a Board of finance [signed T. Case]. Mar. 2nd 1912. [Oxf.], (1912), 8°. 14 pp.
                                               G.A. Oxon c. 310 (91)

1462. CASE, T., The proposed statute concerning a Board of finance, a reply [signed T. Case to a paper by W. R. Anson and W. M. Geldart]. Mar. 4th 1912. [Oxf.], (1912), 8°. 11 pp.   G.A. Oxon c. 310 (92)

1463. University of Oxford. Board of finance. Proceedings for 1917. [Oxf., 1918], 8°. 45 pp.   G.A. Oxon 8° 884 (24)

College contributions

See 6467 [Questions submitted to colleges. 1875].

1464. A statute . . . concerning college contributions for University purposes. (Univ. of Oxf. and Cambr. act, 1877. Oxford. Statutes made by the Univ. of Oxf. commissioners, 1881, p. 1–4.)
Pp. Eng. 1882 vol. 51

1465. Concerning college contributions for University purposes, supplemental statute. (Univ. of Oxf. and Cambr. act, 1877. Oxford. Two statutes made by the Univ. of Oxf. commissioners, 1881, p. 3.)
Pp. Eng. 1882 vol. 51

See 8629 [Case concerning the contribution of Wadham college for University purposes. 1886].

1466. ARMSTRONG, E., A proposal for the alteration of Statute 6, paragraph 3, of the financial statutes made by the University commissioners [signed E. Armstong sic]. Oxf., [1887?], 8°. 9 pp.   G.A. Oxon 8° 424

1467. ARMSTRONG, E., Remarks on the case for the University as to the mode of assessing the college contribution for University purposes [signed E. Armstrong]. n. pl., [1887?], 4°. 7 pp.
G.A. Oxon 4° 186 (17)

1468. [A letter, signed C. B. Heberden, vice-chancellor, dated Dec. 2, 1912, addressed to the colleges, beginning] The Hebdomadal council proposes to take the opinion of the Standing Counsel to the University upon the questions raised in the memorandum below . . . [concerning college 'Disposal of revenue' statutes and any amendment thereto]. [Oxf.], (1912), 8°. 3 pp.   G.A. Oxon c. 153

1469. Proposed memorial to the Hebdomadal council from one hundred members of Congregation [asking for an amendment to Stat. tit. x sect. III § 4, to place the procedure with regard to property on the same level as that for money. Signed W. R. Anson and 17 others.] [Oxf., 1912?], 2 sheets.   G.A. Oxon c. 310 (117)

1470. [Case and opinion of counsel] re college contributions for university purposes. [Oxf.], (1913), 8°. 5 pp.   G.A. Oxon c. 153

Estate acts

1471. [Begin.] A Proposal having been made by the earl of Radnor [to be submitted to Convocation, for an exchange of the estate at Nunton and Bodenham, Wilts, left to the University by the late canon

Bampton, for Tinkersole farm estate, Wing, Bucks] March 26.
[Oxf.] 1804, s. sh.   Don b. 12 (100a)
— [Further particulars.] Mar. 11. [*Begin.*] The exchange proposed last
year . . . [Oxf.], 1805, s. sh.   Don b. 12 (105b)

1472. An act for effectuating an exchange [of land at Nunton and Bodenham, Wilts, for land at Wing, Bucks] between the . . . University of
Oxford and . . . Jacob, earl of Radnor. (45 G. III, c. 82, Private.)
n. pl., 1805, fol. 11 pp.   L.L.

1473. A bill to authorize the raising money on mortgage of the possessions
and revenues of the universities of Oxford and Cambridge, or of the
several colleges or halls therein, to defray the expense of buildings for
the lodging and accommodation of an increased number of students.
31 May. [Lond.], 1825, fol. 5 pp.   Pp. Eng. 1825 vol. 1
— [Another ed.] 6 pp.   G.A. Oxon c. 41 (67b)

1474. A bill to authorize exchanges, to a limited extent, of the land and
possessions of . . . the several colleges or halls within the universities
of Oxford and Cambridge . . . and . . . of the said universities. 27 May.
[Lond.], 1825, fol. 14 pp.   Pp. Eng. 1825 vol. 1
— as amended by the committee. 15 Mar. [Lond.], 1826, fol. 13 pp.
                                  Pp. Eng. 1826 vol. 1

1475. Oxford college estates. A bill to give to colleges in the University of
Oxford power to sell and exchange lands, under certain conditions.
27 June 1856. [Lond.], 1856, s. sh.   Pp. Eng. 1856 vol. 5
— Lords amendments to the Oxford college estates bill. [Lond.],
1856, s. sh.   Pp. Eng. 1856 vol. 5

1476. An act to give to the University of Oxford and to the colleges . . .
power to sell and exchange lands, under certain conditions. (19 & 20
V., c. 95.) Lond., 1856, fol. 3 pp.   L.L.

— 21 & 22 V., c. 44, Pub.   — 5 G.V, c. 22, Pub.
— 23 & 24 V., c. 59, Pub.   — 15 & 16 G.V, c. 24, Pub.
— 43 & 44 V., c. 46, Pub.   — 2 & 3 G. VI, c. 106, Pub.
— 61 & 62 V., c. 55, Pub.

1477. A bill to give to the universities of Oxford and Cambridge and the
colleges in those universities . . . power to sell [&c.] lands under certain
conditions, and also to grant leases [&c.]. 4 May 1858. [Lond.], 1858,
fol. 23 pp.   Pp. Eng. 1857/58 vol. 3
— Lords amendments. [Lond.], 1858, fol. 4 pp.
                        Pp. Eng. 1857/58 vol. 4
— [Act.] (21 & 22 V., c. 44, Pub.)   L. L.

1478. University and college estates act &c. amendment bill. A bill to
extend the provisions of the University and colleges estates act, 1858
[21 & 22 V., c. 44, Pub.] and also the provisions of the act passed in
the 3rd and 4th years of her majesty, chapter 113, so far as the same
relate to universities and colleges. 1 Aug., 1859. [Lond.], 1859, fol.
5 pp.   Pp. Eng. 1859, sess. 2 vol. 2

1479. Universities and college estates bill. A bill to extend the provisions
of the Universities estates act, 1858, and of the Copyhold acts, and
of the act of the 3rd and 4th years of the reign of her majesty, chapter
113, and of the 17th and 18th years of the same reign, chapter 84, so
far as the same relate to universities and colleges. 25 May, 1860. [Lond.],
1860, fol. 7 pp.   Pp. Eng. 1860 vol. 6
— [Act.] (23 & 24 V., c. 59, Pub.)   L.L.

1480. Universities and Colleges estates act amendment. A bill intituled
An act to amend the Universities and College estates act, 1858. 7 July
1880. [Lond.], 1880, fol. 4 pp.   Pp. Eng. 1880 vol. 7
— [Act.] (43 & 44 V., c. 46, Pub.)   L.L.

1481. SKENE, W. B., ed., Handbook of certain acts affecting the universities of Oxford and Cambridge and the colleges therein in the sale,
acquisition and administration of property. Lond., 1894, 8°. 140 pp.
                                                               L.L.
— 2nd ed., enlarged. 1898. 152 pp.   L.L.

1482. Committee on the Universities and college estates acts. Report of
the departmental committee appointed by the Board of Agriculture
to inquire into the working of the Universities and college estates acts,
1858 to 1880, and to report whether any, and if so what, amendments
therein are desirable . . . [and] II. Minutes of evidence, appendices and
index. Lond., 1897, fol. 11+68 pp.   Pp. Eng. 1897 vol. 45

1483. Draft of a bill to amend the Universities and college estates acts,
1858 to 1880. [With] Memorandum. [Lond.], 1898, fol. 7+18 pp.
                                 G.A. Oxon c. 107 (77, 78)

1484. Universities and college estates. A bill to amend the Universities
and college estates acts, 1858 to 1880. [Lond.], 1898, fol. 7 pp.
                                                   Pp. Eng. 1898 vol. 7
— [Act.] (61 & 62 V., c. 55, Pub.)   L.L.

1485. Report from the standing committee on law and courts of justice
and legal procedure, on the Universities and college estates bill; with
the proceedings of the committee. 14 June 1898. Lond., 1898, fol.
7 pp.   Pp. Eng. 1898 vol. 12

1486. GAMLEN, W. B., ed., The Universities and college estates acts 1858
to 1880, and 1898. Oxf. &c., 1898, 8°. 64 pp.   L.L.

1487. SHADWELL, C. L., Dissertatio pro gradu doctoris in jure civili in
qua de statutis regni universitatum et collegiorum fundos concernenti-
bus annis Victoriae XXImo usque ad XLIVum editis tractatur. Oxon.,
1898, 8°. 35 pp.   L.L.
— [Reissue, entitled] The universities and college estates acts, 1858 to
1880, their history and results. Oxf. &c., 1898, 8°. 35 pp.   L.L.

1488. A bill to amend the Universities and college estates acts and to
extend the powers of the universities of Oxford and Cambridge and

the colleges therein to make statutes for purposes connected with the present war. Lond., 1915, fol. 6 pp.   Pp. Eng. 1914/16 vol. 3
— [Act.] (5 G. V, c. 22, Pub.) (Lond.), 1915, 8°. 6 pp.   L.L.

1489. An act to consolidate the Universities and college estates acts, 1858 to 1898, and enactments amending those acts. (15 G.V, c. 24, Pub.) (Lond.), 1925, 8°. 38 pp.   L.L.

1490. A bill intituled An act to consolidate the Universities and colleges estates acts, 1858 to 1898, and enactments amending those acts. 27 March 1925. Lond., 1925, 4°. 37 pp.   Pp. Eng. 1924/25 vol. 5
— [Act.] (15 & 16 G.V, c. 24, Pub.)   L.L.

1491. A bill to provide, in connexion with the present emergency, for amending the Universities and colleges estates act, 1925, and for extending the powers of . . . Oxford and Cambridge, and the colleges therein to make statutes. 7 Sept. 1939. Lond., 1939, 4°. 7 pp.
          Pp. Eng. 1938/39 vol. 5
— [Act.] (2 & 3 G.VI, c. 106, Pub.)   L.L.

1492. Universities and colleges (trusts). A bill to make provision as to trust property held by or on behalf of certain universities and colleges or for purposes connected with those universities and colleges. Lond., 1943, 8°. 3 pp.   Pp. Eng. 1942/43 vol. 1
— [Act.] (6 & 7 G.VI, c. 9, Pub.)   L.L.

Fees and dues

See 1501 [Alteration of fees. 1804].

1493. University dues to be charged on the books of the several colleges and halls. [Oxf.], 1833, s. sh.   G.A. Oxon b. 22

1494. Some unofficial explanations respecting the statute 'De feodis'. [Oxf., 1855], 4°. 8 pp.   G.A. Oxon c. 71 (135**)

1495. On the principles of University taxation [revision of fees and dues]. [Signed A member of council.] [Oxf., 1855], fol. 4 pp.
          G.A. Oxon b. 28

1496. Information collected by a committee of the Hebdomadal council . . . appointed to inquire . . . into the fees and dues paid to the University and its officers. n. pl., 1855, 4°. 19 pp.   G.A. Oxon c. 71 (135*)

1497. Tabula feodorum, &c. &c. n. pl., 1855, s. sh.
          G.A. Oxon c. 71 (196)
— 1860   G.A. Oxon c. 76 (166)
— [3 other undated Tabulae issued between 1860? and 1890?]
          G.A. Oxon b. 137 (18, 19, 21)

1498. [Proposal submitted to Convocation, 6th Dec., that in consideration of the recent reduction of annual dues from £1. 6. 0. to £1. 0. 0, the vice chancellor be authorised to repay the several colleges a proportion of the sum received in composition for every person who has compounded.] Nov. 27, 1866. n. pl., 1866, s. sh.   G.A. Oxon c. 82 (308)

1499. [*Begin.*] Dear Sir, For some time past . . . [Proposal, signed by R. B. Clifton and 10 other heads of scientific departments, for a uniform system of collecting laboratory fees from undergraduates.] [Oxf.], (1896), 4°. 3 pp. G.A. Oxon b. 139 (98*a*)

1500. [Letter to Heads of colleges, signed C. B. Heberden, Vice-chancellor, explaining the proposals of the Hebdomadal council for the revision of the scale of fees and dues payable to the University. May 20.] [Oxf.], (1911), 8°. 3 pp. G.A. Oxon b. 140 (172*c*)

See 2328 [University dues and the M.A. degree fee. 1933].

Salaries and pensions

1501. The following proposals for augmenting the income of certain officers of the University, and regulating certain payments, charged upon the books of the several colleges and halls, are submitted to . . . Convocation. June 11. [Oxf.], 1804, s. sh. Don. b. 12 (102)

See 5849 [Transfer to General fund of the Police pension fund. 1869].
See 949 [Act limiting tenure of certain university and college emoluments. 1880].
See 1934 [Gardner, P., Professorial pensions at Oxford. 1913].

1502. BOYD, J., A sensible pensions scheme. (Oxf. mag., 1950, vol. 69, p. 128–30.) Per G.A. Oxon 4° 141

1503. WILES, P. J. D., Inflation and the FSSU. (Oxf. mag., 1952, vol. 70, p. 195, 96.) Per G.A. Oxon 4° 141

See 6466 [Colleges and University stipends. 1955].

1503.2. KREBS, SIR H., The flexibility of salaries. (Oxf. mag., 1961, N.S., vol. 1, p. 382, 83.) Per G.A. Oxon 4° 141

See 1937.51 [Krebs, Sir H., The salaries of Demonstrators. 1961].

Tithes

1504. An acte concernyng the exoneracyon of Oxford and Cambrydg from payment of there fyrst frutes and tenthe. (27 Hen. VIII, c. 42, Private.) 1535/36.

[Text in Shadwell's Enactments &c. See no. 956.]

See 6473 [Decimae et primitae collegiorum. 1781].

1505. Memorandum on the Tithe bill, 1925, submitted by the Universities and colleges of Oxford and Cambridge. n. pl., [1925], 4°. 3 pp. 1229 d. 11 (1)

1506. Memorandum on tithe, submitted to the Minister of Agriculture by a committee representing the Universities and colleges of Oxford and Cambridge . . . and other charitable corporations owning tithe. n. pl., (1925), 4°. 4 pp. 1229 d. 11 (3)

1507. Memorandum on the Tithe bill as affecting the colleges of Oxford and Cambridge. n. pl., (1925), s. sh. 1229 d. 11 (4)

1508. [Reprint of a letter, signed H. A. L. Fisher and J. J. Thomson, which appeared in The Times, 10 Aug. 1925, headed] The Tithe bill; claims of charitable corporations. n. pl., [1925], s. sh.   1229 d. 11 (2)

1509. SYNNOT, R. HART-, The passing of tithes. (Oxf. mag., 1936, vol. 54, p. 600, 01.)   Per Oxon G.A. 4° 141

Taxation

See also 6470, &c.

1510. Oxford and Cambridge universities. An account of the number of matriculations and degrees conferred . . . for three years (1831–33) with the amount of stamp duty paid thereon. [Lond.], 1834, s. sh.
Pp. Eng. 1834 vol. 43

1511. University matriculations . . . Return 'of the rates of stamp duty upon matriculations in the universities of Oxford [&c.]'. [Lond.], 1854, s. sh.   Pp. Eng. 1854 vol. 50

1512. University degrees . . . Returns of the rates of duty upon the several degrees as conferred by the universities of Oxford [&c.]. [Lond.], 1854, s. sh.   Pp. Eng. 1854 vol. 50

1513. Stamp duties repeal on matriculation and degrees. A bill to repeal the stamp duties payable on matriculation and degrees in the University of Oxford. 5 June 1855. [Lond.], 1855, s. sh.
Pp. Eng. 1854/55 vol. 6
— Act. (18 & 19 V., c. 36, Pub.)   L.L.

1514. Re Common university fund. [Correspondence between the University Chest and the Inland Revenue concerning income-tax assessment.] Apr. 26. [Oxf.], (1890), fol. 4 pp.   G.A. Oxon c. 153

University Grants Committee

1515. Applications for government grants. [Paper signed by C. F. Jenkin and 15 others stating the general requirements of the Natural science departments, and approving a government inquiry into University resources.] [Oxf., 1919], 8°. 3 pp.   G.A. Oxon b. 141 (111a)

1516. VEALE, SIR D., University grants. (Fortnightly, 1952, vol. 177, p. 37–42.)   Per 3977 d. 59

1517. Government assistance to universities in Great Britain, memoranda [Oxford passim] submitted by H. W. Dodds, L. M. Hacker, L. Rogers. (Comm. on financing higher educ.) New York, 1952, 8°. 133 pp.
2625 d. 135

1518. University grants committee. Returns from universities and university colleges in receipt of treasury grant, academic year 1950–1951. (Oxford passim.) Lond., 1952, 8°. 44 pp.
Pp. Eng. 1951/52 vol. 20
— 1951–52. Lond., 1953, 8°. 44 pp.   Pp. Eng. 1952/53 vol. 19
— 1952–1953. Lond., 1954, 8° 44 pp.   Pp. Eng. 1953/54 vol. 19

1519. University grants committee. University development. Interim report on the years 1947 to 1951. (Oxf. univ. *passim*.) Lond., 1952, 8°. 28 pp.   Pp. Eng. 1951/52 vol. 18
— Report. 1947 to 1952. Lond., 1953, 8°. 93 pp.
                                               Pp. Eng. 1952/53 vol. 17

1520. Application for quinquennial grant made to the University grants committee in September 1951 (for 1952–7). [Oxf., 1951], 8°. 224 pp.
                                               G.A. Oxon 8° 1441

1521. Application for the quinquennium 1957/62. 2 pt. [Oxf., 1956–], fol.
                                               G.A. Oxon c. 337

1522.

FIRE PRECAUTIONS

1523. Orders and directions agreed upon by his majesties Justices of the peace of the University and City of Oxford . . . for the prevention of the danger of fire. [Madan 2899.] [Oxf., 1671], s. sh.
                                               Wood 276a (314)

1524. Orders agreed upon by the heads of Houses for the preventing and quenching of fire. [Madan 2901.] [Oxf., 1671], s. sh.
                                               Wood 276a (316)

1525. [March 20, 1809. Report, approved by heads of Houses, and proctors, on the best method of guarding the University against fire.] [Oxf.], (1809), 4°. 4 pp.   G.A. Oxon b. 19

VISITATIONS

1526. An ordinance of the Lords and Commons . . . for the visitation and reformation of the Universitie of Oxford . . . With the names of the committee and visitors. [Madan 1920.] Lond., 1647, 4°. 6 pp.
                                               G. Pamph. 2288 (12)

1527. [*Begin.*] Nos quorum nomina . . . [A citation by the Parliamentary visitors, summoning the University to appear before them.] [Madan 1923.] [Lond.], (1647), s. sh.   Wood 514 (28)

1528. The sworne confederacy between the Convocation at Oxford and the Tower of London [an attack upon the proceedings of leading members of the University who were organising opposition to the Visitors, by F. Cheynell?]. [Madan 1924.] Lond., 1647, 4°. 12 pp.
                                               C 14. 14 Linc.

1529. SANDERSON, R., *bp. of Lincoln*, Reasons of the present judgement of the Vniversity of Oxford concerning The solemne league and covenant, The negative oath, The ordinances concerning discipline and worship. Approved by generall consent in a full Convocation,

1 Jun. 1647. [By R. Sanderson]. [Madan 1926.] [Lond.], 1647, 4°.
44 pp.   Wood 514 (31)
— [Another ed.] [Madan 1927.]   Antiq. f. E. 1647. 1
— [Another ed.] [Madan 1928.]   Pamph. C 80 (40)
— [Another ed.] [Madan 1929.]
— [Another ed.] [Madan 1929*].   G. Pamph. 1053 (10)
— [Another ed.] [Madan 1930.]   B.M.
— [Another ed.] [Madan 1930*.]
— [Another ed.] [Madan 2475.] Lond., 1660, 8°. 35 pp.
— [Another ed.] Repr. 32 pp. [Madan 2475*.]   G.A. Oxon 8° 158
— [Another ed.] 1678. [Madan 3167.]
— [Another ed.] Lond., 1749, 8°. 51 pp.   Gough Oxf. 80
— [Another ed.] (Somers' tracts, 2nd coll., vol. 1, p. 476.) 1750.
                                       GG 136 Art.
— [Another ed.] (Somers' tracts, 2nd ed., vol. 4, p. 606). 1810.
                                      Σ III. 14

1530. SANDERSON, R., *bp. of Lincoln*, Judicium Universitatis Oxoniensis,
de 1. Solenni liga & fœdere. 2. Juramento negativo. 3. Ordinationibus
parlamenti circa disciplinam & cultum, in plena Convocatione i. Junii
1647 . . . promulgatum. [By R. Sanderson. Transl.]. [Madan 1999.]
[Lond.], 1648, 12°. 112 pp.   Mar. 338
— [Another ed.] a Roberto Sandersono. [Madan 2874.] Lond.,
1671, 8°. 64 pp.   G.A. Oxon 8° 266
— [Another ed.] 1682.   Crynes 372
— [Another ed.] 1710.   Antiq. f. E. 1710. 1 (3)
— [Another ed.] 1719.   14198 f. 187

1531. SANDERSON, R., *bp. of Lincoln*, Iugement de l'Vniversité d'Oxford
sur la Lige & Convenant d'Angleterre & d'Escosse. Le sermen négatif
contre le roy. Et les ordonnances touchant la discipline & le service
divin. Approué par . . . Convocation, le 1. Iuin, 1647. [By R. Sander-
son]. Trad. [Madan 2000.] n. pl., 1648, 4°. 45 pp.

1532. CROFTON, Z., Ἀνάληψις Ἀνελήφθη; . . . against . . . the Reasons
of the University . . . for not taking . . . the Solemn league and covenant. Lond., 1660, 4°. 159 pp.   Pamph. C 111 (28)

1533. The remonstrance of the kingdome of England, to the vniversities
of Oxford and Cambridge. With a review of the Covenant. [Madan
1966.] n. pl., 1647, 4°. 4 pp.   Wood 612 (69)

1534. A letter from a scholar in Oxford to his friend in the countrey,
shewing what progresse the visitors have made in the reformation of
that university, and what it is that obstructs it. [Madan 1936.] [Lond.],
1647, 4°. 8 pp.   Gough Oxf. 8 (5)

1535. FELL, J., The privileges of the University of Oxford, in point of
visitation: cleerly evidenced by letter [by J. Fell]. Together with the
Universities answer to the summons of the visitors. [Madan 1955.]
[Lond.], 1647, 4°. 9 pp.   Gough Oxf. 80 (8)
— [Another issue.] [Madan 1956.]   Gough Oxf. 107 (5)

1536. PRYNNE, W., The Vniversity of Oxfords plea refuted. Or, A full answer to a late printed paper [by J. Fell] intituled The priviledges of the Vniversity of Oxford in point of visitation. Together with the Vniversities answer to the summons of the visitors. [Madan 1960.] Lond., 1647, 4°. 68 pp.   Gough Oxf. 107 (6)

1537. WARING, R., An account of mr. Pryn's refutation of the Vniversity of Oxfords plea [signed Basilius Philomusus]. [Madan 1961.] [Lond.], 1648, 4°. 12 pp.   Gough Oxf. 8 (7)

1538. BAGSHAW, E., A short censure of the book of W. P[rynne] entituled The University of Oxford's plea, refuted [by E. Bagshaw]. [Madan 1962.] [Lond.], 1648, 4°. 14 pp.   Gough Oxf. 68 (6)

1539. To the Honourable Visitours appointed . . . for the regulating and reforming of the Vniversity of Oxford. The petition of your friends and servants in the said Vniversity. Iune 2, 1647. [Followed by] Die Veneris. 18. Feb. 1647 [proclamation by Parliament appointing J. Crosse and R. Button proctors. Followed by] At the committee for the Vniversity, Oxford Iuly 2. 1646 [order suspending preferment &c. until the will of Parliament be made known. Followed by] Die Jovis 26 Augusti 1647. An additional ordinance of . . . Parliament for the visitation and reformation of the Vniversity . . . [and] Feb. 18. 1647 [proclamation by Parliament establishing Edward Reynolds as vice chancellor and] March 31. 1648 [order from sir Thomas Fairfax to lt.-col. Kelsay to send troops to Oxford]. [Madan 1973.] [Lond., 1648], fol. 4 pp.   Wood 423 (23–26)

1540. [Begin.] April 13, 1647. Ordered by the lord chancellour and Visitors . . . that no . . . member of Magdalen colledge shall enjoy any benefit . . . untill they give satisfaction to the Visitors . . . [Followed by] Feb. 18. 1647 [Order appointing E. Reynolds as vice-chancellor and] March 31. 1648. [Order by Fairfax to lt.-col. Kelsay to send troops to Oxford.] [Madan 1974.] [Lond.], (1648), s. sh.   Wood 514 (28a)

1541. To the honourable Visitours . . . the petition of your friends and servants . . . (Iune 2, 1647). [Followed by] The protestation of the well-affected against the dis-affected delegacy [and] March 31. 1648. At the committee of the Lords and Commons for the reformation of the University of Oxford [forbidding non-submitters to vote in Convocation or Congregation]. [Madan 1975.] [Lond., (1648)], s. sh.
Wood 514 (28b)

1542. [Begin.] Die Martis, viz: primo die Junii . . . [An account of some of the proceedings of the Parliamentary Visitors at Oxford between June 1, 1647 and Apr. 7, 1648.] [Madan 1976.] [Oxf.], (1648), 4°. 8 pp.
Wood 514 (43b)

1543. SWADLIN, T., Mercurius academicus: communicating the intelligence and affairs of Oxford to the rest of the passive party thorowout the kingdom, from Munday in Easter-week, to Saturday the 15 of April, 1648 [by T. Swadlin. A satirical account of events during the

visit of the Visitors to Christ Church, Magdalen and St. John's].
[Madan 1977.] [Lond.?], (1648), 4°. 8 pp.   Wood 514 (41)

1544. Die Veneris, 21 April. 1648. An order of the commons assembled in
Parliament, enabling the Visitors of Oxford to displace such Fellows,
and other Officers and members of colledges, as shall contemn the
authority of Parliament. [Madan 1979.] Lond., 1648, s. sh.
                                                        Wood 514 (39)

1545. Die Veneris, 21 April. [An order of the Lords and Commons to
bursars and treasurers of colleges to retain their monies till an order
is received from the Committee for reformation of the University.]
[Madan 1980.] [Lond.], (1648), s. sh.   Wood 514 (37)

1546. ✠ Lord have mercy upon us, or The visitation at Oxford. [A satirical
account of the visit to Oxford of the earl of Pembroke, Apr. 11–14,
1648.] [Madan 1981.] [Lond.], 1648, 4°. 8 pp.   G. Pamph. 1524 (11)

1547. BIRKENHEAD, SIR J., Newes from Pembroke & Montgomery, or,
Oxford Manchester'd by Michael Oldsworth and his lord, who swore
he was chancellour of Oxford, and proved it in a speech made to the
new visitours in their new Convocation, April 11, 1648 [by sir J.
Birkenhead]. [Madan 1982.] [Lond.], 1648, 4°. 8 pp.   Wood 614 (5)
— [Another ed.] [Madan 1983.]   Wood 514 (44)
— [Another ed.] [Madan 1984.]   Gough Oxf. 80
— [Another ed.] (Harl. misc., vol. 5, p. 105.) 1745.   GG 128 Art.
— [Another ed.] (Harl. misc., 2nd ed., vol. 5, p. 112.) 1810   Σ III. 5.

1548. Halifax law translated to Oxon: or, The new visitors iustice . . .
more particularly in Brasen-Nose colledge [the dislodgement of dr.
Samuel Radcliffe from the principalship] and S. Johns [where the
president dr. Richard Baylie was also ejected]. [Madan 1985.] [Lond.],
1648, 4°. 8 pp.   Bliss B 64

1549. Die Veneris 21. April. 1648. [An order of the Houses of lords and
commons enabling the Visitors of Oxford to displace Fellows &c.,
also An order to print and publish the above, also An order to bursars
of colleges to retain monies till further order.] [Madan 1986: a repr.
of Madan 1979 and 1980.] [Lond.?], (1648?), s. sh.   Wood 514 (38)

1550. WINYARD, T., An owle at Athens: or, A true relation [in verse] of
the entrance of the earle of Pembroke into Oxford, April xi. 1648 [by
T. Winyard]. [Madan 1987.] [Lond.], 1648, 4°. 8 pp. G.A. Oxon 8° 173

1551. BARLOW, T., and PIERCE, T., Pegasus, or, The flying horse from
Oxford. Bringing the proceedings of the Visitours and other Bedlam-
ites there, by command of the earle of Mongomery [by T. Barlow and
T. Pierce. 2 pt]. [Madan 1988.] [Lond.], (1648), 4°. 22 pp.
                                                        Gough Oxf. 105

1552. PIERCE, T., A third and fourth part of Pegasus [signed Basilius
Philomusus, i.e. T. Pierce]. [Madan 1997.] [Lond.], 1648, 4°. 8 pp.
                                                        Gough Oxf. 80

1553. LITTELTON, A., Tragi-comœdia Oxoniensis [by A. Littelton. A satire in Latin verse on the proceedings of the University Visitors]. [Madan 1989.] [Oxf., 1648], 4°. 8 pp.   G. Pamph. 2288 (2)

1554. HARRIS, R., Two letters written by mr. Harris in vindication of himselfe from the known slanders of an unknown author [in the 2nd part of Pegasus, no. 1551 above]. [Madan 1990.] [Oxf.], 1648, 4°. 8pp.   Wood 514 (51)

1555. The case of the Vniversity of Oxford: or, The sad dilemma that all the members thereof are put to, either to be perjur'd, or destroy'd. [Madan 1992.] [Lond.], 1648, 4°. 8 pp.   Gough Oxf. 8(8)

1556. ALLIBOND, J., Rustica Academiæ Oxoniensis nuper reformatæ descriptio: una cum comitiis ibidem A.D. 1648. habitis, & reliquis notatu non indignis [by J. Allibond]. [Madan 1993.] [Lond.?], (1648), 4°. 8 pp.   Wood 514 (53)
— [Another ed.] s. sh. [Madan 1994.]   Wood 276a (520)
— [Another ed.] Lond., [c. 1700], 4°. 19 pp.   Gough Oxf. 80 (3)
— [Another issue.]   CC 50 (1) Art.
— [Another ed.] 1705, s. sh.   Gough Oxf. 80 (2)
— [Another ed.] [c. 1705], 8°. 12 pp.   G.A. Oxon 8° 1008
— [Another ed., *entitled*] A seasonable sketch of an Oxford reformation . . . now reprinted with an English version [by E. Ward]. Lond., 1717, 8°. 12 leaves.   G.A. Oxon 8° 59 (9)
— [Another ed.] (Somers' tracts, 3rd coll., vol. 1, p. 444–47.) 1751.
                                                        GG 140 Art.
— [Another ed.] (Somers' tracts, 2nd coll., vol. 5, p. 503.) 1811.
                                                          Σ III. 15
— [Another ed., *entitled*] A ballad in macaronic Latin, entitled Rustica descriptio visitationis fanaticæ, the verses being done into doggerel [by V. Thomas]. Oxf., 1834, 8°.
— [Another issue.]   34.376
— 3rd ed. 1850.   29935 e. 8

1557. Pembrokes passe from Oxford to his grave [a poem satirizing the earl of Pembroke's chancellorship of the University]. [Madan 1996.] [Lond.], (1648), s. sh.   Wood 531 (21)

1558. WINYARD, T., Midsummer-moone, or, Lunacy rampant: being a character of master Cheynell, the arch visitor of Oxford, and mungrell president of Saint John baptists colledge. With a survey of the three renegado-fellowes, Web, Inkersell and Lownds [by T. Winyard?]. [Madan 1998.] [Lond.], 1648, 4°. 8 pp.   Wood 514 (44)

1559. PHILANAX ANONOMUS, *pseud.*, Oxonii lachrymæ, Rachell weeping for her children, or, a patheticall relation of the present grievances of the late famous University of Oxford, wherein you have her unjust sufferings manifested, the authours of her miseries characterised, and the ejected loyalists nominated. [A satire.] [Madan 2012.] Lond., 1649, 4°. 8 pp.   Gough Oxf. 80 (1)
— [Variant copy.] [Madan 2012*.]   Wood 514 (54)

1560. The history of the visitation of the University of Oxford by a parliamentary commission in the years 1647, 1648. Abridged from the Annals of Anthony à Wood. Oxf. &c., 1837, 8°. 39 pp.   37.876

1561. An ordinance for appointing visitors for the universities. 2 Sept. 1654. [This ordinance was confirmed by an act, anno 1656, c. 10.] [Texts in Shadwell's Enactments &c., vol. 4. See no. 956.]

1562. The register of the Visitors of the University of Oxford from 1647 to 1658, ed., with some account of the state of the University during the Commonwealth, by M. Burrows. (Camden soc., N.S., vol. 29.) n. pl., 1881, 8°. 593 pp.   2233 e. 54=K.

See 1699 [Heywood, J., Notices of the University and collegiate visitations. 1853].

1563. VARLEY, F. J., The Restoration visitation of the University of Oxford and its colleges. (Camden soc., 1948, vol. 79, no. 3. x+64 pp.) 2233 e. 54=K.

See 7609 [Johnston, N., The king's visitorial power asserted . . . As likewise an historical account of several visitations of the universities and particular colleges. 1688].
See 172 [Reasons for a royal visitation. 1717].

HANDBOOKS

1564. GILBERT, R., Liber scholasticus; or an account of the fellowships, scholarships, and exhibitions . . . at the Universities of Oxford and Cambridge [signed R. G.]. Lond., 1829, 12°. 500 pp.   29.104
— 2nd ed. 1843. 634 pp.   43.1559

1565. HATCH, E., The student's handbook to the University and colleges of Oxford [by E. Hatch]. Oxf., 1873, 8°.   Clar. Press 41 c. 1 [2nd–21st eds. publ. in 1873, 76, 76, 79, 81, 83, 85, 88, 89, 91, 92, 95, 98, 1901, 03, 06/7, 09, 12, 13, 14. From the 19th ed. onwards entitled Oxford university handbook.]
—21st ed., revised. 1917.   G.A. Oxon 8° 983

See 3852, 3872 [Stedman, A. M. M., Oxford: its social and intellectual life. 1878, 1887].

1566. Colonial conference. The following memorandum has been drawn up . . . giving information to the Colonies with regard to Oxford university. n. pl., [1906], 8°. 8 pp.   G.A. Oxon 8° 744 (18)

1567. The illustrated Oxford year book. 1911, 1912. Oxf., 1911, 12, 4°. G.A. Oxon 4° 341

1568. Handbook to the University of Oxford. 1st– ed. Oxf., 1932– , 8°. G.A. Oxon 8° 1156

1568.1. University of Oxford. Prospectus. 1965– . Oxf., 1965– , 8°. Per. G.A. Oxon 8° 1507

LISTS AND STATISTICS

Lists

See also Colleges 6567 &c., and Alumni 1602 &c.

1569. A catalogue of all graduats in divinity, law and physick and of all masters of arts and doctors of musick, who have regularly proceeded or been created in the University, between Oct. 10, 1659 and July 14, 1688. [Compiled by R. Peers.] Oxf., 1689, 8°.　　　　8° F 13 Th.
1659–1705.　　　　　　　　　　　　　　　　　　　　　B.M.
1659–1726 (27–35, 35–47, 47–60).　　　　　　　　Gough Oxf. 35
1659–1770 (70–82, 82–92, 92/93).　　　　　　　　Gough Oxf. 37
1659–1800.　　　　　　　　　　　　　　　　　　　Gough Oxf. 146
1800–10.　　　　　　　　　　　　　　　　　　　G.A. Oxon. 4° 70
1659–1814 (14–20).　　　　　　　　　　　　　　　G.A. Oxon 4° 69
1659–1850 [ed. by P. Bliss].　　　　　　　　　　G.A. Oxon 8° 519

See 2588 [Badger, J., A register of the doctors of physick . . . 1695].
See 2589 [Badger, J., An exact alphabetical catalogue of all that have taken the degree of doctor of physick . . . 1696].

1570. Proceeders between March the 29. 1705. and July 24. 1713. n. pl., [1713?], 8°. 40 pp.　　　　　　　　　　　　　　8° M 16 (5) Linc.

1571. Matriculationes Oxonienses pro com. Wilts. [17th century]. [Middlehill, 18–], fol. 4 pp.　　　　　　　　　　　　　　Caps. 6.26

1572. Matriculationes Oxonienses [1564–1615]. [Middlehill, 18—], fol. 6 pp.　　　　　　　　　　　　　　　　　　Caps. 6.24

1573. List of the members of the University of Oxford. Lond., 1809, 4°. 204 pp.　　　　　　　　　　　　　　　G.A. Oxon 4° 97 (1)

1574. Oxford University calendar. [1810]– . Oxf., 1810– , 8°.
Cal. G.A. Oxon 8° 473=B.

1575. The Oxford university calendar for the year 1814. Oxf. &c., 1814, 8°. 271 pp.　　　　　　　　　　Cal. G.A. Oxon 8° 473*

See 2986 [List of graduates in the Faculty of music, 1830–76].

1576. The Oxford, University, city and county directory for 1835. Oxf., 1835, 16°. 70 pp.　　　　　　　　　　G.A. Oxon 16° 147

See 3710 [Oxford seceders to Romanism, 1841–47].

1577. The Oxford university almanack and register. 1857–1909. [Continued as] The Oxford university sports register. Oxf., 1857–1909, 8°.
Alm. Oxon 8° 529

1578. The Oxford ten year book, to the end of 1860. Oxf. &c., 1863, 8°. 388 pp.　　　　　　　　　　　　　　G.A. Oxon 8° 530
— to 1870. Oxf. &c., 1872, 8°.　　　　　　　　G.A. Oxon 8° 531

1579. The honours register of the University of Oxford, complete to the end of Trinity term 1883. Oxf., 1883, 8°. 605 pp.　　G.A. Oxon 8° 532

— to 1888 [*entitled*] The historical register [&c.] Oxf., 1888, 8°.
460 pp. G.A. Oxon 8° 532*
— to 1900. Oxf., 1900, 8°. 914 pp. G.A. Oxon 8° 1398=B.
— 1st [-3rd] suppl. 1900 (-50). Oxf., 1921-51, 8°.
G.A. Oxon 8° 1398*=B.

1580. A list (complete alphabetical list) of the out-college residents
(resident members) graduate and undergraduate, with their addresses.
(To which is added an alphabetical list of resident members and
students of the recognised societies of women students. Hil. term
1885-Trin. term 1919. [Publ. as a suppl. to the Oxford magazine.]
Oxf., 1885-1919, 4°. Per. G.A. Oxon 4° 141 (3-37)
[See no. 1587 for continuation.]

1581. Oxford honours, 1220-1894. Oxf., 1894, 8°. 282 pp.
G.A. Oxon 8° 534*b*

1582. Register of the University of Oxford, 1449-63, 1505(-1622), ed.
by C. W. Boase (A. Clark). 2 vols. [in 5]. (Oxf. hist. soc., I, 10-12, 14).
Oxf., 1885-89, 8°. G.A. Oxon 8° 360=R.

1583. Oxford & Cambridge yearbook. [Directory of alumni.] 1904, 1906.
London, 1904, 06, 8°. G.A. Gen. top. 8° 1161

1584. CRAIG, E. S., *ed.*, Oxford university roll of service, 1914-1915.
Oxf., 1915, 8°. 255 pp. G.A. Oxon 8° 902
— 1914-1916. 2nd ed., revised. 326 pp. G.A. Oxon 8° 907
— [Another ed.] 1920, ed. by E. S. Craig and W. M. Gibson. 683 pp.
G.A. Oxon 8° 1367=S.

1585. Oxford's sacrifice: short notices of those Oxford men in the service
of their country whose deaths were notified between June 18 and
November 1, 1915. (Oxf. mag. extra no. Nov. 5.) Oxf., 1915, 4°.
32 pp. G.A. Oxon c. 309 (50)

1586. Oxford university roll of honour: a complete list of the killed and
missing with biogr. notes: also a record of military honours, (Special
no. of The Varsity, vol. 15, no. 376.) Oxf., 1916, 4°. 24 pp.
G.A. Oxon c. 309 (53)

1587. Alphabetical list of the resident members of the University of
Oxford. Hilary term, 1920- . Oxf., 1920- , 4°.
[See no. 1580 for preceding years.] Per. G.A. Oxon 4° 402

1588. BEAVEN, A. B., Double firsts at Oxford. [List 1808-91.] (Notes &
queries, 1921, 12th ser. vol. 8, p. 294-296, 334, 396.)
Per. 3974 e. 405=A.

1589. RYAN, P., Diocesan returns of recusants for England and Wales,
1577. (Publ., Cath. record soc., 1921, vol. 22, Oxford city and univ.,
p. 97-101.) Soc. G.A. Gen. top. 4° 220=K.

See 2135 [Successful candidates for the degrees of D.Phil., B.Litt., and B.Sc.,
with titles of their theses. 1940/49-].

1590. CONNELY, W., Colonial Americans in Oxford and Cambridge [1648–1775]. [With Appendix] List of colonial Americans in Oxford and Cambridge. (Amer. Oxon., 1942, vol. 29, p. 6–17, 75–77.)
Per. G.A. Oxon 8° 889

1591. WILLIAMS, F. B., Unrecorded university men. (Notes and queries, 1956, vol. 201, p. 235, 236.)   Per. 3974 e. 405=A.

1592. Protestation returns for the University. (Oxfordshire protestation returns, 1641–2. Oxfordshire record soc., 1955, vol. 36, p. 100–19.)
Per. G.A. Oxon 4° 767=R.

Statistics

1593. An exact account of the whole number of scholars and students . . . anno 1612 in the long vacation. (Collectanea curiosa, by J. Gutch, vol. 1, p. 196–203.) Oxf., 1781, 8°.   Gough Oxf. 65

1594. May 25, 1831. University of Oxford. 11 G. IV. c. 30. Population return. [Schedule.] n. pl., 1831, s. sh.   G.A. Oxon c. 47 (70)

See 1510, 1511 [Account of number of matriculations and degrees conferred, 1831–33; 1854].

1595. HEYWOOD, J., Statistics of the universities of Oxford and Cambridge. (Journ., Statist. soc. of London, 1842, vol. 5, p. 235–44.)
Soc. 24712 e. 80=P.

1596. HEYWOOD, J., Oxford university statistics. (Journ., Statistical soc. of London, 1846, vol. 9, p. 193–203.)   Soc. 24712 e. 80=P.
— Repr. 11 pp.   G.A. Oxon 8° 72 (7)
— [Another repr., with additions.] (Oxf. Protestant mag., 1847, p. 121–34, 255.)   G.A. Oxon 4° 575 (4)

1597. Universities . . . Returns for the last five years, from . . . Oxford and Cambridge . . . of the number of students entered annually in the books of each college or hall . . . the number of candidates . . . for the degree of bachelor of arts, specifying the number both of successful and of unsuccessful candidates [&c.]. 5 February 1850. [Lond.], 1850, fol. 5 pp.   Pp. Eng. 1850 vol. 42

1598. Universities, and Durham university . . . Return of the number of graduates of the different universities of the United Kingdom, distinguishing their several degrees, those admitted ad eundem and those upon whom honorary degrees have been conferred. [The return for Oxford, which pleads the impossibility of compliance and gives no figures, is on p. 4.] [Lond.], 1860, fol.   Pp. Eng. 1860 vol. 53

See 1930 [Number of students. 1886].
See 1889 [Eights week, 1904, 05. Statistics of work].

1599. VENN, J. A., Matriculations at Oxford and Cambridge, 1544–1906. (Oxf. and Cambr. review, 1908, no. 3, p. 48–66.)   Per. 2625 d. 37

1600. VENN, J. A., Oxford and Cambridge matriculations 1544–1906, with a graphic chart illustrating the varying fortunes of the two universities.

Repr. from 'The Oxford and Cambridge review'. Cambr. &c., 1908, 8°. 19 pp. 2625 d. 31 (20)

1601. VENN, J. A., The nation: Oxford and Cambridge. [Comparative statistics of distinguished offices obtained by Oxford and Cambridge alumni.] (Oxf. and Cambr. review, 1908, no. 4, p. 26–45.)
Per. 2625 d. 37
See 3997.1 [Isis survey. 1961].

1601.5. Fellows and undergraduates. (Oxf. mag., 1962, N.S., vol. 2, p. 258, 59.) Per G.A. Oxon 4° 141

Alumni: Biographical registers

1602. EMDEN, A. B., A biographical register of the University of Oxford to A.D. 1500. 3 vols. Oxf., 1957–59, 4°. G.A. Oxon 4° 738=R.

1603. FOSTER, J., Alumni Oxonienses, the members of the University of Oxford, 1500–1714. 4 vols. Oxf. &c., 1891, 92, 4°.
G.A. Oxon 4° 237–240=R.

1604. FOSTER, J., Alumni Oxonienses: the members of the University of Oxford, 1715–1886. 4 vols. Lond., 1887, 88, 4°.
G.A. Oxon 4° 241–244=R.

1605. FOSTER, J., Oxford men & their colleges. Oxf. &c., 1893, 4°. 663 pp.
G.A. Oxon 4° 671

Alumni: Types

1606. WOOD, A., Athenæ Oxonienses, an exact history of all the writers and bishops who have had their education in the University of Oxford, from 1500 to 1690. To which are added the Fasti or Annals. [By A. Wood.] 2 vols. Lond., 1691, 92, fol. Wood 431a
— 2nd ed., corrected and enlarged. 2 vols. Lond., 1721, fol.
MS. Top. Oxon b. 8, 9
— 3rd ed., with additions and a continuation by P. Bliss. [5 vols.] Lond., 1813–20, 4° G.A. Oxon c. 333—R.
— New ed. (Eccles. hist. soc.) vol. 1. [No more publ.] Oxf., 1848, 8°.
Soc. 110 d. 524

1607. GIBSON, S., and M. A., An index to Rawlinson's collections, (circa 1700–50) for a new edition of Wood's Athenæ Oxonienses. (Proc. and papers, Oxf. bibliogr. soc., 1924, vol. 1, p. 67–95.)
Soc. 258 d. 176=A.

1608. Bishop Humphreys's additions to, and corrections of, Athenæ et Fasti Oxonienses. (Thomæ Caii Vindiciæ antiq. Acad. Oxon. contra Joannem Caium, in lucem emisit T. Hearnius, 1730, vol. 2, p. 605–78.) Mus. Bibl. II 92

1609. DAVIES, M., Athenæ Britannicæ: or a critical history of Oxford and Cambridge writers and writings. [7 vols.] Lond., 1716, 8° & 4°. [Bodley wants vol. 7. Vol. 1–3, 5, 6: 12 Θ 1346–1350. Vol. 4: 13 Θ 136.]

1610. FRY, E. H., A list of celebrated English poets, educated at the universities of Oxford and Cambridge. Lond., 1860, 8°. 10 pp.

G.A. Oxon 8° 72 (5)

1611. Oxford honours. [Names extracted from old Oxford class lists &c., with biogr. details.] (Cornhill mag., 1881, vol. 43, p. 183–90.)

G.A. Oxon 4° 582 (2)

1612. Oxford *versus* Cambridge [relative merits of alumni]. (Temple Bar, 1894, vol. 101, p. 371–5.)   Per. 2705 d. 277

1613. HUTTON, L., Literary landmarks of Oxford. [Alumni subsequently men of letters.] Lond., 1903, 8° 274 pp.   G.A. Oxon 8° 697

1614. HAYNES, E. S. P., Oxford and Cambridge: a study in types. (Cornhill mag., 1906, N.S., vol. 21, p. 684–90.)   Per. 2705 d. 213

BENEFACTIONS

GENERAL

Benefactions for a particular purpose are classified accordingly.

See 3692 [Place, J., University tests and their abolition. With a table of pre- and post-Reformation benefactions to Oxford. 1870].

1615. BELLAMY, F. A., Statement and comments upon the result of a proffered gift to the University of Oxford [F. A. Bellamy's library of works on philately.] Oxf., 1926, 8°. 9 pp.   G.A. Oxon 8° 1046 (13)

1615.5 VEALE, SIR D., Lord Nuffield and the University. (Oxf. mag., 1963, N.S., vol. 4, p. 124, 25.)   Per. G.A. Oxon 4° 141

FINCH BEQUEST

1616. Jan. 24, 1831. In a Convocation to be holden 27th inst. . . . it will be proposed to accept the bequest . . . of Robert Finch. [Oxf.], 1831, s. sh.   G.A. Oxon c. 47 (7)

RAWLINSON

1617. The deed of trust and will of Richard Rawlinson of St. John Baptist college . . . containing his endowment of an Anglo-Saxon lecture, and other benefactions to the college and university. Lond., 1755, 8°. xiv+30 pp.   Gough Oxf. 44 (8)

VINER

1618. A copy of such part of mr. Viner's last will and testament, as relates to the University of Oxford. n. pl., [1758?], 4°. 3 pp.
Gough Oxf. 96 (17)
— [Another ed. issued as part of no. 1623.]

1619. Resolutions of the Delegates of Convocation for settling the bene-faction of the late Charles Viner . . . [No date.] [Oxf., 1758], fol. 4 pp.
G.A. Oxon b. 19
— [Another issue] on [   ] day the [   ] of June, 1758. [Part of 1st issue of no. 1623.]
— [Another issue] on Monday the fifth of June, 1758. [Part of 2nd issue of no. 1623.]

1620. [*Begin.*] The resolutions of Mr. Viner's Delegacy . . . [critical observations]. June 3d. [Oxf.], (1758), fol. 3 pp.   Gough Oxf. 96 (20)

1621. [*Begin.*] 'Some doubts having arisen with regard to mr. Viner's intentions . . .' [Oxf., 1758?], fol. 4 pp.   G.A. Oxon b. 19
[Also issued as part of no. 1623.]

1622. The voters. [A poem on the country parsons voting at the Convocation held concerning the Vinerian statutes. Dated June 3, 1758.] [Oxf.], 1758, s. sh.   Gough Oxf. 96 (63)

1623. Papers relating to the benefaction of . . . Charles Viner. n. pl., [1758], fol. ii+4+4 pp.   Gough Oxf. 96 (14)
— [Another issue, the Resolutions dated 5 June 1758. ii+8 pp.]
                                                 Gough Oxf. 96 (14a)

1624. [*Begin.*] It being generally supposed that members of Convocation lately consented [June 13?] that certain articles proposed to them by the Delegates . . . of Mr. Viner's Benefaction, should be drawn up in the form of statutes . . . [7 queries on the supposition.] [Oxf., 1758], s. sh.   Gough Oxf. 96 (35)

1625. An examination of the objections [no. 1620] to the Resolutions of the Delegates of Convocation for settling the benefaction of . . . Charles Viner. (June 23 1758.) n. pl., (1758), fol. 4 pp.
                                                 Gough Oxf. 96 (22)

1626. [*Begin.*] It has been confidently asserted . . . [Observations dated June 30th 'doubting the truth of the assertion of the delegates relating to mr. Viner's benefaction that their resolutions were finally confirmed by the majority of Convocation held June 13th'.] n. pl., (1758), fol. 4 pp.   Gough Oxf. 96 (26)

1627. Short remarks on a paper dated June 30, 1758 [no. 1626]. n. pl., (1758), s. sh.   Gough Oxf. 96 (29)

1628. Forma statutorum ad Domum Congregationis referendorum Jun. 30. 1758, & in Domo Convocationis proponendorum Jul. 3. 1758 [concerning mr. Viner's benefaction]. [Oxf., 1758], fol. 4 pp.
                                                 Gough Oxf. 96 (24)

1629. A reply to the Examiner [of the objections to the Resolutions of Mr. Viner's Delegacy]. n. pl., [1758], fol. 8 pp.   Gough Oxf. 96 (23)

1630. A view of the misrepresentations in the Reply to the Examiner. (July 1st.) n. pl., (1758), fol. 4 pp.   Gough Oxf. 96 (25)

1631. [*Begin.*] It having been advanced . . . 'That the only question to be determin'd by Convocation on the third of July is whether the wording and form of the statutes framed by the heads of houses . . . are or are not agreeable to the resolutions of the Convocation on the 13th June . . .'. [Observations reflecting this assertion.] n. pl., [1758], s. sh.
                                                 Gough Oxf. 96 (34)

1632. [*Begin.*] That it may be . . . apprehended what are . . . the questions to be determined by Convocation, on . . . the third of July, it has been judged proper to throw into one view the following Comparison of mr. Viner's will with the resolutions of the delegacy, confirmed by Convocation, and the statutes now formed upon some of those resolutions. n. pl., [1758], fol. 4 pp.   Gough Oxf. 96 (33)

1633. [9] Queries humbly proposed to members of Convocation [con-
cerning mr. Viner's benefaction]. n. pl., [1758], s. sh.
Gough Oxf. 96 (32)

1634. [8] Queries submitted to the members of Congregation and Convocation [concerning mr. Viner's benefaction]. n. pl., [1758], s. sh.
Gough Oxf. 96 (32*b*)

1635. Extracts from the Resolutions of the Delegates of Convocation
[concerning the duties of the proposed Vinerian professor, and the
establishment of Vinerian fellowships and scholarships: with extracts
from mr. Viner's will, from a former will: and two queries concerning
the office of tutor being combined with that of the professor]. n. pl.,
[1758], 4°. 2 pp.
Gough Oxf. 96 (19)

1636. A serious address to the members of Convocation [suggesting that
Resolutions of Mr. Viner's Delegacy are not in accordance with Stat.
tit. x sect. 2 § 2, concerning the process for enacting new statutes].
n. pl., [1758], s. sh.
Gough Oxf. 96 (18)

1637. A bill to empower the University of Oxford to make statutes as to
the Vinerian foundation in that university. 7 Apr. 1865. [Lond.], 1865,
fol. 4 pp.
Pp. Eng. 1865 vol. 3

— Lords' amendments, 26 May 1865. [Lond.], 1865, s. sh.
Pp. Eng. 1865 vol. 3

— [Act.] (28 & 29 V., c. 55, Pub.)
L.L.

See also 2444 Vinerian scholarships; 2575 &c. Vinerian professor, Vinerian
reader.

REFORM

1638. NEWTON, R., Supplement. Well-wishers to the University of Oxford. [By R. Newton.] No. 1. (General Evening post, Jan. 9/11, 1750.)
G. Pamph. 1690 (8)
— No. 2-5. (Jan. 11/13, Mar. 29/31, Apr. 10/12, June 14/16, 1750.)
G. Pamph. 1690 (9-12)
— No. 6.   5 Δ 90 (18)
— No. 8. (July 9/11, 1751.)   G. Pamph. 1690 (13)

1639. A series of papers on subjects [of reform] the most interesting to the nation in general and Oxford in particular containing Well-wishers to the University of Oxford [number 1-4 by R. Newton] and the answers [signed Oxoniensis, i.e. J. Randolph?] collected together from articles in the General Evening post etc.]. Lond., 1750, 8° 51 pp.
G.A. Oxon 8° 62 (4)

1640. A memorial relating to the universities [sometimes ascr. to the 3rd earl of Macclesfield]. (Collectanea curiosa, by J. Gutch, vol. 2, p. 53-75.) Oxf., 1781, 8°.   Gough Oxf. 66

1641. KNOX, V., A letter to . . . lord North, chancellor of the University [urging various reforms and improvements]. Lond., 1789, 8°. xv pp.
G.A. Oxon 8° 97

See 1846-48 [Suggestions for reform put forward by the Edinburgh review; and answers. 1831 &c.].
See 3818 [Academical abuses. 1832].

1642. Thoughts on reform at Oxford, by a graduate. Oxf., 1833, 8°. 22 pp.
G.A. Oxon 8° 219 (16)

1643. Letters to the English public, on the condition, abuses and capabilities of the national universities. No. 1, by a graduate of Cambridge. Lond., 1836, 8°. 48 pp.   G. Pamph. 2689 (4)

1644. An act for appointing commissioners to inquire respecting the statutes and administration of the different colleges and halls at Oxford and Cambridge. [The Bill was introduced by the earl of Radnor to the House of lords, and ordered to be printed Mar. 7, 1837. The Bill failed.]

1645. An historical vindication of the leading principles contained in the earl of Radnor's bill, entitled 'An act for appointing commissioners to inquire respecting the statutes and administration of the . . . colleges and halls at Oxford and Cambridge'. Lond., 1837, 8°. 24 pp.   37.989

1646. Reform of the University of Oxford. (Eclectic rev., 1837, N.S., vol. 2, p. 121-37.)   Per. 3977 e. 76

1647. The independence of the universities and colleges of Oxford and Cambridge, by a layman. Oxf. &c., 1838, 8°. 43 pp.   Bliss B 216 (5)

1648. WALKER, R., Oxford in 1888, a fragmentary dream [of reform] by
a sub-utopian, publ. from the orig. MS. by the editor, R.P. [By
R. Walker.] Oxf., 1838, 8°. 70 pp.   G.A. Oxon 8° 683 (6)

1649. RICHARDS, A. B., Oxford unmasked; or, An attempt to describe
some of the abuses in that University, by a graduate [A. B. Richards].
Lond., 1842, 8°. 40 pp.   G.A. Oxon 8° 215*b*. (3)
— 2nd ed. 1842.   G.A. Oxon 8° 1033 (7)
— 3rd ed. and 4th ed. 1842.   G.A. Oxon 8° 70 (4, 5)

   See 3660 [Christie, W. D., Speech in the House of commons, 10 Apr., 1845,
   moving that a Royal commission of inquiry be appointed. 1850].

1650. Oxford and Cambridge: University reform. (Brit. quarterly rev.,
1846, vol. 3, p. 358–76.)   Per. 3977 e. 198

1651. Can and will the universities reform themselves? (Oxf. Protestant
mag., 1847, vol. 1, p. 6–14.)   Per. G.A. Oxon 8° 119

1652. To . . . Lord John Russell . . . The memorial of the undersigned
graduates . . . of the universities of Oxford and Cambridge [urging
the institution of a Royal commission of inquiry]. n. pl., [1848], 4°.
4 pp.   G.A. Oxon c. 64 (161)
— [Another ed.]   G.A. Oxon c. 64 (162)

1653. Royal commission of inquiry for the Universities of Oxford and
Cambridge. [Account of the presentation of the Memorial to lord John
Russell on 8th July 1848.] n. pl., [1848], s. sh.
                                                 G.A. Oxon c. 64 (163)

1654. Reform of Oxford university. (Tait's Edinb. mag., 1849, N.S. vol. 16,
p. 702–13.)   Per. 2705 d. 416

1655. The present state of the University of Oxford—its defects and
remedies. (Tait's Edinb. mag., 1849, N.S., vol. 16, p. 525–39.)
                                                    Per. 2705 d. 416

1656. ARMYTAGE, W. H. G., James Heywood's resolution: prelude and
finale. [Reform of universities of Oxford and Cambridge begun by
Heywood's address to the Crown in 1850.] (Universities review, 1950,
vol. 22, p. 139–53.)   Soc. 2625 d. 78

1657. INGLIS, SIR R. H., The universities: substance of a speech, delivered
in the House of commons, 23rd Apr. 1850 [on a motion to institute
a Royal commission of inquiry into the state of Oxford &c.]. Lond.,
1850, 8°. 60 pp.   2625 e. 26 (9)

1658. ROW, C. A., Letter to sir Robert H. Inglis . . . in reply to his speech
on university reform, Apr. 23rd, 1850. Lond., 1850, 8°. 35 pp.
                                                     2625 e. 26 (14)

1659. SEWELL, W., The University commission, or Lord John Russell's
postbag of April 27, 1850. The first instalment [by W. Sewell]. Oxf.,
1850, 8°. vii+35 pp.   G.A. Oxon 8° 92 (9)
— 2nd ed. 1850.   G.A. Oxon 8° 92 (9*)

1660. SEWELL, W., The University commission, or Lord John Russell's postbag of April 27, 1850. The second instalment [by W. Sewell]. Oxf., 1850, 8°. 41 pp.   G.A. Oxon 8° 92 (10)

1661. SEWELL, W., The University commission, or Lord John Russell's postbag of April 27, 1850. The third instalment [by W. Sewell]. Oxf., 1850, 8°. 37 pp.   G.A. Oxon 8° 92 (11)
— 2nd ed. 1850. 40 pp.   G.A. Oxon 8° 1033 (5)

1662. SEWELL, W., The University commission, or Lord John Russell's postbag. The fourth instalment [by W. Sewell]. Oxf., 1850, 8°. 47 pp.
                    G.A. Oxon 8° 92 (12)
See also 1676, 1698.

1663. The proposed Royal commission of enquiry into the state of the universities. 4th May. [Oxf.], (1850), 4°. 4 pp.
                    G.A. Oxon c. 66 (156)

1664. T., E., The expediency, the practicability, and the necessity of University reform, a letter. June 10. Lond., 1850, 8°. 10 pp.
                    2625. e. 112 (12)

1665. GLADSTONE, W. E., Speech on the Commission of inquiry into the state of the universities of Oxford and Cambridge, July 18, 1850. Oxf., 1850, 8°. 51 pp.   G.A. Oxon 8° 659 (3)

1666. [Letter from the Oxford University commissioners setting out the particular points into which they wish to inquire, and requesting information and suggestions about these and other subjects.] Nov. [Lond.], (1850), 2 sheets.   G.A. Oxon b. 26
[*With* Text, dated 31 Aug., of the Commission under which they act.]

1667. BISSET, T., Suggestions on university reform, a letter. Lond., 1850, 8°. 31 pp.   2625 e. 130 (2)

1668. A few plain facts and observations relative to the two universities of Oxford and Cambridge, by an anxious father. [A plea for control of undergraduate extravagance.] Oxf., 1850, 8°. 32 pp.
                    2625 e. 130 (5)

1669. INMAN, J. W., The necessity of a Royal commission of inquiry into the condition of the Universities, a letter. Lond., 1850, 8°. 30 pp.
                    2625 e. 130 (11)

1670. LITTON, E. A., University reform, a letter. Lond., 1850, 8°.   B.M.
— 2nd ed., with a postscript. London. &c., 1850, 8°. 84 pp.
                    2625 e. 112 (11)

1671. MELVILLE, D., A practical question about Oxford, a letter to W. E. Gladstone. [A scheme to increase the number of students, by reorganising the domestic administration of the colleges.] Oxf. &c., 1850, 8°. 24 pp.   G.A. Oxon 8° 1101 (7)

See 1857 [Price, B., Suggestions for the extension of professorial teaching. 1850].

1672. The questioner questioned: or A few inquiries concerning the Commission of inquiry, by a member of Convocation. Oxf. &c., 1850, 8°. 34 pp.   2625 e. 130 (4)

1673. ROW, C. A., Letter to . . . lord John Russell . . . on the constitutional defects of the University and colleges of Oxford, with suggestions for a Royal commission of inquiry into the universities, by a member of the Oxford Convocation [C. A. Row]. Lond., 1850, 8°. 59 pp.
G.A. Oxon 8° 1101 (6)

1674. University reform—Oxford. (Fraser's mag., 1850, vol. 42, p. 86–95.)
Per. 3977 e. 200

1675. COOPER, C. P., Oxford university commission. Mr. Purton Cooper's letter to the duke of Wellington. Lond., 1851, 8°. 8 pp.
G.A. Oxon 8° 1197

1676. LANDON, J. T. B., Eureka; a sequel to [no. 1659 &c.] Lord John Russell's postbag [by J. T. B. Landon]. Oxf., 1851, 8°. 32 pp.
G. Pamph. 2379 (15)
See also 1698.

1677. PYCROFT, J. W., The Oxford university commission, a letter to sir R. H. Inglis, M.P.: being a short enquiry into the nature of the protection afforded by legislative incorporation in relation to the University and colleges of Oxford. Oxf. &c., 1851, 8°. 16 pp.
G.A. Oxon 8° 234 (10)
— 2nd ed. 1851.   G.A. Oxon 8° 234 (11)

1678. The Anglican universities as ecclesiastical training schools. [Article on] The Royal commission for visiting the Universities, 1850. (Dubl. review, 1851, vol. 30, p. 208–53.)   G.A. Oxon 4° 579 (2)

1679. Oxford university commission. Case and opinion [signed G. J. Turner, R. Bethell, H. S. Keating, J. R. Kenyon, dated 3 Mar., 1851] on the part of the University of Oxford. n. pl., (1851), 4°. 16 pp.
G.A. Oxon c. 67 (152)
— [Another ed.]   G.A. Oxon c. 67 (46)

1680. Copy of opinion [signed J. Dodson, A. E. Cockburn, W. P. Wood, dated Apr. 10, 1851] respecting the Oxford university commission, received by the Vice-chancellor from the Commissioners, May 4, 1851. n. pl., (1851), 4°. 3 pp.   G.A. Oxon c. 67 (154)

1681. At a meeting of the Board of Heads of Houses and Proctors . . . [Copy of a petition to Her majesty to annul the Commission of inquiry on the ground that it is unconstitutional, to be submitted to Convocation, 21st May.] May 12. [Oxf.], (1851), 4°. 4 pp.
G.A. Oxon c. 67 (154a)

1682. In the matter of the petition of the University against the Commission of enquiry. [Observations signed C. N. i.e. C. Neate?] May 19. [Oxf.], (1851), s. sh.   G.A. Oxon c. 67 (155)

1683. [*Begin.*] The attention of members of Convocation who may intend to vote for the 'Petition' is invited to the following points . . . n. pl., [1851], s. sh.   G.A. Oxon c. 67 (156)

> See 6791 [Oxford university commission. Case and opinion on the part of Brasenose College. 1851].

1684. The public right to the Universities. By a university man. Lond., 1851, 12°. 47 pp.   2625 e. 31

1685. Oxford university commission. Report of Her majesty's Commissioners appointed to inquire into the state, discipline, studies, and revenues of the University and colleges of Oxford. Together with the Evidence and an appendix. Lond., 1852, fol. 260+7+8+72+387 pp.
Pp. Eng. 1852 vol. 57=R.

1686. The Oxford commission and the memorial for a 'Delegacy' [of Convocation to take into consideration the state of the University]. Three letters [signed A resident] to W. E. Gladstone. Oxf. &c., 1852, 8°. 65 pp.   G.A. Oxon 8° 146 (11)

1687. University reform—the Oxford commission. (Brit. quarterly rev., 1852, vol. 16, p. 289–357.)   Per. 3977 e. 198

1688. Oxford university commission report. (Christ. observ., 1852, p. 739–59, 818–34.)   Per. 971 e. 45

1689. Oxford university commission, 1852. (Eclectic rev., 1852, N.S., vol. 4, p. 223–39.)   Per. 3977 e. 76

1690. The Oxford university commission report. (Edinb. rev., 1852, vol. 96, p. 232–88.)   Per. 3977 e. 190

1691. Oxford and the Royal commission. (North Brit. rev., 1852, vol. 18, p. 1–38.)   Per. 3977 e. 204

1692. Oxford [notes on the Report of the Commission]. (Prospective rev., 1852, vol. 8, p. 347–92.)   Per. 971 e. 131

1693. The Oxford commission [comment on the Report]. (Westm. rev., 1852, vol. 58, p. 317–48.)   Per. 3977 e. 228

1694. HAMILTON, SIR W., On a reform of the English universities, with especial reference to Oxford; and limited to the Faculty of arts. (Oxford as it is; Oxford as it might be.) (Discussions on philosophy and literature, 1852, Appendix, p. 651–740.)   265 i. 61
— 2nd ed. 1853.   265 i. 60

1695. SEWELL, W., Collegiate reform, a sermon. Oxf. &c., 1853, 8°. 40 pp.
100 i. 24 (2)

1696. CHASE, D. P., The University pulpit, observations on certain passages in mr. Sewell's sermon entitled Collegiate reform, by the senior proctor. Oxf. &c., 1853, 8°. 19 pp.   Bliss B 218 (8)

1697. GARBETT, J., University reform, a letter. Lond., 1853, 8°. 36 pp.
G.A. Oxon 8° 63 (4)

1698. LANDON, J. T. B., Eureka, no. II. A sequel to a sequel [no. 1676] to lord John Russell's post-bag [by J. T. B. Landon]. Oxf., 1853, 8°. 42 pp.   G.A. Oxon 8° 63 (19)

1699. The recommendations of the Oxford university commissioners, with selections from their report, and a history of the university subscription tests, including notices of the University and collegiate visitations, by J. Heywood. Lond., 1853, 8°. 559 pp.   G.A. Oxon 8° 34

1700. Report [of a committee of the Hebdomadal board] and evidence upon the recommendations of Her majesty's Commissioners for inquiring into the state of the University of Oxford. Oxf., 1853, 4°. 502 pp.   G.A. Oxon 4° 621

1701. The colleges and the Commission. (Christ. remem., 1853, N.S., vol. 25, p. 192–212.)   Per. 971 e. 44

1702. CLOUGH, A. H., Oxford university commission. (North Amer. rev., 1853, vol. 76, p. 369–96.)   R.H.

1703. Oxford university commission report. (Blackwood's Edinb. mag., 1853, vol. 73, p. 216–34.)   G.A. Oxon 4° 578 (7)

1704. A few more words on University reform. (Blackwood's Edinb. mag., 1853, vol. 74, p. 583–94.)   G.A. Oxon 4° 578 (7*)

1705. The Oxford commission. (Quarterly rev., 1853, vol. 93, p. 152–238.)   Per. 3977 e. 191

1706. Oxford and Cambridge universities. Copies of letters addressed to the Chancellors . . . by the Secretary of State for the Home department. [12 Dec. 1853.] [Lond.], 1854, fol. 4 pp.   Pp. Eng. 1854 vol. 50

1707. COSTIN, W. C., ed., Dean Liddell and Oxford reform. [2 letters to lord Granville, 1853, 1856.] (Oxf. mag., 1943, vol. 62, p. 62, 63.)   Per. G.A. Oxon 4° 141

1708. Papers published by the Tutors' Association.
No. 1. Recommendations respecting the extension of the University, January 1853. (p. 1–34.)
No. 2. Recommendations respecting the constitution of the University, April 1853. (p. 35–54.)
No. 3. Recommendations respecting the relation of the professorial and tutorial systems, November 1853. (p. 55–98.)
No. 4. Recommendations respecting college statutes and the alterations required in colleges, March 1854. (p. 99–151.)
Oxf. &c., 1854, 8°.   G.A. Oxon 8° 85

1709. PALMER, R., Suggestions with regard to certain proposed alterations in Oxford. [In reply to questions circulated by the Tutors' Association.] Oxf. &c., 1854, 8°. p. 1–31.   G.A. Oxon 8° 85

1710. AWDRY, SIR J. W., and PATTESON, SIR J., Suggestions with regard to certain proposed alterations in the University and colleges of Oxford, and to the possibility and advantage of a legal education at the University. [In reply to questions circulated by the Tutors' Association.] Oxf. &c., 1854, 8°. p. 32–72.   G.A. Oxon 8° 85

1711. Suggestions respecting the conditions under which University education may be made more available for clerks in government offices, for barristers, for solicitors [signed by sir F. Rogers and 6 others: in reply to questions circulated by the Tutors' Association]. Oxf. &c., 1854, 8°. p. 73–110.   G.A. Oxon 8° 85

1712. DICKINSON, F. H., and FREEMAN, E. A., Suggestions with regard to certain proposed alterations in the University and colleges of Oxford. [In reply to questions circulated by the Tutors' Association.] Oxf. &c., 1854, 8°. p. 111–168.   G.A. Oxon 8° 85

1713. A bill to make further provision for the good government and extension of the University of Oxford and of the colleges therein. 17 Mar., 1854. [Lond.], 1854, fol. 18 pp.   Pp. Eng. 1854 vol. 5
—As amended in committee. 11 Apr., 1854. 20 pp.
     Pp. Eng. 1854 vol. 5
— As amended in committee and on re-commitment. 1 June, 1854. 12 pp.   Pp. Eng. 1854, vol. 5
— As amended in committee on first and second re-commitment, and on consideration of bill as amended. 23 June, 1854. 14 pp.
     Pp. Eng. 1854 vol. 5
— As amended by the Lords. 12 pp.   Pp. Eng. 1854 vol. 5

1714. In a Convocation to be holden . . . 31st instant . . . it will be proposed to affix the University seal to the following Petition to the . . . House of commons [against the leading principles and provisions of the Oxford university bill]. Mar. 25. [Oxf.], (1854), s. sh.
     G.A. Oxon c. 70 (87)

1715. [Begin.] To the Honourable the House of commons. [Petition by E. H. Cradock and 90 other resident members of Convocation, asking the House to pass the Oxford university bill in its principal provisions.] n. pl., [1854], 4°. 3 pp.   G.A. Oxon c. 70 (257)

1716. Proposed petition of heads and fellows of colleges [against those clauses of the Oxford university bill which alter the method of electing fellows and the tenure of fellowships]. [Oxf., 1854], s. sh.
     G.A. Oxon c. 70 (267)

1717. Proposed petition of resident members of Convocation [against those clauses of the Oxford university bill which impinge on the ancient liberty of the University to make and amend its own laws and constitution]. [Oxf., 1854], s. sh.   G.A. Oxon c. 70 (266)

1718. [Begin.] Insignissime vice cancellarie . . . [A speech, probably prepared for, but not delivered in, the Convocation of 31 March 1854, when a petition to Parliament against the Oxford university bill was discussed.] [Oxf., 1854?], 4°. 4 pp.   G.A. Oxon 4° 119 (20)

1719. [*Begin.*] University of Oxford. The difficulty . . . [Proof copy of a
declaration against the Oxford university bill, which resident and non-
resident members of Convocation are invited to sign.] [Oxf., 1854],
s. sh.   G.A. Oxon c. 70 (263)
— [Declaration, together with List of names supporting it.] Apr. 11.
[Oxf., 1854], fol. s. sh+8 pp.   G.A. Oxon c. 70 (264, 65)

1720. The Oxford protest. The Committee invite the attention of members of Convocation to the following letter [signed 'One of the Committee', urging support for the petition against the Oxford university
bill]. Apr. 22. [Oxf., 1854], s. sh.   G.A. Oxon c. 70 (261)

1721. To the . . . lord John Russell. [An address, signed by numerous
fellows and tutors, protesting against the clause in the Oxford bill
which regulates the residence and employment of fellows of colleges.]
[Oxf., 1854], s. sh.   G.A. Oxon c. 70 (258)

1722. A bill to make further provision for the extension of the University
of Oxford and of the colleges therein. [A satirical parody on the powers
of the commissioners.] [Oxf., 1854], s. sh.   G.A. Oxon c. 70 (268)

1723. Doubts and queries respecting the new act for the University of
Oxford, by a resident fellow. Mar. 31. Oxf., 1854, 8°. 13 pp.
                                              G.A. Oxon 8° 146 (23)

1724. HORSMAN, E., University reform, speech delivered in the House of
Commons on the Oxford bill, on 27th April 1854. Westm., (1854),
8°. 22 pp.   G. Pamph. 2737 (18)

1725. MARRIOTT, C., A letter . . . on some of the provisions of the Oxford
university bill. Oxf. &c., 1854, 8°. 16 pp.   G.A. Oxon 8° 63 (6)

1726. MARSHAM, R. B., A letter relating to the Oxford university bill.
Oxf. &c., 1854, 8°. 20 pp.   G.A. Oxon 8° 63 (7)

1727. The Oxford reform bill. (Blackwood's Edinb. mag., 1854, vol. 75,
p. 507–21.)   Per. 2705 e. 486

1728. An act to make further provision for the good government and
extension of the University of Oxford, of the colleges therein . . .
(17 & 18 V. c. 81, Pub.) Lond., 1854, fol. 17 pp.   L.L.
— 19 & 20 V. c. 31, Pub.
— 20 & 21 V. c. 25, Pub.
— 32 & 33 V. c. 20, Pub.
— 40 & 41 V. c. 48, Pub.

1729. Correspondence respecting the proposed measures of improvement
in the universities and colleges of Oxford and Cambridge. Pt. 1, 3, 4,
6 [relate to Oxford]. Lond., 1854, fol. 101+3+4+2 pp.
                                              Pp. Eng. 1854 vol. 50

See 926, &c. [Proposed new constitution of the Hebdomadal board. 1854].

1730. ACLAND, SIR H. W., A letter to . . . W. E. Gladstone . . . on the formation of the Initiative board [to initiate university legislation] in the University of Oxford. Oxf. &c., 1854, 8°. 18 pp.
G.A. Oxon 8° 71 (2)

1731. BARRY, H. B., Remarks on the three proposals for reforming the constitution of the University of Oxford [those of the Oxford university bill, of the Hebdomadal council in the Petition of Feb. 24, and of the Tutors' Association]. Oxf. &c., 1854, 8°. 24 pp.
G.A. Oxon 8° 46 (21)

1732. NEATE, C., Objections to the government scheme for the present subjection and future management of the University of Oxford. Oxf. &c., 1854, 8°. 40 pp.   G.A. Oxon 8° 63 (9)

1733. VAUGHAN, H. H., Oxford reform and Oxford professors: a reply to certain objections urged against the Report of the queen's commissioners. [With] Postscript. Lond., 1854, 8°. 120 pp.
G.A. Oxon 8° 63 (22)

1734. A reply to professor Vaughan's strictures on the third report of the Oxford Tutors' Association, by one of the committee. Oxf. &c., 1854, 8°. 32 pp.   G.A. Oxon 8° 63 (24)

1735. WALFORD, E., Oxford—its past and present [by E. Walford]. (Dubl. review, 1854, vol. 36, p. 314–51; 1854, vol. 37, p. 68–96.)
Per. 3977 e. 199

1736. WILSON, H. B., A letter . . . on university and college reform. Lond., 1854, 8°. 43 pp.   G.A. Oxon 8° 146 (22)
— 2nd ed. 1854.   G.A. Oxon 8° 63 (25)

1737. WOODGATE, H. A., University reform. National faith considered in reference to endowments. Mar. 27. Oxf. &c., 1854, 8°. 35 pp.
G.A. Oxon 8° 63 (26)

1738. [Begin.] The Vice-chancellor is authorized to print . . . the following correspondence between lord viscount Palmerston, the chancellor of the University, and the Board of heads of houses and proctors. [Concerning University reform.] n. pl., (1854), 8°. 24 pp.
G.A. Oxon 8° 63 (13)

1739. Government education measures for poor and rich [part of which examines and comments on the Report of the Commissioners for inquiring into the state of the University, 1853]. (Edinb. review, 1854, vol. 99, p. 158–96.)   Per. 3977 e. 190

1740. Oxford reform and Oxford professors. (Fraser's mag., 1854, vol. 49, p. 358–68.)   Per. 3977 e. 200

See 7968, 7969 [Oxford reformers, a letter to Endemus and Ecdemus. 1854].

1741. The Oxford reform bill. (North Brit. rev., 1855, vol. 22, p. 413–54.)
Per. 3977 e. 204

1742. PYCROFT, J. W., Observations on Stat. 17 & 18 Vict. cap. 81. for the good government and extension of the University of Oxford and the colleges therein. Lond., 1855, 4°. 40 pp.   G.A. Oxon 4° 45 (1)

> See 6423 [Chase, D. P., The rights of 'indigentes' in respect to college foundations. 1856].

1743. SMITH, G., Oxford university reform. (Oxf. essays, 1858, p. 265–87.)
                                                              270 a. 19

1744. Oxford essays. University reform. (Dubl. univ. mag., 1858, vol. 52, p. 248–56.)   Per. 3977 e. 74

> See 6560 [Report of the Commissioners concerning ordinances framed for colleges. 1858].

1745. BURROWS, M., Is educational reform required in Oxford, and what? [by M. Burrows]. Oxf. &c., 1859, 8°. 56 pp.   G. Pamph. 2499 (17)

> See 6561 [Act providing machinery for appeal against ordinances framed by the University commissioners, particularly in relation to St. John's college. 1860].

1746. HEYWOOD, J., Academic reform and university representation. Lond., 1860, 8°. 335 pp.   232 a. 124

1747. Oxford—its constitutional and educational changes. (Christ. remem., 1860, N.S., vol. 40, p. 303–26.)   Per. 971 e. 44

1748. SMITH, G., The Hebdomadal council and the Oxford bill of last session. [Oxf., 1860], 4°. 4 pp.   G.A. Oxon c. 76 (278)

1749. The Hebdomadal council and the Oxford bill of last session. [A statement in reply to G. Smith by the Council. With a short comment by Smith.] 13 Nov. [Oxf., 1860]. s. sh.   G.A. Oxon c. 76 (322)
— [Another issue.]   G.A. Oxon c. 76 (323)

1750. Special report from the select committee on the Oxford and Cambridge universities education bill, together with the proceedings of the committee, minutes of evidence, and appendix [and] Index. 31 July, 1867. [Lond.], 1867, fol. 307+55 pp.   Pp. Eng. 1867 vol. 13

1751. Draft of a proposed bill [made by baron Coleridge] for the extension and improvement of the University of Oxford and the colleges therein. May 18, 1868. [Lond., 1868], fol. 12 pp.   MS. Top. Oxon e. 100

1752. University extension and improvement. [Notice of a meeting to discuss a draft bill circulated by baron Coleridge.] May 20. [Oxf.], (1868), s. sh.   G.A. Oxon c. 84 (456)

1753. BURROWS, M., University reform [by M. Burrows]. (Quarterly review, 1868, vol. 124, p. 385–422.)   Per. 3977 e. 191

1754. PATTISON, M., Suggestions on academical organisation with especial reference to Oxford. Edinb., 1868, 8°. 348 pp.
                                                    G.A. Oxon 8° 110

1755. [Article on and review of M. Pattison's work] Suggestions on academical organisation. (Fraser's mag., 1869, vol. 80, p. 407–30.)
G.A. Oxon 4° 580 (13)

1756. PRICE, B., Oxford. (Fraser's mag., 1868, vol. 78, p. 545–66.)
G.A. Oxon 4° 580 (6)

1757. SMITH, G., The reorganization of the University of Oxford. Oxf. &c., 1868, 8°. 67 pp.   G.A. Oxon 8° 111

1758. University organisation, by a don. (Fraser's mag., 1868, vol. 77, p. 135–53.)   G.A. Oxon 4° 580 (9)

1759. Reform in Oxford. (Macmillan's mag., 1869, vol. 20, p. 124–29.)
Per. 2705 d. 254

1760. STANLEY, E. L., Oxford university reform. Lond. &c., 1869, 8°. 28 pp.   G.A. Oxon 8° 90 (5)

1761. Oxford reviewed. (Dark blue, 1872, vol. 3, p. 95–102, 219–26).
Per. 270 d. 32

1762. Oxford university reform. To the non-resident members of Convocation. Jan. 1872. [Signed] A senior resident member of the University. [Oxf.], (1872), fol. 4 pp.   Per. G.A. Oxon c. 86 (iii)

1763. SMITH, G., Oxford university and the forthcoming report of the commission. Repr. from the 'Oxford Chronicle', May 30th 1874. [Oxf.], (1874), 4°. 4 pp.   G.A. Oxon b. 140 (30)

See 6630–39 [Suggestions by Fellows of All Souls college concerning possible contributions towards funds for University reform. 1874].

1764. Universities commission. Report of the Commissioners appointed to inquire into the property and income of the Universities of Oxford and Cambridge, and of the colleges and halls therein; together with returns and appendix. 3 vols. Lond., 1874, fol.
Pp. Eng. 1873 vol. 37

1765. BRODRICK, G. C., The Universities and the nation. (Contemp. review, 1875, vol. 26, p. 63–86.)   G.A. Oxon 4° 578 (42)

1766. PRICE, B., Oxford reform. Oxf. &c., 1875, 8°. 26 pp.
200 h. 125 (3)

1767. Report of Committee [of the Hebdomadal council] on University requirements. June 4, 1875. [Oxf.], 1875, 8°. 4 pp.
G.A. Oxon c. 228

1768. WILKINSON, J., Oxford university reform, two letters. (Oxf., 1875), 16°. 16 pp.   G.A. Oxon 16° 136 (1)

1769. BRYCE, J., A few words on the Oxford university bill. (Fortnightly review, 1876, vol. 25, p. 771–76.)   G.A. Oxon 4° 578 (44)

See 6429 [Chase, D. P., Oxford university bill. Suggestions respecting the halls in the patronage of the Chancellor of the University. 1876].

1770. Copy of any memorials or extracts of memorials from colleges in the University of Oxford [presented to the House of lords on the proposed Oxford university bill]. [Lond.], (1876), fol. 16 pp.
G.A. Oxon b. 140 (32)

1771. LAING, R., Some dreams of a constitution-monger: a paper on university and college reforms. Oxf. &c., 1876, 8°. 30 pp.
200 h. 131 (13)

1772. MAGRATH, J. R., University reform, two papers. Oxf. &c., 1876, 8°. 23 pp.
G.A. Oxon 8° 199 (12)

1773. Report of the committee [of the Hebdomadal council] on University needs and their comparative urgency. [Oxf.], (1876), s. sh.
G.A. Oxon c. 33 (155)

1774. STANLEY, E. L., Three letters on Oxford university reform. Republ. from 'The Nonconformist' of Dec. 15, 22, 29, 1875. Lond., 1876, 8°. 19 pp.
G.A. Oxon 8° 341

1775. SMITH, G., The Oxford university bill. (Macmillan's mag., 1876/77, vol. 35, p. 281–90.)
Per. 2705 d. 254

1776. A bill to make further provision respecting the Universities of Oxford and Cambridge. 9 Feb., 1877. [Lond.], 1877, fol. 4 pp.
Pp. Eng. 1877 vol. 6
— As amended in committee. 12 Mar., 1877. 16 pp.
Pp. Eng. 1877 vol. 6
— As amended in committee on re-commitment. 14 June, 1877. 19 pp.
Pp. Eng. 1877 vol. 6
— Lords' amendments. 30 July, 1877. 9 pp. Pp. Eng. 1877 vol. 6
— Memorandum respecting Lords' amendments. 21 July, 1877. 6 pp.
Pp. Eng. 1877 vol. 6

1777. For the Hebdomadal council only. Monday, 12th March, 1877. [Amendments to] Universities of Oxford and Cambridge bill. In committee [of the House of commons.] n. pl., 1877, 8°. 14 pp.
G.A. Oxon 8° 1079 (7)

1778. NEATE, C., The Universities' reform bill. n. pl., [1877], 8°. 15 pp.
G.A. Oxon 8° 399

1779. An act to make further provision respecting the Universities of Oxford and Cambridge, and the colleges therein. (40 & 41 V., c. 48, Pub.) Lond., 1877, 4°. 21 pp.
L.L.
— 43 & 44 V., c. 11, Pub.

1780. PLAYFAIR, L., 1st baron, Universities and universities. (Macmillan's mag., 1877, vol. 35, p. 205–11.)
G.A. Oxon 4° 581 (15)

1781. SNOW, T. C., The endowment of education, an appeal to the governing bodies of colleges in Oxford. n. pl., 1877, 8°. 12 pp.
G.A. Oxon 8° 1079 (6)

1782. Statement of the requirements of the University adopted by the
Hebdomadal council on the 19th of March, 1877, with the papers
upon which it was founded. Oxf., 1877, 8°. III pp.
                                              G.A. Oxon 8° 296 (13)

See 4984 [Hatch, E., Abracadabra, a fragment of University history. 1877].

1783. MACAN, R. W., The Oxford university commission. (Theol. rev.,
1878, vol. 15, p. 388–407.)   Per. 1419 e. 1678

1784. WORDSWORTH, J., Answers to questions of the University of
Oxford commissioners (no. 10). n. pl., (1878), 8°. 8 pp.
                                              G.A. Oxon 8° 1148 (3)

1785. ROGERS, J. E. THOROLD, Reforms in the University of Oxford.
(Brit. quarterly rev., 1879, vol. 70, p. 62–95.)   Per. 3977 e. 198

1786. Economical reform at Oxford, by an Oxford tutor. (Fraser's mag.,
1880, N.S., vol. 22, p. 548–60.)   Per. 3977 e. 200

1787. PELHAM, H. F. and JACKSON, W. W., A few words on the proposals
of the Oxford university commission, by two college tutors [H. F.
Pelham and W. W. Jackson]. n. pl., [1880], 4°. 4 pp.
                                              G.A. Oxon 4° 73

1788. Presented to the Oxford university commission, 6 Dec. 1880.
[Memorial, signed by B. Bosanquet and 75 others, concerning the
Commission's proposals for the future regulation of the professoriate.]
[Oxf.], 1880, s. sh.   G.A. Oxon b. 140 (40a)

1789. The universities and their critics. (Quarterly rev., 1880, vol. 150,
p. 183–204.)   G.A. Oxon 4° 578 (51)

1790. Universities of Oxford and Cambridge (Statutes). A bill intituled
An act to make provision respecting certain statutes made by the
Commissioners under the Universities of Oxford and Cambridge act,
1877. [Concerns those statutes which may not have been approved by
Her majesty in council before the expiration on 31st Dec. 1881 of the
Commissioners' powers.] [Lond.], 1881, fol. 4 pp.
                                              Pp. Eng. 1881 vol. 6

1791. University of Oxford commission. Part 1. Minutes of evidence . . .
together with an appendix and index. Part 2. Certain circulars addressed by the Commissioners to the University and the colleges,
together with the answers, or a digest thereof. (Cd. 2868.) Lond.,
1881, fol. 415+187 pp.   R. 3.593

1792. BRYCE, J., The future of the English universities. (Fortnightly rev.,
1883, N.S., vol. 33, p. 382–403.)   Per. 3977 d. 59

See 1874, 1876–78 [Rogers, J. E. Thorold &c., Oxford professors and Oxford
tutors. 1889, 90].

1793. Oxford, democratic and popular. (Macmillan's mag., 1889/90,
vol. 61, p. 282–87.)   Per. 2705 d. 254

1794. KING, J., Democracy and our old universities. (Contemp. review, 1892, vol. 62, p. 692–708.) Per. 3977 d. 58
[Answered by no. 1431.]

1795. CAMPBELL, L., On the nationalisation of the old English universities. Lond., 1901, 8°. 306 pp. 2625 e. 32

1796. ACADEMICUS pseud., The needs of Oxford. (Blackwood's mag., 1903, vol. 173, p. 419–34.) Per. 2705 d. 386

1797. ZIMMERN, A. E., Oxford in the new century. (Independent rev., 1906, vol. 11, p. 95–104.) Per. 3977 d. 38

1798. CAMPBELL, L., Oxford reform. (Univ. rev., 1907, vol. 5, p. 489–94.) Per. 2625 d. 30

1799. Club. Suggestions regarding certain lines of university reform (as amended). [Oxf., 1907?], 8°. 6 sheets. G.A. Oxon 4° 296 (7–10)
— [Revised ed.] [Oxf., 1907?], 8°. 8 pp. Firth b. 36 (187a)

1800. JAM SENIOR, pseud., Oxford's antiquated machinery. (Oxf. and Cambr. rev., 1907, no. 2, p. 74–92.) Per. 2625 d. 37

1801. Oxford and the nation (by some Oxford tutors). Repr. from The Times. Lond., (1907), 8°. 102 pp. 2625 e. 176

1802. Suggestions towards University reform. [Oxf., 1907?], 8°. 8 pp.
G.A. Oxon 4° 296 (11)

1803. To the chancellor of the University of Oxford. [Begin.] We, the undersigned, being resident members of Convocation . . . [asking for a commission, and suggesting certain principles which should govern it. Signed by H. B. Baker and many others]. [Oxf., 1907?], s. sh.
Firth b. 36 (185b)

1804. [Begin.] The undersigned, being professors . . . [proof copy of a paper to the prime minister seeking a commission to inquire into the organization of the University]. [Oxf., 1907?], s. sh.
Firth b. 36 (183h)

1805. [Begin.] The University commissioners of 1877 . . . [A paper advocating a better central organization of the University.] [Oxf., 1907?], 8°. 3 pp. G.A. Oxon 4° 296 (6)

1806. SPOONER, W. A., Oxford university reform: is a commission necessary? (Church quarterly rev., 1908, vol. 65, p. 415–42.)
G.A. Oxon 4° 575 (41)

1807. CURZON, G. N., 1st marq., Principles & methods of University reform. Oxf., 1909, 8°. 220 pp. G.A. Oxon 8° 762

1808. Oxford university reform assoc. [Miscellaneous papers. 1909.]
G.A. Oxon 4° 275

1809. University reform. Resolutions of Council. (Oxf. mag., 1909, vol. 27, p. 279.) Per. G.A. Oxon 4° 141

1810. URQUHART, F. F., Lord Curzon and Oxford reform. (Dublin rev.,
1909, vol. 145, p. 138–46.)   Per. 3977 e. 199

1811. University reform: (Oxf. mag., 1909, vol. 27.)
    i. The constitution of Council, p. 293
    ii. The abolition of Responsions, p. 311
    iii. Finance, p. 330
    iv. A working men's college, p. 347
    v. What are we to do with our professors? p. 362
    vi. Scholarships and emoluments, p. 376.
                           Per. G.A. Oxon 4° 141

See 6430 [Anson, W. R., The place of the colleges in University reform. 1910].

1812. Principles and methods of University reform, report of the Hebdomadal council. Oxf., 1910, 8°. 98 pp.   G.A. Oxon 8° 870

1813. Oxford university reform. (Quarterly rev., 1911, vol. 214, p. 431–52.)
                           Per. 3977 e. 191

1814. University commission. Draft of proposed letter to the chancellor
[urging that a commission be appointed. Proof copy]. [Oxf., 1912],
fol. 4 pp.   G.A. Oxon b. 141 (39a)
— [Definitive ed.]   G.A. Oxon b. 141 (39b)

1815. TILLYARD, A. I., A history of university reform, from 1800 A.D. to
the present time. Cambr., 1913, 8°. 392 pp.   2625 e. 64

1816. A bill to make further provision with regard to the universities of
Oxford and Cambridge and the colleges thereof. 9 March 1914. Lond.,
1914, fol. 18 pp.   Pp. Eng. 1914 vol. 6

1817. PHELPS, L. R., Thoughts for the times. [A plea for a new order to
embody a greater simplicity in living and a greater industry.] [Oxf.],
1915, 4°. 4 pp.   G.A. Oxon 4° 262 (9)

1818. Royal commission on Oxford and Cambridge universities. Report
[With] Appendices. (Cmd. 1588.) Lond., 1922, 4° & fol. 246+372 pp.
                           2625 c. 16=R.

1819. [Evidence (in typewriting) given before the Royal Commission on
Oxford and Cambridge, 1922, was presented to the Bodleian by the
secretary to the Commission: MS. Top. Oxon b. 104–09; c. 267.]

1820. HENDERSON, B. W., Oxford: some ideals, 'reforms' and realities.
(Nineteenth cent., 1922, vol. 92, p. 625–34, 817–24.)
                           Per. 3977 d. 66

1821. A bill to make further provision with respect to the universities of
Oxford and Cambridge and the colleges therein. Lond., 1922, 4°.
12 pp.   Pp. Eng. 1922 vol. 3
— Brought from the Lords. 9 May 1923. Lond., 1923, 4°. 13 pp.
                          Pp. Eng. 1923 vol. 3
— As amended by Standing committee B. 13 pp.
                          Pp. Eng. 1923 vol. 3

1822. Report from Standing committee B on Universities of Oxford and Cambridge bill [Lords] with the proceedings of the committee. 11 July 1923. Lond., 1923, 8°. 10 pp.   Pp. Eng. 1923 vol. 8

1823. Universities of Oxford and Cambridge bill, 1923. Memorandum on expenditure likely to be incurred. Lond., 1923, s. sh.
Pp. Eng. 1923 vol. 19

1824. An act to make further provision with respect to the universities of Oxford and Cambridge and the colleges therein. (13 & 14 G. V, c. 33, Pub.) (Lond.), 1923, 8°. 14 pp.   L.L.

1825. BRIGGS, A., Oxford reformed: the centenary of the act of 1854. (Oxf. mag., 1954, vol. 72, p. 398–400.)   Per. G.A. Oxon 4° 141

1825.1. University of Oxford. Commission of inquiry. Report of [oral] evidence. [103 pt.] [Oxf.], 1964, 65, fol.   G.A. Oxon c. 341

1825.2. University of Oxford. Commission of inquiry. [Written] Evidence. 14 pt. Oxf., [1964, 65], fol.   G.A. Oxon c. 340

1825.3. University of Oxford. Report of Commission of Inquiry. 2 vols. Oxf., 1966, 8°

TEACHING

GENERAL

1826. BARKSDALE, C., An Oxford-conference of Philomathes and Polymathes [by C. Barksdale]. n. pl., 1660, 8°. 11 pp.   Arch. A. f. 96
[This may be Madan 2422, which Madan never saw.]

1827. JONES, SIR W., An oration intended to have been spoken in the Theatre, 9th of July, 1773, by a member of the University [sir W. Jones: defending learning]. Lond., 1773, 8°. 18 pp.
G.A. Oxon 8° 1046 (16)

1828. Observations on the University of Oxford. (Gents mag., 1780, vol. 50, p. 119, 20, 277, 78.)   Per. 22863 e. 193 = A.

1829. KNOX, V., Liberal education; or, A practical treatise on the methods of acquiring useful and polite learning. 9th ed. 2 vols. [Oxford univ. passim.] Lond., 1788, 8°.   Vet. A. 5. e. 4131, 4132
— [Another ed.] (The works of Vicesimus Knox, vol. 3, 4.) Lond., 1824, 8°.   24. 621, 622

1830. A letter to the rev. Vicesimus Knox on the subject of his animadversions on the University of Oxford [in Liberal education; or A practical treatise on the methods of acquiring useful and polite learning. 9th ed. 1788]. By a resident member of that University [signed Philalethes]. Oxf., 1790, 4°. 36 pp.   G.A. Oxon 4° 42 (2)

1831. M., J., On the proposed regulations in the University of Oxford [to restore its ancient discipline in exercises and examinations. Signed J. M.]. (British mag., 1800, vol. 1, p. 425–27.)   Per. 2705 e. 490

1832. COPLESTON, E., A reply to the calumnies [in several general articles between 1808 and 1810] of the Edinburgh review against Oxford, containing an account of studies pursued in that university [by E. Copleston]. Oxf., 1810, 8°. 190 pp.   8° Y 67 (1) Jur.
— 2nd ed. 1810.   G. Pamph. 2859 (1)

1833. COPLESTON, E., A second reply to the Edinburgh review, by the author [E. Copleston] of a Reply to the calumnies of that review against Oxford. Oxf., 1810, 8°. 118 pp.   8° Y 67 (2) Jur.

1834. DRUMMOND, H. H., Observations, suggested by the strictures of the Edinburgh review upon Oxford, and by the two replies [of E. Copleston] containing some account of the late changes in that university. Edinb. &c., 1810, 8°. 90 pp.   G.A. Oxon 8° 233 (6)

1835. Calumnies against Oxford. [A review of and answer to A reply to the calumnies of the Edinburgh review against Oxford, by E. Copleston.] (Edinb. review, 1810, vol. 16, p. 158–87.)
Per. 3977 e. 190

1836. Replies to the calumnies against Oxford. [A review of E. Copleston's A reply &c. and A second reply &c.] (Quarterly review, 1810, vol. 4, p. 177–206.) Per. 3977 e. 191

1837. COPLESTON, E., A third reply to the Edinburgh review, by the author [E. Copleston] of a Reply to the calumnies of that review against Oxford. Oxf., 1811, 8°. 22 pp. 8° Y 67 (3) Jur.

1838. Three Replies to the calumnies against Oxford, &c. [A review of E. Copleston's Replies to the Edinburgh review.] (British critic, 1811, vol. 37, p. 346–56.) G.A. Oxon 4° 577 (4)

1839. TATHAM, E., Oxonia purgata, consisting of a series of addresses on the subject of the new discipline in the University. Lond., 1812, 4°.
G.A. Oxon 4° 48

1840. Oxoniana, a didactic poem . . . on the late improved mode of study and examination for degrees in the University of Oxford, by a Cambridge master of arts [by — Ward of Peterhouse, Cambr.]. Lond., 1812, 8°. 98 pp. 2804 e. 54 (14)

1841. An enquiry into the studies and discipline, adopted in the two English universities, as preparatory to holy orders in the Established Church. By a graduate. Lond., 1824, 8°. 55 pp. 24. 666 (1)

1842. A letter to the author of An enquiry into the studies and discipline adopted in the two English universities, as preparatory to holy orders in the Established Church. By a graduate of the University of Oxford. Lond., 1824, 8°. 31 pp. 24. 666 (2)

1843. TOWNSEND, W. C., The pæan of Oxford, a poem. To which is prefixed, A reply to the charges adduced against the University in the recent numbers of the Edinburgh [Aug. 1825, p. 346] and Westminster [July 1825, p. 147] reviews. Lond., 1826, 4°. 157 pp. G.A. Oxon 4° 4

1844. [Begin.] It is respectfully suggested . . . [that tutors should specialize in the subjects they teach, and perhaps form their pupils into small classes]. May 25. (Oxf.), 1829, s. sh. G.A. Oxon c. 45 (52)

1845. [Form of supplication 'pro minus diligenti publicorum lectorum auditione'. In use about 1830.] G.A. Oxon b. 111 (237)

1846. HAMILTON, SIR W., Universities of England—Oxford. [Observations demonstrating the illegality of the present academical system, with suggestions for its reform. By sir W. Hamilton.] (Edinb. review, 1831, vol. 53, p. 384–427; 1831, vol. 54, p. 478–504.)
Per 3977 e. 190
— [Repr. in no. 1858.]

1847. INGRAM, J., Apologia academica; or, Remarks on a recent article in [vol. 53 of] the Edinburgh review [by J. Ingram]. Oxf. &c., 1831, 8°. 43 pp. 31. 471

1848. THOMAS, V., The legality of the present academical system of the University asserted against the new calumnies of the Edinburgh

review. By a member of Convocation [V. Thomas. Pt. 1]. Oxf., 1831,
8°. 147 pp.   31. 629
— [Pt. 2]. 1832. 83 pp.   32. 740
— 2nd ed. 2 pt. Oxf. &c., 1853, 8°. 147+80 pp.
      G.A. Oxon 8° 63 (20)

1849. Considerations on the great and various injuries arising from the
course of education pursued in the Universities of Oxford and Cambridge. Lond. &c., 1832, 8°. 39 pp.   32. 449

1850. Attack on the universities—Oxford. [A review of the several
attacks made by the Edinburgh review on the academical system of
Oxford and the admission of Dissenters, 1831 etc.] (British critic,
1837, vol. 22, p. 168–215; 397–438.)   G.A. Oxon 4° 577 (8, 9)

1851. PYCROFT, J., The student's guide to a course of reading necessary
for obtaining university honours. By a graduate of Oxford [J. Pycroft].
Oxf., 1837, 8°. 135 pp.   37. 495

1852. Extracts illustrating the extent of instruction which might be
afforded by the University. Oxf., [1839], 8°. 15 pp.
      G.A. Oxon c. 55 (32)

1853. Oxford—tutors and professors. (Quarterly review, 1840, vol. 66,
p. 162–90.)   Per. 3977 e. 191

1854. OGLE, J. A., A letter . . . on the system of education pursued at
Oxford; with suggestions for remodeling the examination statutes
[signed J. A. Ogle]. Oxf., 1841, 8°. 22 pp.   G.A. Oxon 8° 77 (7)

1855. MANSEL, H. L., A plea for the private tutors; or, Alumnus in search
of a dodge, containing a dissertation on dodges in general and remarks
on the recent pamphlet [Should public examiners be private tutors?
No. 2074] of a Bachelor of arts [D. P. Chase. By H. L. Mansel].
Oxf., 1843, 8°. 13 pp.   G.A. Oxon 8° 1033 (2)

1856. ACLAND, H. W., Remarks on the extension of education at the
University of Oxford, a letter. Oxf. &c., 1848, 8°. 39 pp.
      G.A. Oxon c. 65 (44)

1857. PRICE, B., Suggestions for the extension of professorial teaching in
the University of Oxford. Lond. &c., 1850, 8°. 38 pp.
      G.A. Oxon 8° 1101 (8)

1858. HAMILTON, SIR W., Discussions on philosophy and literature,
education and university reform, chiefly from the Edinburgh review,
corrected, vindicated, enlarged. [Oxf. univ. *passim*.] Lond. &c., 1852,
8°. 758 pp.   265 i. 61
—2nd ed., enlarged. Lond. &c., 1853, 8°. 852 pp.   265 i. 60

1859. PATTISON, M., Oxford studies. (Oxf. essays, 1855, p. 251–310.)
      270 a. 16

1860. CHASE, D. P., 'The voluntary system' applied to academical instruction, suggestions. Oxf., 1859, 8°. 16 pp.   G.A. Oxon 8° 71 (6)

1861. BURROWS, M., Pass and class, an Oxford guide-book through the courses of literæ humaniores, mathematics, natural science, and law and modern history. Oxf. &c., 1860, 8°. 256 pp.   260 g. 110

1862. ROGERS, J. E. THOROLD, Education in Oxford: its method, its aids, and its rewards. Lond., 1861, 8°. 266 pp.   260 f. 70

1863. SEEBOHM, F., The Oxford reformers of 1498 [John Colet, Erasmus &c.]. (Fortnightly review, 1866, vol. 5 and 6, *passim*.)
                                                                   Per. 3977 d. 59

1864. SEEBOHM, F., The Oxford reformers of 1498. Lond., 1867, 8°.
440 pp.   210 e. 173
— 2nd ed., revised. 1869. 551 pp.   210 j. 15
— 3rd ed. 1887.   11117 e. 83
— Repr. 1896.   11117 e. 84
— [Another ed.] (Everyman's libr., 665.) 1914.   11117 f. 25
[This work incorporates the preceding item.]

1865. The paper read at Dundee and the University of Oxford. [A paper, signed A member of Convocation, defending Oxford against alleged shortcomings as a place of education.] Oxf., (1867), 4°. 3 pp.
                                                             G.A. Oxon c. 83 (422)

See 1754 [Pattison, M., Suggestions on academical organisation. 1868].

1866. Oxford studies—mr. Pattison and dr .Gillow. (Month, 1869, vol. 11, p. 100–08.)   Per. 11132 d. 17

1867. Study and opinions at Oxford. (Macmillan's mag., 1869/70, vol. 21, p. 184–92.)   Per. 2705 d. 254

1868. RUMSEY, J., A few words on teaching in Oxford. (Oxf., 1871), 8°.
8 pp.   G.A. Oxon 8° 455 (3)

1869. HOLLAND, T. E., On the ancient organisation of the University of Oxford. (Proc., Oxf. architect. and hist. soc., 1877, N.S., vol. 3, p. 287–94.)   Soc. G.A. Oxon 8° 498=R.
— [Another version.] (Macmillan's mag., 1877, vol. 36, p. 203–10.)
                                                             G.A. Oxon 4° 577 (27)

1870. WORDSWORTH, C., Scholae academicae: some account of the studies at the English universities in the eighteenth century. Cambr. &c., 1877, 8°. 435 pp.   260 e. 45=R.

1871. INCE, W., The education of the clergy at the universities, a sermon. Oxf. &c., (1882), 8°. 16 pp.   100 e. 112 (21)

1872. Teaching at Oxford. i. The University and the colleges. ii. The School of Literae humaniores. [Signed N. T.] (Oxf. mag., 1883, vol. 1, p. 225, 26, 290.)   Per. G.A. Oxon 4° 141

1873. WALLIS, J., Dr. Wallis' letter against mr. Maidwell, 1700 [concerning a proposal to establish an 'academy of exercises, such as riding the great horse, fencing, &c.' The work also contains information on the

University curriculum. Ed. by T. W. Jackson]. (Oxf. hist. soc., 1885, vol. 5, p. 269–337.)   G.A. Oxon 8° 360=R.

See 3871 [Freeman, E. A., Oxford after forty years. 1887].

1874. ROGERS, J. E. THOROLD, Oxford professors and Oxford tutors. (Contemp. rev., 1889, vol. 56, p. 926–36.)   Per. 3977 d. 58

1875. PALGRAVE, F. T., The Oxford movement of the fifteenth century. (19th cent., 1890, vol. 28, p. 812–30.)   Per. 3977 d. 66

1876. Oxford professors and Oxford tutors: reply of the examiners in the School of modern history [to no. 1874]. (Contemp. rev., 1890, vol. 57, p. 183–86.)   Per. 3977 d. 58

1877. ROGERS, J. E. THOROLD, The four Oxford history lecturers. [A reply.] (Contemp. rev., 1890, vol. 57, p. 454–56.)   Per. 3977 d. 58

1878. COURTNEY, W. L., Oxford tutors and their professorial critic [Thorold Rogers]. (Fortnightly rev., 1890, vol. 53, p. 294–96.)
                                                           Per. 3977 d. 59

1879. Report of the committee appointed by the meeting held in . . . Corpus Christi college on February 12, 1891 "to elicit opinions as to alternative schemes for shortening the honours course". March 13, 1891. [Oxf.], (1891), 4°. 2 sheets.   Firth b. 36 (105a)

1880. SAMPSON, E. F., Forms and reforms. [Oxf.], (1892), 8°. 4 pp.
                                                      G.A. Oxon b. 140 (98)

See 3761 [Little, A. G., Educational organisation of the mendicant friars. 1894].

1881. DAVIDSON, J. STRACHAN-, To the teachers in the Faculty of arts (Literae humaniores). The Civil service examination. [Observations and suggested reforms]. May 8. n. pl., (1903), fol. 4 pp.   26326 c. 82

1882. Civil Service examination. [Report of the opinions of the Syndicate of Cambridge university authorised to act in connection with the examination. This report was suppressed.] 5 June. [Oxf.], (1903), s. sh.   26326 c. 82

1883. A memorial to the Civil Service commissioners [by 7 delegates nominated by the Hebdomadal council to negotiate on matters connected with the Joint examination for the Home, Indian, and Colonial services]. June 23. (Oxf., 1903), s. sh.   26326 c. 82

1884. Civil service examinations. [An amended scheme which the Oxford committee of negotiation propose to submit.] Oct. 1903. [Oxf.], 1903, s. sh.   26326 c. 82

1885. To the Secretary, Civil service commission. [Amended scheme and proposed modifications of the syllabus, submitted by the Oxford committee of negotiation.] Nov. 13, 1903. [Oxf.], 1903, fol. 3 pp.
                                                           26326 c. 82

1886. Report on negotiations with Cambridge philosophers [by the representatives of the teachers of philosophy at Oxford, in connection with

the Civil service examinations. Signed S. Ball and J. A. Smith]. n. pl.,
[1903], 8°. 5 pp. 26326 c. 82

1887. To the Secretary, Civil service commission. [Remarks by the Oxford
committee of negotiation on a memorial presented Dec. 17, 1903 by
the Cambridge committee.] Feb. 9, 1904. [Oxf.], 1904, fol. 4 pp.
26326 c. 82

1888. PALMER, E. J., [*Begin.*] While the question of the future arrangement of the events in the Summer term . . . [Request for answers to
the listed questions designed to provide the statistics of work, 1905.]
May 26, 1905. [Oxf.], (1905), 8°. 3 pp. Firth b. 36 (91)

1889. PALMER, E. J., The Eights week, 1904 (1905). Statistics of work.
[Statement exhibiting the unfortunate effect of the week on work and
attendance at lectures.] [Oxf., 1905], 06, fol. 8+8 pp.
G.A. Oxon c. 107 (48, 49)

1890. To the members of Congregation. The rearrangement of the [dates
of examinations in the] summer term [signed A. Hassall, E. J. Palmer].
[Oxf., 1906], 4°. 3 pp. G.A. Oxon c. 153

1891. SAMPSON, C. H., The examinations in the Summer term. [A criticism of the statute to be proposed in Congregation on Feb. 13, which
seeks to alter the dates of examinations.] Feb. 9. [Oxf.], (1906), 4°.
3 pp. G.A. Oxon 4° 186 (16)

See 1801 [Oxford and the nation. 1907].

1892. GRUNDY, G. B., Teaching and teachers in the University of Oxford.
(Oxf., 1910), 8°. 8 pp. G.A. Oxon 8° 761 (29)

1893. CLAYTON, H. E., Oxford as a training ground of candidates for holy
orders, the Latin sermon, Oct. 13, 1911. n. pl., (1911), 8°. 8 pp.
G.A. Oxon 8° 828 (9)

1894. MYRES, SIR J. L., The provision for historical studies at Oxford.
Lond. &c., 1915, 8°. 27 pp. 2625 d. 55 (5)

1895. STEWART, J. A., Oxford after the War & a liberal education. Oxf.,
1919, 8°. 35 pp. G.A. Oxon 4° 399 (13)

1896. Notes sur les universités étrangères: ii. Ce qu'on apprend à l'Université d'Oxford. (Revue des sci. pol., 1920, p. 210–17.) All Souls coll.

See 962 [Case, T., Letters to The Times, 1884–1922. 1927].

1897. The tutorial system. (Oxf. mag., 1932, vol. 50, p. 525, 26.)
Per. G.A. Oxon 4° 141

1898. LINDSAY, A. D., Changes in Oxford schools since the war. (Oxford,
1935, vol. 1, no. 3, p. 39–47.) Per. G.A. Oxon 8° 1141

1899. RICHARDSON, H. G., An Oxford teacher of the 15th century
[Simon O., with notes on the Oxford dictatores, including T. Sampson.]
(Bull., John Rylands libr., 1939, vol. 23, p. 436–57.)
Per. 2590 d. Manch. 2. 5=A.

1900. RICHARDSON, H. G., Business training in mediaeval Oxford [as illustrated by the career of T. Sampson, teacher of writing &c.]. (Amer. hist. review, 1941, vol. 46, p. 259, 60.)   Per. 2231 d. 67=K.

1901. HASKINS, G. L., The University of Oxford and the 'Ius ubique docendi'. (Engl. hist. review, 1941, vol. 56, p. 281–92.)
Per. 2231 d. 342=K.

1902. LAST, H., Courses for the demobilised. (Oxf. mag., 1944, vol. 63, p. 5, 6.)   Per. G.A. Oxon 4° 141

1903. POWICKE, F. M., Ways of medieval life and thought. (Oxford passim.) Lond., [1950], 8° 255 pp.   22215 e. 14

1904. HITCH, C., Reflections on Oxford and education. (Amer. Oxonian, 1959, vol. 46, p. 5–12.)   Per. G.A. Oxon 8° 889

1904.2. QUINTON, A., The tutorial system. (Oxf. mag., 1960, vol. 78, p. 284–86.)   Per. G.A. Oxon 4° 141

1904.21. WARNOCK, G. J., The tutorial system. (Oxf. mag., 1960, vol. 78, p. 286, 87.)   Per. G.A. Oxon 4° 141

See 2570 [Carter, P. B., Law at Oxford: miscellaneous comments. 1960].

1904.4. HEUSTON, R. F. V., How hard do dons work? (Oxf. mag., 1962, N.S., vol. 2, p. 227, 28.)   Per. G.A. Oxon 4° 141

See 6485.1, 6485.2 [Report [and] Further report on the closer integration of university teaching and research with the college system. 1964].
See 6485.3 [Report of the Committee to make detailed proposals for carrying out the policy in the Further report etc. 1964].
See 973.6 [Report of a committee to consider points arising out of the Robbins report. 1964].

PROFESSORSHIPS, READERSHIPS, AND LECTURESHIPS

See also under Faculties, 2448, &c., for works on specific professorships, readerships, and lectureships.
See also Reform, 1638, &c.

1905. Encyclopædia seu orbis literarum prout in florentissima iam et omnium plane celeberrima Academia Oxoniensi singulis terminis publice in scholis auditoribus proponuntur. Cyclus prælectorum tam indotat quam dotat: ex corpore statutorum depromptus et delineatus. [Madan 795.] [Oxf? 1635?], s. sh.   O.U.A.
— [Another issue, 1638.] [Madan 875.]   8° O 19 Jur.
— [Another issue, 1638.] [Madan 876.]

1905.1. Speculum academicum: quadratura circuli, sive Cyclus prælectorum in schema redactus. [Madan 878.] [Oxf., 1638?], s. sh.
Wood 423 (16)

1906. Oxon: studia. Quadratura circuli, Anglor: Athenæ. Studiorum & exercitii academici, pridem editi. In hac forma reduxit W. S. [Designed to show all the statutable lectures, &c.] [Madan 1577.] Lond., 1643, s. sh.   Wood 423 (19)

1907. BURGHERS, M., Venerabili viro Guilielmo Lancaster . . . tabulam hanc disciplinæ publicæ dicat dedicat M. B. Encyclopædia seu orbis literarum prout in florentissima jam et omnium plane celeberrima Academia Oxoniensi, singulis terminis publice in scholis auditoribus proponuntur. [Oxf.], 1709, s. sh.   Gough Maps 57 (7)

1908. [*Begin.*] As an altered form of the statute De lectoribus publicis . . . [A paper on this alteration as it affects lectureships in grammar, rhetoric, logic and metaphysics.] Oxf., [1839], s. sh.
G.A. Oxon c. 55 (30)

1909. DAUBENY, C., To the members of Convocation. [A letter giving support for the revision of the statute De lectoribus publicis, and containing statistics of subscribers to lectures on chemistry during the years 1822/3–1838.] n. pl., 1839, fol. 3 pp.   G.A. Oxon c. 55 (31)

1910. DAUBENY, C., To the members of Convocation. [A letter giving further details of decreased attendance at lectures on subjects alien to those required in the Examination schools.] n. pl., 1839, s. sh.
G.A. Oxon c. 55 (42)

1911. PAYNE, P. S. H., Brief remarks on the revival of the professorial system, proposed in the statute to be submitted . . . on the 15th of March next. By a member of Convocation [P. S. H. Payne.] Oxf. &c., 1839, 8°. 16 pp.   39. 951

1912. [*Begin.*] Many persons . . . [Comments on the proposed statute De lectoribus publicis.] Oxf., [1839], s. sh.   G.A. Oxon c. 55 (29)

1913. Considerations of a plan for combining the professorial system with the system of public examinations in Oxford, by a tutor of a college. Oxf., 1839, 8°. 37 pp.   2625 e. 31 (5)

1914. HUSSEY, R., An examination of the new form of the statutes Tit. IV. Tit. V. with hints for establishing a system of professorial teaching. Oxf. &c., 1839, 8°. 42 pp.   39. 807

1915. TAIT, A. C., Hints on the formation of a plan for the safe and effectual revival of the professorial system in Oxford, by a resident member of Convocation [A. C. Tait]. Oxf. &c., 1839, 8°. 46 pp.   39. 1019 (2)

See 1853 [Oxford—tutors and professors. 1840].

1916. A narrative of the steps lately taken in Oxford towards the revival of the professorial system. (Educ. mag., 1840, N.S., vol. I, p. 85–100.)
Per. 2622 e. 39

1917. Oxford and Cambridge universities . . . Returns relative to the professors of Oxford and Cambridge included in the annual vote in the miscellaneous estimates [&c.]. 24 February 1846. [Lond.], 1846, fol. 6 pp.   Pp. Eng. 1846 vol. 32

See 1857 [Price, B., Suggestions for the extension of professorial teaching. 1850].
See 1428 [Augmentation of professorial salaries. 1851].

1918. DAUBENY, C., Brief remarks on the statute De lectoribus publicis, to be submitted to Convocation on . . . June 17. Oxf., 1851, 8°. 12 pp.
G.A. Oxon 8° 72 (1)

1919. The statute De quibusdam dotationibus, &c. [A criticism of the proposed amendment, signed 'A Rationibus'.] Mar. 5. (Oxf., 1856), 4°. 4 pp.   G.A. Oxon c. 72 (97)

1920. The new professorial statute [signed A member of Congregation. Remarks particularly about the Sedley and Savile professorships]. Oxf., [1857], s. sh.   G.A. Oxon b. 29

See 2018 [Daubeny, C., Attendance on the lectures of professors. 1857].

1921. Members of Congregation are respectfully informed that the following provisions and alterations will be made by the statute 'De lectoribus publicis' which will be promulgated Feb. 8th. [Oxf., 1859], s. sh.   G.A. Oxon a. 15

1922. A bill for enabling the University of Oxford to make statutes for the better regulation of professorships therein, and for other purposes relating thereto; and to retain the custody of certain testamentary documents [of the Court of the Chancellor of the University]. 20 June 1860. [Lond.], 1860, fol. 5 pp.   Pp. Eng. 1860 vol. 5

1923. [Begin.] By a form of statute . . . [Statement of proposed increases in the stipends of the professors of Greek, Logic, Moral philosophy, Geometry, Chemistry, Experimental philosophy, and Geology.] Nov. 19. n. pl., (1861), 8°. 4 pp.   G.A. Oxon c. 77 (364)

See 2572–74 [3 papers concerning the Law and other professorships. 1861].

1924. General notice of lectures of professors. [A statement by the vice-chancellor inaugurating a terminal lecture list in lieu of individual notices.] Mar. 24. [Oxf.], 1866, s. sh.   G.A. Oxon c. 81 (110)

1925. [Replies to a circular letter of enquiry sent by the vice-chancellor in 1873 to the several boards of studies and professors, concerning the number of professors, the distribution of subjects among such professors, distinction between professors, readers, &c.]. n. pl., (1874), 8°. 70 pp.   G.A. Oxon 8° 124 (24)

1926. Oxford and Cambridge universities. Return . . . stating . . . for each year, from 1870–1875 . . . the number, names, and description of professors, and the mode of appointment of each professor; the emoluments of each professor; the number of lectures delivered by each professor; the average number of auditors present at each lecture for 1856 to 1875; [statistics relating to the Press fund]. [Lond.], 1876, fol. 34 pp.   Pp. Eng. 1876 vol. 59

1927. Oxford university follette. Published sans authority. Tuesday, November 30, 1880. Supplement to Supplement to no. 365. [A satire in verse on the proposed statute on the duties of professors.] [Oxf.], 1880, s. sh.   G.A. fol. A 130
[In this copy 23 of the professors lampooned are identified in a MS. footnote.]

1928. ROLLESTON, G., Compulsory attendance on professors' lectures. Dec. 9. (Oxf., 1880), 4°. 3 pp.   G.A. Oxon b. 140 (39*b*)

See 1788 [Proposals for the regulation of the professoriate. 1880].

1929. Universities of Oxford and Cambridge act, 1877. (Oxford.) Forty-one statutes made by the . . . Commissioners, 1881, concerning certain professorships, electoral boards and tenure of professorships, the operation of the statutes . . ., the publication of the accounts of the colleges, the form of the accounts, the audit and publication thereof. Lond., 1882, fol. 36 pp.   Pp. Eng. 1882 vol. 51

1930. Universities (Oxford and Cambridge). Reform of [certain] particulars . . . with respect to each . . . professorship, readership, lectureship . . . the fellows of each college . . . the number of students . . . college and university statutes . . . the Common university fund. Lond., 1886, fol. 74 pp.   Pp. Eng. 1886 vol. 51

1931. Oxford and its professors. (Edinb. review, Oct. 1889, vol. 170, p. 303–27.)   G.A. Oxon 4° 577 (42)

1932. Oxford and its professors. (Nature, 1889, vol. 40, p. 637.)
                Per. 1996 d. 596

See 1874, 1876–78 [Rogers, J. E. Thorold, &c. Oxford professors and Oxford tutors. 1889, 90].

1933. [*Begin.*] The object of the accompanying petition is to induce . . . [A memorial that Oxford is not obtaining the best possible results from the readerships created by the commissioners.] [Oxf., *c.* 1893], fol. 2 sheets.   Firth b. 36 (81)

See 1963 [Certificates of attendance at professorial lectures a necessary condition for obtaining honours in examinations. 1897].
See 1811 [What are we to do with our professors? 1909].
See 1040 [Position of professors and readers upon the Hebdomadal council. 1912].

1934. GARDNER, P., Professorial pensions at Oxford. [Oxf.], (1913), 8°. 3 pp.   G.A. Oxon c. 310 (122)

1935. Draft statutes (Tit. IV, sect. ii) concerning individual chairs. [Oxf., 1923], 8°. 56 pp.   G.A. Oxon 8° 1055 (15)

1936. MCCALLUM, R. B., Lectures and lecturers. (Oxf. mag., 1931, vol. 49, p. 322–26.)   Per. G.A. Oxon 4° 141

1937. MCCALLUM, R. B., Professorships and readerships. (Oxf. mag., 1944, vol. 62, p. 162, 63.)   Per. G.A. Oxon 4° 141

DEMONSTRATORS

1937.5. Oxford life as seen by a University Demonstrator appointed from outside. (Oxf. mag., 1961, N.S., vol. 1, p. 397, 98.)
                Per. G.A. Oxon 4° 141

1937.51. KREBS, SIR H., The salaries of Demonstrators. (Oxf. mag., 1961, N.S., vol. 2, p. 5–9.)   Per. G.A. Oxon 4° 141

1937.52. CHILVER, G. E. F., Demonstrators, colleges and professors. (Oxf. mag., 1961, N.S., vol. 2, p. 30, 31.) Per. G.A. Oxon 4° 141

1937.53. WILLIAMS, E. M. VAUGHAN, Academic freedom. [Comment on nos. 1937.5–1937.52.] (Oxf. mag., 1961, N.S., vol. 2, p. 94–96.)
Per. G.A. Oxon 4° 141

EXAMINATIONS
General

See also Admission of women, 3248, &c.

1938. NAPLETON, J., Considerations on the public exercises for the first and second degrees in the University of Oxford [by J. Napleton]. [Oxf.], 1773, 8°. xiii+61 pp. G.A. Oxon 8° 91 (1)

1939. [*Begin* Sig. B.] The rev. D. Wilson, vice-principal of St. Edmund hall, feels himself called upon to state . . . the circumstances of the examination of his pupil, mr. Cradock Glascott on . . . May 11, 1807. (Oxf., 1807), 4°. 11 pp. G.A. Oxon b. 19

1940. BRICKENDEN, F. H., To the members of Convocation [protesting against the treatment in the examinations of Henry Evans]. Oxf., (1810), s. sh. G.A. Oxon b. 140 (11*b*)

See 7834 [Hare, A. W., A letter on the proposed inclusion of New college in university examinations. 1814].

1941. SHORT, T. V., A letter addressed to . . . the dean of Christ Church on the present state of the public examinations in the University. Oxf., 1822, 8°. 26 pp. G.A. Oxon 8° 66

1942. A brief appeal to the good sense of the University of Oxford on classification of merit: with some hints to the rev. H. A. Woodgate on logic, by Philodicæus. Oxf., 1829, 8°. 18 pp.
G.A. Oxon 8° 215*b* (5)

1943. Suggestions, &c. [*Begin.*] Whilst almost all . . . [A scheme for improving the system whereby candidates proceed to honours.] [Oxf., 1830?], 4°. 3 pp. G.A. Oxon b. 140 (17*a*)

See 1913 [Considerations of a plan for combining the professorial system with the system of public examinations. 1839].

1944. [*Begin.*] A desire having been expressed . . . [Statement 'respecting the subjects in which it may be desirable that candidates should offer to be examined for the Final public examination in each of the four schools, and the books which they may be recommended to read'] n. pl., [1852], fol. 4 pp. G.A. Oxon c. 68 (118)

1945. CHASE, D. P., 'The voluntary system' applied to university examinations, considerations addressed . . . to members of Congregation. Oxf., 1859, 8°. 10 pp. G.A. Oxon 8° 71 (7)

See 2754 [Freeman, E. A., Historical study at Oxford. 1859].

1945.1. On the meaning of the term 'First class in one of the public examinations' [signed 'A member of Convocation']. [Oxf.], (1860), 8°. 8 pp.   G.A. Oxon 8° 208 (6)

1946. CHASE, D. P., [*Begin.*] The following remarks . . . [intended to promote discussion about the manner in which a more convenient distribution of the examinations may be accomplished]. n. pl., (1861), s. sh.   G.A. Oxon c. 77 (37)

1947. Report of the committee [of the Association of professors and tutors] appointed to consider the question of relieving classmen in the final schools from their second pass-school. Oxf., 1862, 8°. 7 pp.
G.A. Oxon c. 250 (vii)

1948. [*Begin.*] For the Hebdomadal council only. The undersigned members of Congregation . . . [Observations on the evil of breaking in upon a 'classman's' time with pass examinations.] Oct. [Oxf., 1862], 4°. 4 pp.   G.A. Oxon c. 78 (341)

1949. The Oxford examinations tabularly arranged, from the latest sources of information. Oxf. &c., [1864], s. sh.   B.M.

1950. [*Begin.*] Members of Congregation engaged in tuition are invited to attend a meeting . . . to consider the subjects touched upon in the following letter from the vice-chancellor [to C. W. Sandford on changes in examinations]. [Oxf., 1864], s. sh.
G.A. Oxon c. 80 (169)

1951. The Oxford examinations [syllabus]. Oxf., 1865, s. sh.
G.A. Oxon 4° 277
— corrected to Oct., 1866, by J. Williams. Oxf., 1866, s. sh.
G.A. Oxon 4° 35

1952. SHIRLEY, W. W., Ought our honours to be given without limit of age? Oxf., 1865, 8°. 12 pp.   G.A. Oxon 8° 296 (8)

1953. In the Schools' quad. (Belgravia, 1867, vol. 1, p. 73–79.)
Per. 256 d. 254

1954. [*Begin.*] The interest which you are known to take . . . [A letter, signed C. H. Hoole, to C. W. Sandford, on the subject of pass grammar papers in pass classical examinations.] Oxf., (1867), 4°. 3 pp.
G.A. Oxon c. 83 (429)

1955. CLARKE, R. F., The influence of pass examinations, with a scheme for their incorporation into the honour schools. Oxf. &c., 1869, 8°. 31 pp.   G.A. Oxon 8° 100 (9)

1956. RUMSEY, J., 'Pass' examinations in Oxford [signed J. Rumsey]. (Oxf., 1876), 8°. 7 pp.   G.A. Oxon 8° 455 (1)

1957. FOWLER, T., On examinations. (Fortnightly rev., 1876, vol. 25, p. 418–29.)   G.A. Oxon 4° 578 (43)

1958. Oxford university examinations [defects and remedies]. n. pl., [1881], s. sh.   G.A. Oxon b. 140 (42*b*)

1959. JACKSON, W. W., [Reprints of 3 letters, of 15 Dec., 1883; 5 Jan. and 17 Jan. 1884, to the Guardian, all headed Divinity examinations at Oxford.] [Oxf., 1883, 84], s. sh.   G.A. Oxon b. 140 (50)

1960. COURTNEY, W. L., Recasting of Schools. (Fortnightly rev., 1884, vol. 41, p. 675–82.)   Per. 3977 d. 59

1961. Oxford Pass schools: 'Smalls': 'Mods': 'Greats'. [An account of the procedure involved in taking the examinations.] (Chambers's journ., 1885, p. 731–33; 1887, p. 310–13; 1888, p. 641–43.)
                                                            Per. 2705 d. 396

1962. UNDERHILL, G. E., Pass and preliminary honour examinations. [The scheme recommended by the committee appointed by the Hebdomadal council to consider the question is also included.] October 24, 1895. [Oxf.], (1895), 8°. 7 pp.   G.A. Oxon 8° 540 (21)

1963. Memorial to the Hebdomadal council [signed D. B. Monro, J. L. Strachan-Davidson, S. H. Butcher, against the resolution of the council suggesting to the University commissioners that certificates of attendance on two courses of Professorial lectures shall be a necessary condition for obtaining honours in examinations]. n. pl., [1897?], 4°. 5 pp.   G.A. Oxon 4° 119 (11)

1964. GROSE, T. H., Faculty of arts. Final examination for the B.A. degree. [Historical account by T. H. Grose.] [Oxf., 1900], 2 sheets.
                                                            G.A. Oxon b. 41 (1)

See also 1888–91 [Rearrangement of events in the summer term, 1905, 06].

1965. RYLE, G., For and against the vivas. [A letter.] (Oxf. mag., 1936, vol. 54, p. 339–41.)   Per. G.A. Oxon 4° 141

1966. A., P. E., "Quousque—?" [An article on viva voce examinations.] (Oxf. mag., 1939, vol. 57, p. 733, 34.)   Per. G.A. Oxon 4° 141

1966.4 BATESON, F. N. W., The fallibility of Finals. (Oxf. mag., 1964, N.S., vol. 4, p. 284–86.)   Per. G.A. Oxon 4° 141

1966.5. HARGREAVES, E. L., Combined schools at Oxford (1914–23). (Oxf. mag., 1966, p. 344–50.)   Per. G.A. Oxon 4° 141

1966.6. Report of the Committee on the structure of the First and Second Public Examinations [the Kneale report]. (Oxf. Univ. gazette, Suppl. no. 3, March 1965.) Oxf., 1965, 8°. 141 pp.   Per. G.A. Oxon c. 86

1966.61. Worcester college tutors on the Kneale report. (Oxf. mag., 1965, vol. 6, p. 91–96.)   Per. G.A. Oxon 4° 141

1966.62. BUXTON, R., The Kneale report: further doubts. (Oxf. mag., 1965, vol. 6, p. 112–14.)   Per. G.A. Oxon 4° 141

1966.621. KNEALE, W. C., The Kneale report. (Oxford, 1965, vol. 20, p. 50–59.)   Per. G.A. Oxon 8° 1141

1966.63. KNEALE, W. C., An answer from Kneale. (Oxf. mag., 1966, p. 201, 02.)   Per. G.A. Oxon 4° 141

1966.64. CALDER, W. M., Colleges and the Kneale scheme: a modern
linguist considers implications of the Report. (Oxf. mag., 1966, p. 234,
35.)   Per. G.A. Oxon 4° 141

1966.65. The opinions of schoolmasters on science courses at Oxbridge
[the Kneale report]. (Oxf. mag., 1966, p. 257–59.)
                                                        Per. G.A. Oxon 4° 141

1966.66. TOMLINSON, M., Oxford Chemistry and the Kneale report.
(Oxf. mag., 1966, p. 292, 93.)   Per. G.A. Oxon 4° 141

Lists

1967. Ordo baccalaureorum determinantium in Quadragesima Oxoniæ.
1668–1855. [Oxf.], 1668–1855, s. sh.
[The following years are in Bodley: 1668, 70, 72, 74–78, 80–95, 1705,
06, 08, 10–13, 15–22, 24–68, 73, 77, 79, 81–83, 90–92, 1809, 11–13,
15, 19, 20. They are to be found in Wood 276a, b; G.A. fol. B 34;
fol. Θ 662; G.A. Oxon b. 13, 19, 111; G.A. Oxon c. 40–71, 250; MS.
Top. Oxon d. 281. For more detailed identification of issues, see the
entry in the Bodleian catalogue.]

1968. Scholares facultatis artium qui se examinatoribus publicis maxime
commendaverunt. 1802–06. [afterw.] Candidatorum termini sti.
Michaelis [&c.] 1807–24. [afterw.] Nomina candidatorum qui honore
digni sunt habiti [&c.] 1825–69. Oxf., (1802–69), s. sh.
[Copies for 1802–06: G.A. Oxon b. 111 (107 &c.); 1807, 08: Don. b.
12 (121b, 128); 1809–23: G.A. Oxon a. 14; b. 19, 20; 1824–69: G.A.
Oxon c. 40–85. Subsequently publ. in the Oxford University gazette.]

1969. Ordo examinandorum. Termino Michaelis [&c.] 1807–52. [afterw.]
Nomina examinandorum in prima (secunda) examinatione [&c.] 1853–
69. [Oxf.], (1807–69), s. sh.
[Copies for 1807, 08: Don. b. 12 (121a, 127); 1809–12: G.A. Oxon a.
14; 1814–23: G.A. Oxon b. 19, 20; 1824–69: G.A. Oxon c. 40–85.
Subsequently publ. in the Oxford University gazette.]

1970. Ordo respondentium. 1809–69. [Oxf.], (1809–69), s. sh.
[Copies may be found passim in G.A. Oxon a. 14; b. 19–32; c. 40–85.
Subsequently publ. in the Oxford University gazette.]

Statutes

General

1971. [Begin.] The undersigned tutors . . . [Paper, signed by H. Kett and
6 other tutors, announcing that they will vote against clauses in the
statute De examinandis graduum candidatis. May 20, 1800.] [Oxf.],
1800, s. sh.   G.A. Oxon b. 19

1972. TATHAM, E., An address [signed E. Tatham] to the members of
Convocation at large, on the proposed statute on examination. (Oxf.,
1807), 4°. 17 pp.   G.A. Oxon 4° 23 (1)

— 2nd ed. [*entitled*] An address . . . on the proposed new statute respecting public examination. Lond., 1807, 4°. 18 pp.

G.A. Oxon 4° 276 (2)

— 3rd ed. 1807.   G.A. Oxon 4° 778

1973. TATHAM, E., A second address . . . on the proposed new statute respecting public examinations by the rector of Lincoln college [E. Tatham]. Oxf., 1807, 4°. 8 pp.   G.A. Oxon 4° 23 (2)

— 2nd ed. 1807.   G.A. Oxon 4° 48

1974. Strictures [signed A member of Convocation] on the new statute 'De examinandis graduum candidatis'; together with remarks on dr. Tatham's First and Second Address. Oxf., 1807, 4°. 10 pp.

G.A. Oxon b. 19

1975. TATHAM, E., A letter to the . . . dean of Christ-Church respecting the new statute upon public examinations. To which is added A third address to the members of Convocation on the same subject. By the Rector of Lincoln college. Oxf., 1807, 4°. 34 pp.

G.A. Oxon 4° 23 (3)

—3rd ed. 1807.   G.A. Oxon 4° 48

1976. TATHAM, E., A fourth address . . . respecting the new statute upon public examination, by the rector of Lincoln college [E. Tatham]. Oxf., 1807, 4°. 8 pp.   G.A. Oxon 4° 23 (4)

— 2nd ed. 1807.   G.A. Oxon 4° 48

1977. TATHAM, E., A fifth address . . . on the new statute respecting public examination; and the alterations to be proposed in Convocation. By the rector of Lincoln college [E. Tatham]. Oxf., 1808, 4°. 11 pp.

G.A. Oxon 4° 23 (5)

— 2nd ed. 1808.   G.A. Oxon 4° 48

1978. PHILALETHES, *pseud.*, A letter to the rector of Lincoln [on the new examination statute]. Oxf., 1807, 4°. 13 pp.   Bliss B 419

1979. To the members of Convocation. [A paper against the proposed new examination statute, signed A member of Convocation.] June 5th. Oxf., (1807), 4°. 3 pp.   G.A. Oxon b. 19

See 1020 [Tatham, E., A new address. 1810].

1980. In the press, and speedily will be published, An account of the proceedings relative to the attempt to change the Examination statute of the University of Oxford. [A satirical prospectus.] Oxf., 1824, 4°. 4 pp.   G.A. Oxon c. 40 (50)

1981. Reflections on the project of changing the present examination statute. Oxf., [1824], 8°. 11 pp.   G.A. Oxon c. 40 (22)

1982. ARNOLD, T., Address to the members of Convocation on the expediency of the proposed statute [signed 'A non-resident member of Convocation']. Mar. 8th. (Oxf., 1824), 4°. 4 pp.

G.A. Oxon c. 40 (23)

1983. Observations connected with the subject of the examination statute submitted to the consideration of the . . . Convocation [signed A member of Convocation]. June 11. Oxf., 1824, 4°. 4 pp.

G.A. Oxon c. 40 (44)

1984. To the members of Convocation. [Observations, signed 'A member of Convocation', on the proposed new examination statute.] June 15. (Oxf., 1824), 4°. 3 pp.   G.A. Oxon c. 40 (47)

1985. To members of Convocation. [Observations, signed 'A resident master of arts', on the proposed new examination statute.] June 16. Oxf., (1824), 4°. 4 pp.   G.A. Oxon c. 40 (48)

1986. To the members of Convocation. [A reply, signed 'A senior member of Convocation' to the papers published on June 15 and 16 by 'A member of Convocation' and 'A resident master of arts'.] June 17. (Oxf., 1824), 4°. 4 pp.   G.A. Oxon c. 40 (49)

1987. The addled egg, a poem. By Non Placet. [A satire on the new examination statute.] (Oxf.), [1824], 8°. 7 pp.

G.A. Oxon c. 40 (51)

1988. [Begin.] One of the objections made against the old examination statute . . . [Listing some objections to the proposed new examination statute.] (Oxf.), [1825], s. sh.   G.A. Oxon c. 41 (24*)

1989. To the Board of heads of Houses and proctors. The report of the committee appointed by a resolution dated March 23, 1829, to discuss the construction of a new examination statute. [With] Memorial annexed to the Report. [And] Appendix to the Report. [Oxf., 1829], 4°. 9+5+3 pp.   G.A. Oxon b. 21

1990. RIGAUD, S. P., [Begin.] It is understood . . . [Observations by S. P. Rigaud on the objections entertained by some members of Convocation to the oral examination in mathematics.] May 20. (Oxf., 1830), s. sh.
G.A. Oxon c. 46 (51a)

1991. [Begin.] It is well known . . . [Observations on the recently proposed examination statute, with reference to candidates for mathematical honours. Signed 'A member of Convocation'.] (Oxf.), [1830], s. sh.
G.A. Oxon c. 46 (51d)
— [Further observations. Begin.] A few observations . . . [signed 'A member of Convocation']. June 8th. (Oxf., 1830), s. sh.
G.A. Oxon c. 46 (52b)

1992. [Begin.] A few observations . . . submitted to . . . those who are engaged . . . in the improvement of the Examination statute [signed 'An old examiner']. May 31. (Oxf., 1830), s. sh.
G.A. Oxon c. 46 (51f)

1993. The new [examination] statute. A Master of arts of old standing begs to offer . . . the following suggestions. June 1st, 1830. (Oxf.), 1830, s. sh.   G.A. Oxon c. 46 (52a)

1994. An address to the members of the lower division of the House of Convocation on the proposed examination statute. Oxf., 1830, 8°. 16 pp.　　　　　　　　　　　　　　　　G.A. Oxon b. 21

1995. [*Begin*.] One who has long been engaged in tuition begs leave to offer a few observations . . . [on the new examination statute. Signed Scrutator]. (Oxf.), [1830], s. sh.　　　　G.A. Oxon c. 46 (53)

1996. [*Begin*.] A paper has been circulated with the signature of Scrutator, which contains remarks of so extraordinary a character that some members of Convocation think they ought not to pass . . . without a protest against them. June 9th. (Oxf., 1830), s. sh.　　G.A. Oxon c. 46 (54)

1997. Agitate! Agitate! Agitate! . . . To the tutors of the several colleges and halls of Oxford. [A letter, signed Didascalus, on the effects likely to ensue from the enactment of the proposed new examination statute.] (Oxf.), [1830], s. sh.　　　　　　　　G.A. Oxon c. 46 (55)

1998. Reasons for the suggestion of certain alterations in the examination statute lately submitted . . . by the public examiners. Feb. 1. Oxf., 1832, 8°. 15 pp.　　　　　　　　　　G.A. Oxon c. 48 (16)

1999. Examination system. [Suggestions for the reform of the statute to include physical and mathematical science among the examination subjects.] Nov. 1. [Oxf.], (1833), 4°. 3 pp.　　G.A. Oxon b. 140 (17*b*)

2000. GORDON, O., Considerations on the improvement of the present examination statute and for the admission of poor scholars to the University. Oxf. &c., 1847, 8°. 38 pp.　　G.A. Oxon 8° 77 (19)

2001. JOWETT, B., and STANLEY, A. P., Suggestions for an improvement of the examination statute [by B. Jowett and A. P. Stanley]. Oxf., 1848, 8°. 33 pp.　　　　　　　　　　G. Pamph. 2905 (19)

2002. HUSSEY, R., Remarks on some proposed changes in the public examinations. Oxf., 1848, 8°. 36 pp.　　　　48. 1413 (17)

2003. WALKER, R., A letter . . . on improvements in the present examination statute, and the studies of the University. Oxf., 1848, 8°. 27 pp.
　　　　　　　　　　　　　　　　G.A. Oxon 8° 77 (33)

2004. Hints to members of Convocation [on the proposed examination statute]. No. 1. First examination. [Queries on paragraphs in notice of 8 March, 1849, i.e. Forms of Statutes to be promulgated, 15 Mar. Bodl. copy G.A. Oxon c. 65 (35)].　　　G. A. Oxon c. 65 (36)
　— No. 2, 3. Second examination. n. pl., [1849], s. sh.
　　　　　　　　　　　　　　　G.A. Oxon c. 65 (37, 38)

2005. Outline of the plan respecting the responsions and the public examinations in the University of Oxford, which is to be submitted to Convocation. [Oxf., 1849], fol. 4 pp.　　　G.A. Oxon b. 26
　— Outline [&c.] of which a part has been adopted by, and the remainder is to be submitted to, Convocation. [Oxf., 1849], fol. 4 pp.
　　　　　　　　　　　　　　　　G.A. Oxon b. 26

2006. To members of Convocation. [*Begin*.] It is conceived . . . [suggesting the rejection of the new statute]. [Oxf., 1849], s. sh.
G.A. Oxon c. 65 (40)

2007. Proposed examination statute. Analysis of votes. [Oxf., 1849], s. sh.
G.A. Oxon c. 65 (39)

2008. The new statute. [Comments, signed 'A tutor who signed the memorial', no. 1652.] Mar. 19. n. pl., (1849), fol. 4 pp.
G.A. Oxon c. 65 (41)

2009. Subjects of consideration for members of Convocation. n. pl., [1849], s. sh.
G.A. Oxon c. 65 (42)

2010. [*Begin*.] 1. What reasons can be given . . . [Comments in support of the proposed alterations in the statute.] Mar. 20. n. pl., [1849], 4°. 3 pp.
G.A. Oxon c. 65 (43)

2011. A few words on 'boards' [of examiners, as proposed in the statute] with an apologue. n. pl., [1849], s. sh.   G.A. Oxon c. 65 (178)

2012. HUSSEY, R., A letter . . . on the proposed three examinations. Oxf., 1849, 8°. 24 pp.   49. 1988 (6)

2013. New examination statutes. [Brief statement of their main provisions.] [Oxf., 1850], fol. 4 pp.   G.A. Oxon c. 66 (91*a*)
— [Another ed.] June 6, 1850.   G.A. Oxon c. 66 (91*b*)

2014. As the provisions of the new examination statute passed last term may not be generally known, the proctors beg to call attention to certain changes. May 13. n. pl., 1854, s. sh.   G.A. Oxon c. 70 (134)

2015. TWEED, J. P., The vote on the Examination statute, a letter by a tutor [signed J. P. T.]. Oxf., 1857, 8°. 10 pp.   G.A. Oxon 8° 459

2016. WALKER, R., Remarks on certain parts of the proposed form of statute respecting the examinations for the degree of B.A. Oxf., 1857, 8°. 14 pp.   G.A. Oxon 8° 179 (11)

2017. Remarks on the proposed changes in our examinations, by a tutor. Oxf., 1857, 8°. 14 pp.   G.A. Oxon 8° 179 (12)

2018. DAUBENY, C., Reasons for voting in favour of clauses 2 and 3 in the Examination statute . . . relative to the attendance on the lectures of professors. 13th June. n. pl., (1857), 4°. 4 pp.   G.A. Oxon c. 73 (187)

2019. The educational changes proposed in the new examination statute. n. pl., [1857], 8°. 16 pp.   G.A. Oxon c. 73 (121)

See 2684 [Ancient history and the new statute. 1857].

2020. TWEED, J. P., The least change which suffices best, two letters on the examinations. Oxf., 1859, 8°. 34 pp.   G.A. Oxon 8° 73 (9)

2021. [*Begin*.] Two propositions were in circulation . . . [Paper, signed An ex-tutor, against certain propositions for altering examination statutes.] May 5. [Oxf.], (1859), 4°. 4 pp.   G.A. Oxon b. 29

2022. The penal statute. [Observations on the proposed amendment to the statute 'which gives for the first time a degree without classics'. Signed Prudens.] Mar. 11. [Oxf.], (1863), s. sh.   G.A. Oxon c. 79 (105)

2023. The new Oxford examination statute. Mar. 23. [Oxf.], (1863), s. sh.
                                                                G.A. Oxon b. 30

2024. CHASE, D. P., The new statute [signed D. P. C.]. Apr. 18. [Oxf.], (1863), s. sh.   G.A. Oxon b. 30

2025. BURROWS, M., On which side is the majority of the professors and tutors? [signed M. Burrows]. Apr. 20. [Oxf.], (1863), s. sh.
                                                                G.A. Oxon c. 78 (165)

2026. Examination statute. [Notice of an amendment. Nov.] n. pl., [1863], s. sh.   G.A. Oxon c. 79 (417)

2027. The new examination statute. Dec. 5. n. pl., (1863), s. sh.
                                                                G.A. Oxon c. 79 (416)

2028. The new examination statute. [Remarks on the amendment submitted on Nov. 1, described in no. 2026. Signed 'A member of Congregation'.] Dec. 16. n. pl., [1863], s. sh.   G.A. Oxon c. 79 (428)

2029. CHASE, D. P., Examination statute. [Approval of an amendment allowing candidates to choose the order in which the two final examinations are taken. Signed D. P. C.] [Oxf.], (1863), s. sh.
                                                                G.A. Oxon c. 79 (418)

2030. Degree statute, Tit. VI. (IX.) iii–vii. [Explanations of proposed changes.] [Oxf., 1863], s. sh.   G.A. Oxon c. 80 (84)

2031. FREEMAN, E. A., The new examination statute [objections, signed E. A. F.]. [Oxf., 1863], 8°. 4 pp.   G.A. Oxon c. 79 (210)

2031.1. ROGERS, J. E. THOROLD, The new examination statute [reply to no. 2031]. [Oxf., 1863], s. sh.   G.A. Oxon b. 30

2032. MICHELL, R., The proposed statute. [Oxf., 1863], s. sh.
                                                                G.A. Oxon b. 30

2033. NEATE, C., On the proposed changes in our scheme of examinations. [Oxf., 1863], s. sh.   G.A. Oxon b. 30

2034. The new examination statute. [Urging that those placed in the first, second, or third class in any final school should be allowed to take their degree without passing in any other school.] [Oxf., 1863], s. sh.
                                                                G.A. Oxon b. 30

2035. Denique sit quod vis simplex dumtaxat et unum [signed M.A. Hon. Lit. Hono. Math.]. [Oxf., 1863], s. sh.   G.A. Oxon b. 30

2036. Reply to mr. Michell . . . Reply to capt. Burrows. [Oxf., 1863], s. sh.
                                                                G.A. Oxon b. 30

2037. Oxford examinations. [*Begin.*] The following change . . . [Oxf., 1863], s. sh.   G.A. Oxon b. 30

2038. Oxford examinations. [*Begin.*] The suggestions circulated under the title of 'Oxford examinations'. . . Oxf., [1863], s. sh.   G.A. Oxon b. 30

2039. The Oxford examination statute. [Repeating the memorial on which the measure was founded, and supporting the statute generally. Signed C. W. Sandford and 82 others.] [Oxf., 1863], s. sh.
G.A. Oxon c. 79 (211)

2040. BUCKLEY, W. E., A new view of the new [examination] statute. Feb. 16. n. pl., 1864, s. sh.   G.A. Oxon c. 80 (384)

2041. X *pseud.*, A true view of the new statute. [An answer to W. E. Buckley.] Feb. 19. n. pl., 1864, s. sh.   G.A. Oxon c. 80 (385)

2042. The new examination statute. [A criticism, signed A college tutor.] Feb. 20. n. pl., 1864, s. sh.   G.A. Oxon c. 80 (386)

2043. The new examination statute. [Arguments in favour.] [Oxf., 1864?], 4°. 4 pp.   G.A. Oxon b. 32 (1)

2044. A. B. C. *pseud.*, The rival lines, or sham and reality. [An answer to 2042.] Feb. 22. n. pl., 1864, s. sh.   G.A. Oxon c. 80 (387)

2045. DODGSON, C. L., Examination statute. A list of those who might, could, would or should have voted thereon in Congregation, Feb. 2, 4681 . . . [An alphabet-poem satirizing the contest. The names, which are left blank in the text, are given in MS. on the verso of this Bodleian copy. By C. L. Dodgson.] [Oxf., 1864], s. sh.
G.A. Oxon b. 140 (20a)

2046. DODGSON, C. L., The new examination statute. [A letter to the vice-chancellor, resigning from the office of examiner in mathematics.] Mar. 2. [Oxf.], (1864), s. sh.   G.A. Oxon c. 80 (393)

2047. MILLER, C., The Oxford examination statute examined by an examiner; or, A plea for moral philosophy and law, a second letter. Lond. &c., 1865, 8°. 16 pp.   G.A. Oxon 8° 92 (13)

2048. PUSEY, E. B., University examination statute. [Paper, signed A member of council, i.e. E. B. Pusey, concerning the examination in the rudiments of faith and religion.] [Oxf., 1865], s. sh.
G.A. Oxon c. 81 (397)

2049. An important principle in danger. [Remarks on the proposed amendment of the examination statute which is said to offend the principle of keeping every man to the study of Divinity through the whole of his academic course.] Mar. 10. [Oxf.], (1865), s. sh.
G.A. Oxon c. 81 (409)

2050. PUSEY, E. B., An answer to the paper, 'An important principle in danger'. [Oxf., 1865], s. sh.   G.A. Oxon c. 81 (408)

2051. The examination statute. [Four comments.] Mar. 14. [Oxf.], 1865, s. sh.   G.A. Oxon c. 81 (401)

2052. CONINGTON, J., The debate on the examination statute. [Arguments against the proposed change.] Mar. 8. [Oxf.], (1866), s. sh.
G.A. Oxon c. 82 (376)

2053. SANDFORD, C. W., The proposed change in the examination statute [allowing undergraduates to offer themselves for Moderations in their 5th instead of 7th term]. Mar. 5. [Oxf.], (1866), s. sh.
G.A. Oxon c. 82 (378)
— [Further arguments in support of the amendment.] Apr. 23. [Oxf.], (1866), 4°. 4 pp. G.A. Oxon c. 82 (359)

2054. CONINGTON, J., The proposed examination statute. [Objections against the clause allowing undergraduates to offer themselves for Moderations in their 5th instead of 7th term.] [Oxf., 1866], 4°. 4 pp.
G.A. Oxon c. 82 (375)

2055. GREEN, T. H., The 'once-a-year examination' statute. Apr. 27th. [Oxf., 1866], s. sh. G.A. Oxon b. 140 (20e)

2056. SANDFORD, C. W., The new pass examination statute. Jan. 23. n. pl., (1868), s. sh. G.A. Oxon c. 84 (403)

2057. MAGRATH, J. R., Reasons for certain amendments to the new examination statute which are to be submitted to Congregation, Nov. 14, 1871. Oxf., 1871, 8°. 15 pp. G.A. Oxon 8° 265

2058. BRAMLEY, H. R., To resident members of Convocation. [A paper against the statute respecting the examination of passmen.] Mar. 4. [Oxf.], (1872), s. sh. G.A. Oxon b. 140 (26h)

2059. To members of Convocation. [*Begin.*] Your attention is earnestly invited . . . [Arguments against a proposed disabling decree to annul a clause in the statute which gives protection to certain candidates during a period of transition. Signed by A. S. Chavasse and 3 others.] [Oxf., 1885], s. sh. G.A. Oxon b. 140 (54c)

2060. To members of Convocation. [*Begin.*] A decree will be presented . . . [Further arguments against the proposed disabling decree: the opinion of Arthur Charles, Q.C., is quoted. Signed by A. S. Chavasse and 3 others.] [Oxf., 1885], 4°. 3 pp. G.A. Oxon b. 140 (54b)
— [Another issue.] G.A. Oxon 4° 255

2061. Postscript to members of Convocation [on the proposed disabling decree. Signed by A. S. Chavasse and 3 others]. [Oxf., 1885], s. sh.
G.A. Oxon b. 140 (54a)

2062. MONRO, D. B., To members of Convocation. [*Begin.*] The legal question . . . [Arguments in favour of the proposed disabling decree, by D. B. Monro. Jan. 26.] [Oxf., 1885], s. sh. G.A. Oxon b. 140 (54d)

2063. GROSE, T. H., and ELLIOTT, E. B., The object of this paper is to call attention to certain important anomalies which have been produced by recent changes in the Examination statutes. [Signed T. H. G. and E. B. E.] [Oxf.], (1886), 4°. 4 pp. G.A. Oxon b. 140 (68a)

2064. MONRO, D. B., The statute on pass examinations. 14 Feb. [Oxf.], (1890), s. sh.   G.A. Oxon b. 140 (95*a*)

2065. A letter [signed Two college tutors engaged in classical honour work] . . . touching certain details in the new statute regulating the first public examination. [*With*] Appendix. Oxf., [1890?], 8°. 12 pp.
G.A. Oxon b. 140 (94*f*)

2066. [*Begin.*] The statute on the first public examination . . . [Statement calling for the rejection of the statute to be proposed in Congregation on Nov. 16th, signed by J. Wells and F. J. Lys.] [Oxf., 1920], s. sh.
G.A. Oxon c. 311 (145)

2066.4. HARDIE, W. F., The Examination statutes. (Oxf. mag., 1963, N.S., vol. 4, p. 6–9.)   Per. G.A. Oxon 4° 141

2066.5. Changes in regulations made by Boards of Faculties. (Oxf. Univ. gazette, suppl. no. 8, June 1965.) Oxf., 1965, 8°. 34 pp.
Per. G.A. Oxon c. 86

2066.51. HARDIE, W. F. R., The Examination statutes again. (Oxf. mag., 1965, N.S., vol. 5, p. 120–22.)   Per. G.A. Oxon 4° 141

Texts

2067. New examination statutes. Abstracts of their principal provisions. Oxf., 1851, 8°. 48 pp.   Per. G.A. Oxon 8° 644
— 2nd ed. 1854. 58 pp.   Per. G.A. Oxon 8° 644

2068. The new examination statutes, together with the decrees of Convocation, and regulations of the Boards of studies. June 1872. Oxf., 1872, 8°. 95 pp.   Per. G.A. Oxon 8° 644

2069. The new examination statutes for the degrees of B.A. and B.C.L., together with the decrees of Convocation, and regulations of the Boards of studies. 1873–77.
— B.A., B.Mus., B.C.L., and B.M. (and M.Ch.) 1878–87.
— 1888– [*entitled*] Examination statutes.
Oxf., 1873– , 8°.   Per. G.A. Oxon 8° 644

Examiners

2070. [*Begin.*] The members of Congregation and Convocation are . . . requested to consider whether the nomination of mr. Shepherd . . . to the office of examining master . . . after having been rejected . . . be not . . . repugnant . . . to . . . the statute . . . [signed A member of Convocation]. (Oxf.), [1807], s. sh.   G.A. Oxon b. 19

2071. Academicus *pseud.*, The following remarks are respectfully submitted to the members of Convocation. [A paper, signed Academicus, in defence of Shepherd.] (Oxf.), [1807], s. sh.   G.A. Oxon b. 19

2072. [*Begin.*] Mr. Shepherd, of University college, having again been nominated as an examining master . . . [A paper against his renomination, signed A member of Convocation.] (Oxf.), [1807], 4°. 3 pp.
G.A. Oxon b. 19

2073. [*Begin.*] The following remarks upon the late rejection of mr. Shepherd . . . [A paper in support of Shepherd.] (Oxf.), [1807], fol. 3 pp.
G.A. Oxon b. 19

2074. CHASE, D. P., Should public examiners be private tutors? A question . . . to members of Convocation by a bachelor of Arts [D. P. Chase]. Oxf., 1843, 8°. 13 pp.
G.A. Oxon 8° 1130* (9)
— A repr. (by the author). Oxf., 1881, 8°. 13 pp.
G.A. Oxon 8° 250 (3)

See 1854 [Ogle, J. A., Suggestions for remodeling the examination statutes. 1841].
See 1855 [Mansel, H. L., A plea for the private tutors, remarks on no. 2074. 1843].
See 2011 [A few words on 'boards' of examiners. 1849].

2075. The professorial boards. [Objections, signed B.D., to the proposed boards for the appointment of examiners in the schools.] Oxf., (1850), 4°. 3 pp.
G.A. Oxon b. 26

2076. The objections of B.D. to the 'professorial boards' answered by M.A. [Oxf., 1850], s. sh.
G.A. Oxon b. 26

2077. The new statute. Boards a third time! [Objections, signed A member of Convocation, to the repeated presentation of the proposal to amend the method of electing examiners.] [Oxf.], (1850), s. sh.
G.A. Oxon b. 26

2078. A statute . . . concerning nomination of examiners. (Univ. of Oxf. and Cambr. act, 1877. Oxford. Statutes made by the Univ. of Oxf. commissioners, 1881, p. 4, 5.)
Pp. Eng. 1882 vol. 51

2079. In the Privy council, Universities committee. In the matter of the Universities of Oxford and Cambridge act, 1877, and in the matter of a statute made by the University of Oxford commissioners . . . concerning the nomination of examiners. The petition of . . . the University of Oxford for disallowance [*and*] Case in support of the petition. (Lond.), [1881], fol. 14 pp.
G.A. Oxon c. 107 (76)

2080. In the Privy council. The universities committee of the Privy council. In the matter of the Universities of Oxford and Cambridge act, 1877, and the humble petition of . . . the University of Oxford [to disallow a statute on the nomination of examiners made by the Oxford university commissioners in 1881]. Case for the . . . commissioners [*With*] Appendix. [Lond., 1882], fol. 7+18 pp.
G.A. Oxon b. 140 (45 a, c)
— Petition [of the University]. [Lond., 1882], s. sh.
G.A. Oxon b. 140 (45b)

See 2507 [Lock, W., Observations on regulations that examiners in the honour school of theology shall be in holy orders. 1904].

Disputations
General

2081. [*Begin.*] At a meeting of the Delegates in d. Staunton's lodgings. [Order of the delegates de negotiis publicis about the expenses &c. of determining bachelors.] [Madan 2219.] [Oxf.], (1653), s. sh.   O.U.A.

2082. [*Begin.*] Cum per nuperam dispensandi . . . [Notice signed Johan. Fell requiring all Bachelors of Arts who intended to determine in Lent to be present at the Festum ovorum, to be placed in various classes for Quadragesimal exercises.] Octob. 25. [Madan 2752.] [Oxf.], (1666), s. sh.   G.A. Oxon b. 111 (20)

2083. [*Begin.*] Quanquam statuta . . . [A Latin programma, about academical exercises, insisting that they are to be strictly and gravely carried out without tumult.] Feb. 16, 1666. [Madan 2775.] [Oxf., 1667], s. sh.   Wood 276a (353)

2084. [*Begin.*] Ut exercitia academica & præsertim Quadragesimalia . . . [Regulations about the order of the Lent academical exercises.] [Madan 3294.] [Oxf.], 1669, s. sh.   Wood 276a (356)
— Programma. Die Martii 13. 1670.   Wood 276a (357)
——. Die Febr. 22. 1671.   Wood 276a (361)
——. Feb. 12. 1672.   Wood 276a (368)
——. Jan. 29. 1673.   Wood 276a (371)
——. [Feb. 7], 16 [77].   Wood 276a (375)

See 1303 [Notice about dress, long hair, and reading from manuscript in disputations etc. 1674].

2085. [*Begin.*] Cum disputationes in parviso . . . [Vice-chancellor's notice about the due observance of the regulations governing the Academical exercises.] [Oxf., c. 1677], s. sh.   Don. b. 12 (30)

2086. HEARNE, T., Editoris dissertatio de codice MS. [early 15th cent.] in bibliotheca collegii Magdalenensis Oxoniæ, modum creandi artium magistros Vesperiarum tempore secundum usum Oxoniæ continente. (Thomæ Caii Vindiciæ antiq. Acad. Oxon. contra Joannem Caium, in lucem emisit T. Hearnius, 1730, vol. 1, p. lxv–lxxxi.)   Mus. Bibl. II 91

2087. [Printed form of licence to determine in the Quadragesima, completed in MS. with the Quæstiones. In use c. 1800.]   G.A. Oxon b. 19

See 927 [Proposed repeal of statute relating to Collectors in Lent. 1854].

2088. GIBSON, S., The order of disputations. (Bodleian quarterly record, 1930, vol. 6, p. 107–12.)   Per. 2590 d. Oxf. 1. 40 = R.

2089. ROBSON, J. A., Wyclif and the Oxford schools, the relation of the 'Summa de ente' to scholastic debates at Oxford in the later 14th century. (Cambr. studies in mediev. life and thought, N.S., vol. 8.) Cambr., 1961, 8°. 268 pp.   26671 d. 281 = S.

Quaestiones

2090. GENTILIS, A., Legalium comitiorum Oxoniensium. Actio. Francisco Bevanno docturæ dignitatem suscipiente. [Madan 59.] Lond., 1585, 12°. 48 pp.   Byw. N 4. 12

2091. BRETT, R., Theses mri. Bret respondentis in comitiis [Madan 170.] Oxon., 1597, s. sh.   C.C.C.

2092. Quæstiones sex, totidem praelectionibus, in schola theologica, Oxoniae, pro forma, habitis discussae et disceptatae anno 1597. [Madan 174.] [1597].

2093. Quæstiones . . . in vesperijs discutiendæ. Iul. 10, 1602 . . . Theses theologicæ discutiendæ in comitijs . . . Iulij 12, 1602 . . . Quæst. in jure civili in vesperijs discutiendæ . . . Quæstiones doctoris King. [Madan 214.] [Oxf.], (1602), 16°. 16 pp.   Denyer 21
— [Another issue.] [Madan 215.]   8° W 61 (3) Th.

2094. Quæstiones, deo propitio, discutiendæ publice in comitiis coram . . . rege . . . 1605. Oxon., 1605, fol. 2 sheets. MS. Tanner 75 (f. 138, 39)

2095. Quæstiones favente Deo in sacra theologia [etc.] discutiendæ Oxoniæ in comitijs An. Dom. 1608. Oxon., 1608, 4°. 8 pp.
                                                  MS. CCC. 257 (f. 156–59)

2096. COOKE, J., Iuridica trium quæstionum ad maiestatem pertinentium determinatio; in quarum prima et ultima processus iudicialis contra H. Garnetum institutus, ex iure civili & canonico defenditur [&c.] . . . habita Oxoniæ in vesperijs comitiorum . . . a Jacobo Cooke. [Madan 305.] Oxon., 1608, 4°. 52 pp.   4° B 93 Th.

2097. Quæstiones in sacra theologia [etc.] discutiendæ Oxoniæ in vesperijs (in comitijs) . . . 1614. [Oxf., 1614], fol. 2 sheets.   Wood 276a (412)

2097.1. [Quæstiones. 1617.] [Madan 3288.] [A fragment in a Bodleian binding, which has not been traced.]

2098. Quæstiones in sacra theologia [etc.] discutiendæ Oxonii in vesperiis (in comitiis) . . . 1618. [Oxf., 1618], fol. 2 sheets.   Wood 276a (413)

2099. Quæstiones in sacra theologia [etc.] discutiendæ Oxonii in vesperiis (in comitiis) . . . 1619. [Oxf., 1619], s. sh.   Wood 276a (414)

2099.1. Quæstiones . . . [Oxf., 1621], s. sh.   S. of A.

2100. Quæstiones in sacra theologia [etc.] discutiendæ Oxonii in vesperiis (in comitiis) . . . 1622. [Oxf., 1622], fol. 2 sheets.   Wood 276a (415)

2100.1. Quæstiones . . . [Oxf., 1624], s. sh.   Harvard

2101. Quæstiones in sacra theologia [etc.] discutiendæ Oxonii in vesperiis (in comitiis) . . . 1627. [Oxf., 1627], fol. 2 sheets.
                                                  MS. Rawl. D 859 (f. 139, 40)

2102. Quæstiones in sacra theologia [etc.] discutiendæ Oxonii in vesperiis (in comitiis) . . . 1628. [Oxf., 1628], s. sh.   Wood 276a (416)

2103. Quæstiones in sacra theologia [etc.] discutiendæ Oxonii in vesperiis (in comitiis) . . . 1629. [Oxf., 1629], s. sh.   Douce fragm. d. 12 (29)

2103.1. Quæstiones . . . [Oxf., 1630], s. sh.   S. of A.

2104. Quæstiones in sacra theologia [etc.] discutiendæ Oxonii in vesperiis (in comitiis) . . . 1632. [Oxf., 1632], s. sh.   Wood 276a (417)

2105. Quæstiones in sacra theologia [etc.] discutiendæ Oxonii in vesperiis (in comitiis) . . . 1633. [Oxf., 1633], s. sh.   C.C.C.

2106. Quæstiones in sacra theologia [etc.] discutiendæ Oxonii in vesperiis (in comitiis) . . . 1634. [Oxf., 1634], s. sh.   Wood 276a (419)
— [Another ed.]   fol. Θ 659 (4)

2107. Quæstiones in sacra theologia [etc.] discutiendæ Oxonii in vesperiis (in comitiis) . . . 1635. (Oxf.), [1635], fol. 2 sheets.   Wood 276a (418)

2107.1. Quæstiones . . . [Oxf., 1639], s. sh.   P.R.O.

2108. Quæstiones in sacra theologia [etc.] discutiendæ Oxonii in vesperiis (in comitiis) . . . 1640. [Oxf., 1640], s. sh.   Wood 276a (420)

2109. Quæstiones in sacra theologia [etc.] discutiendæ Oxonii in vesperiis (in comitiis) . . . 1651. [Oxf.], 1651, s. sh.   fol. Θ 659 (6)

2110. Quæstiones in sacra theologia [etc.] discutiendæ Oxonii in vesperiis (in comitiis) . . . 1652. Oxon., 1652, s. sh.   Wood 276a (421)

2111. Quæstiones in sacra theologia [etc.] discutiendæ Oxonii in vesperiis (in comitiis) . . . 1653. Oxon., 1653, s. sh.   G.A. Oxon b. 137 (3)

2111.5. Quæstiones in sacra theologia [etc.] discutiendæ Oxonii in vesperiis (in comitiis) . . . 1654. Oxon., 1654, s. sh.   G.A. Oxon b. 137 (3)

2112. Quæstiones in sacra theologia [etc.] discutiendæ Oxonii in vesperiis (in comitiis) . . . 1657. Oxon., 1657, s. sh.   Don. b. 12 (3)

2113. Quæstiones in s. theologia [etc.] discutiendæ Oxonii in vesperiis (in comitiis) . . . 1661. Oxon., 1661, s. sh.   Wood 276a (423)

2114. Quæstiones in sacra theologia [etc.] discutiendæ Oxonii in vesperiis (in comitiis) . . . 1663. Oxon., 1663, s. sh.   Wood 276a (414)

2115. Quæstiones in sacra theologia [etc.] discutiendæ Oxonii in vesperiis (in comitiis) . . . 1664. Oxon., 1664, s. sh.   G.A. Oxon b. 111 (19)

2116. Quæstiones in s. theologia [etc.] discutiendæ Oxonii in vesperiis (in comitiis) . . . 1669. Oxon., 1669, s. sh.   Wood 276a (422)

See 594 [Quæstiones discutiendæ in comitiis Oxonii habitis in honorem Gulielmi Henrici principis Arausionensis, 1670].

2117. Quæstiones in s. theologia [etc.] discutiendæ Oxonii in vesperiis (in comitiis) . . . 1671. Oxon., 1671, s. sh.   Don. b. 12 (19)

2118. Quæstiones in s. theologia [etc.] discutiendæ Oxonii in vesperiis (in comitiis) . . . 1672. Oxon., 1672, s. sh.   Don. b. 12 (23)

2119. Quæstiones in s. theologia [etc.] discutiendæ Oxonii in vesperiis (in comitiis) . . . 1673. Oxon., 1673, s. sh. Wood 276a (426)

2120. Quæstiones in s. theologia [etc.] discutiendæ Oxonii in vesperiis (in comitiis) . . . 1674. Oxon., 1674, s. sh. Wood 276a (427)

2121. Quæstiones in s. theologia [etc.] discutiendæ Oxonii in vesperiis (in comitiis) . . . 1675. Oxon., 1675, s. sh. Wood 276a (428)

2122. Quæstiones in s. theologia [etc.] discutiendæ Oxonii in vesperiis (in comitiis) . . . 1676. Oxon., 1676, s. sh. Don. b. 12 (28)

2123. Quæstiones in s. theologia [etc.] discutiendæ Oxonii in vesperiis (in comitiis) . . . 1677. Oxon., 1677, s. sh. Wood 276a (430)

2124. Quæstiones in sacra theologia [etc.] discutiendæ Oxonii in vesperiis (in comitiis) . . . 1679. Oxon., 1679, s. sh. Wood 276a (431)

2125. Quæstiones in s. theologia [etc.] discutiendæ Oxonii in vesperiis (in comitiis) . . . 1680. Oxon., 1680, s. sh. Wood 276a (432)

2126. Quæstiones in s. theologia [etc.] discutiendæ Oxonii in vesperiis (in comitiis) . . . 1681. Oxon., 1681, s. sh. Wood 276a (433)

2127. Quæstiones in s. theologia [etc.] discutiendæ Oxonii in vesperiis (in comitiis) . . . 1682. (Oxf.), 1682, s. sh. Don. b. 12 (32)

2128. Quæstiones in sacra theologia [etc.] discutiendæ Oxonii in vesperiis (in comitiis) . . . 1683. Oxon., 1683, s. sh. Wood 276a (435)

2129. Quæstiones in s. theologia [etc.] discutiendæ Oxonii in vesperiis (in comitiis) . . . 1684. (Oxf.), 1684, s. sh. Don. b. 12 (33)

2130. Quæstiones in s. theologia [etc.] discutiendæ Oxonii in vesperiis (in comitiis) . . . 1693. (Oxf.), 1693, s. sh. Wood 276a (437)

2131. Quæstiones [in vesperiis et in comitiis] discutiendæ An. Dom. 1733. Oxon., 1733, s. sh. G.A. Oxon b. 111 (41)

2132. Quæstiones in Augustinensibus discutiendæ 1774. [Oxf.], (1774), s. sh. G.A. Oxon b. 19

2133. Quæstiones logicæ in parvisiis discutiendæ anno 1774. [Oxf.], (1774), s. sh. G.A. Oxon b. 19

Theses

2134. Abstracts of dissertations for the degree of Doctor of philosophy. Vol. 1–13. (Comm. for advanced studies.) Oxf., 1928–47, 8°.
Per. 3974 d. 439 = R.

2135. Successful candidates for the degrees of D.Phil., B.Litt. and B.Sc., with titles of their theses, 1940/49– . Vol. 1– . (Comm. for advanced studies.) Oxf., 1950– , 8°. Per. 2626 e. 510 = R.

See 2788.3 [Notes for writers of B.Litt. and D.Phil. theses in the Faculty of Modern History. 1964].

Responsions

General

2136. [*Begin.*] Was it ever intended by the framers of the present statute . . . [Observations on the treatment of mathematics in Responsions, signed 'A deeply interested and long experienced member of Convocation'.] [Oxf., 1851], s. sh.   G.A. Oxon c. 67 (156*)

2137. OGLE, O., The Responsions examination, its defects considered, and remedies suggested, a letter. Oxf., 1863, 8°. 30 pp.   2625 d. 5

2138. KING, J. R., Responsions: an answer to the rev. O. Ogle, a letter. Oxf. &c., 1863, 8°. 10 pp.   200 h. 35 (5)

2139. CHASE, D. P., Responsions available as an (optional) entrance examination. [Proposal submitted to members of Congregation.] n. pl., (1868), s. sh.   G.A. Oxon c. 84 (451)

2140. DODGSON, C. L., Algebraical formulæ for responsions. Oxf., 1868.

2141. DODGSON, C. L., Responsions, Hilary term, 1877. [Letter to the Vice-chancellor calling attention to the difference between the percentages of successful candidates passed by different examiners in Responsions. April 18.] [Oxf.], 1877, s. sh.   G.A. Oxon 4° 624

2142. DODGSON, C. L., An analysis of the Responsions-lists from Michaelmas 1873 to Michaelmas 1881. Oxf., 1882, 4°. 4 pp.

See 1961 [Oxford Pass schools: 'Smalls'. 1885].

2143. HIRA LAL KUMAR, Oxford university and the Indian students [by Hira Lal Kumar, suggesting that Indian students should be allowed to offer two Oriental languages instead of Latin and Greek in Responsions]. n. pl., [1892], s. sh.   G.A. Oxon b. 145

2144. GOTCH, F., Letter . . . in reference to a scheme for the modification of Responsions. 25 Feb. [Oxf.], (1902), 4°. 3 pp.
G.A. Oxon b. 141 (181e)

2145. [*Begin.*] The chief object . . . [A paper supporting the proposal to allow an optional alternative to Greek in Responsions. Signed by W. R. Anson and 10 others]. 3 Nov. [Oxf.], (1902), 4°. 4 pp.
G.A. Oxon b. 141 (183a)

2146. [*Begin.*] It appears probable . . . [Letter, signed by W. W. Jackson and ten others, suggesting a meeting of those in favour of the conditional exemption from Greek of some candidates in Responsions.] 3 Dec. [Oxf.], (1902), s. sh.   G.A. Oxon 4° 232 (2)

2147. Exemption from Greek in Responsions. [Oxf., 1903], 8°. 5 pp.
G.A. Oxon b. 141 (183b)

2148. MONRO, D. B., Exemption from Greek in Responsions. The substitute proposed. [Oxf., 1903], 4°. 4 pp.   G.A. Oxon b. 141 (185d)

2149. GODLEY, A. D., [*Begin.*] We are asked to exempt . . . [A paper opposing the exemption from Greek in Responsions for students in science and mathematics. Signed A. D. G.] [Oxf., 1904], s. sh.
G.A. Oxon 4° 232 (21)

2150. Substitutes for Greek and a high standard in Smalls! Jan. 26. [Oxf.], (1904), s. sh.   G.A. Oxon 4° 232 (5)

2151. CASE, T., The uses of Greek to students of mathematical and natural sciences. Jan. 29. [Oxf.], (1904), s. sh.   G.A. Oxon b. 141 (185*a*)

2152. Exemption from Greek [for students in mathematics and science] in Responsions. [Arguments in favour, signed G. C. Bourne and 12 others. Feb.] [Oxf., 1904], 4°. 4 pp.   G.A. Oxon 4° 232 (8)
— [Another ed., signed by W. C. Allen and 55 others.] [Oxf., 1904], 4°. 4 pp.   G.A. Oxon 4° 232 (9)

2153. DYER, L., Modern languages as a substitute for Greek [a protest against]. Feb. 1. [Oxf.], (1904), s. sh.   G.A. Oxon b. 141 (185*b*)

2154. Greek in Responsions. [Observations by W. A. Spooner, C. C. J. Webb, R. T. Günther, J. U. Powell.] Feb. 3. (Oxf. mag., 1904, vol. 22, p. 169–72).   Per. G.A. Oxon 4° 141

2155. MONRO, D. B., Some reasons for rejecting the preamble of the statute concerning Greek in Responsions . . . [Oxf., 1904], s. sh.
Firth b. 36 (111)

2156. Exemption of students of mathematical and natural science from Greek in Responsions. Reply of the committee of opposition to the manifesto of the advocates of the resolutions. Feb. 4. [Oxf.], (1904), s. sh.   G.A. Oxon b. 141 (191*b*)

2157. [*Begin.*] We the undersigned . . . [Declaration of approval for the principle of exemption of students of mathematical and natural science from Greek in Responsions, signed by J. F. Bright and 119 others. Nov.] [Oxf., 1904], 4°. 4 pp.   G.A. Oxon b. 141 (195*c*)

2158. JACKSON, W. W., Some reasons for voting in favour of the preamble of the statute concerning Greek in Responsions. [Nov.?]. [Oxf., 1904], 4°. 3 pp.   G.A. Oxon b. 141 (245*b*)

2159. Some reasons for rejecting the preamble of the statute concerning Greek in Responsions on November 29 [signed D. B. Monro, on behalf of the Greek defence committee]. [Oxf., 1904], s. sh.
G.A. Oxon b. 141 (197*b*)

2160. SNOW, T. C., Greek in Responsions [arguments in favour. Nov.]. [Oxf., 1904], s. sh.   G.A. Oxon 4° 232 (34)

2161. JACKSON, W. W., Exemption from Greek in Responsions [arguments in favour]. Nov. 19. [Oxf.], (1904), 4°. 4 pp.
G.A. Oxon b. 141 (195*d*)

2162. SPOONER, W. A., and NAGEL, D. H., The proposed statute as to exemption from Greek in Responsions. Nov. 23. [Oxf.], (1904), s. sh.
G.A. Oxon b. 141 (195*b*)

2163. WALKER, E. M., Exemption from Greek in Responsions. The meaning and the value of the alternative course. Nov. 23. [Oxf.], (1904), 4°. 3 pp.   G.A. Oxon b. 141 (195*a*)

2164. WEBB, C. C. J., The proposed exemptions from Greek in Responsions. [*c.* Nov. 26.] [Oxf., 1904], s. sh.   G.A. Oxon b. 141 (195*e*)
— [Postscript. 26 Nov.]   G.A. Oxon b. 141 (197*a*)

2165. Why I vote placet. [Verses on the Greek in Responsions controversy. *c.* Nov. 28.] [Oxf., 1904], s. sh.   G.A. Oxon 4° 232 (35)

See 1811 [The abolition of responsions. 1909].

2166. MURRAY, G., [Letter to the Registrar, giving views on the proposal 'that Greek be no longer required as a necessary subject for a degree in Arts'. Reprod. from typewriting.] n. pl., [1910], 4°. 7 leaves.
G.A. Oxon b. 141 (207*a*)

2167. DAVIDSON, J. L. STRACHAN-, Statute on abolition of compulsory Greek in Responsions: letter from Master of Balliol. Oct. 6 [Oxf.], (1910), s. sh.   G.A. Oxon b. 141 (207*b*)

2168. Considerations in favour of the statute to be promulgated on Nov. 22, 1910 [signed by H. B. Baker and 50 others]. (Nov. 14.) [Oxf., 1910], 4°. 3 pp.   G.A. Oxon b. 141 (229*a*)
— [Proof copy with additional matter].   G.A. Oxon 4° 232 (46)

2169. DAVIDSON, J. L. STRACHAN-, and MURRAY, G., To members of Congregation. (The Greek statute.) Nov. 15. [Oxf.], (1910), 4°. 3 pp.
G.A. Oxon b. 141 (217*a*)

2170. Compulsory Greek. The arguments for its abolition briefly considered. Nov. 16. [Oxf.], (1910), s. sh.   G.A. Oxon b. 141 (217*b*)

2171. Greek and the 'excluded'. Nov. 17. [Oxf.], (1910), s. sh.
G.A. Oxon b. 141 (217*c*)

2172. What are Council's real intentions? Nov. 18. [Oxf.], 1910, s. sh.
G.A. Oxon b. 141 (217*d*)

2173. The proposition of the true lovers of Greek! [signed Credat Iudæus Apella]. Nov. 18. [Oxf.], (1910), s. sh.   G.A. Oxon b. 141 (217*e*)

2174. Compulsory Greek [signed: For the Greek defence committee, L. R. Phelps, A. D. Godley, C. T. Atkinson]. [*c.* Nov. 20.] [Oxf., 1910], 4°. 4 pp.   G.A. Oxon b. 141 (229*b*)

2175. GODLEY, A. D., Considerations in favour of opposition to the statute [signed A. D. G. Nov.]. [Oxf., 1910], 4°. 4 pp.
G.A. Oxon b. 141 (229*e*)

2176. WEBB, C. C. J., Considerations in favour of voting against the preamble of the statute to be promulgated on November 22nd, 1910
[signed C. C. J. W.]. Nov. 21. [Oxf.], (1910), 4°. 4 pp.
G.A. Oxon b. 141 (229*d*)

2177. MURRAY, G., The Greek statute of November 22, 1910. [Oxf.,
1910], 4°. 3 pp.   G.A. Oxon b. 141 (217*f*)

2178. Petition by members of Congregation. The undersigned members
. . . petition Council to propose . . . a short statute relieving honour
students in . . . Natural Science and Mathematics from . . . taking two
ancient languages in Responsions. Dec. 7. [Oxf.], (1910), 8°. 4 pp.
G.A. Oxon b. 141 (235*b*)

2179. SNOW, T. C., The statute on Responsions [signed T. C. S. May 6,
1911]. [Oxf., 1911], s. sh.   G.A. Oxon c. 310 (66)

2180. Greek in Responsions. [May 15, 1911.] [Oxf., 1911], s. sh.
G.A. Oxon c. 310 (67)

2181. ELLIOTT, E. B., The Responsions statute [signed E. B. E.]. June 5.
[Oxf.], (1911), 8°. 4 pp.   G.A. Oxon b. 141 (237*a*)

2182. DAVIDSON, J. L. STRACHAN-, and HOW, W. W., To members of
Congregation [propounding an alternative scheme for allowing some
candidates to pass Responsions without a second classical language].
June 7. [Oxf.], (1911), 4°. 3 pp.   G.A. Oxon b. 141 (237*b*)

2183. For members of Congregation. [A paper, signed by C. Cookson and
6 others, opposing the suggestions of no. 2182.] [Oxf., 1911], 8°. 4 pp.
G.A. Oxon b. 141 (245*a*)

2184. For members of Congregation. [*Begin.*] We hope that those members . . . [canvassing votes against the amendments to be proposed by
J. L. Strachan-Davidson on June 13, which seek to extend the exemption from Greek in Responsions, beyond those who intend to study
mathematics and natural science. Signed by C. Cookson and 6 others].
[Oxf., 1911], 4°. 4 pp.   G.A. Oxon c. 153

2185. The preservation of Greek at Oxford [signed T. Case, on behalf of
the Committee for the preservation of Greek]. Nov. 8. [Oxf.], (1911),
4°. 3 pp.   G.A. Oxon b. 141 (251*a*)

2186. The proposed statute as to compulsory Greek at Oxford. [Articles by
E. B. Poulton, W. T. Thiselton-Dyer, sir W. Osler, E. R. Lankester
and R. C. Punnett.] Nov. 23. (Oxf. mag., 1911, vol. 30, p. 102–07.)
Per. G.A. Oxon 4° 141

2187. An answer to professor Murray [his letter in The Times, Nov. 23].
[Oxf., 1911], s. sh.   G.A. Oxon b. 141 (235*c*)

2188. Preservation of Greek at Oxford. [Card commemorating the 'victory' of the Hellenists and recording the relevant votes of Convocation
and Congregation, 1902–1911.] Jan. 24. [Oxf.], 1912, s. sh.
G.A. Oxon 4° 232 (51)

2189. [*Begin.*] It is intended to present the petition printed below to Council . . . [The petition, signed by P. S. Allen and 20 others urges that Responsions should be replaced in ordinary cases by a test at school, and suggests that the School certificate, with modifications, would suffice.] [Oxf., 1912], s. sh.   G.A. Oxon b. 141 (251c)

2190. Committee for the preservation of Greek. [Amendments to the proposed statute concerning Responsions, which the committee resolve to bring forward.] Nov. 4. [Oxf.], (1913), s. sh. G.A. Oxon b. 141 (269a)

2191. [*Begin.*] The statute for the reform of Responsions . . . [Some account of the reasons which may be urged in favour of the proposed statute. Signed E. Barker and 10 others. Jan., 1914.] [Oxf., 1914], 8°. 11 pp.   G.A. Oxon c. 309 (6)

2192. The Responsions statute. [Statement, signed by J. Murray and 5 others. Jan.] [Oxf., 1914], s. sh.   G.A. Oxon b. 141 (275b)

2193. SNOW, T. C., Statute on Responsions, January 27th, 1914. [Amendments to be proposed by T. C. Snow and G. G. A. Murray.] [Oxf., 1914], 4°. 4 pp.   G.A. Oxon b. 141 (283a)

2194. CASE, T., and JACKSON, W. W., The proposed Responsions statute. Clause 5 and amendment (5) on the additional subject. Feb. 28. [Oxf.], (1914), 8°. 3 pp.   G.A. Oxon b. 141 (283b)

2195. ELLIOTT, R. T., Congregation, March 3. Responsions: amendment 3. [Oxf., 1914], s. sh.   G.A. Oxon b. 141 (283c)

2196. JACKSON, W. W., The proposed Responsions statute [arguments against]. June 13. [Oxf.], (1914), 4°. 4 pp. G.A. Oxon b. 141 (307b)

2197. Congregation, June 16. Responsions statute [arguments against, signed by G. Dickins and 8 others.] [Oxf., 1914], s. sh.
                    G.A. Oxon b. 141 (283e)

2198. The Responsions statute [arguments in favour, signed S. Ball and 21 others. June 16, 1914]. [Oxf., 1914], s. sh.   G.A. Oxon c. 309 (29)

2199. Reasons for opposing the new Responsions statute [signed by A. C. Clark and 4 others]. Jan./Feb. [Oxf., 1919], s. sh.
                    G.A. Oxon b. 141 (315c)

2200. PHELPS, L. R., The Responsions statute. Congregation, 6 May 1919 [amendments to be proposed]. Apr. 28. [Oxf.], (1919), s. sh.
                    G.A. Oxon b. 141 (317a)

2201. ELLIOTT, R. T., The proposed statute [Responsions] of May 6 in relation to Greek [arguments against]. May 3. (Oxf., 1919), s. sh.
                    G.A. Oxon c. 311 (22)

2202. Oxford university Responsions statute. Appeal to Convocation, June 17, 1919 [signed by R. W. Macan and 27 others with a list of many members who have expressed an intention of supporting the statute]. [Oxf., 1919], fol. 3 pp.   G.A. Oxon b. 141 (323a)

2203. Greek in Responsions [Arguments supporting an amendment to be proposed on Dec. 2. Signed by A. C. Clark and 4 others]. Oxf., [1919], s. sh.   G.A. Oxon b. 141 (323*b*)

2204. LYS, F. J., The University of Oxford and the nation. [Observations on Greek as a compulsory subject in Responsions.] (Nineteenth cent., 1920, vol. 87, p. 574–81.)   Per. 3977 d. 66

2205. Convocation and the proposed Responsions statute [signed by A. C. Clark and 15 others, calling for a rejection of the statute. Feb.]. Oxf., [1920], 4°. 4 pp.   G.A. Oxon b. 141 (323*c*)

2206. JONES, H. S., Greek at Oxford. The vote on Tuesday [Mar. 2]. [A letter to The Times.] Feb. 25. n. pl., (1920), s. sh.
                                                   G.A. Oxon b. 141 (325*a*)

2207. Convocation: the Responsions statute at Oxford [arguments against, signed by J. Bell and 18 others]. Oxf., [1920], 4°. 4 pp.
                                                   G.A. Oxon b. 141 (329*a*)

2208. Oxford university Responsions statute. Appeal to Convocation, March 2, 1920. [signed by R. W. Macan and 25 others. With a list of resident members who have expressed general approval of the statute]. [Oxf., 1920], 4°. 3 pp.   G.A. Oxon b. 141 (329*b*)

2209. ROSS, W. D., and WILLIAMS, N. P., Holy Scripture in Responsions. 2 Feb. [Oxf.], (1932), s. sh.   G.A. Oxon b. 141 (173*d*)

2210. GARDNER, H., Latin at Oxford. The case for compulsory Latin [as an entrance requirement]. (Amer. Oxonian, 1960, vol. 47, p. 1–5.)
                                                   Per. G.A. Oxon 8° 889

2211. OAKESHOTT, W., The case for change. [Latin as an entrance requirement.] (Amer. Oxonian, 1960, vol. 47, p. 5–7.)
                                                   Per. G.A. Oxon 8° 889

2212. Entrance to Oxford and Cambridge. Reports of committees appointed by the two universities. (Oxf. univ. rept., p. 1–22.) Oxf. &c., 1960, 8°.   2625 e. 241 = S.

Regulations

2213. Statute and regulations respecting Responsions (as amended). (Board of studies.) [Oxf.], 1889, 8°. 8 pp.   G.A. Oxon 8° 455 (2)

2214. Responsions. I. General information. II. Regulations of the Board of studies. 1893/4– . [Oxf.], (1893), 8°. [Bodley has an incomplete set 1893/4–96/7, 1905/06– : Per. 2626 e. 330.]

Examination papers

2215. Examination papers. [Schools' papers.] 1853–99. [Oxf.], 1853–99, fol. &c.   2626 d. 7; b. 2
— [Collected ed.]. 1863– . Oxf., 1863– , 8°   Per. 2626 e. 169

First public examination
General

See 2053, 2054 [Proposal to allow candidates to offer themselves for Moderations in their 5th instead of 7th term. 1866].

2216. [A letter, signed by J. Conington and 7 others, protesting against a change which has been made in the examination papers for the Moderations class schools.] [Oxf., 1867], s. sh.   G.A. Oxon c. 83 (415)

2217. [A letter, signed by North Pinder and 3 others, replying to the letter of J. Conington and his colleagues.] Oxf., [1867], 4°. 4 pp.
G.A. Oxon c. 83 (423)

2218. COPLESTON, R. S., An appeal on behalf of certain candidates for honours in Moderations in Trinity and Michaelmas terms, 1873. [Attacking the result of the Decree of Convocation, Feb. 27, 1872 which settled the effective date of the new statute as Michaelmas 1873, thereby forcing students to sit for their honours degree earlier than hitherto.] Oxf., 1873, 8°. 7 pp.   G.A. Oxon 8° 250 (2)

2219. JACKSON, W. W., Letter to the vice-chancellor on the exemption of candidates for honours from Pass moderations. June 10, 1885. [Oxf.], (1885), 4°. 4 pp.   G.A. Oxon 4° 255

2220. [*Begin.*] Attention is drawn to the fact . . . [Outline of a scheme for the introduction of a new specialized examination for candidates in some Honour schools, in lieu of Pass moderations.] n. pl., [*c.* 1885], 8°. 6 pp.   Acland 14 (17)

See 1961 [Oxford Pass schools: 'Mods.' 1887].
See 2757, 2761–63 [Proposed History moderations. 1886].

2221. WELLS, J., The proposed legislation as to Pass moderations. (Oxf. mag., 1915, vol. 33, p. 159, 60.)   Per. G.A. Oxon 4° 141

2222. MCCALLUM, R. B., The new Pass mods. (Oxf. mag., 1930, vol. 49, p. 50–54.)   Per. G.A. Oxon 4° 141

2223. F., M.B., The reform of Pass mods. (Oxf. mag., 1938, vol. 57, p. 47, 48.)   Per. G.A. Oxon 4° 141

2224. DENNISTON, J. D., Honour moderations. (Oxf. mag., 1930, vol. 48, p. 420–23.)   Per. G.A. Oxon 4° 141

See 2786, 2787 [History moderations. 1938, 39].

Other aspects of the first public examination are classified according to the aspect, e.g. subjects of examinations under the Faculties concerned.

Examination papers

2225. [Examination papers. Schools' papers. Pass and honour.] 1852–99. [Oxf.], 1852–99, fol. &c.   2626 b. 1–4; e. 72a

2226. In literis Graecis et Latinis. [Examination papers. Pass and honour. Collected ed.] 1863–85. Oxf., 1863–85, 8°   Per. 2626 e. 170

— Greek and Latin literature. Honours [Collected ed.]. 1886– . Oxf., 1886– , 8°.   Per. 2626 e. 171
— Greek and Latin literature. Pass [*afterw.*] First public examination. Pass [Collected ed.]. 1886–1942. Oxf., 1886–1942, 8°. Per. 2626 e. 170

2227. In disciplinis mathematicis. [Examination papers. Collected ed.]. 1863– . Oxf., 1863– , 8°.   Per. 18753 e. 102
— [Schools' papers]. 1872–99. [Oxf.], 1872–99, 8°.   2626 e. 50

2228. [A typewritten copy of the first paper set on trigonometry in the pass school of the first public examination.] Trinity term, 1918. [Oxf.], 1918, s. sh.   2626 c. 7

2229. First public examination. Preliminary examination [papers] for theology. Hilary term, 1950– . Oxf., 1950– , 8°.   Per. 2626 e. 490

2230. First public examination [papers]. Honour moderations in theology. 1960– . Oxf., 1960– , 8°.   Per. 2626 e. 562

2230.5. Second [*afterw.*] First public examination [papers]. Honour school of jurisprudence. Preliminary examination [from 1932] Law moderations. 1887– . Oxf., 1888– , 8°.   Per. 2626 e. 186; L.L.

2231. First public examination. Preliminary examination [papers] in classical Greek and Latin and Oriental languages. Hilary term, 1950– . Oxf., 1950–, 8°.   Per. 2626 e. 513

2232. First public examination. Preliminary examination [papers] in modern history. Hilary term, 1949– . Oxf., 1949– , 8°.
Per. 2626 e. 486

2233. First public examination. Preliminary examination [papers] in English language and literature. Hilary term, 1949– . Oxf., 1949– , 8°.   Per. 2626 e. 487

2234. First public examination. Preliminary examination [papers] for modern languages. Trinity term, 1948– . Oxf., 1948– , 8°.
Per. 2626 e. 481

2235. First public examination. Preliminary examination [papers] in Oriental studies. 1960– . Oxf., 1960– , 8°.   Per. 2626 e. 561

See 2249. [First public examination. School of Natural Science. 1854– .]

2235.5. First public examination [papers]. Honour moderations in biochemistry. Trinity term, 1962– . Oxf., 1962– , 8°.   Radcl.

2235.51. First public examination. Preliminary examination [papers] in physiology. Hilary term, 1962– . Oxf., 1962– , 8°.   Radcl.

2235.52. First public examination [papers]. Honour moderations in physics, mathematics and engineering science. 1963– . Oxf., 1963– , 8°.   Radcl.

2235.53. Preliminary examination [papers] for biology. Trinity term, 1964– . Oxf., 1964– , 8°.   Radcl.

2235.54. Preliminary examination [papers] for geology. Trinity term, 1964– . Oxf., 1964– , 8°.   Radcl.

2235.55. First public examination. Preliminary examination [papers] in psychology, philosophy and physiology. Hilary term 1962– . Oxf., 1962– , 8°.   Per. 2626 e. 585

2236. First public examination. Preliminary examination [papers] for philosophy, politics and economics. Hilary term, 1950– . Oxf., 1950– , 8°.   Per. 2626 e. 491

2237. First public examination. Preliminary examination [papers] for geography. Hilary term, 1948– . Oxf., 1948– , 8°.   Per. 2626 e. 479

See 2253 [First and second public examinations, schools of agriculture (and geography) and forestry. 1919].

2238. First public examination. Preliminary examination [papers] in music. Michaelmas term, 1950– . Oxf., 1950– , 8°.   Per. 2626 e. 534

Second public examination

General

2239. [Letter from the chairman, E. Moore, of the Board of studies for the Final Pass school, bringing under the notice of the Hebdomadal council the unsatisfactory nature of the constitution of the board.] Nov. 4. [Oxf.], (1875), s. sh.   G.A. Oxon c. 33 (148)

Other aspects of the second public examination are classified according to the aspect, e.g. subjects of examinations under the Faculties concerned.

Examination papers

2240. Questions at the mathematical examination. Easter term, 1828. [Oxf.], (1828), 8°. 10 pp.   G.A. Oxon c. 44 (65)
— Easter term, 1829.   G.A. Oxon c. 45 (116–25)
— 1830–52, 54.   2626 d. 21

2241. [Final examination, *afterw.*] Second public examination. [Schools' papers.] 1833–74. [Oxf.], 1833–74, fol. &c.   2626 b. 1, 2; d. 8
— [Collected ed.]. 1831, 63–72. Oxf., 1831–72, 8°.   2626 e. 17

2242. [Honour school of theology. Schools' examination papers]. 1872–99. [Oxf.], 1872–99, 8°.   2626 e. 71
— [Collected ed.]. 1872– . Oxf., 1872– , 8°.   Per. 2626 e. 182

2243. School (Honour school) of jurisprudence. [Schools' examination papers.] 1872–99. [Oxf.], 1872–99, 8°.   2626 d. 26; e. 62
— [Collected ed.]. 1872– . Oxf., 1872– , 8°. Per. 2626 e. 186; L.L.

2244. [Literae humaniores. Schools' examination papers.] 1872–99. [Oxf.], 1872–99, 8° &c.   2626 e. 56; b. 2, 7
— [Collected ed.]. 1872– . Oxf., 1872– , 8°.   Per. 2626 e. 173

2245. School of modern history. [Schools' examination papers.] 1872–99.
[Oxf.], 1872–99, 8°. 2626 e. 66
— [Collected ed.]. 1872– . Oxf., 1872– , 8°. Per. 2626 e. 197

2246. Honour school of English language and literature. [Schools'
examination papers.] 1896–99. [Oxf.], 1896–99, 8°. 2626 e. 163
— [Collected ed.]. 1896– . Oxf., 1896– , 8°. 2626 e. 267

2247. Honour school of modern languages. [Examination papers. Collected
ed.] 1905– . Oxf., 1905– , 8°. Per. 2626 e. 332

2248. Honour school of Oriental studies. [Schools' examination papers.]
1885–99. [Oxf.], 1885–99, fol. &c. 2626 c. 12
— [Collected ed.]. 1887– . Oxf., 1887– , 8°. Per. 2626 e. 178

2249. School of natural science [*afterw.*] Natural science school [*afterw.*]
2nd (1st and 2nd) public examination: Honour school of natural
science, preliminary (final) honour examination. [Schools' papers.]
1854–99. [Oxf.], 1854–99, 8°. 2626 e. 59
— [Collected ed.]. 1863– . Oxf., 1863– , 8°. Radcl.

2250. [Honour school of mathematics and physics. Schools' examination
papers.] 1872–99. [Oxf.], 1872–99, 8°. 2626 e. 57
— [Collected ed.] 1873– . Oxf., 1873– , 8°. Radcl.

2251. Second public examination [papers]. Honour school of philosophy,
politics and economics. Trinity term, 1923– . Oxf., 1923– , 8°.
2626 e. 474

2252. Second public examination [papers]. Honour school of geography.
1933– . Oxf., 1933– , 8°. Per. 2626 e. 567 = G.

2253. Second [*afterw.*] First and second public examinations, schools of
agriculture (and geography) and forestry, and examinations for
Diploma in forestry and rural economy. [Examination papers.
Collected ed.] 1919– . Oxf., 1919– , 8°. 2626 e. 348; Radcl.

2254. Second public examination. Final examination [papers] in engineering science. 1943– . Oxf., 1943– , 8°. Radcl.

2255. Second public examination [papers]. Honour school of forestry.
Trinity term, 1945– . Oxf., 1945– , 8°. Radcl.

2256. Second public examination [papers]. Honour school of agriculture.
Trinity term, 1947– . Oxf., 1947– , 8°. Radcl.

2257. Second public examination [papers]. Honour school of psychology,
philosophy and physiology. Trinity term, 1949– . Oxf., 1949– , 8°.
Per. 2626 e. 511

2258. Second public examination [papers]. Honour school of music.
Trinity term, 1952– . Oxf., 1952– , 8°. Per. 2626 e. 537

2259. Pass school, group A (–D). [Schools' examination papers.] 1874–99.
[Oxf.], 1874–99, 8° &c. 2626 d. 9; b. 6
— [Collected ed.]. 1874– . Oxf., 1874– , 8°. Per. 2626 e. 172

2260. Pass school, group E. [Examination papers. Collected ed.] 1906– .
Oxf., 1906– , 8°.   Per. 2626 e. 378

Rudiments of religion examination

See 2048–50 [Papers concerning the Examination in rudiments of faith and
religion. 1865].

2261. [*Begin.*] You are earnestly invited . . . [A letter, Dec. 8, 1883, seeking support to negative the nomination of R. F. Horton as examiner in
the Rudiments of Faith and Religion.] [Oxf.], (1883), 8°. 3 pp.
G.A. Oxon b. 140 (49a)

2262. CHASE, D. P., Concio ad venerabilem Congregationis Domum die
Decembris sexto 1883 de nominatione R. F. Horton, A.M. habita
[signed D. P. C.]. [Oxf., 1883], 4°. 2 sh.   G.A. Oxon b. 140 (49b)

2263. The examination in Holy Scripture. [Suggested amendment to the
statute, to allow an alternative to the Greek translation. Signed
R. Brook, A. E. J. Rawlinson, J. L. Johnston.] [Oxf., 1913], 8°. 3 pp.
G.A. Oxon c. 309 (1)

2264. The proposed statute concerning the examination in Holy Scripture
[arguments against, signed T. Case and 7 others.] Nov. 11th 1914.
[Oxf.], (1914), s. sh.   G.A. Oxon c. 309 (39)

2265. The proposed abolition of the examination in Holy Scripture [signed
V. J. K. Brook and 6 others]. [Oxf.], (1931), 4°. 3 pp.
G.A. Oxon c. 314 (76)

2266. Holy Scripture at Oxford. The real case against a compulsory
examination. (Oxf. mag., 1932, vol. 50, p. 319, 20.)
Per. G.A. Oxon 4° 141

2267. Second public examination. Examination [papers] in the rudiments
of faith and religion [*afterw.*] First public examination. Holy Scripture. [Collected ed.] 1874–1931. Oxf., 1874–1931, 8°.   2626 e. 216
— [Schools' papers]. 1875–99. [Oxf.], 1875–99, fol. &c.
2626 d. 19; b. 5

Special examinations

2268. Special examinations [papers]. Hilary term, 1942–50. [Oxf.], 1942–
50, 8°.   Per. 2626 e. 459; d. 66

2269. [Examination papers for prisoners-of-war.] [Oxf.], 1943, 8°.
Per. 2626 e. 472

2270. Qualifying examination for the shortened final honour school of
English language and literature. 1950. Oxf., 1950, 8°. Per. 2626 e. 492

Oxford Ordination course

2271. HEADLAM, A. C., Memorandum on the proposed course for training
for Orders in Oxford. [Reprod. from typewriting.] n. pl., [1918?], 4°.
20 sheets.   26332 d. 51

2272. Oxford ordination course. (Regulations.) [Oxf., 1919], 8°. 7 pp.
G.A. Oxon 8° 884 (7)

2273. Examination papers. Oxford ordination course. October 1919–
October 1924. Oxf., 1919–24, 4°.   Per. 26332 d. 55

DEGREES, DIPLOMAS, AND CERTIFICATES
General

See also Faculties 2448, &c.
See also Residence 1375, &c.
See also Admission of Women 3248, &c.

2274. Statuta legenda in admissione inceptorum in theologia, ad quorum
observationem singuli tenentur. [Oxf., 17—], s. sh.
MS. Grabe 10 (f. 69)

2275. Statuta legenda in admissione baccalaureorum in theologia ad
quorum observationem singuli tenentur. [Oxf., 17—], s. sh.
MS. Grabe 10 (f. 55)

2276. Statuta legenda in admissione inceptorum in medicina, ad quorum
observationem singuli tenentur. [Oxf., 17—], s. sh.
MS. Grabe 4 (f. 335)

2277. Statuta legenda in admissione baccalaureorum in medicina ad
quorum observationem singuli tenentur. [Oxf., 17—], s. sh.
MS. Grabe 10 (f. 56)

2278. BRETT, T., Of degrees in the universities. [Observations on their
origin.] (Bibliotheca literaria, 1722, num. 1, p. 6–25.)
Per. 3974 d. 291

2279. [Documents showing the procedure of every Degree-day in 1829.
The various Testamurs &c. are given and their use explained.]
MS. Top. Oxon c. 154

2280. Report from the Vice-chancellor . . . to an order of the House of
Lords, dated 24th March 1835 (for a copy and translation of the form
used in applying for and granting dispensations for the degrees of
Bachelor and Master of arts). [Oxf., 1835], s. sh.   G.A. Oxon b. 22

See 1952 [Shirley, W. W., Ought our honours to be given without limit of age?
1865].

2281. [Two newspaper cuttings of 1875 and 1886 relating to the spurious
diploma said to have been given to Samuel ben Menaseh ben Israel in
1655. The text of the diploma is given.]   G.A. Oxon c. 215

2282. FREEMAN, E. A., The proposed degrees of Doctor in letters and in
natural science. n. pl., (1887), 8°. 7 pp.   G.A. Oxon 8° 1055 (9)

2283. To members of Congregation. [A paper, *begin.*] After a discussion
. . . [signed D. B. Monro, W. Odling, J. L. Strachan-Davidson, on
degrees for research.] [Oxf.], (1894), fol. 3 pp.   G.A. Oxon c. 153

2284. GARDNER, P., The proposed degrees for research. [Reasons against defining science, for the purposes of the proposed statute, as including mathematics, natural science, and mental and moral science.] Feb. 16. (Oxf., 1895), 4°. 4 pp.   G.A. Oxon 4° 119 (10)

2285. February 12, 1895. Research degrees [B.Litt. and B.Sc.]. Amendment no. 28 [signed J. Wells, explaining his object in suggesting a residence of 8 terms]. [Oxf.], (1895), s. sh.   G.A. Oxon c. 153

2286. CASE, T., Proposed statute respecting degrees for research [in science or natural science. By T. Case]. Feb. 12. n. pl., [1895], 8°. 16 pp.   G.A. Oxon 8° 540 (15)

2287. CASE, T., Proposed statute concerning degrees for research. Feb. 19. [Oxf.], (1895), s. sh.   G.A. Oxon c. 153

2288. CASE, T., Degrees in science. 3 May. [Oxf.], (1895), fol. 4 pp.   G.A. Oxon c. 153

2289. University degrees. A bill to regulate the use of certain university degrees in the United Kingdom of Great Britain and Ireland. [Lond.], 1898, s. sh.   Pp. Eng. 1898 vol. 7
— 1899.   Pp. Eng. 1899 vol. 7

2290. DAVIDSON, J. L. STRACHAN-, The degrees of Doctor of letters and Doctor of science. [Oxf.], (1900), 4°. 3 pp.   G.A. Oxon c. 153

2291. GARDNER, P., The new degrees in science and letters [signed P. G.]. [The Club.] [Oxf., 1903], 8°. 3 pp.   Firth b. 36 (213c)

2292. GARDNER, P., [Begin.] The present regulations for the Litt.B. and Sc.B. degrees . . . [signed P.G.]. [The Club.] [Oxf., 1903?], s. sh.   Firth b. 36 (213d)

2293. MYRES, J. L., Diplomas and degree examinations. [Suggestion that diplomas should be allowed to count as one of the 'groups' for the B.A. pass degree.] [Oxf., c. 1910], s. sh.   Firth b. 36 (197b)

2294. [Begin.] We venture to appeal for support to the amendments to the statute concerning Diploma students [signed by H. Balfour and 13 others]. [Oxf., 1912], s. sh.   G.A. Oxon c. 153

2295. Statutes concerning the degrees of Bachelor of letters, Bachelor of science and Doctor of philosophy. (Gen. board of Faculties.) n. pl., (1923), 8°. 28 pp.   G.A. Oxon 4° 430 (12)

2296. LEVENS, R. G. C., War degree requirements. (Oxf. mag., 1940, vol. 59, p. 117–19.)   Per. G.A. Oxon 4° 141

Degrees

Bachelor of Arts (B.A.)

2297. BROWN, C. S., The Oxford B.A. and the 'doctorate or its equivalent'. (Amer. Oxonian, 1961, vol. 48, p. 112–15.)   Per. G.A. Oxon 8° 889

See also under Examinations, 1st and 2nd public and all other relevant aspects of the classification scheme.

Bachelor of Civil Law (B.C.L.)

2298. Examination for B.C.L. degree. (Examination in the Faculty of law.) [Schools' examination papers.] 1869–99. [Oxf.], 1869–99, 8°.
2626 e. 65

— [Collected ed.]. 1874– . Oxf., 1874– , 8°.   Per. 2626 e. 187; L.L.

Bachelor of Divinity (B.D.)

2299. Copies of the correspondence in the case of the Regius professor of divinity [dr. Hampden] and mr. Macmullen [concerning the selection of subjects for the divinity exercises for the degree of B.D.]. Oxf., 1844, 8°. 28 pp.   44. 1645 (5)

2300. Examination papers. Qualifying examination for the degree of B.D. July, 1921– . Oxf., 1921– , 8°.   Per. 2626 d. 117

Bachelor of Education (B.Ed.)

2300.5. BARNETT, J. V., Towards a B.Ed. degree. (Oxf. mag., 1966, p. 380–
82.)   Per. G.A. Oxon 4° 141

Bachelor of Letters (B.Litt.)

See 2285, &c. [Research degrees].
See 2314 [Gotch, F., Letter on residential requirements for B.Litt. 1901].
See 2295 [Statutes. 1923].

2301. K., W., The future of the B.Litt. (Oxf. mag., 1938, vol. 57, p. 207–
10.)   Per. G.A. Oxon 4° 141

See 2135 [Successful candidates for the degrees of . . . B.Litt., &c. 1940/49–].

2301.5. Board of Faculty of English. Qualifying examination [papers] for the degree of B.Litt. 1949– . Oxf., 1949– , 8°.   Per. 2626 d. 119

Bachelor of Medicine (B.Med.)

2302. Memorial [to the Hebdomadal council to consider reducing the term of college residence for students supplicating for the degree of B.Med. when certain tuition takes place outside Oxford.] n. pl., [1858], 4°. 2 sheets.   G.A. Oxon c. 74 (367)

2303. Report on the final examination for the degrees of Bachelor of medicine, and Bachelor of surgery of the University of Oxford, held in December 1904, by the visitor . . . and the inspector . . . appointed by the General medical council. n. pl., [1905], 8°. 20 pp.   26322 e. 47 (2)

2304. Report by the examination-committee [of the General medical council] on the Report by the visitor . . . and the inspector . . . n. pl., [1905], 8°. 24 pp.   26322 e. 47 (3)

2305. Examination for the degree of Bachelor of medicine. [Schools' examination papers.] 1858, 59, 61–76. [Oxf.], 1858–76, fol. & 4°.
2626 c. 3; d. 25

2306. Examination papers (1st and 2nd examinations) for the degree of Bachelor of medicine (and Master in surgery). [Collected ed.] 1864–97, 1900– . Oxf., 1864– , 8°.   2626 d. 25; Radcl.

See 3269 [Case, T., Objections to the proposed statute for admitting women to the examinations for the degree of Bachelor of medicine. 1890].

Bachelor of Music (B.Mus.)

2307. STAINER, SIR J., A few words to candidates for the degree of Mus. Bac., Oxon. Lond. &c., [1897], 8°. 27 pp.   26327 e. 6 (4)

2308. Public (First, Second) examination for the degree of Bachelor in music. [Schools' examination papers.] 1867–99. [Oxf.], 1867–99, fol. &c.   2626 b. 8; d. 30

2309. Examination papers . . . for the degree of Bachelor in music (and Doctor in music). [Collected ed.] 1891– . Oxf., 1891– , 8°.
          Per. 2626 e. 319

Bachelor of Philosophy (B.Phil.)

2310. MCCALLUM, R. B., The proposed B.Phil. degree. (Oxf. mag., 1946, vol. 64, p. 320.)   Per. G.A. Oxon 4° 141

2311. KELLY, J. N. D., The B.Phil. degree: some doubts. (Oxf. mag., 1946, vol. 64, p. 336–38.)   Per. G.A. Oxon 4° 141

2312. RYLE, G., The B.Phil. in philosophy. (Oxf. mag., 1952, vol. 70, p. 180, 81.)   Per. G.A. Oxon 4° 141

2313. Examination [papers] for the degree of Bachelor of philosophy. Trinity term, 1948– . Oxf., 1948– , 8°.   Per. 2626 e. 484

Bachelor of Science (B.Sc.)

See 2285, &c. [Research degrees].

2314. GOTCH, F., [Begin.] May I call your attention . . . [A letter on residential requirements for the research degrees of B.Sc. and B.Litt., particularly in vacation.] Feb. 1901. [Oxf.], (1901), 8°. 4 pp.
          Firth b. 36 (213b)

See 2295 [Statutes. 1923].
See 2135 [Successful candidates for the degrees of . . . B.Sc., &c. 1940/49–].

Bachelor of Surgery (B.Ch.)

See 2303 [Report on final examination for the degree of Bachelor of surgery, &c. 1905].

Doctor of Civil Law (D.C.L.)

See also Honorary degrees, 2329, &c.

2315. SWABEY, M., Facts relative to the [period of standing required of candidates for the] law degree [D.C.L. as compared with Cambridge. By M. Swabey?]. (Oxf., 1789), fol. 3 pp.   G.A. Oxon c. 107 (81)

2316. Reasons humbly offered by a member of Convocation why the alteration in the statute Tit. 6. sect. 4. § 3. as promulged in Congregation . . .
28th May, and to be proposed in Convocation . . . 10th June, ought to
pass into law. [Concerns the reduction of the period of standing required of candidates for the degree of D.C.L.] (Oxf., 1789), fol. 3 pp.
G.A. Oxon c. 107 (82)

2317. WILLIAMS, M., [Letter, dated Oct. 11, to the Hebdomadal Council,
requesting that the degree of D.C.L. may now be conferred on him.
This was announced in the Gazette as taking place on June 12, and
was cancelled owing to the opposition of the Faculty of Law.] [Oxf.],
(1875), s. sh.   G.A. Oxon c. 33 (111)

Doctor of Divinity (D.D.)

2318. HOLLAND, T., Oratio Sarisburiæ habita viii. Id. Iun. cum . . . Henricus . . . episcopus Sarisburiensis gradum doctoratus in theologia
susciperet . . . [Madan 190.] Oxon., 1599, 4°. 12 pp.   Gough Oxf. 116

Doctor of Letters (D.Litt.)

See 2282, 2290.

Doctor of Music (D.Mus.)

2319. Examination for the degree of Doctor in music. [Schools' examination papers.] 1873–99. [Oxf.], 1873–99, fol. &c.   2626 c. 4; d. 29

See 2309 [Examination papers. 1891–1959].

2320. Examination [papers] for the degree of Doctor of music. 1960– .
Oxf., 1960– , 8°.   Per. 2626 e. 563

Doctor of Philosophy (D.Phil.)

2321. WALKER, E. M., The new doctorate for research students at the
University. (Amer. Oxon., 1918, vol. 5, p. 43–47.)
Per. G.A. Oxon 8° 889
See 2295 [Statutes. 1923].
See 2134 [Abstracts of dissertations for the degree of Doctor of philosophy.
1928–47].
See 2135 [Successful candidates for the degrees of D.Phil., &c. 1940/49–].

Doctor of Science (D.Sc.)

See 2282, 2284, &c., 2290.

Master of Arts (M.A.)

2322. To the members of Convocation. [Queries as to the legality of candidates for the degree of M.A. after the Act has commenced being
admitted to their regency in the same year.] Oxf., [1803], s. sh.
G.A. Oxon b. 19

2323. FARNELL, L. R., Club. [*Begin.*] In considering by what practical
measures . . . [suggesting the support by the Club for the principle
that M.A.'s should be allowed to keep their names on the books of the
University without necessarily doing so in a college or hall]. [Oxf.,
1905], s. sh.   Firth b. 36 (77*f*)

2324. FIRTH, SIR C. H., The principle of the M.A. statute. [Oxf., 1909],
s. sh.   G.A. Oxon c. 153

2325. The M.A. statute coming before Congregation on March 2nd, 1909,
at 2 p.m. [A call for the rejection of the statute, signed by E. Armstrong
and 30 others.] [Oxf., 1909], 4°. 3 pp.   G.A. Oxon c. 153

2326. ANSON, SIR W. R., [*Begin.*] The discussion which will take place . . .
[A letter on the proposed alteration in the qualifications for the degree
of M.A.] 28 Feb. [Oxf.], (1909), s. sh.   G.A. Oxon c. 153

2327. MYRES, SIR J. L., The M.A. degree. (Oxf. mag., 1912, vol. 30, p. 322,
33.)   Per. G.A. Oxon 4° 141

2328. University dues and the M.A. degree fee. (Oxf. mag., 1933, vol. 51,
p. 497, 98.)   Per. G.A. Oxon 4° 141

Master of Surgery (M.Ch.)

See 2306 [Examination papers].

Honorary degrees

2329. SMALRIDGE, G., Two speeches made in the Theatre at Oxford (the
1st upon presenting J. E. Grabe to the University for the degree of
doctor, the 2nd at his creation). [In Engl. and Lat.] Lond., 1714, 8°.
16 pp.   G. Pamph. 2288 (16)

2330. TRAPP, J., [*Begin.*] Most excellent vice chancellor . . . [Presentation
address to Convocation on the occasion of an hon. D.C.L. being conferred on sir C. Phipps. By J. Trapp.] Dubl., 1714, o. sh.
                                                   G.A. Oxon 8° 147 (3)

2331. KING, W., Tres oratiunculæ habitæ in domo Convocationis Oxon.
(Oratiuncula . . . xviii kalendas April [really May] MDCCXLIII, cum
. . . Jacobus Hamilton, dux de Hamilton & Brandon præsentaretur ad
gradum doctoris in jure civili honoris causa. Oratiuncula . . . xviii
kalendas August. [really viii kal. Sept.] MDCCXLIII cum . . . Georgius
Henricus Lee, comes de Lichfield præsentaretur ad gradum doctoris
in jure civili honoris causa. Oratiuncula . . . viii kalendas August.
[really Sept.] MDCCXLIII cum . . . Johannes Boyle, comes de
Orrery præsentaretur ad gradum doctoris in jure civili honoris causa.)
n. pl., (1743), 4°. 6+8+8+8 pp.   4 Δ 260 (10)
— [Another ed.]. Lond. &c., (1743), 4°. 22 pp.   Gough Oxf. 89 (10)
— [Another ed.] (Opera Gul. King, vol. 1.) Lond. &c., [1754], 4°.
                                                   GG 43 Art.

2332. Installation at Oxford, a letter [signed E. H. H.] to sir William Sidney Smith &c. [on being granted a D.C.L.]. Bangor, [1810], 4°. 4 pp.   G.A. Oxon 4° 44

See 2541 [Law revivals at Oxford. An earnest appeal to the University not to confer honorary degrees in civil law upon insufficient grounds. 1860].

2333. A speech addressed to the . . . prince of Wales, 16th of June, 1863 . . . by Edward Geoffrey, earl of Derby, chancellor of the University [when the degree of D.C.L. was conferred upon the prince]. Now rendered into English. [Pr. on vellum.] [Oxf.], (1863), fol. [8 pp.].
                                                       G.A. Oxon c. 298

2334. Protest of resident Catholic members of the University of Oxford against the recent act of Convocation conferring the degree of D.C.L. on dr. von Döllinger [signed W. H. M. Bliss and 10 others]. [Oxf.], (1871), s. sh.   G.A. Oxon b. 140 (26b)

2335. CLARKE, R. F., [Begin.] The proposal to confer a degree on dr. Döllinger . . . [protest against]. June 3. [Oxf.], (1871), s. sh.
                                                    G.A. Oxon b. 140 (26a)

2336. Rules as to honorary degrees, to be observed by the Hebdomadal council. Nov. 17. [Oxf.], (1873), s. sh.   G.A. Oxon c. 33 (159)

2337. HEURTLEY, C. A., [Begin.] Of the three gentlemen . . . [A protest against the conferment of an honorary degree on J. Tyndall.] June 18. [Oxf.], (1873), s. sh.   G.A. Oxon b. 140 (28a)

See 2615, 2616 [Degree of M.A. honoris causa to be conferred on Wyndham H. Dunstan. 1888].

2338. To the . . . Vice-chancellor. [Memorial expressing regret that mr. Rhodes is included in the list of those who are to receive the degree of D.C.L. at Encænia. Signed by numerous senior members of the University, who ask that their letter be published in the Gazette.] [Oxf., 1897], fol. 3 pp.   G.A. Oxon c. 153
— [Another ed., with additional signatures.]   G.A. Oxon c. 153

2339. BROCHE, G. E., Une antique institution d'Oxford [Public orator] vue à l'occasion de la réception de m. Gaston Doumergue . . . et de m. Aristide Briand . . . à l'Université d'Oxford, 17 mai 1927. Nîmes, 1928, 8°. 32 pp.   G.A. Oxon 4° 403* (16)

2340. A convocation of the University of Oxford to be holden in the precincts of Harvard university, June 19, 1941. [To confer on president Roosevelt the honorary degree of D.C.L. A made-up volume, containing instructions &c. and photographs.]   G.A. Oxon 4° 616

2341. The Convocation at Cambridge [Mass.] [conferring the degree of D.C.L. on the President of the United States]. (Amer. Oxon., 1941, vol. 28, p. 197–201.)   Per. G.A. Oxon 8° 889

2342. WEAVER, J. R. H., The Oxford Convocation at Coimbra [Apr. 19, 1941, conferring the honorary degree of D.C.L. on Antonio Oliveira Salazar, prime minister of Portugal]. (Oxford, 1942, vol. 8, no. 1, p. 75–80.)   Per. G.A. Oxon 8° 1141

2343. Speeches by the public orator [T. F. Higham] in a Convocation held
on St. Crispin's day, 25 October, 1945. [In Latin.] Oxf., 1945, 8°.
13 pp.   G.A. Oxon 8° 1204 (2)
— English versions. 15 pp.   G.A. Oxon 8° 1204 (1)

2344. ANSCOMBE, G. E. M., Mr. Truman's degree. (Oxf.), [1956], 8°. 15 pp.
                                                             26523 e. 149

2345. HIGHAM, T. F., Orationes Oxonienses selectae: short Latin speeches
on distinguished contemporaries [given at the conferment of honorary
degrees]. Oxf., 1960, 8°. 108 pp.   G.A. Oxon 8° 1396

Certificates

Certificates in French and German

2346. Certificates in French and German. [Examination papers. Collected
ed.] 1914–33. Oxf., 1914–33, 8°.   Per. 2626 d. 67

Certificate in preventive medicine

See 2306 [Examination papers. Certificate in preventive medicine and public
health. 1877].

Certificate in public administration

See 2355 [Certificate in public administration. 1937].

Certificate in statistics

See 2366 [Certificate in statistics. 1949].

Diplomas

Diploma in agricultural economics

2347. Diploma in agricultural economics. [Examination papers.] Trinity
term, 1948– Oxf., 1948– , 8°.   Per. 2626 e. 483

Diploma in anthropology

2348. Diploma in anthropology. [Examination papers. Collected ed.]
1908– . Oxf., 1908– , 8°.   Per. 2626 e. 546

Diploma in classical archaeology

2349. Diploma in classical archaeology. [Examination papers. Collected
ed.]. 1910– . Oxf., 1910– , 8°.   Per. 2626 e. 548

Diploma in comparative philology

2350. Diploma in comparative philology. [Examination papers.] Trinity
term, 1951– . Oxf., 1951– , 8°.   Per. 2626 e. 535 = S.

Diploma in economics

2351. The Oxford diploma in economics. n. pl., [1905], 8°.   263334 e. 31

2352. Diploma in economics (and political science and in public and social
administration). [Examination papers. Collected ed.] 1905– . Oxf.,
1905– , 8°.   Per. 2626 d. 54

2353. The Oxford Diploma in economics and political science. Oxf.,
(1913), 8°. 12 pp.   G.A. Oxon 8° 900 (6)

2354. The Oxford Diploma in economics, and political science. [Booklet.]
(Oxf.), [1917], 8°. 12 pp.   G.A. Oxon c. 249 (373)

2355. Committee for economics and political science. The Diploma in
economics and political science; the Diploma in public and social administration; the Certificate in public administration. Regulations for
the examinations in 1937 and after. [Oxf., 1937], 8°. 5 pp.
                                                  2626 e. 439 (1)

Diploma in education

2356. Examination [papers] in the theory, history and practice of education. [Collected ed.] 1897– . Oxf., 1897– , 8°.   Per. 2626 e. 365 = S.
— [Schools' papers.] 1898–1900. [Oxf.], 1898–1900, 8°. 2626 e. 268

Diploma in European archaeology

See 3129 [Hawkes, C. F. C., Archaeology in Oxford university: two recent
developments—the Research laboratory of archaeology and history of art,
and the Diploma in European archaeology. 1958].

2356.5. Diploma in European archaeology. [Examination papers.]
Trinity term, 1964– . Oxf., 1964– , 8°.   Per. 2626 e. 596

Diploma in forestry

2357. Instructions in forestry [*afterw.*] Diploma in forestry. [Examination
papers. Collected ed.] 1906–19. [Later issues were publ. with the
papers of the 1st and 2nd public examinations, school of agriculture
and forestry, no. 2253.] Oxf., 1906–19, 8°.   2626 e. 347

Diploma in geochemistry

2357.5. Diploma in geochemistry. [Examination papers.] Trinity term,
1966– . Oxf., 1966– , 8°.   Radcl.

Diploma and certificates in geography

See 3135 [Diploma and certificates in geography. Examination papers. 1901–
04/5].

Diplomas and certificates in military history

2358. Diplomas and certificates in military history. [Examination papers.]
Trin. term, 1914. Oxf., 1914, 8°.   2626 e. 404

Diploma in ophthalmology

2359. Diploma in ophthalmology. [Examination papers. Collected ed.] 1910– . Oxf., 1910– , 8°.   Radcl.

Diploma in preventive medicine and public health

See 2621 [Diploma in public health. Regulations. 1894].

2360. Oxford university examination papers for the Diploma in preventive medicine and public health. [Collected ed.] 1908–28. Oxf., 1908–28, 8°.   Per. 1672 d. 122

Diploma in psychology

2361. STEPHENSON, W., A diploma in psychology. (Oxf. mag., 1941, vol. 59, p. 341, 42.)   Per. G.A. Oxon 4° 141

Diploma in public and social administration

See 2352 [Diploma in public and social administration. 1905, &c.].

Diploma in public health

See 2360 [Diploma in public health].
See 2621 [Regulations. 1894].

Diploma in rural economy

2362. Diploma in rural economy. [Examination papers. Collected ed.] 1911–19. [Later issues were publ. with the papers of the 1st and 2nd public examinations, school of agriculture and forestry, no. 2253.] Oxf., 1911–19, 8°.   2626 e. 333

Diploma in science materials

2362.5. Diploma in science materials. [Examination papers.] Trinity term, 1966– . Oxf., 1966– , 8°.   Radcl.

Diploma in scientific engineering and mining

2363. Diploma in scientific engineering and mining subjects. [Regulations and statute.] [Oxf.], (1905), 8°. 15 pp.   G.A. Oxon 8° 1055 (11)

2364. Diploma in scientific engineering and mining. [Examination papers. Collected ed.] 1906–08. Oxf., 1906–08, 8°.   2626 d. 34

Diploma in Slavonic studies

2365. Diploma in Slavonic studies. [Examination papers.] Trinity term, 1951– . Oxf., 1951– , 8°.   Per. 2626 e. 536

Diploma in soil science

2365.5. Diploma in soil science. [Examination papers.] Michaelmas term, 1965– . Oxf., 1965– , 8°.   Radcl.

Diploma and certificate in statistics

2366. Diploma and certificate in statistics. [Examination papers.] Trinity term, 1949– . Oxf., 1949– , 4°.   Per. 2626 d. 70

Diploma in theology

2367. Diploma in theology. [Examination papers. Collected ed.] 1919– . Oxf., 1919– , 8°.   Per. 2626 e. 550

POST-GRADUATE RESEARCH

2368. American club of Oxford. Conditions of advanced study in Oxford university. (Oxf., 1900), 8°. 8 pp.   G.A. Oxon 8° 659 (23)

2369. BIGGAR, H. P., On the establishment of a graduate school at Oxford. (University review, 1906, vol. 3, p. 111–32.)   Per. 2625 d. 30

2370. MCCALLUM, R. B., The advance of the advanced students. (Oxf. mag., 1936, vol. 54, p. 512–14.)   Per. G.A. Oxon 4° 141

2371. POWICKE, F. M., Graduate study in Oxford. (Amer. Oxon., 1937, vol. 24, p. 16–20.)   Per. G.A. Oxon 8° 889

2371.2. QUINTON, A., Notes on the graduate problem. 2 pt. (Oxf. mag., 1959, vol. 78, p. 110, 111, 117–20.)   Per. G.A. Oxon 4° 141

2371.21. QUINTON, A., The graduate problem. (Oxford, 1960, vol. 16, p. 79–84.)   Per. G.A. Oxon 8° 1141

2371.31. BURKE, P., Graduate studies in Oxford. (Oxf. mag., 1961, N.S., vol. 2, p. 60.)   Per. G.A. Oxon 4° 141

2371.32. SAYCE, R., The report on postgraduate studies. (Oxf. mag., 1962, N.S., vol. 3, p. 52, 53.)   Per. G.A. Oxon 4° 141

2371.33. DAWES, G., Postgraduate students. (Oxf. mag., 1963, N.S., vol. 3, p. 184, 85.)   Per. G.A. Oxon 4° 141

2371.5. Comments of the General Board of the Faculties on the Report of the Committee on postgraduate studies. [The text of the Report also is printed here.] Suppl. no. 2 to the Univ. Gazette (3185, February 1964). Oxf., 1964, 8°. 34 pp.   G.A. Oxon c. 86

2371.51. MCCALLUM, R. B., A note on graduate study. (Oxf. mag., 1964, N.S., vol. 4, p. 238, 39.)   Per. G.A. Oxon 4° 141

See also 4268 [Society of post-graduate students].

UNIVERSITY FELLOWSHIPS, SCHOLARSHIPS, AND PRIZES

General

2372. GILBERT, R., Liber scholasticus; or, An account of the fellowships, scholarships and exhibitions at the universities of Oxford and Cambridge . . . [signed R. G.]. (Oxf. univ. passim.) Lond., 1829, 8°. 500 pp.
29. 104

— 2nd ed. [*entitled*] The parent's school and college guide (by R. Gilbert). 1843. 634 pp. 43. 1559

2373. 3 Feb., 1840. A convocation will be holden [to accept a prize given by a gentleman of the E. India Co. for a composition 'for the best refutation of Hinduism' etc.]. [Oxf.], (1840), fol. 3 pp.
G.A. Oxon a. 15

2374. JEYES, S. H., A guide to studying for classical entrance scholarships, adapted more especially to those offered at Oxford. (Oxf. study guides.) Oxf., 1881, 8°. 77 pp. 260 g. 442*b*

2375. [A proposal to be submitted to Convocation, 21st May, accepting trusts under the will of George Richards for the establishment of two annual prizes, one for the best scholar examined in the University, the other for the author of the best Greek ode.] May 8. [Oxf.], (1863), fol. 3 pp. G.A. Oxon c. 79 (223)

See 1811 [Scholarships and emoluments. 1909].

2376. Return of entrance scholarships and exhibitions awarded to students beginning residence in . . . October 1911. [*Followed by*] A selection from the special cases reported by the colleges [giving details of achievements and family background of previous recipients]. [Oxf., 1913], 4°. 8 pp. G.A. Oxon 4° 262 (8)

2377. Fellowships, studentships, scholarships, exhibitions & prizes open to undergraduate and graduate members of the University. Oxf., 1930, 8°. 47 pp. G.A. Oxon 8° 1090

2377.5. [Report of] The meeting on scholarships [Feb. 8, 1962]. (Oxf. mag., 1962, N.S., vol. 2, p. 190, 91.) Per. G.A. Oxon 4° 141

External

Fulbright's scholarships

2378. LOOPER, R. B., The Fulbright Oxonian: some impressions. (Amer. Oxon., 1954, vol. 41, p. 136–40.) G.A. Oxon 8° 889

Marshall scholarships

2379. GLASS, L., Marshall scholarships. (Amer. Oxonian, 1960, vol. 47, p. 110–17.) Per. G.A. Oxon 8° 889

2380. FULLER, J. W., The Marshall scholars at Oxford. (Amer. Oxonian, 1961, vol. 48, p. 133–35.)   Per. G.A. Oxon 8° 889

Rhodes scholarships

See 5977.1, &c.

Internal

Abbott's scholarships

2381. Abbott scholarships. [Schools' examination papers.] 1872–99. [Oxf.], 1872–99, 8°.   2626 e. 72*b*
— [Collected ed.]. 1927– . Oxf., 1927– , 8°.   Per. 2626 d. 116 = S

Arnold prize

2382. [*Begin.*] In a Convocation to be holden . . . 17th instant . . [Proposal instituting the Arnold prize, with suggested regulations.] May 8. [Oxf.], (1850), s. sh.   G.A. Oxon c. 66 (75)

Boden Sanskrit scholarship

See 2851 [Regulations for the Boden scholarships in Sanscrit literature. 1830]. See 2857 [Revised scheme regulating the Boden scholarship, &c. Feb. 13, 1860].

2383. Boden Sanskrit scholarship. [Schools' examination papers.] 1864–1927. [Oxf.], 1864–1927, 8°.   2626 d. 3

2384. MACDONELL, A. A., The Boden Sanskrit scholarships. (Oxf. mag., 1911, vol. 30, p. 46, 47.)   Per. G.A. Oxon 4° 141

Brackenbury scholarship

See 6772.

Buchanan prizes, &c.

2385. [Proposal to be submitted to Convocation accepting a benefaction offered by Claudius Buchanan instituting prizes for compositions on subjects relating to the East.] 30 Apr. [The benefaction was declined.] [Oxf.], 1804, s. sh.   Don. b. 12 (100*b*)

2386. [Proposal submitted to Convocation concerning a prize offered by Claudius Buchanan for a work on a subject relating to the dissemination of the Scriptures in the East.] Dec. 9. [Oxf.], 1805, fol. 3 pp.
          Don. b. 12 (108*b*)
— [Regulations for the prize]. Dec. 16. [Oxf.], 1805, s. sh.
          Don. b. 12 (109*a*)

2387. [Proposal submitted to Convocation that a benefaction offered by Claudius Buchanan for two sermons to be preached on the subject of Oriental translations of the Scriptures, be accepted.] June 22. [Oxf.], 1807, s. sh.   Don. b. 12 (120)

Burdett-Coutts scholarships

See 6188 [Angela Burdett-Coutts' foundation of 2 geological scholarships. 1860].

2388. [Proposals for certain alterations in the regulations for the Burdett-Coutts scholarships, submitted to Convocation, 27 Feb.] Feb. 19. [Oxf.], (1866), s. sh.   G.A. Oxon c. 82 (65*a*)

2389. Burdett-Coutts scholarship. [Schools' examination papers.] 1878– 85. [Oxf.], 1878–85, 8°.   2626 e. 72*c*

Charles Oldham prize

2390. Oldham bequest. Draft report [and Revised Draft report] of committee [recommending the institution of the Charles Oldham prize for classics, and the Charles Oldham scholarship for knowledge of Shakespeare]. [Oxf.], 1907, 8°. 2 sheets.   Firth b. 36 (133)

Charles Oldham scholarship

2391. Oldham bequest. Draft report [and Revised Draft report] of committee [recommending the institution of the Charles Oldham prize for classics, and the Charles Oldham scholarship for knowledge of Shakespeare]. [Oxf.], 1907, 8°. 2 sheets.   Firth b. 36 (133)

2392. Charles Oldham scholarship. [Examination papers. Collected ed.] 1909– . Oxf., 1909– , 8°.   Per. 2626 e. 547

Christopher Welch scholarships

2392.5. Examination [papers] for the Christopher Welch scholarship. 1918– . [Oxf.], 1918– , 8°. [Bodleian has 1947– , Radcl.].

Craven fellowships

2393. Craven university fellowship. [Schools' examination papers.] 1886– 89. [Oxf.], 1886–89, 8°.   2626 e. 73*a* — [Collected ed.] 1886–88. Oxf., 1887, 88, 8°.   2626 e. 402

Craven scholarships

2394. [Craven scholarship examination papers. 1829.] G.A. Oxon c. 45 (109–15) [Subsequent papers issued jointly with the Dean Ireland scholarships, no. 2400, &c.].

2395. CHASE, D. P., A plea for John lord Craven and the eleemosynary purpose of founders generally [signed D. P. C.]. [Oxf., 1857], 8°. 8 pp. G.A. Oxon b. 29

2396. Oxford university. Copy of an ordinance framed by the University
. . . in relation to the scholarships of John, lord Craven's foundation.
[Lond.], 1858, fol. 2 pp.   Pp. Eng. 1857/8 vol. 46

2397. An act for removing doubts respecting the Craven scholarships . . .
and for enabling the University to retain the custody of certain testamentary documents. (23 & 24 V., c. 91, Pub.) Lond., 1860, fol. 3 pp.
                                                              L.L.

2398. [Papers relating to the 1817 examination for the Craven scholarship,
ed. by H. G. Liddell.] (Our memories, no. 9.) [Oxf.], 1890, 4°. 6 pp.
                                                 G.A. Oxon 8° 477

Davis Chinese scholarship

2399. Davis Chinese scholarship. [Schools' examination papers.] 1879–99.
[Oxf.], 1879–99, 8°.   2626 e. 73b

Dean Ireland scholarships

2400. [March 17, 1825. Proclamation of a Convocation to be held on April
20 in order to fix the University seal to an indenture for establishing 4
university scholarships under the endowment of the rev. John Ireland.
With a copy of the indenture.] [Oxf.], 1825, fol. 4 pp.
                                                 G.A. Oxon c. 41 (36)

2401. Dean Ireland scholarship [and] Craven scholarship [afterw.]
Ireland and Craven scholarships. [Schools' examination papers.] 1833–
99. [Oxf.], 1833–99, 8°.   2626 e. 78
— [Collected ed.]. 1863, 74– . Oxf., 1863– , 8°.   2626 e. 331

Denyer and Johnson scholarships

2402. [Feb. 11, 1833. Convocation to be holden on 21st inst., the acceptance of the bequest of John Johnson, to provide for two scholarships,
one in theology, the other in mathematics, will be proposed.] [Oxf.],
(1833), s. sh.   G.A. Oxon a. 49 (15)
— [Final acceptance. 21 Feb.]   G.A. Oxon b. 22

2403. Johnson theological scholarship [afterw.] (Junior) Denyer and
Johnson scholarships. [Schools' examination papers.] 1861, 63, 66–99.
[Oxf.], 1861–99, 8°.   2626 e. 74
— [Collected ed.]. 1874– . Oxf., 1874– , 8°.   2626 e. 213

Derby scholarship

2404. Scheme for the Derby scholarship laid before the Derby trustees . . .
by the Hebdomadal council. Mar. 4. n. pl., 1885, s. sh.
                                                 G.A. Oxon c. 153

Eldon law scholarship

2405. Eldon testimonial. The Eldon law scholarship, founded at Oxford,
and list of subscribers. (Lond.), 1830, 4°. Sigs. B–K.
                                                 G.A. Oxon 4° 93

2406. Eldon testimonial. Resolution, orders & forms of declaration and certificates. [Lithogr.] n. pl., [1831], 4°. 12 pp.   G.A. Oxon c. 47 (55*)
— [Corrected ed. 1831].   G.A. Oxon c. 47 (55**)
— [1840].   G.A. Oxon 4° 570
— (1849).   G.A. Oxon c. 67 (160)
— [Other eds. *entitled*] Eldon testimonial. The Eldon law scholarship, Oxford. Rules and by-laws. May, 1864; April, 1874; May, 1881; May, 1888.   G.A. Oxon 4° 570

Ellerton and Pusey Hebrew scholarships

See 2437–38, Pusey and Ellerton Hebrew scholarships.

Ellerton theological prize

2407. [May 30, 1825. Proclamation of a Convocation to be held on June 2, in which the following proposal from dr. Ellerton will be submitted. An annual prize of 20 guineas for an essay on some doctrine of duty of the Christian religion.] [Oxf.], 1825, s. sh.   G.A. Oxon c. 41 (66)

English poem on a sacred subject prize

2408. [Regulations for the prize English poem on a sacred subject offered by an anonymous donor through the dean of Carlisle, proposed for acceptance in Convocation.] Jan. 31. [Oxf.], 1848, s. sh.
G.A. Oxon c. 64 (5)

Fell's exhibitions

See 7087.

Gaisford Greek prizes

2409. The late dean of Christ Church and regius professor of Greek. [Account of a meeting, June 12, 1855, which resolved to found a Greek prize to be called The Gaisford prize.] [Oxf., 1855], s. sh.
G.A. Oxon c. 71 (322)

2410. [Regulations proposed for the establishment of the Gaisford Greek prizes, together with the conditions of acceptance of the donation to be proposed in Convocation. Apr. 17.] Apr. 11. [Oxf.], (1856), s. sh.
G.A. Oxon c. 72 (152)
— Nov. 18. [Regulations and conditions approved.] [Oxf.], (1856), s. sh.   G.A. Oxon c. 72 (338)

Geographical scholarship

See 3135 [Geographical scholarship. Examination papers. 1901–04/5].

George Webb Medley junior scholarship

2411. Oxford university examination papers. George Webb Medley junior scholarship. 1924– . Oxf., 1924– , 8°.   S.Ed. 44 fg

Gibbs scholarships

2412. Examination papers. Gibbs scholarships in modern history and
chemistry (law). Hilary term, 1924– . Oxf., 1924– , 8°.
Per. 2626 e. 573 = S.

Hall and Hall–Houghton prizes

2413. [Proposal submitted to Convocation, 24 Nov. accepting £3,000 from
John Hall and Henry Houghton to provide the Canon Hall Greek
Testament prize, and the Hall–Houghton Septuagint prize. With
regulations.] 16 Nov. [Oxf.], (1868), s. sh.   G.A. Oxon c. 84 (356)

2414. [Regulations for the Hall–Houghton prize to be approved by Convocation, 16th Feb. 1869.] Feb. 8, 1869. [Oxf.], 1869, 4°. 4 pp.
G.A. Oxon c. 85 (59)

2415. [Hall and Hall–Houghton prizes. Schools' examination papers.]
1869–99. [Oxf.], 1869–99, 8°.   2626 e. 34
— [Collected ed.]. 1875– . Oxf., 1875– , 8°.   2626 e. 212

Heath Harrison scholarships

2416. Oxford university examination papers. Heath Harrison scholarships.
Hilary term, 1920– . Oxf., 1920– , 8°.   Per. 2626 e. 574 = S.

Hebrew scholarships

2417. Hebrew scholarship[s]. [Schools' examination papers.] 1855–99.
[Oxf.], 1855–99, 8°.   2626 e. 76
— [Collected ed.]. 1874– . Oxf., 1874– , 8°.   Per. 2626 e. 214

Hertford scholarship

2418. [Form of statute to be proposed in Convocation enabling the University to pay the dividend of certain stock after the death of Richard
Hewitt, the last surviving member of Hertford college [1st foundation],
to an undergraduate who shall be chosen by examination.] Mar. 17.
[Oxf.], 1834, s. sh.   G.A. Oxon c. 50 (36)

2419. Hertford scholarship [afterw.] Hertford and De Paravicini scholarships. [Schools' examination papers.] 1845–99. [Oxf.], 1845–99, 8°.
2626 e. 30
— [Collected ed.]. 1863– . Oxf., 1863– , 8°.   2626 e. 318

Hulme's foundation

See 6883–88.

Ireland scholarships

See 2400, 2401. Dean Ireland scholarships.

James Mew Arabic scholarship

2420. James Mew Arabic scholarship. [Examination papers. Collected ed.]
1912– . Oxf., 1912– , 8°. Per. 2626 e. 549

John Locke scholarship

2421. John Locke scholarship. [Examination papers. Collected ed.]
1899– . Oxf., 1899– , 8°. Per. 2626 d. 55

Johnson memorial prize essay

2422. [Regulations for the Johnson memorial prize for the encouragement
of the study of astronomy and meteorology, to be proposed in Convocation, June 5th.] May 26. [Oxf.], (1862), s. sh.
G.A. Oxon c. 78 (171)

Johnson scholarship in theology

See 2402, 2403. Denyer and Johnson's scholarships.

Johnson scholarship in mathematics

See 2402 [Acceptance by Convocation of bequest. 1833].

Kennicott Hebrew scholarship

2423. [*Begin.*] In a Convocation to be holden . . . 18th [March] . . . it will
be proposed to accept a bequest . . . of the late mrs. Kennicott for
the foundation of two scholarships to promote the study of Hebrew
literature. March 15, 1830. [Oxf.], (1830), s. sh. G.A. Oxon c. 46 (23)

2424. June 6, 1831. In a Convocation to be holden . . . 9th inst., the follow-
ing regulations . . . will be submitted. Regulations for the Kennicott
Hebrew scholarships. [Oxf.], (1831), fol. 3 pp. G.A. Oxon c. 47 (79)
— Oct. 20, 1831. In a Convocation . . . 27th inst. . . .
G.A. Oxon c. 47 (106)
— Nov. 14, 1831. In a Convocation . . . 17th inst. . . .
G.A. Oxon c. 47 (119)

2425. Regulations for the Kennicott Hebrew scholarships, agreed upon in
a Convocation . . . 17th Nov., 1831. [Oxf., 1831], fol. 3 pp.
G.A. Oxon c. 47 (121)

2426. SANDAY, W., To members of Congregation. The amendments to the
statute on the Kennicott scholarships to be considered in Congregation on Tuesday, April 28th. [Oxf.], (1885), 4°. 4 pp.
G.A. Oxon b. 140 (56c)
See also 2417. Hebrew scholarships.

King Charles the first's trust. [*Scholarships etc. at Exeter, Jesus, and Pembroke colleges*]

See 7299, 7318, 7431.

Macbride scholarship

See 7372.

Mathematical scholarships

2427. [Proposal to found mathematical scholarships or prizes for the encouragement of the study of mathematics. With a list of subscribers. Oct. 27.] (Oxf., 1830), s. sh.   G.A. Oxon c. 46 (94)
— [With list of additional subscribers. Nov. 17.] G.A. Oxon c. 46 (102)

2428. Regulations proposed on the endowment of three mathematical scholarships. Nov. 27, 1830. [Oxf.], (1830), fol. 3 pp.
                                                     G.A. Oxon c. 46 (106)
— Feb. 28, 1831 [to be proposed in Convocation, 9th Mar.]. [Oxf.], (1831), fol. 3 pp.   G.A. Oxon c. 47 (32)

2429. Subscribers for the endowment of three mathematical scholarships. Mar. 9, 1831. [Oxf.], (1831), fol. 4 pp.   G.A. Oxon c. 47 (35)

2430. Mathematical scholarships. [Details of the fund transferred to the University by E. Burton and E. Cardwell. June 7, 1831.] (Oxf., 1831), s. sh.   G.A. Oxon c. 47 (80)

2431. Regulations for three mathematical scholarships agreed upon in Convocation, March 9, 1831 and Feb. 15, 1844. n. pl., [1844], s. sh.
                                                     G.A. Oxon c. 60 (29)

2432. [Revised regulations for the Mathematical scholarships to be submitted to Convocation on May 18th.] May 9, 1864. [Oxf.], (1864), s. sh.
                                                     G.A. Oxon c. 80 (208)

2433. [Junior and Senior mathematical scholarships. Schools' examination papers. 1831–]55.   Savile Mm d. 140a
— 1861–71, 82–91.   2626 e. 79
— 1892–99.   2626 d. 27
[Oxf., 1831]–99, 8°.
— [Collected ed.]. 1863, 72– .   2626 e. 80; d. 13; Radcl.
Oxf., 1863– , 8°.
[The Bodleian shelfmark of an unofficial reprint of the questions set from 1828 to 1830 is: 31.544.]

Matthew Arnold prize

2434. [Proposed decree, for consideration by the Hebdomadal council, setting out details of the Matthew Arnold memorial prize for an English essay.] [Oxf.], 1901, s. sh.   G.A. Oxon c. 104 (55)

Meyricke endowment

See 7422, 7424, 7426, 7427, 7429, 7430, 7441–43.

Newdigate prize

2435. Harvard college library. A list of Newdigate prize poems, the gift of
T. K. Lothrop. n. pl., [1899], 8°. 8 pp.   25909 e. Cambr. 1. 3

Passmore Edwards scholarship

2436. Passmore Edwards scholarship. [Examination papers. Collected ed.]
1903– . Oxf., 1903– , 8°.   2626 e. 345

Pusey and Ellerton Hebrew scholarships

2437. Regulations [to be proposed to Convocation in Michaelmas term]
for the Ellerton and Pusey Hebrew scholarships. June 21, 1830. [Oxf.],
(1830), fol. 4 pp.   G.A. Oxon c. 46 (69a)
— [Amended] Regulations for the Hebrew scholarships. [Oxf.],
[1830], fol. 3 pp.   G.A. Oxon c. 46 (76b)
— [Agreed version of the Regulations to be proposed to Convocation
on Mar. 22.] Mar. 19, 1832. [Oxf.], (1832), fol. 3 pp.
                                          G.A. Oxon c. 48 (36)

2438. Pusey and Ellerton scholarships. [Examination papers.] Trinity
term, 1949– . Oxf., 1949– , 8°.   Per. 2626 e. 512

See also 2417. Hebrew scholarships.

Snell exhibitions and charity

See 6717, 6743, 6770.

Somerset scholarships

See 6889.

Squire scholarships

2439. [Squire scholarships in theology. Draft, for consideration of the
Hebdomadal council, of the scheme for the management and regulations
of the scholarships.] [Oxf.], 1901, 8°. 7 pp.   G.A. Oxon c. 104 (10)

2440. Squire scholarships. [Examination papers. Collected ed.] 1903– .
Oxf., 1903– , 8°.   Per. 2626 e. 209

Stanhope historical prize

2441. In a Convocation to be holden . . . December 14 . . . the following
regulations for the (Stanhope) prize . . . will be submitted to the House.
Dec. 6. [Oxf.], (1855), s. sh.   G.A. Oxon 4° 188

2442. [Proposal in Convocation, at the suggestion of earl Stanhope, to
amend article 2 of the regulations of the Stanhope historical prize.]
Nov. 21, 1864. [Oxf.], (1864), s. sh.   G.A. Oxon b. 31

Taylorian scholarships

2443. The examination papers for the Taylorian scholarships in modern languages. [Collected ed.] 1858–99. Oxf., 1858–99, 8°.
Per. 2626 e. 167

Vinerian scholarships

2444. The Vinerian scholarships. [Urging that preference be given to B.A.'s rather than undergraduates, and particularly to those studying law. Signed M.A.] n. pl., [1852], s. sh.   G.A. Oxon c. 68 (51)

2445. Vinerian (law) scholarship. [Schools' examination papers.] 1866–99. [Oxf.], 1866–99, 8°.   2626 e. 81
— [Collected ed.] 1874– . Oxf., 1874– , 8°.   2626 e. 304
See also 1618–37. Viner benefaction.

Winter Williams scholarships

2446. Winter Williams scholarships. [Examination papers.] Michaelmas term, 1925– . Oxf., 1925– , 8°.   Per. 2626 d. 51

Zaharoff travelling scholarships

2447. Oxford university examination papers. The Zaharoff travelling scholarships. October 1921– . Oxf., 1921– , 8°. Per. 2626 e. 575 = S.

FACULTIES

General

See also 1905–37 for works dealing with Professorships, &c., in general.
See also Degrees. 2274, &c.

2448. ARNOLD, T., Revival of the faculties at Oxford. (Dark blue, 1871/72, vol. 2, p. 380–86, 493–509.)   Per. 270 d. 32
— Repr. Oxf. &c., 1872, 8°. 28 pp.   G.A. Oxon 8° 165 (3)

2449. HOLLAND, T. E., The subdivision of the Faculty of Arts [signed T. E. H.]. [Oxf.], (1882), s. sh.   G.A. Oxon b. 140 (45e)

2450. FIRTH, SIR C. H., The faculties and their powers, a contribution to the history of University organization. Oxf. &c., 1909, 8°. 43 pp.
G.A. Oxon 8° 761 (9)

2451. RASHDALL, H., Letter to the chairman of the committee of Council on faculties. The faculties and the colleges [signed H. Rashdall]. [Oxf., 1909], 8°. 9 pp.   G.A. Oxon 4° 275

2452. CASE, T., The disorganization of the colleges by the proposed statute on faculties. Nov. 4, 1910. [Oxf.], (1910), 8°. 12 pp.
G.A. Oxon c. 310 (39)

2453. CASE, T., How can the proposed statute on faculties become law? Nov. 7, 1910. [Oxf.], (1910), 8°. 8 pp.   G.A. Oxon c. 310 (40)

2454. STEWART, J. A., Congregation, Nov. 29, 1910 [really Jan. 24, 1911]. Notes on Amendments 22 and 23 [to the Statute on faculties and Boards of faculties] from the point of view of a delegate of the Common university fund. [Oxf.], (1910), s. sh.   G.A. Oxon 4° 296 (2)

2455. HOLLAND, T. E., The Faculties statute. [Oxf.], (1911), 4°. 4 pp.
G.A. Oxon b. 140 (172*a*)

2456. CASE, T., The proposed statute concerning the faculties, the Boards of faculties, and the Boards of studies. [Oxf.], (1911), 8°. 38 pp.
G.A. Oxon b. 140 (181*a*)

See 7181 [The proposed statute concerning the faculties &c. *Ex parte* the President of Corpus Christi College. Case for opinion (Opinion). 1911].

2457. The Faculties statute: To members of Congregation. [Arguments against the proposed amendment seeking to deny college tutors their *ex officio* membership of the faculty in which they teach. Signed J. L. Strachan-Davidson, A. H. Johnson, W. W. How.] May 31, 1912. [Oxf.], (1912), s. sh.   G.A. Oxon c. 310 (94)

2458. TURPIN, K. C., University government: The General board (of the faculties). (Oxford, 1955, vol. 13, no. 3, p. 84–94.)
Per. G.A. Oxon 8° 1141

Secretary, Board of Faculties

2459. FREEMAN, E. A., The proctors and the secretary to the Boards of faculties ['relieving' the proctors of the task of taking the names of candidates for the examinations for B.A. and giving this duty to the newly-created secretary. Dated Feb. 19th]. n. pl., (1891), 4°. 4 pp.
G.AO. xon 4° 119 (14)

2460. GROSE, T. H., The proctors and the secretary to the Boards of faculties. [An answer to E. A. Freeman.] n. pl., (1891), 4°. 3 pp.
G.A. Oxon 4° 119 (15)

2461. FREEMAN, E. A., The proctors and the secretary to the Boards of faculties. [An answer to T. H. Grose.] Feb. 27. n. pl., (1891), s. sh.
G.A. Oxon 4° 119 (14*)

George Eastman visiting professor

2462. NILES, E. H., The Eastman house [Jowett walk, private residence of the Eastman professor]. (Amer. Oxonian, 1961, vol. 48, p. 54–57.)
Per. G.A. Oxon 8° 889

FACULTY OF THEOLOGY

General

2463. The new degree of Candidate in theology [in the new Divinity statute]. Oxf., [1842], 4°. 4 pp.   G.A. Oxon b. 24

2464. Reasons for hesitating to vote in favour of the proposal to be made in
Convocation on . . . March 17 [relative to the endowment of two new
theological professorships]. Oxf., 1842, s. sh.   B.M.

2465. Oxford, Feb. 21, 1844. [Observations opposing the proposed new
Theological statute.] Oxf., (1844), s. sh.   G.A. Oxon b. 25

2466. An appeal to the statutes [concerning the powers of the Regius professor of divinity in divinity degrees]. Oxf., (1844), 4°. 3 pp.
G.A. Oxon b. 25

2467. MARRIOTT, C., A few words to the resident members of Convocation on the subject of the statute [affecting theology and law] shortly to
be proposed [signed C. M.]. Oxf., (1844), 4°. 3 pp. G.A. Oxon b. 25

2468. The Theological statute. [Observations opposing it.] Oxf., [1844],
s. sh.   G.A. Oxon b. 25

See 925 [Oxford and its governors. 1844].

2469. The new examination for divinity degrees. Some hints as to the
character of the statute now proposed to Convocation. [Signed] A
resident member of Convocation. Oxf., 1844, 8°. 14 pp.
G.A. Oxon 8° 70 (6)

2470. The new Divinity statute. [An answer to 2469.] (Christ. remem.
1844, new ser., vol. 7, p. 426–37.)   Per. 971 e. 44

2471. How shall we examine Dissenters? Considerations suggested by
clause xliv of the Oxford university act, by an examiner. [With] Postscript. Oxf. &c., 1854, 8°. 26+2 pp.   G.A. Oxon 8° 63 (15)

2472. PUSEY, E. B., Summary of objections against the proposed theological statutes. Oxf. &c., 1854, 8°. 14 pp.   G.A. Oxon 8° 63 (18)

2473. HAWKINS, E., A letter . . . upon a recent statute of the University of
Oxford with reference to dissent and occasional conformity. By the
provost of Oriel. Oxf., 1855, 8°. 22 pp.   G.A. Oxon 8° 165 (11)

2474. QUILIBET, pseud., Is the University justified in omitting to instruct
any of her members in theology? [Arguments against clause vi of the
proposed new statute.] [Oxf., 1855], s. sh.   G.A. Oxon c. 71 (308)

2475. HEURTLEY, C. A., An appeal to members of Convocation on the
proposal to alter the statutes relating to theological instruction and
examination. Apr. 20. [Oxf.], 1855, 8°. 4 pp.   G.A. Oxon c. 71 (313)

2476. ACADEMICUS, pseud., To members of Convocation. Is the University
in her new position, called upon to abandon in any case her theological
instruction, and its proper evidence at the public examination? or, if
any modification as to the latter be required, is the proposed mode of
substitution the desirable one? Apr. 20. [Oxf.], 1855, 4°. 4 pp.
G.A. Oxon c. 71 (307)

2477. [Begin.] Members of Convocation are respectfully informed . . .
[Notice from the vice-chancellor of a Case submitted to Sir Richard

Bethell as to whether the statute on the treatment of Dissenters respecting religious instruction etc. is illegal. The notice contains counsel's rejection of this view.] [Oxf.], (1855), s. sh.   G.A. Oxon b. 28

2478. Heads of an answer to the objections of dr. Heurtley and Academicus, by a member of Council. Apr. 23. [Oxf., 1855], 8°. 4 pp.
G.A. Oxon c. 71 (312)

See 3384 [The humble petition of the University against three bills for 'promoting education in England'. 1855].

2479. CHASE, D. P., To members of Congregation. [On the effect of the proposed new regulations affecting theological examinations and Dissenters. Signed D. P. C.] Mar. 10. [Oxf.], (1855), 4°. 2 leaves.
G.A. Oxon c. 71 (314)

2480. EARDLEY, SIR C. E., The rights of the laity in the universities, a letter to lord Monteagle, and a correspondence with the rev. dr. Hawkins, 1854–5 [touching on the Oxford statute concerning religious subscription as affected by the Oxford University act 1854]. Lond., 1856, 8°. 46 pp.   G.A. Oxon 8° 72 (3)

2481. PUSEY, E. B., On the 'honors' proposed to be conferred by the new Theological statute [signed E. B. P.]. [Oxf., 1860], 4°. 4 pp.
G.A. Oxon b. 30

2482. The new Theological statute [signed A member of Congregation]. [Oxf.], (1860), s. sh.   G.A. Oxon b. 30

2483. The chief changes in the proposed Theological statute [signed A member of Council]. n. pl., [1860], s. sh.   G.A. Oxon c. 76 (50)

2484. Degrees in divinity. [Resumé of conditions and fees.] [Oxf., 1868], s. sh.   G.A. Oxon a. 18

2485. BURGON, J. W., Plea for a fifth final school, a letter. Feb. 17. Oxf., 1868, 8°. 27 pp.   G.A. Oxon 8° 105 (15)

2486. The new Theological statute. [Objections.] n. pl., [1868], s. sh.
G.A. Oxon c. 84 (470)

2487. PUSEY, E. B., The board of examiners for the proposed theological school. June 10. n. pl., (1868), 4°. 4 pp.   G.A. Oxon c. 84 (471)

2488. MAGRATH, J. R., A plea for the study of theology in the University, a sermon preached Jan. 19. Lond. &c., 1868, 8°. 16 pp.
G. Pamph. 595 (15)

2489. SMITH, H. J. S., The proposed school of theology [calling attention to opinions of E. B. Pusey in 1853, and to statements by J. W. Burgon. Signed H. J. S. S.] Nov. 18. n. pl., [1868], 4°. 4 pp.
G.A. Oxon c. 84 (534)

2490. PUSEY, E. B., The divinity school [justifying the alteration of the views he held in 1853]. Nov. 19. n. pl., [1868], fol. 4 pp.
G.A. Oxon c. 84 (535)

2491. PUSEY, E. B., Toleration for members of the Church of England [signed E. B. P.]. Nov. 30. [Oxf., 1868], s. sh. G.A. Oxon b. 140 (24*d*)

2492. ROLLESTON, G., The proposed school of theology. Nov. 30. n. pl., (1868), s. sh. G.A. Oxon c. 84 (536)

2493. SMITH, R. P., [*Begin.*] My dear Rolleston, In a paper . . . [An answer to 2492.] Dec. 4. [Oxf.], (1868), s. sh. G.A. Oxon c. 84 (539)

2494. BURGON, J. W., The new divinity school. Mr. Burgon to professor Rolleston. Dec. 4. n. pl., [1868], s. sh. G.A. Oxon c. 84 (541)

2495. CONINGTON, J., The Theological statute. [Observations in favour of the proposed theological honour school.] n. pl., [1869], 4°. 4 pp. G.A. Oxon c. 85 (183)

2496. The Theological statute. Case submitted to mr. George Mellish, Q.C., and mr. Charles Bowen, with their opinion. n. pl., 1869, 8°. 15 pp. G.A. Oxon c. 85 (423)

2497. PUSEY, E. B., The proposed statute for a theological school. May 12. [Oxf., 1869], 4°. 4 pp. G.A. Oxon b. 140 (26*a*)

2498. SMITH, H. J. S., The proposed school of theology. [Observations against, signed H. J. S. S.] Whit Monday, 1869. Oxf., 1869, 4°. 4 pp. G.A. Oxon c. 85 (438)

2499. PUSEY, E. B., The proposed school of theology. [A reply to the observations of H. J. S. Smith.] Whit-Monday, 1869. n. pl., 1869, 4°. 4 pp. G.A. Oxon c. 85 (443)

2500. BURGON, J. W., To professor Henry J. S. Smith [The Theological statute). May 18. [Oxf.], (1869), s. sh. G.A. Oxon b. 140 (25*b*)

2501. Sketch of a case prepared by dr. Pusey. [A paper on technical points connected with the statute constituting a new theology school: undated but apparently May, 1869.] [Oxf., 1869?], 4°. 4 pp.

2502. BURGON, J. W., Plea for the study of divinity in Oxford. Oxf. &c., 1875, 8°. 56 pp. MS. Eng. theol. d. 11 (5)

2503. INCE, W., The past history and present duties of the Faculty of theology, 2 lectures. Oxf. &c., 1878, 8°. 51 pp. 100 f. 169 (24)

2504. WOODS, F. H., A guide to the study of theology, adapted more especially to the Oxford honour school. (Oxf. study guides.) Oxf., 1880, 8°. 80 pp. 260 g. 442*c*

2505. FAIRBAIRN, A. M., Letter to the Regius professor of divinity on the school of theology. Oxf., (1898), 8°. 15 pp. 26332 e. 13 (11)

2506. SANDAY, W., and LOCK, W., Faculty of arts. Honour school of theology. [Historical account by dr. Sanday and dr. Lock.] [Oxf., 1900], s. sh. G.A. Oxon b. 41 (4)

2507. LOCK, W., To the members of the Board of the Faculty of theology. [Observations by W. Lock against the proposal for the removal of the

clause of the statute which requires examiners in the honour school of
theology to be in priest's orders.] n. pl., (1904), 8°. 7 pp.

G.A. Oxon 8° 705 (2)

2508. ALLEN, W. C., The clergy and the honour school of theology. Oxf.,
1904, 8°. 11 pp.   G.A. Oxon 8° 705 (1)

2509. Promulgation of statutes in Congregation. [Arguments against
amendments to be proposed on Dec. 3, that neither the examiners in
the final school of theology nor the candidates for the degrees of D.D.
and B.D. need be in priest's orders.] Nov. 16. [Oxf.], (1912), s. sh.

G.A. Oxon c. 310 (115)

2510. WATKINS, O. D., The Divinity proposals: two letters to the press.
[Oxf., 1912], s. sh.   G.A. Oxon c. 310 (126)

2511. WACE, H., Divinity degrees at Oxford. (Repr. from The Record,
Feb. 21, and abridged.) n. pl., [1913], 8°. 4 pp. G.A. Oxon b. 141 (61a)

2512. STRONG, T. B., Divinity degrees at Oxford. Apr. 17, 1913. [Oxf.],
(1913), s. sh.   G.A. Oxon c. 310 (132)

2513. Oxford divinity degrees and the school of theology. Mar. 31st 1913.
[Oxf.], (1913), 8°. 8 pp.   G.A. Oxon c. 310 (131)

2514. Divinity degrees and theological studies at Oxford. [Statement
signed H. Wace and 40 others against the statutes to be proposed in
Convocation on April 29th.] [Oxf., 1913], 4°. 4 pp.

G.A. Oxon c. 310 (129)

2515. Theological degrees at Oxford. [Statement signed H. S. Holland and
7 others supporting the statutes to be proposed in Convocation on
April 29th.] Mar. 24, 1913. [Oxf.], (1913), 4°. 4 pp.

G.A. Oxon c. 310 (130)

2516. HEADLAM, A. C., The study of theology, an inaugural lecture. Oxf.,
1918, 8°. 31 pp.   2625 d. 55 (2)

2517. STREETER, B. H., Theology. (Oxf. mag., 1930, vol. 48, p. 850–54.)
Per. G.A. Oxon 4° 141

2518. LITTLE, A. G., and PELSTER, F., Oxford theology and theologians,
c. A.D. 1282–1302. (Oxf. hist. soc., vol. 86.) Oxf., 1934, 8°. 389 pp.

G.A. Oxon 8° 360 = R.

2518.1. Faculty of theology. Libraries of the faculty. [Duplicated list of
accessions, 1961/62– .] n. pl., [1962–], fol.   Per. 2590 c. Oxf. 39.1

Bampton lecture

2519. HEURTLEY, C. A., The proposed statute respecting the Bampton
lecture. Oxf., (1857), 8°. 4 pp.   G.A. Oxon c. 73 (157)

Dean Ireland's professor of exegesis of Holy Scripture

2520. [Nov. 21, 1842. Proposed acceptance, in Convocation of 1 Dec., of the legacy left by John Ireland for the benefit of a professor, whose department shall be the 'Exegesis of Holy Scripture'.] [Oxf.], (1842), s. sh.   G.A. Oxon c. 58 (116)

2521. HAWKINS, E., An inaugural lecture upon the foundation of Dean Ireland's professorship, Nov. 2, 1847; with brief notices of the founder. Lond. &c., 1848, 8°. viii+59 pp.   48.1404 (7)

Grinfield lecture

2522. [Proposed acceptance by Convocation on 25 March of the founding of a terminal lecture on the Septuagint version of the Hebrew scriptures, by Edward Grinfield.] n. pl., 1859, s. sh.   G.A. Oxon c. 75 (84)

Margaret professor of divinity

2523. An additional act for providing maintenance for ministers and other pious uses. (Anno 1650, c. 5, Pub.). [This act provides for the compensatory payment of £80 to the Margaret lecturer in divinity.] Lond., 1650, fol. 19 pp.   L.L.

See 7043 [Act annexing a canonry of Christ Church to the Lady Margaret professorship. 1840].

2524. Suggestions respectfully addressed to graduates in divinity connected with the coming election [of the Lady Margaret professor of divinity.] [Oxf.], (1853), s. sh.   G.A. Oxon b. 27

2525. HANSELL, E. H., The Margaret professorship. [Observations on the proposed statute which seeks to vest the election thereof in those members of Congregation who are in holy orders, instead of in all graduates in theology, signed 'A resident'.] Mar. 5, 1856. n. pl., 1856, s. sh.
G.A. Oxon c. 72 (98)

2526. A list of persons believed to be qualified to vote in the election of a Margaret professor of divinity. Trinity term, 1895. Oxf., 1895, 8°. 12 pp.   G.A. Oxon 8° 540 (17)

Regius professor of Divinity

2527. An act for confirming and rendring more effectual certain letters patents of King James the first for annexing a canonry and several rectoryes to the regius professor of divinity in the University of Oxford [&c.]. (10 Anne, c. 12, Private.) n. pl., [1711], fol. 3 pp.
MM 29 (33) Jur. 3rd ser.

See 3487, &c. [Hampden controversy. 1836, &c.].
See 2466 [An appeal to the statutes concerning the powers of the professor in divinity degrees. 1844].

Regius professor of ecclesiastical history

See 7043 [Act annexing a canonry of Christ Church to the Regius professorship of ecclesiastical history. 1840].

Regius professor of pastoral theology

See 7043 [Act annexing a canonry of Christ Church to the Regius professorship of pastoral theology. 1840].

FACULTY OF LAW

General

2528. Some thoughts concerning the study of the laws of England in the two universities, a letter to the reverend —— head of —— college in Oxford [by T. Wood]. Lond., 1708, 4°. 26 pp.   4° W 90 (9) Th.
— 2nd ed., by T. Wood. Lond., 1727, 8°. 62 pp.   G. Pamph. 22 (3)

2529. Oxford, 23 June, 1753. In Michaelmas term next will begin A course of lectures on the laws of England. By dr. Blackstone. (Oxf., 1753), sheets.   All Souls coll.

2530. BLACKSTONE, W., Proposals for a course of lectures on the laws of England. [Oxf.], (1754), 4°. 4 pp.   G.A. Oxon b. 111 (50)

2531. A course of lectures on the civil law [syllabus]. 3 pt. [Oxf.? c. 1760?] 2 sheets.   G.A. Oxon b. 111 (54, 55)

2532. Books recommended as proper to accompany this [law] course [*and*] Scheme of the course. [Oxf., 1764], s. sh.   G.A. Oxon b. 111 (55 b, c)

See 2467 [Marriott, C., A few words . . . on the subject of the statute [affecting theology and law. 1844].

2533. HADDAN, T. H., Remarks on legal education, with reference to the suggested introduction of legal studies into the University of Oxford, a letter. Lond. &c., 1848, 8°. 23 pp.   48. 1413 (1)

2534. The examiners in the school of law and modern history wish to call the attention of students to the following recommendations . . . n. pl., [1854], s. sh.   G.A. Oxon c. 70 (170)

2535. HOOPER, J. J., The establishment of a school of jurisprudence in the University of Oxford: a letter. Lond., 1854, 8°. 16 pp.
G.A. Oxon 8° 63 (5)

See 1710, 1711 [Legal education at the University. 1854].
See 992 [Proposed lectures in English law. 1855].

2536. NEATE, C., Remarks on the legal and other studies of the University. Oxf. &c., 1856, 8°. 16 pp.   G.A. Oxon 8° 63 (10)

2537. TWISS, T., A letter . . . on the law studies of the University. Lond., 1856, 8°. 32 pp.   G.A. Oxon 8° 63 (21)

2538. JOHNSON, M. J., [*Begin.*] It seems to be a privilege . . . [A letter dated Jan. 28 in answer to no. 2537.] n. pl., (1856), s. sh.
G.A. Oxon 8° 63 (21*)

2539. Freeman, E. A. [*Begin.*] I was surprised to find . . . [Letter to the vice-chancellor defending the actions of himself and other examiners in the school of law and modern history, which were said by the vice-chancellor to be without statutable authority.] [Oxf.], (1857), s. sh.
G.A. Oxon b. 29

2540. Correspondence between the 'Protestant alliance' and the examiners in law and modern history [who defend themselves against the charge of recommending a 'Romish writer' i.e. Lingard, as a book for English history.] Oxf. &c., 1858, 8°. 8 pp.   G.A. Oxon 8° 179 (13)

2541. MILLER, C., Law revivals at Oxford. An earnest appeal to the University not to confer honorary degrees in civil law upon insufficient grounds. May 29, 1860. n. pl., (1860), s. sh.   G.A. Oxon b. 30

2542. TWEED, J. P., Our law professorships and the claims of the school of law and modern history, a letter. Oxf. &c., 1863, 8°. 17 pp.
200 h. 35 (6)

2543. ROUNDELL, C. S., [*Begin.*] The following letter to the vice-chancellor is circulated . . . [commenting on the school of law and modern history, and the 'lower level' of law compared with history]. [Oxf.], (1864), 4°. 4 pp.   G.A. Oxon c. 80 (216)

2544. BERNARD, M., A letter . . . on the provision for the teaching of law at Oxford. Oxf., 1864, 8°. 22 pp.   G.A. Oxon 8° 179 (20)

2545. School of law and modern history [list of books recommended by the examiners]. Trinity term 1866. [Oxf.], 1866, s. sh.   G.A. Oxon b. 31

2546. COMPTON, F., and MALCOLM, W. R., A letter . . . on the subject of legal education. Oxf., 1867, 8°. 32 pp.   G.A. Oxon 8° 105 (8)

2547. BERNARD, M., Notes on the academical study of law. Oxf. &c., 1868, 8°. 27 pp.   G.A. Oxon 8° 105 (19)

2548. BRYCE, J., The academical study of the civil law, an inaugural lecture. Lond. &c., 1871, 8°. 39 pp.   26331 e. 18 (2)

2549. POTTINGER, H. A., Letter . . . on the subject of the school of jurisprudence. May 25, 1876. n. pl., (1876), 8°. 11 pp. G.A. Oxon 8° 250 (16)

2550. POTTINGER, H. A., Letter . . . on the subject of the school of jurisprudence. June 6, 1876. n. pl., (1876), 8°. 19 pp. G.A. Oxon 8° 250 (17)

2551. POTTINGER, H. A., Letter . . . on the subject of the recent notice of the Board of studies of the school of jurisprudence [which announced changes in the curriculum to be introduced in Michaelmas term]. n. pl., [1876], 8°. 12 pp.   G.A. Oxon 8° 250 (15)

2552. Grotius tercentenary, 1883. Oxford faculty of law [address]. n. pl., (1883), 4°. 4 pp.   G.A. Oxon 4° 505 (4)

2553. Preliminary examination in the school of jurisprudence [signed by W. R. Anson & 3 others]. [Oxf., 1885], 8°. 3 pp.
G.A. Oxon b. 140 (53c)

2554. FOWLER, T., Preliminary examination in the school of jurisprudence. [An answer to 2553.] [Oxf.], (1885), s. sh.   G.A. Oxon b. 140 (55e)

2555. The study of law in Oxford. (Oxf. mag., 1885, vol. 3, p. 24, 25; 41, 42.)   Per. G.A. Oxon 4° 141

2556. POLLOCK, SIR F., Oxford law studies. (Law quarterly review, 1886 vol. 2, p. 453–64.)   L.L.

2557. BUTLER, A. G., The law preliminary. [Oxf., 1886], s. sh.
G.A. Oxon b. 140 (65d)

2558. MORRELL, F. P., Legal education and the universities. Lond., 1886, 8°. 10 pp.   26331 e. 18 (1)

2559. BRYCE, J., Legal studies in the University of Oxford, lecture. Lond., 1893, 8°. 35 pp.   26331 e. 18 (4)

2560. HOLLAND, T. E., Faculty of law [historical account by T. E. Holland. [Oxf., 1900], s. sh.   G.A. Oxon b. 41

2561. ANSON, SIR W. R., Faculty of arts. The honour school of jurisprudence [historical account by sir W. R. Anson]. [Oxf., 1900], s. sh.
G.A. Oxon b. 41 (5)

2562. BRYCE, J., visct., Valedictory lecture: legal studies in the University of Oxford. (Studies in history and jurisprudence, 1901, vol. 2, p. 887–907.)   L.L.

2563. DICEY, A. V., The extension of law teaching at Oxford. (Harvard law rev., 1910, vol. 24, p. 1–5.)   L.L.

2564. HOLDSWORTH, W. S., The Oxford law school. (Oxf. mag., 1930, vol. 48, p. 386, 87.)   Per. G.A. Oxon 4° 141

2564.1. HANSCHER, V. M., Oxford and American legal education: a contrast. (Amer. bar assoc. journ., 1930, vol. 16, p. 523–29.)   L.L.

See 8535 [Campbell, A. H., Law and lawyers in University college. 1930].

2565. Law and legal research at Oxford [signed W. S. Holdsworth, C. K. Allen, A. L. Goodhart]. (Amer. Oxon., 1937, vol. 24, p. 39–43.)
Per. G.A. Oxon 8° 889

2566. RICHARDSON, H. G., The Oxford law school under [king] John. (Law quarterly review, 1941, vol. 57, p. 319–38.)   L.L.

See 5566 [De Zulueta, F., The Arts End decree and the Law faculty. 1939].

2567. Oxford university law societies. Nisi Prius. Vols. 1–2, no. 3. Oxf., 1950.

2568. MAUDSLEY, R. H., Law at Oxford. (Amer. Oxon., 1957, vol. 44, p. 10–14.)   Per. G.A. Oxon 8° 889

2569. BODINE, J. W., and MCQUADE, L. C., The study of jurisprudence at Oxford. (Amer. Oxonian, 1959, vol. 46, p. 13–18.)

Per. G.A. Oxon 8° 889

2570. CARTER, P. B., Law at Oxford: miscellaneous comments. (Journ., Soc. of publ. teachers of law, 1960, vol. 5, p. 124–29.)

Soc. 26331 d. 21 = L.L.

2570.3. BOYLE, L., The curriculum of the Faculty of Canon law at Oxford in the first half of the 14th century. (Oxf. studies presented to D. Callus; Oxf. hist. soc., 1964, N.S., vol. 16, p. 135–62.)

G.A. Oxon 8° 360 = R.

2570.4. KAYE, J. M., Legal education in Oxford. (Oxf. mag., 1961, N.S., vol. 2, p. 47–49.)

Per. G.A. Oxon 4° 141

2570.6. LAWSON, F. L., The Oxford law school, 1850–1965. Oxf., 1967, 8°. 258 pp.

L.L.

See also 4108 [Blackstone society].
See also 4135 [Maine law society].
See also 4251 [Oxford university moot club].
See also 5779, &c. [Bodleian Law Library].

Regius professor of civil law

2571. The proposed legislation on the Regius professor of civil law [arguments against the 'residence' requirement. Signed A member of Congregation]. Feb. 20, 1856. [Oxf.], (1856), s. sh. G.A. Oxon c. 72 (70)

2572. In a Convocation to be holden . . . May 7 . . . the following . . . decree will be submitted [expressing the wish of Convocation, for a Bill to be brought into Parliament concerning the expediency of uniting the Regius professorship of civil and the Vinerian professorship of common law into one professorship, and concerning various other professorships]. Apr. 22. [Oxf.], (1861), 8°. 3 pp. G.A. Oxon 8° 236 (5*)

2573. Draft of a bill submitted by the Hebdomadal council to lord Palmerston for his approbation; a letter from the vice-chancellor to eminent jurists on the expediency of uniting the Regius professorship of civil, and the Vinerian professorship of common law into one professorship . . . with the answers received [&c.]. n. pl., [1861], 8°. 31 pp. G.A. Oxon 8° 236 (5)

2574. [Begin.] A wish having been expressed . . . [An explanation, signed A member of Council, of the measures proposed to Convocation concerning the professorships of civil and common law.] n. pl., [1861], s. sh. G.A. Oxon c. 77 (345)

Vinerian professor of English law

See also 1618, &c., Benefactions. Viner.

2575. [Begin.] A petition having been propos'd . . . to dispense with the scholars . . . upon mr. Viner's foundation for not attending their pro-

fessor . . . [reasons for Convocation's rejection thereof]. Nov. 20.
[Oxf.], (1758), 4°. 3 pp.   Gough Oxf. 96 (37)

2576. [*Begin.*] Dr. Blackstone, finding himself personally charged . . .
[Statement denying having violated the statutes by changing the day
appointed for his Vinerian lecture.] 22 Nov. n. pl., (1758), s. sh.
                                                        Gough Oxf. 96 (38)

2577. [*Begin.*] Dr. Blackstone having desired the authors of a paper . . .
[Statement substantiating a previous suggestion that dr. Blackstone
had violated the statutes concerning the Vinerian lecture.] n. pl.,
[1758], 4°. 3 pp.   Gough Oxf. 96 (39)

2578. [*Begin.*] The Vinerian professor gives this public notice . . . [Scheme
of the course of private lectures which will be given, 1759.] 18 June.
n. pl., (1759), s. sh.   Gough Oxf. 96 (40)

2579. [*Begin.*] The University-statute having directed the Vinerian professor to read his four solemn lectures . . . [Notice of a proposal to be
put to Convocation, 17th July 'that the gentlemen above named be
approved as persons properly qualified to read the Vinerian professor's
lectures'.] (Oxf., 1761), s. sh.   Gough Oxf. 96 (41)

2580. [*Begin.*] The Vinerian professor is extremely concerned . . . [State-
ment by dr. Blackstone expressing his concern at the controversial
reception accorded to the proposal to appoint deputies to read his lectures.] (Oxf., 1761), fol. 4 pp.   Gough Oxf. 96 (42)

2581. CHAMBERS, R., [*Begin.*] The Vinerian professor being appointed . . .
a judge in . . . Calcutta . . . [Request that a deputy may discharge his
office for no more than 3 years, so that if ill-health compels his return,
he may resume his professorship.] July 5. [Oxf.], (1773), s. sh.
                                                        G.A. Oxon b. 19

2582. TWEED, J. P., The proposed law reader and the Vinerian professorship [suggesting that professor Kenyon should be deprived of his
professorship for failure to deliver the statutable course of lectures.
Signed J. P. T.] Nov. 26. [Oxf.], 1855, s. sh.   G.A. Oxon c. 71 (310)

2583. TWEED, J. P., The Vinerian professorship. [Another attack, signed
J. P. T., on dr. Kenyon.] Nov. 28. [Oxf.], 1855, s. sh.
                                                        G.A. Oxon c. 71 (309)

2584. TWEED, J. P., The proposed law reader and the Vinerian professor of
common law [signed J. P. T., 28 Oct., 1861]. n. pl., (1861), s. sh.
                                                        G.A. Oxon c. 77 (267)

See 2572–74 [Papers on the proposal to unite the Regius professorship of civil
law with the Vinerian professorship of common law. 1861].

2585. The Vinerian professorship and the common law of England. Mar.,
1867. [Oxf.], (1867), s. sh.   G.A. Oxon b. 31

2586. HANBURY, H. G., The Vinerian chair and legal education. Oxf.,
1958, 8°. 248 pp.   26331 d. 41

All Soul's readership in English law

2587. The Law faculty and the All Souls readership in English law [signed
by W. S. Holdsworth and 4 others]. May 10th, 1907. [Oxf.], (1907),
s. sh.   Firth b. 36 (141)

Vinerian reader in law

See 2582 [J. P. Tweed, The proposed law reader and the Vinerian professorship. 1855].
See 2584 [J. P. Tweed, The proposed law reader and the Vinerian professor of
common law. 1861].

FACULTY OF MEDICINE

General

For works on the sciences in general see no. 2863, &c.

2588. BADGER, J., A register of the doctors of physick in our two universities of Cambridge and Oxford [the latter, p. 17–25. By J. Badger].
n. pl., 1695, 8°.   8° L 82 (18) Med.

2589. BADGER, J., An exact alphabetical catalogue of all that have taken
the degree of doctor of physick in our two universities from 1659 to
1695. Lond., 1696, s. sh.   Ashm. 1820 (87)

See 2915 [Cursus chymicus Oxonii in schola Chymiæ habendus, in quo medicamenta pleraque in praxi medica usitatiora fideliter parantur. 1705/6].

2590. Præside . . . sociisque . . . Collegii regalis medicorum Londinensium
s. o. procancellarius . . . & magistri Universitatis Oxoniensis. [A letter
about medical degrees.] n. pl., [c. 1710], s. sh.   G.A. Oxon b. 19

2591. [Begin.] According to the lately altered statute . . . [Regulations respecting medical degrees. Aug. 1, 1840.] [Oxf., 1840], s. sh.
G.A. Oxon c. 59 (133)

See 1856 [Acland, H. W., Remarks on the extension of education. 1848].

2592. PEARSON, C. H., A letter . . . on a scheme for making Oxford more
accessible to medical students generally. Lond., 1858, 8°. 28 pp.
G.A. Oxon c. 74 (354)
— 2nd ed., revised. 1858. 35 pp.   G.A. Oxon 8° 1230 (14)

2593. ACLAND, H. W., [Begin.] 1. Alterations in the Oxford statute respecting degrees in medicine . . . [A paper outlining defects in the existing
statute, and suggesting remedies.] Apr. 7. [Oxf.], (1860), 8°. 3 pp.
G.A. Oxon b. 140 (19b)

2594. [Begin.] Alterations in the Oxford statute . . . [Observations on the
proposed alterations respecting medical degrees.] Apr. 30, 1860.
[Oxf.], 1860, 8°. 7 pp.   G.A. Oxon c. 76 (135)

2595. OGLE, J. W., Proposed Medical statute. [Letter to dr. Acland.]
May 2, 1860. n. pl., 1860, 8°. 4 pp.   G.A. Oxon c. 76 (136)

2596. TEALE, T. P., The Medical statute. [Extracts from a letter objecting to the Thesis test for the M.D.] Oxf., [1860], s. sh.

G.A. Oxon c. 76 (137)

2597. To members of Congregation. The Medical statute [4 opinions, including that of dr. Acland in 1852. n. pl., [1860], s. sh.

G.A. Oxon c. 76 (138)

2598. ACLAND, H. W., [*Begin.*] A paper . . . [An answer to no. 2597 refuting the suggestion of discrepancy between his opinions in 1852 and in 1860.] May 3, 1860. [Oxf.], 1860, s. sh. G.A. Oxon c. 76 (139)

2599. ACLAND, H. W., For Hebdomadal council. Memorandum by the regius professor of medicine on the documents [Reports on the visitations of medical examinations of bodies which give licences in medicine, for 1866–67; Report of a committee of the Medical council on the above reports; Letter from the Medical council requesting the opinion of the University] forwarded for his opinion . . . July 8, 1867. n. pl., [1867], 8°. 11 pp. G.A. Oxon c. 83 (418)

2600. Medical education committee of Hebdomadal council. Memorandum by regius professor of medicine, Nov. 4, 1867 [and] May 7, 1868. Letter of . . . committee . . . thereon, May 13, 1868. [Oxf., 1868], 8°. 23 pp. G.A. Oxon b. 137 (28)

2601. SHADWELL, C. L., To members of Congregation. [A paper calling attention to a precedent which may be established if Congregation and not Convocation is allowed to accept or decline a resolution on the medical statutes.] [Oxf.], (1872), s. sh. G.A. Oxon b. 140 (26g)

2602. Report of medical committee of the Hebdomadal council on recommendations of the Medical council, as regards professional examination. (Revise, Mar. 14, of draft of Feb. 1, 1876.) [Oxf.], (1876), 8°. 4 pp.

G.A. Oxon c. 33 (118)

2603. WEST, S., The proposed establishment of a medical school in Oxford. Apr. 29. [Lond.], (1879), 8°. 12 pp. 26322 e. 26 (11)

2604. SHARKEY, S. J., The University of Oxford and medical education. n. pl., [1879], 8°. 7 pp. G.A. Oxon 8° 683 (9)

2605. To the Vice-chancellor . . . A letter upon the new Medical statute [signed by G. T. Fincham and other medical graduates]. [Oxf., 1885], fol. 4 pp. G.A. Oxon b. 140 (59b)

2606. WEST, S., Postscript to letter to Vice-chancellor [on the proposed new Medical statute]. [Oxf., 1885], s. sh. G.A. Oxon b. 140 (59a)

2607. CHILD, G. W., University medical legislation. [Oxf., 1885], s. sh.

G.A. Oxon c. 221

2608. SANDERSON, J. B., The new Medical statute in its relation to the study of medicine in the University. [Oxf., 1885], 8°. 4 pp.

G.A. Oxon c. 221

2609. The proposed new Medical statute. [Resolutions of a meeting of Oxford Medical graduates held at the Medical society, London, on June 2nd, 1885.] (Lond., 1885), 4°. 4 pp.   G.A. Oxon c. 221

2610. CLARKE, W. B., To the Vice-chancellor . . . A letter concerning the proposed new Medical statute. n. pl., [1885], 4°. 3 pp.
G.A. Oxon b. 140 (58*b*)

2611. To members of Convocation. [Objections signed J. B. Balfour and 5 others, to a decree to be proposed in Convocation requiring candidates for the degree of B.M. to have passed a qualifying examination before 'the examining board in England'.] [Oxf., 1885], s. sh.
G.A. Oxon c. 221

2612. Medical education in Oxford. (Oxf. mag., 1885, vol. 3, p. 309, 10.)
Per. G.A. Oxon 4° 141

2613. SANDERSON, J. S. BURDON-, Medical study in, Oxford [signed J. B. S.]. (Oxf. mag., 1886, vol. 4, p. 4–6.)   Per. G.A. Oxon 4° 141

2614. Teaching, examinations and degrees in medicine, at Oxford. Oxf., 1887, 8°. 42 pp.   26322 e. 49

2615. Protest against degree of M.A. honoris causa to be conferred on Wyndham H. Dunstan [signed Medical student]. [Oxf.], (1888), s. sh.
G.A. Oxon b. 140 (82*b*)

2616. SANDERSON, J. S. BURDON-, Memorandum on the teaching of materia medica in the university, by the Waynflete professor of physiology [signed J. B. S. An answer to 2615]. [Oxf.], (1888), 4°. 3 pp.
G.A. Oxon b. 140 (82*c*)

2617. ACLAND, SIR H. W., Oxford and modern medicine. Oxf. &c., 1890, 8°. 61 pp.   G.A. Oxon 8° 467

2618. NEVINS, W. PROBYN-, Oxford, natural science and the Faculty of medicine, a review of sir H. Acland's Oxford and modern medicine. Oxf. &c., [1890], 8°. 32 pp.   26322 e. 26 (13)

2619. SANDERSON, J. S. BURDON-, The school of medical science in Oxford. Oxf., 1892, 8°. 35 pp.   26322 d. 3 (4)

2620. Lord Salisbury and the medical school at Oxford. (Oxf. mag., 1893, vol. 11, p. 276, 77.)   Per. G.A. Oxon 4° 141

2621. Degrees in medicine and surgery and Diploma in public health [regulations]. [Oxf., 1894], 8°. 8 pp.   26322 e. 26 (12)

2622. SANDERSON, J. BURDON-, Extension of laboratory and lecture-room accommodation for medical students. [Oxf.], (1896), 8°. 3 pp.
G.A. Oxon b. 139 (94*a*)

2623. SANDERSON, J. BURDON-, Medical education in Oxford, a letter to the president of Magdalen college. Nov. 10. n. pl., (1896), 8°. 6 pp.
Acland 14 (10)

2624. SANDERSON, SIR J. BURDON-, Faculty of medicine. Oxford school of medical science [historical account by sir J. Burdon-Sanderson]. [Oxf., 1900], s. sh.   G.A. Oxon b. 14

2625. COLLIER, W., The growth and development of the Oxford medical school. (Brit. med. journ., 1904, vol. 2, p. 221–26.)   Radcl.
— Repr. 1904. 27 pp.   1996 e. 201 (12)

2626. Oxford pathology endowment fund. [Statement of the claims of the science of medicine to a greater share of the resources and sympathy of the University.] [Oxf.], (1906), 4°. 3 pp.   G.A. Oxon b. 139 (98c)

2627. Oxford and medical training for women. Oxf., 1916, 8°. 8 pp.
                                                 2626 e. 401 (19)

2628. Information concerning the school of medicine, medical degrees and diplomas, and post-graduate medical study and research. Dec. 1922. Oxf., 1922, 8°. 14 pp.   26322 e. 115 (1)
— Dec. 1926.   26322 e. 115 (2)

2629. WALKER, E. W. A., The school of medicine. (Oxf. mag., 1930, vol. 48, p. 564–68.)   Per. G.A. Oxon 4° 141

2630. C., H. E., The medical school at Oxford. (Brit. med. journ., 1936, p. 1064–66.)   Radcl.

2631. FRANKLIN, K. J., A short sketch of the history of the Oxford medical school. (Annals of science, 1936, vol. 1, p. 431–46.)   Radcl.

2632. WITTS, L. J., The future of the clinical school [signed L. J. W.]. (Oxf. mag., 1948, vol. 66, p. 252, 53.)   Per. G.A. Oxon 4° 141

2633. The Oxford medical school gazette. Vol. 1– . Oxf., 1949– , 8°. Radcl.

2634. SINCLAIR, H. M., and SMITH, A. H. T. ROBB-, A short history of anatomical teaching in Oxford. Oxf., 1950, 8°. 81 pp.   Radcl.

2635. DAVIDSON, M., Medicine in Oxford, a historical romance, the Fitzpatrick lectures for 1952–53. Oxf., 1953, 8°. 68 pp.   15012 e. 93

2636. SMITH, A. T. ROBB-, Harvey at Oxford. (Oxf. med. sch. gazette, 1957, vol. 9, p. 70–76.)   Radcl.

2637. SMITH, A. H. T. ROBB-, The Oxford medical school and its graduates. 1, 2. (Oxf. med. sch. gazette, 1958, vol. 10, p. 135–40; 1959, vol. 11, p. 15–24.)   Radcl.

2637.1. SMITH, T. G., AND PORTER, R., The study of medicine at Oxford. (Amer. Oxon., 1966, vol. 53, p. 14–21.)   Per. G.A. Oxon 8° 889

See also 4097 [Agenda club].
See also 4129 [Junior physiological club].
See also 4248 [Oxford university junior physiological society].
See also 4262 [Physiological society].

Clinical professor

2638. The clinical professorship. [A paper, dated Oct. 23 and signed A resident M.A., supporting dr. Jackson.] n. pl., 1857, s. sh.

G.A. Oxon c. 73 (269)

2639. The clinical professorship. [A paper, dated Oct. 26 and signed A resident M.A., supporting dr. Jackson.] n. pl., 1857, s. sh.

G.A. Oxon c. 73 (270)

2640. The clinical professorship. [Urging caution against voting for dr. Acland as one appointed by the crown and already holding the professorship of medicine.] n. pl., [1857], s. sh.   G.A. Oxon c. 73 (268)

2641. To the members of Convocation. [A paper, signed Another member of Convocation, supporting dr. Acland.] n. pl., [1857], s. sh.

G.A. Oxon c. 73 (229*b*)

2642. LIDDELL, H. G., To members of Convocation [urging support for dr. Acland in the contest for the clinical professorship with dr. Jackson]. n. pl., 1857, s. sh.   G.A. Oxon c. 73 (229)

2643. To the members of Convocation. [A paper, signed A senior member of Convocation supporting dr. Jackson's nomination for the post of clinical professor, against dr. Acland.] n. pl., 1857, s. sh.

G.A. Oxon c. 73 (228)

Linacre professor of physiology

2644. [Notice concerning the election to the first Linacre professorship of physiology, with regulations.] Apr. 3, 1860. [Oxf.], 1860, s. sh.

G.A. Oxon c. 76 (99)

Regius professor of medicine

2645. Extract of the will of George Aldrich . . . [leaving money to trustees to pay equal parts of the interest to the praelector of anatomy, the professor of chemistry, and the Regius professor of physic.] [Oxf., 1803], 4°. 4 pp.   G.A. Oxon b. 19

2646. Copy of a statute for the application of the gift or endowment of dr. George Aldrich. (Oxford university. Copies of regulations . . . p. 8.)

Pp. Eng. 1857/8 vol. 46

See 2651 [Ogle, J. A., Reduction of income of the Regius professor as a result of the proposed statute de prof. anatom. Tomlinsiano et Aldrichiano. 1857].

2647. The Regius professorship of medicine [signed W. S. Church, J. F. Payne, S. West]. [Oxf.], (1904), 4°. 3 pp.   G.A. Oxon c. 153

2648. SANDERSON, SIR J. BURDON-, A letter . . . on the office of Regius professor of medicine, with a postscript. n. pl., (1904), 8°. 9 pp.

G.A. Oxon 8° 1033 (9)

2649. The Regius professorship of medicine. [Resolutions of a meeting of Oxford medical graduates holding teaching appointments at Medical schools, held Jan. 5th 1904, emphasizing the importance of the professor's being a physician who is representative of medicine in its widest sense.] (Lond. &c.), [1904], 4°. 7 pp.   G.A. Oxon 4° 186 (2)

Tomlinsian and Aldrichian professor of anatomy

See also 2645, &c., Regius professor of medicine.

2650. OGLE, J. A., [Begin.] The vice-chancellor of the University . . . [Open letter about the new statute de professore anatomiæ Tomlinsiano et Aldrichiano.] (Oxf., 1857), s. sh.   G.A. Oxon c. 73 (172)

2651. OGLE, J. A., [Begin.] The Regius professor of medicine . . . [Statement of the reduced state of the professor's income in consequence of the proposed statute de professore anatom. Tomlinsiano et Aldrichiano.] [Oxf.], (1857), s. sh.   G.A. Oxon c. 73 (155)

Professor of social medicine

2652. MACNALTY, A. S., The new chair of social medicine at Oxford. (Oxf. mag., 1942, vol. 61, p. 37, 38.)   Per. G.A. Oxon 4° 141

FACULTY OF LITERAE HUMANIORES
General

See 1849 [Considerations on the great and serious injuries arising from the course of education pursued . . . 1832].

2653. Hints to students in reading for classical honours, by a class man. 2nd ed., revised. Oxf., 1843, 8°. 40 pp.   G.A. Oxon 8° 286 (8)

2654. FARRAR, A. S., Hints to students in reading for classical honours. 2nd ed. Oxf., 1856, 8°. 55 pp.   G.A. Oxon 8° 286 (7)

2655. [Begin.] In order to prevent misapprehension . . . [Correspondence between H. H. Vaughan and J. T. H. Peter &c. concerning an alleged fraud practised by the former on the latter during the final classical honour school examination of Easter term 1833.] (Oxf., 1845), 8°. 13 pp.   G.A. Oxon 8° 77 (15)

2656. A correspondence between . . . [J. T. H.] Peter . . . [H.] Liddell . . . and [H. H.] Vaughan, 8 letters which have been already printed; and 2 now printed between mr. Peter and mr. Liddell. [In which J. T. H. Peter accuses H. H. Vaughan of deceitful conduct to him during the classical examination for honours in 1833.] Oxf., 1845, 8°. 20 pp.
G.A. Oxon 8° 850 (3)

2657. Terminalia; or, Notes on the subjects of the Literæ humaniores and Moderation schools. Oxf., 1851, 8°. 104 pp.   G.A. Oxon 8° 172

2658. GORDON, O., To the members of Convocation. [Protest against innovations by the examiners in literis humanioribus.] n. pl., 1853, s. sh.   G.A. Oxon c. 69 (125)

2659. Reasons for dissenting from the proposed examination statute so far as relates to the final examination of candidates for honours in literis humanioribus. Oxf., [1857], s. sh.   G.A. Oxon c. 73 (340)

2660. PAPILLON, T. L., Oxford scholarship and [classical] Honour moderations. Oxf., 1880, 8°. 11 pp.   G.A. Oxon 8° 296 (5)

2661. FARNELL, L. R., A guide to studying for Honour classical moderations. (Oxf. study guides.) Oxf., 1881, 8°. 74 pp.   260 g. 442a

See 1872 [T., N., The school of Literae humaniores. 1883].

2662. SNOW, T. C., The school of Literæ humaniores, a reply [to no. 1872, signed T. C. S.]. (Oxf. mag., 1883, vol. 1, p. 205, 06.)
Per. G.A. Oxon 4° 141

2663. CASE, T., Proposed scheme of Literæ humaniores. Oxf. &c., 1891, 8°. 9 pp.   G.A. Oxon 8° 524 (6)

2664. CASE, T., A plea for Classical moderations as a necessary preliminary to the English school. [Oxf.], (1894), s. sh.
G.A. Oxon b. 140 (105)

2665. Draft report, by the chairman of committee [of The Club] appointed to consider certain proposed modifications of 'Greats' with a view to the promotion of special or advanced studies. [Jan. 29.] [Oxf., 1897], s. sh.   G.A. Oxon b. 147

2666. Suggested scheme [of The Club] in outline for the fusion of Honour moderations and Greats [Oct. 22]. [Oxf., 1897], s. sh.
G.A. Oxon b. 147

2667. Suggested scheme [by The Club] of a single classical school combining the existing schools of Honour moderations and Literae humaniores. [28 Jan.] [Oxf., 1898], s. sh.   G.A. Oxon b. 147

2668. [Another] Suggested scheme [by The Club] of a single classical school combining the existing schools of Honour moderations and Literae humaniores. [Oxf., 1899?], s. sh.   G.A. Oxon b. 147

2669. Suggested scheme of a single classical school combining the existing schools of Honour moderations and Literae humaniores. [A skit on the scheme produced by The Club.] [Oxf., 1899?], s. sh.
Firth b. 36 (103a)

2670. FARNELL, L. R., The question of a three-years' classical course and a single examination. (Oxf., 1898), 8°. 16 pp.   G.A. Oxon 8° 620 (24)

2671. GROSE, T. H., Faculty of arts. Honour school of Literae humaniores. [Historical account by T. H. Grose.] [Oxf., 1900], 2 sheets.
G.A. Oxon b. 41 (3)

2672. SIDGWICK, A., Faculty of arts. Honour moderations, classical. [Historical account by A. Sidgwick.] [Oxf., 1900], s. sh.
G.A. Oxon b. 41 (2)

See 1881 [Strachan-Davidson, J. L., Reform in allocation of subjects etc. in Lit. Hum. in relation to the Civil service examinations. 1903].

2673. GARDNER, P., Oxford at the cross roads, a criticism of the course of Literae humaniores. Lond., 1903, 8°. 132 pp.   2625 e. 39

2674. E., H. A., Literae humaniores. [An attempt to trace the development of the School from 1636 to circa 1850. Signed H. A. E. i.e. H. A. Evans?] (Oxf. mag., 1908, vol. 27, p. 55, 56, 90, 91, 119, 20, 152, 53, 188, 89, 220, 247, 48.)   Per. G.A. Oxon 4° 141

2675. BAILEY, C., Honour moderations in classics. (Oxf. mag., 1918, vol. 37, p. 78–80, 97–99.)   Per. G.A. Oxon 4° 141

2676. DENNISTON, J. D., Honour moderations and Literae humaniores. (Oxf. mag., 1919, vol. 38, p. 147–49, 225, 26.) Per. G.A. Oxon 4° 141

2677. GARROD, H. W., What is the matter with 'Mods'? (Oxf. mag., 1920, vol. 38, p. 240–42.)   Per. G.A. Oxon 4° 141

2678. OWEN, A. S., Classical moderations and Literae humaniores. (Oxf. mag., 1920, vol. 38, p. 198.)   Per. G.A. Oxon 4° 141

2679. DODD, P. W., Literae humaniores. (Oxf. mag., 1930, vol. 48, p. 495, 96.)   Per. G.A. Oxon 4° 141

2680. CORBET, M., The presumption of Greats. (Oxf. mag., 1931, vol. 49, p. 547–49.)   Per. G.A. Oxon 4° 141

2681. CHILVER, G. E. F., Greats under conscription [signed G. E. F. C.]. (Oxf. mag., 1947, vol. 65, p. 188, 89.)   Per. G.A. Oxon 4° 141

2682. WILLIAMSON, D. M., Record of a B.A. examination [Literae humaniores in 1813]. (Oxoniensia, 1955, vol. 19, p. 122, 23.)
Per. G.A. Oxon 4° 658 — R.

2683. DODDS, E. R., The position of classical studies in Oxford. (Oxf. mag., 1956, vol. 74, p. 372–74.)   Per. G.A. Oxon 4° 141

Ancient history

2684. Ancient history and the new statute [signed M.A.]. [Oxf., 1857], 8°. 3 pp.   G.A. Oxon c. 73 (341)

2685. HAVERFIELD, F., The study of ancient history in Oxford, a lecture. Lond. &c., 1912, 8°. 31 pp.   263334 e. 38 (8)

See 1894 [Myres, sir J. L., The provision for historical studies at Oxford. 1915].

2686. MYRES, J. L., Ancient history. (Oxf. mag., 1930, vol. 48, p. 634–36.)
Per. G.A. Oxon 4° 141

2687. LAST, H., Ancient history and its troubles in Oxford. (Oxf. mag., 1930, vol. 48, p. 814–18.)   Per. G.A. Oxon 4° 141

2688. GRUNDY, G. B., Ancient history in Literae humaniores. (Oxf. mag., 1930, vol. 48, p. 889–91.)   Per. G.A. Oxon 4° 141

2688.5. BRUNT, P. A., Ancient history dinners [1903–]. (Oxf. mag., 1963, N.S., vol. 4, p. 111, 12.)   Per. G.A. Oxon 4° 141

Camden professor of ancient history

2689. Correspondence [dated 18 June 1851] between the Camden professor [E. Cardwell] and the rev. dr. Pusey [concerning the proposed augmentation of the Camden professorship]. [Oxf., 1851], 4°. 3 pp.
G.A. Oxon c. 67 (101a)

2690. [*Begin.*] The following correspondence is published with the consent of professor Rawlinson . . . [relating to a notice of the Camden professor, which was considered to have produced an undesirable impression upon the minds of undergraduates]. [Oxf.], (1869), s. sh.
G.A. Oxon c. 85 (487)

2691. ALLISON, W. H., The first endowed professorship of history [Camden ancient history] and its first incumbent [Degory Whear]. (Amer. hist. review, 1922, vol. 27, p. 733–37.)   Per. 2231 d. 67 = K.

2692. JONES, H. S., The foundation and history of the Camden chair. (Oxoniensia, 1943/44, vol. 8/9, p. 169–92.)
Per. G.A. Oxon 4° 658 = R.

Reader in ancient history

2693. The vacant Readership [in ancient history]. (Oxf. mag., 1887, vol. 5, p. 151, 52.)   Per. G.A. Oxon 4° 141

Archaeology

2694. GARDNER, P., Classical archaeology at Oxford. n. pl., 1889, 8°. 16 pp.
G.A. Oxon 8° 454 (1)

2695. GRUNDY, G. B., The recognition of archaeology as a study in Oxford. [Oxf.], (1900), 8°. 11 pp.   G.A. Oxon b. 140 (116a)

Comparative philology

Professor of comparative philology

2696. DODGSON, C. L., The professorship of comparative philology. Feb. 4, 1876. [Oxf.], (1876), s. sh.

2697. DODGSON, C. L., The professorship of comparative philology. Feb. 12, 1876. [Oxf.], (1876), s. sh.   Arch. AA e. 10 (25)

2698. DODGSON, C. L., The professorship of comparative philology. Feb. 14, 1876. [Oxf.], (1876), s. sh.   Arch. AA e. 10 (28)

Greek

See also 2143, &c., [Greek in Responsions].
See 6739–41 [Works by or concerning Christophoros Angelos].

2699. A plea for the study of Greek at Oxford, a letter . . . in answer to a letter from lord Lyttelton, by M.A. of Wadham college. Lond., 1870, 8°. 11 pp.   G.A. Oxon 8° 1079 (16)

2700. FREEMAN, E. A., Greek in the universities. (Contemporary review, 1891, p. 663–71.)   G.A. Oxon 4° 575 (19)

See 962 [Case, T., Letters to The Times, 1884–1922. 1927].

Regius professor of Greek

2701. CHASE, D. P., Endowment of the Greek professorship [signed D. P. C.]. Oxf., 1861, s. sh.   G.A. Oxon c. 77 (365)

2702. STANLEY, A. P., A speech delivered in the house of Congregation, Nov. 20, 1861, on the endowment of the Regius professorship of Greek, with notes. Oxf., 1861, 8°. 16 pp.   G.A. Oxon 8° 296 (10)

2703. The debate in Oxford Congregation (Nov. 20, 1861) on endowing the professor of Greek [dated Nov. 21, and signed A member of Congregation]. [Oxf.], (1861), 4°. 3 pp.   G.A. Oxon c. 77 (380)

2704. The public teaching of the Regius professor of Greek. [Letters dated Nov. 21 and 22, exchanged between R. Duckworth and H. R. Bramley.] [Oxf.], (1861), s. sh.   G.A. Oxon c. 77 (376)

2705. 'Endowment of the Greek professorship.' [A paper, dated 22 Nov., 1861, animadverting upon certain alternative amendments recently put forward as solutions of the controversy about the Greek professorship. By C. L. Dodgson? Sometimes ascr. to O. Ogle.] [Oxf.], 1861, s. sh.   G.A. Oxon c. 77 (374)

2706. The endowment of the Greek chair [23 Nov.]. Oxf., 1861, s. sh.   G.A. Oxon c. 77 (381)

2707. LIDDON, H. P., The Greek professorship [by H. P. Liddon. 23 Nov., 1861]. Oxf., 1861, 8°. 8 pp.   G.A. Oxon c. 77 (384)

2708. SHORTING, C. G. H., The Greek professorship. (A few lines from an unpublished play 'Oxford in the 19th century' with especial reference to Nov. 25th 1861, by Pacificus.) [This pamphlet was suppressed.] n. pl., [1861], 8°. 16 pp.   G.A. Oxon b. 113 (141)

2709. PUSEY, E. B., Answer to professor Stanley's strictures. 25 Nov. [Oxf.], (1861), 8°. 6 pp.   G.A. Oxon c. 77 (386)

2710. WAYTE, S. W., Mr. Jowett's professorial lectures. [A paper, dated 25 Nov., 1861, signed S. W. W., attacking Montagu Burrows for inconsistencies in his attitude as shown in speeches and in his work 'Pass and Class', no. 1861.]. [Oxf.], 1861, s. sh.   G.A. Oxon c. 77 (377)

2711. BURROWS, M., A letter to the rev. S. W. Wayte [defending apparent inconsistencies between a speech in Congregation and 'Pass and class', no. 1861, in relation to the teaching of the professor of Greek]. [Oxf.], 1861, s. sh.
                                                            G.A. Oxon c. 77 (371)

2712. The endowment of the Regius professorship of Greek. [A paper, dated 25 Nov., 1861, signed M.A.] Oxf., 1861, s. sh.
                                                            G.A. Oxon c. 77 (375)

2713. PUSEY, E. B., With whom lies the responsibility of the approaching conflict as to the Greek chair? [signed Pacificus]. [Oxf., 1861], 8°. 4 pp.
                                                            G.A. Oxon c. 77 (378)

2714. The Greek professorship. [25 Nov.]. Oxf., 1861, s. sh.
                                                            G.A. Oxon c. 77 (370)

2715. PUSEY, E. B., On whom lies the responsibility of the present contest? Answer to M.A. [signed Pacificus]. [Oxf., 1861], s. sh.
                                                            G.A. Oxon c. 77 (373)

2716. To members of Congregation. [A paper, dated 25 Nov., 1861, signed An undergraduate, describing the gradual demoralizing of his Christian faith after attending professor Jowett's lectures.] Oxf., 1861, s. sh.
                                                            G.A. Oxon c. 77 (372)

2717. To members of Congregation. [A paper, dated 26 Nov., signed An undergraduate, urging that the opposition to dr. Jowett's endowment be extended to include other professors, and in particular mr. Mansel.] Oxf., 1861, s. sh.
                                                            G.A. Oxon c. 77 (383)

2718. To members of Congregation. [A paper, dated 26 Nov., signed A graduate, an answer to no. 2716.] [Oxf.], 1861, s. sh.
                                                            G.A. Oxon c. 77 (382)

2719. CHASE, D. P., The Greek professorship. 'Ἐπίλογος. [A paper, dated 27 Nov., signed D. P. C., urging the preparation of a memorial in support of the second 'alternative amendment' to settle the question of the Greek professorship endowment.] Oxf., 1861, s. sh.
                                                            G.A. Oxon c. 77 (385)

2720. CHASE, D. P., Greek professorship. [Proposals, dated 9 Dec., 1861, to found a professorship of Greek distinct from the Regius professorship, as a method of solving the controversy.] [Oxf.], (1861), fol. 2 sheets.
                                                            G.A. Oxon c. 77 (396)

2721. [Begin.] It will be remembered . . . [A paper, intended 'to put a check, if possible, on improper modes of conducting University contests'. The impropriety here is in a letter signed M. Burrows, which contains reflections on Pusey and Keble. Both the latter wrote in refutation of the statements. The texts of the three letters are given. The contest was about the endowment of the Regius professor of Greek.] [Oxf., 1862?], s. sh.   G.A. Oxon b. 140 (19b)

2722. CONINGTON, J., The University of Oxford and the Greek chair. Oxf. &c., 1863, 8°. 21 pp.   G.A. Oxon 8° 397

2723. A reply to professor Conington's pamphlet on the Greek professor-ship at Oxford, by a member of Congregation. Oxf. &c., 1863, 8°. 14 pp.   200 h. 35 (7)

2724. Oxford, Feb. 26, 1864 [urging the rejection of the proposed endow-ment of the professor of Greek. Signed by R. L. Cotton and 9 others]. [Oxf.], (1864), s. sh.   G.A. Oxon c. 80 (397)

2725. An appeal to Congregation against the statute on the Greek pro-fessorship [signed A member of Congregation]. [Oxf.], (1864), s. sh.
                                                      G.A. Oxon c. 80 (378)

2726. W., A. C., Is the University to endow the Greek chair? A few words by a non-resident M.A. [signed A. C. W.]. (Oxf.), [1864], s. sh.
                                                      G.A. Oxon c. 80 (399)

2727. Reasons for voting against the endowment of the Regius professor of Greek. (Oxf.), [1864], s. sh.   G.A. Oxon c. 80 (394)

2728. FREEMAN, E. A., The Regius professorship of Greek. [Repr. of a letter to the Daily news, Oct. 18, 1864, suggesting that an obligation to endow the professorship lies upon the Dean and chapter of Christ Church.] n. pl., (1864), 8°. 8 pp.   G.A. Oxon 4° 13 (10)

2729. LIDDELL, H. G., [*Begin.*] Mr. Freeman has published a letter . . . [Statement refuting that an obligation for the endowment of the Regius professorship of Greek lies upon Christ Church.] (Oxf., 1864), 4°. 3 pp.
                                                      G.A. Oxon 4° 13 (10*)

2730. FREEMAN, E. A., The Chapter of Oxford and the Regius professorship of Greek. [An answer to dr. Liddell. Nov. 22.] n. pl., (1864), 8°. 7 pp.
                                                      G.A. Oxon b. 31

2731. Some remarks on the debate in Congregation upon the proposed endowment of the Regius professorship of Greek, Feb. 4, 1864. Oxf. &c., 1864, 8°. 10 pp.   G.A. Oxon 8° 105 (7)

2732. To non-resident members of the Oxford Convocation. [A paper giving the compromise arrangement by means of which the stipend of the Regius professor of Greek may be increased.] [Oxf.], 1864, s. sh.
                                                      G.A. Oxon c. 80 (396)

2733. [*Begin.*] The vice-chancellor has received the following communica-tion from the Dean of Christ Church [concerning the augmentation of the salary of the Regius professor of Greek from the funds of Christ Church. *Followed by* Epitome of case submitted to the Attorney-general and others *re* the Greek professorship at Oxford, *and* Opinion dated Dec. 23, 1864 and signed by Roundell Palmer, H. M. Cairns, R. Jones-Bateman]. [Oxf.], (1865), 4°. 4 pp.   G.A. Oxon c. 81 (60)

2734. DODGSON, C. L., The new method of evaluation as applied to π. [A satire on the proposed increase of salary for the Greek professor-ship. By C. L. Dodgson.] [Oxf.], (1865), fol.   G.A. Oxon c. 81 (399)
— [Another ed.] First pr. in 1865. (Notes by an Oxf. chiel.) Oxf., 1874, 12°.   G.A. Oxon 8° 161 (24)

— [Another ed.] (The Lewis Carroll picture book, ed. by S. D.
Collingwood, 1899, p. 45–57.)   270 e. 1155
[Also included in no. 807.]

Latin

See also 2210, &c., [Latin in Responsions].

2735. HIGHAM, T. F., Latin. I. In the University. II. In the schools. (Oxf.
  mag., 1938, vol. 56, p. 570–73; 604–07.)   Per. G.A. Oxon 4° 141

Corpus Christi college professor of Latin

2736. CHASE, D. P., Reasons for rejecting the Latin professorship statute
  [signed D. P. C.]. Oxf., (1854), s. sh.   G.A. Oxon b. 27

Logic

See 1942 [Some hints to the rev. H. A. Woodgate on logic. 1829].

2737. The following extract from the preface to dr. Whately's Elements
  of logic is reprinted, with reference to one of the questions now before
  the University. [Concerning the Examination statute of 1807, and
  in particular whether logic should be an indispensable part of the
  examination.] (Oxf.), [1829], 8°. 8 pp.   G.A. Oxon c. 45 (127*)

2738. A few remarks suggested by the reprinting of part of the preface to
  dr. Whately's Elements of logic. Oxf., 1829, 8°. 16 pp.
                                              G.A. Oxon c. 45 (127**)

2739. A dissertation on the heads of predicables, with some remarks on the
  state of logical studies in Oxford. Oxf., 1847, 8°. 60 pp.
                                              G.A. Oxon 8° 250 (21)

2740. LANDON, J. T. B., Grand University logic stakes of two hundred
  and fifty sovereigns . . . ten-mile course, gentlemen riders. [A satire
  concerning the election of a prælector of logic, by J. T. B. Landon.]
  Oxf., (1849), 8°. 8 pp.   G.A. Oxon 8° 135 (6)
  [A key to this satire is to be found in W. Tuckwell's Reminiscences.
  2nd ed. p. 325, no. 3903.]

2740.3. THOMAS, I., Medieval aftermath: Oxford logic and logicians of the
  17th century. (Oxf. studies presented to D. Callus; Oxf. hist. soc.,
  1964, N.S., vol. 16, p. 297–311.)   G.A. Oxon 8° 360 = R.

Numismatics

2741. MILNE, J. G., Numismatics [signed J. G. M.]. (Oxf. mag., 1930, vol.
  49, p. 278–80.)   Per. G.A. Oxon 4° 141

Papyrology

2742. HUNT, A. S., Papyrology. (Oxf. mag., 1930, vol. 49, p. 84–86.)
                                                Per. G.A. Oxon 4° 141

Philosophy

2743. Reflections occasioned by the flirtations of Alma Mater and the Stagyrite, in addition to a collection of opinions. Oxf., 1820, 8°. 15 pp.
G.A. Oxon 8° 219 (13)

See 1427 [Payment of the annuity of £100 to the several readers in moral philosophy for the 8 years, 1832 to 1840, from the estate of Langdon Hills. 1841].

2744. OAKELEY, F., Remarks on the study of Aristotelian and Platonic ethics, as a branch of the Oxford system of education. Oxf., 1837, 8°. 83 pp.
G.A. Oxon 8° 1001 (15)

2745. PATTISON, M., Philosophy at Oxford. (Mind, 1876, vol. 1, p. 82–97.)
Per. 27684 d. 54 = P.
— [Repr.] (Essays by M. Pattison, collected by H. Nettleship, 1889, vol. 1.)
270 d. 20 = A.

2746. MUIRHEAD, J. H., The Oxford chairs of philosophy: the need of reform. (Contemp. rev., 1898, vol. 74, p. 724–36.)   Per. 3977 d. 58

2747. STURT, H., Philosophy in Lit. hum., practical hints . . . Oxf., 1927, 8°. 36 pp.
2626 e. 401 (12)

2748. CALLUS, D. A., Introduction of Aristotelian learning to Oxford. (Proc., Brit. acad., 1943, vol. 29, p. 229–81.)   Soc. 3974 d. 105 = A.

2749. MURE, G. R. G., Oxford and philosophy. (Philosophy, 1937, vol. 12, p. 291–301.)
Per. 26784 d. 126 = P.

2749.5. HARE, R. M., Philosophy and its ancient umbrella. (Oxf. mag., 1965, vol. 6, p. 137–39.)
Per. G.A. Oxon 4° 141

White's professor of moral philosophy

2750 [Correspondence between M. J. Johnson and F. Bulley concerning an amendment to the statute relating to the professorship of moral philosophy submitted by the former, to dispossess the President of Magdalen college of his right to vote in elections to the professorship. With observations on the attitude of the President and Fellows of Magdalen college in relation to the Magdalen praelectorships.] (Mar., Apr., 1855). n. pl., (1855), 4°. 11 pp.   G.A. Oxon 4° 28 (2)

2751. White's professorship of moral philosophy. [Statement concerning foundation, &c.] [Oxf., 1889], 8°. 5 pp.   G.A. Oxon 8° 620 (33)
— [Similar statement with Indenture.] [Oxf., 1889], 8°. 12 pp.
G.A. Oxon 8° 620 (34)

2752. STEWART, J. A., Remarks on certain memorialists, by White's professor of moral philosophy. n. pl., (1899), 8°. 4 pp.
G.A. Oxon 8° 611 (28)

FACULTY OF MODERN HISTORY
General

See also 2528, &c., Faculty of Law [School of law and modern history].

2753. The fourth school. [Objections to the establishment of a Modern history school.] Oxf., [1849], s. sh.   G.A. Oxon c. 65 (179)

2754. FREEMAN, E. A., Historical study at Oxford. (Bentley's quarterly, 1859, vol. 1, p. 282–300.)   Per. 2705 e. 240

2755. STUBBS, W., *bp. of Chester*, Two lectures on the present state and prospects of historical study, delivered on the 17th and 20th of May, 1876. Oxf., [1876?], 4°. 47 pp.   223 e. 58 (1)

2756. STUBBS, W., *bp. of Chester*, An address delivered by way of a last statutory public lecture, by William bishop of Chester and Regius professor of modern history . . . May 8, 1884. [Recollections of his term of office.] Oxf., [1884?], 4°. 10 pp.   223 e. 58 (2)

2757. Proposed scheme for a first public examination in history. [Oxf.], (1885), s. sh.   G.A. Oxon b. 140 (55a)

2758. The new History school [signed Teacher]. (Oxf. mag., 1886, vol. 4, p. 12.)   Per. G.A. Oxon 4° 141

2759. SMITH, A. L., The new History school [an answer signed A. L. S. to no. 2758]. (Oxf. mag., 1886, vol. 4, p. 36, 37.)   Per. G.A. Oxon 4° 141

2760. The new History schools. [An answer signed Teacher to no. 2759.] (Oxf. mag., 1886, vol. 4, p. 76, 77.)   Per. G.A. Oxon 4° 141

2761. ARMSTRONG, E., and SMITH, A. L., The proposed first public examination in Greek and Latin historical writers, &c. [The authors were appointed to form a committee by the teachers in modern history.] [Oxf.], 1886, 8°. 4 pp.   G.A. Oxon b. 140 (67b)

2762. DAVIDSON, J. L. STRACHAN-, The proposed first public examination in Greek and Latin historical writers, &c. [An answer to no. 2761.] [Oxf.], (1886), 4°. 4 pp.   G.A. Oxon b. 140 (67c)

2763. CASE, T., The proposed first public examination in Greek and Latin historical writers &c. [Oxf.], (1886), 4°. 3 pp.   G.A. Oxon b. 140 (67d)

2764. Modern history association. [Miscellaneous papers. 1889–1914.]   G.A. Oxon 4° 602

2765. ASHLEY, SIR W. J., Study of history at Oxford. (Nation, 1895, vol. 60, p. 274, 75.)   R.H.

2766. JOHNSON, A. H., Faculty of arts. Honour school of modern history [historical account by A. H. Johnson]. [Oxf., 1900], s. sh.   G.A. Oxon b. 41 (6)

2767. FIRTH, C. H., Honours in history. [Observations on the standard of the Modern history school, 1893–1903, by C. H. Firth.] n. pl., [1903], 4°. 4 pp.   G.A. Oxon 4° 186 (5)

2768. FIRTH, SIR C., A plea for the historical teaching of history. Oxf., 1904, 8°. 30 pp.   263334 d. 7

2769. Oxford school of historians. (Church quarterly, 1904, vol. 59, p. 92–127.)   Per. 1419 e. 402 = S.

2770. A letter [signed E. Armstrong and 22 others, tutors and lecturers in modern history] to the professor of modern history on the teaching and study of history at Oxford. Oxf., 1905, 8°. 14 pp.   263334 e. 38 (15)

2771. FIRTH, SIR C., Answer to [no. 2770] A letter to the Regius professor of modern history on the teaching and study of history at Oxford. n. pl., [1905], 8°. 8 pp.

2772. Report of the examiners in the School of modern history. 1905, 08, 11, 12, [Oxf.], 1905–12, s. sh.   G.A. Oxon b. 138 (79)

2773. OMAN, SIR C., Inaugural lecture on the study of history. Oxf., 1906, 8°. 30 pp.   2625 d. 55 (3)

2774. FIRTH, SIR C., Memorandum on the present state of the study of modern history and on university reform in general. n. pl., 1907, 8°. 27 pp.

2775. FIRTH, C. H., Memorandum on the organisation of advanced historical training in Oxford. [Oxf., 1908], 8°. 6 pp.   G.A. Oxon b. 138 (82)

2776. BARKER, SIR E., On the need for the redistribution of the work prescribed for the school of modern history. (Oxf.), [c. 1908], 8°. 7 pp.   O.P.L.

2777. FIRTH, SIR C. H., On the desirability of diminishing the work set for the Modern history school, and in particular the amount of early constitutional history. n. pl., [c. 1908], 8°. 8 pp.   263334 d. 64 (8)

2778. FIRTH, C. H., The statute respecting Group B. (i). [A paper, signed C. H. Firth, E. Barker, supporting the transfer of this group to the Modern history board.] [Oxf., 1910], s. sh.   G.A. Oxon 4° 296 (5)

2779. [Begin.] The statute as to the previous examination . . . [Arguments against the statute for a previous examination in modern history: signed A. J. Jenkinson and 6 others.] [Oxf., 1913], s. sh.   G.A. Oxon c. 310 (138)

2780. [Begin.] We venture to address . . . [Considerations in favour of the amended statute for a previous examination in modern history: signed C. Grant Robertson, H. W. C. Davis, E. Barker. June 10, 1913.] [Oxf., 1913], s. sh.   G.A. Oxon c. 310 (137)

2781. MUIR, R., School of modern history. [A letter upon the working of the school.] [Oxf.], (1914), 8°. 21 pp.   G.A. Oxon b. 141 (87a)

See 1894 [Myres, sir J. L., The provision for historical studies at Oxford. 1915].

2782. FIRTH, C. H., Modern history in Oxford, 1724–1841. (Engl. hist. review, 1917, vol. 32, p. 1–21.) Per. 2231 d. 342 = K.

2783. FIRTH, SIR C. H., Modern history in Oxford, 1841–1918. Oxf., 1920, 8°. 51 pp. 263334 e. 80 (2)

2784. POWICKE, F. M., Historical study in Oxford, inaugural lecture. Oxf., 1929, 8°. 24 pp. 223 d. 35

2785. POWICKE, F. M., The school of modern history. (Oxf. mag., 1930, vol. 48, p. 528–30.) Per. G.A. Oxon 4° 141

2786. JONES, I. D., History moderations. (Oxf. mag., 1938, vol. 57, p. 240, 41.) Per. G.A. Oxon 4° 141

2787. PRESTWICH, J. O., The proposed History moderations. (Oxf. mag., 1939, vol. 57, p. 275, 76.) Per. G.A. Oxon 4° 141

See 2954 [Hancock, W. K., Economic history at Oxford. 1946].

2788. BROMLEY, J. S., Honour school of modern history. (Amer. Oxon., 1957, vol. 44, p. 66–72.) Per. G.A. Oxon 8° 889

2788.1. SOUTHERN, R. W., The shape and substance of academic history, an inaugural lecture. Oxf., 1961, 8°. 26 pp. 2232 e. 135

2788.2. Report of the sub-committee of the Student Representative Council to inquire into the History syllabus. [Reprod. from type-writing.] [Oxf., 1963], fol. 8 leaves. 263334 c. 8

2788.3. Notes for writers of B.Litt. and D.Phil. theses in the Faculty of Modern History. Oxf., [1964], 8°. 13 pp. 3972 e. 74

2788.4. THOMPSON, A. F., The History syllabus. (Oxf. mag., 1965, N.S., vol. 5, p. 274, 75.) Per. G.A. Oxon 4° 141

Chichele professor of modern history

2789. BURROWS, M., Inaugural lecture [on the foundation of the Chichele professorship of modern history]. (Oxf.), 1862, 8°. 32 pp.
G.A. Oxon 8° 299

Chichele professor of the history of war

2790. WILKINSON, S., The University and the study of war, an inaugural lecture. Oxf., 1909, 8°. 28 pp. 26324 d. 22

Ford's Lecturer in English history

2791. Ford's professorship of English history [signed T. E. Holland, and 4 others]. [Oxf.], (1893), 8°. 4 pp. G.A. Oxon c. 153

2792. MADAN, F., The Ford professorship [letter on the statute of foundation]. (Oxf. mag., 1893, vol. 11, p. 247.) Per. G.A. Oxon 4° 141

Regius professor of modern history

2793. Modern history and regius professors. [A paper, signed Academicus, on the neglect of the Regius professor of modern history to deliver lectures during last year.] Oxf., (1857), s. sh.   G.A. Oxon c. 73 (331)

2794. VAUGHAN, H. H., [*Begin.*] Some unknown person . . . [Objections to no. 2793.] [Oxf.], 1858, s. sh.   G.A. Oxon c. 74 (23)

2795. ACADEMICUS, *pseud.*, [*Begin.*] A public officer . . . [A reply, signed Academicus, to no. 2794.] Jan. 25. Oxf., (1858), s. sh.
G.A. Oxon c. 74 (24)

2796. [Suggested regulations for the Regius professor of modern history agreed by the Hebdomadal council, 26 May, 1858, to be placed before the chancellor.] n. pl., [1858], s. sh.   G.A. Oxon c. 74 (178)

2797. DUNN, W. H., Valiant professorship [J. A. Froude's, as Regius professor of modern history]. (South Atlantic quarterly, 1951, vol. 50, p. 519–29.)   R.H.

Diplomatic

2798. GALBRAITH, V. H., Diplomatic. (Oxf. mag., 1930, vol. 49, p. 238, 39.)   Per. G.A. Oxon 4° 141

FACULTY OF ENGLISH

General

2799. MURRAY, G., The Oxford Ars poetica: or, How to write a Newdigate [by G. Murray. Attacking, in facetious vein, the low standard of Oxford poetry]. Oxf., 1853, 8°. 38 pp.   G.A. Oxon 8° 135 (2)
— [Another ed. 1853?]   280 f. 2492
— [Repr. in no. 5003. Three Oxford ironies, 1927.]   2704 f. 6

See 2821, &c., [School of modern language and literature 1886, &c.].

2800. A school of English literature. (Oxf. mag., 1887, vol. 5, p. 8, 9.)
Per. G.A. Oxon 4° 141

2801. Memorial [drawn up for The Club, chiefly by H. F. Pelham] addressed to the Hebdomadal council [urging the establishment of a final honour school of English language and literature. April, 1891]. [Oxf., 1891], s. sh.   G.A. Oxon b. 147
— [Another ed.] June, 1891. [Oxf.], 1891, 4°. 4 pp. Firth b. 36 (125)

2802. The proposed final honour school of English language and literature. [Oxf., 1891?], s. sh.   Firth b. 36 (131)

2803. The proposed university scholarship in English language and literature [signed by D. B. Monro and 4 others]. Dec. 4. [Oxf.], (1893), s. sh.   G.A. Oxon c. 153

2804. The proposed university scholarship in English language and literature. [*Begin.*] It seems well to point out . . . [14 Nov.]. [Oxf., 1893],
s. sh.   G.A. Oxon c. 153

2805. The proposed university scholarship in English language and literature. [*Begin.*] Congregation will have . . . [Oxf., 1893], s. sh.
                                                           G.A. Oxon c. 153

2806. English language and literature at Oxford. [A criticism of the members of the Board of studies of the new honour school.] (Sat. rev., 1894,
vol. 78, p. 525, 26.)   N. 2288 c. 8

See 2664 [Case, T., A plea for Classical moderations as a necessary preliminary
to the English school. 1894].

2807. COLLINS, J. C., Language versus literature at Oxford. (19th cent.,
1895, vol. 37, p. 290–303.)   Per. 3977 d. 66

2807.1. Oxford. November, 1909. [*Begin.*] Dear Sir, The statute for establishing an English fund . . . [Letter, signed by A. S. Napier and 6 others,
asking for provision for the continuance and security of the fund.]
[Oxf.], (1909), s. sh.   G.A. Oxon b. 32 (5)

2808. FIRTH, SIR C., The school of English language and literature, a
contribution to the history of Oxford studies. Oxf., 1909, 8°. 55 pp.
                                                           26333 e. 25

2809. TOLKIEN, J. R. R., The Oxford English school. (Oxf. mag., 1930,
vol. 48, p. 778–82.)   Per. G.A. Oxon 4° 141

2810. CRAIGIE, W. A., English at schools and the University [signed
W. A. C.]. (Oxf. mag., 1931, vol. 49, p. 684–88.) Per. G.A. Oxon 4° 141

2811. Notes on the presentation of theses on literary subjects (prepared by
members of the Faculty of English language and literature . . . for the
use of students in that Faculty). Lond., 1952, 8°. 8 pp.
                                                           3962 e. 412 = A.

2811.2. WHITEHEAD, W. V., The study of English language and literature
at Oxford. (Amer. Oxon., 1962, vol. 49, p. 118–21.)
                                                      Per. G.A. Oxon 8° 889

2811.21. PALMER, D. J., The rise of English studies, an account . . . from
its origins to the making of the Oxford English School. Lond. &c.,
1965, 8°. 192 pp.   262225 e. 209

Merton professor of English language and literature

2812. [*Begin.*] The committee appointed to consider the question of the
professorships of English language and literature report— [suggesting
the endowment of a Merton professor of English literature on the first
vacancy of the Professorship of Anglo-Saxon]. [Oxf., *c.* 1899], s. sh.
                                                      G.A. Oxon c. 281 (f. 16)

Professor of poetry

2813. The Poetry professorship, an appeal to members of Convocation [against the election of I. Williams]. (Oxf., 1841), s. sh.
G.A. Oxon 8° 77 (13)

2814. HOOD, T., University feud [the contest for the Professorship of poetry]. (Colburn's New monthly mag., 1842, vol. 64, p. 142–46.)
Per. 2705 d. 393

2815. Oxford professors of poetry in Oxford. Copleston and Keble. (Fraser's mag., 1844, vol. 29, p. 629–39.)   Per. 3977 e. 200

2816. The Poetry chair at Oxford. (Sat. rev., 1885, vol. 60, p. 708, 09.)
N. 2288 c. 8

2817. MACKAIL, J. W., Henry Birkhead and the foundation of the Oxford chair of poetry, a lecture. Oxf., 1908, 8°. 23 pp.   3964 e. 15
[Also issued in 'Oxford lectures on literature, 1907–1920'.] 3966 d. 33

2818. WARREN, T. H., Oxford and poetry in 1911, lecture. Oxf., 1911, 8°. 35 pp.   G.A. Oxon 8° 828 (4)

English library

2819. The Napier memorial library fund. Report of the committee. Nov. 11. (Oxf., 1916), 8°. 4 pp.   G.A. Oxon c. 281 (f. 49)

2820. The Napier memorial library. [Request for subscriptions towards purchasing the library for the University.] June 20. (Oxf., 1916), s. sh.
G.A. Oxon c. 281 (f. 48)

See 5779 [New group for Oxford, English library, &c. 1960].

2820.2. Oxford university English library. Notes for readers and Library regulations. Oxf., [1965], 8°. 6 pp.   2590 e. Oxf. 44. 1

FACULTY OF MODERN LANGUAGES

General

2821. ARMSTRONG, E., The duty of the University in relation to the modern languages [by E. Armstrong]. (Oxf.), [1886], 8°. 8 pp.
G.A. Oxon 8° 1079 (8)

2821.1. [Begin.] We beg to lay before you the following considerations in favour of establishing a final school of modern language and literature. Nov. 2. [Oxf.], (1886), s. sh.   G.A. Oxon b. 140 (66)

2821.2. [Begin.] Dear Mr. Provost, Thinking it might be well for Council to have . . . a fuller statement . . . [Details of the scheme proposed in item no. 2821.1, signed A. N. and F. Y. P., i.e. A. Neubauer? and F. York Powell.] Dec. 1. [Oxf.], (1886), 4°. 3 pp. and Appendix.
G.A. Oxon b. 140 (67)

2821.3. A school of English literature: [article on] Petition addressed to the Hebdomadal council for the foundation of a school of modern literature, 1886 [no. 2821.1]. (Quarterly review, 1887, vol. 164, p. 241–69.)
Per. 3977 e. 191

2822. POWELL, F. Y., A brief statement of the case for the proposed final school of modern language and literature. Oxf., 1887, 8°. 11 pp.
G.A. Oxon 8° 427

2823. NETTLESHIP, H., The study of modern languages and literatures in the University of Oxford. Oxf. &c., 1887, 8°. 20 pp.
G.A. Oxon 8° 455 (4)

2824. The honour school of modern languages. (Oxf. mag., 1887, vol. 5, p. 185, 86, 204.)
Per. G.A. Oxon 4° 141

2825. CASE, T., An appeal . . . against the proposed final school of modern languages. Oxf., (1887), 8°. 14 pp.
G.A. Oxon 8° 426

2826. [Begin.] The curators wish to draw . . . [A letter, signed W. R. Morfill, May 6, 1905, seeking aid to implement their scheme for making teaching provision in the Taylor institution for the new final school of modern languages.] [Oxf.], (1905), 4°. 2 sheets.
Firth b. 36 (41a)

2827. [Begin.] The curators beg to inform you . . . [A letter, signed W. R. Morfill, Dec. 4, 1905, announcing arrangements for carrying out the scheme outlined in no. 2826.] [Oxf.], (1905), s. sh. Firth b. 36 (41b)

2828. GRUNDY, G. B., The honour school of modern languages. (Oxf. mag., 1919, vol. 37, p. 207.)
Per. G.A. Oxon 4° 141

2829. FIRTH, SIR C. H., Modern languages at Oxford, 1724–1929. Lond., 1929, 8°. 151 pp.
S. Ed. 32 h*

2830. FOLIGNO, C., The school of modern languages. (Oxf. mag., 1930, vol. 48, p. 705–08.)
Per. G.A. Oxon 4° 141

2831. ENTWISTLE, W. J., Modern languages. (Oxf. mag., 1935, vol. 54, p. 149, 50.)
Per. G.A. Oxon 4° 141

2832. TIMPSON, G. F., Kings and commoners. (Oxford and modern languages, p. 121–37.) Lond. &c., 1936, 8°.
211 e. 867

Celtic

2833. Committee on Celtic professorship. [Draft of statute establishing the professorship and setting out regulations controlling it.] [Oxf., 1876], s. sh.
G.A. Oxon c. 33 (101)
— [Amended form].
G.A. Oxon c. 33 (102)

French

2834. HALL, H. G., French in the Oxford honour school of modern languages. (Yale Fr. studies, 1959, no. 22, p. 116–21.)
Taylor

German

Taylorian professor of German

2835. Draft statute for the creation of a Taylorian professorship of the German language and literature [and] Draft note to be appended . . Dec. 7. [Oxf.], 1906, 8°. 2 sheets.   Firth b. 36 (43b)

Portuguese

2836. Portuguese studies in Oxford. (Oxf. mag., 1933, vol. 52, p. 221, 22.)
Per. G.A. Oxon 4° 141

Romance languages

Professor of the Romance languages

2837. Professor of the Romance languages. Draft letter and decree. [Oxf.], (1909), 8°. 3 pp.   Firth b. 36 (47)

Russian and Slavonic

2838. Letters addressed to lord Ashley by Henry Hallam . . . and by . . . the chevalier Bunsen . . . on the importance of a Slavonic chair at Oxford. n. pl., (1844), 8°. 4 pp.   G.A. Oxon 8° 234 (7)

2839. HALLAM, H., Reflections on the importance of the Slavonic languages and literature in the present time, with remarks on the establishment of a professor's chair at Oxford [by H. Hallam]. Lond., 1844, 8°. 8 pp.   G.A. Oxon 8° 215b (4)

2840. [Proposal to accept a bequest from William, earl of Ilchester of £1,000 to be used to encourage the study of Slavonic languages, submitted to Convocation, 17th May.] 7th May, 1866. n. pl., 1866, s. sh.
G.A. Oxon c. 81 (160)

2841. To the Delegates of the Common university fund, We the undersigned . . . [asking for some practical recognition of the importance of Russian and Slavonic studies. Oct.] [Oxf., 1889], s. sh.
G.A. Oxon c. 153

FACULTY OF ORIENTAL STUDIES

General

See also 3042, &c., Delegacy for superintending instruction of Civil service of India.
See also 3128.5. Oriental institute.

2842. ROLLESTON, G., The statutes proposed for the establishment of two teacherships of Persian and of Indian languages, and of two readerships in Indian history and Indian law [observations]. [Oxf., 1877], 8°. 20 pp.   G.A. Oxon 8° 199 (23)

2843. [*Begin.*] The letter of mr. Godley ... [An answer to the Secretary of State for India expressing thanks for an offer of financial support; giving details of the Faculty of Oriental languages and offering to continue to devote £500 per annum if the Secretary will grant the same amount.] [Oxf.], (1890), s. sh.   G.A. Oxon c. 25 (7)

Arabic

Laudian professor of Arabic

See 8368–70 [Payment of Laudian professor of Arabic. 1888].

Chinese

Professor of Chinese

2844. Committee on professorship of Chinese language and literature. [Recommendations to Council.] [Oxf., 1876], s. sh.
G.A. Oxon c. 30 (99)
— [Draft of statute.]   G.A. Oxon c. 30 (100)

2845. LEGGE, J., Inaugural lecture, on the constituting of a Chinese chair, delivered Oct. 27, 1876. Oxf. &c., 1876, 8°. 27 pp.
G.A. Oxon 8° 199 (14)

Egyptian

2846. BLACKMAN, A. M., Honour school of oriental studies: Egyptian. (Oxf. mag., 1930, vol. 49, p. 120–22.)   Per. G.A. Oxon 4° 141

Hebrew

Regius professor of Hebrew

2846.5. The Regius professorship of Hebrew. [Proposed severance from the canonry at Christ Church.] (Oxf. mag., 1959, vol. 78, p. 73, 74.)
Per. G.A. Oxon 4° 141

Hindi and Urdu

2847. DEWHURST, R. P., The honour school of Oriental languages: Urdu and Hindi. (Oxf. mag., 1930, vol. 49, p. 195–99.)
Per. G.A. Oxon 4° 141

Hindustani

See 992 [Proposed lectures on the Hindustani language. 1855].

Teachership of Hindustani

2848. MÜLLER, M., Letter to the ... vice-chancellor on the expediency of founding a professorship of Hindustani. n. pl., (1859), 4°. 4 pp.
G.A. Oxon c. 75 (6)

Persian

2849. HASTINGS, W., A proposal for establishing a professorship of the
Persian language in the University of Oxford [by W. Hastings?].
n. pl., [1768?], 8°. 15 pp.   8° Z 459 Th

Sanskrit

2850. THOMAS, F. W., Sanskrit [signed F. W. T.]. (Oxf. mag., 1930, vol. 49,
p. 159–63.)   Per. G.A. Oxon 4° 141

Boden professor of Sanskrit

2851. Dec. 6, 1830. The following regulations for the establishment of the
Boden professorship and scholarships in Sanscrit literature have been
recently confirmed by a decree in the high court of Chancery. [Oxf.],
(1830), fol. 6 pp.   G.A. Oxon c. 46 (109)

2852. Boden professorship. [Observations made in June 1820 by mr.
Haughton.] Lond., [1832], 4°. 3 pp.   G.A. Oxon b. 22

2853. [Letter from the bishop of Calcutta and a Memorandum respecting
Sanskrit literature in England, by H. H. Wilson, circulated by 'A member of Convocation' in connection with the candidature of H. H.
Wilson for the Boden professorship of Sanskrit.] (Oxf.), [1832], fol.
4 pp.   G.A. Oxon b. 111 (261)

2854. [3 letters, by J. H. Alt and F. Holmes discrediting H. Wilson's candidature for the Boden professorship of Sanskrit on the grounds of
irreligion and immorality.] (Oxf.), [1832], s. sh. G.A. Oxon b. 111 (256)

2855. Sanskrit professorship. Mr. Belfour's memorial and testimonials,
Mar. 9, 1832. (Oxf.), 1832, fol. 4 pp.   G.A. Oxon b. 111 (257, 58)

2856. Sanscrit professorship . . . Mr. Wilson's memorial to Convocation.
(Oxf.), [1832], fol. 3 pp.   G.A. Oxon b. 111 (259)

2857. [Begin.] The following decree [Feb. 13] respecting the foundation of
the late colonel Boden is printed for the information of members of the
University. [With the revised scheme regulating the Boden professorship and the Boden Sanskrit scholarships, dated Feb. 13, 1860.] Apr. 5.
[Oxf.], (1860), 8°. 7 pp.   G.A. Oxon c. 76 (97)

2858. PLUMPTRE, F. C., and MEDD, P. G., Boden Sanskrit professorship.
[Defending Monier Williams against the allegation that he 'cannot read
a Sanskrit MS.'.] [Oxf.], 1860, s. sh.   G.A. Oxon c. 76 (346)

2859. Boden professorship of Sanskrit. [Extract from a letter of Sidney
Owen, disclaiming all connection with the cause of Monier Williams.]
(Oxf.), [1860], s. sh.   G.A. Oxon c. 76 (351)

2860. ELLIS, R., Boden Sanskrit professorship. [A paper in answer to no.
2858.] (Oxf.), [1860], s. sh.   G.A. Oxon c. 76 (352)

2861. Boden Sanskrit professorship [signed M.A.]. Oxf., [1860], s. sh.
                                          G.A. Oxon c. 76 (353)
— [Another ed., dated Nov. 30, 1860.]   G.A. Oxon c. 76 (354)

2862. Boden Sanskrit professorship. Dec. 1, 1860. [A paper, signed D.D.,
   answering that of M.A.] [Oxf.], 1860, s. sh.   G.A. Oxon c. 76 (355)

FACULTY OF PHYSICAL SCIENCES

General

2863. POWELL, B., The present state and future prospects of mathematical
   and physical studies in the University of Oxford considered in a public
   lecture. Oxf., 1832, 8°. 45 pp.   32. 809

2864. WALKER, R., A few words in favour of professor Powell and the
   sciences . . . by Philomath. Oxoniensis [R. Walker]. Oxf., 1832, 8°.
   24+1 pp.   G. Pamph. 2832 (11)

2864.1. A short criticism of a lecture published by the Savilian professor of
   geometry [B. Powell]. By a master of arts. Oxf., 1832, 8°. 28 pp. 32. 661

   See 1999 [Examination system to include physical and mathematical science.
   1833].

2865. Mr. Falconer Madan on the past history of science at Oxford. (Oxf.
   mag., 1893, vol. 12, p. 111, 12.)   Per. G.A. Oxon 4° 141

2866. Faculty of natural science. [Historical accounts.]
      Honour school of natural science [by G. C. Bourne].
      The University museum [by G. C. Bourne].
      Chemistry [by W. Odling].
      Geology and palaeontology [by W. J. Sollas].
      The Hope department of zoology [by E. B. Poulton].
      Department of physiology [by F. Gotch].
      Zoology and comparative anatomy [by W. Weldon].
      Physics [by R. B. Clifton].
   [Oxf., 1900], fol. 5 pp.   G.A. Oxon b. 41

2867. PERRY, J., Oxford university and science. (Nature, 1903, vol. 69,
   p. 207–14.)   Per. 1996 d. 596

2868. GOTCH, F., Two Oxford physiologists: Richard Lower, 1631 to 1691,
   John Mayow, 1643 to 1679. Oxf., 1908, 8°. 40 pp.   166 e. 25

2869. GUNTHER, R. T., Early science in Oxford. 14 vols. Oxf., 1923–45, 8°.
                                                      Radcl.
— [Another issue of vol. 1, 2.] (Oxf. hist. soc., vol. 77, 78.)
                                          G.A. Oxon 8° 360 = R.

2870. Physical science. (Oxf. mag., 1930, vol. 48, p. 886–89.)
                                          Per. G.A. Oxon 4° 141

2871. GUNTHER, R. T., Oxford and the history of science, inaugural
   lecture. Lond., 1934, 8°. 49 pp.   1991 d. 156 (1)

2872. GETTING, I. A., Opportunities for research in the physical sciences at Oxford. (Amer. Oxon., 1937, vol. 24, p. 21–24.)
Per. G.A. Oxon 8° 889

2873. TAYLOR, F. SHERWOOD, The teaching of science at Oxford in the nineteenth century. (Annals of science, 1952, vol. 8, p. 82–112.) Radcl.
— [Offpr.]   26223 d. 41 (12)

2874. DICK, W. E., Science in Oxford. (Discovery, 1954, vol. 15, p. 366–70.)   Per. 1996 d. 576

2875. CROMBIE, A. C., Oxford's contribution to the origins of modern science, a paper. Oxf., 1954, 8°.   Radcl.

2876. CHARLTON, M., The scientists at Oxford. (Twentieth century, 1955, vol. 157, p. 585–92.)   Per. 3977 d. 66

2876.3. BREWER, F. M., Science at Oxford since 1945. (Oxford, 1958, vol. 16, p. 49–64.)   Per. G.A. Oxon 8° 1141

2876.4. WILLIAMS, R. J. P., The organisation of a science department. (Oxf. mag., 1961, N.S., vol. 1, p. 334, 35.)   Per. G.A. Oxon 4° 141

2876.5. HOLFORD, SIR W., Future requirements of the Oxford science departments. (Town planning review, 1963, vol. 34, p. 97–118.)
Per. 2479115 d. 4 = G.

2876.51. WILLIAMS, R. J. P., The science area. (Oxf. mag., 1963, N.S., vol. 3, p. 148, 49.)   Per. G.A. Oxon 4° 141

See also 4098 [Alembic club].
See also 4114 [Daubeny club].
See also 4266 [Scientific club].
See also 4273 [Twentieth century club].

Engineering

See also 3083, &c., Department of Engineering Science.

2877. Letter of appeal to the delegates of the Common university fund, and to the colleges, for assistance in starting a professorship of scientific engineering [signed for the Hebdomadal council]. [Oxf., 1906?], 8°.
3 pp.   Firth b. 36 (59b)

2878. JENKIN, C. F., Engineering science, an inaugural lecture. Oxf., 1908, 8°. 22 pp.   2625 d. 55 (10)

2879. Engineering science. [Booklet.] Oxf., 1909, 8°. 8 pp.
2626 e. 401 (18)

2879.3. HOLDER, D., Engineering science at Oxford. (Oxf. mag., 1962, N.S., vol. 3, p. 68, 69.)   Per. G.A. Oxon 4° 141

2879.4. HOLDER, D. W., Engineering science at Oxford. (Oxford, 1964, vol. 19, p. 70–76.)   Per. G.A. Oxon 8° 1141
— Repr. (Amer. Oxon., 1964, vol. 51, p. 124–27.)
Per. G.A. Oxon 8° 889

Mathematics

2880. An essay on the usefulness of mathematical learning, a letter [by J. Keill? Sometimes ascr. to J. Arbuthnot]. Oxf., 1701, 8°. 57 pp.
G. Pamph. 2831 (8)
— 2nd ed. 1721. 37 pp.   G.A. Oxon 8° 59 (19)
— 3rd ed. Lond., 1745, 8°. 37 pp.   G. Pamph. 2831 (9)

2881. [*Begin.*] I am at a loss . . . [Statement, signed S. Love, refuting a charge of negligence in office made against him by mr. Cochrane in connection with S. Love's mathematical lectures.] [Oxf.], (1772), s. sh.
Gough Oxf. 90 (10)

See 1990, 1991 [Examination statute: mathematics. 1830].

2882. Considerations respecting the most effectual means of encouraging mathematics in Oxford. Oxf., 1830, 8°. 16 pp.   G.A. Oxon c. 46 (93)

2883.

2884. COOKE, G. L., A few remarks recommending a geometrical course of mathematical studies for the majority of Oxford students . . . Oxf. &c., 1849, 8°. 38 pp.   49. 1986 (7)

2885. PRICE, B., A letter from the Sedleian professor of natural philosophy, to a candidate disappointed in the late mathematical examination. [Attacking the character of the examination.] Oxf., (1855), 4°. 3 pp.
G.A. Oxon b. 28

2886. Correspondence [between F. Ashpitel and B. Price] on the subject of the late second public examination in the mathematical schools. Oxf. &c., [1856], 8°. 22 pp.   G.A. Oxon 8° 73 (2)

2887. ASHPITEL, F., A reply to the second letter of the Sedleian professor [B. Price] on the subject of the recent examination in the final mathematical schools. Oxf., 1856, 8°. 16 pp.   G.A. Oxon 8° 73 (3)

2888. PRICE, B., A rejoinder to the Reply of . . . F. Ashpitel . . . on the subject of the recent examination in the final mathematical schools. Oxf. &c., 1856, 8°. 18 pp.   G.A. Oxon 8° 73 (4)

See 2046 [Resignation of C. L. Dodgson from the office of examiner in mathematics. 1864].

2889. ACLAND, T. D., The discouragement of elementary mathematics in general education at Oxford considered in a letter. Oxf. &c., 1867, 8°. 32 pp.   G.A. Oxon 8° 105 (9)

2890. ACLAND, T. D., General education and special studies, a letter to . . . professor Liddon on a portion of his evidence [which commented on no. 2889] before the Lords' committee on University tests. Oxf. &c., 1871, 8°. 15 pp.   G. Pamph. 2905 (20)

2891. GEORGE, H. B., Mathematical honours; the true relation between Moderations and the Final school. [A letter to the Vice-chancellor.] 9 Feb. 1869. Oxf., 1869, 4°. 4 pp.   G.A. Oxon c. 85 (60)

2892. ELLIOTT, E. B., Honour school of mathematics and physics. [Historical account by E. B. Elliott.] [Oxf., 1900], s. sh.
G.A. Oxon b. 41 (8)

2893. The proposed statute for changing the time of Mathematical moderations. [Arguments against, signed J. W. Russell and 3 others.] [Oxf., 1914], s. sh.   G.A. Oxon c. 309 (23)

2894. HARDY, G. H., Mathematics. (Oxf. mag., 1930, vol. 48, p. 819–21.)
Per. G.A. Oxon 4° 141

See also 4152 [Oxford mathematical society].

Natural science
General

2895. DAUBENY, C., Brief remarks on the correlation of the natural sciences, drawn up with reference to the scheme for the extension and better management of the studies of the University, now in agitation. Oxf., 1848, 8°. 23 pp.   G.A. Oxon 8° 77 (20)

2896. School of natural science. [Details of the syllabus.] n. pl., [1852], 4°. 4 pp.   G.A. Oxon c. 68 (180)

2897. EARWAKER, J. P., Natural science at Oxford. (Nature, 1870/71, vol. 3, p. 170, 71.)   Per. 1996 d. 596

2898. The Oxford scheme of natural science. (Nature, 1872, vol. 6, p. 57, 58.)   Per. 1996 d. 596

2899. Report of the committee [of the Board of studies, natural science school] on examination in practical physiology. n. pl., (1878), 8°. 4 pp.
G.A. Oxon 8° 659 (8*)

2900. [Begin.] My dear Acland, Of course no Christian . . . [Letter from E. B. Pusey on the subjects required in the school of natural science.] May 1. [Oxf.], (1882), 8°. 4 pp.

2901. Statute, and regulations of the Board of the faculty, respecting the honour school of natural science. Mich. term, 1888. [Oxf.], (1888), 8°. 27 pp.   G.A. Oxon 8° 1055 (10)

2902. The vice-chancellor and professor Ray Lankester. [Letters exchanged concerning the removal of the latter from the office of Examiner in the school of natural science.] (Oxf. mag., 1888, vol. 6, p. 153–56, 246, 47.)   Per. G.A. Oxon 4° 141

2903. WELLS, J., Convocation, June 2nd, 1891. [Urging the rejection of grants proposed to be made for natural science.] May 29. [Oxf.], (1891), s. sh.   Firth b. 36 (59f)

2904. The position of science at Oxford. (Nature, 1896, vol. 54, p. 225–28.)
Per. 1996 d. 596

2905. [Correspondence between G. C. Brodrick and E. R. Lankester about the teaching of natural science at Oxford.] (Sat. rev., 1900, vol. 89, p. 331, 394, 459, 527.)   N. 2288 c. 8

See 1515 [General statement of the requirements of the natural science departments. 1919].

2906. Preliminary examination in natural science. Regulations. 1922/24, 23/24. Oxf., 1922, 23, 8°.   Per. 2626 e. 368

2907. General information concerning courses in natural science at Oxford & Cambridge prepared for the use of candidates for admission to the women's colleges. Oxf. &c., 1949, 8°. 12 pp.   26321 e. 35 (9)

Astronomy

2908. FOTHERINGHAM, J. K., Ancient astronomy and chronology. (Oxf. mag., 1930, vol. 49, p. 48–50.)   Per. G.A. Oxon 4° 141

2909. BELLAMY, F. A., A plea for astronomy in Oxford. (Oxf. mag., 1931, vol. 50, p. 126, 27.)   Per. G.A. Oxon 4° 141

2910. Astronomy in Oxford. I. The astrographic star catalogue. II. A solar telescope for the University observatory. (Oxf. mag., 1933, vol. 52, p. 217–20.)   Per. G.A. Oxon 4° 141

SAVILIAN PROFESSOR OF ASTRONOMY

See 6129, 6130 [Arguments as to whether the place of Keeper of the University archives may be held by the Savilian professor. 1657, 58].

2911. The Savilian professorship of astronomy and Balliol college. [Arguments against the proposal to attach one of the Savilian professorships to a fellowship of Balliol. Signed Philo-professor. Feb. 19, 1856.] n. pl., 1856, 4°. 4 pp.   G.A. Oxon c. 72 (67)

2912. The new professorial statute [as it affects the electors to the Sedley and Savilian professorships. Signed A member of Congregation]. Oxf., [1857], s. sh.   G.A. Oxon c. 73 (156)

2913. CHASE, D. P., Balliol college and the Savilian professorship of astronomy. Reasons for declining at present to sanction the arrangement proposed as vote 7 in the statute de quibusdam dotationibus [attaching the professorship to a fellowship of Balliol. Signed D. P. C. Feb. 20, 1856]. Oxf., 1856, s. sh.   G.A. Oxon c. 72 (68)

2914. SMITH, E. C., The Savilian professorships [of geometry, and astronomy: historical account]. (Nature, 1949, vol. 164, p. 899–901.)   Radcl.

Chemistry

See also 3063, &c., Department of Chemistry.

2915. Cursus chymicus Oxonii in schola Chymiæ habendus, in quo medicamenta pleraque in praxi medica usitatiora fideliter parantur. [Oxf.], 170$\frac{5}{6}$, fol. 3 pp.   G.A. Oxon c. 25 (3)

2916. WALL, M., A syllabus of a course of lectures in chemistry, read at the
Museum, Oxford. Oxf., 1782, 8°. 63 pp.   8° C 103 (2) BS.

2917. A syllabus of a course of chemical lectures read at the Museum . . .
in 1794 [by R. Bourne]. [Oxf.], (1794), 8°. 31 pp. G. Pamph. 2832 (7)

2918. KIDD, J., Syllabus of a course of lectures on chemistry [by J. Kidd].
Oxf., 1808, 8°. 22 pp.   G. Pamph. 1505 (7*)

2919. KIDD, J., An answer to a charge against the English universities contained in the supplement to the Edinburgh Encyclopædia [that
chemistry is neglected as a branch of education]. Oxf. &c., 1818, 8°.
42 pp.   8° A 37 (1) Med.

See 1909 [Statistics of subscribers to lectures on chemistry, 1822/3–1838].

2920. DAUBENY, G. C. B., Syllabus of a course of lectures on chemistry
delivered at the Museum [by G. C. B. Daubeny]. 1824. (Oxf., 1824),
8°. 15 pp.   G. Pamph. 527 (5)
— 1826.   G. Pamph. 1513 (5)
— 1827.31.   Radcl.
— 1853.   3974 e. 83 (20)

2921. BRODIE, B. C., Syllabus of a course of lectures on chemistry, to be
delivered in the Museum, 1864 and 1865. B. C. B. [i.e. B. C. Brodie].
[Oxf.], (1864), 8°. 8 pp.   1933 e. 6

See 2928 [Needs of the professor of chemistry. 1866].

2922. THORPE, SIR T. E., Early chemistry in Oxford. (Nature, 1921, vol.
107, p. 113–15.)   Radcl.

2923. HINSHELWOOD, C. N., The school of chemistry [signed C. N. H.].
(Oxf. mag., 1930, vol. 48, p. 743–46.)   Per. G.A. Oxon 4° 141

2924. TURNBULL, G. H., Peter Stahl, the first public teacher of chemistry
at Oxford. (Annals of science, 1953, vol. 9, p. 265–70.)   Radcl.

2924.5. Chemistry in Oxford. (The development of the University laboratories, by E. J. Bowen: The contribution of the college laboratories, by
sir Harold Hartley: Oxford chemistry 1966, by H. M. Powell.)
(Cambr., 1966), 4°. 16 pp.   26321 d. 57

See also 4227 [Oxford university chemical club].

PROFESSOR OF CHEMISTRY [suppressed 1866]

See 2645 [Extract of will of George Aldrich. 1803].

2925. DAUBENY, C., To the members of Convocation. [Statement of
monies received and disbursed by the professor of chemistry and
botany during 1850.] [Oxf.], (1851), s. sh.   G.A. Oxon c. 67 (145a)

Dr. Lee's readers in anatomy, chemistry, and physics

2926. [*Begin.*] Dr. Lee's reader in anatomy proposes to apply a sum of money . . . [particulars of prizes to be given for the promotion of physiological knowledge]. [Oxf.], (1856), s. sh. G.A. Oxon c. 72 (30)

See 7029 [Statute concerning Dr. Lee's Readers. 1903].

Experimental philosophy

2927. [Proposals embodying certain grants of money for the immediate requirements of the Professor of experimental philosophy, to be submitted to Convocation, 16th March.] Mar. 12, 1866. [Oxf.,] 1866, s. sh.
G.A. Oxon c. 81 (91)

2928. [Report from the Museum delegates respecting the requirements of the professors of experimental philosophy and chemistry, to be submitted to Convocation, 20th Nov.] Nov. 12, 1866. [Oxf.], 1866, s. sh.
G.A. Oxon c. 82 (284)

2929. [9 Dec. 1867. Proposal to accept the offer by the Clarendon trustees to apply their fund to the erection of a building contiguous to the New Museum, for the purpose of providing laboratories &c. for the department of Experimental philosophy.] [Oxf.], (1867), fol. 4 pp.
G.A. Oxon c. 83 (332)

DR. LEE'S PROFESSOR OF EXPERIMENTAL PHILOSOPHY

2930. The professorship of experimental philosophy. [Observations, dating from Wadham college, May 27, in favour of the proposed new statute.] Oxf., [1863], s. sh.   G.A. Oxon c. 79 (252)

2931. The professorship of experimental philosophy. [Observations in answer to no. 2930, against the proposed new statute.] [Oxf., 1863], s. sh.   G.A. Oxon c. 79 (253)

2932. Some grounds for voting against the proposed Board of electors for the professorship of experimental philosophy. n. pl., [1863], s. sh.
G.A. Oxon c. 79 (251)

2933. Some reasons [signed A college tutor] for voting for the proposed Board of electors for the professorship of experimental philosophy. May 27, 1863. Oxf., 1863, s. sh.   G.A. Oxon c. 79 (250)

2934. A statement of the duties and emoluments of the professorship of experimental philosophy. n. pl., [1865], s. sh.   G.A. Oxon c. 81 (290)

2935. The Lee's professorship statute. [Arguments in favour, signed G. C. Bourne and 8 others.] [Oxf., 1914], s. sh.   G.A. Oxon c. 309 (22)

2936. The proposed statute relating to Lee's readerships and professorships [arguments against, signed A. E. H. Love, R. B. Clifton, J. S. E. Townsend]. [Oxf., 1914], s. sh.   G.A. Oxon c. 309 (21)

Geology

2937. STRICKLAND, H. E., On geology in relation to the studies of the University. Oxf., 1852, 8°. 31 pp.   G.A. Oxon 4° 370 (1)
— [Another issue.]   26321 e. 35 (8)

See 2941 [Lankester, E. R., Appeal on behalf of geology. 1892].

2938. SOLLAS, W. J., The influence of Oxford on the history of geology. (Science progress, 1898, vol. 7.)
— Repr. 1898, 30 pp.   G.A. Oxon 4° 382

Natural Philosophy

SEDLEIAN PROFESSOR OF NATURAL PHILOSOPHY

See also 2911, &c., Savilian professor of astronomy.

2939. Report of committee [of Queen's college] (mr. Armstrong, mr. Grose) on [the college's contribution to the stipend of the] Sedleian professorship. [Oxf., 1900], 8°. 6 pp.   G.A. Oxon c. 153

Physics

See also 2999, &c., Clarendon laboratory.
See 1037 [Dodgson, C. L., Facts, figures and fancies. 1874].

2940. To the Warden and Fellows of Merton college. [Letter from the vice chancellor asking for a grant from Merton college University purposes fund, for the purpose of fitting and maintaining a temporary Electrical laboratory]. Feb. 19. [Oxf.], 1900, s. sh.   G.A. Oxon c. 281 (f. 17)

FACULTY OF BIOLOGICAL SCIENCES
General

For works on the sciences in general see 2863, &c.

2941. LANKESTER, E. R., An appeal to the governing bodies of the colleges within the University of Oxford [suggesting the provision of scholarships and fellowships to encourage the study of zoology, botany and geology]. (Oxf., 1892), 8°. 8 pp.   G.A. Oxon 8° 900 (13)

2942. FINNEY, D. J., The place of statistical science in biological research. (Oxf. mag., 1948, vol. 66, p. 374–76.)   Per. G.A. Oxon 4° 141

See 2876.5 [Holford, sir W., Future requirements of the Oxford science departments. 1963].

Botany

See also 3053, &c., Department of botany.
See also 5810, &c. Botanic garden.
See 5833 [Report on the requirements of botany in the University, &c. 1875].

2943. RAMSBOTTOM, J., Early botany at Oxford [the work of J. J. Dillenius]. (Nature, 1940, vol. 145, p. 993–96.)   Radcl.

Sherard professor of botany

2944. CHILD, G. W., [*Begin.*] I beg to ask your serious attention ... [Letter detailing conditions, counsels' opinions, etc. as they relate to the Sherardian professorship of botany.] n. pl., (1868), fol. 4 pp.

G.A. Oxon c. 84 (434)

Zoology

Hope professor of zoology

2945. [17 Dec. 1860. To be proposed to fix the University seal in Convocation of 29 Jan., 1861, to the Deed for foundation and endowment of the Hope professorship of zoology.] [Oxf.], (1860), s. sh.

G.A. Oxon c. 76 (363)

FACULTY OF SOCIAL STUDIES

General

See also 3117.05, &c., Department of social and administrative studies.

2946. RITCHIE, D. G., Political science at Oxford. (Annals, Amer. acad. of pol. sci., 1891, vol. 2, p. 85–95.) R.H.

2947. PRICE, L. L., The present position of economic study in Oxford, a letter. [Oxf.], (1902), 4°. 4 pp. G.A. Oxon c. 104 (159)

2948. Wanted! A new school at Oxford. [A 'modern-side Greats, based on philosophy'.] Oxf., 1909, 8°. 8 pp. G.A. Oxon 8° 761 (12)

2949. Degree in civil science. Draft statute [for the proposed degree of Master of Civil science]. [Oxf.], 1915, 8°. 5 pp. G.A. Oxon c. 249 (2)

2950. PENSON, T. H., A plea for greater recognition of economics in Oxford. [Oxf.], (1920), 4°. 3 pp. G.A. Oxon b. 141 (133*a*)

2951. CLARK, G. N., Social studies in Oxford. (Amer. Oxon., 1934, vol. 21, p. 132–36.) Per. G.A. Oxon 8° 889

2952. GORDON, L., Oxford's place in social science research. (Amer. Oxon., 1937, vol. 24, p. 25–28.) Per. G.A. Oxon 8° 889

2953. HALL, R. L., Economics in Oxford [signed R. L. H.]. (Oxf. mag., 1938, vol. 56, p. 315–17.) Per. G.A. Oxon 4° 141

2954. HANCOCK, W. K., Economic history at Oxford, an inaugural lecture. Oxf., 1946, 8°. 19 pp. 2232 e. 17 (15)

2955.

2956. MCCLELLAND, G., Management studies at Oxford. (Oxf. mag., 1964, N.S., vol. 4, p. 366, 67.) Per. G.A. Oxon 4° 141

Barnett House Library

See 3117.1, &c.

Drummond professor of political economy

2957. [April 25, 1825. Proclamation of a Convocation to be held on April 29 in which it is proposed to accept from Henry Drummond an annual endowment of £100 for a professorship in political economy.] [Oxf.], 1825, s. sh.   G.A. Oxon c. 41 (52)

2958. GRIFFITHS, J., The chair of political economy [signed J. G.] n. pl., (1867), s. sh.   G.A. Oxon c. 83 (391)

2959. The professorship of political economy. [A paper signed by J. E. Sewell and 4 others.] Oxf., 1868, s. sh.   G.A. Oxon c. 84 (402)

2960. SMITH, G., The professorship of political economy. n. pl., (1868), fol. 4 pp.   G.A. Oxon c. 84 (408)

2961. ROGERS, J. E. THOROLD, The election to the chair of political economy. n. pl., [1868], fol. 4 pp.   G.A. Oxon c. 84 (418)

2962. WALL, H., The late election. Oxf., 1868, s. sh.   G.A. Oxon c. 84 (420)

Politics, philosophy, and economics

2963. Report of committee [of the Hebdomadal council] on proposed degree in economics. June 10, 1915. [Oxf.], 1915, 8°. [5 pp.].   G.A. Oxon c. 249 (6)

2964. Economic curricula at Oxford and Cambridge. (Econ. journ., 1921, vol. 31, p. 400–06.)   Per. 23211 d. 81 = P.

2965. JOSEPH, H. W. B., Philosophy, politics and economics. (Oxf. mag., 1930, vol. 48, p. 456–59.)   Per. G.A. Oxon 4° 141

2966. MCCALLUM, R. B., Study of politics in Oxford. 1, 2. (Oxf. mag., 1932, vol. 50, p. 360, 61; 390, 91.)   Per. G.A. Oxon 4° 141

2967. TOMLIN, E. W. F., Scrutiny of Modern Greats. (Scrutiny, 1936, vol. 4, p. 344–58.)   Per. 3977 e. 319 = A.

2968. MORRIS, C. R., Reflections on Modern Greats [signed C. R. M.] (Oxf. mag., 1937, vol. 56, p. 118–20.)   Per. G.A. Oxon 4° 141

2969. BRIGGS, A., Cerberus and the sphinx [Honour school of P.P.E.]. (Twentieth century, 1955, vol. 157, p. 577–84.)   Per. 3977 d. 66

2969.5. CLARK, C., The teaching of economics and related subjects. (Oxf. mag., 1962, N.S., vol. 3, p. 83, 84.)   Per. G.A. Oxon 4° 141

2969.6. MUNBY, D. L., A new School in economics. 2 pt. (Oxf. mag., 1963, N.S., vol. 4, p. 79, 80, 94, 95.)   Per. G.A. Oxon 4° 141

FACULTY OF ANTHROPOLOGY AND GEOGRAPHY

Anthropology

See also 3123. Institute of social anthropology.

2970. Report of the committee on the position of anthropology in the University. [Oxf.], (1905), 8°. 4 pp.   Firth b. 36 (197*a*)

2971. BUXTON, L. H. D., The needs of anthropology [signed L. H. D. B.]. (Oxf. mag., 1934, vol. 53, p. 215, 16.)   Per. G.A. Oxon 4° 141

See 4218 [Anthropology at Oxford. 1953].

Geography

See also 3135, &c., School of Geography.

2972. HEYES, J. F., The beginnings of geography in Oxford. From The Oxford Review, Nov. 2, 1887. [Oxf., 1887], s. sh.
                                                  G.A. Oxon b. 138 (f. 9)

2973. BAKER, J. N. L., Geography. (Oxf. mag., 1930, vol. 48, p. 673–76.)
                                                  Per. G.A. Oxon 4° 141

2974. MASON, K., Geography in Oxford [signed K. M.]. (Oxf. mag., 1935, vol. 53, p. 629, 30.)   Per. G.A. Oxon 4° 141

2974.1. BAKER, J. N. L., The history of geography in Oxford, an address to the . . . Geogr. Assoc. at Oxford, April 14th, 1954. (The history of geography, 1963, p. 119–29.)   2003 e. 61

See also 4122 [Herbertson geographical society].

FACULTY OF AGRICULTURE AND FORESTRY

General

See also 3049, &c., Department of Agriculture.
See also 3088, &c., Department of Forestry.

2975. Report of the committee [of the Hebdomadal council] on agricultural education [to be considered by the council]. [Oxf.], 1891, 8°. 11 pp.   G.A. Oxon 8° 620 (11)

2976. SOMERVILLE, W., The place of rural economy in a university curriculum, an inaugural lecture. Oxf., 1907, 8°. 28 pp.
                                                  2625 d. 55 (9)

2977. [*Begin.*] A statute which proposes . . . [Statement signed by S. Ball and five others, in favour of the proposed statute adding Forestry as a subject in the final honour school of natural science. Feb. 28, 1910.] (Oxf.), 1910, s. sh.   G.A. Oxon c. 310 (17)

2978. [*Begin.*] The undersigned hope ... [Arguments against the proposed statute, signed by W. Ramsden and 7 others. 28 Feb., 1910.] [Oxf.], 1910, s. sh.   G.A. Oxon c. 310 (19)

2979. BENSUSAN, S. L., The study of rural economy at Oxford. (Journ., Min. of agric., 1920, vol. 27, p. 272–76.)   Per. 19192 d. 12

2980. WATSON, J. A. SCOTT, The honour school of agriculture [signed J. A. S. W.]. (Oxf. mag., 1937, vol. 55, p. 668, 69.)
     Per. G.A. Oxon 4° 141

2981. TROUP, R. S., Forestry at Oxford. (Oxf. mag., 1939, vol. 57, p. 676–78.)   Per. G.A. Oxon 4° 141

2982. Agricultural economics research in Oxford. (Oxf. mag., 1938, vol. 56, p. 732, 33.)   Per. G.A. Oxon 4° 141

See also 4234 [Oxford university forest club].
See also 4263 [Plough club].

FACULTY OF MUSIC

General

2983. CROTCH, W., Syllabus of a course of lectures on music [by W. Crotch]. [Oxf., *c.* 1800], s. sh.   MS. Top. Oxon d. 22 (73)

2984. MAURICE, P., What shall we do with music? A letter. Lond., 1856, 8°. 24 pp.   G.A. Oxon c. 72 (395)

2985. Report of the Committee on examination for degrees in music. [Proposed alterations, dated Oct. 28.] [Oxf.], 1875, s. sh.
     G.A. Oxon c. 33 (138)

2986. A list of graduates in the Faculty of music [at Oxford, Cambridge, Dublin & Durham] from 1830 to 1876. (Oxf.), [1877], 4°. 8 pp.
     174 e. 42

2987. Music in Oxford. (Musical standard, 1889, vol. 36, p. 382–84.)
     G.A. Oxon 4° 586 (39)

2988. Directions for candidates for degrees in Music [signed J. Stainer]. [Oxf.], (1891), 8°. 7 pp.   G.A. Oxon 8° 620 (35)

2989. WILLIAMS, C. F. ABDY, A short historical account of the degrees in music at Oxford and Cambridge, with a chronological list of graduates in that faculty from 1463. Lond. &c., [1894], 8°. 167 pp.   26327 e. 34

2990. HADOW, W. H., Faculty of arts. Degrees in music [historical account by W. H. Hadow]. [Oxf., 1900], s. sh.   G.A. Oxon b. 41 (7)

2991. Examinations and degrees in music. Regulations for 1901/1902 (from 1903) together with general information. Oxf., 1901, 03, 8°. 26327 e. 6

2992. Convocation and [degrees in] music. [Arguments against the proposed statute, signed R. M. W. Pope, J. Mitchinson.] [Oxf., 1911], s. sh.
     G.A. Oxon c. 310 (64)

2993. STRONG, T. B., The proposed statute for degrees in music [arguments in favour]. 8 May, 1911. [Oxf.], (1911), 8°. 3 pp.
G.A. Oxon c. 310 (65)

2994. ALLEN, SIR H., Music in the universities: Oxford. (Musical news and herald, 1922, vol. 62, p. 574–76.) N. 17402 d. 36

2995. ALLEN, SIR H., Concerning music in Oxford university. (Oxford, 1944, vol. 8, no. 3, p. 23–28.) Per. G.A. Oxon 8° 1141

2996. CARPENTER, N. C., The study of music at the University of Oxford in the Renaissance. (Musical quart., 1955, vol. 41, p. 191–214.)
Per. 17402 d. 170

2996.1. FORD, W. K., The Oxford music school in the late 17th century. (Journ., Amer. musicological soc., 1964, vol. 17, p. 198–203.)

COMMITTEES, DELEGACIES, TEACHING DEPARTMENTS, &C.

See also 5252, &c., Buildings and Institutions.

BOARD OF STUDIES FOR PSYCHOLOGY

2997. FARRELL, B. A., The development of psychological studies at Oxford [signed B. A. F.] (Oxf. mag., 1951, vol. 69, p. 311–12.)
Per. G.A. Oxon 4° 141

BUREAU OF ANIMAL POPULATION

2998. ELTON, C., The work of the Bureau of animal population. (South eastern naturalist and antiq., 1936, vol. 41, p. 89, 90.) Soc. 18853 e. 6

CLARENDON LABORATORY

2999. The offer of the Clarendon trustees [to employ funds at their disposal to erect buildings for the study of physics. Signed R. B. Clifton].
n. pl., (1868), 4°. 4 pp. G.A. Oxon c. 84 (6)

See 6119 [Claims of the Taylor institution on the funds of the Clarendon trustees. 1868].

3000. DODGSON, C. L., The offer of the Clarendon trustees. [A satire of various arguments in favour of a building for mathematical studies.] [Oxf.], (1868), s. sh. [Also pr. in no. 1037.] G.A. Oxon b. 32 (24)

3001. CLIFTON, R. B., Proposed extension of the Clarendon laboratory. [Oxf.], (1887), 8°. 4 pp. G.A. Oxon b. 139 (89)

3002. CLIFTON, R. B., The proposed additions to the Clarendon laboratory. n. pl., [1887], 8°. 7 pp. G.A. Oxon 8° 420

3003. KEELEY, T. C., Physics in Oxford during the war. The Clarendon laboratory. I. Radar [signed T. C. K.]. (Oxf. mag., 1946, vol. 64, p. 289-91.)   Per. G.A. Oxon 4° 141

3004. SIMON, F. E., Physics in Oxford during the war. The Clarendon laboratory. II. Atomic energy [signed F. E. S.]. (Oxf. mag., 1946, vol. 64, p. 353, 54.)   Per. G.A. Oxon 4° 141

3004.3. WILKS, J., The Clarendon laboratory: physics in Oxford. (Oxford, 1961, vol. 17, p. 58-74.)   Per. G.A. Oxon 8° 1141

3004.4. BLEANEY, B., Financing the Clarendon laboratory. (Oxf. mag., 1964, N.S., vol. 4, p. 314, 15.)   Per. G.A. Oxon 4° 141

COMMITTEE FOR ADVANCED STUDIES

See also 2368, &c., Post-graduate research.

3005. Programme of special studies for the academical year 1904-5 (-07/08). Oxf., 1904-08, 8°.   Per. 2626 e. 243

3006. Facilities for advanced study and research. 1921, 25, 28, 52, 55, 57, 59, 61- . Oxf., 1921- , 8°.   Per. 2626 e. 393

Lists of students under the Committee are printed in the *Oxford University Gazette.*

COMMITTEE FOR APPOINTMENTS

3007. Oxford university appointments committee. [Miscellaneous papers 1893-1927.]   G.A. Oxon 4° 178

3008. Committee for appointments. Annual report. 1916, 20- . [Oxf.], 1917- , 8°.   G.A. Oxon c. 249 (255); Per. G.A. Oxon 4° 178*

3009. Committee for appointments, 1916. Supplementary memorandum and statement of accounts for the information of the Committee. [Oxf.], 1917, 8°. 9+4 pp.   G.A. Oxon c. 249 (270)

3010. KNOX, T. M., The appointments committee [signed T. M. K.]. (Oxf. mag., 1935, vol. 53, p. 504, 05.)   Per. G.A. Oxon 4° 141

3011. HUNT, F. B., and ESCRITT, C. E., Historical notes on the Oxford university appointments committee (1892-1950). [Reprod. from type-writing.] [Oxf., 1950], fol. 20 pp.   2632 c. 17

COMMITTEE FOR THE FINE ARTS

See also 3130, &c., Ruskin school of fine arts.

3012. BURGON, J. W., Some remarks on art, with reference to the studies of the University, in a letter. Oxf., 1846, 8°. 73 pp.   46. 58

3013. TYRWHITT, R. ST. J., Suggestions on the study of art in Oxford, &c. [signed R. St. J. T.]. [Oxf., 1868], 4°. 4 pp.   G.A. Oxon c. 84 (450)

3014. GLEADOWE, R., Oxford university and the fine arts. (Journ., Roy. inst. of Brit. architects, 1928, 3rd ser., vol. 35, p. 636–40, 676–79.)
Per. 17356 d. 27

Slade professor of fine art

3015. For the Hebdomadal council only. Committee on mr. Slade's bequest. . . . Proposed basis of a deed of trust to be made between the University . . . and the executors of the late Felix Slade, esq., for founding a professorship of the fine arts . . . 3 March. [Oxf.], (1869), s. sh.   G.A. Oxon a. 18
— [Revised form of] Proposed basis [&c. For general use]. 8 March. [Oxf.], (1869), s. sh.   G.A. Oxon a. 18

3016. [Proposal in Convocation, 27th May 1869, to accept a trust fund to found a professorship of fine art, offered in pursuance of the will of Felix Slade; together with regulations governing the professorship.] 24 May 1869. [Oxf.], 1869, 4°. 4 pp.   G.A. Oxon c. 85 (218)

3017. Slade professorship of art [proposal for suspension]. (Sat. rev., 1916, vol. 122, p. 78, 111.)   N. 2288 c. 8

DELEGACY FOR MILITARY TRAINING, O.T.C., AND OTHER ARMED ASSOCIATIONS

Delegacy

3018. (Rules and instructions for University candidates for) Commissions in the Army, 1905, 06, 07, 10, 12. Oxf., 1905–12, 8°.
Per. 26324 e. 106

3019. Report. 1906–11, 14. [Oxf.], 1906–14, 8°.   Per. 26324 e. 105

3020. Notice of lectures, etc. 1908–12. [Oxf.], 1908–12, 8°.
Per. 26324 e. 107
— 1913.   G.A. Oxon 8° 900 (7)

Armed associations

3021. [Conditions drawn up by a select committee, for the establishment of an armed association in the University of Oxford.] May 2, 1798. [Oxf.], 1798, 4°. 3 pp.
— Additional regulations. May 5, 1798. [Oxf.], 1798, s. sh.
— Additional regulations. May 11, 1798. [Oxf.], 1798, s. sh.
G.A. Oxon c. 232

3022. University armed association. [Notice.] May 24. [Oxf.], (1798), s. sh.   G.A. Oxon b. 111 (86)

3023. The following statement was this day read in Convocation. Expence of the Military Association . . . [between 1798 and 1802]. [Oxf.], 1804, s. sh.   Don. b. 12 (99b)

3024. University rifle corps. [Notification of the proposed formation of the corps, and appeal for money to purchase arms, etc.] May 24. (Oxf., 1859), s. sh.   G.A. Oxon c. 75 (385)

3025. Oxford university rifle corps. Subscription list. [Oxf., 1859], s. sh.   G.A. Oxon c. 75 (388)

3026. O.U.R.C. [List of senior members of the University who have agreed to pay an annual subscription towards expenses of enrolled members.] May 18, 1862. (Oxf.), 1862, 4°. 2 pp.   G.A. Oxon c. 79 (236)

3027. May 4, 1871. [Résumé of previous contributions and appeal for donations.] [Oxf.], (1871), 4°. 3 pp.   G.A. Oxon c. 92
— June 6th, 1874. [Further appeal.] [Oxf.], (1874), s. sh.
                                                   G.A. Oxon c. 92

3028. To members of the University. [Appeal for new members, with details of certain changes which will be made.] (Oxf.), [1879], s. sh.
                                                   G.A. Oxon c. 92

3029. [Letter from 'A' Company, University Rifle corps asking for recruits, to avoid disbandment. Signed R. Russell, G. R. Scott. March 1889?.] n. pl., [1889?], s. sh.   G.A. Oxon c. 281 (f. 56)

3030. [Notices, Orders for the week, etc. 1879–1908, G.A. Oxon c. 92; 1908–1926, G.A. Oxon c. 121.]

3031. First Oxford university rifle volunteers [afterw.] First Oxford university V.B., Oxfordshire light infantry. (Annual report.) 1882–1907. Oxf., [1883–1908], 8°.   G.A. Oxon 8° 187

3032. First Oxfordshire Oxford University rifle volunteers [afterw.] First Oxford University V.B., Oxfordshire light infantry. Rules. Oxf., 1886, 8°. 19 pp.   G.A. Oxon 8° 1110 (1)
— 1890. 21 pp.   G.A. Oxon 8° 1110 (2)
— 1897. With an appendix. 50 pp.   G.A. Oxon 8° 1110 (3)
— 1900. 45 pp.   G.A. Oxon 8° 611 (31)
— 1903. Rules and instructions. 48 pp.   G.A. Oxon 8° 1002 (2)

3033. ABBOTT, R. L., The muster roll of the 1st (Oxford University) V.B., the Oxfordshire light infantry, from 1859 to 1887. Oxf., 1887, 8°. 108 pp.   G.A. Oxon 8° 447

3034. Memorandum re the proposed formation of a reserve of officers in connection with Oxford university. [Oxf., c. 1908], 4°. 4 pp.
                                                   G.A. Oxon c. 121

3035. Officers' training corps. [Change of name, and details of objects, conditions and curriculum.] 22nd April 1908. n. pl., (1908), s. sh.
                                                   G.A. Oxon c. 121

3036. O.U.V.—O.T.C. [A paper by the commanding officer explaining new regulations, etc.] Oct. 1, 1908. [Oxf.], (1908), 4°. 4 pp.
                                                   G.A. Oxon c. 121

3037. Oxford university officers' training corps. [A paper by the commanding officer, further explaining the new conditions, etc.] Oct. 19, 1908.
[Oxf.], (1908), 4°. 4 pp.   G.A. Oxon c. 121

3038. SHEPPARD, S. T., The first Oxford volunteers. (Blackwood's mag.,
1942, vol. 251, p. 117–23.)   Per. 2705 d. 386

3039. Oxford university officers' training corps. [Booklet.] (Oxf.), [1958],
8°. 11 pp.   G.A. Oxon 8° 1376

3039.2. GUNN, W. S. B., The Officers' training corps. (Oxf. mag., 1960,
vol. 78, p. 271–73.)   Per. G.A. Oxon 4° 141

3040. Oxford university air squadron. Report. 1927/28–1932/33. n. pl.,
1928–33, 4°.   G.A. Oxon 4° 534

DELEGACY FOR SOCIAL TRAINING

See 3117.05, &c., Department of social and administrative studies.

3041.

DELEGACY FOR SUPERINTENDING THE INSTRUCTION
OF CANDIDATES FOR THE INDIAN CIVIL
SERVICE

3042. PUSEY, E. B., Can the instruction necessary for the Indian civil
service students be compressed into two of our academical years?
[Oxf., 1875], s. sh.   G.A. Oxon b. 140 (31)

3043. WILLIAMS, M., Reply by the Boden professor of Sanskrit to dr.
Pusey's question: 'Can the instruction necessary for the Indian civil
service students be compressed into two of our academical years?'
[Oxf.], (1875), s. sh.   G.A. Oxon b. 140 (31)

3044. [Begin.] It appears desirable that the selected candidates for the
Indian civil service . . . [A paper on the proposed change in the time of
residence from 2 years to 3 years, and some suggestions whereby
candidates might proceed to a B.A. degree.] [Oxf.], (1875), s. sh.
                                                    G.A. Oxon c. 33 (115)

3045. Examination for the Civil service of India [signed by H. G. Liddell
and 3 others]. [Oxf.], (1889), fol. 3 pp.   G.A. Oxon b. 140 (87a)

3046. Address from persons engaged in the government or teaching of the
University of Oxford or of its colleges [making some suggestions re-
garding the subjects and scale of marks in the examination for the
Civil service of India]. [Oxf., 1889], fol. 4 pp. G.A. Oxon b. 140 (87b)
— [Another ed.] 7 pp.   G.A. Oxon b. 140 (87c)

3047. [Draft letter dated 21 June, from the Hebdomadal council to the
Secretary of State for India enclosing a Statement relating to the

arrangements made in the University of Oxford for the reception and training of selected candidates for the Indian civil service.] [Oxf.], (1890), 2 sheets.   G.A. Oxon c. 25 (6, 4)
— [Letter and Statement, dated 26 June.]   G.A. Oxon c. 25 (7, 5)

3048. Delegacy for superintending the instruction of selected candidates for the Civil Service of India. Report. 1906–16. n. pl., 1907–17, fol.
G.A. Oxon c. 263

DELEGACY FOR TRAINING OF (PRIMARY, SECONDARY) TEACHERS

See 3065, &c., Department of Education.

DELEGACY OF EXTRA-MURAL STUDIES

See 3177, &c.

DELEGACY OF LOCAL EXAMINATIONS

See 3194, &c., Local examinations.

DELEGATES OF THE SCIENCE AREA

3048.5. First (1964–) annual report. (Oxf. univ. gazette, suppl.) Oxf. 1965– , 8°.   Per. G.A. Oxon c. 86
[The 1st annual report was combined with the 76th annual report of the University Museum.]

DEPARTMENT OF AGRICULTURE

3049. SOMERVILLE, W., University activities. 1. The University farm [Temple farm, administered by the School of rural economy. Signed W. S.] (Oxf. mag., 1920, vol. 38, p. 339, 40.) Per. G.A. Oxon 4° 141

3050. List of periodicals & annual reports held in the library. [Reprod. from typewriting.] [Oxf.], 1952, 8°.   Radcl.
— 4th ed. 1955.   Radcl.

DEPARTMENT OF BIOCHEMISTRY

3051. School of biochemistry. Opening by . . . viscount Cave . . . 21st October, 1927. Oxf., (1927), 4°. 8 pp.   G.A. Oxon 4° 403* (14)

3052. The new School of biochemistry. (Nature, 1927, vol. 120, p. 634, 35.)   Radcl.

DEPARTMENT OF BOTANY

See also 5810, &c., Botanic garden.

3053. DAUBENY, C., [A letter, dated 4 May 1852, to the Board of Heads of houses and proctors detailing the conditions under which the Fielding collection of dried plants is offered to the University, and urging its acceptance.] n. pl., 1852, 4°. 4 pp.　　　　　G.A. Oxon c. 68 (101*a*)
— [Letter dated 8 June 1852 in similar vein.] G.A. Oxon c. 68 (101*b*)
— [June 10, 1852. To be proposed in Convocation of 15 June to accept the Fielding Herbarium.]　　　　　　　　G.A. Oxon c. 68 (102)
— [16 May 1853. Statement of sums proposed to be paid out of the University Chest and by the professor of botany for alterations at the Botanic garden.]　　　　　　　　　　　G.A. Oxon c. 69 (103)

3054. DAUBENY, C., Address . . . May 20, 1853 . . . on the completion of the arrangements for receiving the Fielding Herbarium in the room set apart for it within the Botanic garden. n. pl., [1853], 8°. 15 pp.
G.A. Oxon c. 69 (220)

3055. DRUCE, G. C., An account of the Herbarium of the University of Oxford [by G. C. Druce]. Oxf., 1897, 8°. p. 1–20.　　　191163 e. 3
— Pt. 2, by S. H. Vines and G. C. Druce. Oxf., 1919, 8°. p. 21–55.
191163 e. 3

3056. DRUCE, G. C., The Dillenian herbaria, an account of the Dillenian collections in the Herbarium of the University of Oxford, ed. by S. H. Vines. Oxf., 1907, 8°. cxii+258 pp.　　　　　　191163 e. 27

3057. VINES, S. H., and DRUCE, G. C., An account of the Morisonian herbarium in the possession of the University of Oxford, with . . . the early history of the Physic garden, 1619–1720. Oxf., 1914, 8°. lxviii+350 pp.　　　　　　　　　　　　　　　191163 e. 14

3058. DRUCE, G. C., An addition to Oxford's art treasures. A lucky acquisition by mr. G. Claridge Druce [of 131 sepia botanical sketches by F. Bauer made during the visit to Greece in company with H. Sibthorp. The article mainly written by G. C. Druce]. Repr. from the Oxf. Chronicle. Oxf., 1917, 8°. 7 pp.　　　　G.A. Oxon 8° 900 (30)

3059. DRUCE, G. C., British plants contained in the Du Bois herbarium at Oxford. (Report, Botanical exchange club, 1927, p. 463–93.)　Radcl.
— Repr. 1928.　　　　　　　　　　　　191163 e. 18 (3)

3060. TANSLEY, A. G., The future development and functions of the Oxford Department of botany, an inaugural lecture. Oxf., 1927, 8°. 22 pp.　　　　　　　　　　　　　　26321 d. 21 (4)

3061. Department of botany libr. List of periodicals. Oxf., 1944, 8°. 20 pp.
2590 e. Oxf. 23.1

3062. Catalogue of manuscripts belonging to Oxford university department of botany, deposited in the Bodleian library, referenced MSS. Sherard 1–476. [Reprod. from typewriting.] (Nat. Reg. of Archives.) n. pl., 1958, 4°.　　　　　　　　　　2262 c. 10 = R.

DEPARTMENT OF CHEMISTRY

See 7951.9 [Offer by lord Nuffield to finance the building and equipment of the Physical chemistry laboratory. 1937].

See 3103 [Florey, sir H. W., Penicillin. Account of the work carried out in the School of Pathology and the Dyson Perrins laboratory. 1945].

3063. Lecture theatre for the Organic chemistry department. (Builder, 15 Jan. 1960, p. 104–07.) N. 1863 c. 1

DEPARTMENT OF COMPARATIVE ANATOMY

3064. Anthropometric laboratory, Department of comparative anatomy, University museum. [Objects &c. of the laboratory.] [Oxf., 1908], 4°. 4 pp. G.A. Oxon b. 139 (100a)

DEPARTMENT OF EDUCATION

General

3065. CASE, T., A protest against the proposed statute establishing instruction and examination in the theory, history, and practice of education. (Oxf., 1896), 8°. 7 pp. G.A. Oxon 8° 620 (5)

3066. CASE, T., Questions for members of Convocation regarding the proposed statute for training of teachers, 20 Nov. [Oxf.], (1896), s. sh. G.A. Oxon c. 153

3067. JACKSON, W. W., and WILSON, R. J., The statute for training of teachers. [Arguments in favour, in answer to T. Case.] 23 Nov. [Oxf.], (1896), s. sh. G.A. Oxon c. 153

3068. Training of secondary teachers at Oxford. (Educ. rev., 1904, vol. 28, p. 518 &c.)

3069. Delegacy for training elementary teachers. Prospectus and report. 1906–1907. n. pl., (1906), 8°. 8 pp. G.A. Oxon 8° 900 (9)

3070. Delegacy for the training of secondary teachers. Annual report. 1912. n. pl., 1912, 8°. 6 pp. G.A. Oxon 8° 900 (8)

3071. Delegacy for training of secondary teachers. Memorandum for information of members of Convocation. n. pl., [1912], 8°. 8 pp. G.A. Oxon 8° 900 (8)

3072. HENDY, F. J. R., The universities and the training of teachers, an inaugural lecture. Oxf., 1920, 8°. 28 pp. 2625 d. 55 (8)

See 1394 [Opposition to proposed statute compelling all students reading for a diploma, to matriculate. 1923].

3073. The Department of education. (Oxf. mag., 1937, vol. 56, p. 81–83.) Per. G.A. Oxon 4° 141

3074. JACKS, M. L., The Department of education. (Oxford, 1938, vol. 5, no. 1, p. 62–69.)　　　　　　　　　　Per. G.A. Oxon 8° 1141

3074.5. PETERSON, A. D. C., The future of education at Oxford. (Oxf. mag., 1965, N.S., vol. 5, p. 46, 47.)　　　　Per. G.A. Oxon 4° 141

University day training college

3075. JACKSON, W. W., Proposed statute for establishing a day training college at Oxford. June 6, 1891. [Oxf.], (1891), 4°. 3 pp.
　　　　　　　　　　　　　　　　　　G.A. Oxon b. 138 (f. 53)

3076. Congregation, Tuesday, June 2. Opposition to a proposal to establish in the University 'a day-college for training elementary teachers'. [Oxf., 1891], s. sh.　　　　　　　　　　G.A. Oxon b. 138 (f. 53)
— [Another ed. *entitled*] Congregation, Tuesday, June 9. Proposal to establish in the University 'a day-college for training elementary teachers'. [Arguments against.] [Oxf., 1891], s. sh.
　　　　　　　　　　　　　　　　　　G.A. Oxon b. 138 (f. 53)

3077. Oxford university day training college. Of the Delegacy for the training of teachers. [Oxf., 1892?], s. sh.　　G.A. Oxon b. 138 (f. 54)

3078. Oxford university day training college. [Prospectus, 1892, 1905, 1911?.] [Oxf., 1892–1911?], 8°.　　　　G.A. Oxon b. 138 (f. 53, 54)

3079. [*Begin.*] The Oxford university day training college . . . [Letter, signed R. Carter asking colleges to consider establishing exhibitions for prospective members.] [Oxf., 1898], 4°. 3 pp. G.A. Oxon b. 138 (f. 55)

3080. Oxford university day training college. [Report of H.M. Inspector on his visit in May, 1905.] [Oxf., 1905], 8°. 4 pp.
　　　　　　　　　　　　　　　　　　G.A. Oxon b. 138 (f. 54)

3081. Oxford university day training college. List of members. 1909/10–1911/12. [Oxf., 1909–11], s. sh.　　　G.A. Oxon b. 138 (f. 58)

3082. Oxford university day training college society [*afterw.*] Oxford university elementary training college [sometimes called] The Dominies club. [Miscellaneous papers. 1906–1913.]　　G.A. Oxon 4° 602

DEPARTMENT OF ENGINEERING SCIENCE

3083. Board of Education. Reports for the year 1911–12 from those universities . . . which are in receipt of grant. (Univ. of Oxford, Dept. of engineering, vol. 1, p. 327–32.)　　　Pp. Eng. 1913 vol. 21
— 1912–13, p. 343–49.　　　　　　Pp. Eng. 1914 vol. 26
— 1913–14, p. 404–10.　　　　　　Pp. Eng. 1914/16 vol. 19

3084. The engineering laboratory decree [signed by E. Armstrong and 9 others]. [Oxf., 1912], s. sh.　　　　　　G.A. Oxon c. 153

3085. The proposed new engineering laboratory. [Oxf., 1912], s. sh.
　　　　　　　　　　　　　　　　　　G.A. Oxon c. 153

3086. TOWNSEND, J. S., The proposed engineering laboratory. [Oxf., 1912], s. sh.   G.A. Oxon c. 153

See 6261–65 [The Parks and science. 1912, 13. 5 papers].

DEPARTMENT OF ENTOMOLOGY

3087. The Hope reports, ed. by E. B. Poulton. Vol. 1– . Oxf., 1897– , 8°.
Radcl.

DEPARTMENT OF FORESTRY

3088. Imperial forestry institute. Annual report, 1924/25– . [Oxf.], (1925–), 8°.   Soc. 19182 e. 176

3089. LINDSAY, A. D., The forestry statute and the site [signed A. D. L.]. (Oxf. mag., 1934, vol. 52, p. 398, 99.)   Per. G.A. Oxon 4° 141

3090. TROUP, R. S., The forestry statute. The Department of forestry and the proposed statute. (Oxf. mag., 1934, vol. 52, p. 396–98.)
Per. G.A. Oxon 4° 141

3091. [*Begin.*] In Congregation on February 13th . . . [Objections to the proposed grant of site in the parks to a Government Forestry institute. Signed by E. S. Goodrich and 5 others.] [Oxf., 1934], s. sh.
G.A. Oxon b. 141 (181*b*)

3092. The new Imperial forestry institute. (Oxf. mag., 1950, vol. 69, p. 36–38).   Per. G.A. Oxon 4° 141

3093. CHAMPION, H. G., University of Oxford School of forestry. (Nature, 1955, vol. 176, p. 721.)   Radcl.

3094. Department of forestry libr. List of periodicals and serial publications. Oxf., 1949, 8°. 118 pp.   2590 e. Oxf. 25. 1
— 2nd ed. 2 pt. [Reprod. from typewriting.] Oxf., 1961, fol.
2590 c. Oxf. 25. 1

3095. Library bulletin. Vol. 1, no. 1– . [Reprod. from typewriting.] n. pl., 1951– , fol.   B.M.
[Radcl. Sci. Libr. has vol. 6, no. 3– .]

DEPARTMENT OF HUMAN ANATOMY

3096. Memorandum [signed J. Andrew and 9 others] relating to the proposed grant for the Department of human anatomy. [Oxf., 1891], 8°. 3 pp.   Firth b. 36 (59*e*)

DEPARTMENT OF METALLURGY

3097. Metallurgy laboratory. (Builder, 22 Jan. 1960, p. 166–70.)
N. 1863 c. 1

DEPARTMENT OF PATHOLOGY

3098. GOTCH, F., and THOMSON, A., Memorandum as to pathology. [Oxf., 1899?], 8°. 3 pp.   G.A. Oxon b. 139 (96a)

3099. Oxford pathology endowment fund. [Appeal to the university, signed J. S. Fairbairn and H. French.] [Oxf.], (1906), 4°. 2 sheets.
Firth b. 36 (59d)

3100. Proposed new School of pathology and its site: statement for members of Congregation. [Oxf., 1922], 4°. 3 pp.   G.A. Oxon c. 311 (60)

3101. CROWTHER, C. C., The Oxford school of pathology. (Architects' journ., 1927, vol. 65, p. 415–20.)   N. 1863 c. 12

3102. School of pathology. (Architect, 1928, vol. 119, p. 422–24.)
N. 1731 c. 16

3103. FLOREY, SIR H. W., Penicillin [account of the work carried out at Oxford, mainly in the Sir William Dunn school of pathology and the Dyson Perrins laboratory]. (Oxf. mag., 1945, vol. 64, p. 97, 98.)
Per. G.A. Oxon 4° 141

DEPARTMENT OF PHYSIOLOGY

3104. NICHOLSON, E. B., Reasons for non-placeting the following form of decree in Convocation on June 5 . . . [authorizing the expenditure of £10,000 for the Waynflete professor of physiology. An anti-vivisection pamphlet]. (Oxf., 1883), 4°. 4 pp.   MS. Top. Oxon c. 182 (29)

3105. [Begin.] On June 5 a form of decree was proposed . . . granting £10,000 . . . for the Waynflete professor of physiology . . . [Another attempt to prevent vivisection.] [Oxf., 1883], s. sh.
MS. Top. Oxon c. 182 (75)
— [Revised form.]   MS. Top. Oxon c. 182 (79)
— [Final form.]   MS. Top. Oxon c. 182 (80)

3106. MONRO, S. S., Dr. Burdon Sanderson & vivisection at Oxford. From the London Record. Lond., 1883, s. sh.   1516 e. 9 (8)

3107. A memorial to the Hebdomadal council . . . [asking Council to authorize a decree that buildings etc. provided by the University be not used for vivisection.] [Oxf., 1883], s. sh.
MS. Top. Oxon c. 182 (54)

3108. Copy of the memorial to the Hebdomadal Council presented Nov. 5, 1883, rejected Nov. 19. Copy of paper circulated with the foregoing and some notes to it. [Oxf., 1883], s. sh. MS. Top. Oxon c. 182 (296)

3109. Vivisection in Oxford. [A paper urging members of Convocation to vote against decrees which would establish out of University funds, a centre of vivisection in Oxford.] [Oxf., 1884], 4°. 4 pp.
MS. Top. Oxon c. 182 (294)

3110. FREEMAN, E. A., A speech, made . . . February 5th, 1884, on the vote for the proposed physiological laboratory. (Wells, 1884), 8°. 6 pp.
1516 d. 4 (17)

3111. The physiological laboratory and Oxford medical teaching. [Request for votes in favour of the decree in Convocation of March 10, 1885.] n. pl., [1885], s. sh.   G.A. Oxon 8° 868 (f. 15)

3112. Vivisection in Oxford. [Request for votes against the decree in Convocation of March 10, 1885.] n. pl., [1885], 4°. 3 pp.
MS. Top. Oxon c. 182 (379)

3113. NICHOLSON, E. B., [Letter urging all opponents of vivisection to vote against the decrees of March 10.] [Oxf.], (1885), 8°. 3 pp.
MS. Top. Oxon c. 182 (387)

3114. The proposed grant to the physiological laboratory. [Oxf., 1885], s. sh.   1516 d. 4 (24)

3115. [Paper, signed A resident, against vivisection in the physiological laboratory.] [Oxf., 1885], s. sh.   1516 d. 4 (25)

3116. NICHOLSON, E. B., What the other side are saying. [Oxf.], (1885), s. sh.   MS. Top. Oxon c. 182 (392)

See 2866 [Department of physiology. Historical account. 1900].

3117. New physiology laboratories for Oxford university. (Builder, 12 Mar. 1954, p. 460–68.)   N. 1863 c. 1

DEPARTMENT OF SOCIAL AND ADMINISTRATIVE STUDIES

See also 2946, &c., Faculty of social studies.

3117.05. [Annual report. 1962/3– .] (Oxf. univ. gazette, octavo suppl.)
Per. G.A. Oxon c. 86

Barnett House

3117.1. Barnett House. [Miscellaneous papers. 1913–1919.]
G.A. Oxon b. 145

3117.2. Barnett House. [Account of foundation, aims and appeal for funds.] n. pl., [1915?], 8°. 4 pp.   O.P.L.

3117.3. Barnett House: the Delegacy for social training. (Oxf. mag., 1956, vol. 74, p. 249–52.)   Per. G.A. Oxon 4° 141

DEPARTMENT OF ZOOLOGY

See 2866 [Hope department of zoology. Historical account. 1900].

3117.8. To members of Congregation . . . Resolution on allocation of site for a zoology building. [Open letter, reproduced from typewriting and signed J. R. Baker, W. Holmes, N. Tinbergen, urging the needs of zoology.] [Oxf., 1962], 4 sheets.   G.A. Oxon b. 148

DYSON PERRINS LABORATORY

See 3063, &c., Department of Chemistry.

EDWARD GREY INSTITUTE OF FIELD
ORNITHOLOGY

3118. TUCKER, B. W., Ornithology in Oxford. I, II. [signed B. W. T.].
(Oxf. mag., 1939, vol. 57, p. 304–06; 341–43.) Per. G.A. Oxon 4° 141

3119. NORWOOD, SIR C., The Edward Grey institute of field ornithology.
(Oxford, 1939, vol. 6, no. 1, p. 52–57.)   Per. G.A. Oxon 8° 1141

IMPERIAL FORESTRY INSTITUTE

See 3088, &c., Department of Forestry.

INSTITUTE FOR RESEARCH IN AGRICULTURAL
ECONOMICS

3120. The work of the Agricultural economics research institute. 2nd
issue. Lond., 1926, 8°. 50 pp.   19192 e. 214 (9)

INSTITUTE OF EXPERIMENTAL PSYCHOLOGY

3121. STEPHENSON, W., The Institute of experimental psychology. (Oxf.
mag., 1938, vol. 56, p. 607–09.)   Per. G.A. Oxon 4° 141

3122. OLDFIELD, F. C., The Institute of experimental psychology. (Oxf.
mag., 1958, vol. 76, p. 268–70.)   Per. G.A. Oxon 4° 141

INSTITUTE OF SOCIAL ANTHROPOLOGY

3123. PRITCHARD, E. E. EVANS-, The Institute of social anthropology.
[signed E. E. E.-P.]. (Oxf. mag., 1951, vol. 69, p. 354–60.)
Per. G.A. Oxon 4° 141

INSTITUTE OF (ECONOMICS AND) STATISTICS

3124. MARSCHAK, J., The Institute of statistics [signed J. M.]. (Oxf. mag.,
1936, vol. 53, p. 215, 16.)   Per. G.A. Oxon 4° 141

3125. First(–) annual report, 1935/36 (–). [The first report is reprod.
from typewriting.] [Oxf.], 1936– , fol. & 8°.   Per. 247256 d. 27
[Also publ. in the Oxford University gazette.]

See 5779 [New group for Oxford, including the Institute of statistics. 1960].

MAISON FRANÇAISE

3126. [Exhibition catalogues &c. 1949- .]   G.A. Oxon 8° 1342

3127. Maison française. La bibliothèque [guide]. Oxf., 1956, 8°. 19 pp.
2590 e. Oxf. 26. 1

3128. Maison française. Bibliothèque: supplément au catalogue. No. 1- .
[Reprod. from typewriting.] Oxf., 1956- , 4°.   2590 d. Oxf. 26. 1

ORIENTAL INSTITUTE

3128.5. DRIVER, G. R., Oriental studies and the Oriental institute. (Oxford,
1961, vol. 17, p. 56–67.)   Per. G.A. Oxon 8° 1141

OXFORD UNIVERSITY APPOINTMENTS COMMITTEE

See 3007, &c., Committee for appointments.

PHYSICAL CHEMISTRY LABORATORY

See 3063, &c., Department of Chemistry.

PHYSIOLOGICAL LABORATORY

See 3104, &c., Department of Physiology.

RESEARCH LABORATORY FOR ARCHAEOLOGY AND THE HISTORY OF ART

3129. HAWKES, C. F. C., Archaeology in Oxford university: two recent
developments [i. The Research laboratory for archaeology and the
history of art. ii. The Diploma in European archaeology]. (Antiquity,
1958, vol. 32, p. 123–26.)   Per. 17573 d. 45 = R.

RUSKIN SCHOOL OF FINE ARTS

See also 3012, &c., Committee for the fine arts.

3130. RUSKIN, J., Catalogue [by J. Ruskin] of the Educational series [of
drawings, arranged in the University galleries for the use of the Ruskin
drawing-school]. (Lond., 1871), 8°. 56 pp.   MS. Top. Oxon e. 153
— [Another ed.] (Lond., 1874), 8°. 53 pp.   G.A. Oxon b. 80 (2)

3131. RUSKIN, J., Instructions in the preliminary exercises arranged for
the lower drawing-school, Oxford. (Lond.), 1873, 4°. 55 pp.
G.A. Oxon b. 80 (4)

3132. RUSKIN, J., Catalogue [by J. Ruskin] of the Reference series, including temporarily the first section of the Standard series [of drawings

arranged in the University galleries for the use of the Ruskin drawing-school]. (Lond.), [1874?], 8°. 32 pp.   G.A. Oxon b. 80 (3)

3133. Catalogue of sketches by Turner lent by the Trustees of the National gallery to the University of Oxford. n. pl., [c. 1890], 8°. 11 pp.
MS. Top. Oxon e. 153 (19)

3134. Catalogue of sketches by Turner lent by the Trustees of the National gallery to the University of Oxford. n. pl., [1891], 8°. 14 pp.
MS. Top. Oxon e. 153 (33)

SCHOOL OF BIOCHEMISTRY

See 3051, &c., Department of Biochemistry.

SCHOOL OF FORESTRY

See 3088, &c., Department of Forestry.

SCHOOL OF GEOGRAPHY

3135. School of geography. Regulations and Examination papers [for the Diploma and certificates in geography and the Geographical scholarship]. 1901–04/5. Oxf., 1901–05, 8°.   2626 e. 346

3136. MACKINDER, H. J., Memorandum from the Reader for the geographical committee [concerning the organization of the School of geography]. May 1905. [Oxf.], (1905), s. sh.   Firth b. 36 (155a)

3137. Memorandum of ways in which the School of geography in the University of Oxford could be helped. [Oxf., 1907], 8°. 3 pp.
Firth b. 36 (152)

3138. Memorandum on the requirements of the School of Geography . . . submitted to the chancellor, November 1907. [Oxf.], (1907), 8°. 8 pp.
Firth b. 36 (149a)

3139. School of geography. Statement for the delegates of the Common university fund. [Oxf., 1908], s. sh.   Firth b. 36 (149b)

3140. DARWIN, L., [A letter, begin.] With reference to your letter . . .[from the president of the Royal geographical society renewing the grant of £400 for a further five years, and making suggestions for the School]. Jan. 1, 1909. [Oxf.], (1909), s. sh.   Firth b. 36 (155d)

3141. Delegates of the Common university fund. To the trustees of the Oxford endowment fund. [Statement, signed E. B. Elliott, secretary, of grants made to the School by the Royal geographical society and others, and a request for assistance from the endowment fund.] Feb. 1, 1909. [Oxf.], (1909), s. sh.   Firth b. 36 (155c)
[The letter from L. Darwin was used as an enclosure with this paper.]

3142. FIRTH, SIR C. H., The Oxford school of geography. (Roy. geogr. soc.) Oxf., 1918, 8°. 24 pp.   G.A. Oxon 8° 1033 (8)

3143. Oxford university school of geography. Aspect. Ed., D. R. Diamond.
No. 1. [Reprod. from typewriting.] (Oxf.), 1955, 4°. Per. 2017 d. 438

3143.1. BASSETT, S., Royal marine, the autobiography of colonel Sam
Bassett. [Pp. 164 et seq. describe the installation etc. of the Inter-
Service Topographical Department in the School of Geography and
the New Bodleian building during the 1939–45 war.] Lond., 1962, 8°.
224 pp.   23141 e. 427

SCHOOL OF RURAL ECONOMY

See 3049, &c., Department of Agriculture.

SIR WILLIAM DUNN SCHOOL OF PATHOLOGY

See 3098, &c., Department of Pathology.

UNIVERSITY DAY TRAINING COLLEGE

See 3075, &c., Department of Education.

EXTENSION

GENERAL

3144. WILKINSON, M., Expenses of undergraduates; a few remarks on a recent suggestion that certain means should be adopted for enabling persons of very limited resources to obtain an academical education. A letter. Lond., 1845, 8°. 7 pp.   G.A. Oxon 8° 250 (7)

3145. EDEN, C. P., University extension, a letter to a country vicar. Oxf., 1846, 8°. 12 pp.   G.A. Oxon 8° 234 (9)

3146. Six letters [signed C.] . . . on the subject of an address [the text of which is reprinted here] presented . . . to the heads of colleges in November 1845 [concerning the addition of new departments to existing colleges, or the foundation of new collegiate bodies, to cater for students unable to afford present university expenses]. Oxf., 1846, 8°. 24 pp.   G.A. Oxon 8° 77 (18)

3147. University extension—college revenues. (Oxf. Protestant mag., 1847, vol. 1, p. 506–13.)   Per. G.A. Oxon 8° 119

    See 2000 [Gordon, O., Considerations on . . . the admission of poor scholars. 1847].

3148. WOOLLCOMBE, E. C., University extension and the poor scholar question, a letter. Oxf. &c., 1848, 8°. 34 pp.   48. 1420 (21)

3149. MARRIOTT, C., University extension and the poor scholar question, a letter to . . . E. Woollcombe. Oxf., 1848, 8°. 14 pp.   48. 1942

3150. MARRIOTT, C., [Begin.] My dear mr. justice Coleridge. You have been for some time . . . [A letter, which is to be circulated, appealing for contributions to found an additional college for the use of poorer students.] [Oxf.], (1849), s. sh.   G.A. Oxon b. 26

3151. SEWELL, W., Suggestions for the extension of the University. Oxf., (1850), 8°. 11 pp.   G.A. Oxon 8° 1148 (14)

    See 1428 [Pusey, E. B., On the proposed vote of £53,100 [which the author would prefer to devote to extension]. 1851].

3152. Recommendations respecting the extension of the University [drawn up by a committee appointed Nov. 19th 1852 by the Tutors' association]. n. pl., [1852], 8°. 27 pp.   G.A. Oxon 8° 1175 (4)
— [Another ed.] 32 pp.   G.A. Oxon 8° 160

3153. MARRIOTT, C., A few words on the statute for new halls, to be proposed to Convocation . . . May 23 [signed C.M.]. [Oxf.], (1854), s. sh.   G.A. Oxon b. 27

3154. CHASE, D. P., Education for frugal men at the University of Oxford. An account of the experiments at St. Mary's and St. Alban's Halls, by

the principals of those halls [D. P. Chase and W. C. Salter]. Oxf. &c.,
1864, 8°. 24 pp.   G.A. Oxon 8° 92 (14)
— 2nd ed. 1865. 30 pp.   G.A. Oxon 8° 90 (8)

3155. DAUBENY, C., A letter . . . on University extension. Oxf. &c., 1865,
8°. 20 pp.   G.A. Oxon c. 81 (456)
— 2nd ed.   G.A. Oxon 8° 90 (2*)

3156. ROGERS, B. B., Oxford university extension. [Oxf.], (1865), s. sh.
                                                   G.A. Oxon c. 80 (455)

3157. RUMSEY, J., University extension. [9 letters by J. Rumsey and others
contributed to various newspapers.] n. pl., (1865), 8°. 20 pp.
                                                   G.A. Oxon 8° 705 (12)

3158. General committee for the extension of the University. Private
Reports of the (1st–6th) sub-committees. [Oxf., 1866], 8°. 56+16+15
pp.   G.A. Oxon 8° 90 (1)
[Later issued for the general public. See no. 3159.]

3159. General committee for the extension of the University. Oxford
university extension. Reports.
    1. On the foundation of a new college or hall. 39 pp.
    2. On adapting existing colleges and halls to the object of University
       extension. 16 pp.
    3. On allowing undergraduates to reside in lodgings through their
       whole time. 16 pp.
    4. On allowing undergraduates to reside in lodgings after keeping
       eight terms in college. 1 page.
    5. On extending University education to persons intended for the
       profession of medicine. [Deferred pending publ. of the other
       sub-committees.]
    6. On the extension of the University by the affiliation of other
       places of a liberal education. 15 pp.
Lond., 1866, 8°.   G.A. Oxon 8° 90

3160. RUMSEY, J., Oxford extension [by J. Rumsey]. Lond., 1866, 8° 7 pp.
— [Another ed.] By J. Rumsey. 1866.   2625 e. 31 (8)
— [Another ed.] Oxf. &c., 1868, 8°. 15 pp.   G.A. Oxon 8° 100 (8)

3161. Oxford and Cambridge universities education. A bill to extend the
benefits of education in the universities of Oxford and Cambridge to
students not belonging to any college or hall. 13 March 1867. [Lond.],
1867, s. sh.   Pp. Eng. 1867 vol. 4

3162. MOORE, E., Frugal education attainable under the existing collegiate
system: with an account of the expenses of the system at St. Edmund
Hall. Oxf. &c., 1867, 8°. 20 pp.   G.A. Oxon 8° 90 (7)
— Revised ed. 1868.   G.A. Oxon 8° 659 (11)

3163. Oxford university extension. (North British review, 1867, vol. 46,
p. 223–41.)   G.A. Oxon 4° 575 (7)

See 1407 [The Hebdomadal council and the Lodging statute. 1867].

3164. Draft of A bill for the extension and improvement of the University of Oxford, and the colleges therein. May 18, 1868. (Lond.), 1868, fol. 12 pp.   G.A. fol. A 135

3165. RIVIERE, W., An address to the committee appointed . . . to consider the subject of University extension and national education. Oxf., (1868), 8°. 7 pp.   G.A. Oxon 8° 135 (7)

See 1410 [Admission of unattached students. 1868].

3166. PERCIVAL, J., The connection of the universities and the great towns. [Suggesting the planting of branches or faculties in provincial towns.] Lond., 1873, 8°. 23 pp.   G.A. Oxon 8° 165 (15)

3167. MAYOR, J. B., Affiliation of local colleges to the universities of Oxford and Cambridge. Lond., 1874, 8°. 29 pp.   G.A. Oxon 8° 199 (6)

3168. The proposed statute on affiliated colleges [signed A senior tutor]. [Oxf.], (1876), 4°. 4 pp.   G.A. Oxon b. 140 (34d)

3169. University extension in England. (Quarterly review, 1891, vol. 172, p. 399–430.)   Per. 3977 e. 191

3170. SADLER, M. E., On the eve of change; suggestions for the future development of university extension teaching. Oxf., 1891, 8°. 11 pp.
                                                           26269 e. 38 (2)

3171. E., M. I., Oxford blue versus drab; some ideas on university extension in general, and on the Oxford summer meetings in particular, by an 'extensioner' [signed M. I. E.]. Oxf. &c., 1892, 8°. 16 pp.
                                                           26269 e. 38 (7)

3172. SAMPSON, E. F., The universities & the educational movement. (Oxf., 1893), 8°. 7 pp.   G.A. Oxon 8° 620 (2)

3173. The University extension journal. Vol. 1–9. Westm., 1895–1904, 4°.
                                                           N. 26269 d. 7

3174. Oxford and working-class education, report of a joint committee of University and working-class representatives on the relation of the University to the higher education of the workpeople. Oxf., 1908, 8°. 174 pp.   G.A. Oxon 8° 753
— 2nd ed. 1909.   O.P.L.
— Repr. 1951.   O.P.L.

3175. RYE, J. B., Oxford and working-class education. Oxf., 1909, 8°. 10 pp.   O.P.L.

See 1811 [A working men's college. 1909].

3176. An Oxford association for the consideration and improvement of national education. (Oxf. mag., 1919, vol. 37, p. 174, 75.)
                                                      Per. G.A. Oxon 4° 141

DELEGACY OF EXTRA-MURAL STUDIES

3177. [Papers, reports etc. published by the Extension delegacy. 1885– .]
26269 d. 25, 25*; c. 6, 7; G.A. Oxon 4° 255

3178. Committee of Delegates of local examinations appointed to carry into operation the university statute for the establishment of lectures and teaching in the large towns of England and Wales [*afterw.*] Delegacy for the extension of teaching beyond the limits of the university [*afterw.*] University extension delegacy [*afterw.*] Delegacy for extra-mural studies. Annual report. 1885/6– . Oxf., 1886– , 8° &c.
Per. 26269 d. 6

3179. Delegacy for extra-mural studies. [Lecturers' syllabuses. 1886– .]
[Oxf. &c., 1886–], 8°. 26269 e. 30, 31, 33, 37, 44; 26269 d. 34

3180. (Programme) summer meeting. 1886–1915. Oxf., 1886–1916, 8°.
[The Bodleian has programmes for 1888–1915: 26269 e. 44; d. 25, 25*.]

3181. University of Oxford. Lectures and teaching in large towns. Instructions and suggestions for the use of the local committees and of others engaged in university extension teaching. Oxf., 1887, 8°. 32 pp.
26269 e. 108
— 2nd ed. 1890: 3rd ed. 1892: 4th ed. 1895.

3182. Oxford university extension lectures. Report of a conference . . . of representatives of the local committees . . . and others interested in the extension of university teaching, Apr. 20, 21, 1887. Oxf., 1887, 8°.
104 pp. 26269 e. 110

3183. University extension lectures. [Information.] 1890–1913/14. Oxf., (1890–1914), 8°.
[The Bodleian set is imperf.: 26269 e. 98.]

3184. The Oxford university extension gazette. Vol. 1–5. Oxf., 1890–95, 4°. Per. G.A. Oxon 4° 124

3185. Oxford university extension. Summer meeting 1901 (–15). Report of proceedings. Oxf., 1901–15, 8°.
[The Bodleian set is imperf.: 26269 e. 72.]

3186. Tutorial classes committee. Appeal on behalf of the tutorial classes of Oxford university. n. pl., [1910], 4°. 3 pp.   G.A. Oxon 4° 276 (8)

3187. Tutorial classes committee. Report on the second year's working to May 31, 1910. 26269 e. 109 (1)
— Report, including accounts on the second year's working to September 30, 1910. 26269 e. 109 (2)
— Report on the working of the summer classes. Oxf., 1910, 12, 8°.
26269 e. 109 (3)

3188. (Report of Committee on applications by Extension delegacy.)
[Oxf.], (1912), 8°. 48 pp.   G.A. Oxon 8° 874 (2)

3189. CASE, T., A financial danger to the University [concerning contributions to the Delegacy for the extension of teaching beyond the University.]. May 30, 1913. [Oxf.], (1913), 8°. 7 pp.
G.A. Oxon c. 310 (123)

3190. CASE, T., A financial danger to the University and the omission of a
Statute from the Statuta Universitatis Oxoniensis affecting a decree to
be proposed on Tuesday, June 3, 1913. June 2, 1913. [Oxf.], (1913),
s. sh.   G.A. Oxon c. 310 (124)

3191. Proposed grant to the Tutorial classes committee [signed T. B.
Strong and 6 others]. June 2, 1913. [Oxf.], (1913), 8°. 4 pp.
G.A. Oxon c. 310 (125)

3192. Delegacy for extra-mural studies. Rewley house papers. 1– . Oxf.,
1927– , 4°.   Per. 26269 d. 30

3193. HODGKIN, T. L., Developments in the Oxford university Delegacy
for extra-mural studies. (Oxford, 1948, vol. 9, no. 3, p. 74–79)
Per. G.A. Oxon 8° 1141

3193.4. JESSUP, F., Education regression and Rewley House. (Oxf. mag.,
1962, N.S., vol. 2, p. 356, 57.)   Per. G.A. Oxon 4° 141

3193.45. Rewley house. (Oxf. mag., 1966, p. 203–06.)
Per. G.A. Oxon 4° 141

NON-COLLEGIATE STUDENTS

See 8260, &c., St. Catherine's Society.

LOCAL EXAMINATIONS

3194. Middle-class education. Proposed West of England examination and
prizes . . . With intr. remarks addressed to members of the universities.
Extr. from Journ., Bath and West of Engl. soc. Lond. &c., 1857, 8°.
50 pp.   26269 e. 38 (17)
— 3rd ed. [*entitled*] Scheme of the West of England examination [&c.]
. . . Together with letters from the vice-chancellors and other members
of the universities . . . Lond. &c., 1857, 8°. 65 pp.   26269 e. 38 (21)

3195. Middle-class education, III. Report on the results of the West of
England examination . . . Together with . . . Documents relating to
Middle-class examinations at the universities. Lond. &c., 1857, 8°. 60
pp.   26269 e. 38 (20)

3196. Report of the Committee on middle class examinations. [*With*]
Appendix of letters and memorials. [Oxf., 1857], 8°. 28 pp.
G.A. Oxon b. 29

3197. TEMPLE, F., [*Begin.*] My dear Master, I hear . . . [Letter to the
master of Pembroke on the expediency of granting the proposed title
Associate in Arts to candidates who are not members of the University.] June 8, 1857. Oxf., (1857), 4°. 4 pp.   G.A. Oxon b. 29

3198. HAWKINS, E., [*Begin.*] Dear mr. Vice-chancellor, I am in a small minority . . . [Letter on the proposed conferring of any title, such as Associate in Arts, on successful examinees from middle-class schools.] June 17. [Oxf.], (1857), s. sh. G.A. Oxon b. 29

3199. Oxford, June 19, 1857. [*Begin.*] Within an hour . . . [Suggested representatives for serving on the Delegacy.] (Oxf., 1857), s. sh.
G.A. Oxon b. 29

3200. The Delegacy of Congregation [for the middle-class examinations]. [Oxf., 1857], s. sh. G.A. Oxon b. 29

3201. The Delegacy for the middle class examinations. 20 June. Oxf., (1857), s. sh. G.A. Oxon b. 29

3202. Oxford, June 20, 1857. Members of Congregation are . . . informed that the following . . . will be voted for as Delegates . . . (Oxf., 1857), s. sh. G.A. Oxon b. 29

3203. The new Delegacy [signed A member of Congregation]. [Oxf., 1857], s. sh. G.A. Oxon b. 29

3204. Regulations for carrying into effect the statute 'concerning the examination of those who are not members of the University' [*afterw.*] Oxford local examinations. Regulations. 1858–1917/18. (Oxf., 1857–1917), 8°. 26269 e. 101

3205. University of Oxford. Under the statute 'De examinatione candidatorum qui non sunt de corpore Universitatis'. First (–53rd) annual report of the Delegacy. Oxf., (1858–1910), 8°. 26269 e. 7

3206. ACLAND, T. D., Some account of the origin and objects of the new Oxford examinations for the title of Associate in Arts, and certificates for 1858. Lond. &c., 1858, 8°. 212 pp. 232 a. 1
— 2nd ed. 227 pp. 232 a. 2

3207. HOWSON, J. S., The co-operation of Oxford and Cambridge in local examinations, and the assimilation of their schemes. (Extr. from Occasional papers on university matters, 3.) (Cambr.), [1859], 8°. 12 pp.
2621 e. 505 (2)

3208. PUSEY, E. B., Grounds of objection to details, at least, of the statute, as now proposed, for Middle class examinations. [Oxf., 1860], 8°. 8 pp.
G.A. Oxon b. 30
— [Another ed. 1860]. G.A. Oxon b. 30

3209. PUSEY, E. B., Vindication of 'Grounds of objection . . . ' against a leading article in the Guardian. Oxf., [1861], 8°. 6 pp.
G.A. Oxon c. 77 (340)

3210. GRIFFITHS, J., The Local examinations statute. [Oxf.], (1863), 8°. 8 pp. G.A. Oxon 8° 208 (7)

3211. Local examination fund [to provide prizes for boys examined in Oxford, an account and Subscription list. Signed W. Ward.]. Oxf. 1863, s. sh. G.A. Oxon c. 79 (288)

3212. GRIFFITHS, J., The Local examinations statute. [Oxf.], (1864), s. sh.
G.A. Oxon c. 80 (181)

3213. GRIFFITHS, J., The subject entitled 'Rudiments of faith and religion' in the local examinations [signed J. G.]. [Oxf.], 1864, s. sh.
G.A. Oxon c. 80 (403)

3214. GRIFFITHS, J., A comparison [between the local examinations for religious knowledge in Oxford and Cambridge]. [Oxf.], (1864), s. sh.
G.A. Oxon c. 80 (406)

3215. PUSEY, E. B., Will the plan of the delegates promote or discourage the study of the Bible, or will the proposed statute discourage essential secular knowledge? [signed E. B. P.]. [Oxf.], [1864], s. sh.
G.A. Oxon c. 80 (407)

3216. PUSEY, E. B., Answer to the objections to the Middle class examination statute, and reasons for its acceptance. [Oxf., 1864], 4°. 7 pp.
G.A. Oxon c. 80 (404)

3217. Prize fund for candidates examined in Oxford at the Local examination. [Oxf.], (1864), s. sh.
G.A. Oxon 8° 208

3218. The Oxford local examinations. Regulations. 1865. Oxf., 1864, 8°.
26269 e. 38 (14)

3219. PUSEY, E. B., For the Hebdomadal council only. [Letter concerning the keeping of the 'rudiments of religion' as an essential part of the Middle-class examinations.] [Oxf. 1864?], 4°. 5 pp.
G.A. Oxon a. 16

3220. Reasons for the extension of the University local examinations to girls. [Oxf., c. 1865], 8°. 4 pp.
G.A. Oxon 8° 208

3221. Proposed admission of girls to University local examinations. [Oxf.], c. 1865], 8°. 3 pp.
G.A. Oxon 8° 208

3222. The Local examinations statute [signed by R. L. Cotton and 6 others]. [4 March?] [Oxf.], [1865], s. sh.
G.A. Oxon c. 81 (412)

3223. GRIFFITHS, J., The Local examinations statute. March 6. [Oxf.], (1865), s. sh.
G.A. Oxon c. 81 (414)

3224. The Local examinations statute [opposing no. 3222]. [Oxf., 1865], s. sh.
G.A. Oxon c. 81 (416)

3225. The Local examination statute. [Remarks advocating its rejection.] March 6. [Oxf., 1865], s. sh.
G.A. Oxon c. 81 (415)

3226. PUSEY, E. B., The Local examination statute, March 6. [Oxf.], (1865), s. sh.
G.A. Oxon c. 81 (411)

3227. For Delegates of local examinations. Proposed examination of teachers. n. pl., (1868), 8°. 4 pp.
26269 e. 27 (1)

3228. Oxford local examinations. Report of the Committee appointed to draw up a memorandum on the practicability of giving . . . senior

candidates a certificate of proficiency . . . accepted in lieu of Responsions. [Oxf.], (1875), s. sh.   G.A. Oxon c. 33 (162)
— [Another ed.]   G.A. Oxon c. 33 (168)

3229. The Oxford and Cambridge local examination record. Vol. 2. Lond.
&c., (1875), 8°.   26269 d. 1

> See 3250 [Proposed instructions for the Committee for the examination of
> women. 1875].
> See 3252 [Annual report on the examination of women above the age of
> eighteen years. 1877–1910].

3230. Delegacy of local examinations. Report of the committee appointed
to carry into operation Stat. tit. VIII 1 §5. 1888/89–91/92. [Oxf.],
(1889–92), fol.   26269 c. 1

3231. Oxford local examinations. Examination for commercial certificates.
1891. [Regulations.] [Oxf.], (1890), 8°. 8 pp.   26269 e. 100

3232. Oxford and Cambridge Schools examination board. Decennial
report. 1914–23, 1924–33. Oxf. &c., [1924, 34], 8°.   2624 e. 89 (6, 13)

Examination papers and division lists

3233. University of Oxford. Under the statute De examinatione candidatorum qui non sunt de corpore Universitatis. Examination papers
and division lists [afterw.] Local examinations. Papers of the examinations (Senior and Junior) [afterw.] Papers of the School certificate
examination (and junior examinations) [afterw.] General certificate of
education, ordinary level papers. 1858– . Oxf., 1858– , 8°.
                                                          Per. 26269 e. 3

3234. Oxford local examinations. Division lists for 1858 (1861, 64–66,
1907). [With] Supplementary tables. Oxf., (1858)–1907, 8°.
                                           2626 d. 2; Per. 26269 e. 96

> See 3251 [Examination papers for women above eighteen years of age. 1877
> 1904].

3235. University of Oxford. Local examinations. Papers set for commercial certificates, 1891 (1892). Oxf., 1891, 92, 8°.   26269 e. 100

> See 3272 [Examination for women. Papers of the higher local examinations.
> 1894–1903].

3236. Oxford and Cambridge School examination board. Papers set . . . for
naval cadetships. July, 1903–39. Oxf. &c., 1903–39, 8°. Per. 26325 e. 22

3237. Oxford higher local examination. Papers. 1904–29. Oxf., 1904–29,
8°.   Per. 26269 e. 85

3238. Oxford higher local examination. [Class lists, tables, and examiners'
reports.] 1905–29. (Oxf., 1905–29), 8°.
[The Bodleian set is imperf.: Per. 26269 e. 71.]

3239. Special reports of the examiners in natural science subjects and in drawing. July 1907. Oxf., 1907, 8°.   Per. 26269 e. 75
— Special reports [&c.] in arithmetic, history and mathematics. July 1908. Oxf., 1908, 8°.   Per. 26269 e. 75

3240. Delegacy of Local examinations. Report of awarding examiners, July, 1916. [Oxf.], (1916), 8°. 4 pp.   G.A. Oxon c. 249 (158)

3241. Oxford higher school certificate examination. Papers. [*afterw.*] General certificate of education, advanced and scholarship level papers. July 1918– . Oxf., 1918– , 8°.   Per. 26269 e. 104*a*

3242. Oxford higher school certificate examination. [List of successful candidates.] 1919, 21, 23–39. (Oxf., 1919–39), 8°.   Per. 26269 e. 81

3243. Oxford and Cambridge Schools examination board. Examination papers. School certificate. [Repr. by subjects.] 1918/27–43/49. Cambr., 1928–50, 8°.   26269 e. 113
— Higher certificate. 1918/27–43/49. Oxf. &c., 1928–50, 8°.
                                                              26269 e. 114

3244. Oxford and Cambridge Schools examination board. Examination papers. General certificate, A. & S. levels. [Repr. by subjects.] 1951/55– . (Oxf.), [1956–], 8°.   Per. 2636 e. 59 = S.

3245. Oxford local examinations. Regulations for the examination for the General certificate of education. 1951/52– . Oxf., 1951– , 8°.
                                                              Per. 2636 d. 20

3246. Oxford and Cambridge Schools examination board. Papers set at O. & A. levels in the General certificate examination. July 1951– . Oxf. &c., 1951– , 8°.   Per. 2624 e. 257

3247. Oxford and Cambridge Schools examination board. Papers set in the General certificate examination for advanced and scholarship levels. July 1951– . Oxf. &c., 1951– , 8°.   Per. 2624 e. 258

3247.5. A fine new building for Local examinations delegacy. (Oxf. mag., 1965, vol. 6, p. 115–19.)   Per. G.A. Oxon 4° 141

ADMISSION OF WOMEN

See 3221 [Proposed admission of girls to Local examinations. 1865].

3248. Ladies' classes. Michaelmas term, 1867. [To be held 'in a room in the Taylor buildings'.] n. pl., (1867), s. sh.   G.A. Oxon c. 83 (413)

3249. Oxford lectures for ladies. [Details &c.] 1874–1903. [Oxf., 1874–1903], 4°.   G.A. Oxon b. 125

3250. Oxford local examinations. For Delegates only. Notice of motion for December 4. [Proposed instructions for the Committee for the examination of women.] [Oxf.], (1875), s. sh.   G.A. Oxon c. 33 (167)

3251. Examination of women over eighteen years of age. Examination papers [*afterw.*] Examination for women. Papers of the examinations.

[Including First examination; Second examination, pass and honours.]
1877–88/89.   2628 e. 16
— Papers of the first examination. 1889–96.   2628 e. 16; 34
— Papers of the second examination. Pass. 1890–96.   2628 e. 16
— Papers of the second examination. Honours. 1890–1904. 2628 e. 35
Oxf., 1877–1904, 8°.

3252. University of Oxford. Delegacy of local examinations. First (–34th)
annual report on the examination of women above the age of eighteen
years. Oxf., 1877–1910, 8°.
[The Bodleian set is imperf.: 2628 e. 1.]

3253. Association for promoting the higher education of women in
Oxford. [Account of foundation meeting, June 22, 1878, with resolu-
tions passed, and appeal for a guarantee fund.] [Oxf., 1878], s. sh.
G.A. Oxon b. 125

3254. Association for promoting the higher education of women in Oxford.
[Report of meeting, Dec. 3, 1878.] [Oxf., 1878], s. sh.
G.A. Oxon b. 125

3255. Association for promoting the higher education of women in Oxford. Proposed rules of the Association. Amended copy. [Oxf., 1878],
s. sh.   G.A. Oxon b. 125
— Rules. [1878].   G.A. Oxon b. 125
— Rules. [1895].   G.A. Oxon b. 125

3256. Association for (promoting) the (higher) education of women in
Oxford. Report. 1879–1920. Oxf., 1879–1920, 8°.   G.A. Oxon 8° 1123

3257. Report of the joint committee appointed to consider the relations of
the halls, and the Association for promoting the education of women in
Oxford. [Oxf., 1882?], 4°. 4 pp.   G.A. Oxon b. 125

3258. SIDGWICK, A., Women's examinations [signed A. S.] (Oxf. mag.,
1882, vol. 2, p. 66, 67.)   Per. G.A. Oxon 4° 141

3259. Committee on the admission of women to honours. [Recommenda-
tions. Nov. 3, 1883.] [Oxf.], 1883, s. sh.   G.A. Oxon c. 34 (iii. 1)

3260. Association for education of women in Oxford. [Appeal for support
for the statute allowing Delegates of Local examinations to use the
University examinations (in Honour Mods. and in 3 final schools)
to examine women. Feb. 1884.] [Oxf., 1884], s. sh.   G.A. Oxon b. 125
— 8 March 1884.   G.A. Oxon b. 125
— 25 April 1884.   G.A. Oxon b. 125

3261. Examinations of women at Oxford. [Oxf., 1884], 4°. 4 pp.
G.A. Oxon b. 140 (53a)

3262. [Begin.] The further progress of the statute for opening four of the
University examinations for honours to women, will be resisted . . .
[Oxf., 1884], 4°. 3 pp.   G.A. Oxon c. 34 (iii. 5)

3263. Women and the Oxford examinations. [Reasons in favour of admitting them to the examinations.] [Oxf., 1884], 8°. 2+3 pp.
　　　　　　　　　　　　　　　　　　　　G.A. Oxon c. 34 (iii. 10)
— [Another ed. without title.]　　　　　　G.A. Oxon c. 34 (iii. 9)

3264. Oxford university examination for women: Regulations. 1886–1915/16. (Oxf., 1885–1915), 8°. [Bodleian set imperf.: 2628 e. 26.]

3265. Education of women in Oxford [signed A. Sidgwick, B. J. Johnson]. (Assoc. for the educ. of women in Oxf.) [Oxf., 1888], 8°. 4 pp.
　　　　　　　　　　　　　　　　　　　　G.A. Oxon b. 125
— [Another ed. c. 1888.]　　　　　　　　　G.A. Oxon b. 125
— [Another ed. 1889.]　　　　　　　　　　G.A. Oxon b. 125

3266. Association for (promoting) the education of women in Oxford. Calendar. 1887/8–1920. [Oxf.], 1888–1920, 8°. (Cal.) G.A. Oxon 8° 647

3267. Women students at Oxford. [Oxf., 1889], s. sh.　G.A. Oxon b. 125
— [Another ed. 1895?]　　　　　　　　　　G.A. Oxon b. 125

3268. [Draft of alterations to Statt. Tit. VIII. sect. 1 § 3 to enable Delegates of local examinations to make arrangements for using the examinations for the degree of B.Med. for the examination of women.] May 30, 1890. [Oxf.], 1890, s. sh.　　　　G.A. Oxon c. 34 (iii. 13)

3269. CASE, T., Objections to the proposed statute for admitting women to the examinations for the degree of Bachelor of medicine. Oxf., (1890), 8°. 12 pp.　　　　　　　　　　　　　　G.A. Oxon 8° 455 (6)

3270. Oxford local examinations. Resolution of the Delegacy . . . March 16, 1893 [that a supplementary list of women who have been successful in University examinations be published, and that all honour examinations for B.A. be opened to women]. March 21, 1893. [Oxf.], 1893, s. sh.　　　　　　　　　　　G.A. Oxon c. 34 (iii. 14)

3271. Association for education of women. [Application for a room in the Clarendon buildings. *With*] Memorandum on the need of an office for the Association . . . May 18, 1893. [Oxf.], 1893, 8°. 3 pp.
　　　　　　　　　　　　　　　　　　　　G.A. Oxon c. 34 (iii. 15)

3272. Oxford university. Examination for women. Papers of the higher local examination [*afterw.*] Oxford higher local examination. Papers of the examination. 1894–1903. Oxf., 1894–1903, 8°.　　　2628 e. 16

3273. Draft statute. Admission of women to pass examinations. Apr. 27, 1894. [Oxf.], 1894, s. sh.　　　　　　G.A. Oxon c. 34 (iii. 16)

3274. University education of women. Petition that a candidate studying for a first in Jurisprudence and fulfilling all University conditions as to residence . . . fees, &c., may be allowed to matriculate as a Non-collegiate student [signed G. Williams, urging the matriculation of his daughter, Ivy Williams]. n. pl., [1895], fol. 3 pp.
　　　　　　　　　　　　　　　　　　　　G.A. Oxon c. 107 (11)

3275. The following report was approved by the Council of the Association for the education of women, March 6, 1895. [Oxf., 1895], 4°. 3 pp.
G.A. Oxon c. 34 (1a)

3276. Association for the education of women. [Announcement of meeting on 4 May 1895 and details of resolutions which will be moved.] [Oxf.], (1895), 8°. 2 leaves.
G.A. Oxon c. 34 (1c)

3277. [Resolutions carried at a meeting on May 4 of the Association for promoting the education of women, seeking to enable women to be admitted to the degree of B.A.; and application to the University for such admission.] May 8 [and] Memorial 1, 2. May 15, 1895. [Oxf.], (1895), s. sh.
G.A. Oxon c. 34 (iii. 18)

3278. Memorial [asking for due recognition for women] presented to the Hebdomadal council, May 13, 1895. (Office of Assoc. for the educ. of women.) [Oxf.], (1895), 4°. 4 pp.
G.A. Oxon c. 34 (1k)

3279. [Begin.] 1. The undersigned members of Congregation . . . [Memorial to the Hebdomadal council, proposing not to open the degree of B.A. to women, but to award a university diploma instead.] [Oxf., 1895], 8°. 3 pp.
G.A. Oxon c. 34 (i. 4b)

3280. GROSE, T. H., Memorandum for the committee of Council. Admission of women to the B.A. degree. June 4, 1895. [Oxf.], 1895, s. sh.
G.A. Oxon c. 34 (iii. 22)

3281. WAKEMAN, H. O., RALEIGH, T., and HASSALL, A., Proposed degree for women. [Objections.] [Oxf., 1895], s. sh. G.A. Oxon c. 34 (iii. 24)

3282. Admission of women to the B.A. degree at Oxford. Report on evidence contained in documents, or in answers to . . . letters collected by miss Rogers. (Assoc. for promoting the educ. of women in Oxford.) Oxf., 1895, 4°. 22 pp.
G.A. Oxon c. 34 (5)

3283. CASE, T., Against Oxford degrees for women. (Fortnightly review, 1895, vol. 64, p. 89–100.)
G.A. Oxon 4° 575 (24a)

3284. Oxford degrees for women. [Correspondence between T. H. Grose and T. Case.] (Fortnightly review, 1895, vol. 64, p. 323, 24.)
G.A. Oxon 4° 575 (24b)

3285. Admission of women to the B.A. degree. [Memorial in favour.] (Assoc. for the educ. of women.) January, 1896. [Oxf.], 1896, 4°. 3 pp.
G.A. Oxon c. 34 (17)

3286. Resolutions drafted by the Committee on memorials on the higher education of women. February 1, 1896. [Oxf.], 1896, s. sh.
G.A. Oxon c. 34 (iii. 29)

3287. The following is the report of the committee appointed by Council on memorials respecting degree of B.A. for women. [Repr. from Oxf. univ. gazette, Feb. 4, 1896.] [Oxf., 1896], 8°. 6 pp.
G.A. Oxon c. 34 (42)

3288. Admission of women to the B.A. degree. Resolutions to be submitted to Congregation on Tuesday, March 3, 1896. [Remarks explanatory of the resolutions which the Hebdomadal council sent on to
Congregation.] Feb. 6, 1896. [Oxf.], 1896, 8°. 4 pp.
G.A. Oxon c. 34 (27)

3289. Resolution carried . . . at a meeting . . . Feb. 5 [that a diploma be
granted to women instead of the degree of B.A.]. 7 Feb., 1896. [Oxf.],
1896, s. sh.   G.A. Oxon c. 34 (29)

3290. MACAN, R. W., Diplomas and degrees for women. Feb. 11, 1896.
Oxf., (1896), 8°. 12 pp.   G.A. Oxon c. 34 (77)

3291. Resolutions to be submitted to Congregation on . . . March 3rd . . .
and reasons in favour of Resolution (5). [Against B.A. degree and in
favour of diploma.] Feb. 11, 1896. [Oxf.], 1896, 4°. 3 pp.
G.A. Oxon c. 34 (33)

3292. SIDGWICK, E. M., Proposed degrees for women. Feb. 12, 1896.
[Cambr.], (1896), 4°. 6 pp.   G.A. Oxon c. 34 (36)
— [Another ed.] [Oxf.], (1896), 4°. 7 pp.   G.A. Oxon c. 34 (122)

3293. BAYNE, T. V., To members of Congregation. [A satire signed
[Γυναικονομος]. 14 Feb. 1896. [Oxf.], 1896, s. sh.
G.A. Oxon c. 34 (35)

3294. [Begin.] We, the undersigned, are opposed to admitting women to
the degree of B.A. . . . Feb. 15, 1896. [Oxf.], 1896, s. sh.
G.A. Oxon c. 34 (41)

3295. Resolutions to be submitted to Congregation on . . . March 3. [Some
proposing the admittance of women to the B.A. degree, some proposing alternatives.] [Feb. 16, 1896.] [Oxf., 1896], 8°. 3 pp.
G.A. Oxon c. 34 (46)

3296. Letter by mr. A. Sidgwick of Corpus, which appeared in the 'Times'
of Feb. 11, in answer to professor Gardner's letter of Jan. 31. [Feb. 16,
1896.] [Oxf., 1896], 4°. 7 pp.   G.A. Oxon c. 34 (48)

3297. The due recognition of women by the University of Oxford. Papers
against resolutions (1), (2), (3), & (4) to be submitted to Congregation
on March 3. February 17, 1896. Oxf., 1896, 8°. 32 pp.
G.A. Oxon c. 34 (53)

3298. Proof. [Begin.] We, the undersigned, are in opposition to resolutions
for conferring upon women the degree of B.A., or any diploma . . .
[Feb. 18]. [Oxf., 1896], s. sh.   G.A. Oxon c. 34 (40b)
— [Corrected version. Feb. 19, 1896.]   G.A. Oxon c. 34 (83)

3299. PELHAM, H. F., The new resolution (No. 5). Reasons for voting
against it. [Feb. 18, 1896.] [Oxf., 1896], 4°. 4 pp. G.A. Oxon c. 34 (71)

3300. GROSE, T. H., Can the University stop, if it grants the B.A. degree to
women? [19 February, 1896]. [Oxf., 1896], 8°. 3 pp.
G.A. Oxon c. 34 (90)

3301. WAKEMAN, H. O., To members of Congregation. Some reasons for voting against resolutions i., ii., iii., and iv., and for resolution v. [20] February, 1896. [Oxf.], (1896), 4°. 4 pp.   G.A. Oxon c. 34 (88)

3302. SIDGWICK, A., Admission of women to the B.A. degree [signed A. S.]. [20 February, 1896.] [Oxf., 1896], 8°. 4 pp.
G.A. Oxon c. 34 (92)

3303. CASE, T., A brief history of the proposal to admit women to degrees at Cambridge in 1887–8, with a preface and a note on residence. February 20, 1896. Oxf., 1896, 8°. 28 pp.   G.A. Oxon c. 34 (97)

3304. ANSON, SIR W. R., A reply to the Camden professor [H. F. Pelham]. [21 Feb. 1896]. [Oxf., 1896], s. sh.   G.A. Oxon c. 34 (94)

3305. GROSE, T. H., Is it proposed to matriculate women? [21 February 1896.] [Oxf., 1896], 4°. 3 pp.   G.A. Oxon c. 34 (95)

3306. CASE, T., 'Is it proposed to matriculate women?' February 22, 1896. [Oxf.], 1896, s. sh.   G.A. Oxon c. 34 (111)

3307. The Epicurean. [A quotation from chapter 1 of the work by Thomas Moore, selected by T. Case to illustrate the distraction women would cause to male members of the University.] [24 Feb. 1896.] [Oxf., 1896], s. sh.   G.A. Oxon c. 34 (115)

3308. PELHAM, H. F., A reply to the Warden of All Souls [sir W. R. Anson] by the Camden professor. Feb. 24, 1896. [Oxf.], (1896), s. sh.
G.A. Oxon c. 34 (121)

3309. MAITLAND, A. C., The due recognition of women by the University of Oxford. [25 February, 1896.] [Oxf., 1896], 8°. 4 pp.
G.A. Oxon c. 34 (117)

3310. DAVIDSON, J. L. STRACHAN-, University degrees for women. [25] February 1896. [Oxf.], (1896), s. sh.   G.A. Oxon c. 34 (120)

3311. BRIGHT, J. FRANCK, What is a diploma? (A few words about Resolution 5.) Feb. 25th, 1896. [Oxf.], (1896), 8°. 3 pp.
G.A. Oxon c. 34 (128)

3312. MACAN, R. W., The value of a certificate for 'the strict course', and the justice of the demand for it. 27 Feb., 1896. Oxf., (1896), 8°. 4 pp.
G.A. Oxon c. 34 (131)

3313. A suggestion [signed M.A.]. [28 Feb., 1896.] [Oxf., 1896], s. sh.
G.A. Oxon c. 34 (133)

3314. GROSE, T. H., Some replies. To mr. Wakeman. (To mr. Armstrong. To mr. Strachan-Davidson.) Feb. 27, 1896. [Oxf.], (1896), 4°. 4 pp.
G.A. Oxon c. 34 (134)

3315. Admission of women to the B.A. degree [by J. B. Baker and A. M. A. H. Rogers. Giving supporters and opponents of the proposal]. Feb. 29, 1896. [Oxf.], 1896, s. sh.   G.A. Oxon c. 34 (137)

3316. PELHAM, H., and GROSE, T. H., The B.A. degree for women. Congregation!... March 3 ... [signed H. P. and T. H. G.]. [Feb. 29, 1896.] [Oxf., 1896], s. sh.   G.A. Oxon c. 34 (143)

3317. ROGERS, A. M. A. H., A reply to mr. Strachan-Davidson. February 29, 1896. [Oxf.], (1896), s. sh.   G.A. Oxon c. 34 (144)

3318. CASE, T., An undelivered speech against Resolution (4). Mr. Macan's papers of February 11 and February 27. February 29, 1896. [Oxf.], (1896), fol. 4 pp.   G.A. Oxon c. 34 (145)
— Corrected ed. March 2, 1896.   G.A. Oxon c. 34 (148)

3319. JOHNSON, A. H., 'The strict course' for women. [February 29, 1896.] [Oxf., 1896], s. sh.   G.A. Oxon c. 34 (147)

3320. GROSE, T. H., Reply to professor Case. Feb. 29, 1896. [Oxf.], (1896), s. sh.   G.A. Oxon c. 34 (151)

3321. MACAN, R. W., A soft answer to the Undelivered speech of professor Case. 1 March 1896. Oxf., (1896), fol. 4 pp.   G.A. Oxon c. 34 (161)

3322. CASE, T., To members of Congregation [signed Aristotle]. March 2, 1896. [Oxf.], 1896, s. sh.   G.A. Oxon c. 34 (150)

3323. The due recognition of women in the University. March 2, 1896. [Oxf.], 1896, s. sh.   G.A. Oxon c. 34 (152)

3324. JOHNSON, A. H., Some replies to miss Maitland and mr. Grose. [March 2, 1896.] [Oxf., 1896], 8°. 3 pp.   G.A. Oxon c. 34 (153)

3325. CASE, T., The real issue of resolution (4). March 2, 1896. [Oxf.], 1896, s. sh.   G.A. Oxon c. 34 (155)

3326. DE PARAVICINI, F., Thoughts [signed X] suggested by an Undelivered speech. March 2, 1896. [Oxf.], (1896), 8°. 3 pp.
                                                       G.A. Oxon c. 34 (157)

3327. ARMSTRONG, E., Anecdota apologetica. [March 2, 1896.] [Oxf., 1896], 4°. 3 pp.   G.A. Oxon c. 34 (159)

3328. B., pseud., Resolution 1 in Congregation. (Oxf. mag., 4 March 1896, p. 233, 34.)   Per. G.A. Oxon 4° 141

3329. The due recognition of women by the University of Oxford ... Signed on behalf of the Committee, W. R. Anson [and 4 others]. March 5, 1896. [Oxf.], 1896, s. sh.   G.A. Oxon c. 34 (170)
— [Another ed.]   G.A. Oxon c. 34 (174)

3330. GARDNER, P., Mixed universities: what is the teaching of experience? March 5, 1896. [Oxf.], (1896), 8°. 4 pp.   G.A. Oxon c. 34 (180)

3331. FIRTH, C. H., A personal explanation [signed A.B.C.]. [6 March 1896.] [Oxf., 1896], 8°. 4 pp.   G.A. Oxon c. 34 (172)

3332. PELHAM, H., and GROSE, T. H., Second notice. The B.A. degree for women [signed H. P. and T. H. G.]. [6 or 7 March 1896.] [Oxf., 1896], s. sh.   G.A. Oxon c. 34 (175)

3333. DODGSON, C. L., Resident women-students. Mar. 7th, 1896. (Oxf., 1896), 8°. 3 pp.   G.A. Oxon c. 34 (176)

3334. PELHAM, H. F., An appeal. [7 March, 1896.] [Oxf., 1896], s. sh.   G.A. Oxon c. 34 (178)

3335. BALL, S., and ROGERS, A. M. A. H., The due recognition of women in the University. Reasons for voting for Resolution 5 [signed Y]. [7 March 1896.] [Oxf., 1896], s. sh.   G.A. Oxon c. 34 (179)

3336. ANSON, W. R., Resolution (2). Diploma versus degree. [7 March 1896.] [Oxf., 1896], s. sh.   G.A. Oxon c. 34 (182)

3337. Printed for the use of members of Congregation ... on March 10 ... [Summary of resolutions &c.] [9 March 1896.] [Oxf., 1896], s. sh.   G.A. Oxon c. 34 (187)

3338. The value of a genuine diploma [signed A member of the council of the Association for the education of women in Oxford; of Lady Margaret hall; of Somerville college; of St. Hugh's hall. Really the work of A. M. A. H. Rogers]. March 9, 1896. [Oxf.], (1896), s. sh.   G.A. Oxon c. 34 (188)

3339. FIRTH, C. H., Resolution II. A grievance and its remedies. [9 March 1896.] [Oxf., 1896], 8°. 4 pp.   G.A. Oxon c. 34 (189)

3340. CASE, T., The inferiority of the undergraduate course proposed by Resolutions (2) & (4) to the freedom of education proposed by Resolution (5) in the case of women [signed An old Liberal]. March 9, 1896. [Oxf.], (1896), fol. 4 pp.   G.A. Oxon c. 34 (191)

3341. FIRTH, C. H., Resolution (5). [A satire, by C. H. Firth, on J. Bellamy, T. Case, and W. R. Anson.] [March 9, 1896.] [Oxf., 1896], s. sh.   G.A. Oxon c. 34 (193)

3342. WELLS, J., The question of residence. [9 March 1896.] [Oxf., 1896], 4°. 3 pp.   G.A. Oxon c. 34 (194)

3343. DE PARAVICINI, F., A noble resolution. [A satire, signed Z, on Resolution 5.] [10 March 1896.] [Oxf., 1896], s. sh.   G.A. Oxon c. 34 (196)

3344. FIRTH, C. H., The due recognition of women by the University of Oxford. [In verse, signed Balliolensis.] [10 March 1896.] [Oxf., 1896], s. sh.   G.A. Oxon c. 34 (197)

3345. B., pseud., Resolutions II–V in Congregation. (Oxf. mag., 11 March 1896, p. 249, 50.)   Per. G.A. Oxon 4° 141

3346. Association for the education of women, Oxford. Certificates. June 1896. [Oxf.], 1896, s. sh.   G.A. Oxon c. 34 (217)

3347. Association for the education of women, Oxford. Regulations for the alternative course. June, 1896. [Oxf.], 1896, s. sh.   G.A. Oxon c. 34 (218)

3348. The Association for promoting the education of women in Oxford. Report, October 1895–October, 1896. Oxf., 1896, 8°. 23 pp.

G.A. Oxon c. 34 (224)

3349. ROGERS, A. M. A. H., The position of women at Oxford and Cambridge . . . paper, 15 October. (Women's emancipation union.) (Lond., 1896), 8°. 8 pp.   G.A. Oxon c. 34 (236a)

3350. GARDNER, P., Women at Oxford and Cambridge [by P. Gardner]. (Quarterly review, 1897, vol. 186, p. 529–51.)   Per. 3977 e. 191

See 1807 [Lord Curzon, Degrees for women, being p. 193–200 of Principles & methods of university reforms. 1909].

3351. Report as to the rules of discipline in force for the women students at the University of Oxford. (Assoc. for the educ. of women in Oxf.) [Oxf.], (1909), 8°. 4 pp.   G.A. Oxon b. 125

3352. Statute on the Delegacy for women students [signed by E. Armstrong and 10 others.] [May 1910.] [Oxf., 1910], s. sh.

G.A. Oxon c. 34 (iii. 35)

3353. CASE, T., Statute on the Delegacy for women students. May 9, 1910. [Oxf.], 1910, s. sh.   G.A. Oxon c. 34 (iii. 34)

3354. JACKSON, W. W., LOCK, W., and MACAN, R. W., The amendments to the proposed statute appointing a delegacy for women students. [May 26, 1910.] [Oxf., 1910], 4°. 3 pp.   G.A. Oxon c. 34 (iii. 36)

3355. The amendments to the statute on the Delegacy for women students [signed by C. B. Heberden and twelve others]. [May 29, 1910.] [Oxf., 1910], s. sh.   G.A. Oxon c. 310 (26)

See 2627 [Oxford and medical training for women. 1916].

3356. Proposed admission of women to membership of the University and to degrees in the University. Case for the opinion of Council [and] Counsel's opinion [signed G. J. Talbot, J. Simon]. (Oxf. univ. gazette, 22 Oct. 1919, vol. 50, p. 107–12.)   Per. G.A. Oxon c. 86

3357. ROGERS, A. M. A. H., The admission of women to membership of the University [by A. M. A. H. Rogers]. (Oxf. mag., Jan. 30, 1920, vol. 38, p. 185.)   Per. G.A. Oxon 4° 141

3358. COURTNEY, MRS. W. L., Oxford and women. (N. Amer. review, 1920, vol. 212, p. 200–09.)   R.H.

3359. Statute on degrees for women. Voting on amendments, Tuesday, March 9. [Memorial, urging members to vote against the amendments, signed by 96 members of Congregation.] [Oxf., 1920], s. sh.

G.A. Oxon c. 34 (iii. 48)

3360. To members of Congregation. [A paper, signed by C. Bailey and 38 others, urging the rejection of a statute 'to limit the number of women students'.] [Oxf., 1927], 8°. 4 pp.   G.A. Oxon c. 314 (24)

3361. To members of Congregation. [Another paper signed C. Bailey and 18 others, opposing the limitation of the number of women students.] [Oxf., 1927], s. sh.   G.A. Oxon c. 314 (25)

3362. To the members of Congregation. [Urging the acceptance of the statute to limit the number of women students. Signed by G. B. Allen and 25 others.] [Oxf.], (1927), 4°. 3 pp.   G.A. Oxon c. 314 (26)

3363. FARNELL, L. R., Statute on limitation of numbers (Women). Congregation, June 14. [A paper in support of the statute.] [Oxf.], (1927), s. sh.
                                   G.A. Oxon c. 314 (28)

3364. WELLS, J., Statute on limitation of numbers (Women). Congregation, June 14. [A paper in support of the statute.] [Oxf.], (1927), s. sh.
                                   G.A. Oxon c. 314 (27)

3365. WELLS, J., Women at Oxford. (Engl. review, 1927, vol. 45, p. 436–44.)   Per. 2705 d. 192

See 962 [Case, T., Letters to The Times, 1884–1922. 1927].

3366. ROGERS, A. M. A. H., Degrees by degrees, the story of the admission of Oxford women students to membership of the University. Oxf., 1938, 8°. xxiii+163 pp.   2628 e. 99

3367. The subjection of women. (Oxf. mag., 1957, vol. 75, p. 250–54.)
                          Per. G.A. Oxon 4° 141

3368. BRITTAIN, V., An Oxford anniversary: women's rights in the University. (Nat. and Engl. review, 1959, vol. 153, p. 115–18.)
                          Per. 22775 d. 14

3369. BRITTAIN, V., The women at Oxford. Lond., 1960, 8°. 272 pp.
                          G.A. Oxon 8° 1401

See also 6433–38, &c., [Colleges. Admissions].
See also 7859.51 [Admission to New college].
See also 8720, &c., [Women's colleges, hall, &c.].

RELIGION

3370. De schismate extinguendo, et vere ecclesiastica libertate adserenda epistolæ aliquot mirum in modum liberæ, et veritatis studio strenuæ ... Huttenus in lucem edit. [Letters from the universities of Oxford, Paris and Prague &c. on the schism between the popes Urban VI and Clement VII written *c.* 1380.] [Madan 36.] n. pl., [1520?], 4°. 84 pp.
4° A 37 Th.

3371. The answere of the vicechancelour, the doctors, both the proctors and other the heads of houses . . . to The humble petition of the ministers of the Church of England, desiring reformation of certaine ceremonies and abuses of the Church. [With the text of The humble petition.] [Madan 231.] Oxf., 1603, 4°. [16]+32 pp. G.A. Oxon 4° 14
— [Another issue.] [Madan 232.]
— [Another issue.] [Madan 233.]   Wood 614 (3)
— [Another issue.] [Madan 234.]   Pamph. C 1 (5)
— [Another issue.] [Madan 235.]   4° A 27 (5) Th. BS.
— [Another ed.] 1604. [Madan 248.]   Wood 516 (1)
— [Another ed., *entitled*] The humble petition of the ministers ... with the answer of the vicechancelor . . . [Madan 980.] n. pl., 1641, 4°. 32 pp.
G. Pamph. 1041 (14)

3372. To the high court of Parliament, The humble petition of all colledges and halls . . . throughout the kingdome of England . . . [in favour of the clergy and churches]. [Madan 977.] [Oxf., 1641], s. sh. Wood 423 (18)

3373. To the high . . . court of Parliament, The humble petition of the University of Oxford, in behalfe of episcopacy and cathedralls. [Madan 981.] Oxf., 1641, 4°. 8 pp.   Wood 514 (2)
— [London reprint.] [Madan 982.]   Pamph. C 41 (26)
— [Another London reprint], s. sh. [Madan 983.]   Wood 514 (3)
— [A Dutch translation, *begin*.] d'Ootmoedige request van d'Vniversiteyt . . . [Madan 984.] [Amst.?], 1641, 4°. 8 pp.
Antiq. e. N. 1641. 1

3374. An answer to the petition sent from the Vniversitie of Oxford to . . . Parliament. [Madan 985.] Lond., 1641, 4°. 12 pp.   Wood 514 (4)

3375. HERBERT, T., A reply in the defence of Oxford petition . . . [verses]. [Madan 986.] Lond., 1641, 4°. 8 pp.   G. Pamph. 2132 (2)

3376. To our reverend brethren the ministers of the Gospel in England and Wales [an appeal for money to help the 'promoting and propagating the Gospel in New England', 'that desolate Wildernesse', signed in the name of the Delegates of the University]. [Madan 2018.] [Lond.], (1649), s. sh.   Wood 423 (29)

3377. Literæ a celeberrimis pastoribus & professoribus ecclesiæ & academiæ Genevensis ad Universitatem Oxoniensem transmissæ: una
cum responso ejusdem Universitatis Oxon. ad easdem literas . . . Feb.
5, 1706 [concerning the suggestion that the Church of Geneva is in
opposition to the Church of England]. Oxon., 1707, fol. 6 pp.

V 1. 1 (16) Jur.

3378. A letter from . . . the Church and University of Geneva to the
University of Oxford; together with the answer of the University of
Oxford. Transl. Oxf., 1707, fol. 4 pp.   4 Δ 260 (6)

3379. Several letters from the pastors of the Church of Geneva to the archbishop of Canterbury, the bishop of London, and the University of
Oxford, with their answers to them. Transl. Lond., 1707, 4°. 12 pp.

G. Pamph. 1781 (22)

3380. Stricturæ breves in Epistolas d.d. Genevensium & Oxoniensium
nuper editas. Lond., 1707, 4°. 29 pp.   4° B 76 Jur.

3381. WELLS, E., Epistola ad authorem anonymum libelli non ita pridem
editi: cui titulus, Stricturæ breves in Epistolas d.d. Genevensium &
Oxoniensium [signed E. Wells]. Oxon., 1708, 4°. 22 pp. 4° B 76 Jur.

3382. SPADEMAN, J., Some brief remarks on the letters of the Geneva and
Oxford universities, lately publish'd. Lond., 1708, 4°. 8 pp.

G.A. Oxon 4° 59

See 3705, &c. [Papers connected with the petition against Roman Catholics.
1812, 28].

3383. To the queen's . . . majesty . . . The humble petition of the undersigned members of Convocation and bachelors of civil law in the
University of Oxford. [Asking that questions touching the doctrine of
the Church of England shall be referred to a provincial synod, and not
to courts appointed by the civil power. *With*] To . . . the archbishop
of Canterbury . . . [Another similar but shorter petition.] n. pl., [1855],
fol. 3 pp.   G.A. Oxon b. 143 (4)

3384. To the . . . Commons . . . The humble petition of the University of
Oxford [against three bills for 'promoting education in England',
deprecating the establishment of free schools, and insisting on the need
for specific instruction in religion]. [Oxf., 1855], s. sh. G.A. Oxon b. 28

3385. Welsh church suspensory bill. We, the undersigned resident graduate
members of the University of Oxford . . . protest strongly against the
bill . . . n. pl., [1893], s. sh.   G.A. Oxon b. 143 (276a)
— [Another ed.], (1893), fol. 3 pp.   G.A. Oxon b. 143 (276b)
— [Another ed.] 8°.   G.A. Oxon b. 143 (276c)

RELIGIOUS INSTRUCTION AND PRACTICE

General

3386. LENTHALL, W., A copy of the speakers letter to the . . . Vniversity
of Oxford, together with the Protestation [to maintain the Protestant

religion] and Declaration with it. [Madan 974.] Oxf., 1642 [41], 4°.
14 pp.   Wood 514 (11)

3387. Protestation returns for the University. (Oxfordshire protestation
returns, 1641–2. Oxfordshire record soc., 1955, vol. 36, p. 100–19.)
Per. G.A. Oxon 4° 767 = R.

3388. At a general meeting of the vice-chancellor, heads of houses and
proctors of the University . . . Dec. 2d, 1728 [recommending tutors to
pay particular attention to instruction in the principles of the established Church]. [Oxf.], 1728, s. sh.   G.A. Oxon b. 111 (39)

3389. KENNICOTT, B., A word to the Hutchinsonians: or Remarks on
three extraordinary sermons lately preached before the University of
Oxford, by dr. Patten, mr. Wetherall and mr. Horne. By a member of
the University [B. Kennicott]. Lond., 1756, 8°. 44 pp.
G. Pamph. 766 (13)

3390. HORNE, G., An apology for certain gentlemen in the University of
Oxford aspersed in a late anonymous pamphlet [*entitled* A word to the
Hutchinsonians]; with a short postscript. Oxf., 1756, 8°. 66 pp.
G. Pamph. 275 (11)
— 2nd ed. Lond., 1799, 8°. 87 pp.   G.A. Oxon 8° 234 (1)
[Further items concerned with the theological content of the sermons,
have been ignored.]

3391. An appeal to the heads of the University of Oxford, by an undergraduate. [Concerns compulsory attendance at the sacrament.] Lond.,
1822, 8°. 16 pp.   G. Pamph. 2905 (10)

3392. HAWKINS, E., A letter to the author of 'An appeal to the heads of the
University of Oxford' upon compulsory attendance at the communion.
By a graduate [E. Hawkins]. Oxf., 1822, 8°. 29 pp.
G.A. Oxon 8° 234 (2)

3393. FRY, C., The listener in Oxford, by the author of 'Christ our example'
[C. Fry]. 2nd ed. Lond., 1840, 8°. 182 pp.   G.A. Oxon 8° 101
— 11th ed. 1856.

3394. An apology for the universities; being an attempt to rescue them
from the imputation of criminal neglect . . . recently cast upon them
in certain publications [Letter to the lord bishop of Lichfield, by
C. Perry &c.] issuing from Cambridge. By Oxoniensis. Oxf., 1841, 8°.
32 pp.   G.A. Oxon 8° 77 (5)

3395. Oxford intrigues—past and present. (Oxf. Protestant mag., 1847,
vol. 1, p. 640–42.)   Per. G. A. Oxon 8° 119

See also 2471, &c., Faculty of Theology, 1854, 1855, 56.

3396. OXONIENSIS, *pseud.*, Oxford in 1857 [religious aspect]. (Christ.
obs., 1857, p. 438–45.)   Per. 971 e. 45

See 1863, 1864 [Seebohm, F., The Oxford reformers of 1498. 1866, 67].

3397. Oxford reminiscences. No. i, ii. (The Ecclesiastic, 1868, vol. 30, p. 218–21, 270–79.) Per. 11126 e. 399

3398. ANSTEY, F., Sundays in Oxford [signed F. A.]. (Sunday at home, 1869, p. 724–29, 774–78, 819–22.) G.A. Oxon 4° 578 (29, 30)

3399. The tutor and his pupil in the University of Oxford [signed A senior member of Convocation. Provoked by a statement in the House of Commons on the University Tests bill, no. 3693]. [Oxf.], (1870), s. sh. G.A. Oxon b. 140 (26c)

3400. PUSEY, E. B., Doctrinal or undoctrinal instruction of the undergraduate members of the University belonging to the Church of England [signed E. B. P.]. [Oxf.], 1871, s. sh. G.A. Oxon b. 140 (89b)

3401. Sundays in Oxford. (Christ. obs., 1871, p. 837–42.) Per. 971 e. 45

3402. Oxford in 1871 [the condition of religious belief]. (Month, 1871, vol. 15, p. 103–19.) Per. 11132 d. 17

3403. Religious thought in Oxford. (Christ. obs., 1873, p. 288–99.) Per. 971 e. 45

3404. INCE, W., Religion in the University of Oxford, a paper. Oxf. &c., 1875, 8°. 16 pp. 100 f. 153 (18)

3405. Spiritual destitution at Oxford, a letter to the bishop of Oxford, an appeal to his lordship to provide facilities for divine worship and instruction in the faith for 2,500 undergraduates. By a fellow of a college. Oxf., 1876, 8°. 22 pp. G.A. Oxon 8ᵘ 405

3406. To the Hebdomadal council, and heads and governing bodies of colleges and halls [suggestions by members of the Oxford clerical association and parochial clergy of Oxford, for improving the provision for religious instruction and services in the different colleges]. n. pl., [1878], 4°. 3 pp. MS. Top. Oxon e. 38 (f. 24b)
— [Another ed.] 4 pp. G.A. Oxon c. 153

3407. INCE, W., The internal duties of the university in prospect of external changes, a sermon. Oxf. &c., 1878, 8°. 19 pp.
100 i. 82 (15)

See 6482 [Wordsworth, J., The Church and the universities. II. Lay teaching of theology. 1880].

3408. Recent fortunes of the Church in Oxford. (Church quarterly review, 1881, vol. 12, p. 201–42.) G.A. Oxon 4° 582 (4)

See 8645 [Religious life in Wadham. 1891].

3409. The Evangelical pastorate for undergraduates at Oxford [afterw.] The Oxford pastorate. Annual report. Oxf., 1894– , 16°. [Reports for 1896, 1926 in the Bodleian. Per. G.A. Oxon 16° 199.]

3410. LEGGE, H., The religion of the undergraduate. A reply from Oxford [to a general article on religion in any university]. (19th cent., 1895, vol. 38, p. 861–69.) Per. 3977 d. 66

3411. Christian Oxford. (Congregationalist, 1899, vol. 8, p. 307–13.)
Per. 11138 e. 20

3412. Religion in Oxford. (Church quarterly, 1902, vol. 55, p. 1–24.)
Per. 1419 e. 402 = S.

3413. HORWILL, H. W., Religious life at Oxford. (Meth. rev., 1904, vol. 64,
p. 69 &c.)   L. of C.

3414. CHARTERIS, S., Religion in Oxford, an interview with the rev. W. H.
Hutton. (Treasury, 1907, vol. 8, p. 526–30.)   G.A. Oxon 4° 575 (39)

3415. MACAN, R. W., Religious changes in Oxford during the last fifty
years, a paper read before the Oxf. soc. for hist. theol. Lond. &c., 1917,
8°. 48 pp.   G.A. Oxon 8° 900 (31)
— Revised and repr. 1918.   G.A. Oxon 8° 611 (30)

3416. BAILEY, C., Religion at the universities [mainly assessing the situa-
tion at Oxford]. A paper read to the Conference of college tutors and
schoolmasters. (Westm.), 1927, 8°. 16 pp.   1419 e. 5295 (3)

3417. THOMSON, G. I. F., The Oxford pastorate, the first half century. 1st
ed. Lond. &c., 1946, 8°. 160 pp.   11126 e. 810

3418. REYNOLDS, J. S., The evangelicals at Oxford, 1735–1871, a record of
an unchronicled movement. (Aularian ser.). Oxf., 1953, 8°. 212 pp.
11125 e. 101

3418.1. REYNOLDS, J. S., The Reformation in Oxford [1510–1560]. (The
Churchman, 1962, vol. 76, p. 216–26.)   Per. 1419 d. 31

3418.2. GREEN, V. H. H., Religion at Oxford and Cambridge. Lond., 1964,
8°. 392 pp.   111 d. 84

General religious societies

See also 3721 [Roman Catholic societies].

Association of graduate members of the University desirous of assisting one another to carry on their work in the University on the
principles of the Church of England. See 3421, 3422. Graduates'
association.

See 8071 [Butler society].

3419. Christian social union. Oxford university branch. [Miscellaneous
papers. 1890–1914.]   G.A. Oxon 4° 596

3420. English Church union. Oxford university branch. [Miscellaneous
papers, 1890–1894.]   G.A. Oxon 4° 595

3421. Graduates' association. [*Formerly*] Association of graduate members
... desirous of assisting one another ... on the principles of the Church
of England [*afterw.*] Tutors' association. [Miscellaneous papers. 1871–
1925.]   G.A. Oxon b. 143 (80–132)

3422. Graduates' association. Conditions regulating the Association. Oxf.,
[1893], 16°. 12 pp.   G.A. Oxon 16° 200 (1)

Inter-collegiate Christian union, Oxford. See 3426–28. Oxford inter-
collegiate Christian union.

See 8822 [Martineau club].

3423. Μαθηταί society. Rules. [Oxf.], 1893, s. sh.   G.A. Oxon b. 147

Mission associates. See 3443. Oxford university missionary union.

See 4139 [Newman society].

3424. Nicene society. [3 notices of meetings, 1924–26.]
                                          G.A. Oxon b. 147 (58)

3425. Origen society. [Miscellaneous papers. 1907–1927.]
                                     G.A. Oxon 4° 603; b. 147 (58)

3426. Oxford inter-collegiate Christian union. [Miscellaneous papers.
1883–1915.]   G.A. Oxon 4° 595

3427. Oxford. Inter-collegiate Christian union. Rules. [Oxf.], (1890), 8°.
4 pp.   G.A. Oxon 4° 595
— 1895.   G.A. Oxon 4° 595

3428. Oxford inter-collegiate Christian union. Annual report and list of
members. 1896/7. [Oxf.], (1897), 8°. 19 pp.   G.A. Oxon 8° 695

3429. Oxford laymen's league for defence of the national church. [Mis-
cellaneous papers. 1886–87.]   G.A. Oxon b. 143 (148–72)

3430. Oxford laymen's league for defence of the national church. Proposals of the provisional committee. n. pl., [1903?], 4°. 7 pp.
                                          G.A. Oxon 4° 186 (14)

3431. Oxford missionary association of graduates. [Miscellaneous papers.
1874–1910.]   G.A. Oxon 4° 540, 595

3432. Oxford missionary association of graduates. Report. 1877–1908.
Oxf., [1878–1909], 4°.   G.A. Oxon 4° 539

3433. (Oxford) Society of historical theology. Abstract of proceedings.
1891/92– . Oxf., (1892–), 8°.   Soc. 971 e. 172 = S.

3434. Oxford student Christian union. [Miscellaneous papers. 1904–22.]
                                          G.A. Oxon b. 145

3435. Oxford university church aid association. [Miscellaneous papers.
1857–90.]   G.A. Oxon c. 272 (f. 53, 54); G.A. Oxon 4° 265

3436. Oxford university Church army. [Tract no. 2, 6.] [Oxf., 1882], 4°.
                                          G.A. Oxon b. 143 (256)

3437. Oxford university church society. Rules. May, 1875; May 1877; Jan., 1878; Jan. 1879. (Oxf.), 1875–79, 16°.

G.A. Oxon 16° 200 (2–5)

3438. Oxford university church society. [Miscellaneous papers. 1880–85.]

G.A. Oxon b. 143 (134–42)

3439. Oxford university church union. [Miscellaneous papers. 1897–1938.]

G.A. Oxon 4° 595; b. 144 (65–77)

3440. Oxford university church union. Hand-book. Oxf., 1902, 16°. 12 pp.

13217 f. 15

3441. Oxford university church union. List of members, Hilary term, 1905 (1906, 08). [Oxf.], 1905–08, 8°.

G.A. Oxon b. 144 (63)

3442. Oxford university church union. Report. 1906/07. Oxf., [1907], 8°. 12 pp.

G.A. Oxon 8° 1002 (3)

3443. Oxford university missionary union [*formerly*] The Mission associates. [Miscellaneous papers. 1887–1905.]   G.A. Oxon b. 144; 4° 596

3444. Oxford university missionary union for junior members of the University. [Miscellaneous papers, 1861–63.]   G.A. Oxon b. 144

3445. Oxford university Protestant union. Rules. [Oxf., 1888], folded card.

G.A. Oxon b. 143 (16)

— [1893].

G.A. Oxon b. 143 (16)

3446. Oxford university society for the defence of the Church in Wales. [Miscellaneous papers. 1888–1912.]   G.A. Oxon b. 143 (266–86)

See 4256 [Oxford university Socratic club. Socratic digest. 1943–].

3447. Oxford university student volunteer missionary union. [Miscellaneous papers. 1891–1906.]

G.A. Oxon 4° 596

3448. St. Hilary essay society. Rules. [Oxf., 1888], 16°. 3 pp.

G.A. Oxon b. 147

— [Another ed.] [*c*. 1894], 8°.

G.A. Oxon b. 147

See 4943 [Pretended Oxford branch of the 'Society for the suppression of vice'. 1812].

Society of historical theology. See 3433. Oxford society of historical theology.

3449. Society of the Annunciation [for University women. Objects &c.]. n. pl., [1902], s. sh.

G.A. Oxon 4° 410

Tutors' association. See 3421, 3422. Graduates' association.

See 6893 [Brasenose college missionary assoc.].
See 7091 [Christ Church Bible reading society].
See 7237, 7238 [Corpus Christi college church society].
See 7803, 7804 [Merton college church society].
See 7807 [Merton Melanesian mission society].
See 8654 [Wadham college guild of St. Andrew].

Oxford movement

No attempt has been made to compile a bibliography of the Oxford movement, its complex ramifications being beyond the scope of this work. Only items with a particular Oxford interest have been listed, together with some of the standard general works.

See also 3702, &c., Roman Catholics.
See also 3475, &c., Condemnations and Expulsions.

3450. DICKINSON, C., Pastoral epistle from his holiness the pope to some members of the University. Transl. [really written, by C. Dickinson.] Lond., 1836, 8°. 39 pp.   Bliss B 213 (10)
— 3rd ed.   1307 e. 74 (2)

3451. Oxford theology. (Quarterly review, 1839, vol. 63, p. 525–72.)
         Per. 3977 e. 191

3452. Correspondence illustrative of the actual state of Oxford with reference to Tractarianism, and of the attempts of mr. Newman and his party to unprotestantize the national Church. [Compiled by C. P. Golightly.] Oxf., 1842, 8°. 36 pp.   G.A. Oxon 8° 234 (6)

3453. PALMER, W., A narrative of events connected with the publication of the Tracts for the times. Oxf. &c., 1843, 8°. x+112 pp.   43. 1274 (1)
— 2nd ed., 1843.   8° V 197 (14) Th.
— 3rd ed., with postscript. 1843. x+116 pp.   110 j. 717
— [Another ed.] with intr. and suppl. Lond., 1883, 8°. viii+293 pp.
         110 k. 828

3454. The Oxford Tractarian school. (Edinb. review, 1843, vol. 77, p. 501–62.)   Per. 3977 e. 190

3455. Recent developments of Puseyism. (Edinb. review, 1844, vol. 80, p. 310–75.)   Per. 3977 e. 190

3456. BURDON, R., The Oxford Argo, by an Oxford divine. [A poem, by R. Burdon, sometimes ascr. to H. B. Bulteel, satirizing the papist tendencies of the Tractarian 'ship'.] Lond., 1845, 8°. 24 pp.
         280 j. 693 (13)

3457. The Newmania, or Puseyism, by —— s —— s, A.M. of Oriel and Exeter colleges. [In verse.] 2nd ed. Lond. &c., 1847, 8°. 35 pp.
         G.A. Oxon 8° 135 (4)

3458. GEMINUS, *pseud.*, To Frederic Charles Plumptre . . . vice chancellor of the University . . . a letter [on the spread of Roman doctrine in the Tractarian movement]. Lond. &c., 1852, 8°. 8 pp.
         G. Pamph. 2395 (21)

3459. OAKELEY, F., Historical notes on the Tractarian movement, 1833–1845. Lond., 1865, 8°. ix+113 pp.   110 j. 5

3460. The Oxford school [an outline of the religious movement]. (Edinb. review, 1881, vol. 153, p. 305–35.)   Per. 3977 e. 190

3461. MOZLEY, T., Reminiscences, chiefly of Oriel college and the Oxford movement. 2 vols. Lond., 1882, 8°.　　　　　　110 j. 711, 721
— 2nd ed. 1882.　　　　　　　　　　　11126 e. 191, 192

3462. TAIT, A. C., *abp. of Canterbury*, Thoughts [mainly on the Oxford movement] suggested by mr. Mozley's Oxford reminiscences. (Macmillan's mag., 1882, vol. 46, p. 417–23.)　　G.A. Oxon 4° 582 (7)

3463. WARD, W., William George Ward and the Oxford movement. Lond., 1889, 8°. xxix+462 pp.　　　　　　　　11126 d. 15
— 2nd ed. 1890. xxxi+481 pp.　　　　　　11126 e. 83

3464. CHURCH, R. W., The Oxford movement, 1833–1845. Lond., 1891, 8°. 358 pp.　　　　　　　　　　　　11126 e. 825

3465. WAKELING, G., The Oxford church movement, sketches and recollections. Lond. &c., 1895, 8°. 309 pp.　　　　11126 e. 199

3466. RIGG, J. H., Oxford High Anglicanism and its chief leaders. Lond., 1895, 8°. 348 pp.　　　　　　　　　11126 e. 200

3467. The origin and historical basis of the Oxford movement. (Quarterly review, 1906, vol. 205, p. 196–214.)　　Per. 3977 e. 191

3468. OLLARD, S. L., The Oxford movement, 4 lectures. Lond., 1909, 8°. 60 pp.　　　　　　　　　　　　11126 e. 307

3469. FABER, G., Oxford apostles, a character study of the Oxford movement. Lond., 1933, 8°. 467 pp.　　　　　11126 e. 662

3470. KNOX, E. A., The Tractarian movement, 1833–1845. Lond. &c., 1933, 8°. 410 pp.　　　　　　　　　11126 e. 660

3471. HOLLOWAY, O. E., The Tractarian movement in Oxford. (Bodleian quarterly record, 1933, vol. 7, p. 213–32.)
Per. 2590 d. Oxf. 1. 40 = R.

3472. FLOOD, J. M., Cardinal Newman and Oxford. (Lond.), 1933, 4°. 283 pp.　　　　　　　　　　　11126 e. 648

3473. TRISTRAM, H., The Oxford background [of J. H. Newman and the Oxford movement]. (Dublin review, 1945, new ser., vol. 217, p. 136–46.)　　　　　　　　　　　Per. 3977 e. 199

3474. MIDDLETON, R. D., Newman at Oxford, his religious development. Lond. &c., 1950, 8°. 284 pp.　　　　　11132 e. 153

Condemnations and expulsions
General

3475. Isti sunt errores condemnati a fratre Roberto Kilunardbi [*sic*] archiepis. Cantuariensi de consensu omnium magistrorum tam regentium quam non regentium apud oxoniam die iouis xx. ante festum sancti cuberti in quadragesima. Anno domini. M.CC.lxxvi. (Collectio errorum in Anglia et Parisius [*sic*] condempnatorum, 1483, sig. a ii, iii.) [Proctor 7931.]　　　　　　　　　4° C 15 (4) Th.

— [Another ed. *c*. 1488.] [Proctor 1382.]   Auct. 4 Q VI 20
— [Another ed. *c*. 1490.]   B.M.
— [Another ed.] (Collectio judiciorum de novis erroribus, 1728, tom. I, p. 185, 86.)   II 54 Th.

3476. Judicium & decretum Universitatis Oxoniensis latum in Convocatione habita August. 19., 1610 contra propositiones quasdam impias & hæreticas, exscriptas & citatas ex libello [by A. Bury] . . . cui titulus est The naked Gospel. [In Lat. and Engl.] Oxonii, 1690, fol. 6 pp.
Gough Oxf. 63 (3)

3477. PARKINSON, J., The fire's continued at Oxford: or, The decree of the Convocation for burning the Naked Gospel [of A. Bury] considered, in a letter [by J. Parkinson]. [Lond.? 1690], 4°. 16 pp.
Gough Oxf. 63 (4)

See 7253 [Censure of the University upon the Naked Gospell, by A. Bury. 1690].

3478. At a meeting of the vice-chancellor and the heads of colleges and halls . . . 25. day of Nov., 1695. [Condemnation of words used in a sermon preached by J. Bingham before the University in the church of St. Peter in the East on Oct. 28, concerning the Trinity.] [Oxf.], (1695), s. sh.   G.A. Oxon b. 111 (25)

3479. An account of the decree of the University of Oxford, against some heretical tenets . . . the 25th of November, 1695. [The heresy was spoken in a sermon by J. Bingham, and was inspired by the writings of Dr. Sherlock.] (Lond., 1695), s. sh.   G.A. Oxon b. 137 (1)

3480. SHERLOCK, W., A modest examination of the authority and reasons of the late decree of the Vice-Chancellor of Oxford, and some heads of colleges and halls; concerning the heresy of three distinct infinite minds in the . . . Trinity. Lond., 1696, 4°. 46 pp.   Gough Oxf. 80 (13)

3481. EDWARDS, J., Remarks [by J. Edwards] upon a book lately published by dr. Will. Sherlock . . . entituled A modest examination of the Oxford decree, &c. Oxf., 1695 [*sic*], 4°. 62 pp.   Gough Oxf. 80 (14)

3482. SOUTH, R., Decreti Oxoniensis vindicatio [by R. South] in tribus ad modestum ejusdem examinatorem [W. Sherlock] modestioribus epistolis, a theologo transmarino. [Oxf.?], 1696, 4°. 92 pp.
Crynes 898 (7)

Other works which attempt to impugn the orthodoxy of Sherlock's teaching have not been included.

3483. The vice-chancellorship of dr. Wynter. [Observations on the conduct of dr. Wynter in connexion with the religious condemnations authorized during his period of office.] (Christ. remem., 1845, new ser., vol. 9, p. 133–87.)   Per. 971 e. 44

3484. Case whether professor Jowett in his essay and commentary [in Essays and reviews] has so distinctly contravened the doctrines of the Church of England, that a court of law would pronounce him guilty;

with the opinion of the Queen's advocate [R. Phillimore] thereon.
Lond., 1862, 8°. 40 pp. 100 f. 6 (2)

3485. Case as to the legal position of professor Jowett: with the opinion of
the Queen's advocate [R. Phillimore] thereon. Lond., 1862, 8°. 11 pp.
100 f. 6 (3)

3486. CALLUS, D. A., The condemnation of st. Thomas at Oxford.
(Aquinas papers, no. 5.) Oxf., 1946, 8°. 38 pp. 26671 e. 87 (5)

R. D. Hampden

*No systematic effort has been made to list works relating to the purely
theological aspect of Hampden's writings, but those which seemed concerned
chiefly with providing evidence for the University case against Hampden have
been recorded.*

3487. At a meeting of members of Convocation . . . it was unanimously resolved that a . . . requisition be . . . presented [asking that a certificate of
attendance at the lectures of the Lady Margaret professor be accep-
table instead of at those of the Regius professor, while the latter position
is held by dr. Hampden]. Feb. 24. Oxf., [1836], s. sh. Bliss B 213 (15)

3488. At a meeting of members of Convocation . . . it was resolved . . . [to
present a requisition to the vice-chancellor asking for an opportunity
for Convocation to condemn dr. Hampden's doctrines]. Feb. 25. Oxf.,
(1836), s. sh. Bliss B 213 (16)

3489. Oxford, March 2, 1836. At an adjourned meeting of members of
Convocation . . . in Corpus Common room it was . . . resolved, that the
. . . requisition [asking for a meeting of heads of houses to consider the
Hampden question, &c.] be signed and presented. [54 signatures said
to be added 'in loco'; to await others in Corpus Common room].
[Oxf.], (1836), s. sh. Bliss B 213 (21)

3490. Oxford, March 5, 1836. [Resolutions passed at a meeting held in
Corpus Common room, condemning dr. Hampden's theological
teaching.] Oxf., (1836), s. sh. Bliss B 213 (21b)

3491. [*Begin.*] The Reverend the vice-chancellor having given notice . . .
[Mar. 10, 1836. Declaration of resident members of Convocation upon
the nature and tendency of the publications of dr. Hampden. Also
various papers urging the divestment of certain powers appurtenant to
his office, &c.] Oxf., [1836], 8°. 15 pp. G.A. Oxon 8° 1001 (17)
— Repr. 1842. [June 4?]. G.A. Oxon b. 24

3492. Brief observations upon dr. Hampden's inaugural lecture. March 21.
(Oxf., 1836), 8°. 7 pp. Bliss B 213 (4)

3493. PUSEY, E. B., Dr. Hampden's past and present statements compared
[signed E. B. P.] March 21. Oxf., 1836, 8°. 22 pp. Bliss B 213 (7)
— 2nd ed., revised and enlarged [signed E. B. Pusey]. 1836. 35 pp.
Bliss B 213 (8)

3494. Oxford, March 22, 1836. Requisition to the . . . vice-chancellor. [Petition by members of Convocation requesting that some act of formal censure be made against the opinions expressed in certain publications of dr. Hampden, the Regius professor of divinity.] (Oxf., 1836), fol. 4 pp.   G.A. Oxon 4° 25 (1)

3495. WOODGATE, H. A., A letter to viscount Melbourne on the recent appointment to the office of Regius professor of divinity in the University of Oxford. (Mar. 31.) Lond., 1836, 8°. 32 pp.   Bliss B 213 (11)

3495.1. An elucidation of mr. Woodgate's pamphlet [no. 3495] in a letter to a friend. Lond., 1836, 8°. 29 pp.   G. Pamph. 2904 (4)

3496. MILLER, J., Conspectus of the Hampden case at Oxford. (7 Apr.) Lond. &c., 1836, 8°. 47 pp.   36. 548 (6)

3497. THOMAS, V., Oratiunculæ cum oratiuncula non habitæ cum habita concertatio [by V. Thomas. Apr. 16]. Cui subjiciuntur . . . Johannis Morton et Ricardi Wilbraham . . . de autonomia academica sententiæ. Oxon., 1836, 8°. 36 pp.   Bliss B 213 (13)

3498. The propositions attributed to dr. Hampden by professor Pusey compared with the text of the Bampton lectures, by a resident member of Convocation. (April 16.) Lond. &c., 1836, 8°. 28 pp.
                                                              36. 547 (4)

3499. HULL, W. W., Remarks intended to shew how far dr. Hampden may have been misunderstood and misrepresented during the present controversy at Oxford. (Apr. 20.) Lond., 1836, 8°.   B.M.
— 2nd ed. (May 2) 1836. 64 pp.   36. 548 (3)

3500. Requisition to . . . the Vice-chancellor [protesting against the intervention of the proctors which prevented an opinion being expressed against Hampden; giving the text of a proposed statute censuring him; with an explanatory letter, signed V. Thomas and 5 others.]. (27 April.) Oxf., (1836), 8°. 7 pp.   Bliss B 213 (29)

3501. CAMERON, C. R., Does dr. Hampden's inaugural lecture imply any change in his theological principles? A letter . . . Apr. 29. Oxf. &c., 1836, 8°. 8 pp.   Bliss B 213 (4a)

3502. DUNCAN, P. B., An address [dated May 2] to those members of Convocation who are disposed to support the statute to be submitted to their consideration on Thursday next [May 5th.]. [Oxf.], (1836), 4°. 3 pp.   Bliss B 213 (30)

3503. GRINFIELD, E. W., Reflections after a visit to the University of Oxford, on occasion of the late proceedings against the Regius professor of divinity. (May 11.) Lond. &c., 1836, 8°. 16 pp. 36. 548 (2)

3504. CHURTON, E., A letter to an Edinburgh reviewer on the case of the Oxford malignants and dr. Hampden. Lond., 1836, 8°. 62 pp.
                                                              36. 548 (1)

3505. Copy of a declaration submitted for signature to the governors, fellows, and tutors, of the University of Oxford, by the Corpus Christi committee of censors of the publications of . . . dr. Hampden. [With strictures upon it.] Tunbridge Wells, [1836], s. sh.   B.M.

3506. Correspondence between . . . dr. Hampden . . . and . . . dr. Howley, lord archbishop of Canterbury. Lond., 1838, 8°. 38 pp.
                                                                    G. Pamph. 2840 (13)

3507. COX, W. H., Specimens of the theological teaching of certain members of the Corpus committee at Oxford [by W. H. Cox]. Lond., 1836, 8°. 38 pp.   Bliss B 213 (9)

> See 1057 [Four questions, and counsel's answers, on the power of the University to make statutes which would change the Laudian code. This arose from the proposed decree against Hampden. 1836].

3508. LAURENCE, R. F., Remarks on the Hampden controversy. Oxf. &c., 1836, 8°. 24 pp.   Bliss B 213 (14)

3509. A letter to . . . the archbishop of Canterbury, [W. Howley] explanatory of the proceedings at Oxford, on the appointment of the present Regius professor of divinity. By a member of the University of Oxford. 3rd ed. With a letter to the Corpus committee by Jortin Redivivus. Lond., 1836, 8°. 40 pp.   36. 906

3510. NEWMAN, J. H., Elucidations of dr. Hampden's theological statements [by J. H. Newman?]. Oxf., 1836, 8°. 47 pp.   Bliss B 213 (2)

3511. A non-resident M.A.'s self-vindication for attending to support the vote of censure on dr. Hampden's writings. Oxf., 1836, 8°. 21 pp.
                                                                          36. 547 (10)

3512. Observations on A letter addressed to . . . the archbishop of Canterbury [no. 3509]. By Misopseudes. Oxf., 1836, 8°. 11 pp.   36. 547 (5)

3513. Oxford and dr. Hampden. (Blackwood's Edinb. mag., April and June 1836, vol. 39, p. 425–34, 768–71.)   Per. 2705 e. 486

3514. The Oxford malignants and dr. Hampden. (Edinb. review, April 1836, vol. 63, p. 225–39.)   Per. 3977 e. 190

3515. POWELL, B., Remarks on A letter from the rev. H. A. Woodgate to viscount Melbourne [no. 3495] relative to the appointment of dr. Hampden. Oxf. &c., 1836, 8°. 31 pp.   36. 548 (7)

3516. PUSEY, E. B., Dr. Hampden's theological statements and the Thirty-nine articles compared. By a resident member of Convocation [E. B. Pusey]. With a preface and propositions extracted from his works. (Mar. 12). Oxf., 1836, 8°. xlii+62 pp.   Bliss B 213 (1*)

3517. State of parties in Oxford, from the public prints. With an appendix containing some letters relative to the persecution of the Regius professor of divinity. Lond. &c., 1836, 8°. 61 pp.   36. 547 (6)

3518. Statements of Christian doctrine, extracted from the published writings of R. D. Hampden . . . Lond., 1836, 8°. 36 pp.
Bliss B 213 (6)
— 2nd ed. 1836.   36. 547 (8)

3519. Strictures on an article in The Edinburgh review; entitled 'The Oxford malignants and dr. Hampden', [no. 3514] with some observations on the present state of the Hampden controversy, by a member of Convocation. Oxf., 1836, 8°. 26 pp.   36. 547 (9)

3520. Oxford, May 25, 1842. [*Begin.*] It is with great pain . . . [opposing the proposed statute to abrogate the 1836 statute censuring Hampden]. [Oxf.], (1842), s. sh.   G.A. Oxon b. 24

3521. Oxford, May 26, 1842. The undersigned . . . [Memorial, signed F. A. Faber and others, affirming their opposition to the statute.] (Oxf., 1842), s. sh.   G.A. Oxon b. 24

3522. [*Begin.*] Oxford, May 30, 1842. An unfavourable answer having been returned by the Hebdomadal board to the recent address, it remains that the members of Convocation seriously consider the responsibilities of their present position [regarding the Hampden question]. Oxf., [1842], s. sh.   B.M.

3523. Oxford, June 2, 1842. The Regius professor of divinity . . . [Another paper opposing the statute.] (Oxf., 1842), s. sh.   G.A. Oxon b. 24

3524. The censure of 1836 still necessary: considerations . . . on the subject of the proposed repeal of the statute affecting dr. Hampden. (Oxf.), [1842], 8°. 8 pp.   G.A. Oxon 8° 76 (3)

3525. Considerations submitted to members of Convocation [relative to the proposed repeal of the statute against dr. Hampden]. [Oxf., 1842], s. sh.   B.M.

3526. The Hampden question revived by the Hebdomadal board. (Oxf., 1842), 8°. 7 pp.   G.A. Oxon 8° 76 (2)

3527. A letter to certain members of Convocation [relative to the proposed repeal of the statute passed against dr. Hampden in 1836]. Oxf., [1842], 8°.   B.M.

3528. Letters addressed by large bodies of the clergy to those members of Convocation who met in the common room of Corpus Christi college during the controversy of 1836, together with the answers returned to the same. [Ed. by V. Thomas.] Oxf., 1842, 8°. 30 pp.
G.A. Oxon 8° 76 (1)

3529. The Queen's ball and the Oxford convocation. [Concerning the abrogation of the statute against dr. Hampden.] (Westm. review, 1842, vol. 38, p. 139–52.)   Per. 3977 e. 228

3530. Oxford and dr. Hampden. (Brit. and foreign review, 1843, vol. 15, p. 169–93.)   Per. 2228 e. 240

3531. To members of Convocation. [*Begin.*] Two classes of persons . . . [A paper, signed A lay professor, Dec. 10, 1847, about Hampden's deprivation of privileges in 1836 and his suggested reinstatement.] (Oxf., 1847), 4°. 4 pp.   G.A. Oxon c. 63 (161)

3532. [*Begin.*] Those members of Convocation . . . who may be desirous of recording their adhesion to the following protest . . . [against any steps being taken to prevent dr. Hampden's elevation to the bishopric of Hereford]. Oxf., 1847, s. sh.   B.M.

3533. The University censure on dr. Hampden [signed Clericus]. Lond., 1847, 8°. 7 pp.   11126 e. 93 (6)

3534. CANDLIST, R. S., The Hampden controversy [by R. S. Candlist]. (North Brit. rev., 1848, vol. 8, p. 534–55.)   Per. 3977 e. 204

3535. CHRISTMAS, H., A concise history of the Hampden controversy, from . . . 1832 to the present time, with all the documents which have been published. Lond., 1848, 8°. 172 pp.   48. 97

3536. K., C. E., The bishop of Oxford [S. Wilberforce] and dr. Hampden; with an appendix of correspondence. Lond., 1848, 12°. 12 pp.
48. 1423 (22)

3536.9. The reproof of ignorance and calumny, being a re-print of the addresses of large bodies of the clergy, to those members of Convocation who met in the Common Room of Corpus Christi college during the controversy of 1836, with the answers [signed V. Thomas] to the same. Oxf., 1848, 8°. 23 pp.   11126 d. 34 (2)

3537. LAURENCE, R. F., An inquiry into the circumstances attendant upon the condemnation of dr. Hampden in 1836, in six letters originally addressed to the editor of the Oxford University herald, and now repr. with remarks on the 'Reproof of ignorance and calumny put forth in defence of the Corpus committee'. Oxf., 1848, 8°. xx+73 pp.
48. 1404 (17)

3538. [*Begin.*] Oxford declarations in favour of dr. Hampden. [Memorial from heads of houses; and Protest of members of Convocation.] [Oxf.? 1848], fol.   B.M.

3539. Dr. Hampden and Anglicanism. (Dublin review, 1871, new ser., vol. 17, p. 66–108.)   Per. 3977 e. 199

3540. Some memorials of Renn Dickson Hampden, ed. by H. Hampden. Lond., 1871, 8°. 284 pp.   210 j. 103

E. B. Pusey

Works which comment on the subject-matter of E. B. Pusey's sermon 'The Holy Eucharist a comfort to the penitent', have not been listed.

3541. PUSEY, E. B., Protest [to the vice-chancellor 'against the late sentence against me, as unstatutable as well as unjust']. June 2, 1843. n. pl., (1843), s. sh.   G.A. Oxon 4° 25 (3)

3542. The revised statute [Tit. XVI. § 11]. [Statement suggesting that the terms of the statute under which dr. Pusey's sermon has been condemned, have not been properly observed.] June 3, 1843. (Oxf., 1843), s. sh.   G.A. Oxon 4° 25 (5)

3543. PUSEY, E. B., [Begin.] When I drew up my protest . . . [Letter to the vice-chancellor stating his conviction that, given the opportunity of defending himself, he would have been acquitted.] June 6. (Oxf., 1843), s. sh.   G.A. Oxon 4° 25 (4)

3544. Present position of the six doctors. [Asking the reasons for their condemnation of Pusey's sermon, or for a statement that the statute prevents them from explaining.] June 6. (Oxf., 1843), s. sh.
            G.A. Oxon 4° 25 (6)

3545. Dr. Pusey and dr. Hampden. [Statement signed 'A resident member of Convocation' suggesting that dr. Pusey should have had the same opportunity of answering the charges made against him as was afforded dr. Hampden.] June 13, 1843. (Oxf., 1843), 4°. 4 pp.
            G.A. Oxon 4° 25 (7)

3546. A letter to the . . . vice chancellor of the University . . . and the learned doctors who assisted him on a late occasion, from Torquemada the younger. Lond., 1843, 8°. 16 pp.   43. 1300

3547. GARBETT, J., Dr. Pusey and the University of Oxford, a letter. 2nd ed. Lond., 1843, 8°. 35 pp.   43. 1265 (2)

3548. The plea of the six doctors, examined. Oxf., 1843, 8°. 13 pp.
            43. 1265 (7)

3549. WOODGATE, H. A., Considerations on the position and duty of the University of Oxford, with reference to the late proceeding against the Regius professor of Hebrew [E. B. Pusey]. Oxf. &c., 1843, 8°. 36 pp.
            43. 1265 (8)

Tract no. 90, J. H. Newman and W. G. Ward

Works which treat Tract no. 90 or 'The ideal of a Christian church' from a purely theological view, have been ignored.

Works issued prior to the decision of Convocation on 13 February 1845.

3550. NEWMAN, J. H., [Begin.] I write this respectfully . . . [Letter to the vice-chancellor acknowledging the authorship of Tract no. 90. Mar. 16th, 1841.] n. pl., (1841), s. sh.   G.A. Oxon 4° 25 (1)

3551. WARD, W. G., [Begin.] False impressions seem . . . [Letter of Dec. 3, 1844, to the vice-chancellor, explaining that he has refused to answer questions about 'The ideal of a Christian church' until he is informed what course is to be taken against him.] [Oxf., 1844], s. sh.
            G.A. Oxon b. 25

3552. [Begin.] Whereas it is notoriously reputed . . . [Extracts from 'The ideal of a Christian church' to be submitted to Convocation on 13 Feb. 1845 as evidence for the proposed degradation of W. G. Ward. With

a suggested amendment of the statute De auctoritate et officio vice-cancellarii, to be promulgated in Congregation on Feb. 10.] Dec. 13, 1844. (Oxf., 1844), 4°. 4 pp.   G.A. Oxon 4° 25 (9)
— [Another ed.] fol. 4 pp.   G.A. Oxon b. 25
— Jan. 23, 1845. [As above, but withdrawing the proposal to submit to Convocation the suggested amendment to the statute.] [Oxf.], 1845, fol. 3 pp.   G.A. Oxon c. 61 (15)

3553. [*Begin.*] Saturday, Dec. 14, 1844. Mr. Ward . . . called . . . on the vice-chancellor and presented . . . the following letter [acknowledging authorship of 'The ideal of a Christian church' and expressing his readiness to answer to Convocation for any sentiment occurring therein]. (Oxf., 1844), 4°. 3 pp.   G.A. Oxon 4° 25 (8)

3554. To members of Convocation. Objects of the measures to be submitted to the Convocation on the 13th of February, 1845. Dec. 26. Oxf., (1844), 4°. 3 pp.   G.A. Oxon b. 25

3555. Mr. Ward and the new test; or, Plain reasons why those who censure mr. Ward should not vote for the new statute, which limits the Thirty-nine articles; a letter by M.A. (Dec. 27, 1844.) [Oxf., 1845], 8°. 9 pp.
                     G.A. Oxon 8° 884 (22)

3556. TAIT, A. C., A letter . . . on the measures to be proposed to Convocation on the 13th of February in connexion with W. G. Ward. (31 Dec. 1844). Edinb. &c., 1845, 8°. 22 pp.   G.A. Oxon 8° 705 (7)

3557. BRICKNELL, W. S., Oxford: Tract no. 90: and Ward's Ideal of a Christian church. A practical suggestion respectfully submitted to members of Convocation . . . Oxf. &c., 1844, 8°. 22 [really 60] pp.
                     44. 1644 (4)
—3rd. ed. 1844.   G. Pamph. 2721 (2)
— 5th ed. 1845.   G. Pamph. 2899 (15)

3558. EXPLICATOR, *pseud.*, The case as it is, with reference to the proposed declaration [in the proposed statute, no. 3552] considered in a letter to a friend. [Oxf., 1844], s. sh.   G.A. Oxon b. 25

3559. New form of declaration which the proposed statute [as in no. 3552] will enable the Vice-chancellor to impose. [Some remarks against it.] Oxf., [1844], s. sh.   G.A. Oxon b. 25

3560. PUGH, W., and CHAPMAN, R. G., Henry Wall's notes, 1844 [on the machinations against Ward which took place in the University generally and in Balliol in particular]. (Oxoniensia, 1959, vol. 24, p. 83–97.)
                     Per. G.A. Oxon 4° 658 = R.

3561. MOZLEY, J. B., Observations on the propositions to be submitted to Convocation on Feb. 13 [signed A Tutor of —— college i.e. J. B. Mozley]. (Jan 2.) Oxf., 1845, 8°. 15 pp.   G.A. Oxon 8° 77 (17)

3562. HULL, W. W., MDCCCXLV. The month of January. [The measures to be proposed in Convocation on Feb. 13.] (Jan. 11.) Lond. &c., 1845, 8°. 18 pp.   G.A. Oxon 8° 72 (8)

3563. WARD, W. G., An address to members of Convocation in protest against the proposed statute. (Jan. 14.) Lond., 1845, 8°. 56 pp.
45. 1616

3564. KEBLE, J., Heads of consideration on the case of mr. Ward. (Jan. 16.) Oxf. &c., 1845, 8°. 15 pp.   45. 1614 (2)

3565. MARRIOTT, C., Reasons [signed C. M.] for voting against the proposed censure on certain propositions extracted from a work lately published by the rev. W. G. Ward. Jan. 18. Oxf., 1845, s. sh.
G.A. Oxon b. 25

3566. Case as to the proposed degradation [of W. G. Ward] and declaration in the statute of Feb. 13 submitted to sir J. Dodson and R. Bethell, with their opinions of its decided illegality, accompanied with notes. [c. 20 Jan.] Oxf. &c., 1845, 8°. 52 pp.   G.A. Oxon 8° 82 (1)

3567. [*Begin.*] Members of Convocation are reminded . . . [A paper, pointing out that the charge against Ward is an ill-defined comprehensive indictment that all excerpts from his work are inconsistent with the articles, the declaration to them, etc.] Jan. 21. (Oxf., 1845), s. sh.
G.A. Oxon b. 25

3568. GARBETT, J. The University, the Church, and the new test, with remarks on mr. Oakeley's and mr. Gresley's pamphlets. [c. 24 Jan.] Lond. &c., 1845, 8°. 84 pp.   45. 1613 (10)

3569. OAKELEY, F., A few words to those churchmen being members of Convocation who purpose taking no part in mr. Ward's case. (Jan. 31.) Lond., 1845, 16°. 32 pp.   45. 761

3570. MARRIOTT, C., [*Begin.*] Allow me to lay before you . . . [Letter opposing the proposed censure of Newman.] Ash-Wednesday [Feb. 5]. (Oxf., 1845), s. sh.   G.A. Oxon b. 25

3571. EDEN, C. P., [*Begin.*] To the . . . bishop of Oxford. [A letter protesting against the proposed condemnation of Tract no. 90.] Feb. 6. (Oxf., 1845), 4°. 4 pp.   G.A. Oxon 4° 25 (10)

3572. HUSSEY, R., Reasons for voting upon the third question [condemnation of Tract no. 90] to be proposed in Convocation on the 13th inst. Feb. 8. Oxf. &c., 1845, 8°. 11 pp.   G.A. Oxon 8° 82 (4)

3573. There is no pleasing some folks. [Extract from The Christian remembrancer for Jan. 1845, p. 151, which suggests that the Board condemning Tract XC of J. H. Newman was guilty of gross usurpation and encroachment upon the authority of the University.] Feb. 8, 1845. (Oxf., 1845), s. sh.   G.A. Oxon 4° 25 (12)

3574. ROGERS, F., A short appeal to members of Convocation upon the proposed censure of No. 90. (Feb. 8.) Lond. &c., 1845, 8°. 9 pp.
G.A. Oxon 8° 884 (21)

3575. Difficulties in the matters published in Congregation this day [concerning the arraignment of W. G. Ward]. Feb. 10. n. pl., (1845), s. sh.
G.A. Oxon 4° 25 (14)

3576. Νέμεσις, *pseud.*, Oxford, February 10, 1845. 1. In 1836 Dr Hampden . . . [Remarks on the similarity of the Hampden case and the proposed censure of Feb. 13.] (Oxf., 1845), s. sh.   G.A. Oxon b. 25

3577. MOZLEY, J. B., The proposed decree on the subject of no. XC [signed] An Oxford M.A. [J. B. Mozley. Feb. 11.] Oxf., 1845, 8°. 12 pp.   G.A. Oxon 8° 82 (5)

3578. Oxford, February, 1845. To the . . . proctors. [A memorial thanking them for their resolution that they will put their 'negative' upon the proposal relating to Tract 90. Signed by S. W. Cornish and some hundreds more.] [*c.* Feb. 12]. (Oxf., 1845), fol. 4 pp. G.A. Oxon b. 25

3579. DONKIN, W. F., A defence of voting against the propositions to be submitted to Convocation on Feb. 13, 1845. Oxf. &c., 1845, 8°. 7 pp.
G.A. Oxon 8° 72 (2)

3580. GOULBURN, E. M., A reply to some parts of mr. Ward's defence, justifying certain parties in recording their votes against him. Oxf. &c., 1845, 8°. 31 pp.   G.A. Oxon 8° 82 (2)

3581. MAURICE, F. D., The new statute and mr. Ward, a letter to a non-resident member of Convocation. Oxf. &c., 1845, 8°. 31 pp.
45. 1614 (5)

3582. MAURICE, F. D., Thoughts on the rule of conscientious subscription, on the purpose of the Thirty-nine articles . . . in a second letter to a non-resident member of Convocation. Oxf. &c., 1845, 8°. 52 pp.
45. 1614 (6)

3583. MOBERLY, G., The proposed degradation and declaration considered in a letter. Oxf. &c., 1845, 8°. 29 pp.   45. 1747

3584. Questions submitted to counsel on behalf of the Board of heads ot houses and proctors respecting the propositions to be brought before Convocation in the matter of mr. Ward, and opinion of the solicitor-general, sir Charles Wetherell, dr. Addams, and mr. Cowling. n. pl., [1845], s. sh.   G.A. Oxon c. 61 (28)

3585. [*Begin.*] We the undersigned, strongly disapproving . . . [Four reasons for deprecating the proposed appeal to Convocation on mr. Ward's Ideal of a Christian church.] [Oxf., 1845], s. sh.
G.A. Oxon b. 25

3585.1. Reasons for voting against the measures to be proposed in Convocation at Oxford on Feb. 13, 1845. [By H. A. Woodgate?] Lond., 1845, 8°.   Cardiff Castle

Works issued after the decision of 13 February 1845.

3586. OLLARD, S. L., A famous centenary. [An account of the meeting of Convocation on 13 Feb. 1845 seeking to condemn W. G. Ward's Ideal of a Christian church, to deprive him of his degrees, and to censure Tract 90.] (Oxf. mag., 1945, vol. 63, p. 142–44.) Per. G.A. Oxon 4° 141

3587. WARD, W. G., [*Begin.*] I entertain so much respect . . . [Letter to the vice-chancellor dated 13th Feb. commenting upon the proceeding of Convocation of that day.] (Oxf., 1845), s. sh.   G.A. Oxon 4° 25 (15)

3588. OAKELEY, F., [*Begin.*] The vote of Convocation . . . [Letter to the vice-chancellor referring to the decrees of Feb. 13 against mr. Ward, stating that as his own views are similar, he merits similar penalties.] Feb. 14. (Oxf., 1845), s. sh.   G.A. Oxon 4° 25 (13)

3589. OAKELEY, F., A letter to the lord bishop of London on a subject connected with the recent proceedings at Oxford. (19 Feb.) Lond., 1845, 8°. 39 pp.   45. 1615

3590. Some answers to the question, How did you vote on the 13th? A letter by a junior M.A., one of the 386. Feb. 20. Oxf., 1845, 8°. 15 pp.
G.A. Oxon 8° 77 (16)

3591. Mr. Ward and the Oxford university. (Eclectic rev., May 1845, N.S., vol. 17, p. 509–40.)   Per. 3977 e. 76

3592. Oxford and mr. Ward. (Edinb. review, Apr., 1845, vol. 81, p. 385–98.)   Per. 3977 e. 190

3593. VAUGHAN, R., Oxford and evangelical churchmen. (British quarterly rev., 1845, vol. 1, p. 436–71.)   Per. 3977 e. 198

> See 742 [Mr. W. E. Gladstone's committee make the following statement with regard to 'The ideal of a Christian church'. 1847].

Religious tests

3594. A collection of papers, designed to explain and vindicate the present mode of subscription required by the University of Oxford, from all young persons at their matriculation [*and*] Appendix. Oxf., 1772, 8°. 24+4 pp.   Gough Oxf. 58

3595. A complete and faithful collection of the several papers which have been published in Oxford on the subject of subscription to the XXXIX articles . . . [*and*] An appendix. Oxf., 1772, 8°. 118+4 pp.
G. Pamph. 202 (9)

3596. Origin of subscription to the 39 articles at matriculation in the University of Oxford. Ex regist. Convoc. KK. p. 338, anno Domini 1581. n. pl., [1772], fol. 4 pp.   G.A. Oxon b. 17 (25)

3597. The case of subscription to the thirty-nine articles required of all scholars matriculated in the University of Oxford, stated and considered. n. pl., [1772], fol. 4 pp.   G.A. Oxon b. 17 (26)

3598. Considerations on the expediency of making some alterations in regard to the present mode of subscribing to the XXXIX articles in this university. Mar. 19. n. pl., (1772), fol. 4 pp. G.A. Oxon b. 17 (2)

3599. [*Begin.*] The design of the author . . . [Further remarks by the author of The case of subscription, &c.] n. pl., [1772], s. sh.
G.A. Oxon b. 17 (27)

3600. [*Begin.*] The sedate author . . . [An answer to no. 3598.] Mar. 27.
n. pl., (1772), fol. 3 pp.   G.A. Oxon b. 17 (3)

3601. Observations on two anonymous papers published on March the
21st and 27th [no. 3597? and 3600] against the Considerations on the
expediency, &c., dated March the 19th, 1772. Mar. 28th. n. pl., (1772),
fol. 4 pp.   G.A. Oxon b. 17 (4)

3602. Further considerations upon the expediency of making some alteration in regard to subscription to the XXXIX articles in this university.
Mar. 28. n. pl., (1772), fol. 4 pp.   G.A. Oxon b. 17 (5)

3603. [*Begin.*] The author of the Case . . . [An answer, by the author of The
case, to no. 3602.] n. pl., [1772], s. sh.   G.A. Oxon b. 17 (28)

3604. A vindication of the test at matriculation, in it's present mode, from
the plausible objections that have been raised against it. Apr. 3. (Oxf.,
1772), fol. 3 pp.   Gough Oxf. 96 (4)

3605. [*Begin.*] Our disputes are now come to a crisis. [A paper answering
no. 3602.] April 4. n. pl., [1772], s. sh.   G.A. Oxon b. 17 (7)

3606. [*Begin.*] The affair of the subscription . . . [A recapitulation of the
arguments about subscription, &c.] n. pl., [1772], s. sh.
                                                       G.A. Oxon b. 17 (30)

3607. Objections to the received test at matriculation impartially stated
and examined. Apr. 7. n. pl., (1772), fol. 4 pp.   G.A. Oxon b. 17 (8)

3608. The plain and obvious meaning of the received test at matriculation
examined and vindicated. Apr. 10. n. pl., (1772), fol. 4 pp.
                                                       G.A. Oxon b. 17 (9)

3609. Subscription at matriculation considered, with respect to the nature
of the act, and the extent of its obligation. Apr. 18. n. pl., [1772], fol.
4 pp.   G.A. Oxon b. 17 (10)

3610. Reflections on the impropriety and inexpediency of lay-subscription
to the XXXIX articles in the University of Oxford [by B. Buckler or
T. Fry]. Apr. 22. Oxf., [1772], 8°. 39 pp.   G. Pamph. 202 (6)

3611. An answer [by T. Randolph] to a pamphlet entitled Reflections on
the impropriety and inexpediency of lay-subscription to the XXXIX
articles in the University of Oxford. Oxf., [1772], 8°. 21 pp.
                                                       G. Pamph. 202 (7)

3612. BAGOT, L., *bp. of St. Asaph*, A defence of the subscription to the
XXXIX articles, as it is required in the University of Oxford [by
L. Bagot] occasioned by . . . Reflections on the impropriety . . . of
lay-subscription . . . in the University of Oxford. Oxf., [1772], 8°.
26 pp.   G.A. Oxon 8° 233 (5)

3613. BENTHAM, E., [*Begin.*] It is well known that . . . [Suggested alternative form of subscription to the Church of England, signed E. B.
r.p.d.]. Oct. 27. n. pl., (1772), s. sh.   G.A. Oxon b. 17 (11)

3614. [*Begin.*] The obligations required . . . [Another alternative form of subscription.] Nov. 1. n. pl., (1772), s. sh. G.A. Oxon b. 17 (12)

3615. BENTHAM, E., Reflections [signed E. B. r.p.d.] occasioned by a paper, bearing date November 1 [no. 3614] . . . animadverting upon a proposal dated October 27. Nov. 3. n. pl., (1772), s. sh. G.A. Oxon b. 17 (13)

3616. [*Begin.*] Notwithstanding the great variety . . . [Paper quoting bishop Jeremy Taylor's opinion concerning subscription to the 39 articles.] Nov. 20. n. pl., (1772), s. sh. G.A. Oxon b. 17 (14)

3617. A letter to the reverend **** ***** M.A. . . . on the case of subscription at Matriculation. Oxf., 1772, 8°. 18 pp. G.A. Oxon 8° 121

3618. [*Begin.*] As the day draws near . . . [A paper concerning subscription to the 39 articles.] Jan. 28. n. pl., (1773), s. sh. G.A. Oxon b. 17 (15)

3619. Observations occasioned by a paper dated Feb. 15. 1773 [which seeks to subjoin an explanation to the statute de tempore, &c.] Feb. 25. n. pl., (1773), s. sh. G.A. Oxon b. 17 (16, 17)

3620. Considerations on the proposed Explanation of the statute de tempore et conditionibus matriculationis. Feb. 27. (Oxf., 1773), s. sh.
Gough Oxf. 96 (2)

3621. Observations upon the proposed Explanation of the statute Tit. 2. sect. 3 [concerning subscription at matriculation]. n. pl., [1773], s. sh.
Gough Oxf. 96 (1)

3622. An answer to the question 'Why, if we will retain the old statute, the old form of subscription, which is made simply, and without any declaration of assent at all, is not likewise to be retained?' n. pl., [1773], s. sh. Gough Oxf. 96 (3)

3622.1. HORNE, G., *bp. of Norwich*, A letter to . . . lord North . . . concerning subscription to the XXXIX articles; and particularly the undergraduate-subscription, by a member of Convocation [G. Horne].
Oxf., 1773, 8°. 43 pp. G. Pamph. 2704 (3)
— [Another ed., ed. by V. Thomas, in 1834 and issued as part of no. 3640.]

See 1047 [Case for powers of making or altering royal statutes, with Counsels' opinion; issued in 1759, but re-pr. in 1773 when it was proposed to alter the form of subscription].

3623. An account of the origin of subscriptions to the 39 articles and the 36th Canon, in the University of Oxford. [Lond.? 1774?], 8°. B.M.

3624. WILLIAMSON, J., Opinions concerning the University of Oxford, and subscription to the Thirty-nine articles. By a clergyman [J. Williamson]. Lond., 1774, 4°. G. Pamph. 519 (5)

3625. Religious tests. Return to an order . . . dated 4 July 1833; that . . . the universities of Oxford and Cambridge do communicate . . . copies of the religious tests required of persons on admission . . . or at the time

of taking any degree; as also the dates of the original imposition of
those tests [&c.]. 22 July 1833. [Lond.], 1833, fol. 3 pp.

Pp. Eng. 1833 vol. 27

3626. Universities. Return to an order . . . 13 August 1833; that the . . .
universities of Oxford and Cambridge do communicate . . . copies of
the three articles of the 36th canon, as entered in their books of subscription [&c.]. 28 August 1833. [Lond.], 1833, s. sh.

Pp. Eng. 1833 vol. 27

3627. A bill to remove certain disabilities which prevent some classes of
her majesty's subjects from resorting to the universites of England, and
proceeding to degrees therein. 21 Apr. [Lond.], 1834, fol. 4 pp.

Pp. Eng. 1834 vol. 4

— As amended by the committee. 2 July. [Lond.], 1834, s. sh.

Pp. Eng. 1834 vol. 4

3628. To the members of Convocation. [Text of the Declaration by those
connected with instruction and discipline, and an invitation to other
members of Convocation to add their signature approving it.] Oxf.,
[1834], s. sh.   G.A. Oxon c. 50 (122)

3629. [*Begin.*] The undersigned resident members . . . engaged as private
tutors . . . [Supporting the Declaration by those connected with instruction and discipline.] Oxf., [1834], s. sh.   G.A. Oxon c. 50 (124)

3630. [*Begin.*] Being deeply convinced . . . [Circular letter from the committee acting in behalf of those connected with instruction and discipline who signed the Declaration. The text of the latter is given, and
support for it is sought from parents and guardians of students.] Oxf.,
[1834], fol. 3 pp.   G.A. Oxon c. 50 (125)

3631. Declaration [dated 25 April] of approval and concurrence [of various
members of Convocation to the Declaration of those connected with
instruction and discipline, outlining their sentiments concerning the
admission of Dissenters. The text of the latter Declaration, dated
April 24, is given]. Oxf., [1834], fol. 3 pp.   G.A. Oxon c. 50 (123)
— [Another ed., *entitled*] The Oxford declarations. [With 1447 sig-
natures]. Oxf., 1834, fol. 4 pp.   G.A. Oxon b. 113 (45)
— [Another issue with 1789 signatures.]   G.A. Oxon c. 50 (126)
— [Another issue with 1842 signatures.]   G.A. Oxon c. 50 (121)
— [Another issue with 1909 signatures.]   G.A. Oxon c. 50 (127)

[See also no. 3661 for 1854 reissue.]

3632. DALBY, W., The real question at issue between the opponents and
the supporters of a bill . . . 'to remove certain disabilities which prevent some classes . . . from resorting to the universities . . . and proceeding to degrees . . . ' Lond. &c., 1834, 8°. 24 pp.   34. 447

3633. HAMILTON, SIR W., Admission of Dissenters to the Universities [by
sir W. Hamilton]. (Edinb. review, 1834, vol. 60, p. 202–30, 422–45.)

Per. 3977 e. 190

— [Repr. in his Discussions on philosophy and literature. 1852.]

265 i. 61

3634. Oxford and lord Brougham. [Observations on lord Brougham's comments on the University of Oxford made in the House of Lords, June 24, 1834, occasioned by the petition against the admission of Dissenters, presented by the bp. of Llandaff.] (Fraser's mag., 1834, vol. 10, p. 119–24.) Per. 3977 e. 200

3635. PUSEY, E. B., [*Begin.*] The expediency of substituting a declaration for the signature of the Articles at matriculation . . . [23 questions, signed A bachelor of divinity, i.e. E. B. Pusey.] Oxf., [1834], fol. 3 pp.
G.A. Oxon c. 50 (129)

3636. SEWELL, W., Thoughts on the admission of Dissenters to the University of Oxford; and on the establishment of a state religion, a letter. Oxf. &c., 1834, 8°. 117 pp. 34. 626

3637. SEWELL, W., A second letter to a Dissenter on the opposition of the University of Oxford to the charter of the London college. Oxf. &c., 1834, 8°. 57 pp. 34. 625

3638. SEWELL, W., Thoughts on subscription, in a letter to a member of Convocation. [*With*] Postscript. Oxf. &c., 1834, 35, 8°. 62+28 pp.
34. 627; 35. 790

3639. SEWELL, W., The attack upon the University of Oxford, a letter. 2nd ed. [really a shorter and more general form of an earlier pamphlet]. Lond. &c., 1834, 8°. 63 pp. G.A. Oxon 8° 296 (11)

3640. Pamphlets in defence of the Oxford usage of subscription to the XXXIX articles at matriculation. Oxf. &c., 1835, 8°.
Bliss B 210 (13–28)

[The collection contains 14 pp. of prefatory matter and the following 12 pamphlets. This impression was withdrawn after only 4 or 5 copies had been sold; nos. 10 and 12 and the title and prefatory matter were suppressed: to the remainder were added 3 other pamphlets, forming a second collection: *Note by Philip Bliss.*]

1. Self-protection, the case of the Articles, by Clericus [C. P. Eden]. Oxf., 1835, 8°. 24 pp. Bliss B 210 (17)
2. Subscription no bondage, or The practical advantages afforded by the Thirty-nine articles as guides in all the branches of academical education. By Rusticus [J. F. Maurice]. Oxf., 1835, 8°. 125 pp.
Bliss B 210 (18)
3. Sewell, W., Thoughts on subscription. Oxf. &c., 1834, 8°. 63 pp.
Bliss B 210 (19)
4. A religious reason against substituting a declaration of conformity to the Church for the subscription to the Articles required at matriculation in the University, by a non-resident layman. Oxf. &c., 1835, 8°. 22 pp. Bliss B 210 (20)
5. Subscription to the Thirty-nine articles, questions . . . on the declaration proposed as a substitute for the subscription to the Thirty-nine articles, by a bachelor of divinity [E. B. Pusey]. With answers, by a resident member of Convocation [E. Hawkins] and

brief notes upon those answers by the bachelor of divinity. Oxf. &c., 1835, 8°. 38 pp.   Bliss B 210 (21)

6. Marriott, C., Meaning of subscription [by C. Marriott]. (Oxf., 1835), 8°. 3 pp.   Bliss B 210 (22)

7. Horne, G., A letter . . . concerning subscription to the XXXIX articles and particularly the undergraduate subscription in the University, by a member of Convocation, generally supposed to be George Horne. With a preface and notes by the editor [V. Thomas. A new ed. of no. 3622.1]. Oxf. &c., 1834, 8°. xxi+48 pp.
Bliss B 210 (23)

8. Undergraduate subscription. Extracts from a collection of papers published in Oxford in 1772 on the subject of subscription to the XXXIX articles . . . at . . . matriculation. With a preface by the editor [V. Thomas]. Oxf., 1835, 8°. xix+44 pp.
Bliss B 210 (24)

9. 1835 and 1772. The present attack on subscription compared with the last, by a resident member of Convocation. Oxf. &c., 1835, 8°. 52 pp.   Bliss B 210 (25)

10. The foundation of the earth assailed in Oxford, by a clerical member of Convocation [W. Wilberforce]. Lond., 1835, 8°. 47 pp.
Bliss B 210 (26)

11. The views of our reformers as bearing on religious dissent. Oxf., 1835, 8°. 30 pp.   Bliss B 210 (27)

12. Latitudinarianism in Oxford in 1690, a page from the life of bishop Bull. Oxf., 1835, 8°, 24 pp.   Bliss B 210 (28)

— [The second collection issued with a title [?] 'Just published . . . Pamphlets in defence . . . ' [&c.] and 'Contents' [Bliss B 210 (14)] lists 13 pamphlets comprising no. 1–9, 11 of the first collection, renumbered, together with the following pamphlets, numbered 6, 7 and 13. All appear to have been also available separately.]

6. Questions [on the declaration proposed April 1, 1835, &c. By a bachelor of divinity. E. B. Pusey]. Oxf., [1835], 8°. 8 pp.
Bliss B 210 (3)

7. A few plain reasons for retaining our subscription to the Articles at matriculation, &c. By Quinquagenarius [G. Fausset]. [Oxf.], (1835), 4°. 3 pp.   Bliss B 210 (16)

13. Oakeley, F., A letter . . . upon the principle and tendency of a bill . . . entitled 'An act prohibiting subscription to the Thirty-nine articles in certain cases. 2nd ed. Oxf., 1835, 8°. 29 pp.
Bliss B 210 (15)

3641. Oxford, March 28, 1835. It having been stated . . . [Signatures against the substitution of any declaration for subscription to the 39 articles.] Oxf., (1835), s. sh.   Bliss B 210 (7)
— [Another ed.]   Bliss B 210 (8)

3642. [*Begin.*] I am requested on the part . . . [Circular letter advocating resistance to the proposed substitution of a declaration for the subscription to the Articles. By E. B. Pusey?] [Oxf., 1835], s. sh.
Bliss B 210 (9)

— [Another ed., enlarged. *Begin.*] I am requested (on the part . . .
April 4, 1835. [Oxf.], (1835), s. sh.   Bliss B 210 (10)

3643. FAUSSET, G., A few plain reasons for retaining our subscription to
the Articles at matriculation in preference to the . . . declaration, which
it is proposed to substitute [signed Quinquagenarius]. Apr. 9. Oxf.,
1835, 4°. 3 pp.   G.A. Oxon c. 51 (116)
— [Another issue.]   Bliss B 210 (16)

3644. PUSEY, E. B., Questions respectfully addressed to members of Convocation on the subjoined declaration, which is proposed as a substitute for the subscription to the Thirty-nine articles at Matriculation
[signed A bachelor of divinity. E. B. Pusey]. [April]. (Oxf.), [1835],
8°. 8 pp.   G.A. Oxon 8° 77 (3)
— A second ed. . . . with some additional queries. Oxf., [1835], 8°.
12 pp.   B.M.

3645. [*Begin.*] 'I A. B. declare . . . [Circular letter, dated May 5, giving the
date of the Convocation for the substitution of the proposed declaration.] [Oxf.], (1835), s. sh.   Bliss B 210 (11)

3646. [*Begin.*] Sir, I beg to inform you . . . [A circular letter to non-
resident members of Convocation, by E. B. Pusey.] May 5. [Oxf.,
1835], 8°. 4 pp.

3647. HAWKINS, E., Oxford matriculation statutes, answers to [no. 3644]
the 'Questions addressed to members of Convocation by a bachelor of
divinity' by a resident member of Convocation [E. Hawkins]. May 7.
Oxf. &c., 1835, 8°. 29 pp.   Bliss B 210 (4)

3648. PUSEY, E. B., Subscription to the Thirty-nine articles. Questions . . .
addressed to members of Convocation on the declaration proposed as
a substitute for the subscription to the Thirty-nine articles, by a
bachelor of divinity, with answers by a resident member [E. Hawkins]
of Convocation; and brief notes upon those answers by the bachelor of
divinity [E. B. Pusey]. May 13. Oxf., 1835, 8°. 38 pp.
                                         G. Pamph. 2248 (4)

3649. MARRIOTT, C., Meaning of subscription [to the 39 articles, by
C. Marriott]. May 18. Oxf., 1835, 8°. 3 pp.   G.A. Oxon c. 51 (118)

3650. A bill intituled An act prohibiting subscription to the Thirty-nine
articles in certain cases. (11th June, House of Lords.) [Lond., 1835],
s. sh.   Bliss B 210 (1)

3651. DENISON, E., A review of the state of the question respecting the
admission of Dissenters to the universities. Lond., 1835, 8°. 56 pp.
                                              270 e. 483 (3)

3652. EDEN, C. P., Self-protection. The case of the Articles, by Clericus
[C. P. Eden]. Oxf., 1835, 8°. 24 pp.   G.A. Oxon 8° 70 (3)

3653. HAWKINS, E., A letter to the earl of Radnor upon the oaths, dispensations and subscription to the XXXIX articles at the University of

Oxford, by a resident member of Convocation [E. Hawkins]. Oxf. &c., 1835, 8°. 26 pp. Bliss B 210 (2)

3654. 1835 and 1772. The present attack on subscription compared with the last, a letter to 'A resident member of Convocation' occasioned by some remarks in his [E. Hawkins'] 'Letter to the earl of Radnor'. By a resident member of Convocation. Oxf., 1835, 8°. 52 pp.
G.A. Oxon 8° 77 (2)

3655. MAURICE, J. F., Subscription no bondage, or, The practical advantages afforded by the Thirty-nine articles as guides in all the branches of academical education. With an introductory letter on the declaration which it is proposed to substitute for subscription to the Articles at matriculation. By Rusticus. Oxf., 1835, 8°. 125 pp.
G. Pamph. 2248 (2)

3656. Reasons for preferring a simple declaration, to the present method of exacting signature to the Thirty-nine articles, at matriculation in the University of Oxford; in a letter from a country clergyman to his friend. Speenhamland, 1835, 8°. 19 pp. G. Pamph. 2248 (5)

3657. SYMONS, B. P., A letter to a non-resident friend upon subscription to the Thirty-nine articles at matriculation. By a senior member of Convocation [B. P. Symons]. Oxf., [1835], 8°. 8 pp.
G.A. Oxon c. 51 (117)

3658. The universities and the Dissenters. Lond., 1835, 8°. 66 pp.
G. Pamph. 2248 (1)

3658.1. THOMAS, V., The reasonableness of the Academic ordinance of 1581 requiring subscription at matriculation, proved . . . in a letter. Oxf., 1835, 8°. 31 pp. 35. 800

See 1850 [A review of observations made in the Edinburgh review on the admission of Dissenters. 1837].

3659. The proposed Oxford test. (Christ. rem., 1845, new ser., vol. 9, p. 188–200.) Per. 971 e. 44

3660. CHRISTIE, W. D., Two speeches in the House of Commons on the universities of Oxford and Cambridge . . . 1. On moving for leave to introduce a bill 'to abolish certain oaths and subscriptions in the universities . . . and to extend education . . . to persons who are not members of the Church of England'. May 25th, 1843. 2. On moving 'that an humble address be presented to her majesty . . . praying that she will . . . appoint a Commission to inquire into . . . the universities . . . ' April 10th, 1845. Lond., 1850, 8°. 51 pp. G.A. Oxon 8° 234 (12)

See 1699 [Heywood, J., History of the subscription tests. 1853].

3661. The Oxford declarations against the admission of Dissenters to the University, in the year 1834. [The text of three declarations is given, followed by a statement, signed A member of Convocation, urging a similar declaration in 1854.] June 28. [Oxf.], (1854), s. sh.
G.A. Oxon c. 70 (272)

3662. A few words upon the admission of Dissenters to the University of Oxford, by a priest of the Church of England. Oxf. &c., 1854, 8°. 16 pp.
G.A. Oxon 8° 63 (14)

3663. Universities of Oxford and Cambridge. [Memorial of many members of the House of Commons urging the abolition of a religious test taken at matriculation.] [Lond., 1854], fol. 3 pp. G.A. Oxon b. 137 (23)

3664. To the . . . Lords . . . The humble petition of the undersigned resident [and non-resident] members of the Convocation of the University of Oxford . . . not to alter by compulsory legislation the relations . . . between the University and the established Church. Oxf., [1854], fol. 4 pp.   G.A. Oxon b. 27

3665. HUSSEY, R., University prospects and university duties, a sermon. Oxf., 1854, 8°. 35 pp.   G.A. Oxon 8° 659 (24)

See also Faculty of Theology [No. 2463, &c. 1855].

3666. To the . . . Commons . . . in Parliament assembled; the humble petition of the Chancellor, Masters, and Scholars of the University of Oxford [against the proposed bill to abolish religious tests]. 2nd June, 1863. n. pl., 1863, fol. 4 pp.   G.A. Oxon c. 79 (253)

3667. STANLEY, A. P., A letter to the lord bishop of London on the state of subscription in the Church of England and in the University of Oxford. Oxf. &c., 1863, 8°. 100 pp.   100 f. 12 (4)

3668. Tests abolition. A bill to provide for the abolition of certain tests in connection with academical degrees in the University of Oxford. 12 Feb., 1864. [Lond.], 1864, fol. 4 pp.   Pp. Eng. 1864 vol. 4
— 12 March, 1865. [Lond.], 1865, fol. 4 pp.   Pp. Eng. 1865 vol. 4

3669. GOSCHEN, G. J., Speech . . . on the Oxford university tests abolition bill, June 14, 1865. Lond., 1865, 8°. 31 pp.   G.A. Oxon 8° 1400 (1)

3670. HAWKINS, E., Notes on subscription, academical and clerical. Oxf. &c., 1864, 8°. 69 pp.   1365 e. 8 (4)

3671. LIDDELL, H. G., Subscription no security, by the dean of Christchurch. (MacMillan's mag., 1864, vol. 9, p. 465–72.)
G.A. Oxon 4° 579 (14)

3672. LYGON, F., University tests, substance of a speech, House of commons, July 24, 1863. Oxf. &c., 1864, 8°. 12 pp.   2625 e. 112 (14)

3673. SMITH, G., A plea for the abolition of tests in the University of Oxford. Oxf. &c., 1864, 8°. 103 pp.   G.A. Oxon 8° 202

3674. BRAMLEY, H. R., An answer to professor Goldwin Smith's Plea for the abolition of tests in the University of Oxford. Lond. &c., 1864, 8°. 74 pp.   100 f. 121 (8)

3675. The abolition of religious tests. (Westm. review, 1864, vol. 81, p. 384–97.)   Per. 3977 e. 228

3676. Tests abolition. A bill to provide for the abolition of religious tests in connexion with academical degrees and offices in the University of Oxford. 13 Feb. 1866. [Lond.], 1866, s. sh.   Pp. Eng. 1866 vol. 5
— 12 Feb., 1867. [Lond.], 1867, s. sh.   Pp. Eng. 1867 vol. 6

3677. BRODRICK, G. C., University tests. (Journ. of social sci., 1866, p. 117–36.)   G.A. Oxon 4° 580 (2)
— [Repr.]. 18 pp.   G.A. Oxon 8° 1400 (2)

3678. HAWKINS, E., Additional notes on subscription, academical and clerical. Oxf. &c., 1866, 8°. 66 pp.   1365 e. 8 (1)

3679. Abolition of tests at the universities of Oxford and Cambridge. Report of speeches at a public meeting held in . . . Manchester, April 6, 1866. Lond. &c., 1866, 8°. 55 pp.   G.A. Oxon 8° 1400 (3)

3680. For the Hebdomadal council only. Draft. [*Begin.*] That your petitioners have been informed that a bill has lately been introduced into your honourable House entitled 'A bill to provide for the abolition of religious tests . . . [A petition against the bill.] [Oxf., 1867], s. sh.
       G.A. Oxon a. 17
— Proposed form of petition. [Oxf., 1867], s. sh.   G.A. Oxon a. 17

3681. Oxford and Cambridge universities. A bill to repeal certain tests and alter certain statutes affecting the constitution of the Universities of Oxford and Cambridge. 18 Feb. 1868. [Lond.], 1868, fol. 3 pp.
       Pp. Eng. 1867/68 vol. 3

3682. [Address] To . . . the . . . archbishop of Canterbury [seeking his aid against a bill designed to permit men to proceed to the degree of M.A. without subscribing to the 39 articles. Signed by F[rancis Jeune, bishop of] Peterborough and many others]. n. pl., [1868], 8°. 4 pp.
       G.A. Oxon c. 84 (429)

3683. YOUNG, SIR G., University tests, an apology for their assailants, with facts and documents for their abolition. Lond., 1868, 8°. 55 pp.
       G.A. Oxon 8° 1400 (4)

3684. CHASE, D. P., A few words on the Oxford address to the archbishop of Canterbury, by the principal of St. Mary hall. Oxf., 1868, 8°. 12 pp.
       G.A. Oxon 8° 250 (11)
[Repr. of 2 articles emphasizing the folly of resisting the admission to Convocation of all otherwise qualified persons without religious test.]

3685. University tests. A bill to repeal certain tests and alter certain statutes affecting the constitution of the Universities of Oxford and Cambridge. 23 Feb. 1869. [Lond.], 1869, fol. 3 pp.
       Pp. Eng. 1868/69 vol. 5

3686. Abolition of University and Collegiate [religious] tests. [Proceedings of a meeting held in Corpus Christi college, Dec. 4, 1869.] (Oxf.), [1869], 8°. 8 pp.   G.A. Oxon 8° 1079 (3)

3687. CHASE, D. P., The de-Christianising of the colleges of Oxford. Repr. from the Standard of October 27, 1868. Lond. &c., 1869, 8°. 7 pp.
G.A. Oxon 8° 100 (7)

3688. CHASE, D. P., University tests. Observations upon the bill of the solicitor-general, and upon the counter-proposal of lord Carnarvon, by the principal of St. Mary hall, Oxford. Lond. &c., 1869, 8°. 19 pp.
G.A. Oxon 8° 1400 (6)

3689. University tests. A bill to alter the law respecting religious tests in the Universities of Oxford, Cambridge and Durham, and in the halls and colleges of those universities respectively. 25 Apr. 1870. [Lond.], 1870, fol. 4 pp.   Pp. Eng. 1870 vol. 4

3690. Amendments to the draft of mr. Coleridge's bill, passed by the committee appointed to consider its provisions. [Oxf., 1870], fol. 4 pp.
G.A. Oxon b. 140 (94*b*)
— [Another ed. with 'Scheme for Convocation and Congregation as proposed by the dean of Christ Church and professor Jowett'.] [Oxf., 1870?], fol. 4 pp.   G.A. Oxon b. 140 (94*a*)

3691. University tests. (Blackwood's Edinb. mag., 1870, vol. 107, p. 139–60.)   G.A. Oxon 4° 580 (16)

3692. PLACE, J., University tests and their abolition [signed One of the people and a non-university man]. With a table of pre- and post-Reformation benefactions to Oxford. Lond. &c., (1870), 8°. 31 pp.
G.A. Oxon 8° 90 (6)

3693. University tests. A bill to alter the law respecting religious tests in the Universities of Oxford, Cambridge and Durham, and in the halls and colleges of those universities. 10 Feb. 1871. [Lond.], 1871, fol. 4 pp.   Pp. Eng. 1871 vol. 6
— As amended by the Lords. 16 May 1871. [Lond.], 1871, fol. 4 pp.
Pp. Eng. 1871 vol. 6
— Lords' amendments. 16 May 1871. [Lond.], 1871, s. sh.
Pp. Eng. 1871 vol. 6

3694. Report from the select committee of the House of Lords on university tests; together with the proceedings of the committee, minutes of evidence, and appendix. [Lond.], 1871, fol. 133 pp.
Pp. Eng. 1871 vol. 9

3695. First (Second) report from the select committee of the House of Lords on university tests; together with the minutes of evidence, and appendix. [Lond.], 1871, fol. 361+xii pp.   Pp. Eng. 1871 vol. 9
— Index to Reports. [Lond.], 1871, fol. 64 pp. Pp. Eng. 1871 vol. 9

3696. Abolition of university and college tests. Speeches delivered at Liverpool, March 27th, 1871. Liverpool, 1871, 8°. 42 pp.
G.A. Oxon 8° 1400 (8)

3697. Oxford, as it is and as it was. (Dublin review, 1871, N.S., vol. 17, p. 269–85.)   Per. 3977 e. 199

3698. An act to alter the law respecting religious tests in the Universities of Oxford, Cambridge and Durham, and in the hall and colleges of those universities. (34 V. c. 26, Pub.). Lond., 1871, fol. 4 pp.   L.L.

3699. POTTINGER, H. A., University tests, a short account of the contrivances by which the Acts of parliament abolishing tests and declarations have been evaded at Oxford. Lond., 1873, 8°. 56 pp.
                                                     G.A. Oxon 8° 165 (14)

3700. University tests. A bill to amend the law relating to tests in the Universities of Oxford, Cambridge and Durham, and the colleges therein. 13 Aug., 1878. [Lond.], 1878, s. sh.   Pp. Eng. 1878 vol. 9

3701. BURGON, J. W., The disestablishment of religion in Oxford, the betrayal of a sacred trust: Words of warning to the University, a sermon. Oxf. &c., (1880), 8°. 55 pp.   MS. Eng. th. d. 14 (9)
— [Proof of 2nd ed.]   MS. Eng. th. d. 14 (10)
— 2nd ed. 56 pp.   MS. Eng. th. d. 14 (11)
— 2nd ed. [Another issue.]   MS. Eng. th. d. 14 (12)

Roman Catholics

See also 3758, &c., Religious orders.

3702. ROWLAND, W., The late act [June 1, 1641] of the Convocation at Oxford examined: or, The obit of prelatique Protestancy: occasioning the conversion of W. R. . . . to Catholique union. [Madan 2188.] Rouen [really Oxf.], 1652, 12°. 141 pp.   8° L 108 Th.

3703. The docket of king James the second's licence, dispensation and pardon for Obadiah Walker, Nath. Boyse, Thomas Deane and John Bernard. May 1686. [Permitting them to absent themselves from Church and from administering the sacrament as used in the Church of England, and from taking the oaths of supremacy, &c.] (Collectanea curiosa, by J. Gutch, vol. 1, p. 287, 88.) Oxf., 1781, 8°. Gough Oxf. 65

3704. Mr. Massey's licence, dispensation and pardon [from James II, dated 16 Dec. 1686, excusing him from attendance at church, from taking the oath of allegiance, and from subscribing to the 39 articles]. (Collectanea curiosa, by J. Gutch, vol. 1, p. 294–98.) Oxf., 1781, 8°.
                                                     Gough Oxf. 65

3705. To the members of Convocation. [A paper, signed A member of Convocation, against sanctioning the petition against Roman Catholics.] (Oxf., 1812), fol. 3 pp.   G.A. Oxon b. 140 (12a)

3706. [Begin.] Notice having been given . . . [Queries concerning the annual petition against further concessions to the Roman Catholics.] Mar. 12. Oxf., (1828), s. sh.   G.A. Oxon c. 44 (28)

3706.5. MAURICE, P., The Popery in Oxford. Oxf., 1833, 8°. 16 pp.
                                                     G. A. Oxon 8° 233 (8)
—[Another ed.]. 1133. 23 pp.   G. A. Oxon 8° 233 (9)
—2nd ed. [Pupl. as Appendix I of no. 3707].

3707. MAURICE, P., The popery of Oxford confronted, disavowed, & repudiated. [With Appendix 1–3.] Lond., 1837, 8°. 88+72 pp. 37. 1098

3708. MAURICE, P., A key to The popery of Oxford. Lond., 1838, 8°. 71 pp. 38. 811

3709. Oxford Catholicism. (Edinb. review, 1838, vol. 67, p. 500–35.)
Per. 3977 e. 190

3710. Oxford seceders to Romanism [list 1841–47]. (Oxf. Protestant mag., 1847, vol. 1, p. 245–48.) Per. G.A. Oxon 8° 119

3711. MAURICE, P., Postscript to The popery of Oxford: the number of the name of the beast. [With Appendix.] Lond., 1851, 8°. 60+7 pp.
100 f. 34

3712–14. MAURICE, P., The ritualism of Oxford popery (Postscript *and* Dr. Macbride's legacy). Lond., [1867–69], 8° 191 pp.
100 f. 104 (20); 114 (12); 126 (23)

3715. Catholics and the Oxford examinations. (Month, 1869, vol. 11, p. 213–16.) Per. 11132 d. 17

3716. CLARKE, R. F., Catholics at the English universities. 1–4. (The Month, 1885, vol. 35. p. 345–58, 457–73; vol. 36, p. 1–17, 153–69.)
G.A. Oxon 4° 586 (21–24)

3717. A memorandum on the universities question as affecting Catholics [by 15 English Catholic laymen]. Lond., 1894, 8°. 16+viii pp.
2625 d. 9 (9)

3718. BLAIR, SIR D. O. HUNTER-, Catholics at the national universities. [Oxford *passim*.] Lond., 1906, 8°. 15 pp. 2625 d. 31 (25)
See 3953 [Blair, O. Hunter-, Oxford as it is. 1908].

3719. RYAN, P., Diocesan returns of recusants for England and Wales, 1577. (Publ., Cath. record soc., 1921, vol. 22, Oxford city and univ., p. 97–101.) Soc. G.A. Gen. top. 4° 220 = K.

3720. HEMPHILL, D., Oxford and James II [the installation of Catholics in leading positions]. (Clergy review, 1948, vol. 29, p. 86–94.)
Per. 132 d. 25

3720.3. Catholic activities in Oxford. [Reprod. from typewriting.] n. pl., [1962], 8°. 12 pp. G.A. Oxon 8° 1471

See 242.7 [Hinnebusch, W. A., Foreign Dominican students and professors. 1964].
See 5130.1 [Janus, the Oxford Catholic review. 1965].

3720.4. REYNOLDS, S., The work of Grandpont house [residence for postgraduates run by Opus Dei.] (Oxf. mag., 1965, N.S., vol. 5, p. 258, 59.)
Per. G.A. Oxon 4° 141

Roman Catholic societies

3721. Oxford university Catholic club. (Rules, members.) [Oxf.], (1879), 16°. 8 pp. G.A. Oxon 16° 200 (14)

Dissenters

3722. HUBBERTHORNE, R., A true testimony of the zeal of Oxford-professors and university-men who for zeal persecute the servants of the living God. [Madan 2245.] Lond., 1654, 4°. [2]+14 pp.
Wood 515 (15)

3723. Here followeth a true relation of some of the sufferings inflicted upon ... Quakers, by ... the schollars and proctors of the University of Oxford. [Madan 2250.] [Lond.? 1654], 4°. 8 pp.   Wood 515 (14)

3724. BIDDLE, H., [*Begin.*] Wo to thee City of Oxford ... [An address to Oxford bitterly inveighing against the sins of the City and University, especially in the treatment of Quakers.] [Madan 2268.] [Lond., 1655], s. sh.
B.M.

3725. The Oxford methodists: some account of a society of young gentlemen in that city. A letter. Lond., 1733, 8°. 32 pp. Gough Oxf. 62 (1)
— 2nd ed. To which is prefix'd A short epistle to ... mr. Whitefield. Lond., 1738, 8°. 29 pp.   Gough Oxf. 62 (2)

3726. WHITEFIELD, G., A letter ... occasioned by a late expulsion of six students from Edmund Hall. Lond., 1768, 8°. 50 pp.
Gough Oxf. 61 (4)
— 2nd ed. 47 pp.   11142 f. 4

3727. C., W., Remarks upon ... mr. Whitefield's letter, in a letter, by a late member of the University of Oxford [signed W. C.]. Oxf., 1768, 8°. 62 pp.   Gough Oxf. 61 (5)

3728. BROWNE, W., A vindication of the proceedings against the six members of E—— Hall, Oxford, by a gentleman of the University [W. Browne]. Lond., 1768, 8°. 16 pp.   Gough Oxf. 61 (1)
— 2nd ed., with additions. Lond., 1769, 8°. 39 pp.
G.A. Oxon 8° 70 (1)

3729. HILL, SIR R., Pietas Oxoniensis: or, A full and impartial account of the expulsion of six students from St. Edmund Hall. Lond., 1768, 8°. 85 pp.   Gough Oxf. 62 (4)
— 2nd ed. 102 pp.   G. Pamph. 130

3730. HILL, SIR R., Duwioldeb Rhydychen: neu, Hanes gyflawn a diduedd am chwech o ysgolheigion a swriwyd allan o neuadd-golegol St. Edmund ... gyda llythyr cyflwyniad at yr anrhydeddus iarll Litchffild. Gan athraw'r celfyddydau, brif-ysgol Rhydychen [sir R. Hill]. Caerfyrddin, 1769, 12°. vi+102 pp.   141 n. 91 (1)

3731. A letter to the author of a pamphlet entitled Pietas Oxoniensis [signed: A member of the Church of England]. Lond., 1768, 8°. 26 pp.
Gough Oxf. 62 (8)

3732. NOWELL, T., An answer to a pamphlet, entitled Pietas Oxoniensis, a letter wherein the grounds of the expulsion of six members from St. Edmund Hall are set forth. Lond., 1768, 8°. 150 pp.
Gough Oxf. 62 (5)
— 2nd ed. with additions. 1769. 206 pp.   G.A. Oxon 8° 72 (12)

3733. HILL, SIR R., Goliath slain: a reply to . . . dr. Nowell's answer to Pietas Oxoniensis, by the author of Pietas Oxoniensis. Lond., 1768, 8°. 214 pp.   Gough Oxf. 62 (7)

3734. HILL, SIR R., A defence of the doctrines of sovereign grace: a full answer to a letter [no. 3731] lately addressed to the author of Pietas Oxoniensis. By the author of that book [sir R. Hill]. Lond., 1768, 8°. 48 pp.   G.A. Oxon 8° 72 (11)

3735. MACGOWAN, J., A further defence of priestcraft, by the Shaver [J. MacGowan]. [Five eds. were publ. in 1768, of which Bodley has]:
— 4th ed. Lond., 1768, 8°. 44 pp.   Gough Oxf. 61 (3)
— 5th ed.   G.A. Oxon 8° 154 (2)

3736. HIGGENBROCCIUS, GERARDUS, pseud., Carmen introductorium Pietati Oxoniensi præfigendum auctore Gerardo Higgenbroccio; cum ejusdem annotatiunculis. Subjicitur Epistola gratulatoria ad auctorem missa ab amico anonymo. Cui adjungitur postscriptum de criticis recensoribus. n. pl., [1768?], 8°. 22 pp.   G.A. Oxon 16° 24

3737. MACGOWAN, J., Priestcraft defended, a sermon occasioned by the expulsion of six young gentlemen from the University of Oxford. By the Shaver [J. MacGowan]. Dubl., 1768, 8°. 34 pp.
— 2nd ed. Lond., 1768.   Gough Oxf. 61 (2)
[10 eds. were publ. in 1768. Other eds. in 1769, 71, 87, 88, 96, 1806, 09, 10, 12, and the 21st ed. in 1813: G.A. Oxon 8° 147 (16). Some editions were publ. without the title 'Priestcraft defended'.]

3738. HILL, SIR R., A letter to . . . dr. Nowell: containing some remarks on certain alterations and additions in the second edition of his answer to Pietas Oxoniensis. By the author of Pietas Oxoniensis. Lond. &c., 1769, 8°. 45 pp.   G.A. Oxon 8° 219 (5)

3739. The Oxford expulsion condemned and the gross errors of the Oxonian refuted, in his Remarks on . . . mr. Whitefield's letter [no. 3727]. In a letter to a friend. By a real member of the Church of England. Lond., 1769, 8°. 74 pp.   Gough Oxf. 61 (7)

3740. Strictures on An answer to the Pietas Oxoniensis by Thomas Nowell. By No Methodist. Lond., 1769, 4°. 46 pp.   Gough Oxf. 62 (6)

3741. The Shaver shaved; a macaronic dialogue between B. and S. By a matriculated barber. Lond., 1769, 8°. 24 pp.   G. Pamph. 1352

3742. The contrast: or, The rev. dr. Thomas Nowell public orator . . . against dr. Nowell, principal of St. Mary Hall, concerning the doctrine of justification in his letter to the author of Pietas Oxoniensis. By one who is not a master of arts. Lond., 1769, 8°. 36 pp. Gough Oxf. 61 (8)

3743. [*Begin.*] The reverend dr. Dixon . . . [Notification of the holding of a Convocation on 12 July 1769, to decide whether to matriculate S. Seager of St. Edmund Hall, who was closely connected with the Methodists.] [Oxf.], (1769), s. sh. Gough Oxf. 62 (9)

3744. SEAGER, S., A letter . . . to the . . . Vice-Chancellor [defending himself against dr. Audley's letter, which is quoted in no. 3743]. [Oxf., 1769], s. sh. Gough Oxf. 62 (10)

3745. OLLARD, S. L., The six students of St. Edmund hall, expelled from the University of Oxford in 1768, with a note on the authorities for their story. 1st impr. Lond., 1911, 8°. 59 pp. G.A. Oxon 8° 826

3746. FLETCHER, W. G. D., The expulsion of Oxford students in 1768. (Trans., Shropshire archaeol. soc., 1912, vol. 35, p. 186–92.)
Per. G.A. Salop. 8° 61 = R. Top.
— [Repr.]. 7 pp. G.A. Oxon 8° 828 (23)

3747. OLLARD, S. L., A note on the expulsions of 1768. (St. Edmund Hall mag., 1928, vol. 2, no. 3, p. 63–67.) Per. G.A. Oxon 4° 447

3748. HINTON, J., A vindication of the Dissenters in Oxford . . . in reply to dr. Tatham's sermon. Lond., (1792), 8°. 19 pp.
G.A. Oxon 8° 165 (18)
— 2nd ed. [1793.] Firth d. 9
— 3rd ed. [1793.] 11134 e. 3
— 4th ed. [1793.] G.A. Oxon 8° 215 (10)

3749. MOORE, J. J., Earlier and later Noncomformity in Oxford, revised to 1875. Oxf., 1875, 8°. 32 pp. G.A. Oxon 8° 338

3750. GUMMERE, A. M., Oxford university and the Quakers. (Pennsyl. mag. of hist. and biogr., 1898, vol. 23, p. 273 &c.) B.M.

3751. STRONG, H. W., Modern Oxford and Nonconformity. (Lond. quarterly, 1899, N.S., vol. 2, p. 279–90.) Per. 3977 d. 57

3752. WHITEHORN, R. D., Presbyterians and Baptists in eighteenth-century Oxford. (Journ., Presbyterian hist. soc., 1938, vol. 6, p. 229–32.) Per. 1119 d. 33

3753. STEVENS, W., Oxford's attitude to Dissenters, 1646–1946. (Baptist quarterly, 1949/50, N.S., vol. 13, p. 4–17.) Per. 11133 d. 20

3754. FIRMAN, C. K., Footnote on Methodism in Oxford. (Church history, 1960, vol. 29, p. 161–66.) Per. 110 d. 698 = S.

Jews

3755. Oxford university Hebrew congregation. [Miscellaneous papers. 1902–1923.] G.A. Oxon b. 145

3756. A prayer book printed for the use of the Oxford university Hebrew congregation. Lond. &c., (1914), 8°. 68 pp. 954 e. 21

See 242.69 [Roth, C., The vicissitudes of the first Oxford Jewish graduate. 1963].

Eastern church

3757. Eastern Church theological students at Oxford. Report. Oxf., [1920],
8°. 8 pp.   G.A. Oxon 8° 1002 (11)

Religious orders

3758. Artycles of the great indulgence of plenary remissyon à pena et culpa
graunted for the buyldynge of seynt Peters churche at Rome and the
cõuentuall churchis of freres Augustyns of Oxford . . . [Lond., 1516?],
s. sh.   St. Johns

3758.1. [*Begin.*] Deuot. in Christo Jesu sibi dilect. [A letter of confraternity
issued by the Oxford Friars Preachers.] Oxon., 1520, s. sh.   B.M.

3758.5. The Friars preachers *v.* the University, A.D. 1311–1313 [from
Digby Rolls 1]. (Oxf. hist. soc., vol. 16, Collectanea, 2nd ser., 1890,
p. 193–273.)   G.A. Oxon 8° 360 = R.

3759. WOODBURNE, G. B. LANCASTER, The Friars in Oxford. (Dublin
review, 1893, N.S., vol. 112, p. 84–106.)   Per. 3977 e. 199

3760. LITTLE, A. G., Cistercian students at Oxford in the thirteenth
century. (Engl. hist. review, 1893, vol. 8, p. 83–85.)
                                       Per. 2231 d. 342 = K.

3761. LITTLE, A. G., Educational organisation of the mendicant friars in
England (Dominicans and Franciscans) [Oxford *passim*]. (Trans.,
Roy. hist. soc., 1894, N.S., vol. 8, p. 49–70.)   Soc. 2262 e. 45 = K.

3762. FOWLER, R. C., Cistercian scholars at Oxford. (Engl. hist. review,
1908, vol. 23, p. 84, 85.)   Per. 2231 d. 342 = K.

3763. LITTLE, A. G., The Franciscan school at Oxford in the 13th century.
(Archivum Franciscanum historicum, 1926, annus xix, p. 803–74.)
                                       Per. 1107 d. 113 = K.

3764. PANTIN, W. A., The general and provincial chapters of the English
black monks, 1215–1540. [Oxford *passim*.] (Trans., Roy. hist. soc.,
1927, ser. 4, vol. 10, p. 195–263.)   Per. 2262 e. 45 = K.

3765. BLAIR, D. O. HUNTER-, The Black monks at Oxford university.
(Dublin review, 1933, vol. 192, p. 17–25.)   Per. 3977 e. 199

3766. SMALLEY, B., Robert Bacon and the early Dominican school at
Oxford. (Trans., Roy. hist. soc., 1948, ser. 4, vol. 30, p. 1–20.)
                                       Per. 2262 e. 45 = K.

3767. IRWIN, R., S. Robert of Lincoln and the Oxford Greyfriars. (The
Private library, 1961, vol. 3, p. 110–19.)   Per. 25899 d. 117

See 242.7 [Hinnebusch, W. A., Foreign Dominican students and professors at
the Oxford Blackfriars. 1964].

Preachers

3768. [*Begin.*] It seems to have been . . . [Alterations in the statute De concionibus, submitted to the consideration of members of Convocation. Dated Feb. 16, 1803.] [Oxf.], (1803), 4°. 3 pp. Don. b. 12 (91*b*)
— [Another issue, dated 21 Nov. 1803.]   G.A. Oxon b. 19

3769. Observations [signed A member of Convocation, Dec. 4] on some parts of the statute De concionibus to be proposed. . . Dec. 6th. Oxf., [1803], s. sh.   G.A. Oxon b. 19

3770. To the members of Convocation. [A paper, beginning Strong doubts, signed A member of Convocation, criticizing the expediency of altering the statute De concionibus. Dec. 4.] (Oxf.), [1803], s. sh.
                                                          G.A. Oxon b. 19

3771. [*Begin.*] Two printed papers . . . To the members of Convocation. [An answer, dated Dec. 5th, to nos. 3769, 70.] (Oxf., 1803), 4°. 4 pp.
                                                          G.A. Oxon b. 19

3772. To the members of Convocation. [A paper, *begin.*] The author of a paper . . . [replying to criticisms in no. 3770. Signed A member of Convocation, Dec. 6, 1803.] (Oxf., 1803,) 4°. 3 pp.   G.A. Oxon b. 19

3773. The following account of monies received and paid in pursuance of the statute De concionibus . . . has been examined and approved by the Delegates of accounts. 1804/05–11/12.   G.A. Oxon b. 13
— 1812/13, 17/18, 18/19, 20/21.   G.A. Oxon b. 19
— 1821/22–25/26.   G.A. Oxon b. 20
— 1825/26–44/45.   G.A. Oxon c. 41–61

3774. [*Begin.*] The attention of members of Convocation is invited . . . [Arguments against a proposal to restore the morning sermon at St. Mary's during the Long-vacation, signed A member of Convocation.] June 22. (Oxf., 1830), s. sh.   G.A. Oxon c. 46 (70)

3775. [*Begin.*] A paper having been circulated . . . [An answer to no. 3774 signed Another member of Convocation.] June 23. (Oxf., 1830), s. sh.
                                                          G.A. Oxon c. 46 (71)

3776. [*Begin.*] Cuilibet die Dominico . . . [An objection, dated 7 May, to the proposal to pay five guineas to the dean and canons of Christ Church when they preach to the University in their own cathedral.] Oxf., (1847), s. sh.   G.A. Oxon b. 26

3777. [*Begin.*] The dean and canons of Christ Church . . . [Observations by the Dean refuting comments made in no. 3776]. May 10, 1847. Oxf., 1847, s. sh.   G.A. Oxon c. 63 (76*a*)

3778. To members of Convocation. [*Begin.*] In reply to a paper . . . [A further attack, dated 11 May, on the dean and canons of Christ Church and their attitude to cathedral sermons.] Oxf., (1847), s. sh.
                                                          G.A. Oxon b. 26

3779. BULL, J., To the rev. the vice-chancellor, &c. &c. &c. [*Begin.*] I am sure . . . [A defence, dated May 11, of the dean and canons of Christ Church.] Oxf., (1847), s. sh.   G.A. Oxon b. 26

3780. PHILALETHES, *pseud.*, To members of Convocation, specially to those of Ch. Ch. common room. [Remarks, dated 13 May, on the papers emanating from Christ Church.] Oxf., (1847), s. sh.   G.A. Oxon b. 26

3781. GAISFORD, T., [*Begin.*] The subject of university sermons . . . [An account of the University sermons, with particular reference to the statutes relating thereto.] Oxf., 1847, 8°. 8 pp.   G.A. Oxon c. 63 (81)

3782. Nov. 15, 1847. [Acceptance in Convocation of Nov. 25th of the James Heywood Markland benefaction for a sermon to be preached annually.]   G.A. Oxon c. 63 (141)

3783. [Proposal to accept a benefaction for an annual sermon 'On the application of the prophecies in Holy Scripture respecting the Messiah . . . to confute the arguments of Jewish commentators . . . ' to be submitted to Convocation, Mar. 30.] Mar. 27. [Oxf.], (1848), s. sh.   G.A. Oxon c. 64 (36)

3784. A letter . . . on the subject of the University sermons. By a tutor. Oxf., 1853, 8°. 8 pp.   G.A. Oxon 8° 161 (11)

3785. SANDFORD, C. W., The University sermon and college services, a letter to the vice-chancellor. Oxf., 1865, 8°. 8 pp.   G.A. Oxon 8° 179 (21)
— 2nd ed. 1866.   MS. Eng. th. d 8 (8).

3786. BURGON, J. W., Mr. Sandford and the University sermon, a letter [in answer to no. 3785]. Oxf., 1865, 8°. 8 pp.   G.A. Oxon 8° 105 (11)

3787. KITCHIN, G. W., Mr. Burgon and the University sermon [in answer to no. 3786.] Oxf., 1865, 8°. 8 pp.   G.A. Oxon 8° 105 (10)

3788. BURGON, J. W., Mr. Kitchin, mr. Sandford, and the University sermon, a second letter. Oxf., 1865, 8°. 12 pp.   G.A. Oxon 8° 179 (22)

3789. SANDFORD, C. W., The University sermon and college services, a letter to the vicar of St. Mary-the-Virgin's. Oxf., 1866, 8°. 19 pp.   G.A. Oxon 8° 105 (12)

3790. BURGON, J. W., The Oxford Sunday, a letter to mr. Sandford in reply. Oxf., 1866, 8°. 20 pp.   G.A. Oxon 8° 179 (23)
— [Another issue, the preliminaries dated Feb. 1 and Feb. 5.]   MS. Eng. th. d. 8 (26)

3791. BURGON, J. W., The proposed list of 'selected preachers'. [A letter protesting against the inclusion of bp. F. Temple.] Nov. 25. [Oxf.], (1871), s. sh.   MS. Eng. th. d. 9 (48)

3792. Oxford, Dec. 3, 1872. Sir, The statutes of the University * imposing . . . [An open letter, signed by W. J. Trower and 14 others, opposing

the appointment of dean Stanley as a select preacher.] [Oxf.], (1872),
s. sh.   MS. Eng. th. d. 10 (18)

3793. Correspondence between . . . Henry George Liddell, vice-chancellor
. . . and mr. Burgon, concerning a privilege of Convocation in respect
of the nomination of select preachers. Oxf. &c., 1872, 8°. 12 pp.
                                                  MS. Eng. th. d. 10 (41)

3794. INCE, W., The new statute on University sermons. Feb. 13, 1890.
[Oxf.], (1890), s. sh.   G.A. Oxon c. 153

3795. HEURTLEY, C. A., The proposed changes in the statute on University
sermons. Feb. 14. [Oxf.], (1890), s. sh.   G.A. Oxon c. 153

SOCIAL HISTORY

LIFE AND MANNERS

General and to the sixteenth century

3796. Reminiscences of Oxford, by Oxford men, 1559–1850, selected and ed. by L. M. Quiller Couch. (Oxf. hist. soc., 22.) Oxf., 1892, 8°. 430 pp.
G.A. Oxon 8° 360 = R.

See 4710 [Collins, C. W., Oxford in fact and fiction. 1895].

3797. ALLEN, W. C., Proctorial reminiscences. (Stapeldon mag., 1908, vol. 2, p. 62–66.) Per. G.A. Oxon 8° 713

See 61 [Henderson, P. A. Wright-. The Oxford undergraduate, past and present. 1926]

3798. RAIT, R. S., Life in the medieval university. [Oxford *passim.*] Cambr., 1912, 8°. 164 pp. 2625 f. 7

3799. RUSSELL, G. W. E., Half-lengths [p. 200–33 Oxford]. Lond., 1913, 8°.
2288 e. 715

3800. DUGDALE, E. T. S., Gentlemen commoners. (Oxf. mag., 1937, vol. 55, p. 310, 11.) Per. G.A. Oxon 4° 141

See 8410 [The inventory of John English [1586–1613]. 1946/47].

Seventeenth century

See 7688 [Heylin, P., Memoranda, 1599–1643. 1851].
See 7082 [Taswell, W., Autobiography and anecdotes [1670–82]. 1853].
See 8594 [Paget, F. E., A student penitent of 1695 [R. Graham of University college]. 1875].

3801. PRIDEAUX, H., Letters of Humphrey Prideaux . . . to John Ellis, 1674–1722 [Oxford 1674–81] ed. by E. M. Thompson. (Camden soc., N.S. vol. 15.) (Westm.), 1875, 8°. 221 pp. 2233 e. 54 = K.

3802. Oxford gossip in the seventeenth century [based on extracts from the Letters of Humphrey Prideaux]. (Quarterly review, 1877, vol. 144, p. 81–107.) Per. 3977 e. 191

3803. WOODHOUSE, J., Seventeenth-century scandal at Oxford [based on extracts from A. à Wood and H. Prideaux]. (Gents mag., 1899, vol. 286, p. 553–62.) Per. 2705 e. 327

3804. MAGRATH, J. R., *ed.*, The Flemings in Oxford: documents selected from the Rydal papers, 1650–1700. 3 vols. (Oxf. hist. soc., 44, 62, 79.) Oxf., 1904–24, 8°. G.A. Oxon 8° 360 = R.

3805. NEWTON, E., Oxford university life in the seventeenth century [Extracts from letters written by Richard Taylor between 1608 and 1611.] (Nat. rev., 1907, vol. 50, p. 618–23.) Per. 22775 d. 14

3806. FIRTH, SIR C. H., The 17th century undergraduate. (Oriel record, 1915, vol. 2, p. 251–57, 280–89; 1918, vol. 3, p. 49–54.)
Per. G.A. Oxon 4° 484

See 7538 [Austin, R., Thomas Smyth of Lincoln college [expenses, books &c. 1638]. 1921].
See 8209 [Diary of T. Crosfield, 1626–1653. 1935].
See 6965 [Bennett, J. A. W., ed., Oxford in 1699. 1939].
See 7070 [Hiscock, W. G., Henry Aldrich, 1648–1710. 1960].

Eighteenth century

See 1638, 1639 [A series of papers on subjects the most interesting to the nation in general and Oxford in particular, containing Well-wishers to the University of Oxford, and the answers. 1750].

3807. The Loiterer, a periodical work in two volumes, first publ. at Oxford in 1789 and 1790 [by James Austen. Contains some satirical reflections on life and manners at the University]. Oxf. &c., 1790, 8°.
Hope 8° 582, 583

See 7080 [Colman, G., Random records (Christ Church, 1780's). 1830].

3808. PHILLIPS, J. P., College life at Oxford, one hundred and thirty years ago. [Extracts from the diary of sir Erasmus Philipps in 1720, 21.] (N. & Q., 1860, ser. 2, vol. 10, p. 365, 66; 443–45.)
Per. 3974 e. 405 = A.

3809. COX, G. V., Recollections of Oxford [1789–1860]. Lond., 1868, 8°. 437 pp.   G.A. Oxon 8° 127
— 2nd ed. 1870. 460 pp.   G.A. Oxon 8° 372

3810. WORDSWORTH, C., Social life at the English universities in the eighteenth century. Cambr. &c., 1874, 8°. 728 pp.
G.A. Oxon 8° 194 = R.

3811. JOHNSON, R. B., The undergraduate. From C. Wordsworth's 'Social life at the English universities in the eighteenth century' revised, abridged, and re-arranged by R. Brimley Johnson. Lond., 1928, 8°. 336 pp.   G.A. Gen. top. 8° 1038

See 8207 [Letters of R. Radcliffe and J. James, 1755–83. 1888].
See 4664 [Letters from and to Charles Kirkpatrick Sharpe, 1798–1806. 1888].
See 8208 [Letters of G. and H. Fothergill, 1722–. 1905].
See 7436.5 [Jenkins, D. E., The life of Thomas Charles. At Jesus college, 1775–1778. 1910].

3812. GIBBS, A. H., Rowlandson's Oxford. Lond., 1911, 4°. 210 pp.
G.A. Oxon 4° 312

See 8407 [Extracts from and comments on the 'battle-book' and diary of Thomas Fry, 1744/45–1772. 1923].

3813. Journal of a Somerset rector, John Skinner . . . 1772–1839, ed. by H. Coombs and A. N. Bax. [The Appendix i, p. 313–20, comprises 'Description of a day spent in college during the winter of 1792'. In verse.] 1st ed. Lond., 1930, 8°.   11125 e. 72

See 6867 [Green, R. L., An undergraduate of 1723 [E. Greene]. 1947].
See 8596 [A gentleman commoner at Univ. [letters of N. Toke, 1721–23]. 1959].

3814. MAWDSLEY, W. N. HARGREAVES-, John Skinner's Oxford verses, 1790–3 [short article about them]. (Oxoniensia, 1959, vol. 24, p. 105, 06.) Per. G.A. Oxon 4° 658 = R.

Nineteenth century

3815. A week at Oxford. Oxf., 1817, 8°. 29 pp.   G.A. Oxon 8° 219 (10)

3816. WESTMACOTT, C. M., The English spy, by Bernard Blackmantle. 2 vols. [Chapters on The freshman: Christ Church college: The dinner party: College servants: Taking possession of your rooms: The spread, or wine party at Brasen-Nose: The Oxford rake's progress: Town and gown, an Oxford row: The excursion to Bagley wood.] Lond., 1825, 26, 8°. xxviii+370 pp.   B.M.
— New ed. Lond., 1907, 8°.   247126 f. 33

3817. Three years at Oxford [signed An Oxonian]. (Blackwood's Edinb. mag., 1828, vol. 24, p. 862–69.)   Per. 2705 e. 486

3818. Oxford. Academical abuses disclosed by some of the initiated. Lond., 1832, 8°. 30 pp.   G.A. Oxon 8° 219 (15)

3819. Club laws, a new song to an old tune. [A parody on the types of songs and rules to be found in many clubs.] Oxf., [c. 1835], 4°. 3 pp.
G.A. Oxon b. 140 (18a)

3820. PYCROFT, J., The collegian's guide: or, Recollections of college days . . . by the rev. **** ******, M.A. [J. Pycroft]. Lond., 1845, 8°. 371 pp.   45. 208
— 2nd ed., by J. Pycroft. Lond., 1858, 8°. 356 pp.   270 c. 267

3821. Chapters in the life of an undergraduate. (Oxf. Protestant mag., 1847, vol. 1, p. 69–75, 134–41, 181–88, 235–45, 331–39, 386–93, 441–48, 497–506, 539–51; 1848, vol. 2, p. 11–20.)   Per. G.A. Oxon 8° 119

3822. CLARKE, C., Letters to an undergraduate of Oxford. Lond., 1848, 8°. 77 pp.   48. 750

3823. BRADLEY, E., College life, a series of original etchings. Oxf. &c., [1850], 4°. 23 plates.   G.A. Oxon 4° 369

3824. TLEPOLEMUS, pseud., Touching Oxford, a letter [signed Tlepolemus]. (Blackwood's Edinb. mag., 1856, vol. 19, p. 179–92.)
G.A. Oxon 4° 579 (7)

3825. GARNETT, J., A visit to Oxford thirty years ago. (Garnett's occasional papers, no. 3.) Windermere, 1858, 8°. 8 pp.   270 e. 598

3826. THOMSON, J. C., Almæ matres, by Megathym Splene, B.A., Oxon. Lond. &c., [1858], 8°. 308 pp.   270 c. 344
— New ed., revised, with a suppl. chapter by A. D. Godley. [Wrongly attr. to R. Thompson.] Oxf., 1922, 8°. 322 pp.   O.C.L.

3827. Oxford in undress. (Leisure hour, 1862, vol. 11, p. 420–22.)
G.A. Oxon 4° 578 (12)

See 7081 [Oakeley, F., Personal recollections of an old Oxonian, (1820–39). 1865].

3828. Life at Oxford. (Cornhill mag., 1865, vol. 11, p. 223–32.)
Per. 2705 d. 213

3829. A visit to the English universities [Oxford]. (Hours at home, New York, 1866, June, p. 155–60.)   G.A. Oxon 4° 578 (16)

3830. ANSTEY, F., University life at Oxford [signed F. A.]. (Leisure hour, 1866, vol. 15, p. 664–68, 677–79.)   Per. 2705 d. 33

3831. S., H. J., Once round the clock at Oxford [signed H. J. S.]. (Sharpe's Lond. mag., 1866, vol. 43, p. 84–88.)   Per. 2705 d. 418

3832. HOPPIN, J. M., A visit to Oxford. (Hours at home, 1866, vol. 3, p. 59 &c.; 153 &c.)   B.M.

3833. RUSHER, W. E., To the senior members of the University of Oxford. [A letter protesting that 'a secret persecution is going on against me and against my family'.] [Oxf.], (1867), s. sh. G.A. Oxon c. 83 (365)

3834. ESCOTT, T. H. S., Summer term at Oxford. (Belgravia, 1867, vol. 2, p. 474–79.)   Per. 256 d. 254

See 3809 [Cox, G. V., Recollections, 1789–1860. 1868].

3835. University men in Town. (Belgravia, 1868, vol. 5, p. 471–77.)
Per. 256 d. 254

3836. Oxford before Commemoration. (London society, 1869, vol. 15, p. 481–94.)   G.A. Oxon 4° 580 (12)

3837. Oxford in the scales, by a graduate. (Britannia, 1869, no. 1, p. 30–41.)
G.A. Oxon 4° 580 (10)

3838. LYMAN, A., Reminiscences of Oxford. (Harper's mag., Amer. ed., 1869, vol. 39, p. 397 &c.)

3839. Oxford as it is. (London society, 1869, vol. 16, p. 305–12.)
G.A. Oxon 4° 580 (11)

3840. Oxford revisited. (St. James's mag., 1869, N.S., vol. 3, p. 305–11.)
G.A. Oxon 4° 580 (15)

3841. HARRIS, S. F., University life at Oxford. (Cassell's mag., 1870, N.S., vol. 1, p. 556, 57.)   Per. 256 d. 256

3842. Oxford and the new régime. (London society, 1870, vol. 18, p. 405–13).   G.A. Oxon 4° 578 (32a)

See 7304 [Impressions of one term at Exeter college. 1870].

3843. Young Oxford in 1870. (Belgravia, 1870, vol. 12, p. 438–44.)
Per. 256 d. 254

3844. Oxford chit chat. (Dark blue, 1871, 72, vol. 1–3, *passim*.)
Per. 270 d. 32

3845. COLLIS, J. D., Concio Latina in ecclesia sanctae Mariae virginis coram universitate die XIXmo Aprilis, MDCCCLXXIII. Oxonii, 1873, 4°. 16 pp. G.A. Oxon 4° 13 (4)

3846. MARSHALL, A. F., The Oxford undergraduate of twenty years ago [1845–] by a bachelor of arts [A. F. Marshall]. Lond., 1874, 8°. 99 pp.
270 e. 245

3847. Oxford revisited. (All the year, 1877, N.S., vol. 18, p. 425–28.)
Per. 2705 d. 202

3848. LEFROY, E. C., Undergraduate Oxford: articles re-pr. from The Oxford and Cambridge undergraduates' journal, 1876–7. Oxf. &c., 1878, 8°. 183 pp. 270 g. 808

3849. WILCOX, A., Undergraduate life at Oxford. (Scribner's monthly, 1878, vol. 17, p. 281 &c.)

3850. Reading at Oxford. (Chambers's journ., 1878, p. 609–11.)
Per. 2705 d. 396

3851. HUTTON, M., Many minds. (Some Oxford types [c. 1878], p. 157–90.) Lond. &c., [1928], 8°. 3962 e. 208

3852. STEDMAN, A. M. M.., Oxford: its social and intellectual life. Lond., 1878, 8°. 309 pp. 260 f. 84

See 6757 [Forbes, E. M., A visit to Balliol, 1879. 1921].

3853. HUGESSEN, E. H. KNATCHBULL-, My Oxford days [1847–]. (Time, 1879, vol. 1, p. 682–93.) G.A. Oxon 4° 581 (21)

3854. KEBBEL, T. E., Oxford in the long vacation [signed T. E. K.]. (Cornhill mag., 1879, vol. 40, p. 332–45.) G.A. Oxon 4° 581 (23)

3855. OAKELEY, F., Personal recollections of Oxford from 1820 to 1845. (Time, 1880, vol. 2, p. 675–87.) Per. 2705 d. 278

3856. School and college. (Blackwood's Edinh mag., 1880, vol. 128, p. 62–80.) G.A. Oxon 4° 581 (29)

3857. Young Oxford [signed An Oxford tutor]. (Fraser's mag., 1881, new ser., vol. 23, p. 618–36.) Per. 3977 e. 200

See 8062 [Mozley, T., Reminiscences. 1882].

3858. Oxford reminiscences: vacation. (Chambers's journ., 1882, p. 761–63.) Per. 2705 d. 396

3859. WORDSWORTH, C., A chapter of autobiography, being some account of my Oxford private pupils, 1831–33; with notices of the first athletic contests between Oxford and Cambridge. (Fortnightly rev., 1883, vol. 40, p. 50–71.) Per. 3977 d. 59

3860. Mushroom rings. [Article on the growth of clubs and societies.] (Oxf. mag., 1883, vol. 1, p. 113, 14.) Per. G.A. Oxon 4° 141

3861. PRESTON, H. W., Oxford in winter. (Atlantic monthly, 1883, vol. 52, p. 49–59.) G.A. Oxon 4° 582 (8)

3862. PEARSON, N., Undergraduate life at Oxford. (Lippincott's mag., 1883, vol. 33, p. 66 &c.)

3863. Letters [1826–76] of the rev. J. B. Mozley, ed. by his sister [A. Mozley]. Lond., 1885, 8°. 364 pp. 11125 e. 10

3864. PATTISON, M., Memoirs. Lond., 1885, 8°. 334 pp. 2696 e. 17

See 7536, 7537 [Recollections, etc., of Mark Pattison. 1884, 85].

3865. BRADLEY, E., Oxford revisited, by Cuthbert Bede. (Leisure hour, vol. 34, 1885, p. 817–20.) G.A. Oxon 4° 577 (36)

3866. PARKER, C. P., Reminiscences of Oxford. (Harvard monthly, 1885, vol. 2, p. 127 &c.) L. of C.

3867. DOYLE, SIR F. H., Reminiscences and opinions . . . 1813–1885. Lond., 1886, 8°. 420 pp. 2288 e. 141

3868. PYCROFT, J., Oxford memories, a retrospect after fifty years. 2 vols. Lond., 1886, 8°. G.A. Oxon 8° 389, 390

3869. Oxford memories, by the author of 'Twenty years in the Church'. (London soc., 1886, vol. 49, p. 88–98, 258–72, 348–60.) Per. 2705 d. 200

3870. SMITH, G., Oxford old and new. [Impressions of Oxford as it is, a letter.] (Oxf. mag., 1886, vol. 4, p. 229, 30.) Per. G.A. Oxon 4° 141

See 7641 [Reade, C. L., Charles Reade [reminiscences, 1831–38]. 1887].
See 7542 [Overton, J. H., Lincoln college, thirty years ago. 1887].

3871. FREEMAN, E. A., Oxford after forty years. (Contemp. rev., 1887, vol. 51, p. 609–23, 814–30.) Per. 3977 d. 58

3872. STEDMAN, A. M. M., ed., Oxford: its life and schools, ed. by A. M. M. Stedman, assisted by members of the University. [A re-writing of the 1878 publ., no. 3852.] Lond., 1887, 8°. 359 pp. 2625 e. 22

3873. KEBBEL, T. E., Old [the 1850's] and new Oxford. (National review, 1887, vol. 9, p. 451–64.) G.A. Oxon 4° 575 (18)

3874. KNIGHT, W., Principal Shairp and his friends. [Oxford 1840–46, 77–84 passim.] Lond., 1888, 8°. 457 pp. 26013 d. 2

3875. BATTY, B. BRAITHWAITE-, Some Oxford customs, by Bee Bee. Lond., 1888, 8°. 116 pp. G.A. Oxon 8° 443

3876. A day of his life at Oxford, by an undergraduate. (Murray's mag., 1888, vol. 3, p. 664–77.) Per. 2705 e. 321

3877. PEARSON, A day of her life at Oxford, by a lady undergraduate [— Pearson]. (Murray's mag., 1888, vol. 3, p. 678–88.) Per. 2705 e. 321

3878. HERFORD, W. LL., Undergraduate life at Oxford. (Castle Howell school record, 1888, p. 106–14).　　　　　　　　　G.A. Lancs 4° 56

3879. A past generation at Oxford, by an old Wykehamist. (Month, 1889, vol. 66, p. 26–39.)　　　　　　　　　　　　　　Per. 11132 d. 17

3880. Reminiscences of my time at Oxford [c. 1865–70]. (Temple Bar, 1890, vol. 90, p. 333–48.)　　　　　　　　　　　Per. 2705 d. 277

3881. HOLE, S. R., The memories of dean Hole. Lond., 1892, 8°.　　B.M.
— New ed. 1893. (Oxonians, p. 275–307.)　　　　　　　211 e. 170
— 5th ed. 1893 (p. 314–50).　　　　　　　　　　　　211 e. 163
— [Another ed.] [1909]. (Nelson's shilling libr.)　　　　211 f. 66

3882. WELLS, J., ed., Oxford and Oxford life. Lond., 1892, 8°. 190 pp.
　　　　　　　　　　　　　　　　　　　　　　　Manning 8° 151

3883. Our memories, shadows of old Oxford, ed. by H. Daniel. Ser. 1, no. 1–20 [and] Index; ser. 2, no. 1, 2. Oxf., 1893 [1888–93], 95, 8°.
　　　　　　　　　　　　　　　　　　　　　　G.A. Oxon 8° 477

3884. HEURTLEY, C. A., Oxford in the twenties. (Pelican Record, 1893, vol. 2, p. 9–13.)　　　　　　　　　　Per. G.A. Oxon 8° 588

3885. GODLEY, A. D., Aspects of modern Oxford. (Portfolio, 1893, p. 103–07, 116–20, 136–42, 166–71, 186–93, 197–202, 219–24.) Per. 170 c. 2
— [Repr. with an additional chapter] by a mere don. Lond., 1894, 8°. 135 pp.　　　　　　　　　　　　　　　　　G.A. Oxon 8° 597
— New ed. By A. D. Godley. Lond., 1910, 8°. 215 pp.
　　　　　　　　　　　　　　　　　　　　　　G.A. Oxon 8° 776

3886. Oxford and Oxford life. (Church quarterly, 1893, vol. 36, p. 162–82.)
　　　　　　　　　　　　　　　　　　　　　Per. 1419 e. 402 = S.
See 7224 [F., H., Forty-five years ago. 1893].

3887. DAVIS, R. H., Undergraduate life at Oxford. (Harper's mag., 1893, vol. 87, p. 779–92.)　　　　　　　　　　　Per. 2714 d. 25

3888. Undergraduates on dons, by our donnish contributor. (Oxf. mag, 1893, vol. 11, p. 204.)　　　　　　　Per. G.A. Oxon 4° 141

See 6756 [Henderson, P. A. Wright-, Balliol in the early sixties. 1894].

3889.

3890. ESCOTT, T. H. S., Oxford in the pre-æsthetic age. [Reminiscences of the 1860's.] (Nat. rev., 1894, vol. 24, p. 232–44.)　Per. 22775 d. 14

3891. P., E., Recollections of Oxford in the '70's. (Sunday mag., 1894, vol. 23, p. 764–67.)　　　　　　　　　　　Per. 1419 d. 318

3892. LAKE, W. C., Rugby and Oxford 1830–1850. (Good words, 1895, p. 666–70.)　　　　　　　　　　　　　　Per. 2705 d. 229

3893. LAKE, W. C., More Oxford memories. [1840–55]. (Good words, 1895, p. 828–32.)　　　　　　　　　　　　Per. 2705 d. 229

3894. MAINWARING, R. K., Oxford reminiscences [1866–69]. (Badminton mag. of sports and pastimes, 1895, vol. 1, p. 386–95.)
G.A. Oxon 4° 575 (25)

3895. GORDON, W. J., New Oxford. (Leisure hour, 1895, vol. 44, p. 249–54, 326–32, 387–91.)
Per. 2705 d. 33

3896. GEORGE, H., Oxford at home. (Strand mag., Jan. 1895, vol. 9, p. 109–15.)
G.A. Oxon 4° 575 (23)

3897. HARE, A. J. C., The story of my life. Vol. 1. (Oxford life, 1851–55, p. 402–515.) Lond., 1896, 8°.
203 e. 677/1

3898. MARSHALL, A. F., Forty years ago at Oxford. (Bachelor of arts, 1896, vol. 3, p. 242 &c.)
L. of C.

3899. COLLINS, W. E. W., Oxford then and now [by W. E. W. Collins]. (Blackwood's mag., 1896, vol. 158, p. 420–29.)
Per. 2705 d. 386

3900. CUST, A. P. PUREY-, College influence in the past and present, a sermon. York, 1897, 8°. 15 pp.
G.A. Oxon 8° 683 (10)

See 8280 [Kitchin, G. W., Early reminiscences of non-collegiate life. 1897].
See 8281 [Pope, R. W. M., Reminiscences of non-collegiate life [1887–98]. 1898].
See 8595 [Smith, E., Memoirs of a highland lady. Life in University college in 1810 and 1811. 1898 etc.].
See 8282 [Jackson, W. W., Reminiscences of non-collegiate life [1883–87]. 1898].

3901. BARDOUX, J., Souvenirs d'Oxford [1895]. Coulommiers, 1898, 4°. 118 pp.
G.A. Oxon 4° 315

3901.5. BARDOUX, J., Memories of Oxford [1895] tr. by W. R. Barker. Lond., 1899, 16°. 131 pp.
G.A. Oxon 16° 57

3902. NESTOR, *pseud.*, Oxford in the 'thirties. (Living age, 1898, vol. 218, p. 92–95.)
L. of C.

See 7078 [Bridges, J. A., At 'the House' in the 50's. 1899].

3903. TUCKWELL, W., Reminiscences of Oxford. Lond. &c., 1900, 8°. 288 pp.
G.A. Oxon 8° 670
— [A grangerized copy.]
MS. Top. Oxon b. 164
— 2nd ed. 1907. 348 pp.
G.A. Oxon 8° 749

3904. MÜLLER, F. MAX, My autobiography, a fragment. Lond. &c., 1901, 8°. 312 pp.
3971 d. 9

3905. NARES, E., A versatile professor, reminiscences of the rev. Edward Nares, Regius professor of modern history, 1813–1841, ed. by G. C. White. Lond., 1903, 8°. 308 pp.
211 e. 280

3906. TUCKWELL, W., Reminiscences of Oxford. Addendula quaedam. (Oxf. mag., 1905, vol. 23, pp. 338, 376, 411; vol. 24, pp. 77, 114, 170, 189, 230.) [These additions were included in the 2nd ed. of Tuckwell's Reminiscences, published in 1907, no. 3903.]

— Addendula quaedam. (Oxf. mag., 1913, vol. 31, p. 299, 319.)
Per. G.A. Oxon 4° 141

See 7227 [Strong, H. A., Corpus in the early sixties. 1905].

3907. MEYRICK, F., Memories of life at Oxford [1843–] . . . and elsewhere.
Lond., 1905, 8°. 348 pp. 11126 d. 93

See 7228 [Tuckwell, W., Corpuscular reminiscences. 1906].

3908. BURROWS, M., Autobiography of Montagu Burrows, Chichele professor of modern history, ed. by S. M. Burrows, with a suppl. by
professor Oman. Lond., 1908, 8°. 260 pp. 23141 d. 34

3909. WOODGATE, W. B., Reminiscences of an old sportsman. [Oxford,
p. 102–224, 1859– .] Lond., 1909, 8°. 38442 d. 8

3910. FARNELL, L. R., Reminiscences [1868–]. (Stapeldon mag., 1909,
vol. 2, p. 181–89.) Per. G.A. Oxon 8° 713

See 8063 [Tuckwell, W., Pre-Tractarian Oxford, a reminiscence of the Oriel
'noetics'. 1909].
See 6872 [Ward, T. H., The Nineteenth century. Reminiscences, 1864–1872.
1909].
See 7229 [M., W. A., Corpus fifty years ago. 1910].

3911. SMITH, G., Reminiscences, ed. by A. Haultain. [Oxford, 1841–66.]
New York, 1910, 8°. 477 pp. 2288 e. 777

3912. HARRISON, F., Autobiographic memoirs. 2 vols. [Oxford passim,
1849–1910.] Lond., 1911, 8°. 2288 d. 240, 41

See 6874 [Price, C., Reminiscences of Brasenose (1854–60). 1911].

3913. POULTON, E. B., John Viriamu Jones and other Oxford memories
[1873–]. Lond. &c., 1911, 8°. 339 pp. G.A. Oxon 8° 823

See 6873 [Latham, F. L., B.N.C. in the fifties. 1911].
See 8733.8 [Wordsworth, E., Glimpses of the past, from 1879 onwards. 1912].
See 7642 [Tuckwell, L. S., Old Magdalen days, 1847–1877. 1913].
See 7079 [Brown, G. J. Cowley-, Christ Church, sixty years ago. 1915].

3914. GRAVES, C. L., Oxford in the 'seventies, by C. L. G. [Recollections
of an undergraduate of Christ Church.] (Chambers's journ., 1917,
p. 54–57, 72–74.) Per. 2705 d. 396

3915. WARD, M. A., A writer's recollections [1865–]. Lond. &c., 1918, 8°.
373 pp. 2569 d. 82

3916. MORE, P. E., Oxford, women and God [incl. comments on no. 3915].
(Shelburne essays, 1921, 11th ser., p. 257–87.) 3962 e. 80 (11)

See 7230 [Reminiscences of the late seventies. 1921].
See 7543 [Fowler, W. W., Reminiscences. 1921].

3917. HOPKINSON, SIR A., Oxford fifty years ago. (Contemp. review,
1921, vol. 119, p. 509–18.) Per. 3977 d. 58

See 3958 [Harrison, F., Oxford old and new, 1848 and 1921. 1921].

3918. JONES, C. W. F., Old Oxford memories [1854–57]. (Cornhill mag., 1923, vol. 55, p. 703–10.)   Per. 2705 d. 213

See 6758 [Henderson, P. A. Wright-. Glasgow & Balliol. 1926].

3919. SHERWOOD, W. E., Oxford yesterday, memoirs of Oxford seventy years ago. Oxf., 1927, 8°. 72 pp.   G.A. Oxon 8° 1054

3920. WOODS, F. C., Recollections of Oxford in the eighties. (Oxf. mag., 1928, vol. 47, p. 456–61, 488–90, 526–28, 548–50, 583, 84, 612–14, 646–48, 671, 72, 705, 06.)   Per. G.A. Oxon 4° 141

3921. MACAN, R. W., Oxford in the 'seventies. (Roy. soc. of lit. of the U.K., The Eighteen-seventies, ed. by H. Granville-Barker, 1929, p. 210–48.)
Soc. 3962 e. 161 = S.

3922. GRANT, SIR A. H., 'The Ephemeral': some memoirs of Oxford in the 'nineties. (Cornhill mag., 1931, N.S., vol. 71, p. 641–53.)
Per. 2705 d. 213

See 7231 [Knox, bp., Memories of Corpus Christi college, 1865–8. 1932].

3923. FISHER, H. A. L., Oxford men and manners [in the 1880's]. (Fifty years, 1882–1932, by contributors to The Times, 1932, p. 87–92.)
247126 d. 40

3924. JEUNE, M. D., Pages from the diary of an Oxford lady, 1843–1862, ed. by M. J. Gifford. Oxf., 1932, 4°. 141 pp.   G.A. Oxon 4° 511

3925. BLAIR, O. HUNTER-, Memories of old Oxford [1875]. (Dubl. review, 1934, vol. 195, p. 227–29.)   Per. 3977 e. 199

See 6759 [Ernle, lord, School and college sixty years since. 1933].

3925.1. KNOX, E. A., bp. of Manchester, Reminiscences of an octogenarian. (Oxford 1865–85, p. 64–118.) Lond., (1934), 8°. 336 pp. 11126 d. 173

See 3972 [Farnell, L. R., An Oxonian looks back. 1934].

3926. SWIFT, MR. and MRS. T., Remembrances of Micklem Hall, 1887–1933. Oxf., 1935, 8°. 27 pp.   O.P.L.

3927. SCUDAMORE, C., Oxford in the 'seventies. (Cornhill mag., 1935, N.S., vol. 151, p. 172–80.)   Per. 2705 d. 213

See 6759.5 [Spender, J. A., Balliol in the eighties, 1881–85. 1936].

3928. SMITH, L. P., Unforgotten years. (Chapter 6. Oxford [in 1888 &c.], p. 149–83.) Lond., 1938, 8°. 266 pp.   2142 e. 142

See 7643 [Knight, J. W., A hundred years ago. 1938].

3929. MOORE, H. K., Reminiscences of Oxford and Balliol in the seventies. (Oxford, 1939, vol. 5, no. 3, p. 42–49.)   Per. G.A. Oxon 8° 1141

3930. BIDWELL, E. J., Oxford days in the 'eighties: some recollections. (Nat. review, 1939, vol. 113, p. 74–85.)   Per. 22775 d. 14

3931. THOMPSON, J. M., My apologia, by J. M. T. [Reminiscences in verse, 1897– .] Oxf., 1940, 8°. 112 pp.   28001 e. 6733

3932. FISHER, H. A. L., An unfinished autobiography. [Oxford 1884–88.]
Lond. &c., 1940, 8°. 163 pp. 2625 e. 142

3933. BAILEY, C., Oxford fifty years ago [1890–94]. (Oxford, 1940, vol. 7,
no. 1, p. 33–40.) Per. G.A. Oxon 8° 1141

3934. WOODS, M. L., Oxford in the 'seventies. (Fortnightly, 1941, vol. 150,
p. 276–82.) Per. 3977 d. 59

3935. OMAN, SIR C., Memories of Victorian Oxford. Lond., 1941, 8°. 288
pp. G.A. Oxon 8° 1185
— 2nd ed.
— 3rd ed. 1942. G.A. Oxon 8° 1355

3936. SMITH, J. C., Oxford in my time [1889–92]. (Chambers's journ.,
1944, p. 511–13, 593–95, 641–43.) Per. 2705 d. 396

3937. COUCH, SIR A. T. QUILLER-, Memories & opinions, an unfinished
autobiography by Q, ed. by S. C. Roberts. (Oxford, p. 68–96.) Cambr.,
1944, 8°. 270 e. 1571

3938. GRUNDY, G. B., Fifty-five years at Oxford, an unconventional autobiography. Lond., 1945, 8°. 243 pp. G.A. Oxon 8° 1202

3939. MARRIOTT, SIR J., Memories of four score years [Oxford 1878–]
autobiography [ed. by H. Marriott]. Lond. &c., 1946, 8°. 252 pp.
211 e. 1093

See 8211 [M., H. M., An undergraduate at Queen's a century ago. 1948].
See 6761 [Barker, sir E., Father of the man, memories of . . . Oxford [1893 98].
1948].

3940. GAMLEN, F. M., My memories, 1856–1952. n. pl., [1953], 8°. 40 pp.
211 e. 1282

3941. WRIGHT, E. M., My life in Oxford [1887–]. (Oxford, 1956, vol. 14,
no. 2, p. 72–81; 1956, vol. 14, no. 3, p. 74–96.) Per. G.A. Oxon 8° 1141

3942. SAVORY, SIR D. LL., Oxford at the turn of the century. (Contemp.
review, 1956, vol. 190, p. 335–40.) Per. 3977 d. 58

See 6762 [Boas, F. S., Some Oxford memories, 1881–86. 1956].

3943. HATCH, E. C., Some reminiscences of Oxford [1870 onwards]. (Oxf.
mag., 1956, vol. 74, p. 500–02; 1957, vol. 75, p. 158; 200–02; 368–70;
vol. 76, p. 40–44.) Per. G.A. Oxon 4° 141

3944. DAVIDSON, M., Memoirs of a golden age [1850–]. Oxf., 1958, 8°.
140 pp. G.A. Oxon 8° 1359

3945. CARRITT, E. F., 'And yet what days were those' [recollections 1894–.]
(Univ. coll. record, 1958, vol. 3, p. 183–92.) Per. G.A. Oxon 8° 1086

3946. RICHARDS, G. C., An Oxonian looks back, 1885–1945. [Reprod. from
typewriting.] n. pl., (1960), 4°. 114 pp. G.A. Oxon 4° 769

See 8123.5 [Hatch, E., My visit to Oxford, November, 1853. 1963].

3946.1. MUNFORD, W. A., Edward Edwards, 1812–86, portrait of a librarian. [The Oxford years, 1870–83, at p. 175–95, describe work in the libraries of Queen's college, Corpus Christi college and in the Bodleian, where he compiled the Calendar of the Carte Papers.] Lond., 1963, 8°.   2589 e. 111

3946.2. SIMMONS, J. S. G., A nineteenth-century Oxford quiz [by J. S. G. Simmons. Reprod. from typewriting]. (Oxf.), 1964, 8°. 12 pp.
                                                              G.A. Oxon 8° 1483

3946.3. EDWARDS, G. HAMILTON-, An undergraduate [W. Cotton of Exeter college] in Regency Oxford. (Oxford, 1965, vol. 19, p. 64–71.)
                                                        Per. G.A. Oxon 8° 1141

See 6866.5 [Smith, J. A., John Buchan. Oxford undergraduate, 1895–99. 1965].

Twentieth century

3947. BRODRICK, H., The undergraduate at Oxford. (Nat. rev., 1900, vol. 36, p. 241–50.)   Per. 22775 d. 14

3948. HAY, C., Undergraduate life at Oxford. (Good words, 1901, p. 325–32.)   Per. 2705 d. 229

3949. The undergraduate at Oxford. (Chambers's journ., 1901, p. 526–28.)
                                                              Per. 2705 d. 396

3950. CORBIN, J., An American at Oxford. Lond., 1902, 8°. 325 pp.
                                                                  2625 e. 37
— [Another ed.] Boston &c., 1903, 8°. 325 pp.   O.P.L.

3951. The woman-student at Oxford. (Chambers's journ., 1903, p. 30–32.)
                                                              Per. 2705 d. 396

3952. MCDONNELL, M. F. J., The Oxford man, by a Cambridge man. (Oxf. and Cambr. review, 1908, no. 3, p. 96–104.)   Per. 2625 d. 37

3953. BLAIR, O. HUNTER-, Oxford as it is. (Cath. univ. bull., 1908, vol. 14, p. 627–40.)   G.A. Oxon 8° 761 (30)

3954. HENDERSON, P. A. WRIGHT-, The Oxford undergraduate, past and present, by the Warden of Wadham college. (Blackwood's mag., 1909, vol. 185, p. 335–43.)   Per. 2705 d. 386
— [Repr.] (Glasgow & Balliol and other essays, p. 105–24). Oxf. &c., 1926, 8°.   G.A. Oxon 8° 1050

3955. DE SÉLINCOURT, H., Oxford from within. Lond., 1910, 8°. 181 pp.
                                                              G.A. Oxon 8° 778

See 3912 [Harrison, F., Autobiographic memoirs [1849–1910]. 1911].

3956. NOGUCHI, YONE, My impressions of Oxford. (Blackwood's mag., 1916, vol. 199, p. 535–40.)   Per. 2705 d. 386

3957. Oxford in 1920 [signed Olim co. prae.]. (Oxf. mag., 1920, vol. 38, p. 170, 71.)   Per. G.A. Oxon 4° 141

3958. HARRISON, F., Oxford old and new [1848 and 1921]. (Amer. Oxon., 1921, vol. 8, p. 136–40.)   Per. G.A. Oxon 8° 889

3959. FAYARD, J., Lettres françaises d'un Parisien à Oxford. (Louviers), [1921], 8°.   G.A. Oxon 8° 884 (32)

3960. STREET, G. S., Oxford: a thought or two. (Nineteenth cent., 1921, vol. 89, p. 819–24.)   Per. 3977 d. 66

3961. FISH, W. W. BLAIR-, Oxford ways, a description of undergraduate life, by Blair. Oxf., 1925, 8°. 75 pp.   G.A. Oxon 8° 1043

> See 6754 [Arthur Lionel Smith, 1916–1924, a biography and some reminiscences. 1928].

3962. HALL, J., Alma mater, or, The future of Oxford and Cambridge. (To-day and to-morrow.) Lond., 1928, 12°. 96 pp.   2625 f. 17

3963. DIPLOCK, W. J. K., Isis, or, The future of Oxford. (To-day and to-morrow.) Lond. &c., 1929, 16°. 95 pp.   G.A. Oxon 16° 183

3964. GREENIDGE, T., Degenerate Oxford? A critical study of modern university life. Lond., 1930, 8°. 245 pp.   G.A. Oxon 8° 1070

3965. SINCLAIR, J. G., Portrait of Oxford. Sturry, 1931, 4°. 133 pp.
                                         G.A. Oxon 4° 503

3966. COURTNEY, J. E., The ladies of Oxford. (An Oxford portrait gallery, p. 209–49.) Lond., 1931, 8°.   G.A. Oxon 8° 1083

3967. THOMAS, E., Oxford. Lond., 1932, 8°. 264 pp. G.A. Oxon 8° 1099

3968. SMITH, P. C., Oxford in the melting-pot. Lond., 1932, 8°. 24 pp.
                                    G.A. Oxon 8° 1101 (4)

3969. HARRISSON, T. H., 'Letter to Oxford'. Wyck, 1933, 8°. 98 pp.
                                          Φ e. 37

3970. KARAKA, D. F., The pulse of Oxford. Lond., 1933, 8°. 80 pp.
                                    G.A. Oxon 8° 1106

3971. EAGLESTONE, A. A., A pitman looks at Oxford, by Roger Dataller. Lond., 1933, 8°. 205 pp.   G.A. Oxon 8° 1098

3972. FARNELL, L. R., An Oxonian looks back. Lond., 1934, 4°. 350 pp.
                                    G.A. Oxon 4° 545
— [Another issue.]   G.A. Oxon 4° 545*

3973. CHETTUR, G. K., The last enchantment, recollections of Oxford. Mangalore, 1934, 8°. 200 pp.   G.A. Oxon 8° 1183

> See 3926 [Swift, T., Remembrances of Micklem Hall, 1887–1933. 1935].

3974. KRISTJANSON, W., Glimpses of Oxford. Winnipeg, 1935, 16°. 68 pp.   G.A. Oxon 16° 202

3975. HOLMES, SIR C. J., Self & partners (mostly self) being the reminiscences of C. J. Holmes. [p. 99–111 Brazenose; p. 235–46 Slade professorship]. Lond., 1936, 8°.   17006 d 396

3976. BRIANT, K., Oxford limited. Lond., 1937, 4°. 320 pp.
G.A. Oxon 4° 572

See 8744 [Lodge, E. C., Terms and vacations, 1890–1921. 1938].

3977. MACKENZIE, SIR C., Undergraduates at the beginning of the century. (Oxford, 1938, vol. 5, no. 2, p. 68–74.) Per. G.A. Oxon 8° 1141

3978. COLLINGWOOD, R. G., An autobiography. [Oxford 1910– .] (Lond.), 1939, 8°. 167 pp. 26684 e. 175 = P.

See 3931 [Thompson, J. M., My apologia, 1897–. 1940].

3979. MARETT, R. R., A Jerseyman at Oxford. [Autobiography.] Lond. &c., 1941, 8°. 346 pp. G.A. Oxon 8° 1182

3980. WOODWARD, E. L., Short journey. [Autobiography: at Oxford 1908–13, 1919 onwards.] Lond., 1942, 8°. 247 pp. 2226 e. 10

See 3938 [Grundy, G. B., Fifty-five years at Oxford. 1945].
See 3939 [Marriott, sir J., Memories, 1878–1945. 1946].
See 8593 [Collett, F., From the porter's lodge and buttery, 1907–. 1951].

3981. SWINTON, SIR E. D., Over my shoulder, autobiography [Chichele professor of military history, 1925–1939, p. 255–82.] Oxf., 1951, 8°.
23167 e. 224

See 8065 [Lee, R. W., A German at Oriel, 1903–4. 1952].
See 8744.8 [Peck, W., A little learning. 1952].
See 6875 [Stallybrass, W. T. S., Brasenose in my early years [1911–]. 1953].
See 3940 [Gamlen, F. M., My memories, 1856–1952. 1953].

3982. An act to consolidate certain enactments relating to justices' licences for the sale by retail of intoxicating liquor, and to the registration of clubs and to matters connected therewith . . . (1 & 2 Eliz. II, c. 46, Pub.) [Section 147 concerns University clubs.] Lond., 1953, 8°. 116 pp.
L.L.

3983. LONGMATE, N., Oxford triumphant. Lond., 1954, 8°. 190 pp.
G.A. Oxon 8° 1309

3984. BAILEY, A., The longest days. (Twentieth century, 1955, vol. 157, p. 548–52.) Per. 3977 d. 66

3985. MCMANIGAL, R., Sky-writing with a peace-pipe. (Twentieth century, 1955, vol. 157, p. 553–58.) Per. 3977 d. 66

See 3941 [Wright, E. M., My life at Oxford, 1887–. 1956].

3986. JONES, SIR L. E., An Edwardian youth [1907–]. Lond., 1956, 8°. 249 pp. 211 e. 1365

See 3943 [Hatch, E. C., Some reminiscences of Oxford, 1870–. 1956].

3987. BALSDON, D., Oxford life. Lond., 1957, 8°. 279 pp.
G.A. Oxon 8° 1351
— 2nd ed. 1962. G.A. Oxon 8° 1458

See 3944 [Davidson, M., Memoirs of a golden age, 1850–. 1958].
See 3945 [Carritt, E. F., 'And yet what days were those', recollections, 1894–. 1958].

3988. BACON, M., 'Going down.' Ilfracombe, [1958], 8°. 132 pp.
G.A. Oxon 8° 1358

3989. HILBERT, L. W., Cambridge et Oxford. (Les langues modernes, 1959, année 53, no. 2, p. 20–22.) Per. 26333 d. 48

3990. MCCALLUM, R. B., Oxford now. (Amer. Oxonian, 1959, vol. 46, p. 97–107.) Per. G.A. Oxon 8° 889

3991. Oxford and Cambridge questionnaire. (20th Cent., 1960, vol. 168, p. 410–26.) Per. 3977 d. 66

3992. TOYNBEE, P., Voice from the thirties. [Comment on the questionnaire.] (20th Cent., 1960, vol. 168, p. 503–08.) Per. 3977 d. 66

3993. CARRITT, E. F., Fifty years a don. [Reprod. from typewriting.] [Oxf.], 1960, 4°. 94 leaves. G.A. Oxon 4° 768
[The Oxford magazine printed part of this in vol. 78, 1960, p. 274.]

See 3946 [Richards, G. C., An Oxonian looks back, 1885–1945. 1960].

3994. POTTER, D., The glittering coffin. Lond., 1960, 8°. 159 pp.
22894 e. 40

3995. CARRITT, E. F., Some Oxford reformations. (Univ. coll. record, 1960, vol. 3, p. 330–34.) Per. G.A. Oxon 8° 1086

See 6026 [Allen, D., Sunlight and shadow, autobiography. 1960].

3996. WILLIAMS, E., George, an early autobiography [at Christ Church, 1923–27, p. 270–]. Lond., 1961, 8°. M. adds. 41 c. 130

3997. MASTERMAN, J. C., The changing face of Oxford. (Bits and pieces, 1961, p. 88–92.) 27001 e. 2204

3997.1. Isis survey [on background, political views, career intentions, religion etc. of one in five of 'last-year men']. (Oxf.), 1961, 4°. 15 pp.
G.A. Oxon 4° 781

3997.2. BEADLE, M., These ruins are inhabited. New York &c., 1961, 8°. 359 pp. 204 e. 706
— [Another ed.] Lond., 1963, 8°. 188 pp. 204 e. 713

3997.21. GIPSON, L. H., Reminiscences of a Rhodes Scholar at Oxford in the Edwardian era [1904]. (Amer. Oxon., 1963, vol. 50, p. 64–72.)
Per. G.A. Oxon 8° 889

3997.22. RUSSELL, R., To catch an angel. [A blind student's life at Oxford, 1948–52, p. 161–218.] Lond., 1963, 8°. 2631 e. 80

3997.3. PFAFF, R. W., Oxford and its present-day critics. (Amer. Oxon., 1964, vol. 51, p. 1–5.) Per. G.A. Oxon 8° 889

3997.4. LANGSTAFF, J. BRETT, Oxford—1914. New York &c., 1965, 8°. 317 pp. G.A. Oxon 8° 1506

3997.41. ROWSE, A. L., A Cornishman at Oxford. Lond., 1965, 8°. 319 pp.
G.A. Oxon 8° 1493

3997.42. HICKLIN, S., Two faces of Eve [Oxford in the thirties]. (Oxf. mag., 1965, N.S., vol. 5, p. 12–14.) Per. G.A. Oxon 4° 141

Artistic

General

3998. Georgian club. [Invitation to dinner, 16 May 1914.]
G.A. Oxon 4° 603

3999. Oxford art society. [Objects, list of officers and members, June 1848.] [Oxf.], 1848, 4°. 3 pp. G.A. Oxon c. 64 (89)

Oxford university design society. See 519 [New Oxford. 1961].

4000. Oxford university film society. Flicker. (Croydon), [1944], 8°.
3858 d. 27 (7)

4001. Oxford university photographic club. [Miscellaneous papers. 1886–1897.] G.A. Oxon b. 147 (45 &c.)

Drama

See 4929 [University miscellany. iv. The players epilogue, &c. 1713].
See 8347 [Higgs, G., Christmas prince. 1896, &c.].

4002. BEDFORD, W. K. R., The O.D.A. [Oxford dramatic amateurs] [signed W. K. R. B.]. (Time, 1880, vol. 3, p. 82–87.)
G.A. Oxon 4° 582 (1)

4003. Notes on play-acting in Oxford [signed Foras]. (Oxf. mag., 1883, vol. 1, p. 373.) Per. G.A. Oxon 4° 141

4004. FIRTH, SIR C. H., Annals of the Oxford stage [signed C. H. F.]. (Oxf. mag., 1886, vol. 4, p. 65–67.) Per. G.A. Oxon 4° 141

4005. ADDERLEY, J. G., The fight for the drama at Oxford. (Church reformer, 1887, vol. 6, p. 209–13.) G.A. Oxon 4° 586 (32)

4006. ADDERLEY, J. G., The fight for the drama at Oxford, some plain facts. Oxf. &c., 1888, 12°. xiv+35 pp. M. adds. 124 f. 3

4007. CARR, P., The Greek play, Oxford. (Amateur clubs & actors, ed. by W. G. Elliot, 1898, p. 53–66.) M. adds. 124 e. 38

4008. SCHELLING, F. E., Thalia in Oxford [dramatic performances in 1607/8]. (The queen's progress, and other Elizabethan sketches, p. 203–19.) Boston, 1904, 8°. 22853 e. 40

4009. BOAS, F. S., A 'defence of Oxford plays and players'. (Fortnightly review, 1907, vol. 88, p. 309–19.) Per. 3977 d. 59

4010. HOFFSTEN, E. G., The floating island, by William Strode . . . and a review of the university drama in England chiefly after . . . 1600. (Thesis, Univ. of Penn.] [St. Louis, 1908], 8°. 31 pp.
M. adds. 37 d. 41 (7)

4011. SMITH, G. C. MOORE, Notes on some English university plays. (Mod. lang. review, 1908, vol. 3, p. 141–56.)   Per. 3962 d. 24 = A.

4012. ADDERLEY, J., Amateur acting at Oxford and elsewhere. (Oxf. and Cambr. review, 1908, no. 3, p. 19–29.)   Per. 2625 d. 37

4012.1. SCHELLING, F. E., Elizabethan drama, 1558–1642. 2 vols. (College drama, vol. 2, p. 51 etc.) Boston &c., 1908, 8°. M. adds. 20 d. 33 = A.

4013. BOAS, F. S., James I at Oxford in 1605. (Malone soc., Collections, 1909, vol. I, pt. 3, p. 247–59.)   M. adds. 111 e. 246 = A.

4014. MACKINNON, A., The Oxford amateurs, a short history of theatricals at the University. Lond., 1910, 8°. 309 pp.   M. adds. 124 e. 86

4015. BOAS, F. S., The early Oxford academic stage. (Oxf. mag., 1912, vol. 30, p. 240, 41, 259, 60.)   Per. G.A. Oxon 4° 141

4016. BOAS, F. S., University drama in the Tudor age. Oxf., 1914, 8°. 414 pp.   M. adds. 25 d. 15 = A.

4017. DE SAUSMAREZ, F. B., Early theatricals [1870's] at Oxford, with prologues by Lewis Carroll. (Nineteenth century and after, 1932, vol. III, p. 235–38.)   Per. 3977 d. 66

4018. BOAS, F. S., University plays. (An introduction to Stuart drama, p. 401–12.) Lond., 1946, 8°.   M. adds. 37 e. 53 = S.

4019. Oxford university drama commission. Report. Oxf., 1945, 8°. 28 pp.
    26328 e. 27 (12)
— [Another ed.] [Oxf.], (1945), 8°. 26 pp.   26328 e. 27 (14)

4020. The Oxford drama commission. (Theatre notebook, 1946, vol. I, p. 18.)   Per. M. adds. 20 d. 28

4021. Theatre for Oxford university, designed by F. Gibberd. (Architect's journ., 1948, vol. 108, p. 421–25.)   N. 1863 c. 12

4022. Report of the Oxford University drama commission. With supplementary architectural report, by F. Gibberd. Oxf., 1948, fol. 23 pp.+22 plates.   G.A. Oxon c. 303

4023. COGHILL, N., Notes on the Report of the O.U. Drama commission. (Oxf. mag., 1948, vol. 67, p. 176–82.)   Per. G.A. Oxon 4° 141

4024. ROBERTSON, R., University theatre at Oxford. (Educ. theatre, 1956, vol. 8, p. 194–206.)   L. of C.

4025. The academic drama in Oxford [1480–1650], extracts from the records of four colleges [New, Magdalen, Christ Church, St. John's] ed. by R. E. Alton. (Malone soc., Collections, 1959/60, vol. 5, p. 29–95.)   M. adds. 111 e. 246 = A.

PLAYHOUSE

4025.5. COGHILL, N., The University playhouse. (Oxf. mag., 1960, vol. 78, p. 297–99.)   Per. G.A. Oxon 4° 141

4025.51. HIGGS, J., and SWEETING, E., Profit from the Playhouse. (Oxf. mag., 1963, N.S., vol. 3, p. 262–65.)   Per. G.A. Oxon 4° 141

4025.52. BOASE, T. S. R., The University theatre. (Oxford, 1963, vol. 19, p. 58–66.)   Per. G.A. Oxon 8° 1141

DRAMATIC SOCIETIES

4026. [Rules of a club which 'shall have no name', the object of which was 'to read plays of modern dramatists'. Hilary term, 1903.]
G.A. Oxon 4° 603

4027. CRITICS (THE), [Blank notification of meeting, c. 1906.]
G.A. Oxon 4° 603

4028. Gargoyle club. [Blank notification of meeting, 1905?]
G.A. Oxon 4° 603

4029. Mermaid club. [Miscellaneous papers. 1902–39.] G.A. Oxon 4° 328

See 7103, 7104 [Christ Church Mermaid club].
See 8073 [Newlands society].

4030. Olympia dramatic club. [Miscellaneous papers. 1905, 1906.]
G.A. Oxon b. 147 (34 &c.)
See 7240 [Owlet club].

4031. Oxford drama society. [List of members] 1909. Oxf., 1909, 8°. 18 pp.
M. adds. 41 e. 8

4032. O.U.D.S. [Programmes &c. 1884– .] G.A. Oxon b. 8, 8*; c. 308, 312

4033. The O.U.D.S. souvenir, 1896. Repr. from The Isis. Oxf., 1896, 4°. 7 ff.   G.A. Oxon 4° 262 (26)

4034. NUGENT, C., The O.U.D.S. (Amateur clubs & actors, ed. by W. G. Elliot, 1898, p. 163–92.)   M. adds. 124 e. 38

4035. MACKINNON, A., The O.U.D.S. after 25 years. (Fortnightly review, 1909, vol. 92, p. 875–90.)   Per. 3977 d. 59

4036. PIMBURY, M., A short history of the Oxford university dramatic society. (Oxf., 1955), 4°. 29 pp.

4037. Oxford university experimental theatre club. [Programmes 1936– .]
G.A. Oxon 4° 660

4038. Oxford university philothespian society (club). [Programmes &c. 1880–1883.]   G.A. Oxon b. 147 (29 &c.); MS. Top. Oxon d. 372

4039. Oxford university philothespian club. Rules [and list of members]. Oxf., (1883), 16°. 26 pp.   G.A. Oxon 16° 200 (13)

VISITING PLAYERS

4040. The players turn'd academicks: or, A description, in merry metre, of their translation from the theatre in Little Lincolns-Inn-Fields, to the Tennis-court in Oxford. With a preface relating to the proceedings

of the University the last Act: as also the Wadhamite prologue [by
J. Trapp]. Lond., 1703, fol. 12 pp.   B.M.

4041. A prologue to the University of Oxford spoke by mr. Betterton. [By
J. Trapp, on occasion of the Company of the Theatre in Little
Lincoln's-inn-fields visiting Oxford.] [Lond.? 1703], s. sh.
                                                      Don. b. 15 (8)

4042. A new prologue relating to the Act at Oxford. With an epilogue [&c.].
Lond., [1703], 4°.   B.M.

4043. An act for the more effectual preventing the unlawful playing of
interludes within the precincts of the two universities . . . and for explaining . . . 'An act for laying a duty upon the retailers of spiritous
liquors' . . . as may affect the privilege of the said universities . . . (10
G. II, c. 19, Pub.) Lond., 1737, fol. 8 pp.   L.L.
— 6 & 7 V., c. 68, Pub.

4044. COURTNEY, W. L., Oxford plays down to the Restoration. (Notes and
queries, 1886, 7th ser., vol. 2, p. 464.)   Per. 3974 e. 405 = A.

4045. SCHELLING, F. E., Tabular list of English and Latin plays acted at
Oxford and Cambridge between 1564–1642. Phila., 1904.

4046. LAWRENCE, W. J., Irish players at Oxford in 1677. (The Elizabethan
playhouse and other studies, 1913, 2nd ser., p. 189–200.)
                                                      M. adds. 126 d. 5b

4047. BOAS, F. S., 'Hamlet' at Oxford: new facts and suggestions. (Fortnightly review, 1913, vol. 100, p. 245–53.)   Per. 3977 d. 59
— [Revised and expanded in] Shakespeare & the universities. Oxf.,
1923, 8°.   M. adds. 20 d. 13

4048. LAWRENCE, W. J., Hamlet at the universities, a belated reply [to the
article by F. S. Boas]. (Fortnightly review, 1919, vol. 112, p. 219–27.)
                                                      Per. 3977 d 59

4049. BOAS, F. S., Theatrical companies at Oxford in the seventeenth
century. (Fortnightly review, 1918, vol. 110, p. 256–62.)
                                                      Per. 3977 d. 59

4050. BOAS, F. S., Hamlet and Volpone at Oxford. (Fortnightly review,
1920, vol. 113, p. 709–16.)   Per. 3977 d. 59

4051. BOAS, F. S., Ben Jonson's 'Volpone' at Oxford and Cambridge.
(Shakespeare & the universities, p. 261–66.) Oxf., 1923, 8°.
                                                      M. adds. 20 d. 13

4052. BOAS, F. S., Three hundred years of Shakespeare at Oxford and
Cambridge. (Shakespeare & the universities, p. 42–83.) Oxf., 1923, 8°.
                                                      M. adds. 20 d. 13

4053. MADAN, F., Oxford oddments. 2. Plays acted in or near Oxford in
1653 and 1662. (The Library, 1929, 4th ser., vol. 9, p. 348–50.)
                                                      Per. 258 d. 252 = A

4054. LAWRENCE, W. J., Irish players at Oxford and Edinburgh, 1677–
1681. (Dublin mag., 1932, N.S., vol. 7, no. 1, p. 49–60.)
Per. 2705 d. 384

4055. BOAS, F. S., Stage-plays at Oxford and Cambridge. (An introd. to
Tudor drama, p. 42–57.) Oxf., 1933, 8°.   M. adds. 25 e. 17 = S.

4056. ROSENFELD, S., The players in Oxford, 1661–1713. (Review of
Engl. studies, 1943, vol. 19, p. 366–75.)   Per. 269 d. 168 = A.

Music

*No attempt has been made to record the bills or programmes of the many
concerts and exercises held in the Holywell music room or the Sheldonian theatre.
The Bodleian has a collection of these dating from 1773: see no. 5861.*

See also 5861, &c. Holywell Music Room.

4057. The First (–Third) grand musical festival in the Theatre . . . July 6
(–8) 1791. [Programmes.] [Oxf.], (1791), 8°.   Gough Oxf. 90 (29–31)
— The First (–Third) grand musical festival at the Encænia in the
Theatre . . . July 2 (–4) 1793. [Oxf.], (1793), 8°. Gough Oxf. 90 (32–34)

4058. University musical festival, in the Theatre. First concert, June 10th,
1823. [Programme.] Oxf., (1823), 4°. 16 pp.   G.A. Oxon b. 111 (166)

4059. University musical festival, in the Theatre, Oxford. Grand miscellaneous concert, June 12, 1823. [Programme.] Oxf., 1823, 4°. 16 pp.
G.A. Oxon 4° 186 (11)

4060. University musical festival . . . [First] (Second) Grand miscellaneous
concert, June 27 (28) 1827. Oxf., (1827), 4°. G.A. Oxon b. 111 (190)

4061. Dr. Corfe respectfully solicits the attention of . . . members of Convocation. [Proposal to inaugurate three subscription concerts per year
to encourage study of music.] Nov. 17, 1856. n. pl., 1856, s. sh.
G.A. Oxon c. 72 (334)

4062. Festival of music held at Oxford, on May 7th–13th, 1922. Programme and words of the music. Oxf., 1922, 4°. 56 pp.
G.A. Oxon 4° 432

4063. Oxford festival of music, May 2, 3, 4, 5, 6, 7 & 8, 1926, in commemoration of William Heather. Oxf., (1926), 8°. 52 pp.
G.A. Oxon 4° 399a (12)

4064. HOWES, F., The Heather festival at Oxford. (Mus. times, 1926, vol.
67, p. 537–41.)   Per. 17402 d. 52

MUSICAL SOCIETIES

See 7101 [Harmony club].

4065. Oxford and Cambridge musical club. Report and balance sheet.
1901–07. Lond., [1902–08], fol.   Per. 17402 c. 19

4066. Oxford and Cambridge musical club. [Miscellaneous papers. 1903–07.] G.A. Oxon 4° 599

4067. Oxford and Cambridge musical club. Rules, regulations, and list of members. 1906, 1909, 1913. [Lond.], 1906–13, 16°. G.A. Oxon 16° 116

4068. Oxford Bach choir. Balance sheet, 1897, 98. [*And* Miscellaneous papers.] G.A. Oxon 8° 787

4069. Oxford university amateur musical society. Rules, regulations, &c. n. pl., 1845, s. sh. G.A. Oxon c. 61 (150)

4070. Oxford university gramophone society. Oxford university library of recorded music and music scores: catalogue. Oxf. &c., 1944, 8°. 37 pp. 17434 e. 37

4071. Oxford university gramophone society. Oxford university library of recorded music and scores. Catalogue of long-playing records. Oxf., 1955, 8°. 24 pp. 17434 d. 28

4072. Oxford university gramophone society. Oxford university library of recorded music and scores. Catalogue of works on long-playing records. Oxf., 1957, 8°. 19 pp. 17434 d. 32

4073. Oxford university heritage society. Heritage. [No. 1]– . [Reprod. from typewriting.] Oxf., 1958, 8°. Per. 2806 d. 71

Oxford university library of recorded music and scores. See 4070–72. Oxford university gramophone society.

4074. Oxford university motett and madrigal society. [Prospectus, rules &c.] [Oxf., 1846], 8°. 3 pp. G.A. Oxon 8° 52

4075. Oxford university motett and madrigal society. The first (–eighth) [and last] report. [Oxf.], (1847–54), 8°. G.A. Oxon 8° 52

4076. Oxford university motett and madrigal society. The words of the madrigals for practice (performance) on the open night June 4, 1850 (July 2, 1851, June 15, 1852, May 31, 1853, June 24, 1854). Oxf., 1850–54, 16°. G.A. Oxon 8° 52

4077. Oxford university motett and madrigal society. The words of the anthems, &c. to be sung on the open night, Dec. 5, 1854. Oxf., 1854, 16°. G.A. Oxon 8° 52

4078. Oxford university motett and madrigal society. Catalogue of books in the library. Oxf., 1853, 8°. B.M.

4079. Oxford university musical club. [Miscellaneous papers and programmes. 1872–1916.] G.A. Oxon 4° 292, 292*

4080. Oxford university musical union. [Miscellaneous papers and programmes. 1884–1916.] G.A. Oxon 4° 291, 291*; 8° 788

4081. Oxford university musical union. [List of members.] Lent term, 1889—Lent term, 1905. Oxf., 1889–1905, s. sh. G.A. Oxon b. 124

4082. Oxford university musical union. [Report on the library.] (Oxf.), [1892], 8°. 7 pp.   2590 e. Oxf. 16. 1

4083. Ten years of University music, a brief record of the proceedings of the Oxford university musical union, 1884–1894, compiled by P. C. Buck, J. H. Mee, F. C. Woods. Oxf., (1894), 8°. 224 pp.   17402 e. 133

4084. Ten more years, 1894 to 1904, of University music in Oxford, a continuation of the proceedings of the Oxford university musical union, compiled by E. S. Kemp and J. H. Mee. Oxf., 1904, 8°. xviii+290 pp.
17402 e. 251

4085. Oxford university musical club and union. [Miscellaneous papers. 1916– .]   G.A. Oxon c. 225

4086. Oxford university opera club. [Programmes. 1927–33.]   17405 d. 27

4087. PONSONBY, R., and KENT, R., The Oxford university opera club, a short history, 1925–1950 [by R. Ponsonby and R. Kent]. Oxf., 1950, 8°. 36 pp.

4088. Professor of music's choir. [Notices of meetings &c. 1894–1917?]
G.A. Oxon 4° 609

4089. Society for the study and practice of plain song of the Church. Terminal report (Report) with list of members. Easter, 1854; June 1855. Oxf., 1854, 55, 8°.   G.A. Oxon 8° 1033 (21, 22)

4090. Society for the study and practice of the plain song of the Church. Rules. With list of members. June 1855. [Oxf.], 1855, 8°. 10 pp.
G.A. Oxon 8° 1033 (24)

4091. Society for the study and practice of the plain song of the Church. Rules, together with an account of the second anniversary festival, held on Saint Cecilia's day, 1855. With a list of members. (Oxf., 1855), 8°. 23 pp.   G.A. Oxon 8° 1033 (23)

See also 6778, 6779 [Balliol college musical society].
See also 7098 [Christ Church philharmonic society].
See also 7336 [Exeter college musical society].
See also 7478 [Keble college musical society].
See also 7808 [Merton college musical society].
See also 7910 [New college glee club].
See also 8129 [Pembroke college glee club].
See also 8130 [Pembroke college musical society].
See also 8420, 8421 [St. John's college glee club].
See also 8422 [St. John's college musical society].
See also 8705 [Worcester college musical society].

Commercial

4092. ELDRIDGE, J. M., and GADNEY, H. G., Professors' shop. The grocer's apron at Oxford. [A paper on the Oxford University Co-operative society.] Oxf., [1914], 8°. 4 pp.   G.A. Oxon b. 141 (97a)

Intellectual and literary

4093. JERROLD, D., Oxford conversation. (Oxf. fortnightly, 1913, vol. 2, no. 6, p. 41–43.) Per. 2705 d. 294

4094. CARR, R. C., *ed.*, Red rays, essays of hate from Oxford. Lond., 1933, 8°. 291 pp. 2705 e. 793

See 6514 [Library catalogues and the English Renaissance. 1956].

4095. CURTIS, M. H., Library catalogues and Tudor Oxford and Cambridge. [Intellectual life as reflected in the private library inventories of individual members of the universities.] (Renaissance soc. of America. Studies in the Renaissance, 1958, vol. 5, p. 111–20.) 3975 d. 298

Intellectual and literary societies

4096. Africa society. [Meetings. Hilary term, 1931–Trinity term, 1936.]
G.A. Oxon 4° 664

4097. Agenda club. [Two notices of a meeting. 1912.] G.A. Oxon 4° 603

4098. Alembic club. [Meetings for Michaelmas term, *c.* 1907.]
G.A. Oxon 4° 603

Anglo-German society. See 4146. Oxford Anglo-German club.

See 7090 [Anonym club].
See 7383 [Anthological club].

4099. Arthurian society. [Miscellaneous papers. 1932–1935.]
G.A. Oxon 4° 603

4100. Ascham club. [Miscellaneous papers. 1923–1926.]
G.A. Oxon b. 147 (60)

4101. Ashmolean society. [Resolution made by some friends of science in Oxford to found the Ashmolean society. *With* Rules.] Oxf., [1829], fol. 4 pp. G.A. Oxon b. 21

4102. Ashmolean society. Rules. Oxf., [1831], 4°. 3 pp.
G.A. Oxon c. 47 (136)
— [1832.] G.A. Oxon c. 48 (116)

4103. Ashmolean society. A list of the Ashmolean society for the year 1831. n. pl., [1831], 4°. 4 pp. G.A. Oxon c. 47 (137)
— 1832. G.A. Oxon c. 48 (117)

4104. Ashmolean society. Catalogue of books, pamphlets, &c. presented to the Ashmolean society or purchased out of its funds. [Oxf., 1833?], fol. 3 pp. 2590 e. Oxf. 3. 2 (1)
— [Another ed.] [Oxf., 1840?], 8°. 12 pp. 2590 e. Oxf. 3. 2 (2)
— [Another ed.]. Oxf., 1848, 8°. 35 pp. 2590 e. Oxf. 3. 1
— [Another ed.] Oxf., 1867, 8°. 40 pp. 2590 e. Oxf. 3. 3

4105. Ashmolean society. [Miscellaneous papers. 1876–1937.]
G.A. Oxon 4° 164

4106. Associated [women] students' debating society. Constitution and rules. Oxf., 1891, 16°. 7 pp. G.A. Oxon 4° 410

4107. Associated [women] students' debating society. List of members. Oct. 1892, 1893. n. pl., 1892, 93, s. sh. G.A. Oxon 4° 410

4108. Blackstone society. [Foundation notice. 1908.] G.A. Oxon b. 147 (66)

See 6781 [Brakenbury society].

4109. Bucolic club. Rules. Oxf., 1902, 16°. 11 pp. G.A. Oxon 16° 195 (19)

4110. Burke society. [Miscellaneous papers. 1901–03.] G.A. Oxon 4° 603

Butler's reading room. See 4275, &c. University city and county reading room.

4111. The Cauldron. [Miscellaneous papers. 1901, 02.]
G.A. Oxon b. 147 (73)

4112. Chalet club. [List of members.] 1891–1905. (Oxf., 1905), 8°. 6 pp.
G.A. Oxon 8° 1127 (20)

See 7545 [Crewe society].

4113. Dafydd ap Gwilym society. [Miscellaneous papers. 1892– .]
G.A. Oxon 8° 711; MS. Welsh d. 1

4114. Daubeny club. Rules. [Oxf., 186–], s. sh. G.A. Oxon b. 147 (73)
— [Another ed.] 1869. 8°. 4 pp. G.A. Oxon b. 147 (73)

4115. Davenant literary society. [4 notifications of meetings, 1893–1907.]
G.A. Oxon b. 147 (73)

4116. Decalogue (The). [Blank notification of meeting. 1905.]
G.A. Oxon 4° 603

See 8704 [De Quincey society].
See 6783 [Dervorguilla society].

Deutsche wissenschaftliche Vereinigung. See 4146. Oxford Anglo-German society.

4117. Eaglet club. [2 blank notifications of meetings. 1905.]
G.A. Oxon 4° 603

4118. Edward Lhuyd society. [List of meetings, members &c. 1903/04.]
G.A. Oxon 4° 603

See 8217 [Eglesfield debating society].
See 8072 [Ellesmere society].

4119. English association, Oxford branch. [Miscellaneous papers. 1922–27.] G.A. Oxon b. 147

See 7546, 7547 [Fleming society].

4120. Fortnightly (The). [3 notifications of meetings &c. between 1883 and 1897.] G.A. Oxon b. 147 (28)

German scientific society. See 4146. Oxford Anglo-German club.

4121. Gryphon club. [2 blank notifications of meetings, c. 1905.]
G.A. Oxon 4° 603

4122. Herbertson geographical society. [Notice, 1927.]
G.A. Oxon b. 147 (67)

4123. Hexameron essay society. Rules. [Oxf., c. 1865], 8°. 3 pp.
G.A. Oxon b. 147

4124. History club. [Notification of a meeting, c. 1907.] G.A. Oxon 4° 603

4125. History society. [Miscellaneous papers. 1908–11.] G.A. Oxon 4° 603

4126. Horace club. Rules for the first (second) meeting. [Lond., 1898], 99,
8°. G.A. Oxon b. 147 (74)
— [Rules of] Meeting, 1898 (–1901). G.A. Oxon b. 147 (74)

4127. Horace club. The book of the Horace club, 1898–1901. Oxf., (1901),
8°. 121 pp. 2805 e. 240

4128. Jowett society. [Miscellaneous papers. 1901–07, 24.]
G.A. Oxon 4° 603

4129. Junior physiological club. [Members and programme for 1893/94.]
G.A. Oxon 4° 603

4130. King Alfred club. Rules . . . with a list of debates and essays (1867–
71). Oxf., 1871, 8°. 15 pp. G.A. Oxon 8° 1132 (10)

4131. King's college club. [Miscellaneous papers. 1871, 72.]
G.A. Oxon b. 146

4132. Kitchin club. Rules. [Oxf., 1874], 8°. 3 pp. G.A. Oxon b. 147

4133. Livingstone society. [Miscellaneous papers. 1894–1910.]
G.A. Oxon 4° 602

4134. Lotos [sometimes] Lotus eaters. [Miscellaneous papers. 1893–1905.]
G.A. Oxon 4° 603

4135. Maine law society. [2 notices. 1893, 95.] G.A. Oxon b. 147 (76)
See 8597 [Martlets society].

4136. Medieval society. [Notification of meetings, Hilary term 1934.]
G.A. Oxon 4° 603
[The society was founded c. 1932 and is still active. This card is the
only printed record of the society in the Bodleian.]

4137. Milton club. [Miscellaneous papers. 1893–1903.]
G.A. Oxon b. 147; 4° 603

4138. Milton club. Rules. [Oxf., 1895], 4°. 4 pp. G.A. Oxon b. 147
— [Another ed.]. Oxf., 1901, 8°. 11 pp. G.A. Oxon b. 147

4139. Newman society. [Miscellaneous papers. 1902–1927.]
G.A. Oxon 4° 603

4140. Nucleus. [Miscellaneous papers. 1894.] G.A. Oxon 4° 603

4141. 'The Old Mortality.' [Account, with list of members from its foundation, 1856, signed] T. E. H[olland.] [Oxf.], 1896, s. sh.
G.A. Oxon b. 147 (20)

4142. Organon club. [Miscellaneous papers. 1899–1920.]
G.A. Oxon b. 147 (40)

4143. Orthodox club. [2 blank notifications of meetings, c. 1905.]
G.A. Oxon 4° 603

4144. Oxford ancient history society. [Miscellaneous papers. 1885–1891.]
G.A. Oxon b. 147 (25)

4145. Oxford ancient history society. List of members. May, 1885–June, 1891. [Oxf.], 1885–91, s. sh.   MS. Top. Oxon e. 195

4146. Oxford Anglo-German society (club) [*formerly*] German scientific society [*formerly*] Anglo-German society. [Miscellaneous papers. 1910–14.]   G.A. Oxon b. 147

4147. Oxford Browning society. [Miscellaneous papers. 1881–86.]
G.A. Oxon b. 147 (70); 4° 603

4148. Oxford Dante society. Toynbee, P., The Oxford Dante society, 1876–1920. Oxf., 1920, 8°. 102 pp.   G.A. Oxon 8° 995

4149. Oxford dialectic society. Rules. Oxf., 1873, 8°. 12 pp.
G.A. Oxon 8° 1132 (11)
— 1875.   G.A. Oxon 8° 1132 (12)

4150. Oxford dialectic society. [Miscellaneous papers. 1876–77.]
G.A. Oxon b. 147 (74)

4151. The Oxford historical seminar. (Rules.) [Oxf.], 1882, 8°. 3 pp.
MS. Top. Oxon e. 195 (86)

4152. Oxford mathematical society. [Miscellaneous papers. 1888–95.]
G.A. Oxon b. 147

4153. Oxford modern ethical society. Firminger, W. K., and Gibson, W. The idea of an Oxford modern ethical society, a paper. Oxf., (1891), 8°. 20 pp.   G.A. Oxon 8° 850 (14)

4154. The social question at Oxford. [Observations on the proposed foundation of an Oxford modern ethical society.] (The Lyceum, 1891, vol. 4, p. 189–210.)   G.A. Oxon 4° 586 (44)

4155. Oxford ornithological society. [Miscellaneous papers, 1921–45.]
G.A. Oxon b. 166

Oxford philological society. See 4252, &c. Oxford university philological society.

4156. Oxford philosophical society. [Miscellaneous papers. 1904–1907.]
G.A. Oxon 4° 603

4157. Oxford [women] students' debating society. Rules and regulations.
Oxf., 1897, 8°. 6 pp. G.A. Oxon 8° 1113 (6)

Oxford Union Society.
General 4158–92.
Lists of members 4193–96.
Building 4197–4202.
Fresco and paintings 4203–12.
Library 4213–15.

General

See also 4216 [Oxford united debating society].

4158. Oxford union society. Proceedings. (1826)–1923/24. Oxf., 1841–
1924, 8°. Per. G.A. Oxon 8° 506

4159. Oxford union society. [Miscellaneous papers. 1834– .]
G.A. Oxon a. 29; b. 70

4160. Oxford union society and reading room. Rules and regulations.
1832– . Oxf., 1832– , 8°. G.A. Oxon 8° 505, 1428, 1490

4161. Proceedings of the Star-chamber at Oxford [concerning the expulsion of 'Ramblers' from the Union. In verse]. Oxf., 1833, 8°. 8 pp.
G.A. Oxon 8° 366 (3)

4162. JACKSON, T., Uniomachia, Canino-Anglico-Græce et Latine, an-
notationibus Heavysternii ornavit; et suas insuper notulas adjecit,
Habbakukius Dunderheadius [T. Jackson.]. [A satire on the dispute
between the Union and the Ramblers.] Oxon., 1833, 8°. 8 pp.
G.A. Oxon 8° 366
— Ed. 2a. 1833. G.A. Oxon 8° 253
— Ed. 3a, auctior: et Slawkenbergii [R. Scott] animadversionibus
nunc primum in lucem prolatis illustrata. Oxon., 1833, 8°.
— 5th ed. Repr. from the 3rd ed. By T. Jackson. Oxf., 1875, 8°. 27 pp.
G.A. Oxon 8° 286 (6)

4163. JACKSON, T., Uniomachia, or, The battle at the Union, given to
the world by Habbakukius Dunderheadius [T. Jackson assisted by
W. Sinclair] now rendered into the English tongue by Jedediah Puzzle-
pate [J. D. Giles]. Oxf., 1333 [really 1833], 8°. 8 pp. G.A. Oxon 8° 254

See also 4265 [Dissolution of The Rambler society, in view of bad feeling with
the Union society. 1834].

4164. [Account of a dispute over the accounts of the society for 1833, when
G. Trevor charged the treasurer and former treasurer, W. Hussey and
G. E. Bruxner, with forging and fabricating the accounts, Correspon-
dence, report of a committee, and treasurer's account, is included.]
[Oxf., 1835], fol. 7 pp. G.A. Oxon c. 25 (2)

4165. Oxford union society. [Statement of accounts.] 1849/50.
G.A. Oxon c. 66 (168)

4166. Annual summary of accounts. 1914/15, 15/16. [Oxf.], 1915–16, 8°.
G.A. Oxon b. 70*b*

4167. A night at the Oxford union. (Leisure hour, 1861, vol. 10, p. 5–7.)
Per. 2705 d. 33

4168. A letter to the members of the Oxford union by Philodikaios [concerning a breach of the rules in connection with a 'requisition']. n. pl., (1868), 8°. 10 pp.
G.A. Oxon 8° 326

4169. NICHOLSON, E. W. B., Intellectual self-help at Oxford. Part 1. The Union society [signed D.]. (Oxf. univ. mag. and review, 1869, p. 173–84.)
MS. Top. Oxon c. 181

4170. NICHOLSON, E. B., The Oxford union, by the late librarian of that society. (Macmillan's mag., 1873, vol. 28, p. 567–76.)
G.A. Oxon 4° 577 (26)

4171. NICHOLSON, E. B., A night in the Oxford union. (Lond. soc., 1873, vol. 24, p. 449–59.)
G.A. Oxon 4° 578 (39)

4172. HEURTLEY, C. A., Archbishop Manning and the Union banquet. [Explaining the author's reasons for objecting to the high precedence given the archbishop at the banquet.] [Oxf.], (1873), s. sh.
G.A. Oxon b. 70*d*

4173. Jubilee banquet, 1823–1873. [A description in verse.] Leeds, 1873, 4°. 7 pp.
G.A. Oxon b. 70*d*

4174. A verbatim report of the speeches at the banquet . . . on occasion of the fiftieth anniversary of the Oxford union society. October 22nd, 1873. To which is prefixed a sketch of the history of the society. Oxf. &c., 1874, 8°. 35 pp.
G.A. Oxon 8° 124 (26)

4175. The Oxford union. (Leisure hour, 1874, vol. 23, p. 507–09.)
Per. 2705 d. 33

4176. HUGESSEN, E. H. KNATCHBULL-, The Oxford union. (Time, 1879, vol. 2, p. 146–56.)
Per. 2705 d. 278

4177. Oxford union society. Report of debates, Easter term, 1886. Repr. from the Oxf. univ. herald. [Oxf.], (1886), 8°. 63 pp.
G.A. Oxon 8° 356 (1)
— Michaelmas, 1886. Repr. from The Oxf. review. Oxf., (1886), 8°. 31 pp.
G.A. Oxon 8° 356 (2)

4178. The position of the Union. (Oxf. mag., 1892, vol. 11, p. 147, 48.)
Per. G.A. Oxon 4° 141

4179. WISE, B. R., Reminiscences of the Oxford union. (Nat. rev., 1897, vol. 29, p. 68–83.)
Per. 22775 d. 14

4180. Proceedings of the Oxford union society on May 19th, 1898, being the day of Mr. Gladstone's death. Oxf., 1898, 8°. 11 pp.
G.A. Oxon b. 70*a* (8)

4181. GROSE, T. H., The Oxford union society [historical account by T. H. Grose]. [Oxf., 1900], s. sh.   G.A. Oxon b. 14

4182. Oxford union society. Unveiling of the memorial bust of the late marquess of Salisbury, report of proceedings and speeches. [Oxf.], (1904), 8°. 18 pp.   G.A. Oxon 8° 715 (4)

4183. The Oxford union society. Oxf., 1907, 8°. 11 pp.
                                            G.A. Oxon 8° 1000 (10)

See 4694 [Hall, S. P., Key book to 'Oxford sketches' acquired by the Union society. 1909].

4184. POULTON, E. B., Memories of the union in the seventies. (John Viriamu Jones and other Oxford memories, p. 135–81.) Lond. &c., 1911, 8°.   G.A. Oxon 8° 823

4185. CANNON, P. S., The Union petition [concerning the presidential election of June 1912]: a last word. (Oxf. fortnightly, 1913, vol. 2, no. 5, p. 1–3.)   Per. 2705 d. 294

4186. SMITH, F. E., 1st earl Birkenhead, The Oxford union society. (Points of view, 1922, vol. 1, p. 77–91.)   L.L.

4187. MORRAH, H. A., The Oxford union, 1823–1923. Lond. &c., 1923, 4°. 326 pp.   G.A. Oxon 4° 446

4188. The speeches given at the centenary banquet of the Oxford union society, 29 Feb., 1924, verbatim report. Oxf., 1924, 8°. 66 pp.
                                            G.A. Oxon 8° 1027

4189. HAM, E. B., The Oxford union centenary. (Amer. Oxon., 1924, vol. 11, p. 65–70.)   Per. G.A. Oxon 8° 889

4190. GRIBBLE, F., The Oxford union. (Edinb. review, 1924, vol. 239, p. 41–50.)   Per. 3977 e. 190

4191. HARDIE, F. M., Pacifism at the Oxford union. (Political quarterly, 1933, vol. 4, p. 268–73.)   Per. 24817 d. 148 = P.

See 6541 [Jordan, A. F., The Oxford union society overprint on the rose-red stars. 1953].

4192. Oxford union society v. City of Oxford. (Ryde's rating cases, 1957, vol. 2, p. 54–60.)   L.L.

4192.5. HOLLIS, C., The Oxford union. Lond., 1965, 8°. 281 pp.
                                            G.A. Oxon 8° 1503

Lists of members

4193. Members of the . . . society. Nov. 1836; Feb. 1837; Mar., May 1838. (Oxf., 1836–38), s. sh.   G.A. Oxon b. 70d

4194. Honorary members. Mar., May, 1838; Mar., 1841. (Oxf., 1838, 41), s. sh.
— Corrected to Mar., 1860. (Oxf., 1860), 8°. 20 pp.

— to Jan. 1863. 22 pp.
— to Oct. 1869. 28 pp.
— to Oct. 1876. 24 pp.
— Jan. 1877–Dec. 1881. 8 pp.   G.A. Oxon b. 70*d*

4195. List of subscribing members . . . Feb. 1866. (Oxf., 1866), s. sh.
                 G.A. Oxon b. 70*d*

4196. A list . . . of life members of the Oxford union society resident in
Oxford. January, 1912. [Oxf.], (1912), 4°. 8 pp.   G.A. Oxon b. 70*b*
— Revised. February, 1914. [Oxf.], (1914), 4°. 8 pp.
                 G.A. Oxon b. 70*b*

Building

4197. DIGBY, K. E., The poll at the Union. Plans of the building committee.
[Oxf., 1862], s. sh.   G.A. Oxon b. 113 (159)

4198. GOODWIN, T., The poll at the Union. Answer to mr. Digby's
remarks [concerning the choice of an architect by the building
committee]. Feb. 18. n. pl., [1862], s. sh.   G.A. Oxon c. 78 (363)

4199. Oxford union society. Report of the building committee. Nov. 26,
1869. (Oxf., 1869), 8°. 8 pp.   G.A. Oxon a. 29

4200. FYFFE, C. A., Remarks on the scheme proposed by the building
committee of the Oxford union society, by a member of the committee
[C. A. Fyffe]. n. pl., (1869), 8°. 19 pp.   G.A. Oxon 8° 100 (4)

4201. Oxford union society. Report of the proceedings . . . at the laying of
the foundation stone of the new debating hall, May 8, 1878; together
with the speeches at the luncheon . . . after the ceremony. Oxf., 1878,
8°. 22 pp.   G.A. Oxon a. 29

4202. Oxford union society. New buildings. [Proposals for the reconstruction of the premises, appeal for funds and plan. 25 Mar.] (Oxf.), 1910,
4°. 2 sheets.   MS. Top. Oxon c. 180 (192)

Fresco and paintings

4203. A [humorous] peep at the pictures, and a catalogue of the principal
objects of attraction in the room of the Oxford union society; an explanation of the gallery of painting shortly to be opened. Oxf., 1857,
8°. 8 pp.   G.A. Oxon 8° 124 (6)

4204. SIDEBOTHAM, J. S., A description of the paintings in the debating
room of the Oxford union society. Oxf., 1859, 8°. 26 pp.
                 G.A. Oxon 8° 286 (2)

4205. The fresco question [signed E. P.]. June 5th, 1871. [Oxf.], (1871), 8°.
12 pp.   G.A. Oxon a. 29

4206. Oxford union society. Report of the Fresco committee. (Oxf., 1871),
8°. 12 pp.   G.A. Oxon 8° 327

4207. The wall paintings at the Union. [Observations on the proposed restoration, signed 'Several promoters of the restoration'.] Feb. 9th, 1874. [Oxf.], (1874), 4°. 4 pp.   G.A. Oxon a. 29

4208. The frescoes again! Reasons for voting against the amendment [appointing a committee to report on possible restoration]. [Oxf., 1874], s. sh.   G.A. Oxon a. 29

4209. Oxford union society. Portraits for the debating hall [list of portraits required]. Nov. 7, 1894. [Oxf.], (1894), 4°. 8 pp. G.A. Oxon a. 29

4210. HUNT, W. HOLMAN, Oxford union society: the story of the painting of the pictures on the walls and the decorations on the ceiling of the old debating hall, 1857-8-9. Oxf. &c., 1906, fol. 15 pp.+12 pl. 17006 b. 29

4211. Paintings in the Oxford union, an appeal [signed by Cosmo Cantuar and 8 others]. n. pl., [1935], 4°. 3 pp.+2 plates. G.A. Oxon b. 197

4212. Oxford union society. The Pre-Raphaelite mural paintings, Old library. [An account of the restored murals, by I. Harvey.] [Oxf.], (1936), 4°. 4 pp.   G.A. Oxon b. 197

See 5399 [Alden, J. E., Pre-Raphaelites and Oxford, including the Union frescoes. 1948].

Library

4213. Catalogue of books in the library of the Oxford union society arranged according to their position in the library. Corrected to March, 1836. Oxf., (1836), s. sh.   2590 e. Oxf. 13. 3 (1)
— [Another ed.] . . . and also alphabetically. Corrected to Feb. 1837. Oxf., 1837, 12°. 32 pp.   2590 e. Oxf. 13. 3 (2)
— [Another ed. *entitled*] Oxford union society. Library catalogue. Oxf., 1838, 12°. 71 pp.   2590 e. Oxf. 13. 3 (3)
— [Another ed. *entitled*] Catalogue of the library. Oxf., 1842, 8°. 51 pp.   2590 e. Oxf. 13. 4
— Supplemental catalogue. Jan. 1, 1846. Oxf., 1846, 8°. 14 pp.
      2590 e. Oxf. 13. 3 (4)
— [Another ed.] Oxf., 1847, 8°. 94 pp.   2590 e. Oxf. 13. 5
— 3rd ed. Oxf., 1852, 8°. 207 pp.   2590 e. Oxf. 13. 1
— 4th ed. Oxf., 1858, 8°. 99 pp.   2590 e. Oxf. 13. 6
— Books added. Mich. term, 1861, Lent, Easter and Act term 1862. [Oxf.], (1862), 8°. 8+14 pp.   2590 e. Oxf. 13. 3 (5, 6)
— 5th ed. Oxf., 1864, 8°. 151 pp.   2590 e. Oxf. 13. 7
— Suppl. [Oxf., 1865], 8°. 19 pp.   2590 e. Oxf. 13. 3 (7)
— 6th ed. Oxf., 1875, 8°. 254 pp.   2590 e. Oxf. 13. 8
— Books added, Lent term 1876—Easter term, 1883. [Oxf., 1876–83], 8°.   2590 e. Oxf. 13. 3 (8)

4214. The subject-catalogue of the Oxford union society's library. 2 pt. Oxf., 1883, 85, 8°.   2590 e. Oxf. 13. 2 = R.

4215. First draft of Report of Union library special committee [concerning the creation of the office of Senior librarian]. [Oxf., 1907], 8°. 8 pp.
MS. Top. Oxon c. 180 (166)
— Report. [Oxf.], (1907), 8°. 8 pp.   MS. Top. Oxon c. 180 (176)

4216. Oxford united debating society. [Laws and transactions.] Oxf., [1823], 8°. 14 pp.   G.A. Oxon 8° 544 (1)
— [Another ed.] Laws and transactions. MDCCCXXIV. Oxf., 1824, 8°. 40 pp.   G.A. Oxon 8° 544 (2)
— [Another ed.] MDCCCXXV [and] Suppl. Oxf., 1825, 8°. 68+[22] pp.   G.A. Oxon 8° 544 (3)
— [Repr. of the 1825 ed. and suppl.] Oxf., 1872, 8°. 44 pp.
G.A. Oxon 8° 544 (4)
[The Society was dissolved in 1825 and immediately reformed as the Oxford union leaving out 'obnoxious' members.]

Oxford university Alembic club. See 4098. Alembic club.

4217. Oxford university anthropological society. [Miscellaneous papers. 1910–16.]   G.A. Oxon 4° 603

4218. Oxford university anthropological society. Anthropology at Oxford, proceedings of the 500th meeting. [Oxf., 1953], 8°.   Radcl.

4219. Oxford university antiquarian society. Journal of the Oxford university brass-rubbing society [afterw.] Oxford journal of monumental brasses. Vol. 1, no. 1–vol. 2, no. 3. (Oxf.), 1897–1912, 8°.
Soc. 2184 d. 50

4220. Oxford university antiquarian society [formerly] Oxford university brass-rubbing society. [Miscellaneous papers. 1894–1912.] 218 d. 169

4221. Oxford university archaeological society. [Miscellaneous papers. 1922–30.]   G.A. Oxon b. 147; 4° 601

4222. Oxford university archaeological society. Annual exhibition of members' work, 1957–8. Catalogue and guide. [Reprod. from typewriting.] [Oxf., 1958], fol. 15 leaves.   G.A. Oxon c. 332

4222.1. Oxford university archaeological society. 1961 exhibition of members' work [with an account of the various sites visited]. [Reprod. from typewriting.] n. pl., 1961, fol. 19 sheets.   17581 c. 6

Oxford university brass-rubbing society. See 4219, 4220. Oxford university antiquarian society.

4223. Oxford university British-American club. [Miscellaneous papers. 1919–23.]   G.A. Oxon b. 148 (37–40)

4224. Oxford (university) Caledonian society. [Miscellaneous papers. 1919–21.]   G.A. Oxon b. 147 (56)

4225. Oxford university Cambrian society. [Miscellaneous papers. 1914–27.]   G.A. Oxon b. 148 (22–27); MS. Top. Oxon d. 279

4226. Oxford university Celtic society. Rules. [*c*. 1906 *and* Miscellaneous papers, 1904–06]. G.A. Oxon 4° 603

4227. Oxford university chemical club. [Blank notification of meeting, *c.* 1910.] G.A. Oxon 4° 603

4228. Oxford university cosmopolitan club. [Miscellaneous papers. 1907–26.] G.A. Oxon 4° 603

4228.1. Oxford university cosmopolitan club. The Oxford Cosmopolitan. Vol. 1, no. 1, 2. Oxf., 1908, 8°. Soc. 3977 d. 56

4229. Oxford university English club. [2 notices, 1927.] G.A. Oxon b. 147 (70)

4230. Oxford university entomological society. Rules. Oxf., [*c*. 1854], 8°. 9 pp. G.A. Oxon 8° 1127 (5)

4231. Oxford university entomological society. [3 notices, 1923, 24, 27.] G.A. Oxon b. 147 (68)

4232. Oxford university exploration club. First (–10th) annual report. 1928/29–37/38. [Oxf., 1929–39], 8°. Per. 2031 d. 23

4233. Oxford university exploration club. Bulletin. No. 1– . Cowley, 1948– , 8°. Per. 2031 e. 212 = G.

4234. Oxford university forest club (society). [Foundation notice, and 2 miscellaneous papers, 1919, 20.] G.A. Oxon b. 147 (65)

4235. Oxford university French club (Le Club français). [Miscellaneous papers. 1906–27.] G.A. Oxon b. 148 (6–18)

4236. Oxford university French club. La Chouette aveugle, Rédacteur-en-chef: M. Smithies. No. 1– . [Reprod. from typewriting.] (Oxf.), 1954– , 4°. Per. 2755 c. 3

4237. Oxford university genealogical and heraldic society. Rules. [Oxf.], 1835, s. sh. G.A. Oxon 8° 514
— [Another ed.] Oxf., 1838, 8°. 16 pp. Manning 8° 30 = R. Top.

4238. Oxford university genealogical and heraldic society. Report (–Fifth report) of the proceedings. Oxf., 1835–39, 8°. Manning 8° 30 = R. Top.

4239. Oxford university German club. [Miscellaneous papers. 1911–28.] G.A. Oxon b. 147

4240. Oxford university German literary society. Rules. [Reprod. from typewriting.] n. pl., [1909?], 4°. 3 sh. G.A. Oxon b. 147
— [Another ed.]. (Oxf.), [1909], 8°. 3 pp. G.A. Oxon b. 147
— [Another ed. 1910?]. G.A. Oxon b. 147

4241. Oxford university German literary society. List of members. 1909. (Oxf.), 1909, 8°. 8 pp. G.A. Oxon b. 147
— 1911. G.A. Oxon b. 147

4242. Oxford university German literary society. [Miscellaneous papers. 1909–14.] G.A. Oxon 4° 601; b. 147

4243. Oxford university India society. Rules [1905? *and* Miscellaneous papers, 1905–07]. G.A. Oxon 4° 603

4244. Oxford university invariant society. Invariant. No. 1- . [Reprod. from typewriting.] [Oxf.], 1961– , 4°. Radcl.

4245. Oxford university Irish society. [Miscellaneous papers. 1905–21.] G.A. Oxon 4° 603

4246. Oxford university Italian circle. [Miscellaneous papers. 1919–25.] G.A. Oxon b. 148 (4–5)

4247. Oxford university junior linguistic society. [Miscellaneous papers. 1929–34.] G.A. Oxon 4° 603

4248. Oxford university junior physiological society. [Miscellaneous papers. 1893/4, 96.] G.A. Oxon 4° 603

4249. Oxford university junior scientific club. Journal [*afterw.*] Transactions. 1887–1935. Oxf., 1887–1935, 8°. G.A. Oxon 8° 512

4250. Oxford university junior scientific society. [Miscellaneous papers. 1882–1928.] G.A. Oxon 4° 168*

4251. Oxford university moot club. [A case for argument at a meeting in 1923.] G.A. Oxon 4° 603

4252. Oxford university philological society. [Miscellaneous papers. 1870– 1937.] G.A. Oxon 8° 1121; 4° 167, 597

4253. Oxford university philological society. Rules. 1873, 77. n. pl., 1873, 77, 8°. G.A. Oxon 8° 1121

4254. Oxford university philological society. Transactions. 1879/80–89/90. Oxf., (1880–90), 8°. 2998 e. 3

4255. Oxford university philological society. List of members. 1910, 12, 17. Oxf., 1910–17, 16°. G.A. Oxon 8° 1121

4256. Oxford university Socratic club. Socratic digest [*afterw.*] The Socratic. No. 1- . (Oxf.), 1943– , 8°. Per. 267 e. 20

4257. Oxford university Spanish club. [Miscellaneous papers. 1916–28.] G.A. Oxon b. 148; 4° 602

4258. Oxford university Sudhamma Samiti. [Notification of 1st meeting, 1914.] G.A. Oxon 4° 603
— Extracts from the regulations [1914]. G.A. Oxon b. 147 (61)

Parker's reading room and society. See 4275, &c. University, city and county reading room.

4259. Phasmatological society. [Miscellaneous papers. 1879–82.] G.A. Oxon b. 147 (81)

4260. Phasmatological society. Rules. n. pl., (1882), 8°. 8 pp.
G.A. Oxon 8° 1132 (9)

4261. Philistines (The). [Syllabus for 1907.] G.A. Oxon 4° 603

4262. Physiological society. [Two notifications of meetings in 1899 and 1902.] G.A. Oxon 4° 603

See 8076 [Plantagenet society].

4263. Plough club. Rules. [Oxf., 1922], s. sh. G.A. Oxon b. 147 (63)

4264. Raleigh club. [Miscellaneous papers. 1871–1904.] G.A. Oxon 4° 603

4265. The Rambler society. [Notice of meeting, Nov. 4, 1833.] [Oxf.], (1833), s. sh. G.A. Oxon b. 70d
— [Notice of meeting, Jan. 25, 1834, when the dissolution of the society will be proposed in view of bad feeling with the Union society.] [Oxf.], (1834), s. sh. G.A. Oxon b. 70d

See 4161 [Expulsion of 'Ramblers' from the Union. 1833].

See 7651 [Rupert society].

4266. Scientific club. List of resident members. 1899, 1904, 08. [Oxf.], 1899–1908, s. sh. G.A. Oxon b. 147 (41)
[The same volume in the Bodleian contains miscellaneous papers from 1894–1914.]

4267. The Society. Matheson, P. E., The Society, 1886–1911. (Oxf.), 1932, 16°. 16 pp. G.A. Oxon 16° 176* (6)

4268. Society of post-graduate students. [Miscellaneous papers. 1924–26.] G.A. Oxon b. 147 (62)

4269. Sophists. [Blank notification of meeting. 1907]. G.A. Oxon 4° 603

See 7334, 7345 [Stapledon debating society].

4270. Stubbs society. [Miscellaneous papers. 1906, 07, 19, 21.] G.A. Oxon 4° 603

See 7241 [Tenterden essay club].

4271. Triste Lignum club. [List of meetings for Michaelmas term 1904.] G.A. Oxon 4° 603

4272. Tudor society. [Rules and list of members.] Jan. 1899. Oxf., 1899, 8°. 10 pp. G.A. Oxon b. 147 (80)
— Officers, members and rules. Oct. 1900. Oxf., 1900, 8°. 10 pp. [Also 3 programmes for terms in 1899, 1900.] G.A. Oxon b. 147 (80)

4273. Twentieth century club. Rules. June 1st, 1908. (Oxf.), 1908, folded card. G.A. Oxon 4° 603

4274. Twenty club. List of members, past and present. Michaelmas term, 1899. Hilary term, 1901. Hilary term, 1902. Oxf., 1899–1902, 16°. G.A. Oxon 16° 73

See 7384 [Tyndale literary and debating society].

4275. University, city and county reading room. [Notice of a meeting to be held in the Radcliffe Library with the object of forming a Reading room and society. Oct. 17, 1823.] G.A. Oxon c. 40

4276. University, city and county reading room. [Meeting of subscribers to Butler's reading room, with resolutions and list of members.] Oxf., (1824), 4°. 7 pp. G.A. Oxon b. 19

4277. University, city and county reading room. [Proposal to establish a reading room at mr. Parker's in the Turl.] n. pl., 1830, s. sh.
G.A. Oxon c. 46 (120)

4278. University, city and county reading room. The rules and regulations of the reading room at mr. Parker's in the Turl. To which are prefixed the names of the members. [Oxf.], 1831, 8°. 15 pp.
G.A. Oxon c. 47 (138a)
— 1832. G.A. Oxon c. 48 (118a)
— 1833. G.A. Oxon c. 49 (114)
— 1836. G.A. Oxon c. 52 (133)

4279. University, city and county reading room. Rules and regulations, with the names of members and a catalogue of the books &c. 1847. [Oxf.], 1847, 8°. 31 pp. G.A. Oxon c. 63 (173)
— 1848. G.A. Oxon c. 64 (159)
— 1853. G.A. Oxon c. 69 (234)

4280.

4281. University reading rooms. Rules. n. pl., [1852], s. sh.
G.A. Oxon c. 68 (204)

4282. Verulam essay society. Rules. n. pl., [c. 1860], 8°. 4 pp.
G.A. Oxon 8° 900 (3)

4283. Verulam essay society. List of members for Hilary term, 1866. n. pl., (1866), s. sh. G.A. Oxon 8° 900 (3*)

4284. Womens' inter-collegiate debating society. Rules and regulations. (Oxf.), [c. 1895?], 8°. 7 pp. G.A. Oxon 8° 1113 (5)

4285. Wooden horse. [Blank notification of a meeting, c. 1905.]
G.A. Oxon 4° 603

4286. X club. [A scientific society for University women.] Report, Oct. 1904–July 1905. n. pl., (1905), 8°. 7 pp. G.A. Oxon 4° 410

See 6890 [Brasenose college debating society].
See 6891 [Brasenose college Ingoldsby essay club].
See 7094 [Christ Church debating society].
See 7095 [Christ Church essay club].
See 7099 [Christ Church Shakespeare society].
See 7239 [Corpus Christi college debating society].
See 7333 [Exeter college debating society].
See 7444 [Jesus college common room and debating society].
See 7550 [Lincoln college debating club].
See 7802 [Merton college biological club].
See 7806 [Merton college debating society].

See 7909 [New college discussion society].
See 7914 [New college moot club].
See 8128 [Pembroke college debating society].
See 8214, &c. [Queen's college debating society].
See 8285 [St. Catherine's history society].
See 8287 [St. Catherine's debating society].
See 8333 [St. Edmund debating society].
See 8418 [St. John's debating and book club].
See 8424 [St. John's junior literary society].
See 8651, &c. [Wadham college book club].
See 8702 [Worcester college debating society].
See 8704 [Worcester college literary society].

Political

See 4550 [Oxford: its morals and its politics. 1866].

4287. CURZON, G. N., Conservatism of young Oxford. (Nat. review, 1884, vol. 3, p. 515–27.)   Per. 22775 d. 14

4288. CADOGAN, E., Lament of an Oxford Tory. (Nat. review, 1903, vol. 41, p. 117–26.)   Per. 22775 d. 14

4289. MACDONALD, M. J., What young Oxford is thinking: university politics from the inside. (Review of reviews, 1922, vol. 65, p. 26–28.) Per. 3977 d. 69

4290. HOW, F. MURTHWAITE-, The politics of the undergraduate. (Nineteenth cent., 1928, vol. 103, p. 775–81.)   Per. 3977 d. 66

4291. ASHLEY, M. P., and SAUNDERS, C. T., Red Oxford, a history of the growth of socialism in the University of Oxford. (Oxf. univ. labour club.) Oxf., 1930, 8°.
— 2nd ed. 1933. 46 pp.   G.A. Oxon 8° 1101 (11)

See 160 [Ward, W. R., Georgian Oxford. 1958].
See 216.5 [Ward, W. R., Victorian Oxford. 1965].
See 5130 [Janus, a review of international affairs. 1960].

Political societies

4292. Arnold society. [Blank notification of meeting. 1903.]
G.A. Oxon 4° 603

4293. Cabinet club. [Miscellaneous papers. 1895.]   G.A. Oxon 4° 603

Canning club. See 4301, &c. Oxford Canning club.

Carlton club. See 4306, &c. Oxford Carlton club.

See 6782 [Carlyle society].

4294. Chatham club. [Miscellaneous papers. 1866–1906.]
G.A. Oxon 4° 600

4295. Chatham club. (Rules, members.) Oxf., 1894, 16°. 44 pp.
G.A. Oxon 16° 195 (9)

4296. Chatham club. Lockhart, J. G., The history of the Chatham club, Oxford, and list of members, 1864 to 1922 [signed J. G. L.]. Oxf., 1922, 8°. 116 pp.   G.A. Oxon 8° 1013

4297.

4298. Cobden club. [Miscellaneous papers. 1905.]   G.A. Oxon 4° 603

4299. Commonwealth club. [Notification of a meeting. 1919.]
                                                        G.A. Oxon 4° 603

Economic society. See 4308. Oxford economic society.

4300. Imperial federation league: Oxford university branch. [Miscellaneous papers. 1886–92.]   G.A. Oxon 4° 600; b. 146

See 8415 [King Charles club].

4301. Oxford Canning club. [Miscellaneous papers. 1865–1906.]
                                                        G.A. Oxon 4° 600; b. 146

4302. Oxford Canning club. The Oxford Canning club minute book from October, 1880 to February, 1882. Oxf., [1882], 8°. 208 pp.
                                                        G.A. Oxon 8° 916

4303. Oxford Canning club. Steinhart, H., ed., The history of the Oxford Canning club, from 1861 to 1911. Oxf., 1911, 8°. 558 pp.
                                                        G.A. Oxon 8° 875

4304. Oxford Canning club. [Rules and list of members.] [Oxf.], 1869, 16°. 16 pp.   G.A. Oxon 16° 195 (10)
— [Rules]. [Oxf., 187–], 16°. 6 pp.   G.A. Oxon 16° 195 (11)
— [List of members.] [Oxf., 1877], 16°. 16 pp. G.A. Oxon 16° 195 (13)
— [Rules and list of members.] (Oxf.), [1877], 16°. 23 pp.
                                                        G.A. Oxon 16° 195 (14)

4305. Oxford Canning club. Rules, with a roll of members, from 9th Dec. 1861 to 6th Feb. 1895. Oxf., 1895, 8°. 39 pp.   G.A. Oxon 8° 1127 (4)

4306. Oxford Carlton club. [Miscellaneous papers. 1919–1923.]
                                                        G.A. Oxon b. 146

4307. Oxford Carlton club. Rules and regulations. Oxf., 1922, 16°. 11 pp.
                                                        G.A. Oxon 16° 161 (2)

4308. Oxford economic society. [Miscellaneous papers. 1887–1921.]
                                                        G.A. Oxon 4° 602; b. 147

4309. Oxford graduates' Liberal association. [Miscellaneous papers. 1902, 03.]   G.A. Oxon b. 147

4310. Oxford Individualist club. [Announcement of foundation.] [Oxf., 1893], s. sh.   G.A. Oxon b. 147

4311. The Oxford Knownothings [account of]. (Lond. rev., June 4, 1864, p. 585, 86.)   G.A. Oxon b. 146

Oxford political economy club. See 4331, &c. Oxford university political economy club.

4312. Oxford republican club. Resolutions. [Oxf., 1871], s. sh.
G.A. Oxon b. 147
[A MS. note by F. Madan on the Bodley copy reads] 'On this rule [VIII. That the club shall neither employ nor countenance the employment of any means that are not perfectly legal] the Society split up and faded away.'

4313. Oxford university blue-ribbon club. Right, ed. by P. Unwin and J. S. Bingham. [Oxf.], 1953, 8°. 35 pp.   22894 e. 8 (2)

4314. Oxford university blue ribbon club. Blue ribbon, a pamphlet. Lond., 1960, 4°. 28 pp.   Per. 22894 d. 59

4315. Oxford university colonial club. [Miscellaneous papers. 1899–1926.]
G.A. Oxon 4° 601; b. 147 (52 &c.)

4316. Oxford university Conservative association. [Miscellaneous papers. 1925–27.]   G.A. Oxon b. 146

4317. Oxford university Conservative association. Conservative Oxford, ed. by A. Berry and D. Wilson. [Oxf., 1949], 4°. 168 pp.   22775 d. 79

See 5191 [Oxford Tory, publ. under the auspices of the Oxford university Conservative assoc.].
See 5101 [Oxford university Conservative assoc. Conservative forum. 1961].

4318. Oxford university Fabian society. [Miscellaneous papers. 1895–1914.]   G.A. Oxon 4° 600; b. 147 (1–9); MS. Top. Oxon d. 465, 466

4319. Oxford university free trade league. [Miscellaneous papers. 1908.]
G.A. Oxon b. 147

4320. Oxford university Gladstone club. Rules. (Oxf.), [c. 1905], 12°. 4 pp.
G.A. Oxon 4° 603

4321. Oxford university habitation of the Primrose league. [Miscellaneous papers. 1885–87.]   G.A. Oxon b. 146

4322. Oxford university home rule league. [Miscellaneous papers. 1887–91.]   G.A. Oxon b. 146

4323. Oxford university home rule league. List of members. 1891. Oxf., 1891, 8°. 27 pp.   G.A. Oxon 8° 1127 (19)

4324. Oxford university junior Tory club. [Miscellaneous papers. 1914.]
G.A. Oxon b. 146

4325. Oxford university Labour club. [Miscellaneous papers. 1919–27.]
G.A. Oxon b. 146

See 5141 [The Oxford university Labour club. The New Oxford. 1920].
See 5159 [Oxford university Labour club. Oxford Clarion. 1951].
See 5164 [Oxford university Liberal club. The Oxford Guardian. 1936].

4326. Oxford university Liberal club. [Miscellaneous papers. 1915–26.]
G.A. Oxon b. 146

4327. Oxford university Liberal league. [Miscellaneous papers. 1903–04.]
G.A. Oxon b. 146

4328. Oxford university men's political union for women's enfranchise-
ment. [Miscellaneous papers. 1912–14.]   G.A. Oxon b. 147

4329. Oxford university new reform club. [Miscellaneous papers. 1920–
25.]   G.A. Oxon b. 146

4330. Oxford university new Tory club. [Miscellaneous papers. 1920–24.]
                                                 G.A. Oxon b. 146

4331. Oxford university political economy club. Rules. 1860, 65, [70?], 79,
90, 97, 1912. Oxf., 1860–1912, 8°.   G.A. Oxon 8° 258

4332. Oxford university political economy club. [Miscellaneous papers.
1879–1923.]   G.A. Oxon 8° 258; 4° 499

See 5188 [Oxford university socialist club. Oxford socialist. 1908].

4333. Oxford university socialist society. (Statement of objects.) [Lond.,
1929?], 16°. 4 pp.   MS. Top. Oxon d. 296 (57)

4334. Oxford university tariff reform league. [Miscellaneous papers. 1904–
09.]   G.A. Oxon 4° 600; b. 147 (10–15)

4335. Oxford university tariff reform league. [Roll of members.] n. pl.,
1905, 8°. 33 pp.   G.A. Oxon 8° 1132 (1)
— 1907.   G.A. Oxon 8° 1132 (2)
— 1908.   G.A. Oxon 8° 1132 (3)

4336. Oxford university unionist league. [Miscellaneous papers. 1888–92.]
                                         G.A. Oxon 4° 600; b. 146

4337. Oxford university unionist league. Rules, with list of officers and
members. Lent term, 1889; Mich. term, 1889; Mich. term, 1890. Oxf.,
1889–91, 8°.   G.A. Oxon 8° 1101 (14–16)

4338. Palmerston club. [Miscellaneous papers. 1879–1910.]
                                         G.A. Oxon 4° 600; b. 146

4339. Palmerston club. (The rules.) n. pl., [c. 1880], 16°. 7 pp.
                                         G.A. Oxon 8° 1127 (22)
— (The rules. Members. 1882, 83, 87.) 91, 96. n. pl., (1882)–96, 16°.
                            G.A. Oxon 8° 1127 (21, 23–25, 29)

4340. Palmerston club. [List of members.] 1894–96. n. pl., 1894–96, 16°.
                                         G.A. Oxon 8° 1127 (26–28)

4341. Royalist club. [Miscellaneous papers. 1905–07.] G.A. Oxon 4° 603

4342. Russell club. [Miscellaneous papers. 1883–1911.]
                                         G.A. Oxon 4° 600; b. 146

4343. St. Patrick's club. [Miscellaneous papers. 1903–07.]
                                         G.A. Oxon 4° 603

4344. Shaftesbury club. [Miscellaneous papers. 1893–1910.]
                                         G.A. Oxon 4° 600

4345. Shaftesbury club. (Rules, members.) (Oxf., 1900), 16°. 13 pp.
G.A. Oxon 16° 195 (17)
— Revised. Oxf., 1906, 16°. 14 pp.   G.A. Oxon 16° 195 (18)

4346. Social and political studies association. [Miscellaneous paper. 1911.]
G.A. Oxon 4° 603

4347. Social science club. [Miscellaneous papers. 1887–1914.]
G.A. Oxon 4° 596; b. 147 (38 &c.)

4348. Social science club. List of officers and rules. [Oxf.], (1899), 16°.
11 pp.   G.A. Oxon 16° 200 (10)

Society for the study of social ethics. See 4347. Social science club.

See 8653 [Society for the study of social problems].

4349. Strafford club. [Miscellaneous papers. 1882–1910.]
G.A. Oxon 4° 600

4350. Strafford club. Second annual report. 1882–3. Oxf., (1883), 8°. 15
pp.   G.A. Oxon 8° 1127 (18)

4351. Thomas More society. [Miscellaneous papers. 1923–1926.]
G.A. Oxon b. 147 (61)

Social and general

4352. Considerations why there should be a café for graduates. (Oxford
mag., 1884, vol. 2, p. 112, 113.)   Per. G.A. Oxon 4° 141

4353. Social Oxford. (Macmillan's mag., 1887, vol. 57, p. 105–11.)
Per. 2705 d. 254

4354. ARNOLD, E. M., Social life in Oxford. (Harper's mag., July 1890,
p. 246–56.)   Per. 2714 d. 25

4355. STEVENS, A. M., Social phases of Oxford life. (Amer. Oxon., 1915,
vol. 2, p. 21–27.)   Per. G.A. Oxon 8° 889

See 7503.5 [Bethell, D., The graduate problem. Lincoln M.C.R. 1959].
See 6967.5 [Barrett, G., The graduate common room in Christ Church. 1961].

Social societies

4356. Ad Eundem. [Account signed H. J. and A. S.] 12 June 1907. n. pl.,
1907, 4°. 4 pp.   G.A. Oxon b. 147 (20)
— Repr. with additions. n. pl., 1925, 4°. 4 pp.   G.A. Oxon b. 147 (20)

See 7322 [Adelphi club].

Anonymous club. See 4359, &c. Club (The) *founded c. 1862.*

4357. Arcades (The). [Menu, June 1909.]   G.A. Oxon 4° 603

See 4433 [Bullingdon club].

4358. Charterhouse club. [Miscellaneous papers. 1882–86.]
G.A. Oxon b. 146

Club (The) *founded 1790*. See 4398, &c. THE Club.

4359. Club (The) *founded c. 1862*. [Miscellaneous papers. 1866–1934.]
G.A. Oxon 4° 599

4360. Club (The) *founded c. 1862*. Anonymous club. List of members.
n. pl., [*c.* 1866], s. sh.   G.A. Oxon 4° 599
— The Club. List of members [and] Rules. n. pl., [*c.* 1875], 8°. 3 pp.
G.A. Oxon 4° 599

4360.2. Club (The) *founded c. 1890*. [Miscellaneous papers. 1890–1900.]
G.A. Oxon 4° 599

4360.3. The Club programme [originally drafted by F. Y. Powell and
approved in 1889]. Dec. 1921. n. pl., 1921, s. sh.   G.A. Oxon 4° 599

Cosmopolitan club. See 4228. Oxford university cosmopolitan club.

4361. Degenerates (The). [Menu, 1902.]   G.A. Oxon 4° 603

4362. Epicureans (The). [Menu, Feb. 1894.]   G.A. Oxon 4° 603

Etonian club. See 4383. Oxford Etonian club.

See 7337 [Falernian wine club].

4363. Fellows (The). Rules. n. pl., [1896?], 16°. 4 pp.   G.A. Oxon 4° 603

4364. Freemasons. [Miscellaneous papers relating to University lodges of
Freemasons. 1889–1905.]   G.A. Oxon c. 124

4365. Freemasons. Hawkins, E. L., Two old Oxford lodges [Lodge of
Alfred in the University of Oxford and the Constitution lodge].
(Trans., Quatuor Coronati lodge, 1909, vol. 22, p. 139–87.)
— [Repr.]. 48 pp.   24791 d. 35

4366. Freemasons. *Apollo university lodge*. [Miscellaneous papers. 1857–
1919.]   G.A. Oxon 4° 607; 8° 1120

4367. Freemasons. *Apollo university lodge*. 1819–1919. Centenary meeting.
[Brochure containing a history of the lodge and a list of brethren.]
n. pl., 1919, 8°. 14 pp.   G.A. Oxon 4° 607

4368. Freemasons. *Apollo university lodge*. Bye laws. (List of the brethren.)
Oxf., (1842), 16°. 29 pp.   G.A. Oxon 16° 197

4369. Freemasons. *Apollo university lodge*. By-laws. To which is added a
history of the lodge, a list of members, etc., ed. by G. Fead Lamert.
(Oxf.), 1869, 16°.   G.A. Oxon 16° 184
— 4th ed., by H. A. Pickard, F. P. Morrell, and E. L. Hawkins. (Oxf.),
1881, 16°. 174 pp.   G.A. Oxon 16° 197

4370. Freemasons. *Apollo university lodge*. By-laws. n. pl., [1880], s. sh.
G.A. Oxon 16° 197
— [1881]. 16°. 15 pp.   G.A. Oxon 16° 197
[The Bodleian copies are proof copies.]

4371. Freemasons. *Apollo university lodge.* List of subscribing members, 1909(–1912). Oxf., 1909–12, 16°.   G.A. Oxon 16° 203

4372. Freemasons. *University lodge of Mark masters, no. 55.* By-laws, with list of members, etc., ed. by R. E. Baynes. (Oxf.), 1892, 16°. 35 pp.
G.A. Oxon 16° 33 (39)

4373. Freemasons. *Oxford university rose croix chapter, no. 40.* [Notification of meetings. 1900–03, 07.]   G.A. Oxon 4° 607

4374. Gridiron club. [Miscellaneous papers. 1883–1923.]
G.A. Oxon 4° 601; b. 146

4375. Gridiron club. The rules and members. Oxf., 1888, 8°. 15 pp.
G.A. Oxon 8° 1127 (2)
— 1902. 28 pp.   G.A. Oxon 8° 1127 (3)

4376. Hermitage club. Rules. n. pl., [*c.* 1860], s. sh. G.A. Oxon 8° 900 (4)

4377. Marlborough club. [Miscellaneous papers. 1875–85.]
G.A. Oxon b. 146

See 7102 [Mercury wine club].

4377.5. FIRMAN, C. K., The Mitre Club, 1820–43. [The minute book of this undergraduate dining club is preserved in the Honnold Library, Claremont, Va.] (Amer. Oxonian, 1966, vol. 53, p. 12, 13.)
Per. G.A. Oxon 8° 889

4378. Nauratan dinner. [3 menu cards for Nauratan dinners. 1902, 03.]
G.A. Oxon 4° 603

4379. New Oxford and Cambridge club. [Miscellaneous papers. 1885–1887.]   G.A. Oxon b. 147

4380. Nicotine club. [Blank notification of meeting, *c.* 1906.]
G.A. Oxon 4° 603

See 8513 ['99 club].
See 6892 [Octagon club].

4381. Oxford and Cambridge (university) club. Rules and regulations (list of members). Lond., 1883, 16°. 93 pp.   2479 f. 27
— 1909. 131 pp.   2479 f. 28

4382. Oxford and Cambridge (university) club. Catalogue of the library. [With] Suppl. [Lond.], 1887, 1909, 8°. 527+314 pp.
2590 d. Lond. 138. 1, 2

4383. Oxford Etonian club. Rules of the Etonian club. Oxf., 1839, 8°. 16 pp.   G.A. Oxon 8° 1101 (13)

4384. Oxford Etonian club. [Miscellaneous papers. 1847–1906.]
G.A. Oxon b. 146

4385. Oxford graduates' medical club. [Miscellaneous papers. 1890–1920.]
G.A. Oxon 4° 598

4386. Oxford graduates' medical club. Officers, rules, list of members. 1891, 1893, 1913. (Oxf., 1891–1913), 16°.   G.A. Oxon 16° 161 (11)

4387. Oxford Old Rugbeians club [*formerly*] Rugby club. [Miscellaneous papers. 1874–96.] G.A. Oxon b. 146

4388. Oxford oriental club. [Miscellaneous papers. 1908–12.]
G.A. Oxon 4° 603; b. 147 (82)

4389. Oxford society. First (Second) General meeting [*afterw.*] Annual report 1934/35–36/37. [Oxf.], 1933–37, 8°. G.A. Oxon 8° 1103

4390. Oxford society. [Miscellaneous papers. 1934– .] G.A. Oxon 4° 592

4391. Oxford society. Oxford. Vol. 1, no. 1– . Oxf. &c., 1934– , 8°.
Per. G.A. Oxon 8° 1141

4392. The Oxford society after seven years, by the secretary. (Oxf. mag., 1939, vol. 57, p. 646–48.) Per. G.A. Oxon 4° 141

4393. BRITTAIN, SIR H., The Oxford society: early days. (Oxford, 1964, vol. 19, p. 82–89.) Per. G.A. Oxon 8° 1141

4393.1. VEALE, SIR D., The founding of the Oxford society. (Oxford, 1964, vol. 19, p. 77–88.) Per. G.A. Oxon 8° 1141

4394. Oxford university medical school association. [Miscellaneous papers. 1891–1908.] G.A. Oxon 4° 597

4395. Oxford university B.P. scout club. [Miscellaneous papers. 1919–27.]
MS. Top. Oxon d. 328

4396. The Pentagon. (Oxford club for University women.) Report for the year Feb., 1931–Mar., 1932. (Oxf., 1932), 8°. 16 pp. G.A. Oxon 4° 410

Rugby club. See 4387. Oxford Old Rugbeians club.

4397. Society for post-graduate students. [Miscellaneous papers. 1924–26.] G.A. Oxon b. 147

4398. THE Club *founded 1790*. [Miscellaneous papers. 1891–1905.]
G.A. Oxon b. 147

4399. THE Club. List of members . . . in the regular order of their election. n. pl., [1892], 4°. 2 pp. G.A. Oxon 4° 599

4400. THE Club. Madan, F. *ed.*, Records of THE Club, 1790–1917. Oxf., 1917, 8°. 118 pp. G.A. Oxon 8° 982

4401. THE Club portraits [no. 1–139]. Portfolio 1–5. [Oxf., 1922–38], 4°.
G.A. Oxon 4° 426

4402. Tutors club. [Miscellaneous papers. 1890–1910.] G.A. Oxon 4° 599

4403. Utopian club. Rules. Oxf., 1896, 8°. 8 pp. G.A. Oxon 8° 1127 (1)

See 4435, &c. [Vincent's club].

4404. Winchester club. [Miscellaneous papers. 1870?–1889.]
G.A. Oxon b. 146

See 7242 [The Wasps].

Manuals of behaviour, unofficial handbooks, etc.

4405. WATERLAND, D., Advice to a young student, with a method of study
for the first four years [by D. Waterland]. Lond., 1730, 8°. 32 pp.
G. Pamph. 213 (9)
— 2nd ed. Oxf., 1755, 8°. 34 pp.   G. Pamph. 212 (9)
— 3rd ed. Cambr., 1760, 8°.   B.M.
— [Another] 3rd ed. Lond., 1761, 8°.   B.M.

4406. A few general directions for the conduct of young gentlemen in the
University [a satire]. Oxf., 1795, 8°. 18 pp.   G.A. Oxon 8° 219 (7)

4407. CAMPBELL, J., Hints for Oxford [by J. Campbell]. Oxf., 1823, 8°.
74 pp.   G.A. Oxon 8° 8

4408. Hints on etiquette for the University of Oxford. Oxf., 1838, 8°. 23
pp.   G.A. Oxon 8° 184 (8)
— [Another ed.] n.d. 20 pp.   G.A. Oxon 8° 285 (3)

4409. HOLE, S. R., Hints to freshmen [by S. R. Hole]. Oxf., 1843, 8°. 56 pp.
G.A. Oxon 8° 285 (2b)
— 2nd ed. [1846].   G.A. Oxon 8° 285 (2)
— 3rd ed. 1853.   G.A. Oxon 8° 285 (2c)

4410. Mottoes for crackers, adapted expressly for the use of Oxford men
. . . forming altogether a complete freshman's manual. [In verse.] Oxf.,
1857, 8°. 15 pp.   G.A. Oxon 8° 135 (3)

4411. Des teutschen scholaren Glossarium in Oxford. n. pl., [1913?], 8°.
77 pp.   G.A. Oxon 8° 860

4412. Oxford university what's what. 1st– ed. 1948/1949– . Cowley,
1948– , 8°.   Per. G.A. Oxon 8° 1216

4413. Oxford vade mecum. 1st– issue. (Abingdon), 1954– , 8°.
Per. G.A. Oxon 8° 1322

4414. Univoxon, a guide to freshmen, ed. by S. Cockburn. 1960– .
(Brighton), 1960– , 8°.   Per. G.A. Oxon 8° 1431

Sport and pastimes

*Specific accounts of the annual sporting events between Oxford and Cam-
bridge (other than those embracing a series) have not been recorded.*

GENERAL

See 455 [Vernon, F., Oxonium, poema. 1667].

4415. Oxford and Cambridge men by land and water. (London society,
1865, vol. 7, p. 466–74.)   G.A. Oxon 4° 578 (14)

4416. [*Begin.*] I was told, a few days ago . . . [A letter, signed R. F. Clarke,
opposing the ban on sports' meetings in Oxford between the two
universities.] [Oxf.], (1867), 4°. 4 pp.   G.A. Oxon c. 83 (432)

4417. STEPHEN, L., Athletic sports and university studies. (Fraser's mag., 1870, vol. 2, p. 691–704.)   G.A. Oxon 4° 580 (17)

4418. University matches. (London society, 1871, vol. 19, p. 422–26.)
                                                            G.A. Oxon 4° 581 (1)

4419. Playtime at Oxford. (Chambers's journ., 1877, p. 540–42.)
                                                              Per. 2705 d. 396

> See 3859 [Wordsworth, C. A chapter of autobiography, 1831–33, with notices of the first athletic contest between Oxford and Cambridge. 1883].
> See 1873 [Dr. Wallis' letter against mr. Maidwell, 1700, concerning a proposal to establish an academy of exercises. 1885].

4420. Reminiscences of Oxford varsity [sporting] life, by an undergraduate. [Sketches.] Oxf., [1885?]. fol. [30 pp.]   G.A. Oxon b. 44

4421. [Miscellaneous papers relating to Oxford university sport, athletics, and games. 1893–1923.]   38436 b. 1, 2

4422. GRENFELL, W. H., Oxford v. Yale. (Fortnightly rev., 1894, vol. 62, p. 368–82.)   Per. 3977 d. 59

4423. [Oxford university sporting fixture lists, many of them recommended by the 'Blues' committee of Vincent's club. 1895–1914.]
                                                            G.A. Oxon b. 174

4424. The book of blues, a record of all matches between the universities . . . in every department of sport, ed. by Ogier Rysden. Lond., 1900, 8°. 267+lvi pp.   384 f. 7

4425. Work v. play at Oxford and Cambridge, by an undergraduate. [A protest against the importance given to games in the university curriculum.] (The Treasury, 1906, vol. 6, p. 353, 54.)
                                                          G.A. Oxon 4° 575 (38)

4426. The Oxford university sports register: a full record of the winners in all inter-university competitions since their commencement, and of the competitors in the academic year 1909(–11). [Formerly publ. as The Oxford university almanack and register.] Oxf., 1909–11, 8°.
                                                              Per. 384 e. 32

4427. GULL, C. B., Some aspects of Oxford athletics. (Oxf. and Cambr. review, 1909, no. 7, p. 96–104.)   Per. 2625 d. 37

4428. Fifty years of sport at Oxford, Cambridge and the great public schools, ed. by A. C. M. Croome. Oxford and Cambridge. [Vol. 1–3.] Lond., 1913–22, fol.   384 c. 8

4429. MANNING, P., Sport and pastime in Stuart Oxford. (Oxf. hist. soc., 1923, vol. 75, p. 83–135.)   G.A. Oxon 8° 360 = R.

4430. Oxford amusement guide. Hilary term, 1925. (Oxf., 1925), 8°. 16 pp.
                                                            G.A. Oxon 8° 1035

4431. Blackwell's weekly programme. Oct. 20–27, 1928–June 9th–22nd 1940. [Oxf.], 1928–40, s. sh.   G.A. Oxon 4° 555

4432. ABRAHAMS, H. M., and KERR, J. BRUCE-, *ed.*, Oxford *versus* Cambridge, a record of inter-university contests from 1827–1930. [*With*] Annual suppl. Lond., 1931– , 8°. 384 d. 62, 62*

4432.1. SEAGER, A., The joy of sport at Oxford. (Amer. Oxon., 1963, vol. 50, p. 79–90.) Per. G.A. Oxon 8° 889

GENERAL SPORTING CLUBS

4433. Bullingdon club. Rules. (Oxf.), 1867, 8°. 4 pp.
  G.A. Oxon 8° 1127 (17)

4434. Etcetera club. Rules [and members]. Oxf., 1864, 8°. 6 pp.
  G.A. Oxon 8° 1127 (13)
— 1865. G.A. Oxon 8° 1127 (14)
— 1866. G.A. Oxon 8° 1127 (15)
— 1869. G.A. Oxon 8° 1127 (16)

4435. Vincent's club. Rules. Oxf., 1863, 8°. 8 pp. G.A. Oxon 8° 1127 (6)
— 1865. 7 pp. G.A. Oxon 8° 1127 (7)
— The rules and members. 1867. 12 pp. G.A. Oxon 8° 1127 (8)
— 1869. 14 pp. G.A. Oxon 8° 1127 (9)
— 1872. 15 pp. G.A. Oxon 8° 1127 (10)
— 1893. 33 pp. G.A. Oxon 8° 1127 (11)
— 1903. 44 pp. G.A. Oxon 8° 1127 (12)

4436. Vincent's club. [Miscellaneous papers. 1871–1927.]
  G.A. Oxon b. 146; 4° 601
See 6773, &c. [Balliol athletic clubs].
See 6898, &c. [Brasenose college amalgamated athletic clubs].

ARCHERY

4437. Bowmen of the Isis. Rules. (Oxf.), [1830], 16°. 16 pp.
  G.A. Oxon 8° 1110 (12)

4438. Oxford university bowmen. Rules. [Oxf., 1874], 16°. 8 pp.
  G.A. Oxon 8° 1110 (11)
See 8416, 8417 [St. John's archery club].

ATHLETICS

4439. Oxford university athletic club. [Miscellaneous papers. 1866– .]
  G.A. Oxon b. 31, 66; 38436 b. 2; 38436 e. 2 (5)

4440. EVE, H. T., The Oxford university athletic record for 1878. Oxf., 1878, 8°. 80 pp. 38436 e. 6

4441. JACKSON, C. N., Some notes on the Oxford university athletic club, from its foundation. (Athletics, by W. Beach Thomas, 1901, p. 39–98.)
  38436 e. 11

See 5998, 5999 [Articles on Rhodes scholars in athletics. 1914].

BELL-RINGING

4442. Oxford university society of change-ringers. [Miscellaneous papers. 1872–1926.]   G.A. Oxon b. 147; 8° 1033 (14)

BOATING, ROWING, AND SAILING

General

See 859 [Proclamation that no boatmen or fishermen are to hire out their boats on Sundays. 1673].

4443. The flags and aquatic costumes of the boating societies in the University of Oxford. Oxf., [c. 1850], s. sh.   G.A. Oxon 16° 151

4444. Regulations for boats intended for the use of members of the University. [Oxf.], (1845), s. sh.   G.A. Oxon b. 25

4445. The Isis at Oxford. (Leisure hour, 1861, p. 766, 67.)
                                                       G.A. Oxon 4° 578 (11)

4446. Boating life at Oxford. (Lond. soc., 1867, vol. 11, p. 289 &c.; vol. 12, p. 70–76.) [Repr. in no. 4449.]   Per. 2705 d. 200

4447. Water derbies. (Lond. soc., 1867, vol. 12, p. 65–70.) [Repr. in no. 4449.]   Per. 2705 d. 200

4448. Rowing at the universities. (Pall Mall gazette, June 1, 1868.) [Repr. in no. 4449.]

4449. Boating life at Oxford, with notes on Oxford training and rowing at the universities. [A repr. of nos. 4446–4448.] Lond. &c., 1868, 8°. 118 pp.   250 k. 7 (14)

4450. On the Cherwell. (Chambers's journ., 1876, p. 609–12.)
                                                       G.A. Oxon 4° 578 (45)

4451. Rowing at Oxford. (Chambers's journ., 1886, p. 234–36.)
                                                       G.A. Oxon 4° 586 (28)

4452. BEDFORD, W. K. R., The academical oarsman [by W. K. R. Bedford]. (Blackwood's Edinb. mag., 1887, vol. 142, p. 834–47.)
                                                       G.A. Oxon 4° 586 (33)

4453. GRENFELL, W. H., Rowing at Oxford. (Engl. illustr. mag., 1890, vol. 7, p. 498–506.)   G.A. Oxon 4° 586 (41)

See 7226 [Hext, G., Early memories of Corpus boating. 1896].

4454. T. Tims: an autobiographical sketch. (Oxf. mag., 1896, vol. 14, May 21, p. 4, 5.)   Per. G.A. Oxon 4° 141

4455. SHERWOOD, W. E., Oxford rowing, a history of boat-racing at Oxford from the earliest times, with a record of the races. Oxf. &c., 1900, 8°. 406 pp.   38442 e. 18

4456. MANNING, P., The early days of boating in Oxford. (Oxf. mag., 1903, vol. 22, p. 8, 9; 41, 42; 96, 97.)   Per. G.A. Oxon 4° 141
— Repr. [*entitled*] Some notes on the early history of boating [&c.]. Oxf., 1904, 8°. 15 pp.   G.A. Oxon 8° 683 (30)

See 3909 [Woodgate, W. B., Reminiscences of an old sportsman. 1909].

4457. LEGGE, H., Reflections on Oxford rowing for 70 years or thereabouts. (Oxf. mag., 1925, vol. 44, p. 276, 285, 86, 308, 325, 26.)
     Per. G.A. Oxon 4° 141

4458. The passing of the barges on the Isis. (Amer. Oxon., 1957, vol. 44, p. 86.)   Per. G.A. Oxon 8° 889

4459. Oxford university sailing club. [Miscellaneous papers. 1884–1903.]
     G.A. Oxon b. 174

4460. Oxford university yacht squadron. Full and bye. No. 1– . (Oxf.), 1948– , 4°.   Per. 38443 d. 103

4461. Oxford university yacht club. Newsletter. 1960– . Oxf., 1960– , 4°.
     Per. 38443 d. 135

Eights, etc.

4462. [Spiers and son's] Chart of the Oxford university eight-oared boat races from 1837 to 1844 (45, 46, 48, 49). Oxf., 1844–49, s. sh.
     G.A. Oxon 4° 481
— 1837–60.   G.A. Oxon a. 22 (9)
— 1861/62–1905. [Imperf.].   G.A. Oxon 4° 116

4463. KNOLLYS, C. C., Oxford university challenge races. Oxf. &c., 1873, 8°. III pp.   G.A. Oxon 8° 161 (18)

4464. Taunt's daily chart of the eight-oar boat races. 1886–1925. Oxf., 1886–1925, 16°.   G.A. Oxon 16° 34

4465. [Miscellaneous cards of the eights. 1890–1904.]   G.A. Oxon 16° 74

4466. The visitors' eights' week guide and programme for commemoration [*afterw.*] Eights' week and commem. programme. 1903, 04, 06–11, 13, 23, 32. [Oxf.], 1903–32, s. sh.   G.A. Oxon 8° 905

4467. ANUNDA GRADD, *pseud.*, The quasi-guide to eights' week. Oxf., 1907, 8°. 38 pp.   G.A. Oxon 8° 905

4468. SHERWOOD, W. E., The evolution of the Eights. (Oxf. mag., 1925, vol. 43, no. 20, suppl.)   Per. G.A. Oxon 4° 141

4469. VENABLES, C., Eights and Mays. (Country Life, 1954, vol. 15, p. 1623.)   Per. 384 b. 6

Boat clubs

4470. Oxford university boat club. [Miscellaneous papers. 1848–1934.]
     G.A. Oxon c. 257
[Miscellaneous papers. 1863–1914.]   G.A. Oxon b. 174

4471. Oxford university boat club. Rules. Oxf., [*c.* 1870], 8°. 25 pp. [Bodley has a proof copy, G.A. Oxon 8° 847 (1).]
— Revised, Dec. 1876. Oxf., (1876), 8°. 24 pp. G.A. Oxon 8° 847 (2)
— Revised. Oxf., 1933, 8°. 26 pp.   G.A. Oxon 8° 1129

4472. List of members of the Oxford university boat club . . . to 1889. n. pl., (1889), 8°. 103 pp.   G.A. Oxon 8° 664

See 4459–61 [Oxford university sailing club and yacht club].
See 6903, &c. [Brasenose college boat club].
See 7092 [Christ Church boat club].
See 7326, &c. [Exeter college boat club].
See 7548 [Lincoln college boat club].
See 7908 [New college boat club].
See 8126, &c. [Pembroke college boat club].
See 8700 [Worcester college boat club].

Inter-University boat races

4473. MACMICHAEL, W. F., The Oxford and Cambridge boat races, 1829 to 1869. Cambr. &c., 1870, 8°. 380 pp.   38442 f. 1

4474. The Oxford & Cambridge boat race, by a member of the C.U.B.C., with plans of the courses. Lond., 1877, 8°. 24 pp.   200 i. 56 (21)

4475. TREHERNE, G. G. T., and GOLDIE, J. H. D., Record of the University boat race 1829–1880, and of the commemoration dinner 1881. Lond. &c., 1883, 4°. 207 pp.   G.A. Oxon 4° 80
— New ed. 1884, 8°. 288 pp.   38442 e. 1

4476. PEACOCK, W., The story of the inter-university boat race. Lond., 1900, 8°. 148 pp.   38442 f. 7
— [Another ed.] 1901. 153 pp.   38442 f. 9
— [Another ed.] 1902. 156 pp.   38442 f. 10

4477. PITMAN, C. M., The record of the University boat race, 1829–1909, and register of those who have taken part in it. Lond. &c., 1909, 8°. 348 pp.   38442 d. 10

4478. DRINKWATER, G. C., and SANDERS, T. R. B., The University boat race, official centenary history, 1829–1929, ed. by C. Gardon. Commemorative ed. Lond. &c., 1929, 4°. 244 pp.   38442 d. 19

4479. One hundred years of boat racing, the official centenary souvenir of the Oxford and Cambridge boat race, 1829–1929. Indian ed. Lond., (1929), 4°. 65 pp.   38442 d. 18

4480. W., D. M., The question of boat race training. (Oxf. mag., 1935, vol. 54, p. 212, 13.)   Per. G.A. Oxon 4° 141

4481. DRINKWATER, G. C., The boat race. Lond. &c., 1939, 8°. 226 pp.
                    38442 e. 52

4482. BURNELL, R. D., The Oxford & Cambridge boat race, 1829–1953. Lond. &c., 1954, 8°. 244 pp.   38442 e. 72

4483. ROSS, G., The boat race, the story of the first hundred races. Lond.'
1954, 8°. 256 pp. 38442 e. 73

4484. The Oxford–Harvard boat race [signed E. P. G.]. (St. Cuthbert's
mag., 1870, vol. 2, p. 251–62.) G.A. Oxon 4° 580 (18)

4485. MATHEWS, J. J., First Harvard–Oxford boat race. (New Engl.
quarterly, 1960, vol. 33, p. 74–82.) L. of C.

BOXING AND FENCING

4486. Oxford university fencing club [*afterw.*] Oxford university boxing
and fencing club. [Miscellaneous papers. 1890–1927: 38468 b. 2;
1900–1919: G.A. Oxon b. 174.]

4487. Oxford university boxing and fencing club. Rules. (Oxf.), [*c.* 1900],
8°. G.A. Oxon b. 174
— [Another ed.]. 1903/04. G.A. Oxon b. 174

CHESS

4488. Oxford Hermes chess club. Rules. Oxf., 1855, 12°. 7 pp.
38472 e. 69 (8)

4489. Oxford university chess club. [Miscellaneous papers. 1873–1927.]
38472 b. 1

4490. Oxford university chess club. Rules; with a list of members &
officers of the club from its foundation. Prescot, 1873, 8°. 15 pp.
38472 e. 4

4491. WALKER, J. M., The history of the Oxford university chess club.
Oxf., (1885), 8°. 48 pp. 38472 f. 2

See 6777 [Balliol college chess club].

CLIMBING

4492. Oxford Alpine club. [Miscellaneous papers. 1882, 98.]
G.A. Oxon 4° 603

CRICKET

See also 6246, &c. [University parks].

4493. University cricket. Oxford. (Blackwood's mag., 1910, vol. 187,
p. 821–31.) Per. 2705 d. 386

Clubs

4494. Conservative cricket club. List of members. n. pl., [*c.* 1865], s. sh.
G.A. Oxon 4° 274
— 1867. G.A. Oxon b. 146

4495. Oxford university Authentics cricket club. [Miscellaneous papers.
1885–1930.] G.A. Oxon b. 174

4496. Oxford university Authentics cricket club. [Handbook] 1897, 1921.
[Lond.], 1897, 1921, 16°.   G.A. Oxon 16° 198
— Alphabetical list of members. 1914, 21. [Lond.], 1914, 21, 16°.
                                                         G.A. Oxon 16° 198

4497. Oxford university Authentics cricket club. Rules. (Lond.), 1906, 8°.
4 pp.   G.A. Oxon b. 174

4498. The names of the Oxford university Authentics who died . . . 1914–
1918. (Oxf., 1919), 16°. 26 pp.   G.A. Oxon 16° 200 (19)

4499. STALLYBRASS, W. T. S., The Oxford Authentics and the Oxford
colleges. No. 1, B.N.C. [Oxf.], 1926, 16°. 32 pp.
                                                 G.A. Oxon 16° 200 (20)

4500. LYON, H., and GLASGOW, R. C. ROBERTSON-, The Oxford Authentics and the Oxford colleges. No. 3, Corpus Christi. [Oxf.], 1928, 16°.
31 pp.   G.A. Oxon 16° 200 (21)

4501. Oxford university cricket club. [Miscellaneous papers. 1882–1927:
G.A. Oxon b. 174. 1887–1927: 38454 b. 2.]

4501.1. BOLTON, G., History of the O.U.C.C. Oxf., 1962, 8°. 374 pp.
                                                         38454 d. 100

4502. NUGEE, F. J., ed., The records of the Oxford university Emeriti
cricket club. n. pl., [c. 1932], 4°. 117 pp.   38454 d. 58

See 7097 [Christ Church Nondescripts].
See 8701 [Worcester college cricket club].

University match

4503. PERKINS, H., Scores of the cricket matches between Oxford &
Cambridge. Lond., 1898, 8°. 76 pp.   38454 f. 23

4504. Cricket. Oxford v. Cambridge, from 1827 to 1876. [Scores of the
matches.] Lond., 1877, 8°. 116 pp.   268 c. 500

4505. BETHAM, J. D., Oxford and Cambridge, scores and biographies.
Lond., 1905, 8°. 286 pp.   38454 e. 74

4506. WARNER, P. F., and COOPER, F. S. ASHLEY-, Oxford v. Cambridge
at the wicket. Lond., 1926, 8°. 208 pp.   38454 e. 156

CROQUET

4507. Oxford university croquet and lawn tennis club. [Miscellaneous
papers. 1883–1924.]   G.A. Oxon 4° 541

4508. Oxford university croquet and lawn tennis club. (Rules. Members.)
1883. [Oxf.], (1883), 4°. 3 pp.   G.A. Oxon 4° 541
— Rules, 1886. [Oxf.], (1886), s. sh.   G.A. Oxon 4° 541
— Rules, list of members. [1888/89]–1915. (Oxf.), [1888]–1915, 8°.
[The Bodleian has [1888/89], 95, 98, 99, 1904–08, 10, 14, 15: Per.
38456 f. 22.]

CYCLING

4509. Dark blue bicycle club [*afterw.*] Oxford university bicycle club.
Rules. Oxf., 1877, 16°. 8 pp.   G.A. Oxon 16° 195 (1)
— Rules, bye-laws, report and list of members. Oxf., 1882, 16°. 32 pp.
           G.A. Oxon 16° 176* (2)
— Rules. (Oxf.), [1891], 12°. 9 pp.   G.A. Oxon 8° 1113 (2)
— [1894].   G.A. Oxon 8° 1113 (3)
— 1898, 8°. 6 pp.   G.A. Oxon 8° 1113 (4)

4510. Oxford university bicycle club. [Miscellaneous papers. 1882–1901:
G.A. Oxon c. 257. 1891–1900: G.A. Oxon b. 174.]

FENCING

See 4486, &c. [Boxing].

FIVES

See 8703 [Worcester college fives club].

FOOTBALL: ASSOCIATION AND RUGBY

4511. Oxford university rugby football club. [Miscellaneous papers. 1881–
1924: G.A. Oxon b. 174. 1891–1913: 38457 b. 2.]
— [Match cards. 1905–07.]   38457 f. 30

4512. Oxford university association football club. [Miscellaneous papers.
1883–1919: 38457 b. 1. 1889–1924: G.A. Oxon b. 174.]
— [Match cards. 1902–08.]   38457 f. 30

4513. BROWNRIGG, C. E., The new [football] ground and cup ties [signed
C. E. B.] (Oxf. mag., 1899, vol. 18, p. 135, 36.) Per. G.A. Oxon 4° 141

4514. The new football ground. (Oxf. mag., 1900, vol. 19, p. 99, 100.)
           Per. G. A. Oxon 4° 141

4515. The new football ground. [Letters by C. N. Jackson and C. E.
Brownrigg, the former defending, the latter opposing the introduction
of an entrance fee to the Iffley road ground. With editorial comment.]
(Oxf. mag., 1900, vol. 19, p. 141–43.)   Per. G.A. Oxon 4° 141

4515.5. ROUTLEDGE, G. B., Rugby football blues: biographical record . . .
1872–1911. Lond., 1912, 8°. 162 pp.

4516. MARSHALL, H., and JORDAN, J. P., Oxford *v.* Cambridge, the story
of the University rugby match. Lond., 1951, 8°. 256 pp.   38457 e. 182

GOLF

4517. Oxford university golf club. [Miscellaneous papers. 1882–1927:
38463 b. 1. 1893–1919: G.A. Oxon b. 174.]

4518. Oxford university golf club. Rules. Oxf., [1892], 16°. 40 pp.
           G.A. Oxon 16° 194
— 1893.   G.A. Oxon 16° 194

— 1900. 50 pp.　　　　　　　　　　　　　　G.A. Oxon 16° 194
— 1903. 15 pp.　　　　　　　　　　　　　　G.A. Oxon 16° 194
— 1907. 19 pp.　　　　　　　　　　　　　　G.A. Oxon 16° 194
— 1914.　　　　　　　　　　　　　　　　　G.A. Oxon 16° 194
— 1922. 14 pp.　　　　　　　　　　　　　　38463 e. 28 (15)

4519. Oxford University golf club. List of members, &c. Mich. term, 1892, 93; Hilary term 1895. Oxf., 1892–95, 16°.　　G.A. Oxon 16° 193

4520. Oxford university golf club. Golf: a retrospect to 1887 (1887–89; from 1889). (Oxf. mag., 1896, vol. 14, p. 164, 65, 218, 19, 274, 75.)
Per. G.A. Oxon 4° 141

4521. HENDERSON, P. A. WRIGHT-, O.U.G.C. A restrospect [signed P. A. W.-H.]. (Oxf. mag., 1912, vol. 30, p. 375, 76.)
Per. G.A. Oxon 4° 141

4522. Oxford university golf club, Southfield. Official handbook. Chelt. &c., [c. 1925], 12°. 16 pp.　　　　　　　　　　　　　O.P.L.

4523. The Oxford and Cambridge golfing society, 1898–1948, ed. by E. Prain. Lond., 1949, 8°. 245 pp.　　　　　　　　　38463 e. 225

HOCKEY

4524. [Oxford university hockey club. Miscellaneous papers. 1895–1920.]
38458 b. 1

4525. Etceteras hockey club [women]. Rules. n. pl., 1902, s. sh.
G.A. Oxon 4° 410

4526. Oxford casuals' hockey club. Rules. 1901/02, 1902, 1906/07. (Oxf.), 1901–06, s. sh.　　　　　　　　　　　　　　　G.A. Oxon b. 174

4527. Oxford casuals' hockey club. [Miscellaneous papers. 1901–13.]
G.A. Oxon b. 174

HUNTING

See 7912, 7913 [New college beagles. 1901, 1919].

4528. CHAPMAN, M. C., Beagling and the statutes. (Oxf. mag., 1931, vol. 50, p. 160–62.)　　　　　　　　　　　Per. G.A. Oxon 4° 141

4529. LLOYD, J. I., The Oxford university drag hunt. Lond., [1953], 8°. 12 pp.　　　　　　　　　　　　　　　　　　　　　　B.M.

4530. Oxford university drag hounds. [Miscellaneous papers. 1910–27.]
G.A. Oxon b. 174

4531. Oxford university hare and hounds club. [Miscellaneous papers. 1877–1908.]　　　　　　　　　　　　　　　G.A. Oxon b. 174

4532. Oxford university hare and hounds club. Rules (List of members). (Oxf.), 1877, 8°. 9 pp.　　　　　　　　　　　G.A. Oxon b. 174

4533. BERRY, M. F., Undergraduate memories of Woodperry [sporting recollections]. (Country Life, 1961, vol. 129, p. 592, 93.)　Per. 384 b. 1

LACROSSE

4534. Oxford university lacrosse club. [Miscellaneous papers. 1902–11.]
38459 b. 1

LAWN TENNIS

4535. Oxford university lawn tennis club. Rules. Oxf., 1883, 16°. 18 pp.
G.A. Oxon 16° 195 (2)
— 1891. 10 pp.   G.A. Oxon 16° 195 (3)

4536. Oxford university lawn tennis club. [Miscellaneous papers. 1885–
1925.]   G.A. Oxon c. 26

See also 4507, &c. [Oxford university croquet and lawn tennis club].
See 8786 [Somerville college lawn tennis club].

POLO

4537. Oxford university polo club. Rules. [Oxf., c. 1878], 8°. 4 pp.
G.A. Oxon b. 174

4538. Oxford university polo club. [Miscellaneous papers. 1877–1925.]
G.A. Oxon b. 174

SKATING

4539. Oxford university skating club. List of members and rules. 1880–
1881. (Oxf., 1881), 16°. 16 pp.   G.A. Oxon 16° 176* (1)

4540. H., C. E., The Oxford university skating club. (Oxf. mag., 1930, vol.
49, p. 280–83.)   Per. G.A. Oxon 4° 141

SWIMMING

4541. Notice. The O.U.B.C. propose to undertake the establishment of
a bathing place for the use of members of the University. [Appeal.]
(Oxf.), [1868], s. sh.   G.A. Oxon c. 84 (441)

4542. The Clarendon trustees, the Hebdomadal council and The Swimming bath memorialists [signed W. F. S. and J. R. M.]. n. pl., (1868),
s. sh.   G.A. Oxon c. 84 (409)

4543. Oxford university swimming club. [Miscellaneous papers. 1891–
1927.]   38437 b. 1

4544. Parson's pleasure and a liberal education. (Amer. Oxon., 1945, vol.
32, p. 130.)   Per. G.A. Oxon 8° 889

WAR-GAME

4545. Oxford university war-game society [*formerly*] Oxford university
Kriegspiel club. [Miscellaneous papers. 1889–1903.] G.A. Oxon 4° 602

WHIST

See 8425 [St. John's whist club].

Personal

GENERAL

4546. GRENVILLE, D., Counsel and directions divine and moral: in plain and familiar letters of advice from a divine of the Church of England [D. Grenville] to a young gentleman, his nephew, soon after his admission into a college in Oxford. Lond., 1685, 8°. 14+210 pp.

1419 e. 2753

See 4926 [The servitour. 1709].

4547. BENTHAM, E., Advices to a young man of fortune and rank upon his coming to the university [by E. Bentham]. Oxf., [1759?], 8°. 32 pp.

Gough Oxf. 44 (5)

— [Another ed. *entitled*] Advices to a young man of quality, upon his coming to the university. Lond., 1760, 8°. 34 pp.

Gough Cambr. 66 (3)

4548. A letter to a young gentleman of fortune, just entered at the University. Oxf., 1784, 8°. 38 pp.   Gough Oxf. 7 (2)

4549. DAMAN, C., Ten letters introductory to college residence, by a tutor [C. Daman]. Oxf., 1848, 8°. 48 pp.   G.A. Oxon 8° 600

See 1668 [A few plain facts &c. A plea for control of undergraduate extravagance. 1850].

4550. Oxford: its morals and its politics. (The Ecclesiastic, 1866, vol. 28, p. 543–51.)   G.A. Oxon 4° 575 (6)

See 8366 [Engagement to be signed by tradesmen desirous of being employed by undergraduate members of St. John's. c. 1880].

4551. Æstheticism and intolerance: a protest [against organized attacks on undergraduate æsthetes]. Oxf., 1882, 8°. 12 pp. G.A. Oxon 8° 761 (16)

4552. Decoration in Oxford rooms [signed 'Gina']. (Oxf. mag., 1883, vol. 1, p. 23, 24, 54.)   Per. G.A. Oxon 4° 141

4552.5. AYDELOTTE, F., The Oxford stamp, and other essays. Articles from the educational creed of an American Oxonian. New York &c., 1917, 8°. 219 pp.   27121 e. 399

4553. ANDERSON, C. A., and SCHNAPER, M., School and society in England: social backgrounds of Oxford and Cambridge students. Wash., D.C., 1952, 8°. 34 pp.   2625 d. 187

4553.4. OGILVIE, R. M., When did you last see your tutor? (Oxf. mag., 1965, vol. 6, p. 74, 75.)   Per. G.A. Oxon 4° 141

DIET

4554. [*Begin.*] Sacræ theologiæ professor . . . [form of licence to eat flesh in Lent]. [Madan 2514.] [Oxf.? c. 1660], s. sh. G.A. Oxon b. 111 (14)

4555. COOK, R., Oxford night caps, a collection of receipts for making various beverages used in the University [by R. Cook]. Oxf., 1827, 8°.
38 pp.   G.A. Oxon 8° 71 (9)
— 3rd ed. 1835. 43 pp.   Don. f. 142 (1)
— 4th ed. 1847.   G.A. Oxon 8° 251
— New ed. 1860. 54 pp.   G.A. Oxon 8° 71 (8)
— New ed. 1871.   G.A. Oxon 16° 180
— New ed. [c. 1880]. 56 pp.   1783 f. 50
— [Another ed.]. 1931. 16°. 31 pp.

4556. At a college breakfast-party. (Cassell's family mag., 1884, p. 247, 48.)
G.A. Oxon 4° 586 (6)

4557. Memorial . . . to the . . . vice-chancellor and to the proctors of the University of Oxford and the governing bodies of the colleges [urging various restrictions on purchase and consumption of intoxicating liquors by undergraduates]. n. pl., [1918], 4°. 4 pp.
G.A. Oxon b. 141 (115)
— [Another ed.] fol. 12 pp.   G.A. Oxon b. 141 (119a)
— [Typewritten letter from J. T. Dodd, one of the organizers, giving the text of the vice-chancellor's reply.]   G.A. Oxon b. 141 (119b)

4558. Oxford university total abstinence society. [Miscellaneous papers. 1888–96.]   G.A. Oxon b. 144 (19–33)

DRESS

See also 1297, &c. [Academic dress].

4559. S., V. V., Concerning costume [undergraduate dress. Signed V. V. S.]. (Oxf. mag., 1903, vol. 21, May 21, p. 17–19.)   Per. G.A. Oxon 4° 141

FINANCE

See also 3144, &c. [Extension].
See 8444 [Account book of an undergraduate. 1619–1622].

4560. [Begin.] Walter Blandford, doctor in divinity . . . [Notice that no tradesmen are to allow credit to undergraduates beyond 5/– without the approbation of a tutor or governor.] [Madan 2665.] [Oxf.], 1664, s. sh.
Wood 276a (348)

4561. [Begin.] John Nicholas, doctor in divinity . . . [notice similar to no. 4560]. [Madan 3190.] Oxf., 1678, s. sh.   Wood 276a (376)

4562. WILDING, J., The account book of James Wilding, 1682–1688 [ed.] by E. G. Duff. (Oxf. hist. soc., 1885, vol. 5, p. 249–68.)
G.A. Oxon 8° 360 = R.

4563. [Begin.] At a general meeting . . . June the 23rd. 1701. Whereas all undergraduates . . . [Notice similar to no. 4560.] [Oxf.], 1701, s. sh.
Don. b. 12 (39)

4564. NEWTON, R., The expence of university education, reduced in a
letter to A. B., fellow of E.C. [by R. Newton]. Lond., 1733, 8°. 48 pp.
                                         G.A. Oxon 8° 68 (2)
— 2nd ed. Lond., 1733, 8°. 52 pp.   G.A. Oxon 8° 233 (1)
— 3rd ed. Lond., 1734, 8°. 64 pp.   G.A. Oxon 8° 233 (2)
— 4th ed. Lond., 1741, 8°. 47 pp.   G.A. Oxon 8° 165 (20)

4565. [*Begin.*] The booksellers in this University . . . [Request to the
governors and tutors of halls and colleges, that some action be taken
to ensure the more expeditious discharge of debts for books incurred
by undergraduates. Signed J. & J. Fletcher, S. Parker, D. Prince &
J. Cooke, W. Hayes, R. Bliss, S. Arnold. Jan. 15, 1779.] [Oxf.],
(1779), s. sh.   MS. Top. Oxon d. 247 (f. 50)

4566. To the members of Convocation. [A paper, signed 'A member of
Convocation, not from the Delegates' room, Dec. 10th 1785', commenting on the proposed new statute De reprimendis sumptibus non
academicis.] [Oxf.], (1785), s. sh.   G.A. Oxon b. 19

4567. BERESFORD, J., An undergraduate's [J. C. Millett of Pembroke coll.]
account book, 1789–93. (Oxford, 1937, vol. 3, no. 3, p. 43–50.)
                                         Per. G.A. Oxon 8° 1141

See 1283 [Proposed amendment of those sections of the statute De moribus
conformandis concerned with the granting of credit to undergraduates.
1838].

4568. Tradesmen & undergraduates; or, The present system of debt and
credit at Oxford unveiled, by an Oxford B.A. Lond., 1844, 8°. 16 pp.
                                         G.A. Oxon 8° 48

See 3144 [Wilkinson, M., Expenses of undergraduates. 1845].

4569. CLOUGH, A. H., A consideration of objections against the Retrench-
ment association. Oxf., 1847, 8°. 20 pp.   G.A. Oxon 8° 1130* (5)

4570. The Oxford credit system—its evils and the remedy. (Oxf. Protestant mag., 1847, vol. 1, p. 632–40.)   Per. G.A. Oxon 8° 119

4571. Oxford and college expenses in 1723. [A commoner's expenses at
Hart hall, extracted from dr. Newton's University education, no. 1396.]
(Oxf. Protestant mag., 1847, vol. 1, p. 402, 03.) Per. G.A. Oxon 8° 119

4572. Poor scholars and college expenses. (Oxf. Protestant mag., 1847,
vol. 1, p. 393–401.)   Per. G.A. Oxon 8° 119

4573. Oxford tradesmen versus the insolvent Jennings: a verbatim copy of
the schedule of Edward Napleton Jennings . . . discharged under the
Insolvent act, December 31st, 1847. Oxf., [1848], 8°. 28 pp.
                                         G.A. Oxon 8° 540 (10)

4574. [*Begin.*] At a meeting of the Oxford Tradesmen's association . . . on
. . . October 13 . . . [making suggestions for improving relations between undergraduates and tradesmen]. [Oxf.], (1849), s. sh.
                                         G.A. Oxon c. 65 (125a)

4575. Honesty the best policy. A story of Oxford in February, 1853. [Written to stress the bad effects of 'long credit' on Oxford tradesmen.] Oxf., 1854, 8°. 20 pp. 280 s. 344 (1)

See 4978 [Solon Secundus. A letter containing a scheme for a . . . debt-relief law [a satire]. 1863].

4576. [Miscellaneous papers collected by G. R. Scott relating to the cost of living at Oxford, 1872–1911.] G.A. Oxon c. 241

4577. Economical reform at Oxford, by an Oxford tutor. (Fraser's mag., 1880, vol. 102, p. 548–60.) Per. 3977 e. 200

4578. Thrift at Oxford. [Letter, signed A Protest, concerning unjust charges to which undergraduates are subjected.] (Oxf. mag., 1883, vol. 1, p. 158, 59.) Per. G.A. Oxon 4° 141

4579. SLESSOR, A. K., The cost of an Oxford career. (Nineteenth cent., 1922, vol. 91, p. 1023–34.) Per. 3977 d. 66

4580. GILL, E. W. B., and PERCIVAL, H. F. P., Oxford battels. (Oxford, 1939, vol. 5, no. 3, p. 49–54.) Per. G.A. Oxon 8° 1141

4581. Oxford university adult students' assoc. Financial position of adult students at Oxford university. (Adult educ., 1950, vol. 23, p. 147–52.) Soc. 2627 d 21

HEALTH

4582. University infirmary. [Considerations of alternative schemes for providing a house or infirmary, the probable cost, the means of defraying it, and other particulars.] [Oxf., 1892], fol. 3 pp. G.A. Oxon b. 140 (89a)

4583. The proposed sanatorium. [A scheme for providing the University with its own fever-house.] (Oxf. mag., 1892, vol. 10, p. 188, 189, 209.) Per. G.A. Oxon 4° 141

4584. HOBSON, F. G., A university hospital. (Oxf. mag., 1931, vol. 50, p. 198–200.) Per. G.A. Oxon 4° 141

4585. MCCALLUM, R. B., A university hospital. (Oxf. mag., 1931, vol. 50, p. 162, 63.) Per. G.A. Oxon 4° 141

4586. BUZZARD, E. FARQUHAR, The Oxford university provident association [for undergraduates]. (Oxford, 1935, vol. 2, no. 1, p. 67–73.) Per. G.A. Oxon 8° 1141

4587. PARNELL, R. W., The physique of Oxford undergraduates: relationship with weight variation, schooling and habits. (Journ. of hygiene, 1954, vol. 52, p. 369–78.) Radcl.

4587.2. DAVIDSON, M. A., and HUTT, C., A study of 500 Oxford student psychiatric patients. Extracts from the Brit. journ. of social and clinical psychology, 1964, p. 175–85. (Oxf. mag., 1965, N.S., vol. 5, p. 362–65.) Per. G.A. Oxon 4° 141

4587.21. WHITELEY, D. E. H., Strain & the undergraduate, a sermon. (Oxf. mag., 1965, N.S., vol. 5, p. 253–56.) Per. G.A. Oxon 4° 141

4588. Oxford slang. (Macmillan's mag., 1869, vol. 21, p. 68–72.)
Per. 2705 d. 254

4589. MARPLES, M., University slang. Lond., 1950, 8°. 187 pp.
302505 e. 29

BIOGRAPHY
General

See also 1569, &c. [Lists and statistics].
See also 3796, &c. [for autobiographies and reminiscences].

4590. GORE, M., Character, &c. &c. [Eulogy upon an unidentified undergraduate, probably a nobleman, of Christ Church. By M. Gore?] Oxf.,
[1821], 8°. 12 pp.   G.A. Oxon 8° 1192

4591. MOORE, J. J., Oxford men and manners in past and present periods,
a miscellany of anecdote, biography and historical portraiture. Ser. 1.
Oxf., 1874, 8°. 80 pp.   G.A. Oxon 8° 332

4592. MADAN, F., Index of obituary notices in the Oxford magazine from
vol. i (1883) to xxxiv (1916). (Oxf. mag., 1916, vol. 34, p. 247–49.)
Per. G.A. Oxon 4° 141

4593. SHEPPARD, S. T., Some Oxford celebrities [c. 1900]. (Blackwood's
mag., 1944, vol. 256, p. 318–24.)   Per. 2705 d. 386

4594. MACKENZIE, SIR C., Some Oxford characters of my time [1901–4].
(Oxford, 1941, vol. 7, no. 2, p. 43–51.)   Per. G.A. Oxon 8° 1141

4595. H., E. V., Eccentric dons. (Oxf. mag., 1908, vol. 26, p. 277, 78.)
Per. G.A. Oxon 4° 141

4596. LOCK, W., Oxford memories [of many famous alumni]. Lond., 1932,
8°. 120 pp.   G.A. Oxon 8° 1095

Individual biographies
(in alphabetical order of subject of biography)

4597. ATLAY, J. B., Sir Henry Wentworth Acland [1815–1900], bart. . . .
Regius professor of medicine . . . a memoir. Lond., 1903, 8°. 507 pp.
15085 d. 31

See 7068 [Dean Aldrich, a commemoration speech by H. S. Holland. 1872].
See 7069 [Henry Aldrich, by E. F. A. Suttle. 1940].
See 7070 [Henry Aldrich, by W. G. Hiscock. 1960].

4598. BAILEY, C., Hugh Percy Allen [at Oxf. 1901–46]. Lond. &c., 1948,
8°. 170 pp.   17402 e. 995

4599. FELL, J., The life of Richard Allestree [1619–1680, by J. Fell. First publ. as the preface to Forty sermons, by Richard Allestree, 1684: G 2. 10 Th.]. Lond., 1848, 8°. 30 pp.   48.548

See 6747 [Smith, A. L., Thomas Allnutt, earl Brassey. 1919].
See 6650 [A memoir of sir William Anson. 1920].

4600. BAMFORD, T. W., Thomas Arnold. Lond., 1960, 8°. 232 pp.
                                                          26011 e. 353

4601. HUMPHREYS, A. L., Elias Ashmole. Repr. from the Berks, Bucks and Oxon Archaeological journal. Reading, 1925, 8°. 25 pp.
                                                          1757 d. 28 (5)

4602. GIBSON, S., A neglected Oxford historian [John Ayliffe, 1676–1732]. (Oxford essays in Medieval history, presented to H. E. Salter, 1934, p. 235–41.)   22215 e. 9 = S.

4603. Sidney Ball, memories & impressions [from 1875 to 1918] of 'an ideal don', arranged by O. H. Ball. Oxf., 1923, 8°. 270 pp. 26011 e. 120

See 8509 [Warton, T., The life . . . of Ralph Bathurst. 1761].
See 8410.4 [Morgan, P., Bellamy and his Fellows. 1961].
See 7631 [Paul Victor Mendelssohn Benecke, by M. Deneke. 1954].

4604. HOLLAND, T. E., Notice nécrologique sur m. Mountague Bernard. Extr. de l'Annuaire de l'Inst. du droit internat. Bruxelles &c., 1884, 4°. 8 pp.   211 d. 2

4605. DOUGLAS, S., baron Glenbervie, The biographical history of sir William Blackstone . . . and a catalogue of all sir William Blackstone's works, manuscript as well as printed. By a gentleman of Lincoln's-Inn [S. Douglas]. Lond., 1782, 8°.   8° C 232 BS.

4606. WARDEN, L. C., The life of Blackstone. Charlottesville, Va., 1938, 8°. 451 pp.   L.L.

4607. GIBSON, S., and HINDLE, C. J., Philip Bliss, 1787–1857, editor and bibliographer. (Proc. and papers, Oxf. bibliogr. soc., 1933, vol. 3, p. 173–260, 367, 68.)   Soc. 258 d. 176 — Λ.

4608. BOBART, H. T., A biographical sketch of Jacob Bobart, together with an account of his two sons, Jacob and Tilleman. (Leic.), 1884, 8°. 12 pp.
                                                          1911 d. 11 (4)

For biographies of sir Thomas Bodley see 5406, &c. [Bodleian library] and 7796, 7797 [Merton college].

See 7797.5 [MacNaghten, A., A great Oxford eccentric, G. C. Brodrick. 1966].

4609. Rhoda Broughton. (Things past, by M. Sadleir, 1944, p. 84–116.)
                                                          27001 e. 1578

4610. MOZLEY, T., Letter to . . . Canon Bull . . . by the author of Reminiscences of Oriel college and the Oxford movement [T. Mozley] on two passages in that book relating to dr. Buckland. Lond., 1882, 8°. 24 pp.
                                                          210 p. 63

4611. The life and correspondence of William Buckland, by his daughter mrs. Gordon. Lond., 1894, 8°. 288 pp.   188 e. 126

See 7632 [In memoriam rev. Frederic Bulley, by sir T. H. Warren. 1885].

4612. GOULBURN, E. M., John William Burgon, a biography. 2 vols. Lond., 1892, 8°.   11126 e. 122, 123

See 7220 [John Burton, by H. B. Fant. 1941].

4613. JACKSON, W. W., Ingram Bywater, the memoir of an Oxford scholar, 1840–1914. Oxf., 1917, 8°. 212 pp.   2998 d. 57
— 2nd impr. 220 pp.   2998 d. 58

See 7436.5 [Jenkins, D. E., The life of Thomas Charles. At Jesus college, 1775–1778. 1910].

4614. HARROD, R. F., The prof., a personal memoir of lord Cherwell. Lond., 1959, 8°. 282 pp.   1991 e. 265

See 6651 [Jacob, E. F., Two lives of archbishop Chichele. 1932].
See 8123 [Scheibner, R. O., Dr. Thomas Clayton. 1943].
See 8053 [Copleston, W. J., Memoir of Edward Copleston. 1851].
See 8054 [Remains of Edward Copleston. 1854].
See 8055 [Brock, M. G., The case of dr. Copleston. 1957].

4615. CREIGHTON, L., Life and letters of Mandell Creighton, by his wife. 2 vols. Lond. &c., 1904, 8°.   11126 d. 87, 88 = S.

See 1263, 1264 [Biographies of Nathaniel, lord Crewe. 1893 and 1937].

4616. Obituary notice of Charles Giles Bridle Daubeny [signed J. P.]. (Ashm. soc.) [Oxf.], (1868), 8°. 15 pp.   G.A. Oxon 4° 370 (2)

See 6755 [Mackail, J. W., J. L. Strachan-Davidson, a memoir. 1925].

4617. WEAVER, J. R. H., Henry William Carless Davis, 1874–1928, a memoir . . . [comprising p. 1–60.] Lond., 1933, 8°.   226 e. 117

4618. Henry Carless Davis, 1874–1928. (Things past, by M. Sadleir, 1944, p. 144–52.)   27001 e. 1578

4619. Memorials of Albert Venn Dicey, being chiefly letters and diaries, ed. by R. S. Rait. Lond., 1925, 8°. 304 pp.   L.L.

4620. DREYER, M., Georges Dreyer, a memoir. Oxf., 1937, 8°. 249 pp.   15085 e. 193

4620.3. ROTH, C., Salomon Israel, writing master in Oxford, 1745—alias Ignatius Dumay. (Oxoniensia, 1963, vol. 28, p. 74–78.)
                                    Per. G.A. Oxon 4° 658 = R. Top.

See 5551.3 [Burden, S. G., Herbert Frank Dyer, 1889–1965. Memorial address. 1965].
See 7900 [Herbert Fisher, by D. Ogg. 1947].
See 3804. [Magrath, J. R., The Flemings in Oxford, 1650–1700. 1904].
See 7535 [William Warde Fowler, by R. H. Coon. 1934].

4621. STEPHENS, W. R. W., The life and letters of Edward A. Freeman. 2 vols. Lond. &c., 1895, 8°.   223 e. 51, 52

4622. PAUL, H., The life of Froude. Lond., 1905, 8°. 454 pp.   226 e. 105

4623. SPERANZA, G., Alberico Gentili. Roma, 1876, 8°. 293 pp. 210 j. 543

4624. HUGHES, H., Gladstone, Christ Church and Oxford, an historical local retrospect. Oxf., 1898, 8°. 20 pp. G.A. Oxon 8° 620 (23)

4625. RICHARDS, J. BRINSLEY-, Mr. Gladstone's Oxford days. (Temple bar, 1883, vol. 68, p. 29–47.) G.A. Oxon 4° 586 (4)

See 7634 [The life of George S. Gordon, by M. C. Gordon. 1945].

4626. NETTLESHIP, R. L., Memoir of Thomas Hill Green. Lond. &c., 1906, 8°. 256 pp. 26684 e. 49

See 7072 [An essay on the life of David Gregory, 1696–1767. 1769].
See 8696 [Richard Greswell, by J. W. Burgon. 1888].
See 7799 [Memories of the rev. Moses Griffiths, by G. Rawlinson. 1890].
See 7798 [Recollections of the rev. Moses Edwards-Griffiths, by G. C. Broderick. 1891].
See 7895 [Burrows, M., Memoir of Grocyn. 1890].

4627. Thomas Hodge Grose. [An In memoriam.] (Oxf.), 1906, 8°. 18 pp.
G.A. Oxon 8° 727

4628. CALLUS, D. A., The Oxford career of Robert Grosseteste. (Oxoniensia, 1945, vol. 10, p. 42–72.) Per. G.A. Oxon 4° 658 = R. Top.

See 8766 [Deneke, H., Grace Hadow. 1946].
See 3540 [Hampden, H., Some memorials of Renn Dickson Hampden. 1871].

4629. CRASTER, H. H. E., Francis Haverfield. Repr. from The Engl. hist. review, January 1920 [p. 63–70]. [Lond., 1920], 8°. 1757 d. 10 (20)

See 8056 [Rev. Edward Hawkins, by J. W. Burgon. 1883].
See 8057 [Edward Hawkins, by J. W. Burgon. 1888].

4630. Impartial memorials of the life and writings of Thomas Hearne, by several hands. Lond., 1736, 8°. 66 pp. Mus. Bibl. II 102

4631. The life of mr. Thomas Hearne. (The lives of John Leland, Thomas Hearne and Anthony à Wood, vol. 1.) Oxf., 1772, 8°. 139 pp.
Mus. Bibl. II 103

4632. DOUGLAS, D. C., Thomas Hearne, 1735–1935. (St. Edmund hall mag., 1935, vol. 3, no. 5, p. 16–24.) Per. G.A. Oxon 4° 447

4633. PHILIP, I. G., Thomas Hearne as a publisher. (Bodleian library record, 1951, vol. 3, p. 146–55.) Per. 2590 d. Oxf. 1. 41 = R.

See 7688 [Heylin, P., Memoranda, 1599–1643. 1851].

4634. D., A. G., A seventeenth century don: Griffin Higgs and his friends. (Oxf. mag., 1938, vol. 56, p. 350–52; 379, 80.) Per. G.A. Oxon 4° 141

4635. WHITAKER, A. P., James Hurdis, his life and writings. [At Oxford 1780–84 and 1793–1801.] (Chichester), 1960, 8°. 63 pp.
2796 d. 441

4636. COFFIN, R. P. T., The 'Britter' [Herbert Jackson, Non-coll.]. (Amer. Oxon., 1925, vol. 12, p. 12–15.) Per. G.A. Oxon 8° 889

See 6748, &c. [Biographies of B. Jowett].

4637. WOOD, FREDERICK WILLIAM LINDLEY, 1st earl Halifax, John
Keble. Lond. &c., 1932, 8°. 244 pp.   11126 e. 639

4637.1. BATTISCOMBE, G., John Keble. Lond., 1963, 8°. 395 pp.
                                                       11126 d. 212

4638. KEMP, E. W., The life and letters of Kenneth Escott Kirk, bishop of
Oxford, 1937–1954. Lond., 1959, 8°. 221 pp.   11126 e. 944

See 7075 [Henry George Liddell, a memoir by H. L. Thompson. 1899].

4639. Henry Parry Liddon, D.D., D.C.L., 1829–1929. A centenary
memoir: contributors, the lord bishop of Oxford [T. B. Strong and 4
others]. Lond. &c., 1929, 8°. 52 pp.   11126 e. 609

See 2868 [Gotch, F., Two Oxford physiologists: Richard Lower, 1631 to
    1691 . . ., 1908].
See 7436 [The life of Francis Mansell, by sir L. Jenkins. 1854].
See 8058 [Charles Marriott, by J. W. Burgon. 1888].
See 2868 [Gotch, F., Two Oxford physiologists . . . John Mayow, 1643 to 1679,
    1908].
See 8059 [Wilson, J. C., David Binning Monro, a short memoir. 1907].

4640. NETTLESHIP, M., A memoir of Henry Nettleship. Oxf., 1895, 8°.
37 pp.   2998 e. 25

4641. CHURTON, R., A memoir of sir Roger Newdigate, bart. Repr. from
the Gentleman's magazine, of 1807. (Leamington), 1881, 16°. 25 pp.
                                                       211 f. 20

4642. MARSH, J. E., William Odling. (Trans., Chem. soc., 1921, vol. 119,
p. 553–64.)   193 d. 22

4643. JOYCE, F. W., The life of . . . sir F. A. G. Ouseley. Lond., 1896, 8°.
278 pp.   17402 d. 29

4644. BOAS, G., An Oxford character, S. G. Owen, student and tutor of
Christ Church, 1858–1940. (Oxford, 1945, vol. 9, no. 1, p. 40–47.)
                                            Per. G.A. Oxon 8° 1141

See 7076 [Francis Paget, by S. Paget and J. M. C. Crum. 1912].

4645. TOVEY, SIR D., and PARRATT, G., Walter Parratt, master of the
music. Lond. &c., 1941, 8°. 184 pp.   17402 e. 825

4645.9. WRIGHT, T., The life of Walter Pater. 2 vols. Lond., 1907, 8°.
                                            2696 d. 86, 87 = S.

4646. CECIL, LORD DAVID, Walter Pater, the scholar-artist. The Rede
lecture. Cambr., 1955, 8°. 30 pp.   2696 e. 662 (2)

See 7536 [Mark Pattison, by J. C. Morison. 1884].
See 7537 [Recollections of Mark Pattison. 1885].
See 8331 [Addresses and essays in commemoration of the life and works of
    Peter Payne-Engliš, 1456–1956. 1957].
See 8510 [Henry Francis Pelham, by H. E. D. Blakiston. 1907].

4647. COMBARIEU, L. C., Phillimore (dr. Joseph) [an obituary notice].
(Mémorial hist., Paris, 1856, p. 153–56.)   G.A. Oxon 4° 40 (1)

4648. BROCK, M. G., The vehemence of dr. Phillpotts [1791–]. (Pelican Record, 1950, vol. 29, p. 30–39.)   Per. G.A. Oxon 8° 588

See 8589 [In memoriam, F. C. Plumptre, by P. G. Medd. 1870].

4649. TWELLS, L., The lives of dr. Edward Pocock, by dr. Twells, [and lives of 3 others]. Vol. 1. Lond., 1816, 8°. p. 1–356.   8° X 178 BS

See 8507 [Warton, T., The life of sir Thomas Pope. 1772; 2nd ed. 1780].

4650. PAINTIN, H., Two famous Oxonians [Ronald Poulton, V. Roberts]. [Oxf., 1920], s. sh.   G.A. Oxon c. 250 (ii)

4651. ELTON, O., Frederick York Powell, a life. 2 vols. Oxf., 1906, 8°.
226 d. 142, 143

See 7308 [Prideaux, S. P. T., John Prideaux. 1938].

4652. PRITCHARD, A., Charles Pritchard . . . memoirs of his life . . . Lond., 1897, 8°. 322 pp.   184 d. 24

4653. LIDDON, H. P., Life of Edward Bouverie Pusey, ed. by J. O. Johnston and R. J. Wilson. 4 vols. Lond. &c., 1893–97, 4°.
11126 d. 39–42 = S.
— 2nd ed. Vol. 1, 2. 1893.   11126 d. 196, 197
— 3rd ed. Vol. 3. 1895.   11126 d. 198
— 3rd impr. Vol. 4. 1898.   11126 d. 199

4654. PRESTIGE, L., Pusey. (Tractarian ser.) Lond., 1933, 8°. 176 pp.
11126 e. 652

4655. NIAS, J. B., Dr. John Radcliffe, a sketch of his life with an account of his fellows and foundations. Oxf., 1918, 4°. 147 pp.   G.A. Oxon 4° 395

For biographies of Cecil Rhodes see 5968, &c. [Rhodes House].

See 7437 [Parry-Williams, T. H., John Rhys. 1954].

4656. Stephen Peter Rigaud . . . a memoir [by his son, J. R.]. Oxf., 1883, 8°. 39 pp.   184 e. 124

4657. PAINTIN, H., Two famous Oxonians [R. Poulton and Varley Roberts]. [Oxf., 1920], s. sh.   G.A. Oxon c. 250 (ii)

4658. POULTON, E. B., George Rolleston, Linacre professor of anatomy, 1860–1881. (John Viriamu Jones, and other Oxford memories, p. 183–220.) Lond. &c., 1911, 8°.   G.A. Oxon 8° 823

4658.1. ROUND, J. T., Some distinctive peculiarities of each of the four Evangelists. (Memoir of the author, by J. M. Chapman, p. ix–xxvii.) Lond. &c., 1866, 8°.   101 e. 99

See 7636 [A biographical sketch of dr. Routh, by C. G. B. Daubeny. 1867].
See 7637 [Memoir of Martin Joseph Routh, by J. W. Burgon. 1878].
See 7638 [Martin Joseph Routh, by J. W. Burgon. 1888].
See 7639 [Dr. Routh, by R. D. Middleton. 1938].

4659. Ruskin at Oxford, by an old Corpus man. (Pelican Record, 1904, vol. 7, p. 44–49, 76–82.)   Per. G.A. Oxon 8° 588

4660. CLARK, SIR K., Ruskin at Oxford, an inaugural lecture. Oxf., 1947,
8°. 24 pp.   17006 d. 280 (14)

See 8590 [Sadleir, M., Michael Ernest Sadler. 1949].

4661. WALTON, I., The life of dr. [Robert] Sanderson . . . Lond., 1678, 8°.
                                                                Mar. 231
— 3rd impr. [Pt. of 36 sermons. 8th ed.] 1686.   Vet. A 3 c. 51

4662. Sir John Burdon Sanderson, a memoir by lady Burdon Sanderson,
completed and ed. by his nephew and niece [J. S. and E. S. Haldane].
With a selection from his papers and addresses. Oxf., 1911, 8°. 315 pp.
                                                                166 e. 13

See 7800 [Memoirs of James Robert Hope-Scott, by R. Ornsby. 1884].

4663. JAMES, L., A forgotten genius [William] Sewell. Lond., 1945, 8°.
314 pp.   26011 e. 216

4664. Letters from and to Charles Kirkpatrick Sharpe, ed. by A. Allardyce.
Vol. I. [Sharpe was at Christ Church from 1798–1806]. Edinb. &c.,
1888, 8°. 589 pp.   2696 e. 65

See 8698 [Masterman, J. C., An eighteenth-century provost, William Sheffield.
   1961].
See 8511 [An Oxford tutor, the life of Thomas Short, by C. E. H. Edwards.
   1909].
See 7901 [Alec Halford Smith, tributes. 1959].
See 6754 [Arthur Lionel Smith, a biography and somereminiscences. 1928].

4665. COOPER, J. J., Goldwin Smith . . . a brief account of his life and
writings. [Bibliography, p. 10–14.] (Reading), [1912], 8°. 14 pp.
                                                           25889 S. e. 11

4666. Biographical sketches and recollections (with early letters) of Henry
John Stephen Smith. (Oxf.), 1894, 4°. 99 pp.   187 d. 26

4667. PROTHERO, R. E., and BRADLEY, G. G., The life and correspondence
of Arthur Penrhyn Stanley. 2 vols. Lond., 1893, 8°.
                                                    11126 d. 43, 44 = S.

4668. BAILLIE, A. V., and BOLITHO, H., A Victorian dean, a memoir of
Arthur Stanley. Lond., 1930, 8°. 311 pp.   11126 d. 164

4669. THORNHILL, A., One fight more [a biography of B. H. Streeter].
Lond., 1943, 8°. 64 pp.   13217 e. 136

4670. Letters of William Stubbs, bishop of Oxford, 1825–1901, ed. by
W. H. Hutton. Lond., 1904, 8°. 428 pp.   226 d. 140

4671. EDWARDS, J. G., William Stubbs. (Hist. assoc., G 22.) (Lond.), 1952,
8°. 19 pp.   Soc. 263334 e. 175 (22) = S.

4671.5. JEROME, J., Montague Summers. [Later years in Oxford, 1929–
34, p. 58– .] Lond., 1965, 8°.   26961 e. 595

4672. GIBSON, S., Brian Twyne. (Oxoniensia, 1940, vol. 5, p. 94–114.)
                                Per. G.A. Oxon 4° 658 = R. Top.

4673. BAILEY, C., Francis Fortescue Urquhart, a memoir. Lond., 1936, 8°.
194 pp. G.A. Oxon 8° 1167

4674. DENEKE, M., Ernest Walker. Lond. &c., 1951, 8°. 144 pp.
17402 e. 1128

4675. POPE, W., The life of . . . Seth [Ward], lord bishop of Salisbury . . .
Lond., 1697, 8°. 193 pp. 8° S 84 Art.

See 7640 [Herbert Warren, by L. Magnus. 1932].

4676. RINAKER, C., Thomas Warton. (Univ. of Illinois studies in lang. and
lit., vol. 2, no. 1.) Urbana, 1916, 4°. 241 pp. Soc. 3962 d. 50

See 7541 [Green, V. H. H., The young mr. Wesley. 1961].

4677. WHATELY, E. J., Life and correspondence of Richard Whately, D.D.
2 vols. Lond., 1866, 8°. 210 e. 142, 143

4678. LANGLÈS, L., Nécrologie. Notice sur m. Joseph White. (Extrait du
Mercure étranger, 1814, p. 1–7.) G.A. Oxon 8° 58 (12)

See 8647 [The life and times of John Wilkins, by P. A. W. Henderson. 1910].
See 8698.2 [C. H. Wilkinson, 1888–1960. 1965].

4679. KEMP, E. W., N. P. Williams. Lond., 1954, 8°. 219 pp. 11126 e. 870

4680. GIBSON, S., Francis Wise, B.D., Oxford antiquary, librarian and
archivist. (Oxoniensia, 1936, vol. 1, p. 173–95.)
Per. G.A. Oxon 4° 658 = R. Top.

4681. RAWLINSON, R., The life of mr. Anthony a Wood, [from 1632–
1695] &c. [by R. Rawlinson]. n. pl., [1711], 8°. 18 pp.
MS. Rawl. J 4° 1 (f. 412–20)

4682. CHARLETT, A., Dr. Charlett's letter to archbishop Tenison concerning the death of mr. Anthony à Wood. (Johannis Glastoniensis
volumen secundum, ed. T. Hearnius, 1726, p. 455–58.)
Mus. Bibl. II 83

4683. The life of mr. Anthony a Wood from 1632 to 1672, written by himself, transcr. by the publisher. (Thomæ Caii Vindiciæ antiq. Acad.
Oxon. contra Joannem Caium, in lucem emisit T. Hearnius, 1730, vol.
2, p. 438–603.) Mus. Bib. II 92

4684. The life of Anthony à Wood, from 1632 to 1672, now continued
[by R. Rawlinson] to the time of his death [1695]. (The lives of John
Leland, Thomas Hearne and Anthony à Wood, vol. 2.) Oxf., 1772, 8°.
404 pp. Mus. Bibl. II 104

4685. The life of Anthony à Wood, written by himself. [Pp. 1–16 only of
an edition.] n. pl., [18—], 8°. Bliss B. 147 (20)

See 122–24 [The life and times of Anthony Wood, 1632–1695. 1891–1900, &c.].
See 7902 [Slee, J., The tree warden, Michael Woodward. 1959].

4686. WATSON, E. W., Life of bishop John Wordsworth. Lond. &c., 1915,
8°. 409 pp. 11126 d. 131

4687. WRIGHT, E. M., The life of Joseph Wright. 2 vols. Lond., 1932, 8°.
302 d. 15, 16
— [Abridged ed.] 1934. 279 pp.   302 e. 137

PORTRAITS AND CARICATURES

For works on portraits etc. in Oxford but not exclusively of Oxford alumni
see Pictures, plate, and historic treasures [No. 532, &c.].

4688. [A collection of Oxford portraits, city and university, 1531–1912.]
G.A. Oxon a. 38

4689. [Three volumes of caricatures.]
G.A. Oxon a. 75, 80, 81

4690. [A volume of 25 portraits of college founders, by J. Faber. 1712.]
Gough maps 166

4691. [5 silhouette portraits, 1828, by August Edouart.] G.A. Oxon c. 106

See 3823 [Bradley, E., College life, etchings. 1850].

4692. HALL, S. P., [Oxford sketches Photographs of a series of 100
caricatures drawn between 1864 and 1866.]   G.A. Oxon 4° 99

4693. HALL, S. P., Descriptive key to 'Oxford sketches' [by S. P. Hall].
Oxf., [c. 1870], 8°. 24 pp.   G.A. Oxon 8° 1012 (5)
— [Another ed.] 29 pp.   G.A. Oxon 4° 443

4694. HALL, S. P., Key book to [44 of the original] 'Oxford sketches'
[which the Union society have acquired]. Oxf., 1909, 8°. 11 pp.
G.A. Oxon 16° 33 (26)

4695. ROTHENSTEIN, SIR W., Oxford characters, a series of [12] lithographs. Pt. 1–6. Lond., 1893, fol.   G.A. Oxon b. 14
— [Another ed., *entitled*] Oxford characters, 24 lithographs, with text
by F. Y. Powell and others. [A reissue of the first 12 above, with others
drawn in 1896.] Lond. &c., 1896, fol.   G.A. Oxon b. 104

4696. ASTON, J., Varsity sketches. [Humorous drawings.] Oxf., (1902), 4°.
12 pl.   G.A. Oxon c. 203

4697. [A collection of 1224 caricatures, c. 1868–92, published by Thomas
Shrimpton and son. Photographic reproductions. 7 vols.]
G.A. Oxon 4° 412–18

4698. BROOKING, C., Oxford men [caricatured] in Dighton prints. (Notes
& queries, 1940, vol. 178, p. 201–06.)   Per. 3974 e. 405 = A.

4699. G., N. M., Recent official Oxford portraits. (Oxf. mag., 1941, vol. 59,
p. 213.)   Per. G.A. Oxon 4° 141

4700. GUINESS, J., Portraits of sir Nathaniel Lloyd. (Oxoniensia, 1960, vol.
25, p. 96–101.)   Per. G.A. Oxon 4° 658 = R. Top.

COMMEMORATION

See also Ceremonies [no. 1227, &c.].
See also Act or Encænia [no. 1236, &c.].
See also Terræ filius [no. 5010, &c.].

4701. Oxford commemoration. (Leisure hour, 1861, p. 374–76.)
G.A. Oxon 4° 578 (9)

4702. Commemoration at Oxford. (Living age, 1862, vol. 77, p. 369 &c.).

4703. Oxford doings [a poem on Commemoration]. (London soc., 1863, vol. 4, p. 125–28.) Per. 2705 d. 200

4704. BRADLEY, E., Young Oxford at the Commemoration, by the author of 'Verdant Green'. (Lond. soc., 1864, vol. 6, p. 25–32.)
Per. 2705 d. 200

4705. Commemoration: an Oxford mixture [signed H. E. P. In verse]. (Lond. soc., 1866, vol. 10, p. 43–46.) G.A. Oxon 4° 579 (11)

4706. The Commemoration at Oxford in the 17th and 18th centuries, by a Templar. (Macmillan's mag., 1867/8, vol. 17, p. 234–47.)
Per. 2705 d. 254

4707. [Begin.] At a meeting of representatives of colleges and halls appointed to confer with Council on the subject of Commemoration, it was agreed that the following resolutions should be offered for consideration ... Apr. 30. [Oxf.], (1875), s. sh. G.A. Oxon c. 33 (174)

4708. [Begin.] The following memorial has been presented to the Hebdomadal council [in connection with the Resolution of March 1st concerning Commemoration. And The reply of the Council. 19 April 1875]. n. pl., [1875], 8°. 3 pp. G.A. Oxon 8° 1001 (14*)

4709. Oxford commemoration, by a fellow of experientia. Lond., 1888, 8°. 128 pp. G.A. Oxon 8° 451

FICTION

In this section, the first edition, or earliest recorded edition has been listed. In every case, however, the earliest edition to be found in the Bodleian has been noted. In a few cases, where this seemed desirable, more complete entries have been made.

4710. COLLINS, C. W., Oxford in fact and fiction [by C. W. Collins]. (Blackwood's mag., 1895, vol. 158, p. 880–904.) Per. 2705 d. 386

4711. CLARKE, W. J., Oxford light literature. Notes of fifty books of Oxford life: novels, articles, verses. Oxf., 1897, 8°. 8 pp. G.A. Oxon 8° 611 (19)

4712. HULTON, S. F., The clerk of Oxford in fiction. Lond., 1909, 8°. 390 pp. G.A. Oxon 8° 772

4713. W., G. O., Oxford novels new and old. 1, 2. (Oxf. mag., 1915, vol. 34, p. 92, 93; 109–11.) Per. G.A. Oxon 4° 141

4714. PROCTOR, M. R., The English university novel. (Univ. of Calif., Engl. studies, 15.) Berkeley, &c., 1957, 8°. 228 pp.
Per. 269 d. 146 (15)

4715. QUINTON, A. M., Oxford in fiction. (Oxf. mag., 1958, vol. 76, p. 212–18.)
Per. G.A. Oxon 4° 141

4715.2. STOCKUM, T. C. VAN, De 'colleges' van de oudere Engelse universiteiten in de spiegel van de Engelse roman. (Meded., K. Ned. akad. van wet., afd. lett., n.r., deel 24, no. 6.) Amst., 1961, 4°. 16 pp.
Soc. 397 d. 48 (ii, 24)

4716. PENTON, S., The guardian's instruction, or, The gentleman's romance [by S. Penton]. Lond., 1688, 12°. 90 pp.   Wood 754 (5)
— [Another ed.] Lond., 1688.   Antiq. f. E. 1688. 1
— 2nd ed. Lond., 1697.   Vet. A 3 f. 916
— Repr. With intr. by H. H. Sturmer. Lond., 1897, 12°. xxvii+82 pp.
2621 f. 15

4717. FIELDING, H., The history of Tom Jones. 6 vols. Lond., 1749, 12°.
Vet. A 4 f. 456–61
[Other editions.]

4718. SMOLLETT, T., The adventures of Peregrine Pickle. 4 vols. Lond., 1751, 12°.   Douce SS 1–4
[Other editions.]

4719. Memoirs of an Oxford scholar, containing his amour with the beautiful Miss L——, of Essex. Written by himself. Lond., 1756, 12°. 264 pp.   256 f. 2356

4720. The adventures of Oxymel Classic, esq.: once an Oxford scholar. 2 vols. Lond., 1768.

4721. The Oxonian: or, The adventures of mr. G. Edmunds, student of Brazen-nose college, Oxford. By a member of the University, 2 vols. Lond., 1771.

4722. HOLCROFT, T., The adventures of Hugh Trevor. 3 vols. Lond., 1794, 8°.
— 2nd ed. [consisting of a re-issue of vol. 1–3 and vol. 4–6 issued for the first time]. 6 vols. Lond., 1794, 97, 8°.   249 s. 315–17
— 3rd ed. 1801. 4 vols.

4723. GODWIN, W., Fleetwood. 3 vols. Lond., 1805, 8°.   249 s. 383–85
[Other editions.]

4724. Frederick: or, The memoirs of my youth. 2 vols. Lond. &c., 1811.

4725. Rhydisel. The devil in Oxford. 2 vols. Lond., 1811, 8°.
G.A. Oxon 8° 88, 89

4726. Night sketch of Oxford. Oxf., 1817, 8°. 19 pp.   256 e. 15225

4727. LOCKHART, J. G., Reginald Dalton. 3 vols. Edinb., 1823, 8°.
8° H 106 Art.

4728. Remarks on the novel of Reginald Dalton, with extracts from that work illustrative of life in Oxford. With 5 plates drawn by N. Whittock. Oxf., 1824, 8°. 68 pp.   G.A. Oxon 8° 365
— 2nd ed. [engraved title-leaf]. 1824.   G.A. Oxon 8° 103

4729. WARD, R. P., Tremaine: or, The man of refinement [by R. P. Ward]. 3 vols. Lond., 1825, 8°.   256 e. 15902–04
— 2nd ed. 1825.   25. 697–99

4730. WESTMACOTT, C. M., The Freshman: Christ Church college: The dinner party: College servants: Taking possession of your rooms: The excursion to Bagley wood. (The English spy, by Bernard Blackmantle, *passim*.) Lond., 1825, 26, 8°.   B.M.
— New ed. 1907.   247126 f. 33, 34

4731. LITTLE, T., Confessions of an Oxonian [by T. Little]. 3 vols. Lond., 1826, 8°.   256 e. 14893–95

4732. BEAZLEY, S., The Oxonians; a glance at society, by the author of 'The roué'. 3 vols. Lond., 1830, 8°.   30. 237

4733. Truth without fiction, and religion without disguise: or, The two Oxford students in college, London, and the country. By a country rector. Lond., 1837.   Honnold
— 2nd ed. [Publ. in parts.] Lond., 1838, 8°. 519 pp.   1489 d. 14

4734. The odd fellow, a college sketch. (Bentley's Miscellany, 1839, vol. 5, p. 210–16.)   G.A. Oxon 4° 578 (2c)

4735. Quip, *pseud.*, Vincent Eden; or, The Oxonian, by Quip. (Bentley's Miscellany, 1839, vol. 5, p. 313–26, 390–405.) G.A. Oxon 4° 578 (2b)

4736. HEWLETT, J. T. J., Peter Priggins, the college scout, ed. by Theodore Hook, esq. 3 vols. Lond., 1841, 8°.   41. 330

4737. WARD, R. P., De Clifford: or, The constant man, by the author of Tremaine &c. [R. P. Ward]. 4 vols. Lond., 1841, 8°.   41. 747, 748 [Other editions.]

4738. HEWLETT, J. T. J., College life; or, The Proctor's note book. 3 vols. Lond., 1843, 8°.   43. 370

4739. LISTER, C., The college chums. 2 vols. Lond., 1845, 8°.   45. 564, 565

4740. HEWLETT, J. T. J., Great Tom of Oxford, by the author of 'Peter Priggins' etc. 3 vols. Lond., 1846, 8°.   46. 1000

4741. FROUDE, J. A., Shadows of the cloud, by Zeta. Lond., 1874, 8°. 287 pp.   47. 926

4742. COLLINS, E. M., Colleges and collegians. Bristol, 1848, 8°. 83 pp.   G.A. Oxon 8° 245

4743. NEWMAN, J. H., Loss and gain [by J. H. Newman]. Lond., 1848, 8°. 386 pp.   48. 1336 [Other editions.]

4744. FROUDE, J. A., Nemesis of faith. Lond., 1849, 8°. 227 pp.
256 e. 15499
[Other editions.]

4745. The Undergraduate [at Oxford]. (Dubl. univ. mag., 1849, vol. 34, p. 331–38, 466–74.) Per. 3977 e. 74

4746. HEYGATE, W. E., Godfrey Davenant at college. Lond., 1849, 8°. 268 pp. 49. 1092

4747. An Oxford legend. (Leisure hour, 1852, p. 122–24.)
G.A. Oxon 4° 578 (4)
4748.

4749. BRADLEY, E., The adventures of mr. Verdant Green, an Oxford freshman, by Cuthbert Bede. Lond., 1853, 8°. 118 pp. 249 z. 293
[Other editions.]

4750. BRADLEY, E., The further adventures of mr. Verdant Green, an Oxford undergraduate, by Cuthbert Bede. Lond., 1854, 8°. 108 pp.
B.M.
— 2nd ed. 1854. 249 z. 293*

4751. GRIFFITH, G., The life and adventures of George Wilson, a foundation scholar. Lond. &c., 1854, 8°. 257 pp. 249 v. 523

4752. CONYBEARE, W. J., Perversion, or, The causes and consequences of infidelity. 3 vols. Lond., 1856, 8°. 249 v. 293–95

4753. BRADLEY, E., Tales of college life, by Cuthbert Bede. Lond., 1856, 8°. 115 pp. 249 u. 167 (2)

4754. BRADLEY, E., Mr. Verdant Green married and done for, by Cuthbert Bede. Lond., 1857, 8°. 112 pp. 249 z. 293**

4755. HEYGATE, W. E., The scholar and the trooper; or, Oxford during the Great Rebellion. Oxf., 1858, 8°. 284 pp. 251 g. 442
[Other editions.]

4756. The senior fellow, by the author of 'Squires and parsons'. Lond., 1860, 8°. 390 pp.. 249 x. 269

4757. READE, W. W., Liberty hall, Oxon. 3 vols. Lond., 1860, 8°.
249 x. 509–11

4758. PEACOCK, T. L., Gryll grange, by the author of 'Headlong hall'. Lond., 1861, 8°. 316 pp. 250 b. 50

4759. HUGHES, T., Tom Brown at Oxford, by the author of 'Tom Brown's school days'. 3 vols. Cambr. &c., 1861, 8°. 250 f. 121–23
[Other editions.]

4760. KINGSLEY, H., Ravenshoe. 3 vols. Cambr. &c., 1862, 8°.
250 h. 67–69
[Other editions.]

4761. KINGSLEY, H., Austin Elliot. 2 vols. Lond. &c., 1863, 8°. 250 o. 5, 6

4762. BUXTON, H. J. W., The mysteries of Isis: or, The college life of Paul Romaine. Oxf. &c., 1866, 8°. 230 pp. 251 i. 955

4763. ARNOLD, F., Christ Church days, an Oxford story [by F. Arnold]. 2 vols. Lond., 1867, 8°. 250 u. 303, 304

4764. KINGSLEY, H., Silcote of Silcotes. 3 vols. Lond., 1867, 8°. 250 x. 76–78
[Other editions.]

4765. CLARKE, C. C., Lord Falconberg's heir. [Vol. 1, ch. 1, Oxford as it was.] Lond., 1868, 8°. 250 n. 303

4766. College debts, by an Oxford M.A. 2 vols. Lond., 1870, 8°. 250 y. 137, 138

4767. BRADLEY, E., Little mr. Bouncer and his friend mr. Verdant Green, by Cuthbert Bede. Lond., [1873], 8°. 200 pp. 251 c. 217

4768. USHER, F., The three Oxonians. 3 vols. Lond., 1873, 8°. 249 q. 384–86

4769. READE, C., How mr. Penlake exercised a proctor. (Belgravia, 1874, vol. 22, p. 420–28.) Per. 256 d. 254

4770. READE, C., Oxford raffles [stories]. No. 1–4. (Belgravia, 1875, vol. 26, p. 38–48; 233–42; 322–34; 516–28.) Per. 256 d. 254

4771. My first 'wine' and what came of it, a story of Oxford life. Oxf., 1875, 8°. 31 pp. G.A. Oxon 8° 161 (20)

4772. ADAMS, H. C., Wilton of Cuthbert's: a tale of undergraduate life thirty years ago. Lond., 1878, 8°. 376 pp. 251 c. 616
— [Another issue entitled] College days at Oxford. Lond. &c., [1880], 8°. 376 pp. 251 g. 79
— [Another issue entitled] Wilton of Cuthbert's. Lond., [1905], 8°. 376 pp. 256 e. 13712

4773. STURGIS, J., John-a-Dreams. Edinb. &c., 1878, 8°. 280 pp. 251 e. 899

4774. WEATHERLY, F. E., Oxford days: or, How Ross got his degree, by a resident M.A. [F. E. Weatherly]. Lond., 1879, 8°. 171 pp. 251 c. 921
— [Republ. in 1879 in Cassell's family mag. with the title 'Frank Ross at Oxford'.]

4775. SHORTHOUSE, J. H., John Inglesant [by J. H. Shorthouse]. Birm., 1880, 8°. 577 pp. 251 f. 929

4776. The Oxford and Cambridge eights; or, The young coxwain's career. Lond., [1880?], 4°. 120 pp. 2533 d. 155

4777. TYRWHITT, R. ST. JOHN, Hugh Heron, Ch. Ch., an Oxford novel. Lond., [1880], 8°. 474 pp. 251 f. 564

4778. MERIVALE, H. C., Faucit of Balliol. 3 vols. Lond., 1882, 8°.
— 2nd ed. 1882. B.M.
— 3rd ed. 1882. 251 i. 882–84

4779. TRAILL, W. F., Tales of modern Oxford, by the author of 'Lays of modern Oxford'. Lond., 1882, 8°. 389 pp.   256 e. 15206

4780. Grimm tales. ii. An Oxford mystery. (To-day, 1883, vol. 1, p. 283–99, 432–47; vol. 2, p. 643–54, 756–69 &c.)   Per. 24772 d. 18

4781. BROUGHTON, R., Belinda. 3 vols. Lond., 1883, 8°.   256 e. 10
[Other editions.]

4782. WARD, MRS. H., Miss Bretherton. Lond., 1884, 8°. 297 pp.
256 e. 356
[Other editions.]

4783. LANG, MRS. A., Dissolving views. 2 vols. Lond., 1884, 8°.
256 e. 609, 610

4784. POGES, JEAN F. DARREL, pseud., Sir Jones, a story of modern Oxford, tr. from the French of Jean F. Darrel Poges. Oxf., 1885, 8°. 21 pp.   256 e. 5208 (1)

4785. CHURCH, A. J., The chantry priest of Barnet, a tale of the two roses. Lond., 1885, 8°. 301 pp.   25433 e. 4

4786. ADAMS, H. C., Charlie Lucken at school and university. Lond., 1886, 8°. 408 pp.   2532 e. 29
[Other editions.]

4787. CHURCH, A. J., With the king at Oxford, a tale of the Great rebellion. Lond., 1886, 8°. 298 pp.   25435 e. 12

4788. BATTY, B. BRAITHWAITE-, Passages in the life of an undergraduate, by Bee Bee. Lond., 1887, 8°. 188 pp.   256 e. 2867

4789. Molly at the Mitre. (Argosy, 1887, vol. 44, p. 48–55.)
G.A. Oxon 4° 586 (31)

4790. WARD, MRS. H., Robert Elsmere. 3 vols. Lond., 1888, 8°.
256 e. 3420–22
[Other editions.]

4791. Robert Elsmere and modern Oxford. [A review of mrs. Humphry Ward's book.] (Blackwood's Edinb. mag., 1888, vol. 144, p. 1–20.)
G.A. Oxon 4° 586 (36)

4792. COUCH, SIR A. QUILLER-, The splendid spur. Lond., 1889, 8°. 328 pp.   25435 e. 31

4793. EVANS, A. E., Prince Maskiloff, a romance of modern Oxford by Roy Tellet. Lond., 1889, 8°. 294 pp.   256 e. 4112

4794. KEDDIE, H., A young Oxford maid, in the days of the king and the parliament. By Sarah Tytler. Lond., [1890], 8°. 320 pp.   25435 e. 28

4795. BALFOUR, F. H., The undergraduate, by Ross George Dering. 2 vols. Lond., 1891, 8°.   256 e. 5659, 60

4796. COURTNEY, W. L., Bertha Goodall, a romance of the Cherwell. (Pall Mall mag. 1893, vol. 1, p. 62–69.)   G.A. Oxon 4° 575 (22)

4797. BLEACKLEY, H. W., One culotte, or, A new woman: an impossible story of modern Oxford, by Tivoli. Lond., [1894], 8°. 316 pp.
256 e. 8581

4798. SMITH, L. P., The youth of Parnassus and other stories of Oxford life. Lond. &c., 1895, 8°. 277 pp.   256 e. 9440

4799. ADAMS, H. C., School and university: or, Dolph Woolward. Lond., 1896, 8°. 395 pp.   2532 e. 96

4800. BAKER, J., The gleaming dawn. Lond., 1896, 8°. 391 pp.
1485 e. 85

4801. HEMYNG, S. B., Jack Harkaway at Oxford [by S. B. Hemyng]. Lond., [1897?], 4°. 319 pp.   2533 d. 242

4802. Within sound of Great Tom, stories of modern Oxford. Oxf. &c., 1897, 8°. 309 pp.   256 e. 11554

4803. GREEN, E. EVERETT-, A clerk of Oxford and his adventures in the Barons' war. Lond. &c., 1898 [97], 8°. 461 pp.   25432 e. 60

4804. HEMYNG, S. B., Jack Harkaway's strange adventures at Oxford [by S. B. Hemyng]. (Harkaway ser., no. 5.) Lond., [1898?].

4805. WEYMAN, S. J., The Castle inn. Lond., 1898, 8°. 371 pp.
25438 e. 109
[Other editions.]

4806. GULL, C. A. E. RANGER-, The hypocrite [by C. A. E. Ranger-Gull]. Lond., 1898, 8°. 167 pp.   256 e. 12117
[Other editions.]

4807. MACKIE, G., Charmides, or Oxford twenty years ago. Oxf., 1898, 8°. 71 pp.   280 f. 1035

4808. COUCH, SIR A. QUILLER-, Ship of stars. Lond., 1899, 8°. 312 pp.
256 e. 12480

4809. SERGEANT, A., Blake of Oriel. Lond., 1899, 8°. 311 pp.
256 e. 12266

4810. COLLINS, W. E. W., The don and the undergraduate, a tale of St. Hilary's college, Oxford. Edinb. &c., 1899, 8°. 320 pp. 256 e. 12696

4811. BEDFORD, W. K. R., Outcomes of old Oxford. Lond., 1899, 8°. 242 pp.
256 e. 12525

4812. COLLINS, W. E. W., A scholar of his college. Edinb. &c., 1900, 8°. 379 pp.   256 e. 13254

4813. BELLOC, H., Lambkin's Remains, by H. B. Oxf., 1900, 12°. 137 pp.
270 f. 1040

4814. ALLEN, I., A 'Varsity man'. Lond., 1901, 8°. 318 pp. 2561 e. 41

4815. ALLEN, I., A graduate in love. Lond., 1902, 8°. 320 pp.
2561 e. 870

4816. CORNWALL, N., The little don of Oxford. Lond., [1902], 8°. 224 pp.
1489 e. 1854

4817. CALDERON, G. L., The adventures of Downy V. Green, Rhodes scholar at Oxford. Lond., 1902, 8°. 184 pp.   2561 e. 1309

4818. GREEN, E. EVERETT-, For the faith, a story of the young pioneers of reformation in Oxford. Lond. &c., 1902, 8°. 364 pp.   1485 e. 125

4819. GULL, C. A. E. RANGER-, His grace's Grace. Lond., 1903, 8°. 304 pp.
2561 e. 1709

4820. SMITH, C. T., Godfrey Marten, undergraduate, by Charles Turley. Lond., 1904, 8°. 358 pp.   2561 e. 2929

4821. COKE, D. F. T., Sandford of Merton, by Belinda Blinders, ed. [really written] by D. F. T. Coke. Oxf. &c., 1903, 8°. 171 pp.   2561 e. 1896

4822. COKE, D. F. T., Sandford of the 'smart' set, or, Sin and scandal, by Belinda Blinders, ed. [really written] by D. F. T. Coke. Lond., 1904, 8°. 64 pp.   2561 e. 2351

4823. COKE, D. F. T., Sandford of Merton and The smart set, by Belinda Blinders, ed. [really written] by D. Coke. Complete and revised ed. Lond., 1909, 8°. 122 pp.   2561 e. 6708

4824. Red paint at Oxford, by 'Pish' and 'Tush'. Lond., 1904, 8°. 161 pp.
2561 e. 2566

4825. GOLDIE, V. T., Nigel Thomson. Lond., 1905, 8°. 377 pp.
2561 e. 3669

4826. BAKER, J., The inseparables, an Oxford novel of to-day. Lond., 1905, 8°. 340 pp.   2561 e. 3737

4827. COKE, D. F. T., The comedy of age. Lond., 1906, 8°. 312 pp.
2561 e. 4489

4828. WOODS, M., The invader. Lond., 1907, 8°. 312 pp.   2561 e. 4966

4829. PORTMAN, L., The progress of Hugh Rendal. Lond., 1907, 8°. 313 pp.   2561 e. 5278

4830. ECKERSLEY, A., An Oxford comedy. (English illustr. mag., 1907, vol. 37, p. 173–83, 227–37.)   G.A. Oxon 4° 575 (40)

4831. BALL, O. H., Barbara goes to Oxford, by Barbara Burke. Lond., 1907, 8°. 293 pp.   2561 e. 5137

4832. DICKINSON, H. N., Keddy. Lond., 1907, 8°. 328 pp.   2561 e. 5735

4833. BALL, O. H., Their Oxford year. Lond., 1909, 8°. 311 pp.
2561 e. 6763

4834. FENTON, W. F. DE WEND, The primrose path: being the adventures of Raymond Forsyth at Oxford [&c.]. Lond., 1911, 8°. 279 pp.

25611 e. 401

4835. GIBBS, A. H., The compleat Oxford man. Lond., 1911, 8°. 264 pp.

25611 e. 560

4836. BEERBOHM, M., Zuleika Dobson; or, An Oxford love story. Lond., 1911, 8°. 350 pp. 25611 e. 666
[Other editions.]

4837. BATTY, B. BRAITHWAITE-, Mrs. Fauntleroy's nephew: an episode of Oxford history in the Eights week. Lond., [1912], 8°. 207 pp.

25611 e. 1310

4838. BROSTER, D. K., and TAYLOR, G. W., The vision splendid. Lond., 1913, 8°. 499 pp. 1485 e. 233

4839. John Cope's year at Oxford. (Blackwood's mag., 1913, vol. 194, p. 187–210.) Per. 2705 d. 386

4840. MACKENZIE, SIR E. M. C., Sinister street. [Vol. 2, book 3: Dreaming spires.] Lond., 1914, 8°.
— 2nd. impr. 25611 e. 2781b

4841. PALMER, J., Peter Paragon. Lond., (1915), 8°. 320 pp.

25611 e. 5404

4842. SADLEIR, M. T. H., Hyssop. Lond., (1915), 8°. 318 pp.

25611 e. 4060

4843. BROWN, I., Years of plenty. Lond., 1915, 8°. 340 pp. 25611 e. 3838

4844. WARD, MRS. H., Lady Connie. Lond., 1916, 8°. 429 pp.

25611 e. 5071

[Other editions.]

4845. MCKENNA, S., Sonia. Lond., 1917, 8°. 404 pp. 25611 e. 5217

4846. TAYLOR, G. W., The pearl. [Pt. 2 *entitled* Janet at Oxford.] Oxf., 1917, 8°. 360 pp. 25611 e. 5673
— [Other editions.]

4846.5. HERMANT, A., L'aube ardente. Par., 1919, 8°. 314 pp. B.M.

4847. HOPKINS, G. W. S., City in the foreground, a novel. Lond., (1921), 8°. 318 pp. 25612 e. 56

4848. NICHOLS, B., Patchwork. Lond., 1921, 8°. 305 pp. 25612 e. 498

4849. BURFORD, F. R., Forty years off. Oxf., 1922, 8°. 98 pp. 25612 e. 1253

4850. MILES, H., and MORTIMER, R., The Oxford circus, a novel of Oxford and youth by the late Alfred Budd, ed. by H. Miles and R. Mortimer. Lond., 1922, 8°. 242 pp. 25612 e. 1574

4851. BLOOMFIELD, P., Most loving mere folly. Lond., [1923], 8°. 320 pp.

25612 e. 2050

4852. BRITTAIN, V., Dark tide. Lond., 1923, 8°. 320 pp.   25612 e. 2354

4853. SELIGMAN, V. J., Oxford oddities. Lond., 1923, 8°. 219 pp.
25612 e. 1850

4854. FAYARD, J., Oxford et Margaret. Par., 1924, 8°. 283 pp. Don. e. 729
— Tr. by L. Golding. Lond., 1925, 8°. 304 pp.   Fic. 27526 e. 342

4855. ALLEN, SIR C. K., The judgement of Paris. Lond., 1924, 8°. 305 pp.
25612 e. 4029

4856. CHILDERS, J. S., Laurel and straw. Lond., 1927, 8°. 314 pp.
25612 e. 7306

4857. GIBBS, P., The age of reason. Lond. &c., 1928, 8°. 288 pp.
25612 e. 8489

4858. HAYNES, R., Neapolitan ice. Lond., 1928, 8°. 296 pp. 25612 e. 8592

4859. WINTER, K., Other man's saucer. Lond., 1930, 8°. 331 pp.
25612 e. 11855

4860. PAKENHAM, CHRISTINE, *countess of Longford*, Making conversation, by Christine Longford. Lond., 1931, 8°. 288 pp. 25613 e. 1221

4861. WALLACE, D., A little learning. Lond., [1931], 8°. 288 pp.
25613 e. 722

4862. CANNAN, J., High table. Lond., 1931, 8°. 255 pp.   25613 e. 29
— [Other editions.]

4863. MORLEY, C. D., John Mistletoe [p. 64–82 relate to Oxford University in 1910]. Lond., 1931, 8°.   25613 e. 1049

4864. CANNAN, J., Snow in harvest. Lond., 1932, 8°. 314 pp.
25613 e. 3015

4865. LEAN, E. T., Storm in Oxford, a fantasy. Lond., 1932, 8°. 300 pp.
25613 e. 2951

4866. MASTERMAN, J. C., An Oxford tragedy. Lond., 1933, 8°. 286 pp.
25613 e. 3851

4867. RUMBOLD, R., Little victims. Lond., 1933, 8°. 266 pp.
25613 e. 4100

4868. MORRAH, D., The mummy case mystery. Lond., 1933, 8°. 308 pp.
25613 e. 3172

4869. FRAZER, SHAMUS, Acorned hog. Lond., 1933, 8°. 296 pp.
25613 e. 3909
[Other editions.]

4870. MITCHISON, N., We have been warned. Lond., 1935, 8°. 553 pp.
254392 e. 45

4871. SAYERS, D., Gaudy night. Lond., 1935, 8°. 483 pp. 25613 e. 8958

4872. TEGEN, G., Vägen över Oxford. Uppsala, 1935. 246 pp.
Fic. 27877 e. 123

4873. COLE, G. D. H., Disgrace to the college, by G. D. H. & M. Cole. Lond., 1937, 8°. 127 pp. 25613 e. 12213

4874. WALLACE, D., The time of wild roses. Lond., 1938, 8°. 446 pp. 25613 e. 13518

4875. LIDDELL, R., The almond tree. Lond., 1938, 8°. 285 pp. 25613 e. 14092

4876. GOUDGE, E., Towers in the mist. New York, 1938, 8°. 444 pp. 25434 e. 483

4877. COLE, G. D. H., Off with her head, by G. D. H. & M. Cole. Lond., 1938, 8°. 252 pp. 25613 e. 14929

4878. CANNAN, J., Princes in the land. Lond., 1938, 8°. 288 pp. 25613 e. 13950

4879. KNOX, R. A., Let dons delight, being variations on a theme in an Oxford common-room. Lond., 1939, 8°. 280 pp. 27001 e. 1395

4879.5. HUDSON, D., An Oxford dialogue, and other papers, by D. H. Oxf., 1940, 8°. 32 pp. 25613 e. 15867 (4)

4880. KENNINGTON, A., Murder, M.A. Lond., [1941], 8°. 224 pp. 25614 e. 311

4881. WILSON, GERALD H. TYRWHITT-, 9th baron Berners, Far from the madding war. Lond., 1941, 8°. 193 pp. 25614 e. 376

4882. STACPOOLE, H. DE V., An American at Oxford. Lond. &c., [1941], 8°. 223 pp. 25614 e. 626

4883. STACPOOLE, H. DE V., Oxford goes to war. Lond. &c., [1943], 8°. 160 pp. 25614 e. 2320

4884. MONTGOMERY, R. B., The case of the gilded fly, by Edmund Crispin. Lond., 1944, 8°. 159 pp. 25614 e. 2676
— [Another ed. entitled] Obsequies at Oxford. 1st ed. (Main line mysteries.) Phila., 1945, 8°. 208 pp. L. of C.

4885. COSTAIN, T. B., The black rose. New York, 1945, 8°. L. of C.
— [Another ed.] Lond., 1947, 8°. 383 pp. 25432 e. 302
— [Other editions.]

4886. MURRAY, D. L., Folly bridge. [A novel of 18th-century Oxford.] Lond., 1945, 8°. 335 pp. 25438 e. 587

4887. WAUGH, E., Brideshead revisited. Lond., 1945, 8°. 304 pp. 25614 e. 3685
— [Other editions.]

4888. HARRISON, P., Oxford marmalade. Lond., 1946, 8°. 310 pp. 25614 e. 5289

4889. HARTLEY, L. P., The sixth heaven. Lond., 1946, 8°. 234 pp.
25614 e. 5356

4890. MONTGOMERY, R. B., The moving toyshop, a detective story by Edmund Crispin. Lond., 1946, 8°. 151 pp. 25614 e. 5439

4891. LARKIN, P., Jill. [A novel concerning the education at Oxford of a north-country boy.] Lond., 1946, 8°. 200 pp. 25614 e. 11133

4892. MONTGOMERY, R. B., Swan song, by Edmund Crispin. Lond., 1947, 8°. 189 pp. 25614 e. 6127

4893. MACINNES, H., Friends and lovers. Lond. &c., 1948, 8°. 336 pp.
25614 e. 8104

4894. LIDDELL, R., The last enchantments. Lond., 1948, 8°. 221 pp.
25614 e. 7583

4895. KENNINGTON, A., Pastures new. Lond. &c., [1948], 8°. 223 pp.
25614 e. 6735

4896. MORGAN, W. G. C., An Oxford romance. (A cinematic comedy-drama.) Carmarthen, 1948, 8°. 72 pp. 25614 e. 9444 (4)

4897. MAIS, S. P. B., Who dies? Lond. &c., [1949], 8°. 287 pp.
25614 e. 8269

4898. MAIS, S. P. B., I loved you once. Lond. &c., [1950], 8°. 192 pp.
25614 e. 9728

4899. STEWART, J. I. M., Operation pax, by Michael Innes. Lond., 1951, 8°. 304 pp. 25615 e. 946
— [Another ed. *entitled*] The paper thunderbolt. New York, 1951.

4900. FARRER, K., The missing link. Lond., 1952, 8°. 250 pp.
25615 e. 1848

4901. HOFF, H. S., The struggles of Albert Woods, by William Cooper. Lond., 1952, 8°. 255 pp. 25615 e. 2215

4902. ATIYAH, E., Black vanguard. Lond., 1952, 8°. 288 pp.
25615 e. 2267

4903. HSUING, D., Flowering exile. Lond., 1952, 8°. 288 pp.
25615 e. 2840

4904. BALSDON, D., Freshman's folly. Lond., 1952, 8°. 222 pp.
25615 e. 2084

4904.1. STEWART, J. I. M., The guardians. Lond., 1955, 8°. 253 pp.
25615 e. 7105

4905. HALE, J., A backward glance. (Twentieth century, 1955, vol. 157, p. 522–29.) Per. 3977 d. 66

4906. ROBINSON, R., Landscape with dead dons. Lond. &c., 1956, 8°. 200 pp. 25615 e. 7952

4907. MCINTOSH, L., Oxford folly. Lond., 1956, 8°. 254 pp.
25615 e. 8282

4908. JAMESON, S., A cup of tea for mr. Thorgill. Lond., 1957, 8°. 300 pp.
25615 e. 10413

4908.5. AVERY, G., The warden's niece. Lond., 1957, 8°. 255 pp.
254391 e. 566

4909. GOODMAN, G. J. W., A time for Paris. [Lond.], 1958, 8°. 239 pp.
25615 e. 11808

4910. JONES, D. A. N., Parade in Pairs. [Lond.], 1958, 8°. 190 pp.
25615 e. 11713

4911. SAYERS, D. L., Murder at Pentecost [college]. (A treasury of Sayers
stories, 1958, p. 102–11.)   25612 e. 13297

4911.5. AVERY, G., The elephant war. Lond., 1960, 8°. 256 pp.
254391 e. 594

4912. BUTLER, G., Death lives next door. Lond., 1960, 8°. 192 pp.
25615 e. 13897

4913. MITCHELL, J., Imaginary toys. Lond., 1961, 8°. 207 pp.
1914   25616 e. 317

4915. ROBINSON, T., When scholars fall. Lond. &c., 1961, 8°. 224 pp.
25616 e. 792

4916. SPENCER, P., Full term. Lond., 1961, 8°. 192 pp.   25616 e. 950

4917. BALSDON, D., The day they burned Miss Termag. Lond., 1961, 8°.
251 pp.   254399 e. 913

4918. DAY, L., The looker in. Lond., 1961, 8°. 253 pp.   25616 e. 977

4919. BUCHAN, S. C., baroness Tweedsmuir, A stone in the pool. Lond.,
1961, 8°. 222 pp.   254391 e. 586

4919.1. SHEED, W. J., A middle class education. Lond., 1961, 8°. 387 pp.
25616 e. 199

4919.5. BUTLER, G., Coffin in Oxford. Lond., 1962, 8°. 192 pp.
25616 e. 1742

4919.6. SMITH, M. L., No easy answer. Lond., 1962, 8°. 224 pp.
25616 e. 2027

4919.61. KENNAWAY, J., The mind benders. Lond., 1963, 8°. 158 pp.
25616 e. 2976

4919.611. STEWART, J. I. M, The last Tresilians. Lond., 1963, 8°. 384 pp.
25616 e. 3444

4919.62. TURNER, J., The long avenues. Lond., 1964, 8°. 216 pp.
25616 e. 4200

4919.621. FORSTER, M., Dames' delight. Lond., 1964, 8°. 220 pp.
25616 e. 4275

4919.63. FLEMING, J., Nothing is the number when you die. Lond., 1965,
8°. 192 pp.   25616 e. 5536

4919.64. TRICKETT, R., The elders. [A novel about the election of a Professor of Poetry.] Lond., 1966, 8°. 272 pp.   25616 e. 6952

SATIRES AND FACETIAE

For verses &c. issued for the Encaenia (but not by the Terrae Filius) see Act
or Encaenia [no. 1236, &c.].

4920. DANVERS, A., Academia: or, The humours of the University of
Oxford, in burlesque verse. Lond., 1691, 4°. 67 pp. Gough Oxf. 59 (4)
— [Another ed.] 1716. 8°. 42 pp. [Anon.].   G.A. Oxon 8° 926
— [Another ed.] 1730.   12 θ 1636

4921. BAKER, T., An act at Oxford, a comedy, by the author of the Yeoman
o' Kent. Lond., 1704, 4°. 60 pp.   Mal. 92 (2)

4922. The university ballad, or, The Church's advice to her two daughters,
Oxford and Cambridge. n. pl., [1705], s. sh.   Antiq. b. E. 9 (24)

4923. The university answer to the pretended University ballad. Lond.,
1705, s. sh.   Antiq. b. E. 9 (25)

4924. HARDING, S., This ode on the coffee-house conversation is humbly
presented to all . . . gentlemen of the University. n. pl., [17—], s. sh.
MS. Top. Oxon d. 281 (194)

4925. Æsop at Oxford: or, A few select fables in verse, under the following
heads, viz. Æsop matriculated [p. 1–3] . . . The conclusion [p. 71–76,
in which many colleges are satirized]. Lond., 1709, 8°.   Douce T 168

4926. The servitour, a poem written by a servitour. Lond., 1709, 8°. 16 pp.
G.A. Oxon 8° 39

4927. The commoner, a poem [signed Incognito]. Lond., 1710, 8°. 14 pp.
G. Pamph. 1610 (1)

4928. EVANS, A., Magdalen grove: or, A dialogue between the doctor
[Sacheverel] and the devil. [By A. Evans. In verse.] Lond., [c. 1713],
8°. 22 pp.   G. Pamph. 1267 (5)

4929. The university miscellany: or, More burning work for the
Ox - - f - - - d convocation, containing i. The two speeches spoken
in the Theatre at the publick act, 1703. ii. Ox - - f - - - d intrigues;
a lampoon . . . iv. The players epilogue . . . Lond., 1713, 8°. 27 pp.
Vet. A 4 e. 1162 (1)
— 2nd ed. 28 pp.   G.A. Oxon 8° 59 (2)

4930. The Oxford packet, containing, i. News from Magdalen college.
ii. Antigamus: or, a satire against marriage, by Thomas Sawyer.

iii. A vindication [in verse] of the Oxford ladies, wherein are displayed the amours of some gentlemen of All Souls and St. John's colleges. Lond., 1714, 8°. 30 pp.　　　　G.A. Oxon 8° 59 (3)

4931. DRY, J., Merton walks, or, The Oxford beauties, a poem [by J. Dry]. Oxf., 1717, 8°. 31 pp.　　　　G.A. Oxon 8° 47

4932. AMHURST, N., Strephon's revenge: a satire on the Oxford toasts, inscrib'd to the author of Merton walks. [By N. Amhurst. In verse.]
Lond., 1718, 8°. 47 pp.　　　　Gough Oxf. 113 (8)
— 2nd ed. 1718. 52 pp.　　　　G.A. Oxon 8° 926 (7)
— 3rd ed. 1720.　　　　G.A. Oxon 8° 61 (5)
— 4th ed. 1724. 54 pp.　　　　Gough Oxf. 59 (1)

4933. The Oxford criticks, a satire [in verse]. Lond., 1719, 8°. 17 pp.
G.A. Oxon 8° 59 (6)

4934. Eubulus Oxoniensis discipulis suis, being an imitation of the ... Qui mihi [by W. Map] in praise of drunkenness. In Lat. and Engl. Lond., 1720, 8°. viii+8+8 pp.　　　　G.A. Oxon 8° 926 (9)

See 5229, 5230 [Terrae filius. 1721, 1763].

4935. MILLER, J., The humours of Oxford, a comedy by a gentleman of Wadham-college [J. Miller]. Lond., 1730, 8°. [vi]+83 pp.
Gough Oxf. 59 (7)
— 2nd ed. Lond., 1730, 8°. [vi]+83 pp.　　G.A. Oxon 8° 926 (10)
— [Another ed.] Dubl., 1730, 12°.　　　　M. adds. 108 e. 63 (9)

4936. Alma mater: a satirical poem by a gentleman of New Inn Hall. Lond., 1733, 4°. 36 pp.　　　　Gough Oxf. 90 (16)

4937. The intrigue, a college eclogue by a gentleman of Oxford. Lond., 1750, 4°. 14 pp.　　　　G.A. Oxon 4° 177

4938. Modius salium. A collection of such pieces of humour . . . as prevail'd at Oxford in the time of mr. Anthony à Wood, collected by himself . . . Oxf., 1715, 12°. 36 pp.　　　　Douce W 102

See 298 [A companion to the guide and a guide to the companion. [Humorous comments on the Oxford Guide]. c. 1760].

4939. The Oxford sausage: or, Select poetical pieces written by the most celebrated wits of the University of Oxford. Adorned with cuts. [Ed. by T. Warton.] Lond., 1764, 8°. 203 pp.　　　　2805 f. 14
— [Another ed. Without cuts.] Dubl., 1766, 8°. 190 pp.　　2805 f. 41
— New ed. Oxf. &c., 1772, 8°. 224 pp.　　　　Gough Oxf. 19
[Other eds. in 1777, [177–?], [c. 1800], 1804, 14, 15, 21, 22.]

4940. MAURICE, T., The Oxonian, a poem by the author of the Schoolboy [T. Maurice]. Oxf., 1778, 4°. 18 pp.　　　　Gough Oxf. 90 (17)

4941. Advice to the universities of Oxford and Cambridge. Lond., 1783, 8°. 67 pp.　　　　2625 f. 3
— 2nd ed. 1783. 105 pp.　　　　Vet. A 5 f. 407

4942. POLWHELE, R., The follies of Oxford: or, Cursory sketches on a University education, from an undergraduate to his friend in the country. [By R. Polwhele. In verse.] Lond., 1785, 4°. 40 pp.

G.A. Oxon 4° 13 (14)

4943. Occasional report of the Society for the suppression of vice. No. VI. [At p. 10, 11 is a note by an Oxford humorist, which the Society took seriously, on the pretended establishment of an Oxford branch of the Society, with details of the proceedings of a general meeting purported to have been held on 6 March 1812.] (Lond., 1812), 4°.

G.A. Oxon 4° 276 (10)

4944. An address to the literary members of the University, by counsellor Bickerton. Oxf., 1816, 8°. 19 pp.   G.A. Oxon 8° 1025 (5)

4945.

4946. The epigrammatique garlande. [Oxf.], 1818, 4°.   Arch. AA d. 7 (2)

4947. BOONE, J. S., The Oxford spy; a dialogue in verse [by J. S. Boone]. Oxf., 1818, 8°. 22 pp.   G.A. Oxon 8° 230 (1)
— 2nd ed. 1818.   G.A. Oxon 8° 230 (2)
— 3rd ed. 1818.   G.A. Oxon 8° 230 (7)
— [Another] 3rd ed. 1818. 24 pp.   G.A. Oxon 8° 1345 (1)

4948. BOONE, J. S., The Oxford spy; in verse [by J. S. Boone]. Dialogue the second. Oxf., 1818, 8°. 23 pp.   G.A. Oxon 8° 230 (3)
— 3rd ed. 1818.   G.A. Oxon 8° 230 (8)
— [Another ed. Wanting title. 1818?] 28 pp.   G.A. Oxon 8° 1345 (2)

4949. BOONE, J. S., The Oxford spy; in verse [by J. S. Boone]. Dialogue the third. Oxf., 1818, 8°. 30 pp.   G.A. Oxon 8° 230 (4)
— 2nd ed. 1818.   G.A. Oxon 8° 230 (9)
— 3rd ed. 1818. 32 pp.   G.A. Oxon 8° 1345 (3)

4950. BOONE, J. S., The Oxford spy; in verse [by J. S. Boone]. Dialogue the fourth. Oxf., 1818, 8°. 31 pp.   G.A. Oxon 8° 230 (5)
— 2nd ed. 1818.   G.A. Oxon 8° 230 (10)
— [Another] 2nd ed. 1818. 32 pp.   G.A. Oxon 8° 1345 (4)

4951. BOONE, J. S., An appendix to The Oxford spy [by J. S. Boone]. Oxf., 1818, 8°. 32 pp.   G.A. Oxon 8° 230 (11)

4952. BOONE, J. S., The Oxford spy [by J. S. Boone] in four dialogues. 4th ed. Oxf., 1819, 16°. 159 pp.   G.A. Oxon 16° 75 (1)

4953. BOONE, J. S., The Oxford spy; in verse [by J. S. Boone]. Dialogue the fifth. Oxf., 1819, 8°. 79 pp.   G.A. Oxon 8° 230 (6)
— [Another issue.]   G.A. Oxon 8° 1345 (5)

4953.1. HERBERT, H. J. G., 3rd earl of Carnarvon, A letter [by the earl of Carnarvon, in answer] to the Oxford spy, from the bigwig's friend. [In verse.] Oxf., 1818, 8°. 23 pp.   G.A. Oxon 8° 219 (11)
2nd ed. 1818.   G.A. Oxon 16° 75 (2)

4954. COTTON, H., Eruditis Oxoniæ amantibus salutem. [A squib, by
H. Cotton.] Oxon., (1819), 8°. 4 pp.   G.A. Oxon b. 19
— [Another ed., *entitled*] Ex Academia Oxoniensi deducta quædam
argumenta, perutilia et perjucunda. (The Crypt, 1829, N.S., vol. 1,
pt. 1, p. 150–54.)   Hope 8° 285

4955. JOHNSON, A., Oxford pastorals [by A. Johnson]. Oxf., 1819, 8°. 11
pp.   G. Pamph. 2675 (2)

4956. Fit ut omnis Votiva pateat veluti descripta tabella Vita. Oxford in
epitome. [A satirical map.] [Oxf.], 1819, s. sh.   G.A. Oxon b. 145
— 2nd ed. [with letterpress]. Oxf., 1832, s. sh.   G.A. Oxon b. 145

4957. Oxford aphrodisiacal licenses, by Peter Marvell. Oxf., 1821, 4°. 16
pp.   G.A. Oxon 4° 119 (9)

4958. Oxford, a eulogistic satire, by a member of the University. Oxf.,
1823, 8°. 47 pp.   G.A. Oxon 8° 270

4959. COX, G., Black gowns & red coats, or, Oxford in 1834, a satire [in
verse, by G. Cox]. 6 pt. Lond., 1834, 8°.   280 e. 3452
— [Another ed. Pt. 2 and 3 are of the 2nd ed.] 1834.   34. 729

4960. CASWALL, E., A new art teaching how to be plucked, a treatise . . .
for the use of students in the University, by Scriblerus redivivus. Oxf.,
1835, 12°. viii+39 pp.   B.M.
— 2nd ed. 1835.   2706 f. 18 (1)
— 3rd ed. 1835; 5th ed. 1836; 6th ed. 1836; 7th ed. 1837; 8th ed. 1843;
9th ed. 1851; 11th ed. 1864; 12th ed. 1874; New ed. 1893; 270 f. 999.

4961. GOOCH, R., Oxford and Cambridge nuts to crack, by the author of
Facetiæ Cantabrigienses [R. Gooch]. 2nd ed. Lond., 1835, 8°. 270 pp.
                                                    2706 e. 306

4962. CASWALL, E., Pluck examination papers for candidates at Oxford
and Cambridge in 1836. To which is added a synchronological table of
the principal historical events at Oxford and Cambridge for the last
four years. By Scriblerus redivivus. Oxf., 1836, 12°. 48 pp.
                                            G.A. Oxon 8° 1056 (11)
— 2nd ed., 1836.   G.A. Oxon 8° 204 (14)
— 3rd ed., 1836.   G.A. Oxon 8° 232 (13)
— 12th ed. 1874. 62 pp.   G.A. Oxon 8° 286 (1)

4963. The rime of the new-made baccalere [by J. T. B. Landon?]. Oxf.,
1841, 8°. 31 pp.   G.A. Oxon 8° 1000 (1)
— [Another ed.] 1867.   G.A. Oxon 8° 286 (5)

4964. Martin's vagaries; a sequel to 'A tale of a tub' recently discovered at
Oxford, ed. with notes by Scriblerus Oxoniensis [R. H. Barham?].
Lond., 1843, 8°. 48 pp.   G.A. Oxon 8° 131

4965. COLERIDGE, J. D., *baron*, Memorials of Oxford. [Verses by J. D.
Coleridge.] Oxf., 1844, 32°.   B.M.

4966. PHILOFUNNICULUS, *pseud.*, A new Oxford sausage. Lond., 1844,
8°. 34 pp.   G.A. Oxon 8° 204 (13)

4967. NEMO, *pseud.*, The devil's return from Oxford. [In verse.] Oxf.,
1847, 8°. 13 pp.   47. 1409 (2)

4968. PHOSPHORUS SQUILL, *pseud.*, The devil at Oxford, being a true
and faithful account of a visit recently paid by his satanic majesty . . .
[In verse.] Oxf., 1847, 8°. 27 pp.   47. 1409 (1)

4969. MANSEL, H. L., Scenes from an unfinished drama, entitled Phrontisterion, or, Oxford on the 19th century [by H. L. Mansel]. 2nd ed. Oxf.
&c., 1852, 8°. 24 pp.   M. adds. 109 e. 438
— 3rd ed. 1852.   M. adds. 109 e. 438
— 4th ed. 1852.   M. adds. 109 e. 438
— 5th ed. 1861.   M. adds. 109 e. 438
— 6th ed. 1867.   M. adds. 109 e. 438
— [Repr. in no. 5003, Three Oxford ironies, 1927.]   2704 f. 6

4970. The siege of Oxford; fragments from the second book of the 'Nova
Æneis'. Oxf., 1852, 8°. 7 pp.   280 s. 341 (9)

4971. MURRAY, G., The Oxford ars poetica: or, How to write a Newdigate
[by G. Murray]. Oxf., 1853, 8°. 38 pp.   G.A. Oxon 8° 135 (2)
— [Another ed. 1853?].   280 f. 2492
— [Repr. in no. 5003, Three Oxford ironies. 1927.]   2704 f. 6

4972. MERRY, W. W., A laye concerning ye greate goe, by a member of the
University [attrib. to W. W. Merry]. Oxf., 1855, 8°. 8 pp.
                        280 e. 3437 (14)
— [Revised ed., *entitled*] Lars Porsenna.   280 e. 2346 (7)
— [Another ed. 1899?]   280 e. 2938 (14)

4973. The student's guide to the school of 'litteræ fictitiæ', commonly
called novel-literature. [Probably written jointly by H. E. Tweed and
T. E. Brown.] Oxf., 1855, 8°. 34 pp.   G.A. Oxon 8° 63 (17)
— 2nd ed. 1855.   G.A. Oxon 8° 250 (19)

4974. The Oxford wit. Oxf., 1855, 8°. 31 pp.   G.A. Oxon 8° 1012 (6)

4975. Weeds from the Isis, a miscellany of prose and verse by a few
Oxonians, ed. by Vaughan Dayrell [i.e. W. S. Austin]. Lond., 1866,
8°. 153 pp.   2705 f. 19 (2)

See 4410 [Mottoes for crackers. 1857].

4976. King Alfred contemplating Oxford at the present day. (A rejected
Newdigate in 3 fyttes.) Oxf., 1859, 8°. 40 pp.   G.A. Oxon 8° 135 (5)

4977. Tournaments holden at Oxford, by an old Oxonian. (Boy's own vol.,
1863, p. 151–56.)   G.A. Oxon 4° 579 (13)

4978. SOLON SECUNDUS, *pseud.*, A letter to professor R***** [J. E. T.
Rogers] containing a scheme for a seisachtheia, or modern Solonian
debt-relief law, to be applied to the undergraduates of the University of
Oxford. [A satire.] Oxf., 1863, 8°. 13 pp.   G.A. Oxon 8° 909

4978.5. An epistle to a professor on the characters of dons: by an Oxford
undergraduate [J. H. Williams. In verse.] Oxf., [*c.* 1870], 8°. 12 pp.
                      G.A. Oxon 8° 1449

4979. The Oxford undergraduate zoologically considered, by 'F.' [squib].
Oxf., [1873], 8°. 8 pp.   G.A. Oxon 8° 220 (8)

4980. A German view of Oxford, a letter from Herman Gottlob, Ph.D.
(St. Paul's mag., 1873, vol. 12, p. 664–74.)   G.A. Oxon 4° 581 (6)

4981. TRAILL, W. F., Lays of modern Oxford, by Adon. Lond., 1874, 8°
127 pp.   280 i. 157
— New ed. Oxf. &c., 1887, 8°. 133 pp.   280 e. 2987

4982. Juvenal in Oxford. [In verse.] Oxf., [1875], 8°. 15 pp.
                                G.A. Oxon 8° 412

4983. Town and gown in pre-historic time, a parody on Macaulay's Battle
of the Lake Regillus, by the author of 'Ch. Ch. besieged'. Oxf., 1877,
8°. 22 pp.   G.A. Oxon 8° 1056 (12)

4984. HATCH, E., Abracadabra, a fragment of University history. [A satire
by E. Hatch.] Oxf., 1877, 8°. 18 pp.   G.A. Oxon 8° 761 (5)

4985.

4986. HILL, L. B., Old saints and new demons [by L. B. Hill]. Oxf. &c.,
1886, 8°. 38 pp.   G.A. Oxon 8° 444

4987. Down with the dons! The manifesto of the Oxford undergraduate
revolutionary committee. [Oxf., 1886], 8°. 4 pp.   G.A. Oxon b. 145

4988. LANG, A., and POLLOCK, W. H., He, by the author of It. [A parody of
Rider Haggard's She, by A. Lang and W. H. Pollock. Part of the novel
is a jeu d'esprit on Oxford.] Lond., 1887, 8°. 119 pp.   256 f. 463

4989. Down with the dons! 2nd series. Manifesto of the Oxford undergraduate revolutionary league. [Concerns the sending down of the hon.
L. J. Bathurst by New college in Nov. 1888, for his connexion with the
magazine The Undergraduate.] n. pl., [1888], 8°. 3 pp.
                            G.A. Oxon c. 282 (f. 9)

4990. PIGOTT, M. T., Common-room carols, and other verses and parodies
by M. T. P. Oxf. &c., 1893, 12°. 122 pp.   280 e. 1294

4991. PIGOTT, M. T., Two on a tour, and other papers from The Isis [in-
cluding Garbage; Oxford types; The Freshman's dictionary; Dons I
have dreamt about]. Oxf. &c., 1895, 12°. 200 pp.   270 f. 1009

4992. Giddy Oxon, an Eights week dialogue, and other pieces. Oxf., 1895,
16°. 47 pp.   G.A. Oxon 16° 102

4993. ROBERTSON, C. G., Voces academicæ. [Sketches of Oxford life.]
Lond., 1898, 12°. 266 pp.   270 f. 1021

4994. Nugæ sacræ et philosophicæ, by some members of a common room.
Oxf., 1905, 8°. 27 pp.   G.A. Oxon 8° 1012 (10)

4995. The Oxford revolution of 1906, by a British workman. [An allusion
to Herbert Jackson, who was so nick-named.] Extracts from the note-
book of an M.A., edited (un-expurgated) by Mods. Oxf. &c., [1906], 8°.
16 pp.   2561 f. 132

4996. Cap and gown. Varsity humours, by Graham Hoggarth and others. Oxf. &c., (1906), 4°. 42 pp.   G.A. Oxon 4° 219 (16)

4997. CALDECOTT, A., Oxford, a satire [in verse, by A. Caldecott]. Oxf., 1907, 8°. 16 pp.   28001 e. 631 (3)

4998. HOARE, J. E., Iuvenes dum sumus. [Verses on Oxford] by J. E. H. Oxf. &c., 1909, 8°. 64 pp.   28001 e. 708

4999. MONFRIES, J. D. C., Ye Oxford booke of drivel. Oxf., 1914.

5000. HENREY, T. S., ed., Good stories from Oxford and Cambridge. Lond., 1918, 8°. 255 pp.   2706 e. 197
— Enlarged eds. in 1922, 24, 31.   2706 e. 210, 222, 267

5001. LEACOCK, S., Oxford as I see it. (Harper's mag., 1922, vol. 144, p. 738–45.)   Per. 2714 d. 25
[Also publ. in Leacock Roundabout, 1946.]

5002. GODLEY, A. D., Fifty poems, ed. C. L. Graves and C. R. L. Fletcher. Lond., 1927, 8°. 125 pp.   280 e. 3130

5003. Three Oxford ironies, being Copleston's Advice to a young reviewer; Mansel's Phrontisterion, or Oxford in the nineteenth century; and The Oxford ars poetica [by G. Murray]. Ed. by G. Gordon. Lond., 1927, 12°. 172 pp.   2704 f. 6

5004. MCCORD, D., Oxford nearly visited, a fantasy [in verse.] Privately pr. [in Fell types] for the Cygnet Press of Cambr., Mass. by the Univ. Press, Oxf., 1929, 4°. 13 pp.   O.U.P.

5005. CORBETT, M., Oxford inflated. (Oxf. mag., 1931, vol. 50, p. 95, 96.)   Per. G.A. Oxon 4° 141

5006. Excerpta academica [jeux d'esprit]. (Oxf. mag., 1933, vol. 52, p. 60, 61; 98–100; 135; 177; 256; 292, 93; 1934, 331; 395; 427, 28; 526.)
— Excerpta selecta (partim academica). (Oxf. mag., 1934, vol. 52, p. 762; 797.)   Per. G.A. Oxon 4° 141

5007. Excerpta academica. Repr. from the Oxford magazine. [Selections from no. 5006 by] F. Madan. Oxf., 1934, 8°. 40 pp.   G.A. Oxon 8° 1132 (20)

5008. MASCALL, E. L., Pi in the High [verses]. Lond. &c., 1959, 8°. 63 pp.   28001 d. 762

5009. Oxford university hide and seek club. [Notification of annual outing, 1921.]   G.A. Oxon b. 147 (67)

Terrae Filius

See also 1236, &c., Act.

5010. HARMAR, J., Oratio steliteutica Oxoniæ habita Octobris 14° . . . MDCLVII; sive Stricturæ in hujus ævi delatores & pasquillos, & in Terræ filios, (quos vocant) . . . elisæ . . . [Madan 2365.] Lond., 1658, 12°. 32 pp.   Wood 62 (4)

5011. WILLES, SIR J., The speech that was intended to have been spoken by the Terræ-filius, July 13, had not his mouth been stopp'd by the V. Ch—r [by sir J. Willes]. Lond., 1713, 8°. 30 pp.

G.A. Oxon 8° 59 (1)

See 5229 [Amhurst, N., Terrae filius. 1721].

5012. The Terræ filius's speech as it was to have been spoken at the publick act. Lond., 1733, 8°. 27 pp.　　　　　G.A. Oxon 8° 61 (3)
— 4th ed. 1733. 27 pp.　　　　　　　　Gough Oxf. 59 (3)

5013. The Oxford toast's answer to the Terræ filius's speech. Lond., 1733, 8°. 24 pp.　　　　　　　　　　　　G.A. Oxon 8° 61 (4)

See 5230 [Colman, G., the elder. Terrae-filius. 1763].

5014. SMITH, B., and EHNINGER, D., The terrafilial disputations at Oxford. (Quart. journ. of speech, 1950, vol. 36, p. 333-39.)

G.A. Oxon 4° 821

COLLEGE SERVANTS

5015. Reasons why the 'claim of privilege, and exemption from serving in the militia, of the matriculated servants of scholars, and other matriculated persons in the University of Oxford' should not be allowed; in reply to a paper published last Tuesday. [Oxf.], (1778), fol. 3 pp.

G.A. Oxon b. 19

See 3816 [College servants. 1825].

5016. College scouts, by one of themselves. (Belgravia, 1873, vol. 20, p. 64-68.)　　　　　　　　　　　　Per. 256 d. 254

5017. College servants' benefit society. Articles. Oxf., 1849, 8°. 16 pp.

G.A. Oxon 8° 124 (2)

5018. The College servants' provident institution. Oxf., 1841, 8°. 16 pp.

G.A. Oxon 8° 161 (8)

5019. College servants' provident institution. [Report of foundation, &c.] n. pl., [1841], s. sh.　　　　　　　　G.A. Oxon c. 57 (143)
— Rules and regulations. Oxf., 1841, 8°. 16 pp.

G.A. Oxon c. 57 (145)

5020. College servants' provident institution. Report 1841/42–46/47, 83, 85–87. Oxf., 1842–(88), s. sh.　　　　　G.A. Oxon c. 14

5021. The College servants' provident institution. Oxf., 1850, 8°. 15 pp.

G.A. Oxon 8° 1002 (4)

5022. Oxford college servants' provident institution. Trustees' report upon the proposed transfer to the Legal and general life assurance society. n. pl., 1889, 4°. 4 pp.　　　　　　　　G.A. Oxon c. 14

5023. Oxford and Cambridge college servants. Visit . . . to Cambridge, July 15th, 1850. n. pl., 1850, s. sh.　　　G.A. Oxon b. 113 (60)

See 7338, &c. [Exeter college servants, J. Nutt, T. Hewlett. 1859, 62].

5024. Oxford college servants' society. Rules, regulations and annual report. 1879. Oxf., 1879, 8°. 8 pp.   G.A. Oxon 8° 208

5025. Oxford college servants' society. Rules, regulations [*afterw.* List of members] and Annual report (and balance sheet). 1876–1915. Oxf., 1876–[1916], 8°.   Per. G.A. Oxon 4° 342

5026. Oxford college servants' society. [Miscellaneous papers. 1887–1910.]
                                                     G.A. Oxon 4° 605

5027. CLAYTON, H. E., 'The master & the servant', or, The college servants' Sunday, a sermon. (Oxf., 1892), 8°. 12 pp.
                                              G.A. Oxon 8° 705 (18)

   See 8592 [Bickerton, F., Fred of Oxford. 1953].

   See 8593 [Collett, F., From the porter's lodge and buttery. 1951].

5028. Oxford university and college servants' rowing club. Centenary 1850 to 1950. [Reprod. from typewriting.] [Oxf., 1950], 4°. 18 pp.
                                                     38442 d. 27

University watermen

5029. Rules for the Oxford university watermen. [Oxf.], 1867, s. sh.
                                                     G.A. Oxon a. 17

5030. Rules for the Oxford university watermen. [Oxf.], 1887, s. sh.
                                                  G.A. Oxon c. 25 (8)

5031. [Letter from the Vice-chancellor asking for college contributions towards the cost of keeping a staff of watermen, and river stations for rescue purposes.] [Oxf.], (1914), s. sh.   G.A. Oxon b. 141 (97*e*)

ALMANACS

General

5032. The Oxford university diary, 1877. With an almanack. Oxf., 1877, 8°.   (Alm.) Oxon 8° 1040

5033. (Oxford) University pocket diary for the academical year 1897–8 (–). Oxf., [1897–], 16°.   G.A. Oxon 16° 54, 54*

5034. Terminal diary. Hilary term, 1903–Mich. term, 1935. Oxf., 1903–35, 16°.   G.A. Oxon 16° 94

5035. WORDSWORTH, C., *ed.*, The ancient kalendar of the University of Oxford, from documents of the 14th to the 17th century. Together with Computus manualis ad usum Oxoniensium, from C. Kyrfoth's edition, Oxon., 1519–20. (Oxf. hist. soc., 45.) Oxf., 1904, 8°. 293 pp.   G.A. Oxon 8° 360 = R.

The Oxford almanac

5036. A hue and cry after Good Friday, lost in the Oxford almanack. [A satirical ballad on 5037.] [Madan 2955.] [Lond.? 1672], s. sh.

5037. The Oxford almanack for . . . 1673 [by M. Wheeler]. [Madan 2957.] Oxf., 1673, 16°. 48 pp.   Arch. A f. 9
— [A folio sheet almanack was issued with the above, but no copy is known to survive. Madan 2958.]

5038. The Oxford almanack. 1674, 76– . [Madan 3297.] Oxf., 1674– , s. sh.   G.A. Oxon a. 88a–91
[An explanation, in MS., of the picture is added to many of the almanacks in this set in the Bodleian.]

5039. WALLIS, J., A treatise concerning St. Matthias day, misplaced in the Oxford Almanack for 1684 at Feb. 24. Publ from the orig. MS. [written in 1684]. Oxf., 1719, 12°. 28 pp.   8° O 35 (5) Linc.

5040. Hieroglyphica sacra Oxoniensia, being an explanation of the Christ-Church almanacks since the beginning of this century. [A burlesque description of the designs of the Oxford Almanacks for 1700–1702.] Lond., 1702, s. sh.   Vet. A 3 b. 23 (27)

5041. The Oxford almanack explained. Lond., 1706, s. sh.
    Vet. A 1 a. 3 (23)

5042. An explanation of the design of the Oxford almanack for . . . 1711. Lond., 1711, 8°. 29 pp.   G. Pamph. 1238 (2)

5043. The Oxford almanack of 1712, explain'd: or, The emblems of it unriddl'd. Together with some prefatory account of the emblems of the two preceding years. A letter. Lond., 1711, 8°. 24 pp.
    G. Pamph. 1238 (3)

5044. An explanation of the Oxford Almanack for . . . 1751. [Oxf., 1751],
s. sh.   G.A. Oxon a. 88a

5045. BUCKLER, B., A proper explanation of the Oxford almanack for this
present year 1755 [an election squib by B. Buckler]. Lond., 1755,
8°. 30 pp.   G.A. Oxon 8° 60 (9)

5046. An explanation of the picture over the calendar in the Oxford
almanack for . . . 1761. n. pl., (1761), s. sh.
                                        MS. Gough Oxon 17 (f. 25)

5047. Proposals for an issue by subscription of the prints of the Oxford
almanac [with some historical details]. Oxf., 1866, s. sh.
                                        G.A. Oxon c. 82 (382)

5048. A century and a half of designs engraved for the Oxford almanac for
the years 1716–1865. [Oxf., 1866], fol.   G.A. Oxon a. 92

5049. MADAN, F., On the Oxford almanacs. (Proc., Oxf. architect. and
hist. soc., 1882, N.S., vol. 4, p. 59–61, 64–66.)
                            Per. G.A. Oxon 8° 498 = R. Top.

5050. BELL, C. F., The Oxford almanacks. (Art journ., 1904, p. 241–47.)
                                        G.A. Oxon c. 108

5051. The Oxford almanack, 1674–1946, with an intr. by H. M. Petter.
New York, 1946, 4°. 56 pp.   G.A. Oxon 4° 639

*Other almanacs published at Oxford. We have attempted to record al-
manacks published at Oxford up to 1700.*

5052. RED, W., Almanach Ephemerides in anno domini M.d.vii. in
latitudo Oxonia . . . [Madan 23.] [Lond., 1507], 16°.   B.M.

5053. Almanacke for xii. yere . . . This almanacke and table . . . is calked
after the latytude of Oxenforde . . . in . . . M.CCCC. and viii. [Madan
24.] Lond., 1508, 16°.   Arch. A g. 19 (5)

5054. MOUNSLOWE, A., An almanacke and prognostication for . . . 1561
. . . referred to the meridiane of Oxforde. [Madan 44.] [Lond.? 1561?],
2 sheets.   Univ. libr., Cambridge
— [Another issue. 1579]. [See after Madan 44.]

5055. HILL, T., A newe almanack for . . . M.D.LXXII. calculated for the
meridian of Oxenforde. [Madan 49.] [Lond.?], 1572, fol.
                                        Merton coll., Oxford

5056. HILL, T., A true almanack for . . . M.D.LXXII. calculated for the
meridian of Oxenforde. [Madan 49*.] n. pl., [1572], s. sh.
                            [Fragments at B.M. and Merton.]

5057. HILL, T., A prognostication made for . . . 1572 . . . exactly calculated
for Oxenforde. [Madan 50.] Lond., (1572), 16°.
[The Bodleian copy is imperf.: Antiq. f. E. 1572. 2.]

5058. COWPER, T., Cowper 1637. An almanack . . . referred to . . . Oxford.
[Madan 842.] [Title page only in B.M.] Oxf., 1637, 12°.

5059. BOOKER, J., Almanack . . . anni M.DC.XXXVII. [Madan 848.]
Oxf., 1637, 16°. 48 pp.   Ashm. 69

5060. WYBERD, J., Synopsis . . . 1637. [Madan 869.] Oxf., 1637, 16°. 48 pp.
                                                          Ashm. 69

5061. WHARTON, SIR G., Naworth 1644, a new almanack . . . calculated
. . . for the latitude and meridian of . . . Oxford. [Madan 2060.] Oxf.,
[1644], 16°. 48 pp.   Douce A 638
— [Another ed.] Naworth 1645. [See after Madan 2060.] Oxf., [1645],
16°. 64 pp.   Ashm. 72

5062. WHARTON, SIR G., Wharton 1645. An almanack . . . referred . . . to
the latitude and meridian of Oxford . . . [Madan 2063.] Oxf., 1645, 16°.
48 pp.   Ashm. 76

5063. An almanack for . . . 1652. [Madan 3295.] Oxf., 1652, s. sh.
                                          St. John's coll., Oxford
— 1653.   Antiq. b. E. 1653. 1
— 1655.   Hertford coll., Oxford

5064. BURTON, W., An almanack for the yeare 1655. [Madan 2271.] Oxf.,
1655, 16°.   Alm. f. 1655. 1

5065. ABENDANA, I., The Oxford almanack for . . . 1692 [containing] The
Jewish kalendar [by I. Abendana]. Oxf., [1692], 8°. 48 pp. 8° Rawl. 698
— 1693, 94.   Alm. f. 1693. 1
— 1695, 96, 98.   Opp. adds. 12° 23b–d
— 1699.   MS. Top. Oxon f. 43

5065.1. ABRAHAMS, I., Isaac Abendana's Cambridge Mishnah and Oxford
calendars. (Trans., Jewish hist. soc. of Engl., 1915/17, vol. 8, p. 98–
121.)   Soc. 24559 d. 5

5066. The Oxford almanak for . . . 1703. Oxf., 1703, 12°. [50]+22 pp.
                                                   Gough Oxf. 31

5067. G., M., Mercurius Oxoniensis; or, The Oxford intelligencer for . . .
1707 Lond., 1707, 8°. 48 pp.   Gough Oxf. 107 (8)

PERIODICALS

5068. MARILLER, H. C., University magazines and their makers, a paper read before the Sette of odd volumes. (Privately printed opuscula, 47.) Lond., 1899, 16°. 99 pp.   Soc. 3974 f. 67 (47)
— [Another ed.] Lond., 1902, 16°.   Manning 8° 172

5069. SYMON, J. D., The earlier Oxford magazines. (Oxf. and Cambr. review, 1911, no. 13, p. 39–57.)   Per. 2625 d. 37

5070. WYNDHAM, H., Some old Oxford magazines. (Bookman's journ., 1921, vol. 4, p. 97, 109.)   Per. 25805 d. 52

5071. HUDSON, D., Three hundred years of University journalism. (Oxford, 1940, vol. 7, no. 1, p. 54–64.)   Per. G.A. Oxon 8° 1141

5072. Anti-teapot review. No. 1–19. Lond. &c., 1864–69, 8°.
     Per. 2705 e. 233

5073. The Aunt. November, 1919. Oxf., 1919, 4°.   G.A. Oxon 4° 403 (4)

See 6711 [Balliol college record. 1899.].

5074. The Barge. May 24, 1900; May 19, 1904; May 1905. [Oxf.], 1904, 05, 4°.   Per. G.A. Oxon c. 203

5075. The Best man. [Oxf.], 1906, 4°.   G.A. Oxon 4° 335 (17)

5076. The Birch. No. 1–5. [Each no. is signed Academicus. No. 5 is by a different hand.] Oxf., 1795, 96, 4°.   G.A. Oxon 4° 187, 43
— 2nd ed. No. 1, 2.   G.A. Oxon 4° 43

See 4431 [Blackwell's weekly programme. 1928].

5077. The Blue. Vol. 1, no. 1–vol. 2, no. 15. Oxf., 1893, 4°.
     G.A. Oxon 4° 285

5078. The Blue book, conducted by Oxford undergraduates. Vol. 1. [No more publ.] Oxf., 1912, 13, 4°.   Per. 2705 d. 287

5079. Boomerang, an Oxford and Cambridge miscellany. No. 1. Oxf., [1875], 8°.   G.A. Oxon 8° 577

5080. The Boost. Vol. 9, no. 47. Oxf., 1920, s. sh.   G.A. Oxon 4° 442

See 6796 [The Brazen Nose. 1909].

5081. The Broad. No. 1–3. Oxf., 1901, 4°.   G.A. Oxon 4° 335 (12–14)

See 8734 [The Brown book. 1914].

5082. The Budget. Oxf., 1911, 4°.   G.A. Oxon c. 203

5083. The Bulldog. Vol. 1, no. 1, 2. Oxf., 1896, 4°. G.A. Oxon 4° 219 (15)

5084. The Buller. May 1913. Oxf., 1913, 4°.   G.A. Oxon 4° 219 (13)

5085. The 'Bump'. May 1898, 99, 1902, 03, 09. Oxf., 1898–1909, 4°.
G.A. Oxon 4° 129, 219

5086. Bumps. No. 1, 2. Oxf., 1920, 21, 4°. G.A. Oxon 4° 422

5087. The Bust. May, 1910. (Oxf.), 1910, 4°. G.A. Oxon 4° 335 (6)

5087.4. Carcanet. 1962– . [Oxf. &c.], 1962– , 4°. Per. 2705 d. 663

> See 6961 [The Cardinal's hat. 1919].
> See 8275 [Cats. 1937].

5088. The Censor. No. 1–5. (Oxf., 1813), 8°. Hope adds. 348

5089. COTTON, H., Vox clamantis! or, A peep at the Censor. May 30, 1813 [signed Crab.]. (Oxf., 1813), 4°. 7 pp. Hope adds. 348

5090. HILDYARD, W., To the Anti-Censor [in verse, signed Westmonasteriensis]. (Oxf.), [1813], s. sh. Hope adds. 348

5091. Oxford versus Cambridge: a freshman's letter [concerning The Censor. Signed T. Shandy, secundus: dated 28 June 1813]. Oxf., (1813), 4°. 7 pp.

5092. To the Anti-anti-Censor [in verse signed Q.]. (Oxf.), [1813], s. sh.
Hope adds. 348

5093. To the author of The Censor. [A letter signed Senex.] June 19, 1813. (Oxf., 1813), 4°. 7 pp. Hope adds. 348

5094. What do you think of The Censor? [signed P.]. (Oxf.), [1813], 4°. 7 pp. Hope adds. 348

5095. The Chaperon, an Eights' week magazine by 'Pembie'. (Oxf.), [1910], 4°. G.A. Oxon 4° 335 (16)

5096. The Chaperon, or The Oxford Cherivari. Vol. 1, no. 1–8. Oxf., 1910, 4°. Per. G.A. Oxon 4° 293

5097. The Cherwell. Vol. 1– . Oxf., 1920– , 4°.
Per. G.A. Oxon 4° 448; N.G.A. Oxon b. 181

> See 4236 [La Chouette aveugle. 1954].
> See 6953 [The Christ Church chronicle. 1892].
> See 7468 [The Clock tower. 1912].

5098. The Clown [ed. by M. Beerbohm]. Vol. 1, no. 1–4. Oxf., 1891, 4°.
G.A. Oxon 4° 285

5099. College rhymes, or Blossoms of the flying terms. Vol. 1–14. Lond. &c., 1860–74, 8°.
[Bodley has No. 1, vol. 3–14; Per. 2805 f. 319; 3967 e. 83; 3967 f. 41]

5100. The Comet. No. 1. Oxf., 1886, 4°. G.A. Oxon 4° 127

5101. Conservative forum. No. 1– . (Oxf. univ. Conservative assoc.) Oxf., 1960– , 4°. Per. 22894 d. 58

5102. Contact (an inter-university magazine on race relations). 1– . Oxf., 1960– , 4°. Per. 24873 d. 12

5103. The Cornstalker, a magazine for Eights week. Oxford, 1898, 8°.
Exeter coll.

5104. Cosmopolitan, a periodical miscellany by gentlemen of the University of Oxford. No. 1. Lond., 1788, 8°.   Hope adds. 60 (24)

5105. The Crier, Oxford day by day. [Vol. 1] No. 1– ,vol. 3, no. 36. (Oxf.), 1925–27, 4°.   Per. G.A. Oxon 4° 468
See 8731 [The Daisy. 1890].

5106. Dark blue. No. 1. Oxf. &c., 1867, 8°.   Per. G.A. Oxon 8° 581

5107. Dark blue, ed. by J. C. Freund. Vol. 1–4 [and extra no. Mar. 1873]. Lond., 1871–73, 8°.
[Bodleian set imperfect: Per. 270 d. 32.]
See 7402 [The Druid. 1862].

5108. Eights illustrated. Oxf., 1902, 4°. 18 pp.   G.A. Oxon 4° 219 (12)

5109. Eights' week illustrated. (Oxf.), [1914], 4°.   G.A. Oxon 4° 335 (1)

5110. Eights' week opinions. May 20th, 1909. Oxf., 1909, 4°. 26 pp.
G.A. Oxon 4° 219 (4)

5111. Eights week pie. Lond., 1910, 4°. 56 pp.   2706 e. 84 (15)

5112. The Ephemeral [ed. by lord Alfred Douglas]. No. 1–6. Oxf., 1893, 4°.   G.A. Oxon 4° 285
See 3922 [Grant, sir A. H., The Ephemeral. 1931].

5113. The Farcity, a true forecast of events for the marvellous month of May 1907. Oxf., 1907, 8°. 43 pp.   G.A. Oxon 8° 884 (13)

5114. Farrago [ed. by P. Burra]. No. 1–6. Oxf., 1930, 31, 8°.
Per. 2705 d. 481

5115. The Farrago: or The lucubrations of counsellor Bickerton. No. 1, 2. Oxf., 1816, 8°.   G.A. Oxon 8° 1025 (6)
See 8308 [First words. 1936].

5116. Fords & bridges. Vol. 1, no. 1–vol. 5, no. 2. Feb. 1936–May 1939. Oxf., 1936–39, 4°.   Per. 2625 d. 97

5117. The Fritillary (the magazine of the women's colleges). [Vol. 1]–vol. 37, no. 8. Oxf., 1894–1931, 4°.   G.A. Oxon 4° 181
See 4460 [Full and bye. 1948].

5117.5 Gargoyle. Trinity 1960. (Oxf.), 1960, 8°.   2705 e. 1430
See 8332 [The Glow-worm. 1919].

5118. The Goat. Oxf., 1919, 4°. 8 pp.   G.A. Oxon 4° 262 (32)

5119. Great Tom [ed. by B. Montgomery]. No. 1–4. Oxf., 1861, 8°.
G.A. Oxon 8° 582
See 7405 [Gwyl dewi sant. 1906].

5120. The Harlequin. No. 1–8. Oxf., 1866, fol. & 4°.
G.A. Oxon b. 176; 4° 128
See 8723 [The Heritage. 1922].
See 4073 [Heritage. Oxford university heritage society. 1958].
See 7381 [Hertford college magazine. 1910].

5121. Hush. Vol. 1, no. 1. Feb. 2, 1920. [Comprising 8 blank pages!]
G.A. Oxon 4° 403 (3)

5122. Illuminatio. Vol. 1, no. 1–vol. 2, no. 1. Oxf., 1947, 48, 8°.
Per. G.A. Oxon 8° 1208

5123. The Infant. June, Nov., 1919. Oxf., 1919, 4°. G.A. Oxon 4° 421

5124. Information Gazette, touching divinity, learning and physic. Vol. 1,
no. 1–vol. 2, no. 3. [Gen. ed. C. C. Ord.]
— Vol. 1, no. 1. 2nd ed.
Oxf., 1898, 99, 4°. N. 26011 d. 25

5125. The Inspector. No. 1–3. [Oxf., 1804], 8°. G. Pamph. 1357 (12–14)

The Inspector. See also 5227, The Student.

See 4244 [Invariant. 1961].

5126. The Isis. Vol. 1, no. 1. n. pl., 1839, 8°. Per. 2705 d. 246

5127. The Isis. [Vol. 1] no. 1– . Oxf., 1892– , 4°. Per. G.A. Oxon 4° 145

5128. The Isis theatre supplement, ed. by C. Bell. Vol. 1, no. 1– . Oxf.,
1953– , 4°. Per. M. adds. 124 d. 153

5129. The J.C.R. No. 1–vol. 3, no. 62. Oxf., 1897–99, 4°. G.A. Oxon 4° 193

5130. Janus: a terminal review of international affairs. No. 1. Oxf.,
1960, 4°. Per. 22284 d. 8

5130.1. Janus, the Oxford Catholic review. No. 1– . Oxf., 1965– , 4°.
Per. 971 d. 200

5131. The Jester. Feb. 6, 13, 20, 27; Mar. 7, 1902. Oxf., 1902, 4°.
G.A. Oxon 4° 335 (7–11)
See 7408 [The Jesus college magazine. 1912].

5132. The Jokelet. No. 1–3. 1886.

See 7499 [The Lincoln imp. 1920].

5133. The Loiterer. No. 1–60. [Mostly by J. Austin.] (Oxf.), 1789, 90, 8°.
[Bodley has No. 40, 41, 45; G. Pamph. 1192 (9).]
— [Another ed.] 2 vols. Oxf., 1790, 8°. Hope 8° 582, 583
— [Another ed.] 2 vols. Dubl., 1792, 12°. 2705 f. 140

5134. The Lyre. Gaudy, 1869. [Programme of projected terminal magazine written by a member or members of St. John's.] [Oxf.], 1869, s sh.
G.A. fol. A 130

5135. The Magnum. [No. 1], 2. (Oxf.), 1908, 4°. G.A. Oxon 4° 355 (19, 20)

See 7727 [Mansfield college magazine. 1897].

5136. The May Bee. Buzz 1. Oxf., 1900, 4°.   G.A. Oxon c. 203

5137. The Mayonnaise. May 1907. Oxf., 1907, 4°. 12 pp.
G.A. Oxon 4° 219 (14)

5138. Mesopotamia. May 1959– . (Abingdon), 1959– , 4° &c.
Per. 2705 d. 647

5139. The Meteor. No. 1. (Oxf.), 1911, 4°.   G.A. Oxon 4° 335 (18)

5140. The New cut. (Lond.), [1912], 4°. 40 pp.   G.A. Oxon c. 308 (5)

See 8851 [New epoch. 1949].

5141. The New Oxford, the official organ of the O.U. Labour club. No. 1–
21. Oxf., 1920–23, 8°. & fol.
[Bodley has No. 3, 9, 12, 14–21: G.A. Oxon c. 234.]

5142. The New Oxford outlook, ed. by R. Crossman, G. Highet, D. Kahn.
Vol. 1, 2. Oxf., 1933–35, 8°.   Per. 2705 d. 492

5143. The New Rattle. Vol. 1, no. 1–vol. 4, no. 6. Oxf., 1890–93, 4°.
G.A. Oxon 4° 285

5143.5. The New university messenger. No. 1– . Oxf., 1962– , fol.
Per. 24772 c. 5

See 2567 [Nisi prius. 1950].
See 8267 [The Non-collegiate students' magazine. 1896].

5144. The Octopus [ed. by C. Carr]. No. 1–6. n. pl., 1895, 4°.
G.A. Oxon 4° 200

5145. Olla Podrida. Mar. 17, 1787–Jan. 12, 1788. Oxf., 1788, fol.
Hope fol. 66
— 2nd ed. Lond., 1788, 8°.   Hope essays 746

See 7977 [The Oriel record. 1909].

5146. Our memories, shadows of old Oxford, ed. and pr. by H. Daniel.
No. 1–20; 2nd ser., no. 1, 2. Oxf., 1888–95, 8°.   G.A. Oxon 8° 477

5147. The Ox or the Commemorator's vade-mecum. June 23, 1903. Oxf.,
1903, 4°. 20 pp.   G.A. Oxon 4° 219 (10)

See 4391 [Oxford. 1934].

5148. Oxford and Cambridge. Vol. 1–4. [Lond.], 1927, 28, fol.
Per. 2625 c. 5

5149. Oxford & Cambridge illustrated. Oxf. ed. Vol. 1, 2. Lond., 1907, 4°.
Per. 2625 d. 34

5150. Oxford and Cambridge magazine [ed. by W. Fulford]. Vol. 1. Lond.,
1856, 8°.   Per. 2705 d. 135

5151. The Oxford and Cambridge miscellany. June 1920. Oxf., 1920, 4°.
Per. 2705 d. 353

5152. Oxford and Cambridge review. July 1845–June 1847. No. 1–24.
Lond., 1845–47, 8°.   Per. 3977 e. 222

5153. The Oxford and Cambridge review, ed. by O. R. Dawson (R. J. Walker). No. 1–26. Lond., 1907–12, 4°.   Per. 2625 d. 37

Oxford and Cambridge undergraduates journal. See 5192, Oxford undergraduates journal.

5154. Oxford angle. Vol. 1, no. 1– . (Oxf.), 1952– , 8°.   Per. 22283 e. 620

5155. Oxford broom. 1923. [In February 1924 incorporated with Cherwell.]

5156. Oxford, Cambridge and Middle-class reporter [*afterw.*] Oxford, Cambridge, Bar, Public school, and Middle-class reporter. Vol. 1, no. 1; suppl. no. Feb. 11, 1861; vol. 4, no. 49; 52; suppl. no. Mar. 1862. Lond., 1857–62, fol.   Per. 3974 c. 33 (22)

5157. Oxford camera. No. 1. [No more publ.] Oxf., 1938, fol.
          N.G.A. Oxon a. 109

5158. Oxford circus plus Parson's pleasure. Vol. 1, no. 1– . Oxf., 1961– , fol. & 8°.   Per. G.A. Oxon b. 198; 8° 1433

5159. Oxford clarion. No. 1– . (Oxf. univ. Labour club.) (Oxf.), 1951– , 4° &c. [Bodley has No. 2– : Per. 22775 d. 84.]

5160. Oxford comment. No. 1–5. Oxf., 1938, fol.   N.G.A. Oxon a. 111

See 4228.1 [The Oxford cosmopolitan. 1908].

5161. The Oxford critic and University magazine. No. 1, 3. Oxf., 1857, 8°.
          G.A. Oxon 8° 586

5162. Oxford fortnightly. Vol. 1, no. 1–vol. 2, no. 7. Oxf., 1913, 4°.
          Per. 2705 d. 294

Oxford fortnightly review. See Oxford review.

5163. Oxford forward, the Univesity progressive weekly. New ser., no. 1– 14. Oxf., 1939, fol. & 4°.   G.A. Oxon c. 294

5164. The Oxford guardian, with which is incorporated 'The Rampant Liberal'. Publ. under the auspices of the Oxford university Liberal club. [Vol 1] no. 1– . Oxf., 1936 , 4° &c.   Per. G.A. Oxon 4° 565

5165. The Oxford individual, a new survey of Oxford life. No. 1– . (Lond.), 1960– , 4°.   Per. G.A. Oxon 4° 773

5166. Oxford left. New ser. No. 1– . (Oxf. univ. Socialist club.) [Oxf.], 1951– , 8°.
[Bodley has No. 1, 2; and Trinity term 1953; Hilary–Michaelmas 1954; Michaelmas 1956: Per. G.A. Oxon 8° 1275.]

5167. The Oxford literary gazette, and classical and foreign journal. No. 1– 6. Oxf., 1829, 4°.   G.A. Oxon 4° 11

5168. The Oxford magazine: or, University museum. Vol. 1–12. Lond., 1768–1776, 8°.   Hope adds. 281–288*d*

5169. The Oxford magazine. Vol. 1, no. 1. Oxf., 1845, 8°.
          Per. G.A. Oxon 8° 589

5170. The Oxford magazine. Vol. 1, no. 1- . Oxf., 1883- , 4°.
Per. G.A. Oxon 4° 141

5171. The Magazine: a retrospect. (Oxf. mag., 1933, vol. 51, p. 296, 97.)
Per. G.A. Oxon 4° 141

5172. Early days of the Oxford magazine. (Oxf. mag., 1933, vol. 51, p. 294, 95.)
Per. G.A. Oxon 4° 141

5173. The Oxford magazine, 1883–1933. (Oxf. mag., 1933, vol. 51, p. 293, 94.)
Per. G.A. Oxon 4° 141

5174. MACCOLL, D. S., Birth-pangs of 'The Oxford magazine'. (Oxf. mag., 1944, vol. 63, p. 54–56.)
Per. G.A. Oxon 4° 141

5174.3. MCCALLUM, R. B., Recollections of the Magazine. (Oxf. mag., 1961, N.S., vol. 1, p. 412, 13.)
Per. G.A. Oxon 4° 141

5175. Retrospectus [signed Echo. A parody in verse on the prospectus in the first number of the Oxford magazine]. [Oxf., 1883], s. sh.
G.A. fol. A 130

5176. The Oxford manner. (Oxf.), 1913, 4°. 20 pp.   G.A. Oxon c. 308 (6)

See 2633 [Oxford medical school gazette. 1949].

5177. Oxford miscellany and review. No. 1, 2. Oxf., [1820?], 8°.   B.M.

5178. Oxford monthly programme. No. 1–5. Oxf., 1899, 4°.
Per. G.A. Oxon 4° 463

5179. The Oxford movement. June, 1908. (Oxf.), 1908, 4°. 16 pp.
G.A. Oxon c. 308 (2)

5180. Oxford opinion. Ed., W. Anderson. No. 1–48. [Oxf.], 1956–61, fol.
N. 22894 c. 5
— [Afterw.] Ox. Op. No. 1. (Lond.), 1965, 4°. Per. G.A. Oxon 4° 815

5181. The Oxford outlook, a literary and political review, ed. by Oxford undergraduates. Vol. 1, no. 1–vol. 12, no. 58. Oxf., 1919–32, 8°.
G.A. Oxon 8° 978

5181.3. Oxford poetry, ed. by G. D. H. C[ole], G. P. D. and W. S. V. 1910/13–52. [Publ. annually: 1914–18, 20–32, 36, 37, 47–52. Cumulative vols. for 1910/13, 14/16, 17/19, 42/43.] Oxf., 1913–52, 8°.
Per. 2805 e. 639
— [1922, 1923 also publ. in New York.]   Per. 2805 e. 1593

5182. Oxford point of view (ed. by M. Compton Mackenzie). No. 1–10. Oxf., 1902–04, 8°.   Per. 3977 d. 35

5183. Oxford Protestant magazine, literary, political and religious. Vol. 1, vol. 2 no. 1. [Incorp. in Christian enquirer.] Oxf. &c., 1847, 48, 8°.
G.A. Oxon 8° 119

5184. The Oxford quarterly magazine. Vol. 1. March and June, 1825. Oxf., 1825, 8°. 237+242 pp.   G.A. Oxon 8° 118

5185. The Oxford rambler. No. 1, 2. Oxf., 1882, 8°.   G.A. Oxon 8° 587

Oxford Reformer. See 5188, Oxford Socialist.

5186. The Oxford (fortnightly) review. No. 1–38. Oxf. (Carlton club.) Oxf., 1919–22, 4°.   B.M.; Per. G.A. Oxon 4° 400

Oxford review, a weekly record of university life and thought. See 5192, Oxford undergraduates journal.

Oxford review and undergraduates journal. See 5192, Oxford undergraduates journal.

5187. Oxford review or literary censor. 3 vols. Oxf., 1807, 08, 8°.
Per. 3977 e. 223

5188. Oxford Socialist, ed. by F. K. G. and G. D. H. C. No. 1–3, Mich. term 1908—Summer term 1909. Oxf., 1908, 09, 4°.   Nuffield coll.
— [Afterw.] Oxford Reformer [ed. by G. D. H. Cole and H. Allsopp. No. 1–4] Nov. 1909–Nov. 1910. [No more publ.]. Oxf., 1909, 10, 4°.
Nuffield coll.

5189. The Oxford spectator [by R. S. Copleston, E. N. Nolan and T. H. Ward]. No. 1–31. [Oxf.], 1867, 68, 8°.
G.A. Oxon 4° 262 (1); G.A. Oxon 8° 128
— Repr. No. 1–31. Lond., 1869, 8°. 183 pp.   G.A. Oxon 8° 129
— Facs. ed. Oxf., 1878, 8°. 124 pp.   G.A. Oxon 8° 130

5190. The Oxford tatler. No. 1–3. Oxf., 1886, 4°. Per. G.A. Oxon 4° 130

5191. Oxford Tory. Vol. 1– . [At first publ. under the auspices of the Oxf. univ. Conservative assoc., later independently. The date of the first issue is not known; Bodley has an imperfect set, commencing with volume 10 in 1951: Per. 22775 d. 83.]

5192. Oxford undergraduates journal. Jan. 31, 1866–Oct. 1875 [continued as] Oxford and Cambridge undergraduates journal. Oct. 21, 1875–Nov. 30, 1882 [continued as] Oxford review and undergraduates journal. Dec. 7, 1882–June 14, 1883 [continued as] Oxford and Cambridge undergraduates journal. Oct. 18, 1883–Dec. 4, 1884.
[The Bodleian set is imperfect: N.G.A. Oxon c. 21.]
— [Continued as] Oxford review, a weekly record of University life & thought. Jan. 21, 1885–June 20, 1888.   G.A. Oxon c. 240
— [From Oct. 15, 1888–June 19, 1914 issued daily.]
Oxf., 1866–1914, 4° & fol.   N.G.A. Oxon a 12

5193. Five letters to the 'Oxford undergraduate's journal', by W. E. W. Morrison [and others]. Oxf., [1874?], 8°. 8 pp.   G.A. Oxon 8° 584

See 1574 [Oxford university calendar. 1810].
See 1106 [Oxford university gazette. 1870].

5194. Oxford university magazine. No. 1–4. Oxf., 1834, 35, 8°. [Bodley has no. 1–3, 1834.].   G.A. Oxon 8° 579

5195. The Oxford university magazine and review. No. 1, 2. Oxf. &c., 1869, 8°.
— 2nd ed. No. 1. 1869.   Per. G.A. Oxon 8° 580

5196. Oxford university review. Vol. 1, no. 1-vol. 5, no. 3. Oxf., 1926–28, 4°.   Per. G.A. Oxon 4° 474

See 4426 [Oxford university sports register. 1909].
See 4412 [Oxford university what's what. 1948].
See 4413 [Oxford vade mecum. 1954].

5197. The Oxford viewpoint. Vol. 1, no. 1–6. (Oxf.), 1947, 48, 8°.
                                              Per. 2705 d. 660

5198. The Oxonian. No. 1–3. Oxf., 1817, 8°.   G.A. Oxon 8° 151

5199. Fair play; or, No. 1 of the Oxonian exposed, by a member of the University [signed A]. Oxf., 1817, 8°. 16 pp.   B.M.

5200. The Oxonian. No. 1. Oxf., 1847, 8°.   Per. G.A. Oxon 8° 590

5200.5. Oxymoron. No. 1- . Oxf., 1965- , 4°.   Per. G.A. Oxon 4° 813

5201. The Pageant post, by members of Merton college. June, 1907. (Oxf.), 1907, 4°.   G.A. Oxon 4° 335 (4)

5202. Pan. No. 1, 2. Oxf., 1904, 4°.   G.A. Oxon c. 203

5203. Pantheon. No. 1, 2. [1886?]

5204. Parsons' pleasure. [Oxf.], 1913, 4°. 22 pp.   G.A. Oxon c. 308 (7)

5205. Parson's pleasure, ed.-in-chief, A. Berry. No. 1, 1958–Feb. 22 [really 23], 1961. (Oxf.), 1958–61, 8°.   Per. G.A. Oxon 8° 1395
[Included in 5158.]

5205.5. Peacock, a new Oxford literary magazine, ed. by Sebastian Brett and Crispin Hasler. [No. 1- .] (Leic.), [1964]- , 8°.   Per 2705 e. 1532

See 7170 [The Pelican record. 1891].

5206. The Pipe. No. 1–4. Oxf., 1900, 01, 8°.   G.A. Oxon 8° 672

5207. Smoke: being the four numbers of 'The Pipe' issued in 1900 and 1901. Oxf., 1911, 8°. 172 pp.   G.A. Oxon 8° 827

5208. Playmates, the Oxford 'chums'. May, 1909. Oxf., 1909, 4°. 11 pp.
                                              2706 c. 14
See 7754 [The Postmaster. 1952].

5209. The Proctor. Ser. 1, vol. 1, no. 1. Oxf., 1896, 4°. G.A. Oxon 4° 119 (5)

5210. The Quad, ed. by C. Scott-Moncrieff. No. 1–4. Oxf., 1900, 01, 8°.
                                              Per. 2705 e. 148

5211. The Radcliffe. No. 1–10. Oxf., 1869, 4°.   Per. G.A. Oxon 4° 126
See 5164 [Rampant Liberal].

5212. The Rattle. [Vol. 1], no. 1-vol. 3, no. 6. (Oxf.), 1886–88, 4°.
                                              Per. G.A. Oxon 4° 134

5213. Replies. Mar. 12th, 1913. Oxf., 1913, 4°.   G.A. Oxon 4° 262 (12)

5214. Revolt. No. 1-[8]. (Oxf.), 1930, 4°.   Per. G.A. Oxon 4° 502

5215. The Right thing, by 'It'. (Oxf.), [1916], 4°.   G.A. Oxon 4° 335 (2)

5216. The Round robin. May 1908. Oxf., 1908, 4°. 20 pp.
                                               G.A. Oxon 4° 219 (3)

5217. Ye Rounde table, an Oxford and Cambridge magazine. Feb.–June.
6 nos. Oxf. &c., 1878, 8°.
[No. 6 wanting in the Bodleian set: G.A. Oxon 8° 583.]

See 8275 [St. Catherine's magazine. 1919].
See 8275 [St. Catherine's wheel. 1941/2].
See 8294 [St. Edmund hall magazine. 1920].

5218. The Scarlet runner. No. 1, 2. 1899.

5219. The Scrap book. No. 1-3. 1866.

5220. The Ship. No. 1- [Oxf., 1910-], 8°.
[Bodley has No. 25- : Per. G.A. Oxon 8° 1421.]

5221. The Shotover papers, or, Echoes from Oxford [ed. by W. E. W.
Morrison and others]. Vol. 1, no. 1-13. Oxf., 1874, 75, 8°.
                                               G.A. Oxon 8° 584, 585
See 4256 [Socratic (digest). 1943].

5222. The Souvenir. June 19, 1893. Oxf., 1893, 4°. 8 pp.
                                               G.A. Oxon 4° 219 (9)

5223. The Spirit lamp. [Vol. 1] no. 1-vol. 4, no. 2. Oxf., 1892, 93, 8°.
                                               Per. G.A. Oxon 8° 526

5224. The Spout. Vol. 1, no. 1. [Oxf.], 1919, 4°.   G.A. Oxon 4° 421

5225. The Squeaker. Oxf., 1893, 4°. Vol. 1, no. 2.   G.A. Oxon 4° 285

5226. The Squib. May 1908. Oxf., 1908, 4°. 16 pp. G.A. Oxon 4° 219 (1)

See 7271 [The Stapledon magazine. 1904].

5227. The Student, or, The Oxford (and Cambridge) monthly miscellany
[ed. by C. Smart]. 2 vols. [With] The Inspector, no. 1-3. Oxf., 1750,
51, 8°.   Vet. A 4 e. 388, 389

5228. Ye Tea-potte [ed. by A. F. R. Abbott and L. L. Morrell]. No. 1.
Oxenforde, 1898, 8°.   Per. 2705 e. 133

5229. AMHURST, N., Terrae filius [by N. Amhurst]. No. 1-52. (Lond.),
1721, fol.   Hope fol. 72; Nich. newsp. 48B
— [Another issue entitled] Terrae filius, or, The secret history of the
University of Oxford. No. 1-50. 2 vols. Lond., 1726, 12°.
                                               Hope adds. 323, 324
— 2nd ed. 1726.   Hope adds. 985, 986
— [A separate pr. of the Dedication.] 12 pp.   Gough Oxf. 113 (4)
— 3rd ed. 1754.   G.A. Oxon 8° 307

5230. Terrae-filius [by G. Colman, the elder]. No. 1–4. Lond., 1763, 4°.
                                                                Hope 8° 984
— [Another ed. Repr. in Colman's Prose on several occasions.] Lond.,
1787, 8°.   2699 e. 159

5231. The Themes. No. 1. Oxf., 1930, fol.   Per. G.A. Oxon c. 297

5232. Tuesday review. Vol. 1, no. 1–vol. 2, no. 7. Oxf., 1909, 4°.
                                                        G.A. Oxon c. 122

5233. The Umbrella. (Oxf.), [1905], 4°.   G.A. Oxon 4° 335 (3)

5234. The Undergraduate. No. 1–6. [No. 1 signed N.] Oxf., 1819, 8°.
                                                        Hope 8° 1048

5235. The Undergraduate. Vol. 1, no. 1–21. Oxf., 1888, 4°.
                                                Per. G.A. Oxon 4° 125
   See 8534.8 [University college record. 1929].

5236. The University news. Vol. 1, no. 1–8. [Reading], 1928, 4°.
                                                Per. G.A. Oxon 4° 488
   See 4414 [Univoxon. 1960].

5237. Undergraduate papers [by members of the Old mortality club, ed.
by J. Nichol]. No. 1–4, pt. 2 [really no. 2 pt. 4]. Oxf., 1857 [58], 8°.
                                                        Arch. AA e. 55
— [Another issue]. No. 1–3. Oxf., 1858, 8°.   Arch. AA e. 60

5238. The Usher. June 1907. (Oxf.), 1907, 4°.   G.A. Oxon 4° 335 (5)

5239. The Vacuum. May 1, 1900. Oxf., 1900, 4°. 12 pp.
                                                G.A. Oxon 4° 219 (11)

5240. Il vagabondo, a terminal miscellany. No. 1–8. [Chiefly by
B. Boucher.] Oxf., 1816, 8°.   B.M.
[Bodley has no. 1–7: G.A. Oxon 8° 1025 (1).]

5241. The first epistle, by Junius, to the author of Il vagabondo. Oxf.,
1816, 8°. 15 pp.   G.A. Oxon 8° 1025 (2)

5242. A letter to Junius, in answer to his Epistle to the author of 'Il vagabondo', by Atalba. Oxf., 1816, 8°. 14 pp.   G.A. Oxon 8° 1025 (3)

5243. The 'Varsity (with which during the War is incorporated The Isis).
[Vol. 1] no. 1–vol. 15, no. 376. Oxf., 1901–1916, 4°.
                                                Per. G.A. Oxon c. 211

5244. Varsity characters. No. 1–4. Oxf., 1900, fol.   G.A. Oxon b. 105

5245. Varsity life illustrated. Oct. 22, 29, Nov. 5, 1906. (Oxf.), 1906, 4°.
                                                        G.A. Oxon 4° 248

5246. Varsity life. Vol. 1, no. 1–vol. 2, no. 1. Oxf., 1929, 4°.
                                                Per. G.A. Oxon c. 252

5247. Varsity vices. The Oxford truth. May 1908. Oxf., 1908, 4°. 12 pp.
                                                G.A. Oxon 4° 219 (2)
   See 8614 [Wadham college gazette. 1897].

5248. Waifs and strays, a terminal magazine of Oxford poetry. No. 1–10.
Oxf. &c., 1879–82, 8°.   B.M.
[Bodley has No. 1–9: Per. 2805 e. 378.]

5249. Why not? No. 1. [No more publ.] (Oxf.), 1911, 4°.
G.A. Oxon 4° 335 (15)

5250. The X. No. 1–35. Oxf., 1898–1900, 4°.   G.A. Oxon 4° 510

See 8844 [Young Oxford. 1899].

5251. 'You're another.' No. 1, 2. [A retort by two Balliol men to the Anti-
teapot review.] Oxf., 1864, 8°.
[Bodley has no. 2: G.A. Oxon 8° 659 (22).]

BUILDINGS AND INSTITUTIONS

GENERAL

5252. Reports of University institutions. 1888–95, 99–1913. [1896–98 were never issued.] Oxf., [1889]–1914, 8°.   G.A. Oxon 8° 510
[Also publ. in the Oxford University gazette.]

Libraries

5253. THOMAS, E. C., The libraries of Oxford and the uses of college libraries. (Trans. and proc., 1st annual meeting of the Library assoc., 1879, p. 24–28.)   Per. 25891 d. 1

5254. GIBSON, S., Oxford libraries. (Book-auction records, 1911, p. i–xix).
2590 e. Oxf. 6

5255. Library provision in Oxford. Report and recommendations of the Commission appointed by the Congregation of the University. Oxf., 1931, 4°. 152 pp.+8 plans.   2590 d. Oxf. 1

5256. STREETER, B. H., The chained library. (Chapter III. Nine Oxford libraries, p. 121–256.) Lond., 1931, 4°.   2590 d. 27

5257. HILL, R. H., Library provision in Oxford: the scheme in progress. (Library assoc. record, 1934, 4th ser., vol. 1, p. 103–07.)
Per. 25891 d. 21
— Repr. 1934. 5 pp.   2590 d. Oxf. 1. 23

5258. CRASTER, SIR H. H. E., A note on the early history of libraries in Oxford. (Festschrift Georg Leyh, 1937, p. 169–71.)   2589 d. 107
— Sonderabdr.   2590 d. Oxf. 2

5259. Oxford libraries. Information for undergraduates. (Oxf.), 1961–, 8°.
2590 e. Oxf. 7

5259.2. Printed Book collections in Oxford outside Bodley. A list of catalogues and works in the Bodleian. [Reprod. from typescript.] n. pl., [1965], fol. 14 sheets.   R. 6. 278*d*

5259.4. Report of the Committee on University libraries [Shackleton report]. Suppl. no. 1 to Univ. gazette (no. 3295) vol. 97, Nov. 1966. Oxf., 1966, 8°. 210 pp.   Per. G.A. Oxon c. 86

ASHMOLEAN MUSEUM

General

For details of the founding &c. of the University galleries, see 6107, &c., Taylorian Institution.

For works relating to the Wood, Ashmole, and Lister collections, see Bodleian Library.

5260. [Views and prints, &c. of the Museum]   G.A. Oxon a. 45

5261. Ashmolean museum. [Postcards issued by the Museum.]
G.A. Oxon 16° 127

5262. DUNCAN, P. B., Introduction to the catalogue of the Ashmolean Museum [by P. B. Duncan?]. n. pl., [1826], 8°. 59 pp. G.A. Oxon 8° 223

5263. DUNCAN, P. B., A catalogue of the Ashmolean museum descriptive of the zoological specimens, antiquities, coins, and miscellaneous curiosities [by P. B. Duncan]. Oxf., 1836, 8°. 188 pp.   17582 d. 2

5264. Hand-book guide for the University galleries. Oxf., 1846, 16°. 30 pp.
G.A. Oxon 16° 189
— 1848. 8°. 57 pp.   G.A. Oxon 16° 136 (16)
— 1850. 59 pp.   G.A. Oxon 8° 184 (7)
— 1853. 62 pp.   G.A. Oxon 8° 232 (10)
— 1857. 64 pp.   G.A. Oxon 8° 285 (4)
— 1859. 64 pp.   G.A. Oxon 8° 93 (3)
— 1865.   Taylor
— 1870. 16°. 50 pp.   G.A. Oxon 16° 220

See 6116 [Ingram, J., The University galleries. 1848].
See 5623 [Waagen, G. F., Treasures of art. 1854].

5265. PARKER, J., The Ashmolean museum and the Ashmole collection of antiquities. [A letter by J. Parker.] n. pl., (1858), 8°. 12 pp.
G.A. Oxon 8° 124 (12)

See 6186 [Westwood, J. O., The Hope collections [of natural history and engraved portraits and engravings. 1860].

5266. PARKER, J. H., The Ashmolean museum: its history, present state, and prospects, a lecture. Oxf., 1870, 8°. 36 pp.   G.A. Oxon 8° 146 (8)

5267. PARKER, J. H., On the history and prospects of the Ashmolean museum. [*With*] Suppl. note of recent additions, by mr. Rowell. (Proc., Oxf. architect. and hist. soc., 1870, N.S., vol. 2, p. 227–39.)
Per. G.A. Oxon 8° 498 = R. Top.

5268. PARKER, J. H., The Ashmolean museum of history and archæology; the additions made to it in 1870–1871; together with the progress of archæology during the same period, a lecture. Oxf. &c., 1871, 8°. 39 pp.   G.A. Oxon 8° 165 (6)

5269. The assistant keepership and the new catalogue of the Ashmolean museum. [Correspondence between G. A. Rowell and J. H. Parker.] [Oxf., 1879], 8°. 24 pp.   G.A. Oxon 8° 221 (4)

5270. PARKER, J. H., Ashmolean museum; the keeper's correction of some misstatements in London newspapers in November, 1880 [concerning certain curiosities said to have been part of the Tradescant collection. The misstatements are here reprinted]. [Oxf.], (1880), 8°. 11 pp.
G.A. Oxon 8° 414

5271. ROWELL, G. A., Recent discoveries [concerning the Tradescant collection] in the Ashmolean museum. Re-pr. from the Oxford Times of December 25th, 1880. [Oxf.], 1880, s. sh.   G.A. Oxon 8° 540 (8)

5272. EVANS, E. C., Recent discoveries in the Ashmolean museum. Re-pr. from the Oxford Times of January 8th, 1881. [Oxf.], 1881, s. sh.
G.A. Oxon 8° 540 (8*)

5273. ROWELL, G. A., Recent discoveries in the Ashmolean museum. Re-pr. from the Oxford Times of January 22nd, 1881. [Oxf.], 1881, s. sh.
G.A. Oxon 8° 540 (8**)

5274. ROWELL, G. A., Recent discoveries in the Ashmolean museum. Feb. 25, 1881. [Oxf.], (1881), 8°. 8 pp.   G.A. Oxon 8° 540 (7)

5275. Ashmolean museum. [Correspondence between J. H. Parker and G. A. Rowell concerning the storing in an outhouse of articles said to have been part of the Tradescant collection. Pp. 13–28 of a larger work.] [Oxf., 1881], 8°.   G.A. Oxon 8° 221 (5)

5276. ROWELL, G. A., Remarks on mr. Greville Chester's notes [no. 5313] on the archæological collections of Oxford, and the recent discovery in the Ashmolean museum. Oxf., 1881, 8°. 7 pp. G.A. Oxon 8° 221 (6)

5277. EVANS, A. J., The Ashmolean museum as a home of archæology in Oxford, an inaugural lecture. Oxf. &c., 1884, 8°. 32 pp.
G.A. Oxon 8° 359

5278. EVANS, A. J., The scheme for a new museum of art and archæology in connexion with mr. Fortnum's offer [by A. J. Evans]. [Oxf., 1891], fol. 4 pp.   G.A. Oxon c. 24 (2)

5279. EVANS, A. J., The government of the united Ashmolean Museum and University galleries. Statement made to the visitors and curators by Ashmole's keeper. [Oxf.], (1895), 4°. 4 pp.   G.A. Oxon b. 139 (f. 53)

5280. To members of Congregation. The proposed statute for amalgamating the government of the Ashmolean Museum and University galleries [signed A. J. Evans]. May 20. [Oxf.], (1895), fol. 4 pp.
G.A. Oxon c. 153

5281. The Ashmolean Museum and Universities galleries [urging speedy action to clarify the situation]. [Oxf., 1895], s. sh.
G.A. Oxon b. 139 (f. 53)

5282. To members of Congregation. The proposed new amendment to the statute for uniting the Ashmolean Museum and University galleries [signed A. J. Evans]. June 10. [Oxf.], (1895), s. sh.   G.A. Oxon c. 153

5283. JACKSON, T. W., The amendments to the proposed statute of the Ashmolean Museum and the University galleries. Oxf., (1895), fol. 4 pp.   G.A. Oxon b. 139 (f. 52)

5284. Agreement between the Visitors of the Ashmolean museum and University galleries, and the Oxford architectural and historical society. (Proc., Oxf. architect. and hist. soc., 1900, N.S., vol. 6, p. 195, 96.)   Per. G.A. Oxon 8° 498 = R. Top.

5285. EVANS, A. J., Statement by Ashmole's keeper regarding present and prospective needs of the Ashmolean Museum. [Oxf., 1902], 8°. 11 pp.   G.A. Oxon b. 139 (f. 56)

5286. EVANS, A. J., The proposed reconstitution of the Ashmolean Museum and University picture galleries. Jan. 28. [Oxf.], (1907), fol. 3 pp.   G.A. Oxon b. 139 (f. 56)

5287. The Ashmolean museum and University galleries. Report of the committee nominated to discuss the details of the scheme for reorganizing the institution . . . March 8. [Oxf.], (1907), 4°. 10 pp.   Firth b. 36 (27c)

5288. Report on the proposed Ashmolean amalgamation scheme: Supplementary note by the keeper of the Ashmolean. [Oxf., 1907], s. sh.   Firth b. 36 (31f)

5289. For the Hebdomadal council only. Re Ashmolean museum and University galleries. Draft case for opinion of counsel. [With] Opinion. [Oxf., 1907], 8°. 4+4 pp.   Firth b. 36 (35 b, c)

5290. NICHOLSON, E. B., Principiis obsta! An appeal to every member of Congregation . . . to attend . . . on 2 June, 1908, to placet prof. Oman's amendment [to the statute governing the Ashmolean museum and University galleries]. Oxf., 1908, 4°. 4 pp.   G.A. Oxon 4° 186 (28)

5291. JACKSON, W. W., The proposed amendment to the Ashmolean statute. 11 June. [Oxf.], (1908), s. sh.   Firth b. 36 (29d)

5292. Ashmolean museum. [Resolutions, signed E. W. B. Nicholson, about the duties and attendance of keepers, which will be proposed at the first opportunity.] 4 Nov. [Oxf.], (1908), s. sh.   Firth b. 36 (27a)

5293. Summary guide. Oxf., 1909, 8°. 146 pp.   1706 e. 171
— New ed., revised. Lond., 1912, 8°. 155 pp.   1706 e. 197
— 3rd ed., revised and enlarged. Oxf., 1920, 8°. 178 pp.   G.A. Oxon 8° 1295
— 4th ed. [entitled] Summary guide to the Department of antiquities. Oxf., 1931, 8°. 121 pp.   17582 e. 27
— [Another ed.] Oxf., 1951, 8°. 86 pp.+73 plates.   17582 e. 38
[See also no. 5397. Summary guide, Dept. of fine art. 1931.]

5294. LEEDS, E. T., Memorandum on the present buildings of the Ashmolean museum and future needs. [Oxf.], 1928, 8°. 8 pp.
[See also 6123–26.]   G.A. Oxon c. 314 (42)

See 6122 [J. L. Myres, Taylorian and Ashmolean. 1928].

5294.1. Taylorian decree. [Intimation that the Visitors of the Ashmolean museum will oppose the decree, with their reasons, and the text of 3 documents.] [Oxf., 1928], 8°. 4 pp.   G.A. Oxon c. 314 (46a)

5295. GARDNER, P., The Ashmolean and the Fitzwilliam. (Oxf. mag., 1931, vol. 49, p. 866–68.)   Per. G.A. Oxon 4° 141

5296. THOMPSON, J. M., The robbery [by Peter Le Maître] from the Ashmolean museum, 1776. (Eng. hist. review, 1931, vol. 46, p. 96–117.)   Per. 2231 d. 342 = K.

5297. THOMPSON, J. M., Le Maître alias Mara. [Identity of the robber of the Ashmolean museum in 1776 with Jean Paul Marat 'not proven'.] (Engl. hist. review, 1934, vol. 49, p. 55–73.)   Per. 2231 d. 342 = K.

5298. LEEDS, E. T., The Drapers' wing at the Ashmolean museum. (Museums' journ., 1939, vol. 39, p. 261–64.)   Per. 1758 d. 10

5299. EVANS, J., Time and chance, the story of Arthur Evans and his forebears. Lond. &c., 1943, 8°. 410 pp.   1757 e. 47

5300. WOODWARD, J., Treasures in Oxford [mainly in Ashmolean and Christ Church]. (Brit. council.) Lond. &c., 1951, 8°. 45 pp.
    24725 e. 775 [57]

5301. HARDEN, D. B., The Ashmolean museum—Beaumont street. (Museums' journ., 1953, vol. 52, p. 265–70.)   Per. 1758 d. 10
— Repr.   17582 d. 10
— [Another re-set]. Repr.   17582 d. 10

Regulations

5302. Instituta Ashmoleana. [Orders and statutes. In Latin.] [Oxf.], (1714), s. sh.   Ashm. 1820b (38)

5303. The orders and statutes of the Ashmolean museum (13 Dec. 1714). [Oxf.], (1714), s. sh.   Ashm. 1820b (37)
— 22 May 1749.   G.A. Oxon b. 19

5304. November 6. 1751. At a meeting of the Visitors of the Museum . . . [Regulations respecting the use of books and MSS. in the Museum.] [Oxf.], (1751), s. sh.   G.A. Oxon b. 139 (37)

5305. University galleries. The following regulations respecting the . . . galleries were approved by Convocation, June 6, 1844. [Oxf., 1844], s. sh.   G.A. Oxon c. 60 (126)

See also 6113, etc.

Reports

5306. The Ashmolean museum and the archæological collections of the University, report of the Keeper to the Visitors. [Oxf., 1884], 4°. 24 pp.
    G.A. Oxon 4° 186 (10)

5307. Annual report of the Keeper [*afterw.*] of the Visitors. 1888– . [The Bodleian set is imperfect: G.A. Oxon 4° 105; 8° 671. See also No. 5252 Reports of University institutions. The reports were printed also in the Oxford University gazette and from 1963 as a suppl. to the Gazette in 8° format.]

Department of antiquities and Department of classical archaeology

5308. PAGE, S., A dissertation on an antient jewel of the Anglo-Saxons [the Alfred jewel]. (Archaeologia, 1770, vol. 1, p. 161–67.)
Soc. G.A. Gen. top. 4° 162 = R.

5309. DUNCAN, P. B., A short account of the art of sculpture, to serve as a guide to the statues [then] in the Radcliffe library [by P. B. Duncan]. Oxf., 1826, 8°. 40 pp. G.A. Oxon 8° 232 (9)

See 6521 [H. Shaw and sir S. R. Meyrick, Ancient plate and furniture. 1837].

5310. A list of donations to the antiquarian and ethnological collections in the Ashmolean museum from 1836 to the end of 1868. Oxf., 1870, 8°. 19 pp. G.A. Oxon 8° 164 (3)

5311. VAUX, W. S. W., Catalogue of the Castellani collection of antiquities in the University galleries. Oxf., 1876, 8°. 53 pp. Clar. Press 16 b. 2

5312. CHESTER, G. J., Catalogue of the Egyptian antiquities in the Ashmolean museum. Oxf., 1881, 8°. 104 pp. G.A. Oxon 8° 269

5313. CHESTER, G. J., Notes on the present and future of the archæological collections of the University of Oxford. Oxf. &c., (1881), 8°. 14 pp.
G.A. Oxon 8° 1001 (4)

5314. GARDNER, P., Catalogue of the Greek vases in the Ashmolean museum. Oxf., 1893, fol. 43 pp.+26 pl. 17538 b. 3

5315. A descriptive catalogue of the maiolica and enamelled earthenware of Italy . . . in the Ashmolean Museum Fortnum collection. Oxf., 1897, 4°. 104 pp. 17543 d. 21

5316. FFOULKES, C., European arms and armour in the University of Oxford, principally in the Ashmolean and Pitt-Rivers museums. Oxf., 1912, fol. 64 pp.+19 plates. 23152 c. 7

5317. Theban ostraca, ed. from the originals, now mainly in the Royal Ontario museum of archaeology, Toronto, and the Bodleian library [later transferred to the Ashmolean] by A. H. Gardiner, H. Thompson, J. G. Milne. (Univ. of Toronto studies.) Lond. &c., 1913, 4°. 214 pp.
24671 d. 65

5318. GARDNER, P., Guide to the casts of Greek and Roman sculpture in the Ashmolean Museum. Oxf., 1914, 8°. 52 pp. Ashm.

5319. HOGARTH, D. G., Hittite seals, with particular reference to the Ashmolean collection. Oxf., 1920, fol. 107 pp.+10 plates. 219 c. 4

5320. The H. Weld–Blundell collection . . . by S. Langdon (G. R. Driver). 3 vols. (Oxf. ed. of cuneiform texts, 1–3.) Lond. &c., 1923, 24, fol.
Or. c. 13 (1–3)

5321. Babylonian penitential psalms . . . in the Weld collection . . . , by S. Langdon. (Oxf. ed. of cuneiform texts, 6.) Par., 1927, fol. 106 pp.+ 37 pl.   Or. c. 13 (6)

5322. BEAZLEY, SIR J. D. Corpus vasorum antiquorum. Oxford Ashmolean museum. No. 1, 2 [by sir J. D. Beazley and others]. (Corpus vasorum antiq.) Oxf., 1927, 31, fol.   17542 c. 6 (iii. 3, 9).

5323. THOMPSON, R. C., A catalogue of the late Babylonian tablets in the Bodleian library [later transferred to the Ashmolean]. [The title-leaf is printed, the remaining 80 leaves are reprod. from typewriting.] Lond., 1927, fol.   2590 c. Oxf. 1. 15

5324. The Herbert Weld collection . . . pictographic inscriptions from Jemdet Nasr . . . by S. Langdon. (Oxf. ed. of cuneiform texts, 7.) Lond. &c., 1928, fol. 72 pp.+41 pl.   Or. c. 13 (7)

5325. The Sayce and H. Weld collection . . . Sumerian contracts from Nippur, by G. R. Hunter. (Oxf. ed. of cuneiform texts, 8.) Lond. &c., 1930, fol. 45 pp.+46 pl.   Or. c. 13 (8)

5326. Greek ostraca in the Bodleian library [later transferred to the Ashmolean] and various other collections, ed. by J. G. Tait (and C. Préaux), 2 vols. (Egypt exploration soc.) Lond., 1930, 55, 8°.
24671 d. 20

5327. BARNARD, F. P., The Rawlinson collection of seal matrices. (Bodleian quarterly record, 1930, vol. 6, p. 132–38.)
Per. 2590 d. Oxf. 1. 40 = R.
— Repr.   219 d. 16

See 5293 [Summary guide to Department of antiquities. 1931, 1951].

5328. Syllabaries A, B¹, and B, with miscellaneous lexicographical texts from the Herbert Weld collection, by P. E. Van der Meer. (Oxf. ed. of cuneiform texts, 4.) Lond., 1938, fol. 72 pp.+54 pl.   Or. c. 13 (4)

5329. Guide to an exhibition of air-photographs of archaeological sites, Ashmolean museum. Nov. 1948 to Feb. 1949. Oxf., 1948, 4°. 19 pp.+ 16 pl.   1758 d. 20

5330. KIRK, J. R., The Alfred and Minster Lovell jewels [by J. R. Kirk]. Oxf., 1948, 8°. 12 pp.   1756 e. 59

5331. Sir Arthur Evans centenary exhibition, 4 Oct.–3 Nov., 1951. Ashmolean museum. [Short biography by D. B. Harden.] Oxf., 1951, 8°. 11 pp.   1757 e. 27 (9)

5332. KENNA, V. E. G., Cretan seals, with a catalogue of the Minoan gems in the Ashmolean museum. Oxf., 1960, fol. 163 pp.+25 pl. 219 c. 14

5333. BOARDMAN, J., The Cretan collection in Oxford. The Dictaean cave and Iron Age Crete. Oxf., 1961, 4°. 180 pp.+48 plates.
17582 d. 53

5333.1. British plate in the Ashmolean Museum. [Oxf., 1963], 8°. 4 pp.+ 28 plates.
17552 c. 92

5333.11. BUCHANAN, B., Catalogue of ancient Near-Eastern seals in the Ashmolean Museum. Oxf., 1966, 230 pp.+67 plates.
219 d. 27

Arundel, Pomfret, and other marbles

5334. Marmora Arundelliana . . . publ. & comm. adiecit I. Seldenus.
[Madan 600.] Lond., 1628, 4°. 184 pp.
4° Rawl. 487
— [Reissued.] [Madan 627.] Lond., 1629, 4°.
Antiq. e. E. 1629. 1
— [Another issue.] [Madan 626.]
Gough Oxf. 115
[The Arundel marbles were subsequently given to the University in 1677, after they had suffered from depredation and decay.]

5335. Marmora Oxoniensia, ex Arundellianis, Seldenianis, aliisque conflata, recens. & perpetuo commentario explicavit H. Prideaux . . . Appositis . . . Seldeni & Lydiati annotationibus . . . [Madan 3092.] Oxon., 1676, fol. [20]+173 pp.
D 4. 7 Art.

5336. Marmorum, Arundellianorum, Seldenianorum, aliorumque Academiae Oxoniensi donatorum secunda editio. [by M. Maittaire. *With*] Appendix. Lond., 1732, 33, fol. 667+12 pp.
O. 2. 4 Jur.

5337. CHANDLER, R., Marmora Oxoniensia. 3 pt. [Arundel marbles.] Oxon., 1763, fol.
G.A. Oxon a. 39

5338. Marmorum Oxoniensium inscriptiones Græcæ ad Chandleri exemplar editæ, curante G. Roberts. Oxon., 1791, 8°. xxxii+234 pp.
Gough Oxf. 123

5339. VIVIAN, J., A poem on the countess of Pomfret's benefaction to the University of Oxford [by J. Vivian]. Oxf., 1756, 4°. 12 pp.
Gough Oxf. 142 (11)

5340. THOMPSON, W., Gratitude, a poem on the countess of Pomfret's benefaction to the University of Oxford. Oxf., 1756, 4°. 12 pp.
Gough Oxf. 142 (10)

5340.5. A poem on the Pomfret statues. To which is added another on Laura's grave. [Perhaps by T. Mytton.] Oxf., 1758, 4°. 12 pp.
Gough Oxf. 142 (13)

5341. [*Begin.*] The following copies of papers . . . placed in the hands of the Vice-chancellor by . . . mr. Churton . . . [A paper submitted to members of Convocation detailing sir Roger Newdigate's proposal to move, at his own expense, the Pomfret donation to the Radcliffe library.] [Oxf., 1806], fol. 3 pp.
G.A. Oxon b. 19

5342. HORNSBY, T., [*Begin.*] The proposal of sir Roger Newdigate for removing the Pomfret statues . . . [A paper, dated March 20, opposing the proposal.] [Oxf., 1806], fol. 4 pp.   G.A. Oxon b. 19

5343. CHURTON, R., [*Begin.*] Mr. Churton begs leave . . . [An answer, dated March 21, to no. 5342.] (Oxf., 1806), fol. 4 pp. G.A. Oxon b. 19

5344. [*Begin.*] It having been suggested, that the following extract from the will of dr. Randolph . . . [Statement, indicating that the acceptance of sir R. Newdigate's proposed benefaction might nullify the terms of dr. Randolph's legacy.] Mar. 21. [Oxf.], 1806, s. sh. Don. b. 12 (111*a*)

5345. [*Begin.*] A member of Convocation who wishes to testify . . . [Paper, dated March 22, 1806, opposing sir Roger Newdigate's proposal.] Oxf., (1806), s. sh.   G.A. Oxon b. 19

5346. The following particulars are . . . addressed to the members of Convocation [rejecting the suggestion that the acceptance of sir R. Newdigate's proposed benefaction would conflict with the terms of dr. Randolph's legacy]. Mar. 22. Oxf., 1806, s. sh.   Don. b. 12 (112*b*)

5347. CHURTON, R., [*Begin.*] Sir R. Newdigate (willing to give more . . . [Statement maintaining that the will of dr. Randolph and sir R. Newdigate's proposed benefaction are not inconsistent.] Mar. 24. Oxf., [1806], s. sh.   Don b. 12 (113*b*)

5348. HORNSBY, T., [*Begin.*] The Radcliffe Librarian begs leave to lay before the members of Convocation the following extracts from the will of Dr. Radcliffe . . . [quoted in opposition to sir Roger Newdigate's proposals]. Mar. 24. Oxf., 1806, s. sh.   G.A. Oxon b. 19

5349. The following queries are most respectfully submitted to the members of Convocation, in consequence of the notice promulgated by the Vice-chancellor for a Convocation . . . when it will be proposed to rescind the votes of . . . March 24, 1806. [Signed A member of Convocation. Feb. 24.] Oxf., [1807], s. sh.   Don. b. 12 (125*b*)

5350. [*Begin.*] The attempt to carry . . . [Vice-chancellor's notice of a Convocation where it will be proposed to rescind the acceptance, on 24 March 1806, of sir Roger Newdigate's benefaction for the removal of the Pomfret statues. Feb. 15, 1808.] [Oxf.], 1808, s. sh.
Don. b. 12 (126)

5351. The following queries are most respectfully submitted as supplementary to those already offered to the members of Convocation. [Signed A member of Convocation. Feb. 24.] Oxf., [1808], s. sh.
Don. b. 12 (125*a*)

5352. (Catalogo ragionato di pietre di decorazione.) [A catalogue of a collection of marbles presented in 1828 by Stephen Jarrett to the University of Oxford.] [Rome, 1825], 8°. 236 pp.+28 pp.   1723 e. 26

5353. MICHAELIS, A., Ancient marbles in Great Britain, tr. from the Germ. by C. A. M. Fennell. [Oxford univ., p. 538–95.] Cambr., 1882, 4°.   1723 d. 39

Chantrey bequest

5354. [A notice, dated 25 April 1842, of a Convocation on the 28th instant, when it will be proposed to accept Lady Chantrey's presentation to the University galleries of sir Francis Chantrey's monumental figures.] [Oxf.], 1842, s. sh. MS. Top. Oxon c. 202 (f. 36)

5355. Etched reminiscences of the models by sir Francis Chantrey in the University galleries. Oxf., 1847, 8°. 60 plates. Ashm.
— 2nd ed. [*entitled*] Sixty etched reminiscences . . . 1850. 8°. 4 pp.
G.A. Oxon b. 139 (41)

5356. NICHOLSON, E. B., Council, lady Chantrey, and the Bodleian; an appeal to Convocation to reject . . . the illegal Chantrey casts decree, to be proposed. . . Dec. 1. Oxf., 1896, 4°. 8 pp. G.A. Oxon 4° 119 (13)

Coins

5357. Nummorum antiquorum scriniis Bodleianis reconditorum catalogus. Oxonii, 1750, fol. 343 pp. Gough Oxf. 95

5358. CHANDLER, H. W., The Bodleian coins and medals [by H. W. Chandler]. [Oxf.], (1885), 8°. Library records

5359. POOLE, S. LANE-, Catalogue of the Mohammadan coins preserved in the Bodleian library. Oxf., 1888, 4°. 55 pp. Arch. Num. xv. 36

5360. OMAN, C. W. C., Unpublished or rare coins of Smyrna in the Bodleian cabinet. (Num. chron., 1900, 3rd ser., vol. 20, p. 203–08.)
Num. 03 d. 10
— Repr. Num. 245 e. 1

5361. MILNE, J. G., Catalogue of Alexandrian coins. Oxf., 1933, 4°. lxviii+ 155 pp.+7 pl. Num. 2362 d. 28

5362. MILNE, J. G., Douce as a coin-collector [*part of* Francis Douce centenary]. (Bodleian quarterly record, 1934, vol. 7, p. 376–79.)
Per. 2590 d. Oxf. 1. 41 = R.

5363. MILNE, J. G., Notes on the Oxford collection. [Greek coins] 1–5. (Num. chron., 1935, 5th ser., vol. 15, p. 191–201; 1936, vol. 16, p. 281–87; 1937, vol. 17, p. 153–81; 1938, vol. 18, p. 254–66; 1939, vol. 19, p. 185–98; 1940, vol. 20, p. 213–54.) Num. 03 d. 10

5364. MILNE, J. G., Archbishop Laud and the University collection of coins. (Oxoniensia, 1936, vol. 1, p. 159, 60.)
Per. G.A. Oxon 4° 658 = R. Top.

5365. MILNE, J. G., The coin collections of Browne Willis. (Bodleian quarterly record, 1937/8, vol. 8, p. 449–52.)
Per. 2590 d. Oxf. 1. 40 = R.

5366. SUTHERLAND, C. H. V., Notes on the Oxford collection: Roman imperial coins. 1, 2. (Num. chron., 1939, 5th ser., vol. 19, p. 216–22; 1940, vol. 20, p. 255–64.) Num. 03 d. 10

5367. MILNE, J. G., and SUTHERLAND, C. H. V., The Evans collection at Oxford. (Num. chron., 1943, 6th ser., vol. 3, p. 73–91.) Num. 03 d. 10

5368. SUTHERLAND, C. H. V., The Evans collection at Oxford: Roman coins of the early empire. (Num. chron., 1944, 6th ser., vol. 4, p. 1–26.) Num. 03 d. 10

5369. MILNE, J. G., Some Greek coins in Oxford. (Num. chron., 1947, 6th ser., vol. 7, p. 52–61.) Num. 03 d. 10

5370. Ashmolean museum. Heberden coin room. Guide to the Greek, Roman, English and Chinese coins. Oxf., 1948, 8°. 51 pp. Num. 2233 e. 19

5371. MILNE, J. G., Oxford coin-collectors of the seventeenth and eighteenth centuries. (Oxoniensia, 1949, vol. 14, p. 53–62.) Per. G.A. Oxon 4° 658 = R. Top.

5372. MILNE, J. G., Unpublished coins in the Oxford collection. (Num. chron., 1953, ser. 6, vol. 13, p. 21–26.) Num. 03 d. 10

5373. KRAAY, C. M., Greek coins recently acquired by the Ashmolean museum. (Num. chron., 1954, 6th ser., vol. 14, p. 62–67.) Num. 03 d. 10

5373.1. KRAAY, C. M., The Ashmolean museum. The Heberden coin room. (Oxford, 1964, vol. 19, p. 50–56.) Per. G.A. Oxon 8° 1141

Department of Eastern art

5373.5. DATTA, A. K., The Museum of Eastern art at Oxford. (Art and letters: India and Pakistan, 1952, vol. 24, p. 21–23.) Ind. Inst.

5373.6. COHN, W., The Museum of Eastern art. (Museums' journ., 1953, vol. 52, p. 271–74.) Per. 1758 d. 10
— Repr. 17582 d. 10

5373.7. Oxford's Oriental art treasures. [Appeal, signed by the chancellor, the vice-chancellor and 4 others, for money to allow galleries in the Museum to be reconstructed to house the collection.] Oxf., [1956?], 8°. 4 pp.+4 plates. G.A. Oxon b. 32

5373.8. SWANN, P. C., The Ashmolean museum. The Department of Eastern art. (Oxford, 1963, vol. 19, p. 49–57.) Per. G.A. Oxon 8° 1141

Department of Western art

5374. WHITEHALL, R., To the no less vertuous than ingenious mris. Mary More; upon her sending sir Thomas More's picture [really Thomas Cromwell's], of her own drawing, to the Long gallery at the Public schools in Oxon [signed R. W.]. [Madan 3029.] [Oxf.], (1674), s. sh. Wood 423 (46)

See 5496 [A catalogue of the several pictures, statues and busto's in the picture gallery, Bodleian library, and Ashmolean museum. 1759, &c.].

5375. The history of the celebrated painting in the Picture Gallery at Oxford, called 'The schools of Athens'. 3rd ed. Oxf., 1807, 8°. 26 pp.
G.A. Oxon 8° 308

5376. Catalogue of the Sutherland collection. 2 vols. [*With*] Suppl. Lond., 1837, 38, fol. 2590 b. Oxf. 1 f. 1–3
[Part of this collection was transferred from the Bodleian Library in 1950.]

5377. Catalogues of original designs by Michael Angelo and Raffaelle, proposed to be purchased by subscription, and exhibited in the new University galleries. Oxf., 1842, 8°. 43 pp. G.A. Oxon 8° 146 (2)

5378. Catalogues of original designs by Michael Angelo and Raffaelle in the University galleries. Oxf., 1848, 16°. 64 pp. G.A. Oxon 16° 120

5379. BUTLER, G., The Raphael drawings in the University galleries. (Oxf. essays, 1856, p. 137–92.) 270 a. 17 (3)

5380. [Mar. 18, 1861. Announcement of proposed acceptance in Convocation of 23 March of a collection of drawings by J. M. W. Turner formed by John Ruskin, and donated to the University to be placed in the hands of the curators of the University galleries.] n. pl., 1861, s. sh.
G.A. Oxon c. 77 (85)

See 3130, &c. [Drawings lent to the Galleries for the use of the Ruskin School of fine art. 1871, &c.].

5381. FISHER, J., The University galleries, Oxford. A catalogue of the works of art in sculpture and painting [by J. Fisher]. Oxf., 1878, 16°. 24 pp. 1706 e. 90 (7)
— [Proof of 1879 ed.] G.A. Oxon 16° 121
— [Another ed.]. 1883. 17582 f. 2

5382. A provisional catalogue of the paintings exhibited in the University galleries. Oxf., 1891, 8°. 61 pp. 1706 e. 64 (12)

5383. University galleries, 1895. Loan exhibition of the work of William Turner of Oxford, 1789–1862. n. pl., 1895, 8°. 16 pp.
G.A. Oxon 8° 611 (2)
— 2nd issue. 1706 e. 164

5384. Catalogue. Exhibition of the etchings of Rembrandt at the University galleries, 1895, 1896. Oxf., [1896], 8°. 13 pp. 25889 R. e. 4

5385. University galleries. 1898. Turner and Claude [exhib. catal.]. [Oxf.], (1898), 4°. 3 pp. MS. Top. Oxon d. 140 (100)

5386. EVANS, A. J., Suggestions for the termination of the present provisorium in the University Picture galleries, and for their reconstitution as a new department in the Ashmolean museum. Nov. 16. [Oxf.], (1906), 4°. 4 pp. Firth b. 36 (27*b*)
— [Another ed., *with*] Supplementary observations. [Oxf.], (1906), 4°. 6 pp. Firth b. 36 (31*d*)

5387. First statement by the Picture galleries committee read at the meeting of the visitors on November 22. [Oxf.], (1906), s. sh.

Firth b. 36 (31c)

5388. HOLMES, C. J., [Begin.] I venture to address you . . . [A letter, signed C. J. Holmes, 28 Nov. 1906, concerning the present administration of the University galleries.] [Oxf.], (1906), 4°. 3 pp.   Firth b. 36 (31g)

5389. RICHMOND, W. B., University picture galleries. Jan. 2. [Oxf.], (1907), s. sh.   Firth b. 36 (37a)

5390. Second statement by the Picture galleries committee, as to the work done since 1884. Jan. 23, 1907. [Oxf.], (1907), 4°. 4 pp.

Firth b. 36 (35a)

5391. COLVIN, SIR S., Drawings of the old masters in the University galleries, and in the library of Christ Church. 3 vols. Oxf., 1907, fol.

1707 a. 18

5392. The Combe bequest. (Catalogue.) Oxf., 1909, 8°. 26 pp.

G.A. Oxon 4° 399 (3)

5393. BUSCHMANN, P., Rubens en Van Dyck in het Ashmolean museum. Overgedr. uit 'Onze kunst'. (Nijmegen), 1916, 4°. 35 pp. 1706 d. 157

5394. WILLIAMSON, G. C., The Bentinck–Hawkins collection of enamels at the Ashmolean museum. (Connoisseur, 1920, vol. 56, p. 34–37.)

Per. 175 d. 15

5395. JONES, E. A., Catalogue of the collection of old plate of William Francis Farrer. Lond., 1924, 4°. xxxii+191 pp.+94 pl. 17551 c. 14

5396. Woodcuts of the fifteenth century in the Ashmolean Museum, ed. by C. Dodgson. With notes on similar prints in the Bodleian. Oxf., 1929, fol. 36 pp.+33 plates.   17156 b. 15

5397. Summary guide: Department of fine art. 4th ed. Oxf., 1931, 8°. 81 pp.   1706 e. 331
[For the 1st–3rd eds. see 5293.]

5398. PARKER, SIR K. T., Catalogue of the collection of drawings in the Ashmolean Museum. Vol. 1– . Oxf., 1938– , 8°.   1706 d. 310

5399. ALDEN, J. E., The Pre-Raphaelites and Oxford, a descriptive handbook [of what Oxford has to show of Pre-Raphaelite art, and where it may be seen]. Oxf., 1948, 8°. 40 pp.   17006 e. 384 (3)

5400. Catalogue of the collection of Dutch and Flemish still-life pictures bequeathed by Daisy Linda Ward. Oxf., 1950, 4°. 211 pp. 1706 d. 356

5401. Catalogue of paintings in the Ashmolean museum. Oxf., [1951], 8°. 113 pp.   1706 e. 402
— 2nd ed. (1961). 185 pp.+64 plates.   1706 e. 532

5402. Memorial exhibition of paintings and drawings by Leonid Pasternak, 1862–1945. Oxf., 1958, 8°. 16 pp.   170072 e. 42

5403. Disegni veneti di Oxford [in the Ashmolean museum and Christ Church] catalogo della mostra a cura di K. T. Parker. (Trad. di M. Minio-Paluello.) (Centro di cultura e civiltà, catal. di mostre, 6.) Venezia, 1958, 8°. 94 pp.+120 pl. 1706 e. 466

5403.5. Accessions by bequest, gift and purchase, 1934–1962. (Dept. of western art.) Oxf., 1962, 8°. 12 pp. 17582 d. 61

5403.51. Gallery plans and brief history of the Ashmolean museum. Oxf., 1963, s. sh., folded. 17582 e. 70

5403.55. LOWE, I., The Mitchell collection in the Ashmolean. (Oxf. mag., 1965, vol. 6, p. 68–70.) Per. G.A. Oxon 4° 141

5403.56. HERRMANN, L., The Ashmolean museum. The Print-room. (Oxford, 1965, vol. 20, p. 60–66.) Per. G.A. Oxon 8° 1141

Griffith Institute

5404. LEEDS, E. T., The Francis Llewellyn Griffith and Nora Griffith bequests [the Griffith institute, and the Griffith Egyptological fund]. (Oxf. mag., 1938, vol. 56, p. 348, 49.) Per. G.A. Oxon 4° 141

5405. List of records in the Griffith Institute, Ashmolean museum. Oxf., 1947, 8°. 11 pp. G.A. Oxon 8° 1204 (4)

Library

See 6506 [List of periodicals. 1913].

5405.1. Ashmolean museum. Library development [signed R. F. Ovenell. Reprod. from typewriting]. n. pl., [1963], 4°. 10 sheets.
2590 d. Oxf. 40. 1

BARNET HOUSE

See 3117.1, Department of social and administrative studies.

BODLEIAN LIBRARY

General history 5406–5444
Visitors' guides 5445–5447
Statute 5448–5451
Buildings and fabric 5452–5487
Fresco 5488–5492
Contents other than books 5493–5507
Administration 5508–5514
Finance 5515–5524
Library economy 5525–5535
Staff 5536–5551
Publications 5552–5554
Readers and reading rooms 5555–5567
Bindings 5568–5571
Copyright 5572–5574
Donations 5575–5577
Exhibitions 5578–5592
Loans 5593–5613
Photography 5614, 5615

Purchases 5616–5618
Department of Western Manuscripts 5619–5655
Music manuscripts 5656–5661
Named collections 5662–5706
Department of Printed Books 5707–5709
General catalogues and cataloguing 5710–5730
Cataloguing rules 5731–5739
Special catalogues 5740–5751
Named collections 5752–5770
Classification 5771, 5772
Desiderata 5773
Book rejection 5774–5778
Law Library 5779, 5780
Department of Oriental Books 5781–5807
Friends of the Bodleian 5808, 5809

General history

5406. [Views and prints, &c. of the Library.]   G.A. Oxon a. 44; b. 71

See 1115 [Iusta funebria Ptolemæi Oxoniensis Thomæ Bodleii. 1613].
See 7796 [Bodleiomnema. 1613].

5407. JACOB, L., Traicté des plus belles bibliothèques publiques et par-
ticulières . . . [The Bodleian and Oxford college libraries, p. 252–67.]
Par., 1644, 8°.   258 c. 58

5408. The life of sir Thomas Bodley . . . written by himselfe. [Madan
1925.] Oxf., 1647, 4°. 16 pp.   Gough Oxf. 116
— [Repr.] (Reliquiæ Bodleianæ, by T. Hearne.) Lond., 1703, 8°.
                                                    Gough Oxf. 126
— [Repr.]. (Harl. misc., 1809, vol. 4, p. 314 &c.)   Σ III. 4
— Repr. for [and ed. by] John Lane. Lond., 1894, 16°. viii+16 pp.
                                                    G.A. Oxon 16° 47
— [Another ed., ed. by R. S. Granniss.] (Lit. of libr. in 17th & 18th
cent., 3). Chicago, 1906, 8°.   2590 f. Oxf. 1. 2
— [Another ed.]. (Trecentale Bodleianum, 1913.)
                                                    G.A. Oxon 8° 864 = A.

5409. WROUGHTON, C., Bodleius [a speech by C. Wroughton, at the Act
in honour of sir Thomas Bodley]. [Madan 3149.] [Oxf., 1677], fol. 4 pp.
                                                    Wood 657 (73)

5410. Reliquiæ Bodleianæ: or Some genuine remains of sir Thomas
Bodley [ed. by T. Hearne]. Lond., 1703, 8°. 383 pp. Gough Oxf. 126

5411. A note of the Divinitie schoole and librarye in Oxford. [*And*] Collections relating to the Div. schoole and library of the Univ. of Oxon.
written by dr. Langbaine. (A collection of curious discourses, publ. by
T. Hearne, 1720, p. 300–04.)   Mus. Bibl. II 63
— [Another ed.] (A collection of curious discourses, 1775, vol. 2,
p. 409–12.)   Mus. Bibl. II. 65

5412. INGRAM, J., Bodleian library. (Memorials of Oxford, 1837, vol. 2.
16 pp.)   G.A. Oxon 8° 19
— [Reissued.] (Memorials of the public buildings of Oxford. 1848.)
                                                    G.A. Oxon 8° 17

5413. MACRAY, W. D., Annals of the Bodleian Library, 1598–1867. Lond.
&c., 1868, 8°. 369 pp.   G.A. Oxon 8° 140
— 2nd ed., enlarged and continued from 1868 to 1880. Oxf., 1890, 8°.
545 pp.   2590 d. Oxf. 1. 9 = R.

5413.5. ROBARTS, C. H., University libraries and professional colleges.
(Macmillan's mag., 1876, vol. 33, p. 326–39.)   Per. 2705 d. 254

5414. NICHOLSON, E. W. B., Bodleian notes. i–xvi. [Articles in the Oxford
Review. Vol. 2–4.] 1885–88.   2590 d. Oxf. 1. 10

5415. MADAN, F., The Bodleian library at Oxford, a review repr. from the
'Guardian', Mar. 11, 1891. n. pl., 1891, 8°. 8 pp. 2590 e. Oxf. 1. 20

5416. [Papers and congratulatory messages &c. on the tercentenary of the Bodleian in 1902.] Tercentenary collection

5417. Pietas Oxoniensis, in memory of sir Thomas Bodley, knt., and the foundation of the Bodleian library. Oxf., 1902, fol. 40 pp.+16 plates.
2590 c. Oxf. 1. 16 = R.

5418. CASARTELLI, L. C., Oxford and Louvain [The address from Louvain on the Bodleian tercentenary, with an article setting out various connections between the two.] (Dubl. review, April 1903, p. 285–308.)
G.A. Oxon 8° 683 (25)

5419. DEGENER, H. A. L., Die Bodleian Library in Oxford. (Zeitschr. für Bücherfreunde, 1904, Jahrgang 8, Heft 3, p. 89–163.)
G.A. Oxon 4° 230

5420. BIRRELL, A., In the name of the Bodleian, and other essays. Lond., 1905, 8°. 214 pp. 27001 e. 95

5421. Trecentale Bodleianum, a memorial volume for the three hundredth anniversary of the public funeral of sir Thomas Bodley, March 29, 1613. Oxf., 1913, 8°. 175 pp. G.A. Oxon 8° 864 = A.

5422. Letter from sir Thomas Bodley to the Vice-chancellor offering to refound the University library, February 28, 1598. (Trecentale Bodleianum, 1913, p. 24–26.) G.A. Oxon 8° 864 = A.
[Previously pr. in Hearne's Glastoniensis chronica, 1726, vol. 2, p. 612 seq.; and in Wood's History of the Univ., 1796, vol. 2, p. 265 seq.]

5423. Extracts relating to the Bodleian Library from the will of sir Thomas Bodley. (Trecentale Bodleianum, 1913, p. 65–86).
G.A. Oxon 8° 864 = A.
[Printed in entirety in no. 5413, Annals of the Bodleian library, 2nd ed., 1890, p. 402–12.]

5424. Sir Thomas Bodley. Commemoration service in Merton college chapel, March 29th, 1913. Repr. from the Oxford Times, Apr. 5. [Oxf.], (1913), 16°. 15 pp G.A. Oxon 16° 33 (32)

5425. KOCH, T. W., The Bodleian library. (The Library journal, 1914, vol. 39, p. 739–46, 803–10.) Per. 25891 d. 3
— Repr. 16 pp. G.A. Oxon 4° 276 (22)

5426. MADAN, F., Statistical survey of the Bodleian library, with notes on book standards. By Bodley's librarian. (Bodleian quarterly record, 1916, vol. 1, p. 254–62.) Per. 2590 d. Oxf. 1. 40 = R.

5427. MADAN, F., Annals of the Bodleian library, 1882–1917 (1918). Pt. 1–4. (Bodleian quarterly record, 1917, vol. 2, p. 73–77; 1918, vol. 2, p. 168–78, 198–206, 229–34.) 2590 d. Oxf. 1. 40 = R.

5428. PLOWMAN, T. F., In the days of Victoria, memories. [Bodleian and Radcliffe Camera and general remarks on the city, p. 49–79.] Lond. &c., 1918, 8°. 211 e. 427

5429. WHEELER, G. W., Early Bodleian records. (Bodleian quarterly record, 1918, vol. 2, p. 147–51.)   2590 d. Oxf. 1. 40 = R.

5430. GOSSE, SIR E. W., Leaves and fruit. [Bodley and the Bodleian, p. 345–54.] Lond., 1927, 8°.   3962 e. 206

5431. MADAN, F., The Bodleian library at Oxford. (Lond.), 1919, 8°. 68 pp.   2590 e. Oxf. 1. 21

5432. COWLEY, SIR A. E., Bodleian library: recent history. (Libr. assoc. record, 1921, vol. 23, p. 316–25.)   Per. 25891 d. 21

5433. PARRY, T. GAMBIER-, Flora Bodleiana. [Plants found within the ground falling under the immediate jurisdiction of Bodley's librarian.] (Bodleian quarterly record, 1925, vol. 4, p. 250–52.)
          2590 d. Oxf. 1. 40 = R.

5434. Letters of sir Thomas Bodley addressed to the University of Oxford, 1598–1611, ed. by G. W. Wheeler. (Bodleian quarterly record, 1926, vol. 5, p. 46–50, 72–76, 127–30, 153–61.)   2590 d. Oxf. 1. 40 = R.
— [Repr.]. Oxf., 1927, 4°. 24 pp.   2590 d. Oxf. 1. 45 = R.

5435. Letters of sir Thomas Bodley to Thomas James, first keeper of the Bodleian library, ed. by G. W. Wheeler. Oxf., 1926, 4°. 251 pp.
          2590 d. Oxf. 1. 44 = R.

See 5256 [Streeter, B. H., The chained library. 1931].

5436. HUSSEY, C., The Schools quadrangle and Duke Humphrey's library. (Country Life, 1931, vol. 69, 480–86.)   Per. 384 b. 6

5437. HUSSEY, C., The Bodleian library. (Country Life, 1931, vol. 69, p. 510–16.)   Per. 384 b. 6

5438. Letters addressed to Thomas James, first keeper of Bodley's library, ed. by G. W. Wheeler. Oxf., 1933, 4°. 69 pp. 2590 d. Oxf. 1. 22 = R.

5439. HILL, R. H., The Bodleian since 1882—some records and reminiscences. (Libr. assoc. record, 1940, 4th ser., vol. 7, p. 76–85.)
          Per. 25891 d. 21
— Repr. 12 pp.   2590 d. Oxf. 1. 30

5440. CHAMBERS, SIR E. K., A sheaf of studies. (Ghosts in the Bodleian, p. 144–54.) Lond. &c., 1942, 8°.   27001 e. 1518

5441. GIBSON, S., Royal visits to the Bodleian library. (Oxf. mag., 1946, vol. 65, p. 22, 23.)   Per. G.A. Oxon 4° 141

5442. CRASTER, SIR E., History of the Bodleian library, 1845–1945. Oxf., 1952, 8°. 372 pp.   2590 d. Oxf. 1. 34 = R.

5443. MYRES, J. N. L., The Bodleian library in post-war Oxford. (Oxford, 1952, vol. 11, p. 64–71.)   Per. G.A. Oxon 8° 1141

5444. WEBB, C. C. J., Some Bodleian memories. (Bodleian library record, 1953, vol. 4, p. 277–79.)   2590 d. Oxf. 1. 41 = R.

See 3143.1 [Bassett, S., Royal marine; the installation etc. of the Interservice Topographical Department in the New Bodleian. 1962].

5444.1. BARBER, G., 'Quarta perennis'. [On Sir Thomas Bodley's motto.] (Bodl. libr. record, 1962, vol. 7, p. 46–50.) Per. 2590 d. Oxf. 1. 41 = R.

5444.2. SOWERS, R. V., Oxford revisited [mainly Bodley]. (Book club of California, Quarterly news letter, 1964, vol. 29, p. 51–59.)
Per. 25805 d. 170

Visitors' guides

5445. CLARK, A., A Bodleian guide for visitors. Oxf., 1906, 12°. 128 pp.
G.A. Oxon 16° 93

5446. Bodleian library. Visitors' guide. [Oxf.], 1933, 12°. 15 pp.
2590 f. Oxf. 1. 14

— [Other issues in 1935, 36, 37, 38, 39.]

5447. Bodleian library. Visitors' guide. [2 issues.] Oxf., 1950, 53, 8°. 16 pp.
2590 e. Oxf. 1. 31

Statute

5448. The first draft of the statutes for the public library at Oxon by sir Thomas Bodley. (Trecentale Bodleianum, 1913, p. 27–64.)
G.A. Oxon 8° 864 = A.

5449. Sir Thomas Bodley's 'Heads of statutes'. [Introduction; and Text, written 1602.] (Bodleian quarterly record, 1921, vol. 3, p. 119–21.)
2590 d. Oxf. 1. 40 = R.

5450. [*Begin.*] The following statute . . . [Statutum novum de administratione Bibliothecæ Bodleianæ. The text, with three pages of preliminary comments.] [Oxf., 1813], fol. 14 pp.   Bliss B 417 (6)

5451. Bodleian library statute. Extr. from the Statuta universitatis Oxoniensis, tit. xx, Sectio iii. Repr. [Oxf.], 1920, 12°. 11 pp.
2590 f. Oxf. 1. 13

Buildings and fabric

5452. [Convocation notice about the proposed warming of the Bodleian and the Convocation House by means of a hot air dispenser.] [Oxf.], 1821, s. sh.   Bliss B 417

5453. Communications [by J. W. [*sic*] Gilbert Scott, J. Braidwood, Geo. Gilbert Scott, J. Burlison] respecting the extension and warming of the Bodleian. n. pl., [1856], 8°. 20 pp.   G.A. Oxon c. 72 (325)

5454. WELLESLEY, H., Plans of the Bodleian library, with practical suggestions by one of the curators [signed H. W.]. n. pl., (1858), fol. 8 pp.+ 3 pl.   G.A. fol. A 138

5455. Report of the Bodleian construction committee, together with captain Galton's report, and a letter from the Bodleian librarian. Oxf., 1874, 8°. 39 pp.   2590 e. Oxf. 1. 4

5456. GALTON, D., [Report on the ceiling of the Divinity school, and the floor and roof of the Bodleian.] n. pl., [1875], 8°. 5 pp.
G.A. Oxon c. 33 (85)

5457. SYMM, J. R., AND CO., Messrs. Symm and co.'s report on the Bodleian library. [Oxf.], (1875), 8°. 3 pp.   G.A. Oxon c. 33 (86)

5458. SCOTT, SIR G. G., Sir G. G. Scott's report on the Proscholium. [The proposed conversion of the Proscholium as a fireproof receptacle for the most precious contents of the Bodleian.] n. pl., (1875), 8°. 3 pp.
G.A. Oxon c. 33 (87)

5459. A suggestion for the enlargement of the Bodleian Library. (Archæologia Oxon., 1892–95, p. 81–84.)   G.A. Oxon 4° 148 = R.
— Revised. Repr. from the Archæol. Oxon. [Lond., 1892], 4°. 4 pp.
G.A. Oxon 4° 155

5460. HARRISON, J. P., The architecture of the Bodleian library and the Old Schools. (Archæologia Oxon., 1892–95, p. 253–68, 315–20.)
G.A. Oxon 4° 148 = R.

See 5911, 5912 [Bicycle stands in the Proscholium. 1904, 05].

5461. POOLE, R., The architect of the Schools and the tower of the five orders. (Bodleian quarterly record, 1922, vol. 3, p. 263, 64.)
2590 d. Oxf. 1. 40 = R.

5461.5. The future of the Bodleian. [Five proposals for dealing with the problem of overcrowding of books.] (Oxf.), 1926, 4°. 12 pp.
2590 d. Oxf. 1. 48

5462. The Bodleian. [Arguments, signed by M. V. Clarke and 9 others, opposing the idea of a building on the Broad street site, and proposing a transfer of the whole library to a new building elsewhere. Scheme A.] [Oxf.], (1928), 4°. 4 pp.   G.A. Oxon c. 314 (32)

5463. Bodleian preservation committee. [Observations in support of scheme B as printed in the University Gazette. Signed P. S. Allen and 5 others.] [Oxf.], (1928), 4°. 4 pp.   G.A. Oxon c. 314 (31)
[Scheme A and B printed in The University Gazette 1928, vol. 58, p. 511: both were rejected. The scheme finally passed is printed in vol. 59 at p. 400.]

5464. Bodleian preservation committee. [Urging the support of scheme B. Signed by P. S. Allen and 5 others.] [Oxf., 1928], 4°. 4 pp.
G.A. Oxon c. 314 (35)

5465. GIBSON, S., Bodley's library, founded 1602. [Urging that scheme B should be supported.] [Oxf.], (1928), 4°. 4 pp. G.A. Oxon c. 314 (33)

5466. The Bodleian. [Arguments, signed M. E. Sadler, E. L. Woodward, E. F. Jacob, reiterating their support of 12 March of scheme A.] [Oxf.], (1928), s. sh.   G.A. Oxon c. 314 (34)

5467. Bodleian extension, an impartial statement [summarizing the advantages &c. of both schemes]. [Oxf.], (1928), s. sh.
G.A. Oxon c. 314 (36)

5468. WELLS, J., and LYS, F. J., The Bodleian library [urging the rejection of both schemes, and favouring the transformation from a copyright library into one of selectivity]. [Oxf., 1928], s. sh.
G.A. Oxon c. 314 (37)

5469. The lighting of the Bodleian. (Architect, 1930, vol. 124, p. 851, 52).
N. 1731 c. 16

5469.9. MADAN, F., The Bodleian decree of May 19 and 26, 1931. The Bodleian commission; remarks on the recommendations [in no. 5255]. [Oxf.], (1931), 4°. 4 pp.
G.A. Oxon b. 148

5470. The New Bodleian. (Oxf. mag., 1931, vol. 49, p. 682, 83.)
Per. G.A. Oxon 4° 141

5471. Speech delivered by ... the Warden of New college when proposing the decree acknowledging the offer of the Rockefeller foundation approved by Congregation on 24 May 1932 [to finance the building of the New Bodleian]. [Oxf.], (1932), 4°. 4 pp. G.A. Oxon c. 282 (f. 51)

5472. H., M., The New Bodleian: sir Giles Scott's design. (Oxf. mag., 1935, vol. 54, p. 120, 21.)
Per. G.A. Oxon 4° 141

5473. Bodleian library: Broad street building: architect's preliminary plans. (Libr. assoc. record, 1935, 4th ser., vol. 2, p. 525, 26.)
Per. 25891 d. 21

5474. The New Bodleian. (Architect, 1936, vol. 146, p. 179–82.)
N. 1731 c. 16

5475. CRASTER, SIR H. H. E., Bodleian library extension: plans of the new building. (Libr. assoc. record, 1936, 4th ser., vol. 3, p. 185–90.)
Per. 25891 d. 21

5476. The engineering plant, Bodleian library. (Air treatment engineer, 1938, vol. 1, p. 12, 13, 26.)
Per. 1864 c. 3

5477. ARKELL, W. J., The geology of the site of the Bodleian extension in Broad street. (Oxoniensia, 1938, vol. 3, p. 1–6.)
Per. G.A. Oxon 4° 658 = R. Top.

5478. LEEDS, E. T., Glass vessels of the xvi century and later, from the site of the Bodleian extension in Broad street. (Oxoniensia, 1938, vol. 3, p. 153–61.)
Per. G.A. Oxon 4° 658 = R. Top.

5479. MITFORD, R. L. S. BRUCE-, The archaeology of the site of the Bodleian extension in Broad street. (Oxoniensia, 1939, vol. 4, p. 89–146.)
Per. G.A. Oxon 4° 658 = R. Top.

5480. Bodleian library extension. (Architect, 1940, vol. 163, p. 139, 143–50).
N. 1731 c. 16

5481. Bodleian library extension. (Architect. journ., 1940, vol. 92, p. 149–53.)   N. 1863 c. 12

5482. Bodleian library extension. (Builder, 1940, vol. 159, p. 180, 185–89.)   N. 1863 c. 1

5483. CRASTER, H. H. E., The Bodleian library extension scheme. (Bulletin, John Rylands libr., 1941, vol. 25, p. 83–96.)
Per. 2590 d. Manch. 2. 5 = B.
— Repr. Manch., 1941, 8°. 14 pp.   2590 d. Oxf. 1. 30

5484. PHILIP, I. G., The building of the Schools quadrangle. (Oxoniensia, 1948, vol. 13, p. 39–48.)   Per. G.A. Oxon 4° 658 = R. Top.

5485. PHILIP, I. G., A forgotten gate to the Schools quadrangle. (Oxoniensia, 1952/53, vol. 17/18, p. 185–87.) Per. G.A. Oxon 4° 658 = R. Top.

5486. Some reflections on Bodleian reconstruction. (Oxf. mag., 1956, vol. 74, p. 208–10.)   Per. G.A. Oxon 4° 141

5487. MYRES, J. N. L., The reconstruction of the Bodleian library. (Amer. Oxon., 1957, vol. 44, p. 62–66.)   Per. G.A. Oxon 8° 889

Fresco

See 5495 [Hearne, T., Heads painted upon the wall. 1725].

5488. MADAN, F., The two hundred 'heads' in the old Bodleian picture gallery. (Bodleian quarterly record, 1934, vol. 7, p. 509–12.)
2590 d. Oxf. 1. 40 = R.

5489. MYRES, J. N. L., The painted frieze in the Picture gallery. (Bodleian library record, 1950, vol. 3, p. 82–91.)   2590 d. Oxf. 1. 41 = R.

5490. ROUSE, E. C., The repair of the painted frieze in the Picture gallery. (Bodleian library record, 1951, vol. 3, p. 201–07.)
2590 d. Oxf. 1. 41 = R.

5491. MYRES, J. N. L., Thomas James and the painted frieze. (Bodleian library record, 1952, vol. 4, p. 30–51.)   2590 d. Oxf. 1. 41 = R.

5492. MYRES, J. N. L., and ROUSE, E. C., Further notes on the painted frieze and other discoveries in the Upper reading room and the Tower room. (Bodleian libr. record, 1956, vol. 5, p. 290–308.)
2590 d. Oxf. 1. 41 = R.

Contents other than books

5493. HEARNE, T., A list of the pictures in the gallery of the publick-library at Oxford. (A compleat volume of the Memoirs for the curious, 1708, p. 359–65.)   4° Rawl. 74

5494. WILSON, R., A full . . . account of all the robberies committed by John Hawkins . . . With an account of Hawkins' defacing several pictures in the Bodleian library. 2nd ed. Lond., [c. 1722], 8°. 29 pp.
8° A 11. 127 Jur.

5495. HEARNE, T., A list of the pictures in the gallery of the Publick library [*and*] Heads painted upon the wall. (A letter containing an account of some antiquities between Windsor and Oxford, repr. 1725, p. 25–43.)   Mus. Bibl. II. 13

5496. A catalogue of the several pictures, statues and busto's in the picture gallery . . . Oxf., 1759, 8°. 16 pp.   Gough Oxf. 142 (5)
— 2nd ed. 1760.   Gough Oxf. 7 (5)
— New ed. [*entitled*] A catalogue [&c.] in the picture gallery, Bodleian library, and Ashmolean museum. 1762.   G.A. Oxon 8° 45 (1)
[Other eds. in 1763, 64, 66, 68, 72, 75, 90, 93, 96, 1802, 1806.]
[An imperfect copy, perhaps printed c. 1790, with many MS. notes, is in Library Records.]

See 317 [A description of the models in the Picture gallery. New ed. 1821].

5497. NORRIS, J., A catalogue of the pictures, models, busts, &c. in the Bodleian gallery. Oxf., [1840], 8°. 60 pp.   2590 e. Oxf. 1. 29
— [Another ed.] [1847].   G.A. Oxon 8° 105 (3)

5498. POOLE, R., Catalogue of portraits exhibited in the reading room & gallery of the Bodleian library. Oxf., 1920, 8°. 134 pp.
                                          17091 e. 59 = R.

5499. Catalogue of portraits exhibited to visitors in the Bodleian library. Oxf., 1930, 8°. 19 pp.+12 pl.   17061 d. 30

5500. A list of contributors for the portrait of . . . H. O. Coxe . . . painted in . . . 1877 by G. F. Watts, and placed in the Bodleian Library. Oxf., [1877], 8°. 12 pp.   G.A. Oxon 8° 1199

5501. SHARPE, F., Bodley's bell. (Bodleian library record, 1951, vol. 3, p. 143–46.)   2590 d. Oxf. 1. 41 = R.

See 5357 [Nummorum antiquorum scriniis Bodleianis reconditorum catalogus. 1750].
See 5358 [Chandler, H. W., Bodleian coins and medals. 1885].
See 5362 [Milne, J. G., Douce as a coin-collector. 1934].

5502. MYRES, J. N. L., The Bodleian coin cabinets. (Bodleian library record, 1950, vol. 3, p. 45–49.)   2590 d. Oxf. 1. 41 = R.

5503. HILL, R. H., *ed.*, The inscriptions on the Drake chair. (Bodleian quarterly record, 1931, vol. 6, p. 273, 74.)   2590 d. Oxf. 1. 40 = R.

5504. KNOWLES, J. A., On two panels of glass in the Bodleian library representing scenes from the history of St. Thomas Becket. (Bodleian quarterly record, 1926, vol. 5, p. 100–04.)   2590 d. Oxf. 1. 40 = R.

See 8694, 8695 [Daniel press].

5505. TURNER, W. H., On seals attached to charters preserved in the Bodleian library. (Trans., Roy. soc. of lit., 1874, new ser., vol. 10, p. 505–20.)   Soc. 3962 e. 161
— Repr. 16 pp.   2590 e. Oxf. ii. 1

5506. CRASTER, H. H. E., and WIBLIN, J. G., Discovery [and description] of a nearly complete specimen of the first great seal of Charles ii, A.D. 1649. (Bodleian quarterly record, 1915, vol. 1, p. 199–202.)
2590 d. Oxf. 1. 40 = R.

5507. WIBLIN, J. G., List of great seals of England in the Bodleian library. (Bodleian quarterly record, 1915, vol. 1, p. 197, 98.)
2590 d. Oxf. 1. 40 = R.

See 5356 [Nicholson, E. B., Council, lady Chantrey and the Bodleian. 1896].

Administration
General

5508. BEDDOES, T., A memorial concerning the state of the Bodleian library and the conduct of the principal librarian . . . by the chemical reader [T. Beddoes]. [Oxf., 1787], 4°. 19 pp. Bodl. Library Records

5508.1. Narrative of proceedings relative to the Bodleian library [signed by J. Randolph and 3 other curators]. [Oxf., 1788], fol. 24 pp.
Bodl. Library Records

5508.2. [Begin.] Many members of Convocation attached to no party . . . [An answer to 5508.1.] [Oxf., 1788], s. sh. Bodl. Library Records

5508.3. [Begin.] The regius professors at present in the University . . . [A reply, signed by J. Randolph and 3 others, to no. 5508.2 by the authors of no. 5508.1.] June 21st, 1788. [Oxf.], (1788), fol. 11 pp.
Bodl. Library Records

5509. NICHOLSON, E. B., [Letter complaining of repeated attacks by the Oxford Magazine on himself and the administration of the Bodleian.] (Oxf. mag., 1887, vol. 5, p. 222, 23.) Per. G.A. Oxon 4° 141

5510. The Bodleian library in 1882–7, a report from the librarian. Oxf., 1888, fol. 66 pp. 2590 d. Oxf. 1. 47 = R.
— Annual report of the Curators of the Bodleian library. 1889– . [Publ. as part of the Oxf. Univ. gazette.] Oxf., [1890–], fol.
Per. 2590 c. Oxf. 1. 14 = R.
— [Separate publ.] 1937/38– . Oxf., [1938–], 8°.
Per. 2590 e. Oxf. 1. 51 = R.

5511. CHANDLER, H. W., Memorandum [on the 1884/85 report of Bodley's librarian. By H. W. Chandler]. [Oxf.], (1885), fol. 4 pp.
2590 c. Oxf. 1. 12

5512. Bodleian library, Oxford. A subject index (for the arrangement of [internal] records, correspondence and papers). [Oxf.], 1912, 16°. 36 pp.
2590 g. Oxf. 1. 5
— [Another ed.] [Oxf.], 1914, 8°. 24 pp. 2590 f. Oxf. 1. 9

5513. GIBSON, S., What we do. [An account of work in the Bodleian, signed S. G.] (Bodleian quarterly record, 1921, vol. 3, p. 80–84.)
2590 d. Oxf. 1. 40 = R.

5514. SQUIRE, J. C., Essays at large, by Solomon Eagle. ['The librarian's hard lot', p. 185–90. Inspired by no. 5513.] Lond. &c., [1922], 8°.
27001 e. 626

Finance

See also 5616, &c. [Purchases, Bodleian Library].

5515. SCOTT, W., lord Stowell, [Begin.] No member of a learned society . . . [Proposals for ensuring an annual income for the Bodleian Library. By W. Scott.] [Oxf., 1780?], fol. 4 pp.   Bliss B 417 (1)

5516. On the income and expenditure of the Bodleian library [and] A statement of the income and expenditure, 1873/74. (Hebdomadal council.) [Oxf., 1875], fol. 4 pp.   G.A. Oxon c. 33 (77)
— [Another ed.]   G.A. Oxon c. 33 (78)

5517. Draft. Communication from the curators of Bodley's library to the Hebdomadal council [concerning library finances, particularly affecting purchase of books and repair of Duke Humfrey, &c.]. [Oxf., 1875], s. sh.   G.A. Oxon c. 33 (91)
— [Final form.]   G.A. Oxon c. 33 (92)

5518. An estimate of the income and expenditure of the Bodleian library for . . . 1875–1876. [Oxf., 1875], s. sh.   G.A. Oxon c. 33 (82)

5519. Report on the accounts of the Bodleian library to the curators, Nov. 6, 1875. [Oxf., 1876], fol. 4 pp.   G.A. Oxon c. 33 (79)

5520. The Bodleian finances. (Oxf. mag., 1887, vol. 5, p. 239, 40.)
Per. G.A. Oxon 4° 141

5521. NICHOLSON, E. W. B., Oxford's poverty, a letter to the . . . Daily News of October 6, 1894. Repr. Oxf. &c., [1894], 8°. 8 pp.
G.A. Oxon 8° 540 (13)

5522. NICHOLSON, E. W. B., Mr. Gladstone and the Bodleian. Oxford's poverty (reprinted from the edition of 1894). Bodley and the Bodleian, 1598–1898. Oxf., 1898, 8°. 42 pp.   2590 e. Oxf. 1. 7 (?)
[Bodley has a proof copy in 2590 e. Oxf. 1. 7 (1).]

5523. Appeal on behalf of the Bodleian library. [Oxf.], (1914), 8°. 7 pp.
G.A. Oxon c. 309 (77)

5524. MADAN, F., A survey of Bodleian library finance. 2 pt. (Bodleian quarterly record, 1935, vol. 8, p. 6–15, 55–65.)
2590 d. Oxf. 1. 40 = R.

Library economy

5525. The following correspondence between mr. C. H. Robarts . . . and the curators of the Bodleian library is printed . . . for the information of members of Convocation. [The former proposes an amalgamation of All Souls college and the Bodleian Library.] n. pl., (1877), 8°. 7 pp.
G.A. Oxon 8° 250 (14)

5526. BRIGGS, G. M., 'The general removal 1723.' (Bodleian library record, 1951, vol. 3, p. 213–22.)   2590 d. Oxf. 1. 41 = R.

5527. Observations by the librarians [H. O. Coxe, J. W. Nutt, A. Neubauer] on the report of the Committee of the curators ('upon the general arrangement of the rooms of the library'). n. pl., 1878, 8°. 14 pp.   G.A. Oxon 8° 828 (3)

5528. Reasons [signed H. T. G. but drawn up for The Club] for rejecting the second Bodleian decree on Tuesday next. Feb. 25, 1889. [Concerns the deposit of books in the Sheldonian basement.] [Oxf.], 1889, s. sh.
G.A. Oxon b. 147

5529. BYWATER, I., [Begin.] Being prevented by illness . . . [differing from the answers which the curators of the Bodleian have framed to the questions concerning binding, purchases, and staff propounded by Convocation]. [Oxf.], (1890), s. sh.   Firth b. 36 (7)

5530. NICHOLSON, E. W. B., The crisis of Bodleian history, an appeal to the Convocation . . . June 1, 1909. Oxf., 1909, 4°. 7 pp.
2590 d. Oxf. 1. 7

5531. GIBSON, S., Humphrey Wanley and the Bodleian in 1697. [Memorandum, dated Nov. 10, for the better regulating of the Bodleian.] (Bodleian quarterly record, 1915, vol. 1, p. 106–12, 136–40.)
2590 d. Oxf. 1. 40 = R.

5532. MADAN, F., Bodleian binding [i.e. the general policy of binding]. (Oxf. mag., 1915, vol. 33, p. 207, 08.)   Per. G.A. Oxon 4° 141

5533. MADAN, F., The ideal Bodleian. Oxf. &c., 1928, 8°. 34 pp.
G.A. Oxon 8° 1055 (3)
— Re-issued with addendum.   G.A. Oxon 8° 1055 (4)

See 5255 [Library provision in Oxford. 1931].
See 5257 [Library provision in Oxford: the scheme in progress. 1934].

5534. CRASTER, H. H. E., The Bodleian and its present problems. (Library assoc. record, 1932, 3rd ser., vol. 2, p. 137–43.)   Per. 25891 d. 21
— Repr. 7 pp.   2590 d. Oxf. 1. 21

5535. GILLAM, S. G., and HUNT, R. W., The curators of the library and Humphrey Wanley [incl. his Memorandum, dated 7 June, 1697, 'on the regulating any present disorders in the Library']. (Bodleian library record, 1954, vol. 5, p. 85–98).   2590 d. Oxf. 1. 41 = R.

Staff

5536. PUSEY, E. B., Is there any ground why the librarian and under-librarians of the Bodleian should not have cure of souls? [Signed A curator of the Bodleian library, i.e. E. B. Pusey.] n. pl., [1861], 8°. 4 pp.
G.A. Oxon c. 77 (387)

5537. The sub-librarianship of the Bodleian library. [Paper, signed B.D., advocating that both W. D. Macray and Max Müller be appointed sub-librarians.] Oxf., [1865], s. sh.   G.A. Oxon c. 81 (443)

5538. The Bodleian library. [Reprints of 2 letters in the Standard and the Morning Herald, opposing the appointment of Max Müller and supporting W. D. Macray.] n. pl., [1865], s. sh. G.A. Oxon c. 81 (444)

5539. The Bodleian library. [Corrections, signed H. O. Coxe, to some misstatements of facts in the reprints of letters from the Standard and the Morning Herald.] n. pl., 1865, s. sh. G.A. Oxon c. 81 (445)

5540. The Bodleian library. [Paper, signed A member of Convocation, supporting Max Müller.] n. pl., 1865, s. sh. G.A. Oxon c. 81 (446)

5541. BURGON, J. W., Henry Octavius Coxe, the large-hearted librarian. 1811–1881. (Lives of twelve good men, 1888, vol. 2, p. 123–48.)
2106 e. 27
— New ed. 1891. 11126 d. 20

5542. MADAN, F., Memorandum. The statutable residence of Bodleian officers. n. pl., 1889, 8°. 16 pp. G.A. Oxon 8° 452

5543. Bodleian library. Staff-kalendar [afterw.] Staff manual. 1902–37. Oxf., 1902–37, 16° & 8°. Per. 2590 g. Oxf. 1. 1; Per. 2590 f. Oxf. 1. 3
— Staff calendar. 1938- . Oxf., 1938- , 8°. Cal. 2590 e. Oxf. 1. 26

5544. TEDDER, H. R., E. W. B. Nicholson . . . In memoriam. Aberd., 1914, 8°. 16 pp. 2590 d. Oxf. 1. 11

5545. WHEELER, G. W., The Bodleian staff, 1600–12. (Bodleian quarterly record, 1919, vol. 2, p. 279–85, 310–14.) 2590 d. Oxf. 1. 40 = R.

5546. WHEELER, G. W., Thomas James, theologian and Bodley's librarian. (Bodleian quarterly record, 1923, vol. 4, p. 91–95.)
2590 d. Oxf. 1. 40 = R.

5547. ALLEN, T. W., Arthur Ernest Cowley, 1861–1931 [signed T. W. A.]. From the Proc., Brit. acad. vol. 19. Lond., (1931), 4°. 11 pp.
2590 d. Oxf. 1. 24

5548. Library code. Oxf., [1939], 8°. 56 pp. 2590 e. Oxf. 1. 27

5549. Bodleian library. Staff regulations. Oxf., 1948, 8°. 24 pp.
2590 e. Oxf. 1. 32

5550. GIBSON, S., E. W. B. Nicholson (1849–1912). Some impressions. (Libr. assoc. record, 1949, vol. 51, p. 137–43.) Per. 25891 d. 21

5551. STEPHENS, J. C., Mr. Crab, the librarian [sub librarian, Bodleian]. (Notes and queries, 1956, N.S., vol. 3, p. 105, 06.)
Per. 3974 e. 405 = A.

5551.3. BURDEN, S. G., Herbert Frank Dyer, 1889–1965. Memorial address. [Reprod. from typewriting.] n. pl., 1965, 8°. 4 pp.
2590 e. Oxf. 1. 56

Publications

5552. The Bodleian quarterly record. Vol. 1, no. 1–vol. 8, no. 96. [Continued as The Bodleian library record.] Oxf., 1914–1937/8, 4°.
2590 d. Oxf. 1. 40 = R.

5553. The Bodleian library record. Vol. 1, no. 1– . Oxf., 1938– , 8°.
        2590 d. Oxf. 1. 41 = R.

5554. Bodleian picture books. 1– . Oxf., 1951– , 8°.
        2590 e. Oxf. 1. 41 = R.
1. English Romanesque illumination.
2. Gold-tooled book-bindings.
3. J. C. Buckler. Drawings of Oxford.
4. Zoological illustration.
5. Scenes from the life of Christ in English MSS.
6. Portraits of the 16th and early 17th centuries.
7. Architectural drawings.
8. Byzantine illumination.
9. Mughal miniatures.
10. English illumination of the 13th and 14th centuries.
11. The Kennicott Bible.
12. Humanistic script of the 15th and 16th centuries.
13. An Islamic Book of constellations.
14. English rural life in the Middle Ages.

Readers and reading-rooms

5555. Public libraries. [An article commenting upon various libraries; the Bodleian and Corpus Christi college library are particularly noticed.] (Retrospective review, 1827, 2nd ser., vol. 1, p. 280–89.)
        Per. 269 e. 261 = A.

5556. Public libraries. [Article on the difficulty of obtaining permission to use 'public' libraries.] (Westminster review, 1827, vol. 8, p. 105–27.)
        Per. 3977 e. 228

5557. Public libraries at Oxford. [Letter, signed M.A. Univ. Oxon., commenting on no. 5555 in so far as it relates to the Bodleian.] (The Crypt, 1828, vol. 2, p. 85–91.)
        Hope 8° 280

5558. Overcrowding of the Bodleian by women [3 letters]. (Oxf. mag., 1900, vol. 18, p. 393, 412, 429.)
        Per. G.A. Oxon 4° 141

5559. NICHOLSON, E. W. B., The north wing of the Picture-gallery as an additional Bodleian reading-room—in fulfilment of Bodley's own design [signed E. W. B. Nicholson]. 1 Feb. 1907. [Oxf.], 1907, 4°. 10 pp.
        G.A. Oxon c. 309 (63)

5560. Memorandum on the new Bodleian reading-room. 8 Oct. 1907. [Oxf.], 1907, 4°. 4 pp.
        G.A. Oxon c. 309 (65)

5561. Bodleian library, Oxford. Manual for readers and visitors. October 8, 1912. 1st issue: under revision: not fully authorized. [Oxf.], 1912, 8°.
14 pp.   2590 f. Oxf. 1. 10a
— [Another issue on better paper].   2590 f. Oxf. 1. 10b
— [Another ed.] 1916, 19 pp.   2590 f. Oxf. 1. 10c
— [Another ed.] 1918. 20 pp.   2590 f. Oxf. 1. 10d
— [Another ed.] 1922. 23 pp.   2590 f. Oxf. 1. 10e

— [Another ed.] 1926. 23 pp.   2590 f. Oxf. 1. 10*f*
— [Another ed.] 1930. 25 pp.   2590 f. Oxf. 1. 10*g*
— [Another ed.] 1933. 12 pp.   2590 f. Oxf. 1. 10*h*

5562. Bodleian library. Readers' manual. (Oxf.), 1936, 8°. 35 pp.
          2590 f. Oxf. 1. 10

5563. WHEELER, G. W., Readers in the Bodleian, Nov. 8, 1602–Nov. 7, 1603. (Bodleian quarterly record, 1922, vol. 3, p. 212–17.)
          2590 d. Oxf. 1. 40 = R.

5564. WHEELER, G. W., 'Free-access' in 1613 [containing Twyne's protest against the removal of MSS. from their former places among printed works]. (Bodleian quarterly record, 1924, vol. 4, p. 192–98.)
          2590 d. Oxf. 1. 40 = R.

5565. The Arts End of the Bodleian library. (Oxf. mag., 1937, vol. 56, p. 86, 87.)   Per. G.A. Oxon 4° 141

5566. DE ZULUETA, F., The Arts End decree and the Law faculty. (Oxf. mag., 1939, vol. 57, p. 369–71.)   Per. G.A. Oxon 4° 141

5567. GILLAM, S. G., Bodleian readers [statistical survey]. (Bodleian library record, 1947, vol. 2, p. 158, 59.)   2590 d. Oxf. 1. 41 = R.

Bindings

5568. BRASSINGTON, W. S., Historic bindings in the Bodleian library, with reproductions of twenty-four of the finest bindings. Lond., 1891, fol. xliv+63 pp.   25897 c. 8 = R.

5569. GIBSON, S., Some notable Bodleian bindings, 12th to 18th cents. [Publ. in 3 pts.] Oxf., 1901–1904, fol. 11 pp.+31 plates.
          25897 d. 16 = R.

5570. GIBSON, S., Douce bookbindings [*part of* Francis Douce centenary]. (Bodleian quarterly record, 1934, vol. 7, p. 373–75.)
          2590 d. Oxf. 1. 40 = R.

5571. GIBSON, S., Bookbindings in the Buchanan collection. (Bodleian library record, 1941, vol. 2, p. 6–12.)   2590 d. Oxf. 1. 41 = R.

5571.5. SOMMERLAD, M. J., Scottish 'wheel' and 'herring-bone' bindings in the Bodleian library, an illustr. handlist. Presented to members of the Oxf. bibliogr. soc., 1964. Oxf., (1964), 4°. 10 pp.+3 pages of photogr.   25897 d. 111 = R.

Copyright

5572. An act for preventing the frequent abuses in printing seditious, treasonable and unlicensed bookes and pamphlets and for regulating of printing and printing presses. [Provides for the Bodleian copyright privilege, in continuation of the earlier agreement with the Stationers' Company, made 20 Dec., 1610.] (14 Ch. II, c. 33, Pub.) Lond., 1662, fol. 20 pp.   L. L.

— 16 Ch. II, c. 8, Pub.
— 16/17 Ch. II, c. 7, Pub.
— 17 Ch. II, c. 4, Pub.
[This act expired on 26 May 1679.]

5573. An act for reviving and continuance of several acts. (1 Jas. II, c. 17, Pub.) Lond., 1685, fol. 8 pp.   L. L.
— 4 W. & M., c. 24, Pub. [This act expired on 13 May 1695.]

5574. An act for the encouragement of learning by vesting the copies of printed books in the authors or purchasers of such copies during the times therein mentioned. [Sect. 5 deals with Bodleian copyright privilege.] (8 A., c. 19, Pub.) Lond., 1710, fol. 6 pp.   L. L.
— 15 G. III, c. 53, Pub.
— 41 G. III, c. 107, Pub.
— 54 G. III, c. 156, Pub.
— 5 & 6 V., c. 45, Pub.
— 1 & 2 G. V, c. 46, Pub.

Donations

5575. Munificentissimis atque optimis cuiusvis ordinis, dignitatis, sexus, qui Bibliothecam hanc libris, aut pecuniis numeratis ad libros coemendos, aliove quovis genere ampliarunt, Thomas Bodleius eques auratus, honorarium hoc volumen . . . pietatis, memoriæ virtutisque causa dedit, dedicavit. [Madan 249.] [Lond., 1604], fol. 91 printed pp. continued in MS.   [Bodl. Libr. Records.]

5576. Donations to the Bodleian library. 1862–85. [Some earlier lists of donations are included in No. 5616.] Oxf., 1862–85, 8°.
                                    2590 e. Oxf. 1. 12–14

5577. CRASTER, H. H. E., Miscellaneous donations recorded in the Benefactors' register. Pt. 1–3. (Bodleian quarterly record, 1923, vol. 4, p. 22–24, 43–47, 68–71.)   2590 d. Oxf. 1. 40 = R.

Exhibitions

5578. List of books, manuscripts, portraits, &c. exhibited in the Bodleian library. Oxf., 1881, 8°. 44 pp.   G.A. Oxon 8° 220 (4)

5579. NICHOLSON, E. W. B., A brief conspectus of the [exhibition] cases in the Bodleian arranged to illustrate the history of Latin and West European book-hands, by the librarian. [Oxf.], 1890, fol. 8 pp.
                                    2590 b. Oxf. 1. 2

5580. A catalogue of the Shakespeare exhibition . . . April 23, 1916. Oxf., 1916, 4°. 99 pp.   M. adds. 36 d. 9
— Corrected re-issue.   M. adds. 36 d. 92

5581. Catalogue of classical MSS. exhibited in the Bodleian library. May–July 1919. (Bodleian quarterly record, 1918, vol. 2, p. 253–58.)
                                    2590 d. Oxf. 1. 40 = R.

5582. British Association meeting, Oxford 1926. Exhibition of scientific MSS. and printed books at the Bodleian library. Oxf., (1926), 4°. 22 pp.
2590 d. Oxf. 1. 15

5583. Oxford English dictionary, 1884–1928: an exhibition of books, illustrating the history of English dictionaries. Oxf., 1928, 8°. 20 pp.
2590 e. Oxf. 1. 22

5584. An exhibition in commemoration of the canonization of sir Thomas More and bishop John Fisher, including works of Robert Southwell and the Oxford recusants, 1535–1660. Oxf., 1935, 4°. 7 pp.
2590 d. Oxf. 1. 25

5585. 1837. An exhibition held . . . May to October, 1937. [Reprod. from typewriting.] [Oxf.], 1937, 4°. 9 pp.
2590 d. Oxf. 1. 28

5586. Catalogue of an exhibition of books on medicine, surgery and physiology. Oxf., 1947, 8°. 31 pp.
2590 d. Oxf. 1. 33

5587. Italian illuminated manuscripts from 1400 to 1550. Catalogue of an exhibition held in . . . 1948. [Oxf.], (1948), 8°. 32 pp.+20 plates.
2590 e. Oxf. 1a. 11 = R.

5587.5. Bibliotheca Radcliviana, 1749–1949. Catalogue of an exhibition. Oxf., 1949, 8°. 47 pp.
2590 e. Oxf. 5. 3
— [Another issue with 16 plates.]
2590 e. Oxf. 5. 4

5588. The Bodleian library in the seventeenth century, guide to an exhibition held during the Festival of Britain, 1951. Oxf., 1951, 8°. 53 pp. +21 plates.
2590 e. Oxf. 1. 49 = R.

5589. Latin liturgical manuscripts and printed books: guide to an exhibition held during 1952. Oxf., 1952, 8°. 61 pp.+20 pl.
2590 e. Oxf. 1. 35

See 72 [The history of the University of Oxford, guide to an exhibition. 1953].

5590. English music, guide to an exhibition held in 1955. Oxf., 1955, 8°. 40 pp.+8 plates.
2590 e. Oxf. 1. 45 = R.

See 6513 [Oxford college libraries in 1556. 1956].

5591. English literature in the seventeenth century, guide to an exhibition. Oxf., 1957, 8°. 167 pp.
R. 6. 140

5592. Notable accessions, guide to an exhibition held in 1958. Oxf., 1958, 8°. 64 pp.+20 plates.
2590 e. Oxf. 1. 47 = R.

5592.1. Music in the Bodleian library, a selection of manuscripts, printed music and treatises exhibited . . . 20 April 1963. [Reprod. from typewriting.] n. pl., 1963, 8°. 24 pp.
2590 e. Oxf. 1 h. 3

5592.2. William Shakespeare, 1564–1964, a catalogue of the Quater-centenary exhibition in the Divinity School. Oxf., 1964, 8°. 83 pp.
25889 Shak. e. 28

Loans

5593. [*Begin.*] To morrow at twelve o'clock . . . [Convocation notice proposing to grant a dispensation to the curators of the Bodleian library to lend certain Hebrew MSS. to B. Kennicott for his collation of the Bible.] Dec. 13. [Oxf.], (1768), s. sh.   G.A. Oxon b. 19

5594. Bishop Barlow's state of the case [made *c.* 1654] Whether any books may be lent out of sir Thomas Bodley's library? Occasioned by mr. Selden's soliciting the University for certain MSS. out of it. [Oxf., 1769], fol. 4 pp.   Gough Oxf. 96 (11)

5595. [*Begin.*] Statut. Bodl. 8 . . . [Paper urging that MSS. should be lent from the Bodleian library to dr. B. Kennicott.] (Oxf., 1769), fol. 4 pp.
Gough Oxf. 96 (12)

5596. HEAD, SIR E. W., A few words on the Bodleian library [by sir E. W. Head]. Oxf., 1833, 8°. 14 pp.   G.A. Oxon 8° 83

5597. CHANDLER, H. W., On book-lending as practised at the Bodleian library. Oxf., [1886], 8°. 30 pp.   Bodl. Library records

5598. CHANDLER, H. W., On lending Bodleian books and manuscripts. [Appendix. Barlow's Argument.] Oxf., 1886, 8°. Bodl. Library records

5599. BURTON, SIR R. F., The loan of manuscripts from the Bodleian library. [An article recording, and protesting against, the refusal of an attempted borrowing.] (Acad., 1886, vol. 30, p. 327.)   N. 2696 d. 4

5600. CHANDLER, H. W., Remarks on the practice and policy of lending Bodleian printed books and manuscripts. Oxf., 1887, 8°. 66 pp.
2590 e. Oxf. 1. 5 (1)

5601. ELLIS, R., The lending of manuscripts from the Bodleian. [Arguments against prof. Chandler's Remarks.] (Acad., 1887, vol. 31, p. 146, 47.)   N. 2696 d. 4

5602. CHANDLER, H. W., Further remarks on the policy of lending Bodleian printed books and manuscripts. Oxf., 1887, 8°. 16 pp.
2590 e. Oxf. 1. 5 (2)

5603. CHANDLER, H. W., The Bodleian debate of May 10th. [Remarks on the lending of Bodleian books and MSS.] [Oxf.], (1887), 8°. 6 pp.
2590 d. Oxf. 1. 1 (1)

5604. The proposed amendment of the Bodleian statute. [Remarks, signed by 43 graduates, on Bodleian loans.] [Oxf., 1887], s. sh.
2590 d. Oxf. 1. 1 (2)

5605. CHANDLER, H. W., The amendments of the Bodleian statute. [Answers to the 43 graduates.] [Oxf.], (1887), 8°. 8 pp.
2590 e. Oxf. 1. 52 (5)

5606. CHANDLER, H. W., Decree number four of November 22nd [opposing the application of mr. Abbott for the loan of Bodleian books]. [Oxf.], (1887), s. sh.   2590 e. Oxf. 1. 52 (7)

5607. On lending books from the Bodleian library. [Oxf.], (1887), 4°. 3 pp.
2590 d. Oxf. 1. 1 (3)

5608. The policy of lending from the Bodleian. (Oxf. mag., 1887, vol. 5,
p. 77, 78, 96, 102, 113, 14.) Per. G.A. Oxon 4° 141

5609. CHANDLER, H. W., The Bodleian statute. [Abstaining from opposing
the promulgated form, but announcing opposition to any enlargement.]
[Oxf., 1888], s. sh. 2590 e. Oxf. 1. 52 (8)

5610. MADAN, F., Bodleian lending to special persons in University institutions, an argument addressed to members of Congregation. Oxf.,
1888, 8°. 32 pp. 2590 e. Oxf. 1. 6

5611. CHANDLER, H. W., The Bodleian statute [recording his change of
opinion with regard to the lending statute which he now opposes].
[Oxf.], (1888), s. sh. G.A. Oxon b. 140 (79*b*)

5612. Bodleian lending. (Oxf. mag., 1888, vol. 6, p. 324, 25, 345.)
Per. G.A. Oxon 4° 141

See 5965 [Radcliffe library. Method of borrowing Bodley books by professors
and students at the Museum. 1901].

5613. MADAN, F., On Bodleian lending to University institutions, an argument. Oxf., 1911, 8°. 13 pp. G.A. Oxon 8° 1001 (5)

Photography

5614. CHANDLER, H. W., Memorandum on photography at the Bodleian
library [signed H. W. Chandler]. (Oxf., 1889), 8°. 11 pp.
2590 e. Oxf. 1. 17

5615. Photographic reproductions to be purchased at or from the Bodleian library, Oxford. [Oxf.], 1909, 16°. 8 pp. 2590 g. Oxf. 1. 2

Purchases

5616. A catalogue of books purchased for the Bodleian library in 1780
(–1825) with an account of monies collected for that purpose. [Oxf.],
1780–1825, fol. 2590 c. Oxf. 1. 5

5617. A catalogue of books purchased for the Bodleian library with a statement of monies received and expended. 1826–61. [Oxf., 1827–63], 8°.
2590 e. Oxf. 1. 9–11

5618. The Curators of the Bodleian library submit . . . the following proposal [to borrow money on the credit of the library, & to make further
purchases at the Crevenna and Pinelli sales]. [Oxf.], 1789, s. sh.
Bliss B 417 (4)

See also 5515, &c. Finance.

Department of Western manuscripts

General

See 5710 [Catalogus Bibliothecæ . . . 1605].
See 5712 [Catalogus . . . 1620].

5619. Catalogi librorum manuscriptorum Angliæ et Hiberniæ in unum collecti [ed. by E. Bernard]. Cum indice alphabetico [by H. Wanley]. 2 tom. [Bodleian and Oxford college libraries *passim.*] Oxon., 1697, fol.
Vet. A 3 b. 27 = R.

5620. Catalogi codicum manuscriptorum Bibliothecæ Bodleianæ Pars prima recensionem codicum Græcorum continens, confecit H. O. Coxe. Oxon., 1853, 4°.   2590 d. Oxf. 1a 15 (1) = R.
— Pars secunda codices Latinos et miscellaneos Laudianos complectens, confecit H. O. Coxe. Addito indice [by F. Madan]. Oxon., 1858–85, 4°.   2590 d. Oxf. 1a. 15 (2) = R.
— Pars tertia codices Græcos et Latinos Canonicianos complectens, confecit H. O. Coxe. Oxon., 1854, 4°.   2590 d. Oxf. 1a. 15 (3) = R.
— Pars quarta codices . . . Thomæ Tanneri . . . complectens, confecit A. Hackman. Oxon., 1860, 4°.   2590 d. Oxf. 1a. 15 (4) = R.
— Partis quintæ fasciculus primus (–quintus) . . . Ricardi Rawlinson, codicum classes duas priores (–codicum classis quartæ indicem) . . . complectens, confecit G. D. Macray. Oxon., 1860–1900, 4°.
2590 d. Oxf. 1a. 15 (5) = R.
— Pars nona codices a . . . Kenelm Digby anno 1634 donatos, complectens, confecit G. D. Macray. Oxon., 1883, 4°.
2590 d. Oxf. 1a. 15 (9) = R.

— Pt. 6 See 5784.
— Pt. 7 See 5785.5.
— Pt. 8 See 5801.
— Pt. 10 See 5662.
— Pt. 11 See 5668.
— Pt. 12 See 5794.
— Pt. 13 See 5785.
— Pt. 14 See 5786.

5621. A summary catalogue of Western manuscripts in the Bodleian library. Vol. 1. Historical introduction and conspectus of shelf-marks, ed. by R. W. Hunt. Oxf., 1953, 8°. 141 pp. 2590 e. Oxf. 1a. 12 = R.
— Vol. 2, pt. 1. Collections received before 1660 . . . by F. Madan and H. H. E. Craster. Oxf., 1922, 8°. 654 pp.
— Vol. 2, pt. 2. Collections . . . acquired during the second half of the 17th century, by F. Madan, H. H. E. Craster, N. Denholm-Young. Oxf., 1937, 8°. 1216 pp.
— Vol. 3. Collections received during the 18th century, by F. Madan. Oxf., 1895, 8°. 651 pp.
— Vol. 4. Collections received during the first half of the 19th century, by F. Madan. Oxf., 1897, 8°. 723 pp.
— Vol. 5. Collections received during the second half of the 19th century, by F. Madan. Oxf., 1905, 8°. 934 pp.

— Vol. 6. Accessions, 1890–1915, by F. Madan and H. H. E. Craster. Oxf., 1924, 8°. 498 pp.
— Vol. 7. Index, by P. D. Record. Oxf., 1953, 8°. 580 pp.

5621.1. SPOKES, P. S., Summary catalogue of manuscripts in the Bodleian Library relating to the City, County and University of Oxford. Accessions from 1916 to 1962. Oxf., 1964, 8°. 207 pp.
2590 d. Oxf. 1a. 41 = R.
— [Another issue.] (Oxf. hist. soc., N.S., vol. 17.)
G.A. Oxon 8° 360 = R.

5622. Ad magnificum virum dominum Iohannem Cirenbergium, ob acceptum Synodalium epistolarum Concilij Basileensis Αὐτόγραφον, quod Thomas Roe Oxoniensi Bibliothecæ transmisit ac dono dedit, carmen honorarium. [Madan 671.] Oxon., 1631, 4°. 24 pp.
4° M 14 Th. BS.

5623. WAAGEN, G. F., Treasures of art in Great Britain: an account of paintings, drawings, sculptures, illuminated MSS. &c. (Bodleian, Ashmolean museum, Christ Church and the private collection of prof. G. H. S. Johnson [now dispersed], vol. 3, p. 44–121.) Lond., 1854, 8°.
170 k. 22
See 5724 [Report on the MSS. catalogues, 1864].

5624. STENGEL, E., Die Chansondegeste-Handschriften der Oxforder Bibliotheken. (Rom. Studien, 1871/75, Bd. 1, p. 380–408.)
Per. 3061 d. 20

5625. Calendar of charters and rolls preserved in the Bodleian library, ed. by W. H. Turner under the direction of H. O. Coxe. Oxf., 1878, 8°. 849 pp.
2590 d. Oxf. 1a. 21 = R.

5626. NAPIER, A. S., The Crawford collection of early charters and documents now in the Bodleian library, ed. by A. S. Napier and W. H. Stevenson. (Anecdota Oxon.) Oxf., 1895, 4°. 167 pp.
3963 d. 85 (7) = A.

5627. MADAN, F., Rough list of manuscript materials relating to the history of Oxford contained in the printed catalogues of the Bodleian and college libraries. Oxf., 1887, 8°. 170 pp.
258811 e. 51 = R.

5627.5. To the Curators of the Bodleian library. [A paper, signed by 38 readers, asking for a summary catalogue, no. 5621, of those MSS. not included in the existing catalogues of the Quarto series, no. 5620.] (Oxf., 1890), s. sh.
2590 e. Oxf. 1. 52 (12)

5628. CLARK, A., The cataloguing of MSS. in the Bodleian library, a letter . . . by the outgoing junior proctor. Oxf., 1890, 8°. 58 pp.
2590 e. Oxf. 1a. 1

5628.1. Confidential. Memorandum on the junior proctor's [A. Clark's] motion. 'Summary of MSS. in the Bodleian library.' [Oxf., 1890], s. sh.
2590 e. Oxf. 1. 52 (14)

5628.2. BYWATER, I. [*Begin*.] Being prevented by illness . . . [Comments on the answers in Convocation on Jan. 28 of the Bodleian curators to the questions propounded to them.] [Oxf.], (1890), s. sh.
2590 e. Oxf. 1. 52 (13)

5628.3. JACKSON, T. W., [*Begin*.] The following reply . . . [Notifying the memorialists of February 1890 of the vice-chancellor's letter stating that a summary catalogue of MSS. in Bodley will be produced.] [Oxf., 1890], s. sh.
2590 e. Oxf. 1. 52 (17)

5629. SCHENKL, H., Bibliotheca patrum Latinorum Britannica. Bd. 1, Abtheil. 1. Die Bodleianische Bibliothek in Oxford. Wien, 1891, 8°. 192 pp.
25859 d. 2

5630. FLETCHER, W. G. D., and AUDEN, MISS, Shropshire topographical and genealogical manuscripts preserved in the Bodleian library. (Trans., Shropshire archaeol. soc., 1895, 2nd ser., vol. 7, p. 79–93.)
Per. G.A. Salop. 8° 61 = R. Top.
— [Repr.]
2590 d. Oxf. 1a. 6

5631. ANDREWS, C. M., and DAVENPORT, F. G., Manuscript materials in the Bodleian library for the history of the United States to 1783. Extract from Guide to the manuscript materials for the history of the United States to 1783, in the British Museum, in minor London archives, and in the libraries of Oxford and Cambridge, pages 372–421. Wash., 1908, 8°.
2590 d. Oxf. 1a. 30 = R.

5632. FIRTH, C. H., Papers relating to the navy in the Bodleian library. (Mariner's mirror, 1913, vol. 3, p. 225–29.)   2590 d. Oxf. 1a. 31 = R.

5633. Early Greek Bodleian manuscripts. (Bodleian quarterly record, 1914, vol. 1, p. 73–77.)   2590 d. Oxf. 1. 40 = R.

5634. Early Latin Bodleian manuscripts. (Bodleian quarterly record, 1914, vol. 1, p. 53–56; 1916, vol. 1, p. 344–49.)   2590 d. Oxf. 1. 40 = R.

5635. Manuscripts relating to Barbados preserved at the Bodleian library [ed. by N. D. Davis]. [Oxf., 1914], fol.   R.H.

5636. ROUTLEDGE, F. J., Manuscripts at Oxford relating to the late Tudors, 1547–1603. (Trans., Roy. hist. soc., 1914, 3rd ser., vol. 8, p. 119–59.)   Soc. 2262 e. 45 = K.
— Repr.
2590 e. Oxf. 1a. 4 = R.

5637. Index to duke Humphrey's gifts to the Old library of the University in 1439, 1441 and 1444. (Bodleian quarterly record, 1915, vol. 1, p. 131–35.)   2590 d. Oxf. 1. 40 = R.

5638. Twelfth-century Latin Bodleian MSS. Pt. 1–3. (Bodleian quarterly record, 1915, vol. 1, p. 193–96; 1916, vol. 1, p. 323–26; 350, 51.)
2590 d. Oxf. 1. 40 = R.

5639. CHANTER, J. F., Exeter cathedral library. [List of MSS. presented to the Bodleian library in 1602.] (Devon and Cornwall notes & queries, 1917, vol. 9, p. 139–42.)   Soc. G.A. Devon 8° 226

5640. TROUP, F. ROSE-, Exeter cathedral library. [List of MSS. presented to the Bodleian library in 1602.] (Devon and Cornwall notes and queries, 1917, vol. 9, p. 177, 78, 195, 96.) Soc. G.A. Devon 8° 226

5641. CRASTER, H. H. E., Latin Bodleian manuscript fragments, written before A.D. 1200. (Bodleian quarterly record, 1920, vol. 3, p. 19–22.)
2590 d. Oxf. 1. 40 = R.

5642. LOBEL, E., Palimpsests in the Bodleian library. (Bodleian quarterly record, 1921, vol. 3, p. 166–70.) 2590 d. Oxf. 1. 40 = R.

5643. CRASTER, H. H. E., The Western manuscripts of the Bodleian library. (Helps for students of history, 39.) Lond. &c., 1921, 8°. 48 pp.
2590 e. Oxf. 1a. 10 = R.

5644. CRASTER, H. H. E., Early vellum fragments in the Bodleian library. (Bodleian quarterly record, 1922, vol. 3, p. 287, 88.)
2590 d. Oxf. 1. 40 = R.

5645. DAVIES, G., A student's guide to the manuscripts relating to English history in the seventeenth century in the Bodleian. (Helps for students of history, 47.) Lond. &c., 1922, 8°. 32 pp. 2590 f. Oxf. 1a. 1 = R.

5646. LOBEL, E., Greek scribes. [An index of scribes whose signatures are found, or whose handwriting is recognized, in Bodleian Greek manuscripts.] (Bodleian quarterly record, 1922, vol. 3, p. 235–38.)
2590 d. Oxf. 1. 40 = R.

5647. FISHER, H. A. L., Manuscripts in the Bodleian and college libraries in Oxford bearing on English history from 1485 to 1547. (Bulletin, Inst. of hist. research, 1923, vol. 1, p. 45–48.) Soc. 223 d. 30 = K.

5648. YOUNG, N. DENHOLM-, Dated Western manuscripts in the Bodleian. (Bodleian quarterly record, 1933, vol. 7, p. 169–73.)
2590 d. Oxf. 1. 40 = R.

5649. PHILIP, I. G., Short list of chartularies of religious houses in the Bodleian library. (Bodleian quarterly record, 1936/7, vol. 8, p. 263–68.)
2590 d. Oxf. 1. 40 = R.

5650. BARNICOT, J. D. A., The Slavonic manuscripts in the Bodleian. (Bodleian library record, 1938, vol. 1, p. 30–33.)
2590 d. Oxf. 1. 41 = R.

5651. KIRCHBERGER, C., Bodleian manuscripts relating to the spiritual life, 1500–1750. (Bodleian library record, 1951, vol. 3, p. 155–64.)
2590 d. Oxf. 1. 41 = R.

5652. HOLTZMANN, W., Papsturkunden in England. Bd. 3. Oxford [&c.]. (Abhandl., Akad. d. Wiss. in Göttingen, philol.-hist. Kl., 1952 3. Folge, Nr. 33, p. 7–48.) 3974 d. 846 = C. Acad.

5653. TADIN, M., Glagolitic manuscripts in the Bodleian library. (Oxf. Slavonic papers, 1953, vol. 4, p. 151–58; 1954, vol. 5, p. 133–44.)
2590 d. Oxf. 1a. 33 = R.

5654. SAXL, F., and MEIER, H., Catalogue of astrological and mythological illuminated manuscripts of the Latin Middle Ages, ed. by H. Bober. [Vol. 3]. (Bodleian, Balliol coll., Merton coll., St. John's coll., and University coll. *passim*.) Lond., 1953, 8°.   2590 d. 53 = R.

5655. HASSALL, W. O., Local history sources in the Bodleian library. (Amateur historian, 1955, vol. 2, p. 130–32.)   Per. 2232 e. 80

Music manuscripts

5656. FRERE, W. H., Bibliotheca musico-liturgica, a descriptive handlist of the musical & Latin-liturgical MSS. of the Middle Ages preserved in the libraries of Great Britain and Ireland. [Bodleian, vol. 1, p. 8–145; college libraries, p. 146–64.] Lond. 1901, 4°.   25875 d. 6 = R.

5657. STAINER, J. F. R., and C., Early Bodleian music. Sacred & secular songs, together with other MS. compositions in the Bodleian library. 2 vols. Lond. &c., 1901, fol.   257 b. 31, 32 = R.

5658. NICHOLSON, E. W. B., Early Bodleian music. Introduction to the study of some of the oldest Latin musical manuscripts in the Bodleian library. Lond. &c., 1913, fol. xciv pp.+71 facsimiles.   257 b. 33 = R.

5659. The Bodleian library and its music. (Musical times, 1902, vol. 43, p. 718–25.)   G.A. Oxon 4° 262 (16)

5660. BLAXLAND, J. H., The Heather music collection. (Bodleian quarterly record, 1926, vol. 5, p. 23, 24.)   2590 d. Oxf. 1. 40 = R.

5661. HUGHES, A., Medieval polyphony in the Bodleian library. Oxf., 1951, 8°. 63 pp.   2590 e. Oxf. 1 h. 2 = R.

See 5590 [English music, guide to an exhibition. 1955].
See 5592.1 [Music in the Bodleian library, a selection . . . exhibited. 1963].

Named collections (*in alphabetical order*)

Ashmole

5662. BLACK, W. H., A descriptive, analytical and critical catalogue of the manuscripts bequeathed . . . by Elias Ashmole . . . also of some additional MSS. contributed by Kingsley, Lhuyd, Borlase and others. [*With*] Index [by W. D. Macray]. Oxf., 1845, 66, 4°. 1522 cols.+188 pp. [Pt. 10 of no. 5620.]   2590 d. Oxf. 1a. 15 (10) = R.

5663. MADAN, F., Memorandum by Bodley's librarian about a proposed restoration of a manuscript [MS. Ashm. 794 to Dean & Chapter of Lichfield]. [Oxf.], 1917, 8°. 3 pp.   G.A. Oxon b. 139 (59)

5664. HUNT, R. W., The cataloguing of Ashmolean collections of books and manuscripts. (Bodleian library record, 1952, vol. 4, p. 161–70.)   2590 d. Oxf. 1. 41 = R.

Bankes

5665. BARRATT, D. M., The Bankes papers, a first report. (Bodleian library record, 1953, vol. 4, p. 313–23.)   2590 d. Oxf. 1. 41 = R.

Boreal.

5666. Catalogus criticus et historico-literarius codicum CLIII. manuscriptorum Borealium. Oxonii, 1832, 4°. 56 pp. 2590 d. Oxf. 1a. 29 = R.

5667.

Canonici

See 5620 [Catalogue of Canoniciani Greek and Latin MSS.].

5668. MORTARA, CONTE A., Catalogo dei manoscritti italiani che sotto la denominazione di codici Canoniciani italici si conservano nella Biblioteca Bodleiana. Oxonii, 1864, 4°. 316 cols. [Pt. 11 of no. 5620.]
2590 d. Oxf. 1a. 15 (11) = R.

Carte

5669. HARDY, T. D., and BREWER, J. S., Report . . . upon the Carte and Carew papers in the Bodleian and Lambeth libraries [by T. D. Hardy and J. S. Brewer]. Lond., 1864, 8°. 101 pp.   2590 d. 61 = R.

5670. RUSSELL, C. W., and PRENDERGAST, J. P., The Carte manuscripts, a report. Lond., 1871, 8°. 236 pp.   2590 d. Oxf. 1a. 24 = R.

See 3946.1 [Munford, W. A., Edward Edwards; compilation of the Carte Calendar. 1963].

Clarendon

5671. Calendar of the Clarendon state papers [1523–1660] ed. by O. Ogle [and others]. 4 vols. Oxf., 1872–1932, 8°.   22855 d. 51 = R. [The Calendar is continued in MS. and typescript.]

Clarke

5672. Catalogus sive notitia manuscriptorum qui a cel. E. D. Clarke comparati in Bibliotheca Bodleiana adservantur. 2 pt. Oxon., 1812, 15, 4°. 105+22 pp.   2590 d. Oxf. 1a. 19 = R.

5673.

Digby

See 5620 [Catalogue of Digby MSS.].

Dodsworth

5674. HUNTER, J., Three catalogues; describing the contents of the Red book of the Exchequer, of the Dodsworth manuscripts in the Bodleian library, and of the manuscripts in the library of . . . Lincoln's Inn. Lond., 1838, 8°. 413 pp.   2590 e. 21 = R.

5675. [Prospectus of the Society for publishing] The manuscripts of Roger Dodsworth [signed J. Foster]. n. pl., 1874, s. sh.
MS. Add. A 294 (f. 311)

5676. TURNER, W. H., Index to the first seven volumes of the Dodsworth MSS. [by W. H. Turner]. Oxf., 1879, 4°. Sigs. 1–39.
2590 d. Oxf. 1a. 25 = R.

D'Orville

5677. GAISFORD, T., Codices manuscripti et impressi cum notis manuscriptis olim D'Orvilliani qui in Bibliotheca Bodleiana . . . adservantur. [By T. Gaisford.] Oxonii, 1806, 4°. 100 pp. 2590 d. Oxf. 1a. 26 = R.
— [Another copy on large paper.]   2590 b. Oxf. 1a. 6

Douce

5678. Catalogue of the printed books and manuscripts bequeathed by
Francis Douce to the Bodleian library. Oxf., 1840, fol. 311 pp.
2590 b. Oxf. 1. 4 = R.

5679. LIDDELL, J. R., The illuminated manuscripts of the Douce collection
[*part of* Francis Douce centenary]. (Bodleian quarterly record, 1934,
vol. 7, p. 368–73.)   2590 d. Oxf. 1. 40 = R.
— The Douce correspondence (loc. cit., p. 381).

5680. PARRY, T. R. GAMBIER-, Douce charters and seals [*part of* Francis
Douce centenary]. (Bodleian quarterly record, 1934, vol. 7, p. 379, 80.)
2590 d. Oxf. 1. 40 = R.

Dugdale

5681. Librorum manuscriptorum in duabus insignibus bibliothecis;
altera Tenisoniana, Londini; altera Dugdaliana, Oxonii; catalogus,
ed. E. G. [E. Gibson]. Oxon., 1692, 4°. 31+20 pp.   4° Z 21 (7) Art.

Gough

5682. A catalogue of the books relating to British topography and Saxon
and Northern literature bequeathed to the Bodleian library in
MDCCXCIX by Richard Gough. Oxf., 1814, 4°. 459 pp.
2590 d. Oxf. 1c. 9 = R.

Hamilton

5683. BROAD, J., Catalogus codicum manuscriptorum ex bibliotheca
Hamiltoniana [by J. Broad]. Berol., 1841, 8°. 8 pp.   2590 e. Oxf. 1a. 6

5684.

Holkham

5685. BARBOUR, R., Greek manuscripts from Holkham. (Bodleian library
record, 1954, vol. 5, p. 61–63.)   2590 d. Oxf. 1. 41 = R.

5686. BARBOUR, R., Summary description of the Greek manuscripts from
the library at Holkham hall. (Bodl. library record, 1960, vol. 6, p. 591–
613.)   2590 d. Oxf. 1. 41 = R.

Laud

See 5620 [Catalogue of Laud MSS.].

5687. A letter sent by William Lawd . . . with divers manuscripts to the
Vniversity of Oxford . . . Together with the answer which the Vniversitie sent him . . . [Madan 969.] [Lond.], 1641, 4°. 8 pp.   4° L 71 Th.

Locke

5688. LONG, P., A summary catalogue of the Lovelace collection of the
papers of John Locke in the Bodleian Library. (Publ., Oxf. bibl. soc.,
1956, N. S., vol. 8.) Oxf., 1959, 4°. xii+64 pp.   Soc. 258 d. 176 = A.
— [Another issue, publ. by the Bodleian.]   2590 d. Oxf. 1a. 32

Lyell

5689. HUNT, R. W., The Lyell bequest. (Bodleian library record, 1950,
vol. 3, p. 68–82.)   2590 d. Oxf. 1. 41 = R.

Malone

5690. BANDINEL, B., Catalogue of early English poetry and works illustrating the British drama collected by E. Malone [by B. Bandinel]. Oxf., 1836, fol. 52 pp. 2587998 b. 1

Montagu

5691. List of manuscripts, volumes of autograph letters, illustrated and other books, etc., the bequest of . . . captain Montagu Montagu, to the Bodleian library. Oxf., 1864, 8°. 40 pp. 2590 e. Oxf. 1. 50 = R.

5692.

Rawlinson

See 5620 [Catalogue of Rawlinson MSS.].

5693. [Convocation notice to decide whether to return to Durham Chancery the MS. Register of Richard Kellow, now in the Rawlinson collection.] [Oxf.], 1810, 4°. 3 pp. Bliss B 417

5694. HUNT, R. W., The cataloguing of the Rawlinson manuscripts, 1771–1844. (Bodleian library record, 1947, vol. 2, p. 190–95.)
2590 d. Oxf. 1. 41 = R.

5695. ENRIGHT, B. J., Rawlinson and the chandlers. (Bodleian library record, 1953, vol. 4, p. 216–27.) 2590 d. Oxf. 1. 41 = R.

Rigaud

5696. BEEVOR, R. J., Inventory of Rigaud papers in Bodleian library [by R. J. Beevor, ed. by E. F. McPike]. (Smithsonian miscellaneous collections, 1905, quarterly issue, vol. 48, p. 229–31.) Soc. 1996 d. 322
— Repr. G.A. Oxon 4° 186 (20)

St. Edm. hall

5697. [List of] Manuscripts belonging to St. Edmund hall, deposited in the Bodleian library. [Reprod. from typewriting.] n. pl., 1951, 4°. 12 sheets. 2590 d. Oxf. 1a. 38 = R.

Shelley

5698. The Shelley collection. Conditions proposed by lady Shelley and accepted by the Bodleian curators on June 11, 1892. [Oxf.], (1893), 4°. 3 pp. G.A. Oxon 4° 119 (12)

5699. LOCOCK, C. D., An examination of the Shelley manuscripts in the Bodleian library. Oxf., 1903, 8°. 75 pp. 280 d. 214 = R.

5700. The 'reserved' Shelley papers in the Bodleian library. (Bodleian quarterly record, 1925, vol. 4, p. 218–22, 246–50.)
2590 d. Oxf. 1. 40 = R.

5701. The Shelley correspondence in the Bodleian library, ed. by R. H. Hill. Oxf., 1926, 4°. xv+48 pp. 2796 d. 365 = R.

Sherard

5702. Catalogue of manuscripts belonging to Oxford university department of botany, deposited in the Bodleian library, referenced MSS. Sherard 1–476. [Reprod. from typewriting.] (Nat. Reg. of Archives.) n. pl., 1958, 4°.   2262 c. 10 = R.

Tanner

See 5620 [Catalogue of Tanner MSS.].

5703.

Walker

5704. TATHAM, G. B., Dr. John Walker and the sufferings of the clergy. [Appendix 1, p. 135–370, is the Calendar of the Walker collection of MSS.] Cambr., 1911, 8°.   11122 e. 12 = R.

5705.

Wood

5706. Huddesford, W., Catalogus librorum manuscriptorum . . . Antonii a Wood, a minute catalogue of each particular contained in the manuscript collections of Antony a Wood deposited in the Ashmolean museum. Oxf., 1761, 8°. 84 pp.   G.A. Oxon 8° 928
— [Repr.] Typis Medio-Montanis re-impressus, 1824, fol. 52 pp.
                                                2590 c. Oxf. 1a. 3 = R.

Department of Printed books
General

5707. Catalogue of a . . . collection of . . . books (being purchase-duplicates from the Bodleian Library) . . . which will be sold by auction by messrs. Sotheby & Wilkinson . . . 21st of May and 4 following days. (Long Acre), 1862, 8°. 145 pp.   2591 d. 73

5708. NICHOLSON, E. W. B., Proposed repurchase for the Bodleian of the original Bodleian copy of the 1st folio Shakespeare (1623). 11 Nov. 1905. [Oxf.], (1905), 4°. 4 pp.   Firth b. 36 (15a)
— [Another ed.] March 1906.   Firth b. 36 (15b)

5709. MYRES, J. N. L., Bodleian time-lag [between publication of books and their acquisition by the Library. A letter.] (Oxf. mag., 1948, vol. 66, p. 430.)   Per. G.A. Oxon 4° 141

General catalogues and cataloguing

5710. JAMES, T., Catalogus librorum Bibliothecæ publicæ . . . quam . . . Thomas Bodleius . . . instituit . . . [Madan 264.] Oxon., 1605, 4°. 655+ 67 pp.   2590 e. Oxf. 1. 2

5711. Catalogus vniversalis librorum in Bibliotheca Bodleiana. Accessit appendix. Auctore Thomas Iames. [Madan 482.] Oxon., 1620, 4°. 539+36 pp.   2590 e. Oxf. 1. 2a
— [Another issue.] [Madan 482*.]   Bodl. Library Records

5712. ROUSE, J., Appendix ad Catalogum librorum in Biblioteca Bodleiana, qui prodiit . . . 1620 [by J. Rouse]. Ed. 2a. [Madan 798.] Oxon., 1635, 4°. 208 pp.   AA 50 Jur.

5713. LYELL, J. P. R., King James I and the Bodleian library catalogue of 1620. (Bodleian quarterly record, 1933, vol. 7, p. 271–83.)
2590 d. Oxf. 1. 40 = R.

5714. Catalogus impressorum librorum Bibliothecæ Bodlejanæ, cura & opera Thomæ Hyde. [Madan 2999.] Oxon., 1674, fol. 480+272 pp.
2590 b. Oxf. 1c. 1, 2 = R.

5715. GIBSON, S., Bodleian catalogues of the seventeenth century. [A résumé of the account read before the Bibliographical society, Dec. 20, 1915.] (Bodleian quarterly record, 1915, vol. 1, p. 228–32.)
2590 d. Oxf. 1. 40 = R.

5716. GIBSON, S., Bodleian catalogues of the 17th century; [to accompany] a paper read before the Bibliographical society, Dec. 20, 1915. [2 facs. and 2 pp. of notes.] (Oxf.), 1915, 8°.   2590 e. Oxf. 1. 19

5717. WHEELER, G. W., Preparation of the first printed Bodleian catalogue. (Bodleian quarterly record, 1920, vol. 3, p. 46–50.)
2590 d. Oxf. 1. 40 = R.

5718. WHEELER, G. W., The earliest catalogues [and other records] of the Bodleian library. Oxf., 1928, 8°. 149 pp.+4 facs.
2590 d. Oxf. 1. 18 = R.

5719. Catalogus impressorum librorum Bibliothecæ Bodleianæ. [Begun by T. Hyde, continued by J. Bowles, R. Fysher and E. Langford, ed. by R. Fysher.] 2 vols. Oxon., 1738, fol.   2590 b. Oxf. 1c. 3–6 = R.

See 6502 [Whereas it is in contemplation to prepare a new catalogue of the books in the Bodleian library. Request for list of books in colleges not in the Bodleian. 1794].

5720–21. Catalogus librorum impressorum quibus Bibliotheca Bodleiana aucta est anno MDCCCXXV (–annis MDCCCXXXVII, XXXVIII), [Oxf., 1826–39], fol.   2590 b. Oxf. 1c. 17

5722. Catalogus librorum impressorum Bibliothecæ Bodleianæ. 3 voll. [With] Catalogus impressorum librorum quibus aucta est Bibliotheca Bodleiana annis MDCCCXXXV–MDCCCXLVII. (Vol. 4). Oxon., 1843, 51, fol.   2590 b. Oxf. 1c. 19–22 = R.

5723. COXE, H. O., Note [dated 1 Nov. 1858] to the curators of the Bodleian library [on the cataloguing methods &c. employed there, in the British Museum, and at Cambridge]. [Oxf.], (1858), 4°. 4 pp. G.A. Oxon b. 29

5724. Report [by the Librarian] to the Curators of the Bodleian library, May, 1864 [on the new general catalogue, classification, and MSS. catalogues]. [Oxf.], (1864), 8°. 12 pp.   G.A. Oxon 8° 178

5724.5. The subject-catalogue. [Announcement and explanation by Bodley's Librarian.] [Oxf., c. 1885], s. sh.   2590 e. Oxf. 1. 52 (19)

5725. CHANDLER, H. W., Memorandum on the subject catalogue. [Oxf.], 1885, 8°. 8 pp.	2590 e. Oxf. 1. 30

5726. CHANDLER, H. W., Some observations on the Bodleian classed catalogue. Oxf., 1888, 8°. 31 pp.	2590 e. Oxf. 1. 16

5727. NICHOLSON, E. B., A protest by Bodley's librarian [against H. W. Chandler's Some observations on the Bodleian classed catalogue]. [Oxf.], (1888), 8°. 4 pp.	G.A. Oxon 8° 469 (1)

5728. WHEELER, G. W., An early Bodleian subject-catalogue. (Bodleian quarterly record, 1917, vol. 2, p. 17–24.)	2590 d. Oxf. 1. 40 = R.

5729. NORRIS, D., A history of cataloguing methods, 1100–1850. [Bodleian catalogues, p. 142–59.] Lond., 1939, 8°.	25894 e. 45

5730. CRASTER, SIR H. H. E., The new Bodleian catalogue. (Oxford, 1939, vol. 6, no. 1, p. 62–68.)	Per. G.A. Oxon 8° 1141

Cataloguing rules

5731. Compendious cataloguing-rules for the author-catalogue of the Bodleian library. [Oxf.], 1882, [85], 2 sheets.	2590 c. Oxf. 1. 10

5732. Bodleian library, Oxford. Rules for the author-catalogues of printed books and printed music. [Oxf.], 1912, 8°. 13 pp.	2590 f. Oxf. 1. 6

5733. Bodleian library, Oxford. Rules for author-catalogues. [Oxf.], 1914, 8°. 16 pp.	2590 f. Oxf. 1. 7

5734. Bodleian library, Oxford. Rules for the cataloguing of printed books. [Oxf.], 1918, 8°. 24 pp.	2590 f. Oxf. 1. 8

5735. Bodleian library, Oxford. Rules for the cataloguing of printed books published before 1920. Repr. [Oxf.], 1922, 8°. 23 pp.	2590 f. Oxf. 1. 11

5736. Bodleian library, Oxford. Rules for the author-catalogue of books published in or after 1920. [Oxf.], 1923, 8°.	2590 f. Oxf. 1. 12

5737. Rules for the author-catalogue of books published in or after 1920. (Oxf.), 1930, 8°. 55 pp.	2590 e. Oxf. 1. 23

5738. Rules for the general catalogue of printed books. (Oxf.), 1933, 8°.	2590 e. Oxf. 1. 24

5739. Cataloguing rules. (Oxf., 1939), 8°.	25894 e. 55

Special catalogues

5740. VERNEUIL, J., Catalogus interpretum S. Scripturæ, iuxta numerorum ordinem, quo extant in Bibliotheca Bodleiana olim a D. Iamesio, in usum theologorum concinnatus, nunc vero altera fere parte auctior redditus. Ed. correcta. [An enlarged edition by J. Verneuil of p. 163–179 of no. 5710.] [Madan 799.] Oxon., 1635, 4°. 55 pp.	4° P 68 Art.

5740.5. VERNEUIL, J., A nomenclator of such tracts and sermons as have beene printed or translated into English upon any place of Holy Scripture, opera . . . I.V. [Madan 867.] Oxf., 1637, 12°. [154 pp.]

Bliss B 43

— Ed. secunda. [Madan 1289]. A nomenclator of such tracts [&c.] now to be had in the . . . library of sr. Thomas Bodley [with shelfmarks]. Oxf., 1642, 12°. 211 pp. 8° O 62 Th.

5741. Notitia editionum quoad libros Hebr. Gr. et Lat. quæ vel primariæ, vel sæc. xv. impressæ, vel Aldinæ in Bibliotheca Bodleiana adservantur. Oxon., 1795, 8°. 60 pp. 2590 e. Oxf. 1. 25

5742. Catalogus dissertationum academicarum quibus nuper aucta est Bibliotheca Bodleiana MDCCCXXXII. Oxon., 1834, fol. 448 pp.+ [63 pp.] 2590 b. Oxf. 1c. 27 = R.

5743. Catalogue of periodicals contained in the Bodleian library. Pt. i. English periodicals. Pt. iii. Foreign periodicals &c. Oxf., 1878, 80, 8°. 2590 e. Oxf. 1c. 7

5744. Current foreign & colonial periodicals in the Bodleian library and in other Oxford libraries. Oxf., 1925, 8°. 135 pp. 2590 e. Oxf. 1c. 4

5745. Current foreign and commonwealth periodicals in the Bodleian and in other Oxford libraries. [With] Suppl. no. 1- . Oxf., 1953, 56- , 8°. 2590 e. Oxf. 1c. 9 = R.

5746. MILFORD, R. T., and SUTHERLAND, D. M., A catalogue of English newspapers and periodicals in the Bodleian library, 1622–1800. (Proc. and papers, Oxf. bibliogr. soc., 1936, vol. 4, p. 163–344.)

Soc. 258 d. 176 = A.

— [Repr.] Oxf., 1936, 4°. 184 pp. 2590 d. Oxf. 1c. 5 = B.

5747. PROCTOR, R., An index to the early printed books in the British Museum . . . with notes of those in the Bodleian library. [With] Suppl. for 1899(-1902). Lond., 1898–1902, 4°. 2590 d. Lond. 1c. 20 = R.

5748. POGSON, K. M., A grand inquisitor [F. Martins Mascarenhas, bp. of Faro] and his library [brought from Faro and presented to sir Thomas Bodley. With] List of books presented . . . in 1600, still in the Bodleian. (Bodleian quarterly record, 1922, vol. 3, p. 239–44.)

2590 d. Oxf. 1. 40 = R.

5749. Lists of Burton's library. Two lists of Robert Burton's library as distributed between (a) the Bodleian library (b) the library of his college, Christ Church. [Ed. by S. Gibson and F. R. D. Needham.] (Proc. and papers, Oxf. bibliogr. soc., 1925, vol. 1, p. 222–46.)

Soc. 258 d. 176 = A.

5750. Specimens of Shakespeariana in the Bodleian library . . . (University extension meeting, July–August 1927). [Oxf.], 1927, 8°. 68 pp.

2590 d. Oxf. 1. 17

5751. DODGSON, C., English devotional woodcuts of the late 15th century, with special reference to those in the Bodleian library. (Walpole soc., 1929, vol. 17, p. 95–108.)   Soc. 17006 c. 82

See 5396 [Woodcuts of the 15th century. 1929].

Named collections (in alphabetical order)
Ashmole
5752. GUNTHER, R. T., The Ashmole printed books. (Bodleian quarterly record, 1930, vol. 6, p. 193–95.)   2590 d. Oxf. 1. 40 = R.

5753. GUNTHER, R. T., The Chemical library of the University. (Bodleian quarterly record, 1930, vol. 6, p. 201–03.)   2590 d. Oxf. 1. 40 = R.

5754. GUNTHER, R. T., The library of John Aubrey. (Bodleian quarterly record, 1931, vol. 6, p. 230–36.)   2590 d. Oxf. 1. 40 = R.

Buchanan
5755. GIBSON, S., Bookbindings in the Buchanan collection. (Bodleian library record, 1941, vol. 2, p. 6–12.)   2590 d. Oxf. 1. 41 = R.

D'Orville
See 5677 [D'Orville collection. 1806].

Douce
5756. Catalogue of the printed books and manuscripts bequeathed by Francis Douce to the Bodleian library. Oxf., 1840, fol. 311 pp.
                                                      2590 b. Oxf. 1. 4 = R.

5757. PHILLIPPS, J. O. HALLIWELL-, A handlist of the early English literature preserved in the Douce collection . . . Lond., 1860, 8°. 151 pp.
                                                      2585 d. 28 = A.

5758. HINDLE, C. J., The Douce collection of printed books [*part of* Francis Douce centenary]. (Bodleian quarterly record, 1934, vol. 7, p. 365–68.)   2590 d. Oxf. 1. 40 = R.

Gough
5759. A catalogue of the books relating to British topography and Saxon and Northern literature bequeathed to the Bodleian library in MDCCXCIX by Richard Gough. Oxf., 1814, 4°. 459 pp.
                                                      2590 d. Oxf. 1c. 9 = R.

Holkham
5760. ROGERS, D., The Holkham collection. (Bodleian library record, 1953, vol. 4, p. 255–67.)   2590 d. Oxf. 1. 41 = R.

Hope
5761. Catalogue of a collection of early newspapers and essayists formed by the late John Thomas Hope and presented to the Bodleian library by the late Frederick William Hope. Oxf., 1865, 8°. 178 pp.
                                                      2590 d. Oxf. 1c. 10 = R.

Malone

5762. BANDINEL, B., Catalogue of early English poetry and works illustrating the British drama collected by E. Malone [by B. Bandinel]. Oxf., 1836, fol. 52 pp. 2587998 b. 1 = R.

5763. PHILLIPPS, J. O. HALLIWELL-, A hand-list of the early English literature preserved in the Malone collection . . . Lond., 1860, 8°. 96 pp. 2585 d. 21

Monro

5764. [Proposal to raise a subscription to acquire that part of the library of the late provost of Oriel, D. B. Monro, which relates to Homeric studies, and present it to the Bodleian as a memorial of him.] [Oxf., 1907], s. sh. G.A. Oxon b. 140 (140a)

Montagu

5765. List of manuscripts, volumes of autograph letters, illustrated and other books, etc., the bequest of . . . captain Montagu Montagu, to the Bodleian library. Oxf., 1864, 8°. 40 pp. 2590 e. Oxf. 1. 50 = R.

Mortara

5766. Biblioteca italica ossia catalogo de' testi a stampa citati nel vocabolario degli Accademici della Crusca, e di altri libri italiani pregevoli e rari gia posseduti C. A. M[ortara] ed ora passati in proprieta della Biblioteca Bodleiana. Oxf., 1852, 8°. 91 pp. 2590 e. Oxf. 1c. 6

Savile

5767. [June 23, 1834. To be proposed in Convoc: on 25 June, that the books, instruments &c. given to the University by sir Henry Savile, should be removed to a room at the S.E. angle of the schools, to be prepared at the expense of the Bodleian and called the Savile study and that this should be annexed to the Bodleian.] G.A. Oxon c. 50 (79)

Selden

5768. SPARROW, J., The earlier owners of books in John Selden's library. (Bodleian quarterly record, 1931, vol. 6, p. 263–70.) 2590 d. Oxf. 1. 40 = R.

5769. BARRATT, D. M., The library of John Selden and its later history. (Bodleian library record, 1951, vol. 3, p. 128–42, 208–13, 256–74.) 2590 d. Oxf. 1. 41 = R.

Shelley

See 5698–5701.

Sutherland

5770. Catalogue of the Sutherland collection. 2 vols. [*With*] Suppl. Lond., 1837, 38, fol. 2590 b. Oxf. 1 f. 1–3 = R.
[Part of this collection was transferred to the Ashmolean Museum in 1950.]

Classification

See also 5710, &c. [Department of Printed Books Catalogues.]

5771. WHEELER, G. W., Bodleian press-marks in relation to classification. (Bodleian quarterly record, 1916, vol. 1, p. 280–92, 311–22.)
2590 d. Oxf. 1. 40 = R.

5772. COXE, H. O., To the . . . Vice-chancellor and curators of the Bodleian library. [Report on the manner of arranging the books at the British Museum and its possible application in the Bodleian.] Nov. 24 [Oxf.], (1858), 4°. 7 pp.
G.A. Oxon b. 29

Desiderata

5773. Rough list of works known or supposed to have been published at Oxford, but not in the Bodleian library up to July, 1882. (Oxf.), 1882, 4°. 17 pp.
2590 d. Oxf. 1. 35

5773.1. Bodleian desiderata. August, 1930. Oxf., 1930, 4°. 29 pp.
2590 d. Oxf. 1. 40 = R.
— January 1936. Oxf., 1936, 4°. 35 pp. 2590 d. Oxf. 1. 40 = R.
[The first list of Bodleian desiderata was published in 1925 in no. 40 of the Bodleian Quarterly Record. Subsequent lists are to be found *passim* in this periodical and in the Bodleian Library Record.]

Book rejection

5774. Books not deemed by the curators necessary to be deposited in the library. Michaelmas 1814 . . . to June 1817. (Extracts of so much of the returns made by the universities of Oxford and Cambridge as state whether any books claimed have been omitted to be placed in their libraries, p. 1, 2.)
Pp. Eng. 1818 vol. 15

5775. MADAN, F., Bodleian 'trash'. (Oxf. mag., 1915, vol. 33, p. 238–40.)
Per. G.A. Oxon 4° 141

5776. JENKINSON, A. J., The policy of the Bodleian library [with regard to 'trash' and book selection]. (Oxf. mag., 1915, vol. 33, p. 287–89, 301, 02.)
Per. G.A. Oxon 4° 141
— [Repr. in Oxf. mag., 1928, vol. 46, p. 413, 14.]
— [Repr.] [Oxf.], (1928), s. sh.
G.A. Oxon c. 314 (38)

5777. SADLER, SIR M. E., The Bodleian. [A comment on no. 5776.] (Oxf. mag., 1928, vol. 46, p. 436.)
Per. G.A. Oxon 4° 141

5778. F, M.B., Fallacy underlying the assumption that all books should be preserved. (Oxf. mag., 1931, vol. 49, p. 656, 57.) Per. G.A. Oxon 4° 141

LAW LIBRARY

5779. New group for Oxford [Law library, Institute of statistics, English library]. (Architects' journ., Oct. 6, 1960, p. 494–96.) N. 1863 c. 12

5780. Development of Commonwealth and American legal studies at Oxford university. Memorandum by the Board of the Faculty of law. (Oxf., 1961), 4°. 10 pp.   26331 d. 53

5780.1. Opening of the Bodleian Law library, Law faculty building and Gulbenkian lecture theatre, 17 October 1964. Oxf., (1964), 4°. 16 pp.
                                                                   2590 d. Oxf. 22. 1

Department of Oriental books

5781. BEESTON, A. F. L., The oriental manuscript collections of the Bodleian library. (Bodleian library record, 1954, vol. 5, p. 73–79.)
                                                                   2590 d. Oxf. 1. 41 = R.

5782. Bibliothecæ Bodleianæ codicum manuscriptorum orientalium . . . catalogus a J. Uri confectus. Pars prima. Oxon., 1787, fol. 327 pp.+ index.   Z fol. 1 (1)
— Pars secunda Arabicos complectens, confecit A. Nicoll. Oxon., 1821, fol.   2590 b. Oxf. 1 b. 1
— Pars secunda. Ed. absolvit et emendavit E. B. Pusey. Oxon., 1835, fol. 730 pp.   Z fol. 1 (2)

5783. Catalogus sive notitia manuscriptorum qui a cel. E. D. Clarke comparati in Bibliotheca Bodleiana adservantur. 2 pt. [Part 2 comprises oriental manuscripts.] Oxon., 1812, 15, 4°. 105+22 pp.
                                                                   2590 d. Oxf. 1a. 19 = R.

5784. Catalogi codicum manuscriptorum Bibliothecæ Bodleianæ pars sexta, codices Syriacos, Carshunicos, Mendacos complectens, confecit R. P. Smith. Oxon., 1864, 4°. 679 pp.   2590 d. Oxf. 1a. 15 (6) = Z.

5785. SACHAU, E., ETHÉ, H., and BEESTON, A. F. L., Catalogue of the Persian, Turkish, Hindûstânî, and Pushtû manuscripts in the Bodleian library. 3 pt. (Catal. codd. mss. Bibl. Bodl., pars xiii.) Oxf., 1889–1954, 4°.   2590 d. Oxf. 1a. 15 (13) = Z.

5785.5. Codices Aethiopici, digessit A. Dillmann (E. Ullendorff). 2 vols. (Catal. codd. mss. Bibl. Bodl., pars vii.) Oxon., 1848, 1951, 4°
                                                                   Z. Cat. 3

5786. FARMER, H. G., The Arabic musical manuscripts in the Bodleian library, a descriptive catalogue. (Journ., Roy. Asiatic soc., 1925, p. 639–54.)   Or. Per. 7 = Z.
— [Repr.] 18 pp.   2590 e. Oxf. 1b. 1 = Z.

5787. BARONIAN, S., and CONYBEARE, F. C., Catalogue of the Armenian manuscripts in the Bodleian library. (Catal. codd. mss. Bibl. Bodl. pars xiv.) Oxf., 1918, 4°.   2590 d. Oxf. 1a. 15 (14) = Z.

5788. EDKINS, J., A catalogue of Chinese works in the Bodleian library. Oxf., 1876, 4°. 46 pp.   2590 d. Oxf. 1d. 6

5789. HSIANG TA, and HUGHES, E. R., The Bodleian Chinese collection. (Bodleian quarterly record, 1936, vol. 8, p. 227–33.)
                                                                   2590 d. Oxf. 1. 40 = R.

5790. BEESTON, A. F. L., The earliest donations of Chinese books to the Bodleian. (Bodleian library record, 1953, vol. 4, p. 304–313.)
2590 d. Oxf. 1. 41 = R.

5791. NANJIO, B., A catalogue of Japanese and Chinese books and manuscripts lately added to the Bodleian library. Oxf., 1881, 4°. 28 coll.
2590 d. Oxf. 1d. 5

5792. Collectio Davidis, i.e. Catalogus ... bibliothecae Hebraeae quam ... collegit r. David Oppenheimerus. Hamb., 1826, 8°. 742 pp.
2590 e. Oxf. 1d. 1

5793. STEINSCHNEIDER, M., Catalogus librorum Hebræorum in Bibliotheca Bodleiana. Berolini, 1852–60, 4°.   2590 d. Oxf. 1d. 1 = Z.
— Suppl. (Separatdr., Centralblatt für Bibliothekswesen, 1894, p. 484–508). [Leipz., 1894], 8°.   2590 d. Oxf. 1d. 1 = Z.

5794. NEUBAUER, A., Catalogue of the Hebrew manuscripts in the Bodleian library and in the college libraries of Oxford. (Catal. codd. mss. Bibl. Bodl. pars xii.) Oxf., 1886, 4°.   2590 d. Oxf. 1a. 15 (12) = Z.
— Vol. 2, by A. Neubauer and A. E. Cowley. Oxf., 1906, 4°.
2590 d. Oxf. 1a. 15 (12) = Z.

5795. ROTH, C., An episode in the history of the Oppenheimer collection. (Bodleian library record, 1954, vol. 5, p. 104–08.)
2590 d. Oxf. 1. 41 = R.

5796. COWLEY, SIR A. E., A concise catalogue of the Hebrew printed books in the Bodleian library. Oxf., 1929, 8°. 816 pp. 2590 d. Oxf. 1d. 4 = Z.

5797. NEUBAUER, A., Facsimiles of Hebrew manuscripts in the Bodleian library illustrating the various forms of rabbinical characters. Oxf., 1886, fol. iv pp.+40 plates.   25754 a. 1 = Z.

5798. GREENTREE, R., and NICHOLSON, E. W. B., Catalogue of Malay manuscripts and manuscripts relating to the Malay language in the Bodleian library. Oxf., 1910, 4°. 19 pp.   2590 d. Oxf. 1b. 5 = Z.

5799. ROBINSON, B. W., A descriptive catalogue of Persian paintings in the Bodleian library. Oxf., 1958, 4°. 219 pp.+40 pl.   17008 d. 61

5800. Professor Wilson's Sanskrit manuscripts now deposited in the Bodleian library. [Oxf.], 1842, 4°. 20 pp.   2590 d. Oxf. 1b. 2

5801. Catalogi codicum manuscriptorum Bibliothecæ Bodleianæ pars octava, codices Sanscriticos, complectens, confecit T. Aufrecht. Oxon., 1864, 4°. 578 pp.
— Appendix to vol. 1, by A. B. Keith. Oxf., 1909, 4°. 123 pp.
— Vol. 2, begun by M. Winternitz, continued and completed by A. B. Keith. Oxf., 1905, 4°. 350 pp.   2590 d. Oxf. 1a. 15 (8) = Z.

5802. KEITH, A. B., A catalogue of the Sanskrit and Prākrit MSS. in the Indian Institute library. Oxf., 1903, 8°. 99 pp. 2590 d. Oxf. 8. 1 = Z.

5803. KEITH, A. B., Catalogue of Prākrit manuscripts in the Bodleian library. Oxf., 1911, 4°. 53 pp.   2590 d. Oxf. 1b. 6 = Z.

5804. CLAUSON, G. L. M., Catalogue of the Stein collection of Sanskrit MSS. from Kashmir. (Journ., Roy. Asiatic soc., 1912, p. 587–627.)
Or. Per. 7 = Z.
— [Repr.] 2590 e. Oxf. 8b. 1

5805. PARRY, T. R. GAMBIER-, A catalogue of the Sanskrit manuscripts purchased for the administrators of the Max Müller memorial fund. Oxf., 1922, 8°. 62 pp. 2590 e. Oxf. 1b. 2 = Z.

5806. PARRY, T. R. GAMBIER-, A catalogue of photographs of Sanskrit MSS. purchased for the administrators of the Max Müller memorial fund. Lond., 1930, 8°. 59 pp. 2590 e. Oxf. 1b. 3 = Z.

5807. STOOKE, H. J., Kālighāt paintings in Oxford. (Indian art and letters, 1946, N.S., vol. 20, p. 71–73.) Ind. Inst.

Friends of the Bodleian

5808. Friends of the Bodleian. First(–) annual report. Oxf., 1925/26– , 8°. Per. 2590 d. Oxf. 1. 19 = R.

5809. MYRES, J. N. L., Bodley's American Friends. (Amer. Oxonian, 1957, vol. 44, p. 154–56.) Per. G.A. Oxon 8° 889

BOTANIC GARDEN

See also 3053, &c., Department of Botany.

5810. [Topographical prints, &c. in the Bodleian.] G.A. Oxon a. 47

5811. BOBART, J., Catalogus plantorum Horti medici Oxoniensis [by J. Bobart]. [Madan 2003.] [Oxf.], 1648, 16°. 112 pp.
8° R 16 (3) Art BS.
— [Another issue.] Catologus [sic &c.] [Madan 2003*.] Ashm. 1361

5812. STEPHANUS, P., et BROUNEUS, G., Catalogus Horti botanici Oxoniensis ... priore duplo auctior ... [Madan 2370.] Oxon., 1658, 8°. 214 pp. Gough Oxf. 28

5813. GAYTON, E., Upon mr. Bobard's yew-men of the guards to the Physick garden. [A ballad by E. Gayton.] [Madan 2580.] [Oxf., 1662], s. sh. Wood 416 (93)

5814. GAYTON, E., A ballad on the gyants in the Physick garden in Oxford [by E. Gayton? concerning the yew trees in the Botanic garden]. [Madan 2579.] [Oxf., 1662], s. sh. Wood 416 (92)

5815. DROPE, J., Upon the most hopefull and ever-flourishing sprouts of valour, the indefatigable centrys of the Physick-garden [by J. Drope]. [Madan 2658.] [Oxf.], 1664, s. sh. Wood 423 (41)
— [Another ed.] 1666. [Madan 2740.] Ashm. 37 (285)
— [Another ed.] Repr. with some alterations. 1682. Bagford collection

5816. EVANS, A., Vertumnus, an epistle [in verse] to mr. Jacob Bobart, botany professor to the University of Oxford and keeper of the Physick-garden, by the author of The apparition [A. Evans]. Oxf., 1713, 8°. 33 pp. Gough Oxf. 109 (11)

5817. SIBTHORP, H., To the gentlemen delegates of accounts, and of the committee for the Physick garden. [Address recommending the storage of dried specimens in mr. Musgrove's late house, and the purchase of another house to use its material for building purposes. Signed The Botany Professor.] [Oxf., 1775], s. sh. G.A. Oxon b. 19

5818. [Begin.] In compliance with your request . . . [A letter concerning the Botanic garden and library, and the proposed widening of Magdalen bridge. By H. Sibthorp.] [Oxf., 1778], 4°. 25 pp. Gough Oxf. 103 (5)

5819. [An address against the demolition of the Botanical library and green house in the Botanical garden. Signed A member of Convocation. Feb. 5, 1778.] [Oxf., 1778], s. sh. B.M.

5820. [Begin.] The committee who have undertaken . . . [An appeal on behalf of the Botanic garden, with subscription list.] [Oxf., 1834], s. sh.
G.A. Oxon b. 139 (155a)
— [Another ed.] March 14, 1834. G.A. Oxon b. 139 (155b)
— [Another ed.] Subscriptions up to April 16. [Oxf.], (1834), 4°. 3 pp.
G.A. Oxon b. 139 (155c)

5821. DAUBENY, C. G. B., Copy of a report presented to the Visitors of the Oxford Botanic garden, by the professor of Botany. [Oxf.], 1834, fol. 3 pp. G.A. Oxon c. 50 (116)

5822. DAUBENY, C., [Begin.] Sir, The alterations at the Botanic garden being now nearly completed . . . I am anxious to lay before the subscribers . . . the manner in which the several sums contributed . . . have been expended . . . [Also a Statement of the receipts and expenditure.] Nov. 2. [Oxf.], (1835), fol. 3 pp. G.A. Oxon 4° 255

5823. Regulations . . . [Oxf.], 1835, s. sh. G.A. Oxon c. 51 (77)

5824. INGRAM, J., The Botanic garden. (Memorials of Oxford, 1837, vol. 3. 16 pp.) G.A. Oxon 8° 20
— [Reissued.] (Memorials of the public buildings of Oxford. 1848.)
G.A. Oxon 8° 17

5825. May 25, 1846. [To be proposed in Convocation on June 4 that the Physic garden be exonerated from the repayment of £600 loaned by Convocation in 1841.] G.A. Oxon c. 62 (52)

See 2925 [Daubeny, C., Expenditure on Botanic garden from income of the professor of Botany in 1850. 1851].

5826. DAUBENY, C., Oxford Botanic garden; or A popular guide . . . 2nd ed. To which is appended An address . . . on . . . receiving the Fielding herbarium. With an appendix. [And] Suppl. 1856 [prefixed to the guide]. (Oxf.), 1853, 56, 8°. 12+62+21 pp. G.A. Oxon 8° 824

— 2nd ed. [A re-issue, p. 23–34 of the appendix being printed in 1860 (?) describing re-arrangements made in the Botanical museum in 1859.] (Oxf.), 1853[60?], 8°. 62+34 pp. G.A. Oxon 8° 1169

— [Another issue, of p. 23–34 of the appendix, paginated 1–12.]
G.A. Oxon 8° 161 (13)

5827. GUNTHER, R. T., Oxford gardens, based upon Daubeny's popular guide to the Physick garden of Oxford. With notes on the gardens of the colleges ... Oxf. &c., 1912, 8°. 280 pp. G.A. Oxon 8° 837

5828. The Botanical gardens. [Observations signed B.D., on the payment of admission fees by members of the University.] Feb. 20, 1856. Oxf., 1856, s. sh. G.A. Oxon c. 72 (71)

5829. DAUBENY, C., Botanical gardens. [Reply to no. 5828 by the professor of Botany.] Feb. 21, 1856. [Oxf.], 1856, s. sh.
G.A. Oxon c. 72 (72)

5830. To the members of Convocation. [Report by C. Daubeny on a meeting of the Garden committee in connection with the demand for free admission to the conservatories by members of the University: together with the Botanic garden account for 1855.] 18 Mar., 1856. [Oxf.], 1856, 4°. 4 pp. G.A. Oxon c. 72 (115)

5831. [Regulation made by the Botanic garden committee admitting members of the University to the gardens &c. without payment, and proposing a decree to Convocation to compensate the gardener for loss of fees so incurred.] May 7, 1856. [Oxf.], 1856, s. sh.
G.A. Oxon c. 72 (189)

5832. [Report presented to the Hebdomadal council by the delegates appointed to superintend the Botanic building repairs, Apr. 9, 1856. With recommendations to Convocation, Apr. 28, 1856.] [Oxf.], 1856, s. sh. G.A. Oxon c. 72 (176)

5833. LAWSON, M. A., [Report to the Garden committee of Council on the requirements of botany in the University; and on the question of retaining the Botanic garden on its site or of moving it to the Parks.] [Oxf.], (1875), 8°. 9 pp. G.A. Oxon c. 33 (104)

5834. Committee on the Botanic garden, 1873. [Report on the cost of restoring the present garden, and the cost of making a new garden in the Parks *and* A letter, dated 8 May, 1875, applying for a grant of £900 for the garden. The letter is signed M. A. Lawson.] [Oxf., 1875], s. sh.
G.A. Oxon c. 228

5835. The Oxford Botanic garden. (Nature, 1875, vol. 13, p. 61, 62.)
Per. 1996 d. 596

5836. ACLAND, SIR H. W., A letter to dr. Hooker [concerning 'the long-intended-design of placing our botanical collections and gardens in proximity to the other scientific collections']. [Oxf.], 1875, 8°. 8 pp.
G.A. Oxon 8° 199 (2)

— 2nd ed. 1875. 10 pp. G.A. Oxon 8° 199 (8)

5837. NEMO, *pseud.*, To the president of the University removal co. (limited). [A satire proposing to move the Radcliffe infirmary and other buildings to the Parks : ridiculing the suggested transfer of the Botanic garden.] [Oxf., 1875?], s. sh.   G.A. Oxon c. 228

5838. ACLAND, H. W., The Botanical gardens, and the administration of science apparatus in Oxford. [Oxf.], (1876), 8°. 4 pp. G.A. Oxon c. 228

5839. LAWSON, M. A., [*Begin.*] Professor H. Smith has . . . [Recommendations upon alterations and repairs needed in the Botanic garden. Feb. 14, 1876.] [Oxf.], (1876), 8°. 7 pp.   G.A. Oxon c. 33 (103)

See 4608 [Bobart, H. T., Biographical sketch of Jacob Bobart. 1884].

5840. First(–) Annual report of the Curators. 1888– . (Oxf. Univ. Gazette, 1889– .)   Per. G.A. Oxon c. 86

See 3057 [Vines, S. H., and Druce, G. C., The early history of the Physic garden, 1679–1720. 1914].

5841. POWER, SIR D'A. The Oxford Physic garden. (Annals of medical history, 1919, p. 109–25.)   G.A. Oxon c. 107 (67)

5842. OSBORN, T. G. B., Changes at the Botanic gardens. (Oxf. mag., 1943, vol. 61, p. 241, 42.)   Per. G.A. Oxon 4° 141

5843. OSBORN, T. G. B., The Oxford Botanic garden. (Endeavour, 1951, vol. 10, p. 70–77.)   Radcl.

5844. Oxford Botanic garden. Guide. (Oxf.), 1957, 16°. 48 pp.
                                                    G.A. Oxon 16° 226

5844.2. PHILIP, I. G., The Physic garden gateway. (Bodleian library record, 1964, vol. 7, p. 175, 76.)   2590 d. Oxf. 1. 41 = R.

CLARENDON BUILDINGS

5845. [Topographical prints, &c. in the Bodleian.]   G.A. Oxon a. 45

5846. June 8, 1831. [Proposals to be submitted to Convocation, 11th inst. that the old Clarendon Printing Office should be appropriated and fitted up as offices and lecture rooms of the University.] n. pl., 1831, s. sh.   G.A. Oxon c. 47 (83)

See 5886 [Proposed use of Clarendon building attics for storing the University archives. 1862].

5847. [Grants to be proposed for the alteration of an upper room in the Clarendon buildings and the provision of fire-proof safes for the University archives to be removed from the Schools tower; &c. Mar. 13, 1863.] [Oxf.], 1863, s. sh.   G.A. Oxon c. 79 (107)

5848. Proposed alterations in the Clarendon buildings and in the Schools. [Statement by the vice-chancellor.] Mar. 16, 1863. n. pl., 1863, s. sh.
                                                   G.A. Oxon c. 79 (116)

5849. [Proposed decree in Convocation, June 3, to authorise expenditure on repairs and alterations to the Clarendon Building basement to adapt it as a Proctor's office, a Police station and a dwelling-house for a care-taker. Also the transfer to the General fund of the University of the Police pension fund.] May 31, 1869. [Oxf.], 1869, s. sh.

G.A. Oxon c. 85 (235)

5850. TIPPING, H. A., The Old Clarendon buildings. (Country Life, 1928, vol. 63, p. 800–07.)   Per. 384 b. 6

5851. CRASTER, SIR H. H. E., The Clarendon building. (Oxford, 1948, vol. 9, no. 3, p. 51–53.)   Per. G.A. Oxon 8° 1141

CLARENDON PRESS

See 6270, &c., University Press.

CONGREGATION HOUSE (OLD)

See 6035, St. Mary's Church.

CONVOCATION HOUSE

See Divinity School.

DIVINITY SCHOOL AND CONVOCATION HOUSE

See 5411 [A note of the Divinitie schoole and librarye [and] Collections relating to the Div. schoole and library, by dr. Langbaine. 1720].

5852. EARWAKER, J. P., Divinity school. [Historical account.] (Proc., Oxf. architect. and hist. soc., 1871, N.S., vol. 2, p. 342–44.)

Per. G.A. Oxon 8° 498 = R.

5853. GALTON, D., [Report to the Curators on the groyned ceiling of the Divinity school, and the floor and roof of the Bodleian.] n. pl., [1875], 8°. 5 pp.   G.A. Oxon c. 33 (85)

5854. CLARK, A., [Historical account of the Divinity school and Convocation house.] (Proc., Oxf. architect. and hist. soc., 1891, N.S., vol. 5, p. 344–47.)   Per. G.A. Oxon 8° 498 = R.

5855. HOPE, W. H. ST. JOHN, The heraldry and sculptures of the vault of the Divinity school. (Archaeol. journ., 1914, vol. 71, p. 217–60 and 16 plates.)   Per. G.A. Gen. top. 8° 529 = R.

5856. [199 photographs of the Divinity school, by F. H. Crossley, 1914.]

G.A. Oxon b. 81

5857. LEGGE, H. E., The Divinity school, a guide. Oxf., 1923, 8°. 41 pp.+ 54 plates.   G.A. Oxon 8° 1023

5858. WEBB, G., The Divinity school (and Convocation house). (Country Life, 1929, vol. 65, p. 592–99, 636–41.)   Per. 384 b. 6

5859. COX, A. D. M., An account for the building of the Divinity school. (Oxoniensia, 1956, vol. 21, p. 48–60.) Per. G.A. Oxon 4° 658 = R.

See 6106.4 [The Sheldonian theatre and the Divinity school. Text by H. M. Colvin, photographs by J. Thomas. 1964].

ENGLISH FACULTY LIBRARY

See 2819, &c.

EXAMINATION SCHOOLS

See 6075, &c., Schools (The).

GRIFFITH INSTITUTE

See 5404, Ashmolean museum of art and archaeology

HALIFAX HOUSE

5860. WYLLIE, J. M., The battle of the mice and the elephant [satirical poem on Halifax house] by the Barras Seer. Oxf., 1958, 4°. 8 pp.
28001 d. 716
— Reissue, with an argument [entitled] The rape of the lounge, or The battle of the mice and elephant. 1958.   28001 d. 717

HOLYWELL MUSIC ROOM

See also 4057, Social history, Music.

5861. [Concert programmes, bills, etc. in the Bodleian library.] 1771–1836.
Mus. 1 d. 64
6 Dec. 1773; 21 Feb. 1774.   Gough Oxf. 90 (5)
9 Nov. 1778; 20 Dec. 1779.   MS. Top. Oxon d. 281 (160, 165)

5862. List of subscribers to the Music room. Oct. 14, 1799 to Oct. 14, 1800 (1801/02, 02/03, 04/05). [Oxf., 1800–05], s. sh.   Mus. 1 d. 64
— [List of subscribers, and Resolutions of the stewards about subscriptions etc.] 1808/09–11/12. [Oxf., 1809–12], s. sh.   Mus. 1 d. 64

5863. Music room, Oxford, June 22, 1802. The stewards . . . submit the following articles . . . [Subscription rates and plans for concerts.] Oxf., 1802, s. sh.   Mus. 1 d. 64
— May 29th, 1804. [Fresh proposals.]   Mus. 1 d. 64
— June 10th, 1805. [Further alterations.]   Mus. 1 d. 64
— May 18th, 1808. [Altered regulations.]   Mus. 1 d. 64
— Jan. 18, 1815. [Altered regulations.]   Mus. 1 d. 64
— Nov. 28, 1816. [Appeal for support.]   Mus. 1 d. 64
— Jan. 3, 1818. [New articles, etc.]   Mus. 1 d. 64
— Dec. 29, 1818. [New articles, etc.]   Mus. 1 d. 64

5864. Music room. [The accounts for 1804/05 and 1805/06 published to encourage support from subscribers.] [Oxf., 1806], s. sh. Mus. I d. 64
— January 24, 1817 (Jan. 3, 1818; Dec. 29, 1818). [The accounts for 1816–18.] Mus. I d. 64
— Treasurer's account. 1824/25. G.A. Oxon c. 41 (87)

5865. JUNG, P., Concerts of vocal and instrumental music as performed at the Music room, Oxford, from October 1807 to October 1808. To which is annexed A list of the subscribers, stewards, and performers. Oxf., 1808, 12°. xiv+146 pp. 174 g. 106

5866. MEE, J. H., The oldest music room in Europe. Lond. &c., 1911, 8°. 216 pp. G.A. Oxon 8° 825

INDIAN INSTITUTE

For catalogues &c. of the Oriental manuscripts once the property of the Institute and now taken over by the Bodleian, see under the Oriental department of the latter, 5781, etc.

5867. [Topographical prints, &c. in the Bodleian.] G.A. Oxon a. 47

5868. Proposal for the founding of an Indian Institute at Oxford. [Oxf., 1875], 8°. 5 pp. G.A. Oxon c. 33 (112)

5869. WILLIAMS, M., Statement [concerning the founding of an Indian Institute and the establishment of a school of Indian studies]. Oxf., (1876), 8°. 8 pp. G.A. Oxon 8° 705 (15)

5870. WILLIAMS, M., Second statement by the Boden professor of Sanscrit after his second Indian journey. (Oxf., 1877), 8°. 8 pp.
G.A. Oxon 8° 620 (12)

5871. A statement of the objects to be effected by the establishment of an Indian Institute at Oxford, and a list of those who are supporters of the project. [Oxf., 1880], 4°. 4 pp. G.A. Oxon b. 139 (135c)

5872. WILLIAMS, M., [Begin.] The attention of members of Convocation . . . [Proposal to found an Indian Institute.] 22 May 1880. [Oxf.], (1880), s. sh. G.A. Oxon b. 139 (135b)

5873. WILLIAMS, M., [Begin.] As it has been recommended . . . [A paper opposing the recommendation by some members of Congregation that a separate building for the Indian Institute be dispensed with.] Nov. 12. [Oxf., 1880], 4°. 4 pp. G.A. Oxon b. 139 (135d)

5874. MÜLLER, F. M., The decree on the Indian Institute. [Oxf.], (1880), 8°. 4 pp. G.A. Oxon b. 139 (136a)

5875. WILLIAMS, M., The Indian Institute. Oxf., 1882, 4°. 16 pp.
G.A. Oxon 4° 109
— 4th ed. 1883. G.A. Oxon 4° 262 (27)
— [Another ed.] 1884. G.A. Oxon 4° 262 (28)
— [Another ed.] 1885. G.A. Oxon 4° 262 (29)

5876. The Indian Institute. (Builder, 1883, vol. 44, p. 652.) N. 1863 c. 1

5877. WILLIAMS, SIR M., The Indian Institute. Memorial stone laid by
    H.R.H. Albert Edward prince of Wales on May 2, 1883. [An account
    of the objects and management of the institute and a statement of re-
    ceipts and expenditure.] Oxf., 1883, 4°. 6 pp.
                                                MS. Top. Oxon d. 122 (f. 76)

5878. The form and order of laying the memorial stone of the Indian
    Institute . . . by H.R.H. Albert Edward, prince of Wales, May 2, 1883.
    (Oxf., 1883), 8°. 8 pp.   G.A. Oxon 8° 457

5879. The Indian Institute in the University of Oxford: a record of the
    circumstances which led to its establishment [&c.]. Oxf., 1886, 8°.
    44 pp.   G.A. Oxon 8° 659 (1)

5880. Statement of receipts and expenditure. Oxf., 1886, 4°. 12 pp.
                                                G.A. Oxon 4° 262 (30)

5881. Regulations for the library of the Indian Institute. [Oxf.], (1894),
    s. sh.   G.A. Oxon b. 139 (144b)

5882. Record of the establishment of the Indian Institute. Oxf., 1897, 8°.
                                                          Ind. Inst.

5883. Debate on Redevelopment of the Indian Institute site, held 1st June
    1965. [Issued with Oxf. Univ. Gazette, vol. 95, no. 3240.] Oxf., 1965,
    fol. 15 pp.   Per. G.A. Oxon c. 86

5883.1. Congregation, Tuesday 15 June. [Begin.] Our amendments . . .
    [Flysheet, signed by K. A. Ballhatchet and 9 others. Reprod. from
    typewriting. Issued with Oxf. Univ. Gazette, vol. 95, no. 3240.] n. pl.,
    [1965], s. sh.   Per. G.A. Oxon c. 86

5883.2. [Begin.] We, the undersigned members of Congregation, who are
    also Curators of the Bodleian . . . [Flysheet urging passing of the decree.
    Reprod. from typewriting. Issued with Oxf. Univ. Gazette, vol. 95, no.
    3240.] n. pl., 1965, s. sh.   Per. G.A. Oxon c. 86

5883.3. [Begin.] In view of the importance . . . [Flysheet issued by Council
    before the vote in Congregation on amendments to the decree on Re-
    development of the Indian Institute site. Reprod. from typescript.
    Issued with Oxford Univ. Gazette, vol. 95, no. 3240.] n. pl., 1965, fol.
    6 pp.   Per. G.A. Oxon c. 86

5884. [Begin.] Mr. Ballhatchet has informed . . . [Council's circular of
    23.6.65, in favour of the decree. Reprod. from typewriting. Issued with
    Oxf. Univ. Gazette, vol. 95, no. 3243.] n. pl., 1965, s. sh.
                                                Per. G.A. Oxon c. 86

5884.1. Convocation, Tuesday 29 June 1965, 2.0 p.m. [Begin.] We ask
    members . . . [signed by K. A. Ballhatchet and 13 others, opposing the
    decree concerning the Indian Institute. Reprod. from typewriting.
    Issued with Oxf. Univ. Gazette, vol. 95, no. 3243]. n. pl., 1965, s. sh.
                                                Per. G.A. Oxon c. 86

MUSEUM OF EASTERN ART

See 5373.5, Ashmolean Museum, Department of Eastern art.

MUSEUM OF HISTORY OF SCIENCE

See 5885, Old Ashmolean museum.

NEW EXAMINATION SCHOOLS

See 6075, Schools (The).

OLD ASHMOLEAN MUSEUM

For works on collections once housed in the Old Ashmolean and since transferred to other institutions see these institutions.

See also 5302, &c. [Rules and regulations affecting collections once in the Old Ashmolean].
See 6138 [Musæum Tradescantianum. 1656].

5885. Sheldonian and approaches. [2 plans made *c.* 1830, one showing the stone stairs to the street from the Old Ashmolean.]
G.A. Oxon b. 111 (235, 36)

See 5940 [Ingram, J., The Observatory. Ashmolean museum. 1837].

5886. For the Hebdomadal council only. Schools accommodation committee. [Report concerning alterations in and around the Ashmolean museum, involving the removal of the stairs to Broad street; and the use of the Clarendon attics for storing the University archives. Oct. 28, 1862.] n. pl., 1862, s. sh. G.A. Oxon a. 16
— [Dec. 8, 1862. Proposal to spend £597 on these alterations.]
G.A. Oxon a. 16

5887. HARRISON, J. P., The Old Ashmolean building [by J. P. Harrison]. [Oxf.], (1896), 4°. 3 pp. G.A. Oxon b. 139 (f. 54)

5888. GUNTHER, R. T., The Old Ashmolean building and the Lewis Evans collection of scientific instruments [signed R.T.G.]. [Oxf.], (1922), 4°. 4 pp. G.A. Oxon b. 139 (145c)

5889. FARNELL, L. R., [Letter to R. T. Gunther declining to transfer the Lewis Evans collection to the Old Ashmolean at this time. December 13.] [Oxf.], (1922), s. sh. G.A. Oxon b. 139 (145d)

5890. GUNTHER, R. T., New light on Ashmole's museum. (Oxf. mag., 1923, vol. 41, p. 315, 16.) Per. G.A. Oxon 4° 141

5891. GUNTHER, R. T., The Lewis Evans collection of scientific instruments and the Old Ashmolean museum [signed] A member of Congregation [R. T. Gunther]. [Oxf.], (1924), s. sh. G.A. Oxon b. 139 (146)

5892. GUNTHER, R. T., The Lewis Evans collection of scientific instruments. Appeal for the fund [to provide a permanent endowment]. [Oxf.], (1924), s. sh.   G.A. Oxon b. 139 (147)

5893. WRIGHT, D., Elias Ashmole, founder of the Ashmolean museum. Lond., [1924], 8°. 35 pp.   1757 e. 27 (2)

5894. GUNTHER, R. T., Historic instruments for the advancement of science, a handbook to the Oxford collections. Lond. &c., 1925, 16°. 90 pp.   19982 f. 2

5895. DAWBER, E. G., The Old Ashmolean building. [Presentation of the Wren window.] (Journ., Roy. inst. of Brit. architects, 1927, 3rd ser., vol. 34, p. 523, 24, 28.)   Per. 17356 d. 27

5896. The Wren–Ashmole–Plot memorial windows. (Nature, 1927, vol. 119, p. 798, 99.)   Radcl.

5897. The diary and will of Elias Ashmole, ed. and extended by R. T. Gunther. (Old Ashm. reprints, 2.) Oxf., 1927, 8°. 183 pp.   1757 e. 35

5898. GUNTHER, R. T., The Old Ashmolean. Oxf., 1933, 16°. 151 pp. 19982 f. 3

5899. GUNTHER, R. T., Handbook to the Museum of history of science in the Old Ashmolean building. Oxf., 1935, 16°. 157 pp.   19982 f. 4

5899.1. 1st(–   ) Report of the Committee of the Museum ... (including the 12th(–   ) Annual report of Lewis Evans collection. 1935–   . (Oxf. Univ. Gazette, 1936–   ).   Per. G.A. Oxon c. 86

5900. Friends of the Old Ashmolean. Annual meeting. 1936. Oxf., 1936, 4°.   G.A. Oxon 4° 571

5901. GUNTHER, R. T., The astrolabe of queen Elizabeth [found in the observatory, when refitting, and deposited in the Museum of the history of science, Old Ashmolean]. (Archaeologia, 1937, vol. 86, p. 65–72.) Per. G.A. Gen. top. 4° 162 = R

5902. TAYLOR, F. SHERWOOD, The Museum of the history of science. [Historic apparatus of bygone scientists.] (Endeavour, 1942, vol. 1, p. 67–69.)   Radcl.

5903. Catalogue of an exhibition of scientific apparatus pertaining to medicine and surgery. Oxf., 1947, 4°. 36 pp.   G.A. Oxon 4° 504 (9)

5904. JOSTEN, C. H., Museum of the history of science. (Museums journ., 1953, vol. 52, p. 263–65.)   Per. 1758 d. 10
— Repr.   17582 d. 10

5905. New staircase for the Old Ashmolean. (Builder, 1958, vol. 194, p. 582, 83.)   N. 1863 c. 1

OLD SCHOOLS

See 6092, &c., Schools (The).

PHYSIC GARDEN

See 5810, &c., Botanic Garden.

PITT RIVERS MUSEUM

See 6138 [Musæum Tradescantianum. 1656].

5906. The Pitt-Rivers collection. [Brief account.] [Oxf.], (1883), 8°. 4 pp.
G.A. Oxon b. 139 (118)

5907. The Pitt-Rivers collection [signed H. B.]. (Oxf. mag., 1887, vol. 5,
p. 13, 14.) Per. G.A. Oxon 4° 141

5908. FFOULKES, C., European arms and armour in the University of
Oxford, principally in the Ashmolean and Pitt-Rivers museums. Oxf.,
1912, 4°. 64 pp.+19 pl. 23152 c. 7

5909. PENNIMAN, T. K., The Pitt Rivers museum. (Museums journ., 1953,
vol. 52, p. 243–46.) Per. 1758 d. 10
— Repr. 17582 d. 10

5909.4. FAGG, B., Towards the new Pitt Rivers. (Oxf. mag., 1966, p. 240,
41, 48.) Per. G.A. Oxon 4° 141

PROSCHOLIUM

5910. SCOTT, SIR G. G., Sir G. G. Scott's report on the [proposed conversion of the] Proscholium [as a fireproof receptacle for the most precious
contents of the Bodleian]. n. pl., (1875), 8°. 3 pp. G.A. Oxon c. 33 (87)

5911. NICHOLSON, E. W. B., The bicycle-stands in the 'Proscholium'.
[Oxf.], (1904), s. sh. G.A. Oxon c. 153

5912. NICHOLSON, E. W. B., Pro Bodleio!!! An appeal to every resident
member of Convocation . . . to non-placet decree no. 1 which proposes
to convert sir Thomas Bodley's 'vaulted walke' . . . into a bicycle-
stable!!! Oxf., 1905, 4°. 12 pp. G.A. Oxon 4° 235

RADCLIFFE CAMERA

*For works dealing with the collection of scientific books originally housed in
the Radcliffe Camera see under Radcliffe Science library, 5950, &c.*

*For works on statues and busts at one time housed in the Radcliffe
Camera see Ashmolean Museum, 5260, &c.*

5913. [Topographical prints, &c. in the Bodleian.] G.A. Oxon a. 46

5914. An act to enable any corporations within the University of Oxford,
or any other persons, to sell and convey any messuages and ground . . .
for building a library pursuant to the will of John Radcliffe . . . (7 G. I.
c. 13, Private.) [Lond., 1720/1], fol. 3 pp. C 2. 19 (10) Art.

5915. GIBBS, J., Bibliotheca Radcliviana: or, A short description of the Radcliffe library. Lond., 1747, fol. 12 pp.+21 plates. G.A. Oxon b. 16

5916. To the ... heads of ... colleges and halls ... [Orders and regulations for attendance on Dr. Radcliffe's trustees. Apr. 10, 1749.] [Oxf.], 1749, s. sh.   Don. b. 12 (58)

5917. LEWIS, W., Oratio in Theatro Sheldoniano habita Idibus Aprilis, MDCCXLIX. die dedicationis Bibliothecæ Radclivianæ. Oxon., 1749, 4°. 24 pp.   G. Pamph. 117 (5)
— 2nd ed. 1749.   Gough Oxf. 90 (1)

5918. The opening of the Radcliffe library in 1749. [2 letters by T. Bray and B. Kennicott, describing the scenes and speeches]. (Bodleian quarterly record, 1915, vol. 1, p. 165–72.)   2590 d. Oxf. 1. 40 = R.

For the political speech made by W. King at the dedication ceremonies, and the answers to it see 183, &c.

5919. Plan of the Radcliffe Library . . . with the arrangements for the banquet . . . June 14, 1814. (Lond., 1814), s. sh.
                                                       MS. Top. Oxon d. 281 (144)

5920. HAKEWILL, An architect and a royal visit to Oxford in 1814. [An account of the arrangements for the banquet in the Radcliffe Camera.] (Builder, 1880, vol. 38, p. 339, 40.)   N. 1863 c. 1

5921. INGRAM, J., The Radcliffe library. (Memorials of Oxford, 1837, vol. 3. 16 pp.)   G.A. Oxon 8° 20
— [Reissued.] (Memorials of the public buildings in Oxford. 1848.)
                                                               G.A. Oxon 8° 17

5922. Engraved scraps of Oxford. 2nd ser. Radcliffe library. 4 prints. Oxf., [c. 1840], 8°.   G.A. Oxon 8° 919

See 5953 [Loan of the Camera as a reading room of the Bodleian: with the conditions relating thereto. 1860].

5923. For the Radcliffe Trustees only. [Reporting a request from the Bodleian curators that the Camera reading room be better ventilated, and that the trustees would reconsider making the basement fireproof. With remarks, signed H. W. Acland.] [Oxf.], (1877), 4°. 3 pp.
                                                       MS. Top. Oxon b. 43 (16)

See 6102 [Proposed lighting of the Camera with electric light. 1880].

5924. Information by Bodley's librarian against an undergraduate reading at the Camera. [Oxf., 1893], fol. 7 pp.   G.A. Oxon c. 90 (45)

5925. NICHOLSON, E. W. B., The changes at the Radcliffe Camera. [A letter.] (Oxf. mag., 1898, vol. 16, p. 182, 83.) Per. G.A. Oxon 4° 141

5926. JONES, H. S., The closing of the reference-shelves in the Radcliffe Camera [letters]. (Oxf. mag., 1898, vol. 17, p. 47, 48, 86, 118.)
                                                       Per. G.A. Oxon 4° 141

5927. NICHOLSON, E. W. B., The select library in the Radcliffe Camera. [Letters in answer to H. S. Jones.] (Oxf. mag., 1898, vol. 17, p. 62, 100.)
Per. G.A. Oxon 4° 141

5928. Alphabetical list of periodicals, of which the latest numbers received are exhibited in the Radcliffe Camera. 1st ed. [Oxf.], 1899, fol. 14 pp.
2590 c. Oxf. 1. 13

5929. [Photograph of Underground bookstore, Bodleian library, 1910.]
G.A. Oxon a. 34

5930. MADAN, F., The Bodleian library: a remarkable underground bookstore. Repr. from the Oxford chronicle, Nov. 29th, 1912. [Oxf., 1912], s. sh.
G.A. Oxon c. 309 (69*)

5931. RAYSON, T., 'Bibliotheca Radcliviana'. (The Salon, 1914, vol. 2, p. 376–84.)
2590 c. Oxf. 1. 9

5932. LUCY, W. and CO. LTD., The new underground book-store. Oxf., [1914], 8°. 12 pp.
2590 e. Oxf. 1. 18

5933. HUSSEY, C., The Radcliffe Camera. (Country Life, 1931, vol. 69, p. 548–54.)
Per. 384 b. 6

5934. LEEDS, E. T., Three stoneware flagons found in Oxford. [One in 1914 within the precincts of the Examination schools, High st., the other two in 1910 on the site of the Radcliffe Camera underground bookstore.] (Antiq. journ., 1933, vol. 13, p. 470–73.)
Per. 17572 d. 73 = R.

5935. TROTMAN, R. R., Rearrangements at the Radcliffe Camera. (Libr. assoc. record, 1936, 4th ser., vol. 3, p. 56, 57.)
Per. 25891 d. 21

5936. LANG, S., By Hawksmoor out of Gibbs. [The design of the Radcliffe Camera.] (Architect. review, 1949, vol. 105, p. 183–90.) Per. 17356 c. 8

See 5587.5 [Bibliotheca Radcliviana, 1749–1949. 1949].

5937. GILLAM, S. G., The building accounts of the Radcliffe Camera. (Oxf. hist. soc., N.S., vol. 13.) Oxf., 1958, 8°. 189 pp. +67 pl.
G.A. Oxon 8° 360 = R.

RADCLIFFE OBSERVATORY

5938. [*Begin.*] In the summer of the year 1768 . . . [Proposal, signed T. Hornsby, Savilian professor of astronomy, that Convocation should approve the granting of money on loan by the Delegates of the Press, to purchase, or order from mr. Bird, the necessary instruments to furnish the Radcliffe Observatory, although the building of the Observatory has yet to be started.] [Oxf.], (1771), 4°. 4 pp.
Gough Oxf. 90 (9)

5939. An act for enabling the president and scholars of Saint John baptist college . . . to sell and convey to the trustees of the will of doctor John Radcliffe, a piece of ground in the parish of Saint Giles . . . and the observatory thereon, and for laying out the purchase money in the purchase of lands and for other purposes. (1 G. IV, c. 33, Private.) [Lond.], 1820, fol. 8 pp.   L.L.

5940. INGRAM, J., The Observatory [and] Ashmolean museum. (Memorials of Oxford, 1837, vol. 3, 16 pp.)   G.A. Oxon 8° 20
— [Reissued.] (Memorials of the public buildings of Oxford. 1848.)
                                                              G.A. Oxon 8° 17

5941. (Results of) Astronomical (and meteorological) observations made at the Radcliffe Observatory in . . . 1840(–1931/5). Vol. 1–56. [Title varies.] Oxf., 1842–1937, 4°.   Per. 1843 d. 24

5942. The Radcliffe catalogue of 6317 stars, chiefly circumpolar . . . Oxf., 1860, 8°.   Per. 18428 d. 57
— Second Radcliffe catalogue, containing 2386 stars . . . Oxf., 1870, 8°.
                                                              Per. 18428 d. 57
— Catalogue of 1772 stars, chiefly comprised within the zone 85°–90° N.P.D. . . . Oxf., 1906, 8°.   18428 d. 33

5943. JOHNSON, M. J., [A letter, dated 28 Jan. 1856, addressed to sir Travers Twiss, commenting on the latter's observations on the office of Radcliffe Observer. The observations were contained in no. 2537]. Oxf., (1856), s. sh.   G.A. Oxon c. 72 (34)

5944. Report of the Radcliffe Observer to the Board of trustees.
— 1861–64.   G.A. Oxon c. 80 (428–31)
— 1865.   G.A. Oxon c. 81 (231)
— 1866.   G.A. Oxon c. 82 (324)
— 1867.   G.A. Oxon c. 83 (402)
— 1868.   G.A. Oxon c. 84 (479)
— 1869.   G.A. Oxon c. 85 (468)
— 1870–75, 77, 83.   Per. 184 d. 57

5945. TURNER, H. H., The Radcliffe and University observatories. [Oxf.], (1907), 8°. 5 pp.   G.A. Oxon b. 140 (138e)

5946. The Radcliffe Observatory and its proposed removal. (Nature, 1930, vol. 125, p. 769–71.)   Radcl.

5947. ESDAILE, K. A., The Radcliffe Observatory. (Journ., Roy. soc. of arts, 1930, vol. 78, p. 755–59.)   Soc. 1761 d. 14

5948. HUSSEY, C., The Radcliffe Observatory. (Country Life, 1930, vol. 67, p. 674–81.)   Per. 384 b. 6

5949. GRAY, A. S., The Radcliffe Observatory. (Oxf. med. sch. gazette, 1958, vol. 10, p. 69–73.)   Radcl.

See also 6233, &c., University Observatory.

RADCLIFFE SCIENCE LIBRARY

5950. Catalogue of the works in medicine and natural history contained in the Radcliffe library. Oxf., 1835, 8°. 330 pp.   2590 e. Oxf. 5. 1

5951. Catalogue of books on natural science in the Radcliffe library at the Oxford university museum up to December 1872. Oxf., 1877, 4°. 566 pp.   2590 d. Oxf. 5. 12 = R.
— Catalogue of books added . . . during 1870(–1927). Oxf., 1871 (–1928), 4°.   2590 d. Oxf. 5. 3, 4 = R.

5952. Provisional catalogue of transactions of societies, periodicals, and memoirs available . . . in the Radcliffe library at the University museum [1866–71]. Together with a third (fourth) report . . . by the librarian. Oxf., 1866–71, 8°.   2590 d. Oxf. 5. 5, 6
— 3rd ed. [*entitled*] Catalogue of transactions [&c.]. Oxf., 1876, 8°.
         2590 d. Oxf. 5. 9
— 3rd ed. Together with The students' library, The regulations . . . and The report . . . for 1876. Oxf., 1877, 8°.   2590 d. Oxf. 5. 10
— 4th ed. Oxf., 1887, 8°.   2590 d. Oxf. 5. 17

5953. [Proposal submitted to Convocation, 16th June, to accept the scientific library offered by the Radcliffe trustees, and also the loan of the Radcliffe Camera as a reading room of the Bodleian: with the conditions relating thereto.] June 12, 1860. [Oxf.], 1860, s. sh.
         G.A. Oxon c. 76 (220)

5954. Report to the Radcliffe trustees on the transfer of the Radcliffe library to the Oxford university museum. By H. W. Acland. Oxf., 1861, 8°. 23 pp.   Per. 2590 d. Oxf. 5. 1
— Second report . . . on the progress of the Radcliffe library. By H. W. Acland. Oxf., 1863, 8°. 15 pp.   Per. 2590 d. Oxf. 5. 1
— Report. 1872–74, 76, 94, 97, 1900, 05, 08/09, 10/11. Oxf., 1872– 1911, 8°.   Per. 2590 d. Oxf. 5. 1

5955. Library and reading-room, Oxford university museum. [Description of the new rooms in which the Radcliffe library is housed.] n. pl., 1861, 8°. 11 pp.   G.A. Oxon 8° 93 (10)

5956. The Radcliffe library and reading-room at the Oxford university museum. [By H. W. Acland.] Oxf., 1867, 8°. 11 pp.   2590 e. Oxf. 5. 2

5957. Arrangements and regulations of the Radcliffe library and reading-room [ed. by sir H. W. Acland]. Oxf., 1871, 8°. 8 pp.   B.M.
— 3rd ed. 1871.   2590 d. Oxf. 5. 7

5958. Regulations and arrangements of the Radcliffe library and reading-room at the Oxford university museum. 6th ed. Oxf., 1895, 8°. 12 pp.
         2590 d. Oxf. 5. 18

5959. ACLAND, SIR H. W., The Radcliffe iron bookcase. (Trans. and proc., 1st annual meeting of the Library assoc., 1879, p. 75.) Per. 25891 d. 1

5960. ACLAND, SIR H. W., Foundation and progress of the Radcliffe library. (Trans. and proc., 1st annual meeting of the Library assoc., 1879, p. 29–31.)   Per. 25891 d. 1

5961. Catalogue of books published in the XVIth, XVIIth, & XVIIIth centuries from the Radcliffe library, Oxford, on sale by B. H. Blackwell. June 1894. (No. 41.) Oxf., 1894, 8°. 32 pp.   2590 d. Oxf. 5. 14

5962. ACLAND, SIR H. W., Radcliffe library, Oxford university museum. Memorandum on the library for the use of members of the British medical association on their visit to Oxford, August 3, 1895. Oxf., 1895, 8°. 14 pp. 2590 d. Oxf. 5. 19

5963. Proceedings in Convocation, June 15, 1897 [concerning the erection by the Drapers' company of a new Radcliffe science library]. (Oxf.), 1897, 8°. 8 pp. G.A. Oxon 8° 1079 (10)

5964. JACKSON, W. H., Report to the Radcliffe Trustees on the extract from the minutes of the Delegates of the Oxford university museum in relation to the regulations of the Radcliffe library. Oxf., 1900, 8°. 20 pp. 2590 d. Oxf. 5. 16

5965. JACKSON, W. H., Radcliffe library. Notice [of method of borrowing Bodley books by 'professors and students' at the Museum, signed W. H. J.]. [Oxf.], (1901), s. sh. G.A. Oxon b. 139 (123a)

5966. ALEXANDER, H. F., Radcliffe library extension. (Oxf. mag., 1934, vol. 52, p. 760, 61.) Per. G.A. Oxon 4° 141

5967. Extension to the Radcliffe library. (Architect, 1935, vol. 141, p. 50–53.) N. 1731 c. 16

RHODES HOUSE

General 5968-5977   Lists and Statistics 6028-6034
Rhodes scholars 5978-6027

General

5968. Rhodes House. (Architect, 1929, vol. 121, p. 605–13.) N. 1731 c. 16

5969. Rhodes House; opened 10 May 1929. Oxf., 1929, 8°. 11 pp. G.A. Oxon 8° 1056 (5)

5970. Rhodes House. (United Empire, 1929, vol. 20, p. 339–41.) R.H.

5971. Cecil Rhodes and Rhodes house. Oxf., 1929, 8°. 23 pp. R.H.
— 4th ed. 1935. R.H.
— 9th ed. 1956. R.H.

5972. Research at Rhodes house. Oxf., 1931, 8°. 7 pp. R.H.

5973. Inventory of the collection of books relating to the history of Malta offered to the Rhodes Trustees by Hannibal P. Scicluna. [In typewriting.] n. pl., [c. 1937], fol. 36 sheets R.H.

5974. Records of the Anti-slavery society [purchased by Rhodes House]. [Reprod. from typewriting.] (Nat. Reg. of Archives.) n. pl., [1953], fol. 19 pp. 2262 c. 7 = R.
— Accessions, 1941–1951. 2262 c. 7 = R.

5975. CLARK, G. N., Cecil Rhodes and his college. (Oxf.), 1953, 4°. 13 pp. R.H.

5975.1. BOWRA, SIR C. M., Centenary of Cecil Rhodes and jubilee of the Rhodes scholarships. (Oration delivered by the vice-chancellor, 1 July 1953.) (Oxf., 1953), 8°. 4 pp.   R.H.

5976. FREWER, L. B., Rhodes House library, its function and resources. (Bodleian libra   record, 1956, vol. 5, p. 318–32.)
2590 d. Oxf. 1. 41 = R.
— Repr. 16 pp.   R. 7.3

5977. Papers of the British and foreign anti-slavery and aborigines protection society, kept in Rhodes House library. [Reprod. from typewriting.] [Oxf.], 1956, 4°. 52 pp.   2590 d. Oxf. 27. 1

5977.1. Rhodes House offered to the University. (Amer. Oxonian, 1962, vol. 49, p. 43, 44.)   Per. G.A. Oxon 8° 889

Rhodes Scholars

General

5978. SCHILLER, F. C. S., A cosmopolitan Oxford. [Rhodes scholars.] (Fortnightly rev., 1902, vol. 77, p. 814–20.)   Per. 3977 d. 59

5979.

5980. MACLEAN, G. E., The Cecil Rhodes scholarships. Repr. from The School review, Apr. 1903, p. 246–253. Chicago, (1903), 4°.
2625 d. 10 (6)

5981. Will and codicils of . . . Cecil John Rhodes. Lond., [1904], 4°. 26 pp.
G.A. Oxon 4° 231

5982. Memorandum. 1905, 13, 14, 15, Rhodes scholarships. United States of America. n. pl., [1904–14], 4°.   G.A. Oxon 4° 336

5983. Memorandum. The Rhodes scholarships in Canada. 1905, 1912. n. pl., [1904, 11], 4°.   G.A. Oxon 4° 336

5984. Memorandum. The Rhodes scholarships in New Zealand. [1906?] n. pl., [1905?], 4°.   G.A. Oxon 4° 336

5985. WILLIAMS, C. L., The American student and the Rhodes scholarships, a manual of information. Detroit, 1905, 8°. 46 pp.
G.A. Oxon 4° 399 (15)

5986. LEINDEINER-WILDAU, H. E. VON, A Rhodes scholar from Germany on Oxford university. (Cornhill mag., 1905, N.S. vol. 18, p. 44–52.)
Per. 2705 d. 213

5987. Memorandum. The Rhodes scholarships in Bermuda. n. pl., [1906?], 4°.   G.A. Oxon 4° 336

5988. ASHBY, S. R., An American Rhodes's scholar at Oxford university. (Macmillan's mag., 1906, N.S., vol. 1, p. 181–90.)   Per. 2705 d. 254

5989. Rhodes scholarships. Statement for 1906(–15/16). n. pl., 1906–16, 4°.   Per. G.A. Oxon 4° 330

5990. SCHOLZ, R. F., and HORNBECK, S. K., Oxford and the Rhodes scholarships. Lond. &c., 1907, 8°. 172 pp.   G.A. Oxon 8° 748

See 6089, 6090 [Unveiling of tablet in New examination schools to commemorate the foundation of Rhodes scholarships. 1907].

5991. The Rhodes scholarships in Jamaica. [1910.] n. pl., (1909), 4°.
G.A. Oxon 4° 336

5992. BEHAN, J. C. V., The Rhodes scholarships. (Oxf. and Cambr. review, 1910, no. 10, p. 31–49.)   Per. 2625 d. 37

5993. Memorandum. The Rhodes scholarships in South Africa. 1911. n. pl., [1910], 4°.   G.A. Oxon 4° 336

5994. Memorandum. The Rhodes scholarships in Australia. n. pl., [c. 1910], 4°.   G.A. Oxon 4° 336

5995. Memorandum. The Rhodes scholarships in Newfoundland. [1914]. n. pl., (1913), 4°.   G.A. Oxon 4° 336

5996. PARKIN, G. R., The Rhodes scholarships. Boston &c., 1912, 8°. 250 pp.   L. of C.
— [Another ed.] Lond. &c., 1913, 8°. 250 pp.   G.A. Oxon 8° 863

5997. The American Oxonian, the official magazine of the Alumni association of American Rhodes scholars. Vol. 1– . Bloomington, Indiana, &c., 1914– , 8°.   Per. G.A. Oxon 8° 889

5998. WYLIE, F. J., Rhodes scholars and athletics. (Amer. Oxon., 1914, vol. 1, p. 33–35.)   Per. G.A. Oxon 8° 889

5999. Athletics at Oxford: the new rules [as they affect Rhodes scholars]. I. By L. C. Hull. II. By S. O. Devan. (Amer. Oxon., 1914, vol. 1, p. 21–32.)   Per. G.A. Oxon 8° 889

6000. BALL, S., Oxford's opinion of the Rhodes scholars. (Amer. Oxon., 1914, vol. 1, p. 1–20.)   Per. G.A. Oxon 8° 889

6001. THAYER, W. W., Comments on Rhodes scholarships in American periodicals. (Amer. Oxon., 1915, vol. 2, p. 34–44.)
Per. G.A. Oxon 8° 889

6002. WYLIE, F. J., Rhodes scholarships after the War. (Oxf. mag., 1918, vol. 37, p. 112–14.)   Per. G.A. Oxon 4° 141

6003. PARKIN, G. R., Rhodes scholarships and American scholars. (Atlantic monthly, 1919, vol. 124, p. 365–75.)   Per. 2714 d. 51

6004. BEVINE, F. F., The inadequate Rhodes scholar, a defence [and a reply to G. R. Parkin]. (Atlantic monthly, 1919, vol. 124, p. 665–69.)
Per. 2714 d. 51

6005. HARRISON, J. B., Rhodes scholarships and a Rhodes scholar [Joel Johanson]. (Pacific review, 1920, p. 53–66). G.A. Oxon c. 274 (f. 71, 72)

6006. AYDELOTTE, F., What the American Rhodes scholar gets from Oxford. (Scribner's mag., 1923, vol. 73, p. 677–88.) Per. 2714 d. 28

6007. CROSBY, L. A., and AYDELOTTE, F., Oxford of to-day, a manual for prospective Rhodes scholars. (Alumni soc. of Amer. Rhodes scholars.) New York &c., 1923, 8°. 288 pp.   G.A. Oxon 8° 1019
— 2nd ed. 1927.   G.A. Oxon 8° 1073

6008. CARTER, C. W., Expenses of a Rhodes scholar. (Amer. Oxon., 1924, vol. 11, p. 1–6.)   Per. G.A. Oxon 8° 889

6009. KERR, P., The Rhodes scholarships: some statistics and suggestions. (Amer. Oxon., 1927, vol. 14, p. 85–91.)   Per. G.A. Oxon 8° 889

6010. Reorganisation of American Rhodes scholarships. Statement by the Trustees. (Amer. Oxon., 1929, vol. 16, p. 194–201.)
Per. G.A. Oxon 8° 889

6011. Rhodes scholars attending the reunion at Oxford, July 1929. n. pl., (1929), 8°. 22 pp.   G.A. Oxon 4° 403* (18)

6012. The Reorganisation plan. Mr. Winston's protest. Mr. Moe's rejoinder. A statement from lord Lothian. (Amer. Oxon., 1930, vol. 17, p. 69–97.)   Per. G.A. Oxon 8° 889

6013. THWING, C. F., Record of the American Rhodes scholars. (Hibbert journ., 1933, vol. 31, p. 203–16.)   Per. 96 d. 29 = S.

6014. V., A. C., The first Rhodes scholars [their impact on Oxford]. (Amer. Oxon., 1934, vol. 21, p. 123–31.)   Per. G.A. Oxon 8° 889

6015. The last colony, an answer by an Oxford Oxonian to some of the questions ... on American Rhodes scholarships. (Oxf. mag., 1938, vol. 56, p. 413, 14.)   Per. G.A. Oxon 4° 141

6016. ALLEN, SIR C. K., Forty years of the Rhodes scholarships. Oxf., 1944, 8°. 20 pp.   2625 d. 85 (12)

6017. ALLEN, SIR C. K., Germans at Oxford. (Amer. Oxon., 1945, vol. 32, p. 135–38.)   Per. G.A. Oxon 8° 889

6018. WYLIE, SIR F., Rhodes' final will and its reception in Oxford. (Amer. Oxon., 1945, vol. 32, p. 1–11.)   Per. G.A. Oxon 8° 889

6019. AYDELOTTE, F., The American record at Oxford. (Amer. Oxon., 1945, vol. 32, p. 121–130.)   Per. G.A. Oxon 8° 889

6020. ALLEN, D. F., Housekeeping in Oxford: advice to married Rhodes scholars. (Amer. Oxon., 1946, vol. 33, p. 106–08.)
Per. G.A. Oxon 8° 889

6021. AYDELOTTE, F., The vision of Cecil Rhodes, a review of the first forty years of the American scholarships. Lond., 1946, 8°. 142 pp. R.H.

6022. AYDELOTTE, F., The American Rhodes scholarships, a review of the first forty years. Princeton, 1946, 8°. 208 pp.   R.H.

6023. ELTON, GODFREY, 1st *baron*, The first fifty years of the Rhodes trust and the Rhodes scholarships, 1903–1953. [Oxf.], 1955, 8°. xiv+ 268 pp.   R.H.

6024. ALLEN, SIR C. K., Fifty years of the Rhodes scholarships. (Oxford, 1953, vol. 12, no. 2, p. 67–77.)   Per. G.A. Oxon 8° 1141

6025. The Oxford reunion. (Amer. Oxon., 1953, vol. 40, p. 161–203.)
Per. G.A. Oxon 8° 889

6026. ALLEN, D., Sunlight and shadow, autobiography. Lond. &c., 1960, 8°. 184 pp.   G.A. Oxon 8° 1404

6027. SMITH, C., The selection of Rhodes scholars. (Amer. Oxon., 1960, vol. 47, p. 169–80.)   Per. G.A. Oxon 8° 889

Lists and Statistics

6028. Rhodes scholarships. Record of past scholars, June, 1913. [Oxf.], 1913, 8°. 97 pp.   G.A. Oxon 8° 1145

6029. Rhodes scholarships. Record of past scholars, elected between the years 1903 and 1916. (Oxf.), [1920], 8°. 205 pp.   G.A. Oxon 8° 1145

6030. BURGESS, R. W., The record of the American Rhodes scholars. (Amer. Oxon., 1921, vol. 8, p. 1–36.)   Per. G.A. Oxon 8° 889

6031. Rhodes scholarships: record of past scholars, 1903–1927. Oxf., 1931, 8°. 412 pp.   2601 e. 99

6032. MACNEILLE, H. M., The academic records of American Rhodes scholars, 1904–1908. (Amer. Oxon., 1932, vol. 19, p. 215–28.)
Per. G.A. Oxon 8° 889

6033. Register of Rhodes scholars, 1903–1945. Lond. &c., 1950, 8°. 290 pp.
2601 e. 98 = S.

6034. Addresses and occupations of Rhodes scholars and other Oxonians. Oct. 1960. (Amer. Oxon., 1960, vol. 47, no. 4, pt. 2. 147 pp.)
Per. G.A. Oxon 8° 889

ST. MARY'S CHURCH AND THE OLD
CONGREGATION HOUSE

6035. [Topographical prints, &c. in the Bodleian.]   G.A. Oxon a. 68

6036. May the 11, 1661. [Vice-chancellor's order forbidding unauthorized persons to use seats in St. Mary's church which belong to M.A.'s and Doctors.] [Oxf.], 1661, s. sh.   Don. b. 12 (6a)

6037. The following queries are . . . submitted . . . relative to the proposed improvement of St. Mary's church . . . By a senior member of Convocation. [Oxf.], 1825, s. sh.   G.A. Oxon c. 41 (37)

6038. [*Begin.*] Mr. Plowman the builder having . . . offered a plan for the improvement of the interior of St. Mary's church . . . for the sum of 3295 l. [Two propositions to be submitted to Convocation.] [Oxf.], (1825), s. sh.   G.A. Oxon c. 41 (31)

6039. [*Begin.*] The delegates appointed to report upon the best mode of fitting up the interior of St. Mary's church . . . [recommendations]. Jan. 26, 1826. [Oxf.], 1826, s. sh.   G.A. Oxon c. 42 (11)

6040. Memoir of St. Mary's church. (The Crypt, 1828, vol. 3, p. 162–72.)
Hope 8° 281

6041. Oxonia explicata et ornata. 2. St. Mary's church. (The Crypt, 1828, vol. 2, p. 248–51.)   Hope 8° 280

6042. INGRAM, J., St. Mary the Virgin. (Memorials of Oxford, 1837, vol. 3. 16 pp.)   G.A. Oxon 8° 20

6043. Dec. 9. 1848. [Nomination of a delegacy to be proposed in Convocation on 13th Dec. to superintend the necessary repairs and allocate the additional expenses which are likely to be incurred in the repair of St. Mary's church.] [Oxf.], (1848), s. sh.   G.A. Oxon c. 64 (134)

6044. HARINGTON, R., Remarks on the church of St. Mary the Virgin. (Archaeol. journ., 1851, vol. 8, p. 125–42.)
Per. G.A. Gen. top. 8° 529 = R.

6045. [Report of] The committee appointed to inquire into the cause of the late explosion at St. Mary's church. [*With*] Report by mr. C. W. Siemens. [Oxf., 1860], 8°. 7 pp.   G.A. Oxon b. 30

6046. VARLEY, F. J., A Victorian blitz at St. Mary's [the explosion on 3 Nov. 1860. Signed F. J. V.]. (Oxf. mag., 1944, vol. 63, p. 91, 92.)
Per. G.A. Oxon 4° 141

6047. BUCKERIDGE, C., The restoration of the church of St. Mary-the-Virgin. (Proc., Oxf. architect. and hist. soc., 1862, N.S., vol. 1, p. 173–77.)   Per. G.A. Oxon 8° 498 = R.

6048. Apr. 21, 1863. [Proposals to be submitted to Convocation, 30th Apr., for restoring St. Mary's porch, in accordance with recommendations in a letter from Geo. Gilbert Scott.] n. pl., 1863, s. sh.
G.A. Oxon c. 79 (174)

6049. FOWLER, J. T., [Music on a bell in St. Mary's church.] (Proc., Soc. of antiq., 1867, ser. 2, vol. 3, p. 513, 14.)   Per. G.A. Gen. top. 8° 524 = R.

6050. FOWLER, J. T., A musical inscription on the fourth bell at St. Mary's. (Archaeologia, 1869, vol. 42, p. 491–93.)
Per. G.A. Gen. top. 4° 162 = R.

6051. Angels' music. [Note about the probable composer of no. 6049, Richard Nicholson.] (Proc., Soc. of antiq., 1912, ser. 2, vol. 24, p. 122.)
Per. G.A. Gen. top. 8° 524 = R.

6052. PARKER, J., [Historical account]. (Proc., Oxf. architect. and hist. soc., 1870, N.S., vol. 2, p. 261–68.)   Per. G.A. Oxon 8° 498 = R.

6053. Proclamation, Diocese of Oxford, Parish of St. Mary-the-Virgin [concerning the granting of a Faculty allowing restoration of the church and re-allocation of accommodation by and for the University]. 12th Apr., 1876. n. pl., (1876), s. sh.   G.A. Oxon c. 107 (116)

See 6435 [Blakiston, H. E. D., Oxford monuments in St. Mary's, etc. 1883].

6054. FFOULKES, E. S., A history of the church of S. Mary the Virgin, by the present vicar. Lond. &c., 1892, 8°. 504 pp.   G.A. Oxon 8° 528

6055. CASE, T., St. Mary's clusters, an historical enquiry concerning the pinnacled steeple of the University church. Oxf., 1893, 4°. 112 pp.
                                                        G.A. Oxon 4° 163
— (Advanced-proof 'For the Common rooms'.)   G.A. Oxon 4° 153
— (Advanced-proof 'For the Hebdomadal council'.) G.A. Oxon 4° 154

6056. The statues on the spire of the church St. Mary the Virgin. [Abbreviated report of the inspecting committee of the Society for the protection of ancient buildings.] (Oxf. mag., 1893, vol. 11, p. 243.)
                                                        Per. G.A. Oxon 4° 141

6057. St. Mary's pinnacles [signed T. Case]. [Oxf.], (1893), 4°. 3 pp.
                                                        G.A. Oxon 4° 156 (1)

6058. St. Mary's pinnacles. Practical conclusions [signed T. Case]. [Oxf.], (1893), 4°. 8 pp.   G.A. Oxon 4° 156 (2)

6059. St. Mary the Virgin. A letter from the architect [T. G. Jackson] on the designs for restoring the pinnacles, between which Convocation is to choose on June 7, 1893. [Oxf.], (1893), 8°. 3 pp.
                                                        G.A. Oxon 8° 540 (11)

6060. St. Mary the Virgin's church. Reports on the proposed repairs, with illustrations. (Oxf. univ. gazette, suppl. to no. 769, May 4, 1893.)
                                                        G.A. Oxon c. 29

6061. CASE, T., [List of dates connected with the church]. (Proc., Oxf. architect. and hist. soc., 1896, N.S., vol. 6, p. 112, 13.)
                                                        Per. G.A. Oxon 8° 498 = R.

6062. JACKSON, T. G., The church of St. Mary the Virgin. Oxf., 1897, fol. 231 pp.   G.A. Oxon 4° 192 = R.

6063. University finance and St. Mary's church. The nave parapets. [Oxf., 1897], s. sh.   G.A. Oxon 4° 156 (3)

6064. THOMPSON, C., A short guide to the church of St. Mary-the-Virgin at Oxford. Oxf., 1899, 8°. 41 pp.   Manning 8° 267

6065. THOMPSON, H. L., church of St. Mary the Virgin. (Sat. rev., 1901, vol. 91, p. 630, 31; 664, 65.)   N. 2288 c. 8

6066. King Henry the seventh's pall. [Suggestion, for the Curators of the University Chest, that the pall be transferred from the keeping of the University Verger, to the Picture Gallery in the Bodleian.] [Oxf.], 1901, s. sh.   G.A. Oxon c. 104 (85)

6067. THOMPSON, H. L., The church of St. Mary the Virgin, Oxford, in its relation to some famous events of English history. Westm., 1903, 8°. 196 pp.   G.A. Oxon 8° 701

6068. PAINTIN, H., Brief notes on the church of S. Mary-the-Virgin, Oxford. Repr. from the 'Oxford Chronicle', Feb. 20, 1909. [Oxf., 1909], 4°. 4 pp.   G.A. Oxon c. 107 (4)

6069. PAINTIN, H., The church of St. Mary-the-Virgin. Memorial services and historical associations [by H. Paintin]. Repr. from the Oxford chronicle, May 27th 1910. [Oxf., 1910), 4°. 4 pp.
           G.A. Oxon 4° 276 (3)

6070. RICHARDS, G. C., Notes on the vicars of St. Mary's [signed G. C. R.]. (Oriel record, 1923, vol. 4, p. 143–46.)   Per. G.A. Oxon 4° 484

6070.9. St. Mary the Virgin, Oxford. The University church had to be rebuilt . . . [Appeal for funds to cover expenses of repair and rearrangement of the interior.] n. pl., [1931], 4°. 3 pp. G.A. Oxon b. 141 (173*)

6071. St. Mary the Virgin, Oxford. To (1) The restoration committee . . . (2) The parochial church council . . . [Expressing approval of part of the appeal, but disagreeing with the planned changes in the nave of the church.] [Oxf., 1931], 4°. 4 pp.   G.A. Oxon b. 141 (173a)

6072. St. Mary the Virgin. Order of service at the thanksgiving for the restoration and beautifying of the nave. 16 Oct. (Oxf., 1932), 8°. 7 pp.
           G.A. Oxon 8° 1079 (15)

6073. WALKER, W. C., St. Mary the Virgin church. [Investigation after the fire on Nov. 17, 1946.] (Oxoniensia, 1948, vol. 13, p. 74, 75.)
           Per. G.A. Oxon 4° 658 = R.

6074. The University church of S. Mary the Virgin, Oxford. Glouc., [1950], 8°. 26 pp.   1736 e. 53 (381)
— 2nd ed. [1953]. 25 pp.   1736 e. 53 (493)
— [Another] 2nd ed. [1956].   1736 e. 53 (605)

SCHOOLS, (THE) NEW

6075. [Topographical prints, &c. in the Bodleian]   G.A. Oxon a. 44

6076. New Examination schools. [Comment on the designs of mr. Street and mr. Deane, signed 'One of the committee'.] (Oxf., 1870), s. sh.
           G.A. Oxon 4° 119 (2)

6077. SCOTT, J. O., New Examination schools: copy of a letter from J. O. Scott to the . . . chairman of the Delegacy [answering observations made in a paper signed C. J. F., C. A. F., E. J. P., criticizing Scott's design for the new Schools]. June 5. n. pl., (1873), 4°. 4 pp.

G.A. Oxon b. 138 (86)

6078. DODGSON, C. L., The blank cheque, a fable, by the author of 'The new belfry'. [To emphasize the folly of signing 'a blank cheque for the expenses of building new Schools before any estimate has been made of those expenses' &c.] Oxf., 1874, 8°. 15 pp.   G.A. Oxon 8° 161 (21)
— [Another ed.] (The Lewis Carroll picture book, ed. by S. D. Collingwood, 1899, p. 149–59.)   270 e. 1155

6079. TYRWHITT, R. ST. J., [Letter, dated May 8, to the Vice-chancellor putting forward considerations for the new Schools.] [Oxf.], (1875), s. sh.   G.A. Oxon c. 33 (181)

6080. Instructions. New Examination schools for the University of Oxford. June 12. [Oxf.], 1875, 8°. 3 pp.   G.A. Oxon c. 33 (183)

6081. Oxford Examination schools competition. Report [by the architect himself] upon the designs submitted by Basil Champneys. (White-friars), [1875], 8°. 13 pp.   G.A. Oxon c. 33 (182)

6082. JACKSON, T. G., Proposed New Examination schools ... Description of design submitted in competition. Jan. 25, 1875 [really 1876]. n. pl., [1876], 4°. 13 pp.   G.A. Oxon c. 33 (184)

6083. BODLEY, G. F., and GARNER, T., New Examination schools for the University of Oxford. [Specifications submitted to the Delegates for the selection of the design for building the New Examination schools.] n. pl., (1876), 8°. 6 pp.   G.A. Oxon 8° 164 (9)

6084. The New Examination schools. (Builder, 1882, vol. 42, p. 719, 20.)
N. 1863 c. 1

6085. New Schools. [Report of Delegates on the fitting up and furnishing of the New schools.] Feb. 3. [Oxf.], 1882, 8°. 4 pp.
G.A. Oxon b. 138 (90)

6086. New Schools [Expenditure]. Jan. 27, 1882. [Oxf.], 1882, 8°. 2 pp.
G.A. Oxon b. 138 (86)

6086.5. Report of the Curators. 1888–   . (Oxf. Univ. Gazette. 1889–   .)
Per. G.A. Oxon c. 86

6087. WESTWOOD, J. O., On a sculptured stone from the site of the New Schools, High Street. (Proc., Oxf. architect. and hist. soc., 1890, N.S., vol. 5, p. 297, 98.)   Per. G.A. Oxon 8° 498 = R.

6088. The so-called 'pit-dwellings' on the site of the New Examination Schools in High Street. (Archæologia Oxon., 1892–1895, p. 7–14.)
G.A. Oxon 4° 148 = R.

See 6516–18 [Catalogues of loan exhibitions of portraits, held in the Examination schools. 1904–06].

6089. Programme of proceedings on February 28, 1907, at the unveiling
in the Examination schools of a tablet to commemorate the foundation
of the Rhodes scholarships (Oxf., 1907), 16°. 12 pp.

G.A. Oxon 16° 136 (2)

6090. Proceedings at the unveiling of the Rhodes memorial tablet. Oxf.,
1907, 4°. 18 pp.   G.A. Oxon 4° 262 (10)

6091. LEEDS, E. T., Three stoneware flagons found in Oxford [one in 1914
within the precincts of the Examination schools, High st., the other two
in 1910 on the site of the Radcliffe Camera underground bookstore].
(Antiq. journ., 1933, vol. 13, p. 470–73.)   Per. 17572 d. 73 = R.

SCHOOLS, (THE) OLD

6092. INGRAM, J., The Schools. (Memorials of Oxford, 1837, vol. 2,
32 pp.)   G.A. Oxon 8° 19
— [Reissued.] (Memorials of the public buildings of Oxford. 1848.)
G.A. Oxon 8° 17

See 5848 [Proposed alterations in the Clarendon buildings and in the Schools.
1863].
See 5460 [Harrison, J. P., The architecture of the Bodleian library and the Old
Schools. 1892].

6093. PELHAM, H. F., The [proposed] purchase of the Logic school [from
Magdalen college, who had leased the property to the University for
250 years]. [Oxf., 1893], s. sh.   G.A. Oxon b. 140 (107e)

6094. WARREN, T. H., The proposed decree for the purchase of the Logic
school [from Magdalen college. Proposed May 9, approved May 16].
[Oxf.], 1893, s. sh.   G.A. Oxon c. 279 (f. 5)

See 5461 [Poole, R., The architect of the Schools and the tower of the five
orders. 1922].
See 5484 [Philip, I. G., The building of the Schools quadrangle. 1948].
See 5485 [Philip, I. G., A forgotten gate to the Schools quadrangle. 1952].

SHELDONIAN THEATRE

*For works dealing with the activities of the University Press in the Sheldon-
ian see University Press, 6270, etc.*

6095. [Topographical prints, &c. in the Bodleian.]   G.A. Oxon a. 45

6096. To the . . . heads of . . . colleges . . . [Orders and rules for the cere-
mony of the conveyance of the Sheldonian theatre to the University.]
[Madan 2836.] Oxoford [*sic*], 1669, s. sh.   Wood 276 a (384)
— [Another issue without imprint.] [Madan 2837.]

6097. WHITEHALL, R., Urania, or a description of the painting of the top
of the Theater at Oxon as the artist lay'd his design. [Madan 2818.]
Lond., 1669, fol. 12 pp.   Wood 423 (42)

6098. A discription of the painting of the Theater in Oxford. [Madan
2956.] Oxf., 1673, s. sh.   Wood 423 (50)
— [Another ed.] 1674. [Madan 3020.]   Pamph. A 133 (7)
— [Another ed.] 1742.   Gough Oxf. 142
— [Another ed.] 1756.   G. Pamph. 1580 (2)
— [Another ed.] 1780.   G.A. Oxon 8° 122

6099. To my lord arch-bishop of Canterbury upon his famous erection,
the Theater in Oxford. [A ballad.] [Madan 3040.] Lond., 1675.   B.M.

6100. Sheldonian and approaches. [2 plans, made c. 1830, one shewing the
stone stairs to the street from the Old Ashmolean museum.]
G.A. Oxon b. 111 (235, 36)

6101. CHASE, D. P., ed., The Sheldonian theatre in 1866, a history of the
new seats therein, with documents, ed. by the Principal of St. Mary
hall. Oxf., (1866), fol. 4 pp.   G.A. Oxon c. 82 (335)

6102. [Begin.] The undersigned members of Convocation ... [Proposal to
light the Sheldonian theatre and any rooms in the neighbourhood, in
particular the Camera Radcliffiana, with electric light.] [Oxf.], 18 May
1880, s. sh.   G.A. Oxon b. 140 (38a)
— 22 May 1880, s. sh.   G.A. Oxon b. 140 (38b)
— 22 May 1880. fol. 3 pp.   G.A. Oxon b. 140 (38c)
— 1 June 1880. fol. 3 pp.   G.A. Oxon b. 140 (38d)

6102.5. [Report of the Curators, 1888–   .] (Oxf. univ. gazette, 1889–   .)
Per. G.A. Oxon c. 86

6103. Report of the Curators on the ceiling paintings of the Sheldonian
theatre. [Oxf., 1899?], 8°. 7 pp.   G.A. Oxon 8° 620 (30)

6104. HUSSEY, C., Sheldonian theatre. (Country Life, 1930, vol. 67,
p. 714–20, 750–55.)   Per. 384 b. 6

6105. The Sheldonian theatre repaired. (Journ., Roy. inst. Brit. arch.,
1937, 3rd ser. vol. 45, p. 26–31.)   Per. 17356 d. 27

6106. OAKESHOTT, W. F., The Sheldonian theatre restoration [signed
W. F. O.]. (Oxf. mag., 1957, vol. 75, p. 304–06; 318–20.)
Per. G.A. Oxon 4° 141

6106.2. CLIFFORD, R., Light on the Sheldonian. (Oxf. mag., 1963, N.S.,
vol. 3, p. 346, 47.)   Per. G.A. Oxon 4° 141

6106.3. SUMMERSON, SIR J., The Sheldonian in its time, an oration delivered to commemorate the restoration of the Theatre, 16 November
1963. Oxf., 1964, 8°. 12 pp.   G.A. Oxon 8° 1482

6106.4. The Sheldonian theatre and the Divinity school. Text by H. M.
Colvin, photographs by J. Thomas. Oxf., 1964, 4°. [24 pp.]
G.A. Oxon 4° 801

TAYLOR INSTITUTION

6107. Plan of a freehold estate in the parish of St. Mary Magdalen . . . the property of the University. [General details added as to the nature and requirements of the Taylor and Randolph buildings to be erected on this site. Signed P. Bliss, registrar.] June 10, 1839. n. pl., 1839, s. sh.
MS. Top. Oxon c. 202 (1)

6108. SEWELL, W., [Begin.] The attention of members [&c. Notice querying the appointment of the delegacy touching the Taylor building and University galleries, and the use of money from printing Bibles, to aid in the building of these institutions. By W. Sewell. 20 Feb. 1840]. Oxf., 1840, s. sh.   G.A. Oxon c. 56 (29)

6109. [Begin.] In answer to certain questions touching the Taylor building and the University galleries, the following observations are offered to members of Convocation. Oxf., [1840], s. sh.   G.A. Oxon c. 56 (30)

6110. [Begin.] Question for those who intend to vote in Convocation on Friday, the 21st of February. [Whether money would not better be devoted to professorial endowments rather than an 'empty Picture gallery'. 20 Feb. 1840.] Oxf., 1840, s. sh.   G.A. Oxon c. 56 (31)

6111. Oxford, Feb. 21, 1840. The following brief observations, respecting the Taylor building and the University galleries are . . . submitted to . . . members of Convocation. Oxf., 1840, s. sh.   G.A. Oxon c. 56 (32)

6112. Regulations for sir Robert Taylor's Institution [submitted to Convocation, Apr. 10, 1844]. [Oxf.], (1844), s. sh.   G.A. Oxon c. 61 (41)

6113. Regulations for sir Robert Taylor's Institution (Regulations for the University galleries) [submitted to Convocation, June 6, 1844]. [Oxf.], (1844), fol. 3 pp.   G.A. Oxon c. 60 (70)

6114. Regulations for sir R. Taylor's foundation. [Objections, signed A senior member of Convocation, to the proposed regulation that the Professor of modern European languages may be removed from office with the concurrence of at least five curators.] [Oxf.], (1847), s. sh.
G.A. Oxon c. 63 (31)

6115. Regulations for sir Robert Taylor's foundation, agreed upon in Convocation, April 10, 1845, and March 4, 1847. [Oxf., 1847], fol. 3 pp.
G.A. Oxon c. 63 (48)

6116. INGRAM, J., The Martyrs' memorial [with] The Taylor building [and] The University galleries. (Memorials of the public buildings of Oxford. 1848. 16 pp.)   G.A. Oxon 8° 17

6117. Regulations for the use of books belonging to the Taylor institution. Dec. 15, 1856. [Oxf.], 1856, s. sh.   G.A. Oxon c. 72 (378)

6118. Catalogue of the library of the Taylor institution. [With] Addenda, 1878– (July 1920). Oxf. &c., 1861–1920, 8°. 2590 e. Oxf. 10. 1, 2 = R.

6119. To the members of Convocation. [Urging the claims of the Taylor institution to 'at least some portion of the fund now about to be appropriated by the Clarendon Trustees'.] [Oxf.], (1868), s. sh.

G.A. Oxon b. 32 (24)

6120. A catalogue of the books in the Finch collection, Oxford. Oxf., 1874, 8°. 318 pp.   2590 e. Oxf. 10. 3

6120.5. [First –   report of the Curators.] (Oxf. univ. gazette, 1889– .)

Per. G.A. Oxon c. 86

See 2826 [Provision for final honour school of modern languages. 1905].
See 6506 [List of periodicals. 1913].

6121. A memorandum on [the financial] amendment no. 6 to the proposed form of statute respecting the Taylor institution, by the Curators. To be considered Feb. 22. [Oxf.], (1922), 4°. 8 pp.   G.A. Oxon c. 311 (49)

6122. MYRES, J. L., Taylorian and Ashmolean. [Oxf.], (1928), 8°. 3 pp.

G.A. Oxon b. 139 (f. 57)

6123. SMITH, A. H., The decree in regard to extension of the Taylor institution. [Oxf.], (1928), s. sh.   G.A. Oxon c. 314 (43)

6124. FIRTH, C. H., The Taylorian and its assailants. [Oxf.], (1928), 4°. 3 pp.   G.A. Oxon c. 314 (44)

6125. WRIGHT, J., An open letter to the Vice-Chancellor of Oxford University on the Taylor extension scheme. [Oxf.], (1928), s. sh.

G.A. Oxon c. 314 (46)

6126. WELLS, J., Taylorian extension. Tuesday, October 23. [Oxf., 1928], s. sh.   G.A. Oxon b. 139 (f. 58)

See 5294, 5294.1 [Papers giving the reactions of the Ashmolean museum to the Taylor decree. 1928].

6127. The extension of The Taylorian institution. (Architect, 1933, vol. 133, p. 157–60, 178.)   N. 1731 c. 16

6128. BOYD, J., Extension of the Taylor institution. (Oxf. mag., 1938, vol. 56, p. 667–70.)   Per. G.A. Oxon 4° 141

6128.5. Catalogue of the Fiedler collection, manuscript material and books up to 1850. Oxf., 1962, 8°. 65 pp.   2590 e. Oxf. 10. 5 = R.

6128.51. A catalogue of Hispanic MSS and books before 1700 from the Bodleian Library and Oxford college libraries, exhibited at the Taylor institution, 6–11 September. Oxf., 1962, 8°. 56 pp.

2590 e. Oxf. 1. 53 = R.

UNIVERSITY ARCHIVES

6129. WALLIS, J., Reasons shewing the consistency of the place of Custos archivorum with that of a Savilian professor [by J. Wallis]. [Madan 2325.] [Oxf., 1657], s. sh.   Wood 515 (20)

6130. STUBBE, H., The Savilian professours case stated, together with the severall reasons urged against his capacity of standing for the publique office of antiquary in the University, which are enlarged and vindicated against the exceptions of dr. John Wallis. [Madan 2371.] Lond., 1658, 4°. 28 pp.   4° A 6 Jur. BS.

See 5886 [Proposed use of Clarendon building attics for storing the University archives. 1862].
See 5847 [Grants to be proposed for the alteration of an upper room in the Clarendon buildings, and the provision of fire-proof safes for the University archives to be removed from the Schools' tower. 1863].

6131. POOLE, R. L., The Delegacy of privileges and the Keepership of the archives, a letter [criticizing the provisions of the new statute]. Oxf., 1909, 8°. 11 pp.   G.A. Oxon 8° 761 (21)

6132. POOLE, R. L., A lecture on the history of the University archives. With an appendix. Oxf., 1912, 8°. 107 pp.   G.A. Oxon 8° 862

6133. SALTER, H. E., ed., Mediaeval archives of the University of Oxford. 2 vols. (Oxf. hist. soc., 70, 73.) Oxf., 1920, 21, 8°.
                                                   G.A. Oxon 8° 360 = R.

UNIVERSITY CHEST

6134. The office of secretary to the curators of the University chest. Duties ... Terms of appointment. [Oxf.], (1868), s. sh.   G.A. Oxon a. 18

6135. GAMLEN, W. B., The University chest [hist. sketch, signed W. B. G.]. (Oxf. mag., 1916, vol. 35, p. 31, 32.)   Per. G.A. Oxon 4° 141
— Repr.   G.A. Oxon 900 (20)

6136. LODGE, H. M., Half a century at the Chest. (Oxf. mag., 1948, vol. 66, p. 231, 32.)   Per. G.A. Oxon 4° 141

6136.4. KEEN, H. H., The University chest [signed H. H. K.]. (Oxf. mag., 1960, vol. 78, p. 321–23.)   Per. G.A. Oxon 4° 141

UNIVERSITY GALLERIES

See 5260, &c., Ashmolean Museum.

UNIVERSITY MUSEUM

Fielding herbarium. See 3054, 5826.

6137. [Topographical prints, &c. in the Bodleian.]   G.A. Oxon a. 47

6138. TRADESCANT, J., the younger, Musæum Tradescantianum: or, a collection of rarities preserved at South-Lambeth neer London. [Madan 2292.] Lond., 1656, 12°. 179 pp.   Ashm. 1007
— [A reissue.] [Madan 2473]. 1660.

— [Facs. repr.] (Old Ashm. repr., 1). n.d.   19982 f. 7
[In the 19th century, ethnographical and natural history specimens were transferred to the Pitt Rivers museum and to the Oxford university museum respectively.]

6139. Oxford museum committee. June 15th, 1849. [Names of chairman and committee.] n. pl., 1849, s. sh.   G.A. Oxon c. 65 (96)

6140. Oxford university museum. [Statement and appeal, June 6, 1850.] n. pl., 1850, fol. 4 pp.   G.A. Oxon c. 66 (162)

See 1428 [E. B. Pusey. On the proposed vote of £53,100 of which £30,000 is intended for the Museum. 1851].

6141. GRESWELL, R., Memorial on the (proposed) Oxford university lecture rooms, library, museums, &c. n. pl., [1853], 8°. 20 pp.+3 plans.
G.A. Oxon 8° 124 (16)

6142. The report of the delegates for the Oxford university museum. n. pl., [1853], 8°. 7 pp.   G.A. Oxon 8° 659 (2)

6143. Considerations affecting the Museum report [signed Prometheus]. Oxf., 1853, 4°. 4 pp.   G.A. Oxon c. 69 (109)

6144. Prometheus vinctus. [Answers to the paper signed Prometheus.] [Oxf., 1853], s. sh.   G.A. Oxon c. 69 (110)

6145. Oxford university museum. [Appeal for money to decorate the interior with specimens of rocks, statues and inscriptions.] n. pl., [1853], fol. 3 pp.   G.A. Oxon c. 69 (111b)

6146. [Begin.] The site of the intended museums and lecture rooms . . . [Objections to the selection of a site in the Parks. Feb. 28.] Oxf., (1853), 4°. 4 pp.   G.A. Oxon b. 27

6147. [Begin.] A paper having just been circulated . . . [An answer to no. 6146.] March 1, 1853. [Oxf.], 1853, s. sh.   G.A. Oxon b. 27

6148. Oxford university museum [committee]. Report [on the present state of the undertaking]. May 19, 1853. [Oxf.], (1853), s. sh.
G.A. Oxon b. 27

6149. To architects. [An invitation to send in plans and elevations, with estimates, for the new museum building.] [Oxf.], (1854), s. sh.
G.A. Oxon b. 27

6150. Little O— u— [a criticism in verse of the competition held to select plans for the University museum]. (Builder, 1854, vol. 12, p. 657.)
N. 1863 c. 1

6151. The old English style of architecture, as applicable to modern requirements, or, Suggestions for the new museum at Oxford. n. pl., [1854], 8°. 11 pp.+6 pl.   G.A. Oxon 8° 105 (6)

6152. Oxford university museum [competition and designs]. (Builder, 1854, vol. 12, p. 388, 562, 590–92, 602, 622, 630, 641.)   N. 1863 c. 1

6153. [March 28, 1854. Report to Convocation of the Delegates for the University museum.] n. pl., 1854, s. sh.   G.A. Oxon c. 70 (89)

6154. Report, &c. [of the Delegacy appointed to consider the plans submitted in the open competition for the new University museum]. [Oxf., 1854], 8°. 7 pp.   G. Pamph. 2248 (14)

6155. Statement of the requirements of the Oxford university museum and plan of the site. n. pl., [1854], 8°. 8 pp.   G.A. Oxon c. 70 (254)

6156. Extracts from a statement of the requirements of the Oxford university museum, drawn up by the Museum delegacy, June 1854, for the use of architects; made, Dec. 9th, for the use of members of Convocation. [Oxf., 1854], s. sh.   G.A. Oxon b. 28

6157. Oxford university museum delegacy. Report. December 7, 1854. n. pl., 1854, 8°. 7 pp.   G.A. Oxon c. 70 (253)

6158. ERGATES, *pseud.*, [*Begin.*] In answer to the question . . . [A paper arguing in favour of the plan known as Nisi Dominus and against that known as Fiat Justitia. Signed 'Εργάτης.] Dec. 11. n. pl., 1854, s. sh.
G.A. Oxon c. 70 (245)

6159. Neutrum placet. Reasons for postponing the application of the £30,000 appropriated to the construction of a museum. n. pl., [1854], s. sh.   G.A. Oxon c. 70 (247)

6160. To members of Convocation. [A paper, signed A member of Convocation, urging the rejection of the museum plans.] Dec. 11. n. pl., 1854, s. sh.   G.A. Oxon c. 70 (244*a*)

6161. To members of Convocation. [A paper, signed A member of Convocation, decrying the approval of £30,000 for the museum, and urging that it be made self-supporting in future.] n. pl., [1854], s. sh.
G.A. Oxon c. 70 (244*b*)

6162. What is to be our vote on Tuesday? [A paper, signed M.A., urging the rejection of the plans for a museum, on the grounds of too great an expenditure of money.] n. pl., [1854], s. sh.   G.A. Oxon c. 70 (244)

6163. BUTLER, G., [*Begin.*] In answer to a question 'What is to be our vote on Tuesday'. Dec. 11. n. pl., 1854, s. sh.   G.A. Oxon c. 70 (246)

6164. The new museum. [A paper signed A member of Convocation, and dated 3 May 1855, against the projected building of a museum.] Oxf., (1855), s. sh.   G.A. Oxon b. 28

6165. ALIQUIS, *pseud.*, The new museum. [A paper, dated 7 May 1855, in answer to that of 3 May signed A member of Convocation.] [Oxf.], (1855), s. sh.   G.A. Oxon b. 28

6166. Oxford university museum. [Appeal for private contribution to provide shafts and ornamental capitals for the interior. 1 June.] [Oxf.], (1855), s. sh.+sketch.   G.A. Oxon b. 139 (f. 81)

6167. The new museum. [An undated paper, signed A member of Convocation, in support of the proposed museum. By C. Daubeny?]
[Oxf., 1855], s. sh.   G.A. Oxon b. 28

6168. Form of prayer on occasion of the ceremony of laying the first stone of the new museum, June¦ xx. MDCCC.LV. n. pl., (1855), 4°. 8 pp.
G.A. Oxon 4° 13 (6)

6169. A dream of the new museum. Oxf., 1855, 8°. 14 pp. G.A. Oxon 8° 431

6170. [*Begin.*] Whereas the following report [dated 5 Apr.] of the subdelegacy for the new museum . . . [recommending to the Hebdomadal council additional expenditure on the accommodation of the professor of chemistry, and other improvements to the building: With a letter from the Delegacy for the new museum listing additional expenditure arising therefrom dated May 5, and a copy of the Decree to be submitted to Convocation, 17th May embodying the proposals]. [Oxf.],
(1856), 4°. 4 pp.   G.A. Oxon c. 72 (190)

6171. Oxford university museum. [List of subscribers to the fund for embellishing the interior.] May 31, 1856. n. pl., 1856, fol. 3 pp.
G.A. Oxon c. 72 (229)

6172. The Delegates for the new museum beg to lay before the Hebdomadal council the following report . . . [recommending additional expenditure on heating, lighting, ventilation &c. dated June 19. With the consequent decree to be proposed in Convocation on June 23].
[Oxf.], (1857), s. sh.   G.A. Oxon c. 73 (194)

6173. [*Begin.*] Whereas the Hebdomadal council have received . . . the following report from a committee appointed by them, and have approved the recommendations therein contained; *viz.* Report . . . upon the professors' requirements in connexion with the new museum. [With the consequent decree to be proposed in Convocation on 14th May.] [Oxf.], (1857), 4°. 8 pp.   G.A. Oxon c. 74 (167)

6174. [*Begin.*] Whereas the Hebdomadal council have received the following . . . Report of the sub-delegacy for the new museum [dated Apr. 30, recommending additional expenditure on laying out the ground, fencing, internal fittings, &c. With the consequent decree to be proposed in Convocation on May 14]. [Oxf.], (1858), 4°. 4 pp.
G.A. Oxon c. 74 (168)

6175. [*Begin.*] Whereas the Hebdomadal council have received the following . . . Report of the Museum building delegates [concerning the radical structural alterations required in the ironwork of the roof, with reports from the architects &c. and a Note regarding the probable use of the tower of the museum for experiments in physical science. With the decree for additional expenditure, to be proposed in Convocation on June 3]. [Oxf.], (1858), 4°. [7] pp.   G.A. Oxon c. 74 (186)

6176. w., h., The new museum. [Comments on the cost of the building &c. June 1, 1858]. Oxf., 1858, s. sh.   G.A. Oxon c. 74 (192)

6177. PLUMPTRE, F. C., The new museum. [An answer, dated June 2, to
H. W.'s paper of June 1.] n. pl., 1858, s. sh.   G.A. Oxon c. 74 (195)

6178. [*Begin.*] Whereas the Hebdomadal council has received the following statement [from the Museum building delegacy reporting a de-
ficiency of £400]. In a Convocation to be holden . . . 10th [Dec.] the
following decree will be submitted . . . [Oxf.], (1858), s. sh.
G.A. Oxon c. 74 (313)

6179. Oxford university museum. [Appeal for money to construct an ornamental doorway.] n. pl., (1859), 8°. 4 pp.   G.A. Oxon c. 75 (187)

6180. ACLAND, SIR H. W., The Oxford museum, by H. W. Acland [with
letters from] J. Ruskin [and J. Phillips]. Lond. &c., 1859, 8°. 111 pp.
G.A. Oxon 8° 1
— 2nd ed. Oxf. &c., 1860, 8°. 78 pp.   G.A. Oxon 8° 71 (1)
— 4th ed. 1867. 75 pp.   G.A. Oxon 8° 285 (1)
— [Another ed.] With additions. Lond. &c., 1893, 8°. 112 pp.
G.A. Oxon 4° 173

6181. The Oxford museum. Balliol chapel . . . (Builder, 1859, vol. 17,
p. 401, 02.)   N. 1863 c. 1

6182. [*Begin.*] It has been thought desirable that the following particulars
respecting the grants for the Museum [for gas fittings, doors, windows,
&c.] should be circulated among members of Convocation previous to
the votes being submitted . . . 17th [June] [signed F. C. Plumptre,
chairman of the sub-delegacy]. [Oxf.], (1859), s. sh.
G.A. Oxon c. 75 (215)

6183. Report on the University museum. [A satire, dated Oct. 15, signed
A resident.] n. pl., 1859, s. sh.   G.A. Oxon c. 75 (287)

6184. At a meeting of the Museum building delegacy, October 22, 1859,
it was resolved to lay before . . . Convocation the following report [of
expenses, Oct. 1, 1858 to Oct. 1, 1859]. [Oxf.], (1859), s. sh.
G.A. Oxon c. 75 (312)

6185. To members of Convocation. [Appeal, signed F. C. Plumptre, Nov.
25, 1859. for £350 to complete paving the central court.] n. pl., 1859,
s. sh.   G.A. Oxon c. 75 (352)

6186. WESTWOOD, J. O., The Hope collections. [Statement of the
principal branches, namely: library of natural history; zoological and
entomological collections; engravings and engraved portraits.] [Oxf.],
(1860), s. sh.   G.A. Oxon c. 76 (36)

6187. [*Begin.*] Whereas the Hebdomadal council has received the following statement [of additional expenditure required to hasten the completion of the building of the University museum]. In a Convocation to
be holden . . . 16th [Feb.] . . . the following decree will be submitted . . .
[Oxf.], (1860), s. sh.   G.A. Oxon c. 76 (47)

6188. [*Begin.*] Whereas Angela Burdett-Coutts . . . [Proposal in Convocation, 16th Feb. accepting the Pengelly collection of Devonshire fossils and also the foundation of the two Burdett-Coutts geological scholarships. With the Conditions of and regulations for the scholarships.] [Oxf.], (1860), s. sh.   G.A. Oxon c. 76 (44)

6189. [*Begin.*] Whereas the late Hugh Edwin Strickland . . . [Proposal in Convocation, 10th May, accepting the Strickland collection of birds for the University museum.] [Oxf.], (1860), s. sh.   G.A. Oxon c. 76 (132)

6190. [*Begin.*] Whereas the Hebdomadal council has received . . . the following Report [on additional expenditure required to provide in the University museum suitable accommodation for the Hope collection]. In a Convocation to be holden . . . 31st [May] . . . the following decree will be proposed . . . [Oxf.], (1860), s. sh.   G.A. Oxon c. 76 (173)

6191. Oxford university museum. [Appeal, dated June 4, 1860, for donations of shafts, statues &c. to provide ornaments for the interior: with list of contributors.] [Oxf.], (1860), fol. 4 pp. G.A. Oxon b. 113 (133)

6192. [*Begin.*] Whereas the Hebdomadal council has received . . . the following report [on estimates of expenditure on account of the preparation of the Museum for working purposes] In a Convocation to be holden . . . 16th [June] . . . the following decree will be proposed . . . [Oxf.], (1860), s. sh.   G.A. Oxon c. 76 (209)

6193. [*Begin.*] Whereas the Dean and Chapter of Christ Church, the trustees of the late Matthew Lee . . . have signified their readiness to offer the physiological and anatomical collections formed at the cost of his trust fund, as a loan to the . . . University museum . . . on the following conditions . . . [Proposal in Convocation, 21st June accepting loan.] [Oxf.], (1860), s. sh.   G.A. Oxon c. 76 (223)

See 5955 [Library and reading-room. Oxford university museum. 1861].

6194. [*Begin.*] The following statement (of the accounts of the Museum, with explanatory remarks [listing grants made from 17 May 1856 to June 16, 1860]) having been presented by the Museum sub-delegacy . . . will be submitted to Convocation . . . 19th [Feb.] . . . [Oxf.], (1861), fol. 4 pp.   G.A. Oxon c. 77 (48)

6195. [*Begin.*] The Delegates of the Museum having recommended . . . certain new works . . . In a Convocation to be holden . . . 27th [Nov.] . . . it will be proposed to make the following grants . . . [Oxf.], (1862), s. sh.   G.A. Oxon c. 78 (316)

6196. STEPHENS, F. G., The Oxford university museum. (Macmillan's mag., 1862, vol. 5, p. 525–33.)   Per. 2705 d. 254

6197. [*Begin.*] The following report has been received by the Council from the Museum delegacy, May 1, 1863 [concerning income and expenditure, 1860/61, 1861/62: followed by the decree to be proposed in Convocation on 28 May authorising additional grants]. [Oxf.], (1863), 4°. 4 pp.   G.A. Oxon c. 79 (239)

6198. PHILLIPS, J., Notices of rocks and fossils, in the University
museum. Oxf., (1863), 8°. 93 pp.   G.A. Oxon 8° 73 (1)

6199. For use of the Hebdomadal council only. The Museum delegates
having received the annexed supplementary report [2nd] from the professors teaching in the Museum are of the opinion that some extension
of the building is . . . necessary [to provide rooms for zoology and
experimental philosophy]. Feb. 1. [Oxf.], (1867), 8°. 7 pp.
                                          G.A. Oxon a. 16

6200. Synopsis of the pathological series in the Oxford museum. Oxf.,
1867, 8°. 51 pp.   Clar. Press 11 b. 1

6201. A statement of the sums granted by the University for establishing
and maintaining the Museum down to December, 1867. n. pl., (1868),
4°. 3 pp.   G.A. Oxon c. 84 (176)

6202. [Begin.] In a Convocation to be holden . . . 19th of May . . . it will be
proposed . . . to pay to the credit of the Museum delegates the sum of
£1000 . . . for the maintenance and improvement of the collections . . .
[with a report of expenditure from May 31, 1858 to May 31, 1867].
[Oxf.], (1868), s. sh.   G.A. Oxon c. 84 (177)

6203. University museum. [Accounts of money spent, from inception to
1867.] n. pl., [1868], fol. 2 leaves.   G.A. Oxon c. 84 (452)

6204. ROWELL, G. A., A letter to Henry W. Acland [declining an annuity
conferred by Convocation, 20 May, 1875, and urging an enquiry into
the writer's theory of meteorological phenomena]. n. pl., (1876), 8°.
3 pp.   G.A. Oxon 8° 250 (8)

6205. PRESTWICH, J., A short guide to the geological collections in the
University museum. Oxf., 1881, 8°. 64 pp.   Clar. Press 21 c. 5

6206. Annual report of the Delegates. 1st report, 1888– . (Oxf. univ.
gazette, 1889– .) [From the 75th report, 1963, issued as a suppl. in
octavo format to the Oxford university gazette. The 76th report has
the addition 'and First report of the Delegates of the science area'.]
                                          Per. G.A. Oxon c. 86
— [Also issued in octavo form.]   Radcl.

6207. [Plan of the proposed new buildings of human anatomy section. Feb.,
1891.]   G.A. Oxon 16° 59

6208. The Oxford university museum. (Nature, 1891, vol. 44, p. 619–21.)
                                          Per. 1996 d. 596

6209. LANKESTER, E. R., Memorandum as to the care and arrangement of
collections illustrating animal morphology in the University museum.
[Oxf.], (1891), 8°. 3 pp.   G.A. Oxon b. 139 (90a)

6210. SANDERSON, J. BURDON-, [Begin.] To the delegates of the University museum [Letter dated Feb. 19, commenting on the Memorandum
of E. R. Lankester.] [Oxf.], (1891), s. sh.   G.A. Oxon b. 139 (90b)

6211. Report of the committee on care and arrangement of collections, appointed February 21, 1891. May 1. [Oxf.], (1891), s. sh.
G.A. Oxon b. 139 (90c)

6212. A. Professor Flower's report. Mar. 14. (B. Professor Macalister's report. Mar. 31). [Recommendations for improving the organization &c. of the Museum.] [Oxf.], (1891), 8°. 16 pp. G.A. Oxon b. 139 (90d)

6213. A summary of answers to questions proposed by a committee of the Hebdomadal council to professors lecturing in the Museum, and others [concerning the administration of the Museum and care of its collections]. [Oxf.], 1892, 8°. 11 pp.   G.A. Oxon 8° 884 (16)

6214. Report of the committee on access to Museum. [Oxf., 1893], 8°. 3 pp.
G.A. Oxon b. 139 (92a)
— Further report. May 24, 1893. [Oxf.], 1893, 8°. 4 pp.
G.A. Oxon b. 139 (92b)

6215. Proposals made by professors Lankester and Poulton, relative to the care of certain collections and the assignment of space in the Museum. Oct. [Oxf.], (1893), 8°. 2 pp.   G.A. Oxon b. 139 (92c)

6216. LANKESTER, E. R., [Begin.] I wish to bring before the Delegates of the Museum . . . [Letter to the vice-chancellor alleging the appropriation, by the Keeper of the Museum, of the Bird and Shell rooms and the services of an attendant, all of which are within the province of the Linacre professor.] Feb. 7. [Oxf.], (1894), 8°. 3 pp.
G.A. Oxon b. 139 (92d)

6217. TYLOR, E. B., [Begin.] You will be called upon . . . [Letter to the vice-chancellor and the Delegates of the Museum refuting the statements made by E. R. Lankester in his letter of Feb. 7.] Feb. 26. [Oxf.], (1894), 8°. 6 pp.   G.A. Oxon b. 139 (93a)

6218. LANKESTER, E. R., [Begin.] A brief statement of facts . . . [Concerning the relative claims of the Keeper of the Museum and the Linacre professor to the Bird and Shell rooms of the Museum.] Feb. 23rd. [Oxf.], (1894), fol. 4 pp.   G.A. Oxon c. 153

6219. The unveiling of the statue of Sydenham in the Oxford museum, August 9, 1894. With an address by sir H. W. Acland. Oxf., 1894, 8°. 42 pp.   G.A. Oxon 8° 606

6220. GOODRICH, E. S., Some reforms in the Oxford university museum. (Natural sci., 1894, vol. 5, p. 128–31.)   Per. 1996 d. 126

6221. Report of the committee of delegates appointed Feb. 15, 1896, to consider the Linacre professor's letter as to the need of increased lecture room and laboratory accommodation in the department of comparative anatomy and the similar needs of the other departments of the Museum. [And] Addendum. [Oxf., 1896], 8°. 8 pp.
G.A. Oxon b. 139 (93e)

6222. Report of the committee of delegates of the University museum, appointed November 5, 1898, to consider the question of the provision of accommodation for the teaching of pathology, public health and pharmacology. [Oxf., 1899], 8°. 6 pp.   G.A. Oxon b. 139 (95c)

6223. WELDON, W. F. R., The human crania in the University museum. [Oxf.], (1899), 4°. 3 pp.   G.A. Oxon b. 139 (95a)

6224. Report of the Additional buildings committee to the Delegates of the Museum [with Memoranda from A. H. Green, E. R. Lankester and J. O. Westwood]. [Oxf., 1900?], 8°. 7 pp.   G.A. Oxon b. 139 (96e)

See 2866 [Historical account. 1900].

6225. FOWLER, W. W., The Museum & the park, a letter. Oxf., 1901, 8°. 14 pp.   G.A. Oxon 8° 659 (25)

6226. Draft report. For the Delegates of the Museum. Report of Committee on electric supply and lighting in the University museum. [With plan.] [Oxf., 1901], 8°. 7 pp.   G.A. Oxon c. 104 (123, 124)
— [Final report.]   G.A. Oxon c. 104 (176)

6227. POULTON, E. B., The Museum and the Parks: a neglected chapter of modern history [signed E. B. P. With subsequent correspondence with F. H. H.]. (Oxf. mag., 1908, vol. 27, p. 27–29, 78, 94, 109, 123.)
Per. G.A. Oxon 4° 141

6228. VERNON, H. M., and VERNON, K. D., A history of the Oxford museum. Oxf., 1909, 16°. 127 pp.   G.A. Oxon 16° 108

6229. HARCOURT, A. V., The Oxford museum and its founders. (Cornhill mag., 1910, N.S. vol. 28, p. 350–63.)   Per. 2705 d. 213
— Repr. 16 pp.   G.A. Oxon 8° 1079 (12)

6230. PLANT, S. G. P., The Oxford university museum. (Museums journ., 1953, vol. 52, p. 240–43.)   Per. 1758 d. 10
— Repr.   17582 d. 10

6231. HOLMES, W., The University museum [centenary account and survey]. (Nature, 1955, vol. 176, p. 331–33.)   Radcl.

6232. DE BEER, SIR G. R., The centenary of the Oxford university museum, with thoughts on the teaching of science, a lecture. Lond., 1955, 8°. 14 pp.   17582 d. 10

UNIVERSITY OBSERVATORY

6233. [Begin.] The Observatory committee appointed by the Delegates of the University museum . . . [Report concerning the installation of an equatorial and a reflecting telescope &c.] [Oxf., 1873], 8°. 6 pp.
G.A. Oxon 8° 715 (20)

6234. [1st, 1875/6]–   Report of the Savilian professor of astronomy [afterw.] Annual report of the visitors of the University observatory. [Oxf., 1877–   ], 8°.
[The Bodleian set is imperfect: Per. 1843 e. 10.]
[Also published in the Oxford university gazette.]

6235. Oxford university observatory. (Builder, 1878, vol. 36, p. 484–90.)
N. 1863 c. 1

6236. TURNER, H. H., On the desirability of a residence at the University
observatory. [Oxf.], (1900), 8°. 6 pp.   G.A. Oxon b. 140 (117c)

6237. Proposed residence for the professor of astronomy. [Objections
against the proposal.] [Oxf.], (1901), 8°. 3 pp.   G.A. Oxon b. 139 (97b)

6238. Proposed residence at the University observatory. [Letters supporting H. H. Turner's application.] [Oxf., 1901], s. sh.
G.A. Oxon b. 140 (118a)

6239. The astronomer's house in the Park. Do we really want it? [Oxf.,
1907], s. sh.   G.A. Oxon b. 140 (138f)

6240. Proposed official house for the professor of astronomy [signed by
W. W. Jackson and 4 others]. [Oxf., 1907], s. sh.
G.A. Oxon b. 140 (138d)

6241. The proposal for building a house in the Park [for the professor of
astronomy. Signed by W. W. Jackson and 4 others]. [Oxf., 1907], s. sh.
G.A. Oxon b. 140 (138c)

6242. Proposed official residence at the University observatory [signed by
T. B. Strong and 7 others]. [Oxf., 1907], 8°. 4 pp.
G.A. Oxon b. 140 (138b)

6243. Miscellaneous papers of the University observatory, ed. by H. H.
Turner [and others]. Vol. 1–7. Oxf., 1894–1927, 8°.   Per. 1842 e. 74

6244. Astrographic catalogue 1900–0 Oxford section, dec.+24° to +32°
from photographs taken and measured at the University observatory.
Vol. 1– . Edinb., 1906– , fol.   18428 c. 24

See 5945 [Turner, H. H., The Radcliffe and University observatories. 1907].

6245. PLASKETT, H. H., The Oxford 35 m. solar telescope. (Monthly
notices, Roy. astronom. soc., 1955, vol. 115, p. 542–49.)   Radcl.

See also 5938 &c., Radcliffe observatory.

UNIVERSITY PARKS

6246. An act to empower the warden and scholars of . . . Merton . . . to
sell certain lands [the 'Parks' to the University] situate in the parish of
Holywell . . . and to lay out the monies . . . in the purchase of other
hereditaments. (17 & 18 V., c. 17, Private.) Lond., 1854, fol. 8 pp. L.L.
— [Additional act]. 18 & 19 V., c. 12, Private. Lond., 1855, fol. 7 pp.
L.L.

6247. First report of the Park delegates. June 3. [Oxf., 1864], 4°. 3 pp.
G.A. Oxon c. 80 (13)
— Plan.   G.A. Oxon b. 30
[From 1888 onwards, the official report was published in the Oxford
university gazette.]

6248. [*Begin.*] In a Convocation to be holden . . . 10th [May] . . . [Proposals of the Hebdomadal council for improving the University parks.] [Oxf.], (1864), s. sh.   G.A. Oxon c. 80 (196)

6249. The Parks. [A criticism of the proposed improvements.] n. pl., [1864], s. sh.   G.A. Oxon c. 80 (373)

6250. EQUES, *pseud.*, Laying out The Parks. n. pl., (1864), s. sh.
                                                       G.A. Oxon c. 80 (372)

6251. MITCHELL, R. A. H., Copy of a letter . . . [to E. Palmer, concerning the laying out of The Parks for cricket, to embody 14 college grounds and a University ground]. Mar. 14. n. pl., 1866, 8°. 4 pp.
                                                       G.A. Oxon c. 82 (345)

6252. PALMER, E., Cricket in The Parks. [Arguments, signed E. P., for Convocation rejecting the proposal to be made on 1st June to limit the area to be used for cricket.] May 26. n. pl., [1866], s. sh.
                                                       G.A. Oxon c. 82 (344)

6253. Cricket and The Parks. [Reply, signed A member of Convocation, to no. 6252.] May 28. (Oxf.), [1866], s. sh.   G.A. Oxon c. 82 (339)

6254. METCALFE, F., Cricket and The Parks. [Arguments against using The Parks as cricket grounds.] May 31. (Oxf.) 1866, s. sh.
                                                       G.A. Oxon c. 82 (340)

6255. [29 Apr. 1867. Details of proposed decree affecting the allocation of cricket grounds in The Parks. The report of F. Field on The Parks is appended.] n. pl., (1867), fol. 3 pp.   G.A. Oxon c. 83 (112)
— [27 May 1867. Decree proposed.]   G.A. Oxon c. 83 (161)

6256. DODGSON, C. L., The deserted Parks. [A parody on The deserted village, written in reply to the proposed introduction of sport into The Parks. By C. L. Dodgson.] [Oxf.], 1867, 4°. 4 pp. G.A. Oxon c. 250 (ii)
— [Repr. in Notes by an Oxford chiel.] 1874.   G.A. Oxon 8° 161

6257. Parks completion committee. Recommendations [concerning applications for cricket grounds]. [Oxf., 1867], s. sh.   G.A. Oxon a. 16

  See 5837 ['To the president of the University removal co.' Satirizing the removal of so many institutions to The Parks, and in particular the suggested transfer of the Botanical garden. 1875?].

6258. CASE, T., Report on the proposed enlargement of the cricket ground in The Park. With a plan and report by messrs. Castle, Field and Castle. Oxf., 1886, fol. 22 pp.   G.A. Oxon c. 293

6259. Cricket in The Parks [cons. &] pros. (Oxf. mag., 1887, vol. 5, p. 187, 204, 205, 242, 243.)   Per. G.A. Oxon 4° 141

  See 6225 [W. W. Fowler, The Museum & The Park. 1901].
  See 6227 [Poulton, E. B., Museum and The Parks: a neglected chapter of modern history. 1908].

6260. FOWLER, W. W., Bird-life in The Parks: past and present. [Signed W. W. F.]. (Oxf. mag., 1908, vol. 26, p. 356, 57.) Per. G.A. Oxon 4° 141

6261. The Parks and science. [Appeal for funds to purchase a site for the School of Civil Engineering, outside The Parks: and to start a permanent accumulating fund for purchasing sites in future. Signed W. R. Anson and 20 others.] [Oxf., 1912], fol. 3 pp. G.A. Oxon c. 153

6262. The proposed laboratories in The Parks. [Arguments against the proposed decrees.] Tuesday, Nov. 19, 1912. [Oxf.], (1912), s. sh. G.A. Oxon c. 153

6263. Parks and science [signed W. R. Anson, R. W. Raper, A. H. Johnson]. Feb. 25. [Oxf.], (1913), 2 sheets G.A. Oxon c. 153

6264. Science and The Parks [signed W. R. Anson, R. W. Raper and A. H. Johnson]. [Oxf., 1913], 8°. 4 pp.+2 plans. G.A. Oxon c. 153

6265. Science and The Park [signed W. W. Jackson]. [Oxf.], (1913), 4°. 4 pp. G.A. Oxon c. 153

6266. [*Begin.*] The curators of The Parks . . . [Appeal for funds to establish a wild duck and aquatic bird sanctuary in Mesopotamia. Aug. 1914.] [Oxf., 1914], s. sh. G.A. Oxon c. 309 (35)

6267. Extension of the University park. [Request by the vice chancellor for subscriptions to a fund.] Feb. 20. [Oxf.], (1923), s. sh. G.A. Oxon c. 311 (61)

6268. DUNKLEY, H. L., Handlist of trees and shrubs in the Oxford University park. Prelim. issue. Oxf., 1936, 8°. 52 pp. Radcl.

6269. Guide to the trees and shrubs in the University parks. Lond. &c., 1953, 8°. 55 pp. Radcl.

6269.2. PARKES, G. D., The University parks. (Oxf. mag., 1965, N.S., vol. 5, p. 64, 65.) Per. G.A. Oxon 4° 141

UNIVERSITY PRESS

General 6270–6297
Fabric 6298–6302
Administration and Finance 6303–6316
Paper Duty 6317–6320
Staff 6321–6328
Clarendon Press Institute 6329

Typography 6330–6334.
House Rules 6335–6337
Specimens of Type 6338–6358
Bibles 6359–6378
Press Lists and Catalogues 6379–6400

General

6270. [A volume of miscellaneous papers in the Bodleian.] G.A. Oxon b. 175

6271. A proclamation to inhibit the sale of Latine bookes reprinted beyond the seas, having been first printed in Oxford or Cambridge. [Madan 549.] Lond., 1625, s. sh. Queen's Coll.

6272. A proclamation touching bookes first printed here [in Oxford, Cambridge or London in Greek or Latin] and after reprinted beyond the seas and imported hither. Lond., 1636, s. sh. O.U.A.

6273. A proposal tending to the advancement of learning by an unburden-some and practicable encouragement of the Press. [Madan 3069.] [Oxf., 1675], s. sh. Wood 423 (51)
— [Another ed., with lists of proposed works.] [Oxf., 1681], s. sh. Wood 423 (54)

6274. The state of the affair of printing in the University of Oxford: Jan. 6th, 1679. (Collectanea curiosa, by J. Gutch, vol. 1, p. 271–75.) Oxf., 1781, 8°. Gough Oxf. 65

6275. An account of the state of the Press in the Vniversity of Oxford as it now stands, January 9, 1679 [i.e. 1679/80]. [Madan 3272*.] [Oxf., 1680], s. sh. B.M.

6276. Advertisement to booksellers. [Notice accusing the University press of pirating an edition of Elegantiæ poeticæ.] [Lond., 1680], s. sh. Wood 516 (10)

6277. Reasons for amending the clause for a drawback to be allow'd to the universities, &c. [A petition to the House of Commons.] [Lond., 1712], s. sh. MM 29 (202) Jur., 3rd ser.

6278. To the honourable House of Commons: the humble representation of the booksellers of London and the two universities [against the additional duty on imported books]. n. pl., [1713], s. sh. G.A. Oxon 4° 6 (10)

See 1214 [Inclination of authors to have their books printed at Clarendon Press c. 1730].

6279. INGRAM, J., The University press. (Memorials of Oxford, 1837, vol. 3. 16 pp.) G.A. Oxon 8° 20
— [Reissued.] (Memorials of the public buildings of Oxford. 1848.) G.A. Oxon 8° 17

6280. University press annual entertainment . . . School report. (1872/73–74/75). [Oxf.], 1873–[75], 8°. G.A. Oxon b. 175

6281. HALL, E. P., Printing . . . with some account of . . . the Clarendon press (p. 42–46). Oxf., 1876, 8°. 258 b. 196
— [Another ed. of the account of the Press, *entitled*] Handbook of the Clarendon press (p. 1–7). Oxf., 1883, 8°. 25823 e. 13 (16)

6282. MADAN, F., Some curiosities of the Oxford Press. (The Library, 1889, vol. 1, p. 154–60.) Per. 2589 d. 21 = A.

6283. The University press at Oxford. (Master printer, March/Apr. 1894.) — [Repr. 1894]. 16 pp. G.A. Oxon 4° 175

6284. HART, H., Charles, earl Stanhope, and the Oxford university press. (Oxf. hist. soc., 1896, vol. 32, p. 363–412.) G.A. Oxon 8° 360 = R.

6285. MADAN, F., Some notes on the Oxford Press, with special reference to the fluctuations in its issue. [A summary.] (Trans., Bibliogr. soc., 1903, vol. 7, p. 1–3.) Per. 258 e. 258 = A.

6286. The University press, Oxford. (From the Caxton mag.) [Oxf.], 1906, 16°. 60 pp.   G.A. Oxon 16° 160

6287. MADAN, F., The Oxford Press during the Civil war. [A summary of a paper.] (Trans., Bibliogr. soc., 1908, vol. 9, p. 107–10.)
Per. 258 e. 258 = A.

6288. The Oxford university press. Oxf., [c. 1910], 16°. 24 pp.
25823 f. 15

6289. STEELE, R. L., The Oxford university press and the Stationers' company. (The Library, 1912, ser. 3, vol. 3, p. 103–12.)
Per. 2589 d. 21 = A.

6290. Some account of the Oxford university press, 1468–1921 [by R. W. Chapman]. Oxf., 1922, 8°. III pp.   25823 d. 84
— 2nd ed. 1468–1926. Oxf., 1926, 8°. 133 pp.   25823 d. 97

6291. MADAN, F., The Oxford Press, 1650–75. (Trans., Bibliogr. soc. The Library, 1925, ser. 4, vol. 6, p. 113–47.)   Per. 258 e. 258 = A.

6292. The Oxford university press, 1468–1926. (A brief chronology.) (Oxf., 1926), 8°. 7 pp.   25823 d. 169
— [Another ed.] 1468–1929. (Oxf., 1929), 8°. 8 pp.   25823 e. 122

See 427 [Lamborn, E. A. G., Oxford . . . To which is added A brief chronology of the University press. 1930].

6293. CHENEY, J., Printers and printing in Oxford (The Oxford Press, p. 11–17) and district. (Our bulletin, S.W. alliance of master printers' assoc., 1931.)   G.A. Oxon b. 175

6294. MURRAY, W. G. R., Murray the [Oxford English] dictionary-maker, a brief account of sir J. A. H. Murray. (Oxford p. 83–128.) Wynberg, Cape, 1943, 8°.   302 e. 155

6295. JOHNSON, J., and GIBSON, S., Print and privilege at Oxford to the year 1700. (Oxf. bibliogr. soc., vol. 7.) Oxf., 1946, 4°. 212 pp.
Soc. 258 d. 176 = A.

6296. LONG, P., A note on Joseph Barnes, printer to the University, 1584–1618. (Bodleian library record, 1947, vol. 2, p. 188–90.)
2590 d. Oxf. 1. 41 = R.

6297. BATEY, C., Horace Hart and the University press, 1883–1915. (Signature, 1954, N.S., vol. 18, p. 5–22.)   Per. 2582 d. 80

See 1341.5 [Peter de Walpergen against the executors of John Fell, 1687–88. 1964].

Fabric

6298. Oxonia explicata et ornata. 1. The new Clarendon printing-office. (The Crypt, 1828, vol. 2, p. 105–08.)   Hope 8° 280

6299. Particular and description for building and finishing the premises for the accommodation of the University printing press. (Oxf.), [1829], fol. 6 pp.   G.A. Oxon c. 45 (29)

6300. Proposed superintendents' houses and other works. Extract [inviting tenders] from a minute of the Board of delegates of the University press. Feb. 15, 1831. [Oxf.], 1831, s. sh.   G.A. Oxon c. 47 (26)

6301. Particular and description for building and completely finishing two superintendents' houses and other buildings . . . on the premises of the University printing office. [Oxf., 1831], fol. 10 pp.
G.A. Oxon c. 47 (27)

6302. University press safety manual. Oxf., 1939, 16°. 20 pp.
G.A. Oxon 16° 208

Administration and Finance

6303. HUDDESFORD, G., Observations [signed G. Huddesford] relating to the Delegates of the Press: with an account of their succession from their original appointment. Oxf., 1756, 4°. 16+xviii pp.
G.A. Oxon 4° 6 (10)

6304. A reply [signed The proctors of the former year, dated Nov. 12, 1756] to Dr. Huddesford's Observations . . . with a narrative of the proceedings of the proctors with regard to their nomination of a delegate, April 28, 1756. Oxf., 1756, fol. 35 pp.   G.A. Oxon 4° 6 (8)

6305. BLACKSTONE, W., To the reverend doctor Randolph . . . [A letter about the Oxford Press, of which a few copies only were printed and dispersed. Blackstone uses the copy here cited, as a proof for another edition, which, apparently, was never printed; those items which were 'penned in the heat of controversy' are marked to be omitted.] [Oxf.], (1757), 4°. 32 pp.   MS. Top. Oxon d. 387 (3)

6306. FOWELL, J., [*Begin.*] An accommodation of the matters in dispute . . . [Statement by the junior proctor of differences between the vice-chancellor and himself about the Delegacy of the Press. With two draught statutes the one prepared by the vice-chancellor, the other by the junior proctor.] [Oxf., 1757], 4°. 4 pp. MS. Top. Oxon d. 387 (4)

6307. Ad Statutorum Tit. X. sect. 2. §. 7. [An amendment to the statute concerning the Delegacy of the Press.] [Oxf., 1757], s. sh.
MS. Top. Oxon d. 387 (6)

6307.5. BLACKSTONE, SIR W., The letters of sir William Blackstone in the . . . Free Library of Philadelphia, ed. by H. J. Heaney. [Includes 2 letters, dated 25 Jan. and 8 Feb., 1758, addressed to T. Randolph concerning the reform of the Press, with draft of Randolph's reply to the 1st letter.] (Amer. journ. of legal hist., 1957, vol. 1, p. 363–78.)   L.L.
— Repr. Phila., 1958, 8°. 18 pp.   L.L.

6308. PHILIP, I. G., William Blackstone and the reform of the Oxford university press in the eighteenth century. (Publ., Oxf. bibliogr. soc., N.S., vol. 7.) Oxf., 1957, 4°. 130 pp.   Soc. 258 d. 176 = A.

6309. Proposals for regulating the prices of printing at the University press in Oxford. [Probably printed for the meeting of 8 March 1758, which established the various tables and orders in no. 6310 and 6322.] [Oxf., 1758], fol. 7 pp.   G.A. Oxon b. 19

6310. Orders established by the Delegates . . . March 8, 1758, for regulating the prices of printing at the University-press. [Oxf., 1758], 4°. 3 pp.
MS. Top. Oxon d. 387 (7)

See 1926 [Statistics relating to the Press fund. 1876].

6311. The universities as traders [i.e. the profits derived from their university presses]. (Sat. rev., 1895, vol. 79, p. 181, 82).   N. 2288 c. 8

6312. MADAN, F., Oxford oddments. 1. Oxford university press accounts, 1672–9. (Library, 1929, 4th ser., vol. 9, p. 341–48.)
Per. 258 d. 252 = A.

6313. The first minute book of the Delegates of the Oxford university press, 1668–1756, ed. by S. Gibson and J. Johnson. (Oxf. bibliogr. soc., extra publ.) Oxf., 1943, 4°. 104 pp.   Soc. 258 d. 176 = A.

6314. RAMSAY, G. D., The University press [a criticism of its constitution and conduct, signed G. D. R.]. (Oxf. mag., 1946, vol. 64, p. 162, 63.)
— [An editorial comment on the above.] (p. 177, 78.)
— [Letter from K. Sisam, secretary to the Delegates of the Press.] (p. 197, 98.)
— The University press. II [signed G. D. R.]. (p. 209, 10).
— [An editorial summary.] (p. 237, 38.)
— [Letter from H. Last.] (p. 325.)
— The University press meeting. [Report of a meeting of members of the University to discuss the conduct of the Press.] (Oxf. mag., 1946, vol. 65, p. 99, 100.)   Per. G.A. Oxon 4° 141

6315. NORRINGTON, A. L. P., The University press. [An account of its administration.] (Oxford, 1950, vol. 10, no. 3, p. 66–78.)
Per. G.A. Oxon 8° 1141

6316. Deeds relating to Wolvercote paper mill . . . among the archives of the University press. [Reprod. from typewriting.] (Nat. Reg. of Archives.) n. pl., [1958], fol.   2262 c. 10 = R.

Paper duty

6317. Accounts relating to drawbacks of duty on paper used for books printed at the universities. [Lond.], 1815, fol. 7 pp.
Pp. Eng. 1814/15 vol. 10

6318. A return of all sums of money paid to the printers of the English and Scotch universities, as drawback of duty on paper printed within the said universities during the last seven years; distinguishing the amount to each university, and period when paid:—as far as relates to England. [Lond.], 1815, s. sh.   Pp. Eng. 1814/15 vol. 10

6319. Oxford and Cambridge universities: Paper duties. Returns of any annual payments to the universities . . . charged on the land revenue of the crown; also, of the amount of paper duty remitted to each during the last ten years &c. [Lond.], 1845, fol. 9 pp.   Pp. Eng. 1845 vol. 28

6320. Paper. A return 'of all sums paid as allowances on paper used in the printing of any books in the Latin, Greek, Oriental, or Northern languages within the Universities of Oxford and Cambridge [&c.] for the last ten years'. [Lond.], 1846, s. sh.   Pp. Eng. 1846, vol. 25

Staff

6321. Articles agreed upon by the workmen of the University printing-house . . . subscribed . . . 1711/12 . . . for the more effectual carrying on the contribution begun . . . 1707/8 . . . [towards a staff benefit fund]. [Oxf., 1715], s. sh.   Ashm. 1820 b (23)

6322. Compositor's table . . . March the eighth, 1758 . . . Distribution table . . . [Proportional rates of pay of compositor, pressmen & overseers in the Press.] [Oxf., 1758], fol. 2 sheets. MS. Top. Oxon d. 387 (8)

6323. Oxford university press annual entertainment. Testimonial to Edward Pickard Hall, Feb. 3, 1873 [with list of subscribers, giving their length of service]. [Oxf.], (1873), 8°. 7 pp.   G.A. Oxon 8° 147 (8)

6324. The Clarendon press: scale of prices for compositors' work. April, 1891. Oxf., 1891, 8°. 23 pp.   25835 e. 49 (5)

6325. Men who have been called up or have enlisted for service in H.M. forces, 1914. [Oxf., 1914], 8°. 8 pp.   G.A. Oxon b. 175

6326. War record of the University press, Oxford. [*On cover*] On active service, war work at home, 1914–1919. Oxf., 1923, 8°. 87 pp.
    22281 d. 521

6327. Oxford university press. Commemoration of the members . . . who have laid down their lives in the War. [With list of names.] [Oxf.], 1919, 8°. 13 pp.   G.A. Oxon 8° 895 (9)

6328. The Clarendonian. Vol. 1– . Oxf., 1919– , 8°.   Per. 25823 d. 78

Clarendon Press Institute

6329. Proposed Institute for persons employed at the Press. [Oxf.], (1890), fol. 3 pp.   G.A. Oxon b. 175
[Other papers about the Institute are in the Bodleian in the same shelf-mark.]

Typography

6330. A compleat inventory of the various signs, peculiar characters, and accents in use at the Clarendon press. (Oxf.), 1878, 4°. 26 pp.
    25839 d. 32

6331. REED, T. B., The Oxford university foundry. (A history of old English foundries, with notes on the rise and progress of English typography, p. 137–63.) Lond., 1887, 4°.   25823 d. 9

6332. HART, H., Notes of a century of typography at the University press, 1693–1794. Oxf., 1900, 4°. xvi+172 pp.   25823 c. 8 = R.

6333. MCMURTRIE, D. C., The printing plant of the Oxford university press. Greenwich, Conn., 1923, 4°. 15 pp.   25823 d. 86

6334. ROTH, C., Edward Pococke and the first Hebrew printing in Oxford. (Bodleian library record, 1948, vol. 2, p. 215–19.)
    2590 d. Oxf. 1. 41 = R.

House rules

6335. Friendly advice to the correctour of the English press at Oxford concerning the English orthographie. Lond., 1682, fol. 9 pp.
    Gough Oxf. 80*

6336. Clarendon press, March 1893. Rules for compositors and readers . . . [Signed] H. Hart. (Oxf., 1893), s. sh.   25835 a. 1

6337. HART, H., Clarendon press, Oxford. Rules for compositors and readers [signed] H. Hart. (Oxf., 1893), s. sh.   25835 a. 1
[Editions later publ. in 12° format, and revised by J. A. H. Murray and H. Bradley: latest ed., 37th ed., 1967.]

Specimens of type

6338. A newly-discovered broadside specimen of Fell type, printed at Oxford about 1685. Reprod. in collotype facs., with bibliogr. note by P. Hofer. Cambr., Mass. &c., 1940, 4°. 4 pp.   25839 c. 30

6339. [Specimen of type given by John Fell to the University.] [Oxf., c. 1687], 8°.   Ch. Ch.

6340. A specimen of the several sorts of letter given to the University by dr. John Fell . . . To which is added the letter given by mr. F. Junius. [*Followed by*] An account of the matrices, punchions &c. given by bishop Fell . . . Oxf., 1693, 4°.   Broxbourne Libr., London;
    Bodl. has 2 imperf. copies
    C 1. 24 (1) Art.; Crynes 824 (9)
[Some copies are bound with 'Catalogus librorum in Theatro Sheldoniano Oxon. impressorum' said by Hearne to be by A. Charlett, *and* 'Anno domini MDCXCIV in Theatro . . . jam imprimuntur . . . ' but these are not integral. Bodley has 2 copies: 258 b. 272; Crynes 824 (10).]
— Reprod. in collotype facs., with intr., census and handlist. Lond., 1928, 8°.   25839 d. 31

6341. A specimen of the several sorts of letter given to the University by dr. John Fell . . . To which is added the letter given by mr. F. Junius. Oxf., 1695, 4°. 22 leaves.   O.U.P.
— [Another issue] 1695. 24 leaves.   Gough Oxf. 142 (8) [Imperf.]

6342. A specimen of the several sorts of letter given to the University by dr. John Fell . . . To which is added the letter given by mr. F. Junius. Oxf., 1706, 8°. 25 leaves.   O.U.P.
[The copy in Bodley lacks sig. b. 1: Gough Oxf. 142 (9).]

6343. Characteres Anglo-Saxonici per eruditam fæminam Eliz. Elstob ad fidem codd. MSS. delineati. Quorum tam instrumentis cusoriis, quam matricibus Univ. donari curavit E. R. M. e Collegio Regin. a.m. 1753. [Oxf.], 1753, s. sh.   St. B.T.L.

6344. A specimen of several sorts of letter in the University printing house, Oxford. [Oxf., 1757/58], s. sh.   C 1. 24 (7) Art.

6345. SIMMONS, J. S. G., The undated Oxford broadsheet Specimen [1757/58]. (Trans., Bibliogr. soc. The Library, 1956, ser. 5, vol. 11, p. 11–17.)   Per. 258 d. 272 = A.

6346. A specimen of the several sorts of printing-types belonging to the University of Oxford at the Clarendon printing-house, MDCCLXVIII. [Oxf.], (1768), 8°. Sig. A–D.   St. B.T.L.

6347. A specimen of the several sorts of printing-types belonging to the University of Oxford at the Clarendon printing-house, MDCCLXVIII. [*With*] New letters purchased in the years 1768, 1769, 1770. [Oxf.] 1768(–70), 8°. Sig. A–E. [40 pp.]   G.A. Oxon 8° 45 (3)

6348. New letters purchased in the year 1771, 1772, 1773, 1774. [A suppl. forming sig. F to the 1768 specimen.] (Oxf.), 1775, 8°. 2 leaves. O.U.P.

6349. A specimen of the several sorts of printing-types belonging to the University of Oxford at the Clarendon printing-house, MDCCLXXXVI. [Oxf.], (1786), 8°. 36 pp.   O.U.P.

6350. A specimen of the several sorts of printing-types . . . at the Clarendon printing-house. [Oxf.], 1794, 8°. 47 leaves.   O.U.P.
[Bodley has an imperfect copy: 25839 d. 22.]

6351. HART, H., On some types in use at the Oxford university press. [Reprod. from typewriting.] [Oxf., 1903], fol. 8 pp.+11 pl.
25839 c. 21

6352. HALL, F. J., Examples of some of the types in general use at the Clarendon press, MDCCCCXX [compiled by F. J. Hall]. [Oxf.], 1920, 8°. 31 pp.   25839 d. 14

6353. Specimens of books printed at Oxford with the types given to the University by John Fell . . . Oxf., 1925, fol. 127 pp.   25839 b. 7

6354. MORISON, S., The roman, italic & black letter bequeathed . . . by dr. John Fell (by S. Morison). Oxf., 1950, 8°. 41 pp.   25839 e. 26

6355. CARTER, H., and SIMMONS, J. S. G., A specimen of types cast at the University press, Oxford in matrices believed to have been bought at Leyden in 1637. [Signed H. C. and J. S. G. S.] Oxf., 1957, s. sh.
25839 c. 36 (1)

6356. A specimen of the types attributable to Peter de Walpergen, cut for the University of Oxford, 1676–1702. Oxf., 1957, s. sh.   25839 a. 4
— [Another ed.] 1959.   25839 a. 4

6357. SIMMONS, J. S. G., Specimens of printing types before 1850 in the typographical library at the University press. (Book collector, 1959, vol. 8, p. 397–410.)   Per. 25805 e. 100 = A.
— Repr. 16 pp.   25839 e. 56

6358. The types bought in Holland by John Fell and Thomas Yate for the University of Oxford, 1670–1672. Oxf., 1959, fol. 4 pp.   25839 b. 10

Bibles

6359. The case (Supplement to the case) of mr. Charles Eyre [complaining that his superior offer for a lease of the moiety of the printing house with a privilege of printing Bibles, etc., was not preferred to that of mr. Baskett]. n. pl., 1764, 3 pp. & s. sh.   G.A. Oxon c. 250 (vii)

6360. [Begin.] Messrs. Wright and Gill beg leave to inform . . . that [their proposals for one moiety of the Clarendon printing house with the privilege of printing Bibles are £850 per annum, and an indemnification from any law-suit by mr. Baskett]. Dec. 9. [Oxf.], (1765), s. sh.
                                                                              G.A. Oxon b. 19

6361. WALLIS, J., Letter . . . to archbishop Sancroft, concerning the right of the University of Oxford to the printing of Bibles, and other privileged books. April 15, 1684. (Collectanea curiosa, by J. Gutch, vol. 1, p. 278–81.) Oxf., 1781, 8°.   Gough Oxf. 65

6362. [Begin.] Articles of agreement . . . [between the University and William Jackson of Oxford and Archibald Hamilton of London in connection with the printing of Bibles, &c. To be approved by Convocation June 20, 1788]. [Oxf.], (1788), 4°. 4 pp.   G.A. Oxon b. 111 (75)

6363. Articles of agreement . . . in . . . 1811, between the . . . University of Oxford . . . and Thomas Bentley . . . Joshua Cooke . . . Samuel Collingwood . . . Edward Gardner . . . and Joseph Parker . . . [Oxf., 1811], fol. 4 pp.   G.A. Oxon b. 19
— 1818. Joshua Cooke, Samuel Collingwood, Joseph Parker, Edward Gardner. 7 pp.   G.A. Oxon b. 19
— 1820. Samuel Collingwood, Joseph Parker, Edward Gardner. 7 pp.
                                                                              G.A. Oxon b. 19
— 1830. Samuel Collingwood, Joseph Parker, Edward Gardner, John Collingwood. 6 pp.   G.A. Oxon c. 46 (45)
— Mar. 29, 1841. [Further articles for 14 years between the University and Joseph Parker, Edward Gardner, John Collingwood, and Thomas Combe.]   G.A. Oxon c. 57 (37)
— Nov. 14, 1853. [Further articles for 14 years with Thomas Combe, Edward Bensley Gardner, and Edward Pickard Hall.]
                                                                              G.A. Oxon c. 69 (192)
— 24 June 1867. [Further articles for 14 years with T. Combe, E. B. Gardner, E. P. Hall, and H. Latham.]   G.A. Oxon c. 107 (52)

6364. House of Lords. Between William Richardson, John Richardson, and James Richardson, appellants, and the . . . University of Oxford and the . . . University of Cambridge, respondents. The case of the respondents. [Asserting the right of the Universities and the King's printer to be sole printers and distributors of Bibles etc.] Lond., [1802], fol. 3 pp.   L.L.

6365. [*Begin.*] In Chancery, Easter term, 1808. The Universities of Oxford and Cambridge *v.* Richardsons. [A circular in reference to the sale by the defendants of Bibles printed in Scotland.] July 21. [Lond.], (1808), s. sh.   B.M.

6366. [*Begin.*] Complaints having been made that the English Bibles printed at the universities . . . differed greatly from the Authorized Version . . . [Account of collation of early Bibles to ensure accuracy in the edition publ. in 1833.] [Oxf.], (1834), 4°. 3 pp.   G.A. Oxon b. 175

6367. Bibles, &c. . . . A return of the number of Bibles, Testaments, Prayer Books and Psalms printed, published and sold by the Queen's printer in England from the year 1837 up to the present time . . . and the amount of drawback of paper duty [&c.] . . . A similar return for the University of Oxford . . . 10 February 1848. [Lond.], 1848, fol. 5 pp.   Pp. Eng. 1847/48 vol. 49
— from 1848 to 31 December 1850. 26 May 1851. [Lond.], 1851, s. sh.   Pp. Eng. 1851 vol. 42

6368. Bibles and prayer books . . . Copies of the patents or authority under which the Queen's printer and the Universities of Oxford and Cambridge claim the exclusive right of printing Bibles and prayer books. 7 August 1851. [Lond.], 1851, fol. 8 pp.   Pp. Eng. 1851 vol. 42

6369. The University press. [Notice concerning the amalgamation of management of the 'Bible press' and the 'learned press'.] Jan. 1, 1863. Oxf., 1863, s. sh.   G.A. Oxon c. 79 (2)

6370. LATHAM, H., Oxford Bibles, and Printing in Oxford. Oxf., 1868, 16°. 62 pp.   25823 f 4
— [Another. ed.] 1870.   258874 f. 1

6371. [Papers relating to the agreement between the universities of Oxford and Cambridge regarding the Revised version of the Bible.] [Oxf. &c.], 1871, fol.   1056 c. 1

6372. Revised version of the Holy Scriptures. Correspondence between the two University presses. n. pl., (1872), 4°. 9 pp.   2581 d. 50 (1)

6373. Correspondence between the two University presses concerning the use of the copyright of the Revised version of the Holy Scriptures. n. pl., [1872], 8°. 31 pp. [The Bodley copy in G.A. Oxon 8° 1148 (6) has MS. corrections on what appears to be a proof copy.]

6374. STEVENS, H., The history of the Oxford Caxton memorial Bible, printed and bound in twelve consecutive hours, June 30, 1877. Lond., 1878, 16°. 30 pp.   258 c. 69

6375. Oxford editions of the Book of common prayer, altar services, litanies, etc., also of the Holy Bible, in large type [Specimen pages, &c.] Oxf., [c. 1900], fol. 32 pp.   258875 c. 3

6376. The Oxford trade catalogue of the Holy Bible ... Book of common prayer ... &c. Lond., 1912, 8°. 297 pp.   2595 e. 4g

6377. Oxford Bibles. Specimens of type. Lond. &c., [1912], 8°. 96 pp.
                                                          2595 e. 4g

6378. Oxford editions of the Book of common prayer ... Specimens of types. Oxf., [1912], 8°. 53 pp.   2595 e. 4g

Press lists and catalogues

6379. MADAN, F., The early Oxford press, a bibliography of printing and publishing at Oxford, '1468'-1640. (Oxf. hist. soc., vol. 29.) Oxf., 1895, 8°. 365 pp.   G.A. Oxon 8° 360 = R.
[This could also be obtained from the Clarendon Press in a binding distinct from that of the Society. Subsequently another title-page was added and this book became volume 1 of Oxford books.]

6380. MADAN, F., Oxford books, a bibliography of printed works relating to the University and City of Oxford, or printed or published there. Vol. 1. The early Oxford press, 1468-1640. [See note in previous entry.] Oxf., 1895, 8°. 365 pp.
— Vol. 2. Oxford literature, 1450-1640, and 1641-1650. Oxf., 1912, 8°. 712 pp.
— Vol. 3. Oxford literature, 1651-1680. Oxf., 1931, 8°. 621 pp.
                                                     25823 d. 192 = R.

6381. A chronological list of Oxford books, 1681-1713 (transcript from the notebooks of Falconer Madan, by F. E. L. S. and J. S. G. S.). [Reprod. from typewriting.] [Oxf., 1954], 4°. 72 leaves.   25823 d. 189 = R.

6382. A catalogue of books printed at the Theater in Oxford. [Madan 3154.] [Oxf., 1677], s. sh.   Wood 658 (16)
— [Another ed. 1677.] [Madan 3155.]   Wood 660 b (9)

6383. Catalogus variorum librorum apud Theatrum Sheldonianum novissimis annis impressorum, et aliorum ... exemplarium propriis sumptibus Moses Pitt ... quorum auctio habebitur ... 24 die Februarii 1678/9 ... [Madan 3202*.] [Lond., 1679], 4°. 6 pp.   Wood 660 b (13)

6384. The books following, lately printed at the Theater, are to be sold by Richard Davis ... Febr. 16, 1680 [79/80]. [Oxf., 1679/80], s. sh.
                                                      Wood D 22 (13)

6385. Books printed at the Theatre in the University of Oxford since 1672. (The general catalogue of books printed since ... 1666, collected by R. Clavell, 1680, p. 98, 99.)   Wood 660 b (3)

6386. An advertisement, concerning the printing and publishing of ancient and other usefull books. [Madan 3273.] [Oxf., 1680], s. sh.
                                                      Wood 658 (775)

6387. A catalogue of books printed at the Theatre in Oxford since the first printing there . . . in . . . 1672, to 1682 . . . sold in London by Moses Pitt. [Lond.], 1682, fol. 4 pp. Wood 660 *b* (11)

6387.5, Catalogues librorum in Theatro Sheldoniano Oxon. impressorum [by A. Charlett? Sig. U of a larger work.] [Oxf., *c.* 1694], 8°. [See also no. 6340.] Crynes 824 (10)

6388. Anno Domini MDCXCIV in Theatro Sheldonio apud Oxoniam jam imprimuntur. [Oxf.], 1694, s. sh. Wood 660 *b* (16)
[See also no. 6340.]

6389. Anno Domini MDCXCVI Maii die 4 in Theatro Sheldoniano . . . sub prelo sunt libri sequentes. [Oxf.], (1696), s. sh. Ashm. 1820 *a* (237)
— [Another issue.] Ashm. 1820 *a* (238)
— MDCXCVII Julii die 14 . . . Ashm. 1820 *a* (236)
— MDCCI. Julii die 16 . . . Antiq. c. E. 9 (98)
— MDCCV. Jun. die 12 . . . Ashm. 1818 (78)
— MDCCVIII. Augusti die 6 . . . Ashm. 1818 (77)
— MDCCXVI. Maii die 17 . . . fol. Θ 662 (12)

6390. Books printed at the University press . . . sold by Daniel Prince . . . and Thomas Payne. [Oxf., 1759], s. sh. MS. Top. Oxon d. 387 (13)

6391. Books printed at the University press in Oxford, sold by Joshua Cooke . . . and by Peter Elmsly and David Bremner . . . London . . . n. pl., [*c.* 1805], fol. 2 sheets. Antiq. b. E. 15 (9)

6392. Books printed at the Clarendon press [*afterw.*] Oxford university press: Clarendon press [*afterw.*] Oxford university press: general catalogue. April, 1871– . Lond. &c., 1871– , 8°. 2595 e. 4*a*

6393. One hundred select works suitable for public libraries. Oxf. &c., [1897], 8°. 22 pp. 2595 e. 4*e*

6394. Clarendon press. New and recent books. Oct. 1886–Feb. 1907. Lond., 1886–1907, 8°. 2595 e. 4*b*

6395. Select list of educational books [*afterw.*] Select educational catalogue. 1907, 19, 20, 23. Oxf., 1907–23, 8°. 2595 e.4*e*

6396. Select catalogue of Clarendon press books specially suitable for public libraries and school reference libraries. Oxf. &c., [1910], 8°. 48 pp. 2595 e. 4*e*

6397. Oxford press bulletin. No. 1– . Oxf., 1912– , 4° &c. 2595 d. 5; e. 4*f*

6398. Oxford university (Clarendon) press. (Spring list of) Forthcoming books. 1916– . (Oxf.), 1916– , 8°. 2595 e. 4*d*

6399. Oxford university press. Supplement to the General catalogue. June 1917–Oct. 1941. [Oxf. &c.], 1917–41, 8°. 2595 e. 4*c*

6400. Oxford university press select catalogue. August 1930–39. Oxf., 1930–39, 8°. 2595 e. 4*e*

UNIVERSITY REGISTRY

6401. VEALE, SIR D., Arcana imperii: the organisation of the Registry. (Oxf. mag., 1954, vol. 73, p. 78–80.)   Per. G.A. Oxon 4° 141

6401.2. CLIFFORD, R., Room and the Registry. (Oxf. mag., 1962, N.S., vol. 3, p. 99, 100.)   Per. G.A. Oxon 4° 141

COLLEGES AND HALLS

MEN

General

6402. A catalogue of the colleges and halls in . . . Oxford. [Madan 3166.] Lond., 1678, s. sh.   G.A. Oxon b. 19

6403. WOOD, A., The history and antiquities of the colleges and halls in the University, now first publ. in English, with a continuation to the present time by the editor, J. Gutch. [*With*] Appendix . . . containing Fasti Oxonienses: or A commentary on the supreme magistrates [Chancellors, commissaries, vice-chancellors and proctors] of the University. Oxf., 1786, 90, 4°.   Vet. A 5. d. 772 = R.

[See also no. 13, 14.]

6404. KILNER, J., Of colleges as incorporated: their name, and nature; priority, and precedency. (The account of Pythagoras's school in Cambridge [by J. Kilner] suppl., p. 112–22.) n. pl., [1790?], fol.   Gough Cambr. 97

See 24 [Chalmers, A., A history of the colleges, halls and public buildings attached to the University. 1810].

6405. SKELTON, J., Pietas Oxoniensis, or, Records of Oxford founders. Oxf., 1828, fol. 96 pp.   G.A. fol. A 114

6406. RUNDT, C., Views of the most picturesque colleges in the University of Oxford. Pt. 1, 2. [Text in Engl. and Germ.] (Berl.), [1852?], fol. 10 plates.   G.A. fol. D 25

6407. The colleges of Oxford. (Fraser's mag. 1852, vol. 45, p. 363–79.)   Per. 3977 e. 200

See 3692 [Place, J., University tests and their abolition. With a table of pre- and post-Reformation benefactions to Oxford. 1870].

6408. In the Common room at Oxford. (Belgravia, 1868, vol. 6, p. 354–60.)
Per. 256 d. 254

6409. Oxford sausage. Ladies at Oxford [their presence within college pre-
cincts]. (All the year, 1874, N.S., vol. 12, p. 607–11.)   Per. 2705 d. 202

6410. Consolidation of college clubs. (Oxf. mag., 1887, vol. 5, p. 78.)
Per. G.A. Oxon 4° 141

6411. The colleges of Oxford: xxi chapters contributed by members of the
colleges, ed. by A. Clark. Lond., 1891, 8°. 480 pp.
G.A. Oxon 8° 1393 = R.

6412. MATTHEWS, H. W., Old college customs at Oxford. (Temple Bar,
1899, vol. 118, p. 298–304.)   Per. 2705 d. 277

6413. SYMONDS, R., Oxford church [and college] notes, 1643–4, with additions of 1656–61, ed. by R. Graham. (Oxf. hist. soc., 1905, vol. 47,
p. 99–135.)   G.A. Oxon 8° 360 = R.

6414. How to choose a college at Oxford [signed A recent undergraduate
(not of Balliol)]. (Nat. rev., 1906, vol. 48, p. 282–88.) Per. 22775 d. 14

6415. GRIBBLE, F., The romance of the Oxford colleges. Lond., 1910, 8°.
324 pp.   G.A. Oxon 8° 780

6416. Oxford war memorials. (Oxf. mag., 1923, vol. 41, p. 455–58.)
Per. G.A. Oxon 4° 141

6416.5. ROBERTS, S. C., College alliances. (Oxford, 1935, vol. 2, no. 1,
p. 41–45.)   Per. G.A. Oxon 8° 1141

6417. BURROUGH, P., Shortened halls [i.e. shortened dinners in hall: the
balance between the cost of these and the normal charge was spent for
relief of malnutrition in distressed areas]. (Oxf. mag., 1938, vol. 56,
p. 704, 05).   Per. G.A. Oxon 4° 141

6418. ALLEN, SIR C. K., The Senior common room. (Amer. Oxonian, 1958,
vol. 45, p. 105–08.)   Per. G.A. Oxon 8° 889

6419. LEARY, P., Views of the Oxford colleges, and other poems. (Poets of
today, vii, p. 93–160.) New York, 1960, 8°.   Per. 2814 e. 79 (7)

6419.2. The colleges of Oxford and Cambridge, with 36 reprod. in colour
and monochrome from 19th century prints, and 16 drawings by
B. Cairns. [Oxf., p. 1–41 and 9 colour plates.] Lond., 1963, fol.
G.A. Gen. top. b. 48

See 519.2 [Pantin, W., The halls and schools of medieval Oxford: an attempt
at reconstruction. 1964].

6419.3. PANTIN, W., [History of relations between the University and the
colleges.] (Rept., Keeper of the Archives to Delegates of privileges,
1962/63. Suppl. no. 4, Univ. Gazette, March 1964, p. 23–35.) [Oxf.],
1964, 8°.   Per. G.A. Oxon c. 86

6419.31. OXBURGH, E. R., New graduate colleges. (Oxf. mag., 1964, N.S., vol. 4, p. 368, 69.)   Per. G.A. Oxon 4° 141

Administration and reform

See also 923 etc. [Government].
See also 1638 etc. [Reform].

6420. An address to his grace the archbishop of Canterbury as a visitor of colleges in the University of Oxford and as primate of all England. 2nd ed. With a postscript concerning the author. By a country clergyman. Lond., 1791, 4°. 89 pp.   G. Pamph. 2917 (10)

See 1644, 1645 [Earl of Radnor's bill . . . respecting the statutes and administration of the colleges and halls. 1837].

6421. MARRIOTT, C., A few words on the statute for new halls, to be proposed in Convocation, May 23 [signed C. M.]. [Oxf.], (1854), s. sh.   G.A. Oxon c. 70 (256)

6422. CHASE, D. P., i. General suggestions for the improvement of the Halls in the patronage and under the visitation of the Chancellor of the University of Oxford, submitted Jan. 19, 1854. ii. Supplementary paper containing extracts from correspondence &c. Oxf., 1856, fol. 9+4 pp.   G.A. Oxon c. 72 (293)

6423. CHASE, D. P., The rights of 'indigentes' in respect to college foundations, a letter. Oxf., 1856, 8°. 22 pp.   G.A. Oxon c. 72 (393)

6424. PYCROFT, J. W., A letter . . . to . . . John MacBride . . . and by him laid before the Hebdomadal council of the University of Oxford. [Enumerating his services to the University and asking for support in his attempt to obtain remuneration from public revenue for his efforts.] Oxf., [1865], 8°. 27 pp.   G.A. Oxon 8° 1198 (3)

6425. A correspondence between J. W. Pycroft . . . and . . . Spencer H. Walpole . . . in reference to the adjustment of his, mr. Pycroft's claims on the 'Bishops' trust substitution act' . . . 1858. Oxf., [1865], 8°. 32 pp.   G.A. Oxon 8° 1198 (2)

6426. The bishop of Oxford's Bishops' trust substitution act, session 1858. A correspondence between . . . Philip Wynter . . . and J. W. Pycroft . . . in reference to the above enactment. [An attempt by the latter to obtain recognition and reward from the University for his part in helping to defeat that portion of the act affecting Founders' trusts.] n. pl., [1865], 8°. 20 pp.   G.A. Oxon 8° 1198 (1)

6427. [Associated college lecture lists. 1868–84.]   G.A. Oxon c. 13

6428. Can colleges reform themselves? (Macmillan's mag., 1872, vol. 25, p. 461–71.)   G.A. Oxon 4° 581 (3)

See 6832 [Wordsworth, C., College statutes, college fellowships and college legislation. 1872].

6429. CHASE, D. P., Oxford university bill. Suggestions respecting the halls in the patronage of the Chancellor of the University. Oxf., 1876, 8°. 17 pp. G.A. Oxon 8° 296 (7)

> See 1770 [Memorials from colleges on the Oxford university bill. 1876].
> See 2452 [Case, T., The disorganisation of the colleges by the proposed statute on faculties. 1910].

6430. ANSON, SIR W. R., The place of the colleges in University reform [6 letters]. (Oxf. mag., 1910, vol. 28, p. 143; 157, 58; 175, 76; 191–93; 224–26; 257, 58.) Per. G.A. Oxon 4° 141

6431. BARKER, E., The Oxford and Cambridge colleges. [Observations on their teaching and administrative organization.] (Edinb. rev., 1923, vol. 238, p. 254–69.) Per. 3977 e. 190

6432. STALLYBRASS, W. T. S., The Oxford college system and its preservation. (Amer. Oxon., 1948, vol. 35, p. 18–28.) Per. G.A. Oxon 8° 889

6433. The ending of national service and its implications for Oxford colleges. (Oxf. mag., 1957, vol. 75, p. 545–47.) Per. G.A. Oxon 4° 141

6433.3. KAYE, J. M., Heads of Houses. (Oxf. mag., 1965, N.S., vol. 5, p. 100–02). Per. G.A. Oxon 4° 141

6433.31. HAYTER, SIR W., Are Heads of Houses necessary? (Oxf. mag., 1965, N.S., vol. 5, p. 122–24.) Per. G.A. Oxon 4° 141

6433.32. BRUNT, P. A., College autonomy. (Oxf. mag., 1965, N.S., vol. 5, p. 176–79.) Per. G.A. Oxon 4° 141

Admissions

6433.38. Entrance to Oxford and Cambridge, reports of committees appointed by the two universities. Oxf. &c., 1960, 8°. 51 pp.
2625 e. 241 = S.

6433.39. WATSON, J. S., University admissions. (Oxford, 1960, vol. 17, p. 45–56.) Per. G.A. Oxon 8° 1141
— Repr. (Amer. Oxonian, 1962, vol. 49, p. 39–43.)
Per. G.A. Oxon 8° 889

6433.4. University of Oxford. Admissions to colleges. [Hardie] Report of a working party. (Oxf., 1962), 4°. 68 pp. G.A. Oxon 4° 789
— [Conclusions of the above, without the evidence and arguments, *entitled*] Admissions to Oxford colleges. [Oxf.], 1962, 8°. 8 pp.
G.A. Oxon 8° 1470

6433.41. Hardie report on admissions [a précis]. (Oxf. mag., 1962, N.S., vol. 3, p. 2, 3.) Per. G.A. Oxon 4° 141

6433.42. DAVIS, R., The Hardie report. (Oxf. mag., 1962, N.S., vol. 3, p. 36–38.) Per. G.A. Oxon 4° 141

6433.43. HARDIE, W. F. R., Admissions—a reply. (Oxf. mag., 1962, N.S., vol. 3, p. 54, 55.) Per. G.A. Oxon 4° 141

6433.44. STYLER, L. M., The pattern of admission to the men's colleges. (Oxf. mag., 1964, N.S., vol. 4, p. 254, 55.)　　Per. G.A. Oxon 4° 141

6433.45. BROCK, M. G., Admissions: the state of the case. (Oxf. mag., 1965, N.S., vol. 5, p. 238–40).　　Per. G.A. Oxon 4° 141

6433.46. ADY, P., Mixed education and the women's colleges. (Oxf. mag., 1964, N.S., vol. 5, p. 138–40.)　　Per. G.A. Oxon 4° 141

6433.51. PANTIN, W., [History of the relations between the University and the colleges in the matter of admission and accommodation of under-graduates, and of the government of the University.] (Rept., Keeper of the Archives to Delegates of privileges, 1963/64. Suppl. no. 2, Univ. Gazette, Dec. 1964, p. 10–24.) [Oxf.], 1964, 8°. Per. G.A. Oxon c. 86

Barges

6434. ROWNTREE, D., Oxford college barges: their history and decay, and their successors the boathouses. (Architect. rev., 1956, vol. 120, p. 37–42.)　　Per. 17356 c. 8

Chapels

6435. BLAKISTON, H. E. D., Oxford monuments [in college chapels, St. Mary's and the Cathedral. Signed H. E. D. B.]. (Oxf. mag., 1883, vol. 1, p. 245, 246.)　　Per. G.A. Oxon 4° 141

6436. FOX, A., College chapels. (Church quarterly review, 1933, vol. 117, p. 89–99.)　　Per. 1419 e. 402 = S.

6437. VALLANCE, A., Greater English church screens [Oxford colleges *passim*]. Lond. &c., 1947, 4°. 184 pp.　　137 d. 137

6437.2. QUINTON, A., Thoughts about college chapels. (Oxf. mag., 1961, N.S., vol. 1, p. 350–52.)　　Per. G.A. Oxon 4° 141

Finance and property

General

See also 1425 &c. [University finance].

6438. An acte for the maintenaunce of the colledges in both the Vniversi-ties . . . (18 Eliz., c. 6, Pub.). Lond., 1578, fol.　　L.L.

See 1545 [An order to bursars of colleges to retain their monies till an order is received from the Committee for reformation. 1648].

6439. [*Begin.*] May 22. 1648. At the committee of Lords and Commons for the reformation of the University of Oxford . . . [an order that bursars of colleges shall deliver monies received by them to the new heads. *Followed by* another order that the committee at Haberdashers hall is to assist such heads to obtain the monies. *Begin.*] Die Jovis 21. Septemb. 1648. Whereas by an ordinance of parliament . . . [Madan 2000*.] [Lond.], (1648), s. sh.　　Don. b. 12 (2)

6440. A collection of several acts of Parliament, ordinances, orders, &c. for providing maintenance for ministers, heads of colledges and halls in the universities of Oxford and Cambridge. [Madan 2324.] Lond., 1657, 4°. 371+[4] pp. 35 b. 48

6441. [*Begin.*] Universit. Oxon. To [   ] being by us nominated . . . [Notice by the Oxford commissioners requiring their appointed assessors to collect money due from each college for war-tax.] [Madan 3186.] [Oxf.], (1678), s. sh. 5 △ 90 (2)

6442. [*Begin.*] Univers. Oxon. These are in His Maiesties name . . . [Notice requiring assessed persons to appear before the commissioners in the convocation house on Apr. 30.] [Madan 3187.] (Oxf., 1678), s. sh. O.U.A.

6443. [*Begin.*] To [   ] being by us approved . . . [Notice by the vice-chancellor and three others, commissioners, requiring their collectors to obtain money for the king's use from assessed persons in the University.] [Madan 3188.] (Oxf., 1678), s. sh. O.U.A.

6444. An act to restrain the disposition of lands, whereby the same become unalienable. [The act limits the number of college advowsons.] (9 G. II, c. 36, Pub.) Lond., 1736, fol. 4 pp. L.L.

6445. Reasons humbly offered to the . . . House of Commons against the bill now depending for restraining the disposition of lands whereby the same become unalienable; as far as relates to the University of Oxford. n. pl., [1736], fol. 3 pp. fol. ⊖ 674 (1)

6446. Some plain reasons humbly offer'd against the bill . . . to restrain the disposition of lands, by which the same become unalienable. [Objections by friends of the University against the Mortmain bill as it affected Oxford.] Lond., 1736, 8°. 22 pp. B.M.

6447. Of the annual revenue of the colleges and halls in the University of Oxford, &c. [in the 17th century?] (Collectanea curiosa, by J. Gutch, vol. 1, p. 191–95.) Oxf., 1781, 8°. Gough Oxf. 65

6448. The old rents of every college in Oxford, according to which they were taxed for the entertainment of queen Elizabeth in the 34th year of her reign. (Collectanea curiosa, by J. Gutch, vol. 1, p. 190, 91.) Oxf., 1781, 8°. Gough Oxf. 65

6449. A bill intituled An act to repeal so much of an act [9 G. II, c. 36, Pub.] . . . intituled 'An act to restrain the disposition of lands [&c.]' . . . as restrains colleges . . . from purchasing or holding advowsons. 16th May 1805. [Lond.], 1805, s. sh. Pp. Eng. 1805 vol. 1
— Act. (45 G. II, c. 101, Pub.) 1805. L.L.

6450. [*Begin.*] By a bill . . . entituled 'An act for encouraging planting on church, college and hospital lands . . . ' [A proposal that a petition to the Lords against the bill be authorized by Convocation.] May 18. [Oxf.], 1805, s. sh. Don. b. 12 (106 b)

6451. Valor ecclesiasticus temp. Hen. viii. Vol. 2. (Oxford university, p. 224–88.) [Lond.], 1814, fol.   G.A. Eccl. top. b. 21–26 = R.

See 1473 [Bill to authorize raising of money to defray expense of buildings for the lodging of an increased number of students. 1825].
See 1474 [Bill authorizing exchanges of land and possessions. 1825.].
See 3147 [University extension—college revenues. 1847].

6452. NEATE, C., Observations on college leases. Oxf. &c., 1853, 12°. 22 pp.
                                                                    35 c. 21

See 1475–79 [Bills and Acts giving power to sell and exchange lands. 1856–60].
See 1480 [Bill amending University and college estates act, 1858. 1880].
See 949 [Act limiting tenure of certain university and college emoluments. 1880].

6453. The colleges as landlords [signed Oxoniensis]. (Fraser's mag., 1881, N.S., vol. 23, p. 590–600).   G.A. Oxon 4° 582 (5)

See 1929 [Publication of the accounts of the colleges, the form of the accounts, the audit and publication thereof. 1882].
See 1439 [Accounts of the colleges, 1883–   ].
See 8039 [Price, L. L., The recent depression in agriculture as shown in the accounts of an Oxford college, 1876–90].

6454. PRICE, L. L., The colleges of Oxford and the agricultural depression. (Journ., Roy. statist. soc., 1895, vol. 58, p. 36–74).
                                                   Soc. 24712 e. 80 = P.
— Repr. 1895.   G.A. Oxon 8° 715 (6)

6455. FISHER, H. A. L., A college Progress [by H. A. L. Fisher]. (Macmillan's mag., 1896, vol. 75, p. 22–27.)   Per. 2705 d. 254
— [Also publ. in Fisher's Pages from the past, 1939; 27001 e. 1428.]

6456. PRICE, L. L., Accounts of the colleges ... 1893–1903; with special reference to their agricultural revenues. (Journ., Roy. statist. soc., 1904, vol. 67, p. 585–660.)   Soc. 24712 e. 80 = P.

6457. PRICE, L. L., Oxford college revenues. [Abstract of a paper read before the Royal statistical society, 20 Dec., 1904.] (Oxf. mag., 1905, vol. 23, p. 159, 160.)   Per. G.A. Oxon 4° 141

See 1468 [Questions concerning college 'Disposal of revenue' statutes and any amendments thereto. 1912].

6458. PRICE, L. L., The estates of the colleges of Oxford and their management. (Journ., Statist. soc., 1913, vol. 76, p. 787–90.)
                                                   Soc. 24712 e. 80 = P.

6459. On tuition funds [the adequate payment of tutors &c., signed S. B.]. (Oxf. mag., 1919, vol. 37, p. 154, 55.)   Per. G.A. Oxon 4° 141

6460. Memorandum addressed to the Royal commission on Oxford and Cambridge universities. The ... committee of the estates' bursars of the Oxford colleges ... submit that the landed estates now held by them should ... be retained ... n. pl., (1920), fol. 4 pp.
                                                   G.A. Oxon b. 141 (131a)

6461. HUTCHINSON, G. T., Some aspects of college finances. (Oxford, 1938, vol. 5, no. 2, p. 74–82.)   Per. G.A. Oxon 8° 1141

6462. College charges. (Oxf. mag., 1945, vol. 63, p. 109, 10.)
Per. G.A. Oxon 4° 141

6463. 'The fee rise in Oxford.' [Comments on an open letter from the University branch of the Communist party which suggested state aid to colleges as the best method of avoiding increased fees.] (Oxf. mag., 1945, vol. 64, p. 53, 54.)   Per. G.A. Oxon 4° 141

6464. Increase of fees. (Oxf. mag., 1946, vol. 64, p. 131, 32.)
Per. G.A. Oxon 4° 141

6465. HACKER, L. M., A note on the Oxford colleges (p. 70–76 of Government assistance to universities, no. 1517). New York, 1952, 8°.
2625 d. 135

6466. The colleges and university stipends. (Oxf. mag., 1955, vol. 73, p. 162–64.)   Per. G.A. Oxon 4° 141

6466.5. College autonomy and finance, by an estates bursar. (Oxf. mag., 1965, N.S., vol. 5, p. 221, 22.)   Per. G.A. Oxon 4° 141

Contributions to University purposes

See 1493 [University dues to be charged on the books of colleges. 1833].
See 1498 [Suggested refund to colleges of proportion of annual dues. 1866].

6467. Questions submitted to colleges [as to what sums colleges would be able and willing to contribute to University purposes, and what control they would wish to retain over such sums] and the answers communicated by the several societies. n. pl., [1875], 8°. 24 pp.
G.A. Oxon 8° 1001 (14)

See 1464, 1465 [Statute concerning college contributions for University purposes. 1881].
See 1466 [Armstrong, E., Remarks on the mode of assessing the college contribution for University purposes. 1887].
See 1470 [College contributions to the University funds. 1913].

Ecclesiastical preferment

6468. T., J. M., College livings. (Oxf. mag., 1944, vol. 62, p. 223, 24.)
Per. G.A. Oxon 4° 141

6469. PARKER, T. M., College livings. i. The origins of college ecclesiastical patronage. (Univ. coll. record, 1954/55, p. 96–104.)
Per. G.A. Oxon 8° 1086

6469.1. LAMBRICK, G., Oxford colleges and some country parishes round Oxford in the early 18th century. (Oxoniensia, 1960, vol. 25, p. 109–20.)   Per. G.A. Oxon 4° 658 = R.

Rates

6470. In the matter of the re-assessment [of rates] of certain Oxford colleges [counsel's opinion, signed E. M. Konstam. 21st Oct., 1926]. n. pl., (1926), fol. 3 pp.   G.A. Oxon c. 247 (9)

6471. [Letter to the Committee of bursars, signed C. Gerald Eve, concerning the Rating and valuation act, 1925 in its relation to the colleges of Oxford university. 23rd Apr., 1927.] n. pl., (1927), fol. 8 pp.

G.A. Oxon c. 247 (10)

6472. OVERDRAFT *pseud.* College rateable values. (Oxf. mag., 1952, vol. 70, p. 232.) Per. G.A. Oxon 4° 141

6472.3. COOKE, C. A., Colleges and rating. (Oxf. mag., 1963, N.S., vol. 3, p. 246, 47.) Per. G.A. Oxon 4° 141

Tithes

6473. Decimæ et primitiæ collegiorum [in Universitate Oxoniensi]. (Collectanea curiosa, by J. Gutch, vol. 1, p. 188–90.) Oxf., 1781, 8°.

Gough Oxf. 65

See 1505 &c. [Memoranda on the Tithe bill. 1925].

6474. Royal commission on tithe rentcharge, 1934–35. Statement of evidence submitted by the bursars of the Oxford colleges [*and*] Appendices. Oxf., (1935), fol. 23+22 pp. G.A. Oxon c. 295

Fellowships

6474.5. Reasons for the repeal of that part of the statutes of colleges in the universities of Cambridge and Oxford, which require the taking of orders under a penalty. Lond., [*c.* 1723], 4°. 3 pp. Lambeth [Hearne records that in 1723 the Provost of Oriel declared a fellowship vacant on the orders of the visitor, as the holder was not in orders. The Lambeth MS. comprises a vol. of misc. papers of Edmund Gibson, bp. of London, who was the visitor of the college. A photographic copy of 6474.5 is in the Bodleian: Facs. d. 82.]

6474.6. HARE, A. W., A letter to Daniel K. Sandford . . . in answer to the strictures of the Edinburgh review [1821, vol. 35, p. 310] on the open colleges of Oxford [chiefly in connexion with fellowship elections]. By a member of a close college [A. W. Hare]. Oxf., 1822, 8°. 75 pp.

8° E 91 (6) Art.

6474.7. SANDFORD, SIR D. K., A letter to the reverend Peter Elmsley, A.M., in answer to the appeal made to professor Sandford, as umpire between the University of Oxford & the Edinburgh review. Oxf., 1822, 8°. 73 pp. G.A. Oxon 8° 766

6474.8. New Oxford controversy [concerning the strictures of the Edinburgh review on the open colleges of Oxford. Signed J. C. B.]. (Blackwood's Edinb. mag., 1822, vol. 11, p. 678–80.)

Per. 2705 e. 486

See 1716 [Petition against clauses of the Oxford university bill which alter the method of electing fellows &c. 1854].

6475. MEYRICK, F., Clerical tenure of fellowships, a letter. Oxf., 1854, 8°. 15 pp. G.A. Oxon 8° 63 (8)

6476. Clerical and lay fellowships. (Christ. rem., 1855, N.S., vol. 30, p. 159–73.) Per. 971 e. 44

6477. Uniformity act amendment. A bill to repeal so much of the Act of uniformity [13 & 14 Ch. II, c. 4] as relates to fellows and tutors in any college, hall or house of learning. 5 May, 1863. [Lond.], 1863, s. sh.
Pp. Eng. 1863 vol. 5
— 8 June, 1864. [Lond.], 1864, s. sh. Pp. Eng. 1864 vol. 4

6478. Fellows of colleges declaration. A bill to repeal certain portions of the Act of uniformity relating to the declaration made by fellows of colleges. 20 Feb. 1866. [Lond.], 1866, fol. 3 pp. Pp. Eng. 1866 vol. 3

6479. Uniformity act amendment. A bill to repeal certain portions of the Act of uniformity [13 & 14 Ch. II, c. 4] relating to fellows of colleges. 7 March, 1867. [Lond.], 1867, fol. 3 pp. Pp. Eng. 1867, vol. 6

6480. SIDGWICK, H., Idle fellowships. (Contemp. review, 1876, vol. 27, p. 681–93.) G.A. Oxon 4° 581 (14)

6481. ROUNDELL, C. S., Clerical headships and fellowships at the universities, a speech delivered in the House of Commons, July 9, 1880. Lond., 1880, 8°. 11 pp. G.A. Oxon b. 140 (40b)

6482. WORDSWORTH, J., The Church and the universities, a letter [on clerical fellowships, lay teaching of theology, and the substitution of lay for episcopal visitors] to C. S. Roundell. Oxf. &c., 1880, 8°. 23 pp.
100 f. 177 (21)
— Reissued with a postscript. Oxf. &c., 1880, 8°. 32 pp. 2625 e. 8 (5)

See 7315 [Bywater, I., A letter on the subject of a statement in no. 6482 concerning clerical fellowships in Exeter college. 1880].
See 1930 [Return of particulars . . . with respect to . . . the fellowships of each college [&c.]. 1886].

6483.

6484. OMAN, SIR C., The 'idle Fellows': a memory of Victorian Oxford. (Blackwood's mag., 1937, vol. 241, p. 46–55.) Per. 2705 d. 386

6485. The problem of the married fellow. (Oxf. mag., 1946, vol. 65, p. 81, 82.) Per. G.A. Oxon 4° 141

6485.1. Report on the closer integration of university teaching and research with the college system. [Confidential report to members of Congregation. Nov. 1962.] Oxf., 1962, 8°. 16 pp.

6485.2. Further report on the closer integration of university teaching and research with the college system. Suppl. no. 1 to the Univ. Gazette (3182, January 1964). Oxf., 1964, 8°. 13 pp. Per. G.A. Oxon c. 86

6485.3. Report of the Committee appointed by the Hebdomadal Council to make detailed proposals for carrying out the policy contained in the Further report on the closer integration of university teaching and research with the college system. (Suppl. no. 1, Univ. Gazette, 3214, Nov. 1964.) Oxf., 1964, 8°. 10 pp. Per. G.A. Oxon c. 86

6485.4. ROAF, D. J., Fellows and non-fellows. (Oxf. mag., 1965, N.S., vol. 5, p. 358, 59.)　　　　　　　　　　　　　　　　　Per. G.A. Oxon 4° 141

Founders' kin

6486. BROOKE, H., An appeal to the publick from an unappellate tribunal, or An impartial enquiry into the rise, progress and extent of visitatorial power, a letter, by a senior fellow of a college in Oxford [signed] Oxoniensis. Lond., 1740, 8°. 54 pp.　　　　　　　G.A. Oxon 8° 62 (8)

See also nos. 6654 &c.

6487–9.

Gardens

See 5827 [Gunther, R. T., Oxford gardens. 1912].

6490. ROHDE, E. S., Oxford's college gardens. Lond., 1932, 4°. 193 pp.
　　　　　　　　　　　　　　　　　　　　　　　　　G.A. Oxon 4° 525

6491. WARD, J. D. U., Landscape [gardening] comes to Oxford. (Architect. review, 1948, vol. 104, p. 187–96.)　　　　　　　Per. 17356 c. 8

Heraldry

See also 524–31 [University heraldry].
See 560 [Sansbury, J., Ilium in Italium. 1608].

6492. SHAW, H., The arms of the colleges of Oxford, by H. Shaw: with historical notices of the colleges by J. W. Burgon. Oxf., 1855, 4°.
　　　　　　　　　　　　　　　　　　　　　　　　　G.A. Oxon c. 12

6493. The arms of the colleges and halls of the University of Oxford emblazoned [in colour]. Oxf., 1869, 4°.　　　　　G.A. Oxon 4° 91

6494. LANDON, P., Notes on the heraldry of the Oxford colleges. (Archæologia Oxon., 1892/1895, p. 142–58, 195–210.) G.A. Oxon 4° 148 = R.

6495. CLARK, A., Heraldry of Oxford colleges. [Comments on P. Landon's Notes on the heraldry of the Oxford colleges.] (Engl. hist. review, 1895, vol. 10, p. 333–36, 543–45.)　　　　　Per. 2231 d. 342 = K.

6496. LANDON, P., Heraldry of Oxford colleges [in reply to A. Clark's notes on a previous article]. (Engl. hist. review, 1895, vol. 10, p. 541–43.)　　　　　　　　　　　　　　　Per. 2231 d. 342 = K.

6497. BARNARD, F. P., and SHEPARD, T., Arms & blazons of the colleges of Oxford. Lond., 1929, 12°. 62 pp.　　　　　　　21943 f. 3

6498. EDEN, S. F., Oxford [university] heraldic quarries. (Connoisseur, 1938, vol. 101, p. 78–81, 106.)　　　　　　　Per. 175 d. 15

6499. SQUIBB, G. D., Oxford college arms, an inquiry into the claim of the Oxford colleges to exemption from Heralds' jurisdiction. (Coat of Arms, 1952, vol. 2, p. 101–03.)　　　　　　Per. 21932 e. 42

6500. Oxford and Cambridge: arms of the colleges. Oxf., [1956], 12°.
14 pl.   21943 f. 4

Libraries and Muniment Rooms

6501. JAMES, T., Ecloga Oxonio-Cantabrigiensis, tributa in libros duo;
quorum prior continet catalogum confusum librorum manuscriptorum
in ... bibliothecaris ... academiarum Oxoniæ & Cantabrigiæ, posterior
catalogum eorundem distinctum & dispositum secundum quatuor
facultates ... opera & studio T. J. [Madan 195.] Lond., 1600, 4°.
                                                            4° F 27 Art. Seld.

6502. [*Begin.*] Whereas it is in contemplation to prepare a new catalogue of
the books in the Bodleian library ... [a request to colleges to make out
a list of books not in Bodley to make the Bodley catalogue more com-
plete]. Apr. 9. [Oxf.], 1794, s. sh.   G.A. Oxon b. 19

6503. COXE, H. O., Catalogus codicum MSS. qui in collegiis aulisque
Oxoniensibus hodie adservantur. 2 pt. Oxonii, 1852, 4°.
                                                       2590 d. Oxf. 4 = R.

See 5253 [Thomas, E. C., The libraries of Oxford, and the use of college
libraries. 1879].
See 4 [Madan, F., Rough list of MS. materials relating to Oxford ... in
college libraries &c. 1887].

6504. Classified list of periodicals and serial works taken in by college
libraries, &c., in Oxford. Oxf., 1890, 8°. 15 pp.   2590 e. Oxf. 1

See 5656 [Frere, W. H., Bibliotheca musico-liturgica, a descriptive handlist.
1901].

6505. OMAN, C., The early printed books in college libraries. Report to
librarians who have joined in the scheme for cataloguing the early
printed books in college libraries. [1911]–15. [Oxf.], (1912–16), s. sh.
                                                         2590 e. Oxf. 2, 3

6506. A list of periodicals taken by Oxford college libraries, the Ashmolean, the Taylorian & Indian institute. Oxf., 1913, 8°. 24 pp.
                                                            2590 e. Oxf. 4

6507. Early Oxford college manuscripts. (Bodl. quart. record, 1915, vol. 1,
p. 157–62.)   2590 d. Oxf. 1. 40 = R.

See 5647 [Fisher, H. A. L., MSS. in college libraries relating to history 1485–
1547. 1923].

6508. SALTER, H. E., *ed.*, Facsimiles of early charters in Oxford muniment
rooms. Oxf., 1929, 4°.   25778 c. 22 = R.

6509. HINDLE, C. J., An inter-collegiate catalogue of early printed books
[signed C. J. H.]. (Oxf. mag., 1930, vol. 48, p. 569, 70.)
                                                      Per. G.A. Oxon 4° 141

6510. HILL, R. H., The projected union catalogue of early books in Oxford
college libraries. (Libr. assoc. record, 1931, 3rd ser., vol. 1, p. 1–7.)
                                                            Per. 25891 d. 21

6511. PANTIN, W. A., College muniments. (Oxoniensia, 1936, vol. 1, p. 140–143.)   Per. G.A. Oxon 4° 658 = R.

6512. CRASTER, SIR H. H. E., Co-operation between college libraries. [Reprod. from typewriting.] [Oxf.], (1947), fol. 7 ff.   2590 c. Oxf. 1 — [Printed in 1952 in new series, vol. 4 of the Publ., Oxford bibliogr. soc., at p. 43–52.]   Soc. 258 d. 176 = A.

See 5652 [Holtzmann, W., Papsturkunden in England. 1952].

6513. Oxford college libraries in 1556, guide to an exhibition held in 1956 [in the Bodleian]. Oxf., 1956, 8°. 56 pp.   2590 e. Oxf. 1. 44 = R.

6514. JAYNE, S., Library catalogues of the English Renaissance. [Oxford colleges and private libraries, *passim*.] Berkeley &c., 1956, 8°. 225 pp.
2589 e. 91 = R.

6515. KER, N. R., Oxford college libraries in the sixteenth century. (Bodleian library record, 1959, vol. 6, p. 459–515.)
2590 d. Oxf. 1. 41 = R.

Pictures

6516. Catalogue of a loan collection of portraits of English historical personages who died prior to . . . 1625, exhibited in the Examination schools, April and May, 1904. Oxf., (1904), 8°. 61 pp.   17061 d. 10 (6) — [Illustr. ed.]   17061 d. 13

6517. Illustrated catalogue of a loan collection of portraits of English historical personages who died between 1625 and 1714, exhibited in the Examination schools . . . April and May 1905. Oxf., 1905, 4°. 104 pp.   17061 e. 26 — [Illustr. ed.]   17061 d. 14

6518. Illustrated catalogue of a loan collection of portraits of English historical personages who died between 1714 and 1837, exhibited in the Examination schools . . . April and May, 1906. Oxf., 1906, 4°. 106 pp.
17061 e. 27 (9)
— [Illustr. ed.]   17061 d. 17
— 2nd ed. 8°.   17061 e. 50

6519. POOLE, MRS. R. L., Catalogue of portraits in the possession of the University, colleges, City and County of Oxford. 3 vols. (Oxf. hist. soc., 57, 81, 82.) Oxf., 1912–26, 8°.   G.A. Oxon 8° 360 = R.

Plate and furniture

6520. An abstract of the plate presented to the King's majesty, by the several colleges of Oxford . . . 20th January 1642. (Collectanea curiosa, by J. Gutch, vol. 1, p. 227.) Oxf., 1781, 8°.   Gough Oxf. 65

6521. Ancient plate and furniture from the colleges of Oxford and the Ashmolean Museum, drawn by H. Shaw, with descriptions by sir S. R. Meyrick. Lond. &c., 1837, fol. 10 plates with letterpress.   175 b. 3

6522. SHIRLEY, A., Oxford college silver: the exhibition at the Ashmolean. (Country Life, 1928, vol. 64, p. 573–76, 681–84, 711–14, 866–69.)
Per. 384 b. 6

6523. WATTS, W. W., An exhibition of silver belonging to the colleges of Oxford [at the Ashmolean museum, Nov., 1928]. (Burlington mag., 1928, vol. 53, p. 220–26.)   Per. 170 c. 25

6524. WATTS, W. W., Catalogue of a loan exhibition of silver plate belonging to the colleges of the University of Oxford: November, 1928 [by W. W. Watts]. Oxf., 1928, 4°. 80 pp.+73 illustr.   17551 e. 16

6525. HUGHES, G. R., Silver & the Oxford colleges. (Lond. merc., 1928, vol. 19, p. 60–68.)   Per. 2705 d. 347

6526. HUGHES, G. R., Oxford plate exhibition and the modern silversmith. (Apollo, 1928, vol. 8, p. 335–40.)   Per. 170 c. 43

Postage stamps

A collection of these stamps is preserved by the Oxford University Press.

6527. Report of a meeting of the heads and bursars of colleges and halls appointed to consider a communication from the Post Office [relating to the delivery of notes and letters by college messengers. Among other suggestions, it is recommended by the committee 'that no stamp be used'. The last letter from the Secretary to the Post Office is reprinted here]. [Oxf.], 1886, 8°. 7 pp.   G.A. Oxon b. 140 (65*b*)

6528. The Oxford college stamps [signed A. S.]. (Stamp collector, 1893, vol. 3, no. 3, p. 33, 34.)   G.A. Oxon c. 302

6529. NAPIER, A. S., The Oxford college stamps, read as a paper before the Oxford philatelic society. (Stanley Gibbons monthly journ., 1893, no. 42, p. 120–23.)   G.A. Oxon c. 302

6530. WESTOBY, W. A. S., Infringements of the privileges of the Post-office. (Philatelic record, 1894, vol. 16, p. 51–56.)   G.A. Oxon c. 302

6531. WESTOBY, W. A. S., The Oxford and Cambridge college stamps. (Philatelic record, 1894, vol. 16, p. 127, 128.)   G.A. Oxon c. 302

6532. TURNER, J. R. F., College stamps and infringements of the privileges of the Post-office. (Philatelic record, 1894, vol. 16, p. 101, 102.)
G.A. Oxon c. 302

6533. TURNER, J. R. F., The Oxford university emissions. (London philatelist, 1894, vol. 3, p. 92–94, 129–31, 142, 43.) G.A. Oxon c. 302

6534. TURNER, J. R. F., The private postage stamps, post cards, and envelopes used by some of the Oxford colleges. (Stanley Gibbons monthly journ., 1894, no. 49, p. 11–13.)   G.A. Oxon c. 302

6535. TURNER, J. R. F., The English college stamps. 3 pt. (Philatelists' suppl. to The Bazaar, 1895, Feb. 11, p. 3, 5; Apr. 8, p. 27; June 10, p. 51, 52.)   G.A. Oxon c. 302

6536. CUMMINGS, J. A. H., Oxford college stamps in the recent London philatelic exhibition [signed C. Namyah]. (Philatelists' suppl. to The Bazaar, 1898, Jan. 12, p. 42, 43.) G.A. Oxon c. 302

6537. CUMMINGS, J. A. H., The college stamps of Oxford and Cambridge, their history and use from 1870 to 1886. Oxf. &c., [1904], 8°. 109 pp. 247928 e. 113

6538. SEFI, A. J., College stamps. (Country life, 1921, vol. 49, p. 221–23.) Per. 384 b. 6

6539. BELLAMY, F. A., Oxford and Cambridge college messengers, postage stamps, cards and envelopes, a short account of their origin and use, 1871–1886. Oxf., 1921, 4°. 20 pp. B.M.

6540. BELLAMY, F. A., Keble college, Oxford. Stamps of the fifth issue, 1876. (British philatelist, 1930, vol. 23, p. 1–6.) G.A. Oxon c. 302

6541. JORDAN, A. F., The Oxford Union society overprint on the rose-red stars. (Philatelic adviser, 1953, vol. 16, no. 6, p. 29–31; 1954, vol. 17, no. 1, p. 19, 20; vol. 17, no. 2, p. 13–16; vol. 17, no. 6, p. 15–17.) Per. 247928 d. 162

Scholarships (Combined)

6542. [A collection of papers relating to the combined organization of college scholarships. May 1885–Feb. 1900.] G.A. Oxon c. 212

6543. College scholarships. [Report and recommendations submitted to colleges by Council.] Mar. 9. [Oxf.], 1917, 8°. 10 pp. G.A. Oxon b. 141 (107c)

6544. [Begin.] College scholarships. [Letter dated Nov. 24, from the Vice-chancellor setting out various questions which colleges were asked about college scholarships. And] Second report of committee on college scholarships. [Oxf.], (1917), 8°. 4 pp. G.A. Oxon b. 141 (107b)

6545. CASE, T., An explanation of proposal (A) in the scheme for college scholarships. [Oxf.], (1918), s. sh. G.A. Oxon b. 141 (109a)

6546. CASE, T., Two methods of examining for college scholarships. [Oxf.], (1918), s. sh. G.A. Oxon b. 141 (109b)

Examination papers

6547. Balliol, Magdalen, Trinity, St. John's, Wadham (Pembroke) and Keble colleges. Classical scholarships (demyships) and exhibitions. Dec. 1929– . (Lond. &c.), 1929– , 8°. Per. 2626 e. 422

6548. Examination papers set for scholarships in classics at University, Exeter, Queen's, New, Corpus Christi (Worcester) and Hertford colleges. January 1941– . Oxf., 1941– , 8°. Per. 2626 e. 462 = S.

6549. Examination papers set for scholarships in history at University, Exeter, Queen's, New, Corpus Christi (Worcester) and Hertford colleges. Jan. 1941– . Oxf., 1941– , 8°. Per. 2626 e. 462 = S.

6550. Examination papers set for scholarships in history at Balliol, Magdalen, Trinity, St. John's, Wadham, Pembroke and Keble colleges. March 1941– . Oxf., 1941– . 8°.   Per. 2626 e. 462 = S.

6551. Examination papers set for scholarships in modern languages at (Exeter), Oriel, The Queen's and Brasenose colleges, Christ Church, Trinity and St. John's colleges (St. Catherine's society). Dec. 1941– . Oxf., 1941– , 8°.   Per. 2626 e. 462 = S.

6552. Examination papers set for scholarships in natural science at University, Balliol, New, Trinity and St. John's [and other] colleges. March 1941– . Oxf., 1941– , 8°.   Per. 2626 e. 462 = S. [These are issued biannually by different combinations of colleges.]

6553. Examination papers set for scholarships in classics and history at Merton, Oriel, Lincoln and Brasenose colleges, Christ Church and Jesus college. Dec. 1942– . Oxf., 1942– , 8°.   Per. 2626 e. 462 = S.

6554. Examination papers set for scholarships in modern subjects. [*Afterw.*] modern subjects scholarships at University, Balliol, New, Magdalen and Corpus Christi colleges. Dec. 1942– . Oxf., 1942– , 8°.
    Per. 2626 e. 462 = S.

6555. Examination papers set for scholarships in English at (Brasenose college and) Christ Church. (University and Brasenose colleges and Christ Church.) December 1947– . Oxf., 1947– , 8°.
    Per. 2626 e. 462 = S.

6556. Mathematical scholarships. Balliol, Oriel, Queen's, Magdalen, Corpus Christi, St. John's and Jesus. Dec. 1958.
— Mar., Dec. 1959. Merton, New college, Brasenose, Christ Church, Wadham and Hertford (and Keble). (Oxf.), 1958– , 8°.
    Per. 2626 e. 462 = S.

6557. Balliol, Magdalen, Trinity, St. John's, Wadham, Pembroke and Keble colleges. Classical scholarships, demyships and exhibitions. March 1960– . Oxf., 1960– , 8°.   Per. 2626 e. 462 = S.

Statutes

6558. Statutes of the colleges of Oxford; with royal patents of foundation, injunctions of visitors and catalogues of documents relating to the University preserved in the Public record office. [Ed. by E. A. Bond.] 3 vols. (Commissioners for inquiring into the state of the Univ. of Oxf.) Oxf. &c., 1853, 8°.   G.A. Oxon 8° 24–26 = R.

6559. Points to be dealt with in revising college statutes. n. pl., [1855], fol. 4 pp.   G.A. Oxon c. 71 (44*)

6560. Report of the Commissioners, pursuant to the 33d section of the Act 17 & 18 Vict. c. 81, on Oxford university [concerning ordinances framed for colleges by the Commissioners, and in particular concerning an ordinance made for St. John's college to which objection has been made]. [Lond.], 1858, fol. 24 pp.   Pp. Eng. 1857/58 vol. 20

6561. A bill to provide for the consideration of an ordinance which has been laid before Parliament in a report of the Oxford university commissioners. 30 Jan. 1860. [Lond.], 1860, fol. 3 pp.   Pp. Eng. 1860 vol. 5
— As amended in committee. 28 Feb. 1860. [Lond.], 1860, fol. 3 pp.
Pp. Eng. 1860 vol. 5
— [Act] (23 & 24 V., c. 23, Pub). Lond., 1860, fol. 4 pp.   L.L.
[The act provides machinery for appeal against ordinances framed by the Commissioners in respect of any college, but in particular in the case of St. John's college.]

6562. Ordinances and statutes [relating to the colleges] framed or approved by the Oxford university commissioners in pursuance of the act 17 and 18 Vict., c. 81. Oxf., 1863, 8°. 533 pp.   Clar. Press 31 a. 63

6563. SMITH, G., Old college statutes. (Proc., Oxf. architect. and hist. soc., 1864, N.S. vol. I, p. 310–12.)   Per. G.A. Oxon 8° 498 = R.

6564. New statutes made for the University by the University of Oxford commissioners under the . . . act, 1877. Oxf., 1882, 8°.
G.A. Oxon 8° 425 = R.

6565. Statutes made for the colleges and St. Edmund hall . . . in pursuance of the . . . act, 1923 . . . Oxf., 1927, 8°.   G.A. Oxon 4° 759 = R.

Visitors

See 6486 [Brooke, H., An appeal to the publick from an unappellate tribunal, or An impartial enquiry into the rise of visitatorial power. 1740].
See 6420 [An address to the archbishop of Canterbury as a visitor of colleges . . . 1791].
See 1699 [Heywood, J., Notices of the University and collegiate visitations. 1853].
See 6482 [Wordsworth, J., The Church and the universities. III. The substitution of lay for episcopal visitors. 1880].

6566. MITCHESON, R. E., Opinion [on the law of England concerning the Visitation of charities, including evidence from college records]. n. pl., (1887), 8°. 41 pp.   L.L.

INDIVIDUAL COLLEGES—FOR MEN

All Souls

General 6567–6587
Administration 6588–6597
Statutes 6598–6619
Finance and Property 6620–6629
  Contributions to University purposes 6630–6639

Members 6640–6653
Founder's kin 6654–6659
Chapel 6660–6668
Chaplain 6669–6670
Library and Archives 6671–6683
Glass, Plate, etc. 6684–6687

General

6567. [Topographical prints &c. in the Bodleian.]   G.A. Oxon a. 48

6568. Pro collegio Animarum in Oxonia. (4 Hen. VII, c. 20, Private.) 1488/89.
[Text in Shadwell's Enactments &c. See no. 956].

6569. Thanksgivings [for the founder and benefactors]. [Oxf., late 17th cent.], 2 sheets.   fol. Θ 667 (11)

6570. RANDOLPH, H., Chichlæus [a poem in Lat.]. n. pl., [1721], fol. 8 pp.
C 2. 19 (8) Art.

6571. Orationes duæ Codringtono sacræ in collegio Omnium animarum nuper habitæ, una a D. Cotes, altera ab E. Young. Oxon., 1716, 8°. 34 pp.   8° O 12 (6) Linc.

6572. BUCKLER, B., A complete vindication [by B. Buckler] of the mallard of All-Souls college, against the injurious suggestions of . . . Mr. Pointer [in Oxoniensis Academia, no. 21.] Lond., 1750, 8°. 35 pp.
Gough Oxf. 60 (5)
— 2nd ed. 1751. 64 pp.   Gough Oxf. 60 (6)
— 3rd ed. 1793.   G.A. Oxon 8° 219 (6)

6573. BILSTON, J., and MORES, E. R., Preparing for the press from an ancient MS De fucorum ordinibus continued by a modern hand; A complete history of the Mallardians. [A satire on B. Buckler's A complete vindication of the mallard of All Soul's college, by J. Bilston and E. R. Mores.] Lond., 1751, s. sh.   B.M.
— [Another ed.] Lond., 1752, fol. 4 pp.   G.A. Oxon c. 107 (31)

6574. The swopping-song of the Mallardians: an ode, n. pl., 1752, s. sh.
G.A. Oxon c. 107 (32)

6575. Collectanea ex archivis collegii Animarum omnium fidelium defunctorum de Oxonia. (Collectanea curiosa, by J. Gutch, vol. 2, p. 257–82.) Oxf., 1781, 8°.   Gough Oxf. 66

6576. Oxonia explicata et ornata. No. 4. The new front of All Souls' college. [A new method of refacing.] (The Crypt, 1829, N.S., vol. 1, p. 201–04.)   Hope 8° 285

6577. INGRAM, J., All Souls college. (Memorials of Oxford, 1837, vol. 1. 32 pp.)   G.A. Oxon 8° 18

6578. ROBARTS, C. H., All Souls college. [A letter concerning the future of the college.] Nov. 25th. n. pl., (1874), 4°. 3 pp. G.A. Oxon c. 268 (f. 27)

See 5525 [A proposal to amalgamate All Souls college and the Bodleian. 1877].

6579. ROBERTSON, C. G., All Souls' college. (Univ. of Oxf., college hist.) Lond., 1899, 8°. 234 pp.   G.A. Oxon 8° 651 (7) = R.

6580. FLETCHER, C. R. L., Mr. Gladstone at Oxford [All Souls] 1890, by C. R. L. F. Lond., 1908, 8°. 103 pp.   2288 e. 659

6581. HENRY, R. L., jr., On dining at All Souls. (Amer. Oxon., 1922, vol. 9, p. 108–11.)   Per. G.A. Oxon 8° 889

6582. MAYCOCK, A. L., All Souls. (Blackwood's mag., 1928, vol. 224, p. 371–77, 505–12.)   Per. 2705 d. 386

6583. TIPPING, H. A., All Souls. (Country Life, 1928, p. 896–904, 930–37, 964–73.)   Per. 384 b. 6

6584. JACOB, E. F., The building of All Souls college, 1438–1443. (Historical essays in honour of James Tait, 1933, p. 121–135.) 2262 d. 52 = S.

6585. JONES, A. H. M., All Souls, 1438–1938. (Oxf. mag., 1938, vol. 56, p. 602, 03; 636–38.) Per. G.A. Oxon 4° 141

6586. ROWSE, A. L., All Souls (1945). (The English past, 1951, p. 1–4.) 228 e. 858

6587. Architectural designs for All Souls college, Oxford by Nicholas Hawksmoor. [*With*] Explanation of designs. Oxf., 1960, fol & 8°. 6 pl. +8 pp. G.A. Oxon a. 129

Administration

6588. A few observations on All Souls' college . . . relative to the abuse of charities. [A criticism of the failure of the Warden and fellows to carry out the intention of the Founder.] Lond., 1819, 8°. 32 pp.
G.A. Oxon 8° 219 (12)

6589. Some animadversions on a pamphlet entitled 'A few observations on All Souls' college, Oxford'. Oxf., 1819, 8°. 63 pp. G.A. Oxon 8° 249

6590. To his grace the Archbishop of Canterbury. [Petition, dated May 17, 1859, of A. G. Watson, W. H. Fremantle, G. Lushington, to settle disputes about the rights of fellows to be present at all college meetings, election of fellows, &c.], n. pl., 1859, fol. 12 pp. G.A. Oxon c. 24 (4)
— The answer of the Warden of All Souls college [Aug. 4, 1859]. [Lond.], 1859, fol. 18 pp. G.A. Oxon c. 24 (4a)
— Correspondence [Aug. 25–Oct. 27, 1859]. n. pl., (1859), fol. 5 pp.
G.A. Oxon c. 24 (4b)
— The Queen v. the Archbishop of Canterbury. [May 4, 1860.] Lond., 1860, fol. 7 pp. G.A. Oxon c. 24 (4c)
— The reply of the petitioners to the Answer of the Warden. [June 16, 1860.] Lond., (1860), fol. 38 pp. G.A. Oxon c. 24 (4d)
— Rejoinder of the college to the Reply of the petitioners. [Sept. 28, 1860.] Lond., (1860), fol. 16 pp. G.A. Oxon c. 24 (4e)
— [Further petition, signed A. G. Watson, W. H. Fremantle. June 20, 1863.] n. pl., (1863), fol. 12 pp. G.A. Oxon c. 35 (7a)
— Answer of All Souls college to a complaint . . . by messrs. Watson and Fremantle [signed T. K. Leighton]. Mar. 29, 1864. n. pl., 1864, fol. 11 pp. G.A. Oxon c. 35 (7b)
— The reply of the applicants to the Answer of the Warden. May 2, 1864. Lond., (1864), fol. 7 pp. G.A. Oxon c. 35 (7c)

6591. Bye-laws. n. pl., [c. 1870?], 8°. [20 pp.] G.A. Oxon c. 268 (1)

6592. All Souls' college. Report of the procedure committee, December 1870. [Oxf.], (1870), s. sh. G.A. Oxon c. 268 (f. 16)

6593. To . . . the Archbishop of Canterbury, visitor of All Souls college, Oxford. [A petition of appeal by C. H. Robarts, fellow of All Souls concerning the government of the college.] n. pl., 1876, fol. 7 pp.
G.A. fol. A 139a (1)

6594. [*Begin.*] The following letters and observations . . . [concerning the rejection of C. H. Robarts' claim to the sub-wardenship of All Souls college]. Dec. 28. n. pl., 1876, s. sh.   G.A. fol. A 139 *a* (2)

6595. ROBARTS, C. H., [A letter to the Warden of All Souls college, dated 12 Feb., 1878, concerning C. H. Robarts' Petition of appeal to the Archbishop of Canterbury, visitor of the college.] n. pl., (1878), fol. 4 pp.   G.A. Oxon 4° 408 (1)

6596. All Souls college. [Correspondence between C. H. Robarts, the Warden of All Souls college, and the Archbishop of Canterbury, concerning C. H. Robarts' Petition of appeal to the Archbishop of Canterbury, visitor of the college.] n. pl., [1878], 8°. 7 pp.
          G.A. Oxon 4° 408 (2)

6597. [*Begin.*] All Souls college, Friday night, February 15. [Correspondence between the Warden and C. H. Robarts dated Feb. 15, 16, 18, 1878 in connection with C. H. Robarts' letter dated Feb. 12.] n. pl., [1878], s. sh.   G.A. Oxon c. 268 (f. 34)

Statutes

6598. WARD, G. R. M., *transl.* The statutes of All Souls college. Lond., 1841, 8°. 208 pp.   G.A. Oxon 8° 29
— [Another issue]. 1843.   G.A. Oxon 8° 734

6599. Statutes of the colleges . . . (All Souls college.) Oxf. &c., 1853, 8°. 122 pp.   G.A. Oxon 8° 24 = R.

6600. Oxford university. Ordinances . . . in relation to . . . All Souls [and 10 other] colleges respectively. [Lond.], 1857, fol. 139 pp.
          Pp. Eng. 1857 vol. 32

6601. Ordinances and statutes framed or approved by the . . . Commissioners . . . (All Souls college, p. 241–60.) Oxf., 1863, 8°.
          Clar. Press 31 a. 63

6602. All Souls' college. Report of committee appointed at the November meeting [to consider the Draft Statutes to be submitted to the University Commissioners]. n. pl., [1878], 4°. 4 pp.
          G.A. Oxon c. 268 (f. 34)

6603. All Souls' college. Report of the committee appointed Feb. 15th, 1878 [to consider the resolutions of the University Commissioners with regard to college reform]. n. pl., [1878], 4°. 3 pp.
          G.A. Oxon c. 268 (f. 33)

6604. A paper presented to H.M. University Commissioners by the Warden and seven Fellows of All Souls' college [disagreeing with the majority scheme of college reform to be reported on by the committee appointed on Feb. 15th]. July 23rd. 1878. (Oxf., 1878), 4°. 3 pp.
          G.A. Oxon c. 268 (f. 34)

6605. Reasons to be submitted to the Commissioners in support of Draft Statutes of All Souls college. n. pl., [1878], 4°. 4 pp.
G.A. Oxon c. 268 (f. 34)

6606. Statutes proposed to be made . . . for All Souls' college. Nov. 1880. (Oxf.), 1880, 8°. 22 pp.   G.A. Oxon 8° 425 (3) = R.

6607. Statutes proposed to be made by the University of Oxford commissioners for All Souls' college. April 1881. [Lond.], 1881, fol. 14 pp.
G.A. Oxon c. 8 (36*)

6608. Statutes of All Souls college. (Univ. of Oxf. and Cambr. act, 1877. Oxford. Thirty-six statutes made by the Univ. of Oxf. commissioners, 1881, p. 1–11, 245.)   Pp. Eng. 1882 vol. 51

6609. Statute made by . . . All Souls college, 21st Nov. 1903, amending Statute 12a, clause 2. Lond., 1904, s. sh.   Pp. Eng. 1904 vol. 75

6610. Statute made by . . . All Souls college, 24th Feb. 1906, and sealed 31st Mar. 1906, altering Statute III, clause 7. Lond., 1906, s. sh.
Pp. Eng. 1906 vol. 90

6611. Statute made by . . . All Souls college, 28th Feb. 1908 and sealed 3rd Mar. 1908, amending Statute 12a, clause 2. Lond., 1908, fol. 3 pp.
Pp. Eng. 1908 vol. 86

6612. Statute made by . . . All Souls college, 4th July 1908, and sealed 11th July 1908, altering and amending Statute III, clause 7. Lond., 1908, fol. 3 pp.   Pp. Eng. 1908 vol. 86

6613. Statute made by . . . All Souls college . . . on the 5th June, 1911, and sealed on the 21st July, 1911, making certain alterations in the existing statutes. 9 November 1911. Lond., 1911, fol. 3 pp.
Pp. Eng. 1911 vol. 59

6614. Statute made by . . . All Souls college, 9th Dec. 1911, and sealed 5th Feb. 1912, amending certain of the existing statutes. Lond., 1912, fol. 5 pp.   Pp. Eng. 1912/13 vol. 65

6615. Statute made by . . . All Souls college . . . on the 13th May, 1913 (and sealed on the 3rd June, 1913) amending Statute IV. (1), (2) and (4). 10 Feb. 1914. Lond., 1914, s. sh.   Pp. Eng. 1914 vol. 64

6616. Statute made by . . . All Souls college, 13th June 1916 and sealed 13th July 1916, amending Statutes III and IV. Lond., 1916, fol. 3 pp.
Pp. Eng. 1916 vol. 22

6617. Statute made by . . . All Souls college, 28th Oct. 1916, and sealed 22nd Nov. 1916, amending Statutes III and IX. Lond., 1917, s. sh.
Pp. Eng. 1917/18 vol. 25

6618. Statutes made for the colleges . . . (All Souls college.) Oxf., 1927, 8°. 38 pp.   G.A. Oxon 4° 759 = R.

6619. JACOB, E. F., The Warden's text of the foundation statutes of All Souls college. (Antiq. journ., 1935, vol. 15, p. 420–31.)
Per. 17572 d. 73 = R.

Finance and property

6620. An act for confirmacion of certen landes [in Leicestershire &c.] to the Warden and Colledge of the Soules of all faithful people deceased of Oxon and of other landes to sir William Smith. (4 James I, c. 9, Private.) 1606/07.
[Précis in Shadwell's Enactments &c. See no. 956.]

6621. William Powell alias Hinton esq.; plaintiffe; the Warden and fellows of All-Soules colledge in Oxford defendants. In the Chancellors court of the University . . . in a pretended cause of damage. [Madan 2291.]
[Lond.], (1656), 4°. 8 pp.   Wood 515 (16)

6622. An act for vesting in the Warden and College of All-Souls in Oxford, and their successors, certain houses and ground belonging to the parish of St. Mary in Oxford. (1 G. I, sess. 2, c. 5, Private.) 1714.
[Pércis in Shadwell's Enactments &c. See no. 956.]
— Bill. n. pl., n.d., fol. 7 pp.   MM 31 (109) Jur. 3rd ser.

See 8692 [George Clarke benefactions to All Souls. 1737].

6623. An act for annexing the rectory of East Lockinge . . . to the office of Warden of the College of the Souls of all faithful people deceased. (4 G. III, c. 26, Private.) 1763–4.
[Text in Shadwell's Enactments &c. See no. 956.]

6624. An act for effecting an exchange between . . . All Souls . . . and Thomas Penrice [in Gower, Glam., and Northants]. (1 & 2 V., c. 30, Private.) n. pl., 1838, fol. 10 pp.   L.L.

6625. An act for enabling the Warden and College of the Souls of all faithful people deceased . . . to grant building and improving leases of their estates in . . . Middlesex. (9 & 10 V., c. 389, L. & P.) Lond., 1846, fol. 12 pp.   L.L.

6626. All Souls college. Summary of account, 1870–71 (–72/73). (Lond., 1872–74), 4°.   G.A. Oxon b. 268 (2–4)

6627. FLETCHER, C. R. L., All Souls college versus lady Jane Stafford, 1587 [in connexion with the granting of a lease of woods in Middlesex]. (Oxf. hist. soc., 1885, vol. 5, p. 179–248.)   G.A. Oxon 8° 360 = R.

6628. BLACKSTONE, SIR W., Dissertation on the accounts of All Souls college, Oxford. [Written in 1753 for the Bursar of arts, B. Buckler. Ed. by sir W. Anson.] Lond., 1898, 4°. 52 pp.   Roxburghe club 129

6629. FABER, G., Notes on the history of the All Souls bursarships and the college agency. (Plymouth, 1950), 8°. 92 pp.   G.A. Oxon 8° 1226

CONTRIBUTIONS TO UNIVERSITY PURPOSES

6630. BERNARD, M., [*Begin.*] There is a question . . . [concerning the excessive income of the Chichele professor of international law, with suggestions for its modification and disposal. Signed M. Bernard].
[Oxf.], (1874), 4°. 4 pp.   G.A. Oxon c. 268 (f. 24)

6631. ANSON, W. R., All Souls college. [A letter proposing specific endowments for Modern history and Law, and suggesting amendments to the regulations governing fellowships.] Nov. 26. n. pl., (1874), s. sh.

G.A. Oxon c. 268 (f. 29)

6632. NUTT, J. W., All Souls college. [A letter suggesting an annual college contribution to the funds of the Bodleian library.] Nov. 26. n. pl., (1874), s. sh.

G.A. Oxon c. 268 (f. 29)

6633. MÜLLER, M., All Souls college. [A letter suggesting that the college contribution to University funds should be at the same rate as other colleges, and recommending an alteration in the regulations governing fellowships.] Nov. 25. n. pl., (1874), 4°. 3 pp. G.A. Oxon c. 268 (f. 28)

6634. MONSON, E., All Souls college. [A letter concerning how the college should contribute towards the cost and method of University reform.] Nov. 10. n. pl., (1874), 4°. 3 pp. G.A. Oxon c. 268 (f. 27)

6635. BERTIE, H. W., All Souls college. [A letter concerning how the college should contribute to the cost and method of University reform.] Nov. 10. n. pl., (1874), s. sh. G.A. Oxon c. 268 (f. 26)

6636. BERNARD, M., All Souls college. [Suggestions concerning how the college should contribute towards the cost and method of University reform.] n. pl., [1874], 4°. 3 pp. G.A. Oxon c. 268 (f. 26)

6637. BURROWS, M., All Souls' college. [A letter concerning how the college should contribute towards the cost and method of University reform.] Nov. 25. n. pl., 1874, 4°. 9 pp. G.A. Oxon c. 268 (f. 26)

6638. All Souls college. Abstract of suggestions [of fellows concerning the college contributions towards the cost and method of University reform]. n. pl., [1874], 4°. 3 pp. G.A. Oxon c. 268 (f. 30)

6639. All Souls college. Report of committee appointed 31st October, 1874 [to frame answers to a circular from the Vice Chancellor concerning college contributions to the cost and method of University reform]. n. pl., [1874], s. sh. G.A. Oxon c. 268 (f. 30)

Members

6640. A step to Oxford: or, A mad essay on the reverend mr. Tho. Creech's hanging himself (as 'tis said) for love. With the character of his mistress. In a letter . . . Lond., 1700, 4°. 23 pp. Bliss B 366

6641. GARDINER, B., Reasons against the profession of physick in All-souls college, . . . more especially if used as an argument to release the fellows there, from the obligation of taking upon them holy orders [by B. Gardiner]. n. pl., [1709?], 4°. 13 pp. Gough Oxf. 60 (15)

6642. GARDINER, B., The case of commutation of faculties in All-Souls college, Oxford [by B. Gardiner]. n. pl., 1713, s. sh.

G. Pamph. 2288 (15)

6643. Juramentum Sociorum Coll. Omn. Anim. [and Testimony]. [Oxf., *c.* 1775], fol. 5 pp.   G.A. Oxon b. 19

6644. BURROWS, M., Worthies of All Souls. Lond., 1874, 8°. 452 pp.
G.A. Oxon 8° 191

6645. All Souls college. Selected Indian civil service candidates. Report of committee [of the college appointed to investigate the possibility of admitting candidates to the college]. n. pl., (1875), 4°. 8 pp.
G.A. Oxon c. 268 (f. 31)

6645.5. FIRTH, C. H., Note on fellowship examination in history. [Oxf.], (1903), 8°. 3 pp.   Firth b. 36 (75*b*)

See 3908 [Burrows, M., Autobiography. 1908].

6646. YOUNG, G. M., A provisional list of the members of parliament coming from All Souls college [by G. M. Young]. [Oxf., *c.* 1910], 8°. 12 pp.   22772 e. 66 (15)

6647. The text of the old betting book of All souls college, 1815–1873, with a comm. by C. Oman. Oxf., 1912, 8°. 178 pp.   G.A. Oxon 8° 813

6648. The text of the Second betting book of All Souls college, 1873–1919, with comm. by C. Oman. Oxf., priv. printed, 1938, 8°. 184 pp.
G.A. Oxon 4° 776

6649. All Souls college. Roll of service. Oxf., [1919], 8°. 13 pp.
G.A. Oxon 8° 1230 (4)

6650. A memoir of . . . sir William Anson . . . ed. by H. Hensley Henson. Oxf., 1920, 8°. 242 pp.   26011 d. 52

6651. JACOB, E. F., Two lives of archbishop Chichele, with an appendix containing an early book list of All Souls college. (Bulletin, John Rylands libr., 1932, vol. 16, p. 428–81.)   Per. 2590 d. Manch. 2. 5 = B.
— Repr. 56 pp.   11116 d. 13

6652. BRODRIBB, C. W., Government by mallardry, a study in political ornithology [by C. W. Brodribb]. (Lond., 1932), 8°. 8 pp.
G.A. Oxon 8° 1230 (3)

See 4700 [Guiness, J., Portraits of sir Nathaniel Lloyd. 1960].

6653. ROWSE, A. L., All Souls and appeasement. Lond. &c., 1961, 8°. 122 pp.   2489 e. 285

Founders' kin

6654. CAWLEY, J., The case of Founders kinsmen: with relation to the statutes of - - - - - college [by J. Cawley]. Lond., [1694], 4°. 23 pp.
G.A. Oxon 8° 104

6655. Johannis Anstis ad librum Anglice scriptum, cui titulus The case of founders kinsmen &c. [by J. Cawley]. Latine responsio. n. pl., [1728?], 4°. p. 1–64.   Gough Oxf. 60 (2)

See 6486 [Founders' kin. 1740].

6656. BLACKSTONE, SIR W., An essay on collateral consanguinity ... more particularly as it is regarded by the statutes of All Souls college [by sir W. Blackstone]. Lond. &c., 1750, 8°. 78 pp.   Gough Oxf. 60 (4)

6657. BLACKSTONE, SIR W., [Letter concerning founder's kin in connexion with All Souls college 14 Feb., 1762.] (Amer. journ. of legal hist., 1957, vol. 1, p. 368–70.)   L.L.
— Repr. Phila., 1958, 8°. 18 pp.   L.L.

6658. BUCKLER, B., Stemmata Chicheleana: or, A genealogical account of some of the families derived from Thomas Chichele ... all whose descendants are held to be entitled to fellowships in All Souls college, Oxford, by virtue of their consanguinity to ... the founder. [By B. Buckler. *With*] A supplement. Oxf., 1765, 75, 4°.   2182 C. d. 6

6659. The appeal of John Whalley Master, B.A. of Brasen-nose college to the archbishop of Canterbury, visitor ... of All Souls college ... against the warden and fellows thereof, relative to his right of admission to a fellowship in All-Souls college, as founder's kin. Heard in Doctors Commons, July, 1792. Lond., 1794, 8°. 238 pp.   Gough Oxf. 50 (7)

Chapel

6660. (Report of the) Chapel restoration committee. [1870]; Easter, 1871; Oct. 30, 1871; Easter, 1872; Whitsuntide, 1872; Dec. 14, 1872; Nov. 1873; Whitsuntide, 1874; Oct., 1874; Dec. 1874; Easter, 1875; Dec. 1878; Easter 1879. [Oxf., 1870]–79, 8°.
G.A. Oxon c. 268 (f. 18, 22, 23, 26, 30, 31, 34, 35, 36)

6661.

6662. All Souls' college chapel. [Appeal for funds. Aug. 1871.] n. pl., (1871), 8°. 4 pp.   G.A. Oxon c. 268 (f. 19)

6663. CLUTTON, H., A narrative and correspondence relating to the restoration of All souls college chapel. n. pl., 1872, 8°. 33 pp.
G.A. Oxon 8° 957

6664. All Souls' college chapel reredos. (Builder, 1879, vol. 37, p. 489.)
N. 1863 c. 1

6665. ['Pilgrims bottles' used as altar-cruets in the college chapel.] (Proc., Soc. of antiq., 1887, ser. 2, vol. 11, p. 242–44.)
Per. G.A. Gen. top. 8° 524 = R.

6666. TOYNBEE, M. R., Robert Streater and All Souls chapel. (Oxoniensia, 1943/44, vol. 8/9, p. 205.)   Per. G.A. Oxon 4° 658 = R.

6667. Monumental inscriptions in the chapel of All Souls, transcr. by F. E. Hutchinson, prepared for publication by sir Edmund Craster. Oxf., 1949, 8°. 55 pp.   G.A. Oxon 8° 1228

6668. SPARROW, J., An Oxford altar-piece [note *and*] A further note. (Burlington mag., 1960, vol. 102, p. 4–9; 452–55.)   Per. 170 c. 25

Chaplain

6669. FINCH, L. W., The case of mr. Jonas Proast [who objected to being removed from the post of chaplain of All-Souls college. Signed L. W. Finch]. n. pl., [*c.* 1695], 4°. 17 pp.   Gough Oxf. 60 (16)

6670. PROAST, J., The case of Jonas Proast [against L. W. Finch, who removed him from the post of chaplain of All Souls college]. n. pl., [*c.* 1695], fol. 4 pp.   Wood 657 (55)

Library and archives

6671. Catalogus virorum illustrium quorum iconibus bibliotheca collegii Omnium animarum Oxon. exornatur. n. pl., [17—], 4°. 4 pp.
Gough Oxf. 60 (14)

6672. An account of an ancient marble tripod in the library of All Souls' college. (The Topographer, 1789, vol. 1, p. 513, 14.)   Douce VV 14

6673. COXE, H. O., Catalogue of manuscripts in the library of All-Souls college [by H. O. Coxe]. Oxf., 1842, 4°. 99 pp.   2590 d. Oxf. 2. 3

6674. ROBARTS, C. H., All Souls' college. [Remarks, signed C. H. R., concerning the library.] Dec. 28. [Oxf.], (1867), 4°. 2 leaves.
G.A. Oxon b. 32 (23)

6675. ROBARTS, C. H., Some remarks [signed C. H. Robarts] concerning the library of All Souls' college. (Oxf., 1867), 8°. 13 pp.
G.A. Oxon 8° 105 (2)

6676. All Souls' college. Report (2nd–[6th] report) of the Library committee, 1869(–74); [*and*] 1893– . [Oxf.], (1869–), 8° &c.
G.A. Oxon c. 268 (f. 39–41); Per. 2590 d. Oxf. 2. 2

6677. ROBARTS, C. H., Some further remarks [signed C. H. Robarts] on the administration of the All Souls' library endowment. n. pl., 1869, 8°. 15 pp.   G.A. Oxon 8° 705 (13)

6678. MARTIN, C. T., Catalogue of the archives in the muniment rooms of All Souls' college. Lond., 1877, 4°. 467 pp.
2590 d. Oxf. 2. 1 = R.

6679. Bookbinding in the library of All Souls college, 12 plates drawn by J. J. Wild. n. pl., 1880, fol. 20 sheets.   25897 b. 3

6679.1. P., R. E. The Codrington library. (N. & Q., 1880, 6th ser., vol. 2, p. 421, 22.)   Per. 3974 e. 405 = A.

6680. Catalogue of the books contained in the Codrington library, All Souls college, Oxford. Vol. 1. A–C. [No more publ.] Oxf., 1923, fol. 304 pp.   2590 c. Oxf. 2. 1

6681. Report on the history of the Codrington library. [Oxf.], (1929), 8°. 8 pp.   2590 e. Oxf. 9. 1

See 5256 [Streeter, B. H., The chained library. 1931].

6682. An early book list of All Souls college [ed. by E. F. Jacob]. (Bull., John Rylands libr., 1932, vol. 16, p. 469–81.)
Per. 2590 d. Manch. 2. 5 = B.

6683. WEISS, R., Henry VI and the library of All Souls college. (Engl. hist. review, 1942, vol. 57, p. 102–05.) Per. 2231 d. 342 = K.

Glass, plate, etc.

6684. HOPE, W. H. ST. JOHN, [Mazers at All Souls.] (Archaeologia, 1887, vol. 50, p. 136, 137, 150, 155, 161, 166.)
Per. G.A. Gen. top. 4° 162 = R.

6685. Inventory of jewels and plate at All Souls' college, 1448. (Archaeol. journ., 1894, vol. 51, p. 120–22.) Per. G.A. Gen. top. 8° 529 = R.

6686. EVANS, J., [Note on a 14th-century enamelled lid at All Souls college.] (Proc., Soc. of antiq., 1918, ser. 2, vol. 30, p. 92–97.)
Per. G.A. Gen. top. 8° 524 = R.

6687. HUTCHINSON, F. E., Medieval glass at All Souls college, a history and description, based on notes of G. M. Rushforth. Lond., 1949, 4°. 67 pp.+31 pl. G.A. Oxon 4° 651

Balliol

General

6688. [Topographical prints, &c. in the Bodleian.] G.A. Oxon a. 49

6689. SAVAGE, H., Balliofergus, or, A commentary upon the foundation, founders and affaires of Balliol colledge. Whereunto is added An exact catalogue of all the heads of the same colledge . . . Oxf., 1668, 4°. 129 pp. Gough Oxf. 114
[A ms. index to this work: MS. Bodl. Add. A 204.]

See 8527 [Kilner, J., Of University and Balliol colleges founded subsequent to Merton college. 1790].

6690. INGRAM, J., Balliol college. (Memorials of Oxford, 1837, vol. 1. 16 pp.) G.A. Oxon 8° 18

See 2913 [Chase, D. P., Balliol college and the Savilian professorship of astronomy. 1856].

6691. New buildings at Balliol. (Builder, 1877, vol. 35, p. 89.) N. 1863 c. 1

6692. Heraldic glass, Balliol college [in the new hall]. (Builder, 1877, vol. 35, p. 165.) N. 1863 c. 1

6693. Balliol college new hall. (Builder, 1879, vol. 37, p. 1109–11.)
N. 1863 c. 1

6694. [Appeal for funds to purchase a sports ground, with plan and list of donations.] n. pl., [c. 1890], fol. 4 pp.   G.A. Oxon c. 269 (f. 43)
— [With list of further donations.] n. pl., n. d., fol. 4 pp.
G.A. Oxon c. 269 (f. 44)

6695. PARAVICINI, F. DE, Early history of Balliol college. Lond., 1891, 8°. 370 pp.   G.A. Oxon 8° 476

6696. Some notes on Balliol college in Elizabeth's reign. (Oxf. mag., 1892, vol. 10, p. 332–34.)   Per. G.A. Oxon 4° 141

6697. Domus de Balliolo. [8 facsimiles of charters and seals relating to Balliol college, ed. by sir J. Conroy.] n. pl., [1893], fol.
G.A. Oxon b. 12

6698. DAVIS, H. W. CARLESS, Balliol college. (Univ. of Oxf., college hist.) Lond., 1899, 8°. 237 pp.   G.A. Oxon 8° 651 (11)
— (Revised ed.) revised by R. H. C. Davis and Richard Hunt, and suppl. by H. Hartley and others. Oxf., 1963, 8°. 329 pp.
G.A. Oxon 8° 1469 = R.

6699. SALTER, H. E., ed., The Oxford deeds of Balliol college. Oxf., 1913, 8°. 388 pp.   G.A. Oxon 8° 876
— [Another issue.] (Oxf. hist. soc., 64.) Oxf., 1913, 8°. 388 pp.
G.A. Oxon 8° 360 = R.

6700. Balliol college war memorial book, 1914–1919. 2 vols. Glasg., 1924, 4°.   G.A. Oxon 4° 513

6701. 1284–1931. The site of the college. n. pl., (1931), 4°. 4 pp.
G.A. Oxon c. 269

6702. The Balliol rhymes, ed. by W. G. Hiscock. Oxf., 1939, 8°. 34 pp.
2808 e. 43
— [Another ed.] Oxf., 1955, 8°. 34 pp.   2808 e. 54

See 3560 [Henry Wall's notes, 1844 on the machinations against Ward which took place in the University generally and in Balliol in particular. 1959].

6703. KEIR, SIR D. L., and GREGSON, P., The Atlantic crossing trust [providing travelling scholarships in America for Balliol college undergraduates]. (Amer. Oxonian, 1959, vol. 46, p. 65–70.)
Per. G.A. Oxon 8° 889

6704. Balliol songs. n. pl., n. d., 8°. 4 pp.   G.A. Oxon c. 269

Administration

6705.

6706. To the Master and Fellows of Balliol college. At a meeting of the undergraduate members ... it was ... resolved to present the follow-

ing statement . . . [Complaints about the quality of hall dinners and the commons system, with suggested remedies.] n. pl., [1864], 4°. 3 pp.
G.A. Oxon c. 269 (f. 1)

6707. Memorandum respecting admissions to Balliol college. [1866?], 1879. [Oxf., 1866?], 79, 8°.   G.A. Oxon c. 269 (f. 4, 5)

6708. Rules respecting members of Balliol college. [c. 1868]; 1871, 76, 83. [Oxf., c. 1868]–83, s. sh. &c.   G.A. Oxon c. 269 (f. 3, 43)

6709. Balliol college shop and store list. Oct., 1880, 1896. [Oxf.], 1880, 96, 8°.   G.A. Oxon c. 269 (f. 5, 7)

6710. Balliol college. College charges [food and drink]. 1883, 89. [Oxf.], 1883, 89, 8°.   G.A. Oxon c. 269 (5, 7)

6711. Balliol college (record). [Report.] 1899/1900– . (Oxf.), 1900– , 8°.
Per. G.A. Oxon 8° 510*; 1084

[The Bodleian set is imperfect.]

6712.

6713. ADDISON, W. G., Academic reform at Balliol, 1854–1882: T. H. Green and Benjamin Jowett. (Church quarterly review, 1952, vol. 153, p. 89–98.)   Per. 1419 e. 402 = S.

Statutes

6714. Statutes of the colleges . . . (Balliol college.) Oxf. &c., 1853, 8°. xxii +69 pp.   G.A. Oxon 8° 24 = R.

6715. Copy of an ordinance framed by the Oxford university commissioners . . . for the consolidation of scholarships in Balliol college . . . and for other purposes. 9 June, 1856. (Copies of four ordinances, &c., p. 2–4.) [Lond.], 1857, fol.   Pp. Eng. 1857 vol. 13

6716. Oxford university. Copies of ordinances in relation to . . . Balliol [and other] colleges, respectively. [Lond.], 1857, fol. 17 pp.
Pp. Eng. 1857 vol. 32

6717. Oxford university. Copies of two ordinances . . . in relation to the foundation of mr. John Snell, within Balliol college . . . and amending a former ordinance in relation to that college. [Lond.], 1858, fol. 7 pp.
Pp. Eng. 1857/8 vol. 46

6718. Ordinances and statutes framed or approved by the . . . Commissioners . . . (Balliol college, p. 47–77.) Oxf., 1863, 8°. Clar. Press 31 a. 63

6719. Statutes proposed to be made . . . for Balliol college. Nov. 1880. (Oxf.), 1880, 8°. 33 pp.   G.A. Oxon 8° 425 (4) = R.

6720. Statutes proposed to be made by the University of Oxford commissioners, for Balliol college. May 1881. [Lond.], 1881, fol. 20 pp.
G.A. Oxon c. 8 (65)

See 7950 [Statute: union of New Inn hall to Balliol college. 1881.]

6721. Statutes of Balliol college. (Univ. of Oxf. and Cambr. act, 1877. Oxford. Thirty-six statutes made by the Univ. of Oxf. commissioners, 1881, p. 11–25, 246.) Pp. Eng. 1882 vol. 51

6722. A statute for the union of Balliol college and New Inn hall. (Univ. of Oxf. and Cambr. act, 1877. Oxford. Four statutes made by the . . . Commissioners, 1881, p. 1, 2.) Lond., 1882, fol. Pp. Eng. 1882 vol. 51

6723. Statute made by . . . Balliol college, 14th Nov. 1896, amending the statute concerning 'The Fellows'. Lond., 1897, s. sh.
Pp. Eng. 1897 vol. 70

6724. Statute made by . . . Balliol college, 10th Dec. 1901, amending Statute V. Lond., 1902, s. sh. Pp. Eng. 1902 vol. 80

6725. Statute made by . . . Balliol college, 15th Dec. 1903, amending Statute V, clause 3(a). Lond., 1904, s. sh. Pp. Eng. 1904 vol. 75

6726. Two statutes made by . . . Balliol college, 26th May 1904, amending (i) Statute III, and (ii) Statute IV, and Schedule B. Lond., 1905, s. sh.
Pp. Eng. 1905 vol. 60

6727. Statute made by . . . Balliol college, 23rd Nov. 1904, amending Statute IV and Schedule B. Lond., 1905, s. sh. Pp. Eng. 1905 vol. 60

6728. Statute made by . . . Balliol college, 23rd Nov. 1904, amending Statute IV and Schedule B. Lond., 1906, s. sh. Pp. Eng. 1906 vol. 90

6729. Statutes made for Balliol . . . and A statute made for Balliol college . . . and for New Inn hall . . . by the University of Oxford commissioners acting in pursuance of the Universities of Oxford and Cambridge act, 1877: together with the subsequent amendments. Oxf., 1909, 8°. 39 pp. G.A. Oxon 8° 1374

6730. Statute made by . . . Balliol college . . . on the 9th October 1913, and sealed on the 29th January 1914, amending Statute III. 16 (D) and (E). 11 May 1914. Lond., 1914, s. sh. Pp. Eng. 1914 vol. 64

6731. Statutes made for the colleges . . . (Balliol college.) Oxf., 1927, 8°. 45 pp. G.A. Oxon 4° 759 = R.

Finance and property

6732. An act to ascertain and settle the payment of the impropriate tythes of the parish of Saint Lawrence Old Jury in London to . . . Balliol college . . . and for confirming an award made concerning the same. (7 & 8 Will. III, c. 18, Private.) 1695/6.
[Précis in Shadwell's Enactments &c. See no. 956.]

6733. An act to enable . . . Baliol college . . . to convey certain lands and possessions . . . in the counties of Salop and Radnor, to William Pearce Hall and John Woodhouse, in exchange for other lands in the county of Radnor . . . (14 G. III, c. 104, Private.) n. pl., 1774, fol. 12 pp. L.L.

6734. An act for annexing a portion of the rectory and of the rectory manor
. . . of Huntspill . . . to the office of Master of Baliol college. (18 G. III,
c. 35, Private.) [Lond.], 1778, fol. 5 pp.   L.L.

6735. An act for carrying into execution an agreement between the Master
and scholars of Balliol college . . . and the mayor [&c.] . . . of the City of
London for vesting in the said mayor . . . certain ground and buildings
in the parish of Saint Lawrence, Jewry, London and for securing to the
said Master and scholars . . . certain yearly rents in lieu thereof. (32 G.
III, c. 12, Private.) n. pl., 1792, fol. 9 pp.   L.L.

6736. Balliol college (1904) endowment fund [and] The needs of Balliol.
[Oxf., 1907], 4°. 4 pp.   Firth b. 36 (75a)

6737. FRYDE, E. B., and HIGHFIELD, J. R. L., An Oxfordshire deed of
Balliol college [granting 12 acres of meadow at Steeple Aston to the
college in 1321]. (Oxoniensia, 1955, vol. 20, p. 40–45.)
                                           Per. G.A. Oxon 4° 658 = R.Top.

Members

6738. [*Begin.*] The bearer hereof, Christopher Angell . . . [Testimonials
from Cambridge, Salisbury & Oxford]. [Madan 462.] [Oxf., 1618],
s. sh.   Wood 516 (3)

6739. ANGELOS, C., Ἐγκώμιον τῆς . . . Μεγαλῆς Βρεττανίας . . . An
encomion of . . . Great Britaine, and of . . . Cambridge and Oxford. [In
Gr. and Engl.] [Madan 471.] Cambr., 1619, 4°. 32 pp.
                                                    4° A 57 (4) Art. Seld.

6740. GIBSON, S., Christopher Angel, teacher of Greek. (The glory that is
Greece, ed. by H. Hughes, 1944, p. 57–61.)   247161 e. 15

6741. MAKRYMIKHALOS, S. I., Χριστοφόρος Ἄγγελος, ὁ ἑλληνοδιδάσκαλος
τῆς Ὀξφόρδης, 1575–1638. Βιβλιογρ. μελέτη. Ἀνατυπ. ἀπὸ τὰ "Πελο-
ποννησιακά", τομ. β' (p. 219–46). Ἀθῆναι, 1957, 8°.   2998 d. 171

6742. The case of James Cochrane. 1772.

6743. HEIGHWAY, R., Humbly addressed to the . . . vice-chancellor, the
provost of Queen's, and the president of St. John's college [as trustees
of Snell's charity. A reply by R. Heighway, tutor, to 'The case of James
Cochrane', a commoner of Balliol college]. n. pl., [1772], 4°. 4 pp.
                                                          Gough Oxf. 89 (8)

See 2881 [Love, S., Statement refuting a charge of negligence made by J. A.
Cochrane. 1772].

6744. A true narrative of three wicked and bloody murthers committed in
three several months. The first was at Oxford, committed by Thomas
Hovell, a taylor; upon the body of John White, a scholar, [servitor of
Balliol college]. [Madan 3254.] [Lond.], 1680, 4°. 8 pp.

6745. The masque of B-ll--l. [Epigrams on members of the college.] n. pl.
[1881], s. sh.   G.A. Oxon b. 178

BIOGRAPHY.

6745.5. HARTLEY, SIR H., Balliol men. Oxf., 1963, 8°. 36 pp.
G.A. Oxon 8° 1473

6746. LAWRENCE, SIR A., The masters of Balliol [in the 19th cent.].
(Publ. admin., 1926, vol. 4, p. 107–12.)   Per. 24853 d. 4 = P.

6747. SMITH, A. L., Thomas Allnutt, earl Brassey, address by the Master
of Balliol. Oxf., 1919, 4°. 8 pp.   G.A. Oxon 4° 399 (16)

6748. The life and work of Benjamin Jowett, master of Balliol. Reminiscences and memorials by friends and pupils. (Westminster gazette
'extra', no. 4.) (Lond.), 1893, 4°. 28 pp.   G.A. Oxon 4° 119 (4)

6749. CAMPBELL, L., 'The master of Balliol' an address [on prof. Jowett].
Suppl. to 'College echoes'. [Oxf.]. (1893), 4°. 8 pp.
G.A. Oxon 4° 262 (2)

6750. TOLLEMACHE, L. A., Benjamin Jowett, master of Balliol. Lond.,
[1895], 8°. 141 pp.   G.A. Oxon 8° 614

6751. ABBOTT, E., and CAMPBELL, L., The life and letters of Benjamin
Jowett. 2 vols. Lond., 1897, 8°.   G.A. Oxon 4° 189, 190

6752. JOWETT, B., Letters, arranged and ed. by E. Abbott and L. Campbell. Lond., 1899, 8°. 262 pp.   G.A. Oxon 4° 203

6753. FABER, G., Jowett, a portrait with background. Lond., 1957, 8°.
456 pp.   G.A. Oxon 8° 1352
— 2nd ed. 1958.   G.A. Oxon 8° 1362 = S.

6754. Arthur Lionel Smith, master of Balliol, 1916–1924, a biography and
some reminiscences by his wife. Lond., 1928, 8°. 326 pp.
G.A. Oxon 8° 1060

6755. MACKAIL, J. W., James Leigh Strachan-Davidson, master of Balliol
(1907–1916) a memoir. Oxf., 1925, 4°. 124 pp.   G.A. Oxon 4° 461

See 4673 [Bailey, C., Francis Fortescue Urquhart. 1936].

REMINISCENCES.

See 7081 [Oakeley, F., Balliol under dr. Jenkyns. 1866].

6756. HENDERSON, P. A. WRIGHT-, Balliol in the early sixties. (Blackwood's mag., 1894, vol. 155, p. 349–56.)   Per. 2705 d. 386
— [Repr.] (Glasgow & Balliol and other essays, p. 13–51.) Oxf. &c.,
1926, 8°.   G.A. Oxon 8° 1050

6756.1. VAUGHAN, C. E., Balliol five and twenty years ago [signed Balliol-
ensis]. (S. Wales and Monmouth. Univ. coll. mag., 1899, vol. 11,
p. 137–45.)
[A photogr. reprod. is in Bodley: G.A. Oxon c. 269.]

6757. FORBES, E. M., A visit to Balliol, 1879. (Nineteenth cent., 1921, vol.
90, p. 861–70.)   Per. 3977 d. 66

6758. HENDERSON, P. A. WRIGHT-, Glasgow & Balliol, and other essays. Lond. &c., 1926, 8°. 145 pp. G.A. Oxon 8° 1050

6759. PROTHERO, R. E., 1st baron Ernle, School and college sixty years since [Balliol 1871–   ]. (Quarterly review, 1933, vol. 260, p. 196–208.) Per. 3977 e. 191

6759.5. SPENDER, J. A., Balliol in the eighties [1881–85]. (Oxford, 1936, vol. 2, no. 3, p. 47–53.) Per. G.A. Oxon 8° 1141

6760. SMITH, L. P., Oxford [reminiscences of Balliol, 1888–1892]. (Atlantic monthly, 1938, vol. 161, p. 731–40.) Per. 2714 d. 51

See 3929 [Moore, H. K., Reminiscences of Oxford and Balliol in the seventies. 1939].

6761. BARKER, SIR E., Father of the man, memories of Cheshire, Lancashire and Oxford. [Balliol, 1893–98.] Lond., (1948), 8°. 248 e. 172

6762. BOAS, F. S., Some Oxford memories [Balliol, 1881–86]. (Essays and studies, Engl. assoc., 1956, p. 113–21.) Per. 269 e. 562 = S.

LISTS

6763. Roll of Balliol college. October 1, 1832–October 1, 1893. [Oxf., 1895], 8°. 88 pp. G.A. Oxon 8° 540 (12*)

6764. Roll of Balliol college, October 1, 1832 to April 1, 1908, from the college entry book . . . (Oxf., 1908), 8°. 118 pp. MS. Top. Oxon e. 124, vol. 16

6765. The Balliol college register, 1832–1914, ed. by E. Hilliard. Oxf., 1914, 8°. 420 pp. G.A. Oxon 8° 887

6766. The Balliol college register. 2nd ed., 1833–1933, ed. by sir I. Elliott. Oxf., 1934, 8°. 494 pp. G.A. Oxon 4° 761 = R. Top.

6767. The Balliol college register. 3rd ed., 1900–1950, ed. by sir I. Elliott. Oxf., 1953, 8°. 518 pp. G.A. Oxon 4° 700 = R. Top.

6768. Roll of service, 1914–1918. Balliol college record. [Oxf., 1919], 8°. 22 pp. G.A. Oxon 8° 895 (3)

6769. Balliol society. Address list of old members of Balliol college. 1927, 1929, 1931. Oxf., 1927–31, 8°. G.A. Oxon 8° 1085

Scholarships

6770. ADDISON, W. I., The Snell exhibitions from the University of Glasgow to Balliol college. Glasg., 1901, 4°. 223 pp. G.A. Lanark 4° 23

6771. [Examination papers. Fellowships, scholarships, &c.]. 1838–84. [Oxf.], 1838–84, 8°. [The Bodleian set is imperf. 2626 e. 36]

6772. [Examination papers. Brakenbury scholarships. 1867–1916.] [Oxf.], 1867–1916, 8°. [The Bodleian set is imperf. 2626 e. 36]

6772.I. The right honourable James Hozier, second baron Newlands to the Master & scholars of Balliol college . . . Deed of trust of the Jowett fellowships fund. (Lond.), 1907, 4°. 15 pp.   G.A. Oxon 4° 816

Societies, etc.

6773. Account of Balliol athletic clubs, Jan.–Oct., 1881; Oct. 1889/90; 1893/4 & 1894/5; [Oxf.], 1881–95, s. sh. &c.
G.A. Oxon c. 269 (f. 45–47)

6774. The Club at war; war edition of the Balliol club magazine. No. 1–11. August 1916–April 1919. Oxf., 1916–19, 8°. G.A. Oxon 8° 810 (10–15)

6775. Rules of the Balliol college athletic clubs. Revised, Oct. 1881. [Oxf.], 1881, 8°. 4 pp.   G.A. Oxon c. 269 (f. 38)

6776. Balliol college barge. [Appeal for funds.] [Oxf., 1881], s. sh.
G.A. Oxon c. 269 (f. 38)

6777. Balliol college chess club. Rules. n. pl., [c. 1900], 16°. 4 pp.
G.A. Oxon 16° 33 (46)

6778. Balliol college musical society. [Miscellaneous papers. 1887–1925.]
G.A. Oxon c. 115

6779. BAILEY, C., The Balliol concerts. (Monthly mus. record, 1937, vol. 67, p. 195, 196.)   Per. 17402 d. 47

6780. Balliol junior common room. Rules and regulations. May 1903. (Oxf.), 1903, s. sh.   G.A. Oxon c. 269 (8)

6781. Brakenbury society. [Miscellaneous papers. 1891–1907.]
G.A. Oxon c. 269

6782. Carlyle society. Rules. [A proof copy.] [Oxf., 1882], 8°.
G.A. Oxon 4° 603

6783. Dervorguilla society. [Miscellaneous papers. 1881–1907.]
G.A. Oxon c. 269

Chapel

See 6181 [Balliol chapel. 1859].

6784. Psalms and hymns for Balliol college. Lond., 1877, 12°. 136 pp.
147 g. 546

6785. Order of morning and evening service to be used in Balliol college chapel on week-days. Oxf., [c. 1905], 16°. 125 pp. G.A. Oxon 16° 83

6786. ARNOLD, H., The glass in Balliol college chapel. Oxf., [1914], 8°. 19 pp.   G.A. Oxon 4° 262 (11)

Library

6787. Catalogue of printed books in Balliol college library. Oxf., 1871, 8°. 459 pp.   2590 e. Oxf. 33. 1 = R.

6788. Balliol college. (Hist. MSS. comm., 4th report, 1874, pt. 1, p. 442–51.)   2262 c. 7 = K.

6788.2. CHEYNE, T. K., The library of Balliol College. (N. & Q., 1881, 6th ser., vol. 3, p. 61, 62.)   Per. 3974 e. 405 = A.

> See 5654 [Saxl, F., and Meier, H., Catalogue of astrological . . . manuscripts. 1953].

Beef hall

> See 8095, &c. Pembroke college.

Brasenose

General

6789. [Topographical prints, &c. in the Bodleian.]   G.A. Oxon a. 49

> See 1548 [Halifax law translated to Oxon, an account of the dislodgement of dr. Samuel Radcliffe from the principalship. 1648].
> See 3816 [Wine party. 1825].

6790. INGRAM, J., Brasenose college. (Memorials of Oxford, 1837, vol. 2. 16 pp.)   G.A. Oxon 8° 19

6791. Oxford university commission. Case and opinion [signed G. J. Turner, R. Bethell, H. S. Keating, J. R. Kenyon, dated 10 Mar., 1851] on the part of . . . Brasenose college [suggesting that the Crown be petitioned to annul the commission]. n. pl., (1851), 4°, 16 pp.
          G.A. Oxon c. 67 (153)

> See 7492 [Proposed amalgamation of Brasenose and Lincoln colleges. 1878].

6792. WORDSWORTH, J., Prayers for use in college [by J. Wordsworth]. (Oxf.), [1879], 12°. 11 pp.   G.A. Oxon c. 270 (f. 70)

6793. MADAN, F., On Brasenose hall. (Proc., Oxf. architect. and hist. soc., 1883, N.S., vol. 4, p. 111.)   Per. G.A. Oxon 8° 498 = R.

6794. JACKSON, T. G., The High street of Oxford and Brasenose college. (Mag. of art, 1889, vol. 12, p. 332–40.)   Per. 170 c. 5
— Repr. 11 pp.   G.A. Oxon c. 10

6795. BUCHAN, J., Brasenose college. (Univ. of Oxf., college hist.) Lond., 1898, 8°. 202 pp.   G.A. Oxon 8° 651 (6) = R.

6796. The Brazen Nose. Vol. 1– . Oxf., 1909– , 4°.   G.A. Oxon 4° 282

6797. Brasenose college quatercentenary monographs. 2 vols. [in 3]. (Oxf. hist. soc., vol. 52–54.) Oxf., 1909, 8°.   G.A. Oxon 8° 360 = R.

6798. MADAN, F., The site of the college before its foundation, including Brasenose and Little university halls. (Brasenose coll. quatercent. monogr., vol. I, no. I. Oxf. hist. soc., vol. 52.) Oxf., 1909, 8°. 18 pp.
G.A. Oxon 8° 360 = R.

6799. MADAN, F., The name and arms of the college. (Brasenose coll. quatercent. monogr., vol. I, no. 2. Oxf. hist. soc., vol. 52.) Oxf., 1909, 8°. 20 pp.   G.A. Oxon 8° 360 = R.

6800. ALLFREY, E. W., The architectural history of the college. (Brasenose coll. quatercent. monogr., vol. I, no. 3. Oxf. hist. soc., vol. 52.) Oxf., 1909, 8°. 68 pp.+36 pl.   G.A. Oxon 8° 360 = R.

6801. MADAN, F., Brief annals of the college, with a list of books relating to it. (Brasenose coll. quatercent. monogr., vol. I, no. 8. Oxf. hist. soc., vol. 52.) Oxf., 1909, 8°. 38 pp.   G.A. Oxon 8° 360 = R.

6802. LEADAM, I. S., Early years of the college. (Brasenose coll. quatercent. monogr., vol. 2, no. 9. Oxf. hist. soc., vol. 53.) Oxf., 1909, 8°. 212 pp.   G.A. Oxon 8° 360 = R.

6803. JEFFERY, R. W., History of the college, 1547–1603. (Brasenose coll. quatercent. monogr., vol. 2, no. 10. Oxf. hist. soc., vol. 53.) Oxf., 1909, 8°. 59 pp.   G.A. Oxon 8° 360 = R.

6804. WAKELING, G. H., History of the college, 1603–1660. (Brasenose coll. quatercent. monogr., vol. 2, no. 11. Oxf. hist. soc., vol. 53.) Oxf., 1909, 8°. 70 pp.   G.A. Oxon 8° 360 = R.

6805. LODGE, R., The college under the later Stuarts. (Brasenose coll. quatercent. monogr., vol. 2, no. 12. Oxf. hist. soc., vol. 53.) Oxf., 1909, 8°. 68 pp.   G.A. Oxon 8° 360 = R.

6806. JEFFERY, R. W., History of the college, 1690–1803. (Brasenose coll. quatercent. monogr., vol. 2, no. 13. Oxf. hist. soc., vol. 53.) Oxf., 1909, 8°. 65 pp.   G.A. Oxon 8° 360 = R.

6807. Brasenose college. New buildings, no. XII staircase, bathrooms etc. Statement of account, 1909–11. n. pl., 1912, s. sh.
G.A. Oxon c. 271 (f. 20)

6808. B., A. J., A chimney of the original college building. (The Brazen Nose, 1912, vol. I, p. 234.)   Per. G.A. Oxon 4° 282

6809. Brasenose college. War memorial. [Details of proposed form.] May, 1919. n. pl., 1919, s. sh.   G.A. Oxon c. 270 (f. 89)

6810. OSWALD, A., Brasenose college. (Country Life, 1935, vol. 77, p. 192–97, 216–21.)   Per. 384 b. 6

6811. COXHILL, W. T., and CRACKNELL, H. C., Aeneinasensiana, some old and new facts relating to Brasenose college, by Galli Collis [W. T. Coxhill]. Oxf., 1941, 16°. 32 pp.   G.A. Oxon 16° 207 (I)

— 2nd ed., by Galli Collis and Spira [H. C. Cracknell]. Oxf., 1946, 16°.
40 pp. G.A. Oxon 16° 207 (2)

6811.4. GARDINER, S., A new building for Brasenose. (Oxf. mag., 1961,
N.S., vol. 1, p. 322, 23.) Per. G.A. Oxon 4° 141

Administration

6812. Laundresses charges. Nov. 1867. n. pl., 1867, s. sh.
G.A. Oxon c. 270 (f. 73)
— [1899]. n. pl., [1899], s. sh. G.A. Oxon c. 270 (f. 87)

6813. Rate of the charges in the kitchen, Feb., 1870. n. pl., 1870, s. sh.
G.A. Oxon c. 270 (f. 73)
— Kitchen list. n. pl., [1885], 12°. 3 pp. G.A. Oxon c. 270 (f. 82)

6814. T. Green, Common room, Brasenose college. List of prices [drinks].
n. pl., [1870?], s. sh. G.A. Oxon c. 270 (f. 73)

6815. Provisional regulations for the use of electric light. [Oct.]. n. pl.,
[1892], s. sh. G.A. Oxon c. 270 (f. 84)

6816. Electric lighting notice. 1 Jan. n. pl., 1894, s. sh.
G.A. Oxon c. 270 (f. 84)

6817. Servants' pension scheme (draft). n. pl., [1894], s. sh.
G.A. Oxon c. 270 (f. 86)

6818. Stores price list. 1896. n. pl., 1896, 8°. 4 pp.
— 1910–11. n. pl., 1910, 8°. 4 pp. G.A. Oxon c. 270 (f. 86)

6819. Brasenose college. [Report.] 1899/1900–1922/23. (Oxf.), 1900–23, 8°.
G.A. Oxon 8° 510*
[The Bodleian set is imperfect.]

6820. Some particulars respecting electric light and the charges made for
the same in one of the Oxford colleges [Brasenose]. [Reprod. from
typewriting.] Feb. 1901. n. pl., 1901, s. sh. G.A. Oxon c. 270 (f. 87)

6821. JEFFERY, N. W., A common room account book [1773–1841]. (The
Brazen Nose, 1915, vol. 2, p. 55–59.) Per. G.A. Oxon 4° 282

6822. JEFFERY, R. W., A college butler's [E. Shippary] note-book [1655–
1706]. [A summary signed R. W. J.] (The Brasen Nose, 1920, vol. 3,
p. 86–91.) Per. G.A. Oxon 4° 282

Statutes

6823. Statuta Aulæ regiæ et collegii de Brasennose in Oxonio. Subjiciuntur excerpta ex compositionibus et testamentis benefactorum et alia
quædam notatu digna ad idem collegium pertinentia. [Oxf.], 1772, 8°.
108+(lxx) pp. G.A. Oxon 8° 30

6824. Statuta Aulæ regiæ et collegii de Brasennose in Oxonia coram
scholaribus non sociis ad eorum observantiam iuramenti vinculo ad-
strictis ter quotannis legenda. [Oxf.], 1773, 8°. 31 pp.

6825. Statutes of the colleges . . . (Brasenose college). Oxf. &c., 1853, 8°.
99 pp.   G.A. Oxon 8° 25 = R. Top.

6826. Oxford university. Copy of an ordinance . . . for the conversion of
four fellowships in Brasenose college into scholarships. Lond., 1856,
s. sh.   Pp. Eng. 1856 vol. 46

6827. Oxford university. Copies of ordinances with respect to the fellowships in . . . Brasenose college. [Lond.], 1856, s. sh.
                                            Pp. Eng. 1856 vol. 46

6828. Oxford university. Ordinances . . . in relation to . . Balliol [and 10
other] colleges respectively. [Lond.], 1857, fol. 139 pp.
                                            Pp. Eng. 1857 vol. 32

6829. Oxford university. Copies of four ordinances . . . in relation to
Christ's Church, and Queen's, University and Brazenose colleges.
[Lond.], 1858, fol. 38 pp.   Pp. Eng. 1857/8 vol. 46

6830. Ordinances framed by the University commissioners . . . in relation
to Brasenose college. Oxf., 1862, 8°. 24 pp.

6831. Ordinances and statutes framed or approved by the . . . Commissioners . . . (Brasenose college, p. 285–310.) Oxf., 1863, 8°.
                                            Clar. Press 31 a. 63

6832. WORDSWORTH, C., *bp. of Lincoln,* College statutes, college fellowships and college legislation, a letter to the principal of Brasenose
college [criticizing the action of the college in petitioning her majesty
for leave to alter certain statutes, without reference to the Visitor].
Lond. &c., 1872, 8°. 20 pp.   G.A. Oxon 8° 1055 (8)

6833. WORDSWORTH, C., *bp. of Lincoln,* A letter to the University of
Oxford commissioners on the announcement of their intention to make
statutes for Brasenose and Lincoln colleges. (Lincoln, 1879), 8°. 10 pp.
                                            G.A. Oxon 8° 456

6834. Statutes proposed to be made by the University of Oxford commissioners for Brasenose college. April 1881. [Lond.], 1881, fol. 22 pp.
                                            G.A. Oxon c. 8 (45)

6835. Statutes proposed to be made . . . for Brasenose college. (Oxf.), 1881,
8°. 35 pp.   G.A. Oxon 8° 425 (5) = R.

6836. Statutes of Brasenose college. (Univ. of Oxf. and Cambr. act, 1877.
Oxford. Thirty-six statutes made by the Univ. of Oxf. commissioners,
1881, p. 26–42, 247.)   Pp. Eng. 1882 vol. 51

6837. Statutes made for Brasenose college, by the University of Oxford
commissioners. Oxf., 1882, 8°. 42 pp.   G.A. Oxon 8° 882 (1)
— Amended . . . in Council from 1885 to 1901. Oxf., 1901, 8°. 51 pp.
                                            G.A. Oxon 8° 882 (2)
— Amended . . . in Council from 1885 to 1904. Oxf., 1904, 8°. 64 pp.

6838. Brasenose college. Copy of a statute made . . . 15th December 1886, for alteration of statute 16 of the statutes of the college, as altered by a statute made . . . 22nd Jan., 1885. Lond., 1887, s. sh.
Pp. Eng. 1887 vol. 65

6839. Statute made by . . . Brasenose college . . . 4th Dec. 1889, making certain alterations in Statute III. Lond., 1890, s. sh.
Pp. Eng. 1890 vol. 56

6840. Statute made by . . . Brasenose college, 3rd May 1895, altering Statute 8. Lond., 1896, s. sh.   Pp. Eng. 1896 vol. 65

6841. Statutes made by . . . Brasenose college . . . on 17th March 1897, amending certain provisions in statutes III. and XII . . . 10 February 1898. Lond., 1898, s. sh.   Pp. Eng. 1898 vol. 70

6842. A statute made by . . . Brasenose college . . . on the 15th day of March 1899, altering statutes III. and XVI. . . . 23 October 1899. Lond., 1899, s. sh.   Pp. Eng. 1899 vol. 76

6843. A statute made by . . . Brasenose college, 15th Mar. 1899, altering Statutes III. and XVI. Lond., 1900, s. sh.   Pp. Eng. 1900 vol. 66

6844. Statute made by . . . Brasenose college, 20th Oct. 1899, amending clause 13 of Statute III. Lond., 1900, s. sh.   Pp. Eng. 1900 vol. 66

6845. Statute made by . . . Brasenose college, 20th June 1900, altering Statutes III., V., XIII., and XVI. Lond., 1901, s. sh.
Pp. Eng. 1901 vol. 56

6846. Statutes made by . . . Brasenose college, 9th Dec. 1903, amending Statutes II, III, IV, V, X, XII, XIII, XV, XVI, and XVII. Lond., 1904, fol. 8 pp.   Pp. Eng. 1904 vol. 75

6847. Statute made by . . . Brasenose college, 11th Mar. 1908, amending Statute III, part II, 12. Lond., 1908, s. sh.   Pp. Eng. 1908 vol. 86

6848. Statute made by . . . Brasenose college . . . on the 25th January, 1911, amending certain of the statutes. 8 May 1911. Lond., 1911, fol. 6 pp.
Pp. Eng. 1911 vol. 59

6849. Statute made by . . . Brasenose college . . . on the 18th February, 1914 (and sealed on the same date) altering Statute III., part 1., clause 2, and Statute V., clause 3. 10 June 1914. Lond., 1914, s. sh.
Pp. Eng. 1914 vol. 64

6850. Statutes made for the colleges . . . (Brasenose college). Oxf., 1927, 8°. 56 pp.   G.A. Oxon 4° 759 = R.

6851. Statutes of the King's hall and college of Brasenose, made on 28 April 1954 in the manner provided by the Universities of Oxford and Cambridge act, 1923. To which are added, the college by-laws. Oxf., 1956, 8°. 69 pp.   G.A. Oxon 8° 1337

Finance and property

6852. An act for confirming to . . . King's hall and college of Brazen-nose . . . the purchase of the advowsons of Stepney and other churches and for settling the same to the benefit of the said college. (9 Anne, c. 16, Private.) n. pl., 1710, fol. 8 pp.   G.A. Oxon c. 223

6853. An act to vest in the commissioners for building fifty new churches [&c.] . . . and for restoring to the . . . college of Brazen Nose . . . the . . . right of presentation to churches and chapels in Stepney parish. (12 Anne, Sess. 1, c. 17, Pub.) Lond., 1713, fol. 5 pp.   L.L.

6854. An act for confirming and establishing an exchange of tythes, cottages, and lands [in Middle Aston], for a messuage, farms, lands, and common of pasture in Steeple Aston . . . pursuant to an agreement between the . . . Kings hall and college of Brazen Nose, John Eaton and Francis Page . . . (29 G. II, c. 29, Private.) 1755–6.
[Précis in Shadwell's Enactments &c. See no. 956.]

6855. An act to enable the trustees of the estates devised by William Hulme . . . to grant building leases thereof and to increase the number of exhibitioners in Brasen Nose college . . . (10 G. III, c. 51, Private.) n. pl., 1770, fol. 7 pp.   L.L.
— 35 G. III, c. 62, Private.
— 54 G. III, c. 205, L. & P.
— 7 & 8 G. IV, c. 9, Private.
— 2 V., c. 17, Private.
— 7 Edw. VII, c. 110, L. & P.

6856. An act for establishing . . . certain articles of agreement for an exchange between . . . the King's hall and college of Brazen Nose . . . and Edward Loveden Loveden, of [lands in Eaton Hastings, Buscot, and Stanford, Berks.]. (34 G. III, c. 62, Private.) n. pl., 1794, fol. 12 pp.
                                                              L.L.

6857. An act for enabling . . . Brazen Nose college . . . to sell the manor and farm of Gennings Court, Kent to sir John Gregory Shaw and to apply the money thence arising in the purchase of other estates . . . (53 G. III, c. 98, L. & P.) Lond., 1813, fol. 7 pp.   L.L.

6858. Whitechapel rectory bill. Report and evidence laid before a public vestry-meeting of the inhabitants of the parish of Whitechapel, 25 Jan., 1849, on the claims of Brazen-nose college, Oxford, and the rector of the said parish. Lond., 1849, 8°. 57+xxx pp.

6859. An act to authorise a sale by . . . Brasenose college . . . to the governors of Saint Bartholomew's hospital of two houses situate in Little Britain . . . London. (42 V., c. 22, L. & P.) Lond., 1870, fol. 3 pp. L.L.

6860. BUTLER, A. J., The college estates and the advowsons held by the college. (Brasenose coll. quatercent. monogr., vol. 1, no. 6. Oxf. hist. soc., vol. 52.) Oxf., 1909, 8°. 64 pp.   G.A. Oxon 8° 360 = R.

6861. BUTLER, A. J., An account of the benefactions bestowed upon the college. (Brasenose coll. quatercent. monogr., vol. 1, no. 4. Oxf. hist. soc., vol. 52.) Oxf., 1909, 8°. 75 pp.   G.A. Oxon 8° 360 = R.

6862. JEFFERY, R. W., The Bursars' account books. (Brazen Nose, 1924, vol. 4, p. 19–30.)   Per. G.A. Oxon 4° 282

6863. JEFFERY, R. W., Brasenose college charities during the Commonwealth. (Brazen Nose, 1925, vol. 4, p. 118–29.) Per. G.A. Oxon 4° 282

6864. JEFFERY, R. W., The foundation property of the college. The Priory of Cold Norton. (Brazen Nose, 1928, vol. 4, p. 371–79.)
          Per. G.A. Oxon 4° 282

Members

BIOGRAPHY

6865. CHURTON, R., The lives of William Smyth, bishop of Lincoln and sir Richard Sutton, founders of Brasen Nose college. [*With*] Suppl. Oxf., 1800, 03, 8°. 553+18 pp.   Gough Oxf. 42

6866. BUCHAN, J., The Nineteenth century. Nine Brasenose worthies. (Brasenose coll. quatercent. monogr., vol. 2, no. 14 (2). Oxf. hist. soc., vol. 54.) Oxf., 1909, 8°. (30 pp.)   G.A. Oxon 8° 360 = R.

6866.5. SMITH, J. A., John Buchan. [Chapter 3, p. 47–74 'Oxford undergraduate, 1895–99' at B.N.C.] Lond., 1965, 8°.   26961 e. 583

6867. GREEN, R. L., An undergraduate of 1723 [Edward Greene of Brasenose college]. (Oxf. mag., 1947, vol. 66, p. 88–92.)
          Per. G.A. Oxon 4° 141
— [Repr. *entitled*] Greene of Brasenose: 1723–1725. (Brazen Nose, 1957/58, vol. 11, p. 23–27.)   Per. G.A. Oxon 4° 282

6868. HEBER, R., The Whippiad. A.D. 1802: a satirical poem [on the rev. H. Halliwell, dean of Brasenose college, ed. by A. J. Ram]. (The Brazen Nose, 1910, vol. 1, p. 101–12.)   Per. G.A. Oxon 4° 282

See 8591 [Jeffery, R. W., Dr. Shippen's share in the Cockman–Denison controversy at University college. 1930].

6869. JEFFERY, R. W., More light on the character of Dr. Shippen. (Brazen Nose, 1931, vol. 5, p. 136–47.)   Per. G.A. Oxon 4° 282

6870. JEFFERY, R. W., The family affairs and death of Dr. Shippen. (Brazen Nose, 1931, vol. 5, p. 181–93.)   Per. G.A. Oxon 4° 282

6871. NICHOLSON, J., Pedigree of Thomas Yate, principal of Brasenose college [with notes and an extract from his will, 1680. By J. Nicholson.] [Warrington, 1843], 8°. 9 pp.   G.A. Oxon 8° 620 (4)

REMINISCENCES

6872. WARD, T. H., The Nineteenth-century. Reminiscences, 1864–1872. (Brasenose coll. quatercent. monogr., vol. 2, no. 14 (2). Oxf. hist. soc., vol. 54.) Oxf., 1909, 8°. (11 pp.)   G.A. Oxon 8° 360 = R.

6873. LATHAM, F. L., B.N.C. in the fifties. (The Brazen Nose, 1911, vol. 1,
   p. 158–62.)   Per. G.A. Oxon 4° 282

6874. PRICE, C., Reminiscences of Brasenose. (1854–60). (The Brazen
   Nose, 1911, vol. 1, p. 189–92.)   Per. G.A. Oxon 4° 282

6875. STALLYBRASS, W. T. S., Brasenose in my early years [1911–].
   (Brazen Nose, 1953, vol. 9, p. 321–26; 350–56.) Per. G.A. Oxon 4° 282

LISTS

6876. BUCKLEY, W. E., and MADAN, F., The Brasenose calendar, a list of
   members, 1509–1888. Oxf., 1888, 8°. 226 pp.   G.A. Oxon 8° 445
   — Suppl. Oxf., 1889, 8°. 31 pp.   G.A. Oxon 8° 445*

6877. Brasenose college register. 1509–1909. [Ed. by C. B. Heberden.]
   2 vols. Oxf., 1909, 8°.   G.A. Oxon 8° 767
   — [Another issue] (Oxf. hist. soc., vol. 55).   G.A. Oxon 8° 360 = R.
   — Suppl. additions and corrections. [Oxf.], (1910), 8°. 14 pp.
                                                      G.A. Oxon 8° 767

6878. JENKINSON, A. J., The Nineteenth century. The schools, university
   honours, and professions of Brasenose men. (Brasenose coll. quatercent. monogr., vol. 2, no. 14 (2). Oxf. hist. soc., vol. 54.) Oxf., 1909, 8°.
   (38 pp.)   G.A. Oxon 8° 360 = R.

6879. Brasenose college. Memorial service for the members . . . who fell in
   the war, 1914–1919. [With list of names.] [Oxf.], 1919, 8°. 14 pp.
                                                    G.A. Oxon 8° 895 (6)

6880. Brasenose society. Members' address list [afterw.] List of members.
   June 1939; Hilary term, 1947; 1953–. [Oxf.], 1939– , 4°.
                                                       G.A. Oxon 4° 591

6880.1. List of members. (Edinb.), 1961, 8°. 127 pp.   G.A. Oxon 8° 1446

Scholarships, exhibitions, etc.

GENERAL

6881. [Examination papers. Fellowships, scholarships &c.]. 1852–85.
   [Oxf.], 1852–85, 8°. [The Bodleian set is imperf. 2626 e. 33]

6882. Brasenose college. Scholarships and exhibitions [details]. n. pl.,
   [1884], 8°. 2 pp.   G.A. Oxon c. 270 (f. 81)
   — [1886].   G.A. Oxon c. 270 (f. 82)
   — [1894].   G.A. Oxon c. 270 (f. 86)

HULME EXHIBITIONS
   See 6855 [Hulme exhibitioners. 1770. &c.].

6883. List of books recommended to the students in divinity on mr.
   Hulme's foundation in Brasen Nose college. Oxf., 1815, 8°. 15 pp.

6884. [History of the foundation of the Hulme exhibitions.] (The history
   of Manchester school, by W. R. Whatton, 1828, p. 55–66.)
                                                       G.A. Lancs. 4° 15

6885. HERBERT, HON. W., and HARINGTON, R., Correspondence between . . . the dean of Manchester and the principal of Brasenose college . . . on some proceedings connected with the appointment of exhibitioners on the foundation of the late W. Hulme, esq. With an appendix. Oxf., 1846, 8°. 62 pp. 46. 994

6886. Proposed alterations in Hulme scheme. Jan. 1899. n. pl., 1899, 4°. 3 pp. G.A. Oxon c. 270 (f. 87)

6887. Board of education. In the matter of the Foundation known as the Hulme trust estates (education) . . . (Certificate of approval of scheme, 20 Dec. 1906.) Lond., 1906, fol. 10 pp. G.A. Oxon c. 271 (f. 7)

6888. An act to confirm a scheme of the Charity commissioners for the application or management of the charity called the Hulme trust estates (non-educational) in the County of Lancaster and elsewhere. (3 & 4 G. V, c. 168, L. & P.) (Lond.), 1913, 4°. 4 pp. L.L. — 10 & 11 G. V, c. 168, L & P.

SOMERSET SCHOLARSHIPS

6889. [History of the foundation of the Sarah, duchess of Somerset scholarships.] (The history of Manchester school, by W. R. Whatton, 1828, p. 66–74.) G.A. Lancs. 4° 15

Societies and sport

INTELLECTUAL AND LITERARY SOCIETIES

6890. Rules of the Brasenose college debating society. (Oxf.), [1879], 8°. 4 pp. G.A. Oxon c. 271 (f. 40)

6891. Brasenose college Ingoldsby essay club. Rules. n. pl., 1894, 12°. 4 pp. G.A. Oxon c. 271 (f. 35) — 1897, 1902. G.A. Oxon c. 271 (f. 36)

See 8072 [Ellesmere society 1922 &c.].

6892. Rules of the Octagon club. (List of members.) n. pl., [1895], s. sh. G.A. Oxon c. 271 (f. 44) — 1906. G.A. Oxon c. 271 (f. 45)

RELIGIOUS SOCIETIES

6893. [A letter, signed J. Wordsworth and E. W. D. Manson, proposing the formation of a Brasenose college missionary association.] May 10, 1873. n. pl., (1873), 12°. 3 pp. G.A. Oxon c. 271 (f. 49)

SOCIAL SOCIETIES

6894. The Phoenix common room, Brasenose college, Oxford. Centenary dinner, June 29, 1886. n. pl., (1886), 4°. 7 pp. G.A. Oxon 4° 89

6895. MADAN, F., ed., A century of the Phœnix common room (Brasenose college) 1786–1886. Oxf., 1888, 8°. 140 pp. G.A. Oxon 8° 720

6896. MADAN, F., The Nineteenth century. A short account of the Phoenix common room. (Brasenose coll. quartercent. monogr., vol. 2, no. 14 (2). Oxf. hist. soc., vol. 54.) Oxf., 1909, 8°. (44 pp.) G.A. Oxon 8° 360 = R.

SPORTS SOCIETIES, ETC.

6897. Brasenose college amalgamated [clubs] fund. Treasurer's statement of accounts. 1901/02. [Oxf.], (1902), fol. 3 pp.
G.A. Oxon c. 271 (f. 63)

6898. Brasenose college amalgamated athletic fund. Treasurer's statement of account. 1894/95, 98/99–1900/01, 04/05, 05/06, 07/08, 10/11. [Oxf.], (1895–1911), s. sh.　　　　　　G.A. Oxon c. 271 (f. 64, 65)

6899. Brasenose college. Proposed cricket & athletic ground. Oct. 23, 1894. [Oxf.], (1894), s. sh.　　　　　　G.A. Oxon c. 271 (f. 66)

6900. Brasenose college. New cricket ground. [Report and appeal . . . May, 1895.] [Oxf., 1895], 4°. 3 pp.　　　　　　G.A. Oxon c. 271 (f. 66)

6901. Brasenose college. New cricket and athletic ground. [Report and statement of account.] May 7th, 1896. [Oxf.], (1896), 4°. 3 pp.
G.A. Oxon c. 271 (f. 66)

6902. MADAN, F., The Nineteenth century. Notes on Brasenose cricket. (Brasenose coll. quatercent. monogr., vol. 2, no. 14 (2). Oxf. hist. soc., vol. 54.) Oxf., 1909, 8°. 13 pp.　　　　　　G.A. Oxon 8° 360 = R.

See 4499 [W. T. S. Stallybrass, The Oxford Authentics and the Oxford colleges. No. 1, B.N.C. 1926].

6903. Brasenose college. Rules of the B.N.C. boat club, 1868. (Oxf., 1868), s. sh.　　　　　　G.A. Oxon c. 271 (f. 67)

6904. NUTTER, A. B., B.N.C. Head of the River (1889, 1890, and) 1891 [by A. B. Nutter]. [Oxf.], (1891), 4°. 6 pp.　　　　G.A. Oxon c. 271 (f. 71)

6905. WACE, H. C., Nineteenth century. Brasenose rowing. (Brasenose coll. quatercent. monogr., vol. 2, no. 14 (1). Oxf. hist. soc., vol. 54.) Oxf., 1909, 8°. 188 pp.　　　　　　G.A. Oxon 8° 360 = R.

Chapel

6906. The form of prayer used in . . . 1666, at the consecration of Brazen-Nose college-chapel . . . with the cloister adjoyning for a burial-place, by . . . Walter Blandford, lord bishop of Oxford. (The antiquities of the cathedral church of Worcester, by T. Abingdon, 1723, p. 192–203.)
Gough Worc. 3

6907. [Begin.] It is proposed to erect an organ in Brasenose college chapel . . . [Details and subscription list. Jan.]. (Oxf., 1877), 12°. 3 pp.
G.A. Oxon c. 270 (f. 72)

6908. BUTLER, A. J., [Church plate and an inventory made in 1591 of goods in Brazenose college chapel.] (Proc., Soc. of antiq., 1883, ser. 2, vol. 9, p. 242, 43.)　　　　　　Per. G.A. Gen. top. 8° 524 = R.

6909. MADAN, F., *ed.*, Consecration of Brasenose college chapel, 1666. (Oxf. hist. soc., 1905, vol. 47, p. 157–164.) G.A. Oxon 8° 360 = R.

Library and archives

6910. MADAN, F., The library of Brasenose College. (N. & Q., 1880, 6th ser., vol. 2, p. 321, 22.)   Per. 3974 e. 405 = A.

6910.2. Brasenose college undergraduates' library [regulations]. Oct. 31, 1883. n. pl., 1883, 12°. 3 pp.   G.A. Oxon c. 270 (f. 81)

6911. Brasenose college library. Regulations. Oct., 1897. n. pl., 1897, s. sh.   G.A. Oxon c. 270 (f. 86)

6912. JEFFERY, R. W., Brasenose college underground bookstore. (Brazen Nose, 1933, vol. 5, p. 314–27.)   Per. G.A. Oxon 4° 282
— Repr.   G.A. Oxon 8° 1101 (10)

6913. Calendar of muniments. 36 vols. [Photogr. reprod. of the college catalogue cards.] (Nat. Reg. of Archives.) n. pl., [1957], 4°.
2262 c. 10 = R.

Plate, pictures, glass, etc.

6914. BUTLER, A. J., The college plate, with a complete list of donors. (Brasenose coll. quatercent. monogr., vol. 1, no. 5. Oxf. hist. soc., vol. 52.) Oxf., 1909, 8°. 52 pp.   G.A. Oxon 8° 360 = R.

6915. BUTLER, A. J., The college pictures. (Brasenose coll. quatercent. monogr., vol. 1, no. 7. Oxf. hist. soc., vol. 52.) Oxf., 1909, 8°. 35 pp.
G.A. Oxon 8° 360 = R.

6916. COLE, A. C., New light on old lights [the stained glass in the hall] (Brazen Nose, 1949, vol. 9, p. 63–67; 1950, p. 103–07.)
Per. G.A. Oxon 4° 282
— [Repr.] (Coat of arms, 1950, vol. 1, p. 21–24, 41–44). Per. 21932 e. 42

Brazen Nose

6917. MADAN, F., On the recent discovery of the 'Brazen Nose'. (Proc., Oxf. architect. and hist. soc., 1890, N.S., vol. 5, p. 298–304.)
Per. G.A. Oxon 8° 498 = R.
— [Another ed. *entitled*] The Brazen Nose. [Oxf., 1892], 8°. 4 pp.
G.A. Oxon c. 271 (f. 88)

6918. HURST, H., The four noses of Brasenose college, and a great error. Oxf., (1904), 16°. 7 pp.   G.A. Oxon 16° 77

6919. MADAN, F., Stamford and the Brazen Nose, 1333–5. (Brazen Nose, 1925, vol. 4, p. 75–84.)   Per. G.A. Oxon 4° 282

Brasenose ale and other verses

6920. Eulogy on the Brasenose ale [*afterw.*] Brasenose ale (verses). [1827], 30, 46, 48–54, 56, 57, 59, 60, 62–86, 88, 89, 1909–13, 19–24, 26–35. (Oxf.), [1827–1935], s. sh.   G.A. Oxon 4° 313

6921. Brasenose ale, a collection of poems [1811–56] presented annually by the butler . . . on Shrove Tuesday [ed. by J. Prior]. Oxf., 1857, 16°. 140 pp.   G.A. Oxon 16° 39
— [Another ed., ed. by T. H. Ward. 1709?–1877.] Boston, Lincs., 1878, 4°. 265 pp.   G.A. Oxon 4° 627
— [Another issue] Revised, with additions, 1878–1889. [Ed. by C. B. Heberden.] Oxf., 1901, 8°. 316 pp.   G.A. Oxon 8° 764
— [The additions were also issued separately as a Supplement in paper covers comprising pages 2 a–e, 257–316.]   G.A. Oxon 8° 764*

6922. DUNBAR, T., The Brase Nose garlande, MDCCCXI [by T. Dunbar]. [Liverpool, 1818?], 4°. 7 leaves.   Arch. AA d. 7 (1)

6923. A lay of Brazennose [signed Old incredulity]. Oxf., 1866, 8°. 25 pp.
                                                             G.A. Oxon 8° 891

6924. SMITH, I. G., Brasenose gaudy [by I. G. Smith. In verse]. n. pl., [1901], s. sh.   G.A. Oxon c. 271 (f. 52)

6925. LATHAM, F. L., [Begin.] Grey heads [a Brasenose Gaudy poem, signed F. L. L.]. Oct. 9, 1906. n. pl., (1906), s. sh.
— [Another variant] Oct. 10, 1910. n. pl., (1910), s. sh.
                                                             G.A. Oxon c. 271 (f. 52)

Commemoration of Founders and other Benefactors

6926. [Prayer for the founders and benefactors of the college.] n. pl., [17—], s. sh.   MS. Willis 45 (235)

6927. [Form of prayer to commemorate founders and benefactors, with list of relevant dates.] n. pl., [c. 1800], s. sh.   G.A. Oxon c. 271 (f. 6)
— [Another ed.] n. pl., [c. 1800], s. sh.   G.A. Oxon c. 271 (f. 6)

6928. Brasenose college. A table of the commemorations of founders and benefactors, and the days on which they are commemorated. [Oxf., 1905], s. sh.

Broadgates hall

See 8095 &c. Pembroke college.

Campion (Clarke's) hall

6929. Campion hall. (Architect, 1936, vol. 146, p. 355–60.) N. 1731 c. 16

6930. OSWALD, A., Campion hall. (Country Life, 1936, vol. 79, p. 676–81.)
                                                             Per. 384 b. 6

6931. D., Campion hall. (Oxf. mag., 1936, vol. 54, p. 628, 29.)
                                                             Per. G.A. Oxon 4° 141

Canterbury college

6932. Excerpta e compoto thesaurariæ monasterii sancti Augustini extra muros Cantuariæ A.D. 1432. Accedunt Compoti quidam Willielmi

Chert custodis collegii Cantuariensis Oxoniæ A.D. 1395–6–7. [Ed. by
R. C. Hussey.] Lond., 1881, 8°. 35 pp. G.A. Kent 8° 152

6933. PANTIN, W. A., *ed.*, Canterbury college, Oxford. Vol. 1–3,. (Oxf.
hist. soc., N.S., vol. 6, 7, 8,.) Oxf., 1947– , 8°.

G.A. Oxon 8° 360 = R.

Cardinal college

See Christ Church.

Christ Church

General 6934–6967
Administration 6968–6998
  Expulsions 6999–7002
Statutes 7003–7039
Finance and Property 7040–7048
Fabric, including Bells 7049–7066
Members
  Biography 7067–7077
  Reminiscences 7078–7082

Academic Life 7083–7086
Exhibitions and Scholarships 7087–
  7088
Clubs and Societies 7089–7105
Library and Archives 7106–7119
Pictures, Plate, Coins, etc. 7120–7130
Cathedral 7131–7164
Meadow 7164.9

General

*Works relating to the monastery of St. Frideswide will be listed in a later
volume dealing with the City of Oxford.*

6934. [Topographical prints, &c. in the Bodleian.] G.A. Oxon a. 50, 51

6934.5. [*Begin.*] Vniversis Christifidelibus ad quos præsentes . .
  Cuthbertus [Tunstall] . . .[For the founding of Cardinal college.]
  [Lond.], (1528), s. sh. Gough Maps 46

6935. An acte concernyng the kynges generall pardon for his spirituall
  subiectes [excepting Cardinal's college]. (22 Hen. VIII, c. 15, Pub.)
  (The second volume conteinyng those statutes . . . made in the . . .
  reigne of kyng Henrie the eight.) Lond., 1551, fol. T. T.

6936. Musa hospitalis Ecclesiæ Christi Oxon. in adventum . . . Iacobi regis,
  Annæ reginæ, & Henrici principis ad eandem Ecclesiam. [Madan 262.]
  Oxon., 1605, 4°. 48 pp. 4° H 17 Art.

6937. Death repeal'd by a thankfull memoriall sent from Christ Church in
  Oxford, celebrating the noble deserts of . . . Paule, lord vis-count
  Bayning of Sudbury. [In verse, partly Engl., partly Lat.] [Madan 870.]
  Oxf., 1638, 4°. 42 pp. Tanner 744 (9)

See 1543 [Visitation of 1648].
See 145 [A modell for a colledge reformation. 1659 &c.].

6938. IRELAND, T., Speeches spoken to the king and queen, duke and
  duchesse of York, in Christ-church hall, Sept. 29, 1663. [Madan 2621.]
  Lond., 1663, 4°. 8 pp. Wood 515 (30)
  — [Another ed.] [Madan 2622.] Oxf., 1663, 4°. 8 pp. Wood 515 (29)

6939. WELCH, J., A list of scholars of St. Peter's college, Westminster, as they were elected to Christ Church college, Oxford, and Trinity college, Cambridge, from MDLXI to the present time. To which is prefixed A list of deans . . . of Christ Church college. Lond. &c., 1788, 4°. 172 pp.
[A copy in Bodley is continued in MS. to 1803: Gough Westm. 24.]
— New ed. [*entitled*] The list of the Queen's scholars . . . and of such of them as have been thence elected to Christ Church [etc.]. New ed., by an old King's scholar [C. B. Phillimore]. Lond., 1852, 4°. 630 pp.
G.A. Westm. 4° 2

6940. INGRAM, J., Christ Church. (Memorials of Oxford, 1837, vol. 1. 64 pp.)   G.A. Oxon 8° 18

6941. ACLAND, SIR H. W., Synopsis of the physiological series in the Christ Church museum [by sir H. W. Acland]. Oxf., 1853, 4°. 42 pp.
G.A. Oxon 4° 2

6942. GORDON, O., A letter . . . on clauses xlix. and l. of the Oxford university bill [concerning their effect on Christ Church]. Oxf., 1854, 8°. 8 pp.
G.A. Oxon 8° 250 (5)

6943. A day with the Christ Church drag: recollections of Oxford. (Once a week, 1860, vol. 2, p. 77–80.)   Per. 2705 d. 261

6944. PROUT, J. SKINNER, Six views of Christ College, Oxford. Lond., [*c.* 1860?], fol.   G.A. Oxon b. 97

6945. Christ Church, Oxford; its past, present and prospective changes, by an M.A. of 'the House'. (St. James's mag., 1866, vol. 17, p. 366–83.)
Per. 2705 d. 268
See 4763 [Arnold, F., Christ Church days. 1867].

6946. [*Begin.*] The following objections having been made to the Ch. Ch. ball being conducted in the usual manner . . . [Observations.] [Oxf., *c.* 1870], s. sh.   G.A. Oxon c. 272 (f. 78)

6947. JUPP, E. K., Correspondence of a junior student of Christchurch [E. K. Jupp] 1868–70. n. pl., [1871], 8°. 115 pp.   G.A. Oxon 8° 717

6948. JENKINS, J. H., Cakeless [by J. H. Jenkins. A squib in verse relating to an incident at Christ Church]. [Oxf., 1874], 8°. 15 pp.   2804 e. 3 (4)
[This was printed by Messrs. Mowbray, but suppressed immediately. Another form of the squib, entitled *The adventures of Apollo and Diana* was printed by Shrimpton, but was never issued.]

6949. The babes in the wood: or, The undertaker, a Christ Church tragedy. Oxf., 1877, 8°. 4 pp.   G.A. Oxon 8° 204 (9)

6950. Ch. Ch. besieged! A parody on Macaulay's 'Horatius'. Oxf., 1877, 8°. 11 pp.   G.A. Oxon 8° 204 (8)

6951. The Ch. Ch. hoax: a poem by an eye-witness. Oxf., 1877, 8°. 7 pp.
G.A. Oxon 8° 204 (7)

6952. CHANCELLOR, E. BERESFORD, Christ Church, with illustr. by V. R. Prince. (Lond.), 1891, fol. 21 pp.   G.A. Oxon c. 16

6953. The Christ Church chronicle. Vol. 1, no. 1. Oxf., 1892, 4°.
G.A. Oxon 4° 146

6954. THOMPSON, H. L., Christ Church. (Univ. of Oxf., college hist.) Lond., 1900, 8°. 288 pp.   G.A. Oxon 8° 651 (13) = R.

6955. ASHTON, J., Sketches of Christ Church, Oxford. (Lond., 1901), 4°. 20 pl.   G.A. Oxon 4° 214

6956. The portfolio of Christ Church, Oxford: illustr. in photogravure. Chelt., [1902], obl. 4°.   G.A. Oxon c. 118

6957. Christ Church, Oxford, an anthology in prose and verse selected by A. Hassall. Lond. &c., 1911, fol. 182 pp.+26 pl.   G.A. Oxon c. 139

6958. PAINTIN, H., Extraordinary table made for Christ Church common room [from the acacia tree destroyed by a storm in 1908]. Repr. from the Oxford journal illustrated, Apr. 9th, 1913. [Oxf., 1913], s. sh.
G.A. Oxon c. 272 (f. 39)

6959. Oxford university roll of service, 1914–1917. Christ Church record. 3rd ed., corrected to Aug. 23, 1917. Oxf., (1917), 8°. pp. 140–69.
G.A. Oxon 8° 1327

6960. Christ Church. Commemoration of members of the House who have laid down their lives in the war. [With list of names.] [Oxf.], 1919, 8°. 19 pp.   G.A. Oxon 8° 895 (7)

6961. The Cardinal's hat. Vol. 1, no. 1–Vol. 2, no. 1. (Oxf.), 1919, 20, 4°.
Per. G.A. Oxon 4° 427

6962. 1525–1925. Christ Church, 24 June 1925. Founders' prayers. [Oxf.], (1925), 4°. 9 pp.   G.A. Oxon 4° 403* (1)

6963. Christ Church, 1525–1925. Programme of concert, May 23, 1925. [Oxf.], (1925), 4°. 15 pp.   G.A. Oxon 4° 403*(2)

6964. WHITE, H. J., Christ Church, 1525–1925 [by H. J. White]. n. pl., [1925], 8°. 7 pp.   G.A. Oxon 8° 1000 (16)

6965. BENNETT, J. A. W., ed., Oxford in 1699. [Three letters from William Adams, student of Christ Church.] (Oxoniensia, 1939, vol. 4, p. 147–52.)   Per. G.A. Oxon 4° 658 = R.

See 1707 [Dean Liddell and Oxford reform; 2 letters, the 2nd of which affects Christ Church. 1943].

6966. ROPER, H. R. TREVOR-, Christ Church, Oxford, official guidebook. (Oxf.), 1950, 8°. 32 pp.   G.A. Oxon 8° 1227

6967. Christ Church (Archaeol. notes. Oxoniensia, 1958, vol. 23, p. 135.)
Per. G.A. Oxon 4° 658 = R.

See 2846.5 [The Regius professorship of Hebrew: proposed severance from the Canonry at Christ Church. 1959].
See 4025 [Academic drama. 1480–1650. 1959/60].

6967.5. BARRETT, G., The graduate common room in Christ Church. (Oxf. mag., 1961, N.S., vol. 1, p. 208, 09.)   Per. G.A. Oxon 4° 141

Administration

6968. Christ Church. Regulations for the college messengers. [Oxf., c. 1861], s. sh.   G.A. Oxon c. 272 (f. 12)

6969. Regulations of the hall and kitchen. [Oxf.], 1862, s. sh.
G.A. Oxon b. 113 (255)

6970. Regulations of the buttery, kitchen, and hall. 1864, 65. (Oxf., 1864, 65), 2 sheets.   G.A. Oxon c. 272 (f. 15)

6971. Regulations of the Steward's office. 1866. Oxf., 1866, s. sh.
G.A. Oxon c. 272 (f. 15)

6972. DODGSON, C. L., American telegrams. [A skit, by C. L. Dodgson, on telegrams relating to the American Civil war, transferred under disguised names to proposed regulations at Christ Church.] [Oxf.], 1865, 4°. 4 pp.   Ch. Ch.

6973. Recommendations of the treasurer and censors respecting the general economy of the House. Dec. 9. [Oxf.], (1865), 4°. 3 pp.
G.A. Oxon c. 272 (f. 6)

6974. Christ Church, Oxford. [Proposals made at 'a meeting . . . March 21st, 1865, to which were invited all Senior Students together with the Students on the old foundation' for reforming the governing and management of the House.] n. pl., (1865), 8°. 13 pp.
G.A. Oxon 4° 430 (9)

6975. Correspondence on the 'bread and butter question' at Christ Church. [Concerning prices and profit made on battels of bread and butter.] Oxf., 1865, 8°. 54 pp.   G.A. Oxon 8° 92 (3)

6976. Regulations applying to honorary members of Common room. Nov. 1865. (Oxf., 1865), s. sh.   G.A. Oxon c. 272 (f. 13)

6977. [*Begin.*] At a meeting of the M.A. table . . . Nov. 6th, 1867, the following resolutions were agreed to. (Oxf., 1867), s. sh.
G.A. Oxon c. 272 (f. 13)

6978. Regulations, &c. Christ Church, Oxford. [Oxf.], 1866, 8°. 18 pp.
G.A. Oxon 8° 1110 (4)
— 1869. 24 pp.   G.A. Oxon 8° 161 (5)
— 1885, 95, 1901, 1902.   G.A. Oxon 8° 433
— 1911.   G.A. Oxon 8° 1328

6979. General notice for members of the House in lodgings. Oct. 16. [Oxf.] (1868), s. sh.   G.A. Oxon c. 272 (f. 6)

6980. DODGSON, C. L., Objections submitted to the governing body of Christ Church, Oxford, against certain proposed alterations in the quadrangle. May 16. Oxf., 1873, 4°. 4 pp.

6981. DODGSON, C. L., Twelve months in a curatorship. [An account of the proceedings of Christ Church common room, by C. L. Dodgson.] Oxf., 1884, 8°. 83 pp.
— Suppl. pp. 58–63. 1884.
— Postscript. [Part of preceding item, reprinted.] Oxf., [1884], s. sh.

6982. [*Begin.*] It has long been felt . . . [A letter proposing the formation of a junior common room.] Nov. 1885. (Oxf., 1885), s. sh.
G.A. Oxon c. 272 (f. 46)

6983. DODGSON, C. L., Three years in a curatorship. Oxf., 1886, 8°. 31 pp.

6984. DODGSON, C. L., Remarks on the report of the Finance committee [by C. L. Dodgson]. Oxf., 1886, 8°. 8 pp.

6985. DODGSON, C. L., Remarks on mr. Sampson's proposal [in connection with the policy of the Christ Church common room]. May 27. Oxf., 1886, 8°. 4 pp.

6986. DODGSON, C. L., Observations on mr. Sampson's new proposal [in connection with the policy of Christ Church common room]. June 10. Oxf., 1886, 8°. 10 pp.

6987. Regulations for scouts. [2 issues, Feb. 6, 17.] (Oxf., 1886), s. sh.
G.A. Oxon c. 272 (f. 15, 16)

6988. List of lodgings and residences, Ch. Ch., Oct. term, 1882; Easter and Act terms, 1886; Mich. term, 1891, 99, 1906. [Oxf.], 1886–1906, s. shs.
G.A. Oxon c. 272 (f. 21–23)

6989. [*Begin.*] The governing body . . . [A proposal to change the constitution of the Electoral board, signed by E. F. Sampson and 2 others.] Mar. 4, 1890. [Oxf.], (1890), s. sh.   G.A. Oxon c. 272 (f. 8)

6990. [*Begin.*] As we shall feel it our duty . . . [The text of a statement made on May 21st urging the dissolution of the Electoral board, signed by E. F. Sampson and 9 others.] June 17th. [Oxf.], (1890), 8°. 4 pp.
G.A. Oxon c. 272 (f. 8)

6991. DODGSON, C. L., [A circular addressed to the governing body of Christ Church concerning the proposal to invite M.A.'s to dine at High Table.] 1891.

6992. DODGSON, C. L., [A circular about resignation of curatorship.] 1892.

6993. Curiosissima curatoria [resolutions of the Senior common room, ed.] by 'Rude Donatus' [C. L. Dodgson]. Oxf., 1892, 8°. 47 pp.
G.A. Oxon 8° 687

6994. SAMPSON, E. F., The Electoral board [signed E. F. Sampson]. Oct. 17th. [Oxf.], (1893), 8°. 4 pp.   G.A. Oxon c. 272 (f. 8)

6995. BAYNE, T. VERE, The Electoral board. 20 Nov. [Arguments in favour of the board.] [Oxf.], (1893), 8°. 4 pp. G.A. Oxon c. 272 (f. 9)

6996. Christ Church. [Report.] 1899/1900–1928/29. (Oxf.), 1900–29, 8°.
G.A. Oxon 8° 510*
[The Bodleian set is imperfect.]

6997. [Tutors' lists of students. Hilary term 1907–Trinity term 1920. The Bodleian set is imperfect.] G.A. Oxon c. 272 (f. 23); 4° 732

6998. Christ Church. Address list, 1937. Oxf., 1937, 8°. 186 pp.
G.A. Oxon 8° 1168

EXPULSIONS

6999. GRENVILLE, WILLIAM WYNDHAM, *baron*. Oxford and Locke. [Defending the so-called expulsion of Locke from his studentship against the censures by Dugald Stewart in the preliminary dissertations to the Supplementary volume of Encyclopædia Britannica, 1824.] Lond., 1829, 8°. 87 pp. 29. 818
— 2nd ed. 1829. 24751 e. 14 (5)

7000. BOURNE, H. R. FOX, Locke's expulsion from Oxford. (Macmillan's mag., 1875, vol. 33, p. 63–66.) G.A. Oxon 4° 581 (13)

7001. OSLER, W., Locke's expulsion from Christ Church. (Oxf. mag., 1914, vol. 32, p. 264–66.) Per. G.A. Oxon 4° 141

See 7085 [Expulsion of W. Shipley. 1767].

7002. GEFFEN, E. M., The expulsion from Oxford [Christ Church] of Edmund ('rag') Smith [1705]. (Notes & queries, 1936, vol. 170, p. 398–401.) Per. 3974 e. 405 = A.

Statutes

7003. Statutes of the colleges... (Statutes of Cardinal and King Henry the VIII.th's colleges.) Oxf. &c., 1853, 8°. 211 pp.
G.A. Oxon 8° 25 = R.

7004. Ordinance framed by the Commissioners appointed for the purposes of the statute 17th and 18th Vict. c. 81, in relation to the Cathedral or House of Christ Church in Oxford. Draft. n. pl., [1857], fol. 6 pp.
G.A. Oxon c. 272 (f. 1)

7005. Oxford university. Copies of three ordinances... in relation to certain exhibitions or scholarships in Queen's college, and to the exhibition of dame Elizabeth Holford's foundation at Christ Church. [Lond.], 1858, fol. 9 pp. Pp. Eng. 1857/8 vol. 46

7006. Oxford university. Copies of four ordinances . . . in relation to Christ's Church, and Queen's, University, and Brazenose colleges. [Lond.], 1858, fol. 38 pp. Pp. Eng. 1857/8 vol. 46

7007. Ordinances and statutes framed or approved by the . . . Commissioners . . . (Christ Church, p. 349–66.) Oxf., 1863, 8°.
Clar. Press 31 a. 63

7008. Christ Church, Oxford. Recommendations and proposed statutes. [Proof, signed C. T. Cantuar and 4 others.] [Oxf., 1866], fol. 16 pp.

G.A. Oxon c. 258 (1)

— [Another proof.] 8 pp.   G.A. Oxon c. 258 (2)

— [Another proof.] [18 pp.]   G.A. Oxon c. 258 (3)

7009. A bill to repeal certain ordinances made for . . . Christ Church . . . by the Commissioners appointed under the Oxford university act, 1854, and to substitute a new ordinance in lieu thereof. 6 June, 1867. [Lond.], 1867, fol. 18 pp.   Pp. Eng. 1867 vol. 1

— Act. (30 & 31 V., c. 76, Pub.) Lond., 1867, fol. 18 pp.   L.L.

7010. Statutes proposed to be made . . . for Christ Church. Nov. 1880. (Oxf.), 1880, 8°. 31 pp.   G.A. Oxon 8° 425 (6) = R.

7011. Statutes proposed to be made by the University of Oxford commissioners for the Queen's college, concerning exhibitions; Christ Church concerning Westminster scholarships; Jesus college concerning the Meyricke endowment. (Oxf.), 1881, 8°. 13 pp.

G.A. Oxon 8° 425 (2) = R.

7012. Statutes proposed to be made by the University of Oxford commissioners for Christ Church. April 1881. [Lond.], 1881, fol. 20 pp.

G.A. Oxon c. 8 (39)

7013. Statutes of Christ Church. (Univ. of Oxf. and Cambr. act, 1877. Oxford. Thirty-six statutes made by the Univ. of Oxf. commissioners, 1881, p. 42–56, 248.)   Pp. Eng. 1882 vol. 51

7014. A statute in part for the University and in part for . . . Christ Church concerning Dr. Lee's readers. (Univ. of Oxf. and Cambr. act, 1877, Oxford. Two statutes made by the Univ. of Oxf. commissioners, 1881, p. 1–3.)   Pp. Eng. 1882 vol. 51

7015. A statute for . . . Christ Church, concerning Westminster scholarships within the House. (Univ. of Oxf. and Cambr. act, 1877. Oxford. Five statutes made by the Univ. of Oxf. commissioners, 1881, p. 4, 5.) Pp. Eng. 1882 vol. 51

7016. Statute made by the governing body of Christ Church, on 15th June, 1882, for inserting a clause in Statute XVI of the Christ Church statutes made by the Commissioners of the University of Oxford, under the provisions of 40 & 41 Vict. c. 48. [Lond.], 1882, s. sh.

Pp. Eng. 1882 vol. 51

7017. Christ Church. Additions made on the 25th October 1882 by the governing body to Statute XVI, clauses 11 and 22, of the statutes of Christ Church. 6 March 1883. [Lond.], 1883, s. sh.

Pp. Eng. 1883 vol. 53

7018. Statute made by . . . Christ Church, on the 9th Feb., 1887, altering clause 22 of Statute XVI. Lond., 1887, s. sh.   Pp. Eng. 1887 vol. 65

7019. Statute made by . . . Christ Church on the 4th May 1887 altering Statute XXII . . . and statute made by Pembroke college on the 14th June 1887, altering Statute VI, clause 8 . . . Lond., 1888, s. sh.
Pp. Eng. 1888 vol. 78

7020. Statute made on the 7th December 1887 by . . . Christ Church . . . amending Statute XXVIII . . . Lond., 1888, s. sh.
Pp. Eng. 1888 vol. 78

7021. Statutes passed by . . . Christ Church . . . on the 8th May, 1889, adding at the end of Statute XXIII. a new clause; and . . . on the 29th May, 1889, adding certain words in Statute I, para. 3, after the words 'Treasurer and steward'. Lond., 1890, s. sh.   Pp. Eng. 1890 vol. 56

7022. Statute made by . . . Christ Church, 7th Dec., 1892, amending Statute XXII, clause 9. Lond., 1893, s. sh.   Pp. Eng. 1893/4 vol. 68

7023. Statute made on the 4th May 1892 by . . . Christ Church, for altering Statute XVI. Lond., 1893, s. sh.   Pp. Eng. 1893/4 vol. 68

7024. Statutes made by . . . Christ Church . . . on the 24th January 1894, amending Statutes X., XVI., XX., and XXXIV. of the Statutes of the House, and a statute concerning Dr. Lee's readers. 7 June 1894. [Lond.], 1894, fol. 3 pp.   Pp. Eng. 1894 vol. 66

7025. Statutes made by . . . the House of Christ Church . . . on the 6th December 1893 altering respectively Statute XXII. and Statute XXIII . . . 9 May 1894. Lond., 1894, s. sh.   Pp. Eng. 1894 vol. 66

7026. Statute made by . . . Christ Church, 8th May 1895, altering Statute XXVI. Lond., 1896, s. sh.   Pp. Eng. 1896 vol. 65

7027. Statute made by . . . Christ Church, 23rd Oct. 1895, altering clause 13 of Statute XVI. Lond., 1896, s. sh.   Pp. Eng. 1896 vol. 65

7028. Statutes made by . . . Christ Church, 14th Nov. and 5th Dec. 1900, respectively, amending Statute XXIII. (College exhibitions.) Lond., 1901, s. sh.   Pp. Eng. 1901 vol. 56

7029. Statutes made for Christ Church, and a statute made for the University and for Christ Church concerning dr. Lee's readers by the University of Oxford commissioners . . . as altered . . . in Council up to May, 1903. Oxf., 1903, 8°. 51 pp.   G.A. Oxon 8° 855

7030. Statute made by . . . Christ Church, 7th Dec. 1904, amending clause 3 of the Statute concerning Westminster scholarships. Lond., 1905, s. sh.   Pp. Eng. 1905 vol. 60

7031. Statutes made by . . . Christ Church, 29th June 1905, altering Statutes XI, XVI, and XVIII. Lond., 1906, s. sh. Pp. Eng. 1906 vol. 90

7032. Statute made by . . . Christ Church, 23rd Oct. 1907, altering and amending Statute XVI, clauses 19 and 20. Lond., 1908, s. sh.
Pp. Eng. 1908 vol. 86

7033. Statute made by . . . Christ Church, 11th Mar. 1908, amending Statute XVI, clause 12. Lond., 1908, s. sh.   Pp. Eng. 1908 vol. 86

7034. Statute made by . . . Christ Church, 25th June 1908, amending Statute XVI, clause 9. Lond., 1908, s. sh.   Pp. Eng. 1908 vol. 86

7035. Statutes made by . . . Christ Church, 10th June 1914 and duly sealed, amending certain of the existing Statutes. Lond., 1914, fol. 8 pp.
Pp. Eng. 1914/16 vol. 51

7036. Statute made by . . . Christ Church, 27th June 1912 and 31st May 1913, amending Statute XVII. Lond., 1914, fol. 3 pp.
Pp. Eng. 1914/16 vol. 51

7037. Statutes made by . . . Christ Church, 16th June 1915, amending Statute XVI (23) and (24), and Statute XVII (2), and adding a 12th clause to the last-named Statute. Lond., 1916, s. sh.
Pp. Eng. 1916 vol. 22

7038. Statutes made for Christ Church . . . by the University of Oxford commissioners . . . approved 30th April, 1926. Oxf., 1926, 8°. [48 pp.].
G.A. Oxon 8° 1407

7039. Statutes made for the colleges . . . (Christ Church). Oxf., 1927, 8°. 48 pp.   G.A. Oxon 4° 759 = R.

Finance and property

7040. An acte of exchaung betwene the kynges highnes and the heyres of the lord marques Mountegue [confirming the title in various agreements made by Cardinal's college]. (22 Hen. VIII, c. 21.) 1530/31. [Excerpts from the act were printed in Shadwell's Enactments &c. See no. 956.]

7041. An acte for the assuringe of the patronage of the vicarage of Rotherston in the countie of Chester and a schollars roome in the cathedrall churche of Christe in Oxon . . . by the deane and chapiter of the saide cathedrall churche to Thomas Venables . . . and his heires for ever. (43 Eliz., c. 8, Private.) 1601.
[Text in Shadwell's Enactments &c. See no. 956.]

7042. The case truly stated betwixt the Dean and Chapter of Christ Church in Oxford, and William Adkins butcher, concerning Frideswides meadow near Oxford. [Madan 2777.] [Oxf., 1667], s. sh.
Wood 423 (37)

7043. An act to carry into effect . . . the fourth report of the Commissioners of ecclesiastical duties and revenues. (3 & 4 V., c. 113, Pub.). [The act annexes to the Lady Margaret professorship of divinity a canonry at Christ Church in lieu of a canonry at Worcester: and two further canonries at Christ Church to the Regius professorships of Pastoral theology and Ecclesiastical history, which her majesty intends to found. Also benefices annexed to headships of colleges may be sold.] Lond., 1840, fol. 28 pp.   L.L.
— 23 & 24 V., c. 59, Pub.

7044. An act to enable the dean and chapter of the cathedral church of
Christ ... as owners ... of lands in Kentish Town ... to grant building
leases ... (14 & 15 V., c. 18, Private.) Lond., 1851, fol. 14 pp.   L.L.

See 2728 &c. [Proposal to endow a Greek chair &c. 1864, 65].

7045. [*Begin.*] The governing body of Christ Church ... [regrets its in-
ability to contribute to funds required in connection with proposed
University reform. An answer to the Vice-chancellor's circular of Oct.
22]. Dec. 1. [Oxf.], (1874), s. sh.   G.A. Oxon c. 272 (f. 7)

7046. *Re* The contribution to be made by Ch. Ch. to University purposes.
'Case for the opinion of counsel' [and] Opinion [signed H. A. Giffard].
5th Nov. n. pl., (1886), 4°. 4 pp.   G.A. Oxon c. 272 (f. 7)

7047. PALMER, E., Presentation to livings [signed E. Palmer]. 24 May.
[Oxf.], (1889), 4°. 3 pp.   G.A. Oxon c. 272 (f. 7)

7048. HOOLE, C. H., [*Begin.*] Mr. C. H. Hoole ... having applied for
presentation to a living in the gift of the House, and having received in
reply ... a doubt as to the validity of his claim, wishes to ... submit the
following remarks ... June 6. [Oxf.], (1886), 4°. 3 pp.
                                                  G.A. Oxon c. 272 (f. 7)

Fabric, including Bells

See also 7131 &c. Cathedral.

7049. Out of the journal book of the expences of all the buildings of Christ
Church college Oxon; which I had of mr. Pore of Blechinton. (Collectanea curiosa, by J. Gutch, vol. 1, p. 204–08.) Oxf., 1781, 8°.
                                                         Gough Oxf. 65

7050. Six etchings by William Crotch from sketches by mr. O'Neill of the
ruins of the late fire at Christ Church. To which is prefixed Some
account of the fire and the buildings injured by it. Oxf., 1809, fol. 6 pp.
+6 plates.   G.A. fol. A 121

7051. [March 6, 1809. The Dean and Chapter of Christ Church thank all
who helped during the fire 'on the night of Friday last'.] Oxf., 1809,
s. sh.   G.A. Oxon c. 272 (f. 3)

7052. Letter from cardinal Wolsey to count Beaumont, respecting stone
for building his colleges at Ipswich and Oxford. Ex MSS. Bibl. Reg.
Paris, vol. 8539. (Collectanea topogr. et geneal., 1834, vol. 1, p. 241,
42.)   2184 d. 21 = R.

7053. Great Tom of Oxford. [A short account of the bell. A MS. note on
the Bodley copy runs] 'from the MS. of [? T. C.] Leach of Exeter coll.'
East Bourn, 1835, s. sh.   MS. Top. Oxon d. 22 (f. 9)

7054. SMYTH, W. H., [Note on the old clock of Christ Church, removed in
1838.] (Archaeologia, 1849, vol. 33, p. 14.)
                                        Per. G.A. Gen. top. 4° 162 = R.

7055. CONRADI, On remains discovered in excavation for the foundations of the new buildings at Christ Church. (Proc., Oxf. architect. and hist. soc., 1863, N.S., vol. 1, p. 217–22.)   Per. G.A. Oxon 8° 498 = R.

7056. Oxford. New buildings, Christ Church college; Worcester college chapel. (Builder, 1866, vol. 24, p. 337, 38.)   N. 1863 c. 1

7057. DODGSON, C. L., The new belfry of Christ Church, a monograph by D. C. L. Oxf., 1872, 8°. 24 pp.   G.A. Oxon 8° 147 (10)
— [Another issue, with J. H. Stacey added in the imprint on p. 24.]
— 2nd thousand. 1872.   Arch. AA e. 36
— [Another ed.] 2nd thousand. (The Lewis Carroll picture book, ed. by S. D. Collingwood, 1899, p. 101–17.)   270 e. 1155
— 2nd thousand. 1873.
— [Another ed.] 32 pp.
[Also publ. as pt. of Notes by an Oxford chiel, 1874.] G.A. Oxon 8° 161

7058. DODGSON, C. L., The vision of the three T's, a threnology by the author of The new belfry [C. L. Dodgson]. Oxf., 1873, 8°. 37 pp.
Arch. AA e. 30
— 2nd ed. 1873.   G.A. Oxon 8° 147 (20)
[Also publ. as pt. of Notes by an Oxford chiel, 1873.] G.A. Oxon 8° 161
— [Another ed.] (The Lewis Carroll picture book, ed. by S. D. Collingwood, 1899, p. 118–46.)   270 e. 1155

7059. GRIFFITH, E. F. G., Report . . . on the drainage and sanitary arrangements of Christ Church. n. pl., 1881, fol. 18 pp.
G.A. Oxon c. 107 (26)

7060. IDLETHORNE, O., Great Tom, the curfew bell of Oxford: an historical ballad. Par., 1885, 8°. 31 pp.   280 e. 271

7061. HAVERFIELD, F. J., [Note on a detail in the architecture of Christ Church.] (Proc., Soc. of antiq., 1909, ser. 2, vol. 22, p. 424–30.)
— [Further note] (Proc., Soc. of antiq., 1910, ser. 2, vol. 23, p. 284).
Per. G.A. Gen. top. 8° 524 = R.

7062. 'Tom tower', Christ Church, Oxford: some letters of sr. Christopher Wren to John Fell, bishop of Oxford, set forth and annotated by W. D. Caröe, with a chapter by H. H. Turner, and another by A. Cochrane. Oxf., 1923, 4°. 127 pp.   G.A. Oxon 4° 440

7063. MILNE, J. G., and HARVEY, J. H., The building of Cardinal college. (Oxoniensia, 1943/44, vol. 8/9, p. 137–53.) Per. G.A. Oxon 4° 658 = R.

7064. HISCOCK, W. G., A Christ Church miscellany, new chapters on the architects, craftsmen, statuary, plate, bells, furniture, clocks, plays, the library and other buildings. Oxf., 1946, 4°. xix+260 pp.
G.A. Oxon 4° 636

7065. PEVSNER, N., Reassessment 4. Three Oxford colleges [Christ Church, Corpus Christi, St. Edmund Hall]. (Architect. review, 1949, vol. 106, p. 120–24.)   Per. 17356 c. 8

7066. SHARPE, F., Re-hanging Great Tom. (Country Life, 1953, vol. 113, p. 1694, 95.)   Per. 384 b. 6

7066.4. HEYWORTH, P. L., Christ Church [library building] & Chaucer [John Urry's edition]. (Oxf. mag., 1962, N.S., vol. 2, p. 386, 87.)   Per. G.A. Oxon 4° 141

Members

BIOGRAPHY

7067. FEILING, K., In Christ Church hall. [Biographical sketches of 21 Christ Church men.] Lond. &c., 1960, 8°. 209 pp.   G.A. Oxon 8° 1415

7068. HOLLAND, H. S., Dean Aldrich, a commemoration speech. (Oxf., 1872), 8°. 26 pp.   11124 e. 34

7069. SUTTLE, E. F. A., Henry Aldrich, dean of Christ Church. (Oxoniensia, 1940, vol. 5, p. 115–39.)   Per. G.A. Oxon 4° 658 = R.

7070. HISCOCK, W. G., Henry Aldrich of Christ Church, 1648–1710. Oxf., 1960, 8°. xii+74 pp. +32 pl.   G.A. Oxon 4° 770

7071. LISTER, I., A bear at Oxford [kept by Francis Buckland at Christ Church]. (Country Life, 1956, vol. 109, p. 1043.)   Per. 384 b. 6

See 4624 [Hughes, H., Gladstone, Christ Church and Oxford. 1898].

7072. An essay on the life of David Gregory [1696–1767] late dean of Christ-Church. Lond., 1769, 8°. 30 pp.   Gough Oxf. 110 (2)

7073. GIRTIN, T., Mr. Hakluyt, scholar at Oxford [student of Christ Church]. (Geogr. journ., 1953, vol. 119, p. 208–12.)   Soc. 2017 d. 60

7074. [*Begin.*] The announcement of the resignation . . . [Copy of an address made by members of the University to dr. Liddell on his resignation as Dean, with the dean's answer. Dec. 1891.] [Oxf., 1891], fol. 4 pp.   G.A. Oxon c. 272 (f. 29)

7075. THOMPSON, H. L., Henry George Liddell, dean of Christ Church, a memoir [1811–98]. Lond., 1899, 4°. 288 pp.   G.A. Oxon 4° 202

7076. PAGET, S., and CRUM, J. M. C., Francis Paget . . . sometime Dean of Christ Church. [Chapter 6, Christ Church, 1892–1901.] Lond., 1912, 8°.   11126 d. 126

7077. Collegas discipulos amicos salutat abiturus Thomas B. Strong decanus. (Oxf., 1920), 4°. 8 pp.   G.A. Oxon 4° 399 (19)

REMINISCENCES

See 3880 [Reminiscences. 1865–70].

7078. BRIDGES, J. A., At 'the House' in the 50's. (Cornhill mag., 1899, N.S., vol. 7, p. 65–75.)   Per. 2705 d. 213

7079. BROWN, G. J. COWLEY-, Christ Church, Oxford, sixty years ago. 1–3. (Oxf. mag., 1915, vol. 34, p. 41, 42; 56, 57, 71, 72.)
Per. G.A. Oxon 4° 141

7080. COLMAN, G., *the younger*, Random records. (Christ Church, 1780's. Vol. 1, p. 263–310.) Lond., 1830, 8°.   30. 56

See 3914 [Graves, C. L., Oxford in the 'seventies. 1917].

7081. OAKELEY, F., Personal recollections of an old Oxonian [F. Oakeley]. i. Christ Church under dean Hall. ii. Christ Church under dean Smith. iii. Balliol under dr. Jenkyns. (Month, 1865, vol. 3, p. 508–20, 606–14; 1866, vol. 4, p. 50–59.)   Per. 11132 d. 17
[See also no. 3855.]

7082. TASWELL, W., Autobiography and anecdotes by W. Taswell, sometime student of Christ Church [1670–82] ed. by G. P. Elliott [tr. by H. Taswell]. (Camden soc., 1853, vol. 55, no. 6. 40 pp.)
2233 e. 54 = K.

Academic life

7083. Carmina quadragesimalia ab Ædis Christi Oxon. alumnis composita et ab ejusdem Ædis baccalaureis determinantibus in schola naturalis philosophiæ publice recitata [ed. by C. Este]. Oxon., 1723, 8°. 168 pp.
8° C 89 Jur.
— Volumen secundum [ed. by A. Parsons]. Oxon., 1748, 8°. 155 pp.
8° C 90 Jur.
— Ed. altera. [Vol. 1]. Lond., 1741, 12°. 180 pp.   2995 f. 8
— [Another ed. Vol. 1, 2]. Glasg., 1757, 12°. 112+102 pp.   2995 f. 6
— Ed. 3a. [Vol. 1]. Lond., 1761, 12°.   Vet. A 5 e. 703

7084. Carmina quadragesimalia ab Ædis Christi Oxon. alumnis composita. [Selections, by L. B.] Oxon., 1829, 16°. 40 pp.   2995 f. 17

7085. SHIPLEY, W., Comparative observations on two of the poems which were honoured with prizes in a late certamen at Ch. Ch., by a gentleman [W. Shipley?] of the University. York, 1767, 8°. 29 pp.
G.A. Oxon 8° 91
[Shipley was deprived of his studentship for publishing this libel with the help of W. Crowe. It seems likely that Shipley was also the author, although he was not accused as such. He was subsequently reinstated after appeal to the Visitor.]

7086. SAMPSON, E. F., [*Begin.*] The accompanying list of the classes obtained by undergraduates of Ch. Ch. during the last twelve years [1860–71] is printed as the main argument for the resolutions [concerning Junior studentships] of which notice was given at the last meeting of the Governing body [signed E. F. S.]. [Oxf., 1872?], 4°. 3 pp.
G.A. Oxon c. 272 (f. 11)

Exhibitions and scholarships

7087. Fell's exhibitions, 1830, 32. [Examination papers.] [Oxf.], (1830, 32), 4° &c.   G.A. Oxon c. 272 (f. 4, 5)

7088. [Examination papers]. 1859–74. [Oxf.], 1859–74, 8°. [The Bodleian set is imperf., 2626 d. 31.]

Clubs and societies

7089. Christ Church. Rules of the Amalgamated clubs. [Oxf.], (1896), s. sh.
G.A. Oxon c. 272 (f. 70)

7090. Anonym club. [List of members.] Hilary term, 1895. (Oxf., 1895), s. sh.
G.A. Oxon c. 272 (f. 48)

7091. Christ Church Bible reading. Mich. term, 1900. (Oxf.), 1900, 16°. 4 pp.
G.A. Oxon c. 272 (f. 51)

7092. Christ Church boat club. Rules. Oxf., 1893, 8°. 13 pp.
G.A. Oxon 8° 1113 (22)

7093. List of members of the Christ Church Cardinals, 1866. (Oxf., 1866), 8°. 4 pp.
G.A. Oxon c. 272 (f. 47)

7094. Christ Church debating society. Rules. Oxf., (1872), 8°. 9 pp.
G.A. Oxon 8° 659 (21*)

7095. The Christ Church essay club. [Rules and members.] (Oxf., 1910), 16°. 4 pp.
G.A. Oxon c. 272 (f. 49)

7096. Christ Church mission to East London. [Miscellaneous papers. 1882.]
G.A. Oxon c. 272 (f. 56)

7097. Christ Church Nondescripts. List of members, 1874. [Oxf.], (1874), s. sh.
G.A. Oxon c. 272 (f. 52)

7098. Christ Church philharmonic society. Concert [programme]. 1886, 87. n. pl., 1886, 87, 8°.
G.A. Oxon c. 272 (f. 60)

7099. Christ Church Shakespeare society. [Rules.] (Oxf.), n. d., 16°. 4 pp.
G.A. Oxon c. 272 (f. 50)

7100. Christ Church society. Rules. n. pl., [18—], s. sh.
G.A. Oxon 8° 1113 (7)
— [With list of members.] Oxf., 1850, 12°. 13 pp.
— Christmas 1851; Easter, 1853; Lent, 1855; Mich. 1857; Hilary 1859; Hilary 1861; Hilary 1863; Hilary 1864; Trinity 1864; Mich. 1866; Trinity 1871; Mich. 1875; Easter 1878.
G.A. Oxon 8° 1113 (8–21)

7101. The Harmony club. Rules. n. pl., n. d., 16°. 3 pp.
G.A. Oxon c. 272 (f. 51)

7102. The Mercury wine club. Rules. n. pl., n. d., 8°. 2 pp.
G.A. Oxon c. 272 (f. 51)

7103. The Mermaid club. [Rules]. 1895. Oxf., 1895, 8°. 3 pp.
G.A. Oxon c. 272 (f. 48)

7104. Mermaid club. [List of members.] Hilary term, 1898; Summer, Mich. term, 1899. Oxf., 1898, 99, s. sh.   G.A. Oxon c. 272 (f. 48, 49)

7105. P. List of members. Mich. term, 1903. [Oxf.], (1903), s. sh.
G.A. Oxon c. 272 (f. 52)

Library and archives

7106. KITCHIN, G. W., Catalogus codicum MSS. qui in bibliotheca Ædis Christi . . . adservantur. Oxonii, 1867, 4°. 82 pp.
2590 d. Oxf. 20. 1 = R.

7107. Ch. Ch. library. [Regulations.] Nov. 1, 1869. Feb. 3, 1870. (Oxf., 1869, 70), 2 sheets.   G.A. Oxon c. 272 (f. 13, 14)

7108. HOOLE, C. H., An account of some Greek manuscripts contained in the library of Christ Church. Lond., 1895, 8°. 31 pp. 2590 e. Oxf. 20. 2

7109. The library, 1904. [Report.] [Oxf., 1905], 8°. 4 pp. 2590 e. Oxf. 20. 1

7110. ARKWRIGHT, G. E. P., Catalogue of music in the library of Christ Church. 2 pt. Oxf. &c., 1915, 23, 8°.   2590 d. Oxf. 20. 2 = R.

7111. HIFF, A., *ed.*, Catalogue of printed music published prior to 1800 now in the library of Christ Church. Lond. &c., 1919, 8°. 76 pp.
2590 e. Oxf. 20. 3 = Mus.

See 5749 [List of Robert Burton's books in Christ Church library. 1925].

7112. PULVER, J., Henry Aldrich [the founder of the old music library, Christ Church]. (Mus. news, 1926, vol. 71, p. 302, 303.) N. 17402 d. 36

7113. YOUNG, N. DENHOLM-, Cartulary of the mediaeval archives of Christ Church. Oxf., 1931, 8°. 266 pp.   G.A. Oxon 8° 1205
— [Another issue.] (Oxf. hist. soc., vol. 92.) G.A. Oxon 8° 360 = R.

7114. HUSSEY, C., The library of Christ Church. (Country Life, 1947, vol. 101, p. 612, 13.)   Per. 384 b. 6

7115. BILL, G., Christ Church and Hereford cathedral libraries and the Bodleian. (Bodleian library record, 1952, vol. 4, p. 145–49.)
2590 d. Oxf. 1. 41 = R.

7116. A catalogue of manorial records at Christ Church. [Reprod. from typewriting.] n. pl., [1953], 4°. 280 pp.   MS. Top. Oxon d. 449

7117. A catalogue of maps, plans & drawings at Christ Church. [Reprod. from typewriting.] n. pl., 1953, 4°. 193 pp.   MS. Top. Oxon d. 450

7118. HISCOCK, W. G., The Christ Church supplement to Wing's Short-title catalogue, 1641–1700. Oxf., 1956, 4°. 47 pp. 2582 d. 121 = R.

7119. HISCOCK, W. G., The Christ Church holdings in Wing's Short-title catalogue, 1641–1700, of books of which less than 5 copies are recorded in the United Kingdom. [Reprod. from typewriting.] n. pl., 1956, fol. 165 sh.   2590 c. Oxf. 20. 1 = R.

Pictures, plate, coins, etc.

7120. List of the pictures in Christ-Church library (the benefaction of the late general Guise). n. pl., [*c.* 1770], 8°. 14 pp. G.A. Oxon 8° 68 (7)

7121. A catalogue of the collection of pictures in the library at Christ Church, bequeathed to the college, by the late general Guise. To which is added A catalogue of the portraits in Christ Church hall. [Oxf., 1770?], 8°. 15 pp. G. Pamph. 1431

7122. A catalogue of the collection of pictures in the library at Christ Church, bequeathed by general Guise, 1765, and of the additions made by subsequent donations; also a catalogue of the portraits in Christ Church hall. Oxf., 1833, 8°. 32 pp. G.A. Oxon 8° 357

7123. Brief guide to the portraits in Christ Church hall. (Oxf., 1904), 16°. 30 pp. G.A. Oxon 16° 33 (16)
— 2nd ed. 1906; 3rd ed. 1907. G.A. Oxon 16° 33 (16*, 16**)
— 5th ed. 1912. 17061 e. 27

See 5391 [Colvin, sir S., Drawings of the old masters . . . in the library of Christ Church. 1907].

7124. BELL, C. F., Drawings by the old masters in the library of Christ Church, an alphabetical list. Oxf., 1914, 8°. 93 pp.+125 pl. 1706 f. 50

7125. BORENIUS, T., Pictures by the old masters in the library of Christ Church, a brief catalogue. Lond. &c., 1916, 12°. 117 pp.+64 pl.
1706 f. 58

7126. HISCOCK, W. G., Notes on some Christ Church portraits, including one of Oriel and two of Pembroke. (Oxoniensia, 1946/7, vol. 11/12, p. 147–51.) Per. G.A. Oxon 4° 658 = R.

See 5403 [Drawings of Venetian artists. 1958].

7127. Paintings and drawings from Christ Church, Oxford. An exhibition in aid of the Christ Church united clubs, Kennington, 27th April–11th June, 1960. [Catalogue.] (Lond., 1960), 4°. 85 pl.+letterpress.
1706 d. 510

7128. An account of plate, gold and silver, made for cardinal Wolsey . . . wherein is set forth what he gave to the colleges founded by him. (Collectanea curiosa, by J. Gutch, vol. 2. St. Frideswide's college in Oxford, p. 304–11.) Oxf., 1781, 8°. Gough Oxf. 66

7129. JONES, E. A., Catalogue of the plate of Christ Church. Oxf., 1939, fol. xxi+52 pp.+18 pl. 17552 c. 20

7130. SUTHERLAND, C. H. V., The coin collection of Christ Church. (Oxoniensia, 1940, vol. 5, p. 140–145.) Per. G.A. Oxon 4° 658 = R.

See 5623 [Waagen, G.F., Treasures of art. 1854].
See 5300 [Woodward, J., Treasures in Oxford. 1951].

Cathedral

7131. [Miscellaneous papers in the Bodleian 1880–1935.] G.A. Oxon b. 149

7132. [Topographical prints, &c. in the Bodleian.]   G.A. Oxon a. 67

7133. Liber precum publicarum in usum Ecclesiæ Chathedralis Christi Oxon. [Madan 423.] Oxon., 1615, 16°. [40]+240+[16] pp. 8° L 96 Th. [Many subsequent editions are to be found in Christ Church library.]

7134. The following particulars relating to the will of . . . mrs. Elizabeth Berkeley are submitted to . . . Convocation [relating to the bequest of Vine's Hill, Henley, to provide for 3 annual sermons, one at Christ Church, one at Cheltenham and one at Shottesbrook]. May 28. [Oxf.], 1804, s. sh.   Don. b. 12 (101*b*)

7135. BRITTON, J., The history and antiquities of the Cathedral church of Oxford. Lond., 1821, 4°. 50 pp.+11 pl.   G.A. Eccl. top. 4° 43
— [Another ed. 1836.]   Manning 4° 52

7136. GRAHAM, J. S., Ecclesiæ Oxonienses illustratæ; comprising the Cathedral of Christ Church, the parish churches and other places of worship situated in Oxford and its vicinity. Oxf., 1825, 4°.
                                             G.A. Oxon 4° 357

7137. Sepulchral monuments in Oxford [at Christ Church, Magdalen and New colleges] from drawings by T. F[isher]. (Lond.), [*c*. 1830], fol. plates 1–10.   G.A. fol. A 122

7138. Oxford cathedral. (Architect. and picturesque illustr. of the cath. churches of Engl. and Wales, by B. Winkles, 1836, vol. 2, p. 129–40.)
                                             Manning 4° 53

7139. INGRAM, J., Christ Church cathedral. (Memorials of Oxford, 1837, vol. 1, p. 1–32 of the account of Christ Church.)   G.A. Oxon 8° 18

See also 3777 &c. [The Dean and Canons of Christ Church and Select preachers. 1847].

7140. BLOXHAM, M. H., Sepulchral monuments in Oxford cathedral [signed M. H. Bloxham]. (Archaeol. journ., 1852, vol. 9, p. 150–57.)
                                Per. G.A. Gen. top. 8° 529 = R.
— [Repr.]   G.A. Oxon 8° 947

7141. SCOTT, G. G., Report . . . on the [fabric of the] Cathedral of Christ Church. n. pl., (1869), 8°. 15 pp.   G.A. Oxon 8° 146 (5)

7142. WALCOTT, M. E. C., Inventories and valuations of religious houses at the time of the dissolution, from the Public Record Office. (Archaeologia, 1871, vol. 43. Christ Church, p. 237, 238.)
                                Per. G.A. Gen. top. 4° 162 = R.

7143. Oxford cathedral. (Sunday at home, 1872, p. 453–56.)
                                             G.A. Oxon 4° 578 (35)

7144. RICHARDSON, W. H., Inscriptions on stones on the floor of the cloisters of the Cathedral, Oxford. (Genealogist, 1880, vol. 4, p. 125, 126.)   Per. 2184 d. 34 = R.

7145. The Cathedral church of Christ in Oxford. [Short history, by W. Bright ?] n. pl., 1880, 8°. 4 pp.   G.A. Oxon 8° 250 (1)

See 6435 [Oxf. monuments. 1883].

7146. The register booke of Christ Church in Oxford of all that have been christened, maried and buried since . . . 1633. (Misc. geneal. et herald., 1886, 2nd ser., vol. 1, p. 143–46, 288–95; 1888, vol. 2, p. 198–200, 215–18, 236, 37, 251–54, 268–71.)   Per. 2184 d. 15 = R.

7147. HARRISON, J. P., Recent discoveries in Oxford cathedral. (Archaeol. journ., 1888, vol. 45, p. 271–83.)   Per. G.A. Gen. top. 8° 529 = R.
— Repr. Exeter, 1888, 8°. 15 pp.   G.A. Oxon 8° 1055 (18)

7148. HARRISON, J. P., Some recent discoveries in the Cathedral of Christ Church. (Proc., Oxf. architect. and hist. soc., 1888, N.S., vol. 5, p. 146, 47; 1889, p. 217–22, 267, 68.)   Per. G.A. Oxon 8° 498 = R.
— Repr. [of 1889 proc.]. Oxf., 1890, 8°. 11 pp. G.A. Oxon 8° 1230 (10)

7149. HARRISON, J. P., [Short account of some recent discoveries in Christ Church cathedral, followed by summary of discussion; extracts from Harrison's paper in the Archaeol. journ. (no. 7147) follow.] (Proc., Oxf. architect. and hist. soc., 1887, N.S., vol. 5, p. 88–108.)
                                                     Per. G.A. Gen. top. 8° 529 = R.

7150. Ward and Lock's illustrated historical handbook to Oxford cathedral, comprising also an account of the colleges, and a perambulation of the City. (Cath. cities of Engl. & Wales.) Lond. &c., 1889, 4°. [36 pp.].
                                                     G.A. Eccl. top. 4° 14 (4)

7151. HARRISON, J. PARK, The pre-Norman date of the design and some of the stone-work of Oxford cathedral. Lond. &c., 1890, 8°. 12 pp.
                                                     G.A. Oxon 8° 1055 (19)
— [Another ed.] 1891. 23 pp.+3 pl.   G.A. Oxon 8° 469 (11)

7152. HARRISON, J. PARK, An account of the discovery of the remains of three apses at Oxford cathedral. Lond. &c., 1891, 8°. 23 pp.
                                                     G.A. Oxon 8° 469 (17)

7153. HARRISON, J. PARK, On a pre-Norman window and other early work lately discovered in Christ Church cathedral. (Archaeologia Oxon., 1892 95, p. 23–31.)   G.A. Oxon 4° 148 = R.
— [Another ed.] . . . and some additional early work . . . (Archaeol. journ., 1892, vol. 49, p. 155–60.)   Per. G.A. Gen. top. 8° 529 = R.
— [Another ed.] Lond. &c., [1892], 8°. 11 pp. G.A. Oxon 8° 524 (5)

7154. The three shrines of St. Frideswide. (Archæologia Oxon., 1892–95, p. 304–14.)   G.A. Oxon 4° 148 = R.

7155. BLAKISTON, C. H., Monumental brasses and matrices in the Cathedral church of Christ in Oxford. (Journ., Oxf. univ. brass-rubbing soc., 1899, vol. 1, p. 268–86.)   Soc. 2184 d. 50

7156. CARÖE, W. D., Report upon the Cathedral church of Christ, Oxford. n. pl., (1908), 4°. 4 pp. G.A. Oxon c. 272 (f. 80)

7157. PAINTIN, H., The shrine of St. Frideswide, Christ Church. [Oxf.? 1911?], s. sh. G.A. Oxon 4° 276 (14)

7158. LAY, H. J., Oxford cathedral and its music. (Mus. news, 1916, vol. 50, p. 38, 39.) N. 17402 d. 36

7159. British cathedral organs: Christ Church. (Music student, 1920, vol. 13, p. 25, 26.) Per. 26327 c. 3

7160. WARNER, S. A., Oxford cathedral. Lond. &c., 1924, 8°. 258 pp. G.A. Oxon 8° 1031

7161. CRUM, J. M., The shrine of St. Frideswide in Oxford cathedral. (Oxf. diocesan mag., 1925, vol. 20, p. 119–24.) Per. 11126 d. 78

7162. JAMES, M. R., and TRISTRAM, E. W., Medieval wall-paintings at Christ Church [cathedral]. (Walpole soc., 1928, vol. 16, p. 1–8.) Soc. 17006 c. 82

7163. BULL, W. M., Tomb of St. Frideswide, Cathedral of Christ Church, a pilgrim's handbook. Lond. [1934], 16°. 16 pp. G.A. Oxon 16° 200 (17)

7164. WATSON, E. W., The Cathedral church of Christ in Oxford. Lond. &c., 1935, 8°. 72 pp. G.A. Oxon 8° 1161

7164.1. EVANS, H. F. O., The tomb of James Zouch in Oxford cathedral. (Trans., Monumental brass soc., 1962, vol. 9, p. 509–11.) Soc. 2184 d. 85

Meadow

7164.9. BILL, E. G. W., Christ Church meadow. Oxf., 1965, 4°. 39 pp. G.A. Oxon 4° 804

[Works dealing with proposed roads across the Meadow will be listed in the projected Bibliography of the City of Oxford.]

Corpus Christi

General 7165–7190
Administration, Property, and Finance 7191–7198
Statutes 7199–7219
Members
  Biography 7220–7223

Reminiscences 7224–7231
Lists 7232–7236
Clubs 7237–7242
Library and Archives 7243–7250

General

7165. [Topographical prints, &c. in the Bodleian.] G.A. Oxon a. 52

See 1116 [Carmina funebria in obitum Georgii de Sancto Paulo. 1614].

7166. The proceedings of Corpus Christi college . . . in the case of mr. Ayscough [and his fellowship] vindicated. Lond., 1730, 4°. 42 pp. Gough Oxf. 63 (7)

7167. A vindication of the proceedings in the case of mr. Ayscough of Corpus-Christi-college, Oxon. Lond., 1731, 4°. 40 pp.

Gough Oxf. 63 (8)

7168. INGRAM, J., Corpus Christi college. (Memorials of Oxford, 1837, vol. 2. 16 pp.) G.A. Oxon 8° 19

7169. [Miscellaneous C.C.C. scholarship examination papers. 1879–91.] G.A. Oxon c. 273 (f. 1–4)

7170. The Pelican Record. No. 1– . Oxf., 1891– , 8°.

Per. G.A. Oxon 8° 588

7171. H., The Wager book [c. 1775–1808]. (Pelican Record, 1892, vol. 1, p. 157–62.) Per. G.A. Oxon 8° 588

7172. FOWLER, T., The history of Corpus Christi college, with lists of its members. (Oxf. hist. soc., 25.) Oxf., 1893, 8°. 482 pp.

G.A. Oxon 8° 360 = R.

7173. FOWLER, T., The portraits in the hall. (Pelican Record, 1894, vol. 2, p. 69–73.) Per. G.A. Oxon 8° 588
— The portraits in the college. (Pelican Record, 1894, vol. 2, p. 109–14.) Per. G.A. Oxon 8° 588

7174. FOWLER, T., Corpus Christi. (Univ. of Oxf., college hist.) Lond., 1898, 8°. 252 pp. G.A. Oxon 8° 651 (3) = R.
[A 'reproduction in shorter form' of no. 7172.]

7175. SMITH, G. O., Monumental brasses at Corpus Christi college. (Oxf. journ. of monumental brasses, 1900, vol. 2, p. 40–44.) Soc. 2184 d. 50

7176. ALLEN, P. S., The early Corpus readerships. (Pelican Record, 1904, vol. 7, p. 155–59.) Per. G.A. Oxon 8° 588

7177. CASE, T., Corpus Christi college, Oxford. A chronological list of the buildings [signed T. Case]. n. pl., (1906), s. sh. G.A. Oxon 4° 186 (18)

7178. FISHER, W. W., The sundial. (Pelican Record, 1908, vol. 9, p. 89–93.)

Per. G.A. Oxon 8° 588

7179. [Letter appealing for subscriptions for the purchase of a sports ground.] July 5th 1908. (Oxf., 1908), 8°. 4 pp. G.A. Oxon c. 273 (f. 24)

7180. COTTON, J. J., A book of Corpus verses. Oxf., 1909, 12°. 48 pp.

28001 e. 721

7181. The proposed statute concerning the Faculties, the Boards of Faculties and the Boards of Studies [no. 2456]. *Ex parte* the President of Corpus Christi college, Oxon. Case for opinion [followed by] Opinion [signed A. Underhill]. (Lond., 1911), fol. 6 pp.

G.A. Oxon c. 273 (f. 5)

7182. CASE, T., An appeal to the Royal commissioners [attacking the proposed arrangements contemplated by the Commissioners for holding college scholarship examinations. Signed T. Case]. Apr. 20. [Oxf.], (1921), 8°. 3 pp. G.A. Oxon c. 273 (f. 9)

7183. MILNE, J. G., The collection of coins at Corpus Christi college. (Num. chron., 1927, 5th ser., vol. 7, p. 187–90.)　　Num. 03 d. 10

See 4500 [Lyon, H. and Robertson-Glasgow, R.C., Oxford Authentics and the Oxford colleges. No. 3, Corpus Christi. 1928].

7184. OSWALD, A., Corpus Christi college. (Country Life, 1933, vol. 73, p. 628–33, 652–57.)　　Per. 384 b. 6

7185. WACE, A. J. B., Lining papers for Corpus Christi college. (Oxoniensia, 1937, vol. 2, p. 166–170.)　　Per. G.A. Oxon 4° 658 = R.

7186. HARDEN, D. B., and GROVE, L. R. A., Seventeenth century lining papers [from Corpus Christi college]. (Antiq. journ., 1951, vol. 31, p. 204–06.)　　Per. 17572 d. 73 = R.

7187. MINN, H., Drawings by J. B. Malchair in Corpus Christi college. (Oxoniensia, 1943/44, vol. 8/9, p. 159–68.)
Per. G.A. Oxon 4° 658 = R.

7188. MILNE, J. G., The early history of Corpus Christi college. Oxf., 1946, 8°. 72 pp.　　G.A. Oxon 8° 1207

See 7065 [Architecture. 1949].

7189. THOMPSON, P. R., The president's lodgings. (Pelican Record, 1959, vol. 32, p. 123–42 and 16 plates.)　　Per. G.A. Oxon 8° 588

7190. GIROUARD, M., An Oxford president's [Corpus Christi college] house replanned. (Country life, 1960, vol. 128, p. 1440, 41.)
Per. 384 b. 6

Administration, property, and finance

7191. An acte concernyng an exchaunge of londes [in Surrey and Berks] betwene the kynges highnes and the presydent and scholers of Corpus Christi college . . . (27 Hen. VIII, c. 52, Private). 1535/36.
[Précis in Shadwell's Enactments &c. See no. 956.]

7192. An acte for the president and schollers of Corpus Christi college . . . (3 James I, c. 3, Private.) 1605–06.
[Text in Shadwell's Enactments &c. See no. 956.]

7193. Some notes out of a MS. in Corpus Christi coll. library, Oxon. containing the expenses of the foundation of that college. (History and antiquities of Glastonbury, publisher T. Hearne, 1722, p. 285–89.)
Mus. Bibl. II 73

7194. An act for establishing . . . exchanges of . . . lands . . . within the hamlet of Wighthill . . . between . . . Corpus Christi college . . . and Simon Wisdome . . . (17 G. III, c. 55, Private.) n. pl., 1777, fol. 14 pp.
L.L.

7195. An act to authorise the president and scholars of Corpus Christi college . . . to grant a lease of part of their estates situate in the parish of Temple Guiting . . . (34 & 35 V., c. 3, Private.) Lond., 1871, fol.

7196. Corpus Christi college. [Report.] 1899/1900–1929. (Oxf.), 1900–29, 8°. [The Bodleian set is imperfect.]   G.A. Oxon 8° 510*

7197. General information & college rules. Revised up to January 1904. Oxf., (1904), 8°. 55 pp.   G.A. Oxon 8° 1110 (5)

7198. Kitchen. [Price list.] n. pl., [c. 1907], 8°. 3 pp.
          G.A. Oxon c. 273 (f. 7)

Statutes

7199. WARD, G. R. M., *transl.*, The foundation statutes of bishop Fox for Corpus Christi college, A.D. 1517. With a life of the founder. Lond., 1843, 8°. 235 pp.   G.A. Oxon 8° 31
— [Another issue.]   G.A. Oxon 8° 734

7200. Statutes of the colleges . . . (Corpus Christi college). Oxf. &c., 1853, 8°. 135 pp.   G.A. Oxon 8° 25 = R.

7201. Statutes of Corpus Christi college, as revised and amended, 1855. Oxf., (1855), 4°. 44 pp.   G.A. Oxon 4° 9 (1)

7202. Corpus Christi college. Copy of regulations and ordinances for the amendment of the statutes . . . (tr. from the Latin). Lond., 1856, fol. 27 pp.   Pp. Eng. 1856 vol. 46

7203. Oxford university. Copies of orders in Council referring to a committee of the Privy council, certain regulations and ordinances of Exeter, Lincoln and Corpus Christi colleges . . . in amendment of their respective statutes . . . Lond., 1856, fol. 52 pp. Pp. Eng. 1856 vol. 46
— [Another ed. *entitled*] Oxford statutes. Orders in council [&c.]. 40 pp.   G.A. Oxon c. 35 (4)

7204. Statutes of Corpus Christi college. Order of her majesty in council of the 24th June 1856, declaring her approval thereof. [Lond.], 1856, fol. 5 pp.   G.A. Oxon 4° 9 (2)

7205. Ordinances and statutes framed or approved by the . . . Commissioners . . . (Corpus Christi college, p. 311–48.) Oxf., 1863, 8°.
          Clar. Press 31 a. 63

7206. University of Oxford commission. Statutes of Corpus Christi college, as partly settled by the Commissioners. Draft, as amended, October 1880. (For the use of the . . . Commissioners only.) [The Bodleian copy has MS. corrections and additions by the Commissioners and thereby became the proof for the amended statutes.] Lond., 1880, 8°. 38 pp.   G.A. Oxon c. 8 (18)

7207. Statutes proposed to be made . . . for Corpus Christi college: Nov., 1880. (Oxf.), 1880, 8°. 33 pp.   G.A. Oxon 8° 425 (7) = R.

7208. Statutes proposed to be made by the University of Oxford commissioners for Corpus Christi college. May 1881. [Lond.], 1881, fol. 20 pp.   G.A. Oxon c. 8 (49)

7209. Statutes of Corpus Christi college. (Univ. of Oxf. and Cambr. act, 1877. Oxford. Thirty-six statutes made by the Univ. of Oxf. commissioners, 1881, p. 57–71, 249.) Pp. Eng. 1882 vol. 51

7210. Statute made by . . . Corpus Christi college . . . 8th Feb., 1890, altering Statute 24 and repealing Statute 78. Lond., 1890, s. sh.
Pp. Eng. 1890 vol. 56

7211. The statutes. (Pelican Record, 1891, vol. 1, p. 12–16.)
Per. G.A. Oxon 8° 588

7212. Statute made by . . . Corpus Christi college . . . 7th Nov., 1891, for amending statute 13. Lond., 1892, s. sh. Pp. Eng. 1892, vol. 60

7213. Statutes made by . . . Corpus Christi college, 13th Dec. 1895, amending section 37 of the statute . . . concerning the scholars, exhibitioners, and commoners. Lond., 1896, s. sh. Pp. Eng. 1896 vol. 65

7214. Statutes made by . . . Corpus Christi college, 16th May 1896, to alter the Statutes . . . by substituting in the Statute concerning the administration of the college, an amended section in lieu of section 48. Lond., 1897, s. sh. Pp. Eng. 1897 vol. 70

7215. Statute made by . . . Corpus Christi, 29th Nov. 1902, amending clauses 19, 22, and 77 of the college statutes. Lond., 1903, s. sh.
Pp. Eng. 1903 vol. 52

7216. Statutes made by . . . Corpus Christi college, on (i) 23rd Apr. 1904 and sealed on 13th Dec. 1905, amending Statute 24 (b); and (ii) 2nd Dec. 1905 and sealed on 13th Dec. 1905, amending Statutes 24 (b) and 32 (a). Lond., 1906, s. sh. Pp. Eng. 1906 vol. 90

7217. Statute made by . . . Corpus Christi college, 12th June 1909 and sealed the 26th day of the same month, amending Statutes 22, 23, and 77. Lond., 1910, s. sh. Pp. Eng. 1910 vol. 72

7218. Statutes made by . . . Corpus Christi college, 12th June 1915 and sealed 18th June 1915, amending clause 13 (b) of the Statutes. Lond., 1915, s. sh. Pp. Eng. 1914/16 vol. 51

7219. Statutes made for the colleges . . . (Corpus Christi college). Oxf., 1927, 8°. 40 pp. G.A. Oxon 4° 759 = R.

Members

BIOGRAPHY

7220. FANT, H. B., John Burton, D.D., one of the founders of the colony of Georgia. (Oxoniensia, 1941, vol. 6, p. 70–83.)
Per. G.A. Oxon 4° 658 = R.

See 7199 [Life of bishop Fox. 1843].

7221. BATTEN, E. C., The life of bishop Richard Fox, by the editor. Prefixed to The register of Richard Fox, 1492–4, ed. by E. C. Batten. n. pl., 1889, 8°. 142 pp. Allen d. 119

7222. FOWLER, T., A Corpus scholar of the sixteenth century [J. Jewel, bp. of Salisbury]. (Pelican Record, 1891, vol. 1, p. 48–54.)
Per. G.A. Oxon 8° 588

7223. ALLEN, P. S., Ludovic Vives at Corpus. (Pelican Record, 1902, vol. 6, p. 156–60.)
Per. G.A. Oxon 8° 588

REMINISCENCES

7224. F., H., Forty-five years ago. (Pelican Record, 1893, vol. 1, p. 185–90.)
Per. G.A. Oxon 8° 588

7225. ODDIE, J. W., Ruskin at Corpus [1870–73. Signed J. W. O.]. (Pelican Record, 1894, vol. 2, p. 101–07.)
Per. G.A. Oxon 8° 588
— II. By C. P[lummer]. (Pelican Record, 1894, vol. 2, p. 134–37.)
Per. G.A. Oxon 8° 588

7226. HEXT, G., Early memories of Corpus boating. (Pelican Record, 1896, vol. 3, p. 130–36.)
Per. G.A. Oxon 8° 588

7227. STRONG, H. A., Corpus in the early sixties. (Pelican Record, 1905, vol. 7, p. 178–82; vol. 8, p. 8–11.)
Per. G.A. Oxon 8° 588

7228. TUCKWELL, W., Corpuscular reminiscences. (Pelican Record, 1906, vol. 8, p. 74–79.)
Per. G.A. Oxon 8° 588

7229. MATTHEWS, W. A., Corpus fifty years ago [signed W. A. M.]. (Pelican Record, 1910, p. 38–41, 67–69.)
Per. G.A. Oxon 8° 588

7230. Reminiscences of the late seventies. (Pelican Record, 1921, vol. 15, p. 100–06, 124–26.)
Per. G.A. Oxon 8° 588

7231. KNOX, E. A., bp. of Manchester, Memories of Corpus Christi college, 1865–8. (Pelican Record, 1932, vol. 20, p. 86–92, 106–15, 136–42.)
Per. G.A. Oxon 8° 588

See 3925.1 [Knox, E. A., Reminiscences of an octogenarian. 1934].

LISTS

7232. Brief notices of the writers and bishops, mentioned by Anthony Wood, as having been members of Corpus Christi coll. (Oxf.), [18—], 8°. 20 pp.
G.A. Oxon 8° 524 (3)

See 7172 [Fowler, T., The history of Corpus Christi college, with lists of its members. 1893].

7233. C.C.C. [List of members]. Mich. term, 1905, 07, 08, 10. n. pl., 1905–10, 16°.
G.A. Oxon 16° 192

7234. The Pelican register [1864–70]. (Pelican Record, 1909, vol. 9, appendix p. 1–16.)
Per. G.A. Oxon 8° 588
— 1871–75, 76–80. (Pelican Record, 1911, vol. 10, appendix p. 17–31, 32–47.)
Per. G.A. Oxon 8° 588

7235. Supplement to the Catalogue of presidents, fellows . . . [&c.] of Corpus Christi college, 1903–12. (Pelican Record, 1911, vol. 10, appendix. 7 pp.)   Per. G.A. Oxon 8° 588

7236. Corpus Christi college. Roll of service [1914–1918]. Oxf., [1921], 8°. 25 pp.   G.A. Oxon 8° 895 (11)

Clubs

7237. [*Begin.*] At a preliminary meeting . . . [Account of the formation of the C.C.C. Church society, signed by C. Plummer and 2 others.] Jan. 31. (Oxf., 1893), 8°. 3 pp.   G.A. Oxon c. 273 (f. 19)

7238. C.C.C. Church society. Rules. Dec., 1903. (Oxf., 1903), 8°. 3 pp.
                                                            G.A. Oxon c. 273 (f. 19)

7239. Rules of the C.C.C. debating society. (Oxf., 1877), 16°. 11 pp.
                                                            G.A. Oxon c. 273 (f. 18)
— 1884. (Oxf., 1884), s. sh.   G.A. Oxon c. 273 (f. 18)

7240. Owlet club. [Miscellaneous papers. 1900–09.]
                                                            G.A. Oxon c. 273 (f. 21–24)

7241. Tenterden essay club. (Syllabus for Summer term 1900, Mich. term, 1902.) (Oxf., 1900, 02), 16°.   G.A. Oxon c. 273 (f. 19)

7242. The Wasps. (Rules.) n. pl., (1907), 16°. 3 pp. G.A. Oxon c. 273 (f. 18)

Library and archives

See 5555 [Public libraries, commenting on the Bodleian and Corpus Christi library in particular. 1827].

7243. Corpus Christi college. (Hist. MSS. comm., 2nd report, 1871, p. 126.)   2262 c. 37 = K.

7244. PLUMMER, C., Continuationem catalogi codicum manuscriptorum Collegii Corporis Christi confecit C. Plummer, n. pl., [c. 1887], 4°. 6 pp. [Suppl. to no. 6503].   2590 d. Oxf. 4 — R.

7245. A hand catalogue of the undergraduates' library. Oxf., 1891, 8°. xii+46 pp.   2590 e. Oxf. 5. 1

7246. Junior Library. (Rules.) (Oxf., 1895), 8°. 5 pp. G.A. Oxon c. 273 (f. 5)

See 5256 [Streeter, B. H., The chained library, 1931].

7247. MILNE, J. G., The muniments of Corpus Christi college, Oxford. (Bulletin, Inst. of hist. research, 1933, vol. 10, p. 105–08.)
                                                            Soc. 223 d. 30 = K.

7248. MILNE, J. G., The muniments of Corpus Christi college. (Oxoniensia, 1937, vol. 2, p. 129–33.)   Per. G.A. Oxon 4° 658 = R.

7249. LIDDELL, J. R., The library of Corpus Christi college, Oxford, in the sixteenth century. (Trans., Bibliogr. soc., 1938, 2nd ser., vol. 18, p. 385–416.)   Per. 258 d. 272 = A.

7250. OVENELL, R. F., Brian Twyne's library. (Publ., Oxf. bibliogr. soc., 1952, N.S., vol. 4, p. 1–42.)   Soc. 258 d. 176 = A.

See 3946.1 [Munford, W. A., Edward Edwards; work in Corpus Christi college library. 1870 onwards. 1963].

Durham college

See 8452 &c. Trinity college.

Exeter college

General 7251–7281
Administration 7282–7287
Statutes 7288–7303
Members
   Reminiscences 7304–7308
   Lists 7309–7314
Fellowships 7315–7316

Scholarships 7317–7320
Clubs 7321–7337
College servants 7338–7341
Site and Fabric 7342–7347
Chapel 7348–7353
Hall 7354–7357

General

7251. Threni Exoniensium in obitum . . . Iohannis Petrei baronis de Writtle . . . [Madan 372.] Oxon., 1613, 4°. 48 pp.   Wood 460 (2)
— Oratio funebris in coll. Exoniensi habita a Matthia Style . . . [In Madan 373 this is stated to be practically a part of the Threni.]

7252. BURY, A., [*Begin.*] To avoid the intolerable drudgery of giving full satisfaction by a several letter . . . the rector of Exeter colledge hath taken this way to give an account of the unhappy affair which hath drawn such clamors, as decry him and his assessors in behalf of one of the fellows [J. Colmer] who they say is injuriously . . . expelled [signed A. Bury]. n. pl., [1689/90], s. sh.   Wood 657 (51)

7253. HARRINGTON, J., An account of the proceedings of . . . Jonathan, lord bishop of Exeter [sir J. Trelawney] in his late visitation of Exeter college. [By J. Harrington]. Oxf., 1690, 4°. 58 pp. Gough Oxf. 106 (1)
— 2nd ed. To which is added, the censure of the University of Oxford upon the Naked Gospell [of A. Bury] 1690. 58+8 pp.
Gough Oxf. 106 (1*)

7254. BURY, A., The account examined: or, A vindication of dr. Arthur Bury, rector of Exeter college, from the calumnies of . . . An account [by J. Harrington] of the proceedings of . . . Jonathan, lord bishop of Exon, in his late visitation of Exeter college. [By A. Bury?]. Lond., 1690, 4°. 32 pp.   Gough Oxf. 106 (2)

7255. BURY, A., The case of Exeter-colledge . . . related and vindicated [by A. Bury]. Lond., 1691, 4°. 74 pp.   Gough Oxf. 106 (5)

7256. HARRINGTON, J., A defence [by J. Harrington] of the proceedings of . . . the Visitor [sir J. Trelawney] and fellows of Exeter college [against the Rector, A. Bury] with an answer to 1. The case of Exeter college related [by A. Bury] 2. The account examined [by A. Bury]. Lond., 1691, 4°. 48+8 pp.   Gough Oxf. 106 (4)

7257. HARRINGTON, J., A vindication of mr. James Colmar [sic] ... from the calumnies of ... 1. A paper publish'd by dr. Bury, 1689 [An account of the unhappy affair, no. 7252. 2. The account examin'd. 3. The case of Exeter college [by A. Bury]. To which are annex'd the authentick copies of the affidavits. [By J. Harrington.] Lond., 1691, 4°. 43 pp.
Gough Oxf. 106 (6)

7258. STILLINGFLEET, E., bp. of Worcester, The case of visitation of colleges [speech] in the House of Lords [1694] in Exeter-college case [supporting the Visitor against the Rector, A. Bury]. (The second part of Ecclesiastical cases, p. 411–36.) Lond., 1704, 8°.   8° L 122 Th.

7259. BURY, A., An answer [by A. Bury?] to the late lord bishop of Worcester's speech in the House of Lords [in 1694] concerning the case of Exeter college. n. pl., [1704?], fol. 4 pp.
G.A. Oxon b. 111 (27)

See 7367–69 [Opposition of Exeter college to the incorporation of Hart Hall. 1734, 1735].

7260. WEBBER, F., A defence of the rector and fellows of Exeter college from the accusations brought against them by ... dr. Huddesford ... in his speech to the Convocation, October 8, 1754, on account of the conduct of the said college at the time of the late election for the county [by F. Webber]. Lond., 1754, 8°. 63 pp.   Gough Oxf. 106 (8)

7261. CANTABRIGIENSIS pseud., The conduct of ... coll. consider'd; with some reflections upon a late pamphlet [by F. Webber] entitled, A defence of the rector and fellows of Exeter college. In a letter from a Cambridge soph, to a gentleman in Hampshire [signed Cantabrigiensis]. Lond., (1754), 4°. 16 pp.   Gough Oxf. 106 (10)

7262. A letter to the author [F. Webber] of the Defence of Exeter college, by way of notes on his pamphlet. (10 Jan.) Lond., 1755, 8°. 74 pp.
G.A. Oxon 8° 60 (7)

7263. HUDDESFORD, G., A proper reply to a late pamphlet [by F. Webber] entitled A defence of the rector and fellows of Exeter college, &c. Oxf., 1755, 4°. 17 pp.   Gough Oxf. 106 (7)

7264. An address [by B. Kennicott?] to ... dr. Huddesford ... occasioned by what is called his Proper reply to the Defence of the rector and fellows of Exeter-college, &c. Lond., 1755, 8°. 37 pp.
Gough Oxf. 106 (9)

7265. The last blow: or, An unanswerable vindication of the society of Exeter college, in reply to the vice-chancellor [G. Huddesford], dr. King and the writers of the London Evening Post. Lond., 1755, 4°. 32 pp.   Gough Oxf. 89 (13)
— 2nd ed. 1755.   Gough Oxf. 106 (11)

[For other polemics which extended beyond Exeter college's part in political dissension, see the section on 18th century history, no. 173–204.]

7266. INGRAM, J., Exeter college. (Memorials of Oxford, 1837, vol. 1. 16 pp.)					G.A. Oxon 8° 18

7267. Exeter college [MSS.]. (Hist. MSS. comm., 2nd report, 1871, p. 127–30.)					2262 c. 37 = K.

See 7309 [Boase, C. W., Register, with a history of the college. 1879].

7268. Annals of Exeter college. [Article on the historical aspect of] Register of . . . Exeter college, by C. W. Boase. (Edinb. review, 1880, vol. 152, p. 344–79.)					G.A. Oxon 4° 578 (52)

7269. SANDAY, W., The example of a Christian scholar [A. Edersheim] with some remarks on the state of learning in Oxford, a sermon. Oxf. &c., 1889, 8°. 15 pp.					G.A. Oxon 8° 455 (5)

7270. STRIDE, W. K., Exeter college. (Univ. of Oxf., college hist.) Lond., 1900, 8°. 262 pp.					G.A. Oxon 8° 651 (16) = R.

7271. The Stapledon magazine. Vol. 1, no. 1–   . Oxf., 1904–   , 8°.
					Per. G.A. Oxon 8° 713

7272. JACKSON, W. W., Exeter, old and new. (Stapledon mag., 1904, vol. 1, p. 12–19.)					Per. G.A. Oxon 8° 713

7273. HENDERSON, B. W., Treasures of the college library. (Stapledon mag., 1905, vol. 1, p. 135–44.)					Per. G.A. Oxon 8° 713

7274. SOMERSET, W. H. B., The Exeter Lollards. (Stapledon mag., 1906, vol. 1, p. 217–28.)					Per. G.A. Oxon 8° 713

7275. WINN, C. E., Four years of college music. (Stapledon mag., 1908, vol. 2, p. 111–14.)					Per. G.A. Oxon 8° 713

7276. Six hundredth anniversary of the foundation of Exeter college [pamphlet]. Oxf., 1914, 4°. 11 pp.					Ex. coll.

7277. FARNELL, L. R., Exeter college in the past. (Stapledon mag., 1914, vol. 4, p. 51–58.)
— [Repr. with alterations, *entitled*] An outline of the history of Exeter college. (Stapledon mag., 1922, vol. 6, p. 39–46.)
					Per. G.A. Oxon 8° 713

7278. 1914–1918. Exeter college, commemoration of the fallen. [Oxf.], 1921, 4°. 13 pp.					G.A. Oxon 4° 403 (6)

7279. PRING, C. J., The birds of Exeter college [signed C. J. P.]. (Stapledon mag., 1922, vol. 5, p. 233–35; 1922, vol. 6, p. 16.)
					Per. G.A. Oxon 8° 713

7280. BALSDON, J. P. V. D., Walter de Stapledon and the founding of Exeter college. (Devon & Cornwall notes & queries, 1932, vol. 17, p. 147–52.)					Soc. G.A. Devon 8° 226
— Repr. 8 pp.					G.A. Oxon c. 274 (f. 1)

7281. EGG, J. T., and MADDISON, F., The effigy of John Crocker at Exeter college. (Oxoniensia, 1948, vol. 13, p. 82–84.)

Per. G.A. Oxon 4° 658 = R.

Administration

7282. Rules and regulations. (Oxf.), 1868, 8°. 23 pp. G.A. Oxon 8° 233 (10)
— October 1899. 32 pp.   G.A. Oxon 8° 1000 (12)
— October 1904.   G.A. Oxon 8° 1000 (13)
— October 1919. 28 pp.   G.A. Oxon 8° 810 (9)
— October 1932. 30 pp.   G.A. Oxon 8° 789 (2)

7283. Exeter college. Tariff. 1884, 85. n. pl., 1884, 85, 8°.
G.A. Oxon c. 274 (f. 9)

7284. Exeter college common room. [Price list.] Oct. 1898. n. pl., 1898, s. sh.
G.A. Oxon c. 274 (f. 9)

7285. Rules for Exeter college junior common room. [*Followed by*] Library rules. Oct. 24, 1898. [Oxf.], 1898, s. sh.
G.A. Oxon c. 274 (f. 11)

7286. Exeter college. [Report.] 1899/1900–1937. (Oxf.), 1900–37, 8°.
G.A. Oxon 8° 510*
[The Bodleian set is imperfect.]

7287. Exeter college. [Regulations for admission.] [Oxf., 1909], 12°. 3 pp.
G.A. Oxon c. 274 (f. 18)

Statutes

7288. The statutes of Exeter college, Oxford, printed by desire of the Commissioners under the Act 17 & 18 Vict. c. 81. Lond., 1855, 8°. 52 pp.
G.A. Oxon 8° 415

7289. Copies of Orders in Council referring to a committee of the Privy council certain regulations and ordinances of Exeter, Lincoln, and Corpus Christi colleges . . . in amendment of their respective statutes . . . Lond., 1856, fol. 52 pp.
Pp. Eng. 1856 vol. 46
— [Another ed., *entitled*] Oxford statutes. Orders in council [&c.]. 40 pp.
G.A. Oxon c. 35 (4)

7290. Exeter college. Copy of Regulations and ordinances for the amendment of the statutes . . . under the authority of 17 and 18 Vict. c. 81. [Lond.], 1856, fol. 23 pp.
Pp. Eng. 1856 vol. 46
— [Another ed., *entitled*]. Regulations [&c.] Oxf., [1856], 4°. 26 pp.
G.A. Oxon 4° 736

7291. Copy of an ordinance made by the Oxford university commissioners . . . in place of section 5 of the third chapter, intituled 'Deprivatio' of the regulations and ordinances made by the rector and scholars of Exeter college . . . on the 9th October, 1855, in amendment of the statutes of the said college. 11 July, 1856. (Copies of four ordinances &c. p. 5.) [Lond.], 1857, fol.
Pp. Eng. 1857 vol. 13

7292. Ordinances and statutes framed or approved by the . . . Commissioners . . . (Exeter college, p. 101–25.) Oxf., 1863, 8°.
Clar. Press 31 a. 63

7293. Statutes proposed to be made . . . for Exeter college. Nov., 1880. (Oxf.), 1880, 8°. 36 pp.
G.A. Oxon 8° 425 (8) = R.

7294. Statutes proposed to be made by the University of Oxford commissioners for Exeter college. May 1881. [Lond.], 1881, fol. 23 pp.
G.A. Oxon c. 8 (66)

7295. Statutes made by the University of Oxford commissioners for Exeter college. [Lond.], 1881, fol. 23 pp.
Ex. coll.

7296. Statutes of Exeter college. (Univ. of Oxf. and Cambr. act, 1877. Oxford. Thirty-six Statutes made by the Univ. of Oxf. commissioners, 1881, p. 71–88, 250.)
Pp. Eng. 1882 vol. 51

7297. Exeter college. Amendment made on the 14th November 1882 by the governing body of the college in Statute V. of the statutes of the college. 6 March 1883. [Lond.], 1883, s. sh.
Pp. Eng. 1883 vol. 53

7298. Statute made by . . . Exeter college . . . on the 30th June 1887 amending Statute III, section 7 and Statute V, section 1 . . . Lond., 1888, fol. 6 pp.
Pp. Eng. 1888 vol. 78

7299. Oxford. Statute made by . . . Exeter college, 25th Jan. 1895, amending Statutes II, section 4; III, sections 15 and 27; IV, section 5; V, sections 2 and 3, and 'King Charles the first's trust', section 2. Lond., 1895, s. sh.
Pp. Eng. 1895 vol. 77

7300. Statute made by . . . Exeter college, 25th Jan., 1895, amending Statutes II, III, IV, and V. Lond., 1895, s. sh. Pp. Eng. 1895 vol. 77

7301. Statutes made by . . . Exeter college, 12th Dec. 1902, amending Statutes III and XV. Lond., 1903, s. sh. Pp. Eng. 1903 vol. 52

7302. Statute made by . . . Exeter college and sealed 18th Nov. 1914, amending Statutes II, III, and IV. Lond., 1915, s. sh.
Pp. Eng. 1914/16 vol. 51

7303. Statutes made for the colleges . . . (Exeter college.) Oxf., 1927, 8°. 69 pp.
G.A. Oxon 4° 759 = R.

Members

REMINISCENCES

7304. Impressions of one term at Exeter college, Oxford, by an expelled undergraduate. (Lond. soc., 1870, vol. 17, p. 460–70). Per. 2705 d. 200

7305. INCE, W., Parting words, a sermon [containing some autobiographical reminiscences and some information concerning other Fellows of the college] preached in Exeter college chapel, June 16, 1878. Oxf., 1878, 8°. 19 pp.
G.A. Oxon 8° 761 (8)

7306. BARBER, E. A., Notes on a betting book [of Exeter college common room, 1812–37]. (Stapledon mag., 1921, vol. 5, p. 139–45.)
Per. G.A. Oxon 8° 713

7307. MARETT, R., The [senior] common-room of thirty years ago. (Stapledon mag., 1921, vol. 5, p. 180–83.)   Per. G.A. Oxon 8° 713

See 3972 [Farnell, L. R., An Oxonian looks back. 1934].

7308. PRIDEAUX, S. P. T., John Prideaux. Salisbury, 1938, 8°. 31 pp.
11122 e. 8

See 3979 [Marett, R. R., A Jerseyman at Oxford. 1941].
See 3946.3 [Edwards, G. Hamilton-, An undergraduate, W. Cotton of Exeter coll. in Regency Oxford. 1965].

LISTS

7309. BOASE, C. W., Register of the rectors and fellows, scholars, exhibitioners, and Bible clerks of Exeter college, with illustrative documents and a history of the college. Oxf., 1879, 4°. 272 pp. G.A. Oxon 4° 67
— Ed. 2 [entitled] Registrum collegii Exoniensis. Register [&c.]. [This ed. brings the register up to date, but does not repr. the History.] Oxf., 1893, 4°. 183 pp.   G.A. Oxon 4° 162
— Pars ii. An alphabetical register of commoners. Oxf., 1894, 4°. 391 pp.   G.A. Oxon 4° 162*
— New ed. [entitled] Registrum collegii Exoniensis. Register of the rectors, fellows, and other members on the foundation of Exeter college, with a history of the college and illustrative documents. (Oxf. hist. soc., vol. 27.) Oxf., 1894, 8°. 399 pp.   G.A. Oxon 8° 360 = R.

7310. HOW, A. B., Register of Exeter college, 1891–1921. Oxf., 1928, 4°. 240 pp.   G.A. Oxon 4° 762 = R. Top.

7311. [Tutors' list of undergraduates. Mich. term, 1884, 85, 87.] [Oxf., 1884–87], 4°.   G.A. Oxon c. 274 (f. 2)

7312. A list of members resident in lodging-houses, in Exeter Hall and in private houses. 1885, 86, 88, 91, 93. [Oxf.], (1885–93), s. sh.
G.A. Oxon c. 274 (3–5)

7313. HENDERSON, B. W., Exeter college Service roll, 1914 [by B. W. Henderson]. (Oxf., 1914), 8°. 15 pp.   G.A. Oxon 8° 895 (1)

7314. Oxford university roll of service, 1914–1915. Exeter college record. Corrected to June 1, 1915. Oxf., (1915), 8°. [10 pp.].
G.A. Oxon c. 274 (f. 78)

See 7324 [Exeter college association. Register, 1925–38].

Fellowships

7315. BYWATER, I., A letter to . . . John Wordsworth . . . on the subject of a statement in his recent letter [no. 6482 concerning clerical fellowships in Exeter college]. Oxf., 1880, 8°. 8 pp.   G.A. Oxon 8° 250 (19)

7316. FARNELL, L. R., Bibliography of the fellows and tutors of Exeter college, in recent times [by L. R. Farnell]. (Oxf., 1914), 8°. 67 pp.
G.A. Oxon 8° 899

Scholarships

7317. [Examination papers. Natural science scholarship.] 1873, 74. [Oxf.], 1873, 74, 8°.   2626 e. 94

See also 7422, 7424, 7426, 7427, 7429, 7430 [Statutes affecting the Meyricke endowment. 1881–97].

7318. King Charles the first's trust. Exeter, Jesus and Pembroke colleges. [Regulations of scholarships and exhibitions.] [Oxf., 1884?], s. sh.
G.A. Oxon c. 274 (f. 6)

7319. Exeter college. Scholarships and Exhibitions. [Regulations.] (Oxf., 1888), 4°. 4 pp.   G.A. Oxon c. 274 (f. 6)

7320. Exeter and Lincoln colleges. Scholarship and Exhibition for modern history. [Regulations.] [Oxf., 1889], s. sh.   G.A. Oxon c. 274 (f. 6)

Clubs

7321. SMALLEY, B., An early undergraduate literary society [of Exeter college, 1734/35]. (Bodleian library record, 1941, vol. 2, p. 30–33.)
2590 d. Oxf. 1. 41 = R.

7322. Adelphi club. Rules. (Oxf.), [c. 1869], s. sh. G.A. Oxon c. 274 (f. 49)

7323. Exeter college association. [List of members.] May, 1924. n. pl., 1924, 8°. 4 pp.   G.A. Oxon c. 274 (f. 52)

7324. Exeter college association. Register. 1925–38. Oxf., 1925–38, 8°.
G.A. Oxon 8° 1128

7325. Rules of the Exeter college barge. (Oxf.), [c. 1865], s. sh.
G.A. Oxon c. 274 (f. 43)

7326. Exeter college boat club. [Appeal for funds for new barge, in view of the amalgamation of the Boat and Barge clubs.] Oct. 16. [Oxf.], (1872), s. sh.   G.A. Oxon c. 274 (f. 46)

7327. Exeter college boat club. Rules. [Oxf., 1876], s. sh.
G.A. Oxon c. 274 (f. 46)
— [1881]. 8°. 3 pp.   G.A. Oxon c. 274 (f. 46)

7328. Exeter college boat club. [Appeal for funds to meet the unexpectedly large bill for the new barge. 2 issues.] Nov., Dec. [Oxf.], [1876], s. sh.
G.A. Oxon c. 274 (f. 46, 47)

7329. Exeter college boat club. Rules of college races [1877, 81]. Oxf., [1877, 81], s. sh.   G.A. Oxon c. 274 (f. 44)

7330. Exeter college clubs. Rules. [Oxf.], [c. 1875], s. sh.
G.A. Oxon c. 274 (f. 48)
— [1877?].   G.A. Oxon c. 274 (f. 50)

7331. Exeter college (amalgamated) clubs. Report. Mich. 1885; 1901.
Oxf., 1885, 1901, s. sh.   G.A. Oxon c. 274 (f. 47, 48)

7332. Exeter college clubs. Rules. (Oxf.), [c. 1895], 8°. 3 pp.
                                        G.A. Oxon c. 274 (f. 11)

7333. Exeter college debating society. Rules. Oxf., 1859, 8°. 11 pp.
                                        G.A. Oxon 8° 789 (3)

7334. Stapledon debating society. [Nominal rolls]. 1872–80.
                                        G.A. Oxon 8° 789 (4)

7335. Exeter college, Stapledon debating society. Rules. [1875, 77, 78,]
97, 1905. Oxf., [1895]–1905, 8°.   G.A. Oxon 8° 789

7336. Exeter college musical society. [Programmes &c.]. 1864–1927.
                                        G.A. Oxon 8° 789

7337. Falernian wine club. Rules. [Oxf., 1874], 8°. 4 pp.
                                        G.A. Oxon c. 274 (f. 50)

College servants

7338. INCE, W., Palm Sunday thoughts, a sermon . . . on occasion of the
death of James Nutt, servant of Exeter college. 2nd ed. (Oxf., 1859),
12°. 21pp.   100 f. 445 (1)

7339. INCE, W., Faithfull stewardship, a sermon preached in Exeter college
chapel . . . on occasion of the death of Thomas Hewlett [college ser-
vant]. Oxf., 1862, 12°. 15 pp.   100 e. 1218

7340. INCE, W., Parting counsels, a sermon preached to the college servants
in Exeter college chapel, June 9, 1878. Oxf., 1878, 8°. 18 pp.
                                        247513 e. 21

7341. Messengers. [Amendment of rules.] n. pl., [188–], s. sh.
                                        G.A. Oxon c. 274 (f. 10)

Site and fabric

7342. [Topographical prints, &c. in the Bodleian.]   G.A. Oxon a. 52

7343. [Appeal for funds for new buildings, with subscription list and print.]
Apr. 1858. (Oxf., 1858), 4°. 4 pp.   G.A. Oxon c. 274 (f. 6)

7344. The college buildings in 1675. (Stapledon mag., 1914, vol. 4, p. 59–
61.)   Per. G.A. Oxon 8° 713

7345. QUARRELL, W. H., Engravings of Exeter college [chronological
account]. (Stapledon mag., 1922, vol. 6, p. 5–11; 1923, vol. 6, p. 66,
67.)   Per. G.A. Oxon 8° 713

7346. JACKSON, W. W., The college buildings. (Stapledon mag., 1922, vol.
5, p. 221–29.)   Per. G.A. Oxon 8° 713

7346.5. WARREN, E., The alterations at the east end of the garden.
(Stapledon mag., 1923, vol. 6, p. 47–49.)   Per. G.A. Oxon 8° 713

7347. MARETT, R. R., Ad corneriam [the college acquisition of its corner
    site]. (Stapledon mag., 1931, vol. 8, p. 143–46.) Per. G.A. Oxon 8° 713
    — [Repr.].   G.A. Oxon c. 274 (f. 51)

Chapel

7348. PRIDEAUX, J., A sermon preached on the fifth of October 1624: at
    the consecration of St. Iames chappel in Exceter colledge. [Madan
    551.] Oxf., 1625, 4°. 36 pp.   Antiq. e. E. 1625. 15
    — [Repr.] 1736.

7349. To the former fellows of Exeter college. [An appeal signed J. D.
    Macbride, for funds to enrich the new chapel with a stained glass
    window.] Oct. 27, 1859. (Oxf., 1859), s. sh. G.A. Oxon c. 274 (f. 7)

7350. The chapel of Exeter college. (Builder, 1859, vol. 17, p. 440.)
                                                        N. 1863 c. 1

7351. BOSSOM, T. E., Exeter college chapel. [Short guide.] n. pl., 1884,
    s. sh.   G.A. Oxon c. 274 (f. 8)

7352. BOSSOM, T. E., The new tapestry [in the chapel] of Exeter college.
    Oxf., (1891), s. sh.   G.A. Oxon c. 274 (f. 8)

7353. HUNT, A. A., Monumental brasses in St. Michael's church and
    Exeter college chapel. (Oxf. journ. of monumental brasses, 1900, vol.
    2, p. 90–96.)   Soc. 2184 d. 50

Hall

7354. [Appeal for funds to repair the Hall and to substitute electric lighting
    for gas.] [Oxf., c. 1904], s. sh.   G.A. Oxon c. 274 (f. 16)

7355. BLOMFIELD, R., A note on recent work in the Hall. (Stapledon mag.,
    1904, vol. 1, p. 58–61.)   Per. G.A. Oxon 8° 713

7356. The new window in Hall. (Stapledon mag., 1906, vol. 1, p. 214–16.)
                                                        Per. G.A. Oxon 8° 713

7357. JACKSON, W. W., Windows in the college hall [account of]. (Staple-
    don mag., 1914, vol. 4, p. 72–80.)   Per. G.A. Oxon 8° 713

Frewen hall

See 8431. St. Mary's hall (dissolved 1541).

Gloucester hall

See also 8661 &c. Worcester college.

7358. A model of a college to be settled in the University for the education
    of some youths of the Greek church. [Oxf., c. 1692], s. sh.
                                                        Wood 276a (381)

7359. STEPHENS, E., A good and necessary proposal for the restitution of Catholic communion between the Greek churches and the Church of England [by E. Stephens. A paper about the Greeks at Gloucester hall, with an appeal for money to purchase a house for Greek clergy and scholars in London]. n. pl., [1705], s. sh.   4° Rawl. 564 (23)

7360. FFOULKES, E. S., Establishment of a Greek college at Oxford in the 17th century [by E. S. Ffoulkes]. (Union review, 1863, vol. 1, p. 490–500.)   Per. 130995 d. 13

7361. GALBRAITH, V. H., ed., Some new documents about Gloucester college. (Oxf. hist. soc., 1924, vol. 80, p. 337–86.)
G.A. Oxon 8° 360 = R.

7362. PANTIN, W. A., Gloucester college. (Oxoniensia, 1946/7, vol. 11/12, p. 65–74.)   Per. G.A. Oxon 4° 658 = R.

7363. TAPPE, E. D., The Greek college at Oxford, 1699–1705. [The Greeks formed part of Gloucester hall under Benjamin Woodroffe.] (Oxoniensia, 1955, vol. 19, p. 92–111.)   Per. G.A. Oxon 4° 658 = R.

7364. TAPPE, E. D., Alumni of the Greek college at Oxford, 1699–1705. (Notes and Queries, 1955, vol. 200, p. 110–14.) Per. 3974 e. 405 = A.

Greek college

See 7358 &c. Gloucester hall.

Greyfriars

7365. Greyfriars. (Oxf. mag., 1957, vol. 76, p. 150–52.)
Per. G.A. Oxon 4° 141
See also 3758 &c. [Religious orders].

Hart hall

See also 7370 &c. Hertford college.

7366. NEWTON, R., A scheme of discipline with statutes intended to be established by a royal charter, for the education of youth in Hart-hall. [*Followed by*] An appendix, containing reasons and explications of certain passages [by R. Newton]. n. pl., 1720, fol. 34+4 pp.
Gough Oxf. 97 (1)

See 1398 [Migration of W. Seaman from Hart hall to Oriel college, 1726. 1928].
See 4571 [Oxford and college expenses in 1723, a commoner's expenses: extracted from dr. Newton's University education, 1726. 1847].

7367. NEWTON, R., A letter to . . . dr. Holmes . . . visitor of Hart-hall [asking him to support Hart hall against Exeter college in the former's attempt to become incorporated in the university]. Lond., 1734, fol. 25 pp.   Gough Oxf. 97 (2)

7368. CONYBEARE, J., Calumny refuted: or, An answer to the personal slanders published by dr. Richard Newton in his letter to dr. Holmes.

In which also the conduct of the lord bishop of Exeter and of the society of Exeter-college, in relation to Hart-hall is vindicated. Lond., 1735, 8°. 134 pp. Gough Oxf. 97 (4)
— 2nd ed. 1735. G.A. Oxon 8° 91 (2)

7369. NEWTON, R., The grounds of the complaint of the principal of Hart-hall concerning the obstruction given to the incorporation of his society, by Exeter-college and their visitor . . . in answer to the misrepresentations of dr. C[onybea] re . . . in his pretended vindication of the conduct of the lord bishop of Exeter. Lond., 1735, fol. 64 pp.
Gough Oxf. 97 (3)
— 2nd ed. 1735. G.A. Oxon c. 235

Hertford college

General 7370–7384
Statutes 7385–7389

Dissolution and Refoundation 7390–7394
Library 7395–7397

General

See also 7366 &c. Hart hall.
See also 7693 &c. Magdalen hall.

7370. [Topographical prints, &c. in the Bodleian.] G.A. Oxon a. 53

7371. The state of the case between dr. [R.] Newton principal, and mr. [F.] Comings, A.M., of Hertford college [concerning the removal of Mr. Comings from the office of tutor]. n. pl., [1753], fol. 3 pp.
G.A. fol. A 240 (3)

7372. Macbride scholarship. Subscriptions already announced. [Oxf., 1856], s. sh. G.A. Oxon c. 72 (385)

7373. Hertford college junior common room. Price list of wines. [Oxf.], 1874, s. sh. G.A. Oxon c. 275 (f. 14)

7374. Rules of the Hertford college junior common room. n. pl., n. d., s. sh.
G.A. Oxon c. 275 (f. 15)

7375. COLERIDGE, B., ed., Judgment of the Court of appeal in the case of the Queen v. Hertford college [concerning the election to a fellowship of A. I. Tillyard, and the legal bearing of the University test act, 1871]. Lond., 1878, 8°. 30 pp. G.A. Oxon 8° 236 (4)

7376. HAMILTON, S. G., Dr. Newton and Hertford college. (Oxf. hist. soc., 1896, vol. 32, p. 279–361.) G.A. Oxon 8° 360 = R.

7377. JEANS, G. E., [Account of the remains of the 15th century Chapel of Our Lady at Smith Gate, subsequently incorporated in Hertford college buildings.] (Proc., Soc. of Antiq., 1898, ser. 2, vol. 17, p. 253–58.) Per. G.A. Gen. top. 8° 524 = R.

7378. HAMILTON, S. G., Hertford college. (Univ. of Oxf., college hist.) Lond., 1903, 8°. 175 pp. G.A. Oxon 8° 651 (19) = R.

7379. Hertford college. [*Begin.*] The most pressing thing in the way of building at the present time is the need of a new chapel . . . [Request for funds, signed H. Boyd.] [Oxf., *c.* 1906], 12°. 3 pp.

G.A. Oxon c. 275 (f. 6)

7380. Hertford college, Oxford. Honours gained in the last ten years, 1897–1906. [Oxf., 1907], 4°. 7 pp.   G.A. Oxon c. 275 (f. 8)

7381. The Hertford college magazine. Vol. 1, no. 1–. Oxf., 1910– , 4°.

G.A. Oxon 4° 289

7382. Hertford college. List of members of the college, 1919–32. Oxf., 1933, 8°. 36 pp.   G.A. Oxon 8° 1104

7383. Anthological club. [Miscellaneous papers. *c.* 1883.] G.A. Oxon 4° 603

7384. Tyndale literary and debating society. Rules. Revised Oct. 1901. Oxf., 1901, 12°. 4 pp.   G.A. Oxon c. 275 (f. 14)

Statutes

7385. NEWTON, R., Rules and statutes for the government of Hertford college. Lond., 1747, 8°. 162 pp.   Gough Oxf. 52

7386. Hertford college. Statutes made by the governing body of Hertford college . . . 6th Feb., 1875, for the government of that college; and, Copy of the Order in Council, dated 17th March, 1875, approving the said statutes. [Lond.], 1875, fol. 7 pp.   Pp. Eng. 1875 vol. 58

7387. Statutes made by . . . Hertford college, 7th June, 1893 and sealed 23rd Sept. 1893, to amend the Statutes. Lond., 1893, 3 pp.

Pp. Eng. 1893/4 vol. 68

7388. Statutes made by . . . Hertford college, 21st Mar. 1896, amending the Statutes of the college approved by Order in Council of 17th Mar. 1875. Lond., 1897, fol. 3 pp.   Pp. Eng. 1897 vol. 70

7389. Statutes made for the colleges . . . (Hertford college.) Oxf., 1927, 8°, 49 pp.   G.A. Oxon 4° 759 = R.

Dissolution and refoundation

7390. An act to authorize such person as his majesty shall appoint to transfer a certain sum in three pounds per cent. reduced annuities, now standing in the name of the dissolved college of Hertford . . . and also to receive dividends due upon such annuities. (56 G. III, c. 95, Pub.) Lond., 1816, s. sh.   L.L.

7391. An act to enable his majesty to grant certain lands, tenements and hereditaments, escheated and devolved to his majesty by the dissolution of Hertford college . . . and the site of the said college and buildings thereon to the chancellor, masters and scholars of the . . . University in trust for the principal and other members of Magdalen hall, for the purpose of their removing to such site; and to enable the said chancellor, masters and scholars of the said university, and the president and scholars of Saint Mary Magdalen college, to do all necessary acts for such removal. (56 G. III, c. 136, Pub.) Lond., 1816, fol. 12 pp. L.L.

7392. Hertford college, Oxford bill. A bill intituled An act for dissolving Magdalen hall . . . and for incorporating the principal, fellows, and scholars of Hertford college; and for vesting in such college the lands and other property now held in trust for the benefit of Magdalen hall. 11 May, 1874. Lond., 1874, fol. 5 pp. Pp. Eng. 1874 vol. 2 — Act. (37 & 38 V., c. 55, Pub.) Lond., 1874, 4°. 8 pp. L.L.

7393. Hertford college. [*Begin.*] Dr. Michell wishes to give publicity to the following facts . . . [Concerns a request to bring before Convocation the Hertford college bill.] May 20. [Oxf.], 1874, s. sh.
G.A. Oxon c. 275 (f. 2)

7394. [*Begin.*] The property of old Hertford college . . . [Statement for the curators of the University chest concerning the disbursement of monies accruing from the property of old Hertford college.] [Oxf., 1876], 8°. 4 pp. G.A. Oxon c. 33 (156)

Library

7395. Catalogue [really Shelf-list] of books in the library of Hertford college, 1888. Oxf., 1888, 8°. 258 pp. 2590 e. Oxf. 6. 1 = R.

7396. Catalogue of books in the library of Hertford college, printed in the 15th and 16th centuries. Oxf., 1910, 8°. 16 pp. 2590 e. Oxf. 6. 2 = R.

7397. Catalogue of the old books in Hertford college library. [Reprod. from typewriting.] n. pl., 1947, fol. 363 leaves. R. 6. 285/3

Hunter-Blair's hall

See 8253. St. Benet's hall.

Jesus college

General 7398–7411
Administration 7412–7415
Statutes 7416–7432
Finance and Property 7433–7434
Members 7435–7438

Scholarships and Exhibitions 7439–7443
Societies and Sport 7444–7446
Library 7447–7450
Arms 7451–7452

General

7398. [Topographical prints, &c. in the Bodleian.] G.A. Oxon a. 53

7399. INGRAM, J., Jesus college. (Memorials of Oxford, 1837, vol. 2. 16 pp.) G.A. Oxon 8° 19

7400. DYKE, W., The justice and expediency of preserving for Wales the Welsh fellowships of Jesus college, a letter. Oxf., 1854, 8°. 4 pp.
G.A. Oxon 8° 179 (8)

7401. Thoughts on the proposed reform at Oxford as far as it affects Jesus college, a letter by an ex-fellow. Oxf., 1854, 8°. 11 pp.
G.A. Oxon 8° 296 (9)

7402. 'The Druid', a Jesus college magazine, No. 1–5 [6]. Oxf., 1862, 8°.
Per. 3974 e. 323 (5)

7403. BROWNE, H. LL., Jesus college, a letter [concerning the utilization and reform of the college as a Welsh college]. Denbigh, 1870, 8°. 16 pp.
G.A. Oxon 8° 761 (6)

7404. HARDY, E. G., Jesus college. (Univ. of Oxf., college hist.) Lond., 1899, 8°. 252 pp.   G.A. Oxon 8° 651 (10) = R.

7405. Gwyl dewi sant. [Jesus coll. magazine.] 1906–28. Rhydychain, 1906–28, 8°. [The Bodleian set is imperfect.]   G.A. Oxon 8° 1024

7406. Jesus college, Oxford. The opening of the Sir Leoline Jenkins' laboratories, Tuesday, June 23rd 1908. [Oxf.], (1908), 4°. 4 pp.
G.A. Oxon c. 276 (f. 34)

7407. PAINTIN, H., Oxford ladies' brass-rubbing society. Visit to Jesus college. (Repr. from 'Jackson's Oxford journal, Feb. 6, 1909.) [Oxf., 1909], s. sh.   G.A. Oxon c. 107 (5)

7408. The Jesus college magazine. Vol. 1, no. 1– . Oxf., 1912– , 8°.
G.A. Oxon 4° 314

7409. RICHARDS, T., The Puritan visitation of Jesus college, Oxford, and the principalship of dr. Michael Roberts [1648–57]. (Trans., Cymmrodorion soc., 1922–23, p. 1–111.)   Soc. G.A. Wales 8° 219 = R.
— [Repr.] Lond., 1924, 8°. 117 pp.   G.A. Oxon 8° 1375

7410. HUSSEY, C., Jesus college. (Country Life, 1932, vol. 71, p. 540–45, 568–74.)   Per. 384 b. 6

7411. Short guide for visitors. (Oxf.), [1959], s. sh. G.A. Oxon c. 276 (f. 37)

7411.1. The inside eye, a study in pictures of Oxford college life [in Jesus college]. (Editor, P. Roberts, photographs by T. Gabriel.) 3rd ed. Abingdon, 1961, 4°. 24 pp.   G.A. Oxon 4° 800

7411.2. Jesus college record. [No. 1–]. (Oxf.), 1962– , 8°.
Per. G.A. Oxon 4° 790

Administration

7412. Regulations of Jesus college, Oxford, respecting the admission and residence of undergraduates. (Oxf.), [1890], 8°. 8 pp.
G.A. Oxon c. 276 (f. 33)
— [1892] 11 pp.   G.A. Oxon 8° 540 (9)
— 1897.   G.A. Oxon 8° 715 (14)
— 1902, 10.   G.A. Oxon c. 241

7413. Jesus college. The attention of undergraduate members . . . is directed to the following regulations [dinners in Hall &c.]. Oct. 31st. [Oxf.], 1896, s. sh.   G.A. Oxon c. 276 (f. 33)

7414. Jesus college. [Report.] 1904/05–13/14. (Oxf.), 1904–14, 8°. [The Bodleian set is imperfect.]   G.A. Oxon 8° 510*

7415. Entrance examination [papers]. Feb. 1957– . Oxf., 1957– , 8°.
Per. 2626 e. 558

Statutes

7416. Statutes of the colleges . . . (Jesus college.) Oxf. &c., 1853, 8°. 114 pp.
G.A. Oxon 8° 26 = R.

7417. Oxford university. Ordinances . . . in relation to . . . Jesus [and 10 other] colleges respectively. [Lond.], 1857, fol. 139 pp.
Pp. Eng. 1857 vol. 32

7418. Ordinances and statutes framed or approved by the . . . Commissioners . . . (Jesus college, p. 385–406.) Oxf., 1863, 8°.
Clar. Press 31 a. 63

7419. University of Oxford commission. Statutes of Jesus college, as partly settled by the Commissioners. (For the use of the . . . Commissioners only.) February 1880. [The Bodleian copy has MS. corrections and additions by the Commissioners, thereby becoming the proof for the amended statutes.] [Lond.], 1880, fol. 21 pp.   G.A. Oxon c. 8 (28)

7420. Statutes proposed to be made . . . for Jesus college. Feb. 1880. (Oxf.), 1880, 8°. 36 pp.   G.A. Oxon 8° 425 (9) = R.

7421. Statutes proposed to be made by the University of Oxford commissioners for Jesus college. May 1881. [Lond.], 1881, fol. 22 pp.
G.A. Oxon c. 8 (62)

7422. Statutes proposed to be made by the University of Oxford commissioners for the Queen's college, concerning exhibitions; Christ Church concerning Westminster scholarships; Jesus college concerning the Meyricke endowment. (Oxf.), 1881, 8°. 13 pp.
G.A. Oxon 8° 425 (2) = R.

7423. Statutes of Jesus college. (Univ. of Oxf. and Cambr. act, 1877. Oxford. Thirty six statutes made by the Univ. of Oxf. commissioners, 1881, p. 88–104, 251.)   Pp. Eng. 1882 vol. 51

7424. A statute for Jesus college concerning the Meyricke endowment. (Univ. of Oxf. and Cambr. act, 1877. Oxford. Five statutes made by the Univ. of Oxf. commissioners, 1881, p. 3.)   Pp. Eng. 1882 vol. 51

7425. Statutes made by . . . Jesus college . . . on the 16th January 1888 amending Statute V, clauses 3 and 6 . . . Lond., 1888, fol.
Pp. Eng. 1888 vol. 78

7426. Statute made by . . . Jesus college on the 2d Feb., 1889, amending the Statute of the college concerning the Meyricke endowment. Lond., 1889, s. sh.   Pp. Eng. 1889 vol. 59

7427. Statute made by . . . Jesus college, 2nd May 1890, making an alteration in the Statute relating to the Meyricke fund, clause 3. Lond., 1890,
s. sh.   Pp. Eng. 1890/91 vol. 61

7428. Statutes made by . . . Jesus college, 2nd May 1895, altering Statute
IV, clauses 1, 19, 22, 23, 31 and 36; and Statute IX, clause 7. Lond.,
1895, s. sh.   Pp. Eng. 1895 vol. 77

7429. Statutes made by . . . Jesus college, 22nd June 1895, altering and
amending the statutes . . . in the matter of 'A statute for Jesus college
concerning the Meyricke endowment.' Lond., 1896, s. sh.
                                                  Pp. Eng. 1896 vol. 65

7430. Statutes made by . . . Jesus college, 22nd Feb. 1896, amending
Statute IV, clause 35, and the Statute . . . concerning the Meyricke
endowment, clause 3, as amended by Order in council of 23rd Feb.
1891, and clause 6. Lond., 1897, s. sh.   Pp. Eng. 1897 vol. 70

7431. Statutes made by . . . Jesus college, 6th Dec. 1901, amending Statute
V., and the Schedule relating to King Charles the first trust. Lond.,
1902, s. sh.   Pp. Eng. 1902 vol. 80

7432. Statutes made for the colleges . . . (Jesus college.) Oxf., 1927, 8°.
66 pp.   G.A. Oxon 4° 759 = R.

Finance and property

7433. An act for vesting the inheritance of the rectory and tithes of Bedge-
worth, granted . . . to the late dissolved corporation of Bergavenny,
and by them leased to Jesus college . . . towards maintaining a fellow
and scholars from Bergavenny school . . . (33 G. II, c. 52, Private.)
1759–60.
[Précis in Shadwell's Enactments &c. See no. 956.]

7434. An act for effectuating an exchange of the advowson of the church of
the parish of Bagendon . . . belonging to Joseph Pitt . . . for a right
which the principal, fellows and scholars of Jesus college . . . have in
the nomination of a curate to the curacy of the impropriate rectory of
Cheltenham . . . (56 G. III, c. 74, Private.) [Lond.], 1816, fol. 6 pp.
                                                               L.L.

Members

7435. Jesus college. Decision of the Visitor [affirming the eligibility of the
rev. C. L. Dundas for a fellowship, in spite of his being a childless
widower]. April 8. n. pl., (1873), s. sh.   G.A. Oxon c. 276 (f. 22)

7436. JENKINS, SIR L., The life of Francis Mansell, principal of Jesus
college. [Pr. from MS. Wood F 30.] Lond., 1854, 8°. 56 pp.   210 i. 239

7436.5. JENKINS, D. E., The life of the rev. Thomas Charles, B.A., of
Bala. (At Jesus college, 1775–1778, vol. I, p. 38–84.) Denbigh, 1910,
4°.   112 d. 24

7437. WILLIAMS, T. H. PARRY-, John Rhŷs, 1840–1915. [In Welsh and Engl.] Cardiff, 1954, 8°. 67 pp. 314 e. 6

7438. Jesus college list. Mich. term, 1896. [Oxf.], 1896, 4°. 8 pp.
G.A. Oxon c. 276 (f. 34)

7438.1. Jesus College. List of old members. Supplementary list, October 1932. Oxf., 1932, 8°. 27 pp. G.A. Oxon 8° 1515
— List of old members. 2nd ed. Oxf., 1937, 8°. 56 pp.
G.A. Oxon 8° 1516
— 5th ed. Oxf., 1955, 8°. 79 pp. G.A. Oxon 8° 1517

Scholarships and exhibitions

7439. [Examination papers. Scholarships &c.]. 1840–77. [Oxf.], 1840–77, fol. &c. [The Bodleian set is imperfect.] 2626 c. 1

7440. Jesus college. Scholarships and exhibitions. [Rules.] 1888, 90, 91, 94, 96, 98, 1900–02, 04, 07. (Oxf.), 1887–1906, s. sh.
G.A. Oxon c. 276 (f. 23–30)

7441. Jesus college. (Meyricke endowment.) Return 'of Copy of the correspondence . . . between the Oxford university commissioners, the Charity commissioners, and Jesus college, as to the capital sum of £20,000, part of the endowment . . . at Jesus college, which it was proposed to deal with by a scheme under the Endowed schools act for the benefit of education in Wales. Lond., 1889, fol. 22 pp.
Pp. Eng. 1889 vol. 59

7442. The alienation of the Meyrick fund from Jesus college, proposed in the Bill for intermediate education (Wales). n. pl., [1889], fol. 3 pp.
G.A. Oxon c. 276 (f. 22)

7443. Reply of Fellows of Jesus college, Oxford, to statements on which the members of Parliament for Wales and Monmouthshire have based their resolutions respecting the accumulated portion of the Meyrick fund. Mar. 17. n. pl., 1890, 4°. 4 pp. G.A. Oxon c. 276 (f. 22)

Societies and sport

7444. Jesus college common room and debating society. Rules. Oxf., [1891], 12°. 11 pp. G.A. Oxon c. 276 (f. 3)

7445. [Letter requesting subscriptions to purchase a new barge.] March. [Oxf.], 1909, s. sh.
— April. [Oxf.], 1910, s. sh. G.A. Oxon c. 276 (f. 2)

7446. [Jesus college concert programmes, 1885–1920.] G.A. Oxon 8° 1108

Library

7447. Jesus college. (Hist. MSS. comm., 2nd report, 1871, p. 130.)
2262 c. 37 = K.
See 5256 [Streeter, B. H., The chained library. 1931].

7448. PHILIP, I. G., Sheldon manuscripts in Jesus college library. (Bodl. libr. record, 1939, vol. 1, p. 119–23.) 2590 d. Oxf. 1. 41 = R.

7449. FORDYCE, C. J., and KNOX, T. M., The library of Jesus college. (Proc. and papers, Oxf. bibliogr. soc., 1940, vol. 5, p. 49–115.) Soc. 258 d. 176 = A.

7450. [5 typewritten sheets listing volumes in the Fellows' Library and the Meyricke Library. Jan. 1961.] 2590 d. Oxf. 38. 1

Arms

7451. BAYLEY, A. R., Jesus college: arms. (Notes & queries, 1929, vol. 156, p. 302, 303, 338.) Per. 3974 e. 405 = A.

7452. BAYLEY, A. R., Arms of Jesus college. (Notes & queries, 1939, vol. 176, p. 74–77.) Per. 3974 e. 405 = A.

Keble college

General 7453–7470
Statutes 7471
Members 7472–7476

Societies 7477–7479
Chapel 7480–7485

General

7453. [Topographical prints, &c. in the Bodleian]. G.A. Oxon a. 53

7454. Keble memorial. [Resolutions of meeting held at Lambeth palace, May 12th, 1866, together with list of subscriptions.] n. pl., 1866, 2 sheets. G.A. Oxon c. 82 (327, 28)

7455. Proceedings at the laying of the first stone of Keble college, Oxford, April 25th, 1868. Lond. &c., 1868, 4°. 50 pp. G.A. Oxon 4° 51

7456. WORDSWORTH, J., Keble college and the present University crisis, a letter. Oxf. &c., 1869, 8°. 15 pp. G.A. Oxon 8° 165 (2)

7457. POTTINGER, H. A., The proceedings in Convocation about Keble college, June 16, 1870 [signed A member of Convocation, H. A. Pottinger?, suggesting that Convocation exceeded its powers in admitting students of Keble college to matriculation, pending consideration under what statutory provisions new foundations should be recognized]. June 21. n. pl., (1870), 4°. 4 pp. G.A. Oxon c. 277 (f. 2)

7458. Keble college. Charter of incorporation, June 6, 1870. Lond., [1870], 8°. 12 pp. G.A. Oxon 8° 1132 (18)

7459. POTTINGER, H. A., The University of Oxford and Keble college. No. I. The decree. Oxf. &c., 1871, 8°. 23 pp. G.A. Oxon 8° 165 (4)
— No. II. The statute. 44 pp. G.A. Oxon 8° 165 (5)

7460. Keble college extension fund, 1876. [Account.] n. pl., 1876, 4°. 4 pp. G.A. Oxon 4° 51* (1)

7461. The ceremonial to be observed at Keble college on the occasion of the opening of the hall and library on ... April 25, 1878. n. pl., (1878), 4°. 16 pp. G.A. Oxon 4° 108

7462. [*Begin.*] Case. [Counsel's instructions and opinion as to whether Keble college is included in the operation of the Universities' Tests act, 1871, with regard to scholarships and exhibitions. *Followed by* Correspondence concerning the same.] n. pl., [1879], 8°. 9 pp.
G.A. Oxon 8° 1148 (1)

7463. Keble college occasional papers. No. 1–8. (Oxf.), [1879]–97, 8°.
G.A. Oxon 8° 1149

7464. [*Begin.*] At the April meeting, the council resolved ... [Notes on the proposed system of scholarships.] Oct. 15. [Oxf.], (1880), 8°. 4 pp.
G.A. Oxon 8° 1148 (2)

7465. TALBOT, E. S., [*Begin.*] My dear lord Beauchamp, Your appeal to me ... [A letter dated Oct. 23, 1882 opposing the suggestion that the memorial to dr. Pusey should be connected with Keble college.] n. pl., (1882), 12°. 4 pp. Acland 14 (16)
[See also no. 8830 &c.]

7466. WILSON, R. J., Keble and the revival of religion, a sermon. Oxf., 1891, 8°. 10 pp. G.A. Oxon 8° 659 (7)

7467. Keble college. [Report.] 1899/1900–1913/14. (Oxf.), 1900–14, 8°.
[The Bodleian set is imperfect.] G.A. Oxon 8° 510*

7468. The Clock tower. Vol. 1, no. 1– . Oxf., 1912– , 4°.
Per. G.A. Oxon 4° 406

7469. DAY, E. H., Keble college [history]. (Treasury, 1920, vol. 35, p. 184–90.) Per. 2705 d. 142

7470. Keble college, past, present and future. Oxf., 1933, fol. 8 pp.
G.A. Oxon c. 277 (f. 29)

Statutes

7471. Statutes made for the college ... (Keble college.) Oxf., 1927, 8°.
22 pp. G.A. Oxon 4° 759 = R.

Members

7472. Keble college. Lent term 1877. [College roll.] [Oxf.], (1877), 8°.
9 leaves. G.A. Oxon 8° 708

7473. Keble college jubilee. June 22nd, 1920. . . . Roll of names. Oxf., (1920), 8°. 20 pp. G.A. Oxon 8° 810 (19)

7474. NICOLLS, O. C. C., A register of the alumni of Keble college, 1870 to 1925. Oxf., 1927, 4°. 560 pp. G.A. Oxon 4° 480

7475. MCKENZIE, H. W., Keble college, the first thirty [members] from within [by H. W. McKenzie]. Oxf., [1930], 8°. 13 pp.
G.A. Oxon 8° 1148 (10)

7476. POULTON, E. B., Memories of the first warden of Keble [bp. E. S. Talbot. Signed E. B. P.]. (Oxf. mag., 1934, vol. 53, p. 44, 45.)
Per. G.A. Oxon 4° 141

See 4637, 4637.1 [Biographies of John Keble].

Societies

7477. Keble college amalgamated clubs. Balance sheet. 1902/03, 04/05, 05/06. (Oxf., 1903–06), s. sh. G.A. Oxon c. 277 (f. 13, 14)

7478. Keble college musical society. [Programmes. 1882–1927.]
G.A. Oxon 8° 786

7479. Keble association. Report and list of members. 1938–40. (Oxf., 1938–40), 8°. Per. G.A. Oxon 4° 768

Chapel

7480. The form of service to be used at the laying of the foundation stone of Keble college chapel, April 25th 1873. n. pl., (1873), 4°. 7 pp.
G.A. Oxon c. 277 (f. 3)

7481. Speeches of the warden of Keble college, and of the earl Beauchamp, at the laying of the foundation stone of the college chapel, St. Mark's day, 1873. Oxf., 1873, 8°. 27 pp. G.A. Oxon 8° 394

7482. The ceremonial to be observed at Keble college on the occasion of the opening of the chapel; and of the laying of the foundation stone of the hall and library . . . April 25, 1876. n. pl., (1876), 4°. 15 pp.
G.A. Oxon 4° 51* (2)

7483. Keble college chapel. The venerable donor [&c. An account of the subjects treated in the mosaics and painted glass]. n. pl., [1876?], s. sh.
G.A. Oxon c. 277 (f. 2)

7484. An account of the proceedings at Keble college on the occasion of the opening of the chapel . . . St. Mark's day, 1876 . . . and a description of the chapel. Oxf. &c., 1876, 8°. 107 pp. G.A. Oxon 8° 207

7485. Keble college chapel. Glass in Keble college chapel. (Builder, 1876, vol. 34, p. 402, 495.) N. 1863 c. 1

Linacre college

7485.5. BAMBOROUGH, J. B., Linacre house. (Oxf. mag., 1962, N.S., vol. 2, p. 385.) Per. G.A. Oxon 4° 141

7485.51. BAMBOROUGH, J. B., Linacre house. (Oxf. mag., 1965, N.S., vol. 5, p. 209, 10.) Per. G.A. Oxon 4° 141

Lincoln college

General 7486–7503
Administration 7504–7510
Statutes 7511–7533
Members 7534
  Biography and Reminiscences 7535–
  7543

Lists 7544
Societies 7545–7551
Library 7552–7553

General

7486. [Topographical prints, &c. in the Bodleian.]   G.A. Oxon a. 53

7487. In adventum illustrissimi Lecestrensis comitis ad collegium Lincolniense carmen gratulatorium. [Madan 58.] Oxon., 1585, s. sh.
Wood 516 (2)

7488. An act for establishing . . . articles of agreement between . . . George, duke of Marlborough . . . and . . . Lincoln college [concerning Combe and Blackbourton]. (33 G. III, c. 22, Private.) n. pl., 1793, fol. 6 pp.
L.L.

7489. INGRAM, J., Lincoln college. (Memorials of Oxford, 1837, vol. I. 16 pp.)   G.A. Oxon 8° 18

7490. [Examination papers. Scholarships.] 1840–87. [Oxf.], 1840–87, 8°. [The Bodleian set is imperfect].   2626 e. 20

7491. The substance of a correspondence between the bishop of Oxford and the rector of Lincoln [C. J. Meredith] touching his lordship's claim to license the chaplains of Lincoln college [ed. by J. Radford]. Oxf., 1848, 8°. 55 pp.   G.A. Oxon 8° 77 (31)
— 2nd ed., with appendix. Oxf. &c., 1848, 8°. 77 pp.
G.A. Oxon 8° 77 (32)

7492. PLATT, H. E. P., A plea for the preservation of Lincoln college [from being amalgamated with Brasenose]. Oxf., 1878, 8°. 8 pp. 2625 e. 9

7493. WORDSWORTH, C., *bp. of Lincoln*, A letter to the members of Lincoln college . . . on certain proposed changes in their college. Lincoln &c., 1880, 8°. 13 pp.   G.A. Oxon 8° 215 b (7)

7494. CLARK, A., Lincoln college. [Proof copy, with additional matter, of the chapter on Lincoln college in no. 6411, The colleges of Oxford.] 1891.   G.A. Oxon 4° 122

7495. CLARK, A., Lincoln. (Univ. of Oxf., college hist.) Lond., 1898, 8°. 220 pp.   G.A. Oxon 8° 651 (2) = R.

7496. CLARK, A., *ed.*, Consecration of Lincoln college chapel, 1631. (Oxf. hist. soc., 1905, vol. 47, p. 136–55.)   G.A. Oxon 8° 360 = R.

7497. WARNER, S. A., Lincoln college. Lond., 1908, 4°. 108 pp.
G.A. Oxon 4° 256

7498. PAINTIN, H., Brief notes on Lincoln college. Repr. from 'Packer's Burford almanack'. n. pl., [*c.* 1912], 8°. 14 pp. G.A. Oxon 8° 874 (7)

7499. The Lincoln Imp. Vol. I, no. I– . Oxf., 1920– , 4°.
G.A. Oxon 4° 428

7500. The five centuries of Lincoln college. Fleming to Wesley. [Part of an article from The Times.] (Proc., Wesley soc., 1927, vol. 16, p. 29, 30.)
Per. 11142 d. 21

7501. The visitation of the college of Blessed Mary and all saints, 1445. (Visitations of relig. houses in the dioc. of Lincoln, vol. 3. Canterbury and York soc., 1927, vol. 33, p. 267, 68.)
Soc. G.A. Eccl. top. 4° 32 = R.

7502. Lincoln college. [Handbook.] Oxf., (1948), 8°. 32 pp.
G.A. Oxon 8° 1184 (8)

7502.5. OAKESHOTT, W. F., The college chapel. (Lincoln record, 1956/7, p. 8–13.)
Per. G.A. Oxon 8° 1450

7503. GREEN, V. H. H., Oxford common room: a study of Lincoln college and Mark Pattison. Lond., 1957, 8°. 336 pp.
G.A. Oxon 8° 1354

7503.5. BETHELL, D., The graduate problem. [The Lincoln Middle common room.] (Oxf. mag., 1959, vol. 78, p. 76–78.)
Per. G.A. Oxon 4° 141

Administration

7504. KETTLE, J. L., Letter to the rev. James Thompson, rector of Lincoln college [concerning his election as rector]. Lond., 1851, 8°. 23 pp.
G.A. Oxon 8° 316

7505. ESPIN, T. E., A letter to . . . James Thompson. [An answer to no. 7504.] Oxf. &c., 1851, 8°. 13 pp.
G.A. Oxon 8° 250 (20)

7506. KETTLE, J. L., Letter to the rev. T. E. Espin. [A reply to no. 7505.] Lond., 1851, 8°. 24 pp.
G.A. Oxon 8° 1079 (17)

7507. A voice from the uninitiated; or, The mysteries of the Lincoln Common room. [Observations on two Letters by J. L. R. Kettle concerning 'close fellowships' and the recent election as rector of J. Thompson.] Lond., 1852, 8°. 20 pp.
G.A. Oxon 8° 70 (9)

7508. MICHELL, R., [*Begin.*] The following letter has been addressed to the lord bishop of Lincoln . . . [offering information concerning the late election of a rector of Lincoln college]. Dec. 5. (Oxf., 1851), s. sh.
G.A. Oxon c. 278 (f. 32)

7509. Lincoln college [report. *Afterw.*] Lincoln college record. 1898/99– . (Oxf.), 1899– , 8°.
[The Bodleian set is imperfect: the years partially covered are 1899/ 1900–1937/38, 1950/51– ; G.A. Oxon 8° 510*, G.A. Oxon c. 278; Per. G.A. Oxon 8° 1450.]

Statutes

7511. Statutes of the colleges . . . (Lincoln college.) Oxf. &c., 1853, 8°.
39 pp. G.A. Oxon 8° 24 = R.

7512. Oxford university. Copies of orders in Council referring to a committee of the Privy council certain regulations and ordinances of Exeter, Lincoln and Corpus Christi colleges . . . in amendment of their respective statutes . . . Lond., 1856, fol. 52 pp.
Pp. Eng. 1856 vol. 46
— [Another ed. *entitled*] Oxford university. Orders in council [&c.]
40 pp. G.A. Oxon c. 35 (4)

7513. Lincoln college. Copy of regulations and ordinances for the amendment of the statutes . . . (tr. from the Latin). Lond., 1856, fol. 19 pp.
Pp. Eng. 1856 vol. 46

7514. Copy of an ordinance made by the Oxford university commissioners . . . in place of a clause in the second chapter of the regulations . . . made by . . . Lincoln college, on 8th Oct., 1855, in amendment of the Statutes of the said colleges. (Copies of four ordinances, &c., p. 4.) [Lond.], 1857, fol. Pp. Eng. 1857 vol. 13

7515. Ordinances and statutes framed or approved by the . . . Commissioners . . . (Lincoln college, p. 217–39). Oxf., 1863, 8°.
Clar. Press 31 a. 63

7516. WORDSWORTH, C., *bp. of Lincoln*, A letter to the University of Oxford commissioners on the announcement of their intention to make statutes for Brasenose and Lincoln colleges. (Lincoln, 1879), 8°. 10 pp.
G.A. Oxon 8° 456

7517. Statutes proposed to be made . . . for Lincoln college. Nov. 1880.
(Oxf.), 1880, 8°. 28 pp. G.A. Oxon 8° 425 (10) = R.

7518. Statutes proposed to be made by the University of Oxford commissioners for Lincoln college. April 1881. [Lond.], 1881, fol. 18 pp.
G.A. Oxon c. 8 (36)

7519. A statute for Lincoln college concerning the form of accounts of the college and the audit and publication thereof. (Univ. of Oxf. and Cambr. act, 1877. Oxford. Thirty-six statutes made by the Univ. of Oxf. commissioners, 1881, p. 262.) Pp. Eng. 1882 vol. 51

7520. Statutes made by the Oxford university commissioners on 16th June, 1881 for Lincoln college. [Lond.], 1882, fol. 14 pp.
Pp. Eng. 1882 vol. 51

7521. Statuta collegii Lincolniensis . . . approbata MDCCCLV. (Oxf.), [c. 1882], 8°. 36 pp. G.A. Oxon 8° 594

7522. Lincoln college. [*Begin.*] At a general meeting of the governing body of the college . . . 9th Dec., 1887, the subjoined amendments to the college statutes were voted upon, and passed . . . n. pl., (1887), s. sh.
G.A. Oxon c. 278 (f. 33)

7523. Lincoln college. [*Begin.*] Subjoined are the proposed amendments to the college statutes, with the alterations that have been suggested since their first circulation. [Jan.] n. pl., [1888], s. sh.
G.A. Oxon c. 278 (f. 33)

7524. Statutes made by . . . Lincoln college . . . on the 27th January 1888 amending cap. II, sections 5 and 10 . . . Lond., 1888, fol.
Pp. Eng. 1888 vol. 78

7525. Statutes passed by . . . Lincoln college, 24th Jan., 1890, amending the Statutes. Lond., 1890, s. sh.
Pp. Eng. 1890 vol. 56

7526. Lincoln college, Oxford. Amendments of Statutes, approved by H.M. the Queen in Council, Jan. 12, 1891. n. pl., (1891), s. sh.
G.A. Oxon c. 278 (f. 32)

7527. Statutes made by . . . Lincoln college, 12th June 1896, altering chapter 6, section 4; chapter 7, section 1, and chapter 8, section 2, of the Statutes. Lond., 1897, s. sh.
Pp. Eng. 1897 vol. 70

7528. Statutes made by . . . Lincoln college . . . on 11th June 1897 amending cap. 2, 3, 4, 5, 6 and 10 of the college Statutes. 10 February 1898. Lond., 1898, fol. 4 pp.
Pp. Eng. 1898 vol. 70

7529. Statute made by . . . Lincoln college, 6th Nov. 1909 and sealed on the 15th of the same month, amending chapter 2, section 5; chapter 6, sections 4, 5, and 6; chapter 7, section 1; and chapter 8, sections 1 and 2 of the Statutes. Lond., 1910, s. sh.
Pp. Eng. 1910 vol. 72

7530. Statute made by . . . Lincoln college, 6th May 1912, amending chapters II (10), and VI (2), of the Statutes. Lond., 1912, s. sh.
Pp. Eng. 1912/13 vol. 65

7531. Statute made by . . . Lincoln college . . . on the 10 June 1913, amending Statute cap. 2, sections 1, 9 and 10. 10 Feb. 1914. Lond., 1914, s. sh.
Pp. Eng. 1914 vol. 64

7532. Statute made by . . . Lincoln college, 11th Dec. 1914, amending chapters 2 and 6 of the existing Statutes. Lond., 1915, s. sh.
Pp. Eng. 1914/16 vol. 51

7533. Statutes made for the colleges . . . (Lincoln college.) Oxf., 1927, 8°. 40 pp.
G.A. Oxon 4° 759 = R.

Members

7534. A college betting book [of the 19th and early 20th century preserved in Lincoln college senior common room. Signed] R. W. J[effrey?]. (Oxf. mag., 1919, vol. 37, p. 139–41.)
Per. G.A. Oxon 4° 141

BIOGRAPHY

7535. COON, R. H., William Warde Fowler, an Oxford naturalist. Oxf., 1934, 8°. 366 pp.
G.A. Oxon 8° 1144

7536. Mark Pattison [by J. C. Morison]. (Macmillan's mag., 1884, vol. 50, p. 401–08.)   G.A. Oxon 4° 575 (14)

7537. Recollections of Mark Pattison. (Temple bar, 1885, vol. 73, p. 31–49.)   G.A. Oxon 4° 575 (15)

See 3864 [Pattison, M., Memoirs. 1885].
See 7503 [Oxford common room: a study of Lincoln college and Mark Pattison. 1957].

7538. AUSTIN, R., Thomas Smyth of Lincoln college. [Memoranda of expenses, books &c. on entering college in 1638.] (Notes & queries, 1921, 12th ser., vol. 9, p. 221, 22.)   Per. 3974 e. 405 = A.

7539. (Records preserved by the Wesley historical society of the bicentenary celebration of the admission of John Wesley to his fellowship at Lincoln college, 1725–6) [with a record for the year 1926 of the college]. (Proc., Wesley hist. soc., 1926, vol. 15, p. 141–65, 198–201.)
Soc. 11142 d. 21

7540. John Wesley's rooms in Lincoln college: a record of their reopening on the 10th September 1928 after restoration by the American Methodist committee. Oxf., 1929, 4°. 32 pp.   G.A. Oxon 4° 493

7541. GREEN, V. H. H., The young mr. Wesley [1726–1735. Lincoln college passim. An appendix discusses the location of his rooms]. Lond., 1961, 8°. 342 pp.   11142 e. 196 = S.

REMINISCENCES

7542. OVERTON, J. H., Lincoln college, Oxford, thirty years ago. (Longman's mag., 1887, vol. 9, p. 258–70.)   G.A. Oxon 4° 575 (16)

7543. FOWLER, W. W., Reminiscences. n. pl., 1921, 8°. 87 pp.
G.A. Oxon 8° 1140

LISTS

7544. Lincoln college record [of graduate members on the books] 1897/98, 1900/01. Oxf., 1899, 1901, 8°.   G.A. Oxon 8° 653

Societies

7545. Crewe society. Rules. Oxf., 1895, 8°. 6 pp.   G.A. Oxon 8° 1110 (10)

7546. The Fleming society. Rules. (Oxf.), 1914, 8°. 4 pp.
— 1922.   G.A. Oxon c. 278 (f. 3)

7547. CARPENTER, J. R., A history of the Fleming society of Lincoln college [with some account of other college societies. Reprod. from typewriting]. n. pl., 1937, 4°. 19 pp.   G.A. Oxon 4° 569
— Addendum [by J. P. Marchant. Typewritten]. n. pl., 1947, 4°. 8 pp.
G.A. Oxon c. 278 (f. 44)

7548. Lincoln college boat club. Rules. Oxf., 1867, 8°. 12 pp.
G.A. Oxon 8° 1110 (8)
— 1871.   G.A. Oxon 8° 1110 (9)

7549. Lincoln college combined athletic clubs. Accounts, 1888–89. (Oxf., 1889), 8°. 7 pp.   G.A. Oxon c. 278 (f. 10)

7550. Lincoln college debating club (society). Rules. Revised to Lent term, 1879. [Oxf.], (1879), 8°. 4 pp.   G.A. Oxon 8° 1110 (6)
— Summer term, 1891. 8 pp.   G.A. Oxon 8° 715 (23)
— Summer term, 1895.   G.A. Oxon 8° 1110 (7)
— Trinity term, 1903. 11 pp.   G.A. Oxon 8° 715 (19)

7551. Constitution and rules of the Lincoln college junior common room, with which is incorporated the Lincoln college debating society, and of amalgamated clubs. As amended Hilary–Trinity, 1948. n. pl., (1948), 8°. 23 pp.   G.A. Oxon 8° 1184 (9)

Library

7552. Lincoln college. (Hist. MSS. comm., 2nd report, 1871, p. 130–32.)
2262 c. 37 = K.

See 5256 [Streeter, B. H., The chained library. 1931].

7553. WEISS, R., The earliest catalogues of the library of Lincoln college. (Bodl. quart. record, 1937, vol. 8, p. 343–59.)
2590 d. Oxf. 1. 40 = R.

7553.5. Lincoln college. The Murray library. [Oxf.], 1956, 8°. 8 pp.
G.A. Oxon c. 278 (47)

Magdalen college

General

7554. [Topographical prints, &c. in the Bodleian.]   G.A. Oxon a. 54

7555. Beatæ Mariæ Magdalenæ lachrymæ, in obitum . . . Gulielmi Grey. [Madan 277.] Oxon., 1606, 4°. 46 pp.   Wood 460 (8)

7556. Luctus posthumus sive erga defunctum . . . Henricum Walliæ principem collegij Beatæ Mariæ Magdalenæ . . . mecænatem longe indulgentissimum Magdalenensium officiosa pietas. [Madan 343.] Oxon., 1612, 4°. 62+[8] pp.   4° O 14 Art.

7557. BARON, J., Quæstiones theologicæ in usum coll. Mag. Oxon. [Madan 2320.] Oxon., 1657, s. sh.   fol. Θ 662 (6)

7558. HURDIS, J., A word or two in vindication of the University of Oxford, and of Magdalen college in particular from the posthumous aspersions of mr. Gibbon [by J. Hurdis]. n. pl., [1797?], 4°. 44 pp.
Gough Oxf. 63 (9)

7559. BUCKLER, J. C., Observations on the original architecture of Saint Mary Magdalen college, Oxford; and on the innovations anciently or recently attempted. [By J. C. Buckler]. Lond., 1823, 8°. 182 pp.
G.A. Oxon 8° 306

7560. INGRAM, J., Magdalene college. (Memorials of Oxford, 1837, vol. 2. 32 pp.)
G.A. Oxon 8° 19

7561. WILSON, H. A., Magdalen college. (Oxf. univ. college hist.) Lond., 1899, 8°. 281 pp.
G.A. Oxon 8° 651 (9) = R.

7562. GLASGOW, E., Sketches of Magdalen college, Oxford. Lond., 1901, 4°. 11 pp.+28 pl.
G.A. Oxon 4° 212

7563. WARREN, T. H., Magdalen college. (The College monographs.) Lond. &c., 1907, 16°. 135 pp.
G.A. Oxon 16° 95

7564. Fritillaries in the college meadow. [To preserve them from extinction, no private person is allowed to pick them.] [Oxf.], 1908, s. sh.
G.A. Oxon c. 279 (f. 17)

7565. SALTER, H. E., ed., A cartulary of the Hospital of St. John the baptist. 3 vols. (Oxf. hist. soc., 66, 68, 69.) Oxf., 1914–17, 8°.
G.A. Oxon 8° 360 = R.

7566. WARREN, SIR H., Magdalen college. (Country Life, 1915, vol. 37, p. 897–900.)
Per. 384 b. 6

7567. The Magdalen elms. (Oxf. mag., 1916, vol. 34, p. 212, 13.)
— [Subsequent article by R. T. Günther] The Magdalen elms on the High Street. (Oxf. mag., 1916, vol. 34, p. 228, 29.)
Per. G.A. Oxon 4° 141

7568. Magdalen college. Carols for Christmas eve. [Words only]. (Oxf.), [192–], 8°. 15 pp.
1475 e. 8
[Three programmes with words are in G.A. Oxon c. 279 at f. 84, 85. None is dated; all seem to be of the 1920's.]

7569. Commemoration of the fallen. Magdalen college In Memoriam 1914–18. [Oxf.], 1921, 4°. 16 pp.
G.A. Oxon 4° 403 (5)

7570. Magdalen college. Singing by the choir in the cloisters. [4 progr. with words.] (Oxf., 1925, 27–29), 8°.
2806 e. 91; 109

7571. WARREN, SIR H., Magdalen college. (Country Life, 1928, vol. 64, p. 502–10, 550–56, 586–93, 618–24.)
Per. 384 b. 6

7572. New buildings, Magdalen college. (Architect, 1930, vol. 124, p. 589–91.)
N. 1731 c. 16

7573. MICHELL, G. J., Magdalen college. Oxf., 1931, 16°. 28 pp.
G.A. Oxon 16° 176* (3)

7574. Magdalen college [guide]. (Oxf. univ. archaeol. soc.) Oxf., 1950, 4°.
20 pp.   G.A. Oxon 4° 677 (1)

7575. BOASE, T. S. R., An Oxford college and the Gothic revival. (Journ.,
Warburg and Courtauld inst., 1955, vol. 18, p. 145–88.)
                                       Per. 2998 d. 109 = R.

7576. BOASE, T. S. R., The quincentenary of Magdalen college. (Amer.
Oxonian, 1959, vol. 46, p. 1–5.)   Per. G.A. Oxon 8° 889

Administration

7577. Bylaws. Revised to 1898. Oxf., 1898, 8°. 40 pp.   G.A. Oxon 8° 1385
— Revised to 1908. 49 pp.   G.A. Oxon 8° 1386
— 1946 [and Amendment slips]. (Oxf.), 1946–58, 8°. 35 pp.
                                        G.A. Oxon 8° 1387

7578. Rules with regard to meals in college. [Oxf.], (1900), 8°. 3 pp.
                                G.A. Oxon c. 279 (f. 15)
— (1903).   G.A. Oxon c. 279 (f. 15)

7579. Magdalen college. [Report *afterw.*] Summary of events of the year
. . . 1899/1900– . (Oxf.), 1900– , 8°.   [The Bodleian set is imperfect.]
                              G.A. Oxon 8° 510*, 1388

7580. Magdalen college, Oxford. Regulations and information. 1905.
— 2nd ed. (Oxf.), 1912, 8°. 42 pp.   G.A. Oxon 4° 657 (11)

7581. Alteration of rules as to duties of the college messenger. [Oxf.], 1908,
s. sh.   G.A. Oxon c. 279 (f. 13)

7582. GUNTHER, R. T., [*Begin.*] Magdalen college, 30 Dec., 1920. Dear
[   ], Now that I have at last escaped . . . [A letter of thanks for his
election as Librarian and Research fellow, in which he fulminates
against errors in the college administration etc. during the 26 years of
his connexion with the college.] [Oxf.], (1920), 8°. 23 pp.
                                G.A. Oxon 8° 1230 (11)

Statutes

7583. WARD, G. R. M., *transl.*, The statutes of Magdalen college. Oxf. &c.,
1840, 8°. 168 pp.   G.A. Oxon 8° 32
— [Another issue] 1843.   G.A. Oxon 8° 734

7584. The statutes of Magdalen college, published by G. R. M. Ward.
[An article reviewing the work.] (British critic, 1840, p. 355–96.)
                                G.A. Oxon 4° 577 (12)

7585. Statutes of the colleges . . . (Magdalen college.) Oxf. &c., 1853, 8°.
132 pp.   G.A. Oxon 8° 25 = R.

7586. DEANE, F. H., A letter from a fellow of Magdalen college to Roundell
Palmer. [Really an exchange of letters on the legality of receiving new
statutes, which is perhaps at variance with the fellows' oath. Also

issued with the next item with a general title Correspondence between Roundell Palmer . . . and a fellow of Magdalen college.] Oxf., 1854, 8°. 11 pp. G.A. Oxon 8° 469 (19*)

7587. PALMER, R., A letter to a fellow of Magdalen college . . . on the effect and obligation of the fellows' oath. Oxf., 1854, 8°. 11 pp.
G.A. Oxon 8° 469 (19)

7588. To the right reverend the lord bishop of Winchester. [Appeal by fellows of St. Mary Magdalen college asking his opinion as to the interpretation of the college statutes which might be said to forbid certain schemes for extending the educational scheme of the college.] n. pl., [c. 1855], 8°. 30 pp. G.A. Oxon 8° 1175 (3)

7589. Oxford university. Ordinances . . . in relation to . . . Magdalen [and 10 other] colleges respectively. [Lond.], 1857, fol. 139 pp.
Pp. Eng. 1857 vol. 32

7590. Oxford university. Copies of certain statutes and ordinations . . . in relation to the University . . . and Magdalen college therein. [Lond.], 1857, fol. 31 pp. Pp. Eng. 1857/8 vol. 46

7591. Ordinance framed by the Commissioners appointed for the purposes of the statute 17th & 18th Vict. c. 81, in relation to Magdalen college. n. pl., (1857), 8°. 30 pp. G.A. Oxon 8° 402

7592.

7593. Ordinances and statutes framed or approved by the . . . Commissioners . . . (Magdalen College, p. 261–83). Oxf., 1863, 8°.
Clar. Press 31 a. 63

7594. [Begin.] The committee appointed to take into consideration and report . . . on the addition to the college ordinance proposed on the 15th of May last, beg to submit . . . an amended form of the draft . . . [Oxf., 1880?], fol. 2 leaves. G.A. Oxon c. 279 (f. 6)

7595. Statutes proposed to be made . . . for Magdalen college. Nov., 1880. (Oxf.), 1880, 8°. 31 pp. G.A. Oxon 8° 425 (11) = R.

7596. Statutes proposed to be made by the University of Oxford commissioners for Magdalen college. April 1881. [Lond.], 1881, fol. 19 pp.
G.A. Oxon c. 8 (37)

7597. Statutes of Magdalen college. (Univ. of Oxf. and Cambr. act, 1877. Oxford. Thirty-six statutes made by the Univ. of Oxf. commissioners, 1881, p. 105–19, 252.) Pp. Eng. 1882 vol. 51

7598. Statutes made by . . . Magdalen college . . . 1st Feb., 1888, supplementary to the existing statutes of the college. Lond., 1888, fol.
Pp. Eng. 1888 vol. 78

7599. Statutes made by . . . Magdalen college . . . on 1st February 1898, amending the existing statutes . . . 9 June 1898. Lond., 1898, fol. 5 pp.
Pp. Eng. 1898 vol. 70

7600. Statute made by . . . Magdalen college, 11th Dec. 1901, amending clause 8 of Statute XII (Grammar schools). Lond., 1902, s. sh.
Pp. Eng. 1902 vol. 80

7601. Statute made by . . . Magdalen college, 11th May 1904, amending the existing statutes. Lond., 1905, s. sh.   Pp. Eng. 1905 vol. 60

7602. Statute made by . . . Magdalen college . . . on the 1st February and 26th May, 1909, amending certain of the statutes of the college. [relating to rent-free rooms for chaplains and to tutors' pensions]. 30 Sept. 1909. Lond., 1909, s. sh.   Pp. Eng. 1909 vol. 69
— [Another ed.] 21 Feb., 1910. Lond., 1910, s. sh.
Pp. Eng. 1910 vol. 72

7603. Statute made by . . . Magdalen college, 25th May 1910, amending the Statutes . . . relating to the Waynflete and other professorships. 15 Nov., 1910. Lond., 1910, s. sh.   Pp. Eng. 1910 vol. 72
— [Another ed.] 7 Feb., 1911. Lond., 1911, s. sh.
Pp. Eng. 1911 vol. 59

7604. Statute made by . . . Magdalen college, 20th Nov. 1912, amending certain of the existing Statutes. Lond., 1913, fol. 11 pp.
Pp. Eng. 1913 vol. 50

7605. Statute made by . . . Magdalen college, 4th Nov. 1914, concerning Pensions, and repealing the Statutes of 1888, 1899, and 1910 as to Pensions. Lond., 1915, fol. 4 pp.   Pp. Eng. 1914/16 vol. 51

7606. Statutes made for the colleges . . . (Magdalen college.) Oxf., 1927, 8°. 53 pp.   G.A. Oxon 4° 759 = R.

7607. Statutes made for Magdalen college . . . including all amendments prior to 31 March 1957. [With 3 Amendment sheets.] Oxf., 1956–59, 8°. 63 pp.   G.A. Oxon 8° 1389

Visitations

See 1540 &c. [Visitation of 1648].

7608. FAIRFAX, H., An impartial relation of the whole proceedings against St. Mary Magdalen colledge . . . in . . . 1687 containing only matters of fact as they occurred [by H. Fairfax]. [Lond.], 1688, 4°. 40 pp.
Gough Oxf. 105 (8)
— [Another ed.] 1688.   Ashm. 1019 (11)
— 2nd ed., to which is added the most remarkable passages, omitted in the former by reason of the severity of the press. Collected by a Fellow of the said colledge. Lond., 1689, 4°. 66 pp.
Gough Oxf. 141 (2)

7609. JOHNSTON, N., The king's visitorial power asserted, being an impartial relation of the late visitation of St. Mary Magdalen college in Oxford. As likewise an historical account of several visitations of the universities and particular colleges. Lond., 1688, 4°. 352 pp. 4° I 1 Jur.

7610. COX, N., An account [by N. Cox?] of the late visitation at St. Mary Magdal. colledge . . . by . . . Peter, ld. bish. of Winton., on Thursday the 24th of October, 1688. [Removing the recently appointed Roman Catholic fellows, and reinstating the former fellows.] Lond., 1688, fol. 4 pp. Pamph. 179 (48)

7611. CARE, H., A vindication [by H. Care] of the proceedings of his majesties Ecclesiastical commissioners against the bishop of London and the fellows of Magdalen-college. Lond., 1688, 4°. 78 pp.
Gough Oxf. 141 (3)

7612. The history of King James's Ecclesiastical commission [1686]: containing . . . the proceedings against . . . Magdalen college. Lond., 1711, 8°. 90 pp. B.M.

7613. Attempt of king James the second to force a dissenter [A. Farmer] upon Magdalen college [as president], April 1687. Compiled from Howell's State trials, and other sources. Oxf. &c., 1834, 8°. 26 pp.
34. 457 (7)

7614. CARTWRIGHT, T., bp. of Chester, The diary of dr. Thomas Cart-wright . . . terminating with the visitation of St. Mary Magdalene college, Oct. MDC.LXXXVII [ed. by] J. Hunter. (Camden soc., vol. 22.) Lond., 1843, 4°. xvi + 110 pp. 2233 e. 54 = K.

7615. BLOXAM, J. R., ed., Magdalen college and king James ii, 1686–1688, a series of documents. (Oxf. hist. soc., vol. 6.) Oxf., 1886, 8°. 292 pp.
G.A. Oxon 8° 360 = R.

Finance and property

See 8492 [Compositio quædam collegiorum, coll. Magd. et coll. Trin. Feb. 26, 1558].

7616. Letter to the fellows of a college [Magdalen?] concerning their method of fining; with tables for renewals of years expired in leases of ten and twenty years [&c.] [By H. Homer?]. Lond., [c. 1765], 8°. 25 pp.
Antiq. e. E. 44

7617. An act to enable . . . the college of Saint Mary Magdalen . . . to grant building leases of certain ground, messuages, houses and buildings in the parish of Saint John, Southwark. (17 G. III, c. 56, Private.) n. pl., 1777, fol. 3 pp. L.L.

7618. An act to enable the president and scholars of the college of Saint Mary Magdalen . . . as owners . . . of lands at Wandsworth . . . to grant building leases . . . (15 & 16 V., c. 10, Private.) Lond., 1852, fol. 18 pp.
L.L.

See 6093 [Pelham, H. F., Purchase of the Logic school from Magdalen college. 1893].
See 6094 [Warren, T. H., Proposed decree for the purchase of the Logic school from the college. 1893].

7619. Magdalen college. Report of finance committee [to prepare for the application of prospective future increase in college revenues]. [Oxf.], (1904), 8°. 6 pp. G.A. Oxon c. 279 (f. 15)

Members

7620. DOBSON, J., Dr. Pierce his preaching confuted by his practice. Sent in a letter by N. G. [i.e. J. Dobson] to a friend in London. [Madan 2624.] [Lond.? 1663], 4°. 4 pp. Wood 515 (27)

7621. PIERCE, T., Dr. Pierce his preaching exemplified in his practice, or, An antidote to the poison of a surrilous [*sic*] . . . pamphlet sent by N. G. to a friend . . . [Madan 2625.] [Lond.?], 1663, 4°. 16 pp. Wood 515 (28)

7622. PIERCE, T., A true accompt [by T. Pierce] of the proceedings . . . of the president and officers of st. Mary Magdalen college . . . against dr. Yerburie lately a fellow of the same. [Madan 2626.] [Lond., 1663], fol. 11 pp. Gough Oxf. 141 (1)

7623. KENT, A., A letter to the . . . bishop of Winchester, relative to the case of the rev. Richard Walker . . . amoved from his fellowship in St. Mary Magdalen college, March the 9th; restored on appeal, May 4th, 1769. [Dr. Walker was removed from his fellowship by the college because he had held two ecclesiastical preferments for more than one year.] Oxf., 1769, 4°. 16 pp. Gough Oxf. 141 (4)

7624. The conduct of the . . . bishop of Winchester as Visitor of St. Mary Magdalen college . . . fully stated [in connexion with the restoration of R. Walker to his fellowship]. With brief observations on visitorial power. Lond., 1770, 8°. 79 pp. G.A. Oxon 8° 61 (13)

7625. KENT, A., The appeal; or, Authentic copies of two late addresses [by A. Kent] to the . . . bishop of Winchester as Visitor of Saint Mary Magdalen college [seeking permission to hold two ecclesiastical preferments in addition to a fellowship of the college]. Lond., 1772, 4°. 24 pp. Gough Oxf. 63 (6)

7626. [Examination papers. Fellowships, demyships &c.] 1853–1909. [Oxf.], 1853–1909, 8°. [The Bodleian set is imperfect]. 2626 e. 25

See 2750 [Magdalen college praelectorships. 1855].

7627. [Photographs of Magdalen college men. 1859– .] G.A. Oxon c. 222

7628. [A collection of photographs of University life connected with H. W. Greene, of Pembroke and Magdalen 1876–1926.]
G.A. Oxon b. 119–22

See 4025 [Academic drama. 1480–1650. 1959/60].

7629. Two presidents of Magdalen [J. Hough and M. J. Routh]. (Temple bar, 1879, vol. 57, p. 63–79.) G.A. Oxon 4° 578 (50)

7630. MIDDLETON, R. D., Magdalen studies. [10 biographies of Magdalen men.] Lond. &c., 1936, 8°. 284 pp. G.A. Oxon 8° 1157

7631. DENEKE, M., Paul Victor Mendelssohn Benecke, 1868–1944. (Oxf., 1954), 8°. 60 pp.   G.A. Oxon 8° 1318

7632. WARREN, SIR T. H., In memoriam rev. Frederic Bulley, D.D., president of Magdalen. Rev. Thomas Henry Tovey Hopkins, fellow of Magdalen. [Signed T. H. W.]. Oxf., (1885), 4°. 15 pp.
G.A. Oxon 4° 119 (3)

7633. The letters of George S. Gordon, 1902–1942. Lond. &c., 1943, 8°. 248 pp.   26961 e. 194

7634. GORDON, M. C., The life of George S. Gordon, 1881–1942, by M. C. G. Lond. &c., 1945, 8°. 171 pp.   2625 e. 159

7635. BURGON, J. W., A century of verses in memory of . . . the president of Magdalen college [M. J. Routh]. Oxf., 1855, 4°. 10 pp.
G.A. Oxon b. 113 (77)

7636. DAUBENY, C. G. B., A biographical sketch of . . . dr. Routh, late president of Magdalen. (Miscellanies, by C. Daubeny, 1867, vol. 2, pt. 4, p. 117–22.)   198 e. 27

7637. BURGON, J. W., [Memoir of Martin Joseph Routh, by J. W. Burgon.] (Quarterly review, 1878, vol. 146, p. 1–39.)   Per. 3977 e. 191

7638. BURGON, J. W., Martin Joseph Routh. 1755–1854. (Lives of twelve good men, 1888, vol. 1, p. 1–111.)   2106 e. 26
— New ed. 1891.   11126 d. 20

7639. MIDDLETON, R. D., Dr. Routh. Lond. &c., 1938, 4°. 278 pp.
G.A. Oxon 4° 588

7640. MAGNUS, L., Herbert Warren of Magdalen, president and friend, 1853–1930. 1st ed. Lond., 1932, 8°. 304 pp.   G.A. Oxon 8° 1093

REMINISCENCES

7641. READE, C. L., and C., Charles Reade, a memoir. 2 vols. [Reminiscences of Magdalen college, 1831–38, vol. 1, p. 112–82.] Lond., 1887, 8°.   2569 e. 40, 41

7642. TUCKWELL, L. S., Old Magdalen days, 1847–1877, by a former chorister [L. S. Tuckwell]. Oxf. &c., 1913, 8°. 104 pp.
G.A. Oxon 8° 1238

7643. KNIGHT, J. W., A hundred years ago. [An account of school life as a chorister of Magdalen college school and college life in Magdalen college, by J. W. Knight.] (Oxf. mag., 1938, vol. 56, p. 321–23.)
Per. G.A. Oxon 4° 141

7644. VENABLES, E. M., Sweet tones remembered, Magdalen choir in the days of Varley Roberts. Oxf., 1947, 16°. 78 pp.   G.A. Oxon 16° 21

LISTS

7645. BLOXAM, J. R., A register of the presidents, fellows, demies, instructors in grammar and music, chaplains, clerks, choristers and other members of Saint Mary Magdalen college, Oxford, from the foundation of the college to the present time. 7 vols. [and] Index. Oxf. &c., 1853–85, 8°.   G.A. Oxon 8° 79–81 f = R.

7646. MACRAY, W. D., A register of the members of St. Mary Magdalen college, Oxford, from the foundation of the college. New ser. Fellows. 8 vols. Lond., 1894–1911, 8°.   G.A. Oxon 8° 603 = R.

7647. MURRAY, J., ed., The Magdalen college record, ed. by J. Murray. n. pl., 1909, 8°. 144 pp.   G.A. Oxon 8° 201
— 2nd issue. 1911. 167 pp.   G.A. Oxon 8° 831
— 3rd issue. 1922. 248 pp.   G.A. Oxon 8° 1004
— 4th issue, ed. by P. V. M. Benecke. 1934. 293 pp. G.A. Oxon 8° 1321

7648. List of members of Magdalen college serving in His Majesty's forces or otherwise employed in connexion with the war. December 31, 1914. n. pl., 1914, 8°. 22 pp.   G.A. Oxon 8° 1230 (9)

7649. Oxford university roll of service, 1914–1916. 2nd ed. Magdalen college record. [Pp. 105–22 of no. 1584.] Oxf., [1916], 8°.   G.A. Oxon 4° 657 (44)

Societies and Sport

7650. Rules of the Magdalen college junior common room. [Oxf., c. 1870], 16°. 8 pp.   G.A. Oxon c. 279 (f. 39)
— [Another ed. 1903.] 13 pp.   G.A. Oxon 4° 656 (2)
— [Another ed. 1913.] 14 pp.   G.A. Oxon 4° 657 (13)

7651. Rupert society. [Miscellaneous papers. 1906–1909.]
        G.A. Oxon c. 279 (f. 47–49.)
See 7913 [Magdalen beagles. 1919].

7652. The new cricket and football ground. [Appeal.] [Oxf., 1901], 4°. 3 pp.
        G.A. Oxon c. 279 (f. 17)

7653. Magdalen college, May 1903. [An account of work done towards the construction of a new cricket and football ground; with a list of subscriptions.] [Oxf.], (1903), 8°. 6 pp.   G.A. Oxon c. 279 (f. 15)

7654. Magdalen college commemoration [and ordinary] concert [programmes. 1861–1912.]. G.A. Oxon 8° 1114; G.A. Oxon c. 279 (f. 53)

Chapel

See 7137 [Sepulchral monuments. c. 1830].

7655. A catalogue of the . . . carved oak fittings, marble floor &c. from Magdalene college chapel, Oxford, much of the more modern work by Grinling Gibbons . . . which will be sold by auction . . . December 14th 1837. Oxf., 1837, 8°. 10 pp.   MS. Top. Oxon d. 22 (f. 27–31)

7656. The present windows of Magdalen college chapel. [*Followed by*] Observations upon the stained glass of the 15th and 16th centuries [*and*] Correspondence. (Oxf.), [*c.* 1840], 4°. 8 pp.   G.A. Oxon b. 113 (50)

7657. G ÜNTHER, R. T. [Contribution to the history of the chapel porch of Magdalen college; appendix on the East window of the hall.] (Proc., Soc. of antiq., 1902, ser. 2, vol. 19, p. 153–70.)
Per. G.A. Gen. top. 8° 524 = R.

7658. STEPHENSON, MILL, [Palimpsest brass of Arthur Cole in Magdalen college chapel.] (Proc., Soc. of antiq., 1912, ser. 2, vol. 24, p. 219–21.)   Per. G.A. Gen. top. 8° 524 = R.

7659. GÜNTHER, R. T., A description of brasses and other funeral monuments in the chapel of Magdalen college. Oxf., 1914, 8°. 98 pp.
Manning 8° 219

7660. FREEMAN, A., The organs of the chapel of St. Mary Magdalen. (Organ, 1928, vol. 8, p. 36–45.)   Per. 17426 d. 14

7661. MIDDLETON, R. D., The chapel of Magdalen college in the time of President Frewen. (Church quarterly review, 1949, vol. 149, p. 72–78.)
Per. 1419 e. 402 = S.

Library and muniment room

7662. MACFARLANE, E. M., Catalogus librorum impressorum bibliothecæ collegii B. Mariæ Magdalenæ. 3 vols. [and] Appendix. Oxonii, 1860–62, 4°.   2590 d. Oxf. 3. 1–3 = R.

7663. Catalogus operum ab illustribus alumnis collegii B. Mariæ Magdalenæ . . . scriptorum vel editorum quibus aucta est biliotheca, diligentia maxime Joannis Rouse Bloxam . . . confecit E. M. Macfarlane. Oxon., 1862, 4°. 154 pp.   2590 d. Oxf. 3. 4

7664. Magdalen college. (Hist. MSS. comm., 4th report, pt. 1, 1874, p. 458–65; 8th report, pt. 1, 1881, p. 262–69.)   2262 c. 37 = K.

7665. Rules of Magdalen college library, 1879. (Oxf.), 1879, 8°. 7 pp.
2590 e. Oxf. 22. 1

7666. Magdalen college library. Regulations. [Oxf.], 1883, s. sh.
G.A. Oxon c. 279 (f. 3)
— [*c.* 1890].   G.A. Oxon c. 279 (f. 3)
— Regulations for the reading room. [Oxf., *c.* 1900], s. sh.
G.A. Oxon c. 279 (f. 3)

7667. MACRAY, W. D., Notes from the muniments of St. Mary Magdalen college, from the 12th to the 17th century. Oxf. &c., 1882, 8°. 148 pp.
G.A. Oxon 8° 125

7667.1. COOLIDGE, W. A. B., The library of Magdalen college. (N. & Q., 1883, 6th ser., vol. 7, p. 361–64, 421–23, 441–43.)
Per. 3974 e. 405 = A.

7668. BAIGENT, F. J., and MILLARD, J. E., A calendar of the deeds relating to Basingstoke, preserved in the muniment room of Magdalen college. (A history of Basingstoke, p. 651–59.) Basingstoke &c., 1889, 8°.
G.A. Hants 8° 165

7669. Calendar of charters and documents relating to Selborne and its priory preserved in the muniment room of Magdalen college, ed. by W. D. Macray. (Hampshire record soc.) Lond. &c., 1891, 8°. 177 pp.
Soc. G.A. Hants 8° 182 (4) = R. Top.

7669.6. GÜNTHER, R. T., The row of books of Nicholas Gibbard of Oxford. (Annals of medical history, 1921, vol. 3, p. 324–26.)   Radcl.

7669.65. GÜNTHER, R. T., Goodyer's library. (Early British botanists, 1922, p. 197–32.)   Radcl.

7669.7. GÜNTHER, R. T., The circulating library of a brotherhood of reformers of the 16th century at Magdalen college. (N. & Q., 1923, 13th ser., vol. 1, p. 483, 84.)   Per. 3974 e. 405 = A.

7670. DRIVER, G. R., Magdalen college library [and] List of books printed before 1641 in the library of Magdalen college, of which the Bodleian library has no copy. (Proc. and papers, Oxf. bibliogr. soc., 1929, vol. 2, p. 145–200.)   Soc. 251 d. 176 = A.
— Repr. [of the List]. Oxf., 1929, 4°. 54 pp.   2590 d. Oxf. 3. 5 = R.

Pictures, plate, and treasures

7671. BOASE, T. S. R., Christ bearing the cross, attributed to Valdés Leal, at Magdalen college. (Charlton lects. on art.) Lond. &c., 1955, 8°. 16 pp.   17002 d. 72

7672. DALE, T. C., The plate of Magdalen college [suit against dr. John Dale, 1661]. (Geneal. mag., 1928, vol. 4, p. 58, 59.) Soc. 2183 e. 10

7673. JONES, E. A., Catalogue of the plate of Magdalen college. Oxf., 1940, fol. xxi+103 pp.+7 pl.   17552 e. 21

7674. HOPE, W. H. ST. JOHN, The episcopal ornaments of William of Wykeham and William of Waynfleet . . . (Archaeologia, 1907, vol. 60, p. 465–92.)   Per. G.A. Gen. top. 4° 162 = R.
— [Repr.] 1907. 28 pp.   G.A. Oxon c. 172

Daubeny laboratory

7675. CHAPMAN, E., [*Begin.*] To the chairman of the University of Oxford commission. [Statement giving an account of the work done by Magdalen college for the encouragement of instruction in physical science.] (Oxf., 1877), 8°. 9+[14] pp.   G.A. Oxon 8° 1079 (5)

7676. YULE, C. J. F., Syllabus [signed C. J. F. Yule] of a year's course of practical work in the physiological laboratory of Magdalen college. n. pl., (1878), 8°. 4 leaves.   G.A. Oxon 8° 659 (8)

7677. GÜNTHER, R. T., A history of the Daubeny laboratory, Magdalen college. To which is appended a register of the names of persons who have attended chemical lectures of dr. Daubeny from 1822 to 1867 as well as those who have received instruction up to the present time. Lond., 1904, 8°. 137 pp.   G.A. Oxon 8° 706

7678. GÜNTHER, R. T., The Daubeny laboratory register, 1849–1923 [comprising A history of the Daubeny laboratory, publ. 1904; The Daubeny laboratory register, 1904–1915, publ. 1916; The Daubeny laboratory register, 1916–1923, vol. 3, publ. 1924]. 3 vols. Oxf., 1904–24, 8°. 532 pp.   Radcl.

May day

7679. BURGON, J. W., Magdalen college. The first of May. [A poem, signed J. W. B.] Oxf., [c. 1852], s. sh.   G.A. Oxon b. 113 (101)
— [Another ed. *entitled*] May morning on Magdalen tower. Together with the Hymnus eucharisticus as sung on the tower. Oxf., [c. 1883], 16°. 7 pp.   14770 f. 64
— 2nd ed. With music. Oxf., [1892], 16°. 12 pp.
                    G.A. Oxon 16° 33 (1)

7680. OUTIS *pseud.* May-day on Magdalen tower [signed Οὖτις]. ('Fors togigera', no. 1.) Oxf., 1874, 8°. 12 pp.   G.A. Oxon 8° 286 (3)

7681. MAGDALENENSIS *pseud.*, May day, Magdalen tower. [Pamphlet accompanying the notice of the exhibition at Ryman's of Holman Hunt's picture of the same name.] n. pl., [1891], 8°. 7 pp.
                    G.A. Oxon c. 280 (f. 7)
— [Another ed. 1891.]   G.A. Oxon c. 280 (f. 8)

7682. TAUNT, H. W., Magdalen tower on May morning. Oxf., [1895], 8°. 16 pp.   G.A. Oxon 8° 611 (1)
— 2nd ed. [1896].   G.A. Oxon 16° 33 (2)
— 3rd ed. [1903].   G.A. Oxon 16° 33 (3)
— [Another ed. 1909.] 26 pp.   G.A. Oxon 8° 761 (10)

7683. PAINTIN, H., Magdalen tower and May morning. Repr. from the Oxford chronicle, May 7th 1909. [Oxf.], (1909), 4°. 3 pp.
                    G.A. Oxon 4° 276 (1)

7684. PAINTIN, H., 'May morning' on Magdalen tower. Repr. from Oliver's Oxf. almanack. Oxf., 1914, 8°. 7 pp. G.A. Oxon 8° 900 (10)

7685. PAINTIN, H., Magdalen tower and May morning. (Robinsons' quarterly, 1920, p. 9–11.)   G.A. Oxon c. 280 (f. 8)

7686. BATTY, B. BRAITHWAITE, A Spanish bull-fight, and some strange old customs. [May-day and Xmas eve, Magdalen college.] Reading, 1931, 16°. pp. 22–85.   G.A. Oxon 16° 185

Founder and benefactors

7687. BUDDEN, J., Gulielmi Patteni, cui Waynfleti agnomen fuit . . . vita obitusq; [by J. Budden]. [Madan 212.] Oxon., 1602, 4°. 84 pp.
Gough Oxf. 116 (3)

7688. HEYLIN, P., Memorial of bishop Waynflete [in verse. Prefixed by Heylin's own memoranda, 1599–1643]. (Publ., Caxton soc., 14.) Lond., 1851, 8°. 25+88 pp.
Soc. 2262 d. 31 (14)

7689. CHANDLER, R., The life of William Waynflete . . . Lond., 1811, 8°. 428 pp.
8° U 128 Jur.

7690. [Form of commemoration of the founder and benefactors used by Magdalen college.] [Madan 2519.] [Oxf.? 1660?], s. sh. Wood 515 (24)

7691. [Commemoration of the founder: versicles and prayer.] [Madan 3068.] [Oxf., c. 1675], s. sh.

7692. [Form of prayer &c. in English, in commemoration of the founder. Verso comprises a Latin list of 12 benefactors.] n. pl., [1693?], s. sh.
Wood 276a (513)

Magdalen hall

See also 7370 &c. Hertford college.
See also 7554 &c. Magdalen college.

7693. [Topographical prints, &c. in the Bodleian.] G.A. Oxon a. 53, 62

7694. WILKINSON, H., Catalogus librorum in bibliotheca Aulæ Magdalenæ [by H. Wilkinson]. [Madan 2545.] Oxoniæ, 1661, 8°. 48 pp.
Wood 91 (4)

7695. A fair representation of the case between the principal of M. Hall [W. Denison] and Mr. E---------s late manciple thereof [concerning the manciple's removal from office for failing to pay tradesmen]. n. pl., 1748, 8°. 23 pp.
Gough Oxf. 50 (4)

7696. An act for confirming and establishing an agreement between the principal of Saint Mary Magdalen hall . . . and Ellis Saint John . . for exchanging the advowson of the church of Southmoreton . . . Berks, for the alternate presentation of the church of Finchampstead. (28 G. II, c. 6, Private.) 1754.
— [Précis in Shadwell's Enactments &c. See no. 956.]

7697. [*Begin.*] The principal, vice-principal and resident undergraduates of [old] Magdalen hall . . . [thank all who helped them in the 'late awful fire']. Jan. 13. Oxf., 1820, s. sh. G.A. Oxon b. 19

7698. [Examination papers. Scholarships]. 1833, 50. [Oxf.,] 1833, 50, 8°.
2626 d. 11

7699. INGRAM, J., Magdalene hall. (Memorials of Oxford, 1837, vol. 2. 16 pp.) G.A. Oxon 8° 19

See 6422 [Suggestions for improvement. 1856].

7700. Oxford university. Copies of regulations . . . in relation to certain scholarships in St. Mary hall and St. Mary Magdalene hall . . . [Lond.], 1858, fol. 8 pp.   Pp. Eng. 1857/8 vol. 46

7701. Ordinances and statutes framed or approved by the . . . Commissioners . . . (Magdalen hall, p. 481–85.) Oxf., 1863, 8°.
                                                        Clar. Press 31 a. 63

7702. An act for dissolving Magdalen Hall . . . and for incorporating the principal, fellows, and scholars of Hertford college. (37 & 38 V. c. 55, Pub.) Lond., 1874, fol. 6 pp.   G.A. Oxon c. 107 (63)

7703. Magdalen Hall Derby club. Rules and resolutions. n. pl., n. d., s. sh.
                                                  G.A. Oxon c. 275 (f. 13)
7704–17.

Mansfield college

7718. [Miscellaneous papers about Mansfield college. 1885– .]
                                          G.A. Oxon 4° 604; b. 134, 135

7719. M., A Nonconformist college for Oxford. (Oxf. mag., 1885, vol. 3, p. 232, 33.)   Per. G.A. Oxon 4° 141

7720. Mansfield college. Scheme of management. (Birm., 1885), 8°. 15 pp.
                                                  G.A. Oxon 8° 437 (1)

7721. FAIRBAIRN, A. M., Mansfield college: its idea and aim. Chilworth &c., 1886, 8°. 64 pp.   G.A. Oxon 8° 437 (2)

7722. Mansfield college, Oxford, October 14–16, 1889. Handbook for the use of visitors. Oxf., (1889), 16°. 32 pp.   G.A. Oxon 16° 80

7723. Mansfield college. (Congregational review, 1889, vol. 1, p. 301, 02.)
                                                  G.A. Oxon 4° 586 (40)

7724. Mansfield college, Oxford: its origin and opening. October 14–16, 1889. Lond., 1890, 4°. 250 pp.   G.A. Oxon 4° 113

7725. Mansfield college. Summer school of theology, 1892, programme. Oxf., 1892, 8°. 15 pp.   G.A. Oxon 8° 437 (3)

7726. MYRES, SIR J. L., Description of a Roman vase found at Mansfield college. (Archæologia Oxon., 1892–1895, p. 109, 10.)
                                              G.A. Oxon 4° 148 = R.

7727. Mansfield college magazine. Vol. 1– . Oxf., 1897– , 8°.
                                                    G.A. Oxon 4° 226

7727.5. Paton library for the use of ministers and students, especially of the Free church in England and Wales. Catalogue. 1909.   Mansfield [This college library is now being dispersed.]

7728. DAVIES, W. T. PENNAR, Mansfield college, its history, aims and achievements. Oxf., 1947, 8°. 57 pp.   G.A. Oxon 8° 1184 (6)

7729. MARSH, J., Mansfield college, 1886–1959. (Amer. Oxonian, 1959, vol. 46, p. 114–17.) Per. G.A. Oxon 4° 889

7729.1. Mansfield college (appeal). (Colchester), [1960], 4°. 17 pp.
G.A. Oxon b. 135

7729.2. MARSH, J., Mansfield, 1962. (Oxf. mag., 1962, N.S., vol. 2, p. 370, 71.) Per. G.A. Oxon 4° 141

Merton college

General

See also 2812 &c. Merton professorship of English.

7730. [Topographical prints, &c. in the Bodleian.] G.A. Oxon a. 55

7731. An acte for thincorporation of Merton colledge . . . (1 Mary, sess. 2, c. 24.) 1553.
[Text in Shadwell's Enactments &c. See no. 956.]

7732. Philologiæ ἀνακαλυπτήριον oratione celebratum inaugurali, quam publice habuit ad Oxonio-Mertonenses Henricus Iacobius, publicavit a quindecennio H. B[irkhead]. [Madan 2184.] Oxf., 1652, 4°. 112 pp.
Wood 512 (11)
— [Another ed. Madan 2184*.] B.M.
— [Another ed. Madan 2185.] 4° S 4 Art. Seld.

7733. KILNER, J., Of the House of scholars of Merton, as, in its form, and formation, and whole shew of its foundation, and confirmation, &c. the earliest of the present colleges. (The account of Pythagoras's school in Cambridge [by J. Kilner] suppl. p. 59–97.) n. pl., [1790?], fol. Gough Cambr. 97

7734. KILNER, J., Of the special and appointed patron [Visitor] of Merton college. (The account of Pythagoras's school in Cambridge [by J. Kilner] suppl. p. 103–11.) n. pl., [1790?], fol. Gough Cambr. 97

See 82 [Kilner, J., Of the two universities . . . with something more of the very first of those particular bodies of scholars now incorporated. 1790].
See 8527 [Kilner, J., Of University and Balliol colleges founded subsequent to Merton college. 1790].

7735. INGRAM, J., Merton college. (Memorials of Oxford, 1837, vol. 1. 32 pp.) G.A. Oxon 8° 18

7736. HEYWOOD, J., The foundation documents of Merton college, ed. by J. O. Halliwell. Lond., 1843, 8°. 64 pp. G.A. Oxon 8° 156

7737. The date of the introduction of the decorated style of architecture into England. Illustrated by extracts from the Bursar's accounts of Merton college, Oxford, from 1277 to 1300. (Archaeol. journ., 1846, vol. 2, p. 137–44.)   Per. G.A. Gen. top. 8° 529 = R.

7738. [Examination papers. Fellowships, postmasterships &c.]. 1866–76. Oxf.], 1866–76, 8°. [The Bodleian set is imperfect.]   2626 e. 26

7739. BRUTON, E. G., On Merton college. (Proc., Oxf. architect. and hist. soc., 1871, N.S. vol. 2, p. 272–77.)   Per. G.A. Oxon 8° 498 = R.

7740. BRODRICK, G. C., Merton college before the Reformation. (Nineteenth century, 1882, vol. 12, p. 426–38.)   G.A. Oxon 4° 578 (57)

7741. BRODRICK, G. C., An Oxford college under James i and Charles i. (Macmillan's mag., 1883/84, vol. 49, p. 460–70.)   Per. 2705 d. 254

7742. BRODRICK, G. C., Merton college in the sixteenth century. (Fortnightly review, 1883, vol. 39, p. 25–37.)   G.A. Oxon 4° 586 (2)

7743. BRODRICK, G. C., Memorials of Merton college, with biographical notices of the wardens and fellows. (Oxf. hist. soc., 4.) Oxf., 1885, 8°. 415 pp.   G.A. Oxon 8° 360 = R.

7744. BRODRICK, G. C., The ancient buildings and statutes of Merton college. (Journ., Brit. archaeol. assoc., 1891, vol. 47, p. 1–11.)
Per. G.A. Gen. top. 8° 526 = R.

7745. HENDERSON, B. W., Merton college. (Oxf. univ. college hist.) Lond., 1899, 8°. 294 pp.   G.A. Oxon 8° 651 (8) = R.

See 2940 [Letter from the vice chancellor asking for a grant to assist in the fitting up of a temporary Electrical laboratory. 1900].

7746. WHITE, H. J., Merton college. (Coll. monogr.) Lond. &c., 1906, 12°. 103 pp.   G.A. Oxon 16° 90

7747. PAINTIN, H., Brief notes on Merton college. Repr. from 'Packer's Burford almanack'. n. pl., [c. 1912], 8°. 10 pp.   G.A. Oxon 8° 850 (24)

7748. GORDON, G., Prologue to Philip Massinger's Duke of Milan, written for the tercentenary performance in Merton college. [2 issues.] n. pl., (1923), 8°. 4 pp.   28001 d. 498

7749. SALTER, H. E., ed., Registrum annalium collegii Mertonensis, 1483–1521. (Oxf. hist. soc., 76.) Oxf., 1923, 8°. 544 pp.
G.A. Oxon 8° 360 = R.

7750. GARROD, H. W., Merton college. Injuctions of archbishop Kilwardby, 1276. [Intr. note signed H. W. G.] Oxf., 1929, 4°. 15 pp.
G.A. Oxon 4° 403* (17)

7751. HUSSEY, C., Merton college. (Country Life, 1933, vol. 73, p. 226–31, 250–56.)   Per. 384 b. 6

See 7928 [Garden buildings. 1942].

7752. JOPE, E. M., Mediaeval pottery from Merton college. (Oxoniensia, 1943/44, vol. 8/9, p. 102–06.)   Per. G.A. Oxon 4° 658 = R.

7753. Merton college, 1939–1945. Oxf., 1947, 8°. 28 pp.
            G.A. Oxon 8° 1204 (11)

7754. The Postmaster. Vol. 1, no. 1– . Oxf., 1952– , 8°.
            Per. G.A. Oxon 8° 1442

7754.1. The early rolls of Merton college, with an appendix of 13th century Oxford charters, ed. by J. R. L. Highfield. (Oxf. hist. soc., N.S., vol. 18.) Oxf., 1964, 8°. 484 pp.   G.A. Oxon 8° 360 = R.

7754.11. PANTIN, W. A., The making of an Oxford college. (Oxf. mag., 1964, N.S., vol. 4, p. 380–82.)   Per. G.A. Oxon 4° 141

     See 117.5 [Oxford starrs; some relating to Merton].

Administration

7755. Merton college. Tariff [battels]. 1876, 83. n. pl., 1876, 83, 8°.
            G.A. Oxon c. 281 (f. 13)

7756. Merton college. [Entrance regulations. c. 1880, c. 1885], 1894. [Oxf., c. 1880–94], 8°.   G.A. Oxon c. 281 (f. 11, 12)

7757. Merton college. Postmasterships . . . [regulations]. [Oxf., c. 1883], 8°. 4 pp.   G.A. Oxon c. 281 (f. 18)

7758. [Merton college menus. 1884–1918.]   G.A. Oxon c. 214

7759. [Syllabus for Collections.] 1886, 88, 89, 91–93, 1896–1901, 1903. [Oxf.], 1886–1903, 12°.   G.A. Oxon c. 281 (f. 8–11)

7760. Merton college. [Report.] 1899/1900–1933. (Oxf.), 1900–34, 8°. [The Bodleian set is imperfect.]   G.A. Oxon 8° 510*

Statutes

7761. PERCIVAL, E. F., ed., The foundation statutes of Merton college, A.D. 1270; with the subsequent ordinances of archbishops Peckham, Chichely and Laud. From the Latin. Lond., 1847, 8°. 141 pp.
            G.A. Oxon 8° 33

7762. Statutes of the colleges of Oxford. Merton college. Oxf. &c., 1853, 8°. 70 pp.   G.A. Oxon 8° 1079 (18)

7763. Statutes of the colleges . . . (Merton college.) Oxf. &c., 1853, 8°. 70 pp.   G.A. Oxon 8° 24 = R.

7764. The statutes of Merton college, made by virtue of the . . . act, 1854, and of an order . . . in council, dated the   day of   , 185 . [Draft. 36 art. The blanks not completed.] Oxf., [1854], 8°. 15 pp.
            G.A. Oxon 8° 1175 (12)

— [Another ed. 38 art.] 16 pp.   G.A. Oxon 8° 1175 (13)

7765. Ordinance framed by the commissioners appointed for the purposes of the statute 17th and 18th Vict. c. 81, in relation to Merton college. (Suppl., London gazette, 8 May, 1857.)   G.A. fol. A 132 (11)

7766. Oxford university. Copy of three ordinances . . . in relation to Merton, Pembroke and University colleges . . . [Lond.], 1857, fol. 49 pp.
Pp. Eng. 1857 vol. 32

7767. Oxford university. Ordinances . . . in relation to . . . Merton [and 10 other] colleges respectively. [Lond.], 1857, fol. 139 pp.
Pp. Eng. 1857 vol. 32

7768. Ordinances and statutes framed or approved by the . . . Commissioners . . . (Merton college, p. 79–99.) Oxf., 1863, 8°.
Clar. Press 31 a. 63

7769. Statutes approved . . . 19th August, 1871 [concerning the power to retain certain fellows and tutors notwithstanding marriage or accession to property]. n. pl., (1871), 8°. 4 pp.   G.A. Oxon c. 281 (f. 84)

7770. Statutes proposed to be made by the University of Oxford commissioners for Merton college. April 1881. [Lond.], 1881, fol. 18 pp.
G.A. Oxon c. 8 (43)
— [Another ed.] (Oxf.), 1881, 8°. 27 pp. G.A. Oxon 8° 425 (12) = R.

7771. Statutes of Merton college. (Univ. of Oxf. and Cambr. act, 1877. Oxford. Thirty six statutes made by the Univ. of Oxf. commissioners, 1881, p. 120–32, 253.)   Pp. Eng. 1882 vol. 51

See 8249, 8250 [Proposed statute for the union of St. Alban hall and Merton college. 1881].

7772.

7773. A statute made by . . . Merton college on 22nd [Jan.] in substitution for Statute IV. 6 (A) of the statutes made for that college by the University of Oxford commissioners . . . Lond., 1886, s. sh.
Pp. Eng. 1886 vol. 51

See 7744 [Brodrick, G. C., The ancient buildings and statutes. 1891].

7774. Statute made by . . . Merton college, 31st Oct. 1895, amending Statute III. Lond., 1896, s. sh.   Pp. Eng. 1896 vol. 65

7775. Statutes made by . . . Merton college, 18th Mar. 1904 amending Statutes III and IV. Lond., 1906, s. sh.   Pp. Eng. 1906 vol. 90

7776. Statutes made by . . . Merton college, 9th Dec. 1905 and sealed on 14th Dec. 1905, altering and amending Statutes III, V and VIII. Lond., 1906, fol. 3 pp.   Pp. Eng. 1906 vol. 90

7777. Statute made by . . . Merton college, 3rd Mar. 1906, and sealed 6th Mar. 1906, altering Statute V, 3 (b). Lond., 1906, s. sh.
Pp. Eng. 1906 vol. 90

7778. Statute made by . . . Merton college, 7th May 1914 and sealed 14th May 1914, amending Statutes II, III, V, IX, and XIII. Lond., 1914, s. sh.   Pp. Eng. 1914/16 vol. 51

7779. Statutes made by ... Merton college, 7th Oct. 1914 and sealed 27th of that month, amending Statutes III and IX. Lond., 1915, s. sh.
Pp. Eng. 1914/16 vol. 51

7780. Statute made by ... Merton college, 6th Mar. 1915 and sealed 11th of that month, further amending Statute IV. 6 (a). Lond., 1915, s. sh.
Pp. Eng. 1914/16 vol. 51

7781. Statutes made for the colleges ... (Merton college.) Oxf., 1927, 8°.
40 pp.   G.A. Oxon 4° 759 = R.

Founders and benefactors

7782. PARKER, J., Walter de Merton, as chancellor, founder, architect. (Proc., Oxf. architect. and hist. soc., 1861, N.S., vol. 1, p. 22–26.)
Per. G.A. Oxon 8° 498 = R.

7783. [Begin.] M. In memoria æterna erit justus ... [Form of commemoration of the founder and benefactor of Merton college.] [Madan 2520.]
[Oxf., c. 1660], s. sh.   G.A. Oxon b. 111 (18)

7784. Merton college. [Order of] Commemoration services [for benefactors]. n. pl., [c. 1924], 4°. 4 pp.   G.A. Oxon c. 281 (f. 17)

Finance and property

7785. HASSALL, W. O., Accounting in the year 1290: earliest accounts of Merton college, Oxford. (The Accountant, Sept. 4, 1954, p. 240.)
Per. 1808 d. 24

7786. Merton colledge case [concerning the lease of Malden manor in Surrey]. [Madan 513.] [Oxf., c. 1623], fol. 4 pp.   Wood 423 (12)

7787. An act for confirming articles of agreement and for effecting an exchange of lands [in Hensington and Woodstock] between ... George duke of Marlborough and ... Merton college. (9 G. III, c. 9, Private.)
[Lond.], 1769, fol. 6 pp.   L.L.

See 6246 [Empowering the college to sell the Parks to the University. 1854, 1855].

7788. Merton college. Abstracts of receipts and payments for the year ending Dec. 31, 1883. [Oxf.], 1884, fol. 4 pp. G.A. Oxon c. 281 (f. 14)

7789. Correspondence between a committee of Merton college and lord Curzon of Kedleston ... concerning the financial administration of the college. Oxf., 1909, 8°. 23 pp.   G.A. Oxon 8° 1079 (11)

Members

GENERAL

7790. COPLESTON, R. S., A lay written about the year of the college DCI [a Nov. 5th 'rag', by R. S. Copleston]. n. pl., [1865], 16°. 18 pp.
G.A. Oxon 16° 173.

7791. [Photographs, &c. chiefly of Oxford men who matriculated at Merton college, 1877–1900].　　　　G.A. Oxon 4° 458

7792. Merton college [tutors' list]. Oct., 1883–86, 89. Oxf., 1883–89, 8°.
G.A. Oxon c. 281 (f. 2–4)

7793. Merton college. Dedication of the memorial to members of the college who laid down their lives in the War, 1914–1918. [With list of names.] [Oxf.], 1922, 8°. 12 pp.　　　　G.A. Oxon 8° 895 (15)

7794. Merton college war memorial. Roll of honour [&c.] Oxf., [1924], 8°.
11 pp.　　　　G.A. Oxon 8° 1001 (18)

7795. GARROD, H. W., Genius loci [p. 87–131; an account of some Merton poets] and other essays. Oxf., 1950, 8°.　　　　27001 e. 1858

7795.5. Merton college register, 1900–1964. Oxf., 1964, 8°. 588 pp.
G.A. Oxon 8° 1492 = R.

BIOGRAPHY AND REMINISCENCES

See 7743 [Brodrick, G. C., Memorials . . . with biographical notices of the wardens and fellows. 1885].

7796. Bodleiomnema. [*Followed by*] Oratio funebris habita in Collegio Mertonensi a J. Halesio . . . 1613, Martij 29°; quo die . . . Thomæ Bodleio funus ducebatur. [Madan 374.] Oxon., 1613, 4°. 84+[18] pp.
Gough Oxf. 125 (1)
[Hales's Funeral oration is repr. in no. 5421, Trecentale Bodleianum, 1913, p. 105–44.]

7797. GARROD, H. W., Sir Thomas Bodley and Merton college. (Bodleian quarterly record, 1931, vol. 6, p. 272, 73.)　　　2590 d. Oxf. 1. 40 = R.

7797.5. MACNAGHTEN, A., A great Oxford eccentric [G. C. Brodrick]. (Country Life, 1966, vol. 139, p. 786, 87.)　　　　Per. 384 b. 6

7798. BRODRICK, G. C., Recollections of the rev. Moses Edwards-Griffiths, fellow of Merton college, based on notes by bishop Hobhouse, fellow of the same college, from 1841 to 1858. (Our memories, no. 11.) [Oxf.], 1891, 4°. 10 pp.　　　　G.A. Oxon 8° 477

7799. RAWLINSON, G., [Memories of the rev. Moses Griffiths of Merton college.] (Our memories, no. 7.) [Oxf.], 1890, 4°. 4 pp.
G.A. Oxon 8° 477

7800. ORNSBY, R., Memoirs of James Robert Hope-Scott . . . late fellow of Merton college. 2 vols. Lond., 1884, 4°.　　　　11126 e. 117

Founder's kin

7801. KILNER, J., Of the founder's kindred [Walter de Merton]; and his attention to them both in, and out of, his college foundation. (The account of Pythagoras's school in Cambridge [by J. Kilner] suppl. p. 98–102.) n. pl., [1790?], fol.　　　　Gough Cambr. 97

Societies and sport

7802. Merton college biological club. [Arrangements for picnic, 1894.]
G.A. Oxon b. 147 (72)

7803. Merton college church society. Rules. [1876, 77, 81]. n. pl., [1876–
81], s. sh.   G.A. Oxon c. 281 (f. 37, 38)
— 1890. 8°. 4 pp.   G.A. Oxon 8° 900 (1)

7804. Merton college church society. Commemoration of 300th meeting,
Feb. 8th, 1893. List of officers and members. (Oxf., 1893), 16°. 16 pp.
G.A. Oxon c. 281 (f. 39)

7805. [Merton college concert programmes. 1862–99.] G.A. Oxon 8° 1107

7806. Merton college debating society. Rules. n. pl., [1892], 8°. 8 pp.
G.A. Oxon 8° 850 (13)

7807. Merton Melanesian mission society. [Rules and objects.] [Oxf.,
1881], s. sh.   G.A. Oxon c. 281 (f. 39)

7808. Merton college musical society. [Information for lady members,
signed A. Brodrick.] n. pl., [c. 1895], 8°. 2 pp. G.A. Oxon c. 281 (f. 41)

7809. [Request for subscriptions for the purchase of a college barge.] June.
(Oxf., 1899), 8°. 3 pp.   G.A. Oxon c. 281 (f. 42)

7809.5. Merton head of the river fund. [Appeal, dated May 1952, and
signed by L. Campbell and 2 others; also an account of the response to
the earlier appeal in 1951 with a description of the Merton bowl,
bought to commemorate finishing 'head of the river'.] [Oxf.], (1952),
8°. 4 pp.   G.A. Oxon c. 281 (f. 85)

7810. [Request for subscriptions towards the cost of enlarging the college
playing field.] Nov. 14. (Oxf., 1890), s. sh. G.A. Oxon c. 281 (f. 42)

Chapel

7811. To the parishioners of S. Peter's-in-the-East. [A letter from J. R.
King explaining the proposed union of the parishes of St. Peter-in-the-
East and St. John the Baptist, which would free the latter church for
the use of Merton college.] [Oxf.], (1874), 8°. 3 pp. G.A. Oxon b. 149

7812. EVANS, G. M., Monumental brasses in the chapel of Merton college.
(Journ., Oxf. univ. brass-rubbing soc., 1898, vol. I, p. 215–33.)
Soc. 2184 d. 50

7813. [Copies of 3 inscriptions in Merton college chapel relating to
A. Fisher, J. Earle, R. Spencer.] [Oxf., 1920], s. sh.
G.A. Oxon c. 107 (83–85)

7814. WOODWARD, J., The monument to sir Thomas Bodley in Merton
college chapel. (Bodleian library record, 1954, vol. 5, p. 69–73.)
2590 d. Oxf. 1. 41 = R.

7815. HIGHFIELD, J. R. L., Alexander Fisher, Sir Christopher Wren and Merton college chapel. (Oxoniensia, 1959, vol. 24, p. 70–82.)
Per. G.A. Oxon 4° 658 = R.

7815.1. BOTT, A., The monuments in Merton college chapel. Oxf., 1964, 8°. 173 pp.   G.A. Oxon 8° 1486

Library and archives

7816. Catalogue of the printed books in the library of Merton college. [*With*] Suppl., Mar. 1880(–Mar. 1890). Oxf., 1880[–90], 8°. 605+ 119 pp.   2590 e. Oxf. 7. 1, 2 = R.

7817. Merton college. (Hist. MSS. comm., 6th report, pt. 1, 1881, p. 545– 59.)   2262 c. 37 = K.

7818. BAIGENT, F. J., and MILLARD, J. E., A calendar of the ancient charters, leases, terriers, account rolls &c. relating to the hospital of St. John the baptist at Basingstoke, existing in the treasury of Merton college. (A history of Basingstoke, p. 593–650.) Basingstoke &c., 1889, 8°.   G.A. Hants 8° 165

7819. Photographs of Merton MSS. November, 1899. n. pl., (1899), fol. 6 plates.   G.A. Oxon a. 27

7820. ALLEN, P. S., Early documents connected with the library of Merton college. (Trans., Bibliogr. soc., The Library, 1924, 4th ser., vol. 4, p. 249–76.)   Per. 258 e. 258 = A.
— Repr. Lond., 1924, 8°.   2590 d. Oxf. 7. 2

7821. GARROD, H. W., Curiosities of Oxford libraries. II. Merton [signed H. W. G.] (Oxf. mag., 1925, vol. 44, p. 30, 31.)
Per. G.A. Oxon 4° 141

7822. GARROD, H. W., Library regulation of a medieval college. (Trans., Bibliogr. soc., The Library, 1927, 4th ser., vol. 8, p. 312–35.)
Per. 258 d. 252 = A.

7823. ALLEN, P. S., and GARROD, H. W., *ed.*, Merton muniments. (Oxf. hist. soc., vol. 86.) Oxf., 1928, fol. 47 pp.   G.A. Oxon 8° 360 = R.

7824. POWICKE, SIR F. M., The medieval books of Merton college. Oxf., 1931, 4°. 287 pp.   2590 d. Oxf. 7. 1 = R.

See 5256 [Streeter, B. H., The chained library. 1931].
See 5654 [Saxl, F., and Meier, H., Catalogue of astrological . . . manuscripts. 1953].

7825. Merton college catalogue of MSS., reprod. from the original calendar. 14 vols. (Nat. Reg. of Archives.) n. pl., 1961, fol. 2262 c. 10 = R.

Coins, glass, and plate

7826. THOMPSON, J. D. A., The Merton college coin collection. (Oxoniensia, 1952/53, vol. 17/18, p. 188–92.)   Per. G.A. Oxon 4° 658 = R.

7827. GARROD, H. W., Ancient painted glass in Merton college. Lond., 1931, 4°. 51 pp.   G.A. Oxon 4° 504 (2)

7828. JONES, E. A., Catalogue of the plate of Merton college. Oxf., 1938, fol. xix+58 pp.+12 pl.   17552 c. 19

New college

General

7829. [Topographical prints, &c. in the Bodleian.]   G.A. Oxon a. 56

7830. Peplus illustrissimi viri d. Philippi Sidnæi supremis honoribus dicatus. [Verses by members of New college, ed. by J. Lhuyd.] [Madan 88.] Oxon., 1587, 4°. 54 pp.   4° A 9 Art. BS.

7831. Encomion Rodolphi Warcoppi ornatissimi quem habuit Anglia, Armigeri, qui communi totius patriæ luctu extinctus est. [Madan 263.] Oxon., 1605, 4°. 32 pp.   Wood 460 (7)

7832. Musæ hospitales Wicchamicæ in adventum illustrissimi principis Frederici Vlrici primogeniti Henrici Iulii . . . ducis Brunsuicensis & Luneburgensis. [Lond.?], 1610, 4°. 32 pp.   4° W 7 (1) Art.

7833. REYNELL, W. H., To the members of Convocation. Gentlemen, As I fear . . . [detailing the dispute with H. Peckham as to which should have New college interest in their candidature for a law scholarship. By W. H. Reynell]. [Oxf., 1766], fol. 3 pp.   G.A. Oxon b. 19

7834. HARE, A. W., A letter [signed A. W. Hare] to George Martin, esq. [On the proposed inclusion of New college in University examinations.] (Oxf.), [1814], 8°. 36 pp.   8° P 245 Art.

7835. INGRAM, J., New college. (Memorials of Oxford, 1837, vol. 1. 32 pp.)   G.A. Oxon 8° 18

7836. WALCOTT, M. E. C., William of Wykeham and his colleges. Lond., 1852, 4°. xvi+473+xv pp.   G.A. Gen. top. 4° 32

7837. Enlargement of New college [with plan]. (Builder, 1872, vol. 30, p. 829.)   N. 1863 c. 1

7838. Cartæ de fundatione collegii Beatæ Mariæ Wynton. in Oxon, A.D. MCCCLXXIX. Oxonii, [1879], 8°. 23 pp.   G.A. Oxon 8° 1195

7839. KIRBY, T. F., On some fifteenth-century drawings of Winchester college, New college etc. (Archaeologia, 1892, vol. 53, p. 229–32.)
Per. G.A. Gen. top. 4° 162 = R.

7840. Oxford architectural & historical society. [Account of a visit to New college, Feb. 8, 1896.] Repr. from Oxford journal. [Oxf.], (1896), 8°. 8 pp.   G.A. Oxon c. 282 (f. 13)

7841. [A dumb bell apparatus at New college.] (Archaeol. journ., 1896, vol. 53, p. 24, 25.)   Per. G.A. Gen. top. 8° 529 = R.

7842. WICKHAM, E. C., The glory of service, an address delivered in New college chapel on June 22, 1898, on . . . the opening of the Alfred Robinson memorial tower. Oxf. &c., 1898, 8°. 9 pp.
G.A. Oxon 8° 620 (28)

7843. New college, Oxford. [Account prepared for the Educational exhibition, 1900.] n. pl., 1899, s. sh.   G.A. Oxon c. 282 (f. 14)

7844. RASHDALL, H., and RAIT, R. S., New college. (Univ. of Oxf. college hist.) Lond., 1901, 8°. 256 pp.   G.A. Oxon 8° 651 (17) = R.

7845. PRICKARD, A. O., New college, Oxford. (College monogr.) Lond. &c., 1906, 16°. 99 pp.   G.A. Oxon 16° 91

7846. GEORGE, H. B., New college, 1856–1906. Lond. &c., 1906, 8°. 102 pp.
G.A. Oxon 8° 740

7847. New college. (Architect, 1915, p. 121, 122, 147, 162.)   B.M.

7848. SPOONER, W. A., New college chapel. Founder's commemoration, October 15, 1916. [Speech.] n. pl., (1916), 8°. 4 pp.
G.A. Oxon 8° 900 (19)

7849. A little book of recipes of New college two hundred years ago. 1922. [Privately printed from the Recipe book of Ralph Ayres, cook of New college, 1721; Bodley has a version of the MS. in MS. Don. e. 89.]

7850. GUNSTON, E. L., Measured drawings: the cloisters, New college. (Architects' journ., 1922, vol. 56, p. 404.)   N. 1863 c. 12

7851. MAYCOCK, A. L., New college et cætera. (Blackwood's mag., 1929, vol. 225, p. 570–78, 675–83.)   Per. 2705 d. 386

7852. OGG, D., New England and New college, a link in Anglo-American relations. Oxf., 1937, 8°. 24 pp.   G.A. Oxon 8° 1148 (11)

7853. LEGG, H. W., Windsor castle; New college, Oxford; and Winchester: a study in the development of planning by William of Wykeham. (Journ., Brit. archaeol. assoc., 1938, 3rd ser. vol. 3, p. 83–95.)
Per. G.A. Gen. top. 8° 526 = R.

7854. Mediaeval figures in New college. (Notes, Oxoniensia, 1939, vol. 4, p. 198, 99.)   Per. G.A. Oxon 4° 658 = R.

7855. BINGHAM, B., Mint julep at New college. (Amer. Oxon., 1943, vol. 30, p. 5–8.)   Per. G.A. Oxon 8° 889

7856. HUNTER, A. G., and JOPE, E. M., Excavations on the city defences in New college, 1949. (Oxoniensia, 1951, vol. 16, p. 28–41.)
Per. G.A. Oxon 4° 658 = R.

7857. SMITH, A. H., New college, Oxford and its buildings. Lond. &c., 1952, 8°. 192 pp.   G.A. Oxon 8° 1254

7858. New college, Oxford. An appeal . . . to endow graduate studies and to modernize the college buildings. (Oxf.), [1961], 4°. 13 pp.
G.A. Oxon c. 282 (55)

7859. First(–) progress report on the New college appeal. (Oxf.), [1961–], 4°.   G.A. Oxon c. 282 (56)

7859.5. GIROUARD, M., The warden's lodgings, New College. (Country Life, 1962, vol. 131, p. 769–73.)   Per. 384 b. 6

7859.51. DE STE CROIX, G. E. M., The admission of women to New College. (Oxf. magazine, 1964, N.S., vol. 5, p. 4–7.)   Per. G.A. Oxon 4° 141
— [Another ed.] (Amer. Oxonian, 1965, vol. 52, p. 21–25).
Per. G.A. Oxon 8° 889

Administration

7860. WICKHAM, E. C., 'Why do we want some open scholarships?' a letter to R. D. Thomson. [Advocating some open scholarships while retaining the close connexion between New college and Winchester.] Oxf., 1866, 8°. 14 pp.   G.A. Oxon 8° 1001 (2)

7861. Duties of the bedmakers. (Oxf., 1867), s. sh. G.A. Oxon c. 282 (f. 15)

7862. A facsimile of five pages from the book of the steward of the Hall for the year 1386–7 [ed. by J. E. Sewell]. Oxf., 1886, fol. [8 pp.].
G.A. Oxon b. 43

7863. Regulations relating to undergraduate members of the college. [Oxf., c. 1890?], 8°. 4 pp.   G.A. Oxon c. 282 (f. 17)

7864. New college. [Report. afterw.] New college record. 1904/05–36/37. (Oxf.), 1905–29, 8°.   G.A. Oxon 8° 510*; Per. G.A. Oxon 8° 1429
[The Bodleian set is imperfect.]

7865. [A letter signed W. A. Spooner recording the setting up of a committee to revise the college scholarship system.] Nov. (Oxf., 1906), 8°. 2 pp.   G.A. Oxon c. 282 (f. 17)

7866. New college matriculation. [Regulations.] [Oxf., 1912], 8°. 4 pp.
G.A. Oxon c. 282 (f. 17)

7867. New college. Information and regulations. Revised October 1927. Oxf., (1927), 8°. 24 pp.   G.A. Oxon 8° 1184 (3)

Statutes

7868. [E statutis collegii Novi] Rub. 65. De portis & ostiis dicti collegii statutis temporibus claudendis & serandis. (Adami de Domerham historia, in lucem protulit T. Hearnius, 1727, vol. 1, p. lxi–lxiv.)
Mus. Bibl. II 84

7869. E statutis collegii Novi, Rub. 61. De libris collegii conservandis & non alienandis. (Adami de Domerham historia, in lucem protulit T. Hearnius, 1727, vol. 1, p. lix–lxi.)　　　　　Mus. Bibl. II 84

7870. Statutes of the colleges . . . (New college.) Oxf. &c., 1853, 8°. 121 pp.
G.A. Oxon 8° 24 = R.

7871. Oxford university. Copies of ordinances in relation to . . . Winchester, New . . . colleges, respectively. [Lond.], 1857, fol. 17 pp.
Pp. Eng. 1857 vol. 32

7872. Oxford university. Ordinances . . . in relation to New [and 10 other] colleges respectively. [Lond.], 1857, fol. 139 pp.　Pp. Eng. 1857 vol. 32

7873. Ordinances and statutes framed or approved by the . . . Commissioners . . . (New college, p. 181–203.) Oxf., 1863, 8°.
Clar. Press 31 a. 63

7874. For the use of the University of Oxford commissioners only. New college—Amendments and additions to the proposed statutes. [Lond., 1880], fol. 3 pp.　　　　　　　　　G.A. Oxon c. 282 (f. 15)

7875. Statutes proposed to be made by the University of Oxford commissioners for New college. April 1881. [Lond.], 1881, fol. 20 pp.
G.A. Oxon c. 8 (44)
— [Another ed.] (Oxf.), 1881, 8°. 32 pp. G.A. Oxon 8° 425 (13) = R.

7876. Statutes of the college of St. Mary of Winchester in Oxford, commonly called New college. (Univ. of Oxf. and Cambr. act, 1877. Oxford. Thirty six statutes made by the Univ. of Oxf. commissioners, 1881, p. 133–147, 254.)　　　　　　　Pp. Eng. 1882 vol. 51

7877. Statutes, passed on 22nd Jan. 1896, and sealed on 11th Feb. 1896, to alter and amend Statutes III, clause 32, and XV . . . in the matter of (a) tenure of rooms by fellows, and (b) application of Pension fund. Lond., 1896, s. sh.　　　　　　　　　Pp. Eng. 1896 vol. 65

7878. Statute made by . . . New college, 14th Oct. 1896, and sealed 29th Oct. 1896, amending Statute III, clause 11. Lond., 1897, s. sh.
Pp. Eng. 1897 vol. 70

7879. Statute made by . . . New college . . . on 23rd June 1897, in substitution for clause 23 of statute III . . . 10 February 1898. Lond., 1898, s. sh.　　　　　　　　　　　Pp. Eng. 1898 vol. 70

7880. Statute made by . . . New college, 10th Oct. 1900 and sealed 23rd Oct. 1900, altering Statute III. Lond., 1901, s. sh. Pp. Eng. 1901 vol. 56

7881. Statute made by . . . New college, 15th Jan. 1902, amending Statute III., clause 11 (Marriage and residence of tutorial fellows). Lond., 1902, s. sh.　　　　　　　　　　Pp. Eng. 1902 vol. 80

7882. Statute made by . . . New college, 17th June 1903, amending certain clauses of Statute III. Lond., 1904, fol. 4 pp.　Pp. Eng. 1904 vol. 75

7883. Statute made by . . . New college, 15th June 1904, amending Statute XV (Pension fund). Lond., 1905, s. sh. Pp. Eng. 1905 vol. 60

7884. Statutes made by . . . New college, 21st June 1905, in lieu of Statutes IV and XIV. Lond., 1906, fol. 3 pp. Pp. Eng. 1906 vol. 90

7885. Statutes made by . . . New College . . . on the 13th January 1909, and sealed on the 8th February 1909, amending Statutes IV. (5) and XXIII. (1), and repealing Statutes XXI. (4) & (5), and XXII. 19 May 1909. Lond., 1909, s. sh. Pp. Eng. 1909 vol. 69

7886. Statute made by . . . New College . . . on the 7th October 1908, and sealed on the 26th February 1909, adding a new clause 10 to Statute IV. 23 June 1909. Lond., 1909, s. sh. Pp. Eng. 1909 vol. 69

7887. Statutes made by . . . New college, 14th Jan. 1914 and 28th Apr. 1914 and sealed 15th June 1914, amending Statutes III, IV, VII, and XI. Lond., 1914, fol. 7 pp. Pp. Eng. 1914/16 vol. 51

7888. Statutes made for the colleges . . . (New college.) Oxf., 1927, 8°. 41 pp. G.A. Oxon 4° 759 = R.

Finance and property

7889. BOHUN, W., A letter to . . . Henry Bigg . . . warden of New college . . . [concerning a debt owed by the college to the author]. n. pl., (1726), 4°. 8 pp. Gough Oxf. 107 (4)

7890. An act for annexing the rectory of Colerne . . . to the office of warden of the college of St. Mary of Winchester. (5 G. III, c. 11, Private.) [Lond.], 1765, fol. 4 pp. L.L.

7891. An act for confirming exchanges of lands in . . . Chesterton . . . made between the trustees of the earl and countess of Jersey and the vicar of Chesterton, and between the said trustees and . . . New college. (10 G. IV, c. 47, Private.) [Lond.], 1829, fol. 23 pp. L.L.

See 6455 [A college Progress. 1896].

7892. The annual progress [through the Bucks estates] of New college, by Michael Woodward, warden, 1659–1675 [ed. by G. Eland]. (Records of Bucks, 1935, vol. 13, p. 77–137.) Soc. G.A. Bucks 8° 45 = R.

Members

GENERAL

7893. [Photographs &c., chiefly of Oxford men who matriculated at New college, 1868–1873.] G.A. Oxon 4° 458

7893.3. Inventory of goods belonging to a warden of New college, Oxford [Thomas de Cranleghe] A.D. 1396. (Archaeol. journ., 1871, vol. 28, p. 232–34.) Per. G.A. Gen. top. 8° 529 = R.

7894. Guddyraw or, Wykeham's curse. [Programme of a play satirizing New college dons, performed Mar., 1888.] (Oxf., 1888), 8°. 3 pp.
G.A. Oxon c. 282 (f. 5)

See 4989 [Down with the dons! 2nd series. 1888].

7895. BURROWS, M., Linacre's catalogue of Grocyn's books, followed by a memoir of Grocyn. (Oxf. hist. soc., 1890, vol. 16, p. 317–80.)
G.A. Oxon 8° 360 = R.

7896. Final report of the New college war memorial committee [signed H. T. Baker, W. A. Spooner]. Sept. 12. [Oxf.], (1921), 8°. 3 pp.
G.A. Oxon c. 282 (f. 2)

7897. New college. Roll of service (1914–1918). Oxf., [1919], 8°. 65 pp.
G.A. Oxon 8° 1440
— [Another ed.] [1921], 4°. 67 pp.   G.A. Oxon 4° 420

7898. New college society. Register of addresses of members of New college, Oxford. Bristol, 1933, 8°. 103 pp.   G.A. Oxon 8° 1105

See 4025 [Academic drama. 1480–1650. 1959/60].

7899.

BIOGRAPHY AND REMINISCENCES

See 3932 [Fisher, H. A. L., An unfinished autobiography. 1940].

7900. OGG, D., Herbert Fisher [in Oxford, 1884–1912; 1923–40]. Lond., 1947, 8°. 205 pp.   2226 e. 12

7901. Alic Halford Smith, 1883–1958: a collection of tributes. Oxf., [1959], 8°. 37 pp.   G.A. Oxon 8° 1397

7902. SLEE, J., The tree warden [Michael Woodward]. (Beds mag., 1959, vol. 7, p. 48–52.)   Per. G.A. Beds 8° 61

Founder's kin

7903. PHILLIMORE, J., A report of An appeal to the lord bishop of Winchester . . . promoted by William Augustus Hare . . . against the election to the vacant scholarships at Winchester and New college in 1829. Argued in October and November 1831. Lond., 1839, 8°. 91 pp.
35 a. 13

7904. LEFEVRE, J. G. S., An answer [signed J. G. S. Lefevre] to 'An appeal to the lord bishop of Winchester . . . touching the further admission . . . of persons claiming kindred with William of Wykeham . . . ' Lond., 1830, 8°. 32 pp.   Bliss B 216 (2)

Societies and sport

7905. New college. Rules of the subscriptions of the college clubs. [Oxf., 1886], 8°. 4 pp.   G.A. Oxon c. 282 (f. 26)

7906. Rules suggested by the committee for the re-organization of the subscriptions of the various college clubs. [Oxf., 1886], 8°. 4 pp.
G.A. Oxon c. 282 (f. 26)

7907. [New college concert programmes. 1846–1907.] G.A. Oxon 8° 1111

7908. N.C.B.C. Rowing notes [signed G. M. Graham]. Oxf., 1904, 8°.
7 pp. G.A. Oxon c. 282 (f. 27)

7909. New college discussion society. [Notices of meetings. 1887, 88.]
G.A. Oxon c. 282 (f. 4, 5, 25)

7910. New college glee club. [Song sheets. 1854–56.] [Oxf., 1854–56], 4°.
G.A. Oxon c. 282 (f. 28, 29)

7911. New college, Junior common room. Rules. Oxf., 1882, 8°. 18 pp.
G.A. Oxon 8° 900 (26)

7912. New college beagles. Kennel book, March 1901. (Oxf., 1901), obl.
12°. 12 sheets. 18975 g. 1

7913. New college, Magdalen and Trinity beagles. [Miscellaneous papers.
1919.] G.A. Oxon b. 174

7914. New college moot club. [Synopsis of case for argument. 1921, 1923.]
[Oxf., 1921, 23]. 8° G.A. Oxon c. 282 (f. 26)

Chapel

See 7137 [Sepulchral monuments. c. 1830].

7915. BROWNE, E. H., *bp. of Winchester*, An address by the bishop of Winchester in New college chapel at the commemoration of the founder
and the celebration of the re-opening of the chapel on October 14,
1879. n. pl., (1879), 8°. 13 pp. G.A. Oxon 8° 1196

7916. New college, chapel. (Builder, 1879, vol. 37, p. 1179, 1218.)
N. 1863 c. 1

7917. BRUTON, E. G., On the recent restoration of New college chapel.
(Proc., Oxf. architect. and hist. soc., 1880, N.S., vol. 3, p. 360–64.)
Per. G.A. Oxon 8° 498 = R.

7918. Oxford architectural & historical society. Restoration of New college
chapel. Repr. from the Oxford chronicle, Feb. 28. [Oxf.], (1880), 8°.
4 pp. G.A. Oxon c. 282 (f. 13)

7919. DOBRÉE, H. C. P., A catalogue of the brasses in New college, both
past and present. (Journ., Oxf. univ. brass-rubbing soc., 1897, vol. 1,
p. 41–67.) Soc. 2184 d. 50

7920. GRIFFIN, R., The brass of bishop Yong at New college. (Antiq.
journ., 1934, vol. 14, p. 379–82.) Per. 17572 d. 73 = R.

See also 7929, etc.

Library and archives

7921. New college. (Hist. MSS. comm., 2nd report, 1871, p. 132–36.)
2262 c. 37 = K.

7922. New college library. [General scheme of the library, pending re-arrangement and cataloguing.] Sept. 1884. (Oxf., 1884), s. sh.
G.A. Oxon c. 282 (f. 15)

7923. Wykeham's books at New college, ed. by A. F. Leach. (Oxf. hist. soc., 1896, vol. 32, p. 211–44.)   G.A. Oxon 8° 360 = R.

7924. New college. Rules for the use of the library by the undergraduates. n. pl., [c. 1900?], s. sh.   G.A. Oxon c. 282 (f. 4)

7925. Catalogue [by G. G. Berry] of books bequeathed by T. Fowler . . . to the Wykeham chair of logic [and housed in New college]. Oxf., 1906, 8°. 36 pp.   2590 e. Oxf. 1 c. 3

7926. HOBSON, T. F., A catalogue of 'manorial documents' preserved in the muniment room of New college. (Publ., Manorial soc., no. 16.) Lond., 1929, 8°. 71 pp.   Soc. G.A. Gen. top. 8° 729 (16)

7927. New college. The new library [announcing their intention to commence building 'next year'. With] Names of subscribers, to Nov. 17th, 1937. (Oxf., 1937), 4°. 4+3 pp.   G.A. Oxon c. 282 (f. 58)

7928. New work at Oxford [the Library at New college and the Garden buildings at Merton college]. (Architects' journ., 1942, vol. 95, p. 440–44.)   N. 1863 c. 12

Stained glass

7929. WARTON, T., Verses on sir Joshua Reynold's painted windows at New-college [by T. Warton]. Lond. 1782, 4°. 8 pp.
G.A. Oxon 4° 13 (12)
— [Repr.] 1930.   2799 d. 158
— 2nd ed., by T. Warton. 1783.   G. Pamph. 1726 (11)

7930. New college chapel. [Description of the painted windows.] n. pl., [1785?], 8°. 8 pp.   Gough Oxf. 7 (3)

7931. WINSTON, C., On the painted glass in New college chapel and hall. (Archaeol. journ., 1852, vol. 9, p. 29–59.)
Per. G.A. Gen. top. 8° 529 = R.
— [Repr.] 33 pp.   G.A. Oxon 4° 186 (19)

7932. WOODFORDE, C., The stained glass of New college. Lond. &c., 1951, 4°. 109 pp.+20 pl.   G.A. Oxon 4° 663

7933. KNOWLES, J. A., Sir Joshua Reynolds's window in the ante-chapel of New college, Oxford. (Journ., Brit. soc. of master glass-painters, 1947/51, vol. 10, p. 189–95.)   Per. 17031 d. 6

7933.4. MUSCALUS, J. A., The Oxford paintings of Reynolds virtues in the West window [of New College chapel] on paper money. Bridgeport, Pa., 1965, 8°. 7 pp.   Num. 2333 d. 5

Treasures

7934. WATSON, C. KNIGHT, [A Chrismatory lid and a paxbrede at New college.] (Proc., Soc. of antiq., 1881, ser. 2, vol. 8, p. 500–06.)
Per. G.A. Gen. top. 8° 524 = R.

7935. HOPE, W. H. ST. JOHN, The episcopal ornaments of William of Wykeham and William of Waynflete . . . (Archaeologia, 1907, vol. 60, p. 465–92.) Per. G.A. Gen. top. 4° 162 = R.
— [Repr.] 1907. 28 pp. G.A. Oxon c. 172

7936. FFOULKES, C., [Note on a carved chest front at New college, illustrating the Battle of Courtrai.] (Proc., Soc. of antiq., 1914, ser. 2, vol. 26, p. 135–37.) Per. G.A. Gen. top. 8° 524 = R.

7937. FFOULKES, C., A carved Flemish chest at New college. (Archaeologia, 1915, vol. 65, p. 113–28.) Per. G.A. Gen. top. 4° 162 = R.

7938. The New college treasures. n. pl., [1936], 8°. 4 pp.
G.A. Oxon c. 282 (f. 52)

Relations with Winchester college

7939. BRIDLE, J., A short address [by J. Bridle] to the society of New college . . . occasioned by a paragraph in a late dedication [in bp. R. Lowth's Life of Wykeham, dealing with the election of a warden of Winchester]. Lond., 1758, 8°. 21 pp. Gough Oxf. 67 (1)

7940. BRIDLE, J., A letter [signed O. W., i.e. J. Bridle] to the rev. dr. Lowth . . . in vindication of the conduct of the fellows of New college . . . in their late election of a warden of Winchester. Lond., 1758, 8°. 62 pp. Gough Oxf. 51 (2)
— 2nd ed. Lond., 1759, 8°. 76 pp. Gough Oxf. 67 (2)

7941. GOLDING, C., A defence of the conduct of the warden of Winchester college in accepting of that wardenship [signed C. Golding]. Lond., 1759, 8°. 51 pp. G. Pamph. 108 (3)
— 2nd ed. 1759. 66 pp. Gough Oxf. 51 (6)

7942. LOWTH, R., An answer to an anonymous letter to dr. Lowth concerning the late election of a warden of Winchester college. [Signed R. Lowth.] Lond., 1759, 8°. 68 pp. Gough Oxf. 67 (3)

7943. BLACKSTONE, C., A reply to dr. Golding's and dr. Lowth's answers to the anonymous letter. By a Wykehamist [C. Blackstone?]. Lond., 1759, 8°. 76 pp. Gough Oxf. 67 (5)

7944. SPEED, J., An impartial by-stander's review of the controversy concerning the wardenship of Winchester college [signed Statutophilus]. Lond., 1759, 8°. 51 pp. Gough Oxf. 67 (6)

7945. The law and equity of the late appointment of a warden of Winchester considered. Lond., 1759, 8°. 19 pp. Gough Oxf. 51 (5)

7946. A statement of the objections entertained by the warden and fellows of New college to that part of the 'Public schools bill' which relates to Winchester college. n. pl., [1868], 4°. 3 pp.   G.A. Oxon c. 282 (f. 14)

7947. JENKINSON, H., [Use of New college seal by Winchester college in 1392.] (Antiq. journ., 1938, vol. 18, p. 386, 389, 90.)
Per. 17572 d. 73 = R.

New Inn hall

7948. [Topographical prints, &c. in the Bodleian.]   G.A. Oxon a. 62

7949. INGRAM, J., New Inn hall. (Memorials of Oxford, 1837, vol. 2. 16 pp.)   G.A. Oxon 8° 19
— [Another ed.] Oxf., 1851, 8°.   G.A. Gen. top. 8° 862 (2)

See 6422 [Suggestions for improvement. 1856].

7950. A statute proposed to be made by the University of Oxford commissioners, for the union of New Inn hall to Balliol college. [Lond., 1881], s. sh.   G.A. Oxon c. 8 (33)

7951. A statute for the union of Balliol college and New Inn hall. (Univ. of Oxf. and Cambr. act, 1877. Oxford. Four statutes made by the . . . Commissioners, 1881, p. 1, 2.) Lond., 1882, fol. Pp. Eng. 1882 vol. 51

See 6729 [A statute made for Balliol college and for New Inn hall. 1909].

Nuffield college

7951.9. MORRIS, W., lord Nuffield, [Begin.] My dear vice-chancellor, A year ago I was privileged . . . [Letter, dated 8 Oct. 1937, offering to finance the building and equipment of a laboratory of physical chemistry, and also proferring a site and money for the founding of the college.] n. pl., (1937), 8°. 8 pp.   G.A. Oxon b. 148

7952. Nuffield college. (Oxf. mag., 1937, vol. 56, p. 246–48.)
Per. G.A. Oxon 4° 141

7953. KENWARD, J., Nuffield college. (Lond. Mercury, 1938, vol. 37, p. 621–27.)   Per. 2705 d. 347

7954. B., H. R., Nuffield college. (Oxf. mag., 1939, vol. 57, p. 703, 04.)
Per. G.A. Oxon 4° 141

7955. CHESTER, D. N., Nuffield college [the new college and its future studies]. (Nature, 1949, vol. 163, p. 862, 63.)   Radcl.

7956. Nuffield college, 1949 (foundation, constitution, and aims). Oxf., 1949, 8°. 24 pp.   G.A. Oxon 8° 1325 (6)

7957. Nuffield college. Laying of the foundation stone. Addresses. Oxf., 1949, 8°. 35 pp.   G.A. Oxon 8° 1184 (21)

7958. CHESTER, D. N., Nuffield college. (Amer. Oxonian, 1959, vol. 46, p. 49–53.)   Per. G.A. Oxon 8° 889

7959. PEARL, M. L., Nuffield college, Oxford. Calendar of papers of
William Cobbett, 1791–1835. [Reprod. from typewriting.] n. pl., 1960,
fol.   25889 C. c. 3 = R.

7959.1. Nuffield College library. Accessions. Jan.–Feb. 1963– . [Reprod.
from typewriting.] n. pl., 1963– , 4°.   2590 d. Oxf. 41. 1 = R.

Oriel college

General 7960–7999   Lists 8066–8070
Administration 8000–8007   Societies and Sport 8071–8076
Statutes 8008–8035   Chapel 8077–8079
Finance and Property 8036–8045   Library and Archives 8080–8087
Members 8046–8050   Plate, etc. 8088–8091
  Biography and Reminiscences 8051–   St. Bartholomew's Hospital 8092–8094
  8065

General

7960. [Topographical prints, &c. in the Bodleian.]   G.A. Oxon a. 57

7961. An acte for the confirmation of the kinges . . . letters patentes made
to the provost and schollers of Oriell colledge . . . (3 James i, c. 9,
Private). 1605/06.
[Text in Shadwell's Enactments &c. See no. 956.]

7962. COPLESTON, E., A sermon preached before the members of Oriel
college upon the commemoration festival, June 15, 1826, held to celebrate the completion of five hundred years from the foundation of the
college. Oxf., 1826, 4°. 24 pp.   G.A. Oxon 4° 13 (2)

7963. Oriel college commemoration service, June 15, 1826. n. pl., (1826),
4°. 3 pp.   G.A. Oxon 4° 13 (2*)

7964. HUGHES, J., The Oriel grace-cup song, June 15th, 1826 [by J.
Hughes]. (Oxf.), [c. 1880], s. sh.   G.A. Oxon c. 283 (46)

7965. Oriel grace-cup song. [A version by T. H. Taunton of the original
text by J. Hughes.] (Oriel record, 1927, vol. 4, p. 425–27.)
                                          Per. G.A. Oxon 4° 484
— [Original text, by J. Hughes.] (Oriel record, 1928, vol. 5, p. 45, 46;
1948, p. 15, 16.)   Per. G.A. Oxon 4° 484

7966. Eucharistica Orielensia. (Oxf.), [1826], s. sh. G.A. Oxon 4° 13 (2*)

7967. INGRAM, J., Oriel college. (Memorials of Oxford, 1837, vol. 1. 16 pp.)
                                             G.A. Oxon 8° 18

7968. GRANT, A., and POSTE, E., Common-room common-places. [A
comment on the attitude of Oriel college to reform] by two Oxford
fellows [signed Endemus, i.e. A. Grant? and Ecdemus, i.e. E. Poste?].
Lond., 1854, 8°. 8 pp.   G.A. Oxon 8° 63 (11)

7969. BURGON, J. W., Oxford reformers, a letter to Endemus and Ecdemus
[in answer to no. 7968] by a fellow of Oriel [signed J. W. Burgon].
Oxf., 1854, 8°. 19 pp.   G.A. Oxon 8° 63 (2)
— [Another issue.]   MS. Eng. theol. d. 9 (36)

7970. HAWKINS, E., I. Notices concerning the design, history and present state of Oriel college, with respect to the ecclesiastical character of the institution and of the provostship. II. Notes on the appointment of laymen to the headship . . . and the disannexation from the provost-ship of the clerical preferment. n. pl., (1875), 8°. 27 pp.
G.A. Oxon 8° 683 (24)

7971. University of Oxford bill. To the . . . Lords . . . 'The humble petition of . . . Oriel college . . . ' [praying that the bill may not pass into law as it stands]. [Lond.], 1876, s. sh.   G.A. Oxon b. 140 (34)

7972. HAWKINS, E., Memorandum respecting Oriel college and clauses 25 and 22 of 'The Universities of Oxford and Cambridge act, 1877', submitted by the provost of Oriel to the Commissioners appointed under the act. n. pl., [1879], 8°. 15 pp.   G.A. Oxon 8° 884 (23)

7973. FREMANTLE, H. E. S., Oriel. [A poem, by H. E. S. Fremantle?] n. pl., [c. 1895], 8°. 7 pp.   G.A. Oxon c. 283 (14)

7974. SHADWELL, C. L., The calendar of Oriel college, A.D. 1397. n. pl., 1899, fol. 20 pp.   G.A. Oxon c. 91

7975. SHADWELL, C. L., Clavis calendarii [signed C. L. S.]. n. pl., 1900, s. sh.   G.A. Oxon c. 91

7976. RANNIE, D. W., Oriel college. (Univ. of Oxf., college hist.) Lond., 1900, 8°. 244 pp.   G.A. Oxon 8° 651 (15) = R.

7977. The Oriel record. Vol. 1, no. 1–   . Oxf., 1909–   , 8° & 4°.
Per. G.A. Oxon 4° 484

7978. SHADWELL, C. L., The college buildings—historical, by the Provost. (Oriel record, 1909/10, vol. 1, p. 63–66, 94–96, 123–26.)
Per. G.A. Oxon 4° 484

7979. VALLANCE, A., The college buildings—architectural. (Oriel record, 1909, vol. 1, p. 61–63.)   Per. G.A. Oxon 4° 484

7980. The new buildings. [List of statues and coats of arms which are to decorate the buildings.] (Oriel record, 1911, vol. 1, p. 183, 84.)
Per. G.A. Oxon 4° 484

7981. PHELPS, L. R., The decoration of the hall. (Oriel record, 1913, vol. 2, p. 108–10.)   Per. G.A. Oxon 4° 484

7982. VARLEY, F. J., Old views (drawings) of Oriel. (Oriel record, 1918, vol. 3, p. 16–18; 1925, vol. 4, p. 316–18.)   Per. G.A. Oxon 4° 484

7983. RICHARDS, G. C., Oriel in Tudor and Stuart times. (Oriel record, 1920, vol. 3, p. 135–39, 166–70.)   Per. G.A. Oxon 4° 484

7984. CLARK, G. N., Antiquities of Oriel common room [signed G. N. C.]. (Oriel record, 1925, vol. 4, p. 304–08.)   Per. G.A. Oxon 4° 484

7985. The college buildings. [Report on state and maintenance.] (Oriel record, 1925, vol. 4, p. 299–304.)   Per. G.A. Oxon 4° 484

7986. CLARKE, B., Oxford college mystery; 'Oriel' a nickname: 600 years' secret revealed by Richard Ingrestone. Oxf., [1926], 8°. 12 pp.
G.A. Oxon 8° 1002 (12)

7987. Oriel college records, by C. L. Shadwell and H. E. Salter. (Oxf. hist. soc., vol. 85.) Oxf., 1926, 8°. 528 pp.   G.A. Oxon 8° 360 = R.

7988. [Printed papers and cards connected with the Oriel college sexcentenary commemoration, June 18th & 26th, 1926.] G.A. Oxon 4° 472

See 204 [Varley, F. J., The treasonable riot outside Oriel college, 1747. 1929].

7989. VARLEY, F. J., A collection of views of Oriel college, catalogue. n. pl., [1929], 8°. 11 pp.   G.A. Oxon 8° 1055 (14)

7990. RICHARDS, G. C., Oriel college and the Oxford movement. (Nineteenth cent., 1933, vol. 113, p. 724–38.)   Per. 3977 d. 66

7991. The college flag. (Oriel record, 1935, vol. 7, p. 7–9.)
Per. G.A. Oxon 4° 484

7992. PHELPS, L. R., The new window [in the hall, by sir J. N. Comper]. (Oriel record, 1936, vol. 7, p. 106–08.)   Per. G.A. Oxon 4° 484

7993. The roof of the dining hall [restoration]. (Oriel record, 1936, vol. 7, p. 108–10.)   Per. G.A. Oxon 4° 484

7994. [Notes on Oriel college testudos.] (Oriel record, 1938, vol. 7, p. 316, 17.)   Per. G.A. Oxon 4° 484

7995. Medieval pottery from Oriel college, 1941. (Oriel record, 1942, p. 175–80.)   Per. G.A. Oxon 4° 484

7996. JOPE, E. M., Some mediaeval craftsmen of the building trade connected with the college. (Oriel record, 1946, p. 7–11.)
Per. G.A. Oxon 4° 484

7997. VARLEY, F. J., The college garden. (Oriel record, 1946, p. 11–14.)
Per. G.A. Oxon 4° 484

7998. VARLEY, F. J., The provost's lodgings at Oriel college. (Oriel record, 1946, p. 15–18.)   Per. G.A. Oxon 4° 484

7999. EMDEN, C. S., Oriel papers. Oxf., 1948, 8°. 223 pp.
G.A. Oxon 8° 1213

Administration

8000. Oriel college (passed) January 30, 1868 [specifying the educational staff, their payments, duties etc.]. [Oxf.], (1868), 8°. 3 pp.
G.A. Oxon b. 32

8001. Oriel college. [Report.] 1901/02–1925/26. (Oxf.), 1902–26, 8°. [The Bodleian set is imperfect.]   G.A. Oxon 8° 510*

8002. An inquisition held at Oriel college in Sept. 1411. (Oxf. hist. soc. 1924, vol. 80, p. 194–215.)   G.A. Oxon 8° 360 = R.

8003. The visitation of the college of Blessed Mary of Lyoryelle, 1445. (Visitations of relig. houses in the dioc. of Lincoln, vol. 3. Canterbury and York soc., 1927, vol. 33, p. 268, 69.)
Soc. G.A. Eccl. top. 4° 32 = R.

8004. VARLEY, F. J., The Oriel college lawsuit [between H. Edmunds representing the Fellows and the bishop of Lincoln, to resolve whether the bishop or the crown should enjoy visitorial powers, &c.]. (Oxoniensia, 1941, vol. 6, p. 56–59; 1943/44, vol. 8/9, p. 206–08.)
Per. G.A. Oxon 4° 658 = R.

8005. VARLEY, F. J., The election of a provost in 1727 at Oriel college. (Oriel record, 1942, vol. 8, p. 180–84.)   Per. G.A. Oxon 4° 484

8006. VARLEY, F. J., The common room man [college servant]. (Oriel record, 1948, p. 14, 15.)   Per. G.A. Oxon 4° 484

8007. BRUNT, P. A., The college's fire insurance in the eighteenth century. (Oriel record, 1955, p. 13–15.)   Per. G.A. Oxon 4° 484

Statutes

8008. Ordinationes collegii Orielensis in quibus et statuta Universitatis Oxoniensis ab Eduardo VI. lata ac sancita. (Johannis de Trokelowe Annales Eduardi II, divulgit T. Hearnius, 1729, p. 295–372.)
Mus. Bibl. II 90

8009. Statutes of the colleges . . . (Oriel college.) Oxf. &c., 1853, 8°. 40 pp.
G.A. Oxon 8° 24 = R.

8010. The statutes of Oriel college, printed by desire of the Commissioners under the act 17 & 18 Vict. c. 81. Lond., 1855, 8°. 48 pp.
G.A. Oxon 8° 416

8011. Oxford university. Ordinances . . . in relation to . . . Oriel [and 10 other] colleges respectively. [Lond.], 1857, fol. 139 pp.
Pp. Eng. 1857 vol. 32

8012. Ordinances and statutes framed or approved by the . . . Commissioners . . . (Oriel college, p. 127–47.) Oxf., 1863, 8°. Clar. Press 31 a. 63

8013. University of Oxford commission. Sketch of a statute for the 'complete union' of Oriel college and St. Mary hall. Proposed by the principal of St. Mary hall. n. pl., (1877), 8°. 3 pp.   G.A. Oxon c. 283 (1)

8014. Statutes of Oriel college. [Nov., 1880]. [The Bodleian copy lacks the title-leaf: it is the version of the statutes produced for the use of the University commissioners and bears their MS. corrections and additions.] n. pl., [1880], fol.   G.A. Oxon c. 8 (24)

8015. Statutes proposed to be made . . . for Oriel college. Nov., 1880. (Oxf.), 1880, 8°. 32 pp.   G.A. Oxon 8° 425 (14) = R.

8016. A statute proposed to be made by the University of Oxford commissioners for the union of St. Mary hall to Oriel college. [Lond., 1881], s. sh.   G.A. Oxon c. 8 (58)

8017. Statutes proposed to be made by the University of Oxford commissioners for Oriel college. May 1881. [Lond.], 1881, fol. 20 pp.
G.A. Oxon c. 8 (61)

8018. A statute ... for Oriel college ... as to a canonry in the chapter of the cathedral church of Rochester, now annexed to the provostship of Oriel college. (Univ. of Oxf. and Cambr. act, 1877. Oxford. Five statutes made by the Univ. of Oxf. commissioners, 1881, p. 1.)
Pp. Eng. 1882 vol. 51

8019. Statutes of Oriel college. (Univ. of Oxf. and Cambr. act, 1877. Oxford. Thirty six statutes made by the Univ. of Oxf. commissioners, 1881, p. 148–62, 255.)   Pp. Eng. 1882 vol. 51

8020. Statutes made by the University of Oxford commissioners for Oriel college. June, 1881. [Lond.], 1881, fol. 20 pp.   G.A. Oxon c. 107 (60)

8021. A statute for the union of Oriel college and St. Mary hall. [Lond., 1881], s. sh.   G.A. Oxon c. 283 (27)
— [Another issue.] (Univ. of Oxf. and Cambr. act, 1877. Oxford. Four statutes made by the ... Commissioners, 1881, p. 3, 4.) Lond., 1882, fol.   Pp. Eng. 1882 vol. 51

8022. A statute made by ... Merton college ... and a statute passed by ... Oriel college on the 12th and sealed on the 18th January, 1886, to amend a Statute [IV. 7] made by the University of Oxford commissioners in relation to that college. Lond., 1886, s. sh.
Pp. Eng. 1886 vol. 51

8023. Oriel college. Statute passed ... on the 14th and sealed on the 27th Oct., 1886, to amend Statute XIV. 4. Lond., 1887, s. sh.
Pp. Eng. 1887 vol. 65

8024. Three statutes made by ... Oriel college ... on 20th April, 1888 amending the existing statutes of the college. Lond., 1888, s. sh.
Pp. Eng. 1888 vol. 78

8025. Two statutes made by ... Oriel college, on the 8th and sealed on the 29th Oct. 1890, altering respectively, clauses 12 and 29, Statute III, and clause 5, Statute IV. Lond., 1891, s. sh.   Pp. Eng. 1890/91 vol. 61

8026. Statute made by ... Oriel college, 21st Apr. 1893, and sealed 10th May following, for amending Statute IV, clause 18. Lond., 1893, s. sh.
Pp. Eng. 1893 vol. 68

8027. Statute made by ... Oriel college, 28th May 1896, altering Statute IV. ... by the insertion ... of a new clause 18A. Lond., 1897, s. sh.
Pp. Eng. 1897 vol. 70

8028. Statute made by ... Oriel college ... on 5th May 1897, altering Statute IV ... 10 February 1898. Lond., 1898, s. sh.
Pp. Eng. 1898 vol. 70

8029. Statute made by . . . Oriel college, 24th April 1903, amending Statute IV. 7. Lond., 1904, s. sh. Pp. Eng. 1904 vol. 75

8030. Statute made by . . . Oriel college, 11th Oct., 1906, and sealed 29th Nov. 1906, amending Statute VI, 5. Lond., 1907, s. sh.
Pp. Eng. 1907 vol. 64

8031. Statute made by . . . Oriel college, 24th Nov. 1909 and sealed 14th Dec. 1909, amending Statute III, 10. Lond., 1910, s. sh.
Pp. Eng. 1910 vol. 72

8032. Statute made by . . . Oriel college, 7th Dec. 1914 and sealed 8th of that month, amending Statute II, clauses 6 and 7. Lond., 1915, fol. 2 pp. Pp. Eng. 1914/16 vol. 51

8033. Statute made by . . . Oriel college, 25th Apr. 1917, and sealed on the 30th of the same month, amending Statutes 3 (17) and 11 (1). Lond., 1917, s. sh. Pp. Eng. 1917/18 vol. 25

8034. Statutes made for the colleges . . . (Oriel college.) Oxf., 1927, 8°. 37 pp. G.A. Oxon 4° 759 = R.

8035. Statutes made for Oriel college . . . in pursuance of the Universities of Oxford and Cambridge act, 1923. With amendments to 31st Dec. 1947. (Oxf., 1947), 8°. 52 pp. G.A. Oxon 8° 1225

Finance and property

8036. An early [16th cent.] law suit: Oriel college *v.* Button [concerning Swainswick manor. Signed F. J. L.]. (Oriel record, 1932, vol. 5, p. 243–46.) Per. G.A. Oxon 4° 484

See 8118 [Act annexing prebend of Rochester to the provostship. 1714].

8037. An act for annexing the rectory of Purleigh . . . to the office of provost of . . . Oriel college. (7 G. III, c. 27, Private.) n. pl., 1767, fol. 4 pp.
L.L.

8038. An act for effectuating an exchange between . . . Oriel college . . . and George Harris of certain freehold estates in . . . Kent. (54 G. III, c. 30. Private.) 1814.
[Précis in Shadwell's Enactments &c. See no. 956.]

8039. PRICE, L. L., The recent depression in agriculture as shown in the accounts of an Oxford college, 1876–90. (Journ., Roy. statist. soc., 1892, vol. 55, p. 2–36.) Soc. 24712 e. 80 = P.
— [Repr.] 36 pp. 23231 e. 36 (7)

8040. Proposed scheme of payments from tuition fund. 1 Sept., 1906. [Oxf.], (1906), s. sh. Firth b. 36 (71*d*)

8041. Abstract of receipts and expenditure on tuition fund, 1897 to 1906. [Oxf., 1906], s. sh. Firth b. 36 (71*b*)

8042. Report of the committee appointed to enquire into the present state and future prospects of the tuition fund. [Oxf., 1906], s. sh.
Firth b. 36 (71*a*)

8043. HALL, F. H. [*Begin.*] I wish to put before the college . . . [A paper against the proposed scheme for payments from the tuition fund.] [Oxf., 1906], s. sh. Firth b. 36 (69*b*)

8044. Report of committee on the state of the tuition fund. March 22, 1907. [Oxf.], (1907), s. sh. Firth b. 36 (71*c*)

8045. Memorandum on revision of degree fees and compositions. [Oxf.], (1909), 8°. 4 pp. Firth b. 36 (77*g*)

Members

GENERAL

8046.

8047. SIMPSON, P., Sir Walter Raleigh at Oriel. (Oriel record, 1918, vol. 3, p. 80–83.) Per. G.A. Oxon 4° 484

See 1398 [Migration of W. Seaman from Hart hall to Oriel college, 1726. 1928].

8048. LYON, P. C., Report on the correspondence of . . . L. R. Phelps . . . 1877 to 1936. n. pl., (1939), 8°. 28 pp. G.A. Oxon 8° 1175 (10)

8049. ROSS, SIR W. D., Oriel fellowships [statistics &c.]. (Oriel record, 1953, p. 11–16.) Per. G.A. Oxon 4° 484

8050. ROSS, SIR W. D., The county connexions of Oriel [statistics]. (Oriel record, 1954, p. 19, 20.) Per. G.A. Oxon 4° 484

BIOGRAPHY AND REMINISCENCES

8051. DITCHFIELD, P. H., Famous men of Oriel college. (Oriel record, 1911, vol. 1, p. 159–64.) Per. G.A. Oxon 4° 484

8052. HUDLESTON, C. R., Two provosts of Oriel college [Anthony Blencowe, provost from 1574–1617/18, and John Tolson, provost from 1621–1644.] (Trans., Cumb. & Westmorl. antiq. & archaeol. soc., 1960, vol. 60, p. 55 65.) Soc. G.A. Cumb. 8° 109 = R.

8053. COPLESTON, W. J., Memoir of Edward Copleston, bishop of Llandaff, with selections from his diary . . . Lond., 1851, 8°. 345 pp. 210 a. 97

8054. Remains of . . . Edward Copleston, bishop of Llandaff, with an intr. containing some reminiscences of his life by R. Whately. Lond., 1854, 8°. 327 pp. 270 a. 29

8055. BROCK, M. G., The case of dr. Copleston. (Pelican Record, 1957, vol. 31, p. 193–201; 1958, vol. 32, p. 33–37, 65–68, 85–90.) Per. G.A. Oxon 8° 588

8056. BURGON, J. W., Rev. Edward Hawkins, D.D., provost of Oriel college [by J. W. Burgon]. (Quarterly review, 1883, vol. 156, p. 305–52.) Per. 3977 e. 191

8057. BURGON, J. W., Edward Hawkins, the great provost. 1789–1882.
(Lives of twelve good men, 1888, vol. 1, p. 374–465.)   2106 e. 26
— New ed. 1891.   11126 d. 20

8058. BURGON, J. W., Charles Marriott, the man of saintly life. 1811–1858.
(Lives of twelve good men, 1888, vol. 1, p. 297–373.)   2106 e. 26
— New ed. 1891.   11126 d. 20

8059. WILSON, J. C., David Binning Monro, a short memoir, tr. with
slight alterations, from a notice in the Jahresb. über die Fortschritte d.
klass. Alterthumswiss. Oxf., 1907, 8°. 16 pp.   2998 d. 39

8060. A list of subscribers to the portrait of D. B. Monro, provost of Oriel
college. n. pl., (1897), 8°. 8 pp.   G.A. Oxon 8° 683 (21)

8061. CLARK, SIR G. N., Cecil Rhodes and his college (Oxf.), 1953, 8°.
13 pp.   R.H.

8062. MOZLEY, T., Reminiscences, chiefly of Oriel college and the Oxford
movement. 2 vols. Lond., 1882, 8°.   110 j. 711, 712
— 2nd ed. 1882.   11126 e. 191, 192

8063. TUCKWELL, W., Pre-Tractarian Oxford, a reminiscence of the Oriel
'noetics'. Lond., 1909, 8°. 264 pp.   G.A. Oxon 8° 763
— [The author's grangerized copy.]   MS. Top. Oxon d. 291

8064. RICHARDS, G. C., The Oriel common room in 1833. (Oriel record,
1932, vol. 5, p. 235–39.)   Per. G.A. Oxon 4° 484

8065. LEE, R. W., A German at Oriel, 1903–4. [An Engl. précis of relevant
chapters of] Aus Gärten der Vergangenheit Erinnerungen 1882–1914,
by K. A. von Müller, 1951. (Oriel record, 1952, p. 20–31.)
Per. G.A. Oxon 4° 484

LISTS

8066. SHADWELL, C. L., Registrum Orielense, an account of the members
of Oriel college, 1500–(1900). 2 vols. Lond., 1893, 1902, 8°.
G.A. Oxon 8° 537, 538 = R.

8067. Oriel college. Memorial service for the members . . . who gave their
lives for their country, 1914–1918. [With list of names.] [Oxf.], 1919,
8°. 22 pp.   G.A. Oxon 8° 895 (4)

8068. RICHARDS, G. C., and SHADWELL, C. L., The provosts and fellows
of Oriel college. Oxf., 1922, 8°. 238 pp.   G.A. Oxon 8° 1015 = R.

8069. The Dean's register of Oriel, 1446–1661, ed. by G. C. Richards and
H. E. Salter. (Oxf. hist. soc., vol. 84.) Oxf., 1926, 8°. 408 pp.
G.A. Oxon 8° 360 = R.

8070. Oriel college war record, 1939–1945. Oxf., [1949], 8°. 55 pp.
G.A. Oxon 8° 1204 (10)

Societies and sport

8071. Butler society. Rules. [Oxf., *c.* 1923], s. sh. G.A. Oxon c. 311 (81)

8072. Ellesmere society. [Miscellaneous papers. 1922–1924.]
G.A. Oxon 4° 603

8073. Newlands society, formerly Dramatic reading circle. 100th (150th, 200th) meeting celebrations. n. pl., 1927–32, 8°.
G.A. Oxon 8° 1056 (2)

8074. Oriel college amalgamated clubs. Accounts for the year ending 1890 (95, 99, 1900, 07, 10–12, 13/14 and 14/15. (Oxf.), [1890–1915], 8°.
G.A. Oxon c. 283 (19–23)

8075. VARLEY, F. J., The Oriel college barge. (Oriel record, 1947, p. 6, 7.)
Per. G.A. Oxon 4° 484

8076. Plantagenet society. [Notification of a meeting, 1912.]
G.A. Oxon b. 147 (64)

Chapel

8077. RUSHFORTH, G. MCN., Mediaeval glass in the college chapel: St. Margaret and the dragon. (Oriel record, 1929, vol. 5, p. 84–87.)
Per. G.A. Oxon 4° 484
— [Repr. *entitled*] Mediaeval glass in Oriel college chapel. (Journ., Brit. soc. of master glass-painters, 1930, vol. 3, p. 108–11.)
Soc. 17031 d. 6

8078. CLARK, SIR G. N., The chapel lectern. (Oriel record, 1949, p. 12, 13.)
Per. G.A. Oxon 4° 484

8079. PÄCHT, OTTO, 'The carrying of the cross', by Bernard van Orley [in Oriel college chapel]. (Oriel record, 1952, p. 16–20.)
Per. G.A. Oxon 4° 484

Library and archives

8080. Oriel college. (Hist. MSS. comm., 2nd report, 1871, p. 136, 37.)
2262 c. 7 = K.

8081. A catalogue of books in the library of Oriel college connected with the studies of comparative philology and comparative mythology. [*With*] Addenda [1–3]. Oxf., 1880–1903, 8°. 2590 e. Oxf. 8. 1, 2 = R.

8082. SHADWELL, C. L., The catalogue of the library of Oriel college in the 14th century. (Oxf. hist. soc., 1885, vol. 5, p. 57–70.)
G.A. Oxon 8° 360 = R.

8083. SHADWELL, C. L., Oriel college, Oxford. Catalogue of muniments. 1–10. n. pl., 1893–1905, 4°. G.A. Oxon 4° 157

8084. Incunabula in Oriel college library. [Oxf., 1919], 8°. 4 pp.
2590 d. Oxf. 28. 1

8085. ROBINSON, R., and WATSON, C. I. W. SETON-, The fire in the senior library. (Oriel record, 1949, p. 8, 9.)   Per. G.A. Oxon 4° 484

8086. ROBINSON, R., The restoration of the senior library. (Oriel record, 1951, p. 10–12.)   Per. G.A. Oxon 4° 484

8087. DALE, A., The building of the library. (Oriel record, 1951, p. 13–18.)   Per. G.A. Oxon 4° 484

Plate, etc.

8088. VARLEY, F. J., Oriel college plate. (Oriel record, 1920, vol. 3, p. 170–71; 1924, vol. 4, p. 248–50.)   Per. G.A. Oxon 4° 484

8089. JONES, E. A., Catalogue of the plate of Oriel college. Oxf., 1944, fol. xxviii+96 pp.+20 pl.   17552 c. 27

8090. HOPE, W. H. ST. JOHN, [Mazer at Oriel.] (Archaeologia, 1887, vol. 50, p. 158.)   Per. G.A. Gen. top. 4° 162 = R.

8091. The Oriel sword. (Oriel record, 1938, vol. 7, p. 247–51.)
     Per. G.A. Oxon 4° 484

St. Bartholomew's hospital

8092. St. Bartholomew's hospital. [Reply of Oriel college to the case prepared on behalf of the Corporation of Oxford.] [Oxf.], (1896), 4°. 13 pp.   G.A. Oxon 4° 119*

8093. DODD, J. T., and BROOKS, E. J., Observations on proposals of Oriel contained in the letter of the Charity commissioners of 11th November 1897 to the town clerk of the City of Oxford. [Oxf.], (1897), 4°. 4 pp.   G.A. Oxon 4° 119*

8094. Oriel college and the St. Bartholomew charity. [Question asked in the House of Commons, and the Charity commissioner's reply.] [Oxf., 1899], s. sh.   G.A. Oxon 4° 119*

Parker's hall

See 8253 St. Benet's hall.

Pembroke college

General 8095–8103
Statutes 8104–8117
Finance and Property 8118–8120
Members 8121–8122

Biography and Reminiscences 8123–8124
Societies 8125–8130
Library 8131–8132

General

8095. [Topographical prints, &c. in the Bodleian.]   G.A. Oxon a. 57

See 561 [Eidyllia [by members of Broadgates hall] in obitum Henrici Walliæ principis. 1612].

8096. [Appeal for money to ensure the removal of certain houses in the widening of St. Aldates, and the laying open of the new front of Pembroke college. With plans.] n. pl., [1834], fol. 3 pp.

G.A. Oxon c. 50 (114)

8097. INGRAM, J., Pembroke college. (Memorials of Oxford, 1837, vol. 2, 16 pp.) G.A. Oxon 8° 19
— [Another ed.] Oxf. &c., 1851, 8°. Manning 8° 230

8098. Preces privatae in usum alumnorum collegii Pembrochiae in Universitate Oxoniensi. Lond., 1884, 12°. 5 pp. 14024 f. 45
— [Another copy, pr. on vellum.] 14024 f. 8

8099. BAYLEY, A. R., A catalogue of portraits in the possession of Pembroke college [by A. R. Bayley]. Oxf., 1895, 8°. 73 pp.

G.A. Oxon 8° 620 (8)

8100. MACLEANE, D., A history of Pembroke college, Oxford, anciently Broadgates hall. (Oxf. hist. soc., 33.) Oxf., 1897, 8°. 544 pp.

G.A. Oxon 8° 360 = R.

8101. MACLEANE, D., Pembroke college. (Univ. of Oxf., college hist.) Lond., 1900, 8°. 270 pp. G.A. Oxon 8° 651 (12) = R.

8102. The Besse building, Pembroke college. (Builder, 1955, vol. 188, p. 369–72.) N. 1863 c. 1

8103. Two residential schemes at Oxford university. 1. Development of Pembroke college properties. 2. Undergraduate block for St. John's college. (Builder, 26 Sept. 1958, p. 526–28.) N. 1863 c. 1

Statutes

8104. Statutes of the colleges of Oxford . . . Pembroke college. Oxf. &c., 1853, 8°. xiii × 55 pp. G.A. Oxon 8° 781

8105. Statutes of the colleges . . . (Pembroke college.) Oxf. &c., 1853, 8°. xv + 55 pp. G.A. Oxon 8° 26 = R.

8106. Oxford university. Copies of ordinances in relation to Pembroke [and other] colleges. [Lond.], 1857, fol. 17 pp. Pp. Eng. 1857 vol. 32

8107. Oxford university. Copy of three ordinances . . . in relation to Merton, Pembroke and University colleges . . . [Lond.], 1857, fol. 49 pp.

Pp. Eng. 1857 vol. 32

8108. Copy of an ordinance made by . . . Pembroke college [on 3 June 1858] . . . to amend an ordinance made by the Oxford university commissioners on the 19th February 1857 . . . in relation to the said college. [Lond.], 1859, fol. 3 pp. Pp. Eng. 1859 vol. 21 (2)

8109. Ordinances and statutes framed or approved by the . . . Commissioners . . . (Pembroke college, p. 425–52.) Oxf., 1863, 8°.

Clar. Press 31 a. 63

8110. Statutes proposed to be made . . . for Pembroke college. April, 1881.
(Oxf.), 1881, 8°. 26 pp.   G.A. Oxon 8° 425 (15) = R.

8111. Statutes of Pembroke college. (Univ. of Oxf. and Cambr. act. 1877.
Oxford. Thirty six statutes made by the Univ. of Oxf. commissioners,
1881, p. 162–174, 256.)   Pp. Eng. 1882 vol. 51

See 7019 [Revision of Statute VI, clause 8, 14th June, 1887].

8112. Statute made by . . . Pembroke college, 17th Mar. 1893, for altering
Statute VI (creating a fund to be called the College exhibition fund).
Lond., 1893, s. sh.   Pp. Eng. 1893 vol. 68

8113. Statute made by . . . Pembroke college . . . on the 7th December
1897, making an addition to clause 16, Statute VI . . . 5 May 1898.
Lond., 1898, s. sh.   Pp. Eng. 1898 vol. 70

8114. A statute made by . . . Pembroke college . . . on the 3rd day of March
1899 amending clause 9 of Statute II, and clause 3 of Statute VIII . . .
23 October 1899. Lond., 1899, s. sh.   Pp. Eng. 1899 vol. 76
— 30 Jan. 1900. Lond., 1900, s. sh.   Pp. Eng. 1900 vol. 66

8115. Statute made by . . . Pembroke college, 12th June 1912 and sealed on
the same day, amending Statutes II, III, V, VI, VII, VIII, and X.
Lond., 1912, fol. 5 pp.   Pp. Eng. 1912/13 vol. 65

8116. Statute made by . . . Pembroke college, 23rd Apr. 1913, and sealed
on the same day, amending Statute X, clause 9. Lond., 1913, s. sh.
                                           Pp. Eng. 1913 vol. 50

8117. Statutes made for the colleges . . . (Pembroke college.) Oxf., 1927, 8°.
44 pp.   G.A. Oxon 4° 759 = R.

Finance and property

8118. An act for taking away mortuaries within the dioceses of Bangor
[&c.] and for confirming several letters patents granted by her majesty
for perpetually annexing a prebend of Gloucester to the mastership of
Pembroke college . . . and a prebend of Rochester to the provostship of
Oriel college . . . (12 Anne, sess. 2, c. 6, Pub.) Lond., 1714, fol. 8 pp.
                                                               L.L.

8119. [*Begin.*] Application having been made . . . [Proposal to make a
conveyance of land, the original site of Beef hall, to Pembroke college,
in consideration of an annual rent of £5–5–0, to enable the college to
extend its buildings.] Jan. 27. [Oxf.], 1845, s. sh. G.A. Oxon c. 61 (19)

8120. EYRE, G., To the rate payers . . . in the city of Oxford. Rating of
Pembroke college to the poor. [A letter signed G. Eyre.] (Oxf., 1852),
8°. 12 pp.   G.A. Oxon 8° 884 (5)

Members

GENERAL

8121. The secularization of ecclesiastical foundations and the Roman propaganda in the University of Oxford. Two questions raised by the members of Pembroke college [apropos of the visits to the college of H. de la G. Grissell, a Roman Catholic]. Oxf., [1883], 8°. 4 pp.
G.A. Oxon b. 140 (45f)

See 4567 [Undergraduate's account book, 1789–93. 1937].

8122. Pembroke college. Order of service for the dedication of the memorial to the members . . . who laid down their lives in the War. [With list of names.] [Oxf.], 1921, 8°. 10 pp. G.A. Oxon 8° 895 (13)

BIOGRAPHY AND REMINISCENCES

8123. SCHEIBNER, R. O., Dr. Thomas Clayton [1575–1647]. [Reprod. from typewriting.] n. pl., (1943), 4°. 10 pp. 26322 d. 59

8123.5. HATCH, E., My visit to Oxford, November 1853 [to matriculate at Pembroke college]. (Oxf. mag., 1963, N.S., vol. 4, p. 48.)
Per. G.A. Oxon 4° 141

8124. GILLING, I., The life of . . . George Trosse [p. 17–20 relate his experiences at Pembroke college from 1657–1664]. Lond., 1715, 8°.
8° H 38 Art. BS.

See 3924 [Jeune, M. D., Pages from the diary of an Oxford lady, 1843–1862].

Societies

8125. Rules of the Junior Common room. Oxf., 1856, 8°. 8 pp.
G.A. Oxon 8° 1110 (13)
— 1860. G.A. Oxon 8° 1110 (14)
— 1868. G.A. Oxon 8° 1110 (15)

8126. Pembroke college boat club. History, rules & regulations. Oxf., 1861, 8°. 20 pp. G.A. Oxon 8° 828 (26)
— [Another ed.] Oxf., 1882, 8°. 40 pp. G.A. Oxon 8° 900 (23)
[Editions said to have been publ. in 1848 and 1870].

8127. Pembroke college boat club. Rules and regulations. [Oxf.], 1888, s. sh. G.A. Oxon c. 284 (9)

8128. Pembroke college debating society. Rules and regulations. Corrected to December, 1850. Oxf., 1851, 8°. 19pp. G.A. Oxon 8° 1110 (16)
— Corrected to December 1852. G.A. Oxon 8° 1110 (17)
— Corrected to March, 1857. G.A. Oxon 8° 1110 (18)
— Corrected to October, 1860. G.A. Oxon 8° 1110 (19)
— Corrected to May, 1867. G.A. Oxon 8° 1110 (20)
— Corrected to May, 1871. G.A. Oxon 8° 1110 (21)
— Corrected to November, 1876. With a list of former officers. 23 pp.
G.A. Oxon 8° 1110 (22)

8129. Pembroke college glee club. Programme of an evening concert. June 11, 1868.
— December 7, 1868.
— June 11, 1874.   G.A. Oxon 8° 1110 (24–26)

8130. Pembroke college musical society. [Concert programmes, 1865–1895.]   G.A. Oxon 8° 1112

Library

8131. Pembroke college. (Hist. MSS. comm., 6th report, pt. 1, 1881, p. 549–51.)   2262 c. 37 = K.

8132. Catalogue of the Aristotelian and philosophical portions of the library of . . . Henry William Chandler . . . preserved in the library of Pembroke college. Oxf., 1891, 4°. 182 pp.   2590 d. Oxf. 4. 1

Plater's hall

See 6929 Campion hall.

Queen's college

General 8133–8152
Administration 8153–8163
Statutes 8164–8190
Finance and Property 8191–8202
Members 8203–8211
  Lists 8212–8213

Societies and Sport 8214–8221
Chapel 8222–8224
Library and Archives 8225–8228
Relations with St. Edmund Hall 8229–8236
Boar's Head Song 8237–8245

General

8133. [Topographical prints, &c. in the Bodleian.].   G.A. Oxon a. 58

8134. An act for the confirmacion of her majesties lettres pattents graunted to the Queens colledge in Oxforde. (27 Eliz., c. 2, Private.) 1584/85. [Text in Shadwell's Enactments &c. See no. 956.]

8135. A thanksgiving for the founder and benefactors of this college. [Oxf., 17—?], s. sh.   MS. Top. Oxon d. 281 (f. 73)

8136. An account of the progress made in the new buildings of Queens college . . . and how much remains unfinished for want of abilities in the college to complete that work. (Feb. 18.) n. pl., (1718), 4°. 6 pp.
                                                             Gough Oxf. 143 (1)
— [Another ed., *entitled*] The present state of the new buildings of Queens college . . . with an ichnography of the whole. Dec. 21, 1730. [Oxf.?], (1730), 4°.   Gough Oxf. 143 (2)

8137. TICKELL, T., On her majesty's re-building the lodgings of the Black prince and Henry V at Queens-college, Oxford. [In verse.] Lond., 1733, fol. 7 pp.   Pamph. 400 (15)

8138. HARDING, S., The deplorable state of Queen's college [after the fire there. In verse]. [Oxf., 1778?], s. sh.   MS. Top. Oxon d. 281 (f. 71)

8139. INGRAM, J., Queen's college. (Memorials of Oxford, 1837, vol. I. 16 pp.) G.A. Oxon 8° 18

8140. The complaint of the eagles, lately removed from the gate of Q—'s college. [Verse.] n. pl., [18—], s. sh. G.A. Oxon c. 285 (f. 18)

8141. [Examination papers. Scholarships and exhibitions.] 1871–78. [Oxf.], 1871–78, 8°. [The Bodleian set is imperfect.] 2626 e. 43

8142. University of Oxford bill. To the . . . Lords . . . The humble petition of . . . Queen's college . . . n. pl., 1876, fol. 3 pp.
G.A. Oxon b. 140 (34c)

8143. MAGRATH, J. R., Queen's college, Oxford. [A circular letter, begin. The number of kind letters of condolence on the late fire . . . By J. R. Magrath.] [Oxf., 1887], s. sh. G.A. Oxon c. 285 (f. 9)

8144. THOROLD, A. W., A sermon preached in the chapel of Queen's college, Nov. 2, 1890 [with historical notes on the college]. Oxf., 1890, 8°. 24 pp. G.A. Oxon 8° 469 (2)

See 2939 [Sedleian professorship of natural philosophy. 1900].

8145. Liber obituarius Aulae Reginae in Oxonia, transcr., recogn., illustr. J. R. Magrath. Oxon., 1910, fol. xliii+153 pp. G.A. Oxon c. 129
— [Another issue.] (Oxf. hist. soc., vol. 56.) G.A. Oxon 8° 360 = R.

8146. A Queen's college miscellany. [2 numbers.] Oxf., 1920, 21, 8°. 49 and 64 pp. 2705 d. 503
— Miscellany. [2 numbers.] Oxf., 1934, 36, 8°. 52 and 64 pp.
2705 d. 503

8147. MAGRATH, J. R., The Queen's college. 2 vols. Oxf., 1921, 4°.
G.A. Oxon 4° 423, 24 = R.

8148. TIPPING, H. A., Queen's college. (Country Life, 1928, vol. 63, p. 724–32, 762–70.) Per. 384 b. 6

8149. JONES, E. A., Catalogue of the plate of the Queen's college. Oxf., 1938, fol. xvii+87 pp.+18 pl. 17552 c. 18

8150. TUNSTALL, E. A., and KERR, A., The Painted room at the Queen's college, Oxford. (Burlington mag., 1943, vol. 82, p. 42–46.)
Per. 170 c. 25

8151. HODGKIN, R. H., Six centuries of an Oxford college, a history of Queen's college, 1340–1940. Oxf., 1949, 4°. 224 pp.
G.A. Oxon 4° 649

8152. GIROUARD, M., Architectural scholarship at Oxford, the new provost's lodgings at Queen's. (Country Life, 1960, vol. 125, p. 34–36.)
Per. 384 b. 6

Administration

8153. THOMPSON, F., A true state of the case concerning the election of a provost of Queens-college [by F. Thompson]. Oxf., 1704, 4°. 32 pp.
Gough Oxf. 63 (5)

8154. Queen's college. [Statements, some drawn from the Oxford commission respecting the Tabardships of the college.] n. pl., [1852], s. sh.
G.A. Oxon c. 68 (106)

8155. BARROW, J., The case of Queen's college, a letter [concerning the election of Fellows, and the interpretation of the college statutes. With a postscript]. Oxf. &c., 1854, 8°. 59+3 pp.   G.A. Oxon 8° 71 (3)

8156. THOMSON, W., An open college best for all, a reply to 'The case of Queen's college, by John Barrow'. With an appendix on the Michel foundation. Oxf. &c., 1854, 8°. 49 pp.   G.A. Oxon 8° 1148 (17)

8157. Memorandum respecting admission to the Queen's college. [Oxf., 1865], s. sh.   G.A. Oxon c. 285 (f. 2)

8158. College regulations. 1868, 71, 77, 83. (Oxf., 1868–83), 8°.
G.A. Oxon 8° 432

8159. Queen's college, Oxford. [*Begin.*] An examination will be held for the election of a fellow . . . [Notice of emoluments and conditions.] [Oxf., 1885?], s. sh.   G.A. Oxon c. 285 (f. 3)

8160. Queen's college, Oxford. Michaelmas term. 1894. Changes in the kitchen. [Oxf.]. (1894), 8°. 4 pp.   G.A. Oxon c. 285 (f. 3)

8161. Queen's college. [Report.] 1901/02–1910/11. (Oxf.), 1902–11, 8°. [The Bodleian set is imperfect.]   G.A. Oxon 8° 510*

8162. The Queen's college. [Official booklet.] 1902, 03, 06. [Oxf.], 1902–06, 16°.   G.A. Oxon 16° 176* (7–9)

8163. The deed of foundation of four Laming scholarships at the Queen's college, Oxford, in modern languages. n. pl., (1916), 8°. 4 pp.
G.A. Oxon c. 285 (f. 4)

Statutes

8164. Statutes of the colleges . . . (Queen's college.) Oxf. &c., 1853, 8°. 39 pp.   G.A. Oxon 8° 24 = R.

8165. Oxford university. Copies of three ordinances . . . in relation to certain exhibitions or scholarships in Queen's college, and to the exhibition of dame Elizabeth Holford's foundation at Christ Church. [Lond.], 1858, fol. 9 pp.   Pp. Eng. 1857/8 vol. 46

8166. Oxford university. Copies of four ordinances . . . in relation to Christ's Church, and Queen's, University and Brazenose colleges. [Lond.], 1858, fol. 38 pp.   Pp. Eng. 1857/8 vol. 46

8167. Ordinances and statutes framed or approved by the . . . Commissioners . . . (Queen's college, p. 149–80.) Oxf., 1863, 8°.
Clar. Press 31 a. 63

8168. Ordinances concerning Queen's college, framed by the Oxford university commissioners in pursuance of the act 17 and 18 Vict. c. 81. Oxf., 1863, 8°. 34 pp.   G.A. Oxon 8° 1079 (1)

8169. Ordinance in relation to the exhibitions of the foundation of the lady Elizabeth Hastings within Queen's college. (Oxf., 1869), 8°. 8 pp.
G.A. Oxon 8° 1079 (2)

8170. Statutes of Queen's college ... as approved Dec., 1878. (Oxf., 1878), 4°. 46 pp.
G.A. Oxon 4° 554

8171. Statutes proposed to be made ... for Queen's college. Nov., 1880. (Oxf.), 1880, 8°. 31 pp.
G.A. Oxon 8° 425 (16) = R.

8172. Statutes proposed to be made by the University of Oxford commissioners for the Queen's college. May 1881. [Lond.], 1881, fol. 19 pp.
G.A. Oxon c. 8 (67)

8173. Statutes proposed to be made by the University of Oxford commissioners for the Queen's college, concerning exhibitions; Christ Church concerning Westminster scholarships; Jesus college concerning the Meyricke endowment. (Oxf.), 1881, 8°. 13 pp.
G.A. Oxon 8° 425 (2) = R.

8174. Statutes of the Queen's college. (Univ. of Oxf. and Cambr. act, 1877. Oxford. Thirty six statutes made by the Univ. of Oxf. commissioners, 1881, p. 175–89, 257.)
Pp. Eng. 1882 vol. 51

8175. A statute for the Queen's college, concerning exhibitions within the college. (Univ. of Oxf. and Cambr. act, 1877. Oxford. Five statutes made by the Univ. of Oxf. commissioners, 1881, p. 5–8.)
Pp. Eng. 1882 vol. 51

8176. A statute for the partial union of the Queen's college and St. Edmund hall. (Univ. of Oxf. and Cambr. act, 1877. Oxford. Four statutes made by the ... Commissioners, 1881, p. 4–6.) Lond., 1882, fol.
Pp. Eng. 1882 vol. 51

8177. Statute made by ... Queen's college, 6th Dec., 1889, altering Statute II, clause 20. Lond., 1890, s. sh.
Pp. Eng. 1890 vol. 56

8178. Statute made by ... Queen's college, 6th June 1890, adding certain words at the end of Statute III, clause 10. Lond., 1890, s. sh.
Pp. Eng. 1890/91 vol. 61

8179. Statute made by ... Queen's college, 14th June 1893, for amending Statute II, clause 19. Lond., 1893, s. sh.
Pp. Eng. 1893 vol. 68

8180. Statutes made by ... Queen's college, 28th Oct. 1896, amending Statutes II, XIII, and XXIII. Lond., 1897, fol. 3 pp.
Pp. Eng. 1897 vol. 70

8181. A statute made by ... Queen's college ... on 16th July 1898 altering Statute XV.... 7 Feb. 1899. Lond., 1899, s. sh. Pp. Eng. 1899 vol. 76

8182. Statutes made by ... Queen's college, 26th Nov. 1902, altering Statutes II and XXIII, and the Statute concerning exhibitions within the college. Lond., 1903, s. sh.
Pp. Eng. 1903 vol. 52

8183. Statutes made for the Queen's college, and a statute made for the Queen's college and for St. Edmund hall, by the University of Oxford commissioners, 1877, as altered . . . down to December, 1904. Oxford, 1905, 8°. 59 pp.   G.A. Oxon 8° 747

8184. Statute made by . . . Queen's college, 28th Feb. 1906 and sealed 16th Mar. 1906, altering Statute XIII, 1. Lond., 1906, s. sh.
         Pp. Eng. 1906 vol. 90

8185. Statutes made by . . . Queen's college, 15th June 1906 and sealed on the same day, altering Statute II, 21 and Statute IX, 3. Lond., 1906, s. sh.   Pp. Eng. 1906 vol. 90

8186. Statute made by . . . Queen's college, 19th June 1907, amending and altering Stat. Tit. II, clauses 1, 2, 7, 8, 9, and 15; and Stat. Tit. XXIII, clause 8. Lond., 1908, s. sh.   Pp. Eng. 1908 vol. 86

8187. Statute made by . . . Queen's college, 10th June 1908 and sealed on the same date, altering the Statutes . . . by adding thereto a new Statute, no. XXIV (The Southampton exhibitioners). Lond., 1908, fol. 3 pp.   Pp. Eng. 1908 vol. 86

8188. Statute made by . . . Queen's college . . . on the 7th day of June, 1911 (and sealed on the 13th day of the same month) being a statute additional to the existing statutes. 24 Oct. 1911. Lond., 1911, s. sh.
         Pp. Eng. 1911 vol. 59

8188.5. At the court at Buckingham palace the 11th day of February, 1913 . . . [Preamble and text of] A statute for the Queen's college and St. Edmund hall. [Lond.], (1913), fol. 7 pp.   G. A. Oxon c. 892 (111)

8189. Statutes made by . . . Queen's college, 11th Nov. 1914 and 19th June 1915 and sealed 19th June 1915, amending (a) Statt. Tit. I, clauses 3 and 7, and Statt. Tit. XVI, clauses 1, 3 and 4; and (b) Statt. Tit. III, clause 11. Lond., 1915, s. sh.   Pp. Eng. 1914/16 vol. 51

8190. Statutes made for the colleges . . . (The Queen's college.) Oxf., 1927, 8°. 77 pp.   G.A. Oxon 4° 759 = R.

Finance and property

8191. An act for the founding and incorporating of a free grammar schoole in . . . Northleech . . . [Queen's college appointed to make statutes, to act as visitor, etc. The advowson of the vicarage of Chedworth is given to the college.] (4 James i, c. 7, Pub.) Lond., 1607, fol.   L.L.

8192. AIRAY, H., The iust and necessary apologie . . . touching his suite in law [on behalf of Queen's college] for the rectorie of Charleton. [Followed by] For the farther clearing and inlarging of some passages in the preceding apologetique . . . [signed T. W.] [Madan 491.] Lond., 1621, 8°. 44+13 pp.   Gough Oxf. 7 (1)

8193. BISPHAM, T., Iter Australe, a Reginensibus Oxon. anno 1658 expeditum. [Verses describing the college progress round some of the college property.] [Madan 2364.] [Lond., 1658], 4°. 24 pp.
Bliss B 72 (2)

8194. An act for exchanging lands [in Southampton and Clifton, Bucks] between the earl of Peterborough and . . . Queens college. (8 G. II, c. 4, Private.) n. pl., 1735, fol. 3 pp.
L.L.

8195. To the honourable the Commons of Great-Britain . . . The humble petition of Anne Lush . . . and of . . . her infant children [concerning the rectory of Sparsholt]. n. pl., [c. 1734], fol. 3 pp.
Gough Berks 3 (22)

8196. Observations on mrs. Lush's case. n. pl., [c. 1734], s. sh.
Gough Berks 3 (23)

8197. The case of the provost and scholars of Queen's-college . . . in answer to the petition of Ann Lush . . . and of John and Charles Lush . . . [concerning the rectory of Sparsholt]. n. pl., [c. 1735], fol. 3 pp.
G.A. Berks c. 27

8198. BARNARD, T., An historical character relating to the . . . life of . . . Elisabeth Hastings. To which are added i. One of the codicils of her last will, setting forth her devise of lands to . . . Queen's college . . . for the interest of twelve Northern schools. [&c.]. Leedes, 1742, 12°. 190 pp.
Gough Oxf. 14

8199. An act for the better effecting the purposes mentioned in the will of John Michel . . . for the benefit . . . of Queen's college in the University of Oxford. (24 G. II, c. 21, Private.) n. pl., [1751], fol. 7 pp.
L.L.

8200. An act for the better establishment of the foundation of John Michel . . . in the Queen's college . . . (9 G. III, c. 72, Pub.) Lond., 1769, fol. 42 pp.
L.L.

8201. The case of the provost and scholars of Queen's college, Oxford, and of . . . Philip Brown, clerk, against the Bill [17 G. iii. c. 119. Private] for inclosing the parish of Uffington. [Endorsed title] Heads of the general objections to Uffington inclosure bill. n. pl., [1777], fol. 4 pp.
G.A. Oxon c. 247 (14)

8202. A codicil to be added to the will of me Elizabeth Hastings, containing the devise of my manor of Wheldale to . . . Queen's colledge, Oxford, for the uses herein mentioned. 1739. [Oxf., c. 1800], 4°. 8 pp.
G.A. Oxon 4° 29

Members

GENERAL

8203. An apology for those gentlemen who have seceded from Queen's-college, and are desirous of a liceat migrare to another. May 20. [26 commoners struck their names from the College book, as a result of a dispute about bad provisions and meals in hall.] n. pl., (1748), fol. 4 pp.
fol. Θ 674 (2)

8204. A further vindication of those gentlemen who have endeavoured to obtain a liceat migrare from Queen's college, Oxford. June 3, 1748. n. pl., (1748), fol. 4 pp.　　　　　　　　　MS. Rawl. J fol. 4 (f. 118)

8205. The case of Queen's college . . . in regard to some late irregularities of several of its younger members. [Oxf.], (1748), fol. 4 pp.
　　　　　　　　　　　　　　　　　　　　　　　MS. Willis 45 (237)

8206. MAGRATH, J. R., [Begin.] I have been desired to prepare a narrative of the circumstances under which mr. James Rochfort Maguire was elected . . . scholar of Queen's college . . . (Oxf., 1873), 4°. 4 pp.
　　　　　　　　　　　　　　　　　　　　　MS. Top. Oxon a. 29 (116)

8207. Letters of Richard Radcliffe and John James of Queen's college, 1755–83, ed. by M. Evans. (Oxf. hist. soc., vol. 9.) Oxf., 1888, 8°. 306 pp.　　　　　　　　　　　　　　　　G.A. Oxon 8° 360 = R.

8208. The Fothergills of Ravenstonedale, their lives and letters, transcr. by C. Thornton and F. McLaughlin. [Letters from George and Henry Fothergill describing their life at Queen's college from 1722 onwards.] Lond., 1905, 8°. 249 pp.　　　　　　　　2182 F. d. 11

8209. The diary of Thomas Crosfield [1626–1653] selected and ed. by F. S. Boas. Lond., 1935, 4°. 169 pp.　　　　　G.A. Oxon 4° 559

8210. WEBB, W. P., High table and senior common room at Queen's college. (Amer. Oxon., 1945, vol. 32, p. 66–72.) Per. G.A. Oxon 8° 889

8211. M　　, H.M., An undergraduate [S. H. Fearon] at Queen's a century ago. (Oxf. mag., 1948, vol. 66, p. 472–74; 496.) Per. G.A. Oxon 4° 141

LISTS

8212. Oxford university roll of service, Aug. 4, 1914–Nov. 1, 1918. The Queen's college record. Oxf., [1919], 8°. 16 pp.
　　　　　　　　　　　　　　　　　　　　G.A. Oxon 8° 895 (2)

8213. Collegium Reginae Oxoniense. Liber vitae Reginensium qui pro patria mortem obierunt MCMXIV–MCMXIX. Edini, 1922, 4°. 60 pp.
　　　　　　　　　　　　　　　　　　　　　G.A. Oxon 4° 433

Societies and sport

8214. Queen's college debating society. Minutes. Easter term, 1849; Lent term, 1850. Oxf., 1849, 50. 16°.　G.A. Oxon 16° 176* (13, 14)

8215. Queen's college debating society. Rules and regulations. Oxf., 1860, 16°. 12 pp.　　　　　　　　G.A. Oxon 16° 176* (15)
— [Another ed.] corrected. Oxf., 1861, 16°. 16 pp.
　　　　　　　　　　　　　　　　　　　　G.A. Oxon 16° 176* (16)

8216. Queen's college debating society. Proceedings . . . during Lent term, 1862: Michaelmas term. Oxf., 1862, 16°.　G.A. Oxon 16° 176* (19)

8217. Queen's college. Rules of the Eglesfield debating society. [Oxf.], 1878, s. sh.　　　　　　　　　　　G.A. Oxon c. 285 (f. 31)

8218. M , F. D., The Queen's torpid of '74. [Verses, signed F. D. M.] n. pl., 1874, s. sh. G.A. Oxon c. 285 (f. 18)

8219. A lay of the Queen's eight, 1878. n. pl., (1878), 8°. 8 pp. G.A. Oxon 8° 900 (29)

8220. BOND, R. W., A lay of the Queen's Torpid, 1880 [signed R. W. B.]. Queen's coll.
— Repr. n. pl., 1926, 8°. 12 pp. G.A. Oxon 8° 1046 (8)

8221. [Queen's college concert programmes, 1842–1913.] G.A. Oxon 8° 273

Chapel

8222. MANNING, P., Monumental brasses at Queen's college. (Journ., Oxf. univ. brass-rubbing soc., 1897, vol. 1, p. 67–79.) Soc. 2184 d. 50

8223. Rules for the choristers of the Queen's college [signed J. R. Magrath]. [Oxf.], 1897, s. sh. G.A. Oxon c. 285 (f. 14)

8224. MAGRATH, J. R., Consecration of the chapel of Queen's college, 1717. (Oxf. hist. soc., 1905, vol. 47, p. 165–74.) G.A. Oxon 8° 360 = R.

Library and archives

8225. Queens college. (Hist. MSS. comm., 2nd report, 1871, p. 137–42; 4th report, 1874, p. 451–58). 2262 c. 7 = K.

8225.5. CLARKE, R. L., The library at Queen's college. (N. & Q., 1881, 6th ser., vol. 4, p. 441–43, 461–63.) Per. 3974 e. 405 = A. [Repr. with corrections in no. 8147, 1921, vol. 2, p. 257–66.]

8226. Archives of the Queen's college. 4 vols. [Reprod. from typewriting.] Oxf., [1929]–38, 4°. MS. Eng. misc. d. 202, 203, 340, 344

See 5256 [Streeter, B. H., The chained library. 1931].

8227. Archives of the Queen's college. 3 vols. [In 5]. [Reprod. from typewriting of no. 8226.] (Nat. Reg. of Archives.) n. pl., [1959], 4°. 2262 c. 10 = R.

8228. GIBSON, S., Fragments from bindings at the Queen's college, Oxford. (Trans., Bibliogr. soc. The Library, 1932, ser. 4, vol. 12, p. 429–33.) Per. 258 e. 258 = A.

See 3946.1 [Munford, W. A., Edward Edwards; work in Queen's college library, 1870 onwards. 1963].

Relations with St. Edmund hall

8229. HILL, G., The right of appointment [by Queen's college] to the principality of St. Edmund's hall, a letter . . . Oxf. &c., 1855, 8°. 16 pp. G. Pamph. 2430 (27)

See 8176 [Statute. 1881].

8230. THOMSON, W., St. Edmund hall, a letter to . . . George Hill [commenting on no. 8229. Signed W. Thomson]. n. pl., 1855, 8°. 7 pp.
G.A. Oxon c. 71 (302)

8231. MAGRATH, J. R., Statute for the complete union of Queen's college and St. Edmund hall. [Explanation of the state of affairs under the statute framed by the Commissioners.] [Oxf.], 1903, s. sh.
G.A. Oxon c. 285 (f. 5)

8232. MOORE, E., The proposed extinction of St. Edmund hall by its fusion with Queen's college. [Arguments against the proposed statute.] [Oxf.], 1903, s. sh.
G.A. Oxon c. 107 (24)

See 8183 [Statute. 1905].

8233. CLARK, A. C., Queen's college and St. Edmund hall. [An account of the relations between them.] [Oxf., 1912], fol. 8 pp.
G.A. Oxon c. 107 (21)

8234. Walmesley *versus* Queen's college, A.D. 1600. [Opinions concerning the right of Queen's college to elect the principal of St. Edmund hall. Extract from the College register.] [Oxf., 1912], fol. 8 pp.
G.A. Oxon c. 107 (22)

8235. MOORE, E., and OLLARD, S. L., S. Edmund hall. [History of events prior to approval of the new statute.] [Oxf., 1912], 4°. 3 pp.
G.A. Oxon c. 291 (f. 6)

8236. EMDEN, A. B., Early relations between the Hall and Queen's. (St. Edmund hall mag., 1922, vol. 1, no. 3, p. 27–31.) Per. G.A. Oxon 4° 447

Boar's head song

8237. The boar's head song as annually sung on Christmas day at Queen's college. [Musical score and words. Also words of the version in W. de Worde's Christmasse carols, 1521.] Lond., [c. 1829], fol. 7 pp.
Mus. 5 n. c. 158

8238. The boar's head song. [A short account by A. Wood; extracts from a Rawlinson MS., words of the version in W. de Worde's Christmasse carols, 1521.] [Oxf., 18—], 4°. 3 pp.   G.A. Oxon c. 285 (f. 37)

8239. The boar's head song. [Score and words.] n. pl., [c. 1860], s. sh.
G.A. Oxon c. 285 (f. 38)

8240. BLIND, K., The boar's head dinner at Oxford, and a Germanic sun-god. (Gentleman's mag., 1877, vol. 240, p. 96–108.)
G.A. Oxon c. 285 (f. 19)
— [Another ed., rewritten.] (Saga-book of the Viking club, 1895, vol. 1, p. 90–105.)   Soc. G.A. Orkney 4° 5 (1)

8241. The boar's head carol. [Score and words.] Oxf. &c., [1890], s. sh.
G.A. Oxon c. 285 (f. 39)

8242. TAUNT, H. W., The boar's head at Queen's college, with the authorized words and music sung on the occasion. Oxf., [1904], 8°.
12 pp. G.A. Oxon 715 (8)
— 2nd ed. [1905], 16 pp. G.A. Oxon 8° 715 (9)

8243. BATTY, B. BRAITHWAITE-, A Spanish bull-fight, and some strange old customs. [Boar's head & needle & thread, Queen's coll.; May-day & Xmas eve, Magdalen; St. Giles' fair.] Reading, 1931, 16°. p. 22–85.
G.A. Oxon 16° 185

8244. The boar's head, unison carol, adapated from an arrangement by E. F. Rimbault. (Novello's school songs, 1628.) Lond., [1932], 8°.
Mus. 2 d. 21 (1628)

8245. The boar's head carol. Mixed voices, arr. Malcolm Sargent. (Oxf. choral songs, 805.) Lond., 1937, 8°. Mus. 2 d. 71 (805)

Regent's Park college

8246. Catalogue of the books, pamphlets & manuscripts in the Angus library at Regent's Park college. Lond., 1908, 4° 348 pp.
2590 d. Oxf. 24. 1

St. Alban hall

See also 7730 &c. Merton college.

8247. [Topographical prints, &c. in the Bodleian.] G.A. Oxon a. 62

8248. INGRAM, J., St. Alban hall. (Memorials of Oxford, 1837, vol. 2. 8 pp.) G.A. Oxon 8° 19

See 6422 [Suggestions for improvement. 1856].
See 3154 [Chase, D. P., Education for frugal men . . . experiments at St. Alban's hall. 1864 &c.].

8249. A statute proposed to be made by the University of Oxford commissioners for the union of St. Alban hall to Merton college. [Lond., 1881], s. sh. G.A. Oxon c. 8 (31)

8250. A statute for the union of Merton college and St. Alban hall. (Univ. of Oxf. and Cambr. act, 1877. Oxford. Four statutes made by the . . . Commissioners, 1881, p. 2, 3.) Lond., 1882, fol. Pp. Eng. 1882 vol. 51

8251. ROBINSON, H., St. Alban hall. (London society, 1887, vol. 51, p. 191–98.) G.A. Oxon 4° 575 (17)

St. Anthony's college

8252. MACLAGAN, M., The arms of St. Antony's college. (Coat of arms, 1955, vol. 3, p. 240, 41.) Per. 21932 e. 42

St. Benet's hall

8253. MCCANN, J., St. Benet's hall. (Ampleforth journ., 1926, vol. 31, p. 89–105.) Per. G.A. Yorks 4° 175
— Repr. 17 pp. G.A. Oxon 8° 1230 (2)

St. Bernard's college (dissolved)

8254. D̲ , A. G., St. Bernard's college: the Cistercian ancestor of St. John's.(Oxf. mag., 1937, vol. 56, p. 52–54.)   Per. G.A. Oxon 4° 141

8255. COLVIN, H. M., The building of St. Bernard's college. (Oxoniensia, 1959, vol. 24, p. 37–48.)   Per. G.A. Oxon 4° 658 = R.

St. Catherine's college

8256. BULLOCK, A., The proposal for a new college in Oxford. (Oxford, 1956, vol. 14, no. 3, p. 98–108.)   Per. G.A. Oxon 8° 1141

8257. BULLOCK, A., A new college of Oxford [St. Catherine's college]. (Amer. Oxonian, 1959, vol. 46, p. 49–53.)   Per. G.A. Oxon 8° 889

8258. St. Catherine's college, Oxford. (Architects' journ., 3 Nov., 1960, p. 634–38.)   N. 1863 c. 12

8259. St. Catherine's college. (Builder, 4 Nov. 1960, p. 821–24.)
    N. 1863 c. 1

8259.1. To the Queen's most excellent majesty in council. The humble petition . . . [of the University for a charter for St. Catherine's college]. [Oxf., Daniel press, 1963], s. sh.   G.A. Oxon b. 177*

8259.2. WEBB, M., A jewel amid the dreaming spires, St. Catherine's college. (Country Life, 1966, vol. 139, p. 348–50.)   Per. 384 b. 6

St. Catherine's society

General 8260–8275
Administration 8276–8279
Members
  Reminiscences 8280–8282

Lists 8283–8284
Societies and Sport 8285–8288

General

8260. Unattached students at Oxford [signed F. A. i.e. F. Anstey?] (Leisure hour, 1869, p. 666–69.)   Per. 2705 d. 33

8261. KITCHIN, G. W., The 'scholares non ascripti'. [Suggestions to the University commissioners.] [Oxf.], 1876, 8°. 19 pp. G.A. Oxon 8° 342

8262. RUMSEY, J., The 'unattached students of Oxford'. The paper of suggestions issued by the Censor is so important . . . that I have thought well to offer the following remarks thereon. Oxf., 1876, 8°. 12 pp.   G.A. Oxon 8° 1001 (10)

8263. HATCH, E., The proposed 'University Hall'. [Oxf.], (1881), 4°. 4 pp.
    G.A. Oxon b. 140 (42c)

8264. KITCHIN, G. W., Letter . . . on amendments to the new statute on students not attached to any college or hall. (Oxf., 1881), 8°. 12 pp.
    G.A. Oxon 8° 383

8265. The unattached system at Oxford. [Oxf., c. 1890], 8°. 3 pp.
    G.A. Oxon b. 140 (87d)

8266. ABBOTT, R. L., The Non-collegiate students, a brief sketch of their history. Oxf., 1894, 8°. 28 pp.   G.A. Oxon 8° 540 (2)

8267. The Non-collegiate students' magazine. Vol. 1–vol. 5, no. 68. Oxf., 1896–1919, 8°.   Per. G.A. Oxon 8° 626

8268. OVEREND, T. G., The first four years of the non-collegiate system at Oxford, 1868–1872 (from a Non-Anglican point of view). (Non-coll. students' mag., 1897, p. 36–39, 70–76.)   Per. G.A. Oxon 8° 626

8269. JEANS, G. E., [Origin of the use of 'St. Catherine' in the name of the society.] (Proc., Soc. of antiq., 1898, ser. 2, vol. 17, p. 253.)
    Per. G.A. Gen. top. 8° 524 = R.

8270. PLUMMER, C., The non-collegiate system and preparation for Holy orders. (Non-coll. students' mag., 1898, p. 158–61.)
    Per. G.A. Oxon 8° 626

8271. BAKER, J. B., The Report of the Hebdomadal council on the principles and methods of University reform [as far as it relates to non-collegiate students]. (Non-coll. students' mag., 1910, p. 151–59.)
    Per. G.A. Oxon 8° 626

8272. The name 'Non-collegiate'. (Non-coll. students' mag., 1910, p. 111–14.)   Per. G.A. Oxon 8° 626

8273. BROOK, V. J. K., St. Catherine's society. (Oxford, 1935, vol. 2, no. 1, p. 55–67.)   Per. G.A. Oxon 8° 1141

8274. 1906–1956. Ibsen exhibition at St. Catherine's society. [Catalogue. A hoax.] (Oxf., 1956), 8°. 12 pp.   3876 e. 29

8274.5 TROTMAN, R. R., and GARRETT, E. J. K., The Non-collegiate students and St. Catherine's Society, 1868–1962. (Oxf.), 1962, 8°. 60 pp.   G.A. Oxon 8° 1456

8275. St. Catherine's magazine. Vol. 1, no. 1–vol. 16, no. 48. New ser., vol. 1, no. 1–3. [Afterw.] Cats. New ser., vol. 1, no. 1–vol. 3, no. 2. [Afterw.] St. Catherine's wheel. New ser., vol. 4– . Oxf., 1919– , 8°.
    Per. G.A. Oxon 8° 981

Administration

See 1410 &c. [Information about admission of unattached students. 1868].

8276. Annual report of the Delegacy of students not attached to any college or hall [afterw.] Delegacy of non-collegiate students. 1869/70–1919/20. (Oxf., 1870–1920), 8°.   G.A. Oxon 8° 630

8277. Students' delegacy, Oxford. Permanent library. [Catalogue.] n. pl., 1879, 8°. 17 pp.   2590 e. Oxf. 18. 1

8278. An information paper compiled for the use of students of the University of Oxford who do not belong to any college or hall. 1883–1916. [Oxf.], 1883–1916, 8°.   G.A. Oxon 8° 448
[The Bodleian set is imperfect.]

8279. Non-collegiate students. [Report.] 1899/1900–1909/10. (Oxf.), 1900–10, 8°.   G.A. Oxon 8° 510*
[The Bodleian set is imperfect.]

Members

REMINISCENCES

8280. KITCHIN, G. W., Early reminiscences of non-collegiate life and work in Oxford. (Non-coll. students' mag., 1897, p. 29–34, 66–70.)
Per. G.A. Oxon 8° 626

8281. POPE, R. W. M., Reminiscences of non-collegiate life [1887–1898]. (Non-coll. students' mag., 1898, p. 185–96.)   Per. G.A. Oxon 8° 626

8282. JACKSON, W. W., Reminiscences of non-collegiate life [1883–1887]. (Non coll. students' mag., 1898, p. 129–33.)   Per. G.A. Oxon 8° 626

LISTS

8283. Students' delegacy [afterw.] St. Catherine's society. [List of members.] 1882–1940, [Oxf.], 1882–1940, s. sh.   G.A. Oxon b. 45

8284. Register of old St. Catherine's men. 1932, 34. [Oxf.], 1932, 34, 8°.
G.A. Oxon 8° 1112

Societies and sport

8285. History society. [Miscellaneous papers. 1908–11.] G.A. Oxon 4° 603

8286. St. Catherine's association. [Miscellaneous papers. 1935– .]
G.A. Oxon b. 177

8287. St. Catherine's debating society. Rules. 1889, [1902]. Oxf., 1889, [1902], 16°.   G.A. Oxon 16° 195 (4, 5)

8288. Sports pavilion in modular construction [St. Catherine's]. (Municipal journ., 1955, vol. 63, p. 3281–83.)   N. 22792 c. 1

St. Cross college

8288.5. Saint Cross and its Master. (Oxf. mag., 1966, p. 315.)
Per. G.A. Oxon 4° 141

St. Edmund hall

General

8289. [Topographical prints, &c. in the Bodleian.]   G.A. Oxon a. 62

8290. INGRAM, J., St. Edmund hall. (Memorials of Oxford, 1837, vol. 2. 16 pp.)   G.A. Oxon 8° 19

8291. HILL, G., The Oxford University commissioners and St. Edmund hall, a letter. Truro, 1882, 8°. 7 pp. G.A. Oxon 8° 900 (27)

8292. FFOULKES, E. S., An English saint [st. Edmund, founder of St. Edmund hall.] (Short sermons from Oxf. pulpits.) Oxf., [1886], 16°. 15 pp. G.A. Oxon 16° 31

8293. PAINTIN, H., Brief notes on St. Edmund hall. Repr. from 'Packer's Burford almanack'. n. pl., [c. 1914], 8°. 12 pp. G.A. Oxon 8° 900 (11)

8294. St. Edmund hall magazine. Vol. 1, no. 1– . Oxf., 1920– , 4°.
Per. G.A. Oxon 4° 447

8295. EMDEN, A. B., Thomas Hearne's rooms. (St. Edmund hall mag., 1921, vol. 1, no. 2, p. 22–28.) Per. G.A. Oxon 4° 447
— [Another ed.] (Bodleian quarterly record, 1921, vol. 3, p. 188–91.)
2590 d. Oxf. 1. 40 = R.

8296. MARCHAM, F. G., Prints of St. Edmund hall. [Annotated list.] (St. Edmund hall mag., 1922, vol. 1, no. 3, p. 13–19.)
Per. G.A. Oxon 4° 447

8297. EMDEN, A. B., Airay's or Link lodgings [on the south side of the quadrangle]. (St. Edmund hall mag., 1925, vol. 1, no. 6, p. 18–21.)
Per. G.A. Oxon 4° 447

8298. EMDEN, A. B., An Oxford hall in medieval times, the early history of St. Edmund hall. Oxf., 1927, 8°. 320 pp. G.A. Oxon 4° 763

8299. EMDEN, A. B., The well [in the quadrangle]. (St. Edmund hall mag., 1927, vol. 2, no. 2, p. 15–17.) Per. G.A. Oxon 4° 447

8300. EMDEN, A. B., The vice-principal's study. (St. Edmund hall mag., 1929, vol. 2, no. 4, p. 18–22.) Per. G.A. Oxon 4° 447

8301. EMDEN, A. B., No. 48 High street [now annexed to St. Edmund hall]. (St. Edmund hall mag., 1930, vol. 2, no. 5, p. 11, 12.)
Per. G.A. Oxon 4° 447

8302. EMDEN, A. B., A painted glass panel of St. Edmund [in the chancel of St. Michael's church]. (St. Edmund hall mag., 1930, vol. 2, no. 5, p. 58, 59.) Per. G.A. Oxon 4° 447

8303. EMDEN, A. B., White hall [46 and 47 High street, now annexed to St. Edmund hall]. (St. Edmund hall mag., 1932, vol. 3, no. 2, p. 21–24.)
Per. G.A. Oxon 4° 447

8304. EMDEN, A. B., An account of the chapel and library building, St. Edmund Hall. Oxf., 1932, 8°. 73 pp. G.A. Oxon 8° 1094

8305. EMDEN, A. B., The restoration of the dining hall. (St. Edmund hall mag., 1934, vol. 3, no. 4, p. 18–20.) Per. G.A. Oxon 4° 447

8306. EMDEN, A. B., The opening of the Canterbury building. (St. Edmund hall mag., 1934, vol. 3, no. 4, p. 24–30.) Per. G.A. Oxon 4° 447

8307. St. Edmund hall: the quadrangle completed. (Architect, 1934, vol. 138, p. 372, 73.)   N. 1731 c. 16

8308. First words (a miscellany of verse and prose). June 1936, Summer 1948, [and] 1949/50. (Oxf.), 1936–50, 4° & 8°.   G.A. Oxon 4° 564

8309. EMDEN, A. B., 'Opus Africanum'. [An altar frontal for use in the chapel.] (St. Edmund hall mag., 1936, vol. 4, no. 1, p. 16–18.)
                                                          Per. G.A. Oxon 4° 447

8310. EMDEN, A. B., An historical account of the Hall, 1558–1675. (St. Edmund hall mag., 1938, vol. 4, no. 3, p. 36–44.)
                                                          Per. G.A. Oxon 4° 447

8311. OSWALD, A., St. Edmund hall. (Country Life, 1939, vol. 85, p. 142–46.)   Per. 384 b. 6

8312. EMDEN, A. B., An historical account of the Hall, 1675–1914. (St. Edmund hall mag., 1939, vol. 4, no. 4, p. 38–49.) Per. G.A. Oxon 4° 447

See 7065 [Architecture. 1949].

8313. [List of] Manuscripts belonging to St. Edmund hall, deposited in the Bodleian library. [Reprod. from typewriting.] n. pl., 1954, 4°. 12 sheets.   2590 d. Oxf. 1a. 38 = R.

Administration

See 3162 [Moore, E., Frugal education attainable . . . with an account of the expenses of the system at St. Edmund hall. 1867].

8314. S. Edmund hall. List of changes in the kitchen &c. [Oxf., c. 1883], s. sh.   G.A. Oxon c. 291 (f. 16)

8315. S. Edmund hall, Oxford. [Details of prices under the Fixed payment system, and the Caution deposit system.] [Oxf., 1885], s. sh.
                                                          G.A. Oxon c. 291 (f. 14)

8316. EMDEN, A. B., The vice-chancellor's visitation of 1613. (St. Edmund hall mag., 1929, vol. 2, no. 4, p. 59–66.)   Per. G.A. Oxon 4° 447

8317. EMDEN, A. B., Orders for the butterie [1659?] (St. Edmund hall mag., 1930, vol. 2, no. 5, p. 63–66.)   Per. G.A. Oxon 4° 447

8318. EMDEN, A. B., Scholarships and exhibitions: a prospective retrospect. (St. Edmund hall mag., 1937, vol. 4, no. 2, p. 24–29.)
                                                          Per. G.A. Oxon 4° 447

Statutes

8319. A statute for the partial union of the Queen's college and St.Edmund hall. (Univ. of Oxf. and Cambr. act, 1877. Oxford. Four statutes made by the . . . Commissioners, 1881, p. 4–6.) Lond., 1882, fol.
                                                          Pp. Eng. 1882 vol. 51

8320. Statutes made for the Queen's college, and a statute made for the Queen's college and for St. Edmund hall, by the University of Oxford commissioners, 1877, as altered . . . down to December, 1904. Oxf., 1905, 8°. 59 pp.   G.A. Oxon 8° 747

8321. At the court at Buckingham palace the 11th day of February 1913 . . . [Preamble and text of] A statute for the Queen's college and St. Edmund hall. [Lond.], (1913), fol. 7 pp.   G.A. Oxon c. 292 (111)

8322. Statutes made for . . . St. Edmund hall . . . Oxf., 1927, 4°. 14 pp.
      G.A. Oxon 4° 759 = R.

8323. Statutes and deed of conveyance. (Oxf.), [1937], 8°. 43 pp.
      G.A. Oxon 8° 1427

8324. EMDEN, A. B., The Hall statutes. (St. Edmund hall mag., 1937, vol. 4, no. 2, p. 18–24.)   Per. G.A. Oxon 4° 447

8325. KELLY, J. N. D., A constitutional advance. [A statute granting full collegiate status.] (St. Edmund hall mag., 1953, vol. 6, no. 3, p. 57–60).
      Per. G.A. Oxon 4° 447

Finance and property

8326. An act for severing the rectory of Gatcombe from the office of principal of St. Edmund hall. (3 & 4 G. V, c. 78, L. & P.) (Lond.), 1913, 4°. 7 pp.   L.L.

8327. Appeal [for financial assistance] on behalf of St. Edmund hall. June 5, 1914. [Oxf.], (1914), 4°. 3 pp.   G.A. Oxon c. 309 (25)

8328. An appeal for endowment. (Oxf.), [1938], 8°. 23 pp.
      G.A. Oxon 8° 1439

Members

See 3726 &c. [Expulsion of six students. 1768, etc.].

8329. Aularian directory. 1927/8–36/37. Oxf., [1928–38], 8°.
      G.A. Oxon 8° 1405

8330. EMDEN, A. B., The oldest portrait of a principal of the Hall. [Henry Romworthe, 1395– : a stained glass window in Horley church, Oxon.] (St. Edmund hall mag., 1931, vol. 3, no. 1, p. 56–59.)
      Per. G.A. Oxon 4° 447

8331. Addresses and essays in commemoration of the life and works of the English Hussite Peter Payne-Engliš, 1456–1956, ed. by J. Polišenský. (Universitas Carolina, Prague, 1957, vol. 3, no. 1.) [Articles in Czech, Polish and English.] Prague, 1957, 4°. 83 pp.   1181 d. 32

Societies

8332. The Glow-worm, the terminal magazine of the Honourable and ancient Society of Glow-worms. Second ser., vol. 1, no. 1. Michaelmas term, 1919. (Oxf.), 1919, 4°.   Per. G.A. Oxon 4° 780

— The Glow-worm, the terminal magazine of S. Edmund hall.
Hilary term, 1920 (Oxf.), 1920, 4°.   Per. G.A. Oxon 4° 780

8333. St. Edmund debating society. Rules. (Oxf.), [1838], 8°. 8 pp.
                                        G.A. Oxon c. 292 (2)
— [1882]   G.A. Oxon c. 292 (12)
— [1886?]   G.A. Oxon 8° 850 (6)

8333.1. Essay society of St. Edmund Hall. Five essays. [Oxf.], 1964, 8°.
109 pp.   27041 e. 11

Relations with Queen's college

8334. HILL, G., The right of appointment [by Queen's college] to the
principality of St. Edmund's hall, a letter To which is prefixed a petition on the same question addressed to the Oxford Commissioners.
Oxf. &c., 1855, 8°. 16 pp.   G. Pamph. 2430 (27)

8335. THOMSON, W., St. Edmund hall, a letter to . . . George Hill [com-
menting on no. 8334. Signed W. Thomson]. n. pl., 1855, 8°. 7 pp.
                                    G.A. Oxon c. 71 (302)

8336. MOORE, E., The proposed extinction of St. Edmund hall by its
fusion with Queen's college. [Arguments against the proposed statute.]
[Oxf.], 1903, s. sh.   G.A. Oxon c. 107 (24)

8337. MAGRATH, J. R., Statute for the complete union of Queen's college
and St. Edmund hall. [Explanation of the state of affairs under the
statute framed by the Commissioners.] [Oxf.], 1903, s. sh.
                                    G.A. Oxon c. 285 (f. 5)

8338. St. Edmund hall, Oxford. [A paper, signed by the principal,
E. Moore, and 6 others, detailing events up to 1906 and appealing
for help in endowing the hall.] (Oxf.), [1909], 4°. 4 pp.
                                    G.A. Oxon c. 291 (f. 8)

8339. MOORE, E., and OLLARD, S. L., S. Edmund hall. [History of events
prior to approval of the new statute.] [Oxf., 1912], 4°. 3 pp.
                                    G.A. Oxon c. 291 (f. 6)

8340. CLARK, A. C., Queen's college and St. Edmund hall. [Oxf., 1912],
fol. 8 pp.   G.A. Oxon c. 291 (f. 6)

8341. Walmesley *versus* Queen's college, A.D. 1600. [Opinions concerning
the right of Queen's college to elect the principal of St. Edmund hall.
Extract from the College register.] [Oxf., 1912], fol. 8 pp.
                                    G.A. Oxon c. 107 (22)

8342. EMDEN, A. B., Early relations between the Hall and Queen's. (St.
Edmund hall mag., 1922, vol. 1, no. 3, p. 27–31.) Per. G.A. Oxon 4° 447

See also nos. 8319 &c.

St. John's college

General 8343–8364
Administration 8365–8373
Statutes 8374–8394
Finance and Property 8395–8400

Members 8401–8410
Founder's Kin 8411–8413
Societies 8414–8425
Library 8426–8430

General

8343. [Topographical prints, &c. in the Bodleian.] G.A. Oxon a. 59

See 1543 &c. [Visitation of 1648].

8344. GAYTON, E., Epulæ Oxoniensis, or a jocular relation of a banquet presented to the best of kings, by the best of prelates [W. Laud] in . . . 1636, in the mathematick library at St. John Baptists colledge. [Madan 2544.] [Oxf., 1661], fol. 4 pp. Wood 398 (2)

8345. LAURENCE, T., Verses spoken to the king, queen and dutchesse of Yorke in St. John's library [by T. Laurence?]. [Madan 2623.] [Oxf., 1663], 4°. 4 pp. G.A. Oxon 4° 19

8346. WHITE, SIR T., To mr. president, the fellowes and schollers of St. Johns colledge in Oxon. [Founder's letter, dated 1566.] [Oxf., 17—], s. sh. MS. Top. Oxon a. 29 (33)

8346.2. The Legend, a poem to the memory of sir Thomas White, founder of St. John's college in Oxford. n. pl., [c. 1720], s. sh.
G.A. Oxon a. 22 (33)

8347. HIGGS, G., An account of The Christmas prince, as it was exhibited in the University of Oxford in . . . 1607, now first publ. [by P. Bliss] from the original ms. [of G. Higgs]. (Misc. antiqua Anglicana, vol. 1, no. 3.) Lond., 1816, 4°. xv+76 pp. Douce A 327

8348. INGRAM, J., St. John's college. (Memorials of Oxford, 1837, vol. 2. 16 pp.) G.A. Oxon 8° 19

8349. Romeo and Juliet; or The shaming of the true! An atrocious outrage perpetrated at Oxford, by the St. John's college amateurs, during Commemoration, 1868. Oxf., 1868, 8°. 31 pp. G.A. Oxon c. 84 (486)

See 5134 [The Lyre. Gaudy, 1869. Programme of a projected terminal magazine, written by a member or members of St. John's].

8350. COURTNEY, W. L., Old Oxford revels. [The Christmas prince at St. John's college, 1607.] (Murray's mag., 1887, vol. 1, p. 236–46.)
G.A. Oxon 8° 586 (29)

8351. HUTTON, W. H., S. John Baptist college. (Oxf. univ. college hist.) Lond., 1898, 8°. 274 pp. G.A. Oxon 8° 651 (1) = R.

8352. HOPE, V., The Huchenson brass at St. John's college. (Oxf. journ. of monumental brasses, 1912, vol. 2, p. 157–60.) Soc. 2184 d. 50

8353. BIDDER, H. J., A handlist of alpine and other plants growing on the rockery in the gardens of St. John's college. (Oxf., 1913), 8°. 25 pp.
191163 e. 4

8354. JOURDAIN, M., Embroideries in the possession of St. John's college. (Connoisseur, 1916, vol. 44, p. 27–31.) Per. 175 d. 15

8355. OSWALD, A., St. John's college. (Country Life, 1929, vol. 66, p. 606–14; 640–48.) Per. 384 b. 6

8356. TAYLOR, A. J., A medieval roof in St. John's college. (Journ., Brit. archaeol. assoc., 1932, N.S., vol. 38, p. 278–92.)
Per. G.A. Gen. top. 8° 526 = R.

8357. St. John Baptist college. The Canterbury quadrangle, 1636–1936. Oxf., 1936, 8°. 10 pp. G.A. Oxon 8° 1132 (19)

8358. STEVENSON, W. H., and SALTER, H. E., The early history of St. John's college. (Oxf. hist. soc., N.S., vol. 1.) Oxf., 1939, 8°. 548 pp.
G.A. Oxon 8° 360 = R.

8359. JONES, E. A., An Oxford goldsmith [Lemuel King, engraver of a rosewater basin and a candle cup at St. John's college]. (Oxoniensia, 1941, vol. 6, p. 90, 91.) Per. G.A. Oxon 4° 658 = R.

8360. JOPE, E. M., H. M., and RIGOLD, S. E., Pottery from a late 12th century well-filling, and other medieval finds from St. John's college, Oxford, 1947. (Oxoniensia, 1950, p. 44–62.)
Per. G.A. Oxon 4° 658 = R.

8361. BRIGGS, N., and FARRER, P., St. John's college. [Guide by N. Briggs and P. Farrer.] (Oxf. univ. archaeol. soc.) Oxf., 1951, 4°. 13 pp.
G.A. Oxon 4° 677 (2)
— (Revised repr.) (Oxf.), 1959, 4°. 16 pp. G.A. Oxon 4° 771

8362. OSWALD, A., Two Oxford anniversaries (Trinity and St. John's colleges). (Country Life, 1955, vol. 117, p. 1616–19.) Per. 384 b. 6

8363. COSTIN, W. C., The history of St. John's college, Oxford, 1598–1860. (Oxf. hist. soc., N.S., vol. 12.) Oxf., 1958, 8°. 297 pp.
G.A. Oxon 8° 360 = R.

See 8103 [Undergraduate block for St. John's college. 1958].

8364. New building for undergraduates at St. John's college. (Architects' journ., 17 Nov. 1960, p. 725–34.) N. 1863 c. 12

Administration

8365. The appeal of five fellows of Saint John's college to the Visitor, against the suspension of the election to three open fellowships, together with the answer of the President, the rejoinder of two of the appellants, and the decision of the Visitor. Oxf., 1869, 8°. 24 pp.
G.A. Oxon 8° 146 (1)

8366. Engagement to be signed by tradesmen desirous of being employed by undergraduate members of St. John's college. [Oxf., c. 1880], s. sh.
G.A. Oxon c. 286 (f. 16)

8367. Michaelmas term, 1880. Regulations for the use of members of the college. (Oxf.), 1880, s. sh.   G.A. Oxon c. 286 (f. 17)

8368. [*Begin.*] On Tuesday next the University will be asked to assent to a statute . . . [A fly-leaf seeking to prove that St. John's college is unfairly asking to be relieved of obligations to the Laudian professorship imposed by the University commission. Dated Feb. 7, 1888.] [Oxf.], 1888, s. sh.   G.A. Oxon c. 286 (f. 10)
— [Amended version. Feb. 9, 1888.]   G.A. Oxon c. 286 (f. 10)
[Text of Statute, no. 8382.]

8369. BIDDER, H. J., Proposed statute for St. John's college. [An answer to no. 8368.] [Oxf.], 1888, s. sh.   G.A. Oxon c. 286 (f. 10)

8370. St. John's college and the Laudian professorship [signed A student of college accounts. Another answer to no. 8368]. [Oxf., 1888], 4°. 3 pp.   G.A. Oxon c. 286 (f. 11)

8371. St. John's college. [Report.] 1899/1900– . (Oxf.), 1900–29, 8°.
[The Bodleian set is imperfect.]   Per. G.A. Oxon 8° 510*; 1316

8372.

8373. Regulations of the college. Oxf., 1949, 8°. 15 pp.   G.A. Oxon 8° 1406

Statutes

8374. Statutes of the colleges . . . (St. John's college.) Oxf. &c., 1853, 8°. 141 pp.   G.A. Oxon 8° 26 = R.

8375. Outline of a proposed statute to be substituted for cap. 69. De qualitate et circumstantiis eligendorum in scholares. [Oxf., 1855?], 8°. 4 pp.   G.A. Oxon c. 71 (304)

    See 6560 [Report of the Commissioners [concerning an ordinance made for St. John's college to which objection has been made: with a copy of the ordinance]. 1858].
    See 6561 [Act providing machinery for appeal against ordinances framed by the University commissioners, particularly in relation to St. John's college. 1860].

8376. Copy of an Ordinance framed by the Commissioners appointed for the purposes of the Act 17 & 18 Vict. c. 81, in relation to the college of St. John the baptist . . . and considered and amended by a committee of her majesty's Privy council. [Lond.], 1861, fol. 23 pp.
       Pp. Eng. 1861 vol. 48

8377. Ordinances and statutes framed or approved by the . . . Commissioners . . . (Appendix, p. 487–517. Act of Parliament and Ordinance concerning St. John's college.) Oxf., 1863, 8°.   Clar. Press 31 a. 63

8378. Statutes proposed to be made by the University of Oxford commissioners for St. John's college. April 1881. [Lond.], 1881, fol. 17 pp.
       G.A. Oxon c. 8 (46)
— [Another ed.] (Oxf.), 1881, 8°. 27 pp. G.A. Oxon 8° 425 (17) = R.

8379. A statute for St. John's college, concerning the form of accounts of the college and the audit and publication thereof. (Univ. of Oxf. and Cambr. act, 1877. Oxford. Thirty six statutes made by the Univ. of Oxf. commissioners, 1881, p. 263).   Pp. Eng. 1882 vol. 51

8380. Statutes of St. John's college. (Univ. of Oxf. and Cambr. act, 1877. Oxford. Statutes made by the Univ. of Oxf. commissioners, 1881, p. 5–18.)   Pp. Eng. 1882 vol. 51

8381. Statute made by the University of Oxford commissioners on 5th Oct., 1881, for St. John's college, concerning an exhibition fund. [Lond.], 1882, s. sh.   Pp. Eng. 1882 vol. 51

8382. Statute made by . . . Saint John Baptist's college . . . repealing section 1 of Statute XVI . . . and substituting a section in lieu thereof. Sealed by the college on 12th January 1888, and consented to by the University on 14th February 1888. Lond., 1888, s. sh.
          Pp. Eng. 1888 vol. 78

[See also no. 8368-70.]

8383. Statute made by . . . St. John's college, 9th Dec. 1899, amending Statute III. 1, III. 14, V. 4a, and XV. 2. Lond., 1900, s. sh.
          Pp. Eng. 1900 vol. 66

8384. Statute made by . . . St. John's college, 15th May 1903, amending Statute XV. 1. Lond., 1904, s. sh.   Pp. Eng. 1904 vol. 75

8385. Statutes made by . . . St. John's college, 20th Apr. and 12th Oct. 1904 respectively, (i) amending Statute III. (12); and (ii) amending Statutes III, V, and XV. Lond., 1905, fol. 4 pp. Pp. Eng. 1905 vol. 60

8386. Statute made by . . . Saint John's college, 20th June, 1905, amending Statutes III and XVI. Lond., 1905, s. sh.   Pp. Eng. 1905 vol. 60

8387. Statutes made by . . . St. John's college, 4th May 1906 and sealed 7th June 1906, altering Statute III, clause 8 and Statute XVI, clause 3. Lond., 1906, s. sh.   Pp. Eng. 1906 vol. 90

8388. Statute made by . . . St. John's college, 2nd May 1908 and sealed 6th May 1908, altering and amending Statute XV, clause 4. Lond., 1908, fol. 3 pp.   Pp. Eng. 1908 vol. 86

8389. Statute made by . . . St. John's college . . . on the 6th November 1908, amending Statutes III and XX. 23 March 1909. Lond., 1909, fol. 4 pp.   Pp. Eng. 1909 vol. 69

8390. Statute made by . . . St. John's college, 12th Dec. 1911 and sealed 17th Jan. 1912, amending certain of the existing Statutes. Lond., 1912, fol. 6 pp.   Pp. Eng. 1912/13 vol. 65

8391. Statute made by . . . St. John's college, 29th May 1912 and sealed 27th June 1912, amending Statute V, clauses 1 and 2, and adding Statute VIA. Lond., 1912, fol. 3 pp.   Pp. Eng. 1912/13 vol. 65

8392. Statute made by . . . St. John's college . . . on the 9th October 1913 (and sealed on the 14th November 1913) amending Statute XV. 25 February 1914. Lond., 1914, s. sh. Pp. Eng. 1914 vol. 64

8393. Statute made by . . . St. John's college, 2nd July 1915 and sealed 5th July 1915; amending Statute XVII . . . by adding a new clause numbered 10. Lond., 1915, s. sh. Pp. Eng. 1914/16 vol. 51

8394. Statutes made for the colleges . . . (St. John Baptist college.) Oxf., 1927, 8°. 60 pp. G.A. Oxon 4° 759 = R.

Finance and property

8395. The deed of trust and will of Richard Rawlinson of St. John Baptist college . . . containing his endowment of an Anglo-Saxon lecture, and other benefactions to the college and university. Lond., 1755, 8°. xiv+ 30 pp. Gough Oxf. 44 (8)

8396. An act for exchanging certain lands [in Bedfordshire] and tenements part of the estates comprised in the settlement made on the marriage of . . . George lord viscount Torrington for certain lands and tenements belonging to . . . Saint John Baptist college. (15 G. III, c. 28, Private.) n. pl., 1775, fol. 24 pp. L.L.

8397. An act for effectuating an exchange [of lands in Chiselhurst, Footscray and Bexley, Kent for land at Garsington, Oxon] between . . . Saint John baptist college . . . and Christopher Hull of Footscray. (48 G. III, c. 149, L. & P.) Lond., 1808, fol. 12 pp. L.L.

See 5939 [Sale of land and observatory thereon to the trustees of John Radcliffe. 1820].

8398. Copy of the petition of the poor commoners of Bagley, presented to the visitor of St. John's college. [Petitioning for the right of gathering fuel from Bagley Common to be continued.] n. pl., [1850], s. sh. G.A. Oxon c. 286 (f. 28)

8399. An act to enable the president and scholars of Saint John Baptist college . . . to grant building leases of their lands in the parishes of Saint Giles, Saint Thomas and Woolvercote, Oxford . . . (18 & 19 V., c. 10, Private.) Lond., 1855, fol. 15 pp. L.L.

8400. ADAMS, A. R., [Account of the funds held by St. John's college, for its members, 1861.] n. pl., (1861), 8°. 11 pp. G.A. Oxon 8° 146 (16)

Members

GENERAL

8401. A very true and faithful account of the apparition, or ghost, of mr. John Nailer, fellow of St. John's-college in Oxford, who . . . came to mr. Shaw . . . of the same college . . . in his study . . . Lond., 1707, 8°. 8 pp. G. Pamph. 2288 (13)

8402. AMHURST, N., A letter from a student in Grub-street to a reverend high-priest and head of a college in Oxford. [A bitter attack upon W. Delaune, president of St. John's college; signed Humphry Scribble-wit, i.e. N. Amhurst?] Lond., 1720, 8°. 52 pp.   G.A. Oxon 8° 61 (8)
— [Another issue.]   Vet. A 4 e. 162 (1)

8403. TOOLY, T., Oratio funebris habita in sacello collegii divi Johannis Baptistæ in obitum R. Blunt. Lond., MDDCXXII (sic) [1722], 8°. 27 pp.   G.A. Oxon 8° 61 (10)

8404. The election of scholars to St. John's college . . . 11 June 1778, from Merchant Taylors school . . . n. pl., (1778), s. sh.
                                                      MS. Top. Oxon a. 29 (54)

8405. The election of scholars to St. John's college . . . 11 June, 1796, from Merchant Taylors school. n. pl., (1796), s. sh.   Gough Oxf. 103 (17)

8406. JERMYN, E., ed., Register of St. John's college (1695–1752). (Misc. geneal. et heraldica, 1914, 5th ser., vol. 1, p. 121–28.)
                                                   Per. 2184 d. 17 = R.
— Repr. 1914. 8 pp.   G.A. Oxon 4° 276 (29)

8407. HAYTHORNE, W., The twentieth president of St. John Baptist college. [Extracts from and comments on the 'battle-book' and diary of Thomas Fry, 1744/45–1772.] (Blackwood's mag., 1923, vol. 213, p. 28–36.)   Per. 2705 d. 386

8408. SIMMONDS, M. J., Merchant Taylor fellows of St. John's college. Lond., 1930, 8°. 112 pp.   G.A. Oxon 8° 1072

8409. COSTIN, W. C., William Laud, president of St. John's college and Chancellor of the University of Oxford, lecture. Oxf., 1945, 8°. 20 pp.
                                                     G.A. Oxon 8° 1194 (1)

8410. COSTIN, W. C., The inventory of John English [1586–1613] B.C.L., fellow of St. John's college. (Oxoniensia, 1946/7, vol. 11/12, p. 102–31.)   Per. G.A. Oxon 4° 658 = R.

See 4025 [Academic drama. 1480–1650. 1959/60].

8410.4. MORGAN, P., Bellamy and his Fellows. (Oxf. mag., 1961, N.S., vol. 2, p. 126–28.)   Per. G.A. Oxon 4° 141

Founder's kin

8411. To the . . . Commons . . . in parliament assembled: The humble petition of the kindred of sir Thomas White, founder of St. John's college [against clauses 28 and 29 of the Bill for the good government of the University, under which it is proposed to withdraw the privi-leges of founder's kin]. n. pl., [1854], fol. 4 pp.   G.A. Oxon 4° 28 (1)

8412. DYER, A. STEPHENS, Pedigree shewing the issue of Abraham and Margaretta Mabella Acworth as founders kin to St. John's college, Oxford, through their grandfather Anthony Rodney Buckeridge. (Misc. geneal. et herald., 1910, 4th ser., vol. 3, p. 41–44.)
                                                   Per. 2184 d. 17 = R

8413. DYER, A. STEPHENS, Buckeridge of Lichfield as founder's kin. [St. John's college.] (Notes and queries, 1915, 11th ser., vol. 12, p. 275, 76.)
Per. 3974 e. 405 = A.

Societies

8414. Short account of the chief societies for religious and social objects in the University and college. [Oxf., 1906], 8°. 3 pp.
G.A. Oxon c. 286 (f. 16)

8415. King Charles club. Rules [and list of members]. (Oxf.), [1892–93], 16°. 12 pp. G.A. Oxon 16° 176* (10)

8416. S. John's archery club. Rules. 1865, 73, 80, 85. Oxf., 1865–85, 8°.
G.A. Oxon 8° 852

8417. St. John's archery club. List of members. (May 1893). [Oxf., 1893], 16°. 14 pp. G.A. Oxon 8° 852

8418. Saint John's debating and book club. Rules. Oxf., [1854], 8°. 16 pp.
G.A. Oxon 8° 1113 (31)
— 1862. 15 pp. G.A. Oxon 8° 1113 (32)

8419. St. John's college concert. (Programme) 1885, 1913.
G.A. Oxon 8° 1113 (27, 29)

8420. St. John's college glee club. List of members. Nov., 1884. (Oxf.), 1884, 8°. 8 pp. G.A. Oxon 8° 1113 (26)

8421. St. John's college glee club. Concert (programme). 1878, 79, 82.
G.A. Oxon 8° 1113 (23–25)

8422. St. John's college musical society. Eight's week concert, 1907. (Programme.) G.A. Oxon 8° 1113 (29)

8423. St. John's college society. Register. 1936, 37. Oxf., 1936, 37, 8°.
G.A. Oxon 8° 1162

8424. St. John's junior literary society. Rules. [Oxf.], 1886, 16°. 7 pp.
G.A. Oxon 16° 176* (11)

8425. St. John's whist club. Rules [and list of members]. Oxf., 1880, 8°.
8 pp. G.A. Oxon 8° 1113 (33)
— 1884. G.A. Oxon 8° 1113 (34)
— 1893. 12 pp. G.A. Oxon 8° 1113 (35)

Library

8426. St. John's college. (Hist. MSS. comm., 4th report, pt. 1, 1874, p. 465–68.) 2262 c. 37 = K.

8427. A catalogue of a portion of the library of H. Butler Clarke . . . now in the library of S. John's college. n. pl., [1906], 8°. 30 pp.
2590 e. Oxf. 17c. 1

8428. BOAS, F. S., Recent recovered manuscripts at St. John's college [by
J. Blencowe, J. Crowther, and G. Peele]. (Mod. lang. rev., 1916, vol.
11, p. 298–301.) Per. 3962 d. 24 = A.
— Repr. Cambr., (1916), 8°. 2590 d. Oxf. 10. 1

See 5256 [Streeter, B. H., The chained library. 1931].

8429. COLVIN, H. M., Manuscript maps belonging to St. John's college.
(Oxoniensia, 1950, p. 92–103.) Per. G.A. Oxon 4° 658 = R.

See 5654 [Saxl, F., and Meier, H., Catalogue of astrological . . . manuscripts.
1953].

8430. St. John's college. Summary catalogue of manuscripts 213–305
[really 310] a suppl. to Coxe's Catalogue [no 6503]. [Reprod. from typewriting.] n. pl., (1956), 4°. [41 pp.]. MS. Top. Oxon d. 469 = R.

8430.1. CHAPMAN, C. B., A comment on holdings in old medicine and
science in the St. John's college library. (Amer. Oxonian, 1964, vol.
51, p. 115–23.) Per. G.A. Oxon 8° 889

St. Mary college of Winchester in Oxford

See 7829 &c. New college.

St. Mary's college
(Augustinians: dissolved 1541)

8431. INGRAM, J., St. Mary's college. (Memorials of Oxford, 1837, vol. 3.
Page 15 of St. Martin's church and St. Peter le Bailey.)
G.A. Oxon 8° 20

8432. SHADWELL, C. L., [History of St. Mary's college, later Frewen hall.]
(Proc., Oxf. architect. and hist. soc., 1894, N.S., vol. 6, p. 38–42.)
Per. G.A. Oxon 8° 498 = R.

8433. PAINTIN, H., Historic Oxford houses. No. 1. Frewin hall. n. pl.,
[1912?], 4°. 4 pp. G.A. Oxon 4° 276 (23)

8434. JEFFERY, R. W., A forgotten college of Oxford [St. Mary's college in
New Inn Hall St.]. (Brazen Nose, 1927, vol. 4, p. 260–88.)
Per. G.A. Oxon 4° 282
— Repr. G.A. Oxon 4° 399a (16)

8435. EVANS, E., St. Mary's college in Oxford for Austin canons. (Rept.,
Oxf. archaeol. soc., 1931, p. 367–91.) Per. G.A. Oxon 8° 499 = R.

St. Mary hall
General

See also 7960 &c. Oriel college.

8436. [Topographical prints, &c. in the Bodleian.] G.A. Oxon a. 62

8437. INGRAM, J., St. Mary hall. (Memorials of Oxford, 1837, vol. 2.
16 pp.) G.A. Oxon 8° 19

See 6422 [Suggestions for improvement. 1856].

8438. Oxford university. Copies of regulations . . . in relation to certain scholarships in St. Mary hall . . . [Lond.], 1858, fol. p. 1–5.

Pp. Eng. 1857/8 vol. 46

See 3154 [Chase, D. P., Education for frugal men . . . experiments at St. Mary's hall. 1864].

8439. [Historical account.] (Proc., Oxf. architect. and hist. soc., 1873, N.S., vol. 3, p. 140–43; 1885, N.S., vol. 4, p. 322–24.)

Per. G.A. Oxon 8° 498 = R.

See 8787 [Chase, D. P., Letter allowing former members of Charsley's hall to withdraw their application for admission to St. Mary hall now that C. A. Marcon intends to succeed Charsley. 1891].

8440. STRIDE, W. K., St. Mary hall. (Gents. mag., 1896, vol. 281, p. 494–99.)

Per. 2705 e. 327

8441. VARLEY, F. J., Oliver Cromwell and St. Mary hall. (Oriel record, 1939, vol. 8, p. 28–30.)

Per. G.A. Oxon 4° 484

8442. LECHMERE, W. L., Oxford: 1863–1867, recollections [of St. Mary hall, &c.]. (Oxf. and Cambr. review, 1912, no. 19, p. 73–113.)

Per. 2625 d. 37

8443. PHILIP, I. G., A proposed re-foundation of St. Mary hall [1657?]. (Oxoniensia, 1957, vol. 22, p. 93–97.)   Per. G.A. Oxon 4° 658 = R.

8444. SOMERSET, H. V. F., An account book of an Oxford undergraduate [of St. Mary hall] in the years 1619–1622. (Oxoniensia, 1957, vol. 22, p. 85–92.)   Per. G.A. Oxon 4° 658 — R.

Statutes

8445. Ordinances and statutes framed or approved by the . . . Commissioners . . . (St. Mary hall, p. 473–80.) Oxf., 1863, 8°.

Clar. Press 31 a. 63

8446. University of Oxford commission. Sketch of a statute for the 'complete union' of Oriel college and St. Mary hall. Proposed by the principal of St. Mary hall. n. pl., (1877), 8°. 3 pp.   G.A. Oxon c. 283 (1)

8447. A statute proposed to be made by the University of Oxford commissioners for the union of St. Mary hall to Oriel college. [Lond., 1881], s. sh.   G.A. Oxon c. 8 (58)

8448. A statute for the union of Oriel college and St. Mary hall. [Lond., 1881], s. sh.   G.A. Oxon c. 283 (27)
— [Another issue.] (Univ. of Oxf. and Cambr. act, 1877. Oxford. Four statutes made by the . . . Commissioners, 1881, p. 3, 4.) Lond., 1882, fol.   Pp. Eng. 1882 vol. 51

St. Mildred hall

8449. SALTER, H. E., An Oxford hall [?St. Mildred's] in 1424. (Essays in history presented to R. L. Poole, 1927, p. 421–35.)   2262 d.34 = S.

St. Peter's college

8450. St. Peter's Hall, [Appeal for funds for the foundation of the hall.] Oxf., (1928), 4°. 8 pp.   G.A. Oxon 4° 661

8451. 1st (–22nd) Annual report of St. Peter's House (Hall) [*afterw.*] St. Peter's Hall 1950/51– . [Oxf.], 1929– , 8°.   G.A. Oxon 8° 1078

8451.1. St. Peter's college record. 1965– . (Oxf.), 1965– , 8°.
Per. G.A. Oxon 8° 1509

Stapledon hall

See 7251 &c. Exeter college.

Trinity college

General 8452–8472
Administration 8473–8475
Statutes 8476–8491
Finance and Property 8492–8500
Members 8501–8506

Biography 8507–8511
Societies and Sport 8512–8515
Library 8516–8518
Millard Laboratory 8519–8522

General

8452. [Topographical prints, &c. in the Bodleian.]   G.A. Oxon a. 60

8453. Preamble of letters patent, from Philip and Mary, for founding Trinity college. Mar. viii. 1554–5. (Warton, T. The life of sir T. Pope, 1772, p. 294–96.)   Gough Oxf. 43

8454. Part of the charter of establishment of the . . . college, in consequence of the . . . letters patent. Mar. xxviii. 1555. (Warton, T. The life of sir T. Pope, 1772, p. 297, 98.)   Gough Oxf. 43

8455. Account of the founder's visit to Trinity college . . . 1556. (Warton, T. The life of sir T. Pope, 1772, p. 432–34.)   Gough Oxf. 43

8456. Instrument concerning the recession of Trinity college from the University to Garsington . . . in time of the plague, 1557. (Warton, T. The life of sir T. Pope, 1772, p. 355–58.)   Gough Oxf. 43

8457. INGRAM, J., Trinity college. (Memorials of Oxford, 1837, vol. 2. 16 pp.)   G.A. Oxon 8° 19

8458. STEVENSON, J., Some account of Durham college, Oxford, suppressed by Henry the eighth; together with the priory in Durham with which it was connected [by J. Stevenson]. Durham, 1840, 8°. 14 pp.
G.A. Oxon 8° 611 (24)

8459. [Examination papers. Scholarships.] 1841, 85. [Oxf.], 1841, 85, 8°.
2626 e. 27

8460. Gratiarum formula in usum coll. Trin. Oxon. [Oxf., *c.* 1865], s. sh.
G.A. Oxon c. 287 (2)

8461. Trinity college. Proposed new buildings. [Oxf., 1882], 8°. 3 pp.
G.A. Oxon c. 287 (51)

8462. Trinity college, Oxford. January 1887. [A letter, signed J. Percival, detailing the response to the appeal in 1882, no. 8461 and the extension of buildings effected.] [Oxf.], (1887), 4°. 2 sheets. G.A. Oxon c. 287 (52)

8463. WOODS, H. G., Religio loci, paper read before the Church society of Trinity college. Oxf., 1888, 16°. 23 pp. G.A. Oxon 16° 20

8464. BLAKISTON, H. E. D., Some Durham college rolls. (Oxf. hist. soc., 1896, vol. 32, p. 1–76.) G.A. Oxon 8° 360 = R.
— [Another ed.] n. pl., [1896?], 8°. G.A. Gen. top. 8° 865 (16)

8465. BLAKISTON, H. E. D., Trinity college. (Oxf. univ. college hist.) Lond., 1898, 8°. 248 pp. G.A. Oxon 8° 651 (4) = R.

8466. RONALDSON, T. M., Drawings of Trinity college [with intr. by J. W. More]. Oxf., 1904, 4°. xxvii pp.+20 plates. G.A. Oxon 4° 223

8467. Auction catal. A few pieces of decorative furniture, the property of Trinity college. Dec. 16, 1915. 175003 d. 14 (1915)

8468. OSWALD, A., Trinity college. (Country Life, 1930, vol. 67, p. 318–24, 352–59.) Per. 384 b. 6

8469. OSWALD, A. S., Eighteenth century furniture at Trinity college. (Country Life, 1930, vol. 67, p. 485, 86.) Per. 384 b. 6

8470. C   , S., A gloss on glass. [Letter on the old hand-blown wine-bottles broken and set into cement on the top of the Parks Road wall of Trinity college.] (Oxf. mag., 1938, vol. 56, p. 741.)
Per. G.A. Oxon 4° 141

8471. MACLAGAN, M., Trinity college, 1555–1955. Oxf., 1955, 4°. 38 pp.
G.A. Oxon 4° 729
— Revised ed. 1963. 39 pp. G.A. Oxon 4° 796

8472. OSWALD, A., Two Oxford anniversaries. (Trinity and St. John's colleges.) (Country Life, 1955, vol. 117, p. 1616–19.) Per. 384 b. 6

Administration

8473. WARD, G. R. M., An appeal to the bishop of Winchester, visitor of Trinity college . . . on the misappropriation of the endowments of that society . . . Oxf., 1839, 8°. 80 pp. Bliss B 216 (3)

8474. The recent election to the presidency of Trinity college, Oxford. [A paper regretting the election of J. Percival as president.] [Oxf., 1878?], s. sh. G.A. Oxon c. 287 (158)

8475. Trinity college. [Report.] 1899/1900–1928/29. (Oxf.), 1900–29, 8°.
G.A. Oxon 8° 510*, 849

3 A

722 COLLEGES AND HALLS

Statutes

8476. The statutes of Trinity college, printed by desire of the Commissioners under the act 17 & 18 Vict. c. 81. Lond., 1855, 8°. 97 pp.
G.A. Oxon 8° 417

8477. Oxford university. Ordinances . . . in relation to . . . Trinity [and 10 other] colleges respectively. [Lond.], 1857, fol. 139 pp.
Pp. Eng. 1857 vol. 32

8478. Ordinances and statutes framed or approved by the . . . Commissioners . . . (Trinity college, p. 367–84.) Oxf., 1863, 8°.
Clar. Press 31 a. 63

8479. University of Oxford commission. Statutes of Trinity college, as partly settled by the Commissioners. (For the use of the . . . Commissioners only.) May 1880. [The Bodleian copy has MS. corrections and additions by the Commissioners, thereby becoming the proof for the amended statutes.] [Lond.], 1880, fol. 15 pp. G.A. Oxon c. 8 (21)

8480. Statutes proposed to be made . . . for Trinity college. November, 1880. (Oxf.), 1880, 8°. 30 pp.   G.A. Oxon 8° 425 (18) = R.

8481. Statutes proposed to be made by the University of Oxford commissioners for Trinity college. April 1881. [Lond.], 1881, fol. 18 pp.
G.A. Oxon c. 8 (38)

8482. Statutes of Trinity college. (Univ. of Oxf. and Cambr. act, 1877. Oxford. Thirty six statutes made by the Univ. of Oxf. commissioners, 1881, p. 189–201, 258.)   Pp. Eng. 1882 vol. 51

8483. A statute for Trinity college, concerning certain trust funds and exhibitions. (Univ. of Oxf. and Cambr. act, 1877. Oxford. Five statutes made by the Univ. of Oxf. commissioners, 1881, p. 2.)
Pp. Eng. 1882 vol. 51

8484. Statute made by . . . Trinity college, 15th July 1890, and sealed 25th July 1890, altering Statute II., clause 21A of the Statute (approved by her majesty on 13th May 1887). Lond., 1890, s. sh.
Pp. Eng. 1890/91 vol. 61

8485. Statutes made by . . . Trinity college, 19th June, 1893, for altering . . . Statute II, clauses 2, 6 and 8; Statute III, clause 7; and Statute VI, clause 2. Lond., 1893, s. sh.   Pp. Eng. 1893 vol. 68

8486. Statute made by . . . Trinity college, 26th Feb. 1904, amending Statute VI (Pension fund). Lond., 1904, s. sh. Pp. Eng. 1904 vol. 75

8487. Statute made by . . . Trinity college, 27th May 1907, altering and amending Statute I. Lond., 1908, s. sh.   Pp. Eng. 1908 vol. 86

8488. Statute made by . . . Trinity college . . . on the 29th day of June, 1911 (and sealed on the 1st day of July, 1911) amending Statute III. 24 Oct. 1911. Lond., 1911, s. sh.   Pp. Eng. 1911 vol. 59

8489. Statute made by ... Trinity college ... on the 9th December 1913, the 16th January 1914, and the 4th February, 1914 (and sealed on the 9th February, 1914) substituting a new clause 12 for clause 12 of Statute II. 10 June 1914. Lond., 1914, s. sh.   Pp. Eng. 1914 vol. 64

8490. Statute made by ... Trinity college ... on the 9th December 1913 (and sealed on the 9th February 1914) adding a new clause (numbered 13) after clause 12 of Statute III. 10 June 1914. Lond., 1914, s. sh.
Pp. Eng. 1914 vol. 64

8491. Statutes made for the colleges ... (Trinity college.) Oxf., 1927, 8°. 39 pp.   G.A. Oxon 4° 759 = R.

Finance and property

8492. Compositio quædam collegiorum, coll. Magd. et coll. Trin. Oxon. Feb. 26, 1558. (Warton, T. The life of sir T. Pope, 1772, p. 339–47.)
Gough Oxf. 43

8493. Grant of Durham college in Oxford, from Edward the sixth, to George Owen, and William Martyn. Feb. iv 1553. (Warton, T. The life of sir T. Pope, 1772, p. 281–84.)   Gough Oxf. 43

8494. Purchase of Durham college ... by sir Thomas Pope, of G. Owen and W. Martyn. Feb. xx. 1554. (Warton, T. The life of sir T. Pope, 1772, p. 285–93.)   Gough Oxf. 43

8495. Letter of attorney from Thomas Slythurste, for taking possession of a certain messuage in Oxford, called Trinity college. Mar. xxviii. 1555. (Warton, T. The life of sir T. Pope, 1772, p. 300, 01.)
Gough Oxf. 43

8496. An indenture made May 5, 1556, 'witnessing that the president, fellows and schollers of Trinity college ... have received of their founder, such parcelles of church playte and ornamentes of the church, as hereafter followethe'. (Warton, T. The life of sir T. Pope, 1772, p. 318–23.)   Gough Oxf. 43

8497. Indentura de ornamentis et jocalibus missis per dominum fundatorem, tam ad ornatum sacelli quam aulæ, Jan. xx. (April 12) 1557. (Warton, T. The life of sir T. Pope, 1772, p. 324–32.) Gough Oxf. 43

8498. Decretum de gratiis collegio rependendis. [A decree by the president and fellows of Trinity college compelling all who have been or who are on the foundation of the college to show their gratitude by a proportionate gift of money.] [Madan 213.] [Oxf., 1602?], s. sh.
Wood 276 B (f. 13)
— [Another ed.] [Lond., c. 1700], s. sh.   G.A. Oxon c. 287 (1)

8499. An act for settling upon ... Trinity college ... and upon the rector of the parish of Dumbleton ... certain perpetual rent charges issuing out of the estate of ... John Sommers, earl Sommers in Dumbleton ... and for vesting certain tithes and lands belonging to the said college

and rector respectively in the mortgages of the said earl subject to
equity of redemption. (3 G. IV, c. 31, Private.) n. pl., 1822, fol. 33 pp.
L.L.

8500. WILSON, J., A few words on the subject of third fines [and their
application by the college. Perhaps by J. Wilson, the president]. [Oxf.,
c. 1863], s. sh.   MS. Top. Oxon c. 86 (67)

Members

GENERAL

8501. Admission of the first president, fellows, and scholars of the . . .
college on the eve of Trinity-Sunday, May xxx, 1556. (Warton, T.
The life of sir T. Pope, 1772, p. 302–12.)   Gough Oxf. 43

8502. A letter from a student in Oxford to his friend in the country, con-
taining a short account of the late proceedings of Trinity college in that
University [against J. Budgen and S. Fry &c.]. Lond., 1709, 8°. 15 pp.
G.A. Oxon 8° 219 (1)

8503. An appeal preferred before George, bishop of Winchester, against
the decision [in 1815] of the president and fellows of Trinity college
[not to confirm him in his fellowship] by William Radford. Lond.,
1825, 8°. 51 pp.   Bliss B 216 (1)

8504. Provisional list of members of Trinity college living on Trinity
monday 1892. Oxf., 1892, 8°. 41 pp.   G.A. Oxon 8° 715 (5)

8505. Room list. 1896, 97. n. pl., (1896, 97), s. sh.   G.A. Oxon a. 28

8506. Trinity college. Admissions during the nineteenth century. Oxf.,
1901, 8°. 108 pp.   G.A. Oxon 8° 673

BIOGRAPHY

8507. WARTON, T., The life of sir Thomas Pope, founder of Trinity
college. With an appendix. Lond., 1772, 8°. 438 pp. Gough Oxf. 43
— 2nd ed. 1780. 464 pp.   210 n. 134

8508. Account of the first president, fellows, and scholars, of Trinity
college . . . nominated by sir T. Pope and admitted May 30, 1556: and
of such others as were afterwards nominated by the same authority.
(Warton, T. The life of sir T. Pope, 1772, p. 359–405.)
Gough Oxf. 43

8509. WARTON, T., The life and literary remains of Ralph Bathurst . . .
president of Trinity college. Lond. &c., 1761, 8°. 232+296 pp.
Gough Oxf. 46

8510. BLAKISTON, H. E. D., A short address in memory of Henry Francis
Pelham, president of Trinity. (Trinity coll. mission quarterly mag.,
Apr. 1907.)
— [Repr.] Lond., (1907), 8°. 7 pp.   G.A. Oxon 884 (3)

8511. EDWARDS, C. E. H., An Oxford tutor, the life of the rev. Thomas Short, B.D., of Trinity college [fellow from 1816 to 1879]. Lond., 1909, 16°. 54 pp. G.A. Oxon 16° 106

Societies and sport

8512. Trinity college. Summary and analyses of income and expenditure of consolidated clubs, 1900/1901–1926/1927. [Oxf.], (1901–27), s. sh.
G.A. Oxon 4° 485

8513. '99 club. Rules and list of members. October 1901, Dec. 1902. (Oxf.), 1901, 02, 16°. G.A. Oxon c. 287 (135)

8514. [Letter, dated in MS., Feb. 1888, appealing for subscriptions for a new college barge.] [Oxf., 1888], 8°. 2 sheets. G.A. Oxon c. 287 (100)
— List of subscriptions. Feb. 1888. [Oxf.], 1888, 8°. 4 pp.
G.A. Oxon c. 287 (101)
— November 1889. [Report from Barge committee announcing that the barge is in use. *With* list of subscriptions *and* photograph of barge.] [Oxf.], 1889, 4°. 4 pp. G.A. Oxon c. 287 (103)

See 7913 [Trinity beagles. 1919].

8515. Trinity college, Oxford. The new cricket and football ground. [Appeal. *With*] First list of donations. Jan., 1899. [Oxf.], 1899, 4°. 2 sheets. G.A. Oxon c. 287 (106, 107)
— Second list of donations. July, 1899. G.A. Oxon c. 287 (108)
— [Report, Jan. 1902, and List of subscribers.] [Oxf.], 1902, fol. 3 pp.
G.A. Oxon c. 287 (109)

Library

8516. Trinity college. (Hist. MSS. comm., 2nd report, 1871, p. 142, 43.)
2262 c. 7 = K.

8517. Trinity college. Catalogue of books in the new library. Oxf., [1892], 8°. 56 pp. 2590 e. Oxf. 11. 1
— [Books added Apr. 1891–Apr. 1892.] (Oxf.), [1892], 8°. 8 pp.
2590 e. Oxf. 11. 2
— Books added Oct. 1898 to July 1899. [Oxf.], (1899), 8°. 4 pp.
2590 e. Oxf. 11. 2
— Accessions. 1899 to 1901. [Oxf.], (1901), 8°. 8 pp. 2590 e. Oxf. 11. 2

8518. Trinity college, Oxford. War memorial (new library) fund. [Report, signed H. E. D. Blakiston, and Subscriptions.] [Oxf.], (1921), 4°. 8 pp.
G.A. Oxon c. 287 (64)
— Report to subscribers. September 1928 [signed H. E. D. Blakiston]. (Supplementary list of contributors.) [Oxf.], (1928), 4°. 4 pp.
G.A. Oxon c. 287 (65)

See 5256 [Streeter, B. H., The chained library. 1931].

Millard laboratory

8519. The Millard laboratory, Oxford. [A description and short history.] [Oxf., c. 1890], 4°. 3 pp.   G.A. Oxon c. 287 (55)
— [Another ed. c. 1895.]   G.A. Oxon c. 287 (56)

8520. The Millard engineering laboratory, Oxford. [A description.] [Oxf., 1892], 8°. 4 pp.   G.A. Oxon c. 287 (59)

8521. The Millard mechanical and engineering laboratory, Oxford. [A description.] [Oxf., c. 1900], 4°. 3 pp.   G.A. Oxon c. 287 (60)
— [Another ed.] 4 pp.   G.A. Oxon c. 287 (62)

8522. SMITH, F. J. JERVIS-, Millard mechanical laboratory, Oxford. Electrical engineering, note by the lecturer [signed F. J. J.-S.]. [Oxf., c. 1900], s. sh.   G.A. Oxon c. 287 (61)

University college

General 8523–8545
Administration 8546–8556
Statutes 8557–8584
Members 8585–8587
  Biography and Reminiscences 8588–8596

Societies 8597–8598
Chapel 8599–8600
Library 8601–8605
Plate 8606–8607

General

8523. [Topographical prints, &c. in the Bodleian.]   G.A. Oxon a. 60

8524. [A prayer commemorating the founder and benefactors of University college.] [Madan 2521.] [Oxf., c. 1660], s. sh.   MS. Tanner 338 (f. 216)

8525. [Form of commemoration of the founder.] [Madan 3070.] [Oxf., c. 1675], s. sh.   MS. Rawl. D. 912 (23)

8526. SMITH, W., The annals of University-college, proving William of Durham, the true founder, and answering all their arguments who ascribe it to King Alfred. Newcastle upon Tyne, 1728, 8°. 376 pp.   Gough Oxf. 124

8527. KILNER, J., Of University and Balliol colleges . . . founded . . . subsequent . . . to . . . Merton college. (The account of Pythagoras's school [by J. Kilner] suppl. p. 132–46.) n. pl., [1790?], fol.   Gough Cambr. 97

8528. INGRAM, J., University college. (Memorials of Oxford, 1837, vol. 1. 16 pp.)   G.A. Oxon 8° 18

8529. [Examination papers. Fellowships, scholarships &c.]. 1838, 54, 70. [Oxf.], 1838–70, 8°.   2626 e. 28

8530. SMITH, G., Alfredus rex fundator. (Canadian monthly, 1872, vol. 2, p. 157–69.)   G.A. Oxon 4° 578 (36)

8531. CARR, W., University college. (Oxf. univ. college hist.) Lond., 1902, 8°. 242 pp.   G.A. Oxon 8° 651 (18) = R.

8532. University college, Oxford *v*. The mayor, aldermen, and citizens of the City of Oxford. Judgment [in favour of the college ownership of the soil of Logic Lane, over which they propose to build a bridge]. n. pl., 1904, fol. 8 pp. G.A. Oxon c. 25 (10)

8533. BAXTER, D., The story of an Oxford college [University]. Oxf., 1907, 8°. 12 pp. G.A. Oxon 8° 744 (3)

8534. PAINTIN, H., University college and dr. Radcliffe. (Antiquary, 1915, N.S., vol. 11, p. 297–303.) Per. 17572 d. 32

8534.8. University college (record). 1929/30– . [Oxf.], 1929– , 8°. Per. G.A. Oxon 8° 1086

8535. CAMPBELL, A. H., Law and lawyers in University college. (Univ. coll. record, 1930/31, p. 59–68.) Per. G.A. Oxon 8° 1086

8536. At the admission of a Master. [Form of service.] [Oxf.], 1935, s. sh. G.A. Oxon c. 288 (66)

8537. OSWALD, A., University college. (Country Life, 1937, vol. 81, p. 146–52.) Per. 384 b. 6

8538. ESDAILE, K. A., and TOYNBEE, M. R., The University college statue of James ii. (Oxoniensia, 1951, vol. 16, p. 42–56.) Per. G.A. Oxon 4° 658 = R.

8539. PAUL, G. A., Scheme of shrubs planted in the quadrangles. (Univ. coll. record, 1951/52, p. 33–35.) Per. G.A. Oxon 8° 1086

8540. COX, A. D. M., The French petition. [An account of the claim that King Alfred was the founder of University college.] (Univ. coll. record, 1952/53, p. 14–24.) Per. G.A. Oxon 8° 1086

8541. BOWEN, E. J., The building stones of the college. (Univ. coll. record, 1956, vol. 3, p. 42–48.) Per. G.A. Oxon 8° 1086

8542. FIRTH, A. E., The college feasts [St. Cuthbert's and SS. Simon and Jude]. (Univ. coll. record, 1957, vol. 3, p. 114–18.) Per. G.A. Oxon 8° 1086

8543. The Hall and Chapel range. [Notes on the building.] (Univ. coll. record, 1957, vol. 3, p. 110–14.) Per. G.A. Oxon 8° 1086

8544. The Summer room carvings. (Univ. coll. record, 1958/60, vol. 3, p. 192–201; 252–56; 341–46.) Per. G.A. Oxon 8° 1086

8545. COX, A. D. M., The college at the Restoration. (Univ. coll. record, 1960, vol. 3, p. 324–30.) Per. G.A. Oxon 8° 1086

Administration

8546. NEWTON, R., The proceedings of the Visitors of University college, with regard to the late disputed election of a master vindicated [by R. Newton]. Oxf., 1723, fol. 6 pp. Gough Oxf. 107 (9)
— 2nd ed. 1723. Gough Oxf. 136 (3)

[See also no. 8591.]

8547. A vindication of the proceedings at University college in the late election of mr. Cockman to be master of that college, in answer to . . . The proceedings of the visitors, &c., vindicated [no. 8546]. Lond., 1723, fol. 11 pp. Gough Oxf. 107 (9*)

8548. Memorandum respecting admissions to University college. [Oxf., c. 1860], 8°. 4 pp. G.A. Oxon c. 288 (14)
— [Another ed. c. 1865.] G.A. Oxon c. 288 (15)

8549. College regulations. 1862, 66, 71, 73, 75. [Oxf.], 1862–75, 4°.
G.A. Oxon c. 288 (1–5)

8550. University college kitchen regulations [and] tariff. November 1865. [Oxf., 1865], 8°. 2 sheets. G.A. Oxon c. 288 (7)
— October 1875. G.A. Oxon c. 288 (9)

8551. A petition of the resident bachelors and undergraduates to the master and fellows of University college. [Complaints about expenses, and the slackness of 'scouts' etc.] (Oxf.), [c. 1866], 8°. 7 pp. G.A. Oxon c. 288 (6)

8552. College regulations in regard to gates. [Oxf.], 1866, s. sh.
G.A. Oxon c. 288 (11)

8553. University and Oriel colleges . . . Scholarships and exhibitions . . . 1899. [Oxf., 1898], s. sh. G.A. Oxon c. 288 (18)

8554. BRIGHT, J. F., [Begin.] I shall on Saturday bring forward . . . [Questions involved in the Pension scheme.] [Oxf., c. 1900], 4°. 3 pp.
G.A. Oxon c. 288 (13)

8555. University college. [Report.] 1899/1900–1928/29. [Subsequently publ. in the University college record no. 8534.8.] (Oxf.), 1900–29, 8°. [The Bodleian set is imperfect.] G.A. Oxon 8° 510*

8556.

Statutes

8557. The statutes of University college, printed by desire of the Commissioners under the act 17 & 18 Vict. c. 81. Lond., 1855, 8°. 29 pp.
G.A. Oxon 8° 418

8558. Oxford university. Copies of ordinances with respect to the fellowships in University college. Lond., 1856, s. sh. Pp. Eng. 1856 vol. 46

8559. Copy of an ordinance framed by the Oxford university commissioners . . . for authorising the suspension of one fellowship in University college, for a limited time. 9 June, 1856. (Copies of four ordinances &c., p. 1, 2.) [Lond.], 1857, fol. Pp. Eng. 1857 vol. 13

8560. Oxford university. Copy of three ordinances . . . in relation to Merton, Pembroke and University colleges . . . [Lond.], 1857, fol. 49 pp.
Pp. Eng. 1857 vol. 32

8561. Oxford university. Copies of four ordinances . . . in relation to Christ's Church, and Queen's, University and Brazenose colleges. [Lond.], 1858, fol. 38 pp. Pp. Eng. 1857/8 vol. 46

8562. Ordinances and statutes framed or approved by the . . . Commissioners . . . (University college, p. 25-45.) Oxf., 1863, 8°.
Clar. Press 31 a. 63

8563. Ordinances concerning University college framed by the Oxford university commissioners. Oxf., 1863, 8°. 21 pp. G.A. Oxon 8° 1148 (4)

8564. Statutes of University college. n. pl., (1871), 4°. 25 pp.
G.A. Oxon 4° 505 (8)

8565. BRADLEY, G. G., Two letters to . . . the Lord chancellor . . . Visitor . . . of University college [in answer to a letter from the Fellows of the college addressed to the Visitor on 10th Nov., 1873 in connexion with the revision of the college statutes, particularly with regard to the pension scheme]. n. pl., (1873), 8°. 34 pp. G.A. Oxon 8° 1148 (16)

8566. Statutes proposed to be made by the University of Oxford commissioners for University college. April 1881. [Lond.], 1881, fol. 26 pp.
G.A. Oxon c. 8 (42)
— [Another ed.] (Oxf.), 1881, 8°. 40 pp. G.A. Oxon 8° 425 (19) = R.

8567. Statutes of University college. (Univ. of Oxf. and Cambr. act, 1877. Oxford. Thirty six statutes made by the Univ. of Oxf. commissioners, 1881, p. 201-20, 259.) Pp. Eng. 1882 vol. 51

8568. Three statutes made by the master and fellows of University college, on 16th June, 1882, amending statutes made by the University of Oxford commissioners under the provision of 40 & 41 Vict. c. 48. [Lond.], 1882, s. sh. Pp. Eng. 1882 vol. 51

8569. Statute made by . . . University college . . . to amend a statute in relation to the college. Lond., 1888, fol. 3 pp. Pp. Eng. 1888 vol. 78

8570. Statute passed by . . . University college, 30th Nov., 1889, and sealed 13th Dec., 1889, for amending Statute III, section 22. Lond., 1890, s. sh. Pp. Eng. 1890 vol. 56

8571. Statute made by . . . University college, 31st May 1890, and sealed 4th June 1890, amending Statute V. Lond., 1890, s. sh.
Pp. Eng. 1890/91 vol. 61

8572. Statute made by . . . University college, 8th Mar. 1893, to amend Statute III. 24 of the Statutes of the Commissioners in relation to the college, and the Ordinance in relation to the Travelling fellowships of the Foundation of dr. John Radcliffe. Lond., 1893, s. sh.
Pp. Eng. 1893 vol. 68

8573. Statute made by . . . University college, 9th June 1894, amending Statute III. (ii). Lond., 1895, s. sh. Pp. Eng. 1895 vol. 77

8574. Statute made by . . . University college, 28th Oct. 1896, and sealed 11th Nov. 1896, amending Statutes III, 13, and IV, 2. Lond., 1897, s. sh.   Pp. Eng. 1897 vol. 70

8575. Statute made by . . . University college . . . on 20th March 1897, amending Statute V . . . 10 February 1898. Lond., 1898, s. sh.
Pp. Eng. 1898 vol. 70

8576. Statute made by . . . University college, 20th Mar. 1902, amending Statute III. 12. (Fellowships held by professors.) Lond., 1902, s. sh.
Pp. Eng. 1902 vol. 80

8577. Statute made by . . . University college, 26th Nov. 1904, amending Statute III (The fellows). Lond., 1905, s. sh.   Pp. Eng. 1905 vol. 60

8578. Statute made by . . . University college, 11th March 1905, to amend the Ordinance regulating the Radcliffe travelling fellowships. Lond., 1905, s. sh.   Pp. Eng. 1905 vol. 60
— [Another ed.] Lond., 1906, s. sh.   Pp. Eng. 1906 vol. 90

8579. Statute made by . . . University college, 1st Dec. 1906 and sealed 7th Dec. 1906, amending Statute III, clause 11. Lond., 1907, s. sh.
Pp. Eng. 1907 vol. 64

8580. Statute made by . . . University college, 27th Apr. 1912 and sealed on 17th May 1912, amending Statute III (The fellows). Lond., 1912, s. sh.   Pp. Eng. 1912/13 vol. 65

8581. Statute made by . . . University college, 27th Apr. 1912 and sealed 17th May 1912, amending Statute V (The scholars and exhibitioners). Lond., 1912, s. sh.   Pp. Eng. 1912/13 vol. 65

8582. Statute made by . . . University college, 5th Dec. 1914 and 16th Jan. 1915 and sealed 5th Feb. 1915, amending the pension scheme under Statute VI, section 9. Lond., 1915, fol. 3 pp. Pp. Eng. 1914/16 vol. 51

8583. Statute made by . . . University college, 3rd July 1915, amending Statutes I, 3; III, 13; and IV, 2. Lond., 1916, s. sh.
Pp. Eng. 1916 vol. 22

8584. Statutes made for the colleges . . . (University college.) Oxf., 1927, 8°. 85 pp.   G.A. Oxon 4° 759 = R.

Members

GENERAL

8585. USHER, C., A letter [signed C. U.] to a member of the Convocation . . . containing the case of a late fellow elect [C. Usher] of University college [who was refused a fellowship]. Lond., 1699, 4°. 31 pp.
G.A. Oxon 4° 6 (30)

8586. DAVISON, J., A letter to the master and fellows of University college [signed J. Davison. Detailing the circumstances which led up to the

author's expulsion for (1) Neglect of Divine service (2) Non-atten-
dance in the hall during the time of dinner (3) Contemptuous treatment of the Dean]. n. pl., (1772), fol. 9 pp.   Gough Oxf. 103 (22)

8586.5. BEVERIDGE, W. H., 1st baron, Farewell address to undergraduates
of University college, 11 March 1945. (Oxf., 1945), 8°. 7 pp.
G.A. Oxon c. 288 (74)

8587. The betting book [of the Senior common room, 1785-]. (Univ. coll.
record, 1951/52, p. 25–32; 1953/54, p. 20–29.) Per. G.A. Oxon 8° 1086

BIOGRAPHY AND REMINISCENCES

8588. Three old members [college servants 1887-]. (Univ. coll. record,
1953/54, p. 29–34.)   Per. G.A. Oxon 8° 1086

8589. MEDD, P. G., In memoriam, a sermon preached in the chapel of
University college . . . the Sunday after the funeral of the rev. F. C.
Plumptre [with a biogr. note]. n. pl., (1870), 8°. 11 pp.
G.A. Oxon 8° 620 (3)

8590. SADLEIR, M., Michael Ernest Sadler, 1861–1943, a memoir. Lond.,
1949, 8°. 424 pp.   26011 e. 242

8591. JEFFERY, R. W., Dr. Shippen's share in the Cockman–Denison con-
troversy at University college. (Brazen Nose, 1930, vol. 5, p. 79–90.)
Per. G.A. Oxon 4° 282
[See also no. 8546, 47.]

8592. BICKERTON, F., Fred of Oxford, head porter of University college.
Lond., 1953, 8°. 166 pp.   G.A. Oxon 8° 1276

8593. COLLETT, F., From the porter's lodge and buttery. [Reminiscences
of a University college servant, 1907- .] (Amer. Oxon., 1951, vol. 38,
p. 84–87.)   Per. G.A. Oxon 8° 889

8594. PAGET, F. E., A student penitent of 1695. [A true story of Richard
Graham, describing life in University college. The names are altered.]
Lond., 1875, 8°. 192 pp.   251 c. 192

8595. SMITH, E., Memoirs of a highland lady, the autobiogr. of Elizabeth
Grant, afterwards mrs. Smith, ed. by lady Strachey. [Life in Univ.
college in 1810 and 1811, p. 115–34.] Lond., 1898, 8°.   2112 d. 8
— 2nd ed. 1911 (p. 122–44).   2112 e. 76
— [Another ed.] (Albermarle libr.) Lond., 1950, 8°. (p. 91–100).
2112 e. 164

8596. A gentleman commoner at Univ. [Letters of Nicholas Toke, 1721–
23.] (Univ. coll. record, 1959, vol. 3, p. 257–66.) Per. G.A. Oxon 8° 1086

Societies

8597. Martlets society. [Miscellaneous papers. 1919–23.]
MS. Top. Oxon d. 95

8598. University college club. [List of members. May 1804, March 1805.] n. pl., 1804, 05, s. sh.   G.A. Oxon c. 288 (25, 27)

Chapel

8599. PAUL, G. A., The chapel organ. (Univ. coll. record, 1954/55, p. 70–74).   Per. G.A. Oxon 8° 1086

8600. Chapel windows. (Univ. coll. record, 1956, vol. 3, p. 28–32.)   Per. G.A. Oxon 8° 1086

Library

8601. University college. (Hist. MSS. comm., 5th report, pt. 1, 1876, p. 477–79.)   2262 c. 37 = K.

8602. GIBSON, S., The manuscripts of University college. (Univ. coll. record, 1934, p. 13–16.)   Per. G.A. Oxon 8° 1086

8603. HUNT, R. W., The manuscript collection of University college, Oxford: origins and growth. (Bodl. libr. record, 1950, vol. 3, p. 13–34.)   2590 d. Oxf. 1. 41 = R.

See 5654 [Saxl, F., and Meier, H., Catalogue of astrological . . . manuscripts. 1953].

8604. COX, A. D. M., An inscription from the Old library. (Univ. coll. record, 1956, vol. 3, p. 32–34.)   Per. G.A. Oxon 8° 1086

8605. The new room. [Account of the new Library.] (Univ. coll. record, 1956, vol. 3, p. 34–40.)   Per. G.A. Oxon 8° 1086

Plate

8606. SMITH, H. C., A catalogue of the plate of University college. [Typewritten.] n. pl., 1943, fol. 87 pp.   MS. Top. Oxon c. 370

8607. SMITH, H. C., The plate of University college. (Country Life, 1949, vol. 106, p. 42, 43.)   Per. 384 b. 6

Wadham college

General 8608–8623	Members 8642–8650
Administration 8624–8630	Societies and Sport 8651–8658
Statutes 8631–8641	Library 8659–8660

General

8608. [Topographical prints, &c. in the Bodleian.]   G.A. Oxon a. 61

8609. An acte for the confirmacion of Wadham college . . . and the possessions thereof. (21 James i, c. 1, Private.) 1623–4. [Text in Shadwell's Enactments &c. See no. 956.]

8610. [Examination papers. Fellowships, scholarships.] 1835, 52, 53. [Oxf.], 1835–53, 8°.   2626 d. 32

8611. INGRAM, J., Wadham college. (Memorials of Oxford, 1837, vol. 2.
16 pp.)   G.A. Oxon 8° 19

8612. Wadham college. [Commemoration concert programmes. 1877, 78,
82, 83.] (Oxf., 1877–83), 8°.   G.A. Oxon 8° 1113 (36–39)

8613. JACKSON, T. G., Wadham college. Oxf., 1893, 4°. 228 pp.
                                                   G.A. Oxon 4° 152

8614. Wadham college gazette. No. 1–85. [Oxf.], 1897–1929, 8°.
                                          Per. G.A. Oxon 8° 690

8615. WELLS, J., Wadham college. (Oxf. univ. college hist.) Lond., 1898,
8°. 222 pp.   G.A. Oxon 8° 651 (5) = R.

8616. GLASGOW, E., Sketches of Wadham college. (Lond.), [1900], 4°.
3 pp. + 20 pl.   G.A. Oxon 4° 206

8617. GARDINER, R. B., ed., The letters of Dorothy Wadham, 1609–1618.
Lond. &c., 1904, 8°. 89 pp.   G.A. Oxon 8° 712

8618. PAINTIN, H., Brief notes on Wadham college. Repr. from Packers'
Burford almanack. n. pl., [c. 1912], 8°. 8 pp.   G.A. Oxon 8° 874 (15)

8619. DIXEY, F. A., The early connexion of the Royal society with Wadham
college and the University of Oxford [signed F. A. D.]. Oxf., 1912, 8°.
11 pp.   G.A. Oxon 8° 828 (21)

8620. FISHER, H. A. L., The real Oxford movement. [The 'scientific' movement, 1649–59 and the birth of the Royal society.] (Contemp. review,
1929, vol. 136, p. 712–20.)   Per. 3977 d. 58
— [Also publ. in Fisher's Pages from the past. 1939.] 27001 e. 1428

8621. HUSSEY, C., Wadham college. (Country Life 1932, vol. 72, p. 662–
68.)   Per. 384 b. 6

8622. A Wadham anthology of immature verse. (Oxf.), 1941, 8°. 35 pp.
                                                   2805 e. 1081

8623. DRIGGS, N., The foundation of Wadham college. (Oxoniensia, 1956,
vol. 21, p. 61–81.)   Per. G.A. Oxon 4° 658 = R.

Administration

8624. Letters with a few remarks concerning rumours which have lately
been in circulation calculated to prejudice the appointment of the
warden of Wadham college [B. P. Symons] to the vice-chancellorship
[ed. by J. G. i.e. J. Griffiths]. Oxf., 1844, 8°. 16 pp.
                                          G.A. Oxon 8° 179 (3)

8625. An act for enabling a married person to hold and enjoy the office of
warden of Wadham college. (46 G. III, c. 147. L. & P.) Lond., 1806,
fol. 3 pp.   L.L.

8626. Wadham college. Regulations. Revised ed. [A satire.] n. pl., 1879,
8°. 12 pp.   G.A. Oxon 8° 1056 (15)

8627. Notice respecting degrees to be taken from Wadham college. [Oxf., c. 1880], s. sh. G.A. Oxon c. 289 (f. 9)

8628. Wadham college. College charges and regulations. May, 1884. [Oxf.], 1884, 16°. 15 pp. G.A. Oxon 16° 176* (12)

8629. The University of Oxford and Wadham college. Case submitted to referees pursuant to section 9 of the university statute 'concerning college contributions for university purposes'. n. pl., 1886, fol. 7 pp.
G.A. Oxon b. 140 (65a)

8630. Wadham college. Admission. [Oxf., 1888], 8°. 3 pp.
G.A. Oxon c. 289 (f. 9)

Statutes

8631. The statutes of Wadham college, printed by desire of the Commissioners under the act 17 & 18 Vict. c. 81. Lond., 1855, 8°. 49 pp.
G.A. Oxon 8° 419

8632. Oxford university. Ordinances . . . in relation to . . . Wadham [and 10 other] colleges respectively. [Lond.], 1857, fol. 139 pp.
Pp. Eng. 1857 vol. 32

8633. Ordinances and statutes framed or approved by the . . . Commissioners . . . (Wadham college, p. 407–24.) Oxf., 1863, 8°.
Clar. Press 31 a. 63

8634. Statutes proposed to be made . . . for Wadham college. April, 1881. (Oxf.), 1881, 8°. 30 pp. G.A. Oxon 8° 425 (20) = R.

8635. Statutes of Wadham college. (Univ. of Oxf. and Cambr. act, 1877. Oxford. Thirty six statutes made by the Univ. of Oxf. commissioners, 1881, p. 221–34, 260.) Pp. Eng. 1882 vol. 51

8636. Two statutes made by . . . Wadham college, 6th Dec. 1890, and sealed 16th Jan. 1891, amending Statutes III. and VI. Lond., 1891, fol. 3 pp. Pp. Eng. 1890/91 vol. 61

8637. Statute made by . . . Wadham college, 6th Dec. 1895, amending clause 11 of Statute IV. Lond., 1896, s. sh. Pp. Eng. 1896 vol. 65

8638. Statute made by . . . Wadham college, 5th Mar. 1902, amending clause 11 of Statute II. Lond., 1902, s. sh. Pp. Eng. 1902 vol. 80

8639. Statutes made by . . . Wadham college, 6th Feb. 1903, amending clause 1 of Statute VI. Lond., 1903, s. sh. Pp. Eng. 1903 vol. 52

8640. Statute made by . . . Wadham college, 3rd Mar. 1910 and sealed on the 8th day of the same month, amending Statute 6 (2). Lond., 1910, s. sh. Pp. Eng. 1910 vol. 72

8641. Statutes made for the colleges . . . (Wadham college.) Oxf., 1927, 8°. 50 pp. G.A. Oxon 4° 759 = R.

Members

8642. A faithful narrative of the proceedings . . . between the rev. mr. John Swinton and mr. George Baker, both of Wadham college . . . wherein the reasons, that induced mr. Baker to accuse mr. Swinton of sodomitical practices . . . are . . . set down. To which is prefix'd, A particular account of the proceedings against Robert Thistlethwayte warden of Wadham for a sodomitical attempt. Lond., 1739, 8°. 32 pp.

Gough. Oxf. 50 (3)

8643. College-wit sharpen'd: or, The head of a house, with a sting in the tail. [A satire in verse on the proceedings against R. Thistlethwayte, warden of Wadham.] Lond., 1739, 8°. 22 pp. Gough Oxf. 50 (2)

8644. GARDINER, R. B., *ed.*, The registers of Wadham college, from 1613 to (1871). 2 pt. Lond., 1889, 95, 8°. G.A. Oxon 8° 464, 464* = R.

8645. WELLS, J., Religious life in Wadham fifty years ago. Oxf., (1891), 8°. 15 pp. G.A. Oxon 8° 1132 (16)

8646. HENDERSON, P. A. WRIGHT-, An old [1867] Oxford common-room [Wadham]. (Blackwood's mag., 1896, vol. 159, p. 668–79.)

Per. 2705 d. 386

— [Repr.] (Glasgow & Balliol, and other essays, p. 52–81.) Oxf. &c., 1926, 8°. G.A. Oxon 8° 1050

8647. HENDERSON, P. A. WRIGHT-, The life and times of John Wilkins, warden of Wadham college . . . Edinb. &c., 1910, 8°. 131 pp.

G.A. Oxon 8° 785

8648. Wadham college. Roll of service [1914–1918]. Oxf., [1920], 8°. 28 pp.

G.A. Oxon 8° 895 (14)

8649. SMITH, F. E., 1st earl Birkenhead, Wadham college and the law. [Reminiscences &c. of members.] (Points of view, 1922, vol. 1, p. 191–204.) L.L.

8650. Wadham college. Unveiling of the memorial to the members . . . who laid down their lives in the War, 1914 1918. [With list of names.] [Oxf.], 1923, 8°. 7 pp. G.A. Oxon 8° 895 (12)

Societies and sport

8651. Rules of the Wadham college book club. [Oxf.], (1883), 8°. 4 pp.

G.A. Oxon c. 289 (f. 26)

— 1897. G.A. Oxon 8° 900 (15)

— 1905. G.A. Oxon c. 289 (f. 26)

8652. WELLS, J., The annals of a college book club [1822 onwards]. (Cornhill mag., 1913, p. 802–10.) G.A. Oxon c. 289 (f. 14)

8653. Society for the study of social problems. [Miscellaneous papers. 1906, 07.] G.A. Oxon 4° 603

8654. Manual of the Wadham college guild of S. Andrew. Oxf., 1887, 16°. 16 pp. G.A. Oxon 16° 28

8655. [Appeal, dated October 31, 1885, for money to pay a long-standing debt to Salter's, and to negotiate through that firm the hire of the barge vacated by Corpus Christi boat club.] [Oxf.], (1855), s. sh.
G.A. Oxon c. 289 (f. 32)

8656. [Announcement, dated March 10, 1886, of the payment of the boat club's debt to Salter's, and the hiring of the barge: also an account of subscriptions received.] [Oxf.], (1886), 4°. 3 pp. G.A. Oxon c. 289 (f. 33)

8657. [Appeal, dated December 14, 1896, for subscriptions towards the purchase of a college barge.] [Oxf.], (1896), s. sh.
G.A. Oxon c. 289 (f. 33)

8658. Proposal to acquire a permanent [sports] ground for Wadham college. [Oxf., c. 1907], s. sh.   G.A. Oxon c. 289 (f. 34)

Library

8659. Wadham college. (Hist. MSS. comm., 5th report, pt. 1, 1876, p. 479–81.)   2262 c. 37 = K.

8660. WHEELER, H. A., A short catalogue of books printed in England and English books printed abroad before 1641 in the library of Wadham college. Lond. &c., 1929, 8°. 102 pp.   2590 e. Oxf. 15. 4

Worcester college

General 8661–8677
Administration 8678–8681
Statutes 8682–8691
Finance and Property 8692–8693

Members 8694–8698
Societies and Sport 8699–8707
Chapel 8708–8712
Library 8713–8719

General

8661. [Topographical prints, &c. in the Bodleian.]   G.A. Oxon a. 61

8662. WOODROFFE, B., The case of Worcester-colledge, or Glocester-hall, changed into Worcester-colledge [by B. Woodroffe]. n. pl., [1702], s. sh.   Worc. coll.
— [Another ed., entitled] The case of Worcester colledge as it was presented to the members of the House of commons. 1702, 4°. 4 pp.

8663. BARON, J., The case of Glocester hall, in Oxford, rectifying the false stating thereof by doctor Woodroffe [by J. Baron]. [Oxf.? 1702], 4°.
57 pp.   C 8. 45 (1) Linc.

8664. WOODROFFE, B., A letter from a member of the House of commons, in answer to a letter from a member of the University enquiring, how the Bill for settling sir Thomas Cookes's charity of 10,000 l. for the erecting and endowing of Worcester colledge in Oxford, came to be rejected in their House [by B. Woodroffe]. 1702, 4°. 8 pp.

8665. INGRAM, J., Worcester college. (Memorials of Oxford, 1837, vol. 2.
16 pp.)   G.A. Oxon 8° 19

8666. LANDON, J. T. B., Worcester gaudy, 1858, by A. Latefellow. [In verse.] n. pl., (1858), 4°. 3 pp. G.A. Oxon 4° 13 (5)

8667. Worcester college gaudy, June 14, 1883. [Names of provost and fellows, annals of the college, 1283–1877, and list of guests at the sexcentenary.] [Oxf., Daniel press, 1883], 4°. 4 pp. G.A. Oxon 4° 626

8668. DANIEL, C. H. O., Worcester college. (Trans., Bristol and Glouc. archaeol. soc., 1891/92, vol. 16, p. 103–10.) Per. G.A. Glouc. 8° 94 = R.

8669. DANIEL, C. H. O., [List of important dates in the development of the college, 1175–1877.] (Proc., Oxf. architect. and hist. soc., 1894, N.S., vol. 6, p. 37.) Per. G.A. Oxon 8° 498 = R.

8670. DANIEL, C. H., and BARKER, W. R., Worcester college. (Univ. of Oxf. coll. hist.) Lond., 1900, 8°. 268 pp. G.A. Oxon 8° 651 (14) = R.

8671. In laudationem benefactorum, Preces Vespertinæ coll. Vigorn. [Oxf., C. Daniel], 1906, 4°. [12 pp.]. G.A. Oxon 4° 246

8672. Worcester college v. the Canal company [concerning the drainage of the college grounds and playing-field]. (Oxf. mag., 1913, vol. 31, p. 148, 49.) Per. G.A. Oxon 4° 141

8673. OSWALD, A., Worcester college. (Country Life, 1935, vol. 77, p. 426–31.) Per. 384 b. 6

8674. Worcester college. Residential block. (Architect's journ., 1940, vol. 91, p. 84, 85.) N. 1863 c. 12

8675. LYS, F. J., Worcester college, 1882–1943, and some account of a stewardship. Oxf., 1944, 8°. 60 pp. Worc. coll.

8676. DEVEREUX, R. A., and GRIFFITHS, D. N., Worcester college. [Guide by R. A. Devereux and D. N. Griffiths.] (Oxf. univ. archaeol. soc.) Oxf., 1951, 4°. 30 pp. G.A. Oxon 4° 677 (3)

8677. A reply to the toast of the college, June 29, 1957. [Worcester. By C. H. Wilkinson.] [Oxf., 1957], 8°. [12 pp.]. G.A. Oxon 4° 779

8677.4. CAMPBELL, J., Worcester college and the University election of 1865. (Oxf. mag., 1961, N.S., vol. 2, p. 62, 63.) Per. G.A. Oxon 4° 141

Administration

8678. Worcester college kitchen. Tariff [with prices]. 1889. (Oxf., 1889), s. sh. G.A. Oxon c. 290 (f. 9)

8679. Worcester college. Electric lighting. [Regulations and charges. Signed C. H. Daniel, bursar.] [Oxf., c. 1895], s. sh.
G.A. Oxon 4° 526 (6)

8680. Worcester college. Admission. [Oxf., c. 1895], 8°. 4 pp.
G.A. Oxon 4° 526 (1)

8681. Worcester college. [Report.] 1899/1900–1922/23. (Oxf.), 1900–23, 8°. [The Bodleian set is imperfect.] G.A. Oxon 8° 510*

Statutes

8682. Statutes of the colleges . . . (Worcester college.) Oxf. &c., 1853, 8ᶜ.
47 pp.   G.A. Oxon 8° 26 = R.

8683. Oxford university. Ordinances . . . in relation to . . . Worcester [and
10 other] colleges respectively. [Lond.], 1857, fol. 139 pp.
Pp. Eng. 1857 vol. 32

8684. Statutes and ordinances framed or approved by the . . . Commissioners . . . (Worcester college, p. 453–72.) Oxf., 1863, 8°.
Clar. Press 31 a. 63

8685. Statutes proposed to be made by the University of Oxford commis-
sioners for Worcester college. May 1881. [Lond.], 1881, fol. 15 pp.
G.A. Oxon c. 8 (52)
— [Another ed.] (Oxf.), 1881, 8°. 24 pp. G.A. Oxon 8° 425 (21) = R.

8686. Statutes of Worcester college. (Univ. of Oxf. and Cambr. act, 1877.
Oxford. Thirty six statutes made by the Univ. of Oxf. commissioners, 1881, p. 234–44, 261.)   Pp. Eng. 1882 vol. 51

8687. A statute made by . . . Worcester college, 22nd Feb. 1899 and 8th
Mar. 1899, amending Statute III.10. 23 Oct., 1899. Lond., 1899, s. sh.
Pp. Eng. 1899 vol. 76
— [Another ed.] 30 Jan., 1900. Lond., 1900, s. sh.
Pp. Eng. 1900 vol. 66

8688. Statute made by . . . Worcester college, 24th Jan. 1900, amending
Statute III. 16. Lond., 1900, s. sh.   Pp. Eng. 1900 vol. 66

8689. Statutes made by . . . Worcester college, 4th Mar. 1904, amending
Statutes II, III, IV, V, VI, and VII. Lond., 1904, fol. 4 pp.
Pp. Eng. 1904 vol. 75

8690. Statute made by . . . Worcester college . . . on the 30th November,
1910, and sealed on the 9th December, 1910, amending certain of the
statutes. 25 April 1911. Lond., 1911, fol. 4 pp. Pp. Eng. 1911 vol. 59

8691. Statutes made for the colleges . . . (Worcester college.) Oxf., 1927,
8°. 45 pp.   G.A. Oxon 4° 759 = R.

Finance and property

8692. A true copy of the last will and testament of George Clarke . . . To
which are annex'd the several codicils subsequent thereto, containing
an account . . . of his particular benefactions to Worcester and All
Souls colleges. Lond., 1737, 8°. 60 pp.   Gough Oxf. 60 (13)

8693. An act for sale of certain leasehold estates, late of Sarah Eaton, deceased, and by her devised to the provost, fellows and scholars of
Worcester college . . . (18 G. II, c. 19, Private.) 1744–5.
— 15 G. III, c. 94, Private.
[Précis of both acts in Shadwell's Enactments &c. See no. 956.]

Members

See 8667 [Worcester college gaudy. Names of provosts and fellows. 1883].

8694. MADAN, F., The Daniel press at Frome and Oxford. (Trans., Bibliogr. soc. The Library, 1920, ser. 4, vol. 1, p. 65–68.)
Per. 258 e. 258 = A.

8695. The Daniel press. Memorials of C. H. O. Daniel [by sir H. Warren and others] with a bibliography of the press, 1845–1919 [by F. Madan]. Oxf., Daniel press in the Bodleian Library, 1921, 4°. 198 pp.+16 plates. 25844 d. 17
— Addenda & corrigenda, by F. Madan. Oxf., 1922, 4°. 12 pp.
25844 d. 17

8696. BURGON, J. W., Richard Greswell, the faithful steward. 1800–1881. (Lives of twelve good men, 1888, vol. 2, p. 94–122.) 2106 e. 27
— New ed. 1891. 11126 d. 20

8697. Worcester sauce. [Satirical verses, signed Shake-spear, on W. H. Hadow.] n. pl., (1898), 8°. 3 pp. G.A. Oxon c. 290 (f. 15)

8698. MASTERMAN, J. C., An eighteenth-century provost [William Sheffield]. (Bits and pieces, 1961, p. 15–24.) 27001 e. 2204

8698.2. C. H. Wilkinson, 1888–1960. Oxf., 1965, 4°. 64 pp.
G.A. Oxon 4° 808

Societies and sport

8699. Statement of accounts . . . 1883/4 (84, 85, 88, 88/9, 89/90, 91) by the treasurer of the Worcester college amalgamated clubs. [Oxf.], 1884–91, s. sh. G.A. Oxon c. 290 (f. 36–39)

8700. Worcester college boat club. Rules. 1863, 1866. Oxf., 1863, 66, 8°.
G.A. Oxon 8° 1122 (2)

8701. Worcester college cricket club. Rules, 1863, 1864. Oxf., 1863, 64, 8°.
G.A. Oxon 8° 1122

8702. Worcester college debating society. Rules. Oxf., 1893, 8°. 8 pp.
G.A. Oxon 8° 1122 (1)

8703. Worcester college fives club. Rules. 1869, 1872. Oxf., 1869, 72, 8°.
G.A. Oxon 8° 1122

8704. Worcester college literary society. [*afterw.*] De Quincey society. (Rules, members.) (Oxf.), 1889, 16°. 6 pp. G.A. Oxon 16° 195 (7)
— Revised. (Oxf.), 1894, 16°. 7 pp. G.A. Oxon 16° 195 (8)

8705. Worcester college musical society. [Concert programmes. 1863–1894.) G.A. Oxon 8° 1122

8706. Worcester college, February 1895. [Appeal for the conversion of the provost's meadow into a cricket-ground.] [Oxf.], (1895), s. sh.
G.A. Oxon 4° 526 (12)

8707. Worcester college. New cricket field and pavilion. February, 1900.
[*With*] List of subscriptions. [Oxf.], (1900), 8°. 4 pp.
G.A. Oxon c. 290 (f. 35)
— Further report. June, 1900.   G.A. Oxon c. 290 (f. 35)

Chapel

8708. Proposed restoration of the chapel of Worcester college, Oxford.
[Appeal for funds, signed by the provost, R. L. Cotton.] [Oxf., 1864],
4°. 3 pp.   G.A. Oxon b. 30

See 7056 [Worcester college chapel. 1866].

8709. Worcester college chapel. [Description of the re-styling.] n. pl.,
[*c.* 1870], 16°. 8 pp.   G.A. Oxon 4° 526 (4)

8710. COLLIS, J. D., Mr. Burges, St. Paul's, and Worcester college [the re-
styling of the college chapel]. Repr. from the Guardian. n. pl., (1872),
s. sh.   G.A. Oxon c. 290 (f. 71)

8711. Worcester college. [Appeal, December 1907, for money to pay for
repairs to damage caused when a portion of the chapel cornice fell upon
the roof of the Old buildings.] [Oxf.], 1907, s. sh.
G.A. Oxon c. 290 (f. 5)
— [Another appeal. 30 June 1910.]   G.A. Oxon c. 290 (f. 4)

8712. CAMBRIDGE, W. A. PICKARD-, Twenty-six years (1919–1945) of
music in Worcester college chapel. [Compiled by W. A. Pickard-
Cambridge.] (Oxf., 1945), 8°.   17402 e. 860

Library

8713. Worcester college. (Hist. MSS. comm., 2nd report, 1871, p. 143.)
2262 c. 7 = K.

8714. Notes from a catalogue of pamphlets in Worcester college library
[by C. H. O. Daniel]. Oxon., typis Henrici Daniel, 1874, 12°. 79 pp.
Arch. C f. 1
— [Pt. 2]. [1875?]. 20 pp.   Don. f. 184

8715. Worcester college library. [Rules.] [Oxf.], 1878, s. sh.
G.A. Oxon c. 290 (f. 1)

8716. A catalogue of the books relating to classical archaeology and ancient
history in the library of Worcester college. [With Addenda.] Oxf.,
1878–[80], 8°. 77+12+8 pp.   2590 e. Oxf. 15. 1 = R.

8717. WILKINSON, C. H., Worcester college library. (Proc. and papers,
Oxf. bibliogr. soc., 1927, vol. 1, p. 263–320.)   Soc. 258 d. 176 = A.

8718. A handlist of English plays and masques printed before 1750 in the
library of Worcester college. [*With*] Plays added up to March, 1948.
Oxf., 1929, (48), 8°. 27+7 pp.   2590 e. Oxf. 15. 2 = R.

8719. Principal accessions, 1st October, 1959–30 September, 1960. [Reprod. from typewriting.] [Oxf.], (1960), 8°. 4 leaves.   2590 d. Oxf. 15. 1

8719.5. COLVIN, H. M., A catalogue of architectural drawings of the 18th and 19th centuries in the library of Worcester college. Oxf., 1964, 8°. 69 pp.+130 pl.   2590 e. Oxf. 15. 5 = R.

COLLEGES FOR WOMEN

General

See also 3248 &c. Teaching: Women, admission of.

8720. Report of the Delegacy for women students. 1915, 16. [Oxf.], 1916, 17, 8°.   G.A. Oxon c. 249 (39, 335)

8721. Oxford women's colleges fund. Subscription list, January 1921 to July 1923. n. pl., [1923], 8°. 24 pp.   G.A. Oxon 8° 1001 (19)

8722. MOBERLY, W. H., The Oxford women's colleges. (Contemp. review, 1921, vol. 119, p. 385–88.)   Per. 3977 d. 58

8723. The Heritage, publ. on behalf of Lady Margaret hall, Somerville college, St. Hugh's college, St. Hilda's hall. No. 2–5. Oxf., 1922, 23, 4°.   G.A. Oxon 4° 435

8723.5. SUTHERLAND, L. S., The new status of women. [Colleges given full status.] (Oxford, 1960, vol. 16, p. 72–76.)   Per. G.A. Oxon 8° 1141

8724. [Miscellaneous papers concerning women students.]   G.A. Oxon 4° 410

Home students

See 8746 &c. St. Anne's college.

Lady Margaret hall

8725. Lady Margaret hall. [Miscellaneous papers. 1878–1931.]   G.A. Oxon 4° 204

8726. [*Begin.*] An 'Association for promoting the higher education of women in Oxford' has been formed . . . [Appeal for funds to establish an academical house for students, and list of subscribers.] [Oxf., 1878], 8°. 4 pp.   G.A. Oxon 4° 204 (1)
— [Another ed. 1878.]   G.A. Oxon 4° 204 (2)
— [Another ed. 1878.]   G.A. Oxon 4° 204 (3)

8727. Proposed hall for ladies in Oxford. [Explanation and appeal.] December 1878. [Oxf.], (1878), s. sh.   G.A. Oxon 4° 204

8728. Ladies' hall, Oxford. [Regulations.] February 1879. [Oxf.], (1879), s. sh.   G.A. Oxon 4° 204
— [Another ed.] February 1879.   G.A. Oxon 4° 204

8729. Lady Margaret hall. [History and regulations.] [Oxf., *c.* 1880], s. sh.   G.A. Oxon 4° 204

8730. Lady Margaret hall. Report. 1882/3– . [Oxf.], (1883–), 8°.
                                            G.A. Oxon 8° 654

8731. The Daisy. No. 1– . (Oxf.), 1890– , 4°.
[Bodley has no. 2, 3, 5, 7, 9: Per. G.A. Oxon 4° 462.]

8732. MEADE, L. T., English girls and their colleges. VI. Lady Margaret hall and St. Hugh's hall. (Lady's pictorial, Jan. 9, 1892, p. 48, 49.)
                                            G.A. Oxon 4° 204

8733. Lady Margaret hall. Declaration of trust. n. pl., [1893], 8°. 10 pp.
                                            G.A. Oxon 8° 1033 (10)

8733.8. WORDSWORTH, E., Glimpses of the past [Lady Margaret Hall, 1879 onwards]. Lond. &c., 1912, 8°. 218 pp.   211 d. 122
— New ed. 1913.   211 e. 384

8734. The Brown book, Lady Margaret hall chronicle [*afterw.*] Old students' report. (Winchester), 1914– , 8°.   G.A. Oxon 8° 1080

8735. Lady Margaret hall. Register. 1879–1920. (Oxf.), 1923, 8°. 88 pp.
                                            G.A. Oxon 8° 654*

8736. Dedication of chapel, October 14th, 1922. [Order of service.] [Oxf.], 1922, 8°. 4 pp.   G.A. Oxon 4° 204

8737. Order of service at the dedication of the chapel . . . 14 January 1933. [Oxf.], 1933, 8°. 16 pp.   G.A. Oxon 4° 204

8738. Lady Margaret hall, a short history [ed. by G. Bailey]. Lond., 1923, 8°. 144 pp.   G.A. Oxon 8° 1022

8739. The new block at Lady Margaret hall. (Architects' journ., 1926, vol. 64, p. 233–36.)   N. 1863 c. 12

8740. Lady Margaret hall. Charter and statutes. Oxf., 1926, 8°. 20 pp.
                                            G.A. Oxon 8° 1101 (3)

8741. Statutes made for the colleges . . . (Lady Margaret hall.) Oxf., 1927, 8°. 20 pp.   G.A. Oxon 4° 759 = R.

8742. Abstract of accounts for year ended July 31, 1929 (1931). [Oxf.], 1929, 31, fol.   G.A. Oxon 4° 204

8743. The chapel and new buildings at Lady Margaret hall. (Architect, 1933, vol. 133, p. 129–34.)   N. 1731 c. 16

8744. LODGE, E. C., Terms and vacations [at Lady Margaret hall, 1890–1921, p. 41–196] ed. by J. Spens. Lond. &c., 1938, 8°. 250 pp.
                                            2628 d. 23

8744.8. PECK, W., A little learning, or, A Victorian childhood. [Lady Margaret hall at beginning of 20th century, p. 153–84.] Lond., 1952, 8°. 2569 e. 912

See 3941 [Wright, E. M., My life in Oxford. 1956].

8745. SUTHERLAND, L. S., Lady Margaret hall. (Amer. Oxonian, 1960, vol. 47, p. 70–75.) Per. G.A. Oxon 8° 889

St. Anne's college

8746. Oxford home students. [Miscellaneous papers. 1912– .] G.A. Oxon 4° 532

8747. Association for the education of women, Oxford. Home students [afterw.] Society of Oxford home students. General report, 1879–1895 and first annual report, 1895/6 (–1925). [Oxf.], 1896–1925, 8°. G.A. Oxon 8° 821

See 5220 [The Ship. 1910].

8748. Society of Oxford home-students. [Appeal for endowment fund which would allow payment of a part of the principal's salary to be made.] May 1912. [Oxf.], 1912, s. sh. G.A. Oxon 4° 532

8749. Society of Oxford home-students. [Regulations.] September 1912. [Oxf.], 1912, s. sh. G.A. Oxon 4° 532

8750. Society of home-students. (General information.) [Oxf., 192—], 8°. 4 pp. G.A. Oxon 4° 532

8751. Women at Oxford. Position of home-students. [Principal's letter to The Times, 12 March 1923, with more detailed explanation by the secretary; an appeal for funds.] [Oxf., 1923], 8°. 3 pp. G.A. Oxon 4° 532

8752. Society of Oxford home-students. Members on the books, Hilary term, 1923. [Oxf.], 1923, 8°. 20 pp. G.A. Oxon 4° 532

8753. The Society of Oxford home-students, retrospects and recollections, 1879–1921, ed. by R. F. Butler, M. H. Prichard.
— Vol. 2 [entitled] A history of Saint Anne's society, formerly the Society of Oxford home-students, 1921–1946, by R. F. Butler. [With] Suppl. 1946–53. Oxf., (1930), 49, 57, 8°. G.A. Oxon 8° 1074

8754. Members of the Society of Oxford home-students old students' association. (Oxf.), [1942], 8°. 41 pp. G.A. Oxon 8° 1422

8755. OSWALD, A. S., St. Anne's college [signed A. S. O.]. (Country Life, 1952, vol. III, p. 1746.) Per. 384 b. 6

8756. New dining hall for St. Anne's college. (Builder, 15 Apr. 1960, p. 736–39.) N. 1863 c. 1

8757. OGILVIE, LADY M. E., St. Anne's college. (Amer. Oxonian, 1961, vol. 48, p. 118–22.) Per. G.A. Oxon 8° 889

St. Hilda's college

8758. St. Hilda's hall [afterw.] college. Report. 1900/01– . n. pl., 1901– , 8°.
G.A. Oxon 8° 1158

8759. St. Hilda's [Miscellaneous papers. 1911– .]   G.A. Oxon 4° 531

8760. Saint Hilda's hall, extension fund. [Appeal.] (Lond.), [1921], 4°.
8 pp.   G.A. Oxon 4° 531

8761. St. Hilda's hall [afterw.] Collegium S. Hildae. Chronicle of the Old
students' association [afterw.] of the Association of senior members.
1920/21–35/36. n. pl., 1921–36, 8°.   G.A. Oxon 8° 1159

8762. Statutes made for the colleges . . . (St. Hilda's college.) Oxf., 1927,
8°. 21 pp.   G.A. Oxon 4° 759 = R.

8763. Elizabeth Levett memorial fund. [Appeal for a fellowship for
historical studies.] [Oxf., 1933], 8°. 4 pp.   G.A. Oxon 4° 531

8764. St. Hilda's college. Register of former students. 1933, 34. Oxf., 1933,
34, 8°.   G.A. Oxon 8° 1160

8765. BRINDLEY, B., Porci ante Margaritam, or, The muse's offering, a
masque performed at Saint Hilda's college, 3 June, 1954 before . . .
princess Margaret, written by B. Brindley, with Latin verses by
C. Leach. Oxf., (1954), 8°. 14 pp.   M. adds. 110 e. 2469
— [Programme]. Oxf., New Bodleian libr., (1954), fol.
M. adds. 110 d. 184

8766. DENEKE, H., Grace Hadow. Lond., 1946, 8°. 225 pp.   26011 e. 221

8767. MAJOR, K., St. Hilda's college. (Amer. Oxonian, 1961, vol. 48, p. 57–
60.)   Per. G.A. Oxon 8° 889

St. Hugh's college

See 8732 [Meade, L. T., Lady Margaret hall and St. Hugh's hall. 1892].

8768. St. Hugh's college. [Miscellaneous papers. 1901–.] G.A. Oxon 4° 530

8769. St. Hugh's college. [Begin.] The enclosed short account . . . [Appeal
for money to purchase a site known as The Mount, Banbury road. The
account, which is a separate sheet, is dated January 18th.] [Oxf.],
(1913), 2 sheets.   G.A. Oxon 4° 530

8770. St. Hugh's college. January 1921. [Statement of the position of St.
Hugh's on the occasion of the appeal on behalf of the women's colleges.]
[Oxf.], (1921), 4°. 3 pp.   G.A. Oxon 4° 530

8771. St. Hugh's college. [Report on alleged personal friction among
members of the staff.] (Oxf. mag., 1924, vol. 42, p. 347–50, 372, 73.)
Per. G.A. Oxon 4° 141

8772. Statutes made for the colleges . . . (St. Hugh's college.) Oxf., 1927, 8°. 23 pp. G.A. Oxon 4° 759 = R.

8773. PROCTOR, E. E. S., St. Hugh's college. (Amer. Oxonian, 1961, vol. 48, p. 10–15.) Per. G.A. Oxon 8° 889

Society of Oxford home-students

See 8746 &c. St. Anne's college.

Somerville college

8774. [Miscellaneous papers. 1879–1929.] G.A. Oxon c. 101

8775. Somerville Report (calendar and suppl.) 1883/84– . (Oxf., 1884–), 8°. G.A. Oxon 8° 684

8776. Somerville college. Calendar. 1901/02, 04/05, 05/06. [Afterw. publ. with Report.] Oxf., 1902–06, 8°. G.A. Oxon 8° 684***

8777. Somerville students' assoc. First(–36th) report and Oxford letter. [Oxf.], 1888–1923, 8°.[The Bodleian set is imperf. G.A. Oxon 8° 859.]

8778. Somerville college. Financial report. 1891/92–1923. [Oxf.], 1892–1923, 8°. [The Bodleian set is imperf. G.A. Oxon 8° 664*.]

8779. Somerville college. Memorandum and articles of association. Lond., [1896], fol. 13 pp. G.A. Oxon c. 101 (1)

8780. BYRNE, M. ST. CLARE and MANSFIELD, C. H., Somerville college, 1879–1921. Oxf., [1922], 8°. 99 pp. G.A. Oxon 8° 1005

8781. Charter and statutes. Draft. (Oxf.), [1925], 8°. 24 pp. G.A. Oxon 8° 1033 (12)

8782. Statutes made for the colleges . . . (Somerville college.) Oxf., 1927, 8°. 27 pp. G.A. Oxon 4° 759 = R.

8783. Somerville college. Association of senior members. 4th(–25th) annual suppl. to the report of the college. [Afterw. publ. with the Report, no. 8775.] [Oxf.], 1929–46, 8°. G.A. Oxon 8° 664**

8784. Somerville college. New East buildings. Oxf., 1934, 8°. 4 pp. G.A. Oxon 8° 1132 (14)

8785. FRY, M., Gilbert Murray and Somerville. (Essays in honour of Gilbert Murray, 1936, p. 49–61.) 3977 e. 337

8785.4. VAUGHAN, J., Building at Somerville. (Oxf. mag., 1963, N.S., vol. 3, p. 218, 19.) Per. G.A. Oxon 4° 141

8786. Somerville college lawn tennis club. Rules and regulations. n. pl., [c. 1900], 8°. 7 pp. G.A. Oxon 8° 1113 (1)

PRIVATE HALLS

Charsley's hall

8787. CHASE, D. P., [*Begin.*] In January 1891 I was informed by mr. Charsley . . . [Letter allowing former members of Charsley's hall to withdraw their application for admission to St. Mary hall now that C. A. Marcon intends to succeed Charsley.] [Oxf.], 1891, s. sh.
G.A. Oxon c. 283 (30)

Pope's hall

8788. Report [for the use of the Hebdomadal council and Delegates of lodging houses] of the Delegates of lodging houses . . . on the houses nos. 11 and 13 St. Giles', proposed to be opened as a private hall, with an ædes annexæ thereto, by mr. John O'Fallon Pope. [Oxf.], 1901, s. sh.
G.A. Oxon c. 104 (133)

Turrell hall

8789. [*Begin.*] Dear mr. vice-chancellor, I wish to address you on the constitution of private halls . . . [3 letters signed H. J. Turrell, March 7th, 1887.] [Oxf.], (1887), s. sh.
G.A. Oxon 4° 100 (1)

8790. Copy of a letter from the vice-chancellor without date, but received at the end of April, 1887. [Oxf., 1887], s. sh.
G.A. Oxon 4° 100 (2)

8791. [*Begin.*] Dear mr. vice-chancellor, You appear to have mistaken . . . [An answer, signed H. J. Turrell, May 12th, 1887, to the vice-chancellor's letter.] [Oxf.], (1887), 4°. 2 sheets.
G.A. Oxon 4° 100 (3)

8792. [*Begin.*] Mr. vice-chancellor, I addressed you . . . [signed H. J. Turrell, 3 October 1887]. [Oxf.], (1887), 4°. 4 pp.
G.A. Oxon 4° 100 (4)

8793. [*Begin.*] Mr. vice-chancellor, I have addressed you twice . . . [A letter, signed H. J. Turrell, 22 Oct. 1887.] [Oxf.], (1887), 4°. 3 pp.
G.A. Oxon 4° 100 (5)

8794. [*Begin.*] I beg to thank you for reporting to me the decision of the University council [the Bodleian shelfmark of this letter: G.A. Oxon 4° 100 (6)]. [A letter, signed H. J. Turrell, 2 Nov. 1887.] [Oxf.], (1887), 4°. 4 pp.
G.A. Oxon 4° 100 (7)

8795. [*Begin.*] I have not received . . . [A letter, signed H. J. Turrell, 3 Dec. 1887.] [Oxf.], (1887), 4°. 2 sheets.
G.A. Oxon 4° 100 (8)

8796. [*Begin.*] It is impossible . . . [Letter from the vice-chancellor, 6 Dec. 1887, *and* a reply by H. J. Turrell, dated 10 Dec. 1887.] [Oxf.], (1887), 4°. 4 pp.
G.A. Oxon 4° 100 (9)

8797. Letter [11 Dec., 1887] from sir W. Anson with references to private halls [*and*] Reply to the warden of All Souls [by H. J. Turrell, 15 May 1889]. [Oxf., 1889], 4°. 3 pp.
G.A. Oxon 4° 255

8798. [*Begin.*] My lord, In 1880 I obtained a license . . . [A letter, signed H. J. Turrell, 22 Dec. 1887, to the Marquis of Salisbury.] [Oxf.], (1887), 4°. 4 pp.   G.A. Oxon 4° 100 (11)

8799. To the vice-chancellor and members of the University council. [A letter, signed H. J. Turrell, 2 May 1889.] [Oxf.], (1889), 4°. 4 pp.
                                                         G.A. Oxon 4° 100 (12)

8800. [*Begin.*] Sir, I cannot help expressing my surprise . . . [Exchange of letters between W. R. Anson and H. J. Turrell about private halls, dated severally May 20, 21 and 22.] [Oxf., 1889], 4°. 3 pp.
                                                         G.A. Oxon 4° 255

8801. Letter from sir William Markby to the master of Turrell's hall, May 31st, 1889 [*and*] Reply of the master . . . to the . . . Hebdomadal council, October 18th, 1889. [Oxf., 1889], 4°. 4 pp.   G.A. Oxon 4° 255

8802. TURRELL, H. J., Reply [dated June 12th, 1889] of the master of Turrell's hall to the warden of All Souls' [answering the latter's several letters in no. 8800]. [Oxf.], (1889), 4°. 8 pp.   G.A. Oxon 4° 255

8803. To the rev. the vice-chancellor, Hertford college. [A letter, signed H. J. Turrell, 8 Oct. 1890.] [Oxf.], (1890), 4°. 3 pp.
                                                         G.A. Oxon 4° 100 (16)

8804. TURRELL, H. J., [*Begin.*] Dear mr. vice-chancellor, My purpose in this letter . . . [Further exposition of his case as regards private halls.] April 13th. [Oxf.], (1891), 4°. 3 pp.   G.A. Oxon 4° 255

8805. To the president of the Hebdomadal council, the president of St. John's college, and other members of the council. [A letter, signed H. J. Turrell, 8 Feb. 1894.] [Oxf.], (1894), s. sh. G.A. Oxon 4° 100 (18)

8806. To the provost of Queen's college. [A letter, signed H. J. Turrell, 22 June 1894.] [Oxf.], (1894), s. sh.   G.A. Oxon 4° 100 (19)

8807. To the president and members of the Hebdomadal council. [A letter, signed H. J. Turrell, 20 Nov. 1894.] [Oxf.], (1894), s. sh.
                                                         G.A. Oxon 4° 100 (20)

8808. To the vice-chancellor and the members of the council. [A letter, signed H. J. Turrell, 17 Jan. 1895.] [Oxf.], (1895), s. sh.
                                                         G.A. Oxon 4° 100 (21)

8809. To the Hebdomadal council and the . . . vice-chancellor . . . and the dean of Durham. [A letter, signed H. J. Turrell, 24 Sept. 1895.] [Oxf.], (1895), s. sh.   G.A. Oxon 4° 100 (22)

8810. The vice-chancellor, Queen's college. [A letter, signed H. J. Turrell, 15 Nov. 1895.] [Oxf.], (1895), s. sh. G.A. Oxon 4° 100 (23)

8811. To the reverend the vice-chancellor . . . [A letter, signed H. J. Turrell, 19 May 1896.] [Oxf.], (1896), s. sh. G.A. Oxon 4° 100 (24)

8812. To the Hebdomadal council and the . . . vice-chancellor. [A letter, signed H. J. Turrell, undated.] [Oxf., 1896], s. sh.
                                                         G.A. Oxon 4° 100 (25)

ASSOCIATED INSTITUTIONS

Catholic workers' college

See 8829, Plater College.

Manchester college

8813. [A volume of miscellaneous papers, 1890– .]   G.A. Oxon b. 136

8814. The report of Manchester new college [afterw.] Manchester college. 104th annual meeting, 1890– . [The college moved to Oxford in 1889.] n. pl., 1890– , 4°.   Per. G.A. Oxon 4° 166; 457

8815. Manchester college. 132nd(–142nd) annual meeting. Committee's address and treasurer's accounts. [Also publ. in the Report, no. 7705.] n. pl., 1918–28, 4°.   Per. G.A. Oxon 4° 456

8816. Manchester new college. Revised report of proceedings and addresses on the occasion of fixing and unveiling the stone of dedication of the college buildings, 20th Oct. 1891. Lond. &c., 1891, 4°. 28 pp.
G.A. Oxon 4° 147 (1)

8817. Manchester college, Oxford. Address to the students. [1891–1928. Imperf.] Manchester, 1891–1928, 8°.   G.A. Oxon 8° 536

8818. Manchester college. Opening proceedings, Oct. 18, 19, 1893. Handbook for the use of visitors. Oxf., (1893), 8°. 34 pp. G.A. Oxon 16° 41

8819. DRUMMOND, J., Manchester college: its origin and principles, an address . . . on the opening of the new buildings, Oct. 19, 1893. Manch. &c., 1893, 4°. 26 pp.   G.A. Oxon 4° 147 (2)

8820. Manchester college. List of preachers. [1893–c.1920.] [Oxf., 1893– 1920], s. sh.   G.A. Oxon 4° 604

8821. Manchester college. Proceedings and addresses on the occasion of the opening of the college buildings and dedication of the chapel, October 18–19, 1893. Lond. &c., 1894, 4°. 163 pp. G.A. Oxon 4° 174

8822. Martineau club. [Miscellaneous papers. 1896–1908.]
G.A. Oxon 4° 604

8823. Manchester college. Historical statement issued at a meeting called . . . to consider a resolution affirming the Non-conformist character of the institution. n. pl., 1904, 8°. 36 pp.   G.A. Oxon 8° 715 (7)

8824. JACKS, L. P., Manchester college, Oxford. What does Manchester college mean by religion? An address. Manch., 1915, 8°. 16 pp.
26332 e. 35 (8)

8825. Manchester college, Oxford. Address of the principal to the Trustees . . . in reply to a resolution [expressing dissatisfaction at the low standard of college work and urging a re-institution of graduated courses of work] moved at the annual meeting, June 21st, 1923, by A. S. Hurn. Manchester, 1923, 8°. 7 pp.   G.A. Oxon 8° 1000 (12)

8826. DAVIS, V. D., A history of Manchester college, from its foundation in Manchester to its establishment in Oxford. Lond., 1932, 8°. 216 pp.
26332 e. 80

8827. Manchester college, Oxford. Proceedings at the 150th anniversary, June 21st, 22nd and 23rd, 1936. Manch., 1936, 8°. 35 pp. Manch. Coll.

8828. GARRARD, L. A., Manchester college. (Oxf. mag., 1962, N.S., vol. 2, p. 338, 39.) Per. G.A. Oxon 4° 141

Plater college

8829. Catholic workers' college. Report. 1945/6– . n. pl., 1946– , 8°.
G.A. Oxon 8° 1234

Pusey house

8830. [Miscellaneous papers. 1882– .] G.A. Oxon c. 140; 4° 604

8831. LIDDON, H. P., The proposed memorial to dr. Pusey. [Letter]. November 29, 1882. [Oxf.], (1882), 4°. 3 pp. G.A. Oxon c. 140
— [Another ed.] 4 pp. G.A. Oxon c. 140

See 7465 [Proposed memorial to dr. Pusey. 1882].

8832. Dr. Pusey memorial fund. [Subscription list.] (Lond., 1883), 8°.
20 pp. G.A. Oxon c. 140

8833. Report of the executive committee of the Dr. Pusey memorial fund, June 2, 1886. [Lond.], (1886), 8°. 12 pp. G.A. Oxon 8° 620 (29)

8834. Dr. Pusey memorial fund ... Constitution. [Notification of meeting on 2 June 1886 to discuss the Constitution. *With*] Original bye laws. (Newbury, 1886), 8°. 4 pp. G.A. Oxon c. 140

8835. Dr. Pusey memorial fund ... Constitution [as approved by the meeting of 2 June 1886]. (Newbury, 1886), s. sh. G.A. Oxon c. 140

8836. Appeal for an extension of the Pusey house. [Oxf.], (1889), 8°. 4 pp.
G.A. Oxon c. 140

8837. Benediction of the Pusey house. (Oxf.), [1894], 8°. 7 pp.
G.A. Oxon c. 140

8838. Pusey house. By-laws provisionally adopted ... on June 25th, 1895. [Oxf.], (1895), 4°. 2 sheets. G.A. Oxon c. 140

8839. Form for the dedication of Pusey house chapel ... October 10, 1914. Oxf., 1914, 8°. 11 pp. G.A. Oxon c. 140

8840. Pusey house jubilee [form of service] May 27, 1935. (Oxf., 1935), 8°. 14 pp. G.A. Oxon c. 140

8841. FENWICK, HUGH, Nineteenth century pamphlets at Pusey House, an intr. for the prospective user. Lond., 1961, 8°. 98 pp.
2590 e. Oxf. 39. 1

Queen Elizabeth house

8842. WILCHER, L. C., Queen Elizabeth house. (Oxf. mag., 1962, N.S., vol. 2, p. 223, 24.)   Per. G.A. Oxon 4° 141

Ripon hall

8843. Ripon clergy college corporation. Annual report of the governors. 1920. Oxf., 1920, 4°. 11 pp.   G.A. Oxon 4° 403 (8)

Ruskin college

8844. Young Oxford, a monthly magazine devoted to the Ruskin hall movement. Vol. 1, no. 1–vol. 4, no. 48. Oxf., 1899–1903, 4°.
G.A. Oxon 4° 205

8845. SINCLAIR, W., A note on Ruskin college. (Univ. review, 1907, vol. 5, p. 396–404.)   Per. 2625 d. 30

8846. BUXTON, C. S., Ruskin college, an educational experiment. Repr. from the Cornhill magazine for August 1908. Lond., (1908), 8°. 11 pp.
G.A. Oxon 8° 850 (37)

8847. The dispute at Ruskin college: before and after. [Oxf., 1910], 4°. 40 pp.   G.A. Oxon 4° 504 (14)

8848. Ruskin college and working class education; its trials; a history of the dispute; future development of the college. (Committee of Ruskin coll. students.) n. pl., [1910], 4°. 42 pp.   G.A. Oxon 4° 276 (5)

8849. Ruskin college. Souvenir of the anniversary celebration. Lond. &c., 1914, 8°. 19 pp.   G.A. Oxon 8° 885

8850. The story of Ruskin college, 1899–1949. Oxf., 1949, 8°. 23 pp.
G.A. Oxon 8° 1204 (12)
— Revised 2nd ed. Oxf., 1955, 8°. 25 pp.   G.A. Oxon 8° 1320 (2)

8851. New epoch. College jubilee number [*and*] No. 6– . Oxf., 1949– , 4°.
G.A. Oxon 4° 684

8852. Ruskin college. Report for year ended July 31st, 1952(–) and Statement of accounts. (Reading, 1952–), 4°.   Per. G.A. Oxon 4° 724

8853. Ruskin college. Prospectus & curriculum. 1954/1955– . [Oxf.], 1954– , 8°.   Per. G.A. Oxon 8° 1339

St. Stephen's house

8854. St. Stephen's house. [Miscellaneous papers. 1878–1939.]
G.A. Oxon 4° 550, 604

8855. St. Stephen's house. [Prospectus.] n. pl., [1877?], s. sh.
G.A. Oxon 4° 550

8856. St. Stephen's house. [Revised prospectus.] n. pl., [1879], s. sh.
G.A. Oxon 4° 550
[Other prospectuses current in 1891, 1896, 1904, 1910, and 1914 are in the Bodleian in the same shelfmark.]

8857. Training for missionaries at Oxford. St. Stephen's house. [Missionary candidates' fund appeal.] n. pl., (1878), s. sh. G.A. Oxon c. 550

8858. Balance sheet. 1911/12–13/14. [Oxf.], 1912–14, s. sh.
G.A. Oxon 4° 550

8859. [*Begin.*] As this is the first time that a general appeal . . . has been issued on behalf of St. Stephen's house . . . [Brief history and appeal.] [Oxf., *c.* 1920], 8°. 4 pp. G.A. Oxon 4° 550

Westminster college

8860. Westminster college. (Builder, 27 May 1960, p. 995–98.)
N. 1863 c. 1

Wycliffe hall

8861. GIRDLESTONE, R. B., Wycliffe hall, Oxford: its nature and object. n. pl., [*c.* 1880], 8°. 3 pp. G.A. Oxon 8° 208

8862. [Miscellaneous papers. 1882–1910.] G.A. Oxon 4° 536

8863. Theological halls at Oxford [Wycliffe] and Cambridge [Ridley]. [Appeal for endowment funds. *With*] Subscriptions [list and balance sheet]. n. pl., [1882], 4°. 1 sheet+4 pp. G.A. Oxon 4° 536

8864. GIRDLESTONE, R. B., Four years' work at Wycliffe hall. (Oxf., 1882), 8°. 12 pp. G.A. Oxon 4° 536

8865. Wycliffe hall. The annual report. 1889/90–98/99. Oxf., 1890–99, 8°. G.A. Oxon 8° 668

8866. Form of service to be used at the dedication of the chapel . . . October 13th, 1896. Oxf., 1896, 8°. 16 pp. G.A. Oxon 4° 536

8867. DRURY, R. F., Wycliffe hall, Feb. 25, 1901. Topical song sung . . . at a . . . concert . . . [satirizing members of the hall]. (Oxf., 1901), 8°. 7 pp. G.A. Oxon 4° 536

8868. Wycliffe hall, Oxford. 1877–1927. Order of services for use on June 2, 1927. n. pl., (1927), 8°. 16 pp. G.A. Oxon 8° 1101 (12)

INDEX OF SUBJECT HEADINGS

*References are to item numbers. An item number
in parentheses indicates a duplicate entry.*

INDEX OF TITLES OR FIRST WORDS
OF SELECTED ANONYMOUS WORKS

Works which clearly indicate their subject-matter in the title are not included.
References are to item numbers.

INDEX OF
PERSONAL NAMES AND SOCIETIES
(EXCLUDING THOSE USING THE NAME
OF A COLLEGE)

*References are to item numbers. An item number
in parentheses indicates a duplicate entry.*

A., 5199.
A., F., *see* Anstey, F.
A., P. E., 965, 1198, 1966.
A., T. W., *see* Allen, Thomas William.
A., W. R., *see* Anson, sir William Reynell.
A.B.C., *pseud.*, *1864*: 2044.
A.B.C., *pseud.*, *1896*, see Firth, sir Charles Harding.
A Rationibus, *pseud.*, 1919.
Abbott, mr., 5606.
Abbott, A. F. R., 5228.
Abbott, Evelyn, 6751, 6752.
Abbott, John, 2381.
Abbott, Robert Lamb, 3033, 8266.
Abendana, Isaac, 5065, 5065.1.
Abingdon, James 1st earl of, *see* Bertie, James, 1st earl of Abingdon.
Abrahams, Harold Maurice, 4432.
Abrahams, Israel, 5065.1.
Academicus, *pseud.*, *1795*: 5076.
Academicus, *pseud.*, *1807*: 2071.
Academicus, *pseud.*, *1855*: 2476, 2478.
Academicus, *pseud.*, *1857*: 2793-5.
Academicus, *pseud.*, *1903*: 1796.
Ackerman, Rudolph, 25, 450.
Acland, sir Henry Wentworth, 1st bart., 1730, 1856, 2593, 2595, 2597-600, 2617, 2618, 2640, etc., 4597, 5836, 5838, 5923, 5954, etc., 6180, 6204, 6219, 6941.
Acland, sir Thomas Dyke, 11th bart., 2889, 2890, 3206.
Acworth, Abraham, 8412.
Acworth, Margaretta Mabella, 8412.
Ad Eundem, 4356.
Ada de Marisco, 92.
Adam de Marisco, *see* Ada de Marisco.
Adams, Arthur Robarts, 8400.
Adams, Henry Cadwallader, 4772, 4786, 4799.
Adams, Philip Edward H., 1042.
Adams, William, 6965.
Addams, Jesse, 3584.
Adderley, James Granville, 4005, 4006, 4012.
Addison, William George, 6713.
Addison, William Innes, 6770.
Adelphi club, 7322.
Adkins, William, 7042.
Adon, *pseud.*, *see* Traill, William Frederick.
Ady, Peter Honorine, 6433.46.
Africa society, 4096.

Agenda club, 4097.
Airay, Christopher, 8297.
Airay, Henry, 8192.
Albemarle, George, duke of, *see* Monck, George, 1st duke of Albemarle.
Alden, Edward Cox, 350, 354, 363, 387, 398.1.
Alden, J. E., 5399.
Alden's Oxford guide, 350.
Alden's Sixpenny guide, 354.
Aldrich, George, 2645 etc.
Aldrich, Henry, 7068-70, 7112.
Alembic club, 4098.
Alexander I, emperor of Russia, 639-43.
Alexander, Henry Frederick, 5966.
Alexander, John Huston, 519.1.
Alexandra, consort of Edward VII, king of Gt. Britain, 646.
Alfred, king, 8526, 8530, 8540.
Alfred jewel, 5330.
Aliquis, *pseud.*, 6165.
Allardyce, Alexander, 4664.
Allen, sir Carleton Kemp, 2565, 4855, 6016, 6017, 6024, 6418.
Allen, Dorothy Frances, lady, 6020, 6026.
Allen, Gerald Burton, 3362.
Allen, sir Hugh Percy, 2994, 2995, 4598.
Allen, Inglis, 4814, 4815.
Allen, Percy Stafford, 1013, 2189, 5463, 5464, 7176, 7223, 7820, 7823.
Allen, Thomas William, 5547.
Allen, Willoughby Charles, 2152, 2508, 3797.
Allestree, Richard, 4599.
Allfrey, Edward Wilfrid, 6800.
Allibond, John, 1556.
Allison, William H., 2691.
Allnutt, Thomas, earl Brassey, 6747.
Allsop, Anthony, 920.
Allsopp, Henry, 5188.
Alt, J. H., 2854.
Alton, R. E., 4025.
Amarantes, *pseud.*, *see* Herdegen, Johann.
American club of Oxford, 2368.
Amhurst, Nicholas, 192, 460, 1397, 4932, 5229, 8402.
Anderson, Charles Arnold, 4553.
Anderson, William, 5180.
Andrew, James, 3096.
Andrews, Charles McLean, 5631.
Angelos, Khristophoros, 6738-41.

3 D

Beeston, Alfred Felix L., 5781, 5785, 5790.
Beeverell, James, 289, 292.
Beevor, Ralph I., 5696.
Behan, John Clifford V., 5992.
Beirne, Frank F., 6004.
Belfour, Francis Cunningham, 2855.
Belinda, *fict. name*, 4781.
Bell, Charles Francis, 534, 5050, 7124.
Bell, Christopher Henry R., 5128.
Bell, John, 2207.
Bellamy, Frank Arthur, 1615, 2909, 6539, 6540.
Bellamy, James, 1213, 3341, 8410.4.
Bellingham, Ida, 388.
Belloc, Joseph Hilaire P., 4813.
Benecke, Paul Victor M., 7631.
Benlowes, Edward, 457, 458.
Bennet, Thomas Gromont, 920.
Bennett, Jack Arthur W., 6965.
Benson, Claude E., 852.
Bensusan, S. L., 2979.
Bentham, Edward, 176–80, 539, 3613, 3615, 4547.
Benthem, Heinrich Ludolf, 16.
Bentinck, William Henry Cavendish, 3rd duke of Portland, 1147.
Bentley, Richard, the younger, 248.
Bentley, Thomas, 6363.
Bereblock, John, 291, 546, 547.
Beresford, John, 4567.
Beresford, John Baldwin, 158, 159.
Berkeley, Elizabeth, 7134.
Bernard, Edward, 5619.
Bernard, John, 3703.
Bernard, Mountague, 1001, 1078, 2544, 2547, 4604, 6630, 6636.
Bernart, Jan, 240.
Berners, 9th baron, *see* Wilson, Gerald Hugh Tyrwhitt-.
Berry, Adrian Michael, 5205.
Berry, hon. Anthony George, 4317.
Berry, George Godfrey, 7925.
Berry, Michael F., 4533.
Bertie, Henry William, 6635.
Bertie, James, 1st earl of Abingdon, 148.
Besse, Antonin, 8102.
Betham, John Dover, 4505.
Bethell, Denis Leslie T., 7503.5.
Bethell, Richard, 1st baron Westbury, 1679, 2477, 3566, 6791.
Betjeman, John, 433, 509.
Betterton, mr., 4041.
Bevans, Francis, 2090.
Beveridge, William Henry, 1st baron, 8586.5.
Bevine, Frank F., 6004.
Bibye, Simon, 283.
Bickerton, counsellor, *pseud.*, 4944, 5115.
Bickerton, Percival Frederick, 8592.
Bidder, Henry Jardine, 8353, 8369.
Biddle, Hester, 3724.
Bidwell, Edward John, 3930.

Bigg, Henry, 7889.
Biggar, Henry Percival, 2369.
Bigge, Lewis Amherst Selby-, 212.
Bill, Edward Geoffrey W., 7115, 7164.9.
Bilstone, John, 6573.
Bingham, B., 7855.
Bingham, John Samuel, 4313.
Bingham, Joseph, 3478, 3479.
Bird, mr., instrument maker, 5938.
Birkenhead, 1st earl, *see* Smith, Frederick Edwin, 1st earl of Birkenhead.
Birkenhead, sir John, 1547.
Birkenhead, Henry, of Trinity college, 2817.
Birkhead, Henry, *1617?–1696*: 7732.
Birrell, Augustine, 5420.
Bispham, Thomas, 8193.
Bisset, Thomas, 1667.
Black, William Henry, 5662.
Blackall, W. G., 415.
Blackman, Aylward Manley, 2846.
Blackmantle, Bernard, *pseud.*, *see* Westmacott, Charles Molloy.
Blackstone, Charles, 7943.
Blackstone, sir William, 1047, 1142, 2529, 2530, 2576 etc., 4605, 4606, 6305, 6307.5, 6308, 6628, 6656, 6657.
Blackstone society, 4108.
Blackwell, B. H., 5961.
Blacow, Richard, 194, 201.
Blair, *pseud.*, *see* Fish, Wallace Wilfrid Blair-.
Blair, sir David Oswald Hunter-, 5th bart., 3718, 3765, 3925, 3953.
Blake *of Oriel*, *fict. name*, 4809.
Blake, Robert Norman W., 973.61.
Blakiston, Cuthbert Harold, 7155.
Blakiston, Herbert Edward D., 6435, 8464, 8465, 8510, 8518.
Blandford, Walter, bp. of Oxford, 6906.
Blaxland, John Hemington, 5660.
Bleackley, Horace William, 4797.
Bleaney, Brebis, 1436.3, 3004.4.
Blencowe, Anthony, 8052.
Blencowe, John, 8428.
Blind, Karl, 8240.
Blinders, Belinda, *pseud.*, *see* Coke, Desmond Francis T.
Bliss, Philip, 152, 1569, 1606, 4607, 6107, 8347.
Bliss, R., 4565.
Bliss, William H. M., 2334.
Blomfield, sir Reginald Theodore, 7355.
Bloomfield, Paul, 4851.
Bloxam, John Rouse, 7615, 7645, 7663.
Bloxham, Matthew Holbeche, 7140.
Blundell, Herbert Joseph Weld-, 5320, 5321, 5324, 5325, 4608.
Blunt, R., 8403.
Boardman, John, 5333.
Boas, Frederick Samuel, 4009, 4013, 4015, 4016, 4018, 4047–52, 4055, 6762, 8209, 8428.
Boas, Guy Herman S., 4644.

3 E

3 F

PRINTED IN GREAT BRITAIN
AT THE UNIVERSITY PRESS, OXFORD
BY VIVIAN RIDLER
PRINTER TO THE UNIVERSITY